MAP USE

Reading, Analysis, and Interpretation

Fifth Edition

MAP USE

Reading, Analysis, and Interpretation

Fifth Edition

A. Jon Kimerling
Professor of Geography
Oregon State University
Corvallis, Oregon

Phillip C. Muehrcke
Emeritus Professor of Geography
University of Wisconsin
Madison, Wisconsin

Juliana O. Muehrcke
Editor, *Nonprofit World* Journal
Madison, Wisconsin

JP Publications
P.O.Box 44173
Madison, WI 53744-4173

To our families,
who gave so generously.

JP Publications
Post Office Box 44173
Madison, WI 53744-4173

Phone: (608) 231-2373

Library of Congress Control Number: 2004097178
ISBN 0-9602978-6-3

ACKNOWLEDGMENTS

In previous editions of *Map Use*, we acknowledged the importance of contributions made by special teachers and colleagues, teaching assistants, and students at the University of Washington, University of Wisconsin, and Oregon State University. We continue to be grateful for the inspiration and assistance provided by these people.

To our delight, hundreds of individuals have taken the time to comment on these earlier editions. Some of these people were merely lovers of maps; others were professors responsible for teaching introductory courses in map reading, analysis, and interpretation; and a number were students who had occasion to use the book in their studies. We were especially moved by letters from people who stumbled upon *Map Use* by accident at a friend's house or library and felt compelled to let us know how pleased they were with their discovery.

All these responses were gratefully received, and many were useful in crafting this improved fifth edition. We alone, of course, bear full responsibility for errors in the text and controversial statements. This work reflects our deep love of maps and a desire to help others bring maps into their lives.

A.J. Kimerling
Corvallis, Oregon

P.C. and J.O. Muehrcke
Madison, Wisconsin

My object in living is to unite
My avocation and my vocation
As my two eyes make one in sight.

—Robert Frost

PREFACE

Readers of earlier editions of *Map Use* will notice major differences in this fifth edition. The biggest change is that the torch of lead author has passed to A. Jon Kimerling, a co-author of the fourth-revised edition. He studied with Phillip Muehrcke at the University of Washington as an undergraduate, and at the University of Wisconsin as a graduate student. After receiving his Ph.D., he went on to an active and distinguished career at Oregon State University. There he has made outstanding contributions to the mapping and environmental sciences. He is recognized internationally as a leading scholar in his field.

Jon's love of maps is infectious. His skill with maps is legend. He approaches the subject with a unique grasp of the natural, physical, and mapping sciences. To this perspective he adds exceptional information-age skills. For years Jon's students have enjoyed sharing his vast environmental knowledge through the visual medium of maps and the process of map use. It is that long experience that he now brings to *Map Use*.

Jon's talent has infused this fifth edition with a fresh look. The text and illustrations are updated and revised from cover to cover. Dozens of colorful maps are presented in a special color inset. Since electronic technology continues to have a profound impact on the way maps are made and used, the process of integrating mapping software, GIS mapping applications, map resources on the Internet, and GPS continues in this edition.

Electronic aids for map use have become widely available at prices most people can afford. GPS receivers now vastly simplify position and route-finding for many people, while computers loaded with mapping software and databases let us use maps interactively. Such innovations are rapidly transforming the way we use maps, and those changes are reflected in this edition. And yet, we have retained much information from earlier editions because it is still useful today. Much of what you need to know about using maps isn't new.

The philosophy behind *Map Use* also remains the same. As in earlier editions, we stress that a good map user must understand what goes into the making of a map. From map makers, we ask for little less than a miracle. We want the overwhelming detail, complexity, and size of our confusing surroundings reduced to a simple representation which is convenient to carry around. We also want that abstract map to provide us with a meaningful basis for relating to the environment.

It's fair to say that cartographers have given us what we asked for. They have mapped a vast array of subjects in a variety of clever, even ingenious, ways. Maps not only cover almost any topic of interest for all parts of the world, but they're also remarkably low in cost.

This is no surprise to the many people who love maps and are intrigued with all aspects of the mapping process. Those falling in this group constantly find themselves surrounded by maps, collecting more maps, or daydreaming with a map in hand. If you're one of those people, our aim is to get you to think about maps in still new ways, to broaden your total mapping experience so that you get more pleasure from less activity.

But sadly, many of us have acquired neither the interest nor the basic skills necessary to take full advantage of the broad range of available maps. Too often we blunder through the environment, not appreciating what it has to offer, causing hardship for ourselves and others, and relating to our surroundings in a destructive way. This need not be the case. Learning to use a map is a relatively easy and painless process, with an immense payoff.

Many books have been written on map making. But since map use isn't the simple reverse of map making, most of these books are of limited value to you as a map user. In contrast, this book has been written strictly for the person who wants to use maps. Academics have tended to treat maps as indoor things, rarely including in their textbooks the fact that one of the most exciting ways to use maps is in the field. Conversely, military manuals and field guides to map and compass use have focused narrowly on way finding, virtually ignoring the role maps play in the way we think about and communicate environmental information. In this book, we bridge the gap between these two extremes, pulling fragments of information from many fields into a coherent view of the environment. We offer a comprehensive, philosophical, and practical treatment of map appreciation. To do so, we've had to deviate in several ways from approaches taken in previous cartographic literature.

First, we define a map as a graphical representation of the environment that shows relations between geographical features. This encompassing definition lets us include a variety of important map forms which are otherwise awkward to categorize. Our definition should also accommodate any new cartographic forms which might be developed in the future. Throughout this book, we have integrated discussions of standard planimetric maps, perspective diagrams, environmental photographs, and satellite images, rather than partitioning each into a separate category.

Second, we have made a clear distinction between the tangible cartographic map and the mental or cognitive map of the environment which we hold in our heads. Ultimately, it is the map in our minds, not the map in our hands, with which we make decisions. Throughout the text, we stress the point that cartographic maps are valuable aids for developing better mental maps. We should strive to become so familiar with the environment that we can move through it freely in both a physical and mental sense. Ideally, our cartographic and mental maps should merge into one.

In a third departure from tradition, we have, where appropriate, made extensive reference to commercial products of special interest to the map user. A few years ago this would have seemed strange, since most mapping was done by large government agencies. But times have changed. The field of mapping is rapidly being commercialized. Computer software and digital data for mapping are being developed and sold by private industry. Since what you do with maps in the future will be strongly influenced by the nature of these commercial products, a convenient listing of sources, websites, and other contact information is provided in Appendix B.

Finally, this book is not written in traditional textbook style. Only sparing reference is made within the text to the professional cartographic literature, and the selected readings at the end of each chapter are chosen as much for their general accessibility as their content. Whenever possible, examples and illustrations have been taken from popular sources. Maps touch so many aspects of our daily lives that it is simple and natural to make points and reinforce ideas with advertisements, cartoons, and quotations from everyday communications. These illustrations and examples are included to demonstrate and reinforce basic mapping and map use principles. They are thus an integral part of the book and should be given as much consideration as the text.

The book was designed for both the specialized and the general map user. It could be used as a basic reference work or as the textbook for a beginning map appreciation course in any of the environmental sciences. It has been specifically designed and tested for use in a three-credit semester course of 15 weeks at the college freshman level. Material is presented at the upper high school to intermediate college level.

Our aim has been to cut through the plethora of confusing terms and details that characterize so many cartographic texts. Readers can obtain an overview of the most important concepts and how they fit together by glancing through the beginning outline included for each chapter.

We have structured the material into three main sections under the headings *Map Reading* (Part I), *Map Analysis* (Part II), and *Map Interpretation* (Part III). In most books, these terms have not had more than vague definitions and are often used interchangeably. Here they have been defined precisely, and the relationship of each to the others has been made clear.

The goal of *Part I, Map Reading* is to give you an appreciation of how the map maker represents the environment in the reduced, abstract form of a map. In map reading, in a sense, you're trying to "undo" the mapping process in your mind. We discuss the geographical data that make up a map, the process required to transform that information from environment to map (geographic and grid coordinate systems, map scale, and map projections), mapping techniques (landform portrayal, qualitative and quantitative data mapping, sensing imagery, and image mapping), and map accuracy issues.

Once you grasp the degree to which cartographic procedures can influence the appearance and form of a map, you're in a position to use maps to analyze spatial structures and relationships in the mapped environment. *Part II, Map Analysis* includes chapters on distance and direction finding. Here we explore compass use, position finding, and route planning, including the use of GPS receivers, cartometrics (area, volume, shape, slope, and profile determination), spatial pattern analysis and comparison, software for map analysis, and aerial photo analysis. With each of these topics, the concern is on estimating, counting, measuring, analyzing, and finding patterns in map features.

The results of map analysis come alive when you try to explain why the environment takes on one spatial character over another. This is the subject of *Map Interpretation (Part III).* The material has been divided into five chapters: Image Interpretation, Interpreting the Lithosphere (landforms and geology), Interpreting the Atmosphere and Biosphere, Interpreting the Human Environment, and Maps and Reality. The emphasis in this final section is on environmental comprehension and understanding, for it is our surroundings, not the map, which is the real subject of map use.

These three parts are followed by a series of appendices. Topics include digital cartographic databases, software vendors (including helpful website addresses and other contact information), GPS terminology, and useful mathematical tables. Each appendix is designed to complement material presented in the main body of the text.

Although a systematic development of subject matter is followed throughout this book, each section and chapter is autonomous from, and crossreferenced to, the rest of the material. Therefore, it isn't necessary to read the book in order from cover to cover. The strategy most appropriate for you depends on your background and interests. Generally, the book is organized to provide inexperienced readers with a logical development of concepts. There is a progressive building of skills from beginning to end. More experienced map users may wish to focus initially on sections or chapters of special interest and then refer to other parts to refresh their memories or clarify terms, concepts, and methods.

This book will have served its purpose if you finish it with a greater appreciation of maps than when you began. In even the simplest map, there is much to respect. Map makers have managed to shape the jumble of reality into compact, usable form. They have done a commendable job. Now it is up to you.

CONTENTS

MAP

It tells the truth by lying, like a poem
With bold hyperbole of shape and line—
A masterpiece of false simplicity,
Its secret meanings must be mulled upon,
Yet all the world is open to a glance.
With colors to fire the mind, a song of names,
A painting that is not at home on walls
But crumpled on a station wagon floor.
Worn through at folds, tape patched and chocolate smudged
(What other work of art can lead you home?)
—A map was made to use.

—JULIANA O. MUEHRCKE

INTRODUCTION

Map me no maps, sir, my head is a map of the whole world.
—Henry Fielding

INTRODUCTION

It should be easier to read a map than to read this book. After all, we know that a picture is worth a thousand words. Everyone from poets to politicians (does "Road Map to Peace" sound familiar?) works from the assumption that nothing could be easier to understand and follow than a map. The very term "map" is ingrained into our thinking. We use it to suggest clarification, as in "Map out your plan" or "Do I have to draw you a map?" How ironic, then, to write a book using language that is, supposedly, more complicated than the thing we're trying to explain!

The problem is that maps aren't nearly as straightforward as they seem. Using a map to represent our detailed and complexly interrelated surroundings can be quite deceptive. This isn't to say that maps themselves are unclear. But it's the environment, not the map, that you want to understand. A map lets you view the environment as if it were less complicated. There are advantages to such a simplified picture, but there's also the danger that you'll end up with an unrealistic view of your surroundings. People who manage critical natural and human resources all too often hold such simplified views of the environment.

In this book, we'll define a map as a **spatial representation of the environment**. By "representation," we mean something that stands for the environment, portrays it, and is both a likeness and a simplified model of the environment. This definition encompasses such diverse maps as those on walls and those held solely in the mind's eye. You may envision the environment by using **cartographic maps**, or you can use maps that are strictly in your mind. The maps in your mind, known as **cognitive** or **mental maps**, are often slighted. Yet they are really the ultimate maps that you use to make decisions about the environment. Let's look more closely at mental and cartographic maps.

MENTAL MAPS

As a child, your mental map was probably based on **direct experience**, connected pathways, and an **egocentric** view of the world (in which you related everything to your own position). The cartoon in **Figure I.1** graphically portrays this type of mental map. As an adult, you can appreciate this cartoon because you see how inefficient the child's mental map is. But the truth is that you will often resort to this way of visualizing the environment when thrown into unfamiliar surroundings. If you go for a walk in a strange city, you will remember how to get back to your hotel by visualizing a pathway like that in the cartoon. Landmarks will be strung like beads along the mental path.

Most of your mental maps are more detailed than this, however. For one thing, you take advantage of **indirect** as well as direct experience. You acquire information through TV, conversations, photographs, books and magazines, the Internet, and other secondary sources. You can transcend your physical surroundings and visualize distant environments, even those on the other side of the planet at different historical periods. Your mental map becomes incredibly complex as it expands to encompass places and times you have never seen and may never be able to visit.

At the same time, your egocentric view of the world is replaced by a **geocentric** view. Rather than relating everything to your own location, you learn to mentally orient yourself with respect to the external environment. You learn to assume yourself to be at a distant location, even though you haven't moved physically. Once you learn to separate yourself from your environment, you don't have to structure your mental map in terms of connected pathways. You can visualize how to get from one place to another "as the crow flies"—the way you would go if you weren't restricted to roads and other pathways. It's your ability to visualize the "big picture" that makes the cartoon amusing.

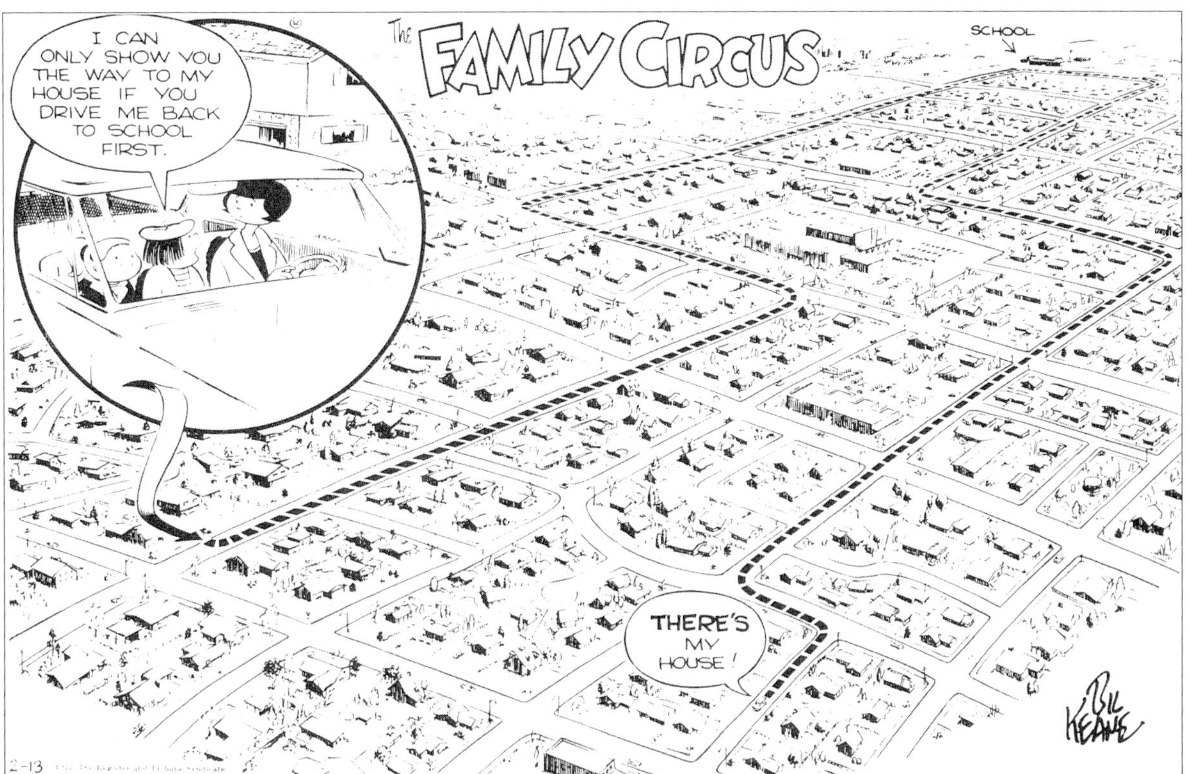

Figure I.1 The geometry of a child's mental map is based on direct experience and connected pathways.

Sharing your mental map with others, either in conversation or on maps that you draw, is much easier when you use a **geometrical reference framework**. The system of **cardinal directions** (north, south, east, and west) is such a framework. You can pinpoint the location of something by stating its cardinal direction and distance from a starting location. You can say, for example, that the pond is five miles north of a particular road intersection.

This visualization of space is based on **Euclidian geometry**, the geometry you learned in elementary and high school. It's the geometry which says that parallel lines never cross, that the shortest distance is a straight line, that space is three-dimensional, and so on. The ability to visualize the environment in terms of Euclidian geometry is an essential part of developing a geocentric mental map. But even if you develop mental maps based on Euclidian geometry, they will only be correct over small areas. That's because the earth is spherical, and the spherical geometry of the earth's surface is inherently non-Euclidian. (We'll see in Chapter 1, for example, that north-south lines on the earth, called meridians, aren't parallel but, rather, converge to a common point at the poles.) Very few of us have well-developed spherical mental maps.

Even if you're able to visualize the world geocentrically in terms of Euclidian or spherical geometry, it's hard for most people to transform their mental map to a cartographic map in a geometrically accurate manner. Try drawing, from memory, a map of the area in which you live. The hand-drawn map will tell you a great deal about the geometrical accuracy of your mental map. Not only will you probably draw the places you know best with the greatest detail and spatial accuracy, you'll probably draw things important to your life and leave off those that you don't care about.

Few people's mental maps correspond with cartographic maps. **Figure I.2** shows the distorted visual image that a person from Michigan's Upper

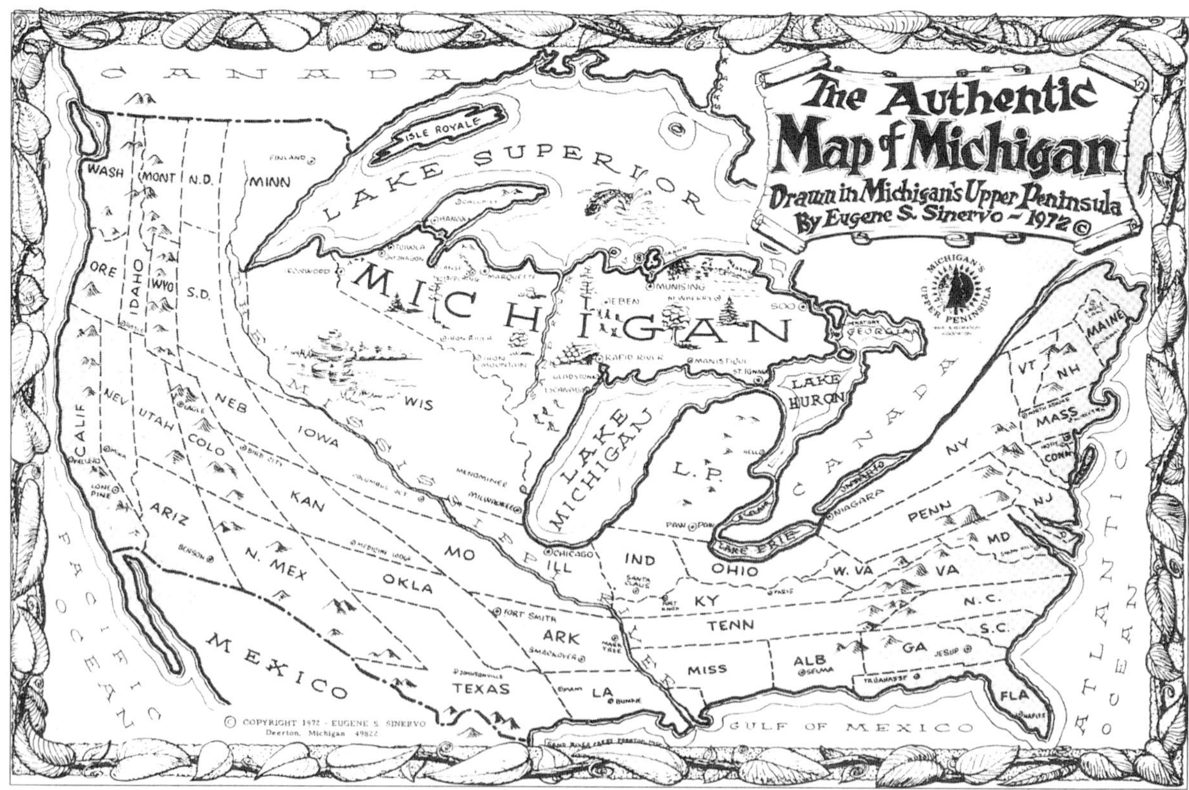

Figure I.2 The United States as seen through the eyes of a resident of Michigan's Upper Peninsula.

Peninsula might have of the country. Tongue in cheek as this map may be, it captures the fact that people visualize their own region as far more important than the rest of the world. In the same way, your mental maps emphasize your own neighborhood, with distant places less well visualized.

It's important to recognize these biases in your mental maps. The quality of your mental maps is crucial, because your behavior in the environment largely depends on them. You relate to your surroundings as you visualize them, not necessarily as they really are. If the discrepancy between your mental maps and the real world is great, you may act in self-defeating or even disastrous ways. Luckily, you don't have to rely solely on mental maps, since cartographic maps have been created for a multitude of places and features in the environment.

CARTOGRAPHIC MAPS

A **cartographic map** is a graphic representation of the environment. By graphic, we mean that a cartographic map is something that you can see or touch. Cartographic databases or digital image files are not in themselves maps, but are essential to the creation of maps. In a similar vein, an exposed piece of photographic film or paper doesn't become a photograph until it has been developed into a slide or paper print.

Cartographic maps come in many forms. Globes, physical landscape models, and Braille maps for the blind are truly three-dimensional objects, but most maps are two-dimensional line drawings or images of the earth taken from aircraft or orbiting satellites. Cartographic maps have been hand-drawn on paper or parchment for thousands of years, and printed maps have been produced for the last five centuries. Today you are just as likely to see maps displayed electronically on a computer monitor or television screen.

What gives a graphic representation of the environment its "mapness"? Many map makers say that cartographic maps have certain characteristics, the four most important being:

1. Maps are **vertical or oblique views** of the environment, not profile views like a photograph of a side of your home taken from the street.

2. Maps are created at a certain **scale**, meaning that there has been a systematic reduction from ground distance to map distance, as we will see in Chapter 1.

3. Except for globes and landscape models faithfully representing the earth's curvature, maps are made on a **map projection** surface. A map projection is a mathematically-defined transformation of locations on the spherical earth to a flat map surface, as we explain in Chapter 2.

4. Maps are **generalized** and **symbolized** representations of the environment. Map makers select a very limited number of features from the environment to display on the map, then display these features in a simplified manner. Insignificant features won't be shown, the sinuosity of linear features and area boundaries will be reduced, and several small ground features may be aggregated into a single feature on the map. The generalized features are then shown graphically with different **map symbols**. The map maker will use different line widths, gray tones, colors, and patterns to symbolize the features, as we describe further in Chapters 6 and 7. Names and numbers that annotate the map are also important map symbols.

A cartographic map need not have all four characteristics of maps, but it should have at least one. You can think of different types of maps as being at different places on a "mapness" continuum defined by the degree to which they exhibit these four characteristics. This continuum is illustrated in **Figure I.3** for a gradation of map types depicting part of Crater Lake National Park in Oregon.

The topographic map in the left quarter of the illustration strongly reflects all four characteristics and is a good example of what most people think of as a map. The orthophotomap in the center of the illustration also has all four characteristics, since topographic map symbols have been printed over a geometrically corrected aerial photo called an orthophotograph (orthophoto for short). We explain in Chapter 9 that an orthophoto is corrected to a constant scale on a map projection surface, and hence has three of the four characteristics. Finally, the aerial photo from which the orthophoto was made is not on a map projection surface and varies in scale with elevation differences on the ground, as we shall see in Chapter 20. The aerial photo only has the characteristic of being a vertical view of the environment, but is still a form of cartographic map.

As you can see from this illustration, there are multitudes of cartographic maps, each somewhere along the "mapness" continuum. The variety is so great that from now on we'll shorten the term "cartographic map" to simply "map," in accord with what you're used to hearing these products called.

WHAT MAKES MAPS POPULAR?

In scrutinizing the nature of maps, the obvious question is, "What accounts for their widespread popularity?" There are four main factors:

Maps are convenient to use. They are usually small and flat for ease of storage and handling. Thus, they bring reality into less unwieldy proportion for study.

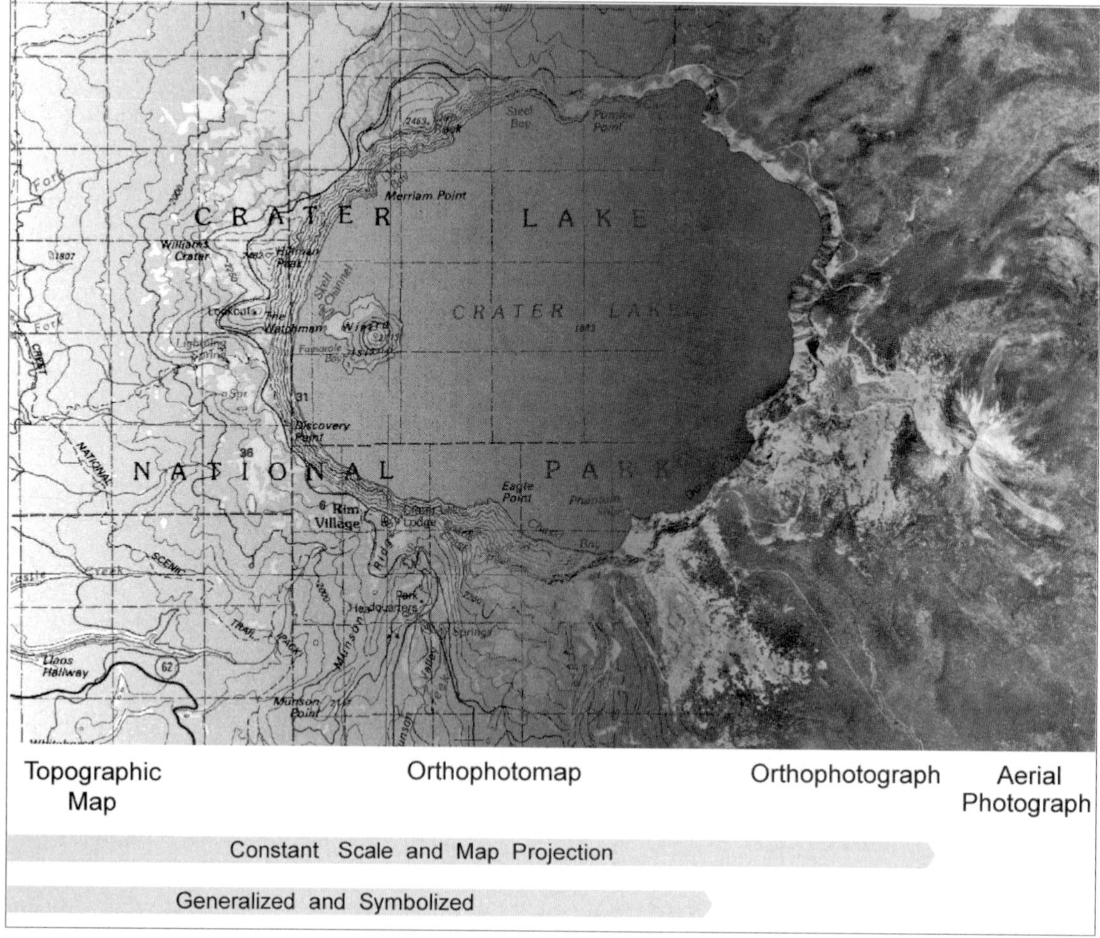

Figure I.3 Different types of maps lie along a "mapness" continuum. Their position on the continuum is defined by how many characteristics of maps they possess.

Maps simplify our surroundings. Without them, our world often seems a chaos of unrelated phenomena, a mass of meaningless events. The selection of information found on a map, on the other hand, is clear at a glance. The world becomes intelligible.

Maps are credible. They claim to show how things really are. The coordination between symbol and reality seems so straightforward that we're comfortable letting maps "stand for" the environment. When we manipulate maps, we expect the results to apply in our surroundings. Maps, even more than the printed word, impress people as authentic. We tend to accept the information on maps without question.

And, finally, **maps have strong visual impact**. Maps create a direct, dramatic, and lasting impression of the environment. Their graphic form appeals to our visual sense. It's axiomatic that "seeing is believing" and "a picture is worth a thousand words."

These factors combine to make a map appealing and useful. Yet these same four factors, when viewed from a different perspective, can be seen as limitations.

Take convenience. It's what makes frozen dinners popular. When we buy processed foods, we trade quality for easy preparation. Few would argue that the result tastes like the real thing made from fresh ingredients. The same is true of maps. We gain ease of handling and storage by creating an artificial image of the environment. This distortion of reality is bound to make maps imperfect in many ways.

Simplicity, too, can be seen as a liability as well as an asset. Simplification of the environment through mapping is nothing but an illusion that appeals to our limited information-processing ability. By using maps, you can avoid facing reality in its overwhelming and confusing natural state. But the environment remains unchanged. It's just your view of it that lacks detail and complexity.

You should also question the credibility of maps. The map maker's invisible hand isn't always reliable or rational. Some map features are distortions; others are errors; still others have been omitted through oversight or design. So many perversions of reality are inherent in mapping that the result is best viewed as an intricate, controlled fiction. Maps are like statistics: People can use them to show whatever they want. And once a map is made, it may last hundreds of years, although the world keeps changing. For all these reasons, a map's credibility is open to debate.

Also, be careful not to confuse maps' visual impact with proof or explanation. Just because a map leaves a powerful visual impression doesn't make it meaningful. Simply because map features are close together doesn't mean they're related. For explanations you must look beyond maps and confront the real world.

FUNCTIONS OF MAPS

Maps function as media for the communication of geographic information, and it is instructive to draw parallels between maps and other communication media. You can first think of maps as a reference library of geographic information. Maps serving this function, called **reference maps**, are more efficient geographic references than written accounts of the locations of different features. Reference maps let you instantly see the position of features and estimate directions and distances between features. Explaining these spatial relationships among features in writing would take hundreds of pages.

Maps also function like an essay on a particular topic. Like a well-written theme, a map can focus on a specific subject and be organized so that the subject stands out above the geographical setting. We call maps that function as geographic essays **thematic maps**.

Maps are **tools for navigation**, equal in importance to a compass or GPS receiver. When you get into your car and drive across your city, you are land navigating. When you step into an airplane and fly to a distant city, you must do air navigation (assuming you are the pilot). And when you motor or sail between two destinations on a body of water, you are sea navigating. In the latter two cases, you will use **navigation charts** to plan your route in advance and to guide you on your trip.

Maps are also **instruments of persuasion**. Like a written advertisement or television endorsement, some maps are made to persuade you to buy a particular product, to make a certain business decision, or to take a political action. These maps often are more sales hype or propaganda than a graphic representation of the environment, and you should view such maps with suspicion.

Let's take a closer look at maps with each of these different functions.

Reference Maps

The earliest known maps, dating back several thousand years, are of the reference type. On reference maps, symbols are used to locate and identify prominent landmarks and other pertinent features. An attempt is made to be as detailed and spatially truthful as possible so that the information on the map can be used with confidence. These maps have a basic "Here is found..." characteristic and are useful for looking up the location of specific geographic features. On reference maps, no particular features are emphasized over the others. As much as possible, all features are given equal visual prominence.

The topographic map and remote sensor images (orthophotomap, orthophotograph, and aerial photograph) in Figure I.3 are excellent examples of reference maps, because they show a variety of phenomena with about the same emphasis given to each. Reference maps are often produced in national mapping series, such as the United States Geological Survey (USGS) **topographic map series**. The topographic map segment in Figure I.3 is from such a series.

Topographic maps show and name **natural features,** including mountains, valleys, plains, lakes, rivers, and vegetation. They also show **cultural features,** such as roads, boundaries, transmission lines, and major buildings. One thing that distinguishes topographic maps from other map types is the use of contour lines to portray the shape and elevation of the land.

The geographic reference information on topographic maps and remote sensor images makes them useful to professional and recreational map users alike. They are used in engineering, energy exploration, natural resource conservation, environmental management, public works design, commercial and residential planning, and outdoor activities like hiking, camping, and fishing.

Globes and atlases are reference maps that show natural and cultural features in more generalized form than topographic maps. School wall maps are another form of reference map, as are the road maps and recreation guides that are produced for each state (**Figure I.4**).

Thematic Maps

Unlike reference maps, which show many types of features but emphasize no particular one over the others, thematic maps show a single type of feature that is the theme of the map. While reference maps focus on the location of different features, thematic maps stress the geographical distribution of the theme. A climate map (**Figure I.5A**), showing how average annual precipitation changes continuously across the state of Oregon, is a good example. A map showing the areal extent of Oregon vegetation provinces (**Figure I.5B**) likewise shows the geographic distribution of physical features.

Many thematic maps show the geographic distribution of concepts that don't physically exist on the earth. One example is a map showing Oregon's rural population with dots and urban population with variations in circle sizes (**Figure I.5C**). Another example is the Oregon population density map in **Figure I.5D**. You can't go into the environment and see population density, but maps showing the spatial distribution of such statistical themes are very useful to experts in demographics and other fields.

Thematic maps ask, "What if we were willing to look at the spatial distribution of some aspect of the world in this particular way?" Figure I.5D, for example, asks, "What if we were willing to look at population density by taking the 2000 population census totals for Oregon counties as truth, dividing each total by the area of the county to get a population density, and then generalizing the densities into seven arbitrarily defined categories?"

Take another look at each map in Figure I.5 and note how each theme is superimposed on a background of county outlines. Most thematic maps have similar background information to give a geographical context to the theme. Be careful not to use the geographical reference information to find specific locations or to make precise measurements. Remember, that's not the intent of thematic maps; it's what reference maps are for. When using thematic maps, focus on their function of showing the geographic distribution of the theme.

Navigation Maps

As you'll see in Chapter 13, several types of maps are specially designed to assist you in land, water, and air navigation. Many of these maps are called

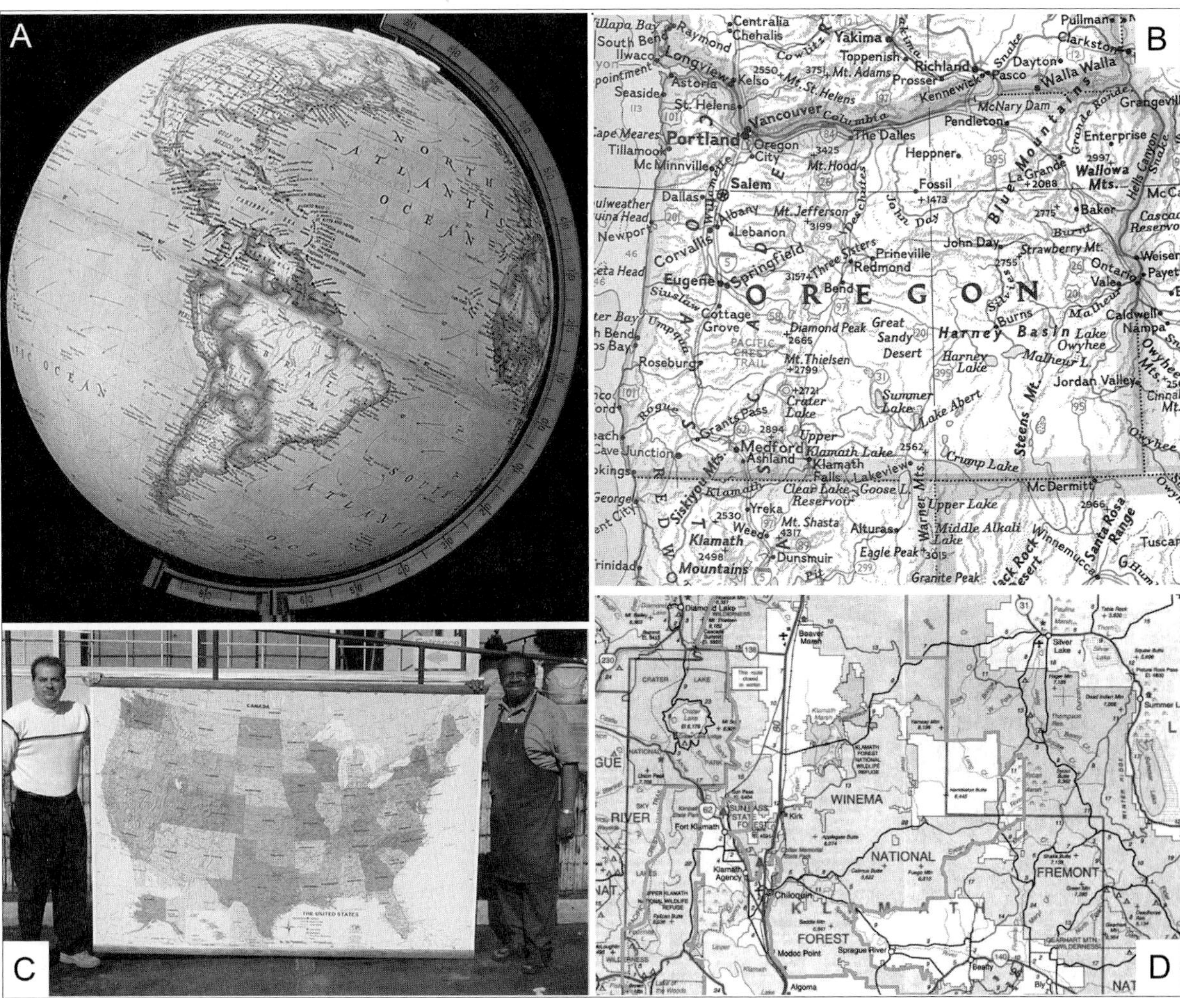

Figure I.4 Reference map examples include the National Geographic Society (NGS) Venture Globe (A), the Oregon section of the United States page from the NGS Atlas of the World (B), the Terra Grande United States wall map (C), and a section of the Oregon State Highway Map.

charts—maps created specifically to help the navigator plan voyages and follow the planned travel route.

A **topographic map**, such as the segment in **Figure I.6A**, not only is a valuable reference map, but also is one of the most important land navigation tools. Hikers, off-road vehicle enthusiasts, and land management professionals use topographic maps to find their way across the land. The topographic map shows ground features such as roads,

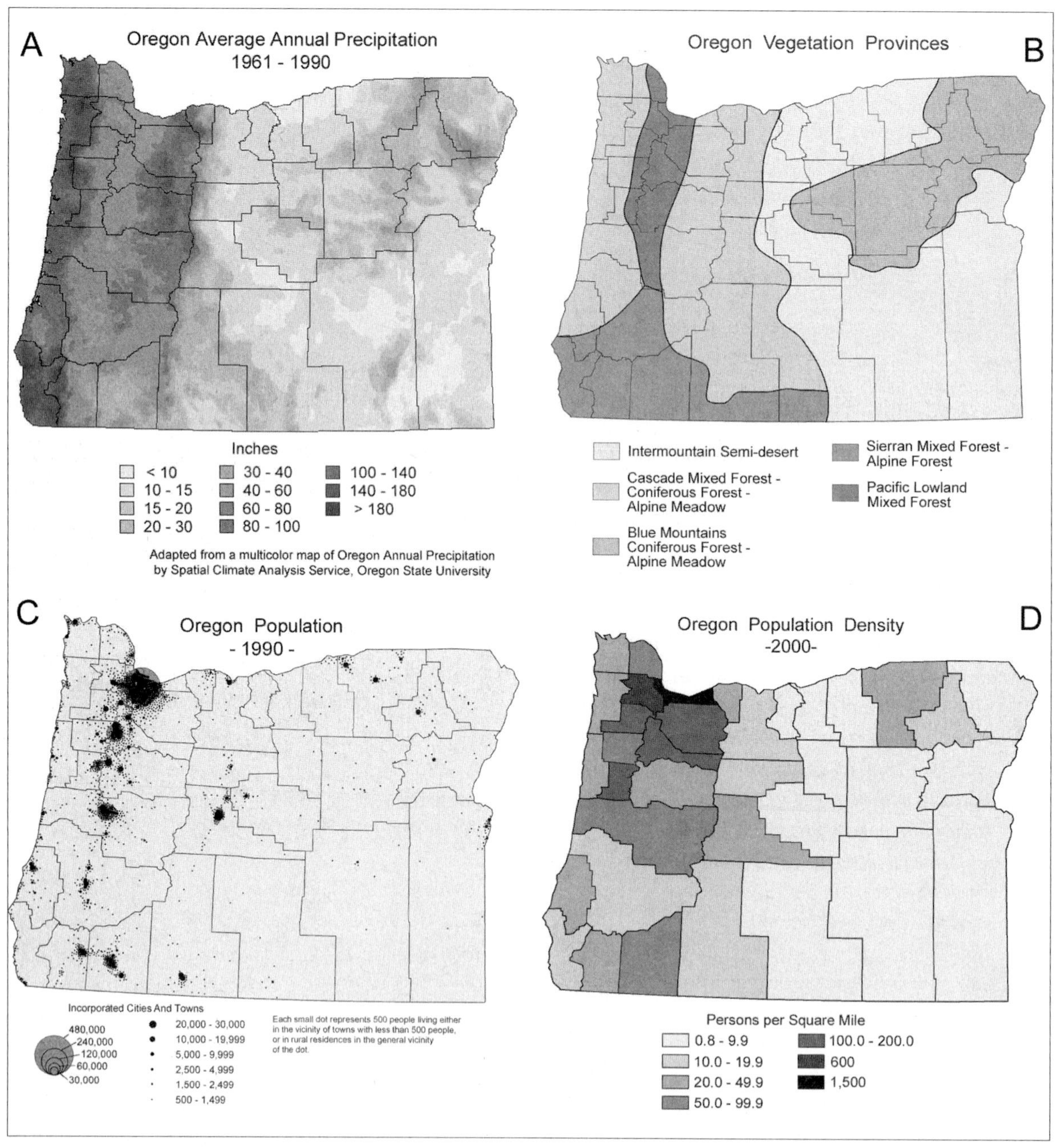

Figure I.5 These four thematic maps for Oregon show annual precipition as a continuous surface (A), vegetation provinces as uniform areas (B), rural and urban population by dots and graduated circles (C), and population density by county (D).

trails, lakes, and streams that are both landmarks and obstacles to be crossed or traveled around. Contour lines on the maps are equally important, as they allow you to determine elevation changes and estimate the slopes you'll encounter along a route. This information will help you estimate the time and physical effort it will take to complete your trip. In addition, topographic maps are drawn on map projections that allow you to measure distances and directions between locations along your route (in Chapters 11 and 12, you'll learn how to make these measurements).

Nautical charts, such as the southeastern corner of the San Juan Islands, Washington, chart copied in **Figure I.6B**, are maps created specifically for water navigation. Recreational and commercial boat navigators use the detailed shoreline, navigational hazard, and water depth information on the chart to plan the "tracks" that they will follow between ports or anchorages. As you'll see in Chapter 13, each chart is made on a special map projection that allows you to quickly and easily measure the distance and direction of each track. Another type of nautical chart gives you information about the currents you must deal with on a particular day and hour. This information is of critical importance in planning your time of departure and estimating the time of arrival at your destination.

Aeronautical charts are maps designed for the air navigator. **Figure I.6C** is a black-and-white reproduction of part of an aeronautical chart covering Wisconsin. Air navigation involves planning and following safe routes between airfields, and the chart is filled with information important to safe flying. Notice the detailed information shown on the chart for the Oshkosh airport. In Chapter 13, you'll learn what these map symbols mean, as you see how pilots use the information on the chart to find distances, directions, and travel times between destinations. Air navigation also involves maintaining a safe altitude above the ground, and you'll see that aeronautical charts show the heights of towers and other obstructions to navigation, as well as contours and special ground elevation symbols that help navigators quickly determine the minimum safe in-flight altitude.

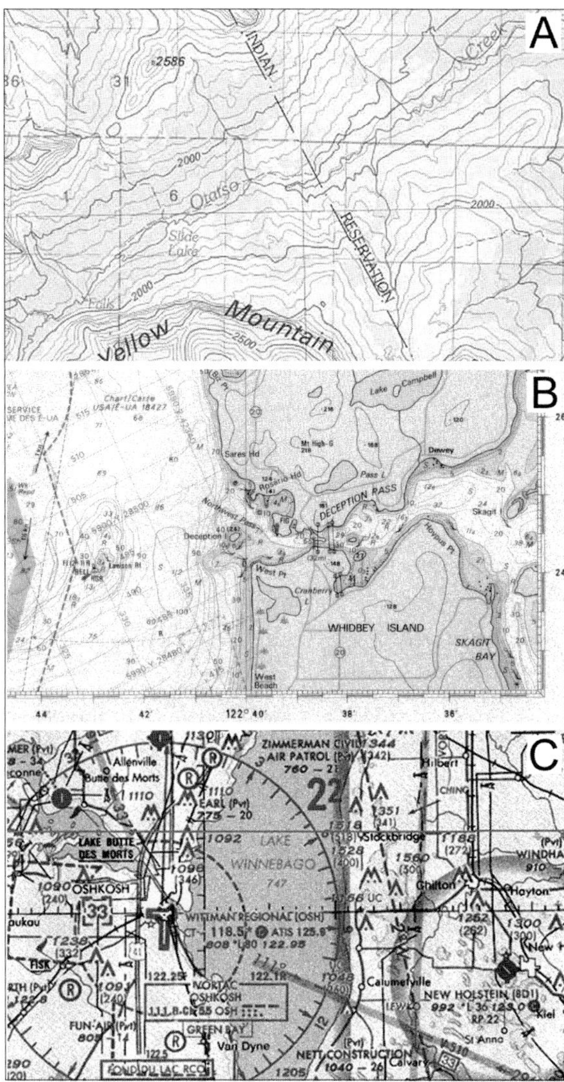

Figure I.6 Topographic maps (A), nautical charts (B), and aeronautical charts (C) are important tools of land, water, and air navigation.

Persuasive Maps

Maps have always played a role in decision-making, and map makers can deliberately try to persuade you to choose a particular product or support a certain position. Some of these maps of persuasion distort or misrepresent to such an extent that they become **propaganda tools**. Such propaganda is common, especially on advertising, political, and religious maps. Since all maps distort reality, what could be easier than to make this distortion serve a special company or organization? And unless we know enough to question every map, how would we suspect anything was wrong? Let's look at several examples of persuasive maps that either are or border on propaganda.

One type of propaganda involves disproportionate symbols as a means of persuasion. Map makers must make symbols overly large. Otherwise, the symbols wouldn't show up at reduced map scales. In propaganda mapping, map makers carry this normal aspect of cartographic symbolization to extremes.

Take the map of Israeli military checkpoints in the West Bank in 2002 (**Figure I.7**) Notice the large, detailed symbol for each checkpoint, and the small square for each city. By using such large symbols, the map maker has made the West Bank appear crowded with military checkpoints. This is an interesting example, because it isn't clear if this propagandizing effect was intended to increase the sense of safety for Israelis, if it was designed to intimidate Palestinians, or if it was inadvertent on the map maker's part.

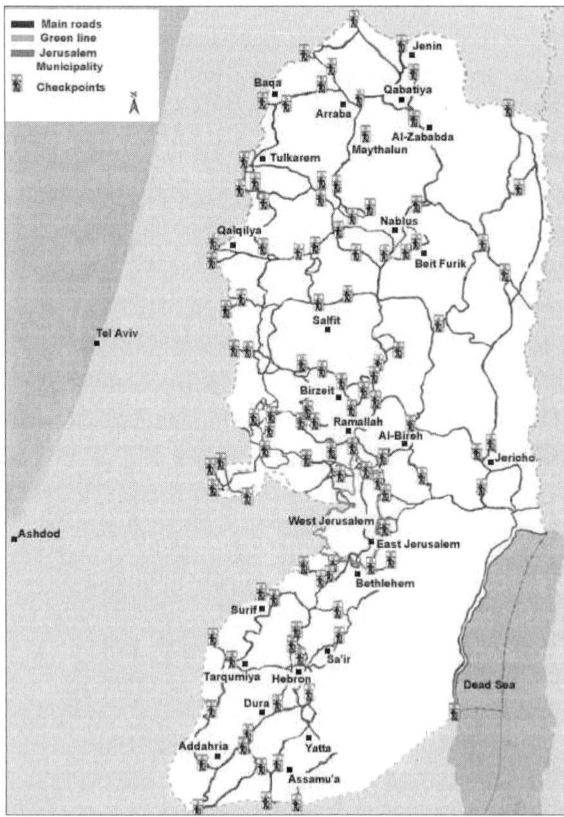

Figure I.7 Disproportionately large map symbols may create the impression that the West Bank was more crowded with Israeli military checkpoints than it actually was at the time the map was made (2002).

Presenting a misleading number of features on a map is another tool of persuasion that grades into propaganda. Nineteenth-century railroad maps such as **Figure I.8** are classic examples. Notice that the map scale has been selectively enlarged along the artificially straight main line from Sault Ste. Marie, Michigan, to Duluth, Minnesota. The map shows several dozen stops along the main and feeder lines, some of which are towns. By mapping every stop, the railroad company is trying to persuade investors, settlers, and riders to choose it over a competing railroad. The following commentary from the *Inland Printer* shows how far this practice of planned map distortion went:

> "This won't do," said the General Passenger Agent, in annoyed tones, to the mapmaker. "I want Chicago moved down here half an inch, so as to come on our direct route to New York. Then take Buffalo and put it a little farther from the lake.
>
> "You've got Detroit and New York on different latitudes, and the impression that that is correct won't help our road.
>
> "And, man, take those two lines that compete with us and make`em twice as crooked as that. Why, you've got one of `em almost straight.
>
> "Yank Boston over a little to the west and put New York a little to the west, so as to show passengers that our Buffalo division is the shortest route to Boston.
>
> "When you've done all these things I've said, you may print 10,000 copies—but say, how long have you been in the railroad business, anyway?"
>
> (*New York Herald*)

Map simplification can also be used for persuasion purposes. **Figure I.9** shows two maps of illegal West Bank settlements in the mid-1980s. Both maps come from the same weekly news magazine. One map depicts 16 settlements, while the

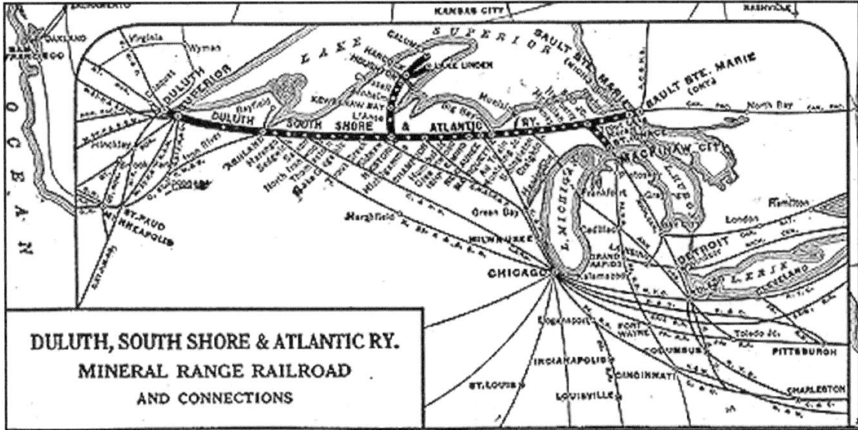

Figure I.8 This portion of the 19th-century Duluth, South Shore & Atlantic railroad map has the area along Lake Superior deliberately distorted to show all stops along the line.

other shows 30 settlements. Which is correct? The truth, revealed deep in the magazine's text, is that there were 45 illegal Israeli settlements in the West Bank region when these maps were made. The legend, at the least, should have provided this information. The makers of these maps, whether intentionally or not, presented a picture that favored the Israeli cause. You should never overlook the possibility for such political bias in mapping.

It pays to be especially cautious of novel or artful advertising maps, because they are invariably more eye-catching than factual. Consider **Figure I.10**, taken from a Columbia City, Indiana, industrial park brochure. Distance rings in 100-mile increments centered on Columbia City have been drawn on the map to show the travel distance to other locales. The idea of drawing equally spaced distance rings outward from Columbia City is absurd, since travel to the city is by road, not air. Notice that the distances to Chicago and Detroit are actually by road and don't agree with the distance rings.

Whether you realize it or not, map makers are constantly molding your attitudes. Of course, they aren't the only people guilty of persuasion and propaganda. But the effect of map propaganda is especially insidious because so many people believe that maps are neutral and unbiased. The consequences are often dramatic: A year's vacation is ruined, or a retirement nest egg is spent on a land parcel in the swamp.

MAP USE

Map use is the process of obtaining useful information from one or more maps to help you understand the environment and improve your mental map. Map use consists of three main activities—reading, analysis, and interpretation.

When **map reading**, you determine what the map makers have depicted and how they've gone about it. If you carefully read the maps in **Figure I.11**, for instance, you can describe the maps as

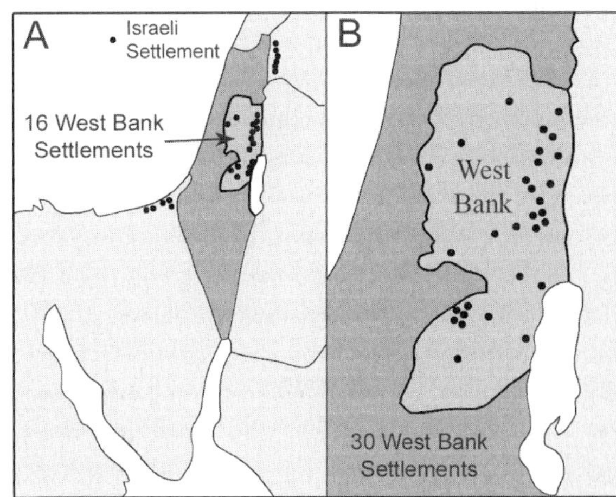

Figure I.9 The need for map simplification can easily be used to create a map that borders on propaganda. Here West Bank settlements on maps of two scales are shown (These examples have been taken from a weekly news magazine in the mid-1980s; in 2005, hundreds of such settlements exist).

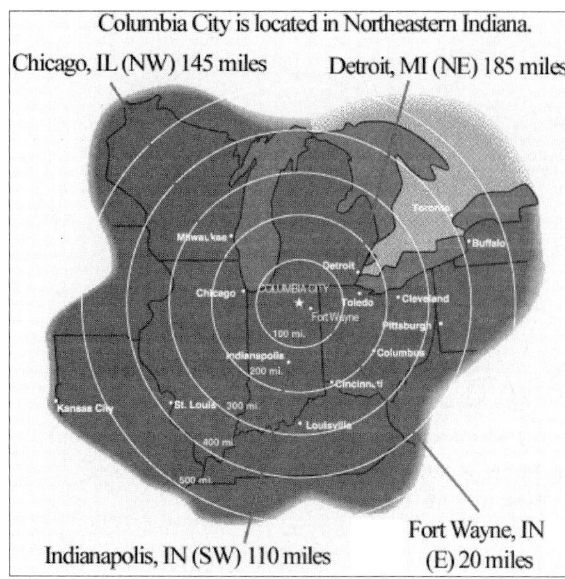

Figure I.10 On this deceptive map, distances to Columbia City, Indiana, are shown by concentric distance circles spaced 100 miles apart. But the travel distances the map purportedly shows are by road, not "as the crow flies."

showing mortality from all types of cancer for males and females from 1980 to 1990 within data collection units called Health Service Areas. Reading the map legends, you learn that the mortality rate is the number of deaths per 100,000 people, and that mortality rates have been generalized into seven categories shown by a gray tone sequence. Light to dark gray represents low to high mortality on both maps, but the range for each category differs on the two maps, showing you that males have higher overall deaths from cancer. There is no explanation of how the category limits were selected, but the maps appear to have about the same number of Health Service Areas in each category. Finally, the legend tells you that areas with sparse mortality data are shown with a diagonal line pattern, and you see a few patterned areas on both maps.

Part I of this book examines these and many other facets of map reading. You will become familiar with map scale, map projections and coordinate systems, land partitioning methods, different ways of portraying landforms, maps that show qualitative and quantitative information, and ways of expressing map accuracy.

Learning to read the information on maps is only the first step. Your curiosity or a work assignment may lead you to go further and analyze the information on one or more maps. *Part II* of this book is devoted to **map analysis**. In this stage of map use, you make measurements and look for spatial **patterns**. We have seen that topographic maps and navigational charts are tools for the measurement of distances, directions, and surface areas.

Analysis of the spatial patterns on the maps in Figure I.11 is particularly thought-provoking. While it's comforting to believe that cancer is unpredictable, analysis of these maps shows that's not true. If you focus on the patterns on these maps, you find that cancer mortality rates are far from random across the country. Regional clustering of high and low rates occurs for both males and females. You see a cluster of high mortality in Kentucky and low mortality in Utah and southeastern Idaho, for example. It's unlikely that this high and low clustering of deaths occurred by chance.

If you next focus on the spatial correspondence of mortality rates on the two maps, you find that eastern Kentucky and western West Virginia appear to have the highest cancer mortality for both men and women. The upper Midwest and Northeast, along with northern California, have the next highest overall male and female mortality. Some areas have high mortality rates for one sex but not for the other. For instance, the Mississippi delta region has high mortality rates for males but not for females.

You may see clusters of high and low mortality on the two maps, but someone else may not see things the same way. Quantitative measures of spatial patterns on a map and spatial association among patterns on two or more maps add rigor and repeatability to your map analysis, and we have devoted two chapters (Chapters 17 and 18) to these important aspects of map analysis.

After analyzing the maps in Figure I.11 and finding spatial patterns of high and low cancer mortality, your curiosity may now be aroused still further. You may wonder how to explain the pat-

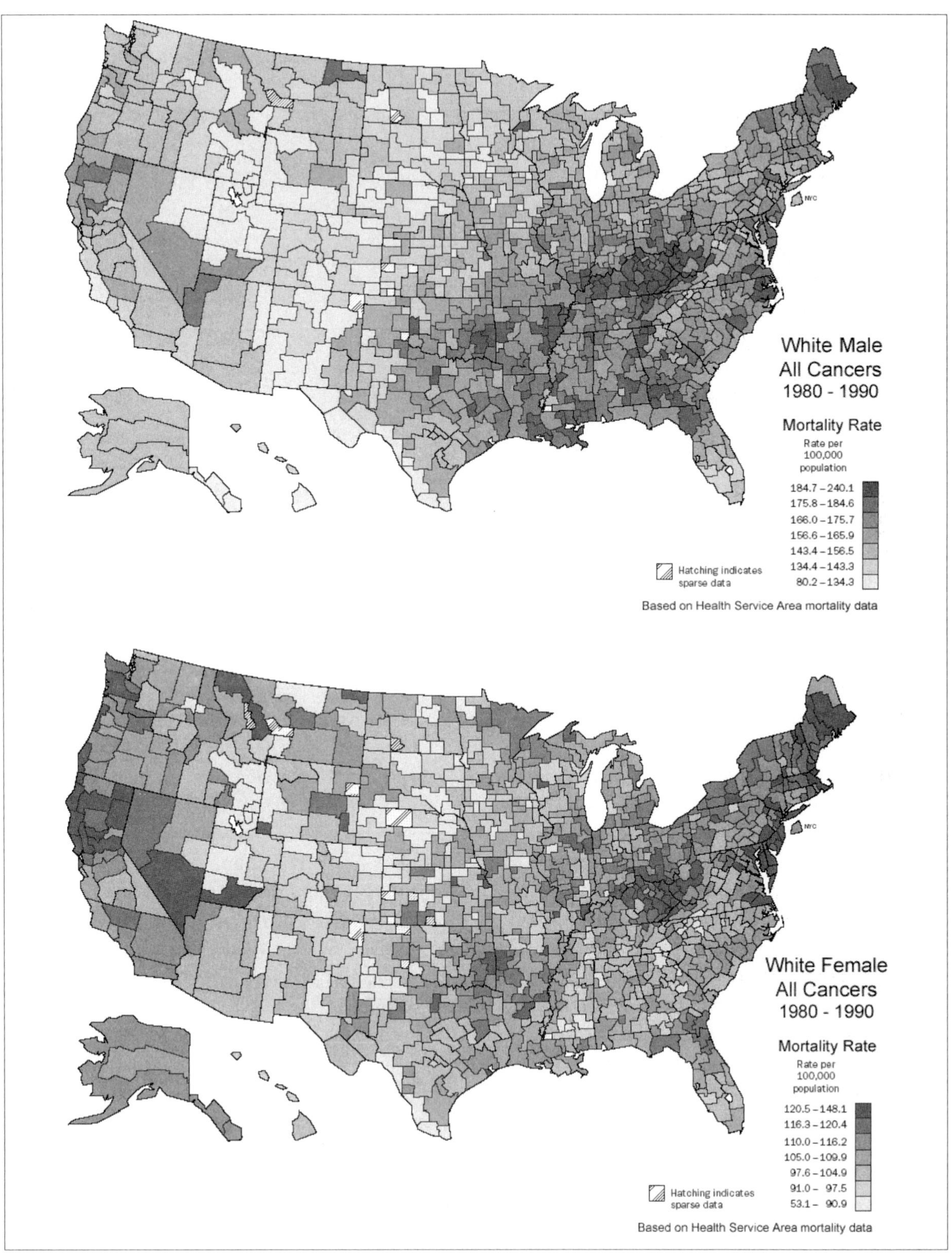

Figure I.11 White male and female 1980-1990 cancer mortality rates in the United States by Health Service Area [adapted from multicolor maps of the same title in the Atlas of United States Mortality].

terns and the spatial correspondences between the two maps. Finding such explanations takes you into the realm of **map interpretation**. To understand why things are related spatially, you have to search beyond the map. To do so, you may draw on your personal knowledge, fieldwork, written documents, interviews with experts, or other maps and images.

In your search, you'll find that cancer deaths are associated with many factors, including industrialized working environments, mining activities, chemical plants, urban areas, ethnic backgrounds, and personal habits of eating, drinking, and smoking. You'll find that people die because of contaminants in their air, water, food, clothing, and building materials. Some local concentrations of high or low cancer mortality, however, don't seem to fit this pattern, suggesting that there must be other causes or that people have migrated in or out of the area. We'll delve into the interpretation of landforms, the physical environment, and the human landscape in *Part III* of this book.

Since maps reflect all aspects of environmental knowledge, map use is intertwined with many disciplines. It is impossible to appreciate them in isolation. The more different fields you study, the better you will be at using maps. Map interpretation grows naturally out of an appreciation of a variety of subjects. The reverse is also true. An appreciation of maps leads to a better understanding of the world around you, for the subject of maps, after all, is the world itself.

This brings us to a final, important point. As you gain an understanding of map use, be careful not to confuse the mapped world with the real world. Remember, the reason you're using maps is to understand the physical and human environment. The ultimate aim of map use is to stimulate you to interact with your environment and to experience more while you do.

SELECTED READINGS

Ames, G.P., "Forgetting St. Louis and Other Map Mischief," *Railroad History*, 188 (Spring-Summer 2003) pp. 28-41.

Arnheim, R., *Visual Thinking* (Berkeley, CA: University of California Press, 1969).

Balchin, W.G.V., "Graphicacy," *The American Cartographer*, Vol. 3, No. 1 (April 1976), pp. 33-38.

Castner, H.W., *Seeking New Horizons: A Perceptual Approach to Geographic Education* (Montreal: McGill-Queen's University Press, 1990).

Dent, B.D., *Cartography: Thematic Map Design*, 5th ed. (New York, McGraw-Hill, 1998).

Downs, R.M., and Stea, D., *Maps in Mind: Reflections on Cognitive Mapping* (New York: Harper & Row Publishers, 1977).

Gershmehl, P.J., and Andrews, S.K., "Teaching the Language of Maps," *Journal of Geography*, Vol. 85, No. 6 (November-December 1986), pp. 267-270.

Head, C.G., "The Map as Natural Language: A Paradigm for Understanding," *Cartographica*, Vol. 21 (1984), pp. 1-32.

Keates, J.S., *Understanding Maps*, 2nd ed. (Essex: Addison Wesley Longman Ltd., 1996).

Kitchin, R.M., "Cognitive Maps: What They Are and Why Study Them?", *Journal of Environmental Psychology*, Vol. 14 (1994), pp. 1-19.

Lloyd, R., *Spatial Cognition: Geographical Environments* (Boston: Kluwer Academic Publishers, 1997).

MacEachren, A.M., *How Maps Work: Representation, Visualization and Design* (New York: The Guilford Press, 1995).

Monmonier, M., *How to Lie with Maps* (Chicago: University of Chicago Press, 1991).

Monmonier, M., and Schnell, G.A., *Map Appreciation* (Englewood Cliffs, NJ: Prentice Hall, 1988).

Pickle, L.W. et al., *Atlas of United States Mortality* (Hyattsville, MD: U.S. Department of Health and Human Services, 1996).

Robinson, A.H., and Bartz-Petchenik, B., *The Nature of Maps: Essays Toward Understanding Maps and Mapping* (Chicago: University of Chicago Press, 1976).

Tufte, E.R., *Visual Explanations: Images and Quantities, Evidence and Narrative* (Cheshire, CT: Graphics Press, 1997).

I

PART ONE

MAP READING

Art, said Picasso, is a lie which makes us realize the truth. So is a map. We don't usually associate the precise craft of the map maker with the fanciful realm of art. Yet a map has many ingredients of a painting or a poem. It is truth compressed in a symbolic way, holding meanings it doesn't express on the surface. And like any work of art, it requires imaginative reading.

To read a map, you translate its features into a mental image of the environment. The first step is to identify map symbols. The process is usually quite intuitive, especially if the symbols are self-evident and if the map is well designed. Obvious as this step might seem, however, you should look first at the map legend, both to confirm the meaning of familiar symbols and to make sure of the logic underlying unfamiliar or poorly designed ones. Too many people look to the legend only after becoming confused. Such a habit is not only inefficient but potentially dangerous.

In addition to clarifying symbols, the map legend contains other information, such as scale, orientation, and data sources important to map reading, and sometimes includes unexpectedly revealing facts. But the legend is still only a starting point. The map reader must make a creative effort to translate the world as represented on the map into an image of the real world, for there often is a large gap between the two. Much of what exists in the environment has been left off the map, while many things on the map do not occur in reality.

Thus, map and reality are not—and cannot—be identical. No aspect of map use is so obvious yet so often overlooked. Most map reading mistakes occur because the user forgets this vital fact and expects a one-to-one correspondence between map and reality.

Since the exact duplication of a geographical area is impossible, a map is actually a metaphor. The map maker asks the map reader to believe that an arrangement of points, lines, and areas on a flat sheet of paper or a computer screen is equivalent to some facet of the real world in space and time. To gain a fuller understanding, the map reader must go beyond the graphic representation to what the symbols refer to in the real world.

A map, like a painting, is just one special version of reality. To understand a painting, you must have some idea of the medium used by the artist. You wouldn't expect a water color to look anything like an acrylic painting or a charcoal drawing, even if the subject matter of all three were identical. In the same way, the techniques used to create maps will greatly influence the final portrayal. As a map reader, you should always be aware of the map maker's invisible hand. Never use a map without asking yourself how it has been biased by the methods used to make it.

If the mapping process operates at its full potential, communication of environmental information takes place between map maker and reader. The map maker translates reality into the clearest possible picture that a map can give, and the map reader converts this picture back into a mental image of the environment. For such communication to occur, the map reader must know something about how maps are created.

The complexities of mapping are easier to study if we break them up into simpler parts. Thus, we have divided Part I into 10 chapters, each dealing with a different aspect of mapping. Chapter 1 examines geographical coordinate systems for the earth as a sphere, an oblate ellipsoid, and a geoid. Chapter 2 looks at ways of expressing and determining map scale. Chapter 3 introduces different map projections and the types of geometric distortions that occur with each projection. Chapter 4 focuses on different grid coordinate systems used on maps in the United States and worldwide. Chapter 5 looks at land partitioning systems used in the United States and how they are mapped. Chapter 6 examines various methods for mapping qualitative information, and Chapter 7 does the same for quantitative information. Chapter 8 is devoted to the different methods of relief portrayal found on maps. Chapter 9 is an overview of remote sensing imagery and image maps. Finally, Chapter 10 presents various aspects of map accuracy.

These 10 chapters should give you an appreciation of all that goes into mapping and the ways that different aspects of the environment will be shown on maps. As a result, you'll better understand the large and varied amount of geographic information that you can glean from a map. In addition, once you realize how intricate the mapping process is, you can't help but view even the crudest map with more respect, and your map reading skill will naturally grow.

CHAPTER ONE

THE EARTH AND EARTH COORDINATES

Latitude and longitude were to the measurement of space what the mechanical clock was to the measurement of time.
—*Daniel J. Boorstin, The Discoverers*

"...but then I wonder what Latitude or Longitude I've got to?" (Alice had not the slightest idea what Latitude was, or Longitude either, but she thought they were nice grand words to say).
—*Lewis Carroll, Alice's Adventures in Wonderland*

1

CHAPTER ONE

THE EARTH AND EARTH COORDINATES

Of all the jobs maps do for you, one stands out. They tell you where things are and let you communicate this information efficiently to others. This more than any other factor accounts for the widespread use of maps. Maps give you a superb **locational reference system**—a way of pinpointing the position of things in space.

There are many ways to pinpoint the location of a feature shown on a map. All of these begin with defining a geometrical figure that approximates the true shape and size of the earth. Once this is done, a system of **parallels and meridians** that we call the **graticule** is draped over the geometrical figure so that we can locate features by their coordinates. In this chapter we will see that maps are based on approximating the earth by either a **sphere** or an **oblate ellipsoid** of precisely known dimensions. Parallels and meridians are then draped over the sphere or ellipsoid, so that we can pinpoint locations by their **latitude and longitude**. The locations of elevations measured relative to the **geoid** can then be defined by three-dimensional coordinates.

THE EARTH AS A SPHERE

We have known for over 2,000 years that the earth is **spherical in shape**. We owe this idea to several ancient Greek philosophers, particularly **Aristotle** (4th century BC) who believed that the earth's sphericity could be proven by careful visual observation. Aristotle noticed that as he moved north or south the stars were not stationary, but new stars appeared in the northern horizon while familiar stars disappeared to the south. He reasoned that this could occur only if the earth were curved north-south. He also observed that departing sailing ships, regardless of their direction of travel, always disappeared from view hull first. If the earth were flat, the ships would simply get smaller as they sailed away—only on a sphere would hulls always disappear first. His third observation was that a circular shadow is always cast by the earth on the moon during a lunar eclipse, something that would occur only if the earth were spherical. These arguments entered the Greek literature and persuaded scholars over the succeeding centuries that the earth must be spherical in shape.

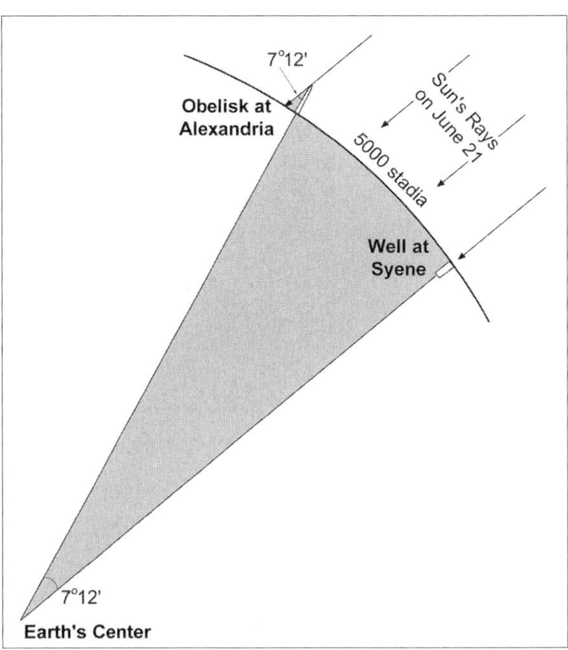

Figure 1.1 Eratosthenes' method for measuring the earth's circumference.

Determining the size of our spherical earth was a daunting task for our ancestors. The Greek scholar **Eratosthenes**, head of the then famous library and museum at Alexandria, Egypt, made the first scientifically based estimate of the earth's circumference around 250 BC. The story that has come down to us is of Eratosthenes reading an account of a deep well at Syene (near modern Aswan about 500 miles south of Alexandria) whose bottom was illuminated by the sun only on June 21, the day of the summer solstice. He concluded that the sun must be directly overhead on this day, with rays perpendicular to the level ground (**Figure 1.1**). Then he reasoned brilliantly that if the sun's rays were parallel and the earth were spherical, a vertical column like an obelisk should cast a shadow in Alexandria on the same day. Knowing the angle of the shadow would allow the earth's circumference to be measured if the north-south distance to Syene could be determined. The simple geometry involved here is "if two parallel lines are intersected by a third line, the alternate interior angles are equal." From this he reasoned that the shadow angle at Alexandria equaled the angular difference at the earth's center between the two places.

The story continues that on the next summer solstice Eratosthenes measured the shadow angle from an obelisk in Alexandria, finding it to be 7°12', or 1/50th of a circle. Hence, the distance between Alexandria and Syene is 1/50th of the earth's circumference. He was told that Syene must be about 5,000 stadia south of Alexandria since camel caravans travelling at 100 stadia per day took 50 days to make the trip to between the two cities. From this distance estimate, he computed the earth's circumference as 50×5,000 stadia, or 250,000 stadia. In Greek times a stadion varied from 200 to 210 modern yards, so his computed circumference is somewhere between 28,400 and 29,800 modern statute miles, 14 to 19 percent greater than the current value of 24,907 statute miles. We now know that the error was due to an under-estimate of the distance between Alexandria and Syene, and to the fact that they are not exactly north-south of each other. However, his method is sound mathematically and was the best circumference measurement until the 1600s. Equally important, Eratosthenes had the idea that careful observations of the sun would allow us to determine angular differences between places on earth, an idea that we shall see was expanded to other stars and recently to artificial satellites such as the **Global Positioning System** (**GPS**) constellation (see Chapter 14 for GPS details).

GEOGRAPHIC COORDINATES

Parallels and Meridians

Once the shape and size of the earth is known, some system for defining locations on the surface is required for maps. We are again indebted to ancient Greek scholars for devising a systematic way of placing reference lines on the spherical earth. Astronomers before Eratosthenes had placed on maps horizontal lines marking the **equator** and the **tropics of Cancer and Capricorn** (marking the northernmost and southernmost positions of where the sun is directly overhead on the summer and winter solstices, such as Syene). Later the astronomer and mathematician **Hipparchus** (190-125 BC) proposed that a set of equally spaced east-west lines called **parallels** be drawn on maps (**Figure 1.2**). To these he added a set of north-south lines called **meridians** that are equally spaced at the equator and converge at the north and south poles. We now call this arrangement of parallels and meridians the **graticule**. His numbering system for parallels and meridians was and still is called **latitude and longitude**.

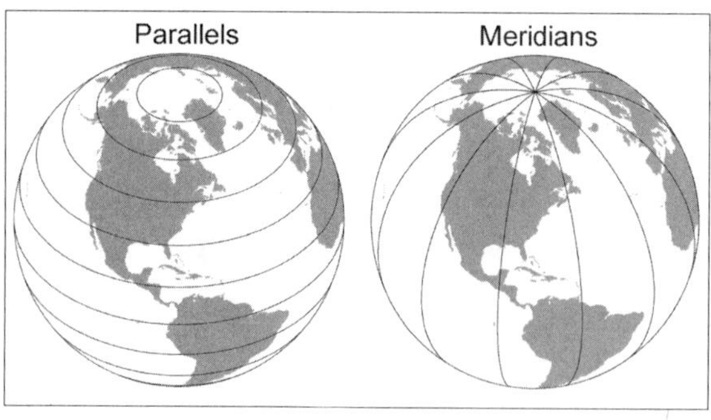

Figure 1.2 Parallels and meridians.

Geographic Latitude and Longitude

Latitude on the spherical earth is the north-south angular distance from the equator to the place of interest (**Figure 1.3**). The numerical range of latitude is from 0° at the equator to 90° at the poles. The letters N and S, such as 45°N for Salem, Oregon, are used to indicate north and south latitude. Longitude is the angle, measured along the equator, between the intersection of the **prime meridian** and the point where the meridian for the feature of interest intersects the equator. The numerical range of longitude is from 0° to 180° east and west of the prime meridian, twice as long as parallels. East and west longitudes are labeled E and W, so that Salem, Oregon, has a longitude of 123°W.

Putting latitude and longitude together into what is called a **geographic coordinate** (45°N, 123°W) pinpoints a place on the earth's surface. There are several ways to write latitude and longitude values. The oldest is the Babylonian sexagesimal system of degrees, minutes, and seconds. The latitude and longitude of the capitol dome in Madison, Wisconsin, is 43°04'29"N, 89°23'03"W, for example. If we can accurately define a location to the nearest 1" of latitude and longitude, we have specified its location to within 100 feet of its true location on the earth.

The choice of prime meridian is entirely arbitrary because there is no physically definable starting point like the equator. Eratosthenes selected Alexandria as the starting meridian for longitude, and in medieval times the Canary Islands off the coast of Africa were used since they were then the westernmost outpost of western civilization. In the 18th and 19th centuries the capital city of many countries was used as the prime meridian for the nation's maps, including the meridian through the center of the White House in Washington, D.C. for our own early 19th century maps (see **Table 1.1** for a listing of historic prime meridians.) You can imagine the confusion that must have existed when trying to locate places on maps from several countries. This was eliminated in 1884 when the **International Meridian Conference** selected as the international standard the British prime meridian de-

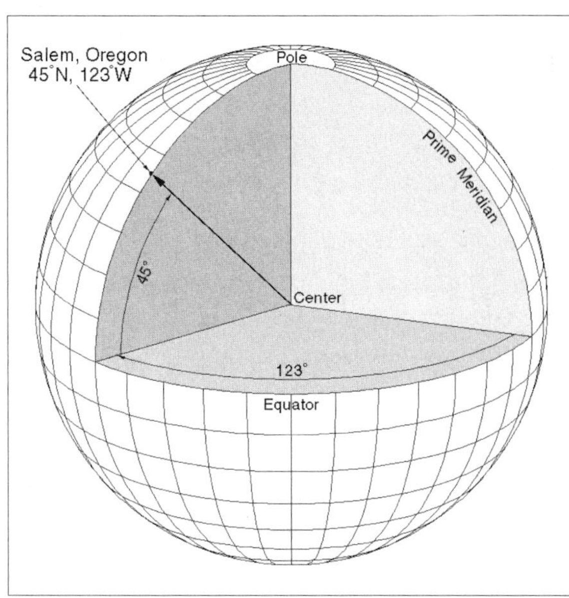

Figure 1.3 Latitude and longitude on the Sphere.

fined by the north-south optical axis of a telescope at the Royal Observatory in **Greenwich**, a suburb of London.

You may occasionally look at historic maps using one of the prime meridians in Table 1.1, at which time knowing the angular difference between the prime meridian used on the map and the Greenwich meridian becomes very useful. As an example, you might see in an old Turkish atlas that the longitude of Seattle, Washington, is 151°16' W (based on the Istanbul meridian) and you know that the Greenwich longitude of Seattle is 122°17' W. You can determine the Greenwich longitude of Istanbul through subtraction: 151° 16' - 122° 17' = 28° 59'E.

This example gives you an idea of how awkward it is to make computations with traditional latitude-longitude coordinates. You're dealing in 60s, not 10s, when changing one unit (degree, minute, second) to another. Fortunately, geographic coordinates can also be written in decimal degrees to simplify many map calculations. We use the formula: decimal degrees = degrees + minutes/60 + seconds/3600 to make the conversion. The capitol dome in Madison, Wisconsin (43°04'29"N, 89°23' 03"W) would be 43 + 4/60 + 29/3600, 89 + 23/60 + 3/3600 or 43.0747°N, 89.3842°W in decimal degrees. Recently, the wide use of digital computers has led us to specify south latitude and west longitude by a negative sign instead of the letters S and W. In this notation, the capitol dome is now at 43.0747, -89.3642.

Table 1.1 Prime Meridians Used Previously on Foreign Maps, along with Longitudinal Distances from the Greenwich Meridian

Prime meridian	Distance from Greenwich
Amsterdam, Netherlands	4°53'01"E
Athens, Greece	23°42'59"E
Beijing, China	116°28'10"E
Djakarta, Indonesia	106°48'28"E
Berlin, Germany	13°23'55"E
Bern, Switzerland	7°26'22"E
Brussels, Belgium	4°22'06"E
Copenhagen, Denmark	12°34'40"E
Ferro, Canary Islands	17°40'00"W
Helsinki, Finland	24°57'17"E
Istanbul, Turkey	28°58'50"E
Lisbon, Portugal	9°07'55"W
Madrid, Spain	3°41'15"W
Moscow, Russia	37°34'15"E
Oslo, Norway	10°43'23"E
Paris, France	2°20'14"E
Rio de Janeiro, Brazil	43°10'21"W
Rome (Monte Mario), Italy	12°27'08"E
St. Petersburg, Russia	30°18'59"E
Stockholm, Sweden	18°03'30"E
Tokyo, Japan	139°44'41"E
Washington DC, USA	77°02'14"W

Determining Latitude and Longitude

The oldest way to determine latitude and longitude is with instruments for observing the **positions of celestial bodies**. The essence of the technique is to establish celestial lines of position (east-west, north-south) by comparing the predicted positions of celestial bodies with their observed positions. A hand-held instrument, called a **sextant**, historically was the tool used to measure the angle (or altitude) of a celestial body above the earth's horizon (**Figure 1.4**).

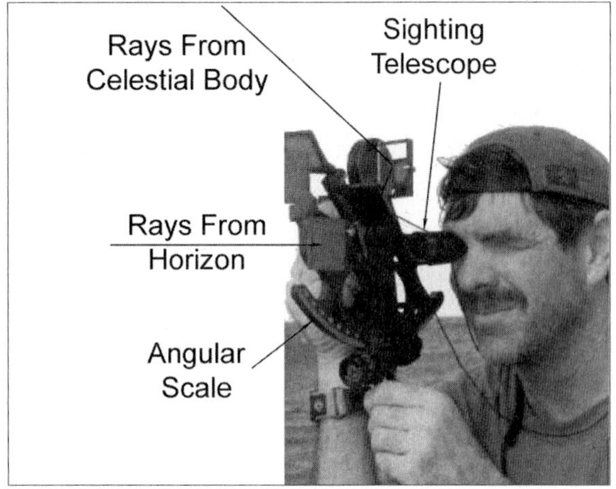

Figure 1.4 A sextant is used at sea to find latitude from the vertical angle between the horizon and a celestial body.

Figure 1.6 The Harrison chronometer allowed longitude to be accurately determined as a time difference between Greenwich, England, and a distant locale.

Astronomers study and tabulate information on the actual motion of celestial bodies to help pinpoint latitude and longitude. But in the northern hemisphere, observing Polaris (the North Star) is far easier. Latitude is simply the angle between the horizon and Polaris (**Figure 1.5**).

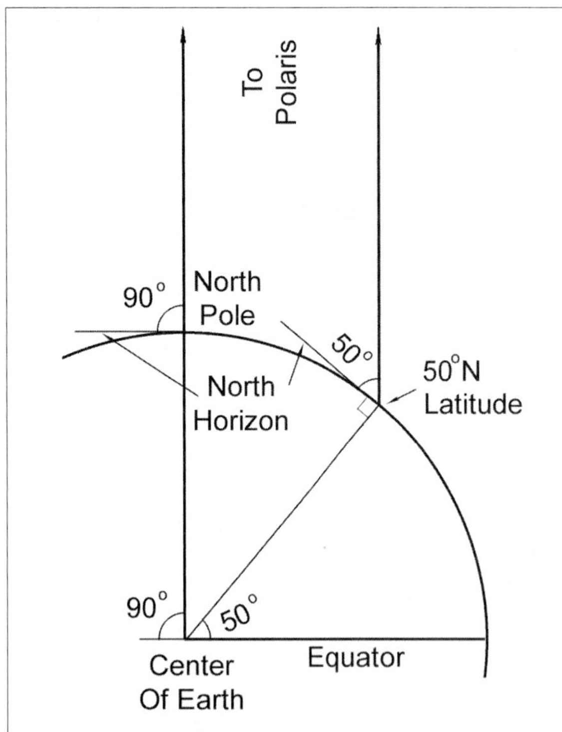

Figure 1.5 It is easy to determine your latitude by observing the height of Polaris above your northern horizon.

Computing longitude is no more complicated. The prime meridian—0 degrees longitude—passes through Greenwich, England. Therefore, each hour difference between your time and that at Greenwich, called **Greenwich Mean Time** or GMT, is equivalent to 15 degrees of longitude from Greenwich. You merely compare your local time with Greenwich mean time. The difficulty is that time is defined by **time zones**, not the exact **local time** at your longitude. Your local time must be determined by celestial observations.

In previous centuries, accurately determining longitude was a major problem in both sea navigation and map making. It was not until 1762 that an accurate enough clock, called a **chronometer**, for longitude finding was invented by the Englishman John Harrison (**Figure 1.6**). The **Harrison chronometer** was set to Greenwich Mean Time before departing on a long voyage. The longitude of a distant locale was found by noting the Greenwich time at local noon (the highest point of the sun in the sky, found with a sextant). The time difference was simply multiplied by 15 to find the longitude.

PROPERTIES OF THE SPHERICAL GRATICULE

Equally Spaced Parallels

On a spherical earth, the north-south ground distance between equal increments of latitude does not vary. Using the most recent spherical earth circumference, latitude spacing is always 24,907 mi./360° or 69.2 statute miles per degree. Expressed in metric and nautical units, it is 111.32 km and 60.12 nautical miles per degree of latitude (see **Table D.1** in Appendix D for the metric and English distance equivalents used to arrive at these values.)

Converging Meridians

A quick glance at any world globe (or Figure 1.2) shows that the length of a degree of longitude, measured east-west along parallels, decreases from the equator to the pole. The precise spacing at a given latitude is found by using the equation: 69.2 mi./deg. × cosine (latitude). At 45 degrees north or south of the equator, for example, cosine (45°) = 0.7071. Therefore, the length of a degree of longitude is 69.2 × 0.7071, or 49.93 statute miles. This is roughly 19 miles shorter than the 69.2 mile spacing at the equator.

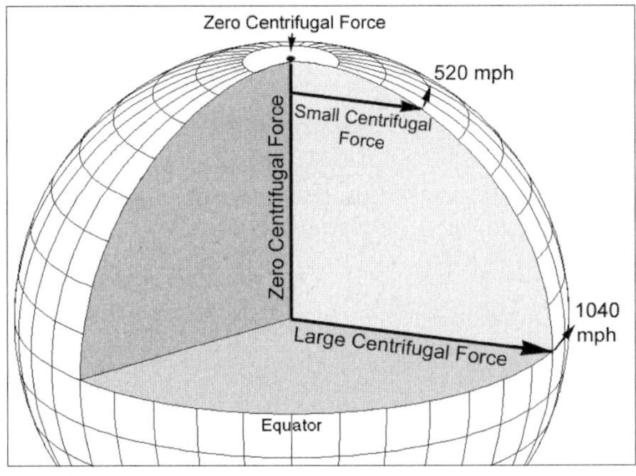

Figure 1.7 A systematic increase in centrifugal force from the pole to equator causes the earth to be an oblate ellipsoid.

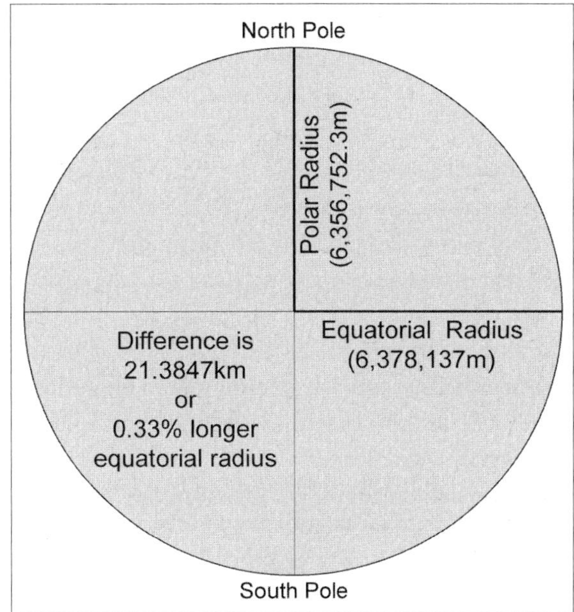

Figure 1.8 Dimensions of the WGS84 oblate ellipsoid, the current best overall fit to the earth.

Great and Small Circles

A **great circle** is the largest possible circle that could be drawn on the surface of the spherical earth. Its circumference is that of the sphere and its center is the center of the earth, so that all great circles divide the earth into halves. The equator is a great circle dividing the earth into northern and southern hemispheres. Similarly, the prime meridian and its opposite 180° meridian (called the **antipodal meridian**) form a great circle dividing the earth into western and eastern hemispheres, as do all other pairs of meridians and antipodal meridians. A great circle is the shortest route between any two points on the earth and hence great circle routes are fundamental to long distance navigation.

Any circle on the earth's surface that is smaller than the circumference is called a **small circle**. All parallels other than the equator are small circles. The circumference of a particular parallel is given by the equation: 24,907 mi. × cosine(latitude). For example, the circumference of the 45th parallel is 24,907 × 0.7071 or 17,612 statute miles.

Quadrilaterals

Quadrilaterals are areas on the earth bounded by equal increments of latitude and longitude, 1° by 1°, for example. Since meridians converge toward the poles, the shapes of quadrilaterals vary from a square on the sphere at the equator to a very narrow spherical triangle at the pole. The equation: cosine(latitude) gives the aspect ratio (width/height) of any quadrilateral. A quadrilateral centered at 45°N will have an aspect ratio of 0.7071, whereas a quadrilateral at 60°N will have an aspect ratio of 0.5. A map covering 1° by 1° will look very long and narrow at this latitude.

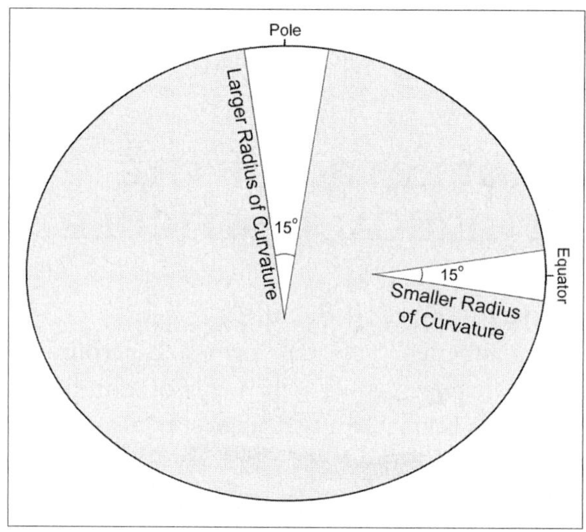

Figure 1.9 Cross-section through a greatly flattened oblate ellipsoid, showing that a larger radius of curvature at the pole results in a larger ground distance per degree of latitude relative to the equator.

THE EARTH AS AN OBLATE ELLIPSOID

Scholars assumed that the earth was a perfect sphere until the 1660s when Sir Isaac Newton developed the theory of gravity. Newton thought that mutual gravitation should produce a perfectly spherical earth if it were not rotating about its polar axis. The earth's 24-hour rotation, however, introduces outward centrifugal forces perpendicular to the axis of rotation. The amount of force varies from zero at each pole to a maximum at the equator, obeying the equation: centrifugal force = mass × velocity^2 /

Table 1.2 Historic and Current Oblate Ellipsoids

Name	Date	Equatorial Radius (m)	Polar Radius(m)	Area of Use
WGS 84	1984	6,378,137	6,356,752.31	Worldwide
GRS 80	1980	6,378,137	6,356,752.3	Worldwide (NAD 83)
Australian	1965	6,378,160	6,356,774.7	Australia
Krasovsky	1940	6,378,245	6,356,863	Soviet Union
International	1924	6,378,388	6,356,911.9	Remainder of world not covered by older ellipsoids
Clarke	1880	6,378,249.1	6,356,514.9	France; most of Africa
Clarke	1866	6,378,206.4	6,356,583.8	North America (NAD 27)
Airy	1849	6,377,563.4	6,356,256.9	Great Britain
Bessel	1841	6,377,397.2	6,356,079	Central Europe; Chile; Indonesia
Everest	1830	6,377,276.3	6,356,075.4	India and the rest of south Asia

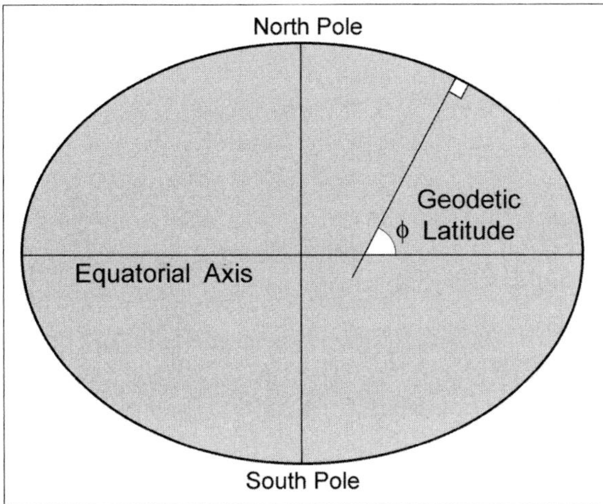

Figure 1.10 Geodetic latitude on a greatly flattened oblate ellipsoid.

Table 1.3 Geographic and Corresponding Geodetic Latitude (WGS 84) at 5° Increments

Geographic	Geodetic	Geographic	Geodetic
0°	0.000°	50°	50.126°
5	5.022	55	55.120
10	10.044	60	60.111
15	15.064	65	65.098
20	20.083	70	70.082
25	25.098	75	75.064
30	30.111	80	80.044
35	35.121	85	85.022
40	40.126	90°	90.000°
45°	45.128°		

distance from the axis of rotation. To understand this, imagine a very small circular disk at the pole and two very thin horizontal cylindrical columns, one from the center of the earth to the equator and the second perpendicular from the axis to the 60th parallel (**Figure 1.7**). The disk at the pole has a tiny mass, but both the velocity and distance from the axis are 0, so the centrifugal force is 0. The column to the equator is the earth's radius in length, and the easterly velocity increases from 0 at the center of the earth to a maximum of around 1,040 miles per hour at the equator. This means that the total centrifugal force on the column is quite large. Between the pole and equator there will be a steady increase in centrifugal force. We see this at the 60th parallel where the column would be half the earth's radius in length and the velocity would be half that at the equator. This column experiences a much smaller centrifugal force.

Newton noted that these outward centrifugal forces counteract the inward pull of gravity, so the net inward force decreases progressively from the pole to the equator. The column from the center of the earth to the equator thus spreads outward slightly due to the decreased inward force. A similar column from the center of the earth to the pole experiences zero centrifugal force and hence does not have this slight outward spread. Slicing the earth in half from pole to pole would then reveal an ellipse with a slightly shorter polar radius and slightly longer equatorial radius (**Figure 1.8**). If we rotate this ellipse 180° about its polar axis, we obtain a three-dimensional solid that we call an **oblate ellipsoid**. The oblate ellipsoid is important to us because parallels are not spaced equally as on a sphere, but vary slightly in spacing from the pole to the equator. This is shown in **Figure 1.9**, a cross-section of a greatly flattened oblate ellipsoid. Notice that near the pole the ellipse curves less than near the equator. We say that on an oblate ellipsoid the **radius of curvature** is greatest at the pole and smallest at the equator. The north-south distance between two points on the surface equals the radius of curvature times the angular difference between them. The distance between two points one-degree apart in latitude near the pole will thus be greater than two points one-degree apart near the equator. This means that the spacing of parallels decreases slightly from the pole to the equator.

Around 1700, scientific expeditions to Ecuador and Finland measured the length of a degree of latitude at the equator and near the Arctic Circle, proving Newton correct. These lengths allowed the semi-major and semi-minor axes of the oblate ellipsoid to be computed, giving about a 15 mile difference between the two, only 1/3rd of one percent.

Figure 1.11 Horizontal control point marker cemented in the ground.

During the 19th century, people with better surveying equipment measured the length of a degree of latitude on different continents. They found from these measurements that slightly different oblate ellipsoids varying by only a few hundred meters in axis length best fit the measurements. **Table 1.2** is a list of these, along with their areas of usage. The **Clarke 1866 ellipsoid** is of particular interest, since it was the best fit for North America and hence was used as the basis for parallels on topographic and other maps produced in Canada, Mexico, and the United States from the late 1800s to about twenty years ago.

By the 1980s, vastly superior surveying equipment coupled with millions of observations of **satellite orbits** allowed us to determine oblate

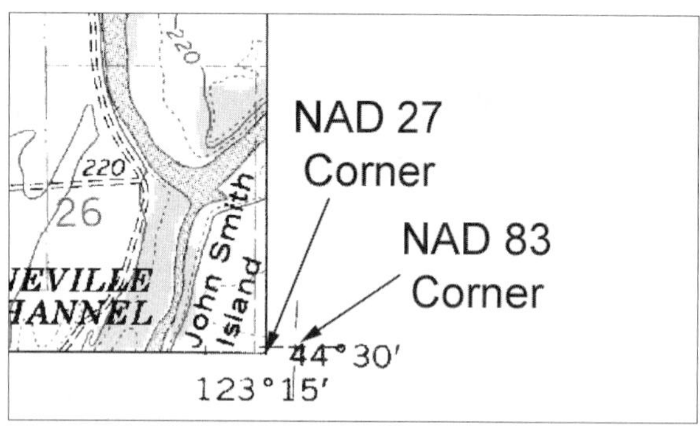

Figure 1.12 Southeast corner of the Corvallis, Oregon, topographic map showing the difference between its NAD 27 and NAD 83 position.

ellipsoids that are excellent average fits for the entire earth. The most recent of these is called the **World Geodetic System of 1984 (WGS 84)**. You'll see in Table 1.2 that the WGS 84 ellipsoid has an equatorial radius of 6378.137 kilometers (3964.038 miles) and a polar radius of 6356.752 kilometers (3950.747 miles). The WGS 84 ellipsoid is what we now use as the basis for latitude and longitude on topographic and similar maps throughout the world.

The equatorial and polar radii of the WGS 84 ellipsoid also are what we need to calculate the radius and circumference of a sphere that best fits the ellipsoid. We find the radius of a sphere that is equal in surface area to that of the WGS 84 ellipsoid. The computations involved are moderately complex and best left to a short computer program, but the result is a sphere of radius 6,371 km (3959.6 miles) and circumference 40,030 km or 24,907 statute miles.

GEODETIC COORDINATES

Geodetic Latitude and Longitude

We call latitude on an oblate ellipsoid **geodetic latitude**. This must differ from geographic latitude on a sphere due to the unequal spacing of parallels on the ellipsoid. Geodetic latitude is defined as the angle made by a line perpendicular to the ellipsoid surface at the parallel and the horizontal equator line (**Figure 1.10**). Lines perpendicular to the ellipsoidal surface only pass through the center of the earth at the poles and equator.

Defining geodetic latitude in this way means that geographic and geodetic latitude are identical only at 0° and 90°. Everywhere else geodetic latitude is slightly greater than the corresponding geographic latitude, as shown in **Table 1.3**. Notice that the difference between geodetic and geographic latitude increases in a symmetrical fashion from zero at the poles and equator to a maximum of just over 1/8th of a degree at 45°.

USE OF GEODETIC COORDINATES ON MAPS

You will always find parallels and meridians of geodetic latititude and longitude on detailed maps of small areas that we call large-scale maps (see the next chapter for further information on map scale.) This is done to make the map a very close approximation to the size and shape of the piece of the ellipsoidal earth that it represents. To see the perils of not doing this, you only need to examine one-degree quadrilaterals at the equator and pole, one ranging from 0° to 1° and the second from 89° to 90° in latitude.

You can see in **Table D.2** (in Appendix D) that the ground distance between these pairs of parallels on the WGS 84 ellipsoid is 68.703 and 69.407 statute miles, respectively. If the equatorial quadrilateral is mapped at a scale such that it is 100 inches high, the polar quadrilateral mapped at the same scale will be 101 inches long. If we mapped both quadrilaterals using the equal surface area sphere having 69.2 miles per degree, both maps would be 100.7 inches long. Having both maps several tenths of an inch longer or shorter than they should really be is an unacceptably large error for maps used to make accurate measurements of distance, direction, and area.

To further understand the use of geodetic coordinates on large-scale maps, we must first look at the collection of very accurate control points upon which all other map data are referenced. Surveyors determine the precise geodetic latitude and longitude of **horizontal control points** spread across the landscape. You may have seen a **control point monument** like **Figure 1.11** on the ground on top of a hill or other prominent feature. From the 1920s to the early 1980s these control points were surveyed relative to the surface of the Clarke 1866 ellipsoid, together forming what was called the **North American Datum of 1927 (NAD 27)**. Topographic maps, nautical and aeronautical charts,

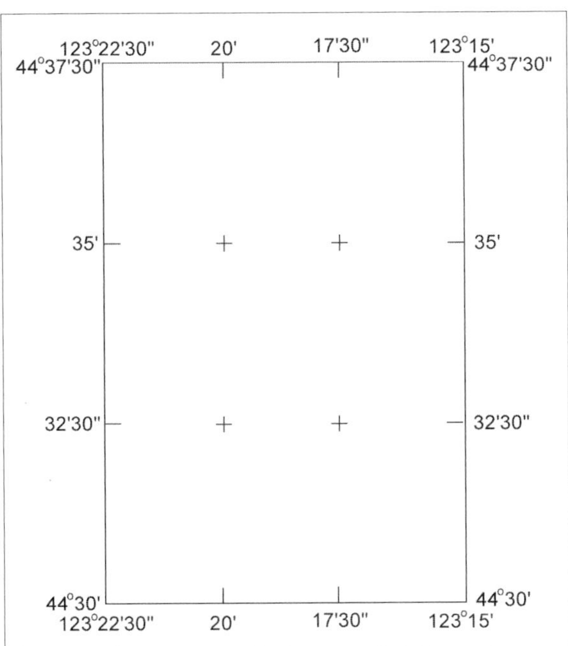

Figure 1.13. Graticule ticks on the Corvallis, Oregon, 7.5-minute topographic map.

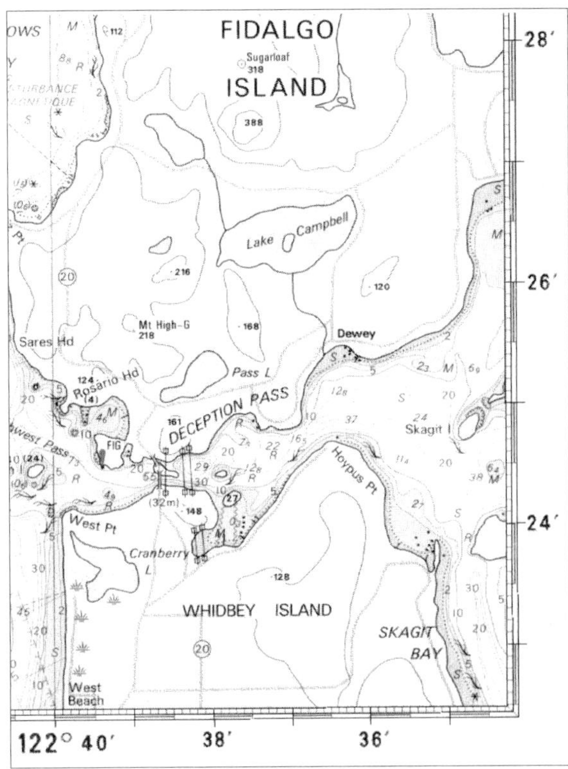

Figure 1.14 Graticule bars on the edges of a nautical chart segment..

and many other large-scale maps of this time period had graticule lines or ticks based on this datum. For example, the southeast corner of the Corvallis, Oregon, topographic map first published in 1969 (**Figure 1.12**) has a NAD 27 latitude and longitude of 44°30'N, 123°15'W.

By the early 1980s, better knowledge of the earth's shape and size and far better surveying methods led to the creation of a new horizontal reference datum, the **North American Datum of 1983** (**NAD 83**). The NAD 27 control points were corrected for surveying errors where required, then were added to thousands of more recently acquired points. The geodetic latitudes and longitudes of all these points were determined relative to the **Geodetic Reference System of 1980** (**GRS 80**) ellipsoid, which is essentially identical to the WGS 84 ellipsoid.

The change of horizontal reference datum meant that the geodetic coordinates for control points across the continent changed slightly in 1983, and this change had to be shown on large-scale maps published earlier but still in use. On topographic maps like Figure 1.12 the new position of the map corner is shown by a dashed "plus" sign. Many times the shift is in the 100 meter range and must be taken into account when plotting geodetic latitudes and longitudes obtained from GPS receivers and other modern position finding devices on older maps.

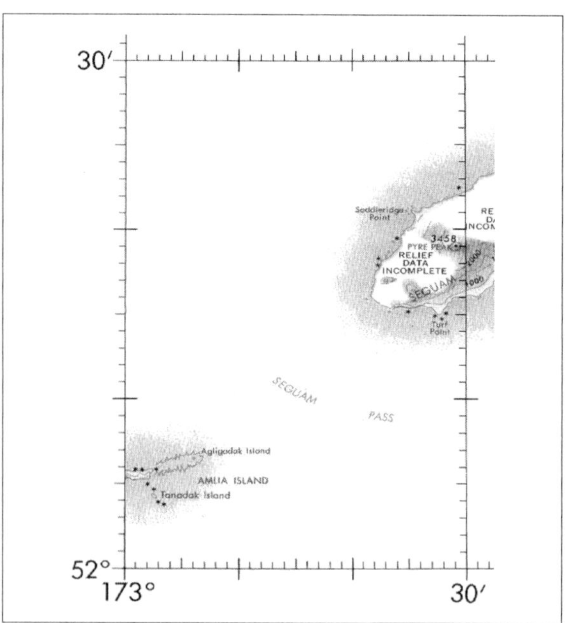

Figure 1.15 Graticule ticks on a small segment of an aeronautical chart.

USE OF GEOGRAPHIC COORDINATES ON MAPS

World or continental maps such as globes and world atlas sheets usually are based on the spherical earth. There are several reasons for this. Prior to using digital computers to make these types of maps numerically, it was much easier to construct them from geographic coordinates. Equally important, the differences in the plotted positions of geographic and corresponding geodetic parallels become negligible on wall-map-sized world maps.

You can see this by looking again at Table 1.3. Earlier we saw that the maximum difference between geographic and geodetic latitude is 0.128 degrees at the 45th parallel. Imagine drawing parallels at 45° and 45.128° on a map scaled at one inch per degree of latitude. The two parallels will be drawn a very noticeable 0.128" apart. Now imagine drawing the parallels on a map scaled at one inch per 10 degrees of latitude. The two parallels will now be drawn 0.013" apart, a barely noticeable difference. This scale corresponds to a world wall map approximately 18 in. high and 36 in. wide.

GRATICULE APPEARANCE ON MAPS

Parallels and meridians are shown in different ways on our major types of large-scale maps. Topographic maps in the United States have **tick marks** showing the location of the gratcule. All U.S. Geological Survey 7.5-minute topographic maps, for example, have graticule ticks at 2.5-minute intervals of latitude and longitude (**Figure 1.13**). The full latitude and longitude is printed in each corner,

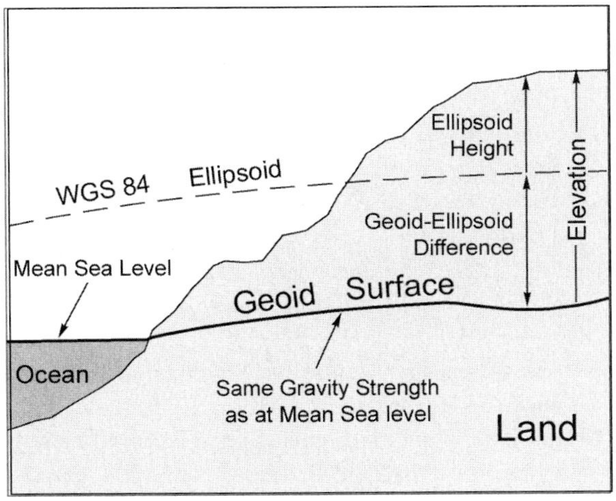

Figure 1.16 The geoid is the surface where gravity is the same as at mean sea level. Elevations traditionally have been measured relative to the geoid, but modern GPS-determined elevations are relative to the WGS 84 ellipsoid.

but only the minutes and seconds of the intermediate edge ticks are shown. Note the four "+" signs used for the interior 2.5-minute graticule ticks.

The graticule is shown in a different way on nautical charts (**Figure 1.14**). Alternating white and dark bars spaced at the same increment of latitude and longitude ring the edge of the chart. Due to the convergence of meridians, the vertical bars on the left and right edges of the chart showing equal increments of latitude are longer than the horizontal bars at the top and bottom. Notice the more closely spaced ticks beside each bar, placed every tenth of a minute on the chart in Figure 1.14. These ticks are used to more precisely find the latitude and longitude of mapped features.

Aeronautical charts contain a third type of graticule. The chart segment for a portion of the Aleutian Islands in Alaska (**Figure 1.15**) shows that parallels and meridians are drawn at 30 minute latitude and longitude intervals. Ticks are placed at 1 minute increments along each graticule line, allowing features to be located easily to within a fraction of a minute.

THE EARTH AS A GEOID

When we treat the earth as a smooth sphere or oblate ellipsoid, we neglect mountain ranges, ocean trenches, and other surface features that have vertical relief. There is justification for doing this, as the earth's surface is truly smooth when we compare the surface undulations to the earth's 7,919-mile (12,742km) diameter. The greatest relief variation is the approximately 12.3 mile difference between the summit of Mt. Everest (29,035ft or 8,852m) and the deepest point in the Mariana Trench (36,192ft or 11,034m). This vertical difference is immense on our human scale, but it is only 1/640th of the earth's diameter. If we look at the difference between the earth's average land height (2,755ft or 840m) and ocean depth (12,450ft or 3,795m), the average roughness is only 1/2,750th of the diameter. It has been said that if the earth were reduced to the diameter of a bowling ball, it would be as smooth as the bowling ball!

The earth's global-scale smoothness aside, knowing the elevations and depths of features is very important to us. Defining locations by their geodetic latitude, longitude, and elevation gives you a simple way to collect elevation data and display this information on maps. The top of Mt. Everest, for example, is located at (27°59'N, 86°56'E, 29035ft.), but what is this elevation relative to?

Elevations and depths are measured relative to what is called a vertical reference datum. The traditional datum used for land elevations is **mean sea level (MSL)**(**Figure 1.16**). Surveyors define MSL as the average of all low and high tides at a particular starting location* over a 19 year lunar period called a **Metonic cycle**.** Early surveyors chose this datum because of the measurement technology of the day. Surveyors could determine elevation by making gravity measurements at different locations on the landform and relating them to the **strength of gravity** at the point used to de-

* *The starting point for the North American Vertical Datum of 1988 (NAVD 88) is a tide gauge at Point-au-Pere, Quebec, Canada.*

* **The* **Metonic cycle** *is the 19 year cycle of the lunar phases and days of the year.*

fine MSL. Gravity differences translate into elevation differences. Later surveyors learned to use the **method of leveling**, where elevations are determined relative to the point where mean sea level is defined, using horizontally aligned telescopes and vertically aligned leveling rods.

Mean sea level is easy to determine along coastlines, but what about inland locations? What is needed is to extend mean sea level across the land. Imagine that mean sea level is extended under the continental land masses, which is the same thing as extending a surface having the same strength of gravity as mean sea level (see Figure 1.16). This imaginary equal gravity surface doesn't form a perfect ellipsoid, however, because differences in earth density affect gravity's pull at different locations. It is this slightly undulating approximation of the earth that we call a **geoid**. The geoid rises above and falls below the oblate ellipsoid surface in an irregular fashion.

The mean sea level datum is so convenient that it is used to determine elevations around the world and is the base for the elevation data found on nearly all maps. But be careful. Better measurements of the geoid have led to updated vertical reference datums. In the United States, for example, the **National Geodetic Vertical Datum of 1929 (NGVD 29)** was adjusted with new data to create the **North American Vertical Datum of 1988 (NAVD 88)**. Be sure you know what vertical datum your map is based upon.

The development of the **Global Positioning System (GPS)** has created a second option for measuring elevation. Here it is easier to measure elevations relative to the surface of the WGS 84 oblate ellipsoid centered at the center of the earth than from the mean sea level geoid surface. Therefore, you must convert raw satellite data to the sea level datum before you can use it with existing maps. You do this by adding or subtracting the **geoid-ellipsoid difference** (Figure 1.16) at a point from the ellipsoid height measured by the GPS receiver.

SELECTED READINGS

Greenhood, D., *Mapping* (Chicago: University of Chicago Press, 1964).

La Condamine, C.M. de. *A Succinct Abridgement of a Voyage Made within the Inland Parts of South America as it was Read to the Academy of Science, Paris, April 28,1745.* London, 1747.

Maling, D.H. *Coordinate Systems and Map Projections,* 2nd.ed. (New York: Pergamon Press, 1992).

Maupertius, P.L.M. de. *The Figure of the Earth Determined from Observations Made by Order of the French King, at the Polar Circle.* Translation. London, 1738.

Meade, B.K., "Latitude, Longitude, and Ellipsoidal Height Changes NAD-27 to Predicted NAD-83," *Surveying and Mapping*, 43 (1983), pp. 65-71.

Robinson, A.H. et al., Chapter 4 ("Basic Geodesy") in *Elements of Cartography,* 6th ed. (New York: John Wiley & Sons, 1995).

Smith, J.R., *Basic Geodesy. An Introduction to the History and Concepts of Modern Geodesy without Mathematics* (Rancho Cordova, CA: Landmark Enterprises, 1988).

Snyder, J.P., *Map Projections - A Working Manual,* U.S. Geological Survey Professional Paper 1395 (Washington D.C.: U.S. Government Printing Office, 1987).

Sobel, D., *Longitude: The True Story of a Lone Genius Who Solved the Greatest Scientific Problem of His Time.* (New York: Walker & Co., 1995).

Wallis, H.M. and A.H. Robinson, eds. *Cartographical Innovations* (London: Map Collector Publications, 1987).

Wilford, J.N., *The Mapmakers* (New York: Alfred A. Knopf, 1981).

U.S. Department of the Army, Chapter 4 ("Grids") in *Map Reading*, FM 3-25.26 (Washington D.C.: Department of the Army, 2001).

CHAPTER TWO

MAP SCALE

EXPRESSING SCALE

Representative Fraction
Word Statement
Scale Bar

LARGE AND SMALL-SCALE MAPS

CONVERTING SCALE

DETERMINING MAP SCALE

Determining Map Scale from a Known Terrestrial Feature
Determining Map Scale from Reference Material
Determining Map Scale from the Spacing of Parallels and Meridians

SELECTED READINGS

"How much further?"
"We've got a hairpin, a thumbnail, and a breathmint to go, according to this map...."
—Erma Bombeck

2

CHAPTER TWO

MAP SCALE

Maps are usually smaller in size than the environment they represent. The amount of size reduction is known as the scale of the map. To use maps effectively, you'll need to convert measurements from map units to ground units. As you might expect, an understanding of map scale is central to performing this task. In this chapter, we'll explore the map-scale abilities needed to become a skilled map user.

EXPRESSING SCALE

Map scale is always given in the form: "This distance on the map represents this distance on the earth's surface." The relationship between map and ground distance can be expressed in three ways—as a representative fraction, a word statement, or a scale bar.

Representative Fraction

A common way to describe scale is with a **representative fraction** (**RF**).You may think of this fraction as the ratio between map and ground distance. An RF is written either as 1/x or 1:x. The numerator is always 1 and represents map distance, while the denominator (x) indicates distance on the ground in the same units of measurement as the map distance. Therefore, 1/x = map distance / ground distance, and the scale denominator x = ground distance / map distance.

The advantage of having identical units on the top and bottom of the fraction is that map measurements may be made in centimeters, inches, or whatever distance unit you choose. For example, an RF of 1/24,000 or 1:24,000 means that the scale reduction is 24,000 to 1. One inch on the map represents 24,000 inches on the ground, one centimeter on the map represents 24,000 centimeters on the ground, and so on.

Word Statement

Another familiar way to express scale is to use a descriptive **word statement**. We express the scale as so many "centimeters to a kilometer" or "inches to the mile" but also as so many "miles to the inch." An RF of 1:24,000 can be expressed as the word statement "one inch to 2,000 feet," while an RF of 1:100,000 could be expressed as "one centimeter to one kilometer." Word statements for commonly used map scales are given in the box below, along with a type of map published at this scale.

Note that some word statements are only close approximations to the RF and should not be used in mathematical calculations. An RF of 1:250,000 is really 3.9457 miles to the inch, but the word statement is much easier to remember if rounded to 4 miles.

At first it may be confusing to find that one map indicates scale as "one centimeter to one kilometer" and another as "four miles to one inch." This lack of consistency should cause little trouble, however, since the smaller unit of measurement (inches or centimeters) always refers to the map while the larger measurement unit refers to the ground.

Scale Bar

A third way to show map scale is to use a **scale bar** (also called a bar scale). The simplest of these looks like a small ruler printed on the map. You'll usually read this scale from left to right, beginning at 0. Sometimes the scale bar is extended to the left of the zero point, using smaller markings (**Figure 2.1**). This allows you to determine distance not only in whole units but also in fractions of units such as tenths of a mile or kilometer.

The marks on the scale bar are arranged so as to provide whole numbers of kilometers or miles of ground distance. This means that the marks won't represent whole numbers of centimeters or inches—there will almost always be some fraction left over. In other words, although the scale bar looks like a ruler, its markings will not coincide with those on your ruler. Rare exceptions would be a scale of 1:100,000, since at this scale one kilometer on the ground would be exactly one centimeter on the map, and 1:63,360, since one inch on the map is exactly one mile on the ground.

The scale bar has three features that make it especially useful. First, if the map is enlarged or reduced using some method of photocopying or screen display, the scale bar changes size in direct proportion to the physical size of the map. The word statement and representative fraction, on the other hand, are incorrect when the map changes size. Second, both kilometers and miles can be shown conveniently on the same bar scale (see bottom of Figure 2.1). And finally, the scale bar is easy to use when figuring distances on a map, as we'll show you in Chapter 11.

On maps showing the whole globe, the scale may vary significantly from one part of the map

Table 2.1 Different Ways Of Expressing Map Scale

RF	Word Statement	Map Type	
1:1200	1 inch to 100 feet	Engineering Plan	large scale
1:4800	1 inch to 400 feet	Surveyor's Plat	
1:24,000	1 inch to 2000 feet	Topographic Map	
1:63,360	1 inch to 1 mile	Topographic Map	
1:100,000	1 cm to 1 kilometer	Topographic Map	
1:250,000	~4 miles to 1 inch	Topographic Map	
1:500,000	1 cm to 5 kilometers	Aeronautical Chart	medium scale
1:1,000,000	~16 miles to 1 inch	Aeronautical Chart	
1:10,000,000	1 cm to 100 kilometers	Continental Maps	
1:100,000,000	~1600 miles to 1 inch	World Maps	small scale

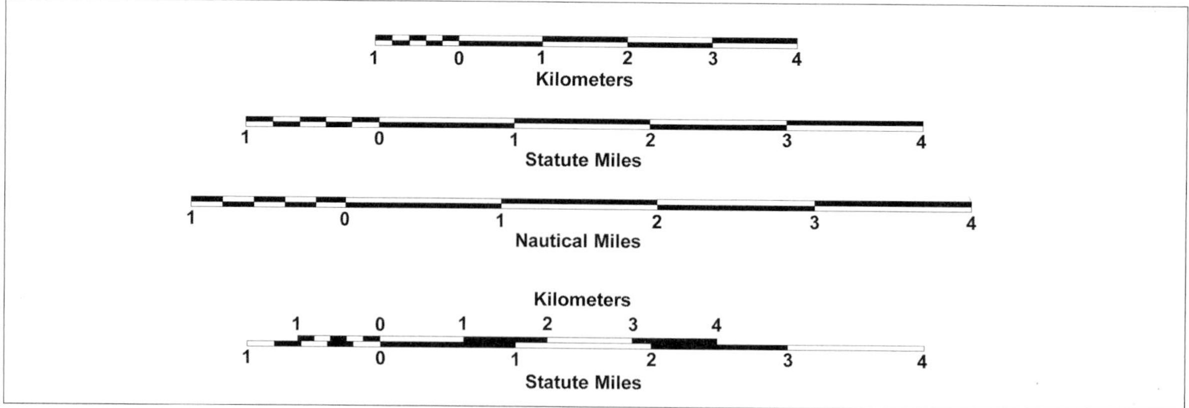

Figure 2.1 Scale bars in kilometers, statute miles, and nautical miles, taken from maps identical in scale. Note the scale bar extensions to the left of the 0 point that are used when making more precise distance measurements.

to another. In such cases, the map maker sometimes replaces the standard scale bar with a variable scale bar. An example of this type of scale bar, taken from a Mercator world map projection, is shown in **Figure 2.2**. Notice that the scale changes systematically in the north-south direction. To use such a scale bar, first decide at what latitude you want to use the map scale, and then find the scale bar for this latitude. In effect, you are working with a scale bar that is stretched to match the local map scale.

LARGE AND SMALL-SCALE MAPS

Since map distance is always stated in the numerator of the RF as 1, it follows that the smaller the denominator (the closer to a 1 to 1 ratio), the larger the scale will be. Thus, a map scale of 1:20,000 is twice as large as a scale of 1:40,000. If that sounds backwards, remember that the terms **large-scale** and **small-scale maps** come from the numerical value of the representative fraction 1/x. The number 1/1,200 is much larger than 1/100,000,000.

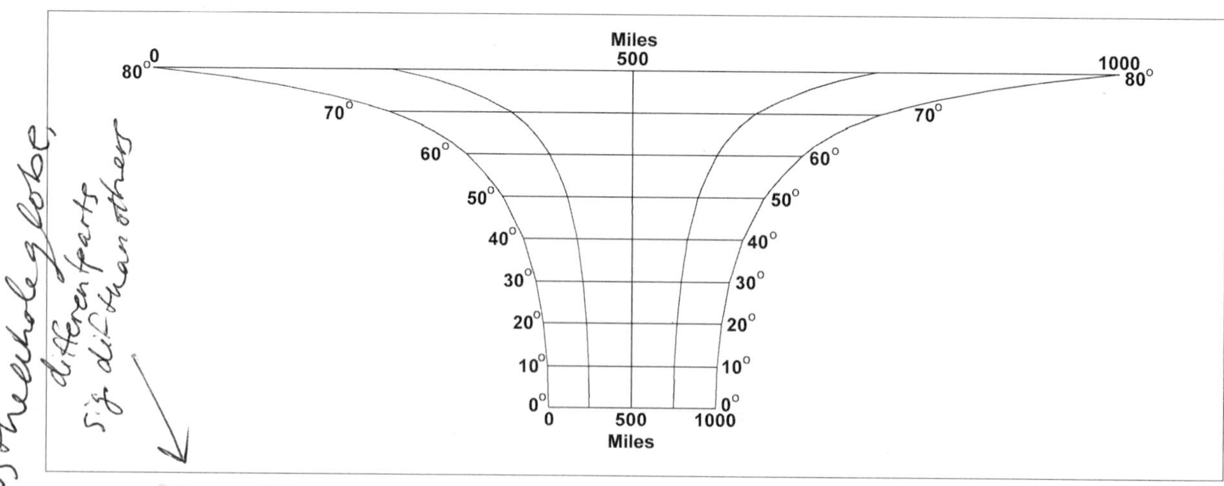

Figure 2.2 Variable scale bar such as seen on a Mercator world map projection.

Thus an engineering plan is a large-scale map, and a page-size world map is a small-scale map.

Common as it is to classify maps by their scales, there is no general agreement as to where the class limits should be set. If we sort maps into two groups—large and small-scale—then 1:1,000,000 would be a likely dividing point between the two. Atlas, textbook, and wall maps of continental coverage would then fall into the small-scale group, while topographic, cadastral, and other maps would be in the large-scale class. If a more detailed three-way grouping is used, maps with scales of 1:1,000,000 and smaller (16 or more miles to the inch) would probably be classed as small-scale and those of 1:250,000 and larger (four or less miles to the inch) as large-scale. Maps ranging in scale between these extremes would then be referred to as medium-scale. The last two columns in **Table 2.1** show the progression of scales from large through medium to small along with the types of maps associated with these scales. Any such classification, of course, is arbitrary and shouldn't be given meaning beyond the organizational convenience it provides.

When you choose a map, be sure to note whether it is a large, medium, or small-scale product. Check that the features of interest to you are displayed at the correct scale for your purposes. If you need to study a small ground area in great detail with little generalization of features, you need a large-scale map. If you are more interested in a generalized presentation of a large area like a state, country, continent, or the entire globe, you need to choose a small-scale map.

CONVERTING SCALE

If the map maker has been at all conscientious, you will find the scale depicted on the map somewhere. At times, however, it may be in the wrong form to best serve your purpose. Therefore, you may need to make conversions between a word statement, RF, and scale bar. Scale conversions are based on applying common distance equivalents such as 1 foot = 12 inches, 1 statute mile = 5,280 feet, 1 statute mile = 63,360 inches, or 1 kilometer = 100,000 centimeters. **Table D.1** in Appendix D is a more complete list of English and metric distance equivalents.

You may, for instance, have a map with a word statement and wish to know the RF. The first thing to remember with any scale conversion is that the ratio 1/x is always map distance (numerator) to ground distance (denominator). Suppose that the word statement is three inches to 10 miles. In converting to an RF, the ratio is 1/x = 3 in./10 mi. But you can't have an RF with different units in its numerator and denominator. So you must convert miles to inches—no problem if you remember that there are 63,360 inches in a statute mile. Thus: 1/x = 3 in./10 mi. = 3 in./(10 mi. × 63,360 in./mi.) = 3/633,600. Remember, too, that the numerator of an RF is always 1. So in this case you will also have to reduce the numerator from 3 to 1 by dividing numerator and denominator by 3 so that the RF is 1/211,200.

Sometimes you may find yourself in the opposite situation. You know the RF but want to know how many miles to the inch or inches to the mile the map scale represents. If it is a miles to the inch word statement that you need, then you merely divide the denominator of the RF by the number of inches in a mile, or 63,360. For example, an RF of 1:500,000 is converted to a "miles to the inch" word statement by dividing 63,360 in./mi. into 500,000 so that the word statement is "7.89 miles to the inch." Similarly, if you want to know kilometers to the centimeter, divide the denominator of the RF by the number of centimeters in a kilometer, or 100,000.

If it is inches to the mile that you wish, divide the denominator of the RF into 63,360. If you want centimeters to the kilometer, divide the RF denominator into 100,000. The above RF of 1:500,000 would then be expressed as 63,360/500,000 or "0.127 inches to the mile," or as 100,000/500,000 or "0.2 centimeters to the kilometer."

Sometimes you may want to create a scale bar from a word statement or representative fraction. Imagine that you have a map at a scale of 3/4 mile to an inch, or 1:47,520. Your scale bar should have mile increments, because this will facilitate ground distance measurements. Since an inch represents 3/4 mile, 1/3 inch represents 1/4 mile, and each mile covers 4/3 inches on the map. So you would mark off 4/3 inch intervals on your scale bar (**Figure 2.3**).

You will have no trouble doing this if your ruler is marked with one-third inch increments. But not all rulers are, so you may have to estimate where one-third of an inch is on your ruler. When you make scale bars, you will often run into this problem of trying to divide a line into segments that aren't found on your ruler. One thing you can do is to fall back on an old trick of plane geometry concerning the relation of parallel lines to equal distance increments.

Let's use our previous example and assume that you want to make a scale bar with 4/3 inches to a mile. First you must decide how long to make the scale bar. Because it would be convenient if your scale showed an even number of inches as well as miles, keep adding 4/3 inches until you come up with a whole number of inches. (If you don't arrive at a whole number within a reasonable amount of time, abandon this method and choose an arbitrary length for your scale bar.) If you add 4/3 + 4/3 + 4/3, you get four inches, which represents three miles. Since four inches is a good length for your scale bar, draw a four-inch horizontal line (Figure 2.3).

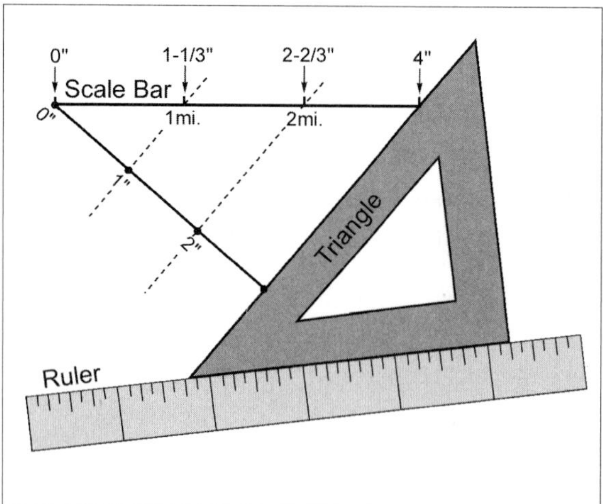

Figure 2.3 A scale bar is divided so that the ground units are whole numbers. The scale bar can be divided into equal segments using a triangle and straightedge. (Caution: This scale bar was not actually drawn to scale.)

Now draw a second line at an acute angle from the left end of your first line. It doesn't matter exactly at what angle you draw it, but an angle of less than 75 degrees will be most convenient. Next, starting at the left edge, mark off three equal divisions on this second line at one-inch intervals.

Now place a right triangle so that its hypotenuse touches the right ends of both lines, and place a ruler along the bottom of the triangle. Slide the triangle along the ruler to the 2" mark on the second line, and draw a line upward to the first line. Slide the triangle to the 1" mark on the second line, and draw another upward line to the first line. What you have done is to draw a series of parallel lines that neatly divide your scale bar into thirds. Since your original line was four inches long, each of those thirds is 4/3 inches.

DETERMINING MAP SCALE

It's good to know that, no matter what sort of map scale you encounter, you can change it to the type of scale you want. But what if you come across a map with no scale depicted at all, or an RF that seems incorrect because the map appears to have been enlarged or reduced? This happens more often than you might expect. You may want to know the scale of a photocopied portion of a map on which no scale has been shown, for instance.

You can figure out the map scale if you know the ground distance between any two points on the map. You just measure the distance between these same two points on the map. The ratio of map to ground distance, in the same units of measurement, will be the map's scale. How, though, do you find the ground distance between the two points? One method is to use some terrestrial feature whose length is known.

Determining Map Scale from a Known Terrestrial Feature

Some features have standard lengths. If you can identify one of these on your map, you can easily figure out the map scale. A regulation U.S. football field, for example, is 100 yards long. If the map distance of the field is 0.5 inch, then 0.5 inch on the map represents 100 yards on the ground. To determine the map scale, you merely convert yards to inches and reduce the numerator to 1 by solving the RF ratio:

$$1/x = 0.5 \text{ in} / (100 \text{ yd} \times 3 \text{ ft/yd} \times 12 \text{ in/ft}) = 0.5 \text{ in} / 3{,}600 \text{ in}$$

$$x = 3600 \text{ in} / 0.5 \text{ in} = 7{,}200$$

This gives an RF of 1/7,200.

Determining Map Scale from Reference Material

If you can't find a feature of standard length on your map, you can still determine scale if you turn to other reference material, such as gazetteers, distance logs, atlases, or other maps of similar scale. From these sources, you should be able to find out the distance of something on your map—the length of a lake, for instance, or the distance between two prominent features such as cities. With this information in hand, you can compute the map scale as you did above when you used a feature of standard length.

You can follow the same procedure to determine the RF of a small-scale world map. Here you can make use of the fact that the earth's circumference is approximately 25,000 statute miles (we saw in Chapter 1 that the actual figure is 24,907 statute miles). If, for example, the equator extends fully across an eight-inch wide textbook page, you can find the map's RF as follows:

$$1/x = 8 \text{ in} / (25{,}000 \text{ mi} \times 63{,}360 \text{ in/mi})$$

$$x = 25{,}000 \times 63{,}360 / 8 = 198{,}000{,}000$$

This gives a RF of 1/198,000,000 and a word statement of 1 inch to 3,125 miles (198,000,000/63,360). Remember that this is only the scale at the equator, since the scale may be much larger or smaller at other places on a small-scale map.

Another procedure is to determine the RF from the length of a feature measured on a reference map of known scale. For example, on a map with a scale of 1:100,000 you measure the distance between two road intersections as 0.7 cm, and as 0.5 cm on your map. Since the ratio of measured distances equals the ratio of the two RFs, you can use the proportion:

$$\frac{1/100{,}000}{1/x} = \frac{0.7\text{cm}}{0.5\text{cm}}$$

This equation reduces to:

$$x / 100{,}000 = 0.7\text{cm} / 0.5\text{cm}$$
$$x = 140{,}000$$

$$RF = 1/140{,}000.$$

Determining Map Scale from the Spacing of Parallels and Meridians

It isn't always convenient or even possible to find a feature such as a football field or a lake of known length on your map. But on many maps, especially those of small scale, parallels and meridians are shown. Thus, you can determine scale by finding the ground distance between these lines.

Finding the ground distance between parallels is quite simple, since a degree of latitude varies only slightly from pole to equator. On a small-scale world map, the earth is assumed to be a sphere so that parallels are equally spaced at 69.2 miles per degree of latitude.

For large-scale maps, an ellipsoidal approximation to the earth's shape has been used. You saw in Chapter 1 that on the WGS 84 ellipsoid, the first degree of latitude is 110.567 kilometers (68.703

statute miles) north or south of the equator, while the 89th parallel adjacent to the North or South Pole is 111.699 kilometers (69.407 miles) from the pole. Thus, the variation in a degree of latitude from equator to pole is only 1.132 km. or 0.704 mile. This difference is so small that for many small-scale maps it can be ignored. We say that a degree of latitude is equivalent to a degree of longitude at the equator, which is 69.2 miles, regardless of where on earth the degree of latitude is found. However, this difference must be taken into account when determining the scale of large-scale maps like topographic sheets. (For lengths of a degree of latitude on the WGS 84 ellipsoid, refer to **Table D.2** in Appendix D.)

In order to use this information in determining map scale, you must be able to find at least two parallels on your map. Let's say that on a small-scale world map you find two parallels separated by two degrees of latitude and a map distance of five inches. To find the ground distance between these parallels, you multiply the number of degrees separating them by the length of a degree. Thus, 2 deg × 69.2 mi/deg = 138.4 miles. Now you can find the ratio between map distance and ground distance:

$$1/x = 5 \text{ in } / 138.4 \text{ miles}$$
$$= 5 \text{ in } / (138.4 \text{ mi} \times 63{,}360 \text{ in/mi}).$$

This gives an RF of 1/1,753,800 or a word statement of 27.7 miles to the inch.

Unfortunately, two parallels are not always shown on a map. You can still compute the map scale, however, if two meridians are shown. The complication is that, because meridians converge at the poles, the distance between a degree of longitude varies from 111.3 kilometers (69.2 miles) along the equator to 0 kilometers at either pole (see **Table D.3** in Appendix D). This means that the distance between meridians, called the longitudinal distance, depends on the mapped region's latitude. Luckily, there's a simple functional relationship between latitude and longitudinal distance: longitudinal distance decreases by the cosine of the latitude. To find the longitudinal distance for a degree of longitude at a given latitude, multiply the length of a degree of latitude (111.3 kilometers or 69.2 miles) by the cosine of the latitude. This relationship is written mathematically as:

$$\text{Longitudinal distance} = \cos(\text{latitude}) \times 111.3 \text{ km.}$$

or

$$\text{Longitudinal distance} = \cos(\text{latitude}) \times 69.2 \text{ miles.}$$

Now how can you use this equation to determine map scale? Although the procedure may at first seem complex, it is actually straightforward if viewed as a series of simple steps. You begin by measuring the map distance between two meridians. Suppose you find that meridians spanning one-half degree of longitude on the map are 10 inches apart. To determine ground distance between these two meridians, first find the latitude of the region on the map, then use your calculator to find the cosine of the latitude. Suppose the latitude is 45°N. In this case,

$$\text{Longitudinal distance} = \cos(45°) \times 69.2 \text{ mi.}$$
$$= 0.7071 \times 69.2$$
$$= 48.9 \text{ miles}$$

Thus, you know that one degree of longitude at 45°N covers a ground distance of 48.9 miles. But since the measured map distance spanned one-half rather than one degree of longitude, the ground distance in this problem would be half the computed value, or 0.5× 48.9 = 24.45 miles. You now have all the information necessary to find the map scale. Simply compute the ratio between map and ground distance:

$$1/x = 10 \text{ in.}/24.45 \text{ mi.}$$
$$= 10 \text{ in.}/(24.45 \text{ mi.} \times 63{,}360 \text{ in./mi.})$$
$$= 10 \text{ in.}/1{,}549{,}000 \text{ in.}$$

$$\text{RF} = 1/154{,}900.$$

SELECTED READINGS

Dickinson, G.C., *Maps and Air Photographs* (London: Edward Arnold Publishers, Ltd., 1969), pp. 99-107, 142-148.

Espenshade, E.B., "Mathematical Scale Problems," *Journal of Geography*, 50, 3 (March 1951), pp. 107-113.

Greenhood, D., *Mapping* (Chicago: University of Chicago Press, 1964), pp. 39-53, 180-184.

Hodgkiss, A.G., *Maps for Books and Theses* (New York: Pica Press, 1970), pp. 37-43, 169-170, 239-242.

Map Uses, Scales, and Accuracies for Engineering and Associated Purposes, ASCE Committee on Cartographic Surveying (New York: American Society of Civil Engineers, 1983).

Quattrochi, D.A., and Goodchild, M.F., *Scale in Remote Sensing and GIS* (Boca Raton, FL: Lewis Publishers, 1997).

Robinson, A.H., et al., *Elements of Cartography*, 6th ed. (New York: John Wiley & Sons, 1995).

U.S. Army, Chapter 4 ("Scale and Distance") in *Map Reading*, FM 21-26, Department of the Army Field Manual, 1969, pp. 4-1 to 4-4.

Gerhardus Mercator, inventor of the Mercator world map projection

CHAPTER THREE
MAP PROJECTIONS

Strike flat the thick rotundity o' th' world!
—William Shakespeare, King Lear

3

CHAPTER THREE
MAP PROJECTIONS

A map projection is a geometrical transformation of the earth's spherical or ellipsoidal surface onto a flat map surface. More has been written about map projections than all other facets of mapping and map use combined, yet people still find the subject to be the most bewildering aspect of map appreciation.

Many people readily admit that they don't understand map projections. This ignorance can have unfortunate consequences. For one thing, it hinders our ability to understand international relations in our global society. It also makes us easy prey for politicians, special interest groups, advertisers, and others who through ignorance or by design use map projections in potentially deceptive ways.

Incorrect use of map projections permeates our lives. An everyday example is major TV news programs using maps designed to serve navigational needs as backdrops for discussing world events. The majority of wall maps sold at retail outlets for home and office display are also of this navigational variety. It would be hard to make a worse choice of projection for either purpose.

What you need to know about projections is neither boring nor mathematically complicated. The secret is to look for similarities rather than focus on differences between projections. Many projections share common features. Once you recognize these, you can group the infinite variety of projections into a few types or families, each of which has a characteristic geometric distortion pattern. It's then quite simple to learn the special properties of interesting individual projections. Rather than trying to recognize a long list of projections by name, you should aim to gain a general understanding of the concepts and problems involved with each projection family.

Before we discuss these major families, we can clarify the whole issue of map projections with a discussion of the logic behind them. Why are projections necessary? We'll begin our discussion with globes, a form of map you have probably looked at since childhood. This familiarity makes it easy for us to compare globes with flat maps on projection surfaces.

GLOBES

Of all maps, globes give us the most realistic picture of the earth as a whole. Basic earth attributes such as distance, direction, shape, and area are preserved since the globe is the same scale everywhere (**Figure 3.1**). Globes have a number of disadvantages, however. They don't let you view all parts of the earth's surface simultaneously, nor are they very convenient. They are bulky and don't lend themselves to convenient handling and storage, especially as the size and weight increase. You can't carry globes around with you or stash them in the glove compartment of your car.

You wouldn't have these handling and storage problems if you used a baseball-sized globe. But such a globe would be of little practical value, since it would have a size reduction of approximately 1 to 125,000,000. Even a globe two feet in diameter (the size of a large desk model) still represents a 1 to 20,000,000 scale reduction. It would take a globe about 40 to 50 feet in diameter—the height of a four-story building! —to provide a map of the scale used for state highway maps. A globe nearly 180 feet in diameter would be required to provide a map of the same scale as the standard 1:24,000-scale topographic map series in the United States.

Figure 3.1 A typical world globe.

Another problem with globes is that the instruments and techniques that are suited for measuring distance, direction, and area on spherical surfaces are relatively difficult to use. Computations on a sphere are far more complex than computations on a plane surface. (For a demonstration of the relative difficulty of making distance computations from plane and spherical coordinates, see Chapter 11.)

Finally, globe construction is laborious and costly. High-speed printing presses have kept the cost of flat map reproduction to manageable levels but have not yet been developed to work with curved media. Therefore, globe construction is not suited to the volume of map production required for modern mapping needs.

It would be ideal if the earth's surface could be mapped undistorted onto a flat medium, such as a sheet of paper or computer monitor screen. Unfortunately, the earth is not what is known as a developable surface. In other words, it cannot be flattened without distorting such geometrical properties as direction, distance, area, and shape. The continuity of the earth's surface also must be violated. Thus, all flat maps geometrically distort reality. It is impossible to transform a spherical surface that curves away in every direction from every point into a plane surface that doesn't exhibit curvature in any direction from any point. This is the map projection problem. There is no true solution, only approximate solutions.

THE MAP PROJECTION PROCESS

The concept of map projections is somewhat more involved than is implied in the previous discussion. Not one but a series of geometrical transformations is required. The highly irregular earth surface is transformed initially into a much simpler three-dimensional surface, and then the three-dimensional surface is projected onto a plane. This progressive flattening of the earth's surface is illustrated in **Figure 3.2**.

The first step is to project the earth's irregular surface topography onto a more regular imaginary surface known as the **geoid.** This is the surface that would result if the average level of the world's oceans were extended under the continents. It serves as the datum, or starting reference surface, for elevation data on our maps (see Chapter 1 for more on the geoid).

The second step is to project the slightly undulating geoid onto the more regular **oblate ellipsoid** surface (see Chapter 1 for further information on the oblate ellipsoid). This new surface serves as the basis for the **geodetic control points** determined by surveyors and as the **datum** for the **geodetic latitude and longitude coordinates** found on maps. An additional step taken in making a small-scale flat map or globe is to mathematically transform geodetic coordinates into geographical coordinates on a sphere equal in surface area to the ellipsoid.

The third step involves projecting the ellipsoidal or spherical surface onto a plane surface using map projection equations that transform geodetic or geographic coordinates into planar (x,y) map coordinates. The greatest distortion of the earth's surface geometry occurs in this step.

CLASSIFYING MAP PROJECTIONS

Potentially, there are an infinite number of map projections, each of which is better suited for some uses than for others. How, then, do we go about distinguishing one projection from another? Our first step is to organize the unlimited variety of projections into a limited number of groups or families on the basis of shared attributes. Two approaches are revealing for those who use maps. One is to look at geometrical distortions in shape, area, direction, distance, and continuity. The other focuses on the nature of the surface used in constructing the projection—a factor central to understanding the pattern of spatial distortion over the map surface. The two approaches go hand in hand, since the map user is concerned, first, with what spatial properties are preserved and, second, with the pattern and extent of distortion.

Geometric Distortions On Map Projections

You can gain an idea of the types of geometric distortions that occur on map projections by comparing the **graticule** (latitude-longitude lines) on the projection surface with a globe. **Figure 3.3** shows how you might make this comparison. (In Figure 3.3, the drawing of a globe on the left is actually a map projection of a hemisphere.) Cartographers place the types of distortion you see on the map projection into the categories of continuity, distance, area, direction, shape, completeness, and preservation of correspondence realtions. Let's look at each of these types of distortion.

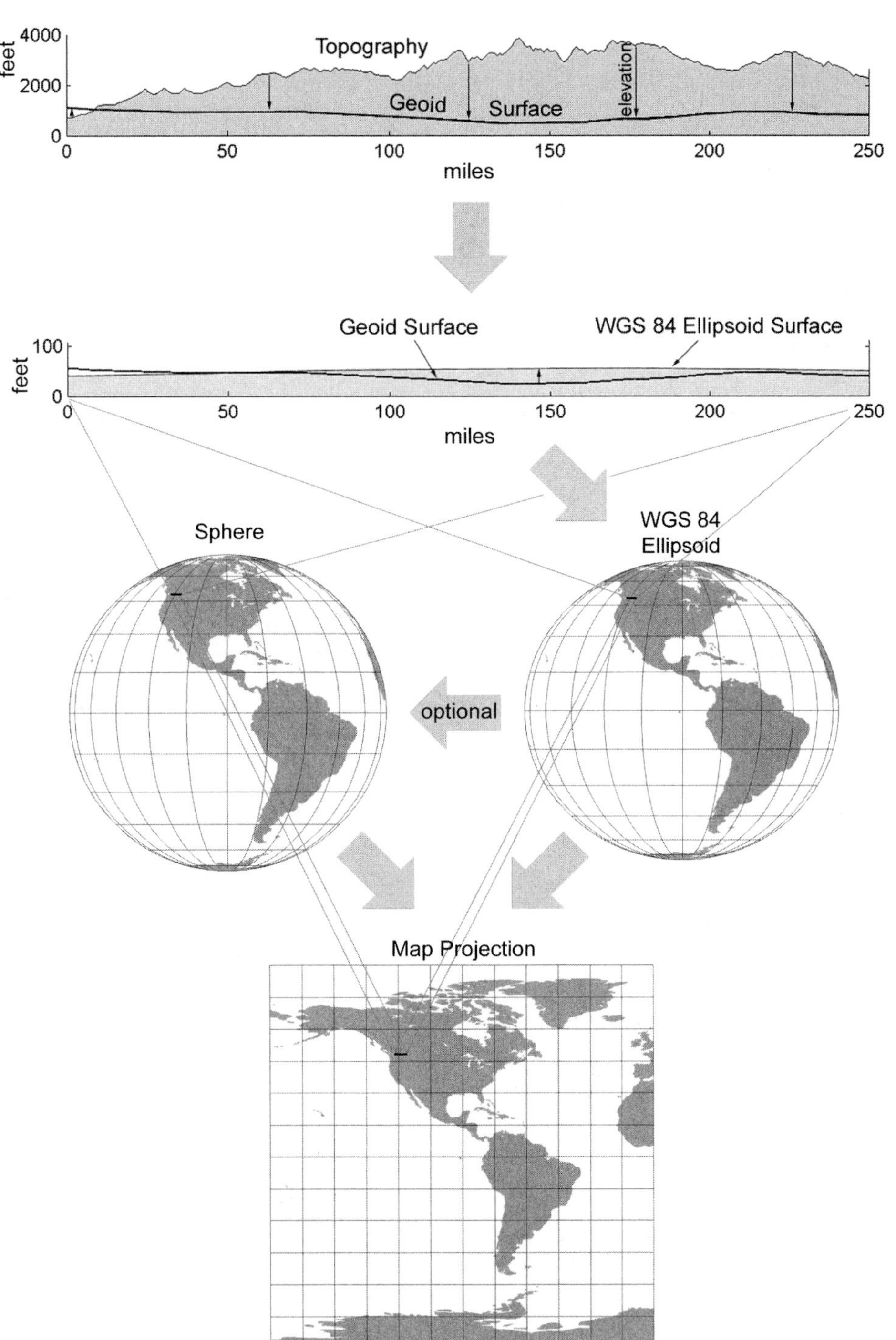

Figure 3.2 The mapping process involves a progressive flattening of the earth's irregular surface. Every point on the earth's surface is vertically lowered or raised so as to be on the geoid surface, with a land elevation or sea depth assigned to an adjusted point. The position on the geoid surface is then adjusted vertically upward or downward so as to be on the WGS 84 ellipsoid surface. The geodetic latitude and longitude of the point is now defined. Geodetic latitudes and longitudes may be converted in geographic coordinates for small-scale maps. Finally, the geodetic or geographic coordinates are transformed into planar (x,y) map projection surface coordinates.

Completeness

You'll find the most obvious geometric distortion on world maps that don't show the whole world. Such incomplete maps occur when the equations used for a map projection can't be applied to the entire range of latitude and longitude. The Mercator world map (Figure 3.18) is a classic example. Here the y coordinate for the north pole is infinity, so the map usually extends to only the 80th parallel north and south. The gnomonic projection (Figure 3.14) is a more extreme example, since it is limited mathematically to covering less than a hemisphere.

Correspondence Relations

You might expect that each point on the earth would be transformed to a corresponding point on the map projection. Such a **point-to-point correspondence** would let you shift attention from a feature on the earth to the same feature on the map, and vice versa, with equal facility. Unfortunately, this desirable property can't be maintained for all points on world map projections. As Figure 3.3 shows, one or more points on the earth are transformed into straight lines or circles on the boundary of the map projection, most often at the north and south poles.

Continuity

To represent an entire spherical surface on a plane, the continuous spherical surface must be interrupted at some point or along some line. These **breaks in continuity** form the map border on a world projection. Where the map maker places the discontinuity is a matter of choice. On some maps, for example, opposite edges of the map are in fact the same meridian. Since this means features next to each other on the ground are found at opposite sides of the map, this is a blatant violation of proximity relations and a source of confusion for map users. Similarly, a map may show the north and south poles with lines as long as the equator. This means features adjacent to each other, but on opposite sides of a pole, will be far apart along the top or bottom edge of the map.

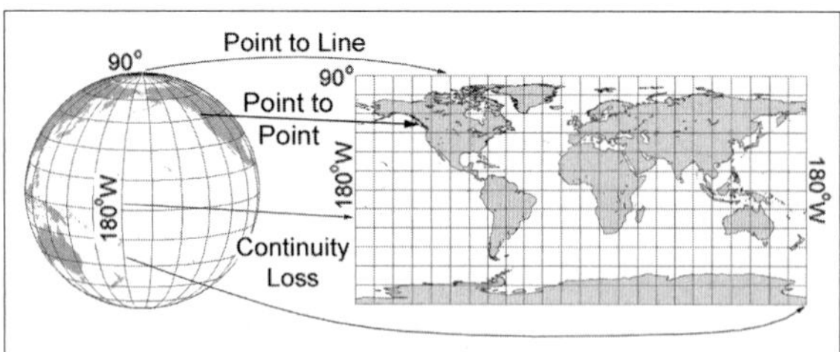

Figure 3.3 The point-to-point correspondence between the globe and map projection may become point-to-line at some locations. There also may be a loss of continuity, where the same line on the globe forms two edges of the map.

Scale and Distance

For a map to be truly **distance-preserving** (equidistant), the scale would have to be equal in all directions from every point. This is impossible on a flat map. Because of the stretching and shrinking that occurs in the process of transforming the spherical or ellipsoidal earth surface to a plane, the stated map scale (see Chapter 2 for more information on scale) is true only at selected points or along particular lines. Everywhere else the scale of the map is actually smaller or larger than the stated scale. Thus, the preservation of distance on a map projection, called **equidistance**, is at best a partial achievement.

To grasp the idea of distance preservation on maps, you first must realize that there are in fact two map scales. One is the **actual scale** at any point on the map, which will differ from one location to another. The other is the **stated scale** of the map.

Next, imagine that the earth is reduced to a **generating globe**. A generating globe is a globe reduced to the scale of the desired flat map. This globe is then transformed into a flat map (**Figure 3.4**). The constant scale of the globe is the scale stated on the flat map. Cartographers call this scale the **principal scale** of the map.

To understand the relation between the actual and principal scale at different places on the map, we compute a ratio called the **scale factor (SF)**, which is defined as follows:

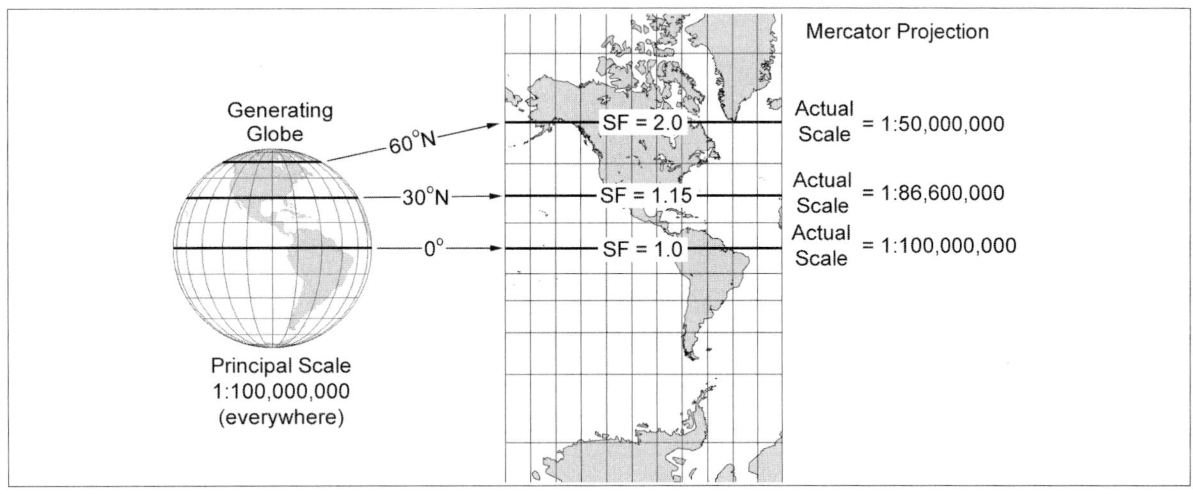

Figure 3.4 Scale factors (SFs) greater than 1.0 indicate that the actual scales are larger than the principal scale of the generating globe.

SF = Actual Scale / Principal Scale.

We use the **representative fractions** of the actual and principal scales to compute the SF. An actual scale of 1/50,000,000 and a principal scale of 1/100,000,000 would thus give an SF of:

$$1/50{,}000{,}000 \;/\; 1/100{,}000{,}000 = 100{,}000{,}000 \;/\; 50{,}000{,}000 = 2.0$$

If the actual and principal scales were identical, then the SF would equal 1.0. But since the actual scale varies from place to place, so does the SF. A scale factor of 2.0 on a small-scale map means that the actual scale is twice as large as the principal scale (Figure 3.4). A scale factor of 1.15 on a small-scale map means that the actual scale is 15 % larger than the principal scale. On large-scale maps, the SF should vary only slightly from unity (1.0), following the general rule that the smaller the area being mapped the less the scale distortion.

Since the scale factor varies from location to location on a map projection, the great-circle distance on the globe between the two locations must also be distorted. The scale factor at a location may also be different in different directions, larger north-south and smaller east-west. On **equidistant projections**, however, cartographers make the scale factor 1.0 radially outward from a single point like the north pole (Figure 3.15). Great-circle distances are correct along the lines that radiate outward from that point.

Shape

When angles on the globe are preserved on the map, the projection is called **conformal**, meaning "correct form or shape." Unlike the property of equidistance, conformality can be achieved everywhere on conformal projections. To attain the property of conformality, the map scale must be the same in all directions from a point. A circle on the ground will thus appear as a circle on the map. But to achieve this characteristic, it is necessary either to enlarge or reduce the scale of the map by a different amount at each location on the map (**Figure 3.5**). This means, of course, that the map area around each location must also vary. Tiny circles on the earth will always map as circles, but their sizes will differ. Typically there will be a smooth increase or decrease in scale across the map. Conformality applies only to directions or angles at points or in the immediate vicinity of points. It does not apply to areas of any great extent; the shape of large regions can be greatly distorted.

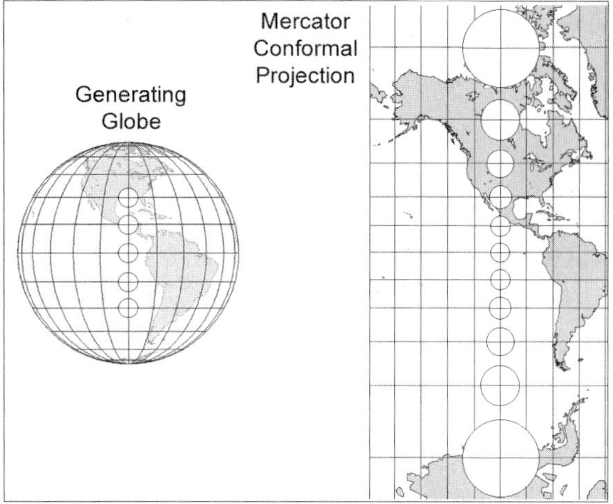

Figure 3.5 On a conformal map projection like the Mercator, identical tiny circles (greatly magnified here) on the generating globe are projected as different sized circles according to the local SF. The direction lines in all projected circles are the same as on the globe.

Conformal maps are best suited for tasks that involve plotting, guiding, or analyzing the motion of objects over the earth's surface. Thus, conformal projections are used for aeronautical and nautical charts, topographic quadrangles, and maps used by meteorologists. They are also employed when the shape of environmental features is a matter of concern.

Direction

While conformal projections preserve angles locally, it's sometimes important to preserve directions globally. Projections that preserve global directions are called **azimuthal** projections. The geometry of an azimuthal projection is symmetrical about a central point.

Unfortunately, no projection can represent correctly all directions from all points on the earth as straight lines on a flat map. But the scales across the map can be arranged so that certain types of direction lines are straight, such as in Figure 3.13 where all meridians radiating outward from the pole are correct directionally. On large-scale conformal map projections, direction distortion will be minimal across the map sheet. On small-scale conformal maps, directions will be preserved locally but not across the entire map.

Area

When the relative size of regions on the earth is preserved everywhere on the map, the projection is said to be **equal area**. Adjusting the scale along meridians and parallels so that shrinkage in one direction from a point is compensated for by exaggeration in another direction creates an equal-area map projection. A small square on the globe is projected as a rectangle with a north-south SF of 2.0 and east-west SF = 0.5, for example. Equal-area world maps, therefore, compact, elongate, shear, or skew the latitude-longitude graticule (**Figure 3.6**). The distortion of shape, distance, and direction is usually most pronounced toward the map's margins. Despite the distortion inherent in equal-area projections, they're the best choice for tasks that call for area or density comparisons from region to region.

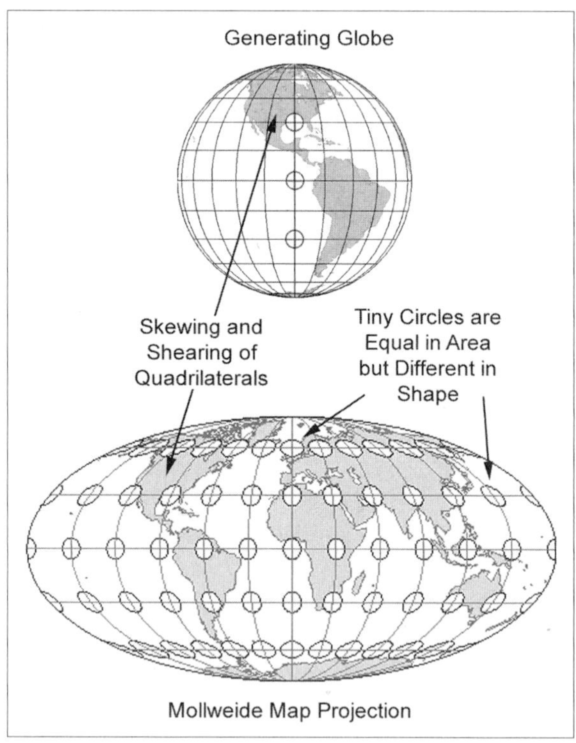

Figure 3.6 Quadrilaterals are skewed and sheared on an equal-area projection. Tiny circles on the generating globe (greatly enlarged here) are projected as ellipses of the same area but different shape. This causes the directions in each ellipse to be skewed.

The demands of achieving equivalence are such that the scale factor can only be the same in all directions along one or two lines, or from at most two points. Since the SF and hence angles around all other points will be deformed, the scale requirements for equivalence and conformality are mutually exclusive. No projection can be both conformal and equal area—only a globe can be.

You can gain helpful clues to all of these geometrical distortions by comparing the projected graticule with a globe. Ask yourself several questions: To what degree do meridians converge? Do meridians and parallels intersect at right angles? Do parallels shorten with increasing latitude? Are the areas of quadrilaterals on the projection the same as on the globe?

Projection Surface

As explained earlier, we will take two interrelated approaches toward understanding projections. So far we've explored the first approach, based on the fact that spatial properties can to some degree be preserved under special circumstances. To further visualize map projection distortions, it is helpful to shift to the second approach and consider the nature of different surfaces used in constructing projections.

As a child, you probably played the game of casting hand shadows on the wall. You were actually making projections, and the wall was your projection surface. You discovered that the distance and direction of the light source relative to the position of your hand influenced the shape of the shadow you created. But the projection surface also had a great deal to do with it. A shadow cast on a corner of the room or on a curved surface was quite different from one thrown upon the flat wall.

You can think of the globe as your hand and the map projection as the shadow on the wall. To visualize this, imagine a transparent generating globe with the latitude-longitude graticule and continent outlines drawn on it in black. Then suppose that you place this globe at various positions relative to a source of light and a projection surface (**Figure 3.7**). This projection surface can either be a plane (planar) surface or a developable surface (a curved form which can be flattened without distortion). There are only two developable surfaces—cones and cylinders. Consequently, there are three basic projection surfaces—**planar, conical, and cylindrical**. Depending on which type of projection surface you use and which way your light is shining, you will end up with different map projections cast by the globe. All projections that you can create in this light-casting way are called **true perspective**.

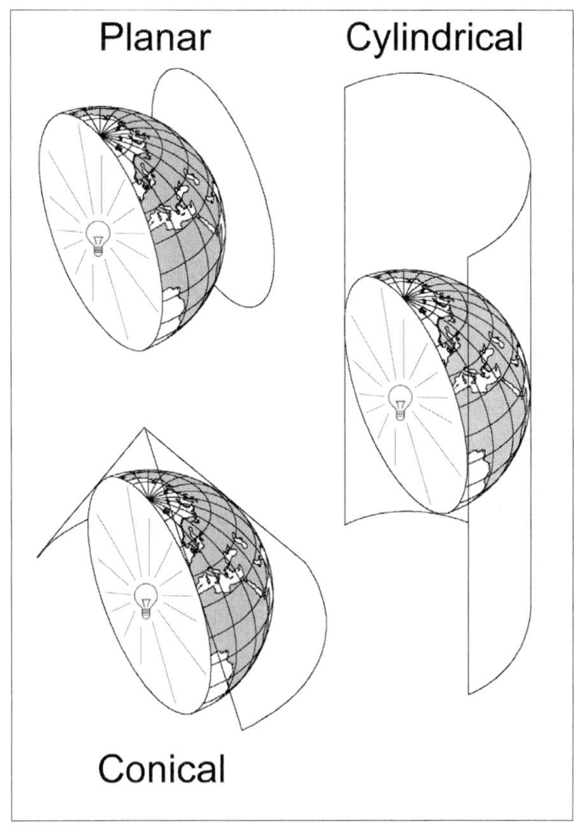

Figure 3.7 Planes, cones, and cylinders are used as true-perspective map projection surfaces.

Most map projections aren't produced this simply. Projections defined by mathematical equations are more common, because they can be designed to serve any purpose desired, can be made conformal, equal-area, or equidistant, and can be readily produced with the aid of computers. Yet even these mathematical projections can usually be thought of as variations of one of the three basic projection surfaces.

Tangent and Secant Case

The projection surface may have either a tangent or secant relationship to the globe. A **tangent-case** projection surface may either touch the globe at a point (called the **point of tangency**) or along a line (called a **line of tangency)**.(see **Figure 3.8**). The general rule is that the SF is 1.0 at the point of tangency for planar projections or along the line of tangency for cylindrical and conical projections. The SF then increases outward from the point of tangency or perpendicularly away from the line of tangency.

A **secant-case** planar projection surface intersects the globe along a small-circle line of tangency (Figure 3.8). Secant-case conic projections have two small-circle lines of tangency, usually mid-latitude parallels, also called **standard parallels**. Secant-case cylindrical projections have two small-circle lines of tangency that are equidistant from the great circle at the projection center. A secant case cylindrical projection centered at the equator, for example, might have the 10°N and 10°S parallels as lines of tangency. All secant-case projections have an SF of 1.0 along the lines of tangency and a systematic change in scale perpendicularly outward from each line of tangency. Between the lines of tangency, the scale factor decreases from 1.0 to a minimum value half way between the two lines, while outside the lines, the scale factor increases from 1.0 to a maximum value at the edge of the map. In other words, the scale is slightly smaller in the middle part of the map and slightly larger than the stated scale at the edges. For planar projections, the SF increases outward from the circle of tangency and decreases inward to a minimum value at the center of the **circle of tangency**.

The advantage of the secant case is that it minimizes the overall scale distortion on the map. This is because the central part of the projection is slightly smaller than the stated scale and the edges don't have SFs as large as with the tangent case, thus providing a greater area of minimum distortion.

Obviously, there is minimal distortion around the point or line of tangency. This explains why earth curvature may often be ignored without serious consequence when using flat maps for a local area. But as the distance from the point or line of tangency increases, so does the degree of scale distortion. By the time a projection has been extended to include the entire earth, scale distortion may have greatly impacted the earth's appearance on the map.

Aspect

Map projection **aspect** refers to the location of the point or line(s) of tangency on the generating globe (**Figure 3.9**). A projection's point or line(s) of tangency can in theory touch or intersect anywhere on the globe. When a tangent-case projection point or line of tangency is at or along the equator, the resulting projection is said to be in **equatorial aspect**. When the point of tangency is at either pole, the projection is said to be in **polar aspect**. With cylindrical projections, the term **transverse aspect** is used. Tranverse aspect occurs when the line of tangency for the projection is shifted 90 degrees so that it follows a pair of meridians (see **Figure 3.10**). Any other alignment of the point or line(s) of tangency to the globe is a projection in **oblique aspect**.

Aspects of secant-case projections are defined similarly. A polar-aspect, secant-case planar projection, for example, has the north or south pole as the center of its circle of tangency. A transverse-aspect, secant-case cylindrical projection has two lines of tangency equally spaced from its central meridian.

Of these three projection aspects, the one that has been used the most historically is referred to as the **normal aspect**. The normal aspect of planar projections is polar; the normal aspect of conical projections is oblique (line of tangency along a parallel); and the normal aspect of cylindrical projections is equatorial. Note the planar projections shown in Figure 3.9. You can see at once why their normal aspect is polar—the graticule is the least complicated of the three to draw, and you are more used to seeing planar projections in this aspect.

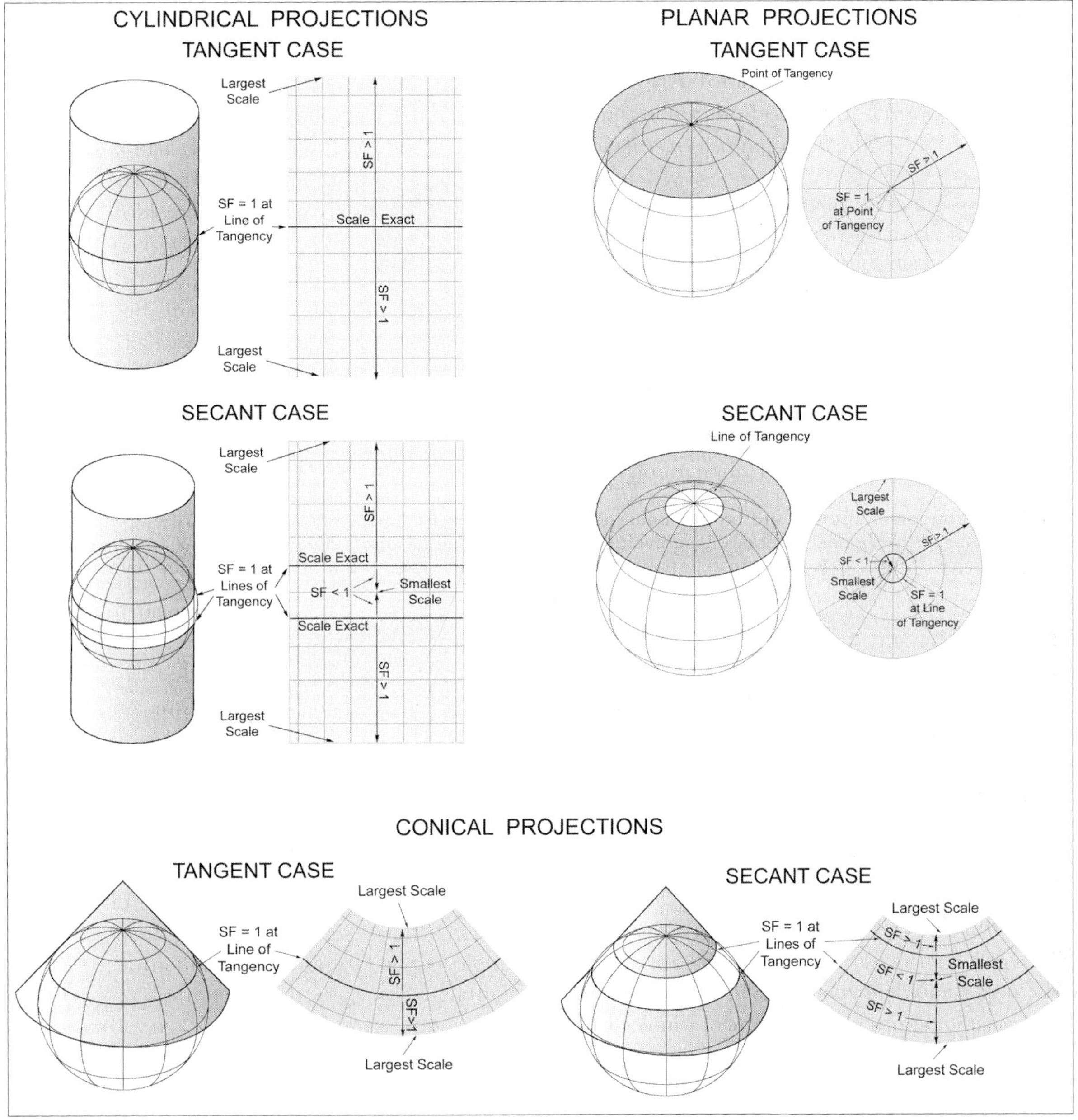

Figure 3.8 Tangent and secant cases of the three basic projection surfaces.

The choice of different projection-surface aspects leads to quite different appearances of the earth's surface (again refer to Figures 3.9 and 3.10). Yet the distortion properties of a given projection surface remain unaltered when the aspect is changed from polar to oblique or equatorial. The cylindrical projection in Figure 3.10 is a good example. In its normal aspect, the SF is 1.0 at the equator and increases north and south at right angles to the equator. In its transverse aspect, the SF is 1.0 along the pair of meridians that form the line of tangency. The SF again increases at right angles to the line of tangency, which is due east and west at the intersection of each parallel and the pair of meridians. The SF will be exactly the same at six inches above and below the equator on the normal aspect and at six inches to the left and right of the meridian pair on the transverse-aspect cylindrical projection.

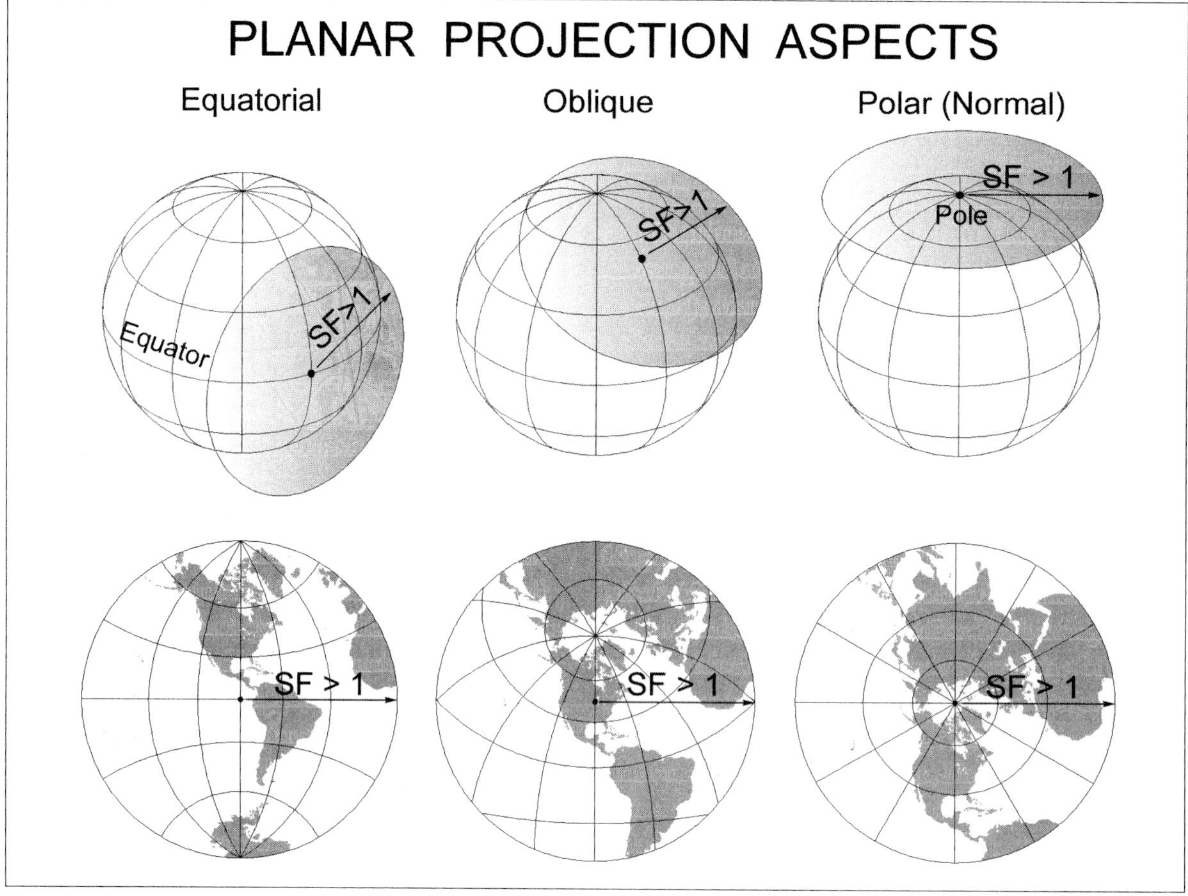

Figure 3.9 Polar, equatorial, and oblique aspects of the planar projection surface dramatically affect the appearance of the graticule and land areas. The pattern of scale distortion increases radially away from the point of tangency and is independent of the location of the point of tangency.

COMMONLY USED PROJECTIONS

We have seen that map projections can be grouped into families based on which projection surface was used—a plane, cone, or cylinder.* Consequently, we can think of most projections as falling into one of three groups: planar, cylindrical, or conical.

Planar Projections

If you remember your childhood shadow-casting game, you will recall that the projection surface was only one of the factors influencing the shape of the shadow you threw upon the wall. The other influence was the distance of the light source from the wall. Thus, there will be basic differences within the planar projection family, depending on where the imaginary light source is located. **Planar projections** (sometimes called **azimuthal projections**) can be thought of as projecting onto a plane tangent to the globe at a point. This family includes three commonly used projections that actually can be created by a light source (**Figure 3.11**): orthographic (light source at infinity),

**Strictly speaking, very few projections actually involve planes, cones, or cylinders in a physical sense. Most, as mentioned earlier, are defined by mathematical equations. But even with these mathematical projections, it is conceptually useful to think of an implied projection surface.*

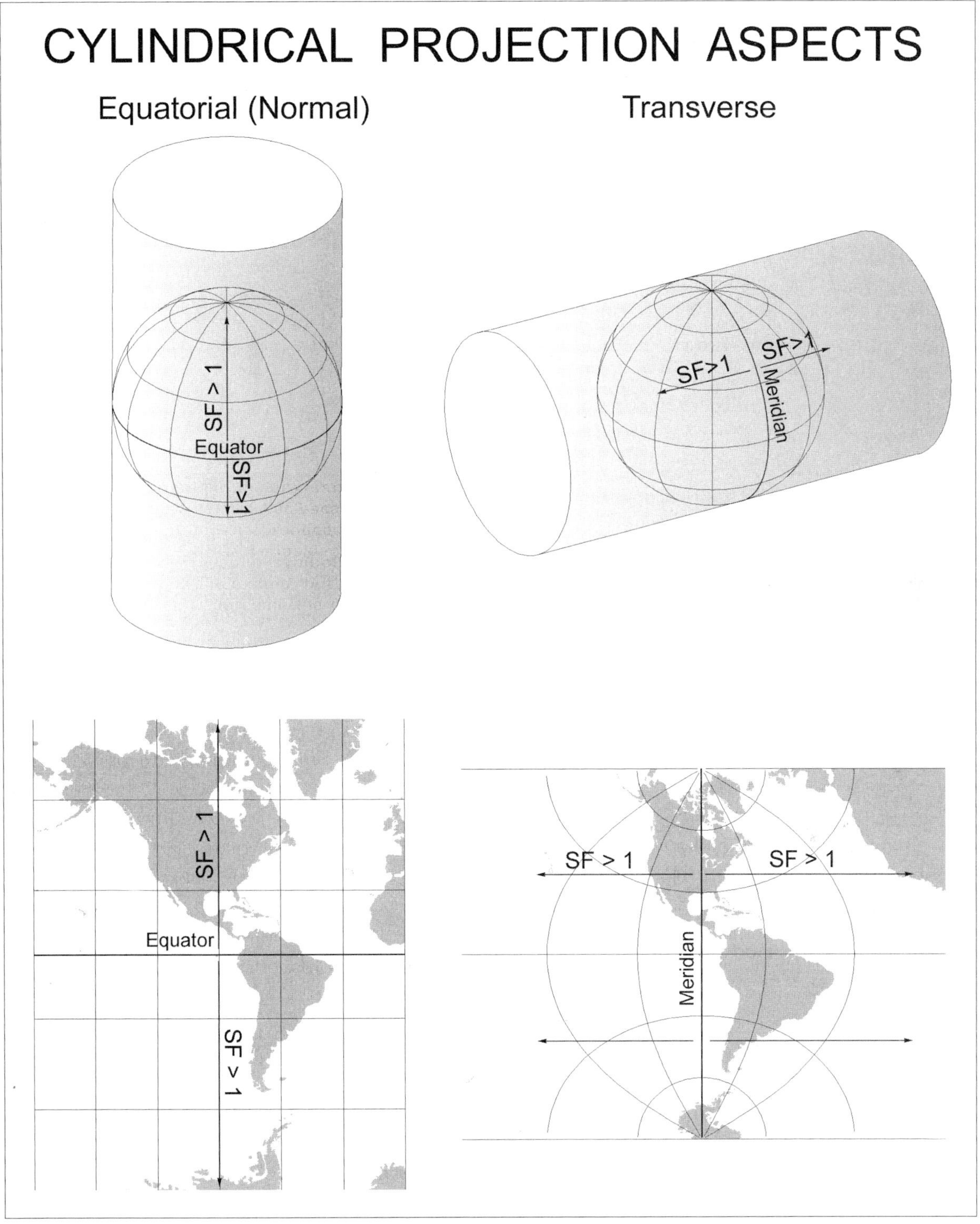

Figure 3.10 Equatorial and transverse aspects of the cylindrical projection surface dramatically affect the appearance of the graticule and land areas. The pattern of scale distortion increases perpendicularly away from the line of tangency and is independent of the location of the line of tangency.

stereographic (light source on the earth's surface opposite the point of tangency), and gnomonic (light source in the center of the globe). Two other projections, the azimuthal-equidistant and Lambert azimuthal equal-area, are mathematical constructs that cannot be created with a light source.

Orthographic

The **orthographic** projection is how the earth would appear if viewed from a distant planet (**Figure 3.12**). Since the light source is at an infinite distance from the generating globe, all rays are parallel. This projection appears to have been first used by astronomers in ancient Egypt, but it came into widespread use during World War II with the advent of the global perspective provided by the air age. It is even more popular in today's space age, often used to show landcover and topography data obtained from remote sensing devices (see Chapter 9 for a discussion of remote sensing devices). The generating globe and half-globe illustrations in this book are orthographic projections. The main drawback of the orthographic projection is that only a hemisphere can be projected. Showing the entire earth requires two maps, often of the northern and southern or western and eastern hemispheres.

Stereographic

Projecting a light source from the antipodal point on the generating globe to the point of tangency creates the **stereographic conformal** projection (**Figure 3.13**). As with all conformal projections, shape is preserved in small areas. The Greek scholar Hipparchus is credited with inventing this projection in the 2nd century BC. It is now most commonly used in its polar aspect and secant case for maps of polar areas. It is the projection surface used for the Universal Polar Stereographic grid system for polar areas, as we will see in the next chapter. A disadvantage of the stereographic conformal projection is that it is generally restricted to one hemisphere. In past centuries, it was used for atlas maps of the western or eastern hemisphere.

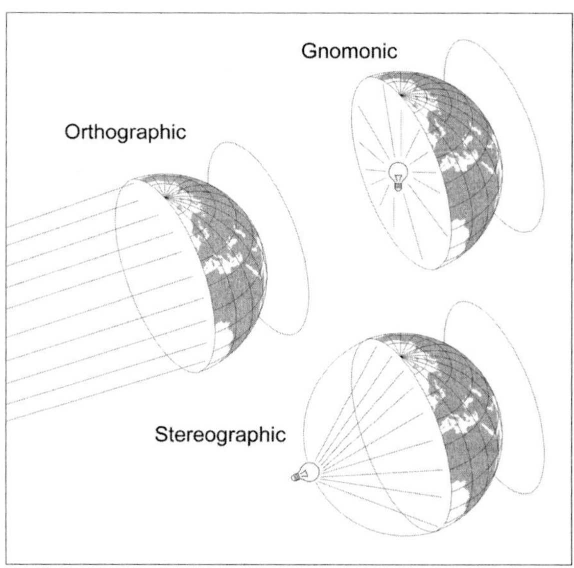

Figure 3.11 Three commonly used true-perspective planar projections are created by changing the light-source distance.

Gnomonic

Projecting with a light source at the center of the generating globe to a tangent plane produces the gnomonic projection. The **gnomonic** is one of the earliest map projections, first used for star maps

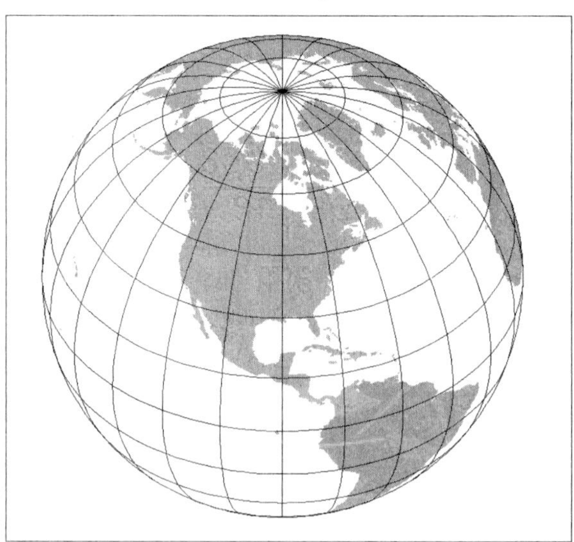

Figure 3.12 The orthographic projection best shows the spherical shape of the earth.

by the Greek scholar Thales of Miletus in the 6th century BC. This is the only projection having the useful property that **all great circles on the earth are shown as straight lines** (**Figure 3.14**). Since a great-circle route is the shortest distance between two points on the earth's surface, the gnomonic projection is especially valuable as an aid to navigation (see Great-Circle Directions in Chapter 12). The gnomonic projection is also used for plotting the global dispersal of seismic and radio waves. Its major disadvantages are extreme distortion of shape and area and the inability to project a complete hemisphere.

Azimuthal Equidistant

This projection in its polar aspect has the distinctive appearance of a dart board—equally spaced parallels and straight-line meridians radiating outward from the pole (**Figure 3.15**). This means that **all straight lines drawn from the point of tangency are great-circle routes**. Equally spaced parallels mean that great-circle distances are correct along these straight lines. The ancient Egyptians apparently first used this projection for star charts, but with the air age it has been used by pilots planning long-distance air routes. In past decades, every major airport had an oblique-aspect azimuthal-equidistant projection centered on the airport. All straight lines drawn from the airport were correctly scaled great-circle routes. This is one of the few planar projections that can show the entire surface of the earth.

Lambert Azimuthal Equal-Area

In 1772 the mathematician and cartographer Johann Heinrich Lambert invented the tangent-case equal-area planar projection that carries his name. The projection is usually restricted to a hemisphere, with polar and equatorial aspects used most often in commercial atlases (**Figure 3.16**). More recently, the Lambert projection has been used for statistical maps of continents and countries that are basically circular in overall extent, such as Australia, North America, and Africa. You will also see maps of the oceans on equatorial or oblique aspects of this projection. The Lambert projection is particularly well suited for maps of the Pacific Ocean, which is almost hemispheric in extent.

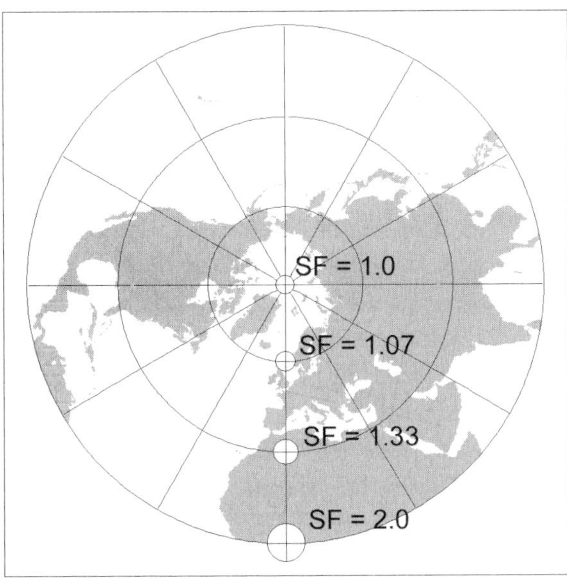

Figure 3.13 Polar stereographic projection of the Northern Hemisphere. Since this is a conformal projection, tiny circles on the generating globe are projected as circles of the same size at the point of tangency to four times as large at the equator.

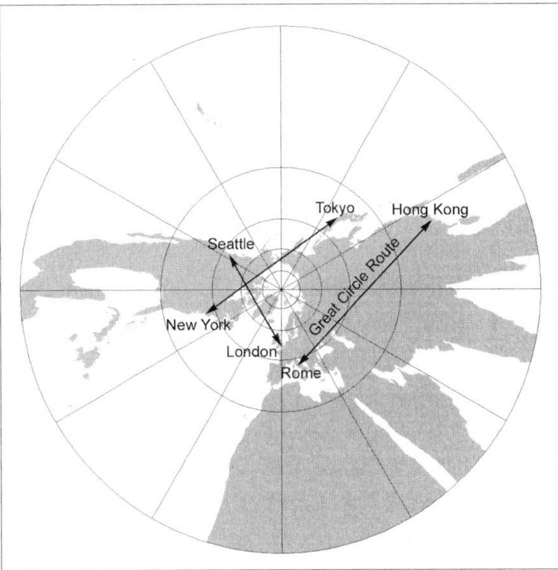

Figure 3.14 Polar gnomonic projection of the Northern Hemisphere from 15N to the pole. All straight lines on the projection surface are great-circle routes. Note the severe shape distortion compared to Figure 3.13.

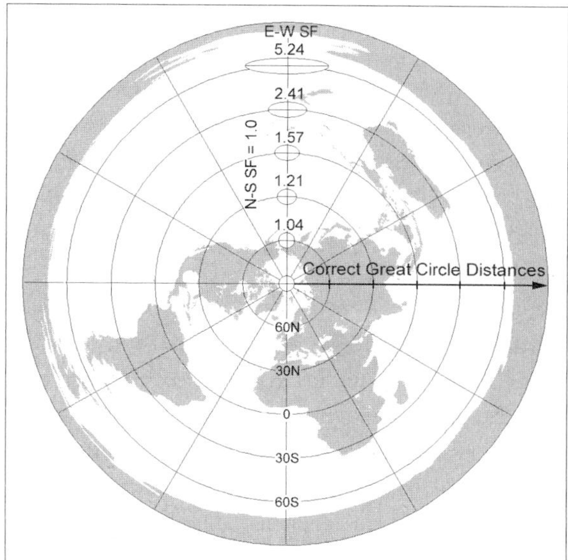

Figure 3.15 Polar-aspect azimuthal-equidistant world map projection. Great-circle distances are correct along straight lines outward from the point of tangency at the north pole since the north-south SF is always 1. The east-west SF increases to a maximum of infinity at the south pole, where we have a point-to-line correspondence.

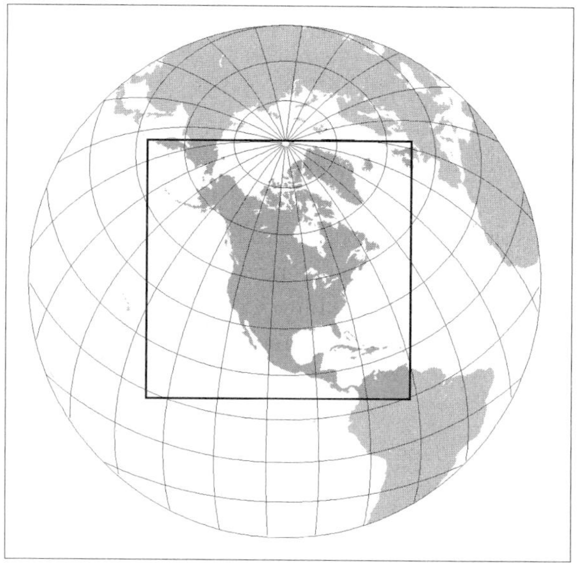

Figure 3.16 The Lambert azimuthal equal-area projection is often used for continental maps, such as this North American map cut out of an oblique-aspect projection centered at 45N, 100W.

Cylindrical Projections

True-perspective cylindrical projections are made by projecting the graticule upon a cylinder of equal diameter to the generating globe and tangent to the globe along any great circle (usually the equator). This family includes the cylindrical equal-area (linear light source along the polar axis) and the central cylindrical (light source at the center of the generating globe) (**Figure 3.17**). The whole world can't be projected onto the central cylindrical projection because the polar rays will never intersect the cylinder. The equal-area cylindrical projection, on the other hand, does cover the entire world, albeit with major shape distortion in the polar regions.

The graticule appears entirely different on normal-aspect and transverse-aspect cylindrical projections. You can recognize cylindrical projections in normal aspect by horizontal parallels of equal width, equally spaced vertical meridians of equal length, and right-angle intersections of meridians and parallels. Transverse-aspect cylindrical projections look quite different. The straight parallels and meridians on the normal-aspect projection become curves in the transverse aspect. These curves are centered around the vertical line of tangency (Figure 3.10).

Mercator

The tangent-case, cylindrical, conformal projection invented by Gerhardus Mercator in 1569 is a classic example of how the same projection can be used poorly and well. Looking at the projection (**Figure 3.18**), we can imagine Mercator starting with a horizontal equator line and equally spaced vertical meridian lines. Mercator knew that meridians on the globe converge toward the poles, so that meridians drawn as parallel vertical lines become progressively more widely spaced toward the poles. He progressively increased the spacing of parallels away from the equator so that the increase matched the increased widening of meridians. This not only produced a conformal map projection, but also the only projection where all lines of constant

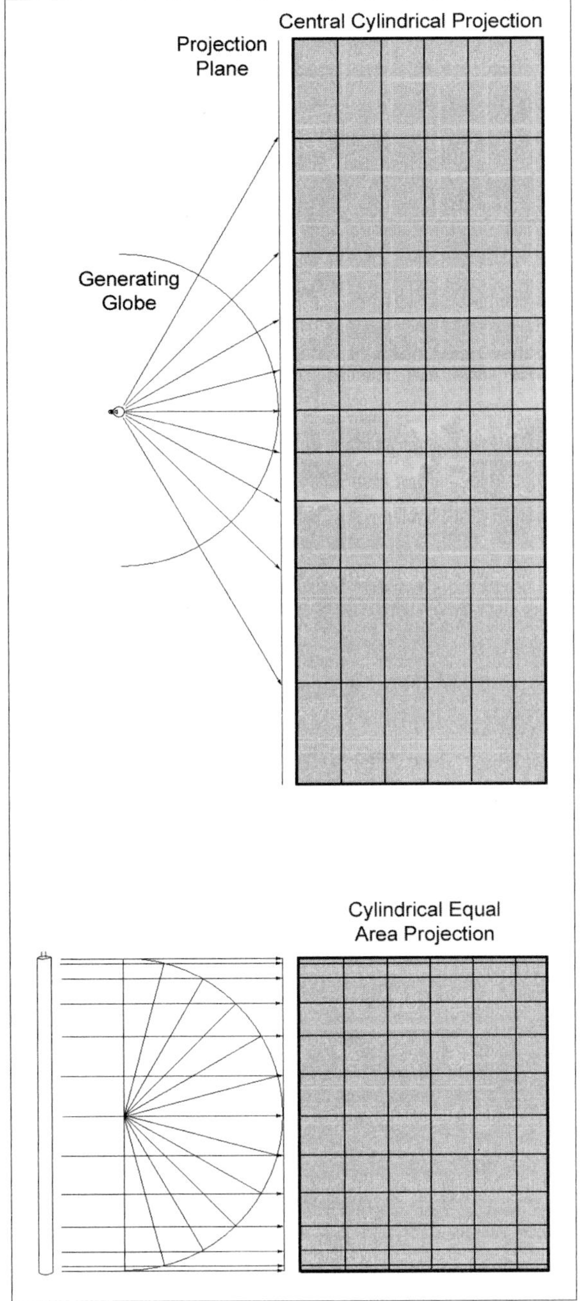

Figure 3.17 True-perspective central and equal-area cylindrical projections.

compass direction, called **rhumb lines**, are straight lines on the map.

Navigators who used a magnetic compass immediately saw the advantage of plotting courses on the Mercator projection, since they needed a map on which compass bearings would appear as straight rhumb lines (see Chapter 13 for more on rhumb line plotting). The Mercator projection has been used ever since for nautical charts, such as small-scale pilot charts of the oceans. The large-scale nautical charts used in coastal navigation can be thought of as being small rectangles cut out of the Mercator world projection.

The use of the Mercator projection in navigation is an example of a projection used for its best purpose. A poor use of the Mercator projection is for wall maps of the world. We saw previously that this projection cannot cover the entire earth, often ending at 80°N and S. Cutting off part of the world does create a rectangular projection surface with a height-to-width ratio that fits walls very well. The problem, of course, is the extreme scale enlargement and consequent area distortion at higher latitudes. The enlargement of North America, Europe, and Russia gives many people an erroneous impression of the land masses.

Peters

The **Peters-projection world map** (**Figure 3.19**) is one of the most controversial images of the world. When the German historian and journalist Dr. Arno Peters introduced the projection in 1973 it generated intense debate due to Peters' assertion that this was the only "non-racist" world map. Peters claimed that his map showed third-world countries more fairly than the Mercator projection, which distorts and dramatically enlarges the size of Eurasian and North American countries. The first English version of the Peters-projection map was published in 1983, and it continues to have passionate fans as well as staunch detractors.

The Peters projection is a secant-case cylindrical equal-area projection that lessens shape distortion in high latitudes by shifting the standard parallels to 45°N and 45°S. Although the relative areas of continents are maintained, their shapes are still distorted. According to prominent cartographer Arthur Robinson, the Peters map is "somewhat reminiscent of wet, ragged long winter underwear

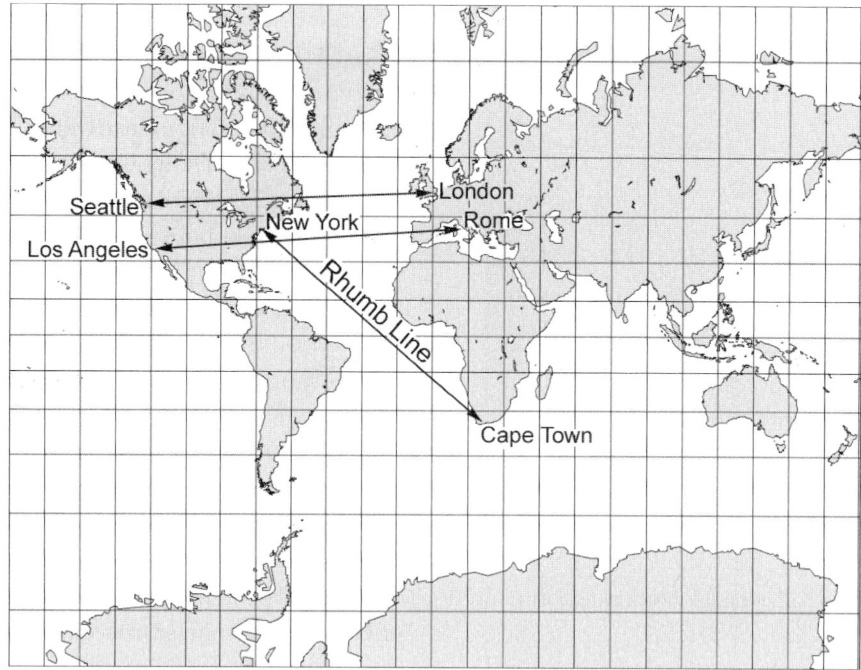

Figure 3.18 Mercator cylindrical conformal world projection, including selected rhumb lines between major world cities.

hung out to dry on the Arctic Circle." Although several international organizations have adopted the Peters map, there are other equal-area world projections, such as the Mollweide elliptical (see Figure 3.23), that distort continental shapes far less.

Transverse Mercator

J.H. Lambert invented the Transverse Mercator projection in 1772, along with the Lambert azimuthal equal-area projection and several others described in this chapter. Lambert's idea was to rotate the Mercator projection by 90 degrees so

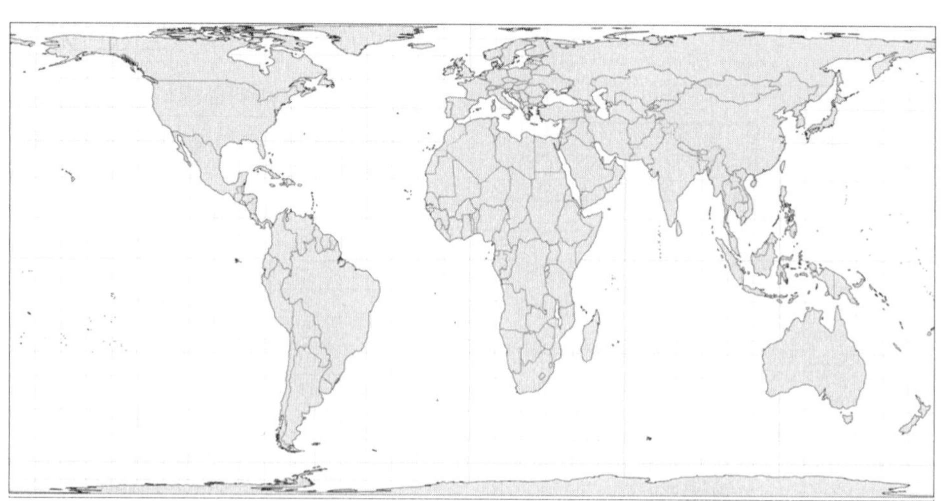

Figure 3.19 Peters-projection world map.

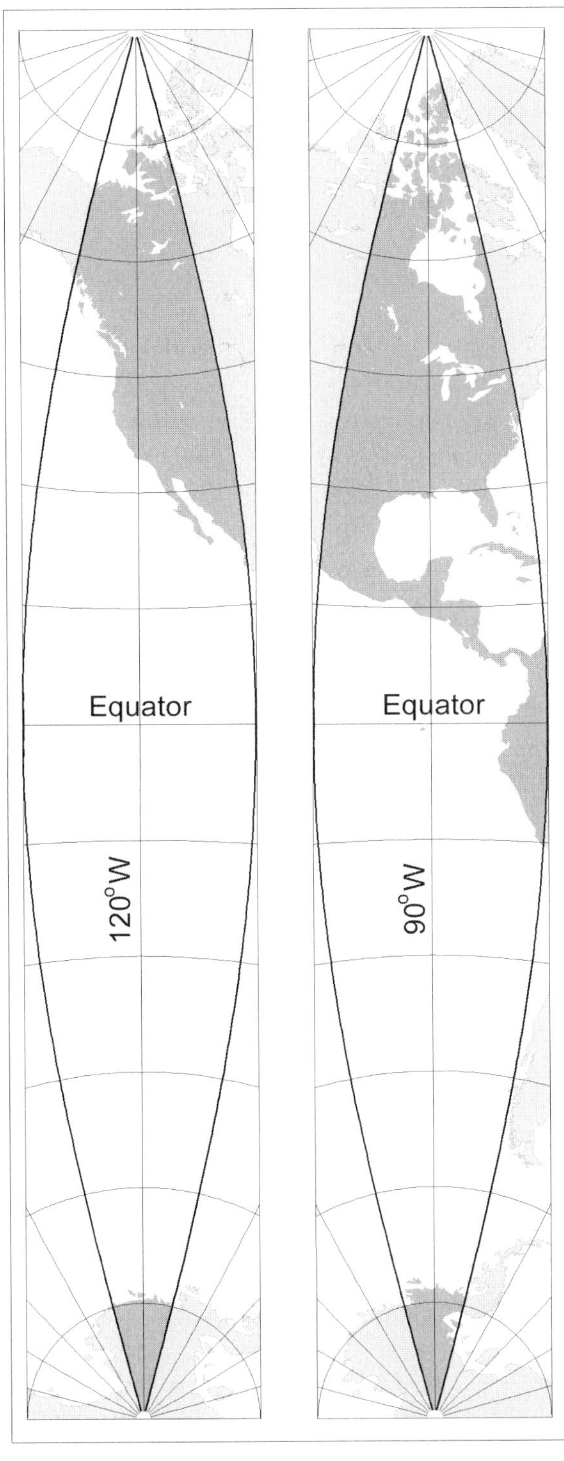

Figure 3.20 Gores of the globe on Transverse Mercator projections thirty degrees wide at the equator centered at 90 and 120 degrees west longitude. To make a world globe, the darkened portion of each map would be cut out and pasted onto the globe.

that the line of tangency became a pair of meridians (see Figure 3.10, bottom right). The resulting projection is still conformal, but rhumb lines no longer are straight lines. The central meridian of the projection has an SF of 1.0, and the scale increases perpendicularly outward. Thus, narrow north-south strips of the earth are projected with no local shape distortion and little distortion in area.

You're likely to see the Transverse Mercator projection used to map north-south strips of the earth. For example, strips 30 degrees wide in longitude from pole to pole, called gores, are cut out and glued onto a sphere to make world globes (**Figure 3.20**). The narrow, six-degree-wide zones of the Universal Transverse Mercator grid system are based on a secant-case Transverse Mercator projection. North-south trending zones of the U.S. State Plane Coordinate system also use secant cases of the projection. Most 1:24,000-scale topographic maps are projected on these State Plane Coordinate system zones.(See Chapter 4 for more on the Universal Transverse Mercator grid and the State Plane Coordinate system.)

Conical Projections

The characteristics of conical map projections are illustrated by the true-perspective central-conical projection. This projection is created by projecting the graticule onto a cone with the line of tangency on the generating globe along any small circle (usually a mid-latitude parallel—hence the name standard parallel). In normal aspect, parallels are projected as concentric arcs of circles, and meridians are projected as straight lines radiating at uniform angular intervals from the apex of the cone (Figure 3.8).

True-perspective conical projections are little used in mapping, as their relatively small area of minimal scale distortion limits their practical value. For this reason, secant-case conic projections with two standard parallels are used most frequently (Figure 3.8). Even then, however, the scale of the map quickly becomes exaggerated with distance from the correctly represented standard parallels.

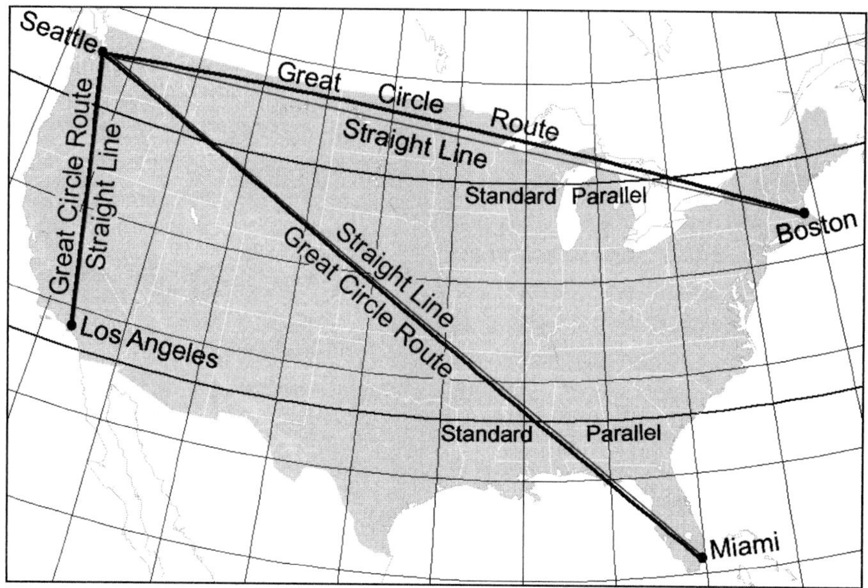

Figure 3.21 Lambert conformal-conic projection of the United States. Straight lines are very close to great-circle routes, particularly on north-south paths.

Because of this problem, conic projections are best suited for maps of mid-latitude regions, especially those elongated in an east-west direction. The United States meets these qualifications and therefore is frequently mapped on one of two conical projections—the Lambert conformal conic and Albers equal-area conic.

Lambert Conformal Conic

The Lambert conformal conic is another of the widely used map projections published by J.H. Lambert in 1772. It is a secant-case, normal-aspect conic projection with its two standard parallels placed so as to minimize the map's overall area distortion. The standard parallels for maps of the conterminous United States are placed at 33°N and

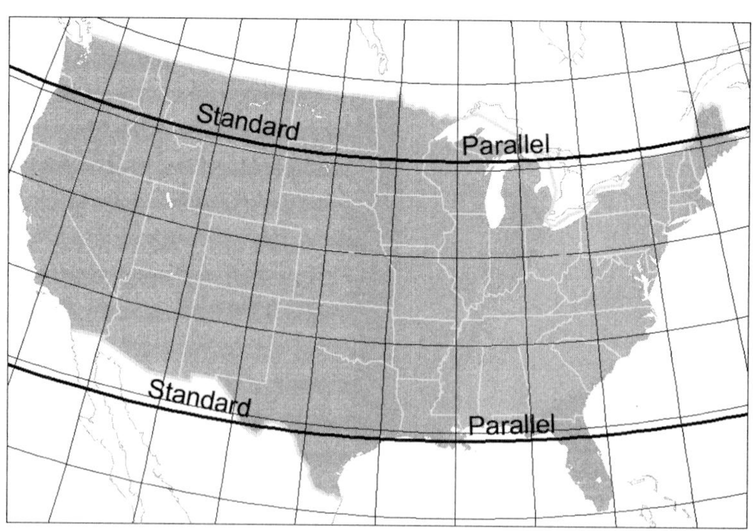

Figure 3.22 Albers equal-area conic projection of the United States.

45°N to keep area distortion at the map's edges to less than 3% (**Figure 3.21**). The Lambert conformal-conic is used as the basis for State Plane Coordinate system zones in east-west trending states like Oregon and Wisconsin. Each zone has its own secant-case projection. These projections are in turn used for the 1:24,000-scale topographic maps within the state.

The other major use of the Lambert conformal-conic projection is for aeronautical charts. All U.S. 1:500,000-scale sectional charts can be thought of as being cut out of the national map described in the above paragraph. Aviators prefer aeronautical charts on conformal projections, which preserve shapes and compass direction locally. Equally important is the fact that straight lines drawn on the 1:500,000-scale charts are almost great-circle routes on the earth (Figure 3.21).

Albers Equal-Area Conic

The Albers equal-area conic is probably the projection used most often for maps of the conterminous United States. Invented in 1805 by the mathematician Heinrich C. Albers, the projection was first used publicly in 1817 for a German map of Europe. The secant-case version that has been used nearly 100 years for the conterminous U.S. has standard parallels placed at 29.5°N and 45.5°N (**Figure 3.22**). This placment reduces the scale distortion to less than 1% at the 37th parallel in the middle of the map, and to 1.25% at the northern and southern edges of the country.

You will see this projection used for U.S. statistical maps created by the Census Bureau and other federal agencies. U.S. Geological Survey products, such as the national tectonic and geologic maps, use the Albers projection, as do recent reference maps and satellite image mosaics of the country at a scale of around 1:3,000,000. The reason for the widespread use of the Albers projection is simple —people looking at these products can assume that the areas of states and counties on the map are true to their areas on the earth.

Other Projections

We have organized projections as being in planar, conic, and cylindrical families. But these three families constitute only a small portion of the vast array of projections that have been created by cartographers. The reasons for using other projections vary. Some preserve areas or shapes. Others have no special property other than holding overall scale distortion to a minimum or presenting a pleasing visual image. For many purposes, a projection that "looks right" is more important than a projection that rigidly provides area, distance,

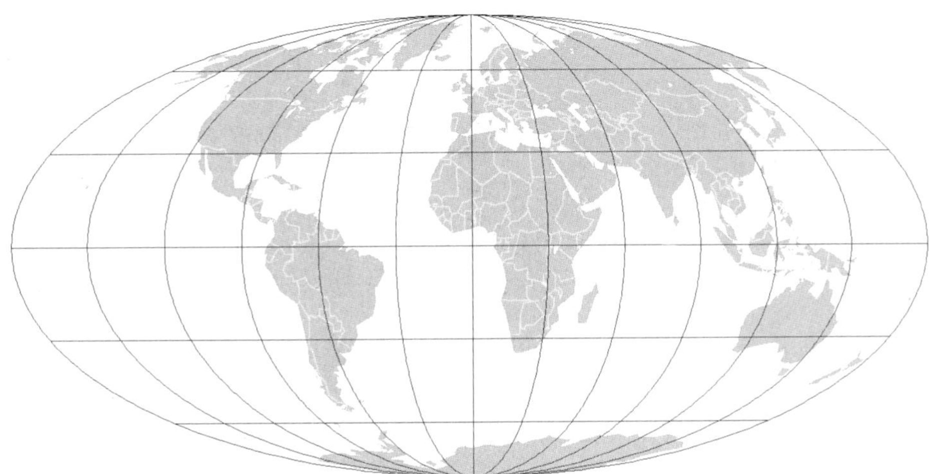

Figure 3.23 Mollweide elliptical equal-area world map projection.

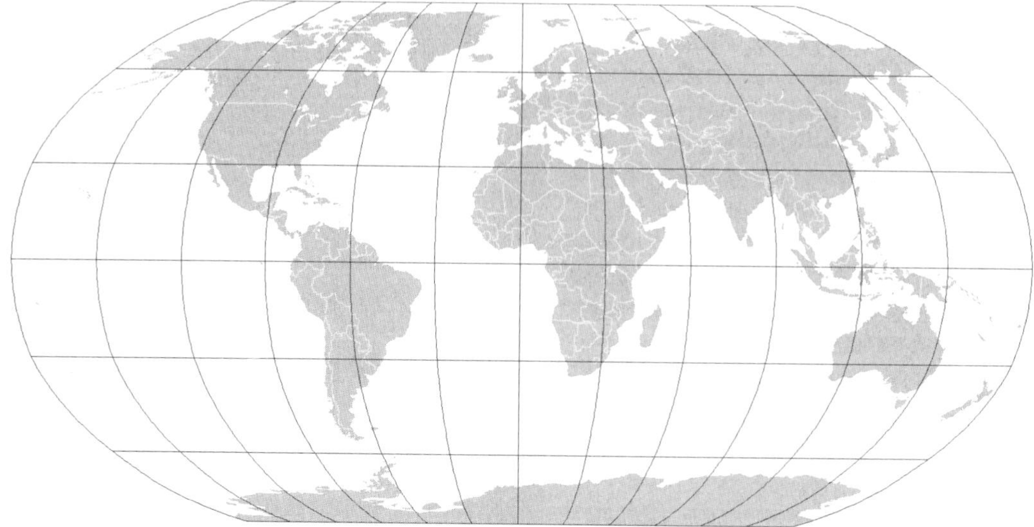

Figure 3.24 Robinson world map projection.

shape, or direction fidelity. Let's look at two unique projections that are of special interest.

Mollweide Elliptical

You've probably seen world maps in the shape of an ellipse twice as wide as high. Most likely you were looking at the **Mollweide elliptical equal-area** projection, invented in 1805 by the German mathematician Carl B. Mollweide. The normal form of the projection has the equator as the major axis and the prime meridian as the minor axis of the ellipse (**Figure 3.23**). Parallels are horizontal lines, but not equally spaced as on the spherical earth. This elliptical shape looks "earth-like," and the overall distortion in shape is less than on other equal-area world projections like the Peters.

You'll find the Mollweide projection used to show a wide range of global phenomena, from population to landcover and major diseases. Cartographers have devised other orientations of the graticule within the ellipse to better show the oceans or to center attention on a particular continent by adjusting the projection's central meridian.

Robinson

In 1963 the American academic cartographer Arthur H. Robinson created a projection that is neither equal-area nor conformal but that makes the continents "look right" (**Figure 3.24**). Robinson visually adjusted horizontal-line parallels and curving meridians until they appeared suitable for a world map projection. Notice that to do this Robinson changed the poles into horizontal lines a little over half the length of the equator. You probably have seen this projection used on world maps created by the National Geographic Society. It has also been used for wall maps of the world that show the shape and area of continents far better than the Mercator projection wall map.

PROJECTIONS AND COMPUTERS

Until digital computers became widely available in the 1960s, computing a map projection graticule and plotting geographical details in the appropriate locations were long, tedious tasks. One consequence was that cartographers had great incentive to use available projections rather than create new ones "from scratch." For the most part, available projections were those that were relatively easy to construct by hand. Usually this meant a projection in normal aspect, aligned so as to accommodate the largest possible user group. In short, projections seldom were tailored to the specific needs of the map user, because the extra costs couldn't be justified.

This situation has improved immensely in the age of computer mapping. Projections can now be tailor-made if three items are available: (1) a computer hooked to a printer or plotter, (2) a map projection program that includes the mathematical definitions (equations) for the desired projections, and (3) a digital cartographic database containing coastlines, political boundaries, and other geographical details. If these three criteria are met, then projections can be created at will. Indeed, all of the projections used as illustrations in this book were constructed using a map projection program and a digital database.

CONCLUSION

Every map projection has its own virtues and limitations. You can evaluate a projection only in light of the purpose for which a map is to be used. You shouldn't expect that the best projection for one situation will be the most appropriate in another. Fortunately, the map projection problem effectively vanishes if the cartographer has done a good job of using projection properties and if you are careful to take projection distortion into consideration in the course of map use.

Since most map use takes place at the local level, where earth curvature isn't a big problem for most purposes, global map projections aren't usually a great concern. With regions as small as those covered by topographic map quadrangles in the United States, your main projection-related problem is that, while the individual sheets match in a north-south direction, they don't fit together in an east-west direction. Yet even this difficulty won't be a serious handicap unless you try to create a large map mosaic.

The age of computers has changed the face of map projections. Map users no longer need to "make do" with inappropriate projections. Computer-generated projections are available for almost any use. Furthermore, it is now practical for map users to sit down at a computer and create their own projections. Most important, perhaps, map users can manipulate projection parameters on the computer in search of the ideal projection base for a given application. All these benefits can only be realized, of course, if map users know enough about projections to take advantage of the opportunity computers provide.

SELECTED READINGS

American Cartographic Association, *Which Map is Best? Projections for World Maps* (Bethesda, MD: American Congress on Surveying and Mapping, 1986.

American Cartographic Association, *Choosing a World Map—Attributes, Distortions, Classes, Aspects* (Bethesda, MD: American Congress on Surveying and Mapping, 1988.

American Cartographic Association, *Matching the Map Projection to the Need* (Bethesda, MD: American Congress on Surveying and Mapping, 1991.

Bugayevskiy, L.M., and Snyder, J.P., *Map Projections: A Reference Manual* (London: Taylor & Francis, 1995).

Canters, F., and Decleir, H., *The World in Perspective: A Directory of World Map Projections* (New York: John Wiley & Sons, 1989).

Chamberlin, W., *The Round Earth on Flat Paper: A Description of the Map Projections Used by Cartographers* (Washington, DC: National Geographic Society, 1947), pp. 39-126.

Dent, B.D., *Cartography: Thematic Map Design, 4th ed.* (Dubuque, IA: Wm. C. Brown Publishers, 1996), pp. 24-48.

Hsu, M.L., "The Role of Projections in Modern Map Design," *Cartographica*, 18, 2 (1981), pp. 151-186.

Maling, D.H., *Coordinate Systems and Map Projections, 2nd ed.* (New York: Pergamon Press, 1992).

Pearson, F., *Map Projections: Theory and Applications* (Boca Raton, FL: CRC Press, 1990).

Richardus, P., and Adler, R.K., *Map Projections: For Geodesists, Cartographers and Geographers* (New York: American Elsevier Publishing Co., 1972).

Robinson, A.H., et al., *Elements of Cartography, 6th ed.* (New York: John Wiley & Sons, 1995), pp. 59-90.

Snyder, J.P., *Flattening the Earth: A Thousand Years of Map Projections* (Chicago: University of Chicago Press, 1993).

Snyder, J.P, and Voxland, P.M., *An Album of Map Projections* (Washington: U.S. Geological Survey Professional Paper 1453, 1989).

Snyder, J.P., and Steward, H., eds., *Bibliography of Map Projections* (Washington: U.S. Geological Survey Bulletin 1856, 1988).

Snyder, J.P., *Map Projections—A Working Manual* (Washington: U.S. Geological Professional Paper 1395, 1987).

Tobler, W.R., "A Classification of Map Projections," *Annals of the Association of American Geographers*, 52 (1962), pp. 167-175.

CHAPTER FOUR
GRID COORDINATE SYSTEMS

The Cartesian coordinate system was developed by the mathematician Descartes during an illness. As he lay in bed sick, he saw a fly buzzing around on the ceiling, which was made of square tiles. As he watched he realized that he could describe the position of the fly by the ceiling tile it was on. After this experience he developed the coordinate plane to make it easier to describe the position of objects.
—Possibly apocryphal

4

CHAPTER FOUR

GRID COORDINATE SYSTEMS

Most of the time, we feel comfortable thinking of our environment in only two dimensions. In other words, we relate to the earth's surface as though it were basically flat. Maps encourage this "flat earth" thinking because they're eminently suited to providing static pictures of the environment on flat media. We have seen in Chapter 3 that most maps are created by projecting geographic features onto a flat surface, such as a sheet of paper. The advantage of the flat earth concept is that we can locate something by using a simple two-axis reference system.

There are many ways to pinpoint location. We have seen in Chapter 1 that the latitude-longitude graticule has been used for over 2,000 years as the worldwide locational reference system. Geographic or geodetic coordinates, still key to modern position finding, are not as well suited for making measurements of length, direction, and area on the earth's surface. The basic difficulty is the fact that latitude-longitude is a spherical coordinate system giving positions on a rounded surface. It would be much simpler if we could designate location on a flat surface using horizontal and vertical lines spaced at regular intervals to form a square grid. We could then simply read coordinates from the square grid of intersecting straight lines. The square grid idea is not new; it has been a prominent feature on Chinese maps since the 3rd century AD.

To devise such a system for large areas, we have to deal somehow with earth curvature. We know that transferring something round to something flat always causes distortion. But we also know that map projection distortion due to earth rotundity is minimal for fairly small regions. If we superimpose a square grid onto flat maps of small areas, we can achieve positional accuracy good enough for many purposes. All grid coordinate systems are based on **Cartesian coordinates**, invented in 1637 by the famous French philosopher and mathematician René Descartes.

CARTESIAN COORDINATES

If you superimpose a square grid on the map, with divisions left to right labeled on a horizontal X axis and divisions bottom to top labeled on a vertical Y axis, you have established the familiar **Cartesian coordinate system** (**Figure 4.1**). You can now pinpoint any location on the map precisely and objectively by giving its two coordinates (x, y). The Cartesian coordinate system is divided into four quadrants (I-IV) based on whether the X and Y-axes are positive or negative. Map makers use only quadrant I for grid coordinate systems so that all coordinates will be positive numbers relative to the (0,0) grid origin.

GRID COORDINATES

Such a simple way of defining map positions has definite advantages over the spherical graticule. Measuring x and y coordinates from horizontal and vertical axes with equally spaced distance increments greatly simplifies locating environmental features.

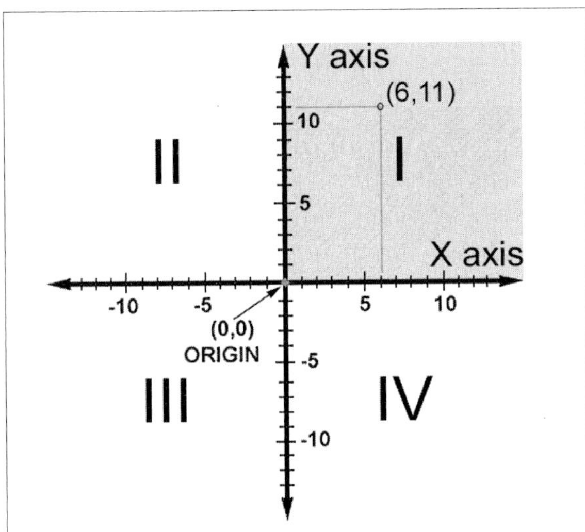

Figure 4.1 The structure of the Cartesian coordinate system, including basic notation. Notice the different signs of the x and y coordinates in the four quadrants. We use only quadrant I (shaded) on maps because it is desirable to have all coordinates as positive numbers.

Cartesian grids are especially handy for such map analysis procedures as finding the distance or direction between locations or the area of a mapped feature like a lake. Two types of **grid coordinates** —State Plane and Universal Transverse Mercator —are found on many large-scale maps in the United States.

State Plane Coordinate (SPC) System

The State Plane Coordinate (SPC) system was created in the 1930s by the land surveying profession in the United States as a way to define property boundaries that would simplify computation of land parcel perimeters and areas. The idea was to completely cover the United States and its territories with grids laid over map projection surfaces so that the maximum scale distortion error would not exceed one part in 10,000. Thus, a distance measured over a 10,000-foot course would be accurate within a foot of the true measure. This level of accuracy could not be achieved if only one grid covered the whole country; the area is too large. The solution was to divide each state into one or more **zones** and make a separate grid for each zone.

The country was divided originally into 125 zones, each having its own projection surface based on the Clarke 1866 ellipsoid and NAD 27 geodetic latitudes and longitudes (see Chapter 1 for further details). Most states have several zones, as **Figure 4.2** shows. Secant-case Lambert conformal conic projections are used for states of predominantly east-west extent, and secant-case Transverse Mercator projections are used for states of greater north-south extent. This explains the orientation of the individual zones. For states with more than one zone, the names North, South, East, West, and Central are used to identify zones, except in California where Roman numerals are used.

The logic of the SPC system zones is quite simple. Zone boundaries follow state and county boundaries because surveyors have to register land surveys in a particular county. Each zone has its own **central meridian** that defines the vertical axis for the zone. An **origin** is established to the west

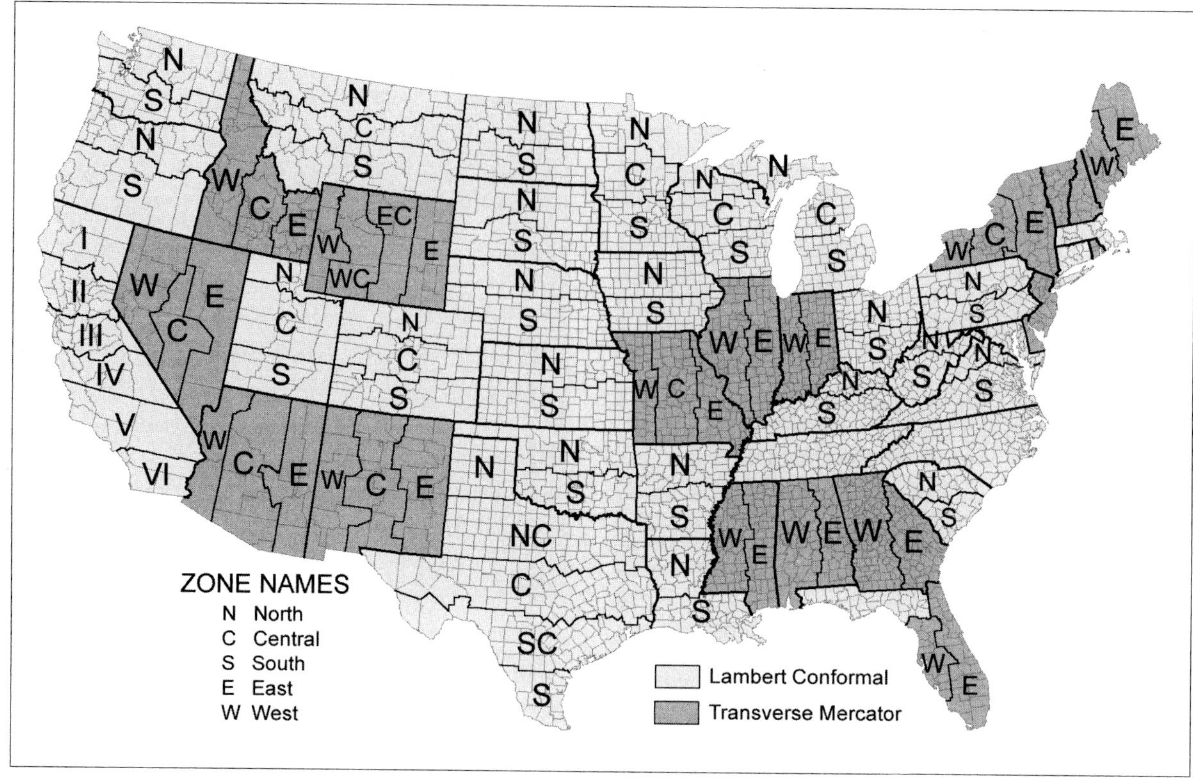

Figure 4.2 Zones of the State Plane Coordinate System for the contiguous United States. Notice that the Transverse Mercator zones are oriented north-south and the Lambert conformal conic zones east-west, depending on the shape of the state. Multi-zone states have zones identified by North, South, Central, East, and West except for the Roman numerals used in California. States without letters have only one grid zone.

and south of the zone, usually 2,000,000 feet west of the central meridian for Lambert conformal conic zones and 500,000 feet west of the central meridian for Transverse Mercator zones (**Figure 4.3**). This means that the central meridians will usually have an x coordinate of either 500,000 or 2,000,000 feet. These large numbers for zone centers were selected so that all x coordinates will be positive numbers. Having the origin to the south of every zone insures that all y coordinates will be positive numbers.

You read x coordinates first to the east of the origin and then y coordinates to the north of the origin, giving rise to the terms **eastings** and **northings** for the x and y coordinates. Since north is conventionally at the top of the map, it may be helpful to remember a simple rule: that you always read coordinates right-up. Specifically, the correct form of SPC notation is to give the easting in feet, the northing in feet, the state, and the zone name. For example, you would give the location of the state capitol dome in Madison, Wisconsin, in abbreviated form as:

2,164,600 ft E, 392,280 ft N,
Wisconsin, South Zone.

In the case of Oregon, the Lambert conformal conic projection is the base surface for the North and South SPC zones (Figure 4.3). The central meridian is the same for both zones, with an easting of 2,000,000 feet in the original system. The origin for northings in each zone is a parallel just south of the counties in the zone, called the parallel of origin. The intersection of this parallel and central meridian has a northing of 0 feet.

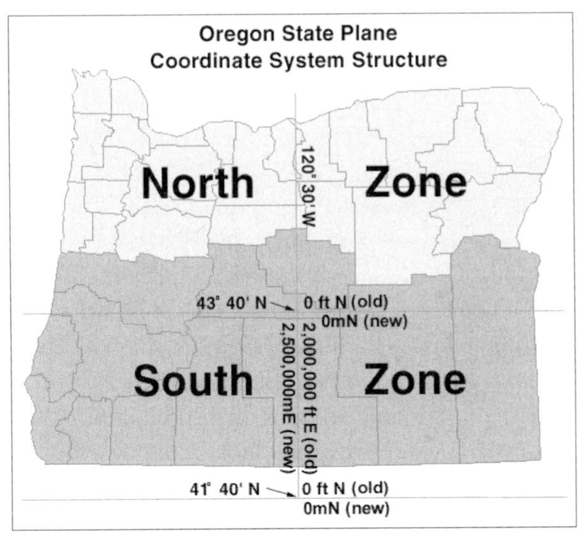

Figure 4.3 North and South zones of the Oregon State Plane Coordinate system.

In 1983 the SPC system was modernized by switching to NAD 83 and the GRS 80 ellipsoid. Zones were redefined in metric units, so the Oregon central meridian now has an easting of 2,500,000 meters, and the intersection of the parallel of origin and central meridian has a northing of 0 meters. This means that you will need to check the map legend material to find out if old or new SPC system coordinates are used on the map.

The SPC system served the needs of the states when it was created, and State Plane Coordinates have been widely used for public works and land surveys. However, the SPC system is now largely obsolete as far as surveyors and other professional map users are concerned. One reason is that accuracy of 1 part in 10,000 in locating points is now easily exceeded using modern surveying methods. Also, each SPC zone is a separate entity with its own defining characteristics—a fact that frustrates and discourages uses across zone boundaries. Nevertheless, the SPC grid is useful for analyzing maps in the laboratory, and you can enter SPC zone parameters into your GPS receiver as a **user-defined grid** (see Chapter 14: GPS and Maps for more information).

Universal Transverse Mercator (UTM) System

The convenience of grid coordinates can also be enjoyed worldwide if enough zones are used to ensure reasonable geometric accuracy. Probably the best-known grid coordinate system of international scope is the **Universal Transverse Mercator (UTM)** grid. The UTM grid extends around the world from 84° North to 80° South latitude. Sixty north-south zones are used, each six degrees in longitude (**Figure 4.4**). A secant-case Transverse Mercator projection centered on the zone's central meridian is used for each of the 60 zones. This projection makes it possible to achieve a geometrical accuracy level of one part in 2,500 maximum scale error within each zone.

Each zone is individually numbered from west to east, beginning with Zone 1 from 180° to 174° West longitude. Zones 10 through 19 cover the conterminous United States. Each zone has separate origins for the northern and southern hemispheres. Taking Zone 10 as an example (**Figure 4.5**), the origin for the northern hemisphere lies on the equator 500,000 meters west of the central meridian at 123°W. In the southern hemisphere, the zone origin lies 500,000 meters west and 10,000,000 meters south of the intersection of the equator and central meridian. These numbers were selected to guarantee that all UTM eastings and northings are positive numbers.

An interesting aspect of UTM zones is that the equator has two northings:

0mN in the Northern Hemisphere
and
10,000,000mN in the Southern Hemisphere.

This means that every location on the equator has two sets of grid coordinates. For example, the coordinates for each central meridian are:

500,000mE, 0mN in the Northern Hemisphere
and
500,000mE, 10,000,000mN in the Southern Hemisphere.

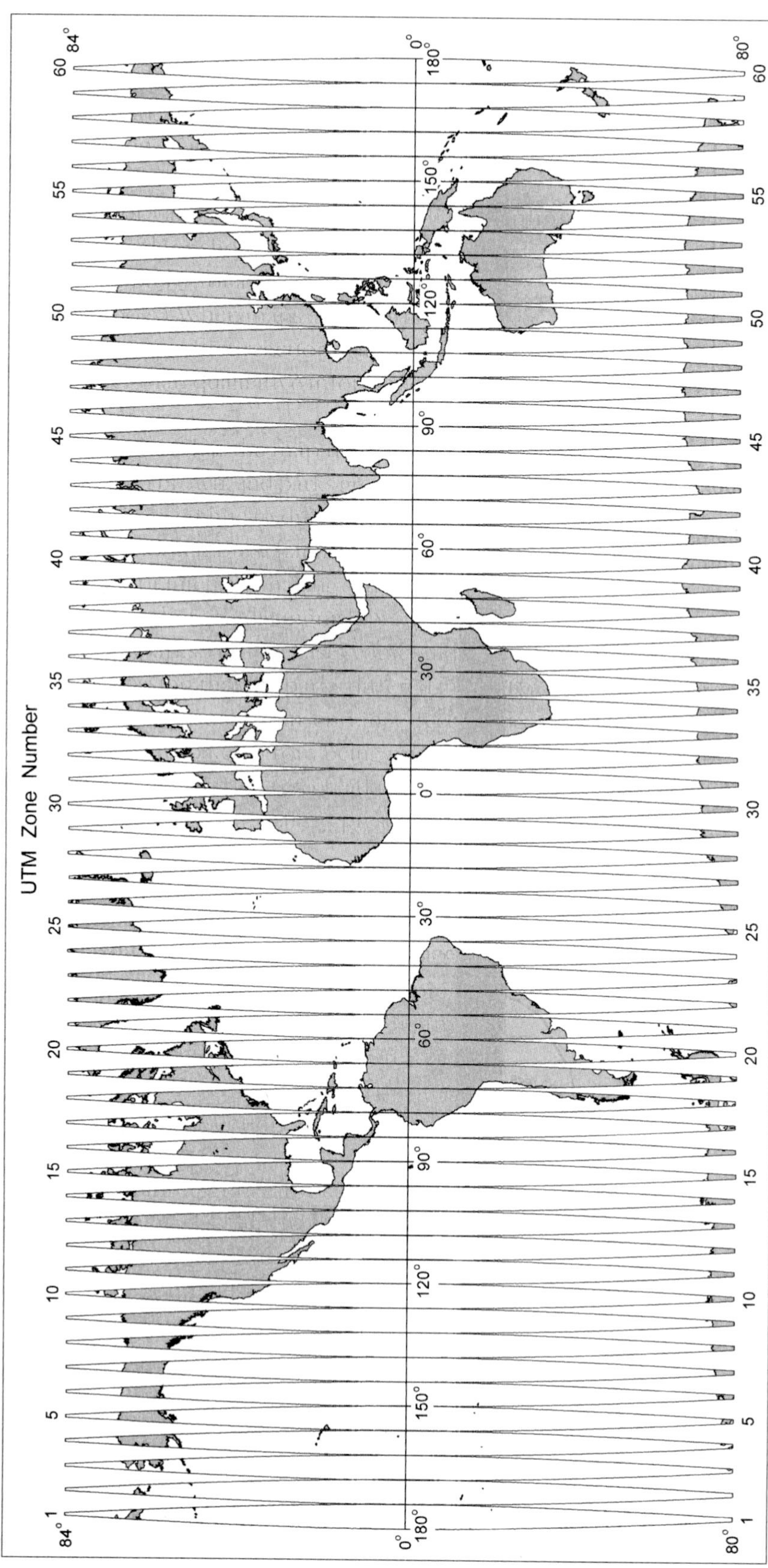

Figure 4.4 The 60 zones of the Universal Transverse Mercator (UTM) grid system.

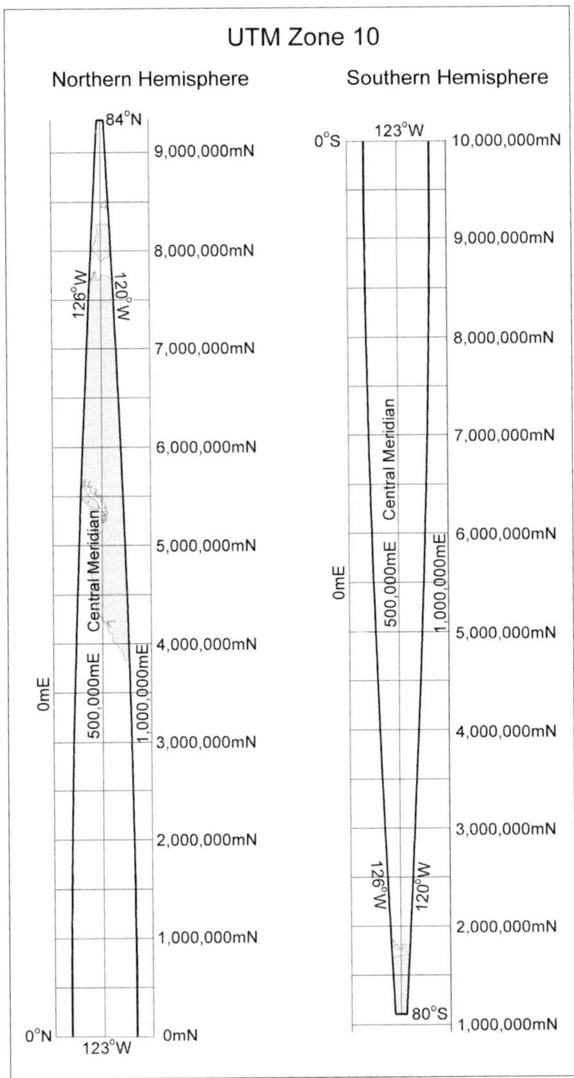

Figure 4.5 The complete Universal Transverse Mercator grid for zone 10.

You read and record UTM coordinates in the same manner as SPC coordinates—first to the east and then to the north of the zone origin. You give the easting in meters, the northing in meters, the zone number, and the zone hemisphere (north or south). Thus, you would designate the location of the capitol dome in Madison, Wisconsin, as:

305,900mE, 4,771,650mN, Zone 16 North.

The near-global extent of the UTM grid makes it a valuable worldwide referencing system. The UTM grid is indicated on many foreign maps and on all recent USGS quadrangles in the topographic, orthophotoquad, and orthophotomap series. All vendors program its specifications into their GPS receivers. Because meridians and not state boundaries bound UTM zones, it usually takes more than one UTM zone to cover a state completely. Oregon falls into zones 10 and 11, while Wisconsin falls into zones 15 and 16 (see Figure 4.4)

Universal Polar Stereographic (UPS) System

As mentioned above, UTM grid zones extend from 84°N to 80°S latitude. To have complete global coverage, a complementary rectangular coordinate system called the **Universal Polar Stereographic (UPS)** grid was created. The UPS grid consists of a North Zone and a South Zone. Each zone is superimposed upon a secant-case polar stereographic projection and covers a circular region. The North Zone (**Figure 4.6**) extends from 84°N to the pole, where the UPS coordinate at the grid center is 2,000,000mE , 2,000,000mN. These large numbers were selected so that all eastings and northings would be positive numbers.

Virtually all large-scale maps of these high latitudes, such as topographic sheets for Antarctica, are based on the UPS grid. The UTM grid system was not extended to each pole because the 60 zones converge at the poles, meaning that a new zone would be encountered every few miles.

State Grids

The widespread use of computer mapping and geographic information systems in state and local government has kindled the desire for grids tailored to each state's specific needs. States that fall into two UTM zones, for example, often create a special state coordinate grid by shifting the central meridian of a UTM zone to the center of the state. Thus, Wisconsin routinely records and reports data formatted in the **Wisconsin Transverse Mercator**

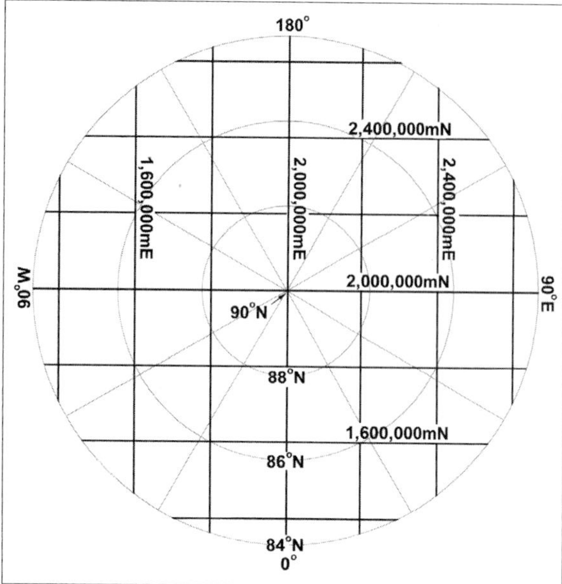

Figure 4.6 North zone of the Universal Polar Stereographic (UPS) grid system.

(WTM) coordinate system (**Figure 4.7**). The UTM and WTM grids have the same geometric accuracy, but WTM avoids the problem of two UTM zones covering the state.

Another possibility is to cover an entire state with one instead of several state plane zones. The

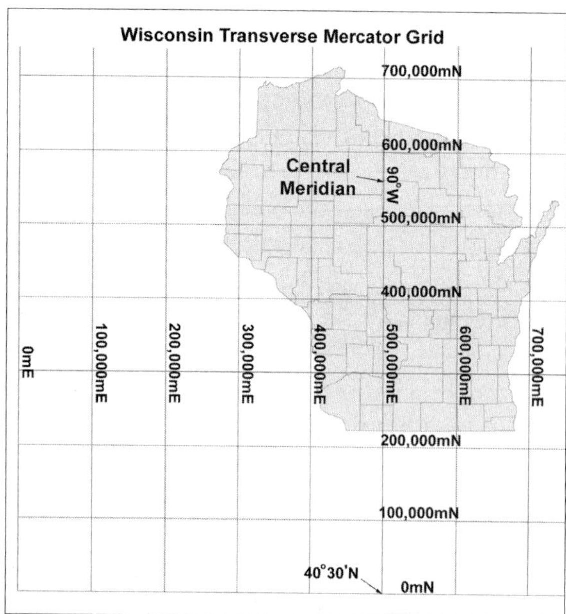

Figure 4.7 The Wisconsin Transverse Mercator grid shifts the UTM zone to the center of the state.

Oregon Lambert coordinate system is a good example (**Figure 4.8**). A single grid has replaced Oregon's two SPC zones. The new grid has the same central meridian but a different parallel of origin. The easting value at the central meridian (400,000mE) is entirely different from the SPC values.

GRID COORDINATE DETERMINATION ON MAPS

Grid Coordinate Appearance on Maps

We have seen that UTM grid coordinates appear on U.S. and foreign topographic maps and that State Plane coordinates are printed on USGS quadrangles of the topographic, orthophotoquad, and orthophotomap series covering our states. The grid appearance varies among map series, so let's focus on our large-scale topographic maps. Military topographic maps have UTM grid lines superimposed at one-kilometer intervals, whereas civilian maps show both UTM and SPC grids by grid ticks along the edges of each map. **Figure 4.9** shows how State Plane and UTM grid ticks appear on two sections of the Madison West 1:24,000 topographic map, illustrated in black and white instead of color.

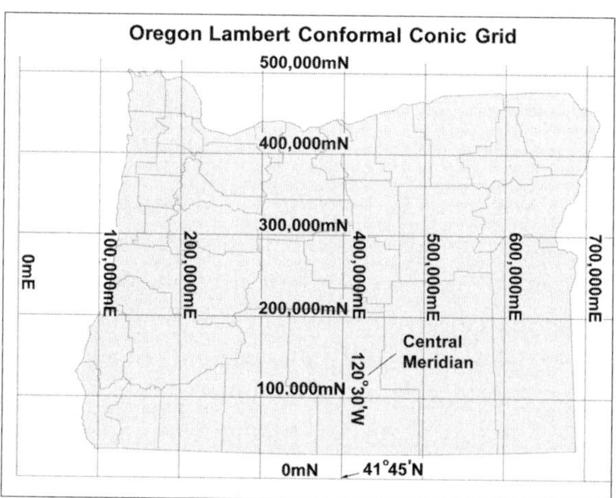

Figure 4.8 The Oregon Lambert conformal conic grid combines two SPC grids into a single grid covering the entire state.

Black ticks along the outer margin of USGS topographic maps indicate SPC 10,000-foot grid lines. The northings or eastings of these ticks are given by the value at one tick on each edge of the map (a 370,000-ft. northing at the tick on the left edge of the Madison West quadrangle in Figure 4.9, for example.) Other ticks are spaced every 5 inches on the 1:24,000 (1 in. to 2,000 ft.) topographic maps. UTM grid ticks are spaced at 1,000 or 10,000 meter intervals, depending on the map scale. On USGS quadrangles of the 1:24000 scale topographic series, 1,000-meter grid ticks are printed in blue (but copied in black on Figure 4.9). These ticks are labeled (in black) with their easting and northing values along the map margin. The **principal digits**—those showing the eastings and northings in kilometers—are printed in larger type with the trailing digits (000) dropped from all but one label along each edge of the map.

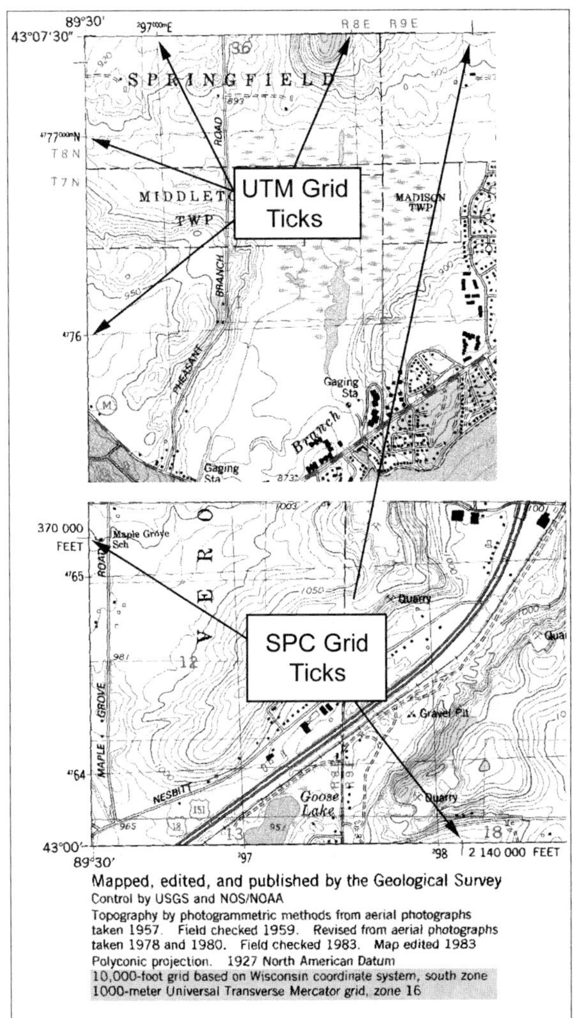

Figure 4.9 Appearance of 1,000m and 10,000ft grid ticks on a 1:24,000 topographic map (printed in black and white).

Grid Orientation

Grid lines or ticks are rarely oriented parallel to the edges of topographic and other quadrilateral-formatted maps. We can see the reason for this by looking at UTM zone 10 in Figure 4.5. Notice that only at the equator do horizontal UTM grid lines intersect the zone edges perpendicularly. Moving toward either pole, the converging edge meridians intersect the horizontal grid lines at increasingly acute angles to a maximum of slightly less than three degrees from perpendicular at the top and bottom of the zone. Let's now look at a map centered on a UTM zone boundary, such as the 90°W boundary between zones 15 and 16 at 45°N latitude (**Figure 4.10**). The zone boundary is a vertical line, and the slight rotation of the edge meridian means that the grid lines are now slightly rotated (2° at this latitude). This slight clockwise rotation to the easterly grid lines at zone edges creates what is termed **grid convergence**.

Grid convergence, then, is zero at the equator and maximum at the top and bottom of the UTM zone. The non-perpendicular intersection of grid lines with latitude-longitude graticule lines also varies longitudinally, being zero at the central meridian of the zone and maximum at the zone edges. East-west grid lines are thus horizontal only on maps at the equator and the central meridian of each UTM zone.

You may wonder how we specify grid coordinates on a map like Figure 4.10 that spans two grid zones. Measuring half of our coordinates in each zone would be very confusing and difficult to work with if we wanted to calculate lengths, directions, and areas from the coordinates. The solution is to extend the zones outward to cover the entire map. This allows us to choose one of the two zones for our map work. UTM zones, for example, can be overlapped up to 30 minutes of longitude with their neighboring zones. For the same reason, State Plane Coordinate system zones also extend above and below or to each side of the counties they cover.

Grid Coordinate Determination

Although the structure of grid coordinate systems is relatively easy to understand, it may take practice to gain skill in using coordinates on maps. Sometimes you'll want to determine an environmental feature's SPC or UTM coordinates. At other times you'll need to find the position on the map of a feature whose coordinates are given.

Say, for instance, that you want to determine the UTM coordinates of the gravel pit on the 1:24,000-scale topographic map segment in **Figure 4.11**. If UTM grid lines aren't printed on the map, use the marginal grid ticks and a straightedge to construct the grid lines lying immediately to the south and north, and east and west, of the gravel pit. Note the coordinate values of the grid lines lying to the west and south of the gravel pit (497,000mE and 4,764,000mN). Next, measure the map distance from these lines to the gravel pit (3.73 and 1.00 cm), and form ratios between these values and the grid interval distance in map units (4.17 cm per kilometer for a 1:24,000-scale map). Multiply these proportions (0.894 and 0.240) by the grid interval distance in ground units (1,000m), and add the results to the west and south grid line values.

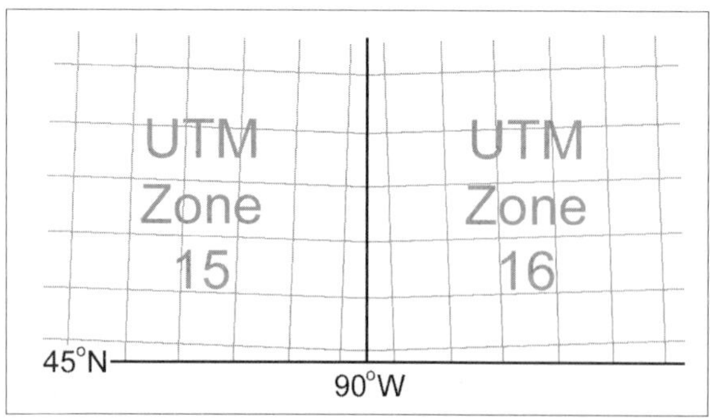

Figure 4.10 UTM grid lines usually are not parallel with graticule lines, but intersect at a slight angle. Maps that span two grid zones will have grid convergence, a problem solved by extending one or both grids across the entire map.

Thus, the UTM coordinate of the gravel pit is:

Easting = 497,000m + 894m = 497,894mE
and
Northing = 4,764,000m + 240m= 4,764,240mN.

Now imagine that you want to plot the location of a feature for which you know the grid coordinates. This problem is essentially the reverse of determining the UTM coordinates of a mapped feature such as the gravel pit in Figure 4.11, which we know is at 497,894mE, 4,764,240mN.

First, determine the UTM northings and eastings for the grid lines falling immediately below and to the left of the coordinate (4,764,000mN and 497,000mE). If these grid lines aren't drawn on the map, use the grid ticks and a straightedge to draw them.

Next, subtract the grid line value immediately west of the easting from the easting (497,894m - 497,000m = 894m), and subtract the grid line value immediately south of the northing from the northing (4,764,240m - 4,764,000m = 240m). Form proportions between these differences and the 1,000m grid interval distance (0.894 and 0.240). Now multiply these proportions by the grid interval in map units (4.17 cm per kilometer) to obtain the easterly and northerly differences in map units (3.73cm and 1.0cm). Finally, plot these distances from the western and southern grid lines. The two plotted lines will intersect at the gravel pit.

If you'll be working with a single coordinate system on maps of a certain scale over and over, it may pay to construct a simple measurement aid called a **roamer**.* You can make this graphic device using the right-angle corner of an ordinary sheet of paper, although you may wish to use more durable material (**Figure 4.12**). To construct a roamer, merely mark off the grid interval distance along

**Many map-scale and grid-using aids are available commercially. These clear plastic devices have calibrated rulers etched into their surface. The rulers match standard topographic map scales. Check your local map or outdoor recreation store to get one of these handy ready-made products.*

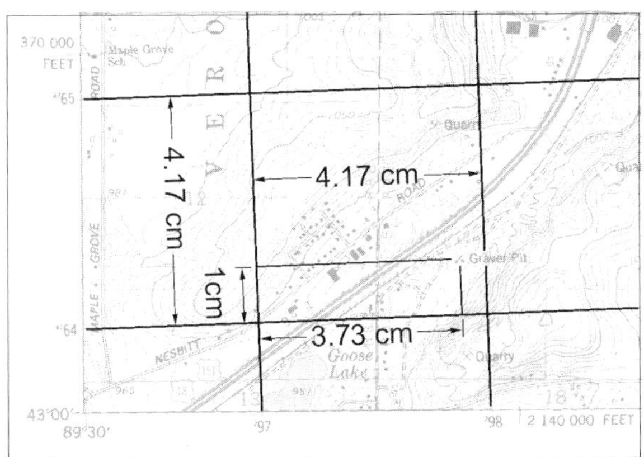

Figure 4.11 To determine the UTM coordinates of the gravel pit or to plot the gravel pit's location from UTM coordinates, follow the steps outlined in the text.

each edge of the paper, starting at the corner. Then divide these distances into units fine enough for the precision of your measurements. Millimeters or tenths of inches normally suffice.

By aligning the roamer with the north-south and east-west grid lines, you can determine map references and plot coordinate locations quickly and accurately (**Figure 4.13**). You'll need a separate roamer for each map scale and grid system, of course. Therefore, you may want to put UTM and SPC roamers for standard USGS quadrangles on opposite corners of the same sheet of paper.

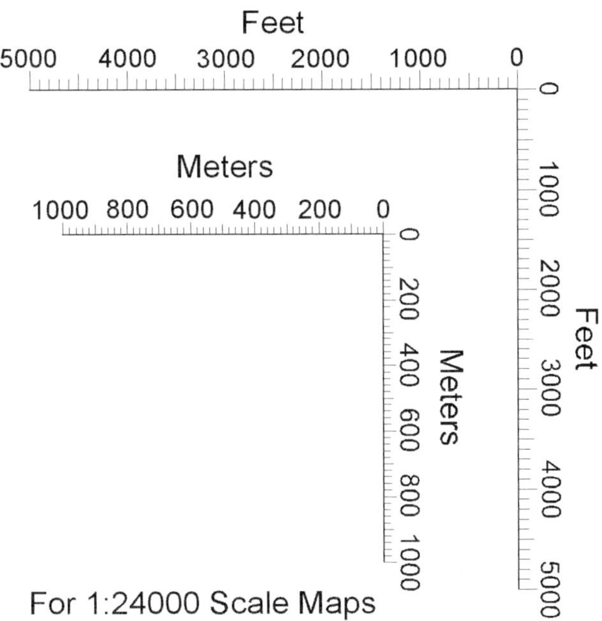

Figure 4.12 Roamers for determining State Plane and UTM coordinates on 1:24,000 scale topographic maps. You can copy this illustration onto a transparency and use it in your map reading work.

GRID CELL LOCATION SYSTEMS

The grid coordinate systems that we've discussed all use point coordinates. Several other reference grids found on maps provide grid cell locations rather than point coordinates. These grid cell coordinates consist of an alphanumeric code that locates cells by their column and row. In this section, we'll explore several such systems.

Arbitrary Grid Cell Systems

You have probably seen grid cell locator systems superimposed over city, state highway, recreational, and atlas maps (**Figure 4.14**). It is common for grid columns to be numbered and rows lettered, so that a cell might have a row, column identification like "C 5". The grid cells are usually keyed to a place name index. If you're looking for a particular street, you simply look it up in the index, where you'll find its grid cell identification.

You now have to locate the feature within the grid cell. This can become difficult if the density of names is great or the cell is large relative to the extent of the feature. The problem of searching for a difficult-to-spot street name is even greater when only marginal ticks indicate grid lines. Remember, too, that each grid cell is specific to the map for which it was drawn. If your friends ask you where a street is and you tell them, "C 5," the information won't be of any help unless they have the same map you do. Keep this in mind when you use maps that include insets. Since each inset may have its own grid cell locator system, the same place may be represented in several grid cells.

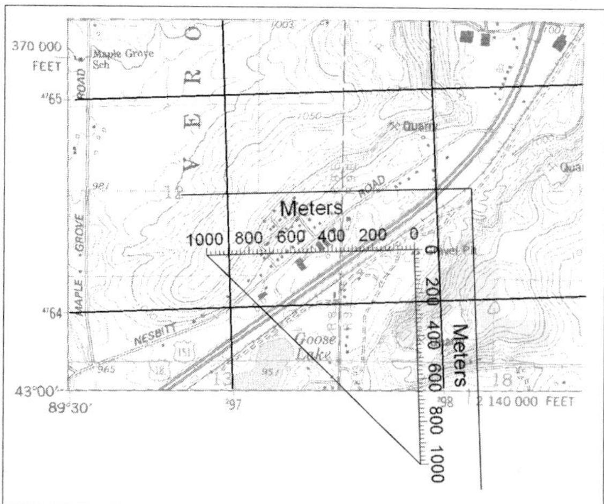

Figure 4.13 You can use a roamer to determine rectangular coordinates for a feature or to plot a feature's position from known coordinates, such as the gravel pit on this topographic map.

Military Grid Reference System

Another grid cell location scheme is the **U.S. Military Grid Reference System** used with UTM and UPS grids. In devising this system, the military aimed to minimize confusion when using long numerical coordinates (up to 15 digits may be required) and numerical grid zone specifications. This was achieved by substituting single letters for several numerals.

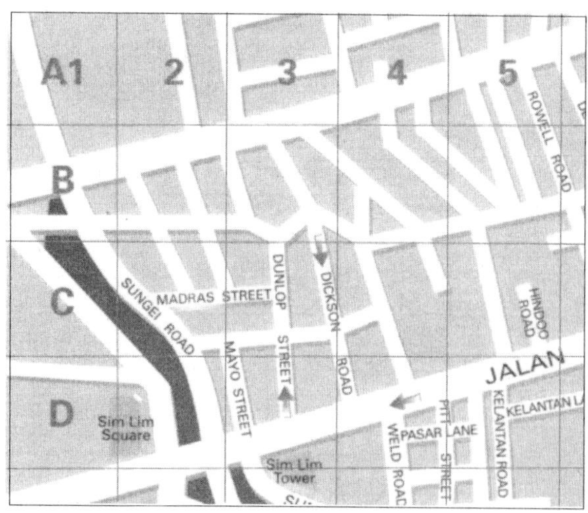

Figure 4.14 An arbitrary grid cell locator system identifies streets by row letter and column number. In this Singapore example, Hindoo Road would be listed as in cell C 5.

In the Military Grid, each of the 60 UTM zones is divided into 19 quadrilaterals covering 8° and one (the northernmost) covering 12° of latitude*. Quadrilaterals are assigned the letters C through X consecutively, beginning at 80°S latitude (**Figure 4.15**). Letters I and O are omitted to avoid possible confusion with similar-appearing numerals. Each grid cell is designated by the appropriate alphanumeric code, referring first to the zone number (column) and next to the row letter. Madison, Wisconsin, for example, is located in the quadrilateral designated 16T (UTM zone 16 and quadrilateral T).

Each quadrilateral is next divided into 100,000-meter square cells, and each cell is identified by a two-letter code. The first letter is the column designation; the second letter is the row designation. The letters I and O are again omitted to avoid possible confusion with numerals. The 100,000-meter-square cell containing Madison, Wisconsin, is designated 16TCC, for example. To assist the user, the 100,000-meter-square cell identification letters for each map sheet are generally shown in the sheet miniature, which is a part of the grid reference box found in the lower margin of the map (**Figure 4.16**).

For more precise designation of grid cells, the Military Grid uses the standard UTM numerals. Thus, the regularly spaced lines that make up the UTM grid on any large-scale map are divisions of the 100,000-meter square cell. These lines are used to locate a point with the desired precision within the cell. Dividing the cell by 10 adds a pair of single-digit numerals which designate a cell of 10,000 meters on a side (**Figure 4.17**). Wisconsin's capitol dome is located in the 10,000-meter cell designated 16TCC07. Further division by 10 requires a pair of two-digit numbers, yielding the designation 16TCC0571 for the 1,000-meter cell containing the capitol. The process can be continued until the desired level of precision is achieved.

**Only the UTM version of the Military Grid will be discussed in detail, since most map users have little call for making coordinate references in polar regions.*

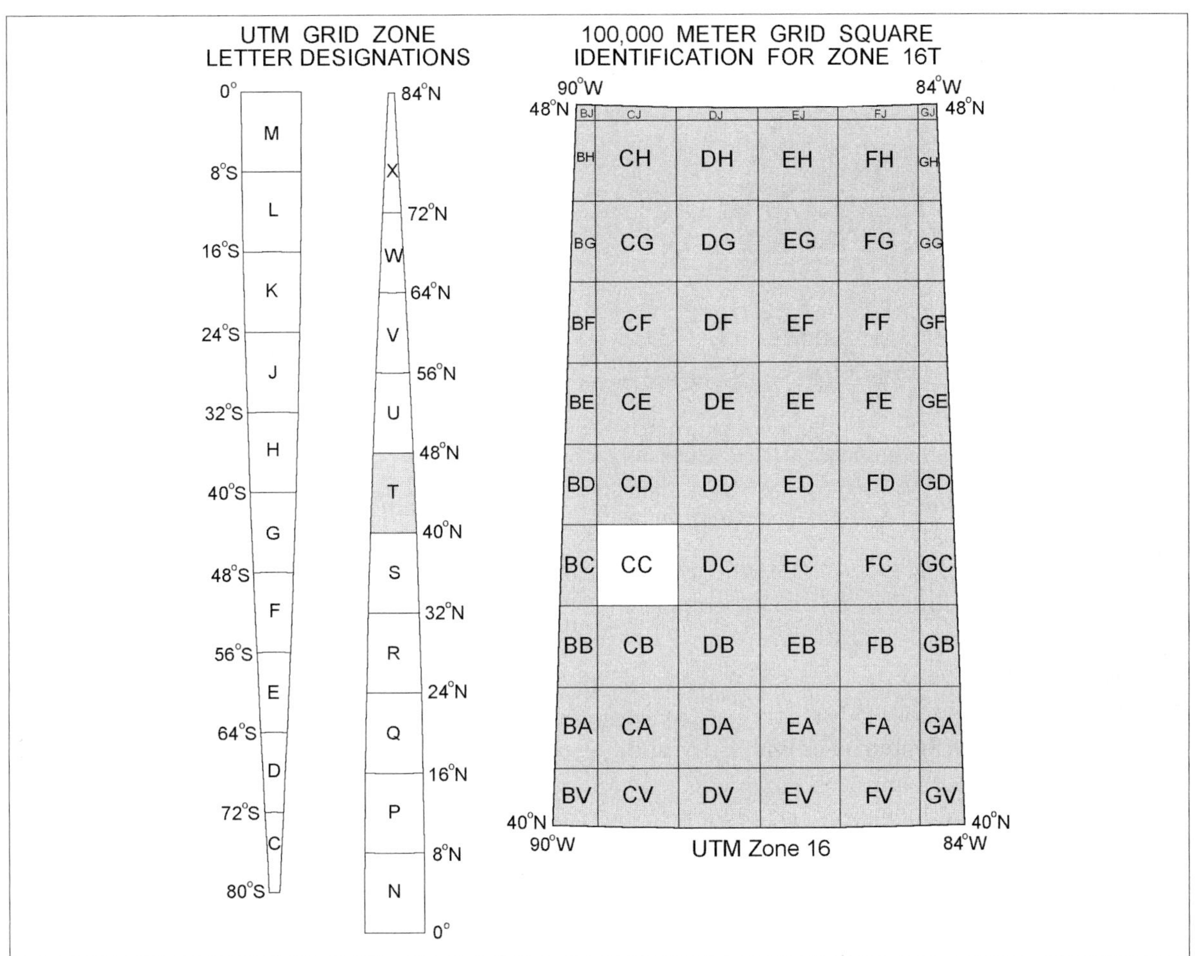

Figure 4.15 With the Military Grid, each of the 60 UTM zones is first divided into 8° latitude quadrilaterals and lettered from south to north. Each of these quadrilaterals is divided into 100,000-meter squares that are given a two-letter code.

In each instance, the coordinate pair designates the southwest corner of the grid cell at the specified level of precision.

Military Grid coordinate system cells are printed on 1:25,000, 1:50,000 and 1:250,000-scale military topographic maps. The 10,000 or 1,000 meter cell row and column numbers are printed over the UTM grid lines for easy identification, along with the two-letter code for the 100,000 meter square. This allows grid cells like the two 10,000 meter squares in the corner of the McDermitt 1:250,000 military topographic map (**Figure 4.18**) to be easily identified as 11TMS23 and 11TMS24.

Proprietary Grids

In recent years, mapping has become more and more commercialized. Commercial vendors have developed and marketed several zone reference systems for use with their products. These proprietary grids may be map related, or they may be related to the use of maps in conjunction with specialized instruments. Let's look at a few examples.

Map Publishers

Atlases have their own version of local grid zone referencing. To complete the spatial reference, you need the name of the atlas and the page number

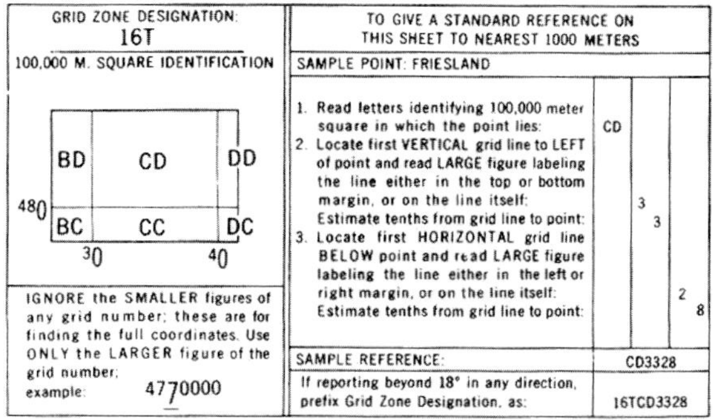

Figure 4.16 A map sheet miniature showing the 100,000-meter-square identification letters can be found in the marginal grid reference box on maps that use the Military Grid.

of the gridded map. The index might indicate, for example, that you'll find London at M-5 on page 12 of the atlas.

This scheme is the basis for **proprietary grid systems** packaged with GPS equipment from some vendors (see Chapter 14: GPS and Maps). For example, the well-known map publisher Thomas Brothers Maps® has created the Page and Grid™ system for use with their three scales of maps covering the continental United States (see Appendix B for contact information on these products). Through special arrangement with the GPS vendor Trimble Navigation, Thomas Brothers Maps® supplies a grid-related product called Thomas Guides™. Trimble, in turn, markets a coordinate extension called Trimble Atlas™ (supplied by Thomas Brothers Maps®) which is designed to increase the locational precision of Page and Grid™ references.

The more specific the zone reference, the larger the scale of the map that is referenced. The

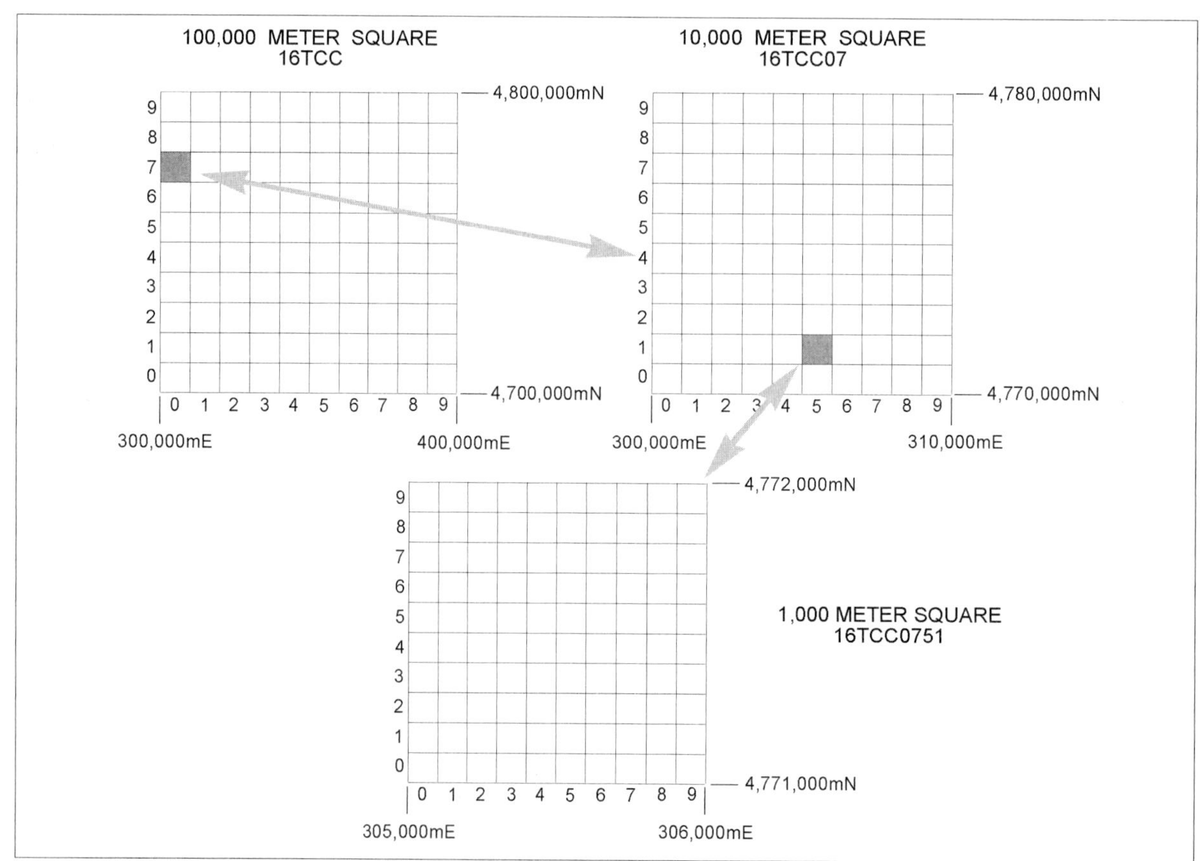

Figure 4.17 Military Grid coordinate designations within 100,000-meter-square cells involve progressive subdivision by 10 and use standard UTM numerals.

result is a tailored package. Your GPS receiver locates you on your map, letting you zoom in or out in scale to see the desired level of detail. As more vendors market electronic navigation systems that display maps on a portable computer screen, such linking of zone coordinates to map features will become more common.

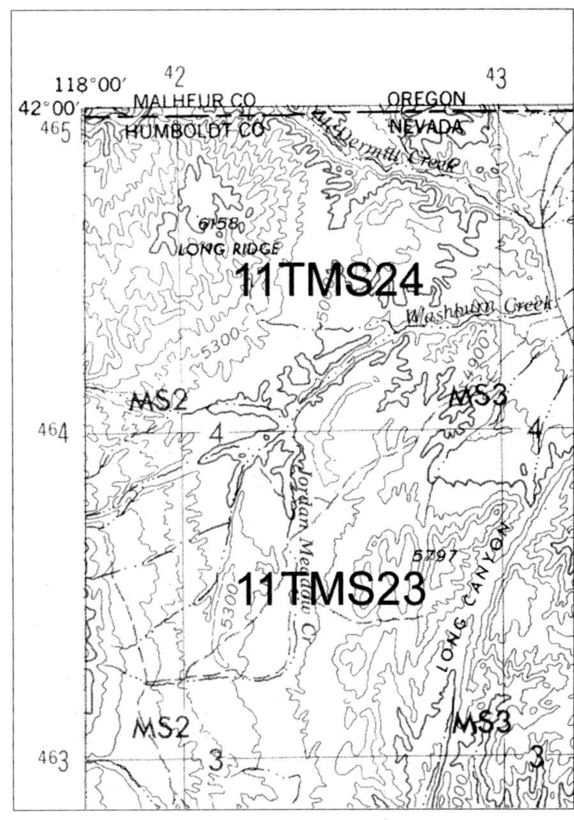

Figure 4.18 Military Grid Reference System (MGRS) cell boundaries are printed on military topographic maps, along with column and row identifiers. The full MGRS identifiers have been added to two 10,000 meter squares.

Amateur Radio Operators

Another proprietary grid is developed and used by amateur (ham) radio operators. This terrestrial reference scheme is based on the **Maidenhead global system**, which partitions the earth into progressively smaller quadrilaterals of latitude and longitude. The first two letters in the reference divide the earth into 20° by 10° fields. Pairs of numbers designate 2° by 1° squares within these fields. Two more letters are used to define 5' × 2.5' sub-squares within each square. Thus a six-character code can locate any place on earth within a rectangular zone of up to 5½ by 3 miles.

As with the Page and Grid™ scheme, Trimble has extended the Maidenhead grid so that it provides more precise spatial referencing. This extension makes the grid more suitable for use with their GPS receivers. The extension, called the Trimble Grid Locator™, adds a pair of numbers and a pair of letters to the six-character Maidenhead code.

SELECTED READINGS

Atwill, L., "What's Up (and Down) at the USGS," *Field & Stream* (May 1997), pp. 54-55.

Department of the Army, *Universal Transverse Mercator Grid*, TM 241-8, Washington, DC, 1958; Departments of the Army and Air Force, TM 5-241, Washington, DC, 1951.

Department of Commerce, Coast and Geodetic Survey, *Plane Coordinate Intersection Tables (2 Minute): Wisconsin*, Special Publication No. 308, Washington, DC, 1953 (series to cover each state).

Hsu, M.L., "The Han Maps and Early Chinese Cartography," *Annals of the Association of American Geographers* (1978), Vol. 68, pp. 45-60.

Maling, D.H., *Coordinate Systems and Map Projections*, 2nd ed. (New York: Pergamon Press, 1992).

Mitchel, H.C., and Simmons, L.G., *The State Coordinate Systems: A Manual for Surveyors*, U.S. Department of Commerce, Coast and Geodetic Survey, Special Publication No. 235, 1945.

Robinson, A.H., et al., "Scale, Reference, and Coordinate Systems," Chapter 6 in *Elements of Cartography*, 6th ed. (New York: John Wiley & Sons, 1995), pp. 92-111.

CHAPTER FIVE
LAND PARTITIONING SYSTEMS

METES AND BOUNDS SYSTEM

French Long Lots
Spanish and Mexican Land Grants
Donation Land Claims

UNITED STATES PUBLIC LAND SURVEY SYSTEM

Townships and Sections
Fractional Divisions
Survey Irregularities
USPLSS Boundaries on Maps

LAND RECORDS

Types of Land Records
- Subdivision Plats
- The Cadastre and Cadastral Maps
- Engineering Plans

Land Information Systems

SELECTED READINGS

"I declare, it's marked just like a large chessboard."
—Alice looking over the country in
Lewis Carroll, Through the Looking Glass

5

CHAPTER 5

LAND PARTITIONING SYSTEMS

Since the beginning of recorded history people have created spatial reference systems convenient for land partitioning. One of the first steps in gaining control of an area is to divide it into tracts that are recorded on maps. Land ownership, zoning, taxation, and resource management are just a few purposes served by such a system. The system has to be simple enough conceptually so that it can be generally understood and simple enough technically so that it can be readily implemented in the field at the time of settlement.

When European settlers first arrived in the United States, they brought a host of land partitioning methods. Two distinct systems were soon in vogue in the colonies. An unsystematic scheme called the **metes and bounds system** prevailed in the South and Southwest, while a systematic plan of **towns** was more common in New England.

METES AND BOUNDS SYSTEM

Much land in the United States colonized before 1800 was characterized by scattered settlements. This was particularly true in the South, where climate was moderate and agriculture was practiced on a large scale. These conditions encouraged people to settle far apart rather than to cluster together as they did in the North. A family usually acquired a grant of a certain size, say 400 acres, through a gift or purchase. The family was then permitted to select a 400-acre parcel to their liking on any part of the unsettled area.

English settlements in the relatively humid Northeast and Southeast were located mainly with respect to soil and timber resources. Consequently, the shape of parcels was decided mainly by the geography of the local setting; people naturally picked the best land they could, regardless of its shape. Convenience of land parcel description was only an afterthought. An irregular parcel was harder to describe than a simple geometrical figure such as a square, but the extra effort would be worthwhile if the parcel contained substantially higher quality land. Some of the lots people created had strange shapes indeed.

The problem, then, was to define these asymmetrical parcels well enough to make clear whose land began where. The solution was to follow a connected path around a parcel's boundaries, noting landmarks along the way. A parcel might be described, using only natural features, as:

> That parcel of land enclosed by a boundary beginning at the falls on Green River, thence downstream to the confluence of the North Fork, thence up the North Fork to the first falls, thence along Black Rock Escarpment to the point of beginning.

This form of land description is referred to as the **metes and bounds system**. With this method, little surveying skill was required to delineate a property boundary. The legal property description was tied to earth features and remained useful as long as neighbors agreed with the place names and accepted the boundaries.

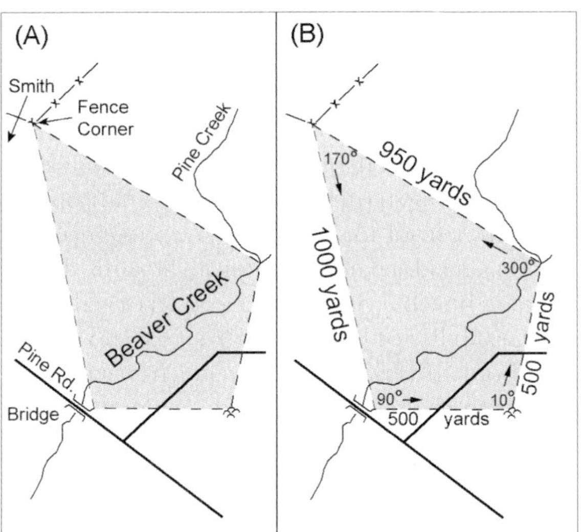

Figure 5.1 Metes and bounds descriptions may consist of landmarks and approximate directions (A) or precise distance and direction readings (B).

Parcels didn't have to be described using only natural features, of course. The parcel shown in **Figure 5.1A**, for instance, could be given the following metes and bounds description, based on artificial as well as natural features:

> Parcel beginning at the point where Pine Road crosses Beaver Creek, thence due east to the big rock pile, thence northeasterly to the confluence of Beaver Creek and Pine Creek, thence northwesterly to the N.E. corner of Tom Smith's fence, thence back to the point of beginning.

After land survey methods arrived, it became less common to use environmental features in land parcel descriptions. Descriptions became more abstract, based on distances and directions from an established point. The land survey form of the feature-based parcel description shown in **Figure 5.1B** would read as follows:

> Parcel beginning at the N.E. corner of the Pine Road bridge over Beaver Creek, thence along a compass sighting of 90° for 500 yards, thence along a compass sighting of 10° for 500 yards, thence along a compass sighting of 300° for 950 yards, and thence along a compass sighting of 170° for 1,000 yards back to the point of beginning.

The description would likely include the parcel's size in common area units, such as acres, as well.

Areas that have been surveyed by metes and bounds are easily identified on topographic maps and aerial photographs (**Figure 5.2**). The characteristic pattern of irregular fields and winding roads intersecting at oblique angles tells you that this is a metes and bounds survey area.

French Long Lots

French settlements had a unique land parcel arrangement. Settlement usually took place along rivers or lakes, which provided the chief source of transportation and communication for the French. Boundaries ran back from the waterfront as paral-

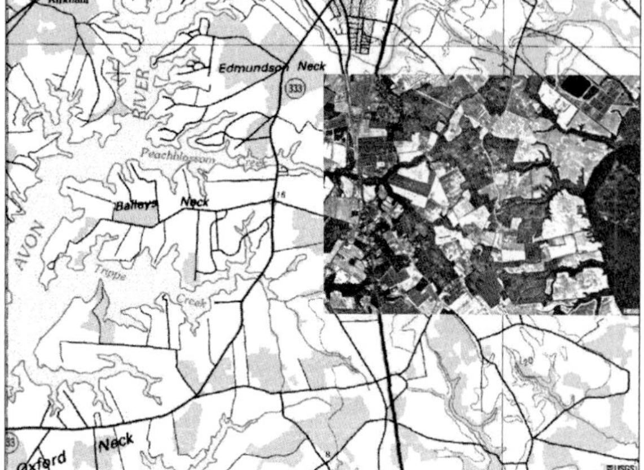

Figure 5.2 Topographic map segment and air photo overlay for an area just south of Easton, Maryland, showing the appearance of metes and bounds surveys. Irregular roads and field boundaries reflect the land survey.

lel lines, creating narrow ribbon farms or long lots. This allowed the settler to have a dock on the river, a home on the natural levee formed by the river, and a narrow strip of farmland that often ended at the edge of a marsh or swamp. Through subsequent subdivision, the parcels often became so narrow that they were no longer practical to farm, but their boundaries still exist legally and are plotted on maps.

Figure 5.3 French long lot boundaries and lot numbers like these along the Mississippi River in Louisiana are shown on topographic maps.

In the United States, long lot boundaries are often shown on topographic maps (**Figure 5.3**). Long lots are particularly apparent along the Mississippi River in Louisiana, but you will also see them in other areas of early French settlement.

Spanish and Mexican Land Grants

During the period from the late 1600s to around 1850, when much of the southwestern United States was part of Spain and later the Mexican Republic, three types of land grants were issued by these governments:

1. Pueblo grants issued to communities of Native Americans were among the earliest, and today Indian reservations in New Mexico and other states are often based on these grants.
2. Private grants, private property that could be sold by the owner, were made to individuals as a reward for service to the government.
3. Community grants were made to groups of settlers. Individuals in the group were given small tracts to settle and cultivate, but most of the grant was held in common for grazing, timber, and other purposes.

To receive a land grant, you had to physically step on the land, run your fingers through the soil, and make a commitment to live on the land, cultivate it, and defend it with your life if necessary.

Land grant boundaries were made easy to recognize. Physical features like hilltops, rivers, and arroyos always defined boundaries. Settlers were very concerned with water resources and many grants straddle rivers and lakes. Descendents of the original settlers still live on these grants, and the boundaries of large grants appear on 1:24,000-scale topographic maps such as **Figure 5.4**.

Donation Land Claims

The Donation Land Claim Act of 1850 granted 320 acres of federal land to any qualified settler who had resided on public lands for four years or more in the Oregon Territory (Idaho, Oregon, Washington, and Montana west of the continental divide.) The metes and bounds property lines of these earliest settlers became Donation Land Claim

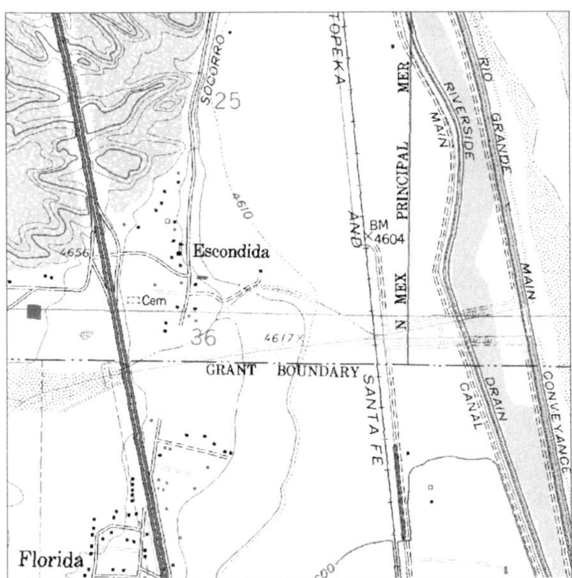

Figure 5.4 Spanish and Mexican land grant boundaries are shown on 1:24,000-scale topographic maps as dashed red lines (reproduced in black) and the words GRANT BOUNDARY inside the grant (near Socorro, New Mexico).

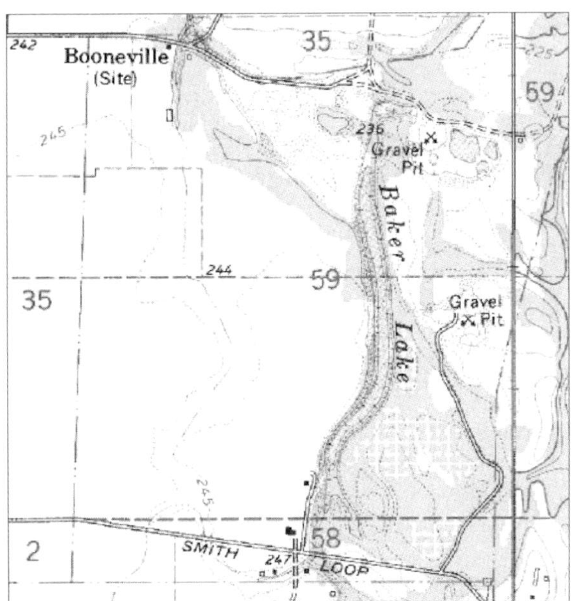

Figure 5.5 Donation land claims south of Corvallis, Oregon, are shown with dashed red boundary lines and claim numbers, always greater than 36. Notice that claims 58 and 59 have north-south and east-west boundaries except for the line for claim 59 at the right edge.

(DLC) parcels. Settlers claiming public lands between 1851 and 1856 were awarded a 160 acre parcel that had to be surveyed with north-south and east-west boundaries. These boundaries had to conform with the Public Land Survey if the survey had already been made. Donation Land Claims were numbered and shown on U.S. Government Land Office maps. DLC boundaries and parcel numbers appear on large-scale topographic maps of the region, such as **Figure 5.5**.

All the land partitioning systems we've discussed so far are unsystematic settlement schemes, in which the land was settled before surveys were made. This free-for-all system encouraged inefficient partitioning of area—at least from the government's point of view. The first people into a region had a virtual monopoly over the choicest lands. Later settlers found only swamps, steep slopes, or poor soils available. In many areas, fragments of poor land remained unowned and unwanted long after a region was "fully" settled.

Furthermore, land claims often overlapped, and boundary errors were common. In homogeneous environments, it was hard to establish accurate borders in the first place. In any setting, boundary mistakes naturally occurred as the land passed through various owners and environmental changes. Good fences, as Robert Frost pointed out, did make good neighbors, because they clarified irregular boundaries. It used to be the custom for neighboring landowners to walk together around their lots each spring. The excursion was far more than a social outing; it made sure that all owners agreed on the borders between their land. Problems arose, however, when later generations ignored the boundary-walking tradition. Many markers were shifted or destroyed through time: Fences fell away; trees died or were cut down; lakes dried up; rock piles were moved. The result has been a host of legal battles over property boundaries of unsystematically settled land.

The alternative to the scattered settlement of irregular parcels was to survey and divide the land systematically before settlers arrived. This practice was followed for towns in many of the colonies, occasionally in the South but mostly in the North. Town sites were laid out and surveyed, and maps of the parcels (called **plats**) prepared and recorded, all prior to settlement. These were part of the foundation for the United States Public Land Survey System, the dominant land partitioning system in the United States.

UNITED STATES PUBLIC LAND SURVEY SYSTEM

In 1783, the United States Congress of the brand-new confederation of 13 states was faced with an urgent need for a national land policy. They had to devise some way to manage the vast lands east of the Mississippi River that had been ceded by Great Britain to the United States after the Revolutionary War. Quick action was important for several reasons. Land had been promised to Revolutionary War soldiers; a source of income was necessary to run the new country; and future states had to be carved out of the wilderness. Most important, the country needed a land policy that the people on the frontier could understand.

By the time the lands west and north of the Ohio River (the Northwest Territories) were opened to settlement in the late 1700s, the newly formed United States government had come up with what seemed to be an orderly way to transfer land to settlers. The solution was called the **Land Ordinance of 1785**, which established the **United States Public Land Survey System (USPLSS)**, otherwise known as the Township and Range System. This plan called for regular, systematic partitioning of land into easily understood parcels prior to settlement and required that all grants be carefully recorded. Settlers were able, however, to select previously surveyed parcels to their liking.

The USPLSS was first implemented in the Northwest Territories and subsequently in the even vaster territories acquired by the United States through the Louisiana Purchase, Red River Cession, Florida Cession, Texas Annexation, Oregon Country Cession, Mexican Cession, Gadsden Purchase, and Alaska Purchase. In these areas the first step was to select arbitrarily an **initial point (Figure 5.6)** for the public land survey. Government land surveyors determined the parallel and meridian that intersected at the initial point. The parallel was called **the base line** or geographer's line (surveyors were called geographers in those days) and the meridian was called the **principal meridian**.

Thirty-five principal meridians and base lines were established within the conterminous United States (**Figure 5.7**) and five within Alaska. The testing ground was Ohio, where seven methods were tried before the final system structure was developed for the 1st Principal Meridian and Base Line in the northwest corner of the state. Notice that at first small areas were surveyed from the initial point, but that later surveys in the West covered large areas, often a territory that was subsequently divided among one or more states. The small surveys in the West were for Indian reservation lands. Each principal meridian was given a name, which was used to identify surveyed parcels within the region. For example, as Figure 5.7 shows, parts of Wisconsin, Minnesota, and Illinois were surveyed using the 4th Principal Meridian.

In Figure 5.7, it appears that the entire area covered by a principal meridian and base line has

Figure 5.6 Initial points were surveyed and defined physically with survey markers. This is the marker at the intersection of the Willamette Meridian and Base Line in Portland, Oregon.

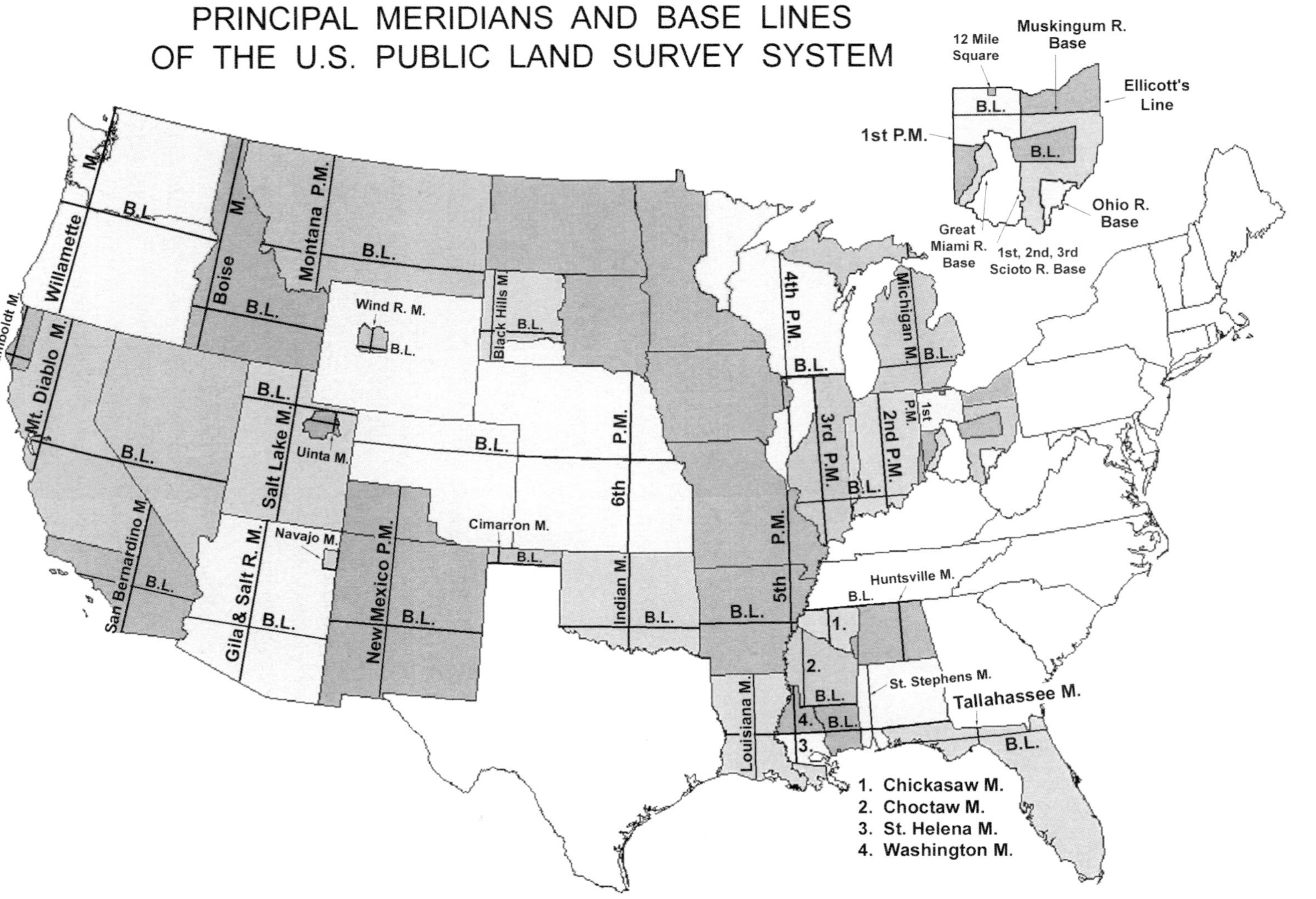

Figure 5.7 Principal meridians and base lines of the Public Land Survey system for the conterminous United States. An initial point marks the intersection of these two lines. Areas surveyed from each initial point are shown with different gray tones.

been surveyed completely, but this is not the case. Some land has never been surveyed under the USPLSS system, mainly because it was reserved for national forests, Indian reservations, or other government use. Setting aside these regions eliminated the need to partition these areas for subsequent land grants or purchases.

Townships and Sections

Once an initial point was established, **range lines** were surveyed along meridians at six-mile intervals east and west of the principal meridian. **Township lines** were surveyed along parallels at six-mile intervals north and south of the base line (**Figure 5.8**). The 6 × 6 mile quadrilaterals bounded by these intersecting township and range lines were called survey or congressional **townships**.

Townships are identified by the number of columns and rows they are away from the initial point. Rows are called townships and columns ranges, corresponding to the surveyed township and range lines. These are usually abbreviated to T and R, so that T3N, R5W identifies the township at the intersection of the third row north and fifth column west of the initial point.

The surveyors encountered a problem, however. We saw in Chapter 1 that meridians converge toward the north pole, so that the east-west distance between the meridians decreases. Thus, the township grid couldn't be extended indefinitely north or south from the initial survey point without townships becoming distorted in shape and area. To reduce the problem of unequal township dimensions**, correction lines** were established at every fourth township (24 miles), where range lines were re-established at six-mile intervals. The effect of this pattern of surveying is seen in Figure 5.8. The range lines north of the Base Line narrow progressively until the correction line is reached, at which time they are resurveyed and hence appear progressively offset to the east or west. This means that townships are neither truly six miles on a side nor 36 square miles in area, since their areas progressively decrease northward from the base line and correction lines.

Each township was partitioned into 36 square-mile parcels, ideally of 640 acres, called **sections**. Every section was then given a number from 1 to 36, depending on its position in the township (Figure 5.8). A zig-zag method of numbering sections was adopted, beginning with section 1 in the upper-right corner of the township and ending with section 36 in the lower-right corner. This was done so that every section would share a common side with its preceding and succeeding section.

Fractional Divisions

A section could be divided successively into **half** or **quarter sections**. An easy way to correctly identify quarter sections is to think of a compass placed at the center of the section. Clockwise from north, the compass direction to the center of each quarter section is northeast, southeast, southwest, or northwest. With this fractional division system, each land parcel's legal description is unique and unambiguous. The 10-acre piece of land in Section 24 (parcel 4) in Figure 5.8, for example, would be described in abbreviated form as:

NE¼, NW¼, SE¼, Sec. 24, T.2N, R.7E, 1st P. M.

In expanded form, the description reads:

> The Northeast quarter of the Northwest quarter of the Southeast quarter of Section 24 of Township 2 North, Range 7 East, 1st Principal Meridian.

To locate a parcel from its legal description, the trick is to read backwards, beginning with the principal meridian and working back through the township and range, the section, and the fractional section. To give the parcel's legal description, you simply reverse the above procedure and work up from the smallest division to the principal meridian. Study the examples in Figure 5.8 until you feel comfortable with the system, because the USPLSS is the basis for abstracts, deeds, and most other land ownership documents in the United States.

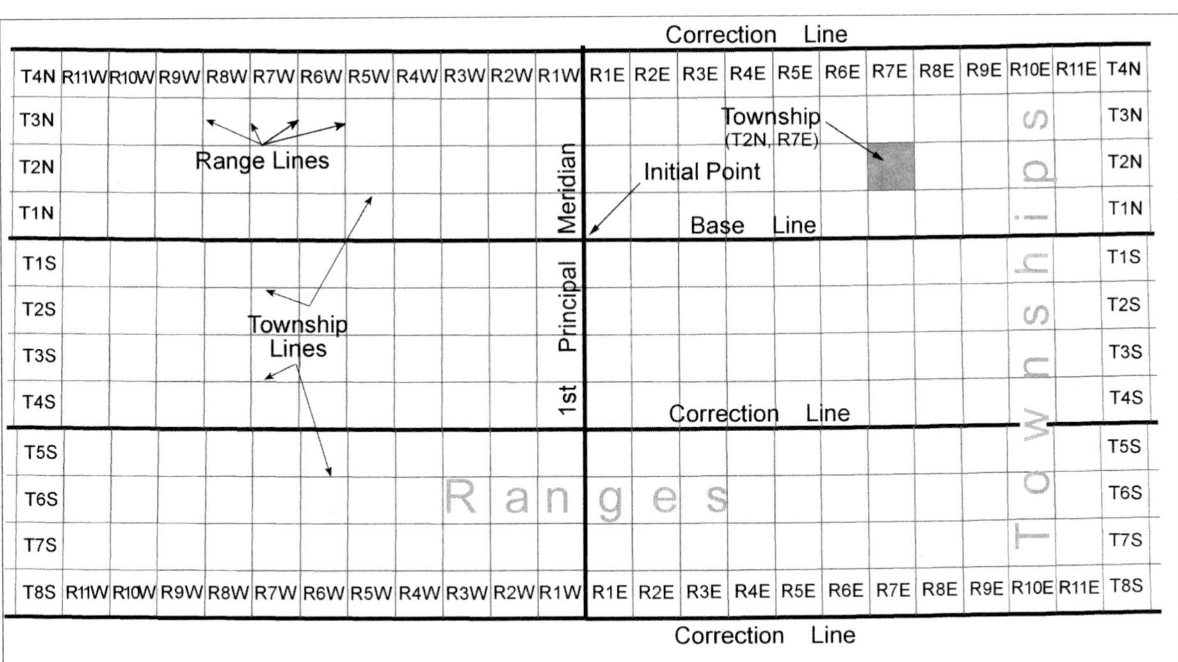

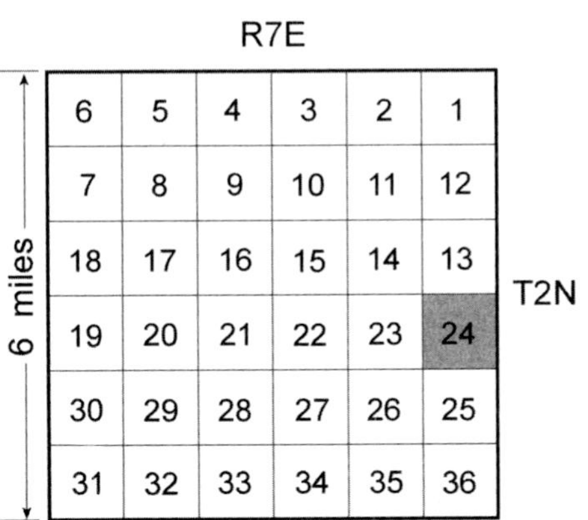

Township Section Numbering

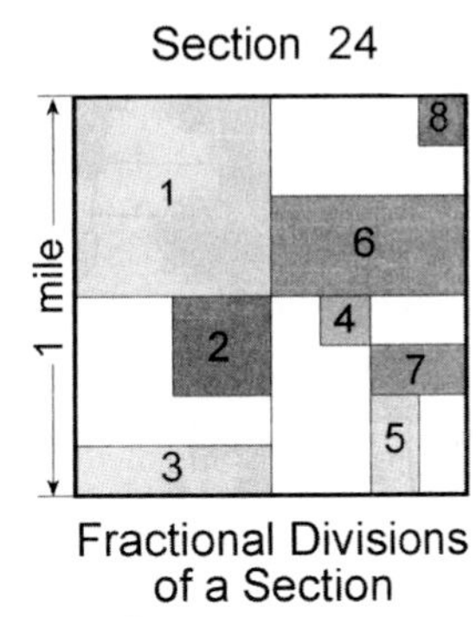

Fractional Divisions of a Section

TYPICAL FRACTIONAL LAND DIVISIONS

(1) NW1/4, Sec. 24, T2N, R7E, 1st P.M.
(2) NE1/4, SW1/4, Sec. 24, T2N, R7E, 1st P.M.
(3) S1/2, S1/2, SW1/4, Sec. 24, T2N, R7E, 1st P.M.
(4) NE1/4, NW1/4, SE1/4, Sec. 24, T2N,R7E, 1st P.M.
(5) W1/2, SE1/4, SE1/4, Sec. 24, T2N,R7E, 1st P.M.
(6) S1/2, NE1/4, Sec. 24, T2N,R7E, 1st P.M.
(7) S1/2, NE1/4, SE1/4, Sec. 24, T2N,R7E, 1st P.M.
(8) NE1/4, NE1/4, NE1/4, Sec. 24, T2N,R7E, 1st P.M.

Figure 5.8 The structure and notation of the United States Public Land Survey provides a systematic means of describing land parcels as small as 10 acres.

There are some exceptions to the use of the USPLSS fractional land division in areas covered by the system. One exception occurs when most of a small parcel falls under a water body. Such a parcel, called a government lot, is usually described solely by a number (**Figure 5.9**). Parcels in a platted subdivision of building sites are also specified by lot numbers. Other exceptions are small (less than 10 acre) and irregular land parcels, which were often given metes and bounds, rather than USPLSS, descriptions.

Survey Irregularities

In practice, the idealized structure of the USPLSS frequently broke down. Errors in the original survey occurred due to poor instrumentation, rugged terrain, or just plain sloppy work by surveyors, who were paid on the basis of total miles surveyed (**Figure 5.10**). These survey errors have persisted, largely because historical boundaries hold legal precedence over new survey evidence.

Variations in the shape and size of sections resulting from survey errors weren't the only obstacles to partitioning land into square mile sections. The pinching effect of converging meridians on the ellipsoidal earth complicated the surveyor's job of laying out a regular grid of sections within a township. To systematize the distribution of shape and area distortions, the order that surveyors de-

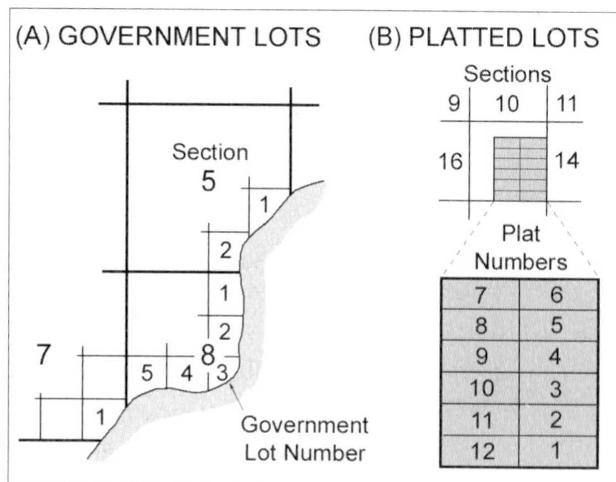

Figure 5.9 Small parcels, such as government lots (A) and platted lots (B), are numbered separately in the USPLSS.

	33	34	35	36	31	32	33	34	
5	4	3	2	1	6	5	4	3	2
8	9	10	11	12	7	8	9	10	
17	16	15	14	13	18	17	16	15	
20	21	22	23	24	19	20	21	22	
29	28	27	26	25	30	29	28	27	
32	33	34	35	36	31	32	33	34	
				Correction Line					
5	4	3	2	1	6	5	4	3	2

Figure 5.10 Survey errors are evident in this segment of the USPLSS section line grid.

termined section corners was standardized so that survey errors accumulated along the western and northern tiers of sections within each township, particularly in sections 5-8.

An irregular pattern of township and section lines occurs at the boundary between the areas surveyed under different principal meridians, particularly if the boundary is an irregular feature like a river. The boundary between areas surveyed under the Michigan Meridian and 4th Principal Meridian follows the Michigan-Wisconsin state line, for example, and you will find offset and partial townships all along the boundary between the two states (**Figure 5.11**).

Another source of deviations from the ideal pattern of townships is the fact that in some areas townships were not surveyed systematically outward from the initial point. A good example is the surveying of townships in Oregon along the base line for the Willamette Meridian. The earliest townships were surveyed outward from the initial point in Portland, but independent surveys were also completed at the coast and from three separate starting points along the Base Line in eastern Oregon. The starting points were calculated so that in theory they would mesh perfectly with the surveys from the initial point, but errors in surveying made this impossible to achieve. You can see on topographic maps the shortened and elongated town-

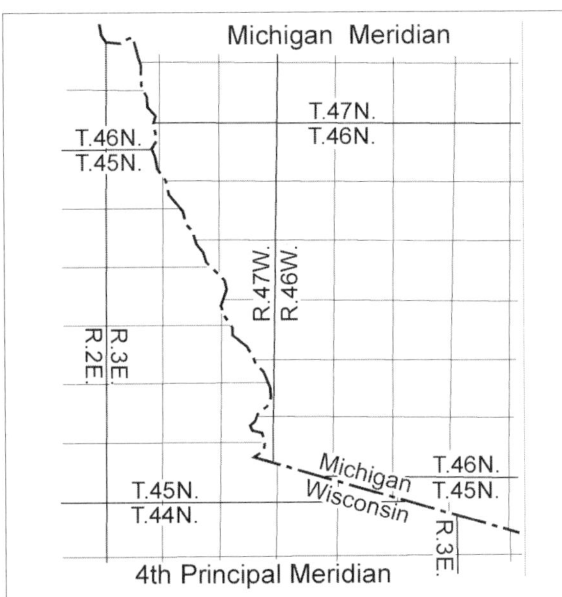

Figure 5.11 Irregularities in USPLSS township boundaries may be due to the convergence of surveys from different principal meridians.

ships that mark the places where these independent surveys came together. The result is many independently surveyed parts of USPLSS grids which, where they come together, rarely mesh. At the contact zone between these independent surveys, some confusing USPLSS descriptions can occur. This is especially true for land parcels straddling the contact zones, since for them two deeds are required.

A similar problem may occur when the USPLSS grid comes into contact with earlier land partitioning systems; this can happen in regions not surveyed at the time of settlement or where boundaries were defined in an older system like long lots or Spanish land grants. The prior Spanish land grant boundary in Figure 5.4 is a classic example—both section lines and the principal meridian stop at the land grant boundary.

USPLSS Boundaries on Maps

The USPLSS grid is found on many different types of maps. On maps made by government agencies, for example, townships and sections are often included because they are so closely associated with the boundaries of civil townships, counties, and other political units. The USPLSS grid probably finds its fullest expression on USGS quadrangle maps in the topographic series. On these maps, township and section lines, section corners, section numbers, and marginal township-range notations are all printed in red (shown in black in **Figure 5.12**). Dashed red lines indicate section lines with doubtful locations.

Township and section lines are also found on a host of governmentally produced maps dealing with land resources, such as U.S. Forest Service and Bureau of Land Management ownership maps. Privately produced road and recreation atlases, some available in digital as well as paper form, also include the USPLSS grid as a handy reference system tied to the ground. Surveys of city and rural lots in USPLSS areas are also tied to section or fractional section corners. These are commonly shown on land subdivision plat maps and tax assessor cadastral maps used as land records.

As we've seen, the USPLSS grid shown on these topographic and land resource maps lets us partition a region into easily defined area parcels. By slightly modifying the USPLSS, you can also use it as a crude point referencing system. To do so, you state the location of environmental features with reference to the corner or center of a standard USPLSS parcel. You can pinpoint many features this way, since the cultural landscape has been aligned to the USPLSS grid in many parts of the country. For instance, Wisconsin's capitol dome is centered on the northeast corner of section 23, T.7N, R.9E, 1st P.M.

LAND RECORDS

Collecting and maintaining land records is common to all civilizations, past and present. Physical features, resource reserves, market value, ownership, improvements, accessibility, and restrictions on land use are but a few of the items entered in these records. Traditionally, the basic spatial unit for this record keeping is the land parcel. A land parcel is the smallest unit of ownership or, as in the case of a farm field, a unit of uniform use.

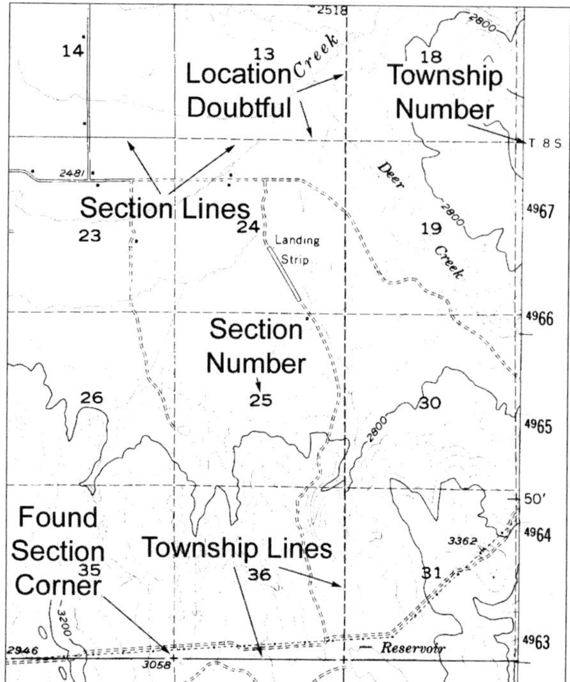

Figure 5.12 Appearance of USPLSS township and section information on a typical USGS topographic map.

Types of Land Records

Subdivision Plats

The land surveying profession carries out the subdivision of USPLSS fractional lots and other land parcels. The boundaries of your lot were probably determined using plane surveying methods similar to the metes and bounds survey described in Figure 5.1. Property boundary corners are defined by the distance and direction from the previous corner, with the first corner defined by the distance and direction from a previously surveyed point, such as a USPLSS section corner. The corner-by-corner survey is called a **traverse**.

Surveyors usually carry out closed traverses (**Figure 5.13**) on land parcels, meaning that the last corner surveyed is the same as the first corner. Unfortunately, the first and last corners rarely match up exactly. But, fortunately, this error lets surveyors check on the accuracy of their work and make adjustments to all the points along the traverse to force an exact fit. This accuracy check makes the extra effort of closing the traverse worthwhile.

Land subdivision surveys are recorded on **subdivision plats** that must be legally recorded in the city or county surveyor's office or an equivalent bureau. A typical subdivision plat map (**Figure 5.14**) shows each property line along with its distance and angle from the previous survey point. In addition to these property line dimensions, the area of each lot and lot numbers must be shown, along with the names and dimensions of proposed and existing streets. Proposed building setback lines and easements must also be shown, making the subdivision plat map the best source of detailed information about any land parcel you are interested in purchasing. Subdivision plat measurements are generally tied to the ground through a system of field markers at the time of survey. Thus, at least in theory, you can use the plat to trace a parcel's boundaries in the field.

The Cadastre and Cadastral Maps

We call the written records kept on land parcels the **cadastre**. **Fiscal cadastres** are among the oldest (not surprisingly, since governments have taxed

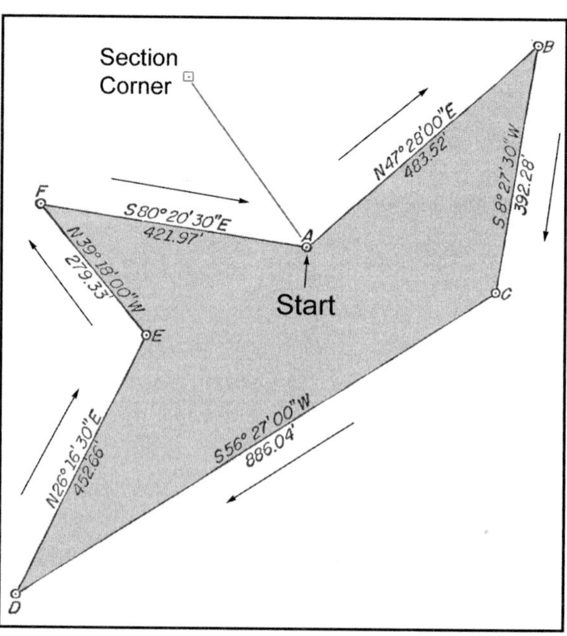

Figure 5.13 A typical closed traverse, with bearings and distances for each property line shown.

property since the beginning of recorded history). Fiscal cadastres include the owner's name and address, parcel description and size, the parcel's assessed value and any improvements, and the current tax levy. In the United States, the fiscal cadastre for rural areas is the responsibility of county government and is housed in the county treasurer's office in the county seat (often the courthouse). The fiscal cadastre for city property is the responsibility of municipal government.

Another type of cadastre is the **legal cadastre**, which consists of records concerning proprietary interests in land parcels.* These records contain the current owner's name and address, legal description of the property, deed, title, abstract, and legal encumbrances (such as easements, mineral rights, and transfer restrictions). In the United States, some of this information is held by the property taxing authority, but the rest may be scattered among several agencies. Property abstract and title companies do a booming business helping people track down these elusive records.

Fiscal and legal cadastres are of limited value for administrators, managers, and planners who make decisions involving natural resources, land use, or infrastructure considerations (fire, police, ambulance, disaster relief services) in the course of

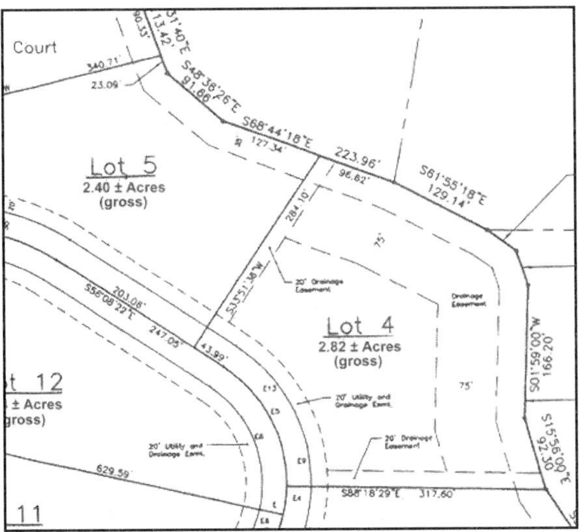

Figure 5.14 Subdivision plats show detailed land survey information for individual lots.

their work. These land information specialists need extensive, reliable attribute (or feature) information about land parcels, including land slope and aspect, soil characteristics, drainage, vegetation cover, number of residents, building construction, access road width and surface material, utility service, and zoning restrictions. The body of land records containing this information is called the **multipurpose cadastre**. It is this third type of cadastre that is currently attracting the most attention. Environmental administrators, managers, and planners realize that they could do their jobs better if this information was reliably recorded and accessible.

Cadastres are generally made up of two complementary parts. One part contains the written record, or **register**, which provides information concerning land ownership. It may include all manner of documents, forms, official seals, and stamps of approval that characterize bureaucratic activities. These written records have traditionally been widely scattered among government offices, each with a different mission and authority. Assembling the register material can therefore be frustrating, time consuming, and costly.

The second part of most cadastres, thoroughly cross-referenced with the first part, contains detailed descriptions of each parcel. These descriptions may be in the form of the original subdivision plat or in the form of **cadastral maps** made from the subdivision plats (**Figure 5.15**). In either case, you can determine the location and areal extent of each parcel from these records.

A key function of cadastral surveys is to provide the foundation for a system of land rights transfer. It is necessary to know a parcel's boundaries before it can be conveyed without ambiguity from one owner to the next. Land conveyance involves more than a geographic description of a parcel, of course, because such a description says nothing about possible restrictions or encumbrances on the property. It is for this reason that the cadastral survey is cross-referenced with the register, and

**In practice, there is a great deal of overlap and duplication between fiscal and legal cadastres.*

it is important to consult both land records when transferring property rights.

Engineering Plans

City engineering or public works departments maintain a series of very large-scale engineering plans. A city might be covered by 1:1,200 (1" to 100') scale map sheets, each covering a 2,000' by 3,000' rectangle defined by State Plane Coordinates. Each sheet is typically a set of map overlays for features such as property boundaries, streets and sidewalks, building footprints and street addresses, water and sewer lines, telephone and power poles, detailed elevation contours, and others. A typical engineering plan (**Figure 5.16**) will include several, but not all, of these features.

The information for engineering plans comes from subdivision plats, engineering records, and interpretation of large-scale aerial photography covering the city. These map overlays are part of a city's multipurpose cadastre, with each overlay stored as a data layer in a **land information system**. Today many city engineering and public works departments have websites where engineering plan overlays can be viewed and downloaded to home computers.

Land Information Systems

Computerized land information systems represent a recent attempt to integrate the various cadastres into a useful whole. Such systems stress data compatibility, sharing, and cooperation. They also incorporate powerful statistical and graphic tools to help users analyze data, generate land information, and make decisions (see Geographic Information Systems in Chapter 19).

The cadastre represents an important part of the database used in a modern land information system. As such, it must meet two requirements:

1. All entries should be spatially referenced, using some form of coordinate referencing system. In other words, there must be some provision for moving from the data records to the appropriate ground positions.

Figure 5.15 A cadastral map shows property boundaries and tax lot numbers that are tied to the fiscal and legal cadastre.

2. There must be compatibility among the spatial referencing entries. It is preferred that all spatial reference data be identified with some terrestrial system. Latitude-longitude coordinates are ideal because they are universal, but State Plane Coordinates and Universal Transverse Mercator coordinates are also acceptable if we're willing to accept the zone boundary problems they introduce. If several spatial reference systems are used in recording data, they should at least be transformable from one to the other. Part of the rationale for developing state grids was to eliminate these zone boundary problems.

Here we have a major problem. Land partitioning systems that accommodated the early settlers aren't best suited today when land records management is the primary concern. The USPLSS is a case in point. It was an excellent system when the government's main concern was selling or giving away land parcels as quickly and efficiently as possible. It also served land transfer needs fairly well in subsequent years.

But for purposes of land management, the USPLSS has been an administrative nightmare. The problem is that locations of township and section corners were not originally defined by their latitude and longitude. Rather, these locations are

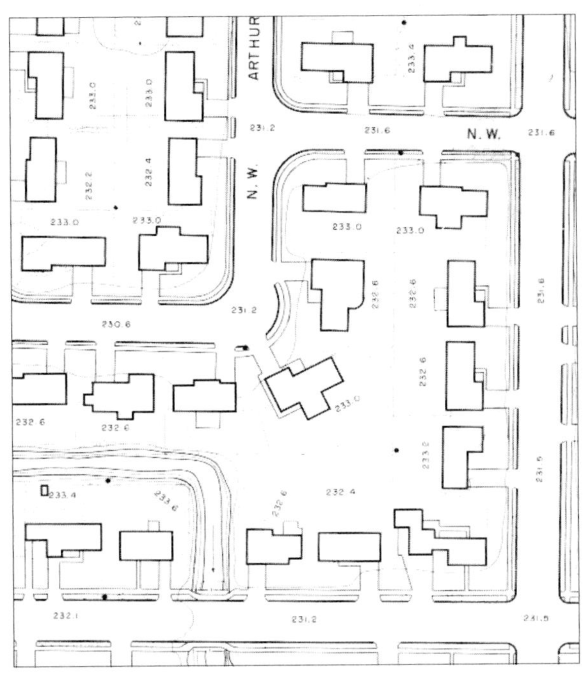

Figure 5.16 An engineering plan such as this 1:1,200 scale segment for Corvallis, Oregon, shows property boundaries and other features critical to public works management.

known only in reference to other points and boundaries in the system. This means that there is no convenient way to determine which parcel contains a particular location or what resources are found in a specific parcel. Learning whose land has been damaged by a flood, for example, usually involves rescaling and overlaying several maps, as well as searching through a diversity of textual and tabular records.

Today we can perform overlay and correlation operations much more quickly and accurately with computers running GIS software than we can manually. For this reason, many thousands of USPLSS section corners have been located on the ground and given latitude-longitude, UTM, or State Plane Coordinates. Although the old system will undoubtedly persist for years to come, we can expect land parcels in the future to be described by geographic or grid coordinates. We'll return to this topic in Chapter 19, where we discuss automated geographic information systems.

SELECTED READINGS

Crossfield, J.K., "Evolution of the United States Public Land Survey System," *Surveying and Mapping*, 44, 3 (1984), pp. 259-265.

Estopinal, S.V., *Guide to Understanding Land Surveys* (Eau Claire, WI: Professional Education Systems, 1989).

Hart, J.F., "Land Division in America" in *The Look of the Land* (Englewood Cliffs, NJ: Prentice-Hall, 1975), pp. 45-66.

Johnson, H.B., *Order Upon the Land: The U.S. Rectangular Land Survey and the Upper Mississippi Country* (London: Oxford University Press, 1976).

National Research Council, *Modernization of the Public Land Survey System* (Washington, DC: National Academy Press, 1982).

National Research Council, *Need for a Multipurpose Cadastre* (Washington, DC: National Academy Press, 1980).

National Research Council, *Procedures and Standards for a Multipurpose Cadastre* (Washington, DC: National Academy Press, 1982).

Thrower, N.J.W., "Cadastral Survey and County Atlases of the United States," *The Cartographic Journal*, 9, 1 (June 1972), pp. 43-51.

Trewartha, G.T., "Types of Rural Settlement in Colonial America," *Geographical Review*, 36, 4 (1946), pp. 568-596.

Ventura, S.J., *Implementation of Land Information Systems in Local Government—Steps Toward Land Records Modernization in Wisconsin* (Madison: Wisconsin State Cartographer's Office, 1991).

Vonderohe, A.P., et al., *Introduction to Local Land Information Systems for Wisconsin's Future* (Madison: Wisconsin State Cartographer's Office, 1991).

CHAPTER SIX
QUALITATIVE THEMATIC MAPS

QUALITATIVE INFORMATION
Point-Feature Information
Line-Feature Information
Area-Feature Information

SINGLE-THEME MAPS
Point-Feature Maps
Line-Feature Maps
Area-Feature Maps

MULTIVARIATE MAPS
Point Symbols
Line Symbols
Area Symbols

QUALITATIVE CHANGE MAPS
Point Symbols
Line Symbols
Area Symbols
Three-Dimensional Features

SELECTED READINGS

Miss Dove had seen paintings done in the art class—
great, free, brilliant blobs of color running into the margins,
and had shuddered to imagine maps executed with such techniques!
—Frances Gray Patton, Good Morning, Miss Dove

6

CHAPTER SIX

QUALITATIVE THEMATIC MAPS

In the introductory chapter, we saw that maps can be divided into two broad categories—reference and thematic. Topographic quadrangles, nautical and aeronautical charts, road maps, and world atlas sheets are examples of reference maps used to locate features, learn the basic geography of a region, and plan travel routes. All of these maps contain basic geographic information such as coastlines, rivers, roads, political boundaries, and topography. Each of these is given equal visual prominence on the map, so that no feature is seen as more important than the others.

In contrast, **thematic maps** show the geographical distribution of a particular theme. A map showing different climate zones within a country is a good example, as is a landcover, vegetation zone, species range, and population density map. Basic geographical reference information will, of course, appear on a thematic map, but the theme will stand out visually as the most important thing on the map.

Thematic maps can show both qualitative and quantitative information. Population density is a quantitative theme, and in Chapter 7 we'll see the methods map makers use to portray quantitative information. In this chapter, we'll focus on the ways map makers show **qualitative themes** such as landcover categories. First, we'll look at the basic types of qualitative information for point, line, and area features. Next, we'll examine the ways that map makers show a single point, line, or area feature. We'll also see examples of how map makers create **multivariate thematic maps** showing the geographical relationships between two themes. Finally, we'll explore qualitative thematic maps that focus on changes in feature locations over time.

QUALITATIVE INFORMATION

Qualitative information tells you only where different things exist—lakes, rivers, roads, cities, farms, an so on. In contrast, quantitative information consists of data giving you the magnitudes of these things. The magnitude data tell you how many of the things exist, or how large, wide, fast, or high they are. This simple dichotomy between qualitative and quantitative information pervades our descriptions of the environment. But to categorize all information as either qualitative or quantitative is needlessly restrictive, since scientists think of data as being at one of four **measurement levels**. The **nominal** level of measurement is associated with qualitative information, whereas quantitative data can be at the **ordinal**, **interval**, or **ratio** measurement levels (see Chapter 7 for details about the three quantitative measurement levels).

Nominal level information tells you simply which category (class) a feature belongs to. Features within a category are assumed to be relatively similar, whereas differences between categories should be quite large. Different types of nominal level data are collected for point, line, and area features, and this information is the basis for qualitative thematic maps.

Point-Feature Information

What is a point feature? This question is harder to answer than you might think, because two types of point features are mapped using similar point symbols. The first type of point feature is a zero-dimensional entity (without width or area) defined solely by its geographic location. The horizontal survey control points discussed in Chapter 1 are an example of zero-dimensional point features. Although a metal control point marker is placed in the ground, geographic coordinates define the control point. The latitude and longitude data for the control points will be the most geometrically accurate information on the map, since each point is determined with care by professional surveyors using high-accuracy surveying equipment.

The second and far more common type of point feature is something having areal extent that is mapped as if it were at a point. A large-scale thematic map showing the locations of several species of individual trees, for example, treats each tree as a point feature. A tree covers an area and has a height, of course, but on the map the center of its crown is shown by a point symbol that represents its species. This example shows you that features with areal extent may be mapped either as points or areas depending on the map's scale and purpose. A large-scale landscape plan for your yard will show the crown area and shape of each plant, while a small-scale world population map will show cities as points on the earth.

Data describing the locations and attributes of this second type of point feature are collected in two basic ways. In our tree-mapping example, the species of each tree may have been determined by direct **field observation**. If a professional botanist looked at each tree and carefully recorded its species and location in a database, great faith can be placed in the accuracy of the mapped information. But it is also possible that lower-accuracy methods such as recreational-grade GPS receivers were used to determine the location of each tree trunk. In this case, you can be confident of the tree species shown on the map, but you should assume that the mapped position of each tree is only approximately correct.

Point data are also collected through **image interpretation** (see Chapter 21 for a detailed description of image interpretation methods). In our tree-mapping example, a botanist interpreting large-scale aerial photographs covering the area may have determined the location and species of each tree. Different tree species are usually determined with the aid of tree identification keys that show the typical appearance of each species on an air photo. Identifying different types of trees from the typical appearance of their crowns on air photos usually is less accurate than direct field observation, but the geographic locations of crown centers may be easier to measure accurately. In this case, you can place more faith in the mapped position of the tree than in the species it is assigned.

Line-Feature Information

Line-feature information is similar to point-feature data in several ways. Surveyed lines such as property boundaries are true one-dimensional features having length and direction but no width. Boundaries are composed of straight line segments whose endpoints are surveyed locations defined by coordinates. Most line features, however, have a width but are mapped as if they were one-dimensional lines. Different types of roads, for example, have standard design widths and surface compositions such as asphalt and concrete. Actual road widths are shown on a few maps such as large-scale engineering plans. But most maps show different types of roads with similar-width line symbols.

Like point-feature data, line feature information is commonly collected through field observation and image interpretation. A person can drive each road and note if it's made of dirt, gravel, asphalt, or concrete. An image interpreter can determine road surface composition from air photos of the area using a road-type interpretation key. The road surface type may also have been included on the original engineering plan for the road. Regardless of the data collection method, surface compositions are probably stored by road segment in a city or county public works or engineering department database. Map makers regularly use these digital data to create road-type maps.

Homogeneity within line features is another important type of information. In the previous example, many road segments probably are completely asphalt or totally gravel. When these homogeneous segments are shown on the map as asphalt or gravel roads, they agree with what's on the ground. However, other road segments may have more than one surface type, such as a forest road segment that's mostly gravel with short sections of asphalt. In this case, the material covering most of the road is likely used as the category for the entire road segment. You can see that roads classified in this way will appear uniform in composition on the map, an inaccuracy that may cause travel problems for the unwary map reader.

In regions where a large number of road segments have more than one surface type, the dataset used for map making may include the percentage of the road segment in each surface type. The map maker may have used this information to define a mixed-type category, based on a criterion such as "No more than 60% of the road segment length is of a single surface type." The map may also show several mixed-type categories such as gravel-asphalt, asphalt-concrete, or dirt-gravel. These categories better capture the dominant surface types in each road segment.

Area-Feature Information

Map makers commonly divide a region into two-dimensional **data collection areas** defined by the qualitative features within their boundaries. The areas are two-dimensional in the sense that data are collected as if the ground were a flat plane. Map makers use qualitative area-feature data collected by ground survey, image interpretation, or other methods to determine the category for each data collection area. The idea is that qualitative features of a certain category share some common trait, while differing significantly from the features in another category. The category is then mapped as if it were homogeneous within the data collection area, with no internal variation.

The qualitative area-feature data may give the map maker information about the actual **degree of homogeneity** within each data collection area. The data might show some areas to be truly homogeneous, such as a clear mountain lake bounded by a steep rocky shoreline devoid of aquatic vegetation. If the lake's surface is categorized as water, its shoreline drawn on an air photo is the boundary of a completely homogeneous water area. Another example is a grove of trees determined by field observation to be entirely of the same species. The grove is a completely homogeneous qualitative area feature since all of its defining objects (trees) are of the same category (species).

The interesting thing about features mapped as homogeneous areas is that most are not actually homogeneous throughout. Let's return to the lake example. For many lakes, the boundary between land and water isn't a sharp line, because a narrow transition zone lies between the clear water and solid land. This transition zone may be wetland (marsh, bog, swamp) or aquatic vegetation (water lilies, reeds, cattails). Is this transition zone part of the lake, part of the shore land, or neither? Including the transition zone as part of the lake means that water is being mapped together with wetland or aquatic vegetation. Adding the transition zone to the shore land means that the land category now includes wetland or aquatic vegetation as well as dry land.

Map makers deal with this problem in several ways. They may add a note to the map explaining that they've included the transition zone as part of the lake or shore land. They could also decide to define the land-water boundary as the middle of the transition zone. Now neither the water nor the land are homogeneous area features, although they are mapped as being so. Another possibility is to define the transition zone as a separate category. This decision increases the complexity of the map, but allows the water and land to be mapped as homogeneous areas that more accurately reflect what's on the ground.

SINGLE-THEME MAPS

The simplest and most common qualitative thematic maps are those that show a single theme. To read these **single-theme maps**, you must first determine what features have been shown with point, line, or area symbols. These symbols are easiest to read if the map maker has used the correct **graphic elements**. The graphic elements that evoke in our mind qualitative differences among features are **shape**, **orientation**, and color **hue** (**Figure 6.1**). A shape can also be repeated along a line or across an area to create a **pattern**. Each of these elements

Feature Type	Graphic Element		
	Shape	Orientation	Color Hue
Point	Spring House Mine	Live Tree Dead Tree	(green) Live Tree (brown) Dead Tree
Line	National Border Trail Section Line	Asphalt Road Concrete Road	(red) National Border (orange) State Border
Area	Gravel Sand	Orchard Field Crop	green Land blue Water

Figure 6.1 The graphic elements that naturally evoke qualitative differences among features are shape, orientation, and color hue. A shape repeated across an area creates the element of pattern.

gives the impression that features are different in type or kind but not more or less in magnitude.

Keep in mind, however, that map makers don't always design maps as well as they might. Thus, they may use some other graphic element (size, texture, color value, or color intensity) that really should be used for showing quantitative differences. (See Chapter 7 for a discussion of quantitative map symbols.) When maps are incorrectly made in this way, your first reaction will be that quantitative rather than qualitative information is being shown.

Say, for instance, that the map makers have made lakes blue, land brown, and parks green. They have quite properly used hue to differentiate one area feature from another. But what if they've also varied the parks' color intensity, making some parks deeper green than others to distinguish between public and private parks? In this case, you could easily get the impression that the parks differed in some quantitative way, such as in entrance fees charged. The only way to keep from being misled by such poorly designed maps is to read the legend to see what the symbols actually represent.

Point-Feature Maps

Point-feature maps contain **point symbols** that show the existence of something at a specific location. The word "point" has a rather loose interpretation here. It isn't being used in the strict mathematical sense of a one-dimensional figure but, rather, as the center of a circle, square, or some other map symbol representing a point feature found at this location.

Qualitative point features are usually represented with point symbols somewhere on a continuum between **pictographic** and **geometric**. Pictographic symbols are designed to "look like" miniature versions of the features represented. They give the map a light, childlike appearance (**Figure 6.2A**) and are commonly used on maps for children and tourists.

A special type of pictographic symbol is the **standard symbol**. Sets of standard symbols have been created to show different categories of transportation, recreation, and other activities (**Figure 6.3**). Standard symbols have a more professional, less childlike look than most pictographic symbols. But they still suffer problems associated with pictographic symbols in general. They have to be relatively large for details to be apparent, which means the map must be rather simple. In addition, only a

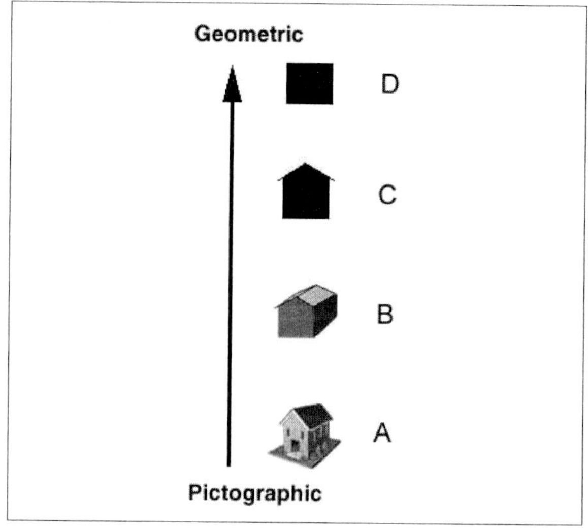

Figure 6.2. Qualitative point symbols for a feature range on a continuum from pictographic (A) to geometric (D).

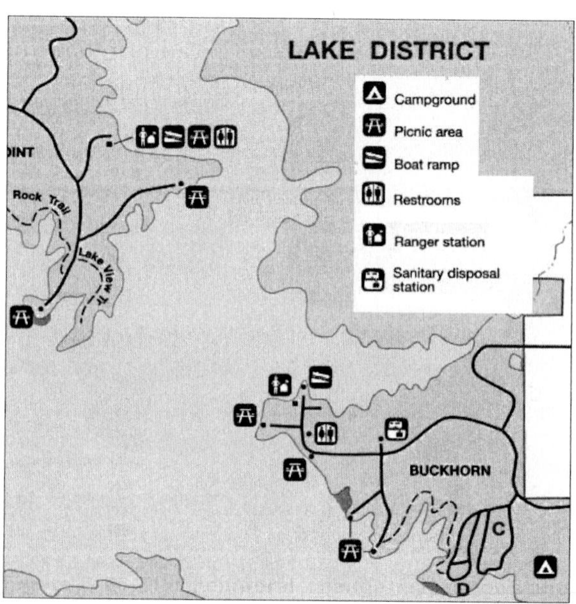

Figure 6.3 Standard pictographic symbols have been used on this map showing different facilities at a lakeside recreation area.

limited number of environmental features can be successfully symbolized pictographically. What, for example, is an obvious icon for a museum? Although these symbols are intended to be intuitive at a glance, you'll often have to check the map legend to determine what is symbolized.

Map makers sometimes cleverly change the orientation or hue of a pictographic symbol to show two or more **attributes** of the point feature. Notice in Figure 6.1 that the orientation or hue of the pictographic symbol for a coniferous tree can be changed to show the tree as alive (vertical or green) or dead (horizontal or brown). The map maker sometimes will use both orientation and hue differences to make sure that you see the attributes of each feature.

The drawbacks of pictographic symbols are overcome by using geometric shapes such as circles, squares, triangles, and so forth (**Figure 6.2D**). Although these symbols may look sterile, they can be read correctly even when very small. This lets map makers pack more information into the map than they can with larger pictographic symbols. Furthermore, since the correspondence between real-world feature and geometric symbol is strictly arbitrary, any feature can be represented in this way. The greater level of abstraction embodied in geometric symbols increases their flexibility as feature display tools. It also requires close study of the legend to determine what is being symbolized.

Line-Feature Maps

Map makers make **line-feature maps** with qualitative **line symbols** showing linear features, such as roads, streams, or boundaries. As with point symbols, the word "line" isn't used here in the strict mathematical sense of a one-dimensional figure. Line symbols usually have obvious width as well as length. If the lines are wide enough, map makers may add graphic elements such as color hue and shape to show different types of linear features.

Shape repetition (line pattern) is commonly used to distinguish different categories of line features (see Figure 6.1). The individual shapes usually are geometric, but also can be pictographic. Pictographic shapes may be easier to read than geometric shapes, but they're more difficult to miniaturize and repeat along a line. Therefore, with the exception of the pictographic symbols used to depict tangible features such as railroads, fences, and powerlines, most line symbols use repetitions of geometric shapes.

Different hues are also used to show different categories of line features. The hues used have been standardized for certain features. For example, water features are usually shown with blue lines, boundaries are depicted with red lines, roads are drawn in black, and different types of contour lines are shown in brown.

Area-Feature Maps

Qualitative **area-feature maps** use **area symbols** to portray area features as extending homogeneously over regions. On such thematic maps, area features are best symbolized using the graphic elements that give the impression of differences in kind. For example, a map maker might use two area patterns to show the states carried by the Democratic and Republican party presidential candidate (**Figure 6.4**).

If map makers instead use visual elements that give a magnitude impression, such as lightness, color intensity, texture, or size, you're likely to find the map confusing. You may think that one sym-

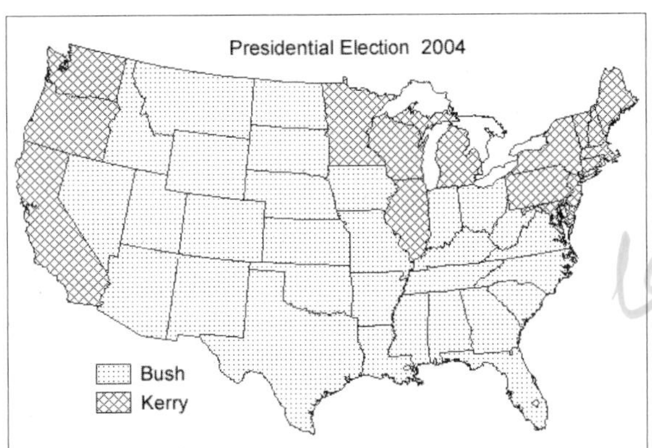

Figure 6.4 Area symbols can be used to distinguish regions from each other on the basis of attributes such as states won by the Democratic and Republican party presidential candidates.

bol depicts more of something than another symbol, when this wasn't the map maker's intent. Look, for instance, at **Figure 6.5**. This map shows three categories of aquifers by lightness levels from light to dark gray. Without reading the legend, your first impression from the gray tones might be that the map is showing minor, intermediate, and major aquifers.

Figures 6.4 and 6.5 exemplify two basic types of qualitative thematic maps. Two different kinds of data collection areas are being mapped using the same graphic elements. The presidential-election map in Figure 6.4 is based on legislatively-defined data collection areas (states). On the map, states are given one of two patterns, depending on which candidate received the most votes. The areas are rightfully portrayed as homogeneous, since the candidate with the most votes receives all the state's electoral-college votes. This type of map is very similar in concept to the choropleth maps for quantitative data described in Chapter 7, but it is often called a **categorical map**.

The aquifer map in Figure 6.5 is an example of mapping area features that are inherently homogeneous in some way, such as having the same bedrock geology. This map is very similar in concept to the dasymetric maps for quantitative data discussed in Chapter 7, but many map makers again call it a categorical map. Notice that the different categories may be purely of one feature (volcanic rocks) or of two or more intermixed features found in certain regions (alluvial and sedimentary deposits). You can see that the map maker can define inherently homogeneous areas in many ways, so you should carefully read the map legend to understand what each category means.

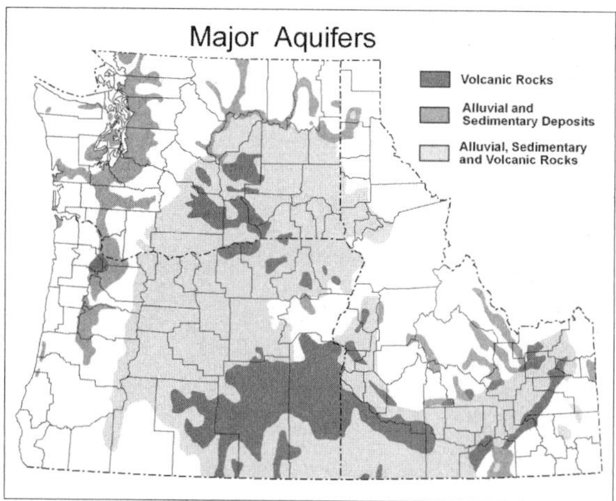

Figure 6.5 The three graytones used to show categories of major aquifers on this map incorrectly connote a magnitude progression from minor to major (from Atlas of the Pacific Northwest, 9th ed.).

MULTIVARIATE MAPS

Most qualitative thematic maps use a separate symbol to represent each feature. But sometimes map makers show several attributes of the feature with the same symbol. They accomplish this feat in two ways.

One method is to use a different graphic element to show each attribute. In theory, map makers could show four different attributes at once by varying the symbol's shape, hue, pattern, and orientation. In practice, symbols showing more than two or three feature attributes are rarely made, because they're very difficult to read. You'll usually have no trouble telling when multivariate information has been mapped, because the symbols will appear more complex than those showing a single feature.

With the second method of symbolizing multivariate information, map makers show composite rather than raw data. Thus, they may combine a number of feature attributes and show them with a single symbol. It is here that map reading becomes especially tricky, for these multivariate symbols look exactly like those on single-feature maps. Only the nature of the information symbolized, not the form of the symbols, has been changed. Therefore, it is essential to check the legend as your initial step in map reading.

Point Symbols

Map makers like to use point symbols to show multivariate qualitative information because they can pack information into each symbol by combining several graphic elements. Some multivariate point symbols are pictographic, but most are geometric. For example, the multivariate symbols for landfills and dumps shown in **Figure 6.6** are based on circles and squares. Arrows in two directions indicate the status of operation, and different hues represent ownership.

Map makers sometimes use the same graphic element more than once to create multivariate symbols. For instance, they may use two shapes, such as a square within a circle. Although they should use graphic elements with qualitative connotations to construct these symbols, they don't always do so. One reason is that they may not be aware of the proper cartographic language. Another is that they often try to show so many attributes with a single point symbol that they can't adhere to using the correct graphic elements.

Line Symbols

Map makers don't often use line symbols to portray multivariate qualitative data. One reason is that their options are limited to using the graphic elements of hue and shape (repeated in a line pattern). But occasionally you'll find such maps.

For example, highway maps may be enhanced with multivariate data. It's common to see highway maps with blue lines for freeways, red lines for state highways, and green lines for scenic routes. Sometimes these single-variable line symbols are augmented to show a second variable. For instance, dash or dot patterns may be added to each line to show the type of road surface lies between the clear water and solid land—dashed for gravel, dotted for dirt.

You may also see multivariate line-feature maps with double-line symbols wide enough to have different hues and line patterns within the two bounding lines. Highway categories might be shown by different hues, and the bounding lines could be solid, dashed, or dotted to show different road surfaces. These double-line symbols tend to cover a larger amount of map space, however. Map makers normally would rather make separate maps of the individual feature attributes than clutter a single map with lines so wide that they distract you from seeing the rest of the map information.

Area Symbols

Map makers can make multivariate area symbols by overlapping two types of area symbols. This technique is quite effective if one category of features is shown with hue differences and the second by different area patterns. For example, the map in **Figure 6.7** shows the type of ocean bottom off the Oregon coast by using a light gray for sand, dark gray for bedrock, and a light brown hue (shown as medium gray here) for silt and mud.

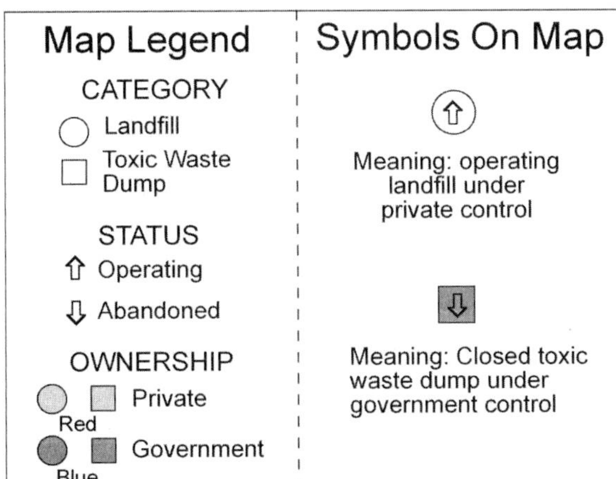

Figure 6.6 A great deal of attribute information can be shown on a map through use of multivariate point symbols.

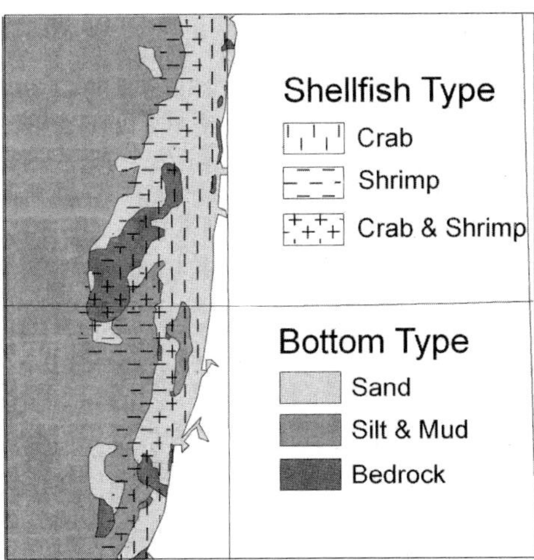

Figure 6.7 The overlap of separate area symbols can create a multivariate symbol showing places where different features overlap.

Vertical and horizontal dashed-line patterns are overlaid to show where crab or shrimp are harvested. The area patterns overlap to form "+" signs that show areas where both crab and shrimp are found. This map lets you see if there is any geographical relationship between bottom type and the harvest of shellfish.

On other maps, hues such as yellow and blue are used for different categories so that their area of overlap is seen as green. However, the overlap area may go unrecognized, because green is normally seen as a separate color, not a mixture of yellow and blue. In such cases, it's necessary to refer to the map legend to see what each hue represents.

At first glance, many qualitative thematic maps seem to show a single theme when they may actually show multivariate information. This is the case with climate and soils maps, for example. Climate zone borders are defined by temperature and precipitation ranges as well as by typical vegetation. You may think of climate as a single theme, but each component of climate plays a crucial part. Similarly, a soil class is defined by a set of soil attributes, including slope, depth, drainage, color, and texture (**Figure 6.8**). You can probably think of other examples of environmental phenomena that are determined by a composite of attributes.

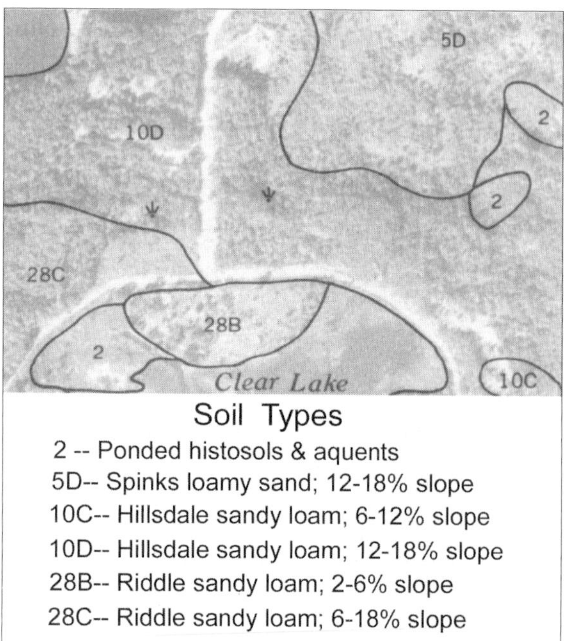

Figure 6.8 Symbols representing soil classes on a map signify areas on the ground where certain combinations of soil attributes exist.

QUALITATIVE CHANGE MAPS

Mapping changes in our environment has long frustrated map makers. Until recently, it took so much time, effort, and money to make maps that dynamic features weren't attractive candidates for cartographic representation. However, modern high-speed computer mapping procedures have simplified the creation of **time-related maps**—maps that deal with time explicitly. In other words, time is actually built into these maps, not simply added on as a date in the map's margin.

Qualitative change maps are an important category of time-related map. One type of qualitative change map shows only features that have changed category over a certain time period. **Figure 6.9**, for instance, shows landcover change from agriculture, forest, or wetlands to urban over a decade in a small watershed. From this figure, it's

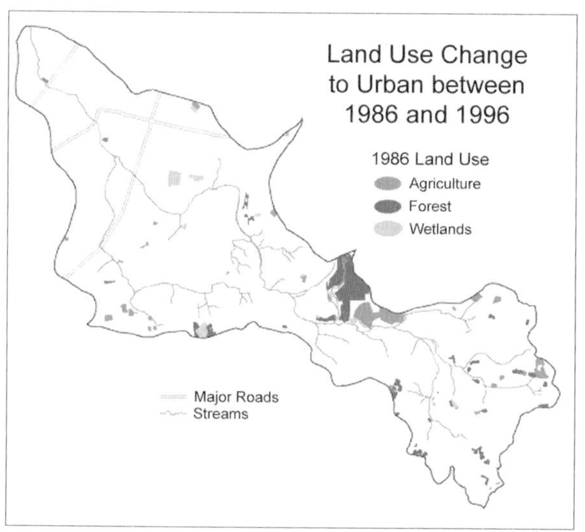

Figure 6.9 This qualitative change map depicts change to urban landcover from agriculture, forest, and wetlands between 1986 and 1996 in a small New Jersey watershed.

obvious that most of the change was from forest to urban land.

Qualitative change maps are easy to make if maps or images are available for both time periods. They can show changes for many environmental phenomena simultaneously, especially if each feature category is given a separate map symbol. Such maps are often of limited use, however, because only the changed features are shown. Thus, it's hard to place these changes in the broader geographical context.

You can circumvent the shortcomings of a single change map by superimposing a map of one date on that of another. You can then see exactly what changes have taken place since the earlier map was made. By doing this for maps produced through a succession of time intervals, you can study the long-term historical pattern of change in the region.

A second type of qualitative change map shows the **movement of features** over time. Since point, linear, area, and three-dimensional features vary in the way they change location through time, we'll consider them separately.

Point Symbols

Movements of point features are often mapped as annotated route lines tracing the paths along which the features move. For instance, **Figure 6.10** shows the westward route taken in 1805 by Lewis and Clark through present-day Oregon and Washington on their historic journey to the Pacific coast.

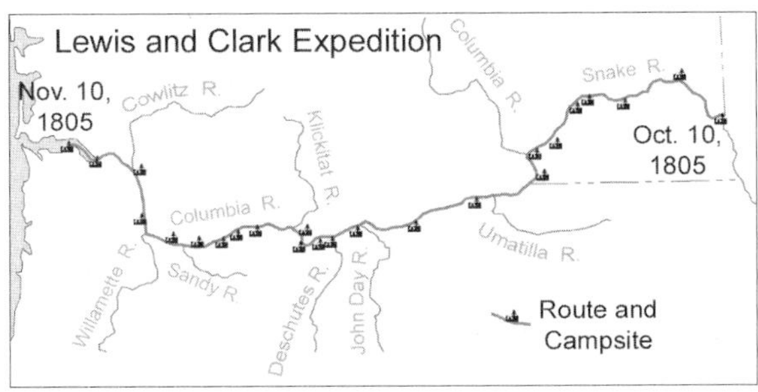

Figure 6.10 This map shows the westward route taken by the Lewis and Clark expedition through Oregon and Washington, including their campsites from October 10 to November 10, 1805.

Their westward movement is shown by a series of point symbols indicating their campsites beside the Snake and Columbia rivers from October 10 to November 10, 1805. The map appears to give you a full picture of their rate of travel, but notice that only 24 campsite symbols are on the map. Since no information is given as to where they camped more than one night, your understanding of their actual westward rate of movement is incomplete.

Map makers can also use thousands of individual point features to show routes, such as those followed by migrating birds or fish. But since the exact route followed by each individual differs slightly and is hard to determine with high accuracy, the route data are usually generalized to broad paths or **corridors of movement**. Thus you might find a map of "Tornado Alley" or the "Mississippi Flyway" (**Figure 6.11**) on which a composite of individual paths is depicted. Be sure you recognize that this type of movement map is intended to show only the general geographic pattern of movement over a certain time period.

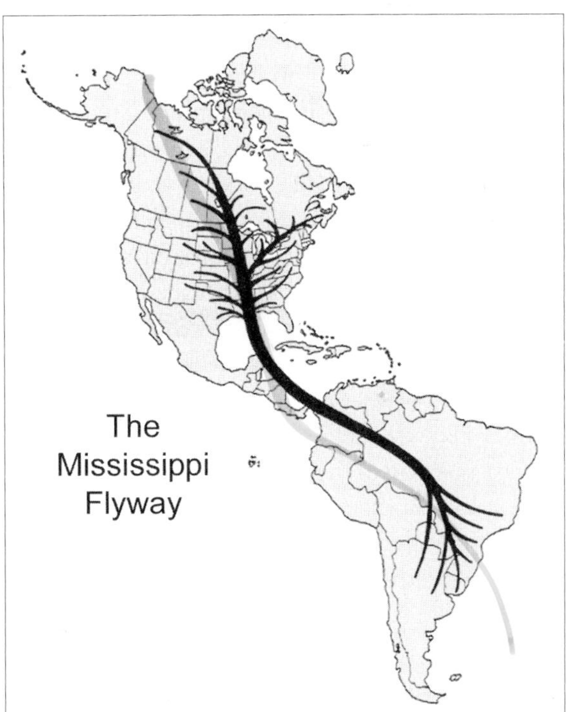

Figure 6.11 Route data are often generalized to broad paths or corridors, such as the Mississippi Flyway for migratory birds.

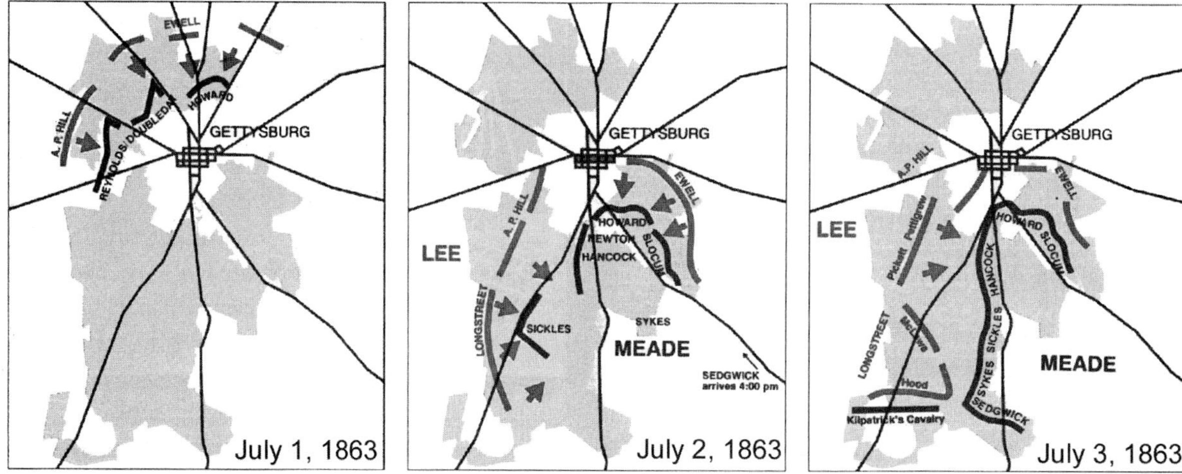

Figure 6.12 The movements of troop lines during the Battle of Gettysburg are shown on these three maps (based upon a National Park Service brochure for the Gettysburg National Military Park).

Line Symbols

There are several ways to show the movement of qualitative line features. The simplest method is to create a set of maps that show the positions of the same features at different dates. You may have seen military maps showing the daily positions of fronts or troop lines during the course of a battle. One of the best known military maps shows the daily position of Union and Confederate troops during the Civil War Battle of Gettysburg on July 1-3, 1863 (**Figure 6.12**). Notice that the map doesn't simply show the advance or retreat of the same battalions over the three days, since new troops arrived and reserves were called into battle.

Another way to show change in position over time is to combine the line features on a single **time composite map**. For instance, your TV weather channel may use a map showing the current and forecast position of the jet stream (**Figure 6.13**) to help explain the changing weather conditions. It is now common to show the continual movement of the jet stream and other weather elements in an animated time sequence .

Area Symbols

Since the movement of qualitative area features occurs at their edge, they move along a linear front that is shown on maps in several ways. The first possibility is to map a zone or area of change. A map of the tidal zone is an example, since it reflects the daily fluctuation in the area covered by seawater due to tidal changes.

Changes over time in qualitative area features that are more concepts than physical phenomena can also be mapped as **spatial diffusions** of discrete point phenomena that occupy an area. **Figure 6.14**, for example, shows the systematic areal expansion of gypsy moths in the northeastern United States from 1890 to 1971. The acres of forest land defoliated by this imported insect pest appear to be expanding at an accelerating rate in

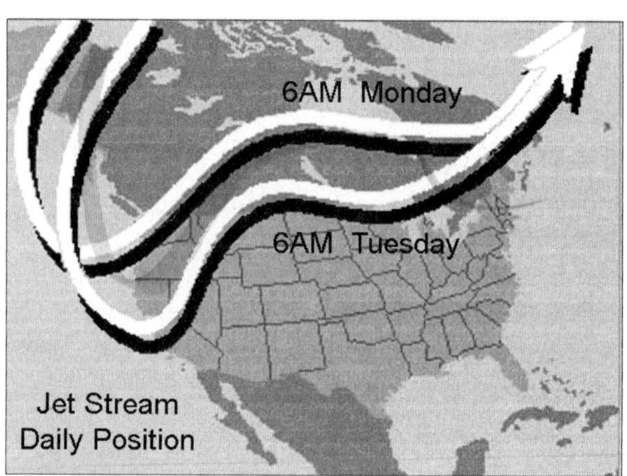

Figure 6.13 Time composite maps of qualitative linear features such as the jet stream allow you to better understand a weather forecast.

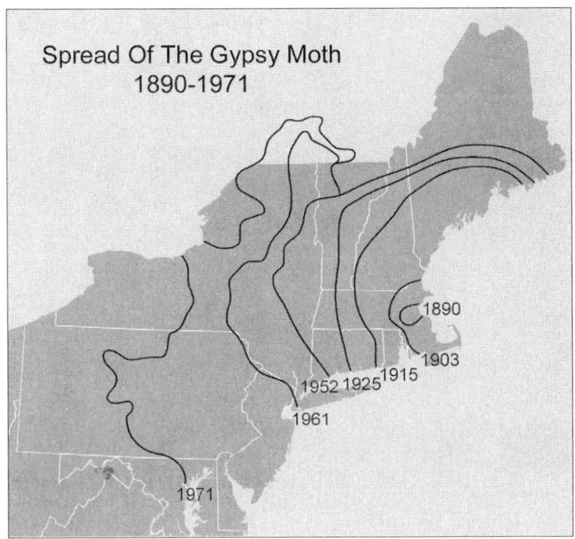

Figure 6.14 The progressive change over time of an areal feature can be shown as an expanding or contracting front. This map depicts the spread of gypsy moths in the northeastern United States at various points in time from 1890 to 1971.

recent decades. Since the mapping method is perfectly general, the inland movement of European settlers from the eastern seaboard in the 18th and 19th centuries could be similarly shown. So could the retreating snow cover in the upper Midwest during a typical spring thaw. When reading this map, remember that you're dealing as much with a concept or theory of movement as with actual movement verified by data collected in the field.

Map makers also try to suggest **spatial process** when designing symbols for area features formed by the movement of materials. Symbols for lava flows or glaciers are examples (**Figure 6.15**). Although the symbol depicts the current extent of the feature, it also gives the impression that the feature was formed by a flow process.

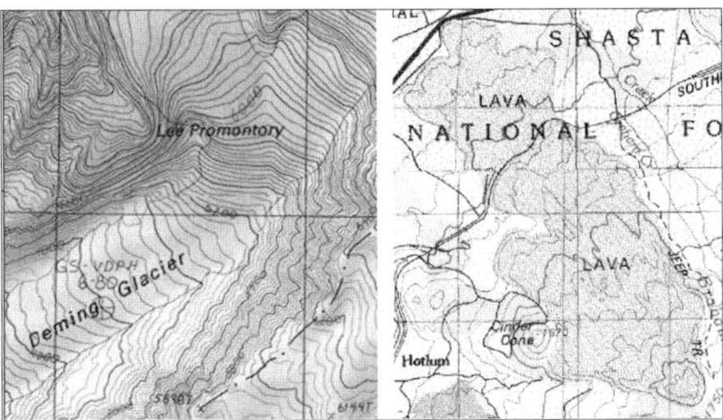

Figure 6.15 Overlaying contour lines on topographic map area symbols for glaciers (left) and lava flows (right) is done to suggest their spatial path of flow over time.

Three-Dimensional Features

Three-dimensional features such as air masses move along a two-dimensional front which is difficult to show on a flat map. Thus, true volumetric change mapping is limited to 3-D models or animated 3-D perspective views such as those discussed in Chapter 8. Instead, the three-dimensional feature is commonly collapsed into a two-dimensional outline by projecting the two-dimensional feature boundary down or up onto the ground-level surface. The feature outlines for different dates are then superimposed on the base map to show changes over time. This is a standard method of mapping air mass movement (**Figure 6.16A**). Sometimes even greater cartographic abstraction

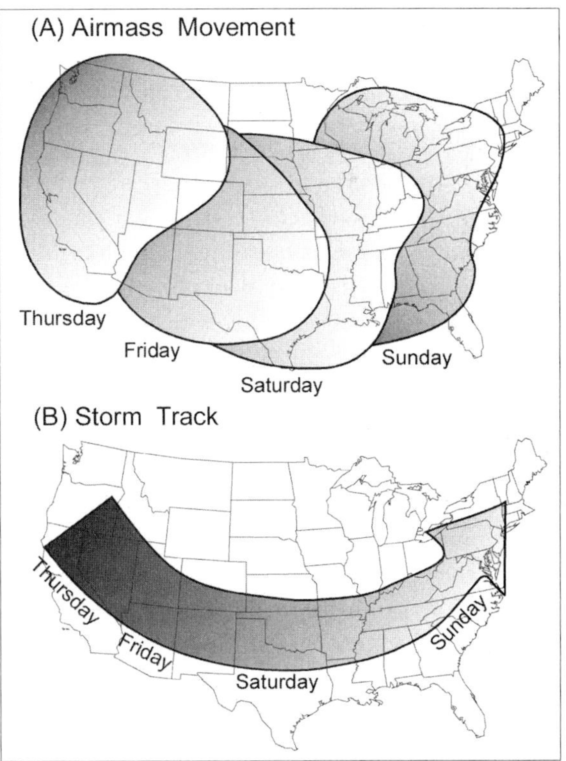

Figure 6.16 Three-dimensional features are commonly depicted on maps by a series of area symbols (A) or a linear flow symbol (B).

is used, and the movement of the feature is shown only by a linear flow symbol (**Figure 6.16B**). You're probably familiar with this conceptual leap through maps of storm tracks on TV weather reports.

SELECTED READINGS

Bertin, J., *Graphics and Graphic Information-Processing* (New York: Walter de Gruyter, 1981).

Carnachan, R., *Wisconsin Soil Mapping*, Guide 4 (Madison, WI: Wisconsin State Cartographer's Office, 1993).

Chaston, P.R., *Weather Maps: How to Read and Interpret All Basic Weather Charts* (Kearney, MO: Chaston Scientific, Inc., 1995).

Dent, B.D., *Cartography: Thematic Map Design*, 4th ed. (Englewood Cliffs, NJ: Prentice-Hall, Inc., 1996).

Hole, F.D., and Campbell, J.B., *Soil Landscape Analysis* (Totowa, NJ: Rowman & Allanheld, Publishers, 1985).

Holmes, N., *Pictorial Maps* (New York: Watson-Guptill Publications, 1991).

Jackson, P.L., and Kimerling, A.J, *Atlas of The Pacific Northwest*, 9th ed. (Corvallis, OR: Oregon State University Press, 2003).

Monmonier, M., and Schnell, G.A., *Map Appreciation* (Englewood Cliffs, NJ: Prentice Hall, 1988).

Robinson, et al., *Elements of Cartography*, 6th ed. (New York: John Wiley & Sons, 1995).

Robinson, V.,ed., *Geography and Migration* (Brookfield, VT: Edward Elgar Publishing Co., 1996).

Saint-Martin, F., *Semiotics of Visual Language* (Bloomington, IN: University Press, 1990).

Tufte, E.R., *Visual Explanations: Images and Quantities, Evidence and Narrative* (Cheshire, CT: Graphics Press, 1997).

Wrigley, N., *Categorical Data Analysis for Geographers and Environmental Scientists* (New York: Longman, Inc., 1985).

CHAPTER SEVEN
QUANTITATIVE THEMATIC MAPS

QUANTITATIVE DATA

- Measurements and Counts
  - Measurement and Count Accuracy
- Spatial Samples
- Measurement Levels

SINGLE-THEME MAPS

- Point Features
- Line Features
  - Flow Maps
- Area Features
  - Choropleth Maps
    - Number of Classes
    - Class Interval Selection
    - Unclassed Choropleth Maps
  - Dasymetric Maps
  - Area-Feature Point Symbols
  - Area Cartograms
    - Non-Contiguous
    - Pseudo-Contiguous
    - Contiguous
  - Stepped-Surface Maps
- Continuous Surface Maps
  - Isoline Maps
    - Isopleth Maps
    - Layer-Tinted Isoline Maps
  - Dot Maps
  - 3-D Perspective Maps

MULTIVARIATE MAPS

- Point Features
- Line Features
- Area Features

TEMPORAL CHANGE MAPS

- Time Composite Maps
- Time Series Maps

SELECTED READINGS

One of the trickiest ways to misrepresent statistical data is by means of a map.
A map introduces a fine bag of variables in which facts
can be concealed and relationships distorted.
—*Darrell Huff, How to Lie With Statistics*

7

CHAPTER SEVEN

QUANTITATIVE THEMATIC MAPS

In the previous chapter, we discussed qualitative thematic maps that emphasize the location of different kinds of environmental features. Sometimes we want to know not only what and where but also how much of something exists at some location. In such cases, we turn to **quantitative thematic maps**.

On quantitative thematic maps, cartographers use a variety of symbols to depict **magnitude information** telling you how many, large, wide, fast, high, or deep things are. The **graphic elements** that inherently connote differences in magnitude are size, pattern texture, gray-tone or color lightness, and color saturation (**Figure 7.1**). A well-designed series of symbols using variations in one or more of these elements will appear to you as a progression of magnitudes from small to large or low to high.

Many types of quantitative thematic information can be portrayed using these graphic elements. Data for a **single-theme map**, such as annual precipitation for different cities, can be shown. You could also be looking at a **multivariate map** that is a composite of several themes, such as a ranking of cities by desirability for raising a family. Although these two maps may look practically identical, the conceptual basis, the meaning of the symbols on each map, and the accuracy of the two maps are very different. Part of the difference is due to the different ways quantitative data are collected for each map, and to the **measurement level** at which the data are presented on the map.

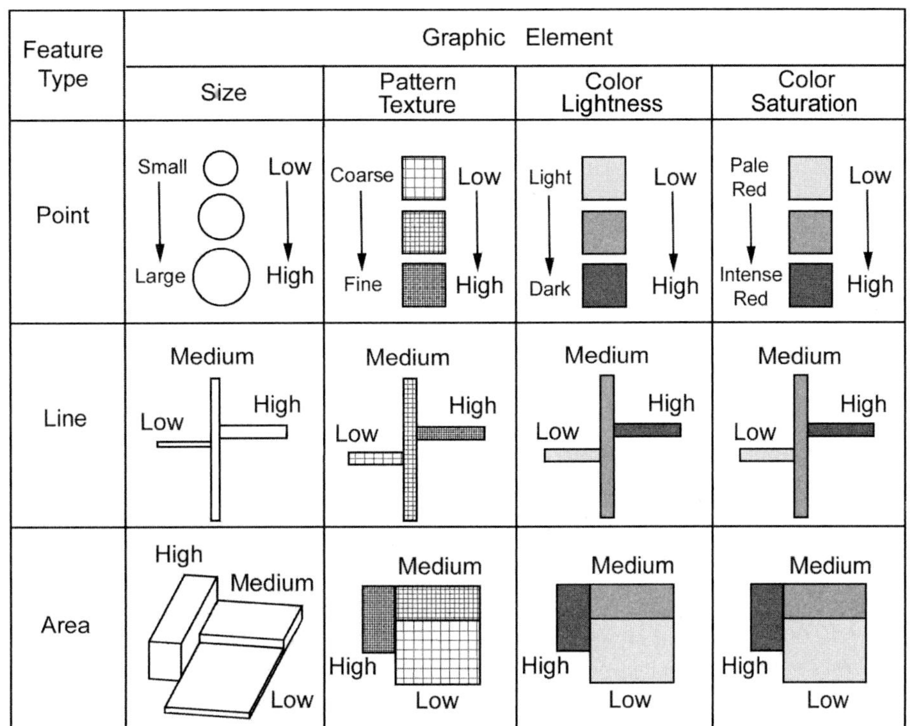

Figure 7.1 The graphic elements that inherently impart a magnitude message are variations in size, pattern texture, gray-tone or color lightness, and color saturation.

QUANTITATIVE DATA

Data collectors have several choices. They can take **physical measurements** describing a theme at different locations within a region. They can collect **statistical data** for every element of a theme and obtain what is called a **population count**. Or they can collect data for only a portion of the region or population, which is called taking a **sample**.

Quantitative thematic maps can be created from all or a part of the measurements, population counts, or sample data. For instance, a map of city population within a state may include all the cities or a selection of major cities, depending on the map's scale and purpose. Let's look more closely at these different types of quantitative data.

Measurements and Counts

Maps are made from a wide variety of measurements and counts. For instance, one way to make measurements for maps is to use data points that describe individual **point features**. A map of tree heights in a forest, for example, could be made from height measurements taken in the field or from aerial photographs. The entire population of trees may have been measured, although more likely the map was made from a sample of trees in the forest.

Physical characteristics of **line features** such as rivers (neglecting their width) are measured in several ways. Say you are looking at a map of water temperature along a river. It is possible that temperatures were measured continuously along the river from thermal-infrared remote sensing data collected in minutes over the entire portion of the river (see Chapter 9 for details on thermal-infrared remote sensing systems). Although the sensing device was operating continuously, the data from the sensor are usually recorded as values for grid cells of a certain spatial resolution that make up the thermal image. The temperature mapped at any point along the river may be an average of the grid cells perpendicular to the direction of flow, or the value for the grid cell at its center.

It is more likely that the river temperatures were obtained from thermometer measurements taken at a small number of **sample sites** along the river's course. The map may only show the temperatures at these points, or the map maker may have interpolated between the measured values to create a continuous dataset for the river. Only by looking at explanatory notes on the map can you tell how the data for the map were obtained.

Counts within sections of a line feature are common. An example for a river is the number of fish caught per river miles. Catch data from your state fish and game department may have been used to make maps showing fishing success in the river. The total number of fish in each river mile could also be estimated from counts taken at sample points using nets or other methods to trap or stun all the fish living at each point.

Area features can also be measured in a variety of ways. Let's take a lake as an example. The average temperature of the lake at a particular time can be obtained from a thermal-infrared image by finding the average value of all cells falling within the lake's boundary. Limnologists (scientists who study lakes and streams) may have taken a large number of surface temperature measurements at different sample points on the lake, from which an average temperature was computed. A map showing average temperatures of lakes within a region may have been created from the average values for image data grid cells or actual temperature measurements taken in each lake.

When you are more interested in understanding the spatial nature of a distribution of features than the location of individual features, a map showing counts of features within **data collection areas** will better suit your needs The count of individual features is called a **census**. Federal, state, and local government agencies conduct censuses to learn basic population characteristics. Private firms focus their census taking on product advertising and marketing. Census maps are produced to make it easier for you to visualize the spatial pattern of high and low counts. The census map will show you how many features were counted in each data collection area, but not where each feature was located at the time of the census.

Maps are made from a variety of census data. U.S. Census Bureau data collectors determine the number of people within households, from which the total **population count** within different data collection areas (blocks, census tracts, cities, counties, and states) can be determined by simple summation. The areas usually are irregular in shape and size, and maps made from population count data inherently show the irregularities among areas. Population counts can also be based on a grid of identical square or triangular cells covering a region. A variety of biological phenomena are counted within square grid cells. Maps of biomass, animal density, insect infestation intensity, and many other themes are made from biological census data.

Data describing phenomena that map makers think of as **continuous surfaces** are also obtained from remote sensing or direct measurement at a number of sample points. You can think of the average annual temperature across your state as a continuous surface. The average value at each point in the state could be obtained from thermal-infrared meteorological satellite imagery taken daily. But more often an average temperature map is made by interpolating between the averages computed for the weather stations within the state. Each weather station, of course, is a sample point from which the surface is inferred.

Measurement and Count Accuracy

It seems logical that a map showing the measured values or population counts for a theme would be accurate. This is true in most cases, but not always. A number of errors may reduce the quality of measurements or counts. The errors are due to **instrumental**, **methodological**, and **human deficiencies** during data gathering. Such errors are usually well disguised on maps.

Take the case of the United States Census of Population and Housing, conducted each decade by the U.S. Census Bureau. Since every household

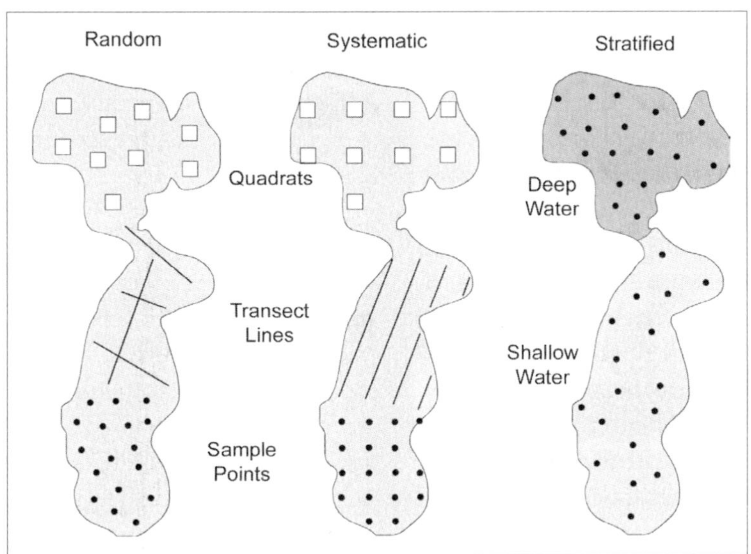

Figure 7.2 Different spatial sampling methods have be used to find the average temperature of this lake. Sample points, transect lines, and quadrats have been randomly and systematically located across the lake, and a point sample stratified by water depth was also taken.

in the country is supposed to be surveyed, maps produced from the counts will be faultless…or will they? A full head count of nearly three hundred million people is an immense job. Let's look at how the data are gathered.

Once every 10 years, the Census Bureau pulls together a nation-wide team from the ranks of the unemployed to track down nonresponders to mailed questionnaires. These census takers are asked to put their hearts into a low-paying job that lasts only a few weeks. They must brave strange neighborhoods, sometimes repeatedly. The people to be interviewed often aren't home, and when they are home they may be hostile. They're supposed to respond truthfully even though this means telling secrets that could get them into trouble with their landlords, the welfare office, or local authorities. Finally, after all the information has been gathered, it still has to be processed, analyzed, and mapped.

You can see the potential for all three types of errors: instrumental (interviewer), methodological (questionnaire method), and human (interviewer and respondent). Yet the Census Bureau has an electronic display and website which at any time will give you the "actual" number of people in the United States. Be your own judge of how accurate and current this population count is.

Physical measurements are subject to these same sources of error. Imagine determining the number of fish in a stream by netting at several locations. The net may not be fine enough to capture all species (instrumental), the sample locations may not be representative of the entire stream (methodological), and the person doing the netting may be too fatigued to complete the job (human deficiency).

Spatial Samples

Quantitative thematic maps are often based on a **spatial sample** of features rather than a full population count. The idea behind sampling is to use a small part of the population to find out what you want to know about the entire population. There are several reasons that samples are used to estimate what the entire population is like. For one thing, the time and cost involved in obtaining a full population count may be prohibitive, so only a sample can be taken. There are also continuous physical phenomena like surface temperature that exist everywhere and change in magnitude from moment to moment. It is impossible to measure their values constantly at every point on the earth, but a spatial sample of temperatures obtained from weather stations can be used to estimate the temperature at any location.

Maps are made from several types of spatial samples, as shown in **Figure 7.2**. Data for a map showing average temperature of this lake and others in the region may have been collected using one of three basic **sampling methods**. The simplest method would be to travel by boat to the pre-defined geographic positions of **sample points** and measure the temperature at each position. A more difficult method is to have the boat slowly follow a **transect line** and obtain temperature measurements along the line either continuously or at a constant time interval. The third method is to navigate the boat to square or circular **quadrat** sampling areas pre-defined on a chart of the lake. With careful navigation, a number of temperature readings can be taken within each quadrat.

The arrangement of sample points, transect lines, or quadrats can be **random** or **systematic**, as seen in Figure 7.2. Systematic samples are usually arranged as a square or triangular grid of sample points or quadrats, or as equally spaced parallel transect lines. A **stratified sample** can also be taken to make sure that certain characteristics of the population are adequately sampled. In our lake example, the sample points were stratified by water depth, since the shallow and deep portions of the lake were thought to be equally important to estimating the average temperature. Notice that the same number of sample points is randomly placed in the deep and shallow sections of the lake, reflecting their equal importance.

Statisticians argue about which form of sampling gives the best data for estimating the true average temperature of the lake. But one thing is certain—a higher density of randomly or systematically sample points, transect lines, or quadrats should give a better estimate, particularly if the sample is stratified in an appropriate manner.

Measurement Levels

The qualitative data for the maps described in the previous chapter were at the nominal measurement level. **Nominal level** data (also called categorical data) consist of categories used to distinguish different features within a map theme. Familiar nominal categories include land and water bodies, different nationalities and religions, or different types of trees. At the nominal level, there is no information about the relative size or importance of each category.

In contrast to qualitative data, the data for a quantitative thematic map are at the ordinal, interval, or ratio measurement levels. **Ordinal level** information is ranked according to a "less than" to "greater than" system. How much more or less one class is than another isn't specified, since there are no numerical values. Examples of ordinal data include small, medium, and tall trees; minor and major highways; and one-star through five-star hotels.

Interval level data consist of numerical values on a magnitude scale that has an arbitrary zero point. Land elevations are an excellent example of interval level data, since the zero datum is arbitrarily defined as mean sea level (see Chapter 1 for more on the definition of mean sea level). To see how arbitrary mean sea level is, you only have to think about how sea level rises and falls in the past and present—the zero point shifts over time and doesn't denote absence of elevation.

When looking at interval level data on a map, you should realize that only the numerical intervals between classes are valid mathematically. A map of average temperature in degrees Fahrenheit, another interval level dataset, may have classes such as 0° to 32°F, and 32° to 64°F. You can correctly conclude that the difference in temperature for the two classes is the same, since the temperature interval is the same. However, it is incorrect to say that a temperature of 64°F is twice as warm as a temperature of 32°F.

Ratio level data also consist of numerical values on a magnitude scale. But, in contrast to interval level data, the zero point isn't arbitrary. Instead, the zero point denotes absence of the phenomenon. You will find many quantitative thematic maps showing ratio level data. Themes such as population density (or any other density), annual precipitation, crime rate, tree heights, or temperature in degrees Kelvin have zero points that denote

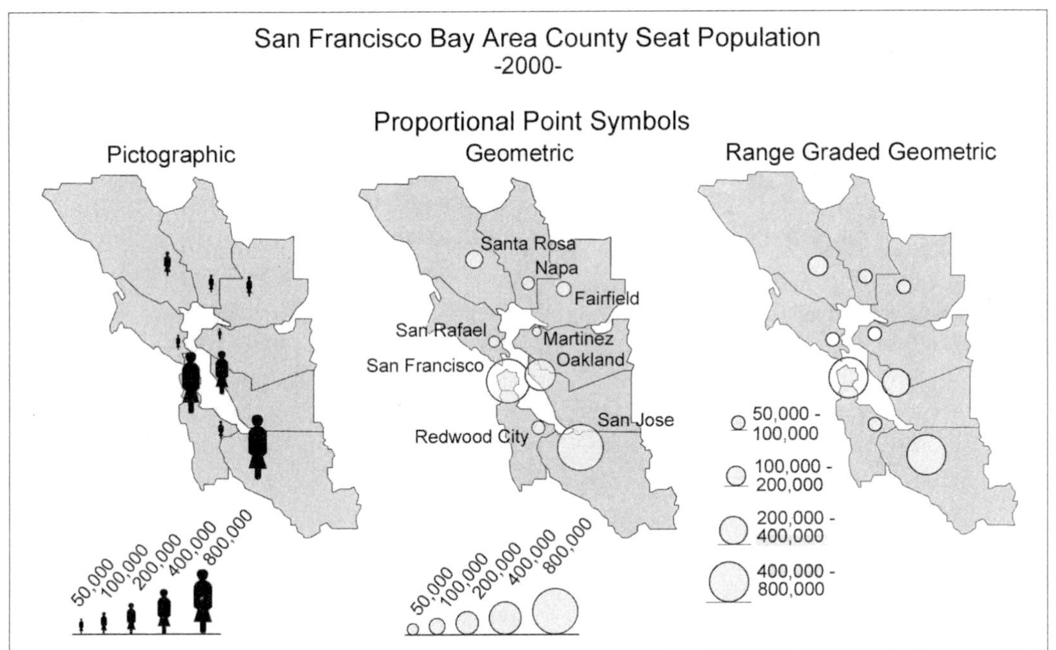

Figure 7.3 Proportional point symbols are commonly used to show quantitative information. Pictographic symbols (A) may look interesting, but simple geometric symbols (B) are usually easier to read. Range graded geometric symbols (C) aggregate the data into a small number of classes to make the symbols easier to read.

total absence. A zero population density, for example, means that there is a total absence of people within the data collection area.

With ratio level data, both the numerical intervals and the ratios between values are mathematically correct. When you look at a population density map with classes such as 0-30 and 30-60 people per square mile, you can conclude that the density range is the same for both classes. You can also assume that a population density of 45 people per square mile is three times as dense as 15 people per square mile.

SINGLE-THEME MAPS

The simplest quantitative thematic maps are those that show a single theme at the ordinal, interval, or ratio measurement level. It is convenient to subdivide map themes into point, line, and area features. Map makers have devised special ways of using graphic elements to create sets of quantitative point-feature, line-feature, and area-feature symbols.

Point Features

To show quantitative information at specific points, map makers vary one or more graphic elements in proportion to the magnitude at each location on the map. Symbols that are varied in this way are called **proportional point symbols**. Proportional point symbols may be **pictographic**—miniature caricatures of the features shown—or **geometric** forms such as circles, squares, or triangles.

If the proportional point symbols are pictographic, they will usually be varied only in terms of size (**Figure 7.3, left**). For example, if a human figure of one size indicates a city population of 100,000 people, the same figure eight times as large shows a city with 800,000 residents.

If proportional point symbols are geometric forms like circles (**Figure 7.3, center**), their texture, lightness, and color saturation, as well as their size, may be varied to show different magnitudes. More saturated shades of red, for instance, could indicate larger populations. But the most common way of showing changes in magnitude is to vary the size of the geometric form.

Figure 7.4 This section of the Washington state highway map shows freeways, U.S. highways, state highways, and county roads by progressively narrower lines.

Reading geometric symbols isn't as straightforward as it might seem. The difficulty arises because of the way the human eye and brain work. The brain doesn't perceive signals from our eyes in a linear fashion; instead, the size of geometric symbols is progressively underestimated as the area or volume of the symbols increases. This discrepancy between the apparent size and absolute size of map symbols is minimal with respect to symbol height, is worse with respect to area, and becomes a major problem with three-dimensional symbols. We judge the magnitude of three-dimensional symbols by their area rather than their volume. Thus, the area that a cube covers on the map, not its volume, is what you're likely to see.

It's most difficult to read proportional point symbols when a continuous sequence of symbols has been used. The human eye simply doesn't function precisely enough to differentiate between such slight variations in symbol size. The inevitable result is that the map user doesn't appreciate much of the effort that went into making the map. In fact, continuous gradation of magnitude symbols may actually contribute to map reading error because of the increased confusion it may cause.

Proportional point symbol reading difficulties are largely avoided when symbols are limited to a small number of classes. With this approach, called **range grading**, the symbols are usually different enough in size so that the eye can easily tell them apart (**Figure 7.3, right**). Although information has been lost by reducing the magnitude data to a few classes, range graded maps are generally the easiest to read of the single-variable quantitative point symbol type.

Line Features

Map makers use a variety of **proportional line symbols** to show quantitative information associated with linear features. With proportional line symbols, map makers first decide where they want the lines to go and then show how some phenomenon changes along a line or between lines.

Two types of proportional line symbols are used to show quantitative data. With the first type, lines representing different features that vary in magnitude are designed to form a **visual hierarchy**. The visual hierarchy is created by systematically increasing the width (size) of the line, often accompanied by a change in the lightness or saturation of the color used for the line. An example is the road symbols found on the typical state highway map (**Figure 7.4**). You will often find an ordinal level hierarchy of expressways, U.S. highways, state highways, and county roads shown by progressively narrower lines.

Alternatively, map makers can create a visual hierarchy by using different textures, lightnesses, or color saturations as "fills" within double line symbols. For instance, the degree of traffic congestion on central Seattle freeways and major highways is illustrated in **Figure 7.5** with a lightness progression from light to dark gray. As with other proportional line symbols, data are usually grouped

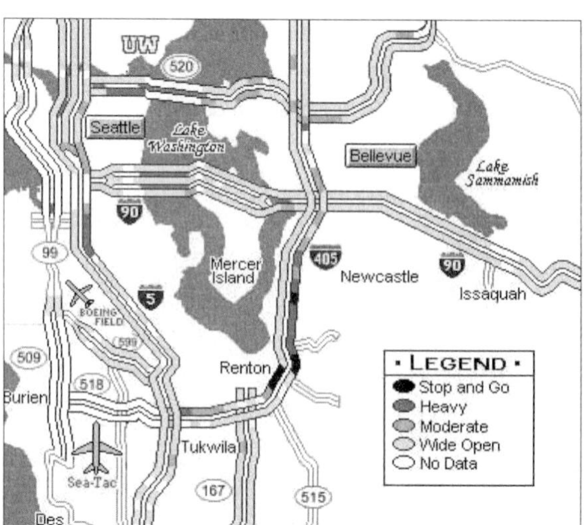

Figure 7.5 This monochrome version of the Seattle traffic flow map from the Internet shows four ordinal levels of congestion with a lightness progression from light to dark gray.

into a small number of classes to simplify map reading.

A problem with proportional line symbols from your perspective as a map user is that the symbols are disproportionately wide, covering large areas on the map. Hence, only a limited number of symbols can be used, and lines that are close together may have been displaced. For the map to make sense, the geographical base features may have been displaced as well to accommodate the proportional lines.

Flow Maps

Flow maps show ratio level changes in magnitude along a line feature using a proportional line symbol called a **flow line**. On most flow maps, the line's width is made proportional to some magnitude, such as river discharge, waterborne commerce, traffic deaths, or speed of travel. The more water that flows down a segment of a river, for instance, the wider that part of the flow line on the map will be (**Figure 7.6**). The **direction of flow** may also be important, and arrows are often added to one end of the flow line to show flow direction.

The magnitude at any point along a proportional flow line is difficult to read because the human eye isn't sharp enough to discriminate between slight changes in width. One solution is to divide the information into a small number of classes. The thinnest line might indicate 0-1 million gallons of water per minute, the next thinnest line 1-2 million gallons per minute, and so on.

When flow lines are made constant in width, changes in amount of flow are shown by varying the texture, color value, or lightness of the lines. Say that a map maker wants to show how many artichokes are being freighted along a railway line from southern California to Chicago. One portion of the line could be shown three times darker than another to show that three times more artichokes are being shipped along it. The problem is that the lines have to be quite wide to make these differences clear.

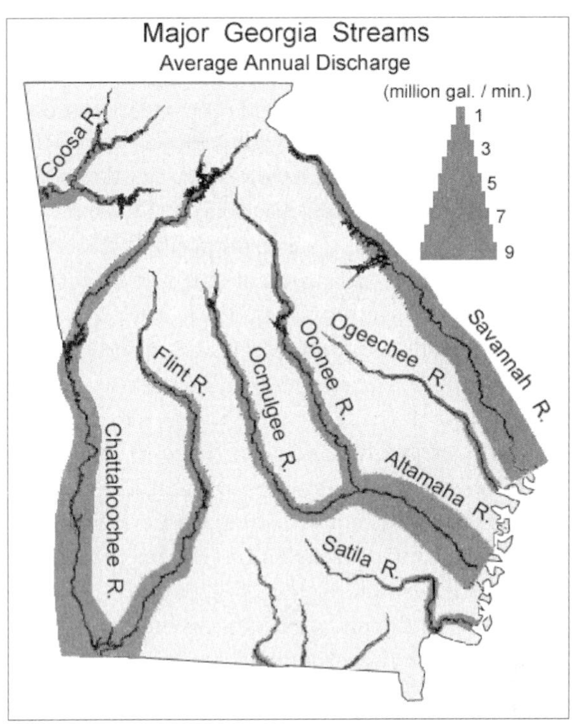

Figure 7.6 Flow map showing the average annual discharge of major streams in Georgia by varying line widths.

When you read a flow map, focus your attention on the magnitude information, not on the flow line's precise location. Map makers often distort geography to accommodate flow lines. A flow line showing the volume of ship traffic through the Strait of Gibraltar, for example, might be too wide to fit into the small space. Thus, the strait must be widened on the map; otherwise, it will look as if the ships are traveling over land.

Area Features

Quantitative area features vary in magnitude "steps" from place to place in patchwork-like fashion. A region may be partitioned, for example, so that data collection areas have a constant magnitude within, with abrupt changes at the borders. Map themes related to human activity, such as tax rates by state, commonly have a pronounced stepped character. More commonly, the quantity within each data collection area is assumed to be distributed homogeneously so that it can be mapped. Homogeneous area symbols are being used to show what in reality is a continuously changing distribution. In other words, they gives the impression that the mapped theme is evenly distributed within the data collection areas and that sharp breaks in the distribution occur at area boundaries. This rarely, if ever, occurs. The population distribution pattern is a reflection of environmental and social factors, not of data collection areas. Population doesn't change abruptly at county boundaries, although the uncritical map user might get this idea from the map.

You probably have seen maps having data collection areas such as states or counties colored or shaded according to the quantity of some feature occurring within each area. To show changes in magnitude on maps, map makers can vary the size, texture, lightness, or saturation of the symbol. Eye-catching area-feature maps are made by varying the height of individual areas, or changing the map area of data collection units to be proportional to their magnitude. There are standard names for the **mapping methods** associated with these ways of varying the graphic elements for area features. Let's look at five common mapping methods: choropleth, dasymetric, area-feature point symbol, value-by-area cartogram, and stepped surface.

Choropleth Maps

Many quantitative thematic maps of ordinal, interval, or ratio level area data are made using the **choropleth** mapping method. With this method, each data collection area is given a particular lightness, color saturation, or texture depending on its magnitude. Choropleth maps showing ratio level Oregon county population density data are shown in **Figure 7.7** and **Figure 7.8**.

On each map, **population density** (people per square mile) and not total population is being mapped. The map maker has **normalized** for the area of each county. In other words, the map is made to look as if the population is uniform throughout the county—a constant number of people per square mile. You'll find densities, percentages, rates (such as incidence of disease per 10,000 people), and other quantities on similar choropleth maps.

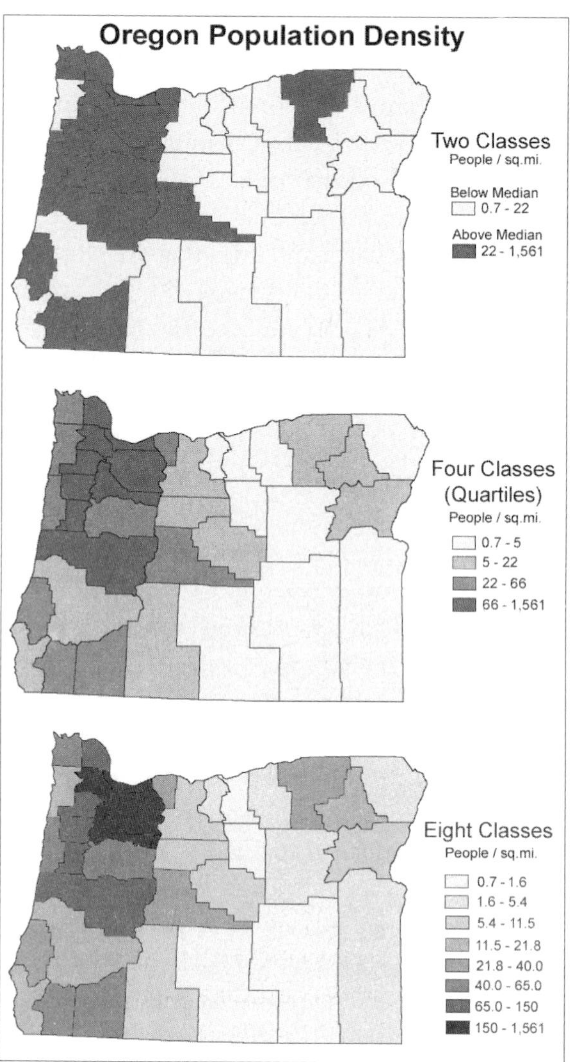

Figure 7.7 Choropleth maps of Oregon population density with two, four, and eight data classes.

Number of Classes. Notice that the choropleth maps in Figure 7.7 have two, four, and eight population density classes. You will likely see choropleth and other quantitative thematic maps having from two to eight classes for a theme. Progressive subdivision of the data range into classes simply involves reducing the numerical intervals between class limits. The simplest map has only two classes—above and below the median in our example. More information is shown if four classes (quartiles) are used. The map would show the most information if the population density for each county was its own class.

You can see that quantitative thematic maps made with different numbers of classes vary greatly in appearance. The number of classes has little to do with the nature of the mapped information; rather, you are looking at the map maker's arbitrary design decision.

You may wonder how meaningful the map classes you see really are, particularly when the range of data values is divided into a small number of classes. Look again at the two-class population density map in Figure 7.7. The "above median" and "below median" classes may tell you all you need to know, but the information content of the map is minimal. When only a few classes are used on the map, there's likely to be significant within-class variation that you can neither see nor assess.

Map makers increase the information content by using more classes, but this solution creates its own problems. Each additional class makes the graphic portrayal of the data more complex, as the eight-class map in Figure 7.7 illustrates. When many classes are used, there is less within-class variability, but the visual complexity of the map makes it very difficult to read.

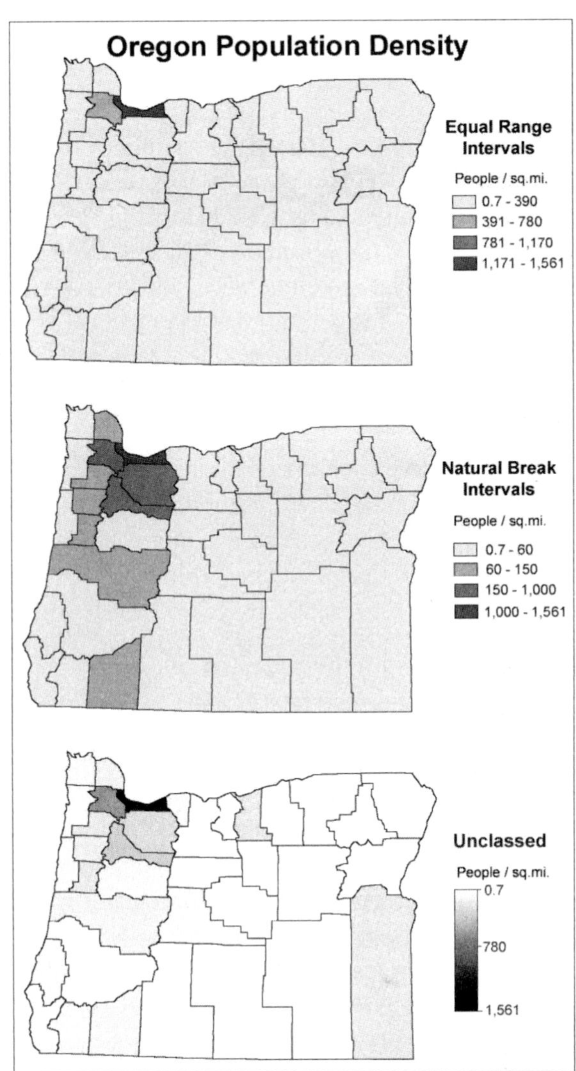

Figure 7.8 Choropleth maps of Oregon population density made using equal-range intervals (top), natural-break intervals (middle), and the unclassed method with gray tones proportional to county population densities.

Class Interval Selection. The impression of magnitude variation you get from the map depends not only on the number of classes, but also on the method used to define the **class intervals**. Let's look at the types of class intervals you are likely to see on choropleth and the other types of quantitative thematic maps discussed in this chapter.

Equal-Frequency Intervals. The three maps in Figure 7.7 have two, four, and eight **equal-frequency** class intervals, with as close as possible to an equal number of counties in each class. The three maps give the impression of high population density throughout northwest Oregon and low population density in the southeast quarter of the state. Are these maps a realistic portrayal of the distribution of people in Oregon? To answer this question, you need to look carefully at the range for each class. Look again at the eight-class map. Values ranging from 150 to 1,561 people per square mile may not be particularly high population densities, since the average county density for the nation is a little under 100 people per square mile. The maps make much of Oregon appear too high in population density.

The Oregon example shows you that equal-frequency interval choropleth maps give the most faithful portrayal of the data when the range of values for each class is approximately the same. To have similar class ranges, the number of low, medium, and high values in the data must be about the same.

Equal-Range Intervals. A second way for the map maker to group quantitative data is by **equal-range** intervals (**Figure 7.8, top**). The range of data values is merely divided by the desired number of classes to obtain equal intervals. For example, dividing the 1,560 (1,561-0.7) Oregon population density range by 4 gives a constant interval of 390, or upper class limits of 390, 780, 1,170 and 1,561.

Equal-range intervals are intuitively meaningful and easy to understand. Numerically-constant intervals appeal to the same basic human data-handling mechanism that makes percentage figures so attractive to us. Our minds are comfortable with the idea of segmenting the number 100 into equal fractional parts.

Equal-range intervals give the most meaningful map if an approximately equal number of data collection areas are in each class. For this to occur, data values must be equally distributed throughout their range. When data values are equally distributed across their range, choropleth maps made with equal-frequency and equal-range intervals should look identical.

The problem is that for many themes the data values are unevenly distributed across their range. Using Oregon population density as a typical example, there are many counties with a low population density and few with a high population density. In this situation, equal-range intervals produce a strange map indeed. Most counties fall into one class, while some classes are empty, with no counties at all. Oregon population density appears to be uniformly low throughout the state, except for the two counties that contain Portland and much of its large suburban area. Although this map may be useful in showing the vast differences in county populations, it poorly communicates the actual variation in population density.

Natural-Break Intervals. Instead of defining classes according to equal-data frequencies or ranges, the map maker may have established class limits at **natural breaks** in the distribution of data values. One way that map makers find natural breaks in a set of data is by creating a **frequency diagram (histogram)** for the data, such as the diagram for Oregon population density in **Figure 7.9**. The map maker looks for clusters of data values with large intervals between clusters. Natural breaks between classes are placed in the middle of the interval between each cluster. The idea is to minimize the variation in population density within each class while maximizing the variation between classes.

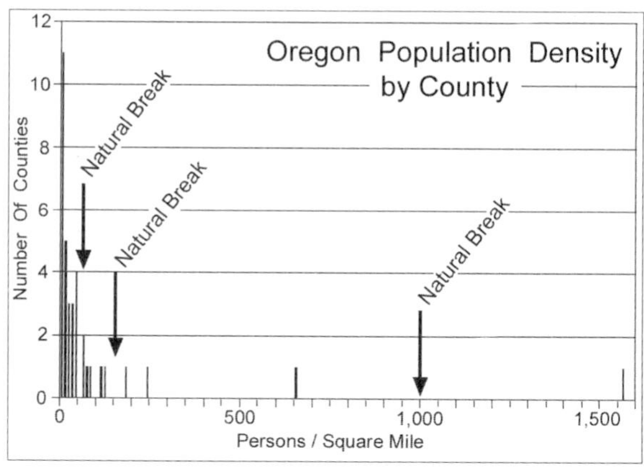

Figure 7.9 Frequency diagram of Oregon population density. Natural clusterings in the data and breaks between clusters can be seen on the diagram.

For the Oregon population density data shown in Figure 7.9, natural breaks were placed at 60, 150, and 1,000 persons per square mile. The choropleth map made with these class limits (**Figure 7.8, middle**) has the county containing Portland in the highest class, three suburban counties in the next highest class, most of the Willamette Valley in the third class, and the rest of the state in the lowest class. This map, based on natural breaks in the data, shows the nature of population variation in Oregon better than the previous maps, which were based on equal-data frequencies or ranges.

Critical-Value Intervals. The map maker may have used **critical values** to determine class limits. A critical value is one that has special relevance to the map's theme. It may be a physical aspect of the theme itself, such as the temperature below which a crop will freeze. Or it may a politically defined dividing point, such as the income level at which counties fall below an artificially devised "poverty" line and are thus eligible for government assistance. If we defined median population density for Oregon as a critical value, the map at the top of Figure 7.7 would be based on critical-value intervals.

Unclassed Choropleth Maps. On unclassed choropleth maps, each data collection area is given a lightness, saturation, or texture according to its magnitude. An unclassed choropleth map of Oregon population density (**Figure 7.8, bottom**), has a continuum of gray-tone lightness ranging from white for the lowest density county to black for the highest density. The intermediate population densities are linearly scaled between these two extremes. This map gives you an unbiased picture of Oregon population, since the map maker has not generalized the values into a small number of classes.

The difficulty with reading unclassed choropleth maps is that unless the data collection area values are more or less evenly distributed through their range, the map will show most areas to be either high or low in value with only a few areas at the opposite extreme. The Oregon map is a classic example, with one county solid black, one county medium gray, and the others a very light gray. The map looks similar to the equal-range map, except that your discerning eye can see small variations among the light tones.

Dasymetric Maps

On **dasymetric maps**, the mapped areas aren't political data collection units such as counties but, rather, areas of inherent homogeneity in the data. The idea is that each mapped area will have small internal magnitude variations, while there will be large magnitude variations between mapped areas. There are several types of homogeneity within areas.

As with choropleth maps, each homogeneous area can have a single value or an average value

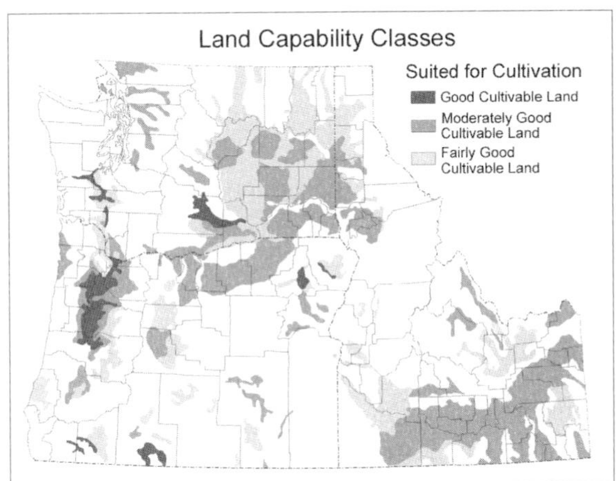

Figure 7.10 Land capability classes in the Pacific Northwest are portrayed using the dasymetric mapping technique. The ordinal level data consist of land that's good, moderately good, and fairly good for cultivation (from Atlas of the Pacific Northwest).

with little variation about the average within the area. Land capability classes in the Pacific Northwest (**Figure 7.10**), for example, are mapped as ordinal level areas of suitability for cultivation ranked from good to fair. Notice how detailed the areas in each class are relative to the counties in the region. You can see that a dasymetric map should give a more faithful representation of land capability than a choropleth map showing the dominant capability class for each county.

An area can be homogeneous in the sense that all values in it are within a certain numerical range. A slope zone map, such as Figure 16.7 in Chapter 16, is a good example of a dasymetric map having areas of homogeneity defined by numerical ranges. For instance, areas mapped in the lowest slope category should have slopes between 0 and 7% throughout, and no slopes should be greater than 7%.

Area-Feature Point Symbols

Possibly the most confusing quantitative thematic maps are those that use proportional point symbols to represent quantities within data collection areas. The problem is that you are led to think you're looking at data for a point feature when this isn't the case. The cartographer has placed the point symbol in the center of each data collection area.

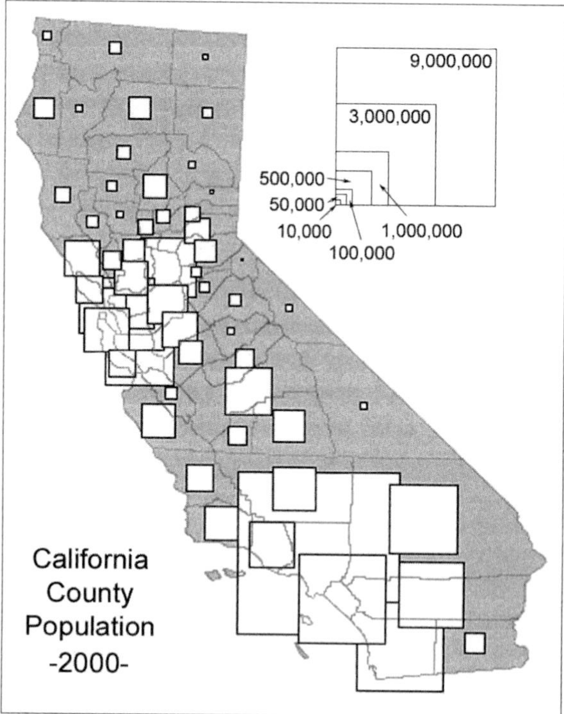

Figure 7.11 California population data from the 2000 census have been aggregated by county, with proportional squares located at county centroids used to show the total county population.

The proportional point symbols will be easiest to read when data collection areas are approximately equal in size on the map and when the range of data values is small. A map of California county population (**Figure 7.11**) illustrates map reading difficulties when both the range of county areas and the data range are large. The map shows total county population with area proportional squares placed at the center of each county. The very large population data range (from 1,500 to 9,000,000) results in a range of squares from barely visible to covering several counties. Many of the squares extend past their county's boundaries and overlap with the squares for neighboring counties. Reading the map is particularly difficult in the San Francisco Bay region, where small counties and large populations have resulted in numerous symbol overlaps.

Area Cartograms

There may be times when you'd like to view an eye-catching portrayal of the relative magnitudes of area features rather than their exact spatial locations. At such times, you might turn to an odd-looking map called an **area cartogram**. Map makers create area cartograms by distorting the geographical size of data collection areas in proportion to their magnitudes. The size of each state, for example, might be made proportional to its population rather than its geographical area.

To use an area cartogram effectively, you must compare sizes of data collection areas on the cartogram with the same areas shown on an equal-area map projection. If the shapes and relative sizes of data collection areas in a region aren't familiar to you, an area cartogram can be difficult to use because you'll need to compare two unfamiliar-looking maps. For this reason, area cartograms are most successful when the size of familiar features such as countries, states, and counties are made proportional to their magnitude rather than their geographical area. This explains why "world by country," "country by state," or "state by county" area cartograms are so common.

Ideally, when enlarging or reducing data collection unit areas in proportion to their magnitudes, map makers retain as many spatial characteristics of conventional maps as possible. Preserving the shape of data collection areas, as well as their proximity and contiguity (boundary connectedness) to neighboring areas will make it easier to compare a cartogram with a standard map. But shapes cannot be preserved without altering the proximity and contiguity of neighboring areas, and vice versa.

Non-contiguous area cartograms are the most commonly produced, because they're the easiest to make. To create a non-contiguous cartogram for the population of California counties (**Figure 7.12, left**), the map maker enlarged or reduced each county in proportion to its 2000 population. The transformed data collection areas were then replaced as closely as possible in their relative geographical positions on the map. Preserving the shapes of data collection areas makes it easy to recognize and compare them with their counterparts on a conventional map. But as Figure 7.12 also shows, proximity relations are only roughly maintained, and contiguity is sacrificed completely.

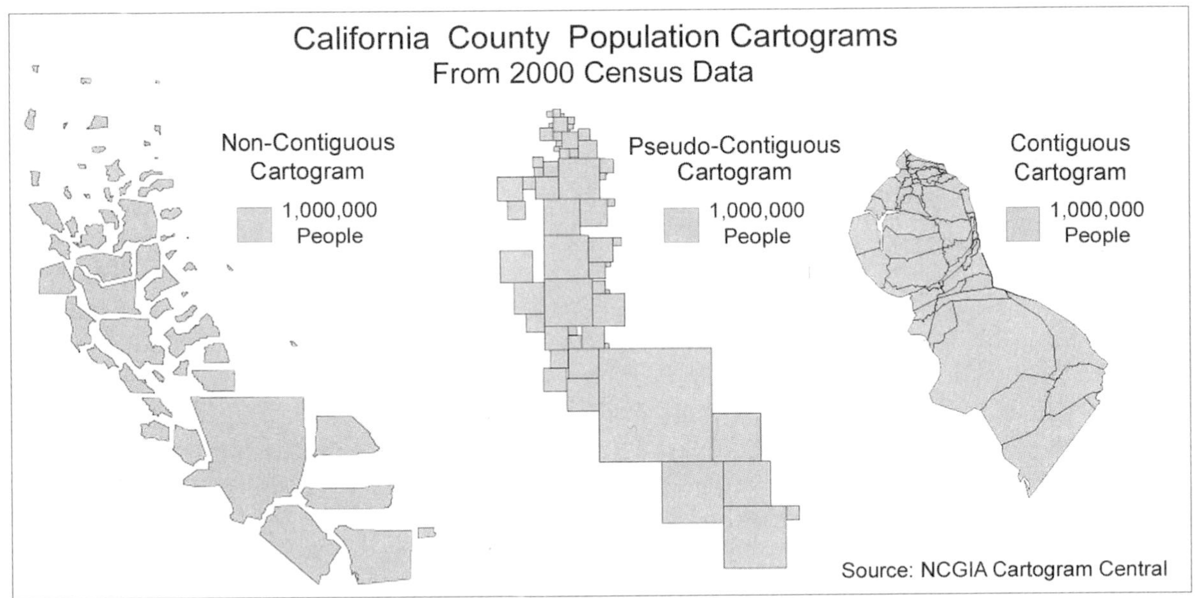

Figure 7.12 Non-contiguous, pseudo-contiguous, and contiguous area cartograms for California county population (based on 2000 census data).

Pseudo-contiguous area cartograms appear contiguous at first glance but upon closer inspection turn out only to give the illusion of contiguity (**Figure 7.12, middle**). The transformed data collection areas share common boundaries, but the boundaries aren't the same as on a conventional map of the region.

A pseudo-continuous cartogram is made by transforming each data collection area into a simple geometrical shape proportional in size to the magnitude being shown. Rectangles are the shapes most commonly used. The new shapes are then arranged in what resembles their relative geographical position. When rectangles are used, the result is called a **rectangular area cartogram**. By sacrificing shape and proximity, these cartograms can maintain a considerable degree of contiguity.

Pseudo-contiguous area cartograms may actually be no better than non-contiguous cartograms—perhaps worse, because some map readers may believe them to be truly contiguous when in fact they aren't. The popularity of pseudo-contiguous cartograms is probably better explained by the fact that they are easy to construct (only graph paper is needed) than by any map reading advantage they might possess.

Contiguous area cartograms are by far the most interesting to look at. On these cartograms, the proximity and contiguity of neighboring areas are maintained, although this is accomplished at the expense of shape distortion. The shapes of regions are usually distorted in a subjective, apparently uncontrolled manner. Therefore, cartograms of the same theme created by different map makers would likely look dissimilar.

This lack of rigid geometrical mapping control is evident in the contiguous area cartogram of California county population in **Figure 7.12, right**. Notice that while the shapes of some counties are fairly well preserved, other counties don't look like themselves at all. Yet, despite this shape distortion, the cartogram is effective; with only a glance, you can see precisely which counties have the greatest population. This would seem to indicate that the variable quality of shape preservation from one region to the next isn't always a major distraction. We appear able to accept a fair degree of shape distortion before areas become unrecognizable.

The biggest problem with contiguous area cartograms is that they are difficult and time-consuming to make. To draw even a simple cartogram well requires a vast amount of labor, not to men-

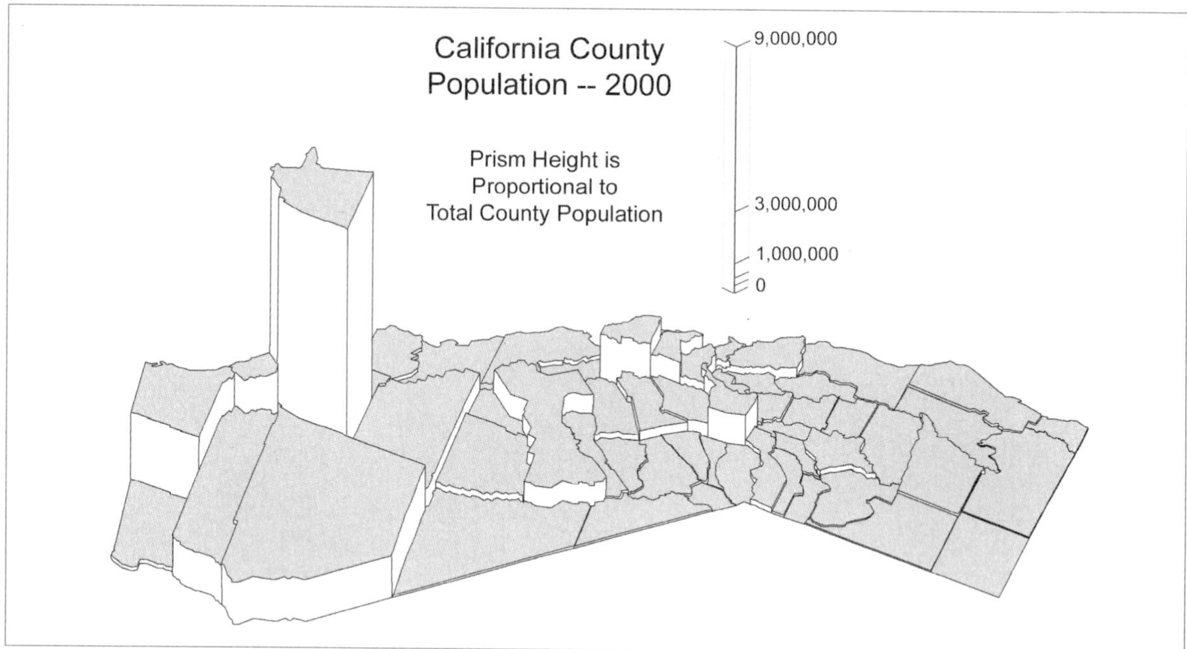

Figure 7.13 Three-dimensional stepped-surface map of California population by county. The height of each county is proportional to its total 2000 population.

tion artistic talent. As a result, area cartograms have, in the past, been regarded more as a novelty than as valuable tools for environmental understanding.

But both problems—uncontrolled geometric distortion and difficulty of construction—have been solved by computer mapping software. It now takes little effort or artistic talent to create contiguous cartograms like that for California population in Figure 7.12. Although county shapes have been distorted, the distortion has been done in a recognizable way.

With increasing use of computer mapping software, area cartograms of all types will become more available each year. In deciding whether to look at a cartogram or a conventional choropleth or point symbol map of a theme, you must decide if you prefer emphasis on the variation in magnitude among areas or on the region's geography. With conventional quantitative maps, you face the problem of decoding magnitude information from map symbols. Cartograms make these magnitudes obvious, but in distorting physical space, they force you to rely on your own familiarity with the geography of the region. The optimal solution, of course, is to use a conventional base map as a reference for understanding the distorted geography seen on the cartogram.

Stepped-Surface Maps

A **stepped-surface map** is made by dividing the mapped region into data collection areas and showing how much of something exists in the areas by varying their heights. Since the information to be mapped is usually collected in areas such as states, counties, or census tracts, it is easiest for map makers to divide the map into these same areas. Such a map, showing California population by county, is shown in **Figure 7.13**. Each county boundary has been raised vertically above the base level to a height proportionate to its total population. The resulting map looks like a three-dimensional, stepped surface.

Stepped-surface maps are visually impressive, but there are several problems with them. One drawback is that, although highs and lows are apparent, the exact height of the surface at a given location is difficult to determine. In addition, if the information that is mapped ranges greatly in magnitude, map makers may have transformed the data values to a more convenient mathematical form. For example, if the population of the United States by state were mapped as raw data, the few very populous states would be so much greater in magnitude than the majority of the low-population states that the map would show little magnitude variation between most states. But by mapping the square root of the state population, differences among the low-population states are exaggerated. Considering the impact of such data transformations on the appearance of a map, you should check the map legend and explanatory notes to see if the data values have been transformed by the map maker and, if so, in what manner.

Another potential drawback of stepped-surface maps is that they are drawn in oblique perspective. This means that the vantage point taken when the map was made is crucial to their appearance. A poor choice of viewpoint may cause important data collection areas to be obscured from view. For instance, the relatively low-angle, east viewpoint used for the map in Figure 7.13 caused two important counties, San Francisco and Santa Cruz, to be obscured.

Continuous Surface Maps

A fourth type of quantitative map shows a theme as a **continuous surface**. A continuous-surface map is like a stepped-surface map in that it portrays the changing magnitude of some phenomenon from one place to another. It differs from a stepped-surface map in that the changes are gradual rather than abrupt. Atmospheric temperature, barometric pressure, humidity, and landform elevation are examples of continuous surfaces that change gradually from place to place. In theory, you can measure their magnitude at all locations on the earth's surface.

Continuous-surface maps can also be created from a sparse set of data values by interpolating between values in such a way that a smooth surface results. An average annual precipitation map created by interpolating between weather station rainfall data is an example. Another example is a population surface map for a state created by interpolating between total population values placed at the centerpoint of each county.

Density distributions are also continuous surfaces. Rather than think of trees as discrete entities, you can count how many are found in a small data collection area (say a square kilometer) and assign that quantity to the center of each area. By performing this operation for all data collection areas, you can create a continuous tree density surface.

There are several ways to map a continuous surface. Many of the mapping methods were originally devised to portray the elevation surface, and these are described in Chapter 8. In this chapter we are focusing on the mapping of other types of continuous surfaces defined by sparser sets of quantitative data. The most important methods for mapping these continuous surfaces produce isoline (including isopleth and layer-tinted isoline maps), dot maps, and 3-D perspective maps. Let's look at each in turn.

Isoline Maps

The most common method used to map continuous data surfaces is to connect points of a selected value with **isolines*** (the prefix iso means equal). Isolines have been given different names according to what type of information they show—isotherms are lines of equal temperature, isobars are lines of equal atmospheric pressure, isohyets are lines of equal precipitation, and so on.

To create an isoline map, map makers must decide how many isolines to draw and how close together to place them. In other words, they must decide what the interval between successive isolines will be. Map makers can choose a constant or variable isoline interval. This choice will have a major effect on the map's appearance.

In **Figure 7.14**, isoline mapping has been used to show average annual hours of sunshine in the Pacific Northwest. Each isoline is labeled with its value so that regional variations in sunshine hours

**Isolines are also known as isarithms.*

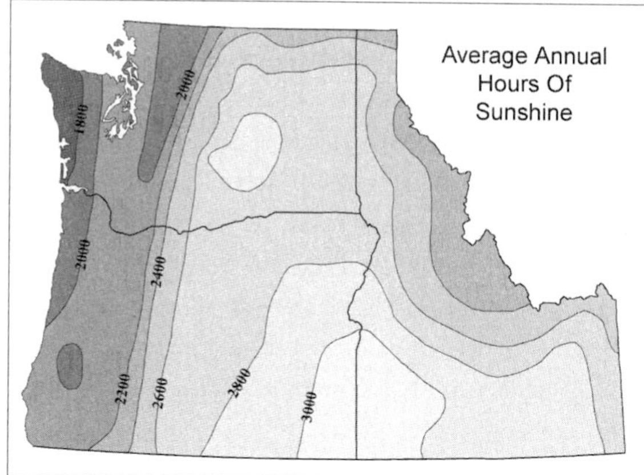

Figure 7.14 This isoline map shows average hours of sunshine received in the Pacific Northwest (adapted from the Atlas of the Pacific Northwest, 9th ed.)

can be studied. A strong regional pattern is evident. Hours of sunshine clearly decrease as you move from west to east across the region, with a rapid increase to the east of the Cascade Range.

In creating this map, the map makers had to make a series of choices. They decided that 1,800 average annual hours of sunshine would be the lowest value they showed, and they chose a constant class interval of 200 hours. Changing either of these factors will alter the appearance of the map. If more isolines were shown, for instance, you would see more detail than the seven isolines on the map, although the regional pattern of sunshine would remain the same.

Isopleth Maps. An isoline drawn across a density surface created from statistical data is called an **isopleth**. Isopleths look identical to standard isolines, but they differ in that they show a density or rate surface where the values can't physically exist at points (**Figure 7.15**). It's impossible, for instance, that 500 people per square mile can exist at one spot.

A common way to create the continuous surface for an isopleth map is to collect data by census units and then assign these data to the center of each unit. Each value is then divided by the census unit area, creating a density. The density values are then mapped using isopleths.

An isopleth map is at best an abstract, generalized representation of the data. Suppose, for example, that an isopleth shows the population density as 1,000 people per square mile. At a given position along the 1,000 isopleth, you may find no people, or you may find 5,000. The map is only intended to give a general impression of varying density over space. It is not to be analyzed location by location.

Layer-Tinted Isoline Maps. The way to read an isoline map is to ignore individual isolines and focus on the overall isoline pattern so that you can visualize the surface. Some people find this hard to do, however. To assist map users who have trouble focusing on the pattern rather than on separate isolines, some maps are made with a progression of gray-tone lightnesses, color intensities, or textures added between isolines (see Figure 7.14). If the tints are selected properly, you will see a magnitude progression from low to high, with the isolines seen as outlining different magnitude zones. The isolines often aren't labeled with numbers, which further encourages you to see the general pattern of highs and lows on the surface rather than to concentrate on individual isolines. Numerical range information for each color, tint, or texture is found solely in the map legend.

One drawback of tinted isoline maps is that when only a small number of isolines are drawn, only a few tints will be used on the map and it will look highly generalized. Furthermore, even though a continuous surface is being mapped with isolines, the progression of tints may leave you with the false impression of a stepped surface or distribution. Fortunately, modern computer mapping software makes it possible for map makers to create a large number of isolines and a continuous-appearing lightness or saturation progression . These modern tinted isoline maps enhance the impression of a continuous surface.

Dot Maps

Just as a series of isolines can be used to show a continuous surface, so can a set of point symbols.

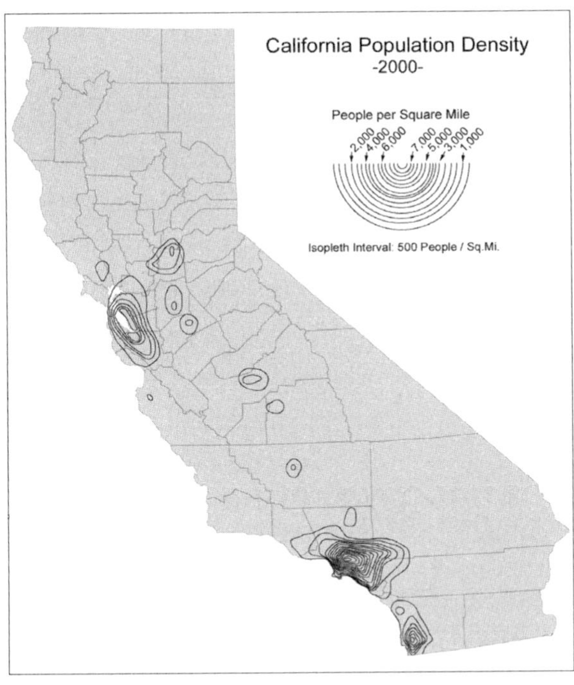

Figure 7.15 This isopleth map of California population density was created by drawing isopleth lines through a set of density values placed at the center of each county.

In fact, point symbols are the basis for one of the most effective ways of showing variations in density across a surface. The procedure is called **dot mapping**.

When producing a dot map, the map maker repeats the same point symbol as many times as necessary to show the variations in density across the surface (**Figure 7.16**). Although the circular dot is the most common symbol used in dot mapping, any geometric figure, such as a square or triangle, may be used. The shape is irrelevant, since the symbol's meaning lies solely in the changes in dot density produced by its repetition.

An understanding of the difference between a point symbol map and a dot map is crucial to map reading. On point symbol maps, each symbol represents only one feature, such as a city. Changing the form of the symbol—making it larger or darker, for instance—shows the change in magnitude from one feature to another.

While point symbol maps show where individual features are located and their magnitudes, the dots on a dot map can't exist at the same locations as the features do in reality, because each symbol represents more than one feature. The aim of dot maps isn't to give precise locational information but to present an image of changing density across the region. Thus, if the dot map is well made, your eye won't be attracted to individual dots but to a general impression of changing spatial density. Not all dot maps meet this criterion, however. The dots may be too large or too small in size, or too few or too many in number. When this happens, you may receive a mistaken impression of the changes in density.

To create a dot map, map makers first choose a **unit value** for each dot. For example, they may decide, as they did for the California population map in Figure 7.16, that each dot represents 10,000 people. They then divide the number of features in the region by this unit value. The resulting number tells them how many dots to put on the map. Dot maps usually include a legend defining the unit value of a dot.

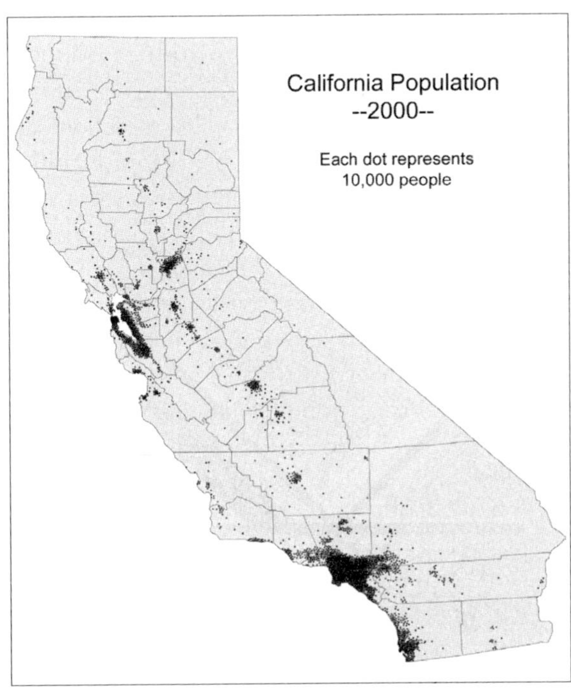

Figure 7.16 Dot map of California population. Each dot represents 10,000 people in the surrounding area.

Dot maps look simple, but they can be some of the most difficult maps to read. For one thing, as we've already seen, the human eye tends to underperceive magnitudes. Psychological experiments have shown that as the density of dots increases, our estimates of the density tend to fall below the actual density at an increasing rate. The result is that people viewing dot maps typically receive the impression that the range in dot density—and therefore the contrast in density from one region to another—is less than it really is. For this reason, you may find it necessary to compensate mentally for underperception in your own density judgments to gain a true picture of the mapped distribution.

A well-made dot map will have variations in dot density within the data collection area boundaries that correspond to variations in magnitude within each area. Notice the within-county variations in dot density on the map in Figure 7.16. To make this map, the map maker used city population statistics along with maps showing the terrain, land use, and transportation features within each county to determine where people most likely lived. Dots placed according to this information are seen as smooth gradations from low to high population density.

Incorrectly made dot maps can be confusing, if not downright misleading. The more clustered the distribution, the more pronounced the discrepancy between reality and the dot map. For example, a poorly created dot map of California population might give the impression that population is scattered evenly within each county, with sharp breaks in density between counties. In reality, most of California's population is clustered within parts of the San Francisco Bay area and southern California counties. The classic mapping problem is San Bernadino County, which stretches from the eastern edge of the Los Angeles metropolitan area to the Arizona and Nevada borders. If dots were placed evenly within the county, you would conclude that most of the Mojave Desert has a medium population density. As you see on the correctly made dot map in Figure 7.16, most of the Mojave Desert is unpopulated, and the vast majority of people live in the far southwestern corner of the county that's part of the Los Angeles metropolitan area.

3-D Perspective Maps

A continuous surface can also be shown as a **three-dimensional (3-D) perspective map**. If the map maker constructs closely spaced line profiles in two directions and in perspective view, you gain an impression not of individual lines but of a continuously varying 3-D surface called a **fishnet** (**Figure 7.17**). The fishnet surface is another example of lines used effectively as continuous surface symbols. Notice how your attention is focused not on any one line but on vertical undulations in the surface. Note, too, how much more realistically this map shows the variability in California population density than does the stepped-surface map in Figure 7.13. Maps that add relief shading to the fishnet create an even more visually effective portrayal of the California population.

Your ability to see all locations on the map is determined by the viewpoint and viewing angle selected by the map maker. In Figure 7.17, the California population density surface is shown at a 30° angle above the horizon from both a north and south viewpoint. Notice that different peaks and valleys in the surface are hidden from view on each map. Two maps are often required to see all parts of the surface. Animated 3-D perspective maps that you appear to fly over are ideal for viewing the details of the continuous surface.

MULTIVARIATE MAPS

Sometimes map makers show magnitude variations in more than one theme on a single **multivariate map**, using a different graphic element to show each theme. The best map designs use combinations of symbol size, texture, lightness, and color intensity. The symbol's size might represent per capita income, for example, while changes in color intensity within the symbol outline might represent years of education.

A second type of multivariate map shows magnitude information for **sub-categories** of the map theme. A typical example is to subdivide a symbol for total county population so as to show the racial or ethnic composition within the county. **Composite data** rather than raw data for each theme can also be shown. For instance, you might see a single symbol showing the ratio of data values for two themes.

Again, let's look at point, line, and area features in turn. We'll begin by considering map symbols for multivariate point-feature information.

Point Features

Quantitative multivariate point-feature information is most often mapped using point symbols varying in size according to their total magnitude. You may see sub-categories of a theme shown by bar graphs (**Figure 7.18**), circles (pie graphs), or other regular geometrical shapes. The symbol may be **segmented** to represent the proportion of the total magnitude in each sub-category (**Figure 7.19**). The use of any of these symbols requires judging the relative length or area falling within each segment. Adjacent vertical bars are somewhat easier for most people to read and analyze with precision than segmented circles, because bars require only the estimation of relative height. The problem with bar graphs is that they often extend outside their data collection areas, because only their height can be varied.

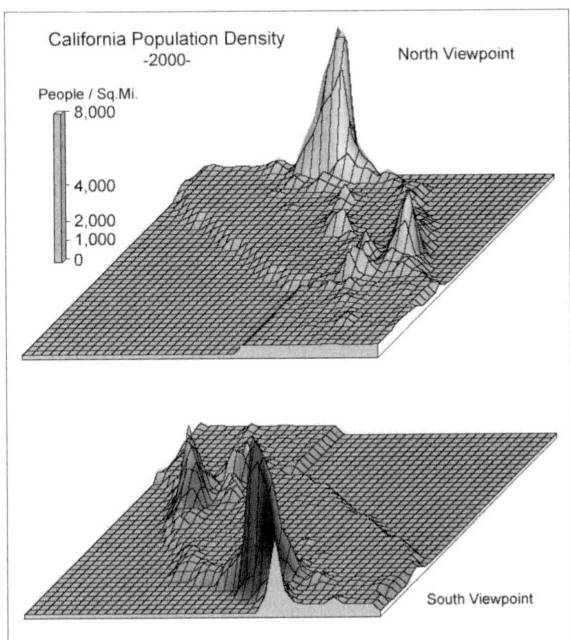

Figure 7.17 3-D perspective views of California population density from the north and south viewpoint. Adding relief shading to the fishnet surface makes the surface easier to visualize.

Another type of multivariate point symbol shows you the percentage of time that a physical phenomenon like wind comes from different directions. The wind roses in **Figure 7.20** show you the July pattern of prevailing surface wind directions in the Pacific Northwest. From the few weather stations shown on the map, you can see that certain areas (the Columbia river gorge, for example) have a strong dominant wind direction relative to other parts of the region.

On other point-feature maps, quantitative multivariate point information is depicted in composite form using a single graphic element. For example, the simple ratio between crop yield and land value may be mapped as proportional circles for a selection of farms. More complex composite indexes involve the weighting of several factors. The categories of California city safety shown on the map in **Figure 7.21**, for instance, involved creating a safety index by weighting the incidence of six basic crime categories.* The index values for the 80 cities on the map were sorted from low to high so that quartiles could be determined. The quartiles were given the names safest, safe, less safe, and least safe, and the city circles in each class were mapped by differences in gray-tone lightness.

At first glance, these circles look no different from circles showing a simple ratio—or even from circles showing only the size of cities. To completely understand what the circles are showing, you will need to look carefully at the legend and explana-

**The data for the map were taken from the 2000 Morgan Quitno national awards for 322 cities. The six basic crime categories—murder, rape, robbery, aggravated assault, burglary, and motor vehicle theft—were inserted into a formula that measured how a particular city compared to the national average for each crime category. The outcomes for the six categories were weighted equally to obtain the safety index.*

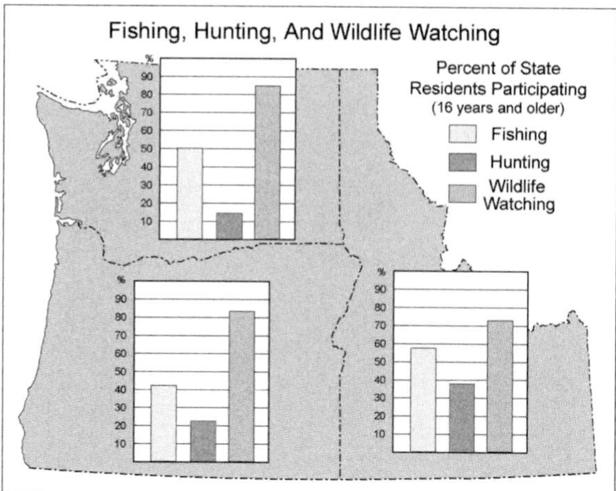

Figure 7.18 Bar graphs can be placed in data collection areas to show sub-categories of a theme such as major outdoor recreation activities. The graph often extends outside the data collection areas because only the height of bars can be varied (from Atlas of the Pacific Northwest 9th ed.).

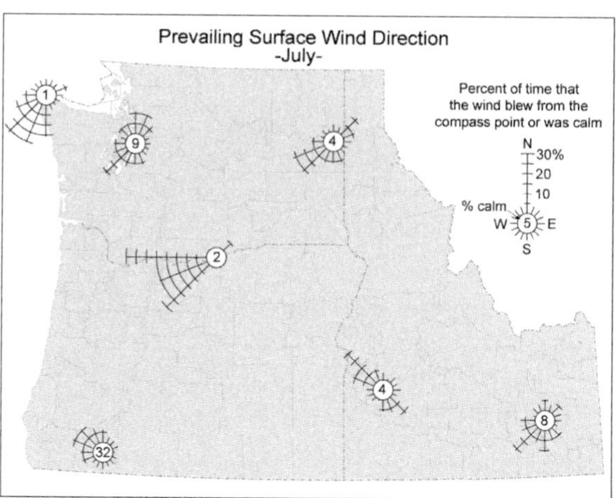

Figure 7.20 Multivariate maps can show sub-categories of directional information, such as prevailing surface wind direction during July in the Pacific Northwest.

tory notes on the map. For example, only California cities greater than 75,000 in population that reported the crime rate in all six categories appear on the map. In addition, the factors used to define the index and the weighting of factors may not be what you expected. You may have wanted to look at a map where murder and rape were weighted much higher than automobile theft, for example. You also may have been looking for a map that included additional city safety factors, such as earthquake or flooding frequency.

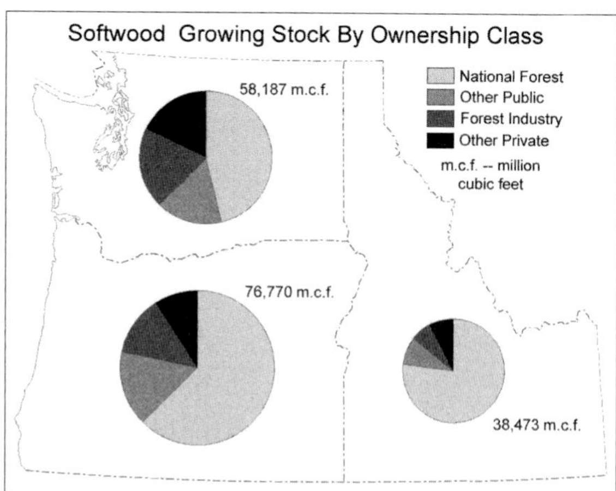

Figure 7.19 Pie graphs placed in data collection areas allow you to estimate the proportion of the total magnitude, softwood growing stock in this example, in sub-categories such as land ownership types (adapted from Atlas of the Pacific Northwest 9th ed.).

Line Features

Quantitative multivariate line symbols are relatively uncommon for the same reason qualitative ones are: If they're made large enough to be easily readable, they take up too much room on the map. But you may occasionally encounter route or flow maps that show multivariate information. You may sometimes see **double flow lines**, with different widths for each line indicating the magnitude of flow in each direction. A common example is a freeway flow map showing the traffic volume in each direction at a particular hour. Since this category of line symbols is relatively neglected by map makers, we won't pursue it further here.

Area Features

Multivariate maps of homogeneous area features commonly show ratios or indexes rather than raw data. For instance, the seismic risk map for Alaska shown in **Figure 7.22** takes into consideration a number of physical factors which combine to cause earthquake damage. These factors are weighted and summed to give a seismic risk index that is used to define the seven risk categories from low to high shown on the map.

Figure 7.21 Categories of California city safety as defined by a safety index based on weighting the incidence of six basic crime categories.

Multivariate area-feature data can also be shown with point symbols. Most maps use segmented geometric symbols such as the familiar pie graph. But a few maps, such as the example in **Figure 7.23**, show several related categories of quantitative data with a single pictographic point symbol. In this example, the quality of life in Los Angeles is shown by different facial expressions depicting four social status factors. The shape of the face shows levels of affluence; the mouth indicates unemployment rate; the eyes represent urban stress; and the tone of the symbol represents the proportion of the population that is white. The combined effect is so striking that you can almost sense how people in different sections of the city might feel.

A third form of multivariate area-feature map combines stepped surface and choropleth mapping. A good example is **Figure 7.24**, which shows two important parts in the story of the spreading West Nile virus. The height of each prism is proportional to the number of confirmed human cases in each state. The top of each prism is given a gray tone according to its approximate dis-

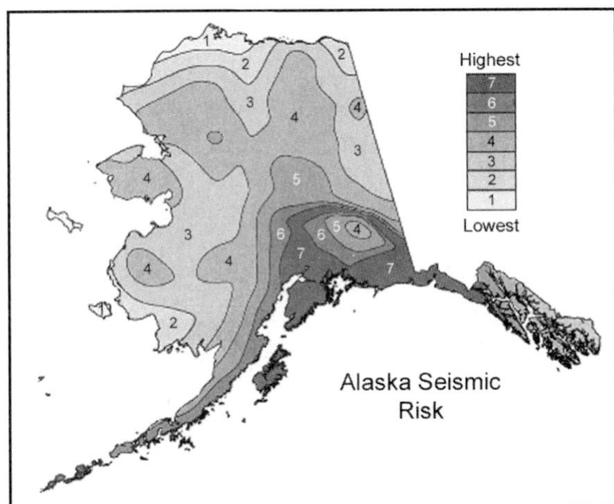

Figure 7.22 Seismic risk map for Alaska showing areas of lowest to highest risk. The risk index used takes into consideration a number of physical factors which combine to cause earthquake damage.

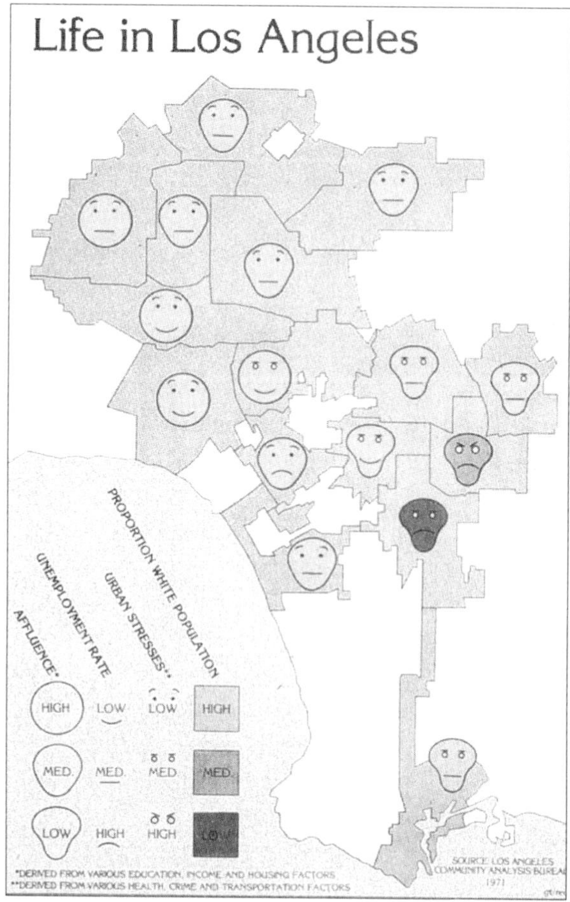

Figure 7.23 This map of life in Los Angeles shows four social status factors, each divided into three classes (low, medium, high) (courtesy of Eugene Turner).

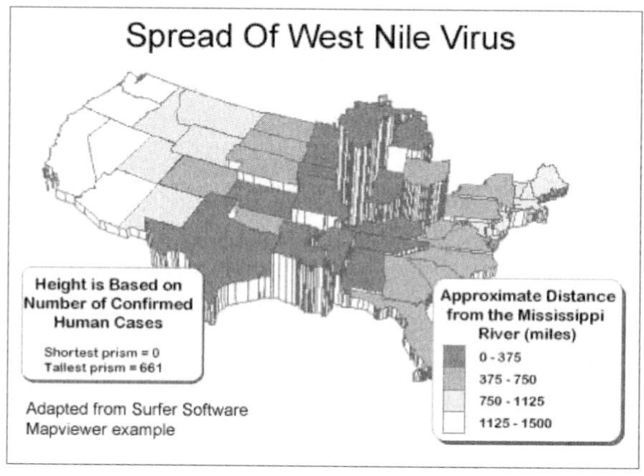

Figure 7.24 This multivariate map combines stepped surface and choropleth mapping to show you the strong relationship between human cases of West Nile virus in 2002 and distance from the Mississippi River.

tance from the Mississippi River. The map clearly shows you the strong relationship between the incidence of the virus and proximity to the Mississippi River.

TEMPORAL CHANGE MAPS

Temporal change maps show the increase or decrease in a theme over a specified time period, as in **Figure 7.25**. This population change map was made by finding the percent change in state populations between 1990 and 2000 as reported by the Census Bureau. If a state had 10 million people in 1990 and 11 million 10 years later, the ratio would be 11/10 million, a 10% increase.

You have to be careful when reading this type of map, because the same percentage of change doesn't mean that the same number of people have been added or lost. If a populous state such as California increases its population by 15%, it is gaining far more people than if a sparsely populated state such as Nevada adds 50% to its population.

Temporal change maps also can show **cyclical** phenomena. The climate of a region, for instance, can be described by a map composed of **annual graphs** showing the yearly cycle of temperature and precipitation at different locations

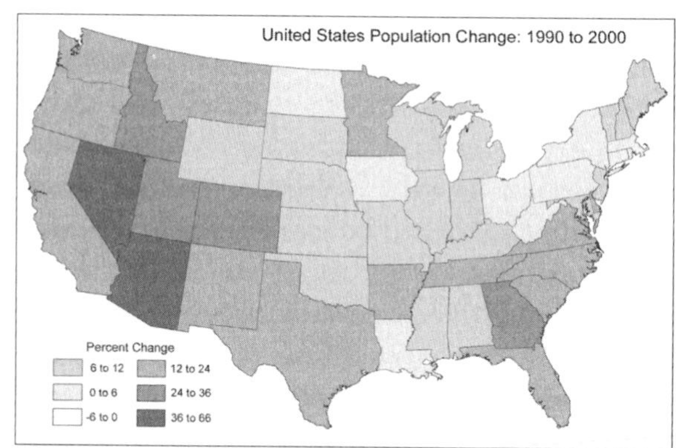

Figure 7.25 This temporal change map shows the percent change in U.S. population by state between 1990 and 2000. Note that the base populations upon which these percentage changes are figured vary greatly.

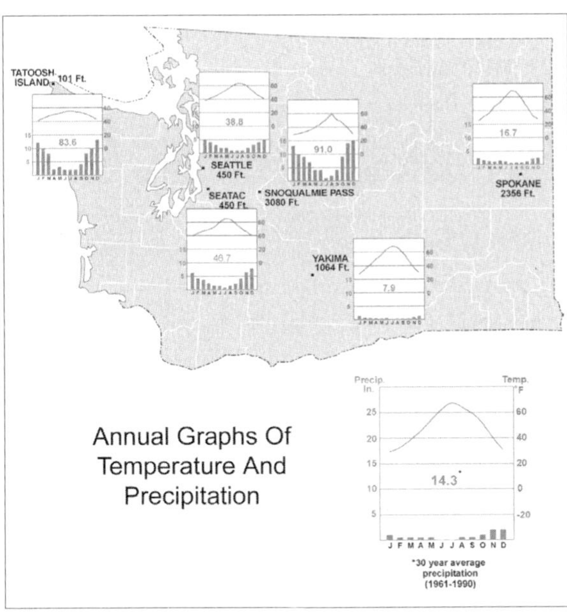

Figure 7.26 Annual graphs showing the yearly cycle of temperature and rainfall at selected Washington weather stations (adapted from the Atlas of the Pacific Northwest).

(**Figure 7.26**). The six annual graphs for Washington allow you to compare seasonal variations at the different weather stations, or to study seasonal variations at a single station. Notice, for instance, the dramatic decrease in monthly precipitation and the greater range of monthly temperature in the eastern half of Washington.

Time Composite Maps

Another way to show changes over time is by superimposing data for several dates on a **time composite map**. You can then see exactly what changes have taken place over the time span covered by the map. Time composite maps are often used to trace the path along which some quantitative feature moves. One of the most famous quantitative time change maps was made in 1861 by Charles Minard. The map uses a sequence of flow lines to portray the disastrous losses suffered by Napoleon's army in the Russian campaign of 1812 (**Figure 7.27**). Beginning at the Polish-Russian border, the textured gray line width shows the size of the army at dif-

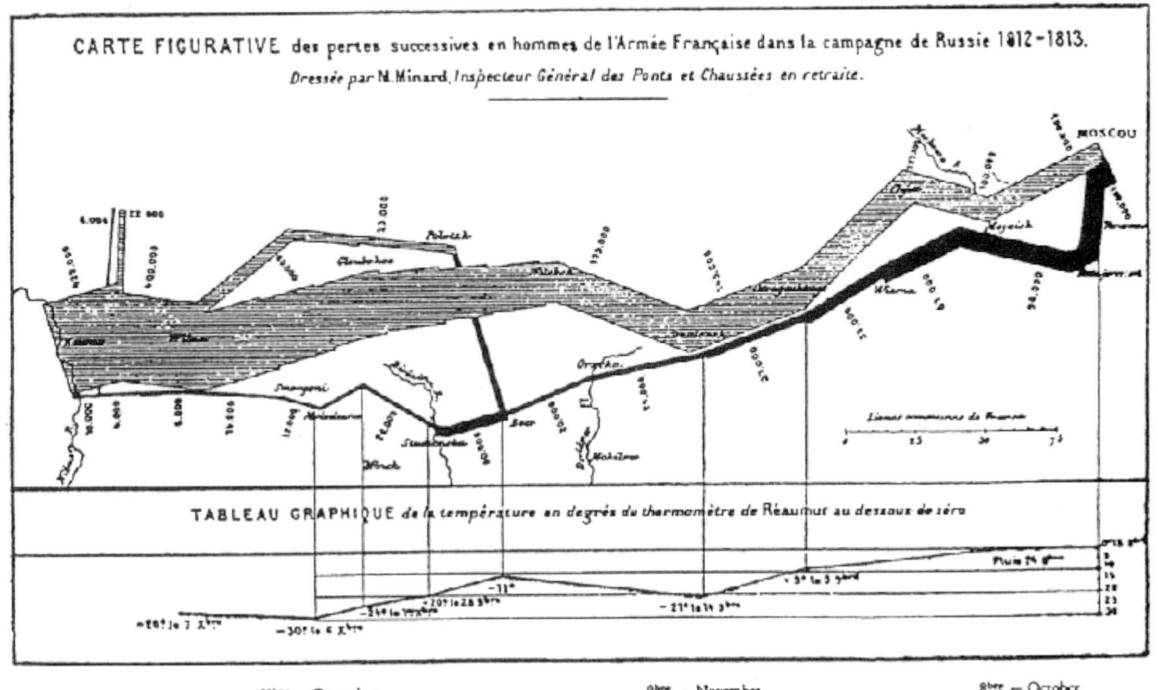

Figure 7.27 One of the most famous quantitative time change maps was made in 1861 by Charles Minard. A sequence of flow lines is used to portray the disastrous losses suffered by Napoleon's army in the Russian campaign of 1812.

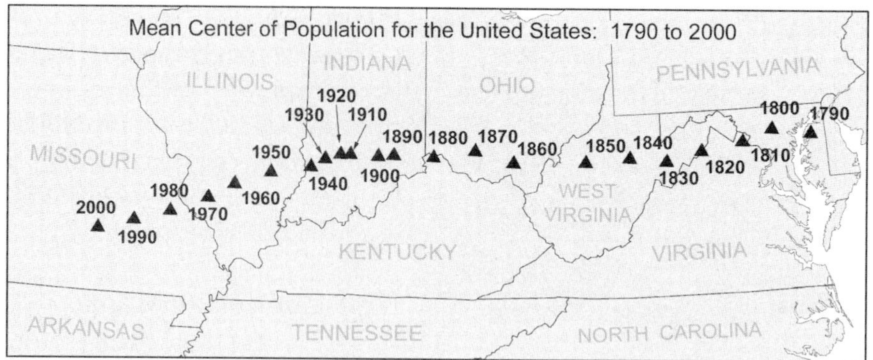

Figure 7.28 This map shows the continual westward shift in the mean center of population for the United States from 1790 to the present.

ferent positions and dates. The path of Napoleon's retreat from Moscow in the bitterly cold winter is depicted by the black lower flow line sequence, below which is a graph of minimum temperature.

Time composite maps can also show the change in position of a geographical measure over time. A classic example is a map showing the position of the **mean center of population** as determined by the Census Bureau after tabulating the results of each census* (**Figure 7.28**).

Each triangle in Figure 7.28 represents the sequential population center of the United States calculated from that decade's census. The map shows a plot of population centers calculated for each decade from 1790 to 2000. You can see that during the 20th century, the mean center of population shifted southwest, from south-central Indiana to its present position in south-central Missouri.

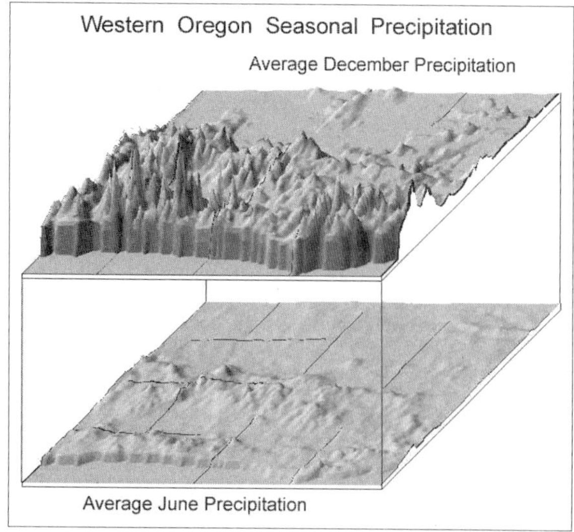

Figure 7.29 December and June precipitation surfaces for western Oregon have been overlaid to show the large seasonal differences in rainfall.

Time Series Maps

A series of choropleth or stepped-surface maps can be made with computer mapping software to show changes over time for the data collection areas on the map. On some time sequences, such as the six maps showing western U.S. population density at ten-year increments from 1850 to 1900 (see **Color Plate 7.1**), the choropleth and stepped surface methods are combined to create visually striking maps. The six maps are actually snapshots taken from an animated map showing the continuous change in U.S. population density from 1790 to the present. You are likely to see an increasing number of animated quantitative maps as movie clips that can be downloaded from the Internet.

Another way to map a time series is by stacking maps vertically so that more than one map can be seen at the same time. This is an effective way to show a set of continuous surfaces, such as average December and June precipitation surfaces for west-

**The Census Bureau defines the mean center of population to be: "the point at which an imaginary, flat, weightless, and rigid map of the United States would balance perfectly if weights of identical value were placed on it so that each weight represented the location of one person on the date of the census."*

ern Oregon (**Figure 7.29**). The 3-D perspective views of the two precipitation surfaces are shown from the same viewpoint and on the same vertical scale. Drawing a line vertically downward from the December surface shows you the corresponding point on the June surface. You can easily see that the amount of precipitation in western Oregon is much greater in December, and that the overall geographical pattern of precipitation is similar in December and June.

SELECTED READINGS

Bertin, J., *Semiology of Graphics* (Madison: University of Wisconsin Press, 1983).

Dent, B.D., *Cartography: Thematic Map Design*, 4th ed. (Dubuque, IA: Wm. C. Brown Publishers, 1996).

Jackson, P.L. and Kimerling, A.J., *Atlas of The Pacific Northwest*, 9th ed. (Corvallis,OR: Oregon State University Press, 2003).

Robinson, A.H., "The Thematic Maps of Charles Joseph Minard," *Imago Mundi*, 21 (1967), pp. 95-108.

Robinson, A.H., et al., *Elements of Cartography*, 6th ed. (New York: John Wiley & Sons, 1995).

Slocum, T.A., and Egbert, S.L., "Cartographic Data Display," Chapter 9 in D.R.F. Taylor, *Geographical Information Systems: The Microcomputer in Modern Cartography* (New York: Pergamon Press, 1991).

Tyner, J., *Introduction to Thematic Cartography* (Englewood Cliffs, NJ: Prentice-Hall, 1992).

Tufte, E.R., *The Visual Display of Quantitative Information* (Cheshire, CT: Graphics Press, 1983).

Tufte, E.R., *Envisioning Information* (Cheshire, CT: Graphics Press, 1990).

Wesson, R.L., et al., *Probabilistic Seismic Hazard Maps of Alaska,* U.S. Geological Survey Open-File Report 99-36 (1999).

Wright, J.K., "The Terminology of Certain Map Symbols," *The Geographic Review*, 34, 4 (1944), pp. 654-655.

Relief Shading (courtesy Mountain Relief)

CHAPTER EIGHT
RELIEF PORTRAYAL

When you get down to it, a map is something impossible,
because it transforms something elevated into something flat.
—Sten Nadolny, The Discovery of Slowness

8

CHAPTER EIGHT

RELIEF PORTRAYAL

The **terrain surface** provides the foundation upon which we play out our lives. Nothing in the environment is immune from the vertical differences we call **relief.** Our mobility, orientation, and environmental understanding are all affected by relief. Yet it's easy to forget the significance of relief in our environment, because many of us live in an essentially flat world. The floor of our house is flat; most yards and streets are flat. Thus, we tend to think of geographical position in purely horizontal terms. This is often a perfectly good way to simplify our world, but ignoring or misunderstanding the terrain surface can have tragic consequences. Ships run aground, airplanes crash into mountainsides, and lost hikers die of exposure—all because the terrain wasn't understood properly.

Maps treat relief in several ways. Some maps ignore it and give only horizontal information. These **planimetric maps** are useful when the mapped area is essentially flat or when facts about an area's relief aren't important to your needs. In such situations, relief information would merely clutter the map with unnecessary detail.

At other times, understanding the terrain surface is crucial to establishing your position and studying spatial associations with other things like vegetation and patterns of rainfall. When relief information is important, it's best to turn to topographic and other maps that show the three-dimensional nature of the terrain surface. There are two types of **relief portrayal—absolute-relief methods** for showing precise elevation information and **relative-relief methods** for showing different landform features and giving a general impression of their relative heights.

ABSOLUTE-RELIEF METHODS

Engineers, scientists, surveyors, and other map users who work analytically with the terrain surface require maps that show more than the general form of terrain features. Absolute-relief methods provide the numerical elevation and water depth information they need. The most accurate elevation and depth data shown on maps are surveyed elevations at individual points on the earth.

Spot Elevations, Bench Marks, and Soundings

On aeronautical charts, topographic maps, engineering plans, and other large-scale maps, the elevation of the surface is given numerically at individual points. These elevation values relative to the **mean sea level (MSL)** datum (see Chapter 1 for more on mean sea level) are called **spot elevations**. On topographic maps like **Figure 8.1**, spot elevations are shown by an "×" followed by the elevation above MSL.

At some of these locations, the elevation has been determined by precise leveling methods (see Chapter 1 for more on leveling), and a permanently fixed brass plate, called a **bench mark**, has

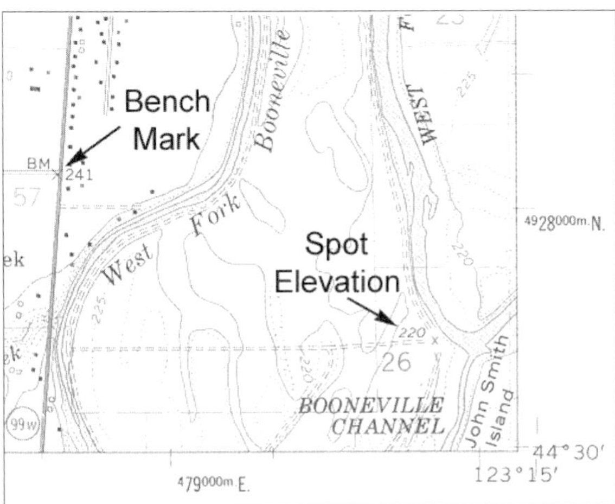

Figure 8.1 Spot elevations and bench marks as portrayed on a 1:24,000-scale topographic map.

Figure 8.2 Precisely surveyed elevation points are identified on the ground by circular brass bench marks.

been installed in the ground (**Figure 8.2**). Bench marks are symbolized on USGS topographic quadrangles by a small "×" next to the elevation value (see Figure 8.1), with the identifier "BM" (for bench mark) preceding the "×".

Water depth readings are called **soundings**. For thousands of years mariners have measured shallow water depths using poles or **lead lines*** marked with depth values. Today soundings are obtained by **electronic depth-measuring instruments** that determine the time that acoustic pulses take to reach the bottom and return to the instrument. This travel time is then converted to distance above the bottom since the velocity of acoustic waves is a known quantity. Our modern electronic instruments collect soundings more rapidly, accurately, and at greater depths than poles or lead lines allowed. **Global positioning system** (see Chapter 14 for more on GPS) receivers integrated into the instruments also give the exact latitude and longitude at the instant each sounding is obtained.

Sounding values are not relative to MSL, but rather to low water. The two datums used in North America are the arithmetic average of all the low tide levels recorded over a 19-year period, called **mean low water** (MLW), and the arithmetic average of the lower of the two daily low tides re-

**A line with a lead weight tied to one end that is lowered into the water to determine depth.*

corded over the same 19-year period, called **mean lower low water** (MLLW). Canadian nautical charts use MLW, whereas in the United States MLLW is the official U.S. National Ocean Service (NOS) nautical chart datum. To support harbor and river navigation, bridge clearances are referenced to a **mean high water** (MHW), and not MLLW.

The MLLW datum is used on nautical charts for water depths because ship captains need to decide whether there is enough clearance for their vessels between the changing water surface and a fixed submerged obstacle, such as the harbor bottom or a wreck. To do so, they must determine the minimum depth likely to be encountered at a given position. If overhead clearance is the concern, as when moving under a bridge, the situation is reversed and the MHW datum is more useful.

Sounding values have been printed on nautical charts since the early 1600s. Charts covering the coastline of the United States (**Figure 8.3**) have used the **fathom** (6 feet) as the unit of measurement for depth. The one exception is the use of **fathoms and feet** in areas shallower than 11 fathoms where more exact depths are required for safe navigation. The value 1_5, for instance, is read as one fathom and five feet, or 11 feet. Nautical charts made in Canada and most other nations show depths in **meters**, and recent U.S. charts are using meters as well.

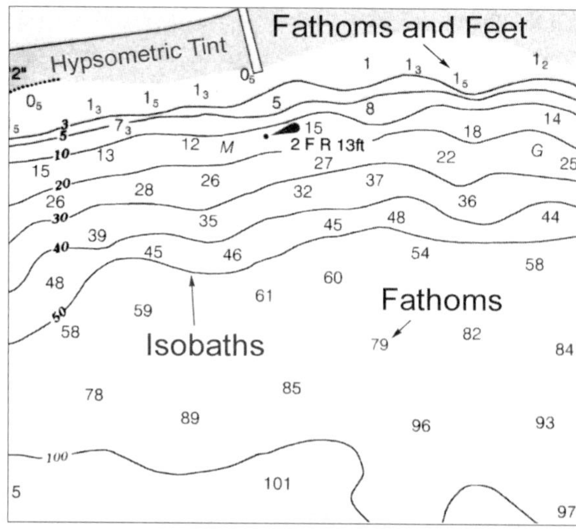

Figure 8.3 Soundings on United States nautical charts usually are shown in fathoms for depths greater than 11 fathoms. Fathoms and feet are used for shallower areas.

Contour Lines

Contours are lines of equal elevation above a datum. If these lines were actually drawn on the earth, they would follow the contour of the terrain. Many countries use contours on their topographic maps to show variations in relief and landform features like hills and valleys. The portion of a 1:24,000-scale USGS topographic quadrangle in **Figure 8.4** is representative of this type of map.

To understand the logic behind contour lines, imagine that you are on a small sandy island in the ocean. If you walked around the island at the shoreline when the tide was at mean sea level, you would trace out the zero or datum contour and would return precisely to your starting point. This is important to remember, since all contour lines eventually close, although the closed curve won't always be seen on a single map sheet.

Now suppose that you climb the side of the island until you reach an elevation of 100 feet above

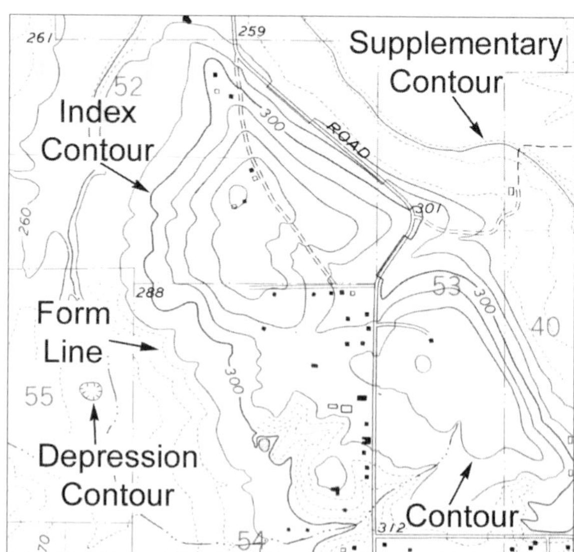

Figure 8.4 A portion of a 1:24,000-scale USGS topographic quadrangle with a 20-foot contour interval. Depression contours, form lines, supplementary contours, and index contours are used to portray special landform features and to make the map easier to analyze.

mean sea level. If you again follow the contour around the island, all points on your path will be at the same elevation, and again you will return to your starting point. The effect is the same as if you had walked along the shoreline after the ocean surface was raised 100 feet. If you did the same thing for elevations of 200 feet, 300 feet, and so forth, and the paths you walked were projected vertically onto a flat map, the result would be something like **Figure 8.5**. If the island were viewed in profile, it would look as though it had been sliced into layers by imaginary horizontal planes. (The procedure used to create a profile from a contour map is explained under Profiles in Chapter 16.)

In our island example, the vertical distance between contours, called the **contour interval**, is 100 feet. The map maker, of course, may select a contour interval of 20 feet, 50 feet, or whatever seems appropriate. The smaller the interval used, the more detailed the relief portrayal will be. Once you know the contour interval, it's a simple matter to "read between the lines." If the spot in which you're interested lies halfway between the 500-foot and 600-foot contours, you can conclude that it's around 550 feet high.

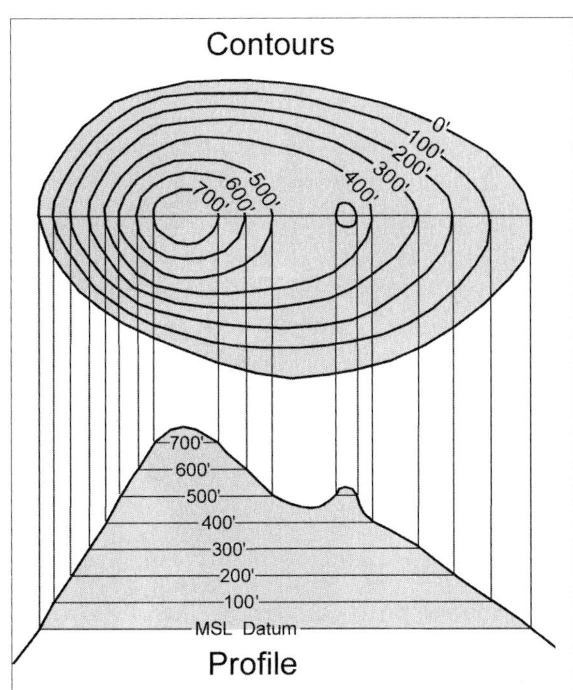

Figure 8.5 The logic of the contour method of relief portrayal is illustrated here by converting the contour intersections with a straight transect (top) into a profile (bottom).

On most maps showing contours, the MSL datum and a constant contour interval are used, regardless of the nature of the terrain on the map. You are usually safe in treating these factors as constants. This leaves only the size of the interval as a variable factor. In general, you will find that the greater the relative relief on a map, the larger the contour interval. Map makers use this relationship between relief and contour interval to keep contour lines from becoming too dense in areas of high relief and too sparse in areas of low relief.

Variable contour line density is desirable on maps because it provides important information about changing terrain slope, but closely spaced contour lines clutter the map and become difficult to differentiate. In contrast, widely spaced contour lines make it hard to determine slopes and to predict elevations at points falling between contours.

A special problem arises when the terrain changes markedly from one part of the map to another. When this occurs, it is quite possible that several different but constant intervals may have been used on the same map. This might happen, for example, with map sheets spanning high to low relief, as is the case along the Rocky Mountain front in the Denver area.

Types of Contours

Several modifications of standard contours are used to portray special aspects of the land surface and to simplify map reading. To aid in identifying closed depressions or basin-like features, for instance, small ticks may be added to the downslope (or inside) of contour lines (Figure 8.4). These **depression contours** help to focus the map user's attention when the depression is small relative to the size of the map sheet. Depression contours are especially useful in distinguishing between small hills and depressions, since there is seldom enough space for the map maker to label the contours of these features with their elevation values.

When depression contours are used, they are sometimes labeled, sometimes not. In either case, note that the first (outside) depression contour is always of the same elevation as the adjacent standard contour. Moreover, depression contours merely represent special cases of the standard contour lines on the map and thus share the same interval and elevation values.

Sometimes you will come across dashed segments of standard contours or will find dashed lines falling between the standard contour lines. These line segments are called **form lines**. They are used to indicate the approximate location of contours where the information isn't reliable, as might be the case in extending standard contour lines across a glacial or sand dune surface.

Supplementary contours provide important topographic detail that otherwise wouldn't be shown by the standard contour lines. These lines are often used in floodplain areas where a slight change in relief might have a major impact on the stream channel and flooding pattern. Although supplementary contours contribute valuable terrain information, they should be viewed with caution. Although sometimes labeled with an intermediate elevation, they are intended to give a general impression of the terrain, not precise elevations.

On most maps, you'll find that not every contour line is marked with its elevation value; instead, every fourth, fifth, or tenth line is labeled, depending on the scale of the map. These labeled contours, called **index contours**, are usually thicker than the standard contours (Figure 8.4) so that they are easily seen. The elevation labels are spaced widely in most cases, meaning that you may have to trace the index contour for some distance before you see its value.

Isobaths

Isobaths, also called depth contours or depth curves, are lines of equal water depth found on nautical charts and other **bathymetric maps** (maps that show water depths). The first isobaths appeared on European charts of river estuaries in the late 1500s. By the end of the 18th century, enough soundings were taken that isobaths could be drawn on a large number of nautical charts. In this century, electronic depth sounders have provided detailed information for drawing isobaths on virtually all nautical charts. In addition, information on deep ocean depths collected by sonar methods and detailed analysis of artificial satellite data have allowed isobaths to be accurately drawn on bathymetric maps of the oceans (**Figure 8.6**).

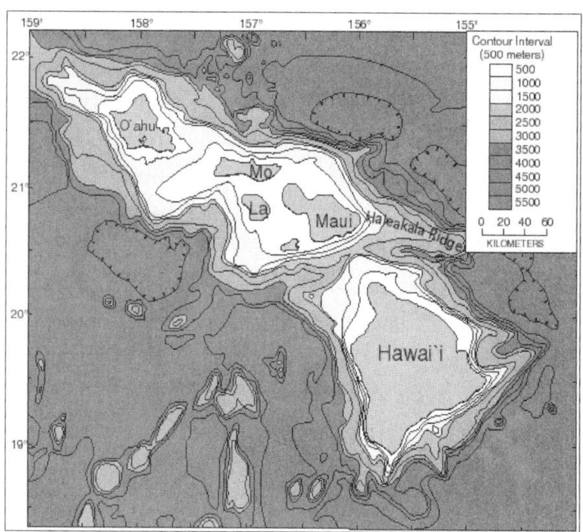

Figure 8.6 Isobaths and hypsometric tinting are used on this bathymetric map of the Hawaiian Islands.

Isobaths on large-scale nautical charts differ from contour lines not only in being based on the MLW or MLLW datum, but also by the use of uneven depth intervals (Figure 8.3). Charts produced by the U.S. NOS, for instance, show isobaths for 1,2,3,5, and 10 fathoms, with greater depths shown in multiples of 10 fathoms, typically 20, 50, and 100. Shallow-water isobaths appear on charts for the same reason that shallow water depths are shown in fathoms and feet—mariners need this information for safe coastal and harbor navigation.

Hypsometric Tinting

Hypsometric tinting (also called **layer tinting**) gives maps using contours or isobaths a stepped appearance, much like a layer cake. On these maps, the space between contour lines is given a distinct gray tone or color, called a hypsometric or layer tint. Enhancing the elevation zones between contours helps show differences in relief. The simplest hypsometric tinting is on U.S. nautical charts, where a light blue tint is usually added to all water areas within the 3-fathom isobath.

When map makers use a series of gray tones to tint between contours or isobaths, the usual rule is: "The darker the tone, the higher the elevation or deeper the water " (Figure 8.6). If the map is well designed, hypsometric tinting should produce a stepped surface impression. But gray tones aren't always properly chosen by map makers, nor do darker tones always signify higher elevations. Thus, it's especially important to check the legend before using these maps.

If map makers use a series of colors, they may assign tints of a single hue but of different intensities to the elevation zones. More intense blues are often used for deeper ocean depths, for example. The effect is the same as that achieved with gray tones. Higher intensities usually signify higher elevations or greater water depths, but there are exceptions. Again, you should routinely consult the map legend.

Sometimes a series of tints composed of different hues are assigned to different elevation zones. This technique is called a **spectral color progression**. It is frequently used in making wall maps for schools. The highest elevation zone is usually shown in dark brown or red, the intermediate zones in buff and light brown, and the lowest zone in dark green. Water is blue.

The spectral color progression is based on the perceptual phenomenon that some colors such as blue appear to visually fall away from you, while others such as red visually rise toward you. Although this spectral scheme is widely used, its visual effectiveness hasn't been satisfactorily proven.

The abrupt change between hypsometric tints can be minimized by gradually merging one tint into the next. This technique, called feathering or **vignetting** (**Figure 8.7**), is readily achieved using computer mapping software and **digital elevation model (DEM)** data, which we'll explore later in this chapter. The key idea is that each elevation in the DEM grid can be assigned a color corresponding to the exact elevation and not a range of elevations as in traditional hypsometric tinting. This creates a continuous progression of color from low to high elevation or from shallow to deep water. It's especially helpful to show water depth in this way since isobaths aren't usually shown.

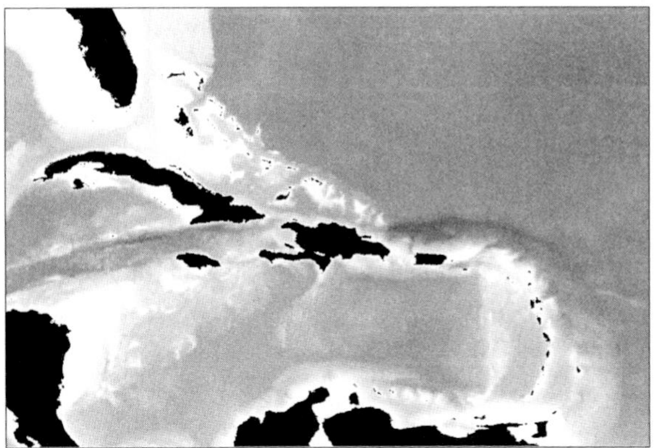

Figure 8.7 Vignetted hypsometric tints (blue tints in the original) create a continuous progression of water depths on this bathymetric map of the Caribbean Sea.

RELATIVE-RELIEF METHODS

In our day-to-day life, we're usually concerned with the local range between high and low heights, or the relative relief. We think of relief in terms of terrain features like plains and hills, mountains and valleys. Relative-relief methods are used on many maps to give a visual three-dimensional effect that makes terrain features easy to see. The ultimate in realism is achieved when the landform surface is depicted in raised relief, as is done on raised-relief globes.

Raised-Relief Globes

Since globes present the truest picture of the earth as a whole, we might conclude that **raised-relief globes** provide the most realistic and useful portrayal of the vertical dimension. But there is a flaw in this reasoning. We saw in Chapter 1 that if the earth were reduced to the size of a bowling ball (a common globe size), the earth would be "smoother" than the ball.

Exaggeration of the actual relief differences on the earth is necessary to make landforms visible and somewhat realistic in appearance (**Figure 8.8**). In practice, a **vertical exaggeration** of about 20 to 1 is typical on relief globes of a 60-centimeter (24-inch) diameter. Therefore, in addition to the highly generalized nature and the handling and storage inconvenience of globes, users of raised-relief globes also face the problem of large vertical distortion.

Relief Models

We can minimize the problem of high vertical distortion by using physical **relief models** rather than globes. Relief models are in effect chunks of a giant raised-relief globe, often constructed to show the curvature of the earth. They let us focus on one small portion of the earth at a larger scale, allowing relief to be shown with less vertical exaggeration than on globes.

Some relief models are constructed with discrete elevation layers (**Figure 8.9A**). The stepped effect usually is a result of the mapping technique, not the nature of the landform surface. Although layered landforms do occur in regions of terraced agriculture, open pit mining, and horizontal sedimentary beds of varying resistance to erosion, these landscapes are relatively rare.

Figure 8.8 Elevation variations on a raised relief globe have to be greatly exaggerated to give a reasonable impression of the landform (courtesy NutriSystems Raised Relief Globes).

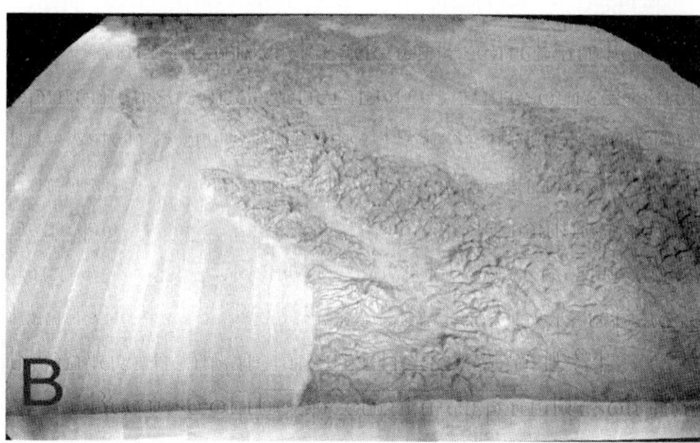

Figure 8.9 The layer by layer construction of relief models often leaves them with a stepped surface (A), although smoothing out the "cliffs" creates a more realistic portrayal, as does showing the earth's curvature (B).

More realistic models are constructed with a smooth, continuous landform surface (**Figure 8.9B**). Of all maps, these relief models probably provide the clearest picture of the terrain. Unfortunately, like all physical models, they suffer the disadvantages of bulk, weight, and high cost of production.

For these reasons, relief models are usually used only in permanent or semi-permanent displays. They are frequently found in the lobbies of government and private agencies that deal with environmental problems, in city-regional planning exhibits, and in university geology, geography, and landscape architecture departments. People working on promotional schemes or research projects are especially fond of using relief models. Parks, urban renewal projects, malls, and dam sites are favorite subjects. For these purposes, the inconvenience of models is offset by the true-to-life impression of the landscape they provide.

There is one type of relief model that partially sidesteps the problems of weight and high cost. This is the **raised-relief topographic map**. It is made by taking an ordinary flat map printed on a sheet of plastic and using heat to vacuum-form it into a three-dimensional model (**Figure 8.10**). The resulting map isn't a curved piece of the globe, as are many relief models. It is really just a flat map sheet with an undulating landform surface.

The raised-relief topographic map is widely available from private mapping firms. It costs about 10 times more than a conventional map of the same size, and it is relatively fragile and difficult to store. But the realism of its relief often compensates for these drawbacks. A more serious concern is that the horizontal position of geographical features may not be portrayed accurately. This is inevitable because of the displacement caused by stretching the flat plastic map into a three-dimensional model. The inaccuracy problem is compounded by the fact that this type of relief map is usually produced at medium to small scale so as to have wider sales appeal.

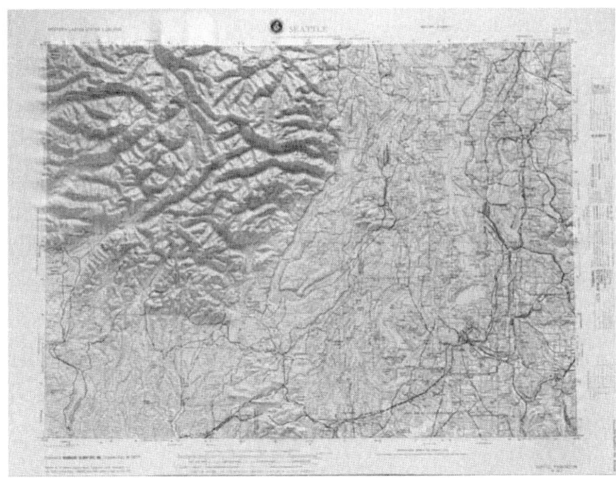

Figure 8.10 A raised relief topographic map is printed on a sheet of plastic molded to form a raised surface.

Figure 8.11 Stylized hills on old maps like this rendition of the California coastline resemble mole hills or haystacks.

Oblique Perspective Views

The stylized drawing of hills from an oblique "bird's eye" perspective is one of the oldest ways to show relief. From the medieval period until the mid-1800s, hills and mountain ranges on both large- and small-scale maps were represented by crude line drawings of highly **stylized hills** (**Figure 8.11**). These drawings look like conical mole-hills or haystacks that bear little resemblance to the features symbolized. Yet, even today, these simple drawings are an effective way to show the general nature of the terrain, particularly on medium-scale to

Figure 8.12 A modern version of stylized hills on a tourist map of the San Juan Islands, Washington.

small-scale maps. They are commonly found on recreational, advertising, and similar maps designed for the public, where only a general impression of landform character is needed (**Figure 8.12**).

Oblique perspective views have strong intuitive appeal and a high level of readability. This accounts for their popularity on everyday maps. But there is a problem. On these maps, you can't place features at their true location. Positional displacement of a terrain feature occurs in direct proportion to the height of its symbol. The true map position can be located for the top, bottom, or middle of the feature—but not all three at once.

Landscape Drawings

Artistically rendered, oblique-perspective maps, called **landscape drawings**, can provide nearly photo-realistic terrain portrayals. Due to the immense amount of hand labor involved in their construction, the best examples are found for regions of special interest, such as national parks and popular mountain resorts. Landscape drawings have become popular as ski area posters like the Mt. Bachelor, Oregon, poster in **Figure 8.13**.

Terrain Profiles and Fishnet Maps

Oblique perspective surfaces can be produced with sets of parallel lines called **terrain profiles** that follow the surface of the terrain (see Profiles in Chapter 16). In **Figure 8.14**, for example, parallel terrain profiles are drawn horizontally or vertically across the terrain surface. More typically, these are combined into profiles drawn across the landform at right angles to each other. The result is called a **fishnet map** or **wireframe**, because it resembles a net or wire draped over the terrain.

More closely spaced profiles produce a smoother surface. But they also take more time to construct and require a higher-resolution grid of digital terrain data (see Digital Elevation Model Data later in this chapter). Now that computer software is used routinely to create fishnet maps, they're increasing in popularity even though they aren't realistic representations of the terrain.

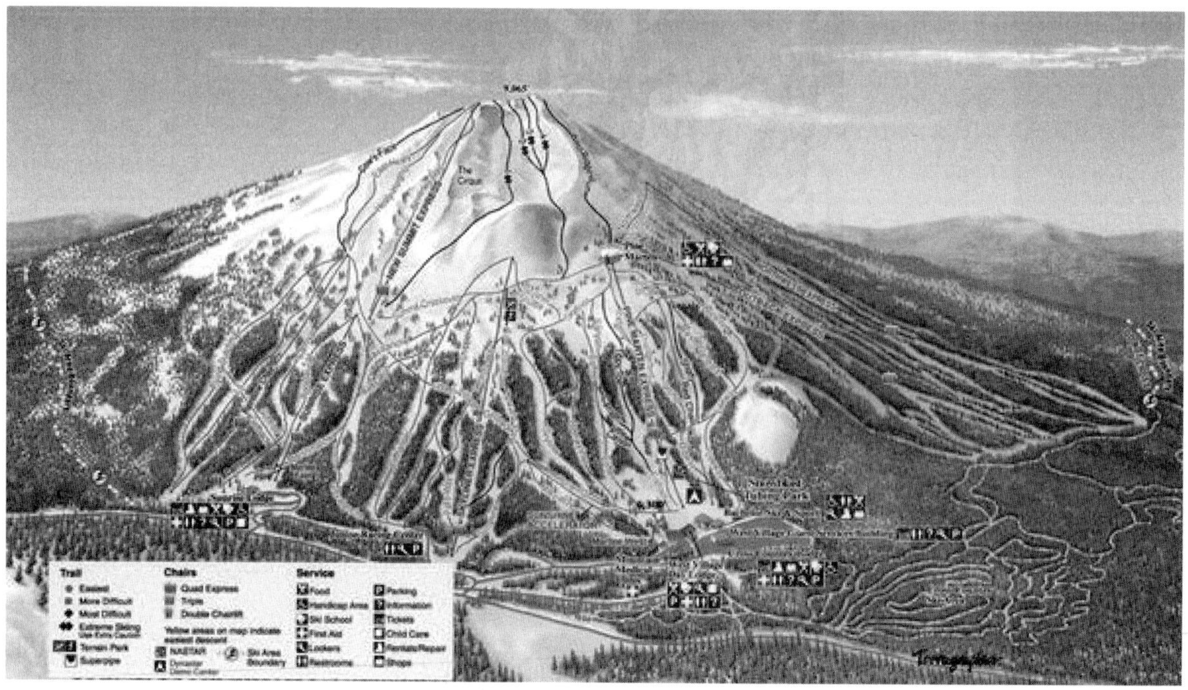

Figure 8.13. Landform drawings like this view of Mt. Bachelor, Oregon, represent the highest achievement in artistic rendering of the terrain surface.

Block Diagrams

A block diagram portrays a piece of terrain as if it were cut out of its adjacent area. The vertical sides of the block allow the underlying rock formations or other subsurface geologic information to be shown (**Figure 8.15**). Block diagrams reach their highest degree of sophistication in their smooth, continuous surface form, where an attempt is made to give an artistic picture of the actual land surface. The natural appearance of the landform can be achieved in two ways—by using sketch lines to accentuate those terrain features which give distinct form to the landscape or by shading the surface continuously. Either technique makes the terrain easily understandable.

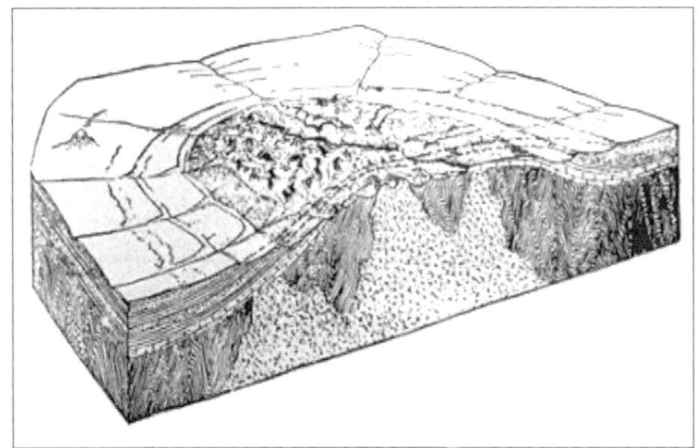

Figure 8.15 A line drawing block diagram showing terrain features and sub-surface geology.

Popular magazines and advertisements take advantage of the realistic terrain picture provided by block diagrams. The illustrations in geology, physical geography, and other environmental textbooks are also commonly of this type.

With fishnet maps and block diagrams, the quality of relief depiction depends on the vantage point taken by the map maker. An oblique vantage point around 45° above horizontal is generally the most useful.

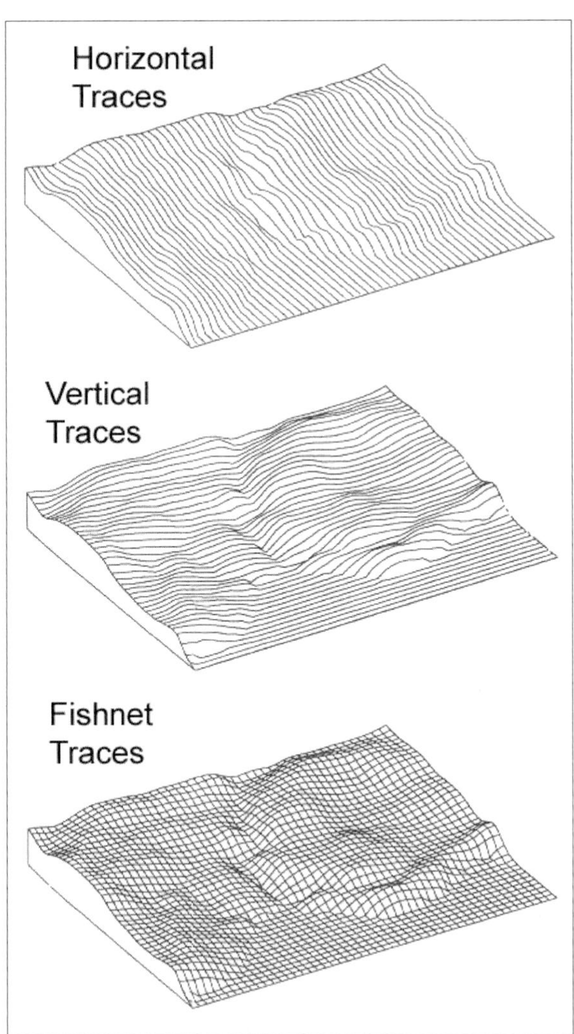

Figure 8.14 Horizontal and vertical traces can be combined into a fishnet map.

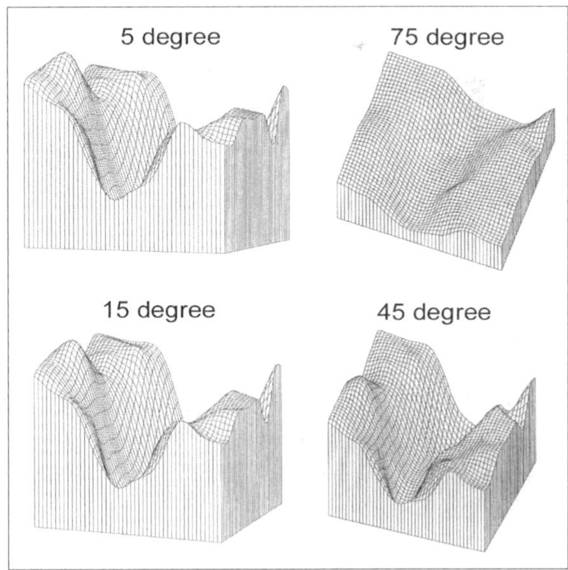

Figure 8.16 Changing the vantage point viewing angle may drastically alter the terrain portrayal, as this sequence of 5°,15°, 45°, and 75° viewing angles demonstrates.

Notice in **Figure 8.16** that as the vantage point viewing angle decreases, the problem of terrain blocking increases. To circumvent the blocking problem, you can sometimes "look behind the hill" if you use two maps, each with a different viewing direction.

To create a realistic impression of relief, map makers exaggerate the vertical scale (make the vertical scale larger than the horizontal scale) of most block diagrams. A **vertical exaggeration** between 2 and 3 is common with large-scale block diagrams, while a 50 to 1 exaggeration is often used for mapping states or countries. Regions of little relief are vertically exaggerated more than regions of substantial relief. Since different degrees of vertical exaggeration can produce quite different relief impressions, you should make it a practice to check the legend of block diagrams to see if the vertical exaggeration factor has been indicated.

Hachures

On large-scale maps, the terrain is sometimes rendered with tiny, short lines called **hachures**, arranged so that they face downhill. Each hachure line lies in the direction of the steepest slope, showing the amount of slope with some accuracy. The best known hachuring method is called the **Lehmann system**, after its founder Johann G. Lehmann, a Saxon military officer who introduced the method to Europe in 1799.

In the Lehmann system, the thickness of hachures is varied—the steeper the slope, the wider the hachures (**Figure 8.17A**). At times, the hachure technique has been so rigorously applied that you can derive numerical slope values by comparing a zone of uniform slope with the map legend. More commonly, only a general impression of steepness was intended.

Hachuring is a poor method when applied to small-scale maps, as it was in the 19th century (**Figure 8.18**). The hachure lines for mountain ranges had to be so simplified and stylized that they look like hairy caterpillars crawling across the map. If you see these creatures on modern maps, realize that they're intended to show only the general location of hills and mountain ranges.

Figure 8.17 With the Lehmann hachure method (A), relief is portrayed by increasing the width of hachures with increasing slope. The Dufour method (B) eliminates hachures on the northwest sides of hills to give a three-dimensional appearance to the terrain.

In the mid-nineteenth century the Lehmann system was largely replaced by the **partial hachuring method** of the Swiss cartographer Guillaume H. Dufour. In Dufour's method, hachures are eliminated on the northwest sides of hills on north-oriented maps (**Figure 8.17B**). This greatly improves the three-dimensional impression of relief and makes terrain features far easier to identify. The problem with Lehmann and Dufour hachures is that they are tedious to execute, and they obscure other map features. Hence, hachures are rarely used in the United States today, but the Dufour system is the predecessor of the relief shading method so widely used throughout the world.

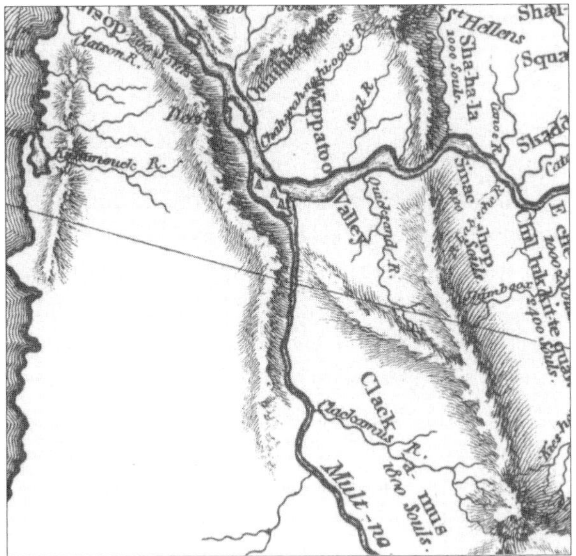

Figure 8.18 Hachures on 19th century small-scale maps, like this piece of the Lewis and Clark Expedition map, look like caterpillars crawling across the map.

Relief Shading

Relief shading, also called hill shading or plastic shading, has been used on maps since the late 19th century to enhance the three-dimensional appearance of terrain features. We know from looking down at the earth from an airplane that patterns of light and shade on hills give us the strongest impression of relief. Relief shading attempts to recreate these tonal variations on maps to give the same three-dimensional effect.

The principle underlying relief shading is that drawings of three-dimensional objects appear correct to us when we use an imaginary light source from the upper-left corner of the drawing surface. If the opposite lower-right light source position is used, objects will appear inverted. The Dufour hachuring method was based on this principle and hence is a crude form of relief shading.

On north-oriented maps, relief shading is based on an imaginary light source at a fixed position off the northwest corner of the map (**Figure 8.19, left**). The lightest shading occurs on northwest-facing slopes, which are at right angles to the imaginary light-source rays. The darkest shadows are cast over southeast-facing slopes, with darker tones assigned to steeper slopes. Lightness and darkness, then, is determined not only by slope steepness but also by terrain orientation with respect to the light source.

Relief shading is not the same as the **shadowing** that appears on real earth features. For instance, compare a mid-morning vertical photograph of a terrain feature (**Figure 8.19, right**) to its shaded representation. On the photo, shadows cast by hills are equal in darkness throughout. These shadows also cross valleys to darken adjacent hillsides. In contrast, the relief shading varies in darkness within shaded areas and stops at the base of valleys.

Relief reversal will occur if you turn a relief-shaded map upside-down so that the imaginary light rays are from the lower right. An upside-down relief-shaded map will produce exactly the opposite effect from what was intended—hills will look like valleys and stream channels will look like ridge tops. Place names, of course, will usually provide an obvious clue to proper map orientation. Still, you should develop the habit of checking the map orientation before interpreting any relief-shaded map.

Another problem with relief-shaded maps is more serious. Relief features oriented roughly parallel to the imaginary light rays (northwest to southeast) aren't shaded enough to give proper relief cues. To circumvent this problem of insufficient shading, map makers often let the imaginary light source "float" around to the map's west and north sides so that terrain with north-south and east-west

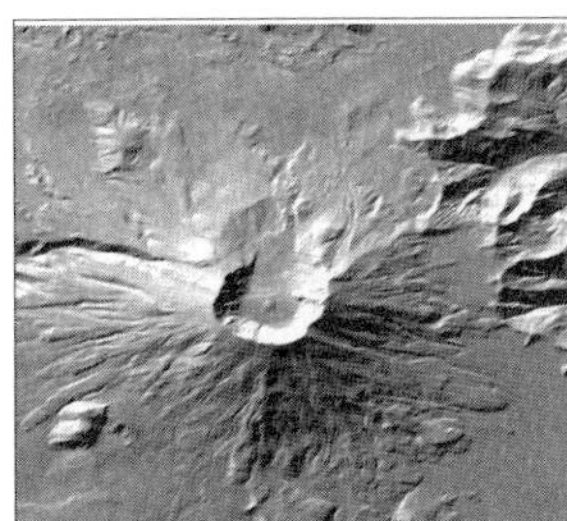

Figure 8.19 Relief shading (left) of Mount St. Helens, Washington, using oblique illumination with a fixed light source at the upper left, and a vertical aerial photograph (right) of the same area illustrate the differences between shading and shadowed terrain.

Figure 8.20 The use of artistic shading from the north to the west depending on the orientation of ridges gives an excellent impression of a continuous landform surface on this Swiss 1:100,000-scale topographic map. Rock outcrop drawings also enhance visual realism. If you turn this illustration upside-down, relief reversal will cause the hills to look like valleys.

orientation also receives sufficient shading. This use of a variable light source, known as **artistic shading**, is probably the best way of all to show relative relief on a flat map (**Figure 8.20**). The map may look as real as a picture of a physical relief model of the landform.

Until recently, relief shading was a laborious manual chore that required a great deal of artistic skill and a thorough understanding of geomorphology (the study of landforms and terrain-forming processes). The expense involved in producing shaded-relief maps by hand could rarely be justified. Thus, despite the dramatic visualization relief shading affords, for practical reasons not many such maps were made. This situation has changed dramatically, however, since relief shading by computer is now feasible. Relief shading can now be produced in seconds using computer mapping and GIS software (see Chapter 19: GIS and Map Analysis Software) and digital elevation model data.

COMBINING METHODS ON MAPS

Cartographers often combine different relief-portrayal methods to enhance the three-dimensional appearance of the terrain while also making it possible for map users to determine elevations or depths. Examples include contours and isobaths combined with spot elevations and soundings, hypsometric tinting applied to contours and isobaths, and relief-shaded block diagrams.

Relating contour lines to terrain features challenges even the most skilled map users. The reason is that it can be difficult to visualize the terrain when relative-relief cues are lacking. To remedy this problem, yet maintain the metric character of the landform portrayal, some form of contour-line enhancement is common. We'll discuss two techniques here—shading and contours, then illuminated contours.

Shading and Contours

A skillful combination of contours and relief shading is one of the most effective relief-portrayal methods. The U.S. Geological Survey and National

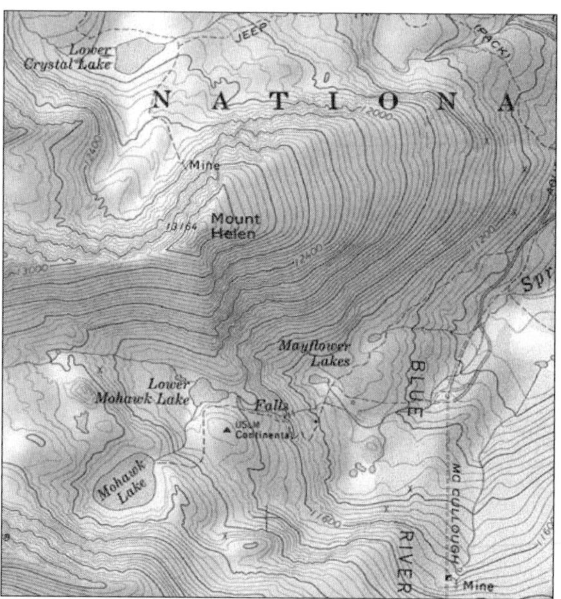

Figure 8.21 Relief-shaded contour maps are produced by the USGS for certain topographic map sheets.

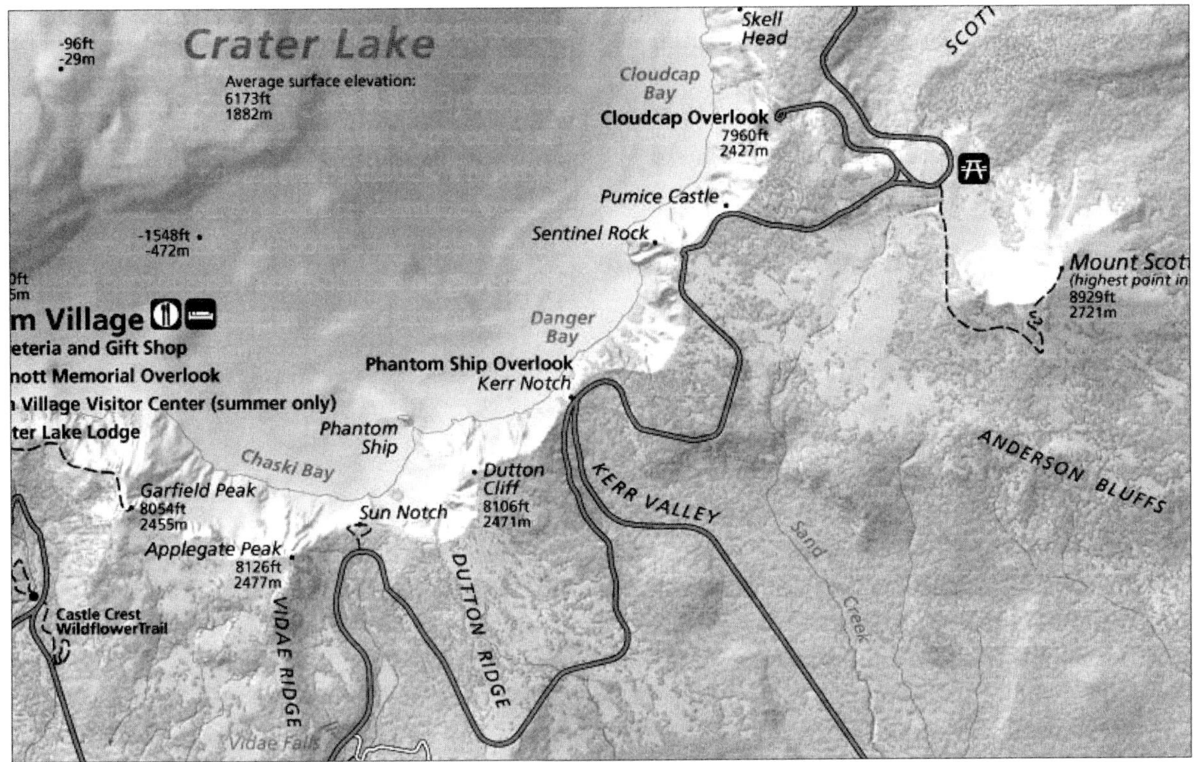

Figure 8.22 A forest texture has been added to this relief-shaded tourist map of Crater Lake, Oregon.

Park Service produce maps like **Figure 8.21** for national park maps and topographic quadrangles containing classic examples of different terrain features. Producers of commercial travel and recreation atlases have also created relief-shaded topographic maps for entire states, some available in digital form*.

Further enhancements are possible for maps combining relief shading and contours to show the terrain. Large-scale Swiss topographic maps like Figure 8.20 are noted for combining contours and relief shading with line drawings of rock outcrops and ridges. These manually produced maps are truly works of art, yet elevations can be determined easily from the contour lines.

Recently, maps have been produced with surface textures added to relief shading, such as the textured relief shading for Crater Lake National Park seen in **Figure 8.22**. The idea is to give a general indication of the surface texture or landcover, adding to the visual realism of the relief shading. This is similar to European topographic maps where symbols for trees and other vegetation types are added to the relief shading.

**The Delorme state atlas and gazetteer series is a good example.*

Illuminated Contours

The illuminated contour method was perfected in Japan by Kitiro Tanaka in the 1950s (**Figure 8.23**). The effect is similar to the stepped-relief model you saw in Figure 8.9, and is reminiscent of the terraced hillsides in Japan and other Asian countries. Illuminated contours are created by making contour line segments on the lower-right face of terrain features (as you view the map) black and segments on the upper-left side white. If the map background is medium gray, this produces a visual impression that the contour lines are stacked, layer upon layer, since the black and white lines simulate a shaded stepped terrain. The upper-left-facing and lower-right-facing contour segments are also made

Figure 8.23 By making contour lines on the lower-right side of terrain features black and those on the upper-left side white, an impression of shading a stepped terrain occurs, giving contours a three-dimensional appearance.

thicker, further accentuating the three-dimensional effect. Since black and white contour lines are easy to produce with the aid of computers and digital contour line data, maps using them are becoming more common.

Shaded and Textured Fishnet Maps

You will note that the fishnet maps in this chapter show bald terrain, denuded of landcover features. With the aid of computer mapping software, map makers have recently overcome this problem. It is now common to drape relief shading over the underlying fishnet to create a **relief-shaded perspective view** (**Figure 8.24**). You will notice on this illustration that contour lines and other map symbols can be draped as well.

Another combination is aerial photography or satellite imagery draped over the fishnet (see Chapter 9 for more on aerial photography and imagery) to create a **perspective-view image map**. Map makers also drape other information—everything from land-use categories to surface geology data—over fishnets. These combinations will only expand in the future as sophisticated surface rendering software allows three-dimensional digital trees and other realistic map symbols to be draped on the fishnet surface. And since all data are in digital form, we can view the terrain from any number of different vantage points (see Dynamic Relief Portrayal later in this chapter).

Figure 8.24 Fishnet map of Mt. Olympus, Washington, draped with contours and other topographic map information.

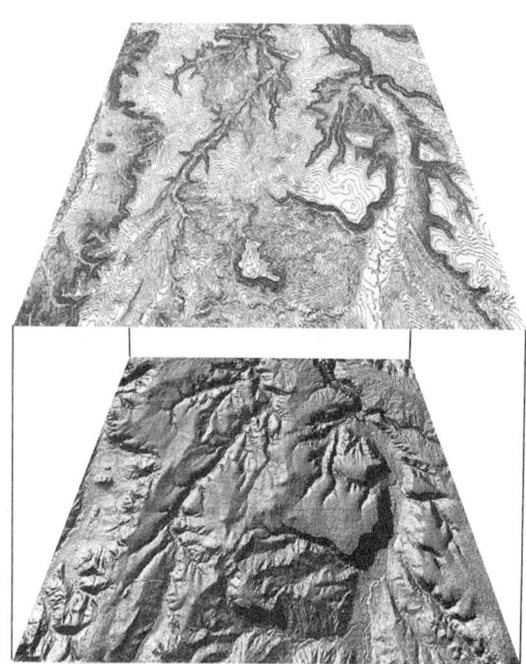

Figure 8.25 A vertical layering of contours and relief shading provides more information than either method by itself.

Dual Representations

Another combined-relief method is to display the landscape in dual form, using two different techniques. Commonly, a contour map is "floated" directly over or under a relief-shaded map, both being oblique perspective views (**Figure 8.25**). By looking back and forth from the contours to the relief shading, you can have the best of both worlds (absolute-relief and relative-relief information). However, since both maps are oblique views, you can't use them to make scale-related measurements of distance and area.

STEREOSCOPIC VIEWS

You can visualize the terrain even more clearly by viewing **stereopairs** of relief shading or oblique perspective views (**Figure 8.26**). The **stereovision** mechanism is the same as that used to view photographic stereopairs (see Stereoviewing and Height Measurement in Chapter 20). In this case, you're viewing relief-shaded maps of the terrain surface from two vantage points. When you view these two maps with a stereoscope, your mind merges them into a single three-dimensional mental image of the terrain.

A special form of stereopair is produced by printing the maps constructed from two vantage points in red and blue and then superimposing one upon the other. The resulting stereopair is called an **anaglyph**. When you view the anaglyph through special glasses equipped with red and blue lenses, you see the red map with one eye and the blue map with the other (see **Color Plate 8.1**). This allows you to see the landform stereoscopically.

The newest way to display the terrain stereoscopically is to view a special computer monitor that alternates the two maps at least 30 times a second. The first map is displayed with horizontally-polarized light, the second with vertically-polarized light. Map viewers wear special goggles with polarizing filters that allow the right eye to see only the horizontally polarized map and the left eye the vertically polarized map, so that the terrain is seen stereoscopically.

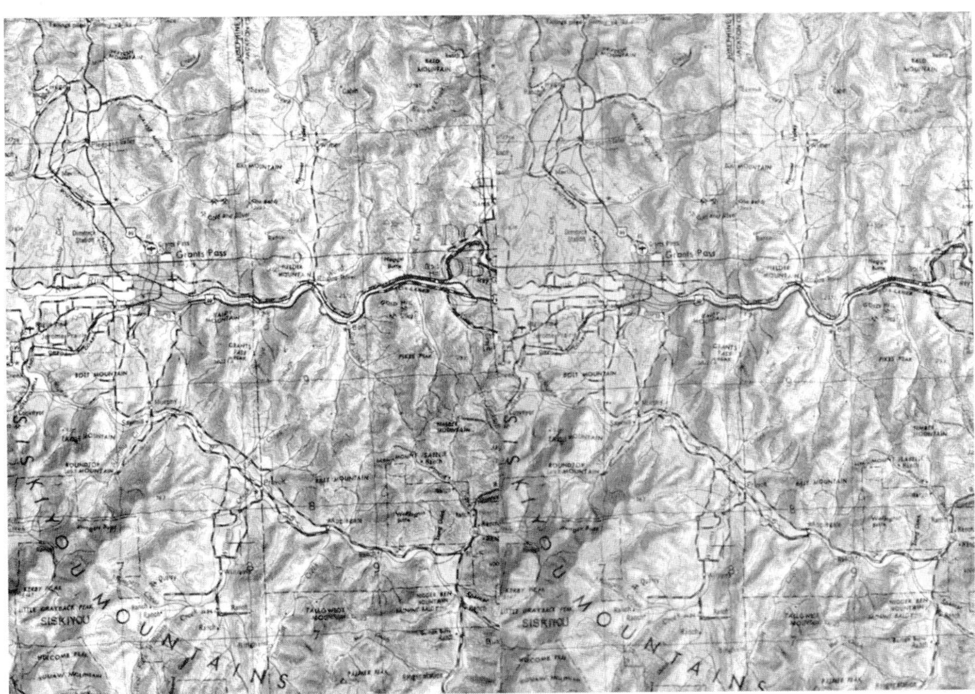

Figure 8.26 When you view relief-shaded map stereopairs stereoscopically, you see a truly three-dimensional image of the terrain. Try viewing this with a pocket stereoscope.

Although stereopairs, anaglyphs, and polarized computer monitor displays are effective visually and fun to look at, they are also somewhat impractical. They cost more to produce and require more viewing effort than standard relief-shaded or oblique-perspective maps. And because the relief impression is created in the brain, not on a sheet of paper, the image is ephemeral and not subject to analytical map-use procedures. Despite these drawbacks, however, anaglyphs and other stereoscopic viewing methods are used extensively in certain earth sciences, such as geology. These stereographic views are also destined to become more common in the future, since they are easily produced by computer.

DYNAMIC RELIEF PORTRAYAL

Computer technology has made it possible to put relief portrayal into motion. If relief portrayals from a sequence of vantage points are animated, you get the impression that you're flying and that the terrain is passing under and around you. The visualization of space and movement can be so realistic that you may actually feel pangs of airsickness! This fly-over effect occurs because your mind finds it easier to accept your body moving than the terrain moving.

Animated Methods

Cinema has introduced the potential of animated mapping. By viewing a motion picture taken by flying a camera over and around a region, you can gain a dramatic, dynamic impression of the landform. The effect is similar to that achieved by viewing a physical model. In both cases, you have the advantage of being able to change vantage points and, therefore, change perspectives (although in the cinema version the sequence of movement is preprogrammed). In fact, animated terrain maps are commonly made by rotating a movie camera over and around a physical model of the terrain rather than the landform itself. Simulators to train pilots and astronauts, for example, have used this dynamic mapping method.

Inexpensive video (television) cameras have brought new life to animated mapping in recent years. But the most important advance came with the advent of high-speed, digital computers and high-resolution color monitors. With the aid of computers and sufficient numerical data representing the terrain, there is no longer a need to photograph or videotape a physical model or the terrain surface itself. Instead, the images can be created from the digital database through a series of calculations that take into consideration the vantage point of the observer, the orientation of the surface, and the nature of the illumination source. The images are then displayed on the monitor screen and may be recorded electronically in video mode or digitally for subsequent playback.

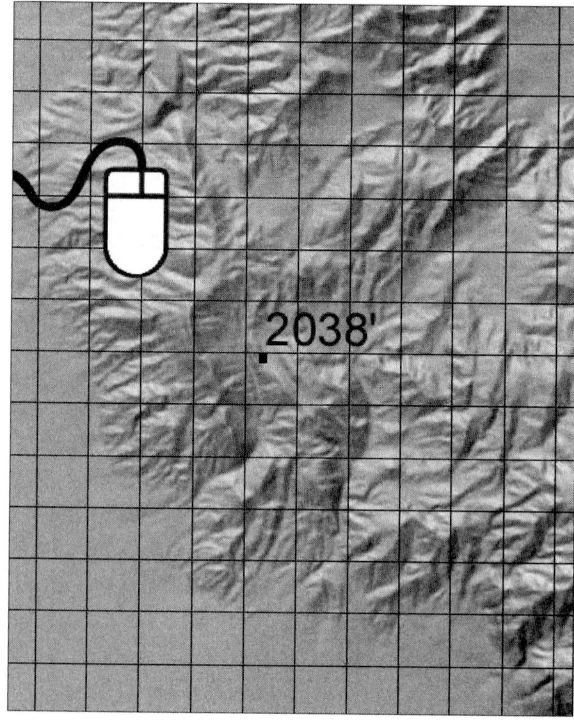

Figure 8.27 When a map displayed on an electronic screen is queried about the elevation at a point, the computer can search the database used to make the map to receive the answer (from MicroDEM program).

Interactive Methods

Interactive maps take animated methods one step further. While animation takes you over the terrain on the path chosen by the animator, interactive relief maps put you in control. You can call up any image onto the screen, in any sequence. If you operate the controls, you can simulate movement realistically from one vantage point to any other. You control the fly-over path. You might start up high to get the overall view, then fly in closer to get a better look at features of special interest. You can view the terrain from as many heights and directions as needed to get a feel for the nature of the landform. You get the sensation of flying over a static terrain, but of course it's the changing view of the terrain that is creating that effect.

Relief-portrayal methods can also be viewed interactively (**Figure 8.27**). The interaction takes place in a series of steps. First, terrain data are displayed on an electronic screen using a relative-relief technique, such as relief shading. Second, you "point" at the location whose elevation you are seeking. The pointing may be done by touching a touch-sensitive screen or by moving a mouse or similar electronic device.

Next, you "ask the map" what the elevation is at the indicated point or what the terrain profile is like along a given path. You may be able to do so through a keyboard, by verbal query, or by pointing to an electronic menu of questions displayed on the side of the screen. Finally, the computer system will note the location or path you indicated, search through the elevation data records used to make the map, perform the necessary computations, and provide you with the requested elevation data or profile.

With these "point and ask" portrayals, the map merely provides a graphic version of the landform, and you direct analytical questions to the underlying digital terrain data. In other words, the map serves as a window on the data. By not burdening the map with the need to portray absolute-relief information, the quality of visualization can be improved. At the same time, elevation values can be determined with greater precision than would be possible with a graphic portrayal alone. (Also see Chapter 19: GIS and Map Analysis Software.)

DIGITAL ELEVATION MODEL DATA

Most of the relief-portrayal methods discussed in this chapter are now carried out on computer mapping software that relies on **digital elevation model** (**DEM**) data. A DEM is a sample of elevations or depths taken on a regular grid. Digital elevation models are tremendously important in modern mapping and map use, because computers can easily carry out computations on a matrix of digital terrain data.

A number of government and private organizations are involved in creating regular grids of elevation values. The most ambitious project is a spin-off of the digital orthophoto quadrangle program (see Chapter 9 for more on orthophotos). In this project, the USGS and cooperators are rapidly completing DEM coverage of the country at a spatial resolution of roughly one second in latitude (approximately 100 feet) and longitude (approximately 90 feet at the south border of the conterminous U.S. and 65 feet at the north border). The USGS is also well along in sampling the terrain surface portrayed on its 1:24,000 topographic quadrangles at an interval of 30 meters in UTM coordinates. DEMs for the entire United States with a three arc-second (latitude and longitude) resolution created from 1:250,000-scale topographic quadrangles have been available for some time. A 30 arc-second resolution DEM for the land areas of the world is also available on compact disks and the Internet, as are 2 and 5 minute global DEMs.

A DEM isn't a map in the sense we are using the term in this book, since a DEM is a digital database of elevation values. Thus, it's better to think of a DEM as a cartographic product, rather than as a map. From this perspective, DEMs serve the same role as other forms of digital cartographic data, such as those generated by electronic image scanners and digitizing tablets.

Surface Mapping Software

Surface mapping software allows you to convert digital elevation model (DEM) and any other (x,y,z) coordinate data for an area into contour, layer tinted, shaded relief, or 3-D perspective maps depicting a continuous surface (**Figure 8.28**). The Surfer mapping package* is a robust program of this type. You can select from a variety of interpolation methods that will turn your irregularly spaced (x,y,z) data set into a regular grid. This grid or a DEM that you have imported is then used to make the continuous surface map type that you specify. It is also possible to import a vector or raster format base map and drape the continuous surface map over the base map.

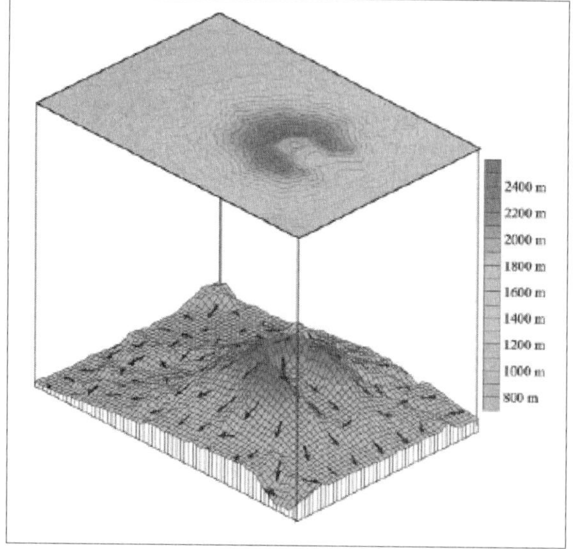

Figure 8.28 Layer tinted and 3-D perspective surface maps of Mt. St. Helens, Washington, created by the Surfer mapping package.

**See Appendix B for ordering information.*

SELECTED READINGS

Baldock, E.D., "Cartographic Relief Portrayal," *International Yearbook of Cartography*, 11 (1971), pp. 75-78.

Castner, H.W., and Wheate, R., "Reassessing the Role Played by Shaded Relief Methods in Topographic Scale Maps," *The Cartographic Journal*, 16 (1979), pp. 77-85.

Curran, J.P., "Cartographic Relief Portrayal," *The Cartographer*, 4, 1 (June 1967), pp. 28-38.

Grotch, S.L., "Three-Dimensional and Stereoscopic Graphics for Scientific Data Display and Analysis," *IEEE Computer Graphics and Applications*, 3, 11 (1983), pp. 31-43.

Imhof, E., *Cartographic Relief Representation*. Translated and edited by H.J. Steward (New York: Walter de Gruyter, 1982).

Irwin, D., "The Historical Development of Terrain Representation in American Cartography," *International Yearbook of Cartography*, 16 (1976), pp. 70-83.

Kraak, M.J., "Cartographic Terrain Modeling in a Three-Dimensional GIS Environment," *Cartography and Geographic Information Systems*, 20 (1993), pp. 13-18.

Kumler, M.P., *An Intensive Comparison of Triangulated Irregular Networks (TINs) and Digital Elevation Models (DEMs)* (Toronto: University of Toronto Press, Inc., 1995).

Lobeck, A.K., *Block Diagrams and Other Graphic Methods Used in Geology and Geography*, 2nd ed. (Amherst, MA: Emerson-Trussel Book Co., 1958).

Petrie, G., and Kennie, T.J.M., eds., *Terrain Modelling in Surveying and Civil Engineering* (New York: McGraw-Hill, Inc., 1991).

Robinson, A.H., et al., "Portraying the Land-Surface Form" in *Elements of Cartography*, 6th ed. (New York: John Wiley & Sons, 1995), pp. 527-548.

Ryerson, C.C., "Relief Model Symbolization," *The American Cartographer*, 11, 2 (1984), pp. 160-164.

Schou, *The Construction and Drawing of Block Diagrams* (London: Thomas Nelson & Sons, Ltd., 1962).

Tanaka, K., "The Relief Contour Method of Representing Topography on Maps," *The Geographical Review*, 40 (1950), pp. 444-456.

Watson, D.F., *Contouring* (New York: Pergamon Press, 1992).

Yoeli, P., "Digital Terrain Models and their Cartographic and Cartometric Utilization," *The Cartographic Journal*, 20, 1 (1983), pp. 17-23.

CHAPTER NINE
REMOTE SENSING IMAGERY AND IMAGE MAPS

THE ELECTROMAGNETIC SPECTRUM
- Spectral Reflectance from Objects
- Spectral Regions for Imaging

AERIAL PHOTOGRAPHY
- Black-and-White Photography
- True-Color Photography
- Color-Infrared Photography
- Low, Medium, and High-Altitude Photography
- Space Photography
- Vertical and Oblique Photography
- Geometric Distortions
- Orthophotography
  - Digital Orthophotoquads
- Photo Mosaics
  - Photo Indexes

ELECTRONIC IMAGING
- Thermal-Infrared Sensors
- Side-Looking Airborne Radar
- Space Imaging Radar
  - Shuttle Imaging Radar
  - RADARSAT
- Shuttle Radar Topography Mapping

MULTISPECTRAL IMAGING
- Earth Resources Satellites
  - Landsat
  - SPOT
  - IRS
  - Ikonos and Quickbird
  - AVHRR
- Geostationary Weather Satellites
- Hyperspectral Imaging
  - MODIS

IMAGE MAPS
- Animated Fly-overs

SELECTED READINGS

What we experience is only a small part of what matters about objects.
—R.L. Gregory, *The Intelligent Eye*

Our maps...are drawn by computers from satellite photos, and that suggests that the Earth has lost its capacity to keep secrets.
—Peter Steinhart, *Names on a Map*

9

CHAPTER NINE

REMOTE SENSING IMAGERY AND IMAGE MAPS

Although people have relied primarily on their own eyes to learn about the environment, they haven't done so exclusively. Indirect experience has always been an important source of information for mapping. Reports of distant places have traveled by word of mouth and other forms of communication since the beginning of humankind. But such methods of gathering data remotely provide information only for specific sites and routes.

In the last century, the significance of collecting images of the earth (and other planetary bodies) from a distance, called **remote sensing**, has grown enormously. We are now inundated with a vast array of remotely sensed images of our surroundings. Remote sensing lets us observe features in the environment by using materials (films) or recording instruments (electronic sensors) which are sensitive to the energy emitted or reflected from objects.

Remote sensing opens up the mapping of our environment in regions of **the electromagnetic spectrum** invisible to us. A wide variety of **images*** are produced from remote sensor data. Some images come directly from the sensor system. Others represent elaborate computer manipulations of the energy recorded by the sensor. These remote sensor images also provide the basic information source for the many **image maps** that we use.

**In the past, the term "photo" was used instead of "image." But with today's electronic technology, many images that look like photos really aren't. Thus, the more general terms "image" and "image map" are more appropriate and will be used throughout this book.*

It's important to realize that, while remote sensing methods produce images that seem to capture the environment as it is at the moment, these images are in fact elaborate technological creations. They contain method-produced artifacts characteristic of the photo-chemical or electronic processes involved. Furthermore, many factors can influence the appearance of the resulting image. Such factors include: the sensor vehicle's vantage point, the sensor's spectral sensitivity, the image's spatial resolution, the sensing instrument's technical quality, and atmospheric conditions.

THE ELECTROMAGNETIC SPECTRUM

All objects emit and reflect **electromagnetic radiation (EMR)** in the form of waves of different lengths. The range of wavelengths, called the **electromagnetic spectrum**, is immense (**Figure 9.1**). Remote sensing devices collect images of reflected or emitted energy from small portions of the electromagnetic spectrum, called **spectral bands**, rather than energy of a specific wavelength. The most important of these spectral bands have been given names. At the short wavelength end of the spectrum are deadly gamma rays, which are about one billionth of a millimeter long, while at the long end of the spectrum are useful radio waves, which are about 10 kilometers (6.2 miles) long. Between these extremes, from short to long, are the visible light, near-infrared (IR), thermal-infrared (TIR), and microwave bands used in remote sensing.

Figure 9.1 provides insight into how little of our environment we see with our eyes. Visible light falls in the spectral range of 0.4 (blue) to 0.7 (red) micrometers. A **micrometer**, or micron (abbreviated μm) is a millionth of a meter (m.) You can see that visible light is only a tiny portion of the electromagnetic spectrum. Yet until a few decades ago, we could only create images of the earth from visible light.

Spectral Reflectance from Objects

The primary source of visible light is energy emitted from hot objects. This fact is evident when a heated piece of black iron progressively changes color from red to orange to yellow to white. The characteristic color of objects as seen by the human eye is primarily the result of **selective reflection** of visible light emitted by the sun. An object appears red, for instance, because it reflects red wavelengths and absorbs blue and green wavelengths (**Figure 9.2**).

Typical reflectance curves for several environmental features are illustrated in **Figure 9.3**. Note that these curves have been extended beyond the visible light portion of the electromagnetic spectrum. Also notice that each curve is distinctly different in form. In fact, the reflectance curves for environmental features are so distinctive that they

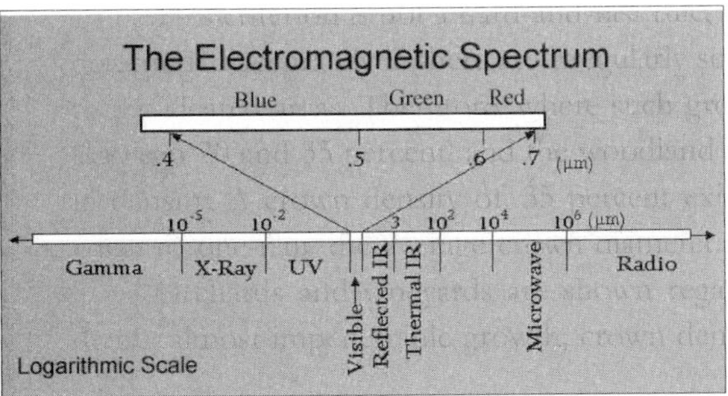

Figure 9.1 The electromagnetic spectrum has been divided into spectral bands. The microwave, infrared, and visible bands are used in remote sensing.

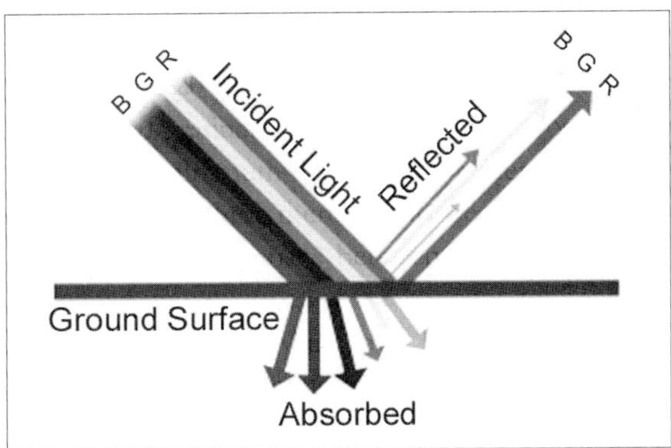

Figure 9.2 The color of an object depends on which visible wavelengths are reflected and which are absorbed. Here a red object is shown.

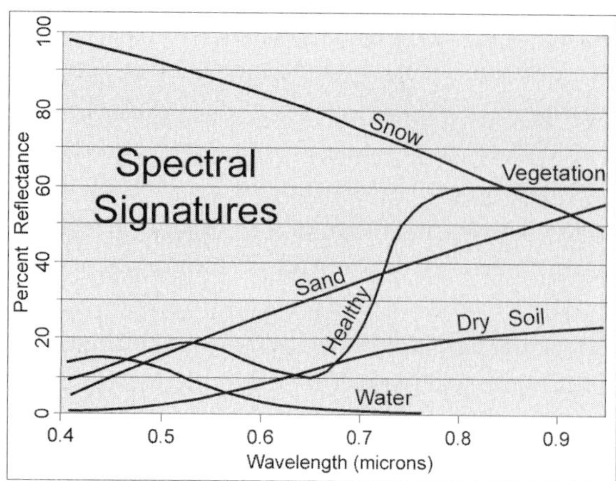

Figure 9.3 The spectral signatures of different terrestrial objects vary considerably in the visible and near-infrared wavelengths.

are referred to as **spectral signatures**. The signature analogy is apt, for every object's curve, like each person's handwriting, is unique.

Spectral Regions for Imaging

Spectral signatures also depend on how the atmosphere absorbs incoming energy from the sun. Water vapor, carbon dioxide, ozone, and solid particles (dust and pollen, for example) in the atmosphere absorb electromagnetic radiation at certain wavelengths. Other wavelengths pass through the atmosphere in what are called the visible, near-infrared (near-IR) , thermal-IR, and microwave **atmospheric windows** (**Figure 9.4**).

The effect of these atmospheric windows is that what we see is based on highly selected electromagnetic energy. But there is far more to the world than meets the eye. **Photography** extends our vision into the near-infrared atmospheric window. **Electronic imaging** allows us to create images of EMR emitted by objects in the thermal-infrared and microwave atmospheric windows.

AERIAL PHOTOGRAPHY

The development of cameras and photographic films began in the early 1800s. At first the visible light portion of the spectrum was imaged as shades of gray. Later photographic films not only came close to duplicating the color sensing capability of the human eye but also extended our imaging capability into the near-ultraviolet and near-infrared portions of the spectrum at both ends of the eye's sensitivity range. In addition to broadening our image of the environment, these different films, when combined with filters for blocking out unwanted wavelengths, made it possible to image specific bands of visible and near-visible light energy like blue, green, or red.

What is imaged on an aerial photograph depends on a number of factors. One is the type of camera used. In taking aerial photos for mapping

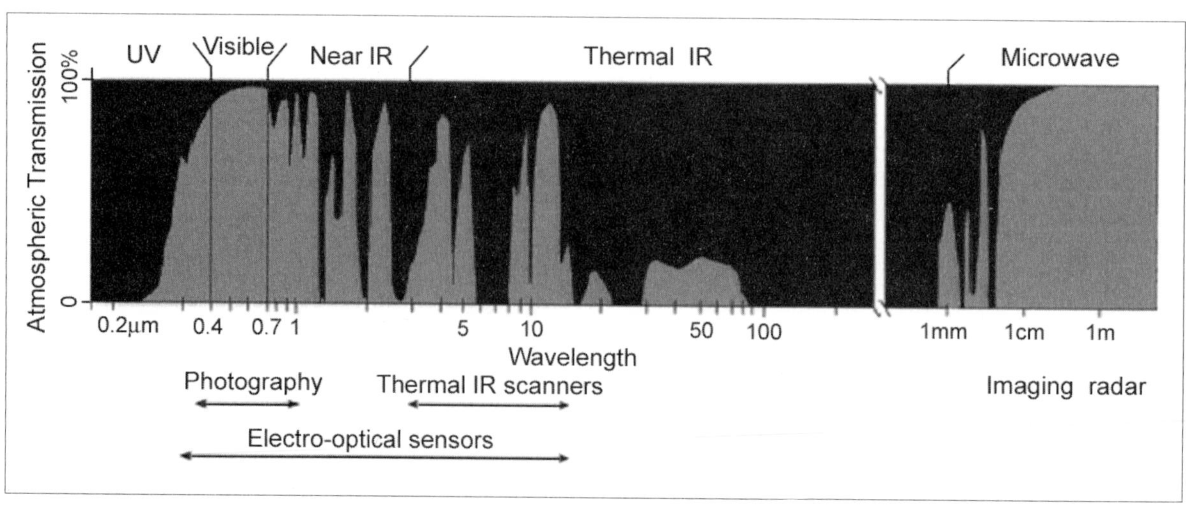

Figure 9.4 Atmospheric windows and the types of remote sensing used in each window.

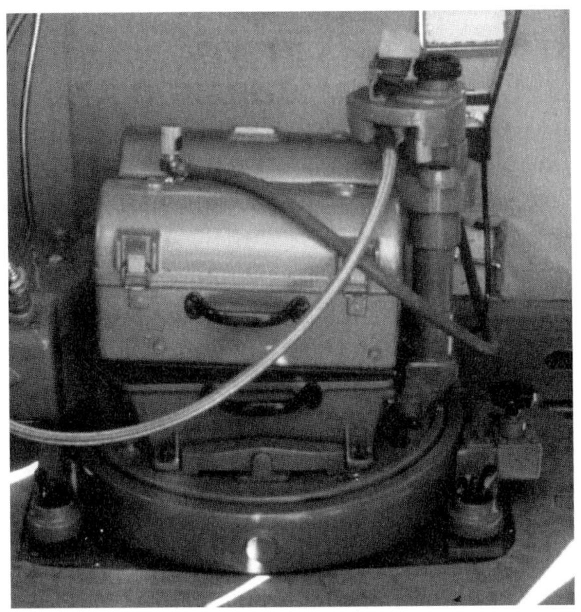

Figure 9.5 A typical aerial mapping camera placed vertically in an airplane.

purposes, photographers usually use the familiar kind of camera that produces individual pictures called **frames. Aerial mapping cameras** (**Figure 9.5**) are specially designed so that they will expose large (9" × 9") frames. Larger film makes it possible to image a larger area in detail on the photo. Complex, expensive camera lenses are used to minimize geometric distortion due to lens defects. Such cameras are so large and heavy, however, that they must be used in a fixed position. Therefore, it is also common to use smaller hand-held cameras that expose 70-millimeter (mm.) wide film.

The **spatial resolution** (or resolving power) of an aerial photo is determined mainly by the quality of the camera and its lens, and by **film emulsion** characteristics. Film emulsions are made up of one or more (in the case of color film) layers of densely packed light-sensitive silver halide crystals (**Figure 9.6 top**). When the emulsion is exposed to light reflected from ground objects, each tiny crystal responds to the light in an all-or-nothing manner. Those crystals struck by a sufficient amount of light change their chemical make-up, changing to black or another color upon development. Those not activated by enough light remain unaltered.

Black-and-White Photography

Standard **black-and-white aerial photographs** are based on a film emulsion which records electromagnetic radiation in the 0.4 to 0.7 μm visible spectrum. Because of its sensitivity to visible light, black-and-white film is often called **panchromatic** (meaning "all-colors") film. Unfortunately, the shorter blue wavelengths are scattered by the atmosphere, reducing the clarity of the photo. This explains why black-and-white photos taken from commercial airliners flying at 35,000 feet are so often hazy.

The greater the amount of visible light gathered by the camera lens onto the film emulsion, the lighter its tone on the final photographic print (see **Figure 9.7**). The moisture content, surface roughness, and natural color of objects all influence a

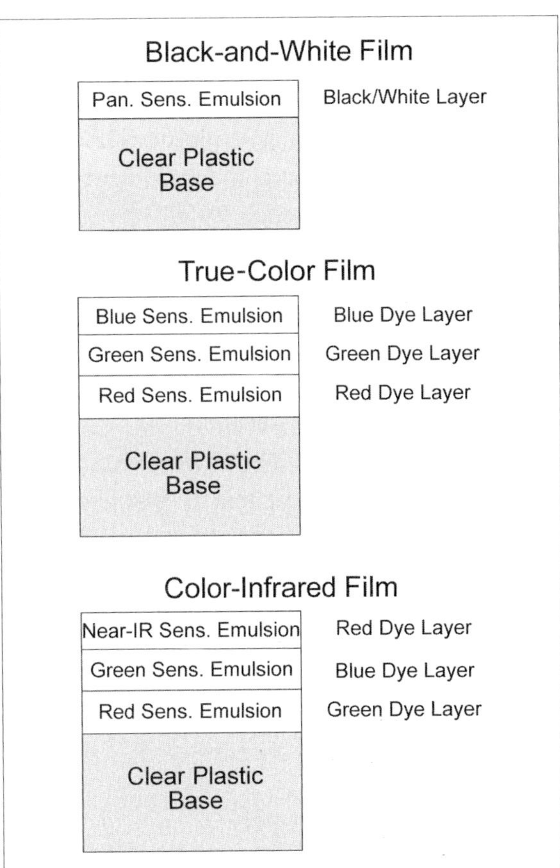

Figure 9.6 Film emulsion diagrams for black-and-white panchromatic, true-color, and color-infrared films.

Figure 9.7 Standard black-and-white panchromatic 9" × 9" aerial photograph of central San Diego, California (scale reduced by two-thirds).

feature's tone on a black-and-white photo. Moist soils, marshlands, and newly plowed fields tend to be darker than surrounding features, while human constructions such as roads and buildings tend to appear lighter (see Chapter 21 for details on image interpretation).

Standard black-and-white photos have been put to many uses. The Forest Service uses them in making timber inventories and in mapping national forests. They are used by the United States Geological Survey (USGS) for topographic mapping in its quadrangle series. The Natural Resources Conservation Service uses them for mapping soils and agricultural activities. They are also used widely for road building, recreation, and forestry planning purposes. Indeed, by far the largest amount of remote sensing has been done using standard black-and-white photography. This type of aerial photography is also used most often to create image maps.

True-Color Photography

True-color film contains three separate emulsion layers sensitive to the blue, green, and red portions of the visible spectrum (see **Figure 9.6, middle**). Upon development, these emulsion layers are transformed into blue, green, and red dye layers. Therefore, blue, green, and red objects on the ground appear blue, green, and red on the photograph.

Image clarity of color film has improved so dramatically in recent years that it is comparable in quality to black-and-white film. In fact, color photos are usually easier to read than black-and-white photos, because they capture the colors uniquely associated with special landscape features. It is easier to distinguish subtle differences in colors than between shades of gray (see **Color Plate 9.1**).

Color is especially useful in revealing the condition of objects, such as the stage of a crop in its maturation cycle. For such applications as vegetation and soils classification, geologic mapping, and surface water studies, using color photos has proven simpler and more accurate than working from equivalent black-and-white photos alone. Despite its extra cost, true-color film is an important source of information for better understanding the environment.

Color-Infrared Photography

During World War II, military researchers developed **color-infrared (CIR) film**. This special film is sensitive to near-infrared wavelengths (0.7 to 0.9 µm) as well as visible light. One of the highest reflecting materials in the near-IR region is the cellular structure in the leaves of plants. Generally speaking, the healthier the vegetation, the higher the near-IR reflectance (see **Color Plate 9.2**). This property turned out to be extremely useful for the military, since on a color-infrared photograph, artificial camouflage materials could be distinguished from live, healthy vegetation. Because color-infrared film is still used for this purpose, it is called **camouflage detection film** by military image interpreters.

Color-infrared film is also known as **false-color film**, since the spectral sensitivities of the dye layers in the film bear no relation to the natural colors of environmental features (**Figure 9.6, bottom**). The explanation for this lack of natural color association can be seen by comparing the emulsion layer diagrams for true-color and color-infrared film shown in Figure 9.6. Upon development, the green, red, and near-IR sensitive emulsion layers are transformed into blue, green, and red dye layers. Therefore, green, red, and highly reflecting near-IR objects on the ground appear blue, green, and red on the color- infrared photograph.

An environmental feature that absorbs a great deal of near-IR energy, such as clear water, appears black on color-infrared photos. Features such as buildings and unhealthy vegetation absorb less near-IR energy and appear blue or blue-gray. The most obvious feature on color-infrared photos is healthy vegetation, which appears bright magenta-red rather than green due to its high near-IR reflectance. The cut vegetation, green paint, and rope netting used to conceal military installations are recorded in pinkish to bluish tones, in stark contrast to the background of bright reds produced by the surrounding healthy vegetation.

Although the first important applications of color-infrared film were in military reconnaissance, many uses in vegetation, geologic, and urban studies have also been found. The film is now used for such applications as crop inspection, tree-growth inventories, and damage assessment of diseased flora. Plant diseases can often be detected on color-infrared photographs well before they would be visible to the unaided eye.

Geologists have found color-infrared photos useful, too, in locating near-surface structural features such as faults, fractures, and joints. These features can be detected because they often collect water, encouraging lusher vegetation growth than in the surrounding area. Color-infrared film also enhances boundaries between bare soil and vegetation and between land and water, making it useful in mapping these features. In addition, the film is valuable for urban mapping because it shows a sharp contrast between vegetation and cultural features, and because the near-IR wavelengths penetrate smog easily.

Low, Medium, and High Altitude Photography

The most detailed images are **low-altitude aerial photographs** taken anywhere from just above the ground surface to around 1,500 feet above ground level. Towers and balloons provided convenient sensing platforms in the 1800s, but these devices were superseded in the 20th century by light aircraft, particularly helicopters. Low-altitude photos usually cover a small ground area at a large map scale (**Figure 9.8**).

Photographs taken at medium altitudes (1,500-10,000 feet) provide less environmental detail than those taken at low altitudes since the image scale is much smaller. But **medium-altitude aerial photography** has the advantage that more ground area can be covered on a single photo. Conventional aerial photography of the type used to obtain basic elevation data for topographic mapping is usually taken from an altitude of about 10,000 feet (**Figure 9.9, top**). These photos are available in a standard 9"× 9" frame format. Systematic coverage of the United States in this format began in the 1930s and has been repeated in many areas at intervals of five to 10 years.

Figure 9.8 Low-altitude aerial photograph of the Memorial Union quad at Oregon State University, Corvallis, Oregon. Notice the students resting in the quad.

In 1987, the **National Aerial Photography Program (NAPP)** was established to develop an aerial photography database of consistent scale, orientation, and image quality. The aim of this federal and state program is to provide complete coverage of the United States, updated every five years. The photographs are taken from 20,000 feet and are oriented to the format of USGS 7.5-minute quadrangles. Ten 9" × 9" photos at a 1:40,000 scale are needed for complete stereoscopic coverage of each quad.

Figure 9.9 Medium (top) and high (bottom) altitude aerial photographs of Corvallis, Oregon (both reduced in scale from the original).

If there are advantages to taking pictures from several miles above the ground, then why not even higher? It is now common to take **high-altitude photographs** from special aircraft flying at altitudes as high as 10 to 20 miles. Examples are the National Aeronautics and Space Administration (NASA) ex-spy plane, the U-2, and the SR-71 military reconnaissance aircraft.

The advantage of high-altitude photography is that a large ground area can be covered in a single photo. The rapid, high-quality photo coverage has many mapping applications. The damage caused by earthquakes, floods, and droughts, for instance, can be monitored. Experiments involving forest resources, snow cover, crop yields, and many other environmental features are being conducted to determine additional uses of high-altitude photography. The USGS uses high-altitude photographs to make image maps and revise existing topographic quadrangles.

An illustration of the quality of high-altitude aerial photography is provided by the photo of Corvallis, Oregon, shown in **Figure 9.9, bottom.** This photograph was taken from an altitude of approximately 20 kilometers (13 miles). For most purposes, this photograph is equivalent in geometry to the standard topographic quadrangle of the area, although the image map shows far more detail.

Space Photography

Space photography is the ultimate high-altitude imagery. Extensive coverage of ground features has been obtained since the 1960s through NASA's manned space flight program, beginning with the race to the moon. Astronauts in **Gemini** and **Apollo** spacecraft found time to take many photographs, albeit in a rather casual manner. When an astronaut observed an interesting ground scene and had time, he would simply point his camera out a window of the spacecraft and snap a picture.

The pictures taken during these manned space flights were often quite dramatic (**Figure 9.10**). But the equipment and manner used to gather the imagery limited the quality and extent of ground coverage obtained. For one thing, the position of the window on the side of Gemini spacecraft meant that only oblique views could be obtained.

Second, the cameras used in all Gemini and most Apollo missions were 70-mm Hasselblad cameras loaded with true-color film, not the precision mapping cameras which were being used at the time for high-altitude photography.

A third factor was that the manned spacecraft orbits only allowed the low- and mid-latitude regions (35°N to 35°S) to be photographed. Within these latitudes, rather complete coverage could be obtained, but the coverage was by no means systematic. To determine the coverage of a particular region, you must search through catalogs for each manned spacecraft mission. Considering that there are over 900 photos available from Gemini flights and over 1,400 photos from Apollo flights, searches through the imagery catalogs are no simple chore, even at the website for manned space program photography (see Appendix B).

Figure 9.10 Gemini 11 true-color space photograph of the Indian subcontinent (shown here in black and white).

A second major source of historic space photography available to the public is from the 1973-74 NASA **Skylab** space laboratory placed in a near-equatorial orbit 270 miles above the earth (see Appendix B for ordering information). In addition to Hasselblad cameras like those used by Gemini and Apollo astronauts, Skylab carried a high-resolution **Earth Terrain Camera**. This camera had an 18-inch focal length lens and used three 114-mm (5-inch) films: true-color, color-infrared, and a high-definition green-through-red-sensitive black-and-white film (see **Color Plate 9.3**). Depending on atmospheric conditions and film processing quality, these films provided a spatial resolution of approximately 10 to 38 meters (33 to 125 feet).

Vertical and Oblique Photography

In addition to the camera's height above the earth, the camera's **vantage point** also affects the resulting image. The most unfamiliar, yet most useful, view of the landscape is provided by **vertical photography** taken with the camera looking straight down at the earth's surface (see Figure 9.9). The advantage of this vantage point is that feature blocking is minimized—it's hard for one feature to hide behind another. But at the same time, relief isn't readily apparent unless features vary greatly in height and unless shadow conditions are optimal (preferably with the sun at a low angle).

A great advantage of vertical photography is that scale variation is minimized. When it does occur, features are displaced radially from the center of the picture, as we'll see in the next section. The tops of features such as buildings or hills may appear more distant from the photo center than they really are, while the bottoms of buildings or valleys may be displaced toward the center.

Aerial photographs taken with the sensor at an oblique angle provide a more familiar view of the world than vertical photography (**Figure 9.11**) But on oblique photography, far greater scale distortion and feature blocking can occur. These problems are greatest on **high oblique photos** obtained when the camera is inclined between 0° and 45° above the horizon. High oblique photographs are distinguished by the fact that the horizon is visible. Features are easily seen in the foreground of such images, but progressive scale reduction and blocking toward the background of the image makes it hard to identify features.

Scale distortion and blocking of features will be balanced more evenly over an oblique image if the camera is tilted somewhere between 45° and 90° above the horizon. The result is a **low oblique photograph**, which can be quite effective in portraying the landscape. On these photos, the horizon isn't visible, and scale reduction toward the background of the image isn't as pronounced as on high oblique photos.

Figure 9.12 Format of a standard vertical aerial photograph (scale reduced by two thirds) with the principal point and fiducial marks identified.

Figure 9.11 High and low oblique aerial photographs of the Shenandoah River Valley, Virginia.

Geometric Distortions

On vertical photos, the photo's scale will most likely be distorted radially away from its center. To provide a simple way to determine the photo center, precision aerial cameras contain **fiducial marks** placed at the midpoint of each edge (**Figure 9.12**). If you draw lines between opposite pairs of fiducial marks, these lines will intersect at the center of the photo. This is the point directly below the camera when the photo was taken and is called the **principal point** of the photo.

The primary reason that radial scale distortion is characteristic of vertical photos is that objects of different heights are displaced radially away from the principal point. If the top of a feature is higher than average ground level, it will be displaced outward (**Figure 9.13**). Inward displacement occurs with objects lying below average ground level. The geometric explanation for this pattern of radial displacement is provided in Chapter 20.

The amount of radial distortion is also influenced by the height of the camera above the ground. The higher the camera, the less the radial distortion. Thus, satellite photos may exhibit so little

Figure 9.13 This vertical aerial photo of Chicago, Illinois, shows radial displacement of buildings away from the principal point (center left edge of photo).

distortion that they can be overlaid on planimetrically correct maps with only small geometric discrepancies visible. In contrast, displacement is great on low-altitude vertical photos; features such as buildings and trees seem to be leaning out from the center of the photograph. If the region is hilly or if the camera is tilted when the photo is taken, scale distortion may be so great that the resulting image map will be difficult or impossible to use. In such cases, aerial photos can be rectified to eliminate these geometric distortions, as we'll see in the next section.

Orthophotography

Scale distortions in a vertical aerial photo due to camera tilt can be removed from raw image maps by physically altering the geometry of the photo. The process is called **photo rectification** and is relatively simple to execute.

Rectified aerial photos still contain radial displacement due to difference in the heights of features, however. To remove this radial distortion, it is necessary to turn the central perspective photo into a **planimetrically correct photo**. Rather than looking outward from the principal point to each feature, you will then be looking directly down on the landscape. Thus, all features will appear in true planimetric position.

The conversion from central to parallel perspective on vertical aerial photography is a demanding process. Fortunately, it is readily accomplished with computers and is therefore increasingly common. The resulting planimetrically correct photo is called an **orthophotograph** (or **orthophoto**). Orthophotos can be laid directly over other planimetrically correct maps, such as topographic quadrangles, with no positional discrepancies between features.

Figure 9.14 Section of a 1:24,000 digital orthophoto quadrangle (DOQ) for Rochester, Minnesota.

Digital Orthophotoquads

Orthophotos represent such an important breakthrough in image mapping technology that federal agencies in the United States are cooperating with state and local governments, as well as the private sector, to create nationwide coverage. The products, called **digital orthophoto quadrangles (DOQs)**, are derived from 1:40,000-scale black-and-white photography (**Figure 9.14**). These 1:24,000-scale image maps are available for you to display and manipulate on desktop computers. Thus, they serve as a uniform, high-quality base for a variety of mapping, geographical study, and planning activities.

Photo Mosaics

Sometimes several aerial photographs are spliced together to show a broader area than could be covered by one alone. This collage of photos is called a **mosaic**.

Mosaics may be created in several ways. With one method, the photos are trimmed to the middle of their area of overlap with adjacent photos, visually aligned, glued together, and then re-photographed (**Figure 9.15**). These are called **uncontrolled mosaics**, because no adjustments have been made for geometric distortion on the component photos.

On most uncontrolled mosaics, precise matching of features along the edges of individual images is lacking. On a few, the photos are physically stretched and shrunk when making the collage so that edge features do match. These uncontrolled mosaics may give a good overall picture of a region (**Figure 9.16**). But, due to the geometric distortions associated with each photo in the mosaic, they aren't suitable for any sort of precision measurements.

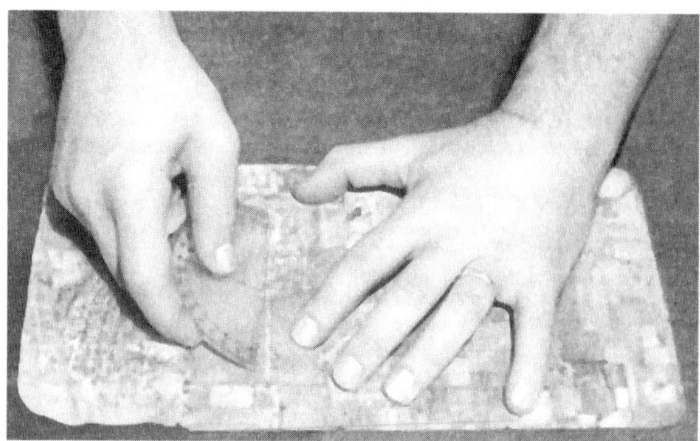

Figure 9.15 Matching and gluing together the first two trimmed photos in an uncontrolled mosaic.

Figure 9.16 Part of an uncontrolled photo mosaic for San Nicholas Island, California.

With **controlled mosaics**, each photo is matched to ground control points seen on the photo and drawn in correct planimetric position on an underlying base sheet. This procedure produces a far more geometrically accurate mosaic relative to the uncontrolled method. You can easily make your own highly accurate controlled mosaic if you use vertical satellite photography or orthophotos as your component images. Since both are planimetrically true for small regions, they will fit together perfectly when laid side by side and matched to control points. This is how space image maps, such as the one in **Color Plate 9.4**, are created.

Mosaics made by hand from existing photos suffer one flaw that may cause confusion for the unwary user. Since each component photograph is created under different light and shadow conditions, tones and contrast may vary from image to image. The consequence is that even the most carefully made mosaic has a mottled appearance (refer again to Figure 9.16). This appearance is especially pronounced if the photos have been taken at different times of the year or (as is the case with many photos taken from satellites) over several years.

Image-to-image tonal variation can be smoothed out using digital image-editing software, thus avoiding the mottled appearance of handmade mosaics. As more photos are available in electronic form, you can expect most medium-scale to small-scale mosaics to look like a single image rather than a collage.

Photo Indexes

One of the difficulties in using aerial photography is to find the correct photo for a given location. When photographs are taken from aircraft, atmospheric turbulence prevents precise camera positioning and alignment. Photography is often obtained along north-south or east-west flightlines, but typically without a standardized photo numbering format. As a result, ground coverage of the aerial photography varies from project to project. To find the appropriate photo for a site, you'll have to refer to some map-based indexing system.

Two forms are common. Most widespread are **photo index maps**. These are conventional maps on which the center of each image is indicated. You merely find your location and count image frames along the appropriate flightline.

A second form of index is a mosaic of actual photos overlapped so as to be approximately correct geometrically, then re-photographed at a much smaller scale. These **photo mosaic indexes** give you image identification information directly, since you can read the identifier code printed along the top edge of each photo (**Figure 9.17**).

Figure 9.17 Photo indexes make it possible to determine the ground coverage and identification code of individual images.

ELECTRONIC IMAGING

The wavelength limitations of photography were circumvented several decades ago by replacing aerial cameras and photographic film with **electronic imaging devices** equipped with small energy detectors called **photocells**. As an electronic imaging-equipped aircraft or spacecraft moves along its flight path, the electromagnetic energy received from the earth is recorded as an electrical voltage of varying strength within **picture elements (pixels)**. There are three basic types of electronic imaging devices—"whiskbroom," "pushbroom," and "area array."

With **whiskbroom** scanners, a continuous electrical voltage signal is recorded by a photocell sensitive to a certain spectral band as the ground scene is scanned line-by-line (**Figure 9.18**). This signal is then digitally sampled at extremely short time intervals to produce individual pixels along each scan line. The electromagnetic energy associated with a pixel is then transformed into discrete intensity levels, typically ranging from 0-255. The number of levels determines the **radiometric resolution** of the sensor. These intensity levels are subsequently represented with gray tones from black (0) to white (255). The greater the number of levels, the better the image quality.

The second type of electronic imaging device, the **pushbroom** scanner, directly records the voltage signals simultaneously for all pixels in a **scan line** (see Figure 9.18). With this type of sensor, the detector does not move. The narrow ground swath passing under the detector at each instant is focused onto the detector by a lens. The pushbroom detector is a linear array of photocells called a **Charge-Coupled Device (CCD)** that may have several thousand photocells per inch. **Multiband pushbroom sensors** require additional linear arrays of detectors for the different bands imaged.

The third type of electronic imaging device is the common **digital camera**. The camera detector is a two-dimensional **area array** of photo-

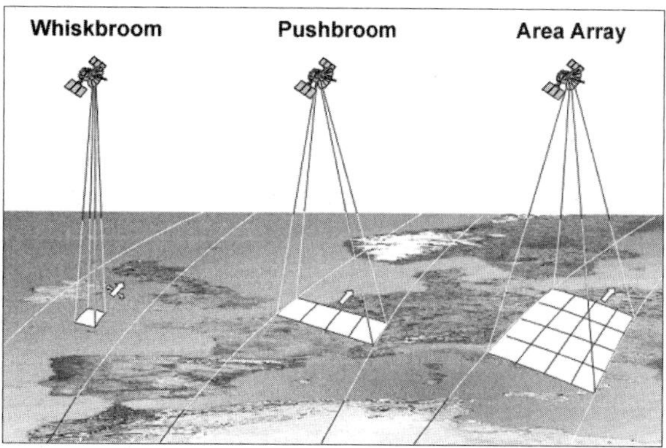

Figure 9.18 Whiskbroom, pushbroom, and area array sensors sample electromagnetic energy in selected spectral bands in different ways.

cells (once again see Figure 9.18), allowing the entire ground scene to be captured at the same instant.

With all three types of electronic images, the ground size of the pixel determines the spatial resolution of the image. Smaller pixels yield greater image detail, but they also mean more data to transmit and process.

The effect of electronic imaging is to paint an image cell-by-cell and line-by-line, just as an image is created on a TV screen. Although electronic images are comparable to photographs in many respects, there are some basic differences. For one thing, the cell size of electronic images tends to be substantially larger than the grain size of photographic film. As a result, most electronic images have a fuzzy appearance unless reduced in scale, and the resolution of landscape detail is relatively poor. The large size of sensor cells also means that scan lines are visible in the image. Fortunately, as technology develops, the cell size has been progressively reduced, yielding images of improved clarity. Another problem is that on electronic scanner images taken from a moving aircraft, scan lines aren't always parallel and hence are very prominent on the image.

Despite these problems, electronic imaging devices have two major advantages over conventional film cameras. For one thing, film handling is eliminated. Only an electronic connection between the sensor and image-processing facility is needed. As a result, sensors carried aboard unmanned spacecraft gather data until there is an equipment malfunction or loss of power, which may not occur for many years. This electronic capability is so important when dealing with spacecraft that most satellites designed for earth monitoring have carried scanners set to record information in the spectral range open to photography.

More important is the capability of electronic sensors to record electromagnetic energy beyond the visible portion of the spectrum. In recent years, many images have been produced in the thermal-infrared portion of the EMR spectrum. These images differ markedly from anything seen with the eye or camera.

Thermal-Infrared Sensors

Sensors designed to detect and record thermal-infrared energy we sense as heat usually operate in the 3-5 or 8 -14 μm spectral range. This means that there is no dependence on reflected visible light, so images can be obtained at any time of day or night. The 3-5 μm band is used to detect hot objects, such as volcanoes or forest fires, whereas the 8-14 μm band is used for thermal mapping when objects are expected to be at normal earth temperatures.

Resolution of landscape detail on thermal-IR images tends to be inferior to photography. This is due in part to the use of longer wavelengths by heat-sensitive detecting devices. It is also due to the lack of adequate thermal contrast between many features and their surroundings.

Thermal sensing is growing rapidly in importance, especially since modern sensors provide temperatures to within 0.1°C, as well as indicate relative heat contrasts. Thermal images have been particularly useful in detecting thermal water pollution from power generating plants and industries that use water for cooling purposes. Successful applications of infrared imagery also include the detection and delineation of potential geothermal energy areas, the edges of forest fires, the boundaries of ocean currents, and cold underground streams. Perhaps the most vital application of all is

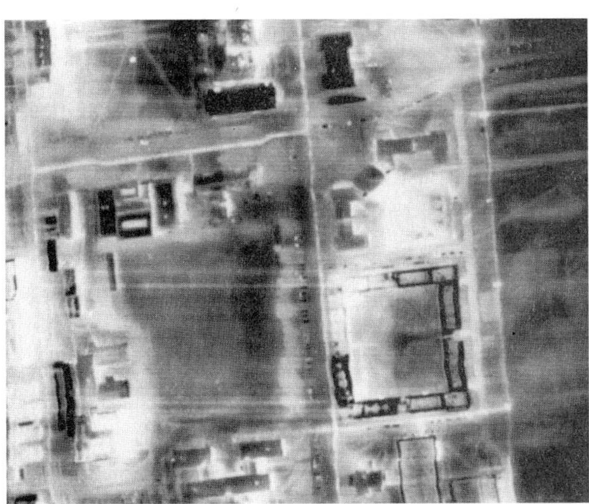

Figure 9.19 Early morning thermal-IR image of the central Oregon State University campus. Notice the white areas showing heat loss from buildings and the white lines showing heat from underground steam lines.

the measurement of heat loss through the roofs of urban dwellings (**Figure 9.19**). Considering the need for energy conservation, this fast and inexpensive way to see which buildings need more insulation is of great value.

Side-Looking Airborne Radar

It is possible to remotely sense the environment by using an antenna to emit pulses of microwave energy (in the 1 to 30 cm wavelength range) and then measure the energy reflected back from the landscape. The strength of the returned signal can then be converted to gray tones. This is how **side-looking airborne radar (SLAR)** works. It is called an active sensor system because it depends on energy emitted by the sensing device rather than the environment. Major advantages of the SLAR system are that it isn't dependent on an external energy source and that it provides an all-weather, day-or-night mapping capability.

An SLAR image is made up of scan lines perpendicular to the aircraft's flight path (**Figure 9.20**). An antenna on the airplane's belly directs short pulses of microwave energy in a narrow fan-shaped beam at right angles (called the look direction) to the aircraft's flight direction (azimuth). As each pulse strikes the earth's surface, a portion of the backscattered energy is returned to the aircraft antenna. As the airplane moves forward, the pulsed signal transmission-reception process is repeated, creating a continuous image of the ground area. Differences in the return signal strength, representing feature reflectance and orientation characteristics, appear on the SLAR image as different gray tones.

An SLAR image may look like a conventional photo or electronic image (**Figure 9.21**), but this appearance is deceptive. Imagery obtained by SLAR depicts the landscape in a far different way than does photography or electronic imaging. Return signal strength depends primarily on object orientation with respect to the aircraft's position. Since radar signals travel in straight lines out from the aircraft, areas obscured by hills or other vertical features aren't illuminated by the radar signal. Ra-

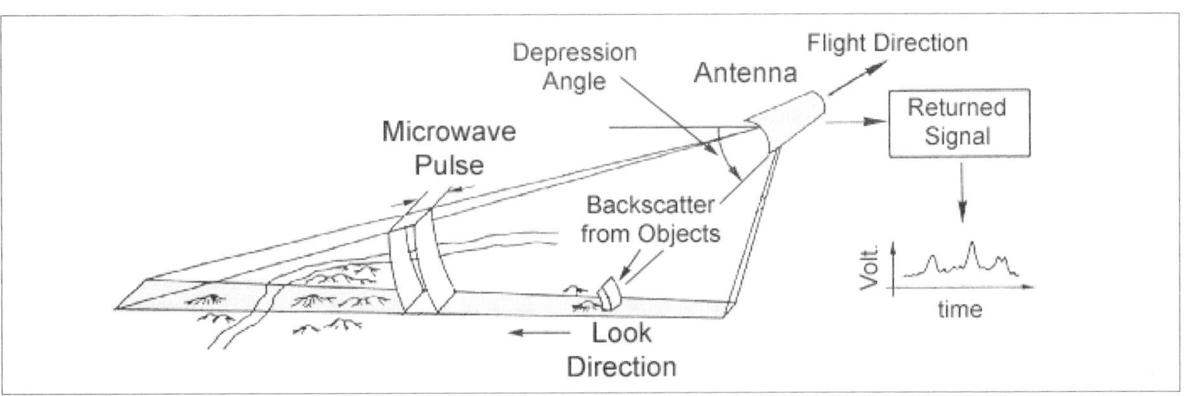

Figure 9.20 Side-looking airborne radar (SLAR) emits microwave pulses and receives backscattered energy from one side of the aircraft.

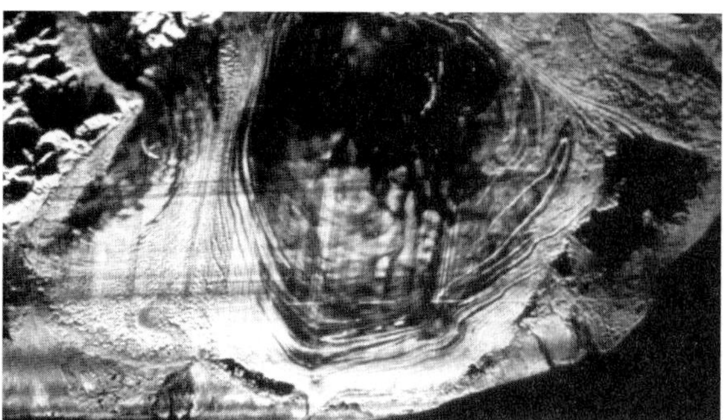

Figure 9.21 SLAR image of the Malaspina Glacier in Alaska.

dar shadows cast beyond these obstructions appear extremely dark on the SLAR image.

Surface roughness relative to the radar pulse's wavelength will also alter an SLAR image's appearance. If the ground surface is rough, it will scatter the radar signal in all directions, returning only a small portion to the antenna. Such diffuse reflectors will appear as a dull gray spot on the SLAR image.

Smooth surfaces, on the other hand, will act like a mirror, reflecting the radar signal in only one direction. If such a mirror-like surface, called a **specular reflector**, happens to lie at a right angle to the radar beam, the energy returned to the antenna will be intense, creating a bright spot on the SLAR image. If the smooth surface lies at any other angle to the radar beam, however, no energy will be returned, and a dark spot will show up on the SLAR image.

Sometimes related horizontal and vertical surfaces (such as a building next to a parking lot) will work together to form a **corner reflector**. When this happens, a large proportion of the radar signal may be returned to the antenna, creating an intense light spot, far out of proportion to the object's size, on the SLAR image.

Another aspect of the radar signal which influences the appearance of an SLAR image is the **depression angle** between the aircraft and the ground feature which is returning a radar signal (see Figure 9.20). The smaller the depression angle, the greater the radar shadow cast by relief features. Thus, small depression angles have proven quite effective in accentuating subtle vertical changes in the landscape. The problem is that the larger the radar shadows, the greater the chance that important features will be hidden within a dark zone on the image. In addition, the lower the depression angle, the lower the intensity of return signals from specular reflectors.

SLAR has tremendous potential for mapping applications, especially in regions of perpetual cloud cover. Due to the low angle of the system's illumination source, SLAR images highlight subtle relief features. This characteristic has proven valuable in detecting fractures, faults, stream patterns, and other features of significance in geologic studies. SLAR images are also useful in distinguishing between different urban land use zones and in detecting variations in vegetation type.

Space Imaging Radar

Side-looking radar is also used aboard satellites and the **Space Shuttle**, where it is called **Space (or Shuttle) Imaging Radar (SIR)**. Technical trickery, called **Synthetic Aperture Radar (SAR)** is commonly used to extend the "effective length" of the antenna. This extension enhances signal transmission and reception and, thus, image quality. SIR has shown dramatic ground penetration ability. This capability has led to a host of new remote sensing applications, especially in archaeology.

Shuttle Imaging Radar

The Shuttle Imaging Radar system received much attention when it was first used on the Space Shuttle. The SIR system is an L-band (23cm wavelength) side-looking radar. The sensor (SIR-A) was initially flown in 1981, and an upgraded version (SIR-B), incorporating several new features, was first flown in 1984. With SIR-B, the depression angle was selectable between 15° and 60°. This permitted ground resolutions from 20 to 100 m. (66 to 328 ft.) while mapping a ground swath 25 to 60 km. (16 to 37 mi.) wide, depending on the shuttle's orbital altitude.

The Space Shuttle Endeavour carried even more refined radar sensors, beginning in 1994. The

Spaceborne Imaging Radar (SIR-C) sensor system used wavelengths of 6 (C-band) and 24 (L-band) centimeters. The same flight also carried an X-band (3 cm.) Synthetic Aperture Radar (X-SAR).

The computer-processed SIR signals can be used to generate black-and-white images highlighting the terrain in sharp relief (**Figure 9.22**). These images can be further computer-processed and rendered in false colors to enhance features of interest. Indeed, the primary aim of SIR-C was to see if it was possible to reveal geologic features such as faults, folds, and drainage patterns which could help scientists locate important mineral resources. Results indicate that SIR imagery can also be used to emphasize subtle differences in vegetation, soil moisture, and ocean waves.

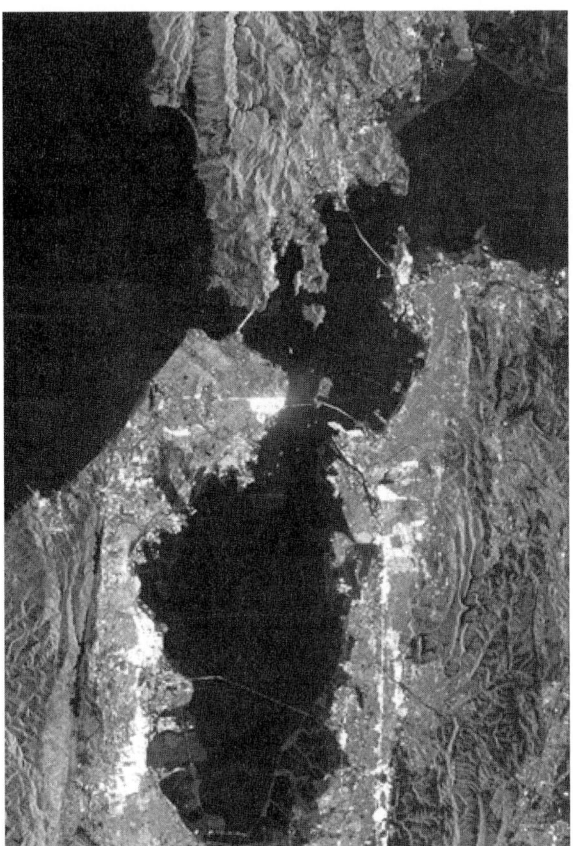

Figure 9.22 Shuttle Imaging Radar (SIR-C L-band) image of the San Francisco Bay area highlighting the terrain and corner reflection from buildings.

RADARSAT

The Canadian Space Agency launched **RADARSAT** in 1995 as a Synthetic Aperture Radar (SAR) satellite system designed to monitor global environmental change and natural resources. Synthetic Aperture Radar is a microwave instrument that sends pulsed signals to earth where the received reflected pulses are processed by computer to create an image. Like side-looking airborne radar, SAR provides its own microwave illumination and thus operates day or night, regardless of weather conditions.

RADARSAT circles the earth at an altitude of 798 km. in a sun-synchronous orbit, meaning that the satellite overpasses are always at the same time of day. Unlike SLAR, RADARSAT has a user-definable microwave beam width (45 to 500 km. wide). Incidence angles anywhere from 10 to 60 degrees can also be selected, giving spatial resolutions ranging from 8 to 100 meters.

RADARSAT is an important source of environmental information. It provides the first systematic imaging of the entire Arctic and Antarctic regions, with daily coverage regardless of weather conditions (**Figure 9.23**). This information is useful to shipping companies in North America, and to government agencies involved with ice identification and mapping. SAR has also been used to map geological features such as faults, folds, and lineaments. These features provide clues to the distribution of groundwater, mineral deposits, oil, and gas in the earth's crust. In addition, RADARSAT imagery has assisted the mapping of land use and the monitoring of disasters such as oil spills, floods, and earthquakes.

Shuttle Radar Topography Mapping

The **Shuttle Radar Topography Mission (SRTM)** was an international project lead by the U.S. National Imagery and Mapping Agency (NIMA) and NASA. The SRTM radar device was carried on the Space Shuttle Endeavor in February, 2000, and acquired enough data during its 10 days of operation to create a near-global high-resolution database of the earth's topography.

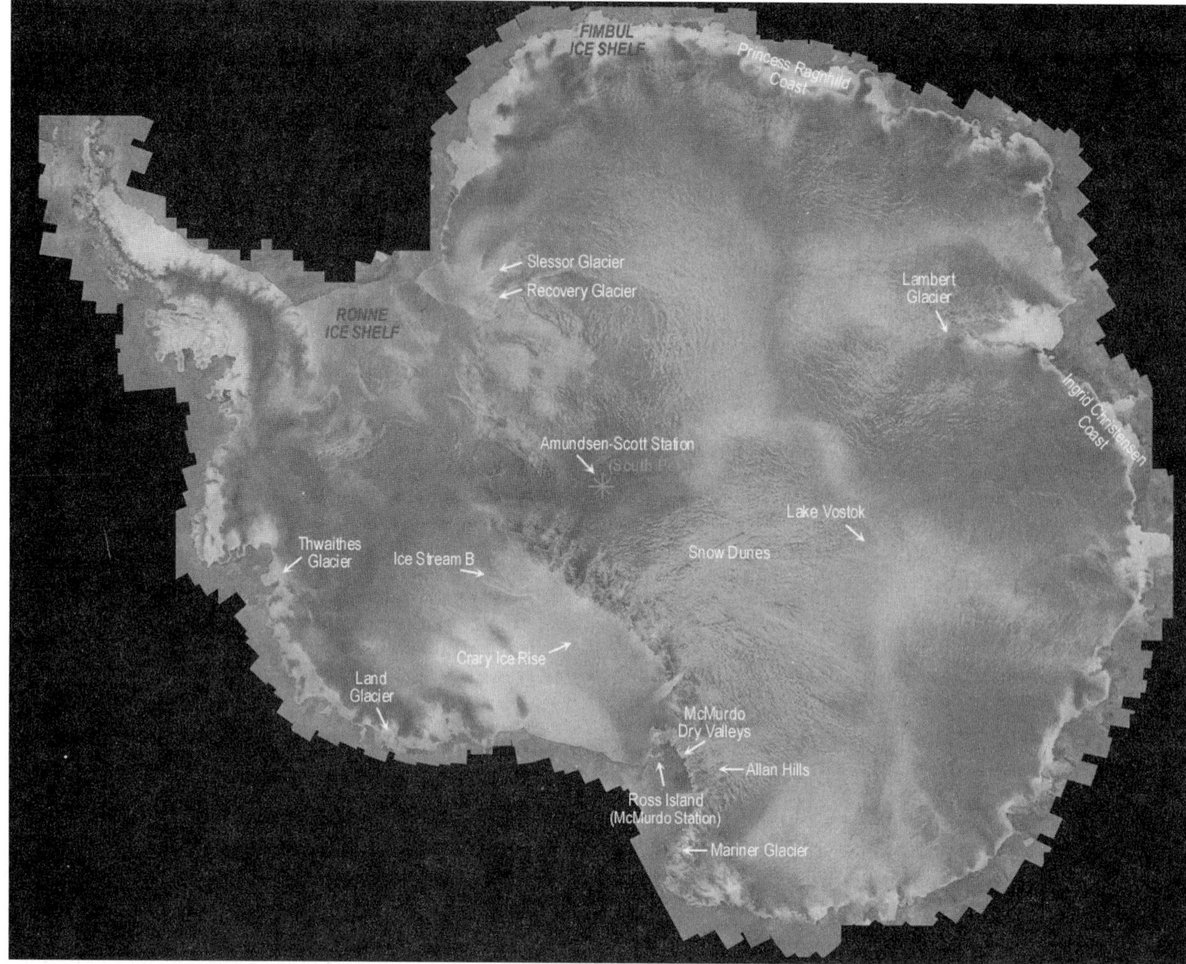

Figure 9.23 RADARSAT image mosaic of Antarctica. Note that the geometric edge of Antarctica is an artifact of the mosaicking process.

Two radar antennas were used, one located in the Shuttle's payload bay, the other on the end of a 60-meter (200-ft.) mast that extended from the payload bay once the Shuttle was in space. The Shuttle's 233-km. (145-mi.) orbital height allowed high-resolution elevation data to be collected between 60° north and 56° south latitude. Elevations for land areas within these latitudes were mapped with a horizontal accuracy of better than 30 meters (100 feet). An extremely large amount of data was collected—enough to fill more than 20,000 CDs.

To date, SRTM data have been released at 30-meter grids for the United States and as images of interesting terrain features such as **Color Plate 9.5**. Most images have been oblique perspective views, often draped with other satellite images of similar spatial resolution such as Landsat Thematic Mapper scenes. When released, a degraded 90-meter global digital elevation model will be still by far the highest resolution dataset available for most foreign countries.

MULTISPECTRAL IMAGING

The electromagnetic spectrum is broad and rich in environmental information throughout its range. In the past several decades, we have learned to use images obtained simultaneously in several spectral bands, each of which gives us valuable insights into the nature of our surroundings. Interpretation problems, which are difficult or impossible to solve when we are restricted to the information provided by a single spectral band, are often simplified if we look at images from several portions of the spectrum.

Multispectral sensing devices are used to capture a ground scene in different spectral bands so that the resulting images are geometrically identical. Artificial satellites are the most recent multispectral sensing platforms. Images acquired several hundred miles above the earth's surface cover a relatively large ground area at a small scale if a sensor with coarse spatial resolution is used. High-resolution multispectral imaging devices record a small ground area at a very high spatial resolution. Most images we see come from what we call **earth resources satellites**.

Earth Resources Satellites

Landsat

In the late 1960s, NASA began a program titled Earth Resources Observation Systems (EROS) to explore the potential for monitoring the earth from space. The first satellite was placed in orbit in 1972. Initially called the Earth Resources Technology Satellite (ERTS-1), it was later renamed **Landsat 1**. Subsequent successful launches in the Landsat series took place in 1975 (Landsat 2), 1978 (Landsat 3), 1982 (Landsat 4), 1984 (Landsat 5), and 1999 (Landsat 7)*. Landsat 5 and 7 are currently in operation. Technologically and functionally, these six satellites represent three generations of environmental remote sensing from space.

The first three Landsat satellites were an experimental, first-generation effort at environmental remote sensing from space. All three satellites were placed in a sun-synchronous circular orbit 917 km. above the earth. A near-polar orbit was used so that global coverage was possible due to earth rotation under the satellite (**Figure 9.24**). A sun-synchronous orbital period was set so that the satellites would circle the earth roughly 14 times per day and would pass over the same spot on earth at the same time of day every 18 days. On each descending orbit (daylight pass from north to south), sensors carried aboard the spacecraft were capable of recording the ground scene over a strip 185 km. wide (**Figure 9.25**). Each image covered a

**Landsat 6 failed to reach orbit.*

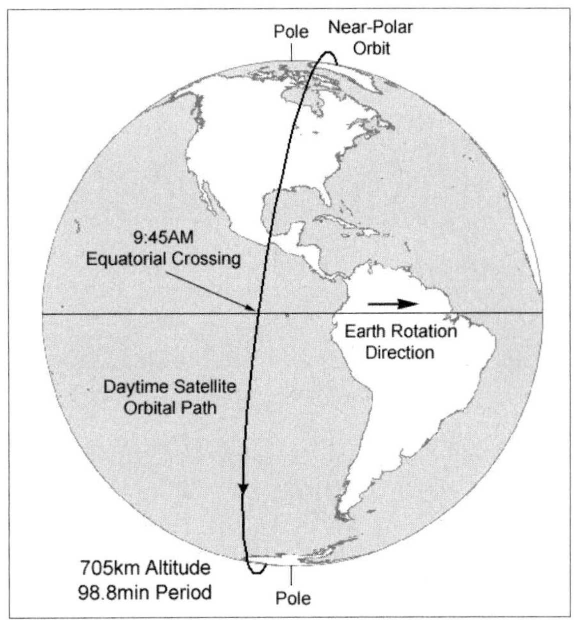

Figure 9.24 The sun-synchronous, near-polar orbit of early Landsat satellites made it possible to provide complete imagery of the earth's surface every 18 days.

185 × 185 kilometer ground area with an 80-meter pixel resolution. Images were recorded digitally and transmitted to ground receiving stations.

A whiskbroom sensor called the **Multispectral Scanner (MSS)** was the primary system on Landsats 1-3. This sensor produced four images of the same ground scene in the green, red, and two near-IR spectral bands numbered 4 through 7. The green radiation (0.5 to 0.6 μm) recorded on Band-4 images was found useful in determinining the depth and turbidity of water bodies (**Figure 9.26**).

Band-5 images in the red (0.6 to 0.7 μm) part of the spectrum were found to clearly show topographic and cultural features such as drainage patterns, roads, buildings, and parking lots. As a rule, this band gives the best general-purpose view of the earth's surface.

Band 6, the first near-IR band, spans the 0.7 to 0.8 μm range. These images have the best tonal contrast and are useful in identifying different land use practices, types of vegetation, landforms, and the boundary between land and water.

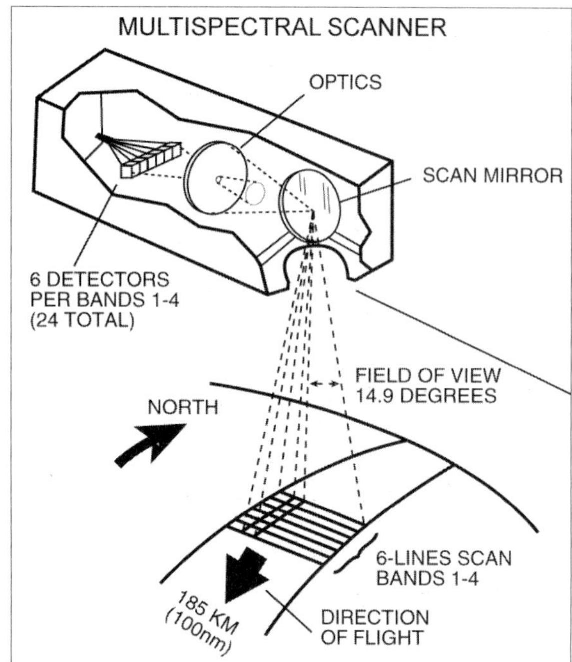

Figure 9.25 The Landsat Multispectral Scanner (MSS) imaged a 185-km.-wide ground swath in four spectral bands.

The second near-infrared band, called Band 7, covers the 0.8 to 1.1 μm wavelength range. This band provided the best penetration of atmospheric haze and the best land-water discrimination. As on Band 6, vegetation and landforms are easily seen on Band-7 images.

These four MSS bands are also used in different combinations to produce a false-color composite image, with blue, green, and red image separations assigned to Bands 4, 5 and 7, respectively. The resulting image (**Color Plate 9.6**) of this band combination shows healthy vegetation as red rather than green. The healthier the vegetation, the redder the image. Since water strongly absorbs near-IR wavelengths, clear water appears black. Sediment-laden water (highly reflective in Band 4) is powder blue in color, while urban centers (highly reflective in Band 5) usually appear blue or blue-gray.

Between Landsats 2 and 3, a significant improvement was made in the MSS scanner so that the sensor on Landsat 3 was equipped with a fifth band, designated Band 8. This fifth band recorded thermal-infrared radiation at a coarser 237-m. spatial resolution, compared with the other four spectral bands.

Band 8 didn't necessarily make recordings of ground scenes simultaneously with the other bands. It was principally designed to make recordings at night during the satellite's ascending orbit on the dark side of the earth. Indeed, this nighttime sensing capability turned out to be one of the sensor's major advantages. In spite of its coarse resolution, Band 8 imagery was found helpful in identifying agricultural crops and providing information on the thermal characteristics of rocks and soils. In addition, it is useful in monitoring volcanic action, geothermal activity, forest fires, and industrial thermal pollution.

After nearly a decade of research and development, a second-generation earth resources satellite system was initiated in 1982 with the launch of Landsat 4*. This satellite was placed in a 705-km., near-polar, sun-synchronous orbit, making nearly total global coverage possible every 16 days. Landsat 4 soon malfunctioned and was replaced by an identical satellite, **Landsat 5**, in 1984.

Because of the spectral and spatial resolution limitations of the MSS sensor, an improved sensor, called the **Thematic Mapper (TM)**, was designed for Landsat 5. The design of the TM was influenced by the technology of the first-generation MSS sensor, but the TM is more effective, because of the following improvements:

- The TM sensor has a finer spatial resolution (30 m.)
- Spectral resolution was increased to seven bands. Bands 1-3 span the blue, green, and red portions of the spectrum; three bands (4, 5, and 7) are in the near to mid-infrared portion of the spectrum; and one channel (Band 6) is in the thermal infrared region(see **Table 9.1**. and **Figure 9.27**).

**To provide continuity with previous Landsat missions, a four-band MSS sensor similar to those flown before was also carried aboard Landsats 4 and 5. A new numbering system was used to designate the four spectral bands of the Landsat 4 and 5 MSS, however. What are known as bands 4, 5, 6, and 7 on the previous MSS sensors are now labeled, respectively, as Landsat 4 and 5 MSS bands 1, 2, 3, and 4.*

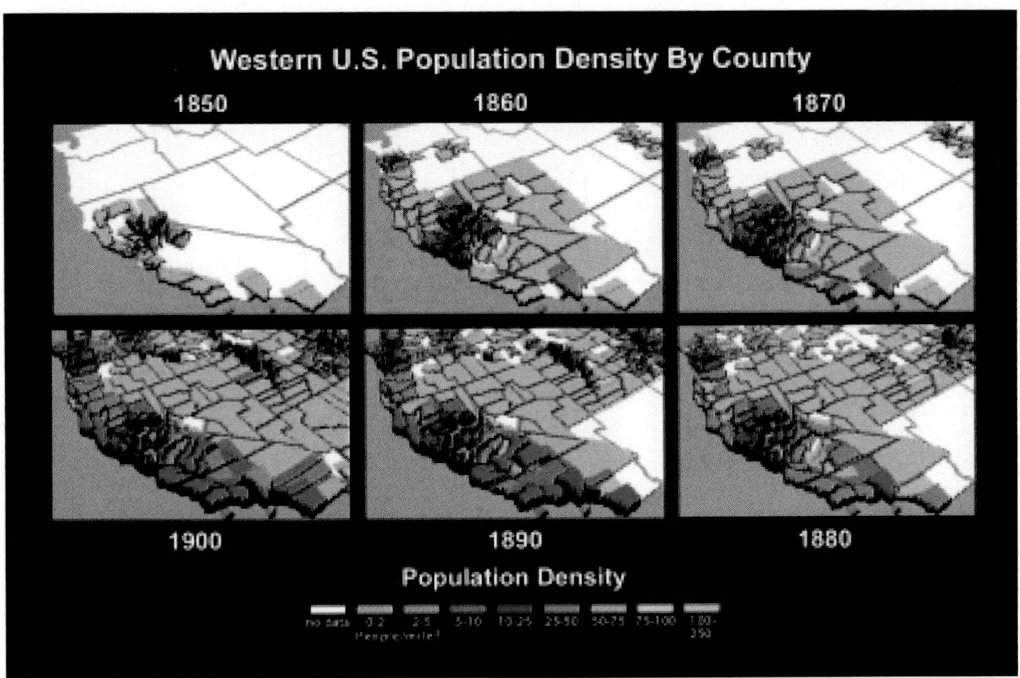

Color Plate 7.1 Time series maps of population density change in the western United States 1850-1900.

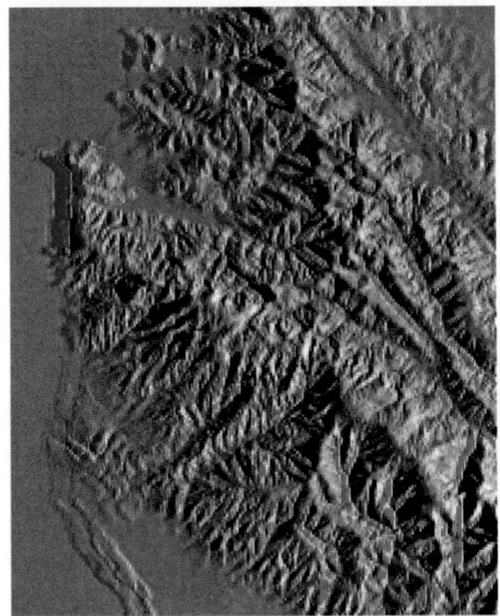

Color Plate 8.1. Anaglyph of a relief shaded image of the Pacifica area near San Francisco, California.

Color Plate 9.1 True color aerial photograph of the World Trade Center site in New York taken immediately after 9-11-01.

Color Plate 9.2 The Pentagon and vicinity, Washington, D.C., portion of a National Aerial Photography Program 9-inch color-infrared aerial photograph, 1:40,000-scale, March 1994.

Color Plate 9.3 Portion of a Skylab Earth Terrain Camera true color photograph of Chicago, Illinois, and vicinity.

Color Plate 9.4 Portion of a 1:250,000 scale satellite image map of the Las Vegas, Nevada, area.

Color Plate 9.5 Landsat Thematic Mapper image of Santa Barbara, California, draped over a SRTM digital elevation model and shown in oblique perspective view.

Color Plate 9.6 Landsat Multispectral Scanner band 4,5,7 color composite of Lake Tahoe, California and Nevada.

Color Plate 9.7 Landsat Thematic Mapper true (top) and false color (bottom) composite images of Tampa Bay, Florida.

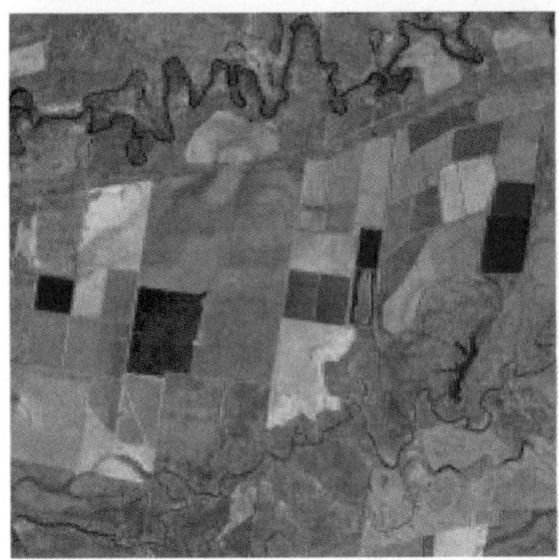

Color Plate 9.8 SPOT 20m-resolution multispectral image of an agricultural area.

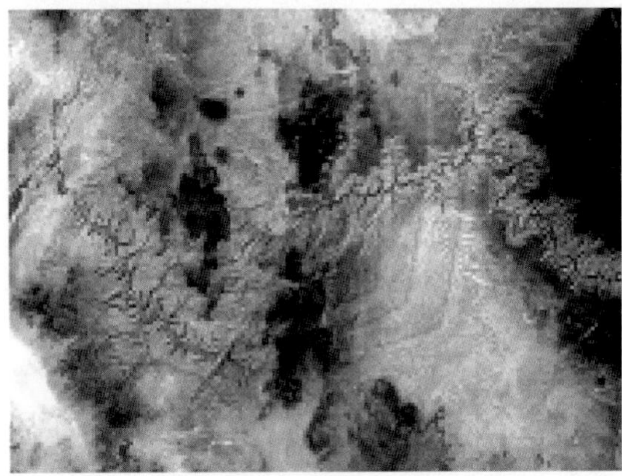

Color Plate 9.9 IRS WiFS image of the Grand Canyon in Arizona.

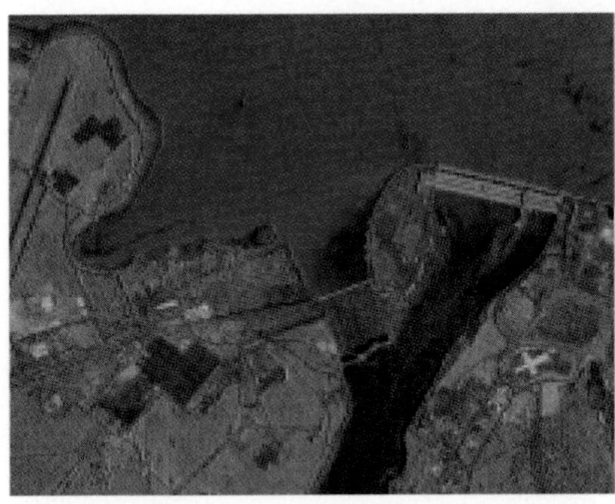

Color Plate 9.10 IKONOS 4m-resolution multispectral image of the Itaipu Dam on the Brazil/Paraguay border.

Color Plate 9.11 Quickbird 2.8m-resolution true color image of central Tampa, Florida.

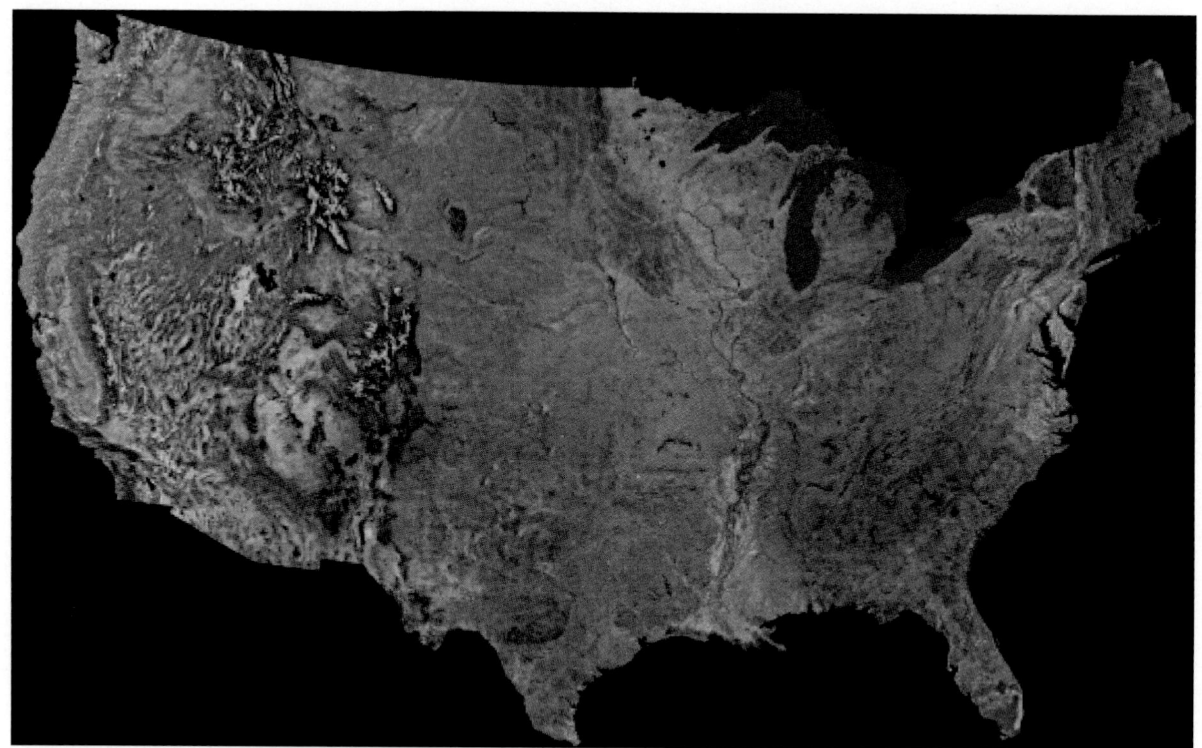

Color Plate 9.12 AVHRR false color mosaic of the United States.

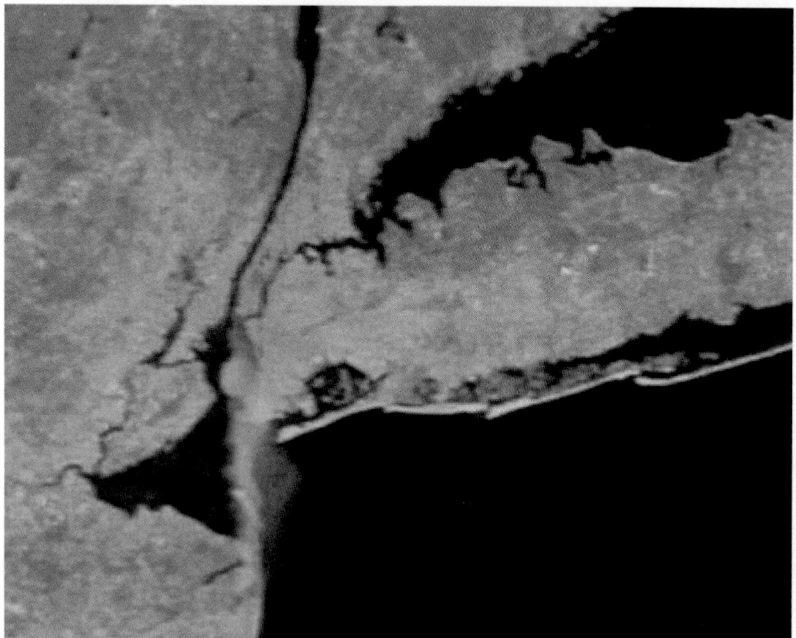

Color Plate 9.13 MODIS 500m-resolution false color image of New York and vicinity taken September 11, 2001. Notice the smoke plume from the World Trade Center site.

Color Plate 9.14 Portion of a USGS 1:24,000-scale orthophotomap of Key West, Florida.

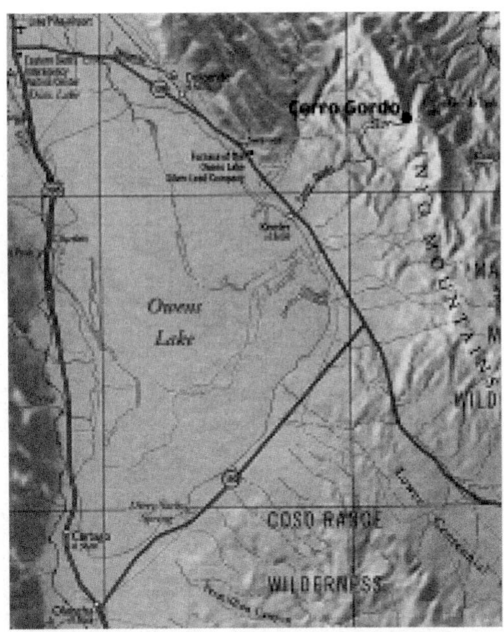

Color Plate 13.1 Portion of a page from the *Benchmark Road & Recreation Atlas* for California.

Aeronautical Chart Series

Sectional Aeronautical Chart (1:500,000)

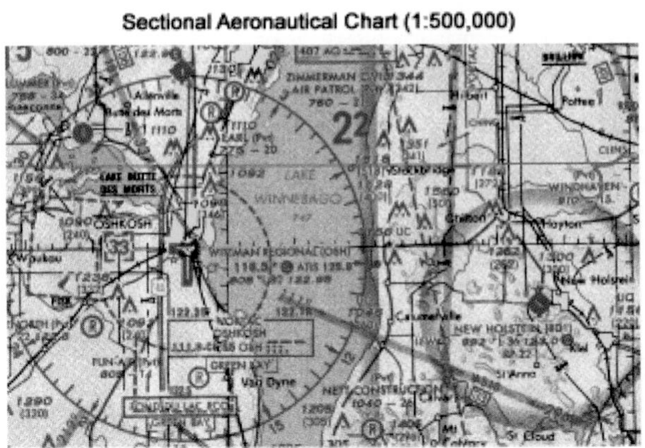

World Aeronautical Chart (1:1,000,000)

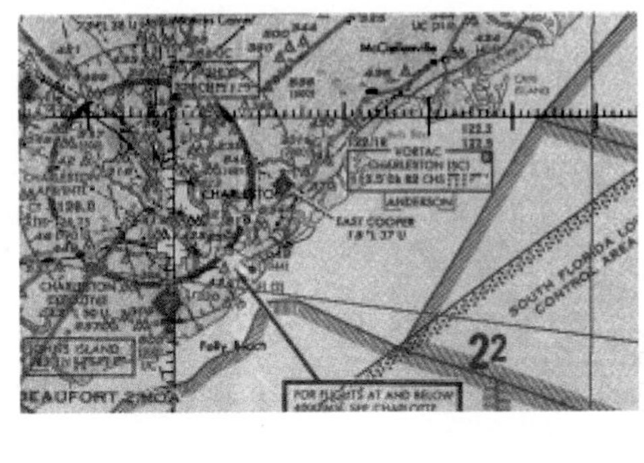

Instrument Flight Rules Low Altitude Chart

Terminal Area Chart (1:250,000)

Color Plate 13.2 Portions of charts from four different United States aeronautical chart series.

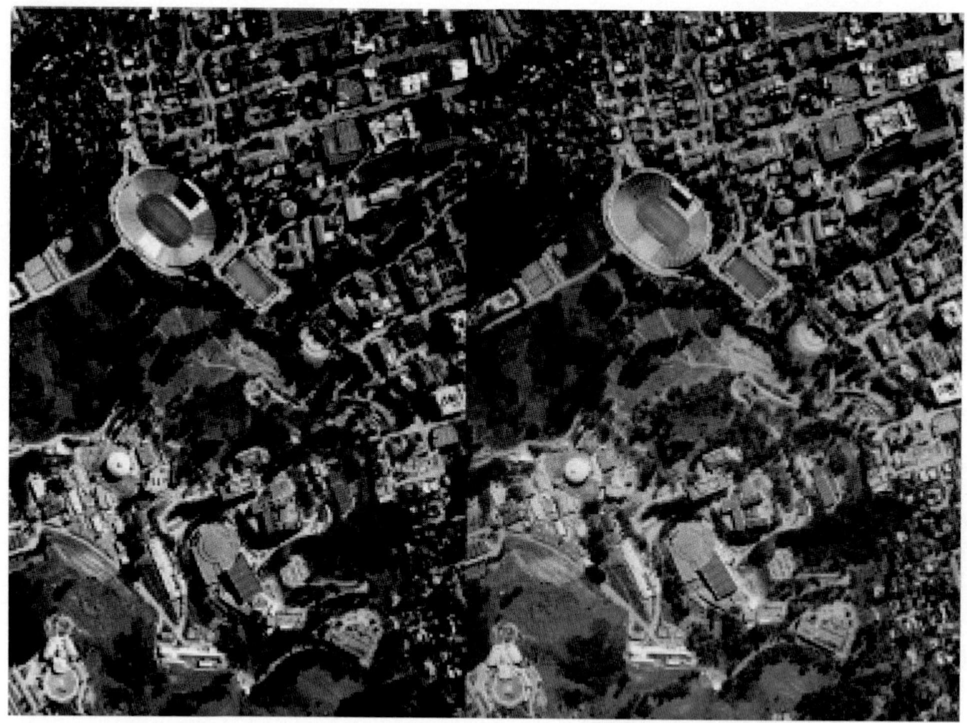

Color Plate 21.1 True-color stereopair of the central UC-Berkeley campus.

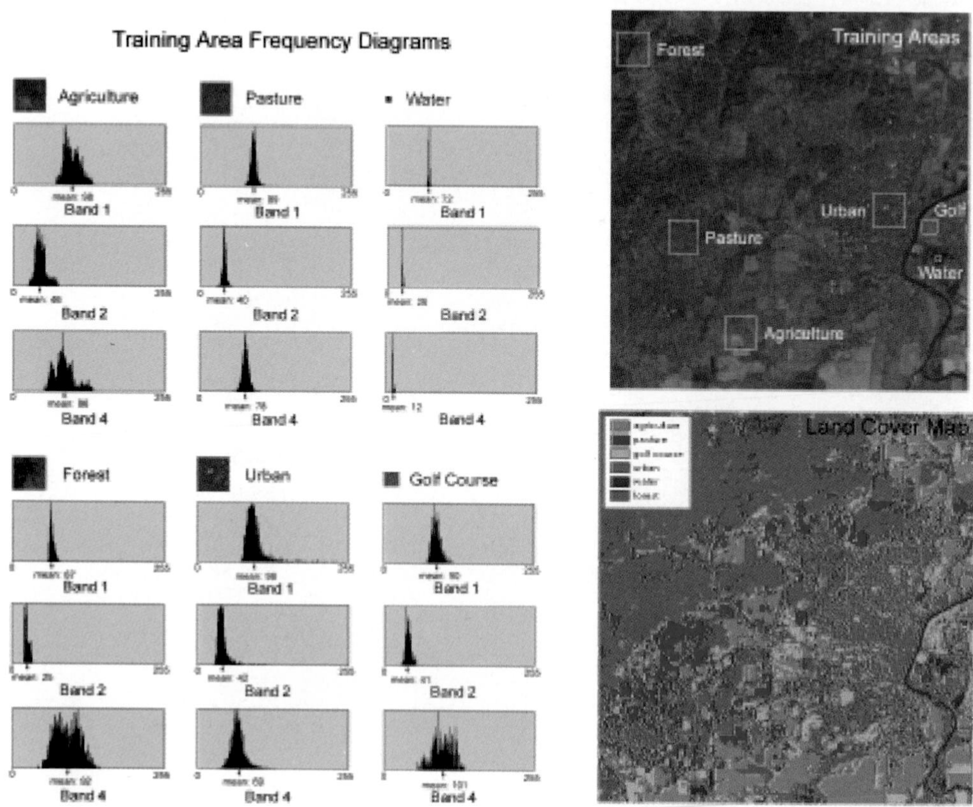

Color Plate 21.2 Landcover training areas, frequency diagrams, and Corvallis landcover map.

Washington Vegetation Zones

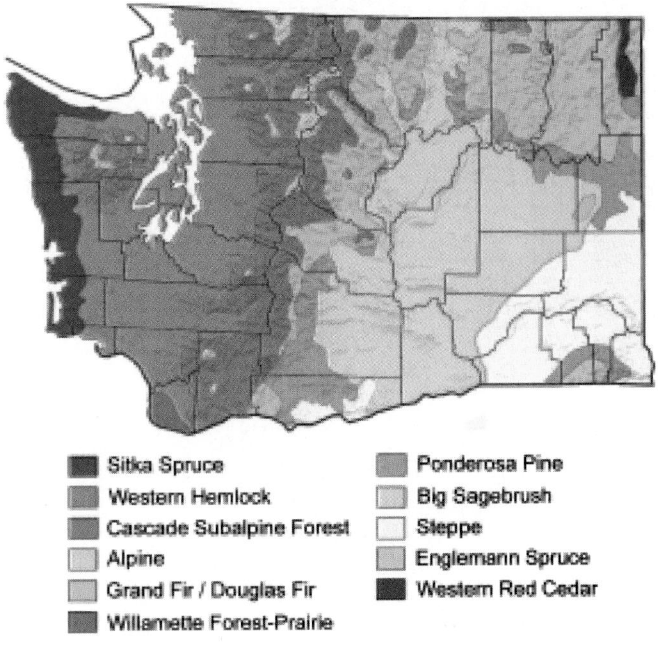

Color Plate 23.1 Vegetation zones for Washington state (taken from the *Atlas of the Pacific Northwest*).

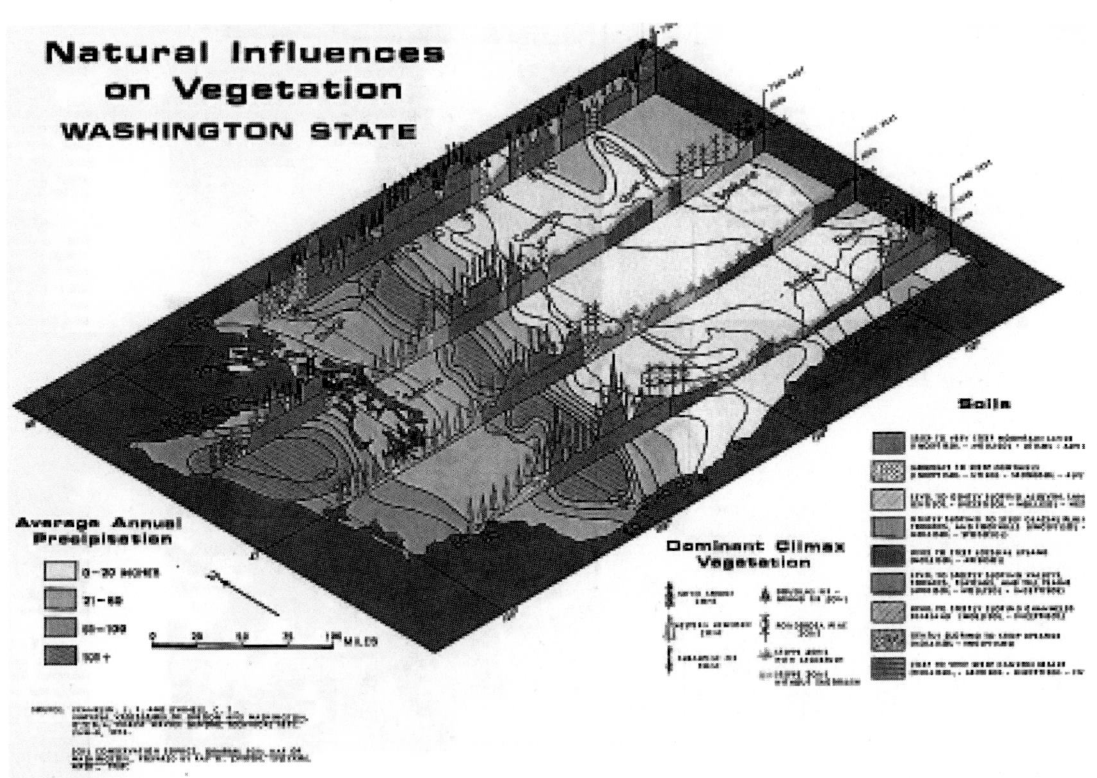

Color Plate 23.2 Natural influences on vegetation in Washington state (courtesy Eugene Turner).

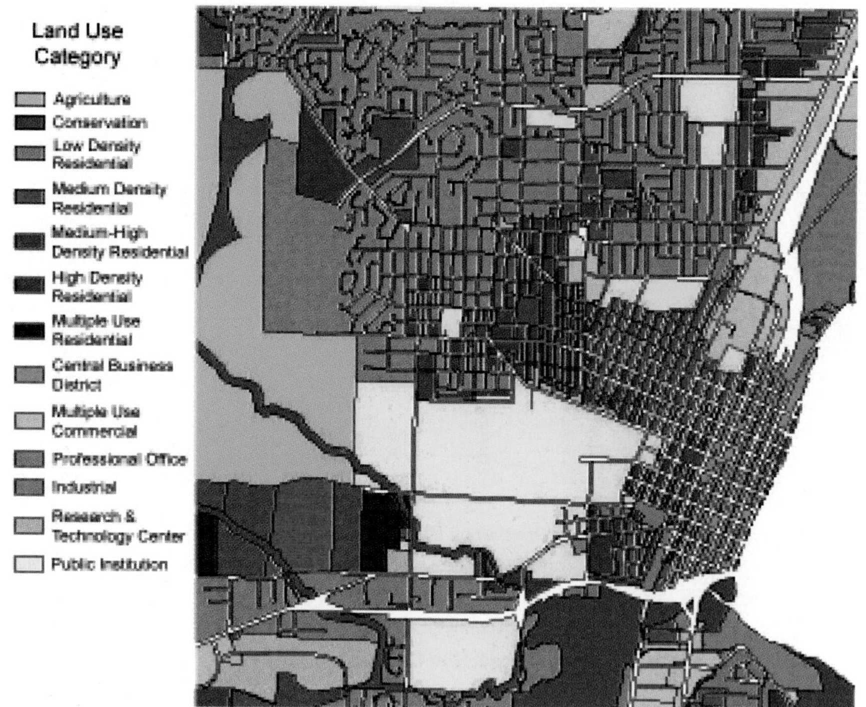

Color Plate 24.1 The spatial mix of residential, commercial, public, industrial, and agricultural land uses reflects urban settlement patterns and zoning policies designed to keep human activities in desired locations.

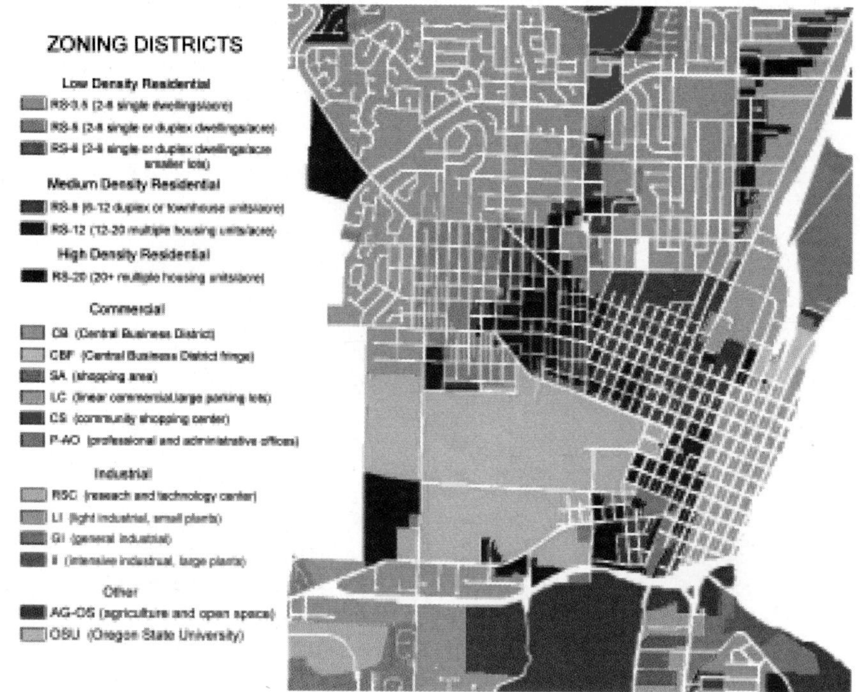

Color Plate 24.2 Zoning districts are legally prescribed areas to be used for residential, commercial, public, industrial, and agricultural land uses.

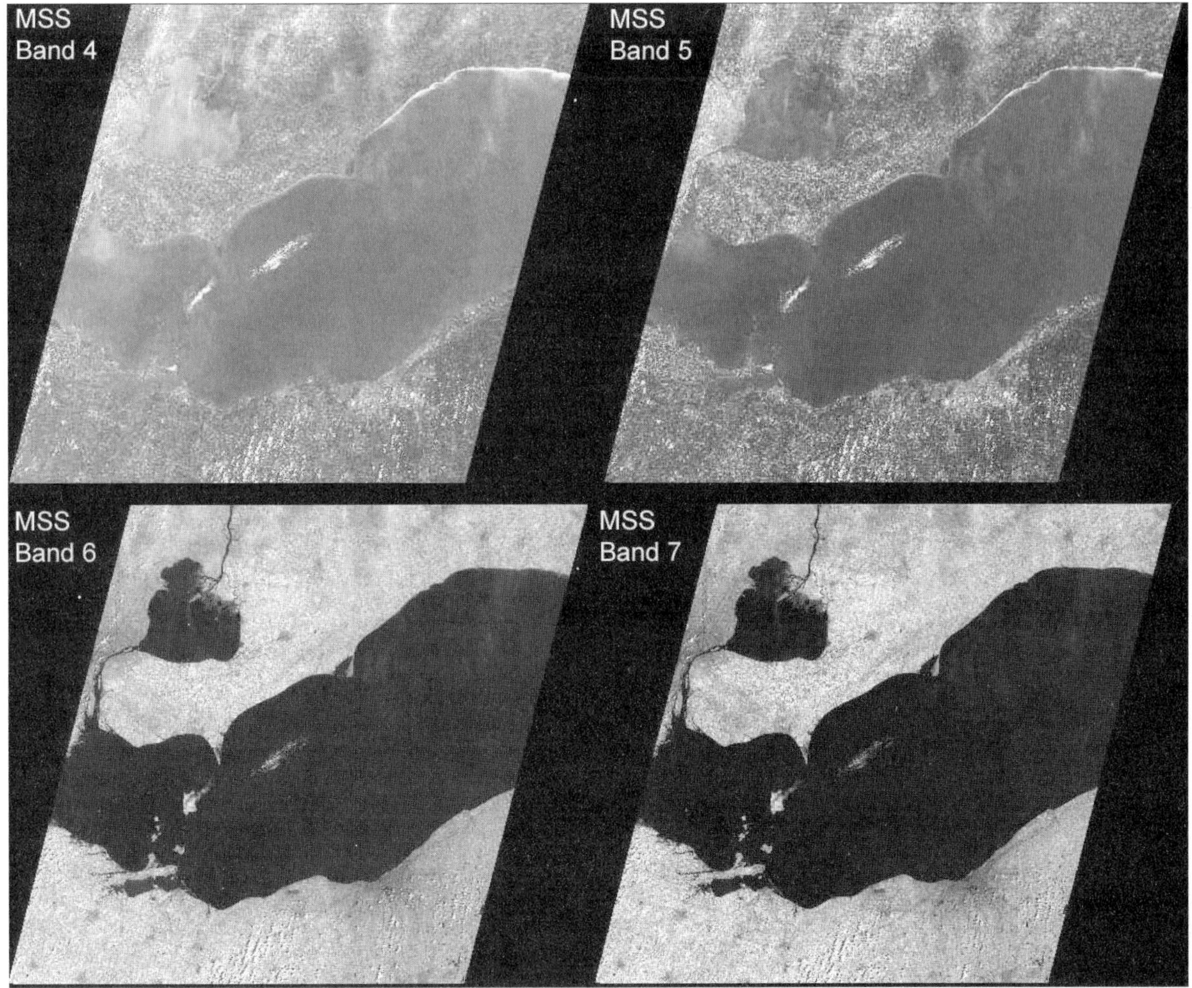

Figure 9.26 The four MSS bands of this Landsat 1 image show different aspects of the western Lake Erie area. Band 4 is green; Band 5 is red; and Bands 6 and 7 are near-infrared.

- The thermal channel has a coarser pixel ground resolution of 120 m.
- Through improved satellite guidance control and more precise positioning data, the data's geometric fidelity was enhanced.
- The ground processing capability for handling TM data was highly automated and streamlined over what was available for earlier MSS data.

The TM spectral bands were chosen primarily for vegetation monitoring. The one exception is Band 7, which is included primarily for geologic applications. The 30-m. pixel resolution in all but Band 6 allows landcover classification of areas as small as 6 to 10 acres (2 to 4 hectares). In contrast, with the MSS in earlier Landsats, it wasn't possible to classify fields of less than about 40 acres (16.2 hectares). Three TM bands are often combined into true-color (Bands 1,2, and 3) and false-color-infrared (Bands 1,2,and 4) images (see **Color Plate 9.7**).

Landsat 7 matches the multispectral capability of Landsat 5, with two significant improvements. The **Enhanced Thematic Mapper Plus (ETM+)** sensor has an additional panchromatic band (Band 8) in the 0.5 to 0.9 μm range (**Figure 9.28**) with 15-meter resolution. The second improvement was increasing the spatial resolution of the thermal-IR band from 120 meters to 60 meters. Other image acquisition parameters are the same as Landsat 5, including a 705-km. sun-synchronous, near-polar orbit and 185-km. image width.

Table 9.1 Landsat 4 and 5 Thematic Mapper Bands

Band Name	Spectral Range
1 – Blue	0.45 – 0.52 μm
2 – Green	0.52 – 0.60
3 – Red	0.63 – 0.69
4 - Near IR	0.76 – 0.90
5 – Mid IR	1.55 – 1.75
6 – TIR	10.4 – 12.5
7 – Mid IR	2.08 – 2.35

SPOT

Landsat isn't the only earth resources satellite program. The "commercialization of space" is well underway. The French have launched a series of land resources satellites known as the **Systeme Probatoire d'Observation de la Terre (SPOT)**. **SPOT 1** was placed in a sun-synchronous polar orbit at an altitude of 822 km. in 1986, followed by **SPOT 2** in 1990, and **SPOT 3** in 1993.

The sensors aboard SPOT 1-3 were two identical linear array **High-Resolution Visible (HRV)** imaging devices of the pushbroom type (see Figure 9.18), which could be operated simultaneously or independently. These solid-state sensors were sensitive to one near-infrared and two visible (green, red) spectral bands optimized for vegetation differentiation and Landsat TM compatibility. The sensors operated in two modes: black-and-white (panchromatic) with a 10-m. ground resolution (**Figure 9.29**), and multispectral with a 20-m. resolution (**Color Plate 9.8**). Each SPOT scene covered a 60×60 km. ground area. Deducting for a

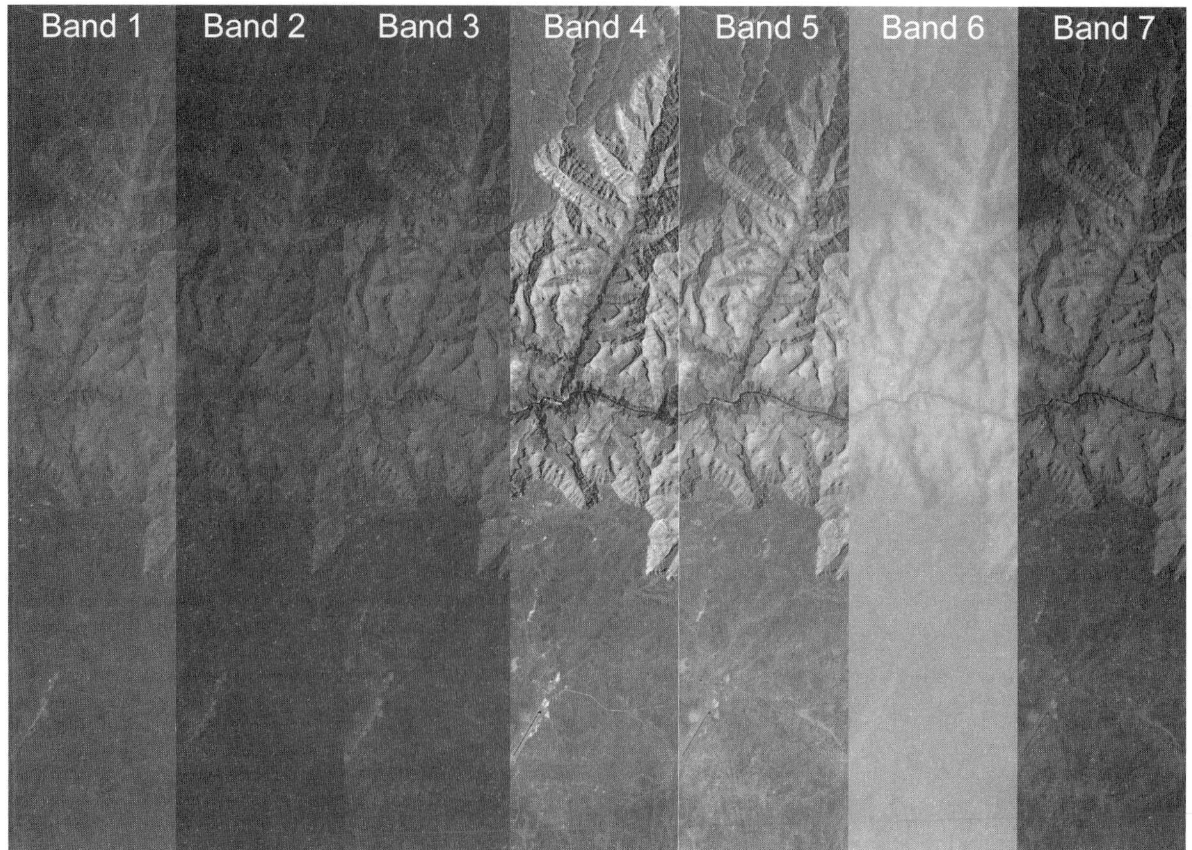

Figure 9.27 Each of the seven bands of the Landsat Thematic Mapper provides different information about the environment, such as the central portion of the Grand Canyon in Arizona.

Figure 9.28 Landsat 7 ETM+ panchromatic band 8 images have a 15-meter spatial resolution.

Figure 9.29 This 10-meter-resolution SPOT panchromatic-band image of central Dallas, Texas, shows the level of detail obtainable with the HRV sensor.

three-kilometer image sidelap, a single pass of the satellite covered a ground swath 117 km. wide.

To provide continuity in SPOT imagery over the long term, **SPOT 4** was launched in an identical orbit in 1998, followed by **SPOT 5** in 2002. The **HRVIR sensor** aboard SPOT 4 is similar to the earlier HRV instrument, but with an additional short-wave-infrared band sensitive to the 1.58-1.75 μm wavelength range. The satellite also carries a new broad-coverage Vegetation 1 sensor with a 1.15-km. spatial resolution that images a 2,250-km. swath width. These changes make SPOT 4 imagery more useful for ocean and vegetation studies.

SPOT 5 is an improved version of its predecessor. Its Vegetation 2 sensor is identical to the Vegetation 1 instrument on **SPOT 4**, but the green, red, and near-IR multispectral images from its two **High-Resolution Geometric (HRG)** sensors are now at a 10-m. spatial resolution. Panchromatic images with a spatial resolution of five meters are obtained with the HRG sensors, and these can be combined to create 2.5-meter images (**Figure 9.30**).

All SPOT satellites can aim their sensors up to 400 km. on either side of their ground tracks using pointable optics. As a result, each satellite can view the same ground scene at one to five day intervals, depending on the latitude. Having a short revisit period permits SPOT to gather more imagery in heavily clouded areas and to monitor environmental phenomena of shorter duration (floods, fires, pollution, natural hazard damage, and the like).

SPOT also has a stereoscopic imaging capability. This permits 10-m. (33-ft.) landform contouring from stereopairs using conventional stereoplotting instruments. Indeed, SPOT data are of sufficient quality to support 1:100,000 topographic mapping, 1:50,000 topographic map revision, and 1:25,000 thematic mapping.

SPOT has higher spatial resolution and more continual coverage than Landsat. It also has the advantage of stereoscopic imagery, which Landsat doesn't have. Furthermore, SPOT's state-of-the-art linear array sensors are based on solid-state electronics, in contrast to the mechanical scanning technology used in Landsat. This means that SPOT should be able to avoid the mechanical malfunctions which have plagued Landsat. It also means that SPOT can provide improved image geometry, something of great interest to map makers and users.

Figure 9.30 SPOT HRG 2.5-meter-resolution panchromatic image of central Stockholm, Sweden.

IRS

The Indian Space Research Organization (ISRO) joined the commercial remote sensing community in 1988 with the launch of its first earth resources satellite. ISRO now has four satellites in its **Indian Remote Satellite (IRS)** program (See **Table 9.2**).

The rapid succession of launches allowed ISRO to respond to user needs with quick design changes. The IRS-1A and -1B satellites carried two versions of the **Linear Imaging Self-Scanning Sensor (LISS)**. LISS-I and -II were both four-band pushbroom sensors with spectral bands matching Landsat Thematic Mapper Bands 1-4. The spatial resolution of LISS-I (72.5-m.) was roughly equivalent to Landsat MSS imagery, whereas LISS-II resolution (36-m.) approximates that of the Thematic Mapper. Both sensors have a ground swath of 148-km., but it takes four LISS-II images to cover the ground area of one LISS-I image. Repeat coverage is 22 days at the equator, and less elsewhere.

IRS-1C and -1D carry three sensors. The LISS-III has four spectral bands, but they differ somewhat from those of the earlier LISS sensors (see **Table 9.3**). The blue band was dropped and a short-wave-infrared (SWIR) capability (Band 5) with 70-m. pixels, similar to TM Band 5, was added. LISS-III bands 2-4 have a finer spatial resolution (23.5-m.) than earlier LISS sensors. This spatial resolution is roughly equivalent to multispectral SPOT imagery (20-m.). The Pan (panchromatic) sensor has a 5.8-m. spatial resolution, ushering in a new generation of high-resolution remote sensing images (**Figure 9.31**).

The **Wide Field Sensor (WiFS)** aboard IRS-1C and -1D has 180-m. resolution, a 810-km. ground swath, and two spectral bands (red and near-IR). This sensor provides regional imagery that falls between the spatial resolution of the Landsat MSS (80-m.) and NOAA's AVHRR (1.1-km.) sensors. WiFS provides repeat coverage every five days

Table 9.2 Indian Remote Satellite (IRS) Program

Satellite and Type	Date	Sensors* Resolution	Bands
IRS 1A	1988	LISS-I	4
Multispectral		72.5 m	
		LISS-II	4
Multispectral		36.25 m	
IRS 1B	1991	LISS-I	4
Multispectral		72.5 m	
		LISS-II	4
Multispectral		36.25 m	
IRS 1C	1995	Pan.	1
Panchromatic		5.8 m	
		LISS-III	4
Multispectral		23.5 m	
		70 m (SWIR)	
		WiFS	4
Multispectral		188 m	
IRS 1D	1997	LISS-II	4
Multispectral		36.25 m	

**See text for definitions of sensor terms.*

Table 9.3 Spectral Characteristics of IRS Sensors

Sensor	Band	Spectral Range	
LISS-I and -II	1	Blue	0.45-0.52μm
	2	Green	0.52-0.59
	3	Red	0.62-0.68
	4	Near-IR	0.77-0.86
LISS-III	1	(Not included)	
	2	Green	0.52-0.59
	3	Red	0.62-0.68
	4	Near-IR	0.77-0.86
	5	Mid-IR	1.55-1.70
WiFS	1	Red	0.62-0.68
	2	Near-IR	0.77-0.86

(compared to several times a day for AVHRR). The sensor was designed to monitor floods, droughts, forest fires, and other dynamic natural events covering broad areas **(see Color Plate 9.9)**.

Figure 9.31 The 5.8-meter-resolution panchromatic imagery from India's IRS-1C and -1D satellites, such as this image of the Tucson airport, ushered in a new generation of advanced remote sensing devices that facilitate applications in urban areas.

IKONOS and Quickbird

Two new commercial satellite systems, **IKONOS** and **Quickbird**, give us images from space at the spatial resolution of aerial photography. In 1999 the Space Imaging Corporation launched the IKONOS satellite into a sun-synchronous 680-km. (423-mi.) orbit. This orbit and the pointable sensor make it possible to image the same area every three days in an 11-km.-wide swath.

The IKONOS sensor collects panchromatic (0.45-0.9 μm) images with 1-meter spatial resolution (**Figure 9.32**). In multispectral mode, blue, green, red, and near-IR images are collected at a 4-meter resolution (see **Color Plate 9.10**).

In 2001, the DigitalGlobe Corporation launched the Quickbird satellite into a 470-km. sun-synchronous orbit. Its high-resolution sensor collects 0.7-m.-resolution panchromatic (0.45-0.9 μm) images as 11×11 km. frames or 11×225 km. strip maps (**Figure 9.33**). In multispectral mode, blue, green, red, and near-IR images are generated at 2.8-m. resolution (see **Color Plate 9.11**).

This high-resolution imagery will open remote sensing to a wide range of new uses. Past applications of civilian space imagery were largely restricted to landcover and general thematic analysis. The spatial detail (shape, size, texture, pattern) that can be

Figure 9.32 IKONOS satellite 1-meter-resolution panchromatic image of the Great Pyramid at Giza, Egypt.

Figure 9.33 Quickbird satellite 0.7-meter-resolution panchromatic image of the Washington Monument.

Figure 9.34 This AVHRR mosaic of California and Nevada shows the general structure of the physical landscape as well as a smoke plume from a fire at Pt. Reyes (center of image).

seen in high-resolution space imagery will make it possible to identify individual features. This will make space imagery suitable for creating large-scale topographic maps, whereas cartographic use of imagery from prior generations of civilian space sensors was restricted to smaller-scale mapping of landcover, ocean temperatures, and other surface features.

AVHRR

The NOAA series of sun-synchronous meteorological satellites has now gone through several generations of technology. The most recent satellites carry an **Advanced Very-High-Resolution Radiometer (AVHRR)** in an 833-km., near-polar orbit. A ground swath 2,400 km. wide allows each satellite to cover the entire surface of the earth every 12 hours. Directly below the spacecraft, ground resolution is 1.1 km., and it decreases rapidly away from this point. This means a raw AVHRR image exhibits severe scale distortion. The images you see have usually undergone geometrical manipulation so that the spatial resolution is approximately 4 km. (**Figure 9.34**).

The AVHRR sensor records five spectral bands: a panchromatic band, near-IR, mid-IR, and two in the thermal-infrared bands. The relatively poor spatial resolution of AVHRR imagery is balanced by its high temporal resolution global coverage. Thus, it has proven useful in regional and global studies. It is particularly suited to monitoring vegetation changes and has been used to make global portraits of vegetation conditions and national or continental image mosaics in true color or false color (see **Color Plate 9.12**).

Geostationary Weather Satellites

The space imagery with the broadest coverage is that from weather satellites positioned in an easterly orbit above the equator at an altitude of 35,680 km. (22,300 mi.). These **Geostationary Operational Environmental Satellites (GOES)** have a 24-hour orbital period in the same direction as the earth's rotation and hence maintain a "fixed" position with respect to the equator. The **GOES West** and **GOES East** satellites obtain the weather images of the United States you see on television. These two satellites record images of the western and eastern U.S. every 15 minutes and the entire hemisphere every three hours.

A single GOES image covers millions of

square miles of ground surface, making it possible to see the cloud patterns over half of the United States instantaneously (**Figure 9.35**). By studying images taken every fifteen minutes, you can easily see the detailed movement of clouds. This imagery has been used to produce dramatic weather system videos that are commonly seen on TV weather broadcasts. The resolution of ground details on weather satellite imagery is extremely poor, however. Consequently, the use of the imagery is essentially restricted to broad-scale atmospheric phenomena.

Hyperspectral Imaging

As the spatial resolution of imagery increases, so does the need for greater spectral resolution. While pixel size is crucial in identifying features by their spatial form, spectral resolution helps us identify objects by their composition. For technical reasons, space sensors to date have had only limited spectral resolution. Less than 10 spectral bands is the current standard.

For some time, researchers have been experimenting with sensors having tens to hundreds of separate, very narrow spectral bands. Technical development has now progressed to the point where these **hyperspectral sensors** are flown in aircraft and on new earth resources satellites, such as MODIS.

MODIS

The **Moderate Resolution Imaging Spectroradiometer (MODIS)** is one of the five sensors aboard NASA's Terra satellites. Terra's 705-km. sun-synchronous orbit around the earth is timed so that the entire earth's surface is imaged every 1 to 2 days. Data are acquired in 36 spectral bands ranging from blue through thermal IR. Most of these bands have a 1-km. spatial resolution, although two are at 250-m. and five at 500-m. resolution **(see Color Plate 9.13)**.

MODIS images help improve our understanding of global dynamics and physical processes occurring on the land, in the oceans, and in the lower atmosphere (**Figure 9.36**). Digital image data from MODIS play an important role in the development of earth system models. These models predict global change accurately enough to help policy makers arrive at sound decisions to protect our environment.

Figure 9.35 A single image taken from a GOES geosynchronous weather satellite covers half of the United States.

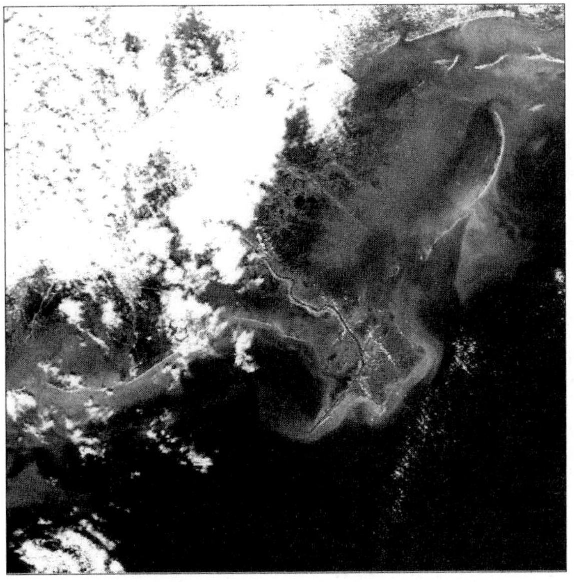

Figure 9.36 MODIS image of the Mississippi River delta.

IMAGE MAPS

Although remote sensor images are excellent at showing many aspects of the landscape, they may fail to depict others. Intangible features, such as political boundaries, aren't commonly picked up on photographic or electronic images. Such useful aids as geographical names, map scale, direction indicators, and positional reference grids are absent from raw images. Features on raw images aren't classified and identified in a key or legend. Features that do appear on images are sometimes so subtle or obscure that they are difficult to identify.

For all these reasons, remote sensor images are often made more interpretable and useful by cartographically enhancing them with lines, words, numbers, and colors. These features are laid over the image base, producing an **image map**. **Orthophotomaps** produced by the USGS to supplement its 1:24,000 topographic map series, provide an example. On these image maps, grids, boundaries, and geographical names have been added; features have been outlined; classes of roads have been indicated with different symbols; and colors have been used to differentiate between classes of features (see **Color Plate 9.14**). Grasslands are yellow, brush and forest green, lakes blue, and contours red.

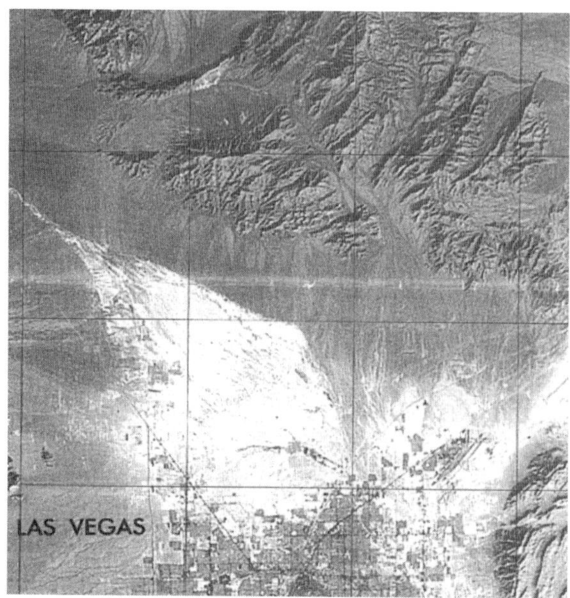

Figure 9.37 Portion of a 1:250,000-scale relief-shaded satellite image map of Las Vegas, Nevada.

Figure 9.38 A Landsat image of the Los Angeles basin has been draped over a digital elevation model and shown in oblique perspective.

There is an important difference between orthophotoquads and orthophotomaps. On the orthophotoquads, all photographic information remains intact, whereas on the orthophotomaps some of this information has been removed and shown in some other way. For instance, major roads have been symbolized with lines and colors, while open water has been colored a flat blue. If this practice of substituting abstract symbols for photographic tones were carried to its logical extreme, the result would no longer resemble the original image and would be more like a topographic map.

Traditional map linework and lettering is also commonly added to geometrically corrected satellite images, creating what we call **satellite image maps**. Very realistic satellite image maps result from combining digital elevation model (DEM) data with the images as relief shading (**Figure 9.37**). The ultimate enhancement is to drape the images over the DEM to create a satellite image map in oblique perspective view (**Figure 9.38**). A series of these image maps can be put together into an animated sequence that appears to be a flight through the area.

Animated Fly-overs

Programs that simulate flight over the landscape are finding many uses. Multimedia atlases boast of dozens of fly-over clips. Scientists use fly-overs to

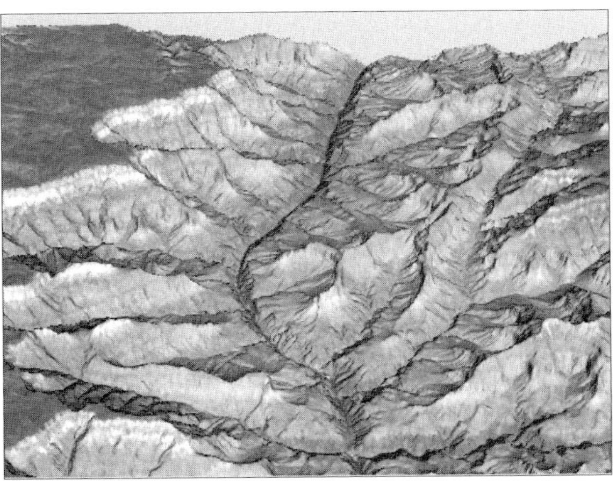

Figure 9.39 One frame from a predetermined full-motion fly-over of the Grand Canyon in Arizona.

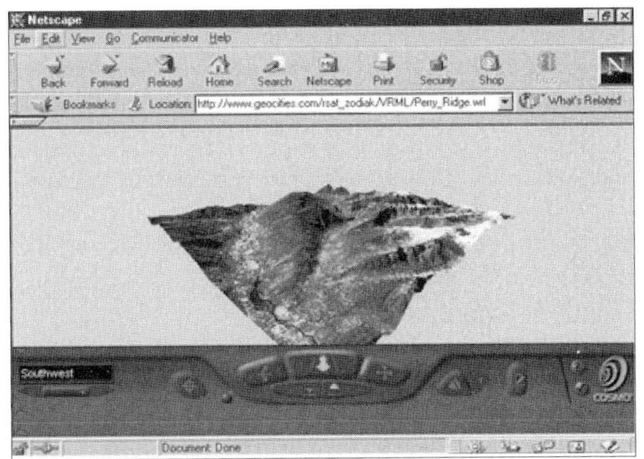

Figure 9.40 Screen shot of an interactive virtual reality system real-time fly-over. The controls below the image allow you to pan, zoom, rotate, and tilt the image.

study the landscape from all angles to better grasp the nature of their subject.

For such fly-overs to be realistic, full-motion video is required. Thus, a powerful computer is needed to produce the 30 or so frames a second required for smooth motion. A database holding the digital image information must be available, along with a digital elevation model needed to create the fly-over. Supporting software must be able to produce an image of the landscape from any vantage point.

The least flexible and most inexpensive fly-over systems display images from vantage points in a pre-selected flight path. The most primitive products generate only still pictures. Although a number of such images can be created by repeating the commands with new vantage points, rarely would more than a few images be called for by a map user.

The exception is when someone puts together a large sequence of images to simulate a full-motion fly-over. This was done, for example, with the Grand Canyon in Arizona (**Figure 9.39**) using Landsat images draped over a digital elevation model.

The inflexibility and lack of user control that characterizes predetermined sequences is overcome in more sophisticated interactive **virtual reality** systems that contain the software and image database needed to compute a sequence of views as you specify new vantage points. You may perform such a **real-time fly-over** by moving a joystick or entering a series of vantage point coordinates from a keyboard (**Figure 9.40**). The advantage of this approach is that you have complete flexibility in choosing a flight path. You can continuously pan, zoom, rotate, and tilt the image so that it appears you are flying over the image.

SELECTED READINGS

Barrett, E.C., and Curtis, L.F., *Introduction to Environmental Remote Sensing*, 3rd ed. (London: Chapman & Hall, 1992).

Carleton, A.M., *Satellite Remote Sensing in Climatology* (CRC Press, Inc. 1991).

Campanella, R., "High-Resolution Satellite Imagery for Business," *Business Geographics* (March 1996), pp. 36-39.

Campbell, J.B., *Introduction to Remote Sensing*, 2nd ed. (New York: The Guilford Press, 1996).

Chedin, A., *Microwave Remote Sensing of the Earth System* (Hampton, VA: A. DeePak Publishing, 1989).

Chien, P., "High Spies," *Popular Mechanics* (Feb. 1996), pp. 47-51.

Ciciarelli, J.A., *Practical Guide to Aerial Photography: With an Introduction to Surveying* (New York: Van Nostrand Reinhold, 1991).

Cook, W.J., "Ahead of the Weather: New Technologies Let Forecasters Make Faster, More Accurate Predictions," *U.S. News & World Report* (April 29, 1996), pp. 55-57.

Corbley, K.P., "Applications of High-Resolution Imagery," *Geo Info Systems* (May 1997), pp. 36-40.

Corbley, K.P., "Multispectral Imagery: Identifying More than Meets the Eye," *Geo Info Systems* (June 1997), pp. 38-43.

Corbley, K.P., "Regional Imagery: Wide Angle Advantages, Wide-Ranging Applications," *Geo Info Systems* (April 1997), pp. 28-33.

Cracknell, A.P., and Hayes, L.W., *Introduction to Remote Sensing* (New York: Taylor & Francis, 1991).

Dickinson, G.C., *Maps and Air Photographs*, 2nd ed. (New York: John Wiley & Sons, 1979).

Evans, D.L., et al., "Earth from the Sky," *Scientific American* (Dec. 1994), pp. 70-75.

Falkner, E., *Aerial Mapping* (Boca Raton, FL: CRC Press, Inc., 1994).

Hamit, F., "Where GOES Has Gone: NOAA's Weather Satellite Imagery and GIS-Marketed," *Advanced Imaging* (Nov. 1996), pp. 60-64.

Jensen, L.C., et al., "Side-Looking Airborne Radar," *The Scientific American*, 237, 4 (October 1977), pp. 84-95.

Lillesand, T.M., and Kiefer, R.W., *Remote Sensing and Image Interpretation*, 3rd ed. (New York: John Wiley & Sons, 1994).

Nicolson, I., *Sputnik to Space Shuttle: The Complete Story of Space Flight* (New York: Dodd, Mead & Co., 1985).

Office of Technology Assessment, U.S. Congress, *The Future of Remote Sensing from Space: Civilian Satellite Systems and Applications* (Washington, DC: U.S. Gov. Printing Officer, 1993).

Rees, W.G., *Physical Principles of Remote Sensing* (New York: Cambridge University Press, 1990).

Silverman, J., Mooney, J.M., and Shepherd, F.D., "Infrared Video Cameras," *Scientific American*, 266, 3 (March 1992), pp. 78-83.

Uhlir, D.M., "Hyperspectral Imagery: On the Brink of Commercial Acceptance," *Earth Observation Magazine* (Feb. 1995).

CHAPTER TEN
MAP ACCURACY

Thinking they were in Canada, and not the area which is now Maine, the McKinnon Brothers settled at the head of the Mattagash River. Oral history says they stopped where they did because one of the women had to pee. In truth, it may have been inaccurate maps.
—Cathie Pelletier, The Funeral Makers

10

CHAPTER TEN

MAP ACCURACY

Mapping, like architecture, is an example of functional design. Unlike an artist's representation of the environment in which geometric liberties are taken in order to convey an idea or emotion, a map is expected to be true to the location and structure of our surroundings. Indeed, our willingness to let maps "stand in" for the environment is due to this adherence to reality.

All graphic representation involves distortion, of course. You either deal directly with reality, or you deal indirectly with a fake version of reality. Fakes by nature are unreal and, therefore, distorted. Since maps are a form of representation, they're no exception. What, then, do we mean by adherence to reality in mapping?

The term **map accuracy** refers to the degree to which a map is true to reality. Map accuracy turns out to be a complex topic, especially since maps are increasingly made from digital data taken from existing maps. In this chapter, we'll consider what we mean by map accuracy and how accuracy information is conveyed to the map user.

TRUTH OR REPRESENTATION?

Beware of the trap of thinking the map shows the truth. Those creating spatial databases by scanning or digitizing maps, and those using computer analysis to extract details from these cartographic databases, need to stop and reflect on the nature of mapping. If you want truth, you should embrace reality directly. If you want the convenience of maps representing reality, then you should consider what it means to map the environment.

The map lets you escape the complexity of the environment and look at a simplified, scale-reduced version of your surroundings. This version of reality may be useful for many purposes, but don't pretend it is true. Using maps helps you to be objective and analytical. Maps let you see the effects of playing out countless "what if..." scenarios—what would the environment look like if you did this? It is these ways of using maps that make them such a powerful tool for thought and communication.

ACCURACY OR PRECISION?

The words "accuracy" and "precision" have different definitions. **Accuracy** means fidelity to the truth. How well, for example, do measured map coordinates conform to the true coordinates of a position? It sounds simple. But which datum do we use to establish true coordinates? Obviously, truth in this case is defined relative to some agreed-upon standard.

Precision is more complicated. It's often used synonymously with accuracy, but there is an important distinction between the two. Precision has three meanings:

• the number of significant digits reported for a measurement
• the repeatability of measurements or the agreement among measurements
• the rigor and sophistication of the measuring process.

Be careful when using the terms "accuracy" and "precision," even though many people use them interchangeably. The topic of map accuracy is confusing enough without the added problem of sloppy language usage. Analyzing what is meant when you see or hear the term "accuracy" or "precision" will help you deal with the subject more effectively.

TYPES OF MAP ACCURACY

Many subjects that seem simple turn out, upon closer inspection, to be surprisingly complex. This is the case with map accuracy. The more you think about the topic, the more facets you discover. Rather than treat map accuracy as a single issue, we'll approach the topic from the perspective of types of accuracy. We'll discuss five aspects of map accuracy: positional errors, conceptual effects, generalization effects, factual errors, and timeliness.

Positional Accuracy

We depend on maps to give us the locations of things. In many cases, location means the horizontal position of an object—its latitude and longitude, for example. But, since we live in a three-dimensional world, location also has a vertical component. Thus, we speak of the elevation of the land surface, or the altitude of an aircraft or spacecraft. Any discussion of **positional accuracy** is with reference to horizontal position, vertical position, or both.

Many maps produced in the United States include the marginal notation, **"This map complies with National Map Accuracy Standards."** To learn what this statement really means, read the explanation in **Box 10.1**. Here you'll find that, as far as **National Map Accuracy Standards (NMAS)** are concerned, both horizontal and vertical map accuracy is measured statistically. You will see that acceptable accuracy decreases progressively as map scale decreases. Horizontal accuracy also pertains only to "well-defined points," such as surveyed triangulation points and bench marks. Since only a few points on a map are actually tested to see if the map meets National Map Accuracy Stan-

Box 10.1 UNITED STATES NATIONAL MAP ACCURACY STANDARDS

With a view to the utmost economy and expedition in producing maps which fulfill not only the broad needs for standard or principal maps, but also the reasonable particular needs of individual agencies, standards of accuracy for published maps are defined as follows:

1. Horizontal accuracy. For maps on publication scales larger than 1:20,000, not more than 10 percent of the points tested shall be in error by more than 1/30 inch, measured on the publication scale; for maps on publication scales of 1:20,000 or smaller, 1/50 inch. These limits of accuracy shall apply in all cases to positions of well-defined points only. Well-defined points are those that are easily visible or recoverable on the ground, such as the following: monuments or markers, such as bench marks, property boundary monuments; intersections of roads, railroads, etc.; corners of large buildings or structures (or center points of small buildings); etc. In general, what is well defined will also be determined by what is plottable on the scale of the map within 1/100 inch. Thus, while the intersection of two roads or property lines meeting at right angles would come within a sensible interpretation, identification of the intersection of such lines meeting at an acute angle would obviously not be practicable within 1/100 inch. Similarly, features not identifiable upon the ground within close limits are not to be considered as test points within the limits quoted, even though their positions may be scaled closely upon the map. In this class would come timber lines, soil boundaries, etc.

2. Vertical accuracy, as applied to contour maps on all publication scales, shall be such that not more than 10 percent of the elevations tested shall be in error more than one-half the contour interval. In checking elevations taken from the map, the apparent vertical error may be decreased by assuming a horizontal displacement within the permissible horizontal error for a map of that scale.

3. The accuracy of any map may be tested by comparing the positions of points whose locations or elevations are shown upon it with corresponding positions as determined by surveys of a higher accuracy. Tests shall be made by the producing agency, which shall also determine which of its maps are to be tested, and the extent of such testing.

4. Published maps meeting these accuracy requirements shall note this fact on their legends, as follows: "This map complies with National Map Accuracy Standards."

5. Published maps whose errors exceed those aforestated shall omit from their legends all mention of standard accuracy.

6. When a published map is a considerable enlargement of a map drawing (manuscript) or of a published map, that fact shall be stated in the legend. For example, "This map is an enlargement of a 1:20,000-scale map drawing," or "This map is an enlargement of a 1:24,000-scale published map."

7. To facilitate ready interchange and use of basic information for map construction among all federal map making agencies, manuscript maps and published maps, wherever economically feasible and consistent with the uses to which the map is to be put, shall conform to latitude and longitude boundaries, being 15 minutes of latitude and longitude, or 7.5 minutes, or 3-3/4 minutes in size.

Issued June 10, 1941
Revised April 26, 1943
Revised June 17, 1947

U.S. BUREAU OF THE BUDGET

Source: Thompson, *Maps for America*, p. 104

Box 10.2 VEGETATION ON STANDARD TOPOGRAPHIC MAPS

Many of the intricate vegetation patterns existing in nature cannot be depicted exactly by line drawings. It is therefore necessary in some places to omit less important scattered growth and to generalize complex outlines.

Types

The term "woodland" is generally used loosely to designate all vegetation represented on topographic maps. For mapping purposes, vegetation is divided into six types, symbolized as shown, and defined as follows:

- Woodland (woods-brushwood). An area of normally dry land containing tree cover or brush that is potential tree cover. The growth must be at least 6 feet (2 m.) tall and dense enough to afford cover for troops.
- Scrub. An area covered with low-growing or stunted perennial vegetation, such as cactus, mesquite, or sagebrush, common to arid regions and usually not mixed with trees.
- Orchard. A planting of evenly spaced trees or tall bushes that bear fruit or nuts. Plantings of citrus and nut trees, commonly called groves, are included in this type.
- Vineyard. A planting of grapevines, usually supported and arranged in evenly-spaced rows. Other kinds of cultivated climbing plants, such as berry vines and hops, are typed as vineyards for mapping purposes.
- Mangrove. A dense, almost impenetrable growth of tropical maritime trees with aerial roots. Mangrove thrives where the movement of tidewater is minimal—in shallow bays and deltas, and along riverbanks.
- Wooded marsh. An area of normally wet land with tree cover or brush that is potential tree cover.

Density

Woods, brushwood, and scrub are mapped if the growth is thick enough to provide cover for troops or to impede foot travel. This condition is considered to exist if density of the vegetative cover is 20 percent or more. Growth that meets the minimum density requirement is estimated as follows: If the average open-space distance between the crowns is equal to the average crown diameter, the density of the vegetative cover is 20 percent.

This criterion is not a hard-and-fast rule, however, because 20 percent crown density cannot be determined accurately if there are irregularly scattered trees and gradual transitions from the wooded to the cleared areas. Therefore, where such growth occurs, the minimum density requirement varies between 20 and 35 percent, and the woodland boundary is drawn where there is a noticeable change in density. A crown density of 35 percent exists if the average open space between the crowns is equal to one-half the average crown diameter.

Orchards and vineyards are shown regardless of crown density. Mangrove, by definition, is dense, almost impenetrable growth; crown density is not a factor in mapping mangrove boundaries.

(continued..)

Box 10.2 *continued*

Areas

On 7.5- and 15-minute maps, woodland areas covering 1 acre (0.4 ha.) or more are shown regardless of shape. This area requirement applies both to individual tracts of vegetation and to areas of one type within or adjoining another type. Narrow strips of vegetation and isolated tracts covering areas smaller than the specified minimum are shown only if they are considered to be landmarks. Accordingly, shelterbelts and small patches of trees in arid or semiarid regions are shown, whereas single rows of trees or bushes along fences, roads, or perennial streams are not mapped.

Clearings

The minimum area specified for woodland cover on 7.5- and 15-minute maps—1 acre (0.4 ha.)—also applies to clearings within woodland. Isolated clearings smaller than the specified minimum are shown if they are considered to be landmarks.

Clearings along mapped linear features, such as power transmission lines, telephone lines, pipelines, roads, and railroads, are shown if the break in woodland cover is 100 feet (30 m.) or more wide. The minimum symbol width for a clearing in which a linear feature is shown is 100 feet at map scale. Clearings wider than 100 feet are mapped to scale.

Landmark linear clearings 40 feet (12 m.) or more wide, in which no feature is mapped, are shown to scale. Firebreaks are shown and labeled if they are 20 feet (6 m.) or more wide and do not adjoin or coincide with other cultural features. The minimum symbol width for a firebreak clearing is 40 feet at map scale; firebreaks wider than 40 feet are shown to scale.

Source: Thompson, *Maps for America*, pp. 70-71

dards, even the accuracy of most well-defined points is unknown. And, since map accuracy is statistically defined, the standards say nothing about the accuracy you can expect to find with respect to a specific point.

If you feel National Map Accuracy Standards are a bit vague about how close a map feature is to its ground location, you're on even shakier ground with maps that don't meet National Map Accuracy Standards. There is simply no way to ascertain the accuracy of data taken from these maps. We can expect, however, that the larger the map scale, the more reliable the plotted positions of features will be.

Conceptual Accuracy

The second aspect of map accuracy is called **conceptual accuracy**, because it concerns features that are mental abstractions rather than concrete objects with clearly defined boundaries. Soil, wetland, and forest boundaries meet this criterion. They all have boundaries that are transitional and difficult to find in the field.

To appreciate what we mean by conceptual accuracy, read the material concerning vegetation mapping on standard topographic maps provided in **Boxes 10.2** and **10.3**. Notice that the definitions of vegetation type, density, vegetated areas, and clearings are all human creations. The intricacy of the pattern to be mapped, the map scale, and the importance assigned to features all enter into the cartographer's judgment of how the mapping should be carried out.

Box 10.3 WOODLAND BOUNDARY ACCURACY ON STANDARD TOPOGRAPHIC MAPS

- **Clearly defined woodland boundaries** are plotted with standard accuracy, the same as any other well-defined planimetric feature. If there are gradual changes from wooded to cleared areas, the outlines are plotted to indicate the limits of growth meeting the minimum density requirement. If the growth occurs in intricate patterns, the outlines show the general shapes of the wooded areas. Outlines representing these ill-defined or irregular limits of vegetative cover are considered to be approximate because they do not necessarily represent lines that can be accurately identified on the ground. The outline of a tract of tall, dense timber represents the centerline of the bounding row of trees rather than the outside limits of the branches or the shadow line.
- **In large tracts of dense evergreen timber**, sharp dividing lines between different tree heights may be shown with the fence- and field-line symbol. Published maps containing fence-line symbols that represent fences and other landmark lines in wooded areas bear the following statement in the tailored legend: "Fine red dashed lines indicate selected fence, field, or landmark lines where generally visible on aerial photographs. This information is unchecked."
- **Woodland** is not shown in urban-tint areas, but it is shown where appropriate in areas surrounded by urban tint if such areas are equivalent to or larger than the average city block.
- **Mangrove** is shown on the published map with the standard mangrove pattern and the green woodland tint. Breaks in the mangrove cover usually indicate water channels that provide routes for penetrating the dense growth.

Source: Thompson, *Maps for America*, pp. 71-72

The accuracy of conceptual boundaries such as those surrounding forested areas on topographic maps means something quite different from the accuracy of discrete features, such as roads, on the same map. National Map Accuracy Standards for positional accuracy don't apply to these conceptually defined features.

Generalization and Map Accuracy

Even environmental features that are well defined, such as roads, rivers, or coastlines, don't get mapped in all possible detail. These linear features and edges of areal features are smoothed on the map. We call this loss of detail **line generalization**. The degree of generalization is proportional to a feature's spatial detail, and inversely proportional to map scale (**Figure 10.1**). Thus, on a state highway map, a smooth high-speed expressway is likely to be less generalized than a sinuous low-speed county road.

Generalization causes a displacement of features as smoothing cuts off natural irregularities. But is this shift of a linear feature's position an example of positional error? Is a map of the world on a postage stamp best critiqued in terms of its generalization errors? We think not.

To say generalization is error misses the point. You might better think in terms of generalization effects, not generalization errors. By concentrating on generalization effects, attention is focused on the necessity of cartographic generalization rather than on the inevitable positional distortions. And, as you've probably guessed by now, U.S. National Map Accuracy Standards make no attempt to address the effects of generalization on map accuracy.

Factual Errors

Sometimes features are left off a map by mistake. A lake or town may have been overlooked by the

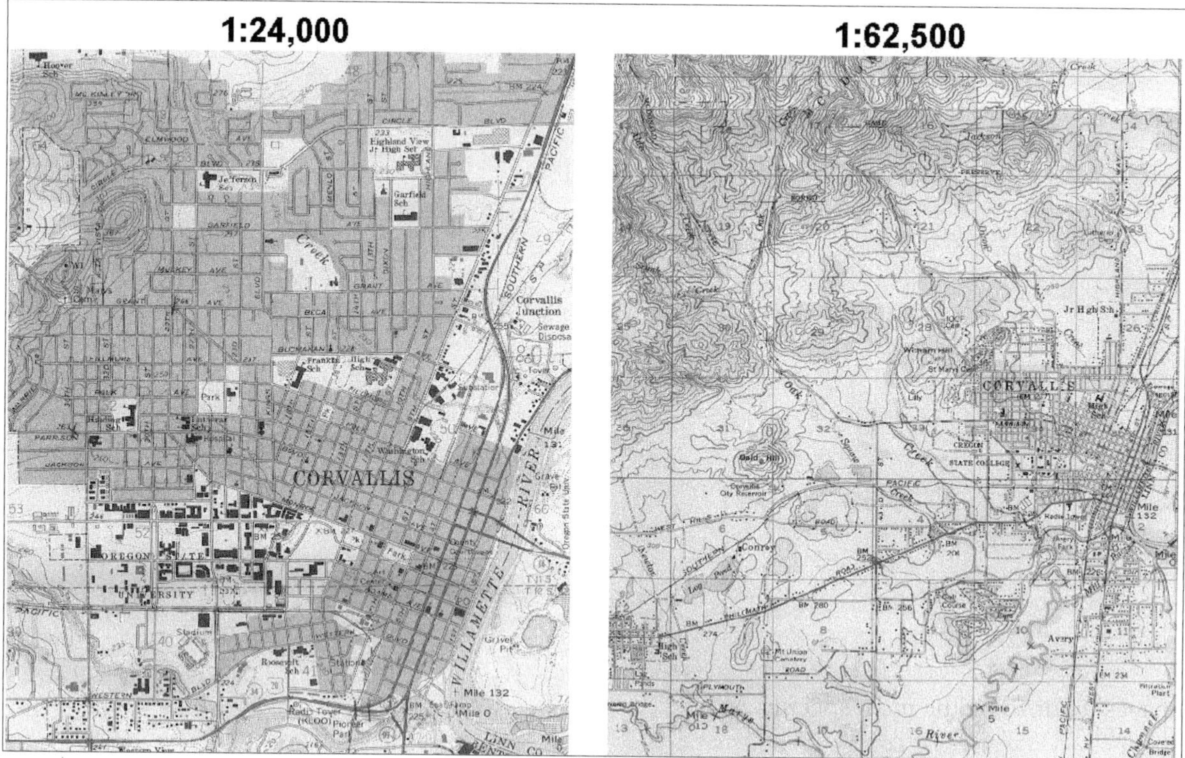

Figure 10.1 The degree of positional inaccuracy due to line generalization is proportional to a feature's spatial detail, and inversely proportional to map scale. Notice the progressive smoothing of linear features as the map scale is reduced.

cartographer.* In other cases, features found on the map don't exist in the environment. Sometimes a name or symbol is misplaced on the map. At other times a feature has disappeared from the environment, but its map symbol persists. Still other errors occur when a feature is misclassified by its map symbol, as when a railroad is shown as a road. These are all examples of **factual errors**. Thorough map editing can minimize errors of this type, but since map makers rely on data from diverse sources, mistakes can be made at many levels. Cartographers rely on feedback from map users to keep from repeating mistakes in subsequent map editions.

The previous comments refer to mapped features, such as roads, towns, or rivers. Image processing, on the other hand, yields a pixel-by-pixel landcover classification, not a set of features defined by boundary coordinates. Mistakes in classifying pixels represent a special type of factual error, called **attribute error**. Most pixels falling in a feature such as a lake may be classified correctly, but pixels falling partly on the shoreline may be misclassified. Pixels within a lake that fall on a boat or weedbed may also be misclassified, since they won't exhibit the spectral characteristics of open water.

We must assess factual or attribute errors differently from positional errors. In contrast to positional errors, which vary in size, factual errors either occur, or they don't occur. If factual errors were known, they would be corrected as a matter of professional pride. In the case of misclassification errors on image maps, a report of the average number of attribute errors counted

**Features left off the map on purpose by the cartographer for design or copyright reasons aren't included in this "overlooked" feature category.*

on similar maps is sometimes given. Thus, testing may show that pixel classification is subject to an approximate error rate of, say, 15%.

Datedness

One of the first things you should do when you pick up any map is to look at the date it was completed. Here you may immediately run into trouble, for many maps aren't dated. At times the date is left off inadvertently. At other times, map makers deliberately avoid adding dates so that maps won't appear outdated through long revision cycles. Even if there is a date, it may be hidden in a corner of the map, written in a cryptic code. Tracking down the approximate date of these maps may take some detective work, such as looking on the map for a spot you know has been altered recently.

On many maps, of course, the completion date is clearly shown. The date on remote sensing images tends to be the most specific. Most dates on standard low-altitude photographs, for instance, are given to the nearest day. Dates on conventional maps are usually less specific, as you would suspect, since the features shown on most maps don't represent data gathered at one instant in time. The completion date may be one of several dates connected with making the map.

Problems of timeliness increase when maps and other sources of information used in mapping aren't properly dated. The map may have been compiled, unknowingly, from information collected at very different times. The growing use of digital information records in mapping invites problems of this sort, because the source date of these records may not be recorded in the description (called **metadata**) for the digital file.

Another thing that contributes to factual errors on maps is the fact that environmental features change through time. The map may have been correct when made but now is outdated. Or the map may have been out-of-date at the time of production. This happens when the map maker isn't aware that features have been added or deleted from the environment since data for mapping were gathered. Even maps which are changed at short intervals, such as special navigational charts, are never truly up to date. Most ephemeral features, such as icebergs or severe storms, are inaccurately shown or remain unmapped and must be dealt with directly in the field or through supplementary sources of information.

An outdated map can lead to serious, even deadly, confusion. For instance, if new interchanges have been constructed since information was collected for a road map, you may miss the correct exit and become disoriented. Map makers sometimes try to extend a map's practical life by mapping interchanges which have been planned but not yet built. The problem is that if the proposed roads are never constructed or aren't completed on schedule, as often happens, the map will be more misleading than ever.

The question, then, is how "dated" a map can be and still be accurate enough to be useful. As usual, there is no one answer. You probably can tolerate different degrees of datedness with respect to different features and in different circumstances. Map datedness depends on both the rate and pattern of change of environmental features and on your ability to imagine how the environment might look 5, 10, or 25 years after the map was made. Most of all, your tolerance of map datedness depends on the consequences of arriving at a wrong conclusion about the environment through map use. Sometimes an outdated map may merely be inconvenient; at other times, it may be fatal.

Three factors can make a map outdated. First, the time it took to complete the map, or the mapping period, might have been excessive. Second, a long time may have elapsed since the map was made. Finally, the varying temporal stability of environmental features must be considered. Let's examine each of these factors in turn.

Mapping Period

The first factor in map datedness, **mapping period**, is often overlooked, but it can have a major effect on map use. If the time between initial data collection and final map printing is lengthy and if phenomena change rapidly, the map can be badly out of date before it is even completed.

You can see that a map's completion date tells only part of the story. It is equally important to know the mapping period. But if the completion date isn't always given directly on a map, the length of the mapping period almost never is. Some maps do include the dates of source information, though, and these dates will give you a clue to the mapping period. Notes on USGS topographic quadrangles, for example, tell when photographs were taken and when field checking of the map compilation was completed. Maps that use census information usually give the date of data collection. Most maps, however, don't include even this basic information.

Look at the corner of the topographic quadrangle in **Figure 10.2**. The publication and map editing date is 1992, but the map was compiled from 1985 aerial photography. In many respects, then, the map was effectively seven years old when first published! It's important to realize that even a new map may, in a sense, be old if the mapping period was long.

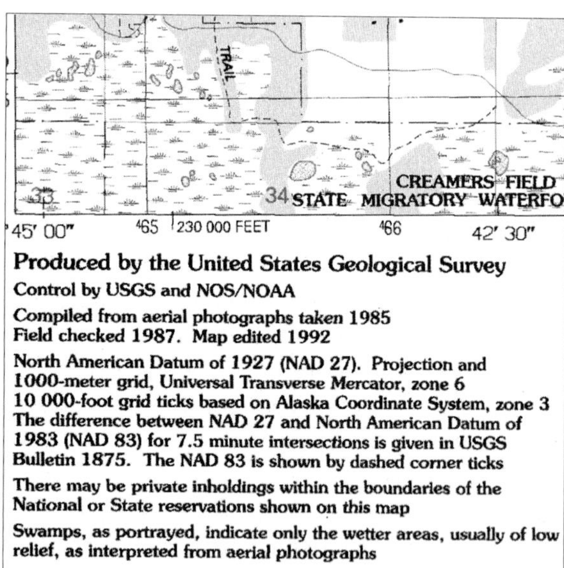

Figure 10.2 It's good practice to pay attention to the dates printed on maps. The publication date on this USGS topographic quadrangle is 1992, but the date of the aerial photography used to compile the map is 1985.

Confusion over mapping period sometimes arises where least expected. Image maps are a good example. It is true that individual aerial photos give you an instantaneous view of the environment. But image maps covering large ground areas at smaller scales are often created by taking a number of photos and then putting them together into an image mosaic. (See Chapter 9 for more on image mosaics.) The photos used to make the mosaic may have been gathered over a period of hours, days, months, or—in the case of space image maps made up of several satellite images—years.

Usually, however, image maps have a shorter mapping period than conventional maps. This means that image maps are generally better than conventional maps at representing rapidly changing features such as plant diseases or water pollution.

When conventional maps are produced with a fully computerized system, however, their mapping period can be shortened remarkably. Computer maps can be completed only minutes after information is collected, especially if automated recording stations send information directly to the computer. Computer maps of a short-lived or rapidly changing feature can be in the user's hands while the feature still exists—not after it is of only historical interest, as with most handmade maps.

Elapsed Time

The second factor in map datedness is the **elapsed time** since the map was completed. A map which provided an accurate picture of conditions when it was printed may be of little use to you today because too many features have changed. The faster environmental features change, the shorter the acceptable elapsed time since mapping.

Sometimes an elapsed time problem is caused by the fact that maps of a certain region haven't been revised for a long time. Map makers tend to give higher priority to mapping hitherto unmapped regions than to updating old maps. Their logic is that it's easier for the user to cope with an outdated map than no map at all.

At other times, the trouble is that, although updated maps have been made, you don't happen to have one. Who hasn't known the frustration of trying to use a 20-year-old road map unearthed from the depths of the glove compartment? These outdated maps can cause no end of confusion. If you are such a skilled map user that you instantly spot changes in the environment and know what decisive action to take, you may be able to manage with an old map. But most people caught in this situation could better spend their effort locating a new map.

The elapsed time problem can be circumvented by producing maps on display screens from current information stored in computer memory. Since you view the screen directly, there is no lapse in time. There are difficulties with these electronic maps, however, primarily because not enough information has yet been stored in computers and because display units are still bulky and expensive. It shouldn't be long, though, before you'll be able to create up-to-date maps at will on your home television screen or on a display console in your car.

Temporal Stability of Features

Map use problems stemming from mapping period and elapsed time are complicated further by the varying **temporal stability** of features. Different features on the same map change at different rates. As a result, some features will hardly have changed since the map was begun, while others will be vastly different or will have disappeared altogether.

Some features are also more sensitive than others to short-term, intermittent datedness. Roads are temporarily closed, for example, due to routine roadbed and bridge maintenance. Storms may cause temporary highway blockages. Rivers swollen by spring runoff or storm-induced flooding may be unnavigable for short periods. Certain soils may become impassable to farm equipment or recreational vehicles during spring break-up and periods of rainfall. To read maps effectively, we must grasp the effects of these and similar short-term conditions.

COMMUNICATING MAP ACCURACY

Symbols and Notations

The most direct way cartographers communicate varying degrees of map accuracy to users is with symbols that indicate differences in accuracy. They may make line symbols for less accurately known boundaries broken instead of solid, for example (**Figure 10.3A**). On topographic maps, you'll find dotted and dashed lines used for less accurately positioned supplemental contour lines and form lines. Another map design strategy is to make the clarity or sharpness of symbols increase with higher accuracy data. Less accurately located features are portrayed with blurred or fuzzy symbols.

A method almost as direct as using map symbols for inaccurate information is to add notes describing areas of lower accuracy on the map. A note such as "This region was not field checked" serves this purpose (**Figure 10.3B**). On aeronautical charts, it's common to find notations of this sort, especially to warn that the general magnetic declination information given on the map may be subject to local disturbance.

Legend Disclaimer

Sometimes a note in the map legend is the only indicator of map accuracy. The statement, "This map meets National Map Accuracy Standards," is an example of this approach. Of course, you have to know what such a statement means. Remember, there are no rules saying that you must be warned of an inaccurate map.

A **legend disclaimer** is commonly found on commercial maps that use government maps as a base. For example, someone may enhance nautical charts with direction and distance information and then market this value-added product. You're likely to find the statement, "This map is for reference only and should not be used for navigational purposes." The aim, of course, is to avoid lawsuits resulting from accidents attributed to the map. It's a curious kind of message, however, since the map is clearly intended for navigational use.

The most common types of legend notes tell you the date of map production and source of the data. The date is especially useful if the mapped region is undergoing rapid change. The source of data gives a hint of its reliability, since some data-gathering organizations have better reputations than others for doing professional quality work. Data from promotional and private-survey groups should be viewed with suspicion.

Reliability Diagram

The third way to communicate map accuracy is through a **reliability diagram**. This is a simple outline map showing variation in source data used to produce the map (**Figure 10.3C**). The diagram may appear in the legend or as an inset near the map margin. The date and source of the data used in mapping are usually provided. You're left to draw your own conclusions about the relative accuracy of information in different parts of the map.

LIABILITY ISSUES

Map accuracy is a concern for both the map maker and map user in a society quick to sue. You compound your problems if you are both map maker and user, as is often the case when working with digital maps. The question is to what degree you place yourself at legal risk when making and using maps. Let's consider map liability issues from the perspective of both maker and user.

Map Maker Responsibility

The interpretation of liability law makes the responsibility of the map maker quite clear. In essence, "every reasonable effort" must be made to ensure map or cartographic database quality. What is reasonable is judged by contemporary professional standards.

Additionally, the map maker must inform or warn map users of potential problems and hazards in using the product. We discussed ways this can be done in the earlier section on Communicating Map Accuracy.

Map User Responsibility

The legal responsibility of the map user is less well-defined than that of the map maker. But the same advice holds true, especially if careless map use on your part has the potential to harm someone else. If your business is to market map-use products, then your responsibility to conduct yourself professionally is increased.

Speaking ethically rather than legally, you probably have no business using maps if low skill on your part could harm others or the environment. You especially have an obligation to get beyond thinking of the map as always showing the truth.

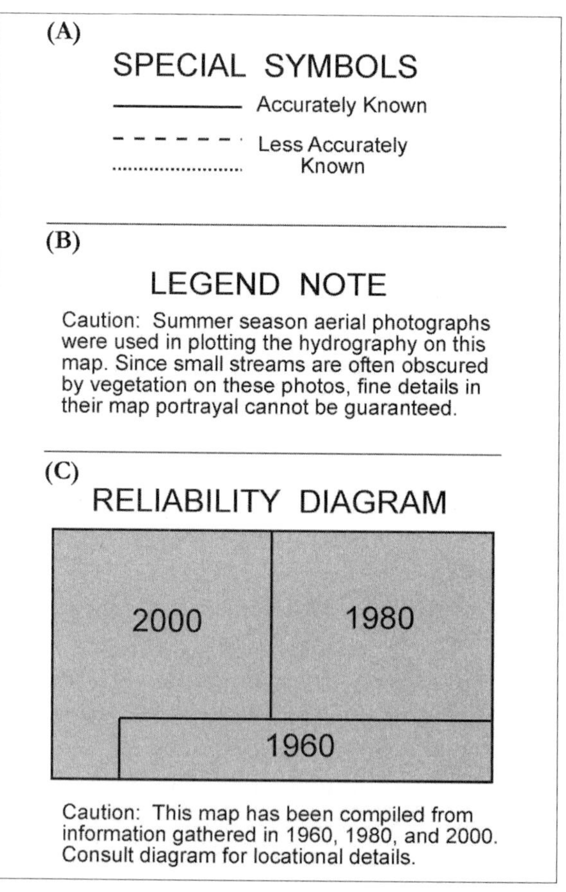

Figure 10.3 The accuracy of mapped features is often indicated by dotted or dashed symbols (A), legend notes (B), or reliability diagrams (C).

CONCLUSION

This discussion of map accuracy isn't meant to scare you away from using maps. As we've noted, maps are graphic representations of the environment, and graphic representation by its very nature involves distortion. This is the paradox of cartography. We're using a distorted representation to make accurate decisions about spatial issues.

Inaccuracies are the price we must pay to obtain the convenience of using maps. Since accuracy problems can't be eliminated, or we would have no map, we must learn to live with them.

Each time you use a map, you should evaluate its accuracy in light of the task at hand. You'll want to ask, "Can I live with the accuracy of this map in this situation?" Or, "What special care should I take if I use this map for this purpose?"

SELECTED READINGS

Buckner, B., "The Nature of Measurement, Part II: Mistakes and Errors," *Professional Surveyor* (April 1997), pp. 19-22.

Buckner, B., "The Nature of Measurement, Part IV: Precision and Accuracy," *Professional Surveyor* (July-August 1997), pp. 49-52.

Chrisman, N.R., "A Diagnostic Test for Error in Categorical Maps," *Proceedings of AUTO-CARTO 10* (Baltimore, MD: American Congress on Surveying and Mapping, 1991), pp. 330-348.

Congalton, R.G., and Green, K., *Assessing the Accuracy of Remotely Sensed Data: Principles and Practices* (Boca Raton, FL: Lewis Publishers, 1997).

Frans, J.M, et al., "Visualization of Data Quality," in A. MacEachren and D.R.F. Taylor, eds., *Visualization in Modern Cartography* (New York: Pergamon Press, 1994), pp. 313-331.

Guptill, S.C., and Morrison, J.L., eds., *Elements of Spatial Data Quality* (London: Elsevier Science Ltd., 1995).

Hopkins, L.D., "Methods of Generating Land Suitability Maps: A Comparative Evaluation," *Journal of American Institute of Planners*, 43, 4 (1977), pp. 386-398.

Lodwick, W.A., Monson, W., and Svoboda, L., "Attribute Error and Sensitivity Analysis of Map Operations in Geographical Information Systems: Suitability Analysis," *International Journal of Geographical Information Systems*, 4, 4 (1990), pp. 413-428.

MacEachren, A.M., *Some Truth with Maps: Primer on Symbolism and Design* (Washington, DC: AAG, 1994).

Monmonier, M., *How to Lie With Maps*, 2nd ed. (Chicago: University of Chicago Press, 1996).

Thompson, M.M., *Maps for America*, 3rd ed. (Washington, DC: U.S. Geographical Survey, 1988).

This map user is converting features on the map into digital form so that distances and areas can be computed.

II

PART TWO
MAP ANALYSIS

In your study of map reading in Part I, you've learned what you might expect to find on a map and gained an appreciation for the mapping process. This information provides the necessary background for the second phase of map use—analysis. Here your goal is to analyze and describe the spatial structure of and relationships among features on maps.

Theoretically, you could carry out spatial analysis directly in the environment. This is rarely done, however—and rightly so, since the same results can be obtained much more easily and inexpensively by analyzing features on maps. A map cuts through the confusion of the environment and makes spatial relationships easier to see. Even a map, however, doesn't make everything apparent at a glance. The purpose of map analysis, therefore, is to reduce the muddle of information on a map to some sort of order so that you can understand it and describe it to other people.

It is possible to do this visually—to view mapped information and describe it by saying, for example, "This area looks hilly" or "That pattern is complex" or "There seems to be a strong correlation between those variables." Traditionally, map analysis has been performed in just such a way. There are problems, however, with a visual approach to map analysis. First of all, such terms as "hilly," "complex," or "correlated" are subjective and vague. They are merely estimates based on personal experience. Two or more people looking at the same map would probably use different terms to describe it. You would also have a hard time conjuring up an image of the landscape on the basis of their nebulous descriptions. What picture comes to mind, for instance, if someone says that a hillside is "steep"? Your mental image of steepness may be quite different from that of the person sitting next to you. Besides, how do you know that you can trust the person who described the hill as steep in the first place? Perhaps his judgment was biased by his poor physical condition and the hill isn't steep at all. Furthermore, all these problems with visual analysis are compounded as patterns grow more complex, as details on maps become more subtle, and as the number of mapped features increases.

Obviously, then, if you're to extract information from a map so that someone else will understand what you have in mind, you need an objective way to describe mapped phenomena. By "objective," we mean repeatable: Two people looking at the same map pattern would describe it in the same way, and you could be sure that their descriptions were trustworthy. Such objectivity is provided by quantitative analysis, in which you use numbers rather than words and replace visual estimation with counting, measurement, and mathematical pattern comparison. These activities let you convert mapped information to numerical data in a rigorous way. You may be satisfied simply with raw numbers—the area and depth of a lake, say, or the measurement of its shoreline, or the number of houses along it. But it's often more interesting to combine raw numbers to obtain more sophisticated information. You might, for instance, want to add up the incomes of people in a state to acquire a state average. You could then compare this figure with average incomes from other states. There are hundreds of similar ways to combine, compare, and manipulate quantitative spatial information.

In theory, quantitative analysis is strictly repeatable. Using the same map and analytical procedures, each map user should arrive at the same conclusions. But there's no limit to the number of mathematical methods from which to choose. Moreover, the choice of best or most appropriate method is by no means obvious, even for someone knowledgeable about quantitative analysis. This means that even with rigorous analysis, there's no guarantee that two or more people will come to identical conclusions when working from the same map.

In general, however, variations in conclusions are far less with quantitative than with visual analysis. You must decide whether the added objectivity and precision gained by using quantitative methods will be great enough to warrant the extra effort required. In many situations, estimates based on simple observation are all you need. You can capitalize on the advantages of quantitative procedures more easily, of course, by letting computers do the mathematical work for you.

In theory, too, quantitative methods are absolute and precise. In practice, however, there are several potential sources of error. As we saw in our discussion of map reading in Part I, the map itself is not error-free. The tools, materials, and techniques of the data collector and the map maker lead to many distortions of mapped information. Even if the map is perfect, map analysts add their own errors. Some of these errors are random and can be minimized only by exercising great care while figuring. Other potential errors are systematic. Some of these are caused by inaccuracies built into our tools of analysis. Others can be attributed to human bias, such as the fact that human vision has resolution limits. You can compensate for both types of systematic error once you know they exist.

Two other cautionary notes are warranted. First, map analysis is based on the assumption that we're working with Euclidian physical space, but the earth's surface is basically spherical and thus non-Euclidian. This problem has plagued nearly everyone who has tried to conduct analytical studies based on map information. The second caution is that map analysis gives you descriptions, not explanations or interpretations. Analyzing a map's geometry is designed to facilitate map interpretation, not to substitute for it. Map analysis merely converts the complex pattern of symbols to more usable numerical form.

A fascinating thing about map analysis is that you can, in a sense, get more out of a map than was put into it. When map makers show a few features in proper spatial relationship, they allow you to determine all sorts of things—directions, distances, densities, and so on—that they may not have had specifically in mind. This is one of the beauties of map analysis. It can make complex geographic relations more readily understandable.

The following discussion of map analysis is divided into 10 chapters. The first two chapters describe how to determine distances (Chapter 11), and directions (Chapter 12) from maps. Next, we discuss how to use distance and direction information in position finding and route planning (Chapter 13). Chapter 14 explores various ways to measure the surface area, volume, and shape of features on maps. In Chapter 15, we show how to compute slope and create profiles from the contours shown on topographic maps. In Chapter 16, we look at spatial pattern analysis of features found on a map, and in Chapter 17 we move our focus to ways of analyzing spatial associations among patterns. Chapter 18 deals with using a global positioning system (GPS) in route planning and navigation. Chapter 19 covers geographic information systems (GIS) and map analysis software. And in Chapter 20, we examine the specialized methods used in aerial photo analysis.

As we move from map reading to analysis, we're shifting our attention from the theory behind maps to their practical use. It is here that the real fun of maps begins. However beautiful a map may be in theory and in design, it is at its most beautiful when it is being used.

CHAPTER ELEVEN
DISTANCE FINDING

How far is a mile?
Well, you learn that right off.
It's peculiarly different from ten tenths on the odometer.
It's one thousand seven hundred and sixty steps on the dead level . . .
It's at least ten and maybe a million times that on the hills
And no river bed ever does run straight.
—Jerry & Renny Russell, On the Loose

11

CHAPTER ELEVEN

DISTANCE FINDING

In our fast-moving society, we sometimes overlook the importance of distance. However, knowing the distance between points can be very important. Travel time and fuel consumption are closely tied to distance traveled, for instance, so that distance measurement is crucial when planning hikes, wilderness road trips, and voyages by sea or air.

As we discuss this important aspect of map use, keep in mind that you can interpret "distance" in two ways. When working with maps, we usually think of the **physical distance** between places. Since we assume that the map shows locations correctly, we expect a close relation between map and ground distance. We measure map distance with a ruler and ground distance in kilometers or miles—usually along the shortest practical route for travel.

In our everyday lives, however, it's also natural to think not of physical but of **functional distance**. Most of us have little notion of how long a kilometer or mile is. Instead, we view distance in terms of the time or energy we must expend to get from here to there. We ask not "How many miles?" but "How long does it take?" or "How hard is it to get there?" Although a few maps do provide information on functional distance, most are based on physical distance. Our first concern, therefore, is to learn to determine physical distance from maps. Then we'll see how we can use special maps to determine functional distance.

PHYSICAL DISTANCE

We measure physical distance in standardized units of measurement. Some of these units are based on the size of the earth, while others are purely arbitrary. Distance units in our familiar **English system of measurement**, for example, are arbitrary. The **yard** (three feet or 36 inches) was decreed by King Henry I to be the distance from the tip of his nose to the end of his thumb with arm outstretched—clearly an arbitrary way of defining distance!

When people talk about a mile, they usually mean a **statute mile** (1,760 yards or 5,280 feet). And when we use the term "mile" in this book, unless otherwise noted, we are referring to this familiar statute mile. But as you use maps, you'll discover other types of miles. Unlike the arbitrary statute mile, these are based on the earth's circumference and represent a specific part of a degree. One such measure is the **geographical mile** (6,087.1 feet), which is one minute of longitude along the equator. The British **admiralty mile** has been rounded off to 6,080 feet. The widely used **international nautical mile** (6,076.1 feet or 1,852 meters) is one minute of latitude on a perfect sphere whose surface area is equal to the surface area of the ellipsoidal earth (see Chapter 1 for more information on the earth's shape).

Although not as familiar to most of us, the international nautical mile is important because it serves as the standard unit of distance in water and air navigation. It also provides the basis for the mariner's **knot**, which is the velocity of one nautical mile per hour. Knots are used in computing the speed of ships, planes, and wind.

In contrast to the English system, all distance units in the **metric system** were originally based on the earth's circumference. The **meter** (39.37 inches), which is roughly equivalent to the yard, represents a physically meaningful distance on the earth's surface. A meter was first defined as one ten-millionth of the distance from the equator to north pole along a meridian.*

When you use the metric system to work with maps, you'll usually measure ground distance in **kilometers** (km.) and map distance in **centimeters** (cm.) Conveniently, each kilometer equals 1,000 meters, and each centimeter is one-hundredth of a meter. Indeed, convenience is the metric system's great advantage. It's much easier to use than the English system because all units are in multiples of 10.

The overwhelming convenience and worldwide use of the metric system is hard for us to ignore. The United States is one of the few nonmetric countries, and we are drifting toward the metric standard for our official government maps.

You should be familiar with both the metric and English systems, because there are situations in which one is more convenient than the other. This means you'll often have to convert from one system to the other. **Table D.1** in Appendix D will help you make these conversions.

All these distance units have little real meaning in themselves, of course. They take on significance only when we use them to specify the distance between geographical locations. Let's look now at this important map analysis activity—determining distance.

Determining Distance

When you need distance information, it's usually impractical to measure distance between places in the environment directly. Nor is it often practical to look up distance information in logs or tables. The solution is to turn to maps. Map and earth space are so closely related that measurements made on the right type of map can be nearly as accurate as ground measurements of distance.

Using maps to measure distance isn't always straightforward, however. A map is always smaller in scale than the environment it depicts. Map distances of centimeters or inches represent ground distances of kilometers or miles. To convert map to ground distance, you need to know the map's

**Today the meter is defined relative to the speed of light, and is 1/299,792,458th of the distance light travels in a vacuum in one second.*

scale (see Chapter 2 for more about map scale). An understanding of scale is vital in using maps to measure distances.

There are two ways to use a large-scale map to find distances between places. You can use the map's scale bar to measure the distance, or you can compute the distance using simple algebra applied to grid coordinates. Let's look at each of these methods.

Determining Distance by Physical Measurement

The easiest way to figure distance is to use the **scale bar**, the ruler-like markings found on most maps. To do so, mark the distance between two map locations with ticks on a piece of paper or string. Then place this map distance next to the scale bar (**Figure 11.1A**). No ruler or mathematical computation is necessary. The distance value you obtain may not be very accurate, however, especially if you try to determine the length of a winding route (**Figure 11.1B**).

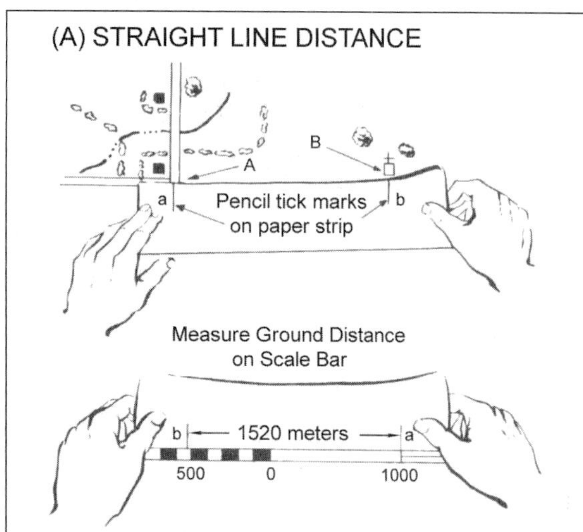

(B) CURVED LINE DISTANCE

Figure 11.1 You can use the scale bar to compute the ground distance between two map features along a straight line (A) or a curved line (B).

You can also compute ground distance using the **representative fraction** (**RF**) printed on most large-scale maps. Simply measure the distance between two points with a ruler and then multiply the number of inches or centimeters by the denominator of the RF. For instance, if the RF is 1:24,000 and the distance between points is 3.3 inches, then:

$$24{,}000 \times 3.3 \text{ in.} = 79{,}200 \text{ in.}$$

You'll want to convert this distance to more familiar ground units such as miles or kilometers. Thus:

$$79{,}200 \text{ in.} \div 63{,}360 \text{ in./mi.} = 1.25 \text{ miles, and}$$
$$1.25 \text{ mi.} \times 1.609 \text{ km./mi.} = 2.01 \text{ km.}$$

You can buy special map rulers that have scale bars for common map scales. The Topo Companion ruler (**Figure 11.2**), for instance, has UTM metric scale bars for four map scales from 1:24,000 to 1:250,000. You simply place the ruler for your map scale on the map and directly read the ground distance between two points.

You can speed your measurement of curved lines with a **map measurer**. This device consists of a wheel and one or more circular distance dials (**Figure 11.3A**). Simply set the needle to 0, then roll the wheel along the desired path. The dials will give you the map distance in inches or centimeters. To convert this value to ground distance, multiply it by the denominator of the map's RF. Many map measurers have dials that directly give the ground distance at several common map scales. On the distance measurer in Figure 11.3A, for example, there are dials for 1:25,000, 1:50,000, 1:75,000, and 1:100,000 scale maps.

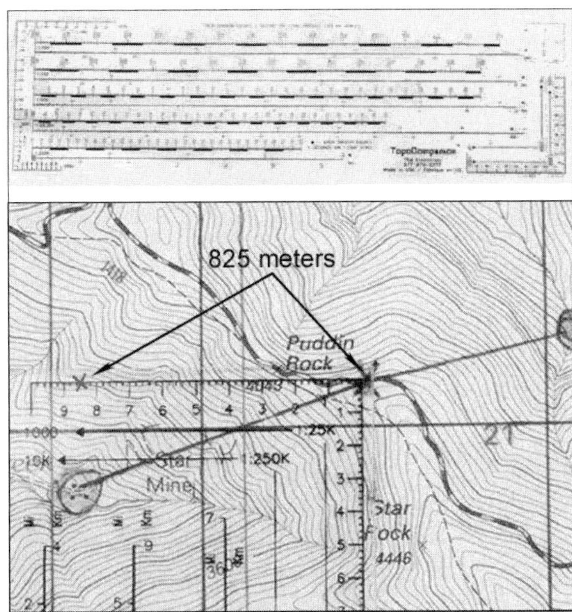

Figure 11.2 Map rulers like the Topo Companion allow you to measure ground distance directly from scale bars for common topographic map series scales.

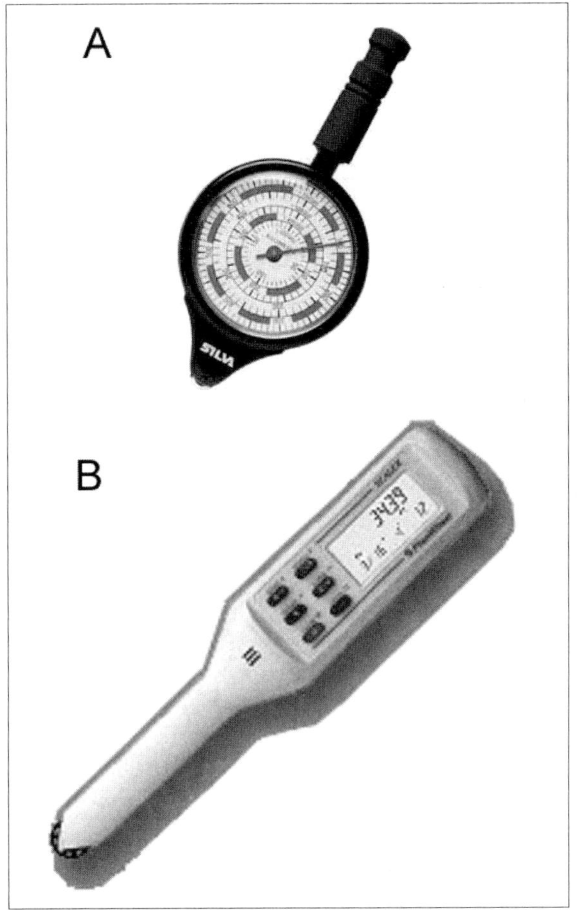

Figure 11.3 Mechanical measuring devices, such as the Silva Mechanical Map Measure (A) and Scalex MapWheel (B), can make accurate distance measurements in ground units if the route isn't intricately detailed.

Mechanical map measurers work best when the path between the two points is relatively smooth. Keeping the small wheel on a winding road or stream is a real exercise in finger control. If the wheel slips or binds on tight curves, errors result.

More sophisticated (and expensive) map measurers (**Figure 11.3B**) have digital displays and built-in functions that let you enter the map scale before you make measurements. Ground distances are displayed, and you can connect the device to your personal computer so that you can download measurements.

Determining Distance by Coordinates

Distance computations become tedious if you must do many of them. If you wanted to know the distance from each of 10 houses to each of the other nine, you would have to make 45 calculations—quite a chore. But there is an alternative. If you use **grid coordinates** to determine distance, you need only figure out the coordinates of the houses once and then use them over and over in your distance computations (see Chapter 4 for more on grid coordinates). You can save even more time and effort if you have access to a computerized mapping system. In that case, you simply use your computer's mouse to find grid coordinates on digital maps displayed on your monitor, and then use the mapping software to process these coordinates and give you the distance values you want.

You can also use your GPS receiver as a convenient distance calculator. To do so, you merely enter the coordinates of the two points, press a few buttons, and the receiver will display the distance between the two points (see Chapter 14: GPS and Maps).

Such modern procedures eliminate the need to know a great deal about either mathematics or computers. You'll feel more comfortable with the techniques, however, if you understand the basic mathematical process behind them. Thus, we'll work through some coordinate distance computations so that you'll know how to do them, although you may never have to perform them by hand.

Grid Coordinates. Assume that the distance you want to measure is the hypotenuse of a right triangle. The Pythagorean theorem tells us that if a, b, and c represent the sides of a right triangle, and c is the hypotenuse, then $c^2 = a^2 + b^2$ (**Figure 11.4A**). To find the distance between two points, we restate the Pythagorean theorem,

$$d = \sqrt{a^2 + b^2}$$

or

$$d = \sqrt{(x_2 - x_1)^2 + (y_2 - y_1)^2}$$

changing c to d, which will represent distance. So: where (x_1,y_1) and (x_2,y_2) are the (easting, northing) coordinates of the locations between which the distance is to be determined. This formula is called the **distance theorem**. It states that you can determine the distance between any two points on your map by taking the square root of the sum of the squares of the differences in the x and y coordinates of the two points (**Figure 11.4B**).

The usefulness of the distance theorem is demonstrated in **Figure 11.5**, using data derived from UTM and State Plane Coordinate (SPC) systems found on the Madison West, Wisconsin, 7.5' topographic quadrangle (UTM and SPC grid systems are discussed in Chapter 4). Let's say we want to find the distance between a corner of the University of Wisconsin Arboretum (P_2) and a building to the southwest (P_1).

Step 1: Extend the marginal ticks on the map to form boundaries around the UTM and SPC grid cells in which the two places are located.

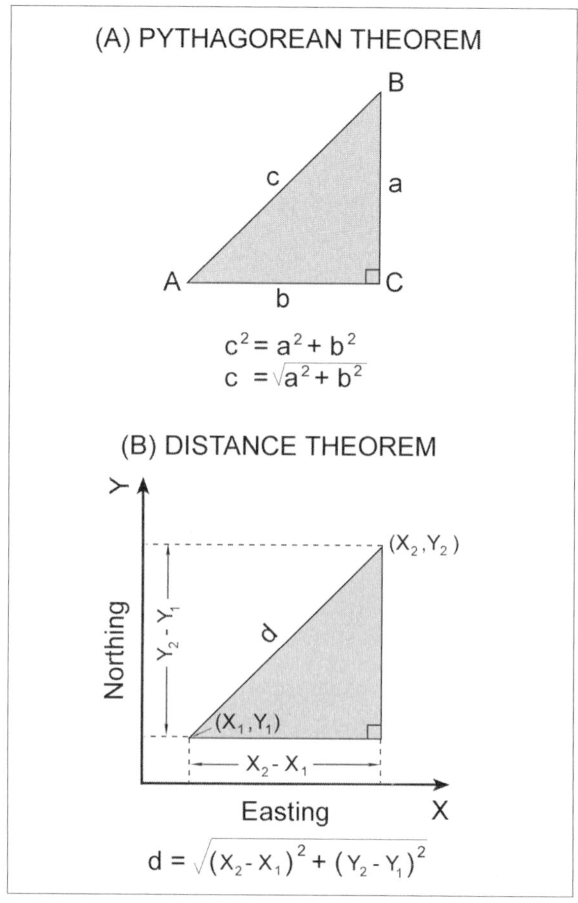

Figure 11.4 You can compute the distance between two points from their coordinates using the distance theorem that is the grid coordinate version of the Pythagorean theorem.

Step 2: Determine the UTM and SPC easting (x) and northing (y) for each point (as was explained in Chapter 4). These are:

$$P_1 \left\{ \begin{array}{l} SPC \left\{ \begin{array}{l} x = 2{,}153{,}600' \\ y = 373{,}320' \end{array} \right\} \\ UTM \left\{ \begin{array}{l} x = 302{,}348m. \\ y = 4{,}766{,}000m. \end{array} \right\} \end{array} \right\}$$

$$P_2 \left\{ \begin{array}{l} SPC \left\{ \begin{array}{l} x = 2{,}156{,}800' \\ y = 379{,}100' \end{array} \right\} \\ UTM \left\{ \begin{array}{l} x = 303{,}384m. \\ y = 4{,}767{,}726m. \end{array} \right\} \end{array} \right\}$$

$$d_{SPC} = \sqrt{(2{,}156{,}800 - 2{,}153{,}600)^2 + (379{,}100 - 373{,}320)^2}$$
$$= \sqrt{3{,}200^2 + 5{,}780^2}$$
$$= \sqrt{10{,}240{,}000 + 33{,}408{,}400}$$
$$= \sqrt{43{,}648{,}400}$$
$$= 6607' or 2013.7m.$$

$$d_{UTM} = \sqrt{(303{,}384 - 302{,}348)^2 + (4{,}767{,}726 - 4{,}766{,}000)^2}$$
$$= \sqrt{1{,}036^2 + 1{,}726^2}$$
$$= \sqrt{1{,}073{,}296 + 2{,}979{,}076}$$
$$= \sqrt{4{,}052{,}372}$$
$$= 2013m. or 6604'$$

Step 3: Now transfer the numerical values determined in Step 2 to the distance formula

Thus, the computed distance from the UTM coordinates is 2,013 meters or 6,604 feet. State Plane Coordinates yielded a distance of 2,013.7 meters or 6,607 feet—a discrepancy of only three feet between the two computations. These computed distances also compare favorably with the distance we obtain by using the map scale. The measured map distance is 3.3 in., which, at a map scale of 1:24,000, yields a ground distance of 3.3 in. × 24,000 = 79,200 in.÷ 12 in./ft. = 6,600 feet. The close agreement between the distances computed from coordinates and measured on the map is remarkable considering the difficulties of making precise measurements on maps.

There's no doubt that using grid coordinates to find distances is a simple, accurate method. Its disadvantage is that you can use it only for relatively small regions: Both places must lie within a single grid zone. Your use of State Plane Coordinates is thus limited to areas the size of a small

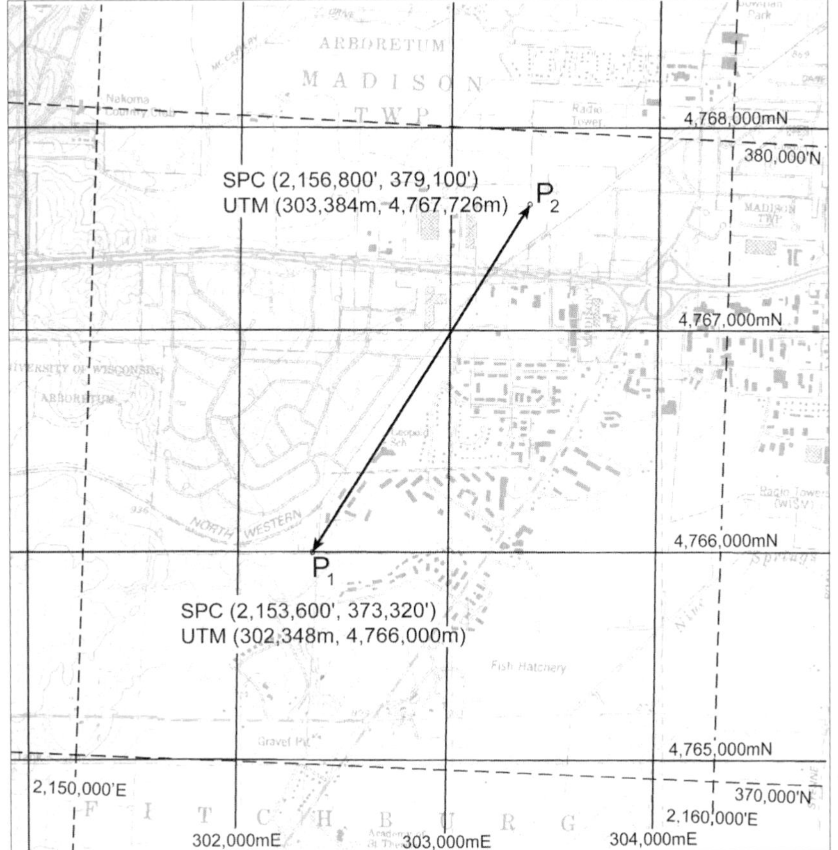

Figure 11.5 Using coordinates to compute the distance between two points on the Madison West, Wisconsin, quadrangle (see text for explanation).

state, while UTM coordinates are restricted to zones of 6° longitude.

Nor can you solve this problem by extending plane coordinates over larger regions. Larger grids incorporate greater scale distortion, since the earth curves progressively away from a plane surface. Grids of greater extent decrease the accuracy of distance computations.

Spherical Coordinates. Fortunately, there is a solution to computing longer distances. You can find the distance between any two places on earth by using spherical geographic coordinates. To find the distance between two locations, you need only know the latitude and longitude of each place and use basic spherical trigonometry. GPS receivers perform this task automatically, but it's good to understand the procedure used.

Suppose you want to know how far it is from Seattle to Miami along a great-circle route (**Figure 11.6**). Follow these steps:

1. Look up the latitude and longitude of the two cities, using Table 5 in Appendix D. This table shows that Seattle is located at 47°36'N,122°20'W, and Miami is located at 25°45'N,80°11'W.

2. Form a triangle, the sides of which are arcs of great circles. Construct this spherical triangle by connecting Seattle and Miami with the arc of a great circle. Extend arcs of great circles along meridians from each city to the north pole. These are called **meridional arcs**.

3. Consider what you know about this spherical triangle. You know that the distance from equator to pole is 90°. Thus, you can calculate side c by subtracting the latitude of city B (Miami) from 90°. Or, c = 90° - 25°45' = 64°15'. Similarly, side b = 90° - 47°36' = 42°24'. Angle A is the difference in longitude between the two cities. Thus, 122°20' (Seattle) - 80°11' (Miami) = 42°09'.

4. Convert the angles determined in Step 3 to decimal degrees and determine the sines and cosines for b,c, and A:

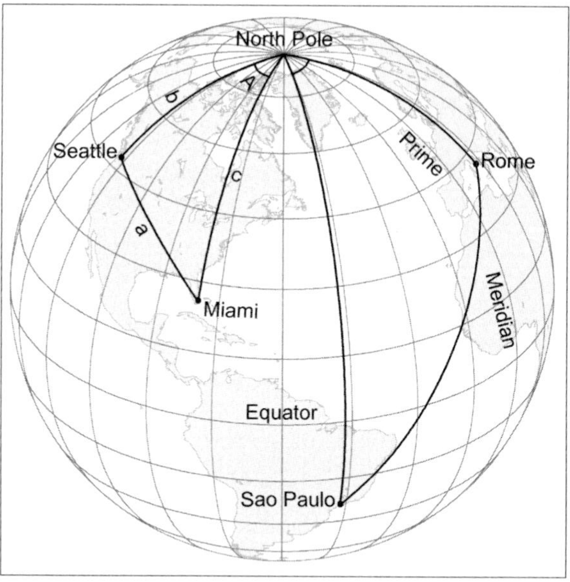

Figure 11.6 You can find the distance between widely separated points by using spherical coordinates.

A = 42°09' = 42.15°
b = 42°24' = 42.40°
c = 64°15' = 65.25°

cos(A) = cos(42.15°) = 0.74139
cos(c) = cos(64.25°) = 0.43445
sin(c) = sin(64.25°) = 0.90070
cos(b) = cos(42.40°) = 0.73846
sin(b) = sin(42.40°) = 0.67430

5. Transfer the numerical values from Step 4 to the **Law of Cosines** from spherical trigonometry:

$$\begin{aligned}\cos(a) &= \cos(b)\times\cos(c)+\sin(b)\times\sin(c)\times\cos(A)\\ &= (0.73846)\times(0.43445)+(0.67430)\times(0.90070)\times(0.74137)\\ &= 0.32082+0.45028\\ &= 0.77110\\ a &= \cos^{-1}(0.77110) = 39.547° = 39°32'50''\end{aligned}$$

6. Convert this angular distance to ground distance by finding the proportion of a circle of the earth's circumference spanned by the angle, using the equation:

$$Dist. = a° / 360° \times circumference$$
$$= 39.547° / 360° \times 24{,}902mi.$$
$$= 2{,}736mi.$$

The great-circle route from Seattle to Miami is 2,736 miles.

You'll have to adjust the trigonometric equation if the two cities fall in different **hemispherical quadrants**. This situation occurs when the great-circle route crosses the 180° meridian, the prime meridian (0°), or the equator (Figure 11.6). If one city is north and the other south of the equator, (such as Sao Paulo and Rome, for example), you'll have to add, rather than subtract, the latitude of the southern hemisphere city to 90° to obtain its meridional arc.

When both cities lie south of the equator, you can either add both latitudes to 90° or use the south rather than the north pole as a meridional reference point. If one city is east and the other west of the prime meridian, again like Sao Paulo and Rome, you add rather than subtract their respective longitudes to obtain angle A. Except for these slight changes, you compute spherical distance just as you did when both cities fell in the same hemispherical quadrant.

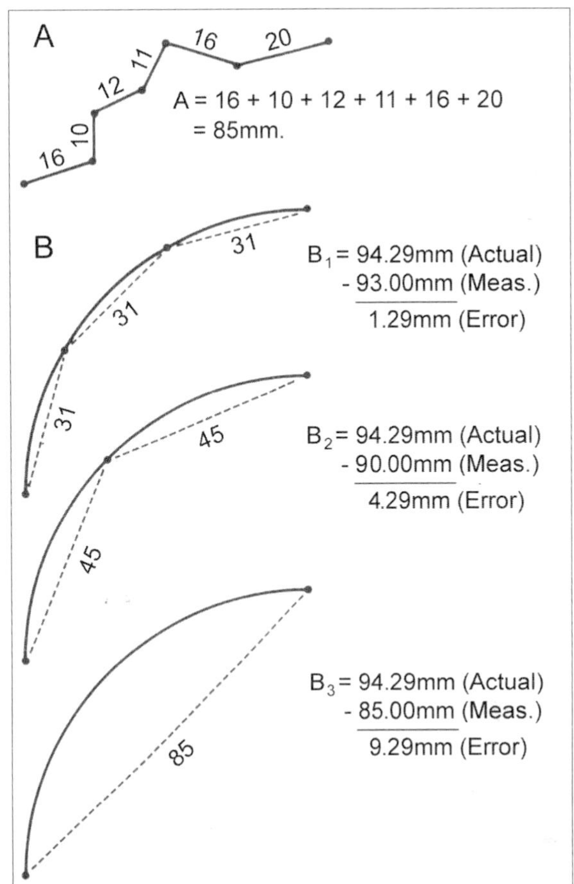

Figure 11.7 You can figure out the length of a complex line if you break it into short, straight segments (A). You can also approximate curved lines with straight line segments (B).

Finding Complex Line and Perimeter Distance

You've now seen how to measure or compute distances along straight lines and great circles. You can also find the length of a **complex line** or the **perimeter** of the boundary line for an irregular area by breaking the line into short, straight segments. You then either physically measure, or compute line segment lengths using the equations presented above for grid and geographic coordinates. Finally, you add the segment lengths to obtain the total distance **(Figure 11.7A)**.

You can use the same method to determine the length of a smooth curved line. All you do is approximate the curve with a series of straight lines (**Figure 11.7B**). You must decide how long to make the line segments, of course, and this decision will affect the accuracy of your results. Although shorter line segments lead to less error, they also require more measurements or computations. You must reach a balance between accuracy and effort.

Error Factors

No matter how you determine distance from maps, some error is bound to slip into your results. The methods you use, the judgments you make, or the calculations you do may be faulty. These are called **external errors**, since you impose them on the map from the outside. To minimize external errors, use only proven techniques and instruments, and take care to avoid mistakes in computation.

But even if you make no external errors, your final distance figure is still likely to be inaccurate. The reason is found in the nature of the map itself. A variety of distance distortions are built into the process of transforming reality to a map. Fortunately, you can compensate to some degree for these **internal errors** if you're aware of their existence. Let's look at some of these internal errors and see how you can compensate for them.

Slope Error. Your first problem is that you have measured or calculated ground distance as if the surface were flat. This distance is always shorter than true ground distance—except in the rare case of perfectly flat terrain. As **Figure 11.8A** shows, the steeper the slope and the longer the ground distance over which slopes occur, the greater the error between true and computed distance.

To compensate for this **slope error**, recall the Pythagorean theorem discussed earlier in this chapter. Consider **Figure 11.8B**. To compute ground-distance c between points A and B, use the horizontal (map) distance (b) and the vertical (elevation) distance (a), both of which you can determine from a topographic map. In this example, the discrepancy between horizontal and slope ground distance is five meters.

In theory, then, it's not much trouble to compensate for slope error. If the terrain undulates quite a bit, however, there will be many slope adjustments to make. If you aren't concerned with high accuracy, you can avoid all these computations by making one overall (but highly approximate) correction. Just determine the region's approximate percent slope and then compensate for this slope by using the information in **Figure 11.9**. From this graph, for instance, you can see that if you walk 10 miles along a 40 percent slope, you'll travel a ground distance of 10 × 1.077 = 10.77 miles, or about three-fourths mile farther than the map scale suggests.

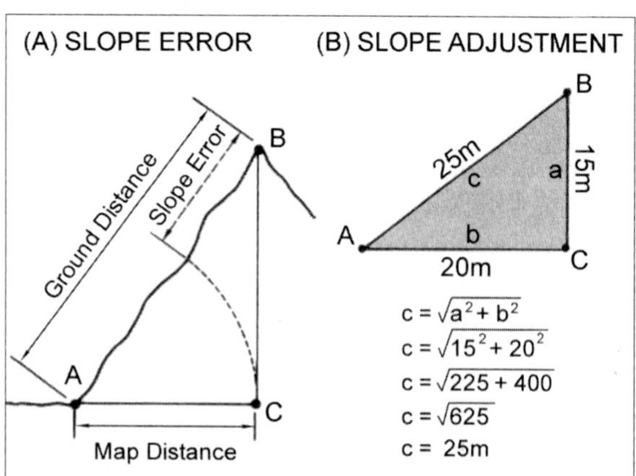

Figure 11.8 When computing distance between two points (A), it may be necessary to adjust for ground slope (B).

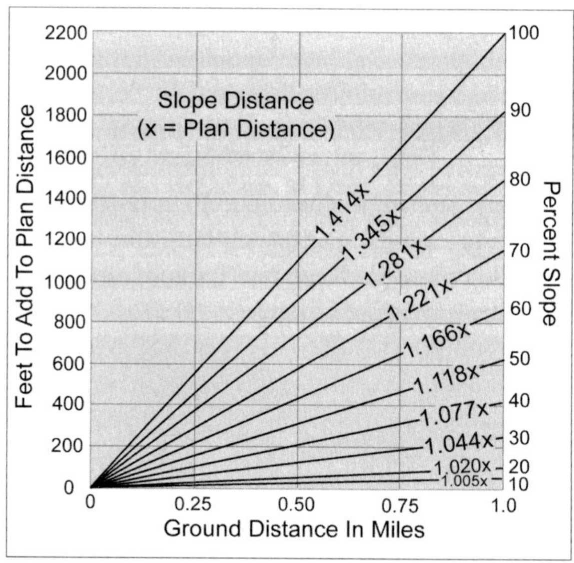

Figure 11.9 Use the slope error figures on this graph's vertical axis to adjust ground distance (horizontal axis) for slope.

Smoothing Error. A second type of distance error can be traced to smoothing of line symbols on maps. When they show linear features such as roads and rivers, map makers straighten curves and smooth irregularities. As a result, the measured route along a highway, railroad, or hiking trail may deviate from the ground distance. Likewise, map distance along a shore or down a stream may mislead a canoeist.

This **smoothing error** has something in common with slope error: Both add to the measured map distance. A ground distance route may be the same length or longer than the map distance estimate, but it can never be shorter. Unless the ground is completely flat and the route perfectly straight, your computed distance will always fall short of true ground distance.

Although elevation information may be available to help you overcome slope error, you have no way of knowing how much map makers have smoothed linear features. There are, however, a few useful guidelines. One good rule to remember is that the smaller the map scale and the more irregular the ground route, the more smoothing map makers use. Thus, the discrepancy between map and ground distance increases as map scale decreases. This means you can minimize the problem if you use large-scale maps.

It's not quite that simple, however. Even on large-scale maps, some roads, rivers, and boundaries will be more smoothed than others. The more detailed and intricate the feature, the more it will be simplified. County roads, for instance, usually will be more smoothed than freeways, because they are more convoluted to start with. The map legend is rarely of much help in sorting out the effects of this **variable smoothing** of line symbols. Intuition is your best guide. You would naturally expect highways to curve more (and therefore be more smoothed by the map maker) than railroads, streams to be more sinuous than roads, and state highways to be less straight than freeways. Additionally, linear features in rugged, rocky regions will be more irregular (and thus more smoothed on the map) than the same features in flat, sandy regions. As you use your common sense and anticipate these differences within the same map, you'll be able to estimate ground distance better.

Scale Variation. The larger the mapped region, the greater the **scale variation** across the map. If you are measuring distances from small-scale maps of continents or hemispheres, it is good advice to trust the scale only near the center of the map or along certain lines, such as meridians or parallels.

Since distances are such an important aspect of our environment, aren't there any small-scale maps designed to keep distances correct? The answer is yes and no. Spherical **globes** faithfully represent distances, except for small errors introduced by the earth being ellipsoidal in shape. But for a small-scale map projection to preserve distance relations perfectly, it would have to show the shortest spherical distance between any two points as a straight line—and do so at true scale. That's a mathematical impossibility on a flat surface. We can, however, make measurements on map projections that have true distances along certain lines.

Recall from Chapter 3 that the **azimuthal equidistant projection** transforms great circles passing through the projection center into straight lines on the map. Distances from all points to the projection's center are true to scale, but distances between all other points are incorrect. This creates a problem: To use the azimuthal equidistant projection to find distances from different starting points, you will need a map for each starting point.

When there is a systematic pattern of scale variation over the map, you'll sometimes find a **variable scale bar** on the map. Figure 2.2 shows a variable scale bar for a Mercator world projection. This scale bar lets you measure distances along parallels, despite the great scale distortion on the Mercator projection.

Disproportionate Symbol Error. A fourth source of error in figuring distance arises because most map features aren't symbolized in correct scale. If they were, the symbols wouldn't be large enough to see. Take, for instance, a road which is 30 feet wide. It might be shown by a thin line (0.01 inch wide) on a map with a scale of 1:125,000. This would give it an effective ground width of 104 feet!

This **disproportionate symbol error** becomes more extreme when a feature such as a political boundary, which has no width, is shown by a symbol which is effectively several miles wide. And the trouble becomes worse as map scale decreases. There's simply not enough space to include everything. As a result, cartographers over-emphasize features selected for the map. By the very na-

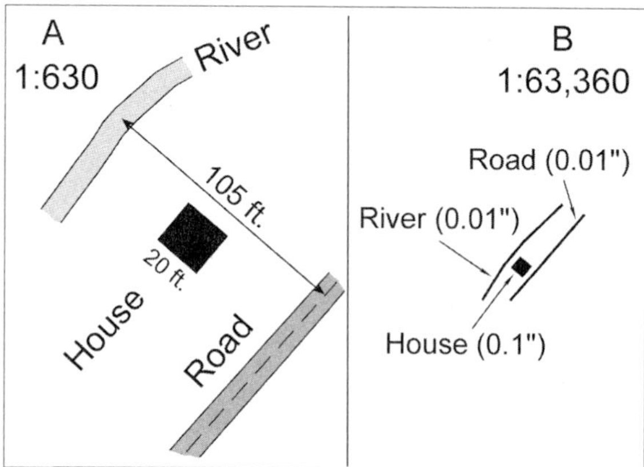

Figure 11.10 Disproportionate map symbols can have a major distorting effect on distance determinations between closely spaced features, as these 1:630 and 1:63,360 ways of depicting the same setting demonstrate.

ture of symbolism, depicting one feature leads to excluding, distorting, or displacing its neighbor.

Consider the case of a house on a 105-foot lot between a road and a river (**Figure 11.10A**). If the river and road were both symbolized by lines 0.01 inch wide at a map scale of 1:63,360, they alone would use up 52.8 feet, or half the space available. There wouldn't be enough room for the building symbol, which at 0.1" × 0.1" would itself take up 528 feet, five times the ground distance between the center of the river and road.

To make all three features visibly distinct, the map maker "pulls them apart". Such **positional modification** is essential to retain the relative spatial relations between features: We can't have the road and river running through the house. But the result is that distance accuracy is compromised.

Be wary, then, of any distance measurements involving closely placed map symbols. If, in **Figure 11.10B**, you computed the distance between the centers of the river and road from the map, you would come up with a ground figure of 686 feet, while the two are really 105 feet apart. If you didn't know about disproportionate map symbols and positional modification, you might even try to measure the distance across the river and find that the river is 52.8 feet wide when it is actually only 10 feet across.

Map users who recognize the problems of disproportionate symbols on conventional maps sometimes overlook the fact that the same thing occurs on air photos and scanner images (see Chapter 9 for more on images). Contrary to what you might think, a photograph doesn't show all environmental features in correct proportion. Since photography is based on reflected light, a shiny, highly reflective object is imaged disproportionately large on a photograph. Mapping teams have made use of this fact for years. Before taking photos, they place highly reflective targets on the ground. These targets stand out on air photos, helping the mappers locate known positions and correct distance distortions when using the photos to compile topographic maps.

The same thing happens with images from non-visible parts of the electromagnetic spectrum. An extremely hot object will appear overly large on a thermal image. Buildings made of certain materials and oriented in certain ways appear on radar images as large bright spots.

If these occurrences seem to defy logic, even more baffling is the fact that linear features appear on photos at far larger than their natural size. Powerlines are often visible on a photo even though the high transmission towers holding them up are not. Railroad tracks can be seen when a car can't. On satellite images with a scanner cell size of 200 by 200 feet, there is no logical way that a 60-foot-wide road would show up—yet it does! These examples should remind us to keep disproportionate symbol error in mind when we make measurements on images as well as conventional maps.

Dimensional Instability Error. Unless maps are printed on a dimensionally stable material such as plastic, glass, or metal, they will stretch and shrink with changes of temperature and humidity. A map the size of a USGS 1:24,000 topographic map, if printed on paper, can change as much as one percent in length or width when moved from a cool and dry to a hot and wet environment. This stretching and shrinking introduces errors in your distance measurements, especially if you're measuring a long distance on the map.

Like slope, smoothing, scale, and symbol error, paper instability error can play havoc with distance calculations. No matter how precisely you compute distance from maps, no matter how carefully you wheel your mechanical distance finder along wiggles in the road, your final distance figure will be only approximate.

Pre-Measured Ground Distances

Map measurement errors occur because map distance isn't the same as ground distance. Such problems are eliminated if someone physically measures distances on the ground and puts the distance figures on the map. That's just what has been done on some maps—road maps in particular. **Pre-measured ground distances** are an invaluable aid in determining route length and choosing between routes. Let's look at some of the ways that ground distances have been added to maps.

Segment Numbers. On some highway maps, ground distances are added between such places as towns or highway intersections (**Figure 11.11A**). Routes are thus divided into segments, with the length of each segment given. To find the distance between two points, you merely add up all the **segment numbers** along the route.

If your route is very long, of course, you'll soon tire of adding numbers. To help you out, map makers may provide a second level of distances.

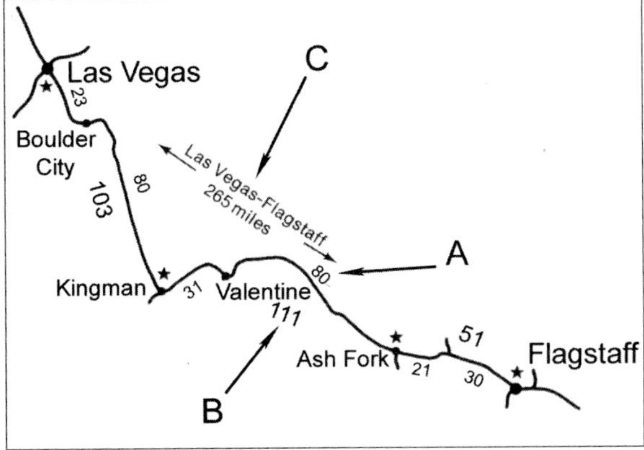

Figure 11.11 Road segment distance numbers (A), second-level route segments (B), and distance insets (C) are often incorporated into the design of road maps to help in determining route length.

Second-level route segments are longer than the first and have as their end points major cities and intersections. These special points are shown by such symbols as stars or tick marks (**Figure 11.11B**). The symbols and segment numbers are usually printed larger and in a different color to reduce confusion with the first-level figures.

Distance Insets. To show the distance between widely separated points, map makers often include **distance insets**. Insets are usually double-ended arrows with names of features, such as cities, and distances between them **(Figure 11.11C)**. Insets can be useful, though they may be hard to locate and are far from complete. All too often you'll find that the map maker ignored the route length of interest to you.

Distance Diagrams. In addition to segment numbers and distance insets, a **distance diagram** may be added to the highway map (**Figure 11.12**). On such a diagram, routes between major features are shown by straight lines, with the length of each route given. These lines aren't meant to duplicate real roads but only to show that one point is connected to another.

The main disadvantage of distance diagrams is their size. They are usually relegated to a corner of the map and are so small that most cities must be left off. Furthermore, you have the same problem you did with segment numbers: You must add a lot of numbers together. To find the distance from Portland to Ashland in Figure 11.12, for instance, you must add at least six numbers.

Distance Tables. The problem of having to add a great many numbers is avoided if distance figures are arranged in tables. There are two types of **distance tables**. On a **rectangular distance table**, key features are listed alphabetically along the top and side. To find the distance between two cities, look up one name along the top and the other along the side. Then follow down the column and across the row to where they intersect. To find the

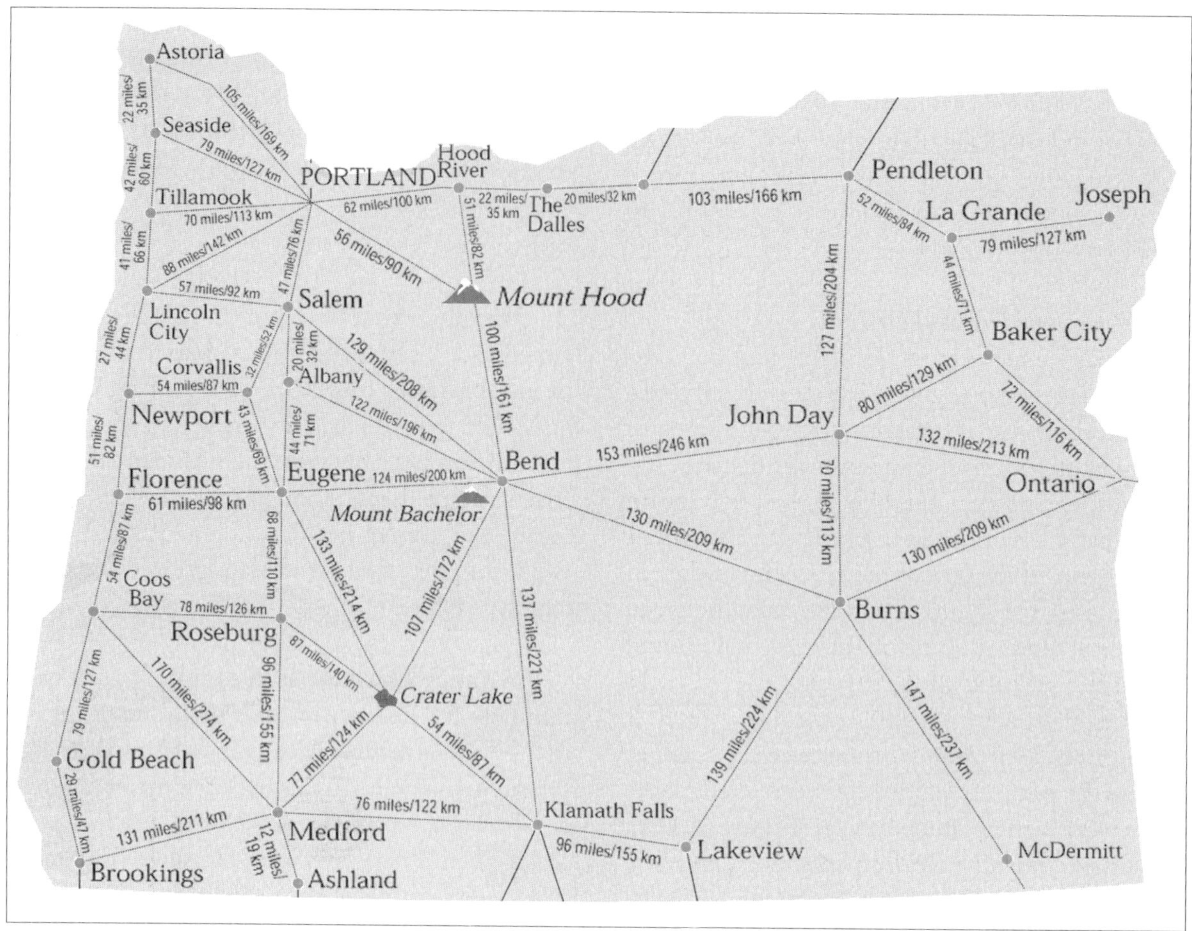

Figure 11.12 A distance diagram, such as this one for Oregon, makes it possible to compute the road distance between selected cities in the state.

distance from Chicago to Fairbanks in **Figure 11.13A**, locate Chicago in the left margin and Fairbanks on the top, and read the row-column intersection as 3,804 miles. Or look up Fairbanks on the left and Chicago on the top—the result will be the same.

Notice that the rectangular distance table is 50 percent redundant. To let you look up either name in either margin, the table's upper-right half is the same as the lower-left half. To avoid this duplication and to save space, map makers often use a **triangular distance table**. On this table, feature names need occur only once. In **Figure 11.13B**, you can find the distance between Chicago and Fairbanks by following down the column from Chicago until it intersects the row opposite Fairbanks. The distance again is 3,804 miles.

Distance tables aren't all-inclusive. You may find one of the cities you're looking for but not the other, or both places may be missing from the table. On such occasions, you can sometimes arrive at an approximate figure by looking up the distance between nearby places.

Distance Databases. The modern way to determine the distance between cities and other "official" geographical places such as national parks, is to access a computer database holding this information. These databases come bundled with route-finding software for your personal computer (see Chapter 19: GIS and Map Analysis Software). You can also find this information at sites on the Internet (see Appendix A). Both sources may have the option of straight-line or routed distances.

FUNCTIONAL DISTANCE

Physical distances tell only a part of the story. Consider the following example:

> In Los Angeles, with everybody traveling by car on freeways, nobody talks about "miles" anymore, they just say "that's four minutes from here," "that's twenty minutes from here," and so on. The actual straight-line distance doesn't matter. It may be faster to go by a curved route. All anybody cares about is the time.
>
> (Wolfe, McLuhan: *Hot & Cool*, p. 38)

There's more to distance than physical miles on the ground or measured miles on the map. Physical distance may not be as germane to our lives as **functional distance**. As the above example illustrates, functional distance depends on many factors—mode of travel, frame of mind, external conditions—the list is endless.

A	Alaska Bdry.	Anchorage	Chicago, Il.	Circle	Dawson Ck.	Delta Junct.	Eagle	Edmonton, Al.	Fairbanks	Glennallen
Alaska Bdry.		421	3506	463	1221	201	242	1591	298	232
Anchorage	421		3927	523	1642	340	503	2012	358	189
Chicago, Il.	3506	3927		3969	2285	3707	3748	1915	3804	3738
Circle	463	523	3969		1684	262	545	2054	165	413
Dawson Ck. B.C.	1221	1642	2285	1684		1422	1463	370	1519	1453
Delta Junction	201	340	3707	262	1422		283	1792	97	151
Eagle	242	503	3748	545	1463	283		1833	380	314
Edmonton, Alta.	1591	2012	1915	2054	370	1792	1833		1889	1823
Fairbanks	298	358	3804	165	1519	97	380	1889		248
Glennallen	232	189	3738	413	1453	151	314	1823	248	

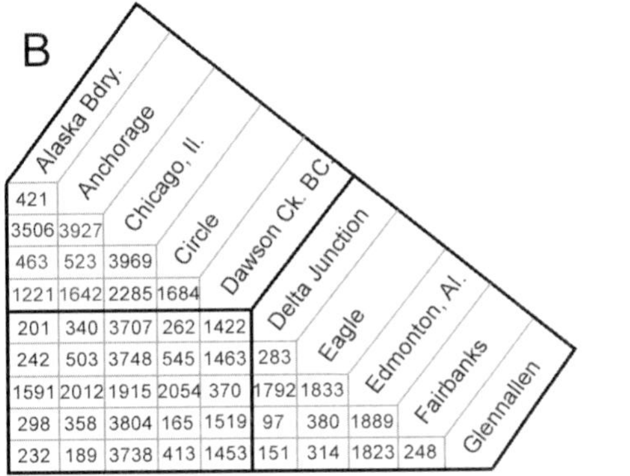

B	Alaska Bdry.	Anchorage	Chicago, Il.	Circle	Dawson Ck. BC	Delta Junction	Eagle	Edmonton, Al.	Fairbanks
Anchorage	421								
Chicago, Il.	3506	3927							
Circle	463	523	3969						
Dawson Ck. BC	1221	1642	2285	1684					
Delta Junction	201	340	3707	262	1422				
Eagle	242	503	3748	545	1463	283			
Edmonton, Al.	1591	2012	1915	2054	370	1792	1833		
Fairbanks	298	358	3804	165	1519	97	380	1889	
Glennallen	232	189	3738	413	1453	151	314	1823	248

Figure 11.13 Rectangular (A) and triangular (B) distance tables for Alaska (adapted from Alaska road map).

Sad to say, map makers have found it difficult to respond effectively to our concern with functional distance. In large part it is their shortsightedness which is at fault. They have concentrated on making maps ever more geographically accurate, thereby satisfying the demands of engineers, land surveyors, and military strategists. In the process, they often overlook the day-to-day needs of the rest of us.

But partly the fault rests with the nature of functional distance. While physical distance is always the same, distance measured in time or energy depends on many factors. Maps based on physical distance, therefore, aren't only simpler and less costly to make but are also more general in purpose. They can be used by anyone at any time. Maps showing functional distance may be more meaningful for specific purposes, but to be effective they must be tailor-made for each situation.

Faced with this problem, what have map makers done? When they have dealt with functional distance at all, they have done so in several ways. One approach is to add functional distance values as supplementary information on conventional maps. Another is to make maps showing only functional distances.

The most common functional distance added to maps is travel time, because it's the easiest to measure. Map makers can determine average travel times simply by studying speed limits along a route. They add this information to maps in two ways —by route segments or with isochrones.

Route Segments

One method, as shown in **Figure 11.14A**, is to give the travel time as well as distance for each **route segment**. The same thing may be done in a distance diagram, rather than on the map, as in **Figure 11.14B**. This procedure is used in road atlases, trip maps produced by the American Automobile Association, and maps in hiking guidebooks. You find your total travel time by summing the numbers of the segments, just as you do to determine physical distance.

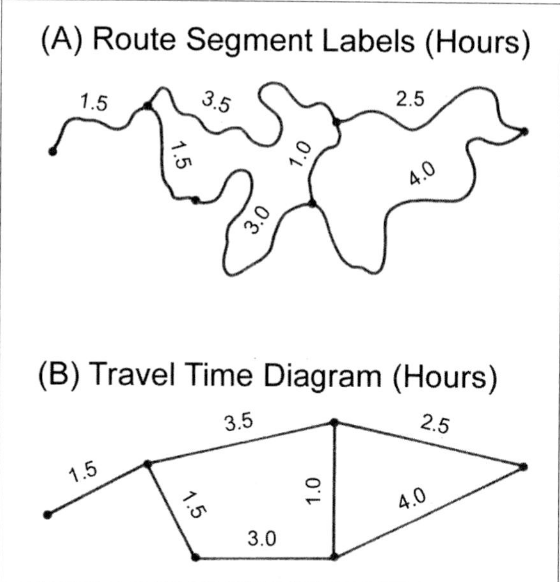

Figure 11.14 Functional distances may appear directly on maps as route segment labels (A) or as a travel time diagram (B).

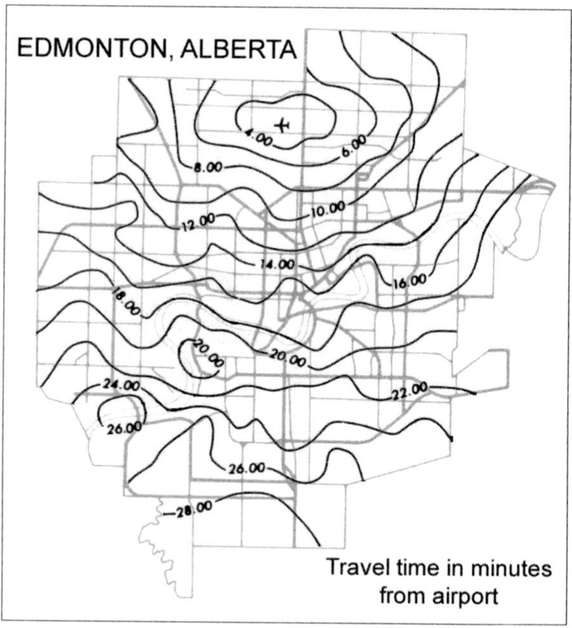

Figure 11.15 Isochrone map of Edmonton, Alberta, showing lines of equal travel time in minutes from the airport (adapted from Muller 1978).

Isochrones

The second method is to give travel time information continuously in all directions from a central point. Travel times are usually shown by lines of equal time-distance, called **isochrones** (see **Figure 11.15**). Isochrones are arranged concentrically around the central point, with the spacing between them directly proportional to travel time. They'll be close together in congested traffic areas, far apart along open stretches of road.

This second way of showing travel times is more restrictive than the first, since only time to and from the central point is meaningful. But both methods are useful because they combine physical and functional distance measures on the same map. You are given the best of both worlds: You can use physical distance units to compute gas mileage and travel time figures to estimate arrival times, travel fatigue, and other such factors.

All travel time figures are approximate, of course. They will vary with weather, time of day, route, and vehicle. Maps provide average figures, and averages seldom correspond to individual cases.

If maps showing travel times are few, those giving other types of functional distance information are nearly nonexistent. Such details as travel comfort, energy consumption, and route safety would all be of interest to map users. The core of the problem is that such information is difficult to gather. And here again, average figures aren't always helpful in individual cases. As widespread automated mapping becomes practical, however, we can envision maps being tailor-made for a particular person and trip. You'll give a computer all the information related to your journey and be presented with your own special and truly functional map.

Functional Distance by Inference

In the meantime, the burden lies with you, the map user, to translate physical into functional distance. You could do this by searching out the information elsewhere and adding it to your maps, but such a process is usually too involved to be worth the effort. Your alternative is to determine functional distances through a process of inference. You can conjure up a great deal of information from past experience stored in your mental maps.

You probably use the inference process frequently without realizing it. When figuring the length of a trip, for instance, you take traffic conditions into account. You know that a drive across town will take longer during rush hour than at other times. Holiday and weekend traffic is equally predictable, so you leave earlier or stay longer and thus shorten your travel time.

You can probably think of many other functional distance measures. Travel time is merely the starting point for a person with imagination. By drawing on your experience and intuition, in combination with careful map study, you can make many inferences that broaden your use of functional distance. Your imagination can add more to maps than cartographers can show.

SELECTED READINGS

Atwill, L., "What's Up (and Down) at the USGS," *Field & Stream* (May 1997), pp. 54-55.

Bovy, P.H.L., and Stern, E., *Route Choice: Wayfinding in Transport Networks* (Boston: Kluwer Academic Publishers, 1990).

Buttenfield, B.P., and McMaster, R.B., *Map Generalization: Making Rules for Knowledge Representation* (Essex: Longman Scientific & Technical, 1991).

Maling, D.H., "The Methods of Measuring Distance," Chapter 3 in *Measurement from Maps* (New York: Pergamon Press, 1989), pp. 30-52.

McMaster, R.B., and Shea, K.S., *Generalization in Digital Cartography* (Washington, DC: Association of American Geographers, 1992).

Muehrcke, P.C., "Functional Map Use," *Journal of Geography*, 77, 7 (December, 1978), pp. 254-262.

Muller, J.C., "The Mapping of Travel Time in Edmonton, Alberta," *The Canadian Geographer*, 22 (1978), pp. 195-210.

Muller, J.C., Lagrange, J.P., and Weibel, R., eds., *GIS and Generalization* (London: Taylor & Francis, 1995).

Monmonier, M.S., *Maps, Distortion and Meaning* (Washington, DC: Association of American Geographers, 1977).

Olsson, G. *Distance and Human Interaction*, Bibliography Series No. 2 (Philadelphia: Regional Science Research Institute, 1965).

Peters, A.B., "Distance-Related Maps," *The American Cartographer*, 11, 2 (1984), pp. 119-131.

Watson, J.W., "Geography: A Discipline in Distance," *Scottish Geographical Magazine*, 71 (1955), pp. 1-13.

Witthuhn, B.O., "Distance: An Extraordinary Spatial Concept," *Journal of Geography*, 78, 5 (1979), pp. 177-181.

This fire lookout volunteer is determining the direction from the fire tower to a plume of smoke.

CHAPTER TWELVE
DIRECTION FINDING AND COMPASSES

GEOGRAPHICAL DIRECTION SYSTEMS

- True North
- Grid North
- Magnetic North
  - Magnetic Declination
  - Annual Change
  - Declination Diagram
- Compass Points
- Azimuths
- Bearings
- Conversions

MAGNETIC COMPASSES

- Types of Compasses
  - Rotating Needle
  - Rotating Card
  - Reversed Card
  - Electronic
- Compass Deviation

DIRECTION FINDING ON LARGE-SCALE MAPS

- Topographic Quadrangles
- Nautical Charts
- Computing Directions from Grid Coordinates

DIRECTION FINDING ON SMALL-SCALE MAPS

- Great-Circle Directions
  - Measuring Directions on a Globe
  - Measuring Directions on the Gnomonic Map Projection
- Rhumb-Line Directions
- The Navigator's Dilemma
- Computing Directions from Geographic Coordinates

SELECTED READINGS

"I'll go steadily south-west," says Tweedledum, "while you go steadily north-east, and when we meet we'll have a battle."
"Very well," replied Tweedledee. "It suits me, because I haven't got my armour today."
—F. Debenham

12

CHAPTER TWELVE

DIRECTION FINDING AND COMPASSES

Some people like to think that animals have an inborn sense of direction that the true outdoorspeople among us have somehow retained. If this is true, however, how do we account for the many animals as well as famed backwoods guides who become lost? A better explanation for the direction-knowing powers of animals, "primitive" people, and guides is that they have learned to be more observant than the rest of us. This is good news, for it means that anyone can learn to tell direction and, with practice, can share the distinction of having a "sense of direction."

If we say that certain people have a "sense of direction," what do we mean? That they always know where the North Star is? Or the North Pole? Or that, like Lassie, they can always find their way home? Direction, by definition, can only be determined with reference to something. The reference point may be near at hand or far away, concrete or abstract. This reference point, whether it is some object or some known position, establishes a **reference line**, sometimes called a base line, between you and it. Direction is measured relative to this reference line.

In its simplest form, direction is determined **egocentrically**. Your reference line is established by the way you are facing. You go left or right, "this way" or "that way," straight ahead or back, up or down the road—all in relation to an imaginary line pointing out from the front of your body.

A common form of egocentric direction is to use a symbolic clock face. You are assumed to be located at its center, facing 12:00. Your reference line is the line projected from your position straight ahead to 12:00. Now say that you want to find the direction to a distant object. The line from you to the object is called the **direction line**. Direction is given in hourly angular units as the difference between the reference line and the direction line. Something directly to your right would be located at 3:00, something behind you at 6:00, and something directly to your left at 9:00 (**Figure 12.1A**).

GEOGRAPHICAL DIRECTION SYSTEMS

Your direction-finding ability will improve if you learn to think **geocentrically** in terms of a **geographical direction system.** In a geographical system, as with the clock face, direction is measured in angular units of a circle (**Figure 12.1B**) with north at the top. In other words, north is equivalent to 12:00 on the clock face. This is probably why we tend to think of north as "up" and why north is customarily placed at the top of maps. Oddly enough, the convention of orienting maps with north at the top is also used in the Southern Hemisphere—most likely because early European settlers carried the custom there.

The north reference point is useful because the reference line is no longer oriented to your own body, as it is with egocentric directional methods. No matter which way you turn, north remains the same. To make this system valuable in direction finding, all you need do is find some reference line on the earth's surface which ties north to the ground. The direction to a distant object can then be given as the angle between the north-south reference line and your direction line.

There is no single north reference line used on all maps, because there are actually three types of north. Each has its advantages and disadvantages as a reference point, and each is best suited for certain purposes. The reference point used on most maps is called **true north**.

True North

True (or geographical) north is a fixed location on the earth—the north pole of the axis of earth rotation. A great-circle line from any point on earth to the North Pole—that is, a meridian —is known as a true-north reference line. Thus, any meridian can serve as your reference line in finding true north.

The advantage of true north is that you can find it in the field without using any special instruments. You can determine direction simply by making reference to natural features, much as animals do. People have used the sun and other stars as directional reference points since they first began observing nature. North was probably chosen as the reference point on maps because there are such good celestial ways to help us find it.

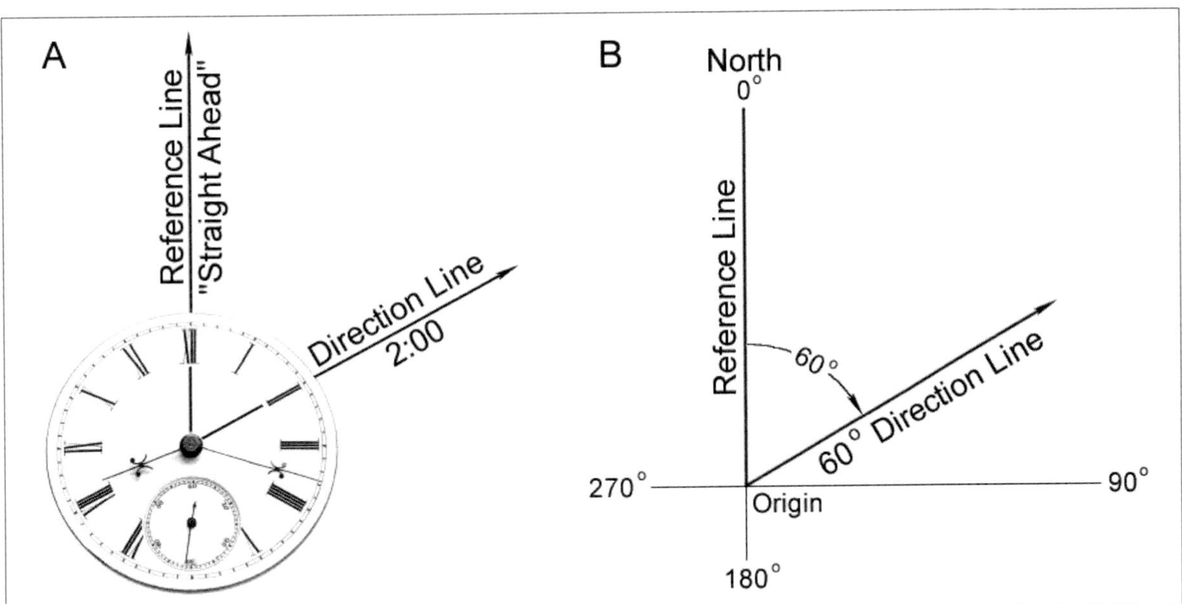

Figure 12.1 Direction is defined as the angular deviation from a base line. Sometimes a clock face is used as a directional reference system (A), but more commonly direction is measured in degrees from north (B).

One of the oldest and most reliable ways to find true north is to find the **North Star (Polaris)**. It is positioned in the Northern Hemisphere sky less than one degree away from the **North Celestial Pole** (the spot in the sky directly above the North Pole). Finding Polaris is a simple matter since it is one of the brightest stars in the sky and is conveniently located at the tip of the handle of the Little Dipper (**Figure 12.2**). Because the earth is rotating on its axis, all the stars seem to move in concentric paths around Polaris (**Figure 12.3**). We could hardly ask for a better true-north reference point.

You can use the sun as well as the stars to tell direction. For thousands of years, people have found the direction of true north by noting the position of the sun at noon (or at 1:00 p.m. daylight saving time). At other times of day, you can use the shadow cast by an object, and a bit of patience, to find true north. Here's how.

The first step is to find an object that casts a well-defined shadow on level ground (**Figure 12.4A**). Next, mark the spot at which the top of the shadow touches the ground. After waiting 30 minutes or so, again mark the tip of the shadow. A line drawn between your two marks is a true east-west line. Since the sun rises in the east and sets in the west, the shadow travels from west to east. Therefore, your first mark will be on the west end of the line and your second mark on the east end. With west to your left and east on your right, draw a perpendicular line. True north is at the top of the line.

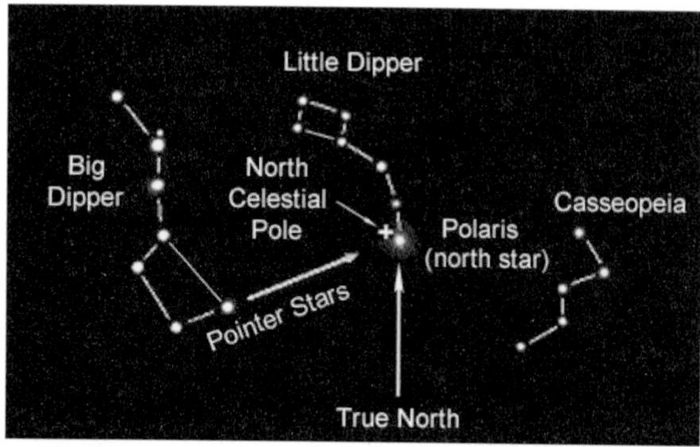

Figure 12.2 True north can easily be determined by observing the stars in the Northern Hemisphere sky at night to find Polaris, the North Star.

Figure 12.3 A time-lapse photo of the night sky in the Northern Hemisphere captures the apparent circular movement of stars around the North Celestial Pole and Polaris, the North Star. In fact, the earth, not the stars, is rotating.

The direction to true north can be determined in a few seconds if you are wearing a watch with hour and minute hands. Simply hold the watch horizontally at eye level, and then turn the watch until the hour hand points to the sun (**Figure 12.4B**). Now picture a spot on the dial halfway between the hour hand and 12:00 (1:00 for daylight saving time). In the northern hemisphere, a line from the center of the dial through that spot will point to true south, so the opposite direction is true north. In the southern hemisphere, the line points to true north. This method works best if you are located at the center of a time zone where the sun truly faces south at noon.

The problem with relying on the sun or Polaris as a reference point for true north is that the sun is visible only during the day and Polaris only at night. Also, they can be hidden by clouds. To overcome these difficulties, people have created their own "artificial stars" in the form of **navigation satellites**. The constellation of satellites developed and operated by the U.S. military is called the **Glo-**

bal Positioning System (GPS) (see Chapter 14 for more on GPS).

Since GPS satellites transmit signals to the earth continuously on a 24-hour basis, we now have an all-weather, day-or-night ability to determine the direction of the true-north reference line. It couldn't be easier. You merely turn on your GPS receiver, enter the latitude and longitude of a distant feature, and in seconds the GPS receiver gives you the direction to the feature with respect to true north.

Grid North

True north isn't always the most useful direction reference line. On maps that have a rectangular grid overprinted, you will find a second north—**grid north**. Unlike true north, it doesn't refer to any geographical place. It is purely artificial, established for the convenience of those who work with maps in the laboratory. Rectangular grids are often superimposed on maps to make it easier to use a protractor when measuring directions. The vertical lines on these grids point to grid north.

The Universal Transverse Mercator (UTM) and State Plane Coordinate (SPC) grids (see Chapter 4 for more on UTM and SPC grids) are standardized systems in which the lines of constant easting running from top to bottom are oriented to grid north. Grid-north lines usually aren't the same direction as true-north-pointing meridians on the map. Grid-north lines are straight and parallel, whereas meridians converge toward the north and south poles. If a map is centered on a vertical meridian, the grid line in the center of the map will also be vertical. It will point to true north only if the meridian is the central meridian for the UTM or SPC zone. The farther east or west the mapped area is from the center of the grid zone, the greater the difference will be between grid and true north (**Figure 12.5**). The angular difference between these two norths is called **grid declination.**

Grid north is defined by a single grid-coordinate system. When two or more grid systems occur on a single map, the system selected for grid north may be difficult to determine. On USGS quads, for example, the grid lines on the SPC system probably won't be at the same angle as the

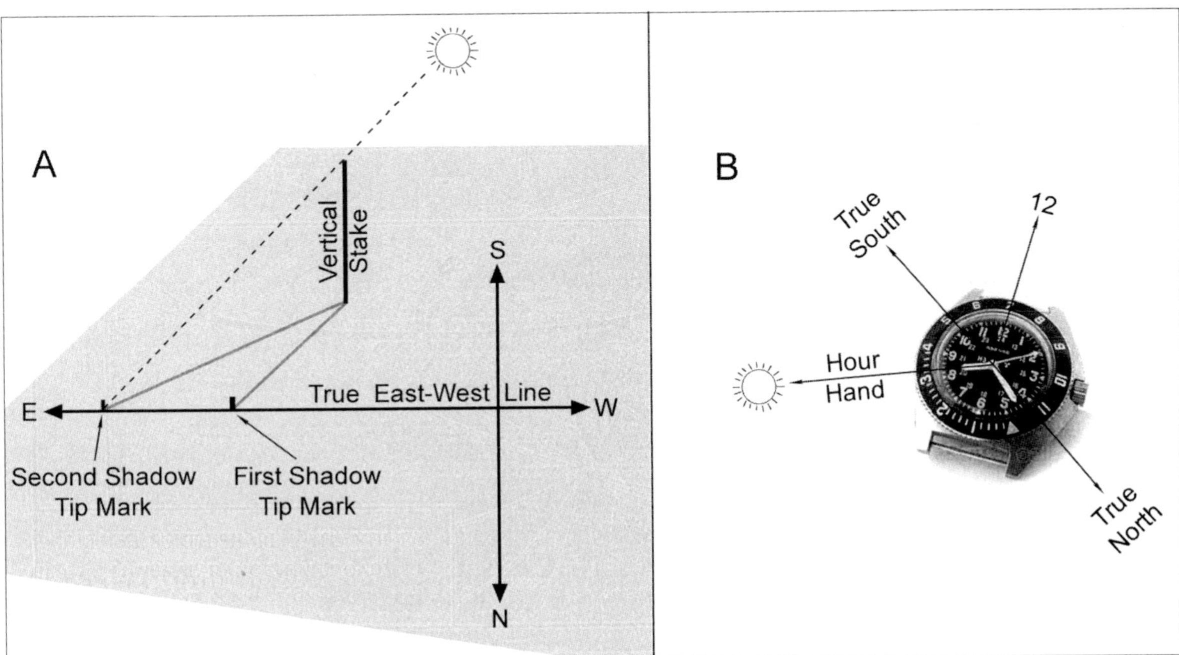

Figure 12.4 True north can be determined in the daytime by using shadows cast by the sun in conjunction with stakes placed in the ground (A) or with a clock face (B).

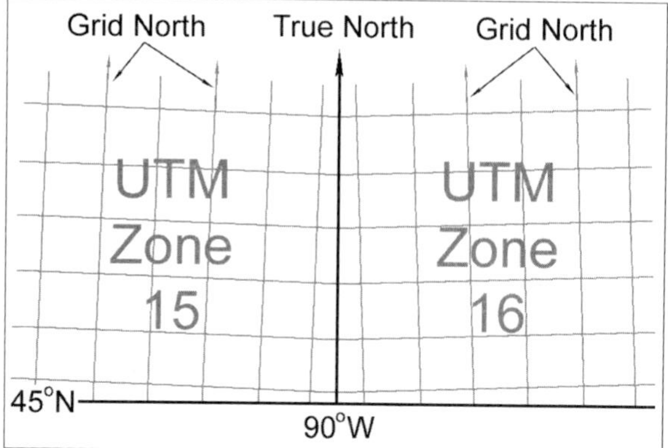

Figure 12.5 There can be a considerable angular difference between true north and grid north away from the center of a UTM grid zone. The maximum grid declination is at the edge of zones.

grid lines on the UTM system. The angular difference between these two grid norths on the Madison West, Wisconsin, quadrangle is illustrated in **Figure 12.6**.

Clearly, using a map with several grid orientations can be confusing. Fortunately, we can avoid this confusion because UTM grid lines are used as the standard grid north on UGSG topographic maps and other large-scale products.

Magnetic North

True north is valuable to map makers and GPS users, and grid north is a helpful aid to map study in the laboratory. The third north—**magnetic north**—is convenient for the map user in the field who has a magnetic compass.

The reason for using magnetic north as the directional reference point is its global utility. In effect, the earth is a giant magnet, with its **magnetic field** running roughly north and south (**Figure 12.7**). A small magnet also has a magnetic field running between its north and south poles. The magnetic property which makes a compass work is that when two magnets are put together, their like poles repel and unlike poles attract. Thus, a freely moving magnetized needle will align itself with the earth's magnetic field. The needle's south pole will point to the earth's north magnetic pole. If this end of the needle is marked distinctly, say with red paint or with the letter N, it will show us the magnetic reference line at our location.

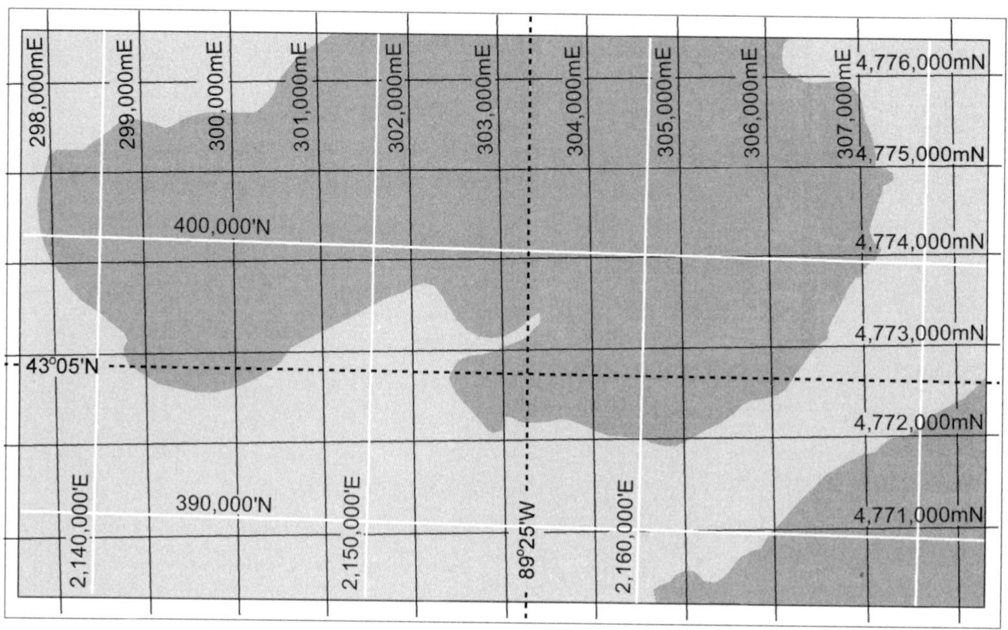

Figure 12.6 Grid north differs substantially from true north (indicated by a dashed meridian) for the UTM (black) and SPC (white) grid lines on this Madison West, Wisconsin, USGS 1:24,000 quadrangle. The near-vertical UTM easting lines are the standard grid north.

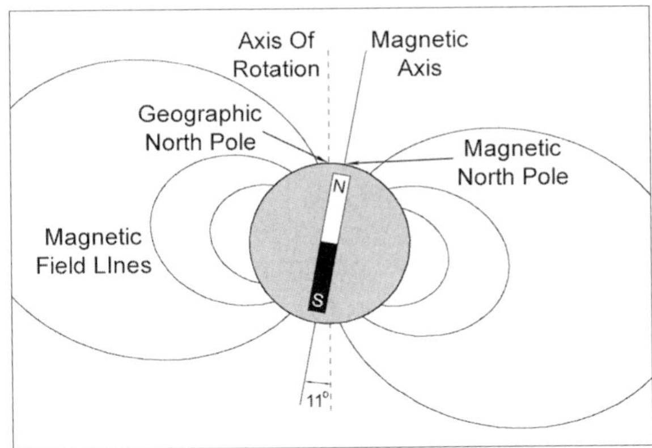

Figure 12.7 The earth's magnetic field resembles that of a simple bar magnet. There is a difference of approximately 11 degrees between the magnetic and geographic poles.

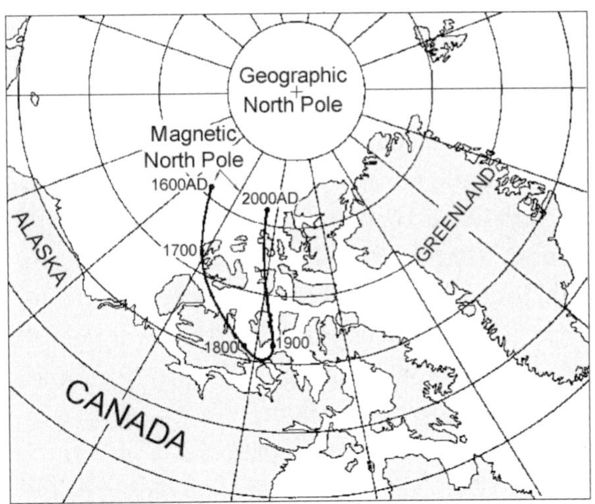

Figure 12.8 This map shows that magnetic north and true north rarely coincide at a location and that the magnetic north pole shifts greatly over time. In 2000, when this map was made, the magnetic north pole was located about 1,300 kilometers south of the geographic north pole.

Theoretically, the needle of a magnetic compass will point to the magnetic north pole from any place on the earth's surface. In practice, however, it doesn't always work out this way, as we'll see later in the chapter.

Magnetic Declination

We've already seen that grid north usually differs slightly from true north. Greater angular differences occur with magnetic north. The north pole of the earth's magnetic field is currently located in the Nunavut Territory of Canada (north of Bathurst Island), approximately 1,300 kilometers (800 miles) south of the true North Pole (**Figure 12.8**). This large distance between the positions of the two poles means that the true-north and magnetic-north reference lines rarely coincide, so the magnetic compass needle rarely points to true north. **Magnetic declination** (called **compass variation** on charts) is the angular difference between true and magnetic north.

The magnetic declination is so predictable that maps are available which show **isogonic lines**, or lines of constant angular difference between the two norths. Such an **isogonic map** is shown in **Figure 12.9**. Note that a line of "no declination" runs through the east-central part of the United States. At any position along this **agonic line**, the true and magnetic north poles are aligned and the compass needle points to true north. In contrast, magnetic declination exceeds 22° in the northwestern and northeastern corners of the country.

In Washington State's Puget Sound, the compass needle points to the east of true north and has **easterly declination**, while in Maine the needle points to the west of true north and has **westerly declination**. If you live in the east-central United States, you'll have little problem with magnetic declination for everyday purposes. But when you use a compass in the northwest or northeast parts of the country, you can't ignore the large difference between true and magnetic north. Compass users in Illinois may be blithely unaware of magnetic declination, but if they go for a backpacking vacation in the Washington Cascades they could be in for a shock.

Annual Change

To make matters worse, the magnetic declination for a given location changes slightly from year to year. The magnetic poles wander across the earth's surface, albeit in a somewhat predictable manner (see Figure 12.8). For this reason, the date shown on a topographic map or nautical chart is a critical piece of information for map users. If the map is used a decade or so after it was created, the declination may have changed significantly.

Nautical charts, which strive to give up-to-date direction information, tell exactly how much the variation is changing each year and in what direction. Charts for the United States give the **annual increase or decrease** in minutes of a degree per year. Canadian charts indicate the amount and direction of annual change (13'W, for example), then leave it to you to figure out if this is an increase or a decrease in declination.

A 1994 nautical chart of Vancouver, British Columbia, for instance, shows a magnetic variation of 20°30'E with an annual change of 7'W. The annual change is in the opposite direction of the variation, so it is a decrease. By 2000 the annual change had accumulated over six years to 42'W, so that the variation was 20°30' - 0°42', or 19°48'.

Declination Diagram

Declination is important to keep in mind, especially when you're in the field or navigating a boat or airplane. It will, of course, be more critical to take note of declination at some times than others, depending on how much accuracy is needed. Surveyors and other professionals who work with precise directional information must always be conscious of declination. Someone building a solar house would also want a precise determination of true north so that the structure could be aligned as effectively as possible. The rest of us may sometimes disregard declination, sometimes not.

Large-scale nautical and aeronautical charts are designed to be used with a compass in a boat or aircraft. **Compass variation (declination)** is shown by circular **compass roses** printed in one or more places on these charts (**Figure 12.10**). The outer compass circle in the compass rose is ori-

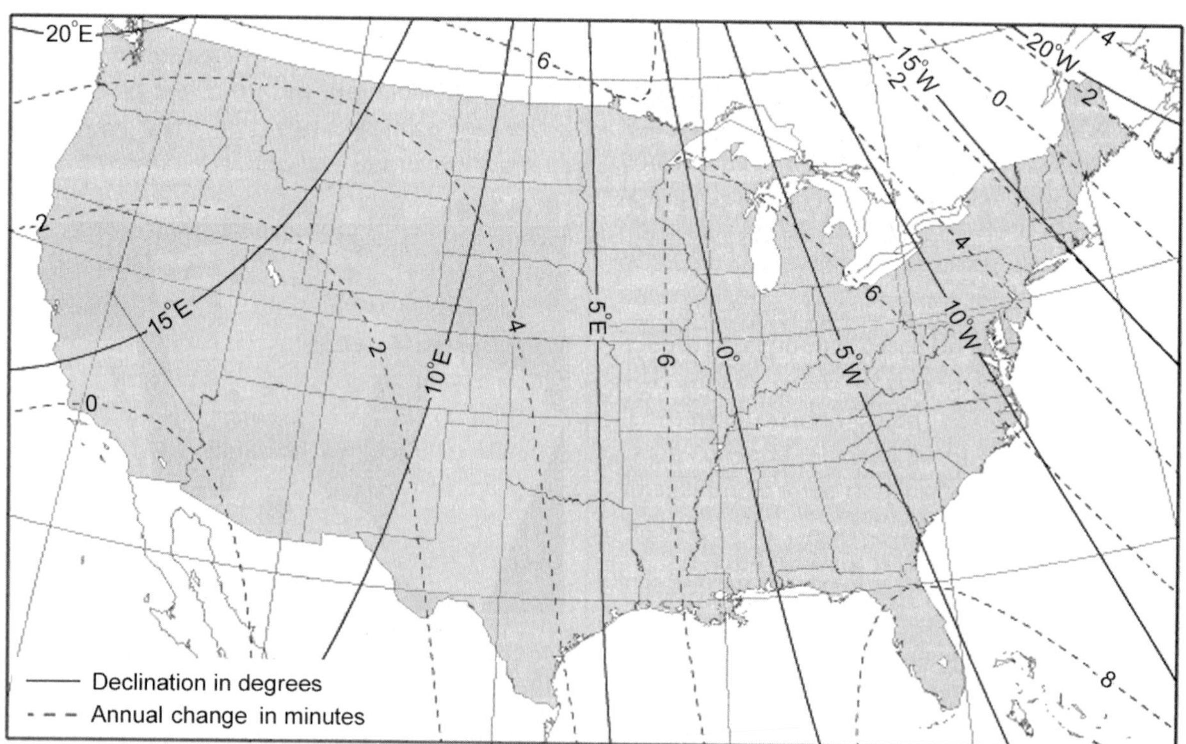

Figure 12.9 Isogonic map of the contiguous United States (1995). The zero-declination agonic line is slowly shifting to the west.

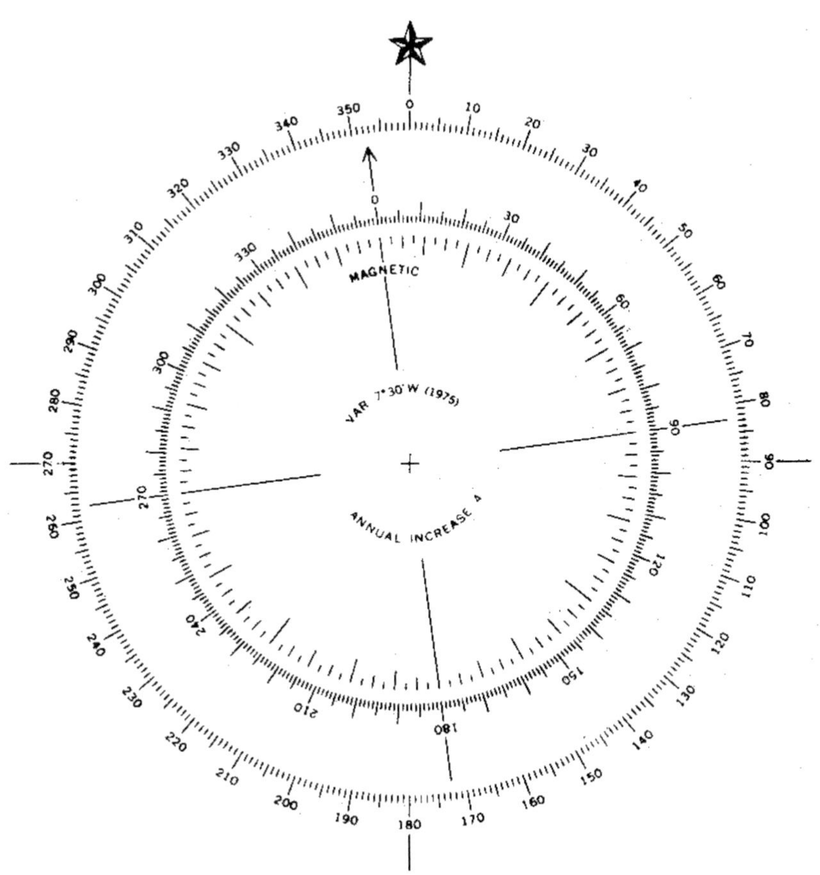

Figure 12.10 A typical compass variation (declination) diagram from a modern nautical chart. The diagram is positioned on the chart so that 0 degrees on the outer circle shows true north, while 0 degrees on the inner circle shows magnetic north. Compass variation and its annual change are also indicated near the center of the diagram.

ented to true north, while the inner ring is oriented to magnetic north. The angular difference between the zero-degree north points on the two rings indicates the compass variation (declination) at the time the chart was made. Notice that the annual change in compass declination is also shown near the center of the diagram so that the navigator may update the chart if necessary.

The standard topographic quadrangle series for the United States published by the USGS is another good example of a large-scale map designed for use with a compass in the field. On these maps a **declination diagram** is shown at the lower left margin of the map. Notice that the true, magnetic, and grid north reference lines are marked at the top with a star, fishhook barb, and the letters GN, respectively (**Figure 12.11**). Always use the

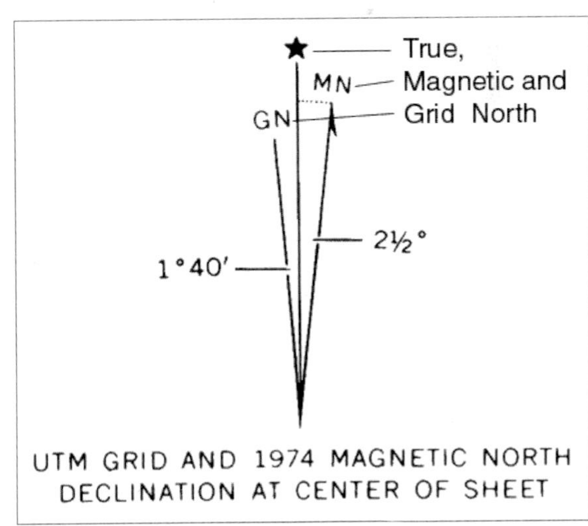

Figure 12.11 Declination diagram showing relations among true, grid, and magnetic north base lines on the Madison West, Wisconsin, USGS 1:24,000 quadrangle.

declination values printed on the diagram, and don't measure the angles on the diagram with a protractor. Small angular differences are often exaggerated on the declination diagram to make them more discernible.

The angular differences among the three north reference lines, taken from the Madison West, Wisconsin, USGS 1:24,000 quad, are illustrated in Figure 12.11. Notice that UTM grid declination and magnetic declination are given for the center of the sheet. Declination in areas toward the sides of the map could be slightly different. The larger the area covered by the map, the greater the change in declination from one side of the map to the other.

By comparing the three reference lines in the declination diagram, you can tell where the region covered by the map is located relative to the central meridian of the UTM grid and the isogonic chart of the country. If the north-south UTM grid lines tilt to the east, you know that the mapped region lies to the east of the central meridian. If the magnetic north lines slant to the east, you know that your mapped region is west of the agonic line. The reverse is true, of course, if the lines slant to the west. In the declination diagram shown in Figure 12.11, for example, grid lines tilt west and magnetic lines east. Consequently, you can tell that the Madison West quadrangle is located west of both the agonic line and the central meridian of the UTM zone.

Compass Points

The oldest compass-direction system is the use of **compass points** (**Figure 12.12**). Early mariners, who used the winds to find their way, devised compass points. The first mariner's compass card had eight points, representing the directions of the principal winds. But eight directions, sailors found, weren't exact enough. So they split their compass card further—first into eight additional "**half-points**" and later into 16 more "**quarter-points**."

The mariner's compass card thus came to have 32 points. The card, which looks something like a 32-petaled flower, is called a **compass rose**. The points on the card are named using a standard lettering system for the common cardinal directions.

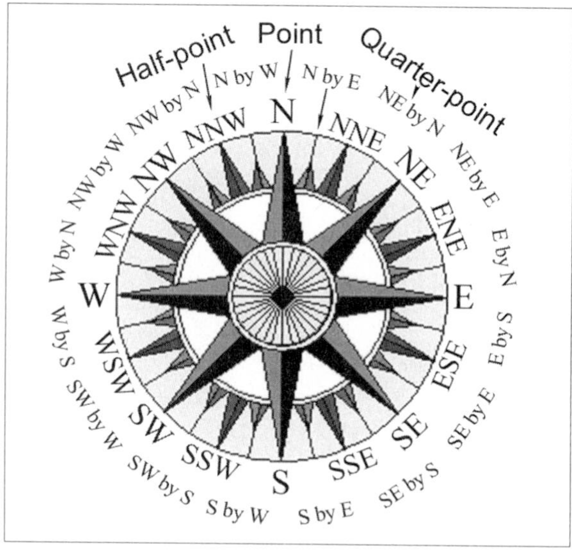

Figure 12.12 There are 32 points on the standard compass card: 8 points, 8 half-points, and 16 quarter-points.

Figure 12.12 shows how it's done. The sizes of the compass-rose points establish the priority system used to name direction. North, northeast, east, southeast, south, southwest, west, and northwest have first priority; the eight half-points have second; and the 16 quarter-points have third priority. A compass-rose reading is therefore of the form NE (verbally stated as "northeast"), ENE (stated as "east-northeast"), and so forth. Each of these terms, of course, has a direct numerical counterpart in degrees, since half-points are 45 degrees and quarter-points are 22.5 degrees apart.

In modern times, the mariner's compass-point system has been largely replaced by azimuth and bearing readings. Not only are azimuths and bearings less awkward and confusing to use, they are far more accurate.

Azimuths

The most common system of compass directions is the use of **azimuths**. An azimuth is the horizontal angle measured in degrees clockwise from a north reference line to a direction line (**Figure 12.13**). Azimuths range from 0° to 360° and are written either in decimal degrees (45.375°) or in degrees, minutes, and seconds (45°22'30").

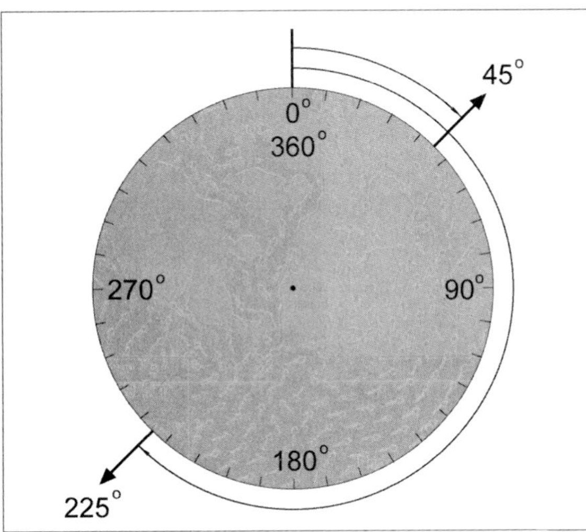

Figure 12.13 Azimuths are measured in degrees clockwise from a reference line at the top of the azimuth circle.

Azimuths are named according to which north reference line is used. Thus, there are **true, magnetic**, and **grid azimuths.** Compass roses for nautical and aeronautical charts (see Figure 12.10) have both true and magnetic azimuth circles to simplify navigation by either true or magnetic directions.

Bearings

The third compass-direction system is the use of **bearings** (**Figure 12.14**). Like azimuths, bearings are horizontal angles given in degrees. The difference is that azimuth readings go through the entire circle from 0° to 360°, while bearing readings range only from 0° to 90°. Bearings are measured clockwise (eastward) or counterclockwise (westward) from either a north or south reference line, whichever is closer to the direction line. To avoid ambiguity with this method, it's essential to give both the reference line (north or south) and an orientation (east or west) in addition to the angular measure in degrees. Therefore, bearings are written as N30°E (meaning 30 degrees east of north), S25°W (meaning 25 degrees west of south), and so on.

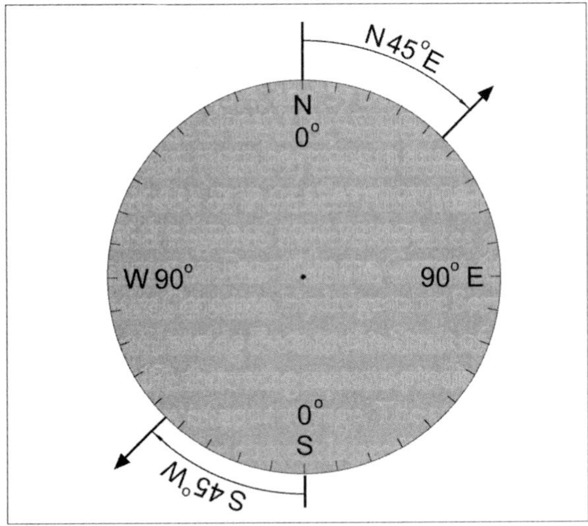

Figure 12.14 Bearings range from 0 to 90 degrees and are measured from north or south toward east or west.

A compass with a bearing card is frequently referred to as a surveyor's compass because it has long been preferred as a surveying instrument. Surveyors like the bearing system because specifying the opposite direction (called a **back-bearing**) is simply a matter of changing letters. For example, the back-bearing of N45°E is S45°W. But since surveyors often must convert bearings to azimuths in their record keeping, it's common for bearings to be augmented with azimuths on the compass card.

Conversions

With three systems for specifying direction, sooner or later you'll want to convert one type of compass reading to another. When you do so, remember the declination diagram discussed earlier. Also keep in mind the mathematical relationships between the three systems of specifying direction. For instance, a true azimuth of 85° converts to a true bearing of N85°E, and both may be roughly described by the "east" compass point.

The declination information provided on large-scale topographic maps and nautical charts lets you convert true, magnetic, and grid azimuths from one form to another. To make the declination information easier to understand, it's a good idea to make an enlarged sketch of the declination diagram and an approximately correct direction line. For example, in **Figure 12.15A** we have sketched a direction line for a 65° true azimuth in a locale with a 17°E magnetic declination and 3°W grid

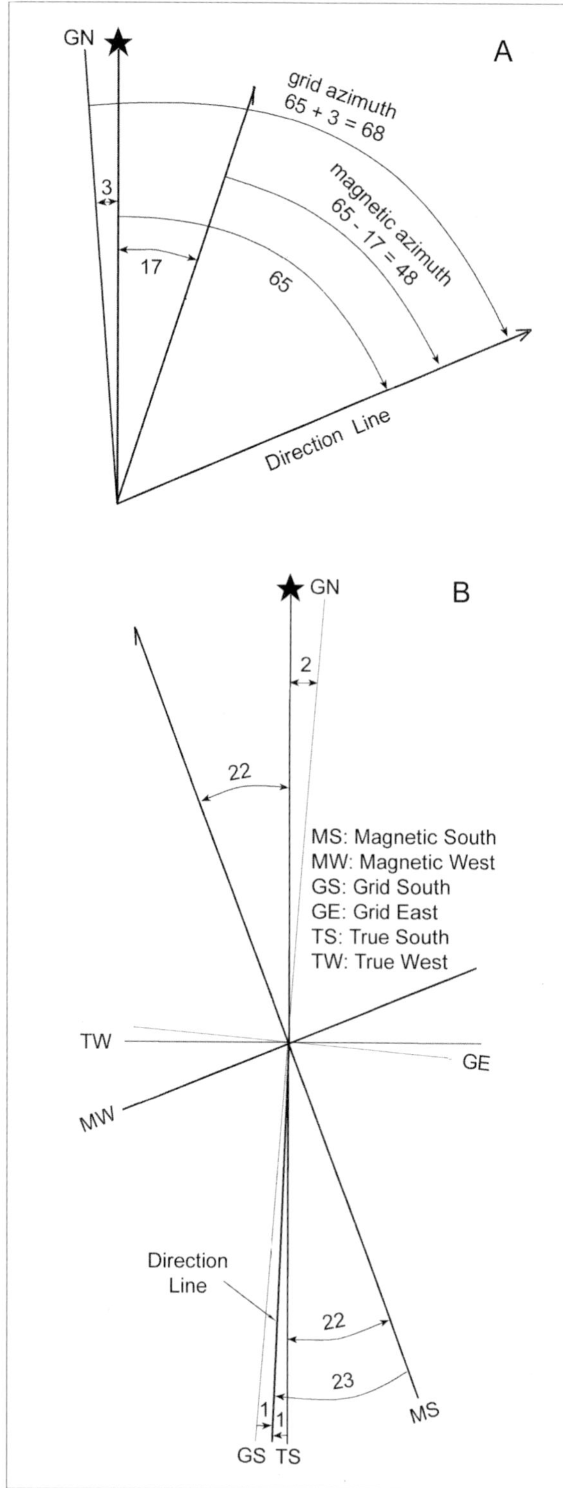

Figure 12.15 It is sometimes necessary to make conversions from one direction system to another. Conversions to azimuths (A) and bearings (B) are described in the text.

declination. By marking the two declinations and the true azimuth with arcs, you can easily see that the magnetic azimuth for this direction must be 65° minus the 17° magnetic declination, or 48°. Similarly, you can see that the grid declination must be added to the true azimuth when converting to a grid azimuth. In this example, the grid azimuth is 65° plus 3°, or 68°.

Converting bearings to and from true, magnetic, and grid reference lines is more complex, but a sketch of the angles involved again clarifies what needs to been added and subtracted. In **Figure 12.15B**, we have sketched a magnetic bearing of S23°W at a locale with a magnetic declination of 22°W and grid declination of 2°E. The diagram includes both magnetic and true south and the 22° angular difference between the two. Notice that the magnetic bearing is 1° west of true south, so the true bearing must be S1°W.

Now let's consider **grid-bearing** notation. Figure 12.15B shows magnetic and grid south, and the 2° difference between them. The direction line for the magnetic bearing is 1° to the east of grid south, so the grid bearing must be S1°E.

MAGNETIC COMPASSES

One of the most useful aids in navigation and map work is the **magnetic compass.** This clever device has three main parts—a balancing needle or floating disk, which has been magnetized so that it will align itself with the earth's magnetic field; a jewel pivot or fluid bowl, which allows the needle or disk to float freely; and a dial, called a compass card, marked with directions (**Figure 12.16**). Some compasses also have a damper button, which locks the needle in place when the compass isn't in use and can help stabilize the needle while the compass is being used. Sometimes a sighting device is also added for convenience. The case that encloses all these parts is known as the compass housing.

Types of Compasses

Compass quality varies greatly, in rather direct relation to the price (currently $5 to $1,200). You may be confused by the wide range in prices and designs, but you don't need to be, especially if you

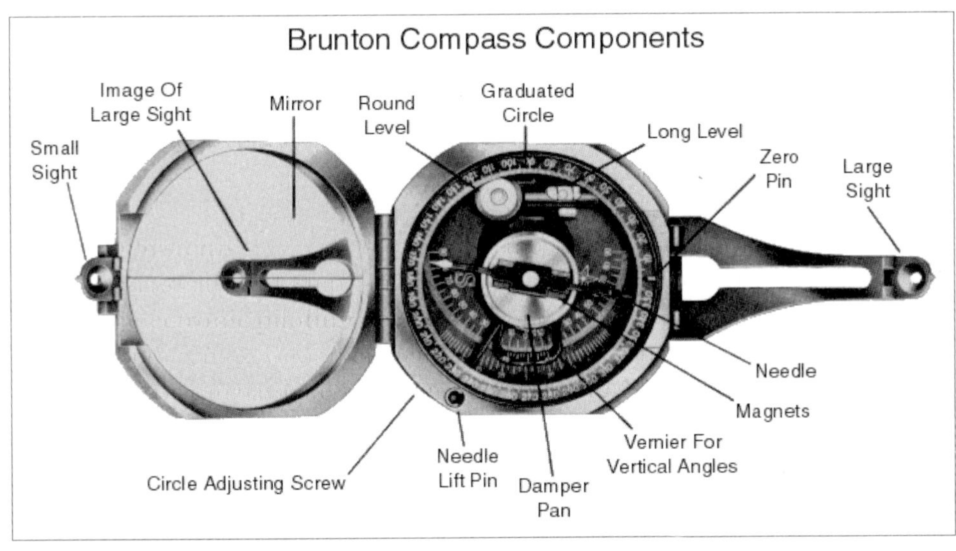

Figure 12.16 Basic components of a Brunton precision magnetic compass.

remember that there are only four basic types of compasses. For convenience, we'll refer to these as rotating-needle, rotating-card, reversed-card, and electronic compasses.

Rotating Needle

Rotating-needle compasses have the direction system inscribed clockwise on the compass card (**Figure 12.17** top). The compass needle is balanced on a center pin and rotates independently of the compass card. This design has the advantage that you can make either magnetic or true readings. To find magnetic north, rotate the compass card slowly until north on the dial is lined up with the needle. With your compass set this way, you can take a sighting on any object and the reading on the compass will be relative to magnetic north.

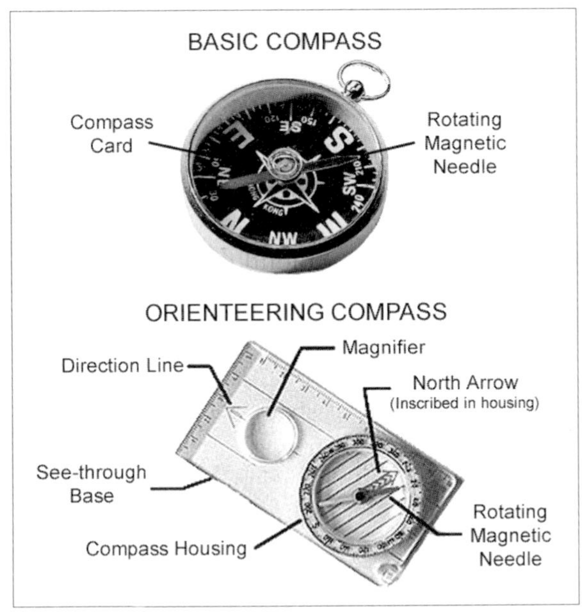

Figure 12.17 Rotating-needle compasses.

Suppose, for instance, that you want to find the direction to a distant tree. With the needle stabilized on north, face the tree and project an imaginary direction line (sight line) from the center of the compass to the tree. You will now be able to read from the dial the number of degrees between magnetic north and the tree.

Your reading will, of course, be approximate. A more precise reading is possible if a sighting aid has been added to the compass. Sighting devices are of two forms. One type, resembling a standard raised gunsight, is mounted on opposite sides of the housing, as on the compass in Figure 12.16. Instead of peering over your compass at the tree, you simply rotate the sighting device until you can see the tree through it. You can then read the angle between the sight line and magnetic north. Readings are thus made easier and more accurate. Most rotating-needle compasses don't include these raised sights, however, because they increase the cost and bulk of the compass and because approximate readings are usually good enough.

A second form of sighting aid is that found on **orienteering compasses**. On these compasses, the housing (consisting of a compass card, an orienting arrow, and a floating magnetic needle) is mounted on a transparent rectangular base (Figure 12.17 bottom). To use an orienteering compass, you merely align the direction line, which is etched into the base, with your destination, and then rotate the compass housing until the orienting arrow is aligned with the magnetic needle. Now read the direction on the compass card beneath the sight line. This is the direction to your destination.

A major advantage of rotating-needle compasses is that they allow you to make true as well as magnetic readings. To find true rather than magnetic north, first look at a declination diagram or compass rose to find the local magnetic declination. Then rotate your compass card east or west until the needle points to the amount of declination for your area. If the local declination is 5°E, you will line up the needle with 5°E on the dial. Now when you take a sighting to an object, you will obtain a true reading, because you have compensated for magnetic declination. Therefore, a rotating-needle compass is easy to use with maps when a true reading is most useful, as well as in the field when a magnetic reading is of the most use.

Rotating Card

On the **rotating-card compass**, the magnetic needle and compass card are joined and work as a single unit floating in a bowl. Consequently, you don't have to bother with aligning the needle and compass card, as you did with the rotating-needle compass. As soon as the disk stabilizes and the needle points to north, you're set to make your sightings. Magnetic readings are thus simplified—an advantage when you are in the field without maps.

But the rotating-card compass points only to magnetic north, not to true north. Therefore, it isn't well suited for use with maps oriented to true north, particularly if there is significant magnetic declination in the local area. To obtain a true reading, you'll have to add (or subtract) local declination to (or from) your reading.

The **mariner's compass** is probably the most widely used rotating-card compass. Since medieval

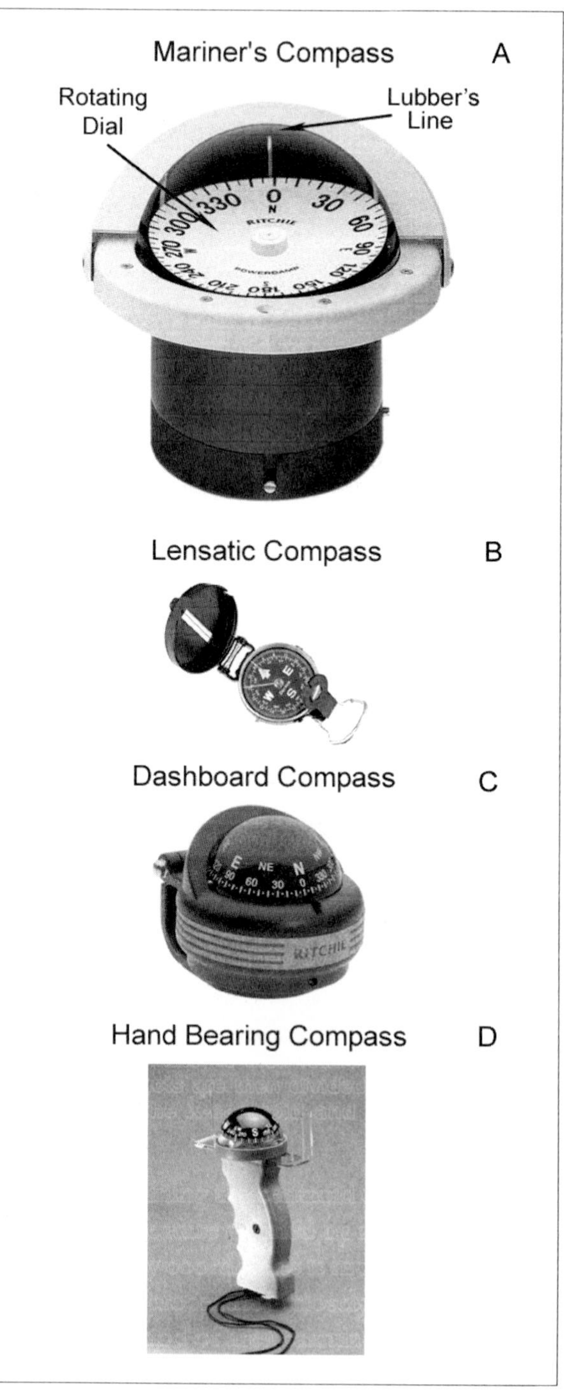

Figure 12.18 Rotating-card compasses.

times, mariners have placed a floating magnetized compass card in a bowl of clear liquid (**Figure 12.18A**). A vertical pin in the middle of the bowl centers and stabilizes the compass card while allowing it to turn freely to magnetic north with changes in boat heading. The compass is suspended so that it remains horizontal as the ship pitches and rolls in the water. A **lubber's line** parallel to the centerline of the ship is marked on the edge of the bowl to allow directions to be read relative to the direction of travel.

Lensatic compasses, available as military surplus items, also fall into the rotating-card group (**Figure 12.18B**), as do the common floating-dial compasses placed on the dashboard of your car (**Figure 12.18C**). Mariners usually have onboard a floating-dial **hand bearing compass** (**Figure 12.18D**). The compass may be mounted on a pistol grip and have a vertical lubbers line and rifle-like sights, all to help you point the compass quickly and accurately.

Reversed Card

With either a rotating-needle or rotating-card compass, you'll have to figure out the angle between true north and the object toward which you are sighting. A **reversed-card compass** directly displays this angle for you. You'll have to pay more for such convenience, of course. But for some people, particularly surveyors and others who make a living with map and compass, the ease of making readings is worth the extra cost.

Reversed-card compasses, like rotating-needle compasses, have a freely rotating needle and independent compass card. They are almost identical to rotating-needle compasses, except that they include a number of refinements which make them more useful. The first thing you'll notice about a reversed-card compass is that the direction system seems to be backward—west and east are reversed on the compass card (see **Figure 12.19**). The manufacturer hasn't made a mistake; there is a good reason for this design.

To visualize the logic behind the reversed direction system, imagine yourself with a rotating-needle compass. Assume that you are facing north and that the needle on your compass is also pointing north. Now turn slowly to face the object whose direction you are seeking. Although the needle actually remains stationary, it will look as though it is moving around the compass card in the opposite direction from which you move. If you turn directly to the east, the needle will point due west. You can see how awkward it would be to substitute west for east mentally each time you made a reading. On reversed-card compasses, therefore, west and east have been switched on the compass card. If you hold a reversed-card compass and turn to the east, the needle will also point east, and you can directly read the direction to which the compass needle points.

The reversed-card compass is the most sophisticated, expensive, and versatile of the three types we've discussed so far. Like the rotating-needle compass, it can be set for local magnetic declination, thereby permitting true readings. While rotating-needle compasses sometimes include a sighting device, reversed-card compasses always do. In

Figure 12.19 Reversed-card compass.

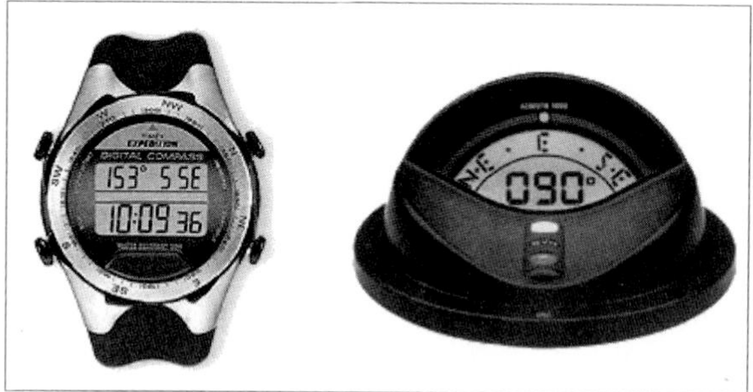

Figure 12.20 Electronic compasses with digital displays, including a watch-compass combination.

addition, a damper button is usually included, as you can expect precision craftsmanship. More than one direction system is often incorporated onto the compass card to make several different types of readings possible. All these features make for a very accurate compass. To take advantage of this accuracy potential, most professionals use a tripod with reversed-card compasses, just as photographers do with very expensive and sensitive cameras.

Reversed-card compasses are used almost exclusively by professionals. **Cruiser or forester compasses** (so named because foresters use them to plan timber-cutting lines) fall into this class. The best known example of a forester compass is the Brunton Pocket Transit (see Figures 12.16 and 12.19).

Electronic

Electronic compasses measure the relative strengths of magnetic fields passing through two wire coils. Sophisticated electronics convert these measurements into a continuous determination of the direction of the earth's magnetic field, and hence magnetic north. The instrument then computes the azimuth between magnetic north and the direction of travel.

Electronic compasses use digital displays to show headings (**Figure 12.20**). Most allow you to enter the magnetic declination so that you can determine and display true azimuths.

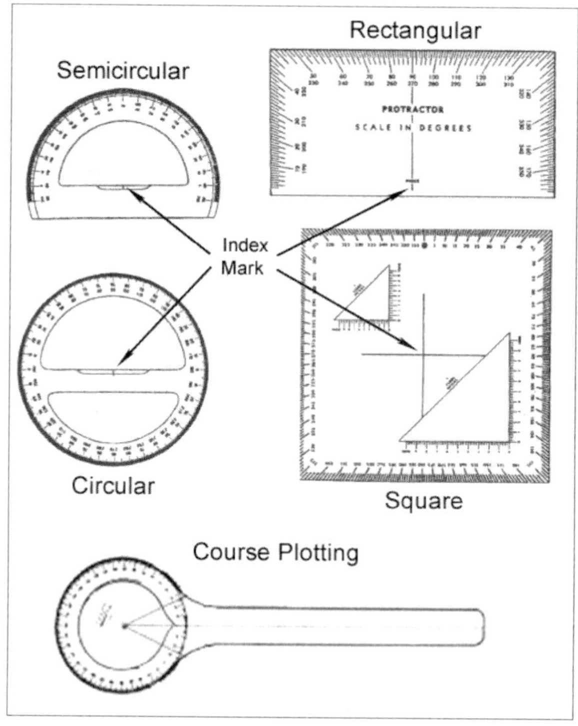

Figure 12.21 Types of protractors used to measure azimuths and bearings from maps.

Compass Deviation

Notice on the isogonic map (Figure 12.9) how in certain areas the isogonic lines appear to wiggle back and forth rather than head straight for the magnetic pole. These are areas of **compass deviation** where the compass needle is strongly affected by **local anomalies**. These anomalies may be caused by non-magnetic forces, such as regional variation in earth density, or by additional local magnetism, such as that produced by magnetic ore bodies. Localized **magnetic anomalies** that shift the compass needle thirty degrees in less than a mile exist on the earth but cannot be plotted on the small-scale isogonic map. The exact location of these anomalies may be described in notes printed on the navigational chart covering the area.

Compass deviation isn't always so predictable, though. It may also be caused by **local dis-**

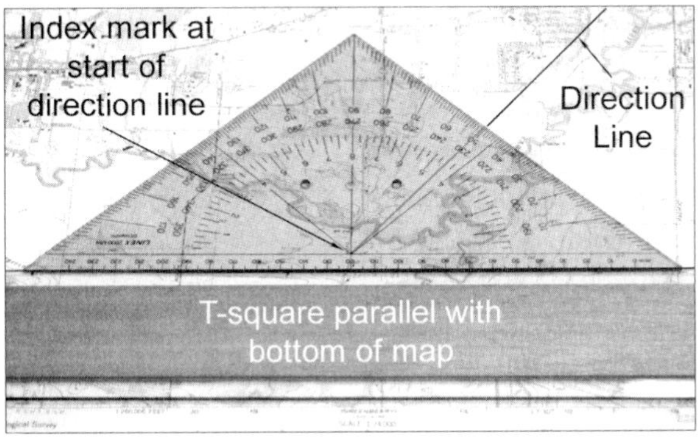

Figure 12.22 Finding the true azimuth of a direction line on a topographic map. See the text for the steps in the measurement procedure.

turbances, such as powerlines, thunderstorms, and iron objects. Since this second source of deviation won't show up on isogonic maps, you must constantly watch for it. Try to keep away from known disturbances and be on the lookout for unknown ones, which may make your compass needle pull "off" north or act erratically.

DIRECTION FINDING ON LARGE-SCALE MAPS

You can accurately measure the azimuth or bearing of a direction line if you can plot its endpoints on a large-scale map designed for navigation purposes. Topographic quadrangles and nautical charts are good examples, since both are made on conformal map projections that preserve the geometry of the azimuth and bearing systems on the earth's surface. A **straightedge** and **protractor** are all you need to measure these angles.

A protractor divides a circle into equal angular intervals, usually degrees. You are probably already familiar with semi-circular and circular protractors used in basic geometry. You can use these for direction finding, along with square, rectangular, and course-plotting protractors specially made for measuring directions on maps (**Figure 12.21**). All protractors have the **angle scale** along their

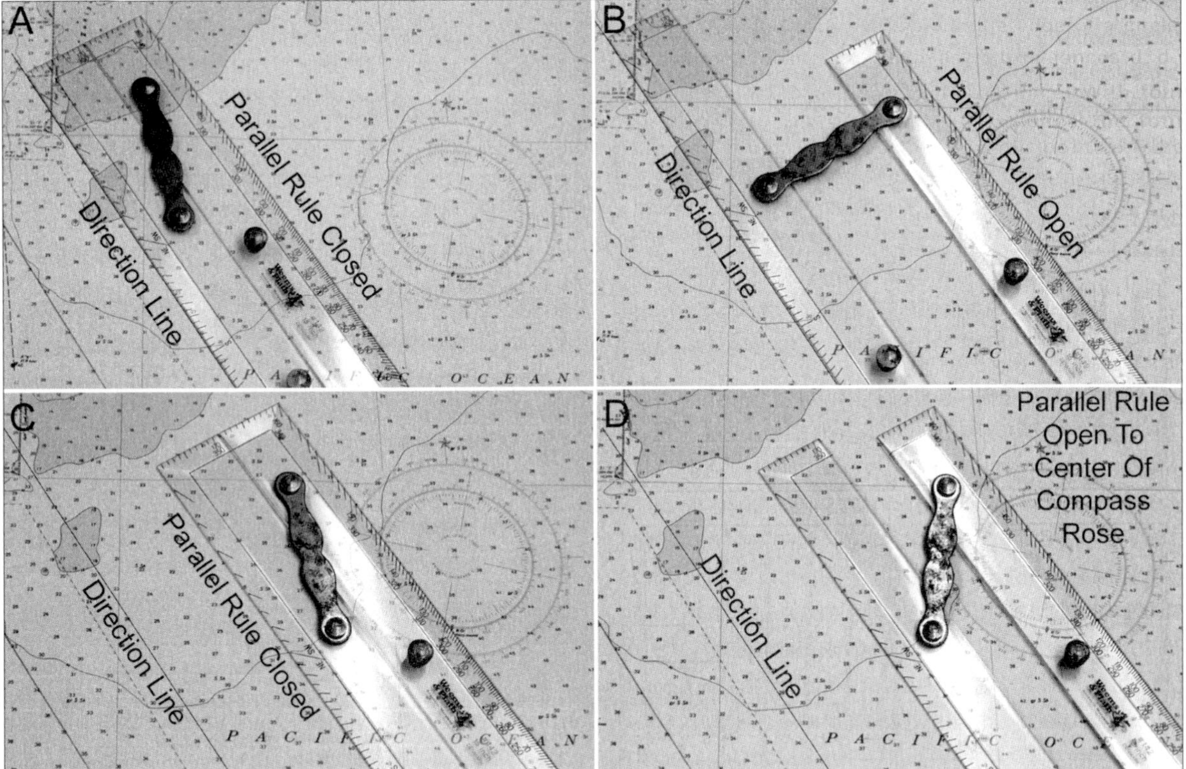

Figure 12.23 Finding the true or magnetic azimuth of a direction line by using a parallel rule on a nautical chart. See the text for the steps in the measurement procedure.

edge and an **index mark** at the center of the protractor circle.

Topographic Quadrangles

To determine the true azimuth for the direction line between points A and B on a topographic quadrangle, you can use the following procedure (see **Figure 12.22**):

1. Place the map on a rectangular table so that the bottom edge of the map is parallel with the bottom of the table. Align the bottom of the map with the top edge of a T-square straightedge placed on the left edge of the table. The map is now oriented to true north.
2. Lightly draw the direction line on the map.
3. Place a semi-circular or rectangular protractor along the top edge of the T-square, then move the T-square vertically and the protractor horizontally so that the index mark is over the start of the direction line.
4. Read the true azimuth from the angle scale on the protractor.

You can use the same procedure to determine a grid azimuth, except that you must first orient the map to grid north. To do so, rotate the map on the table until either a northing line or edge ticks for the same northing are aligned parallel to

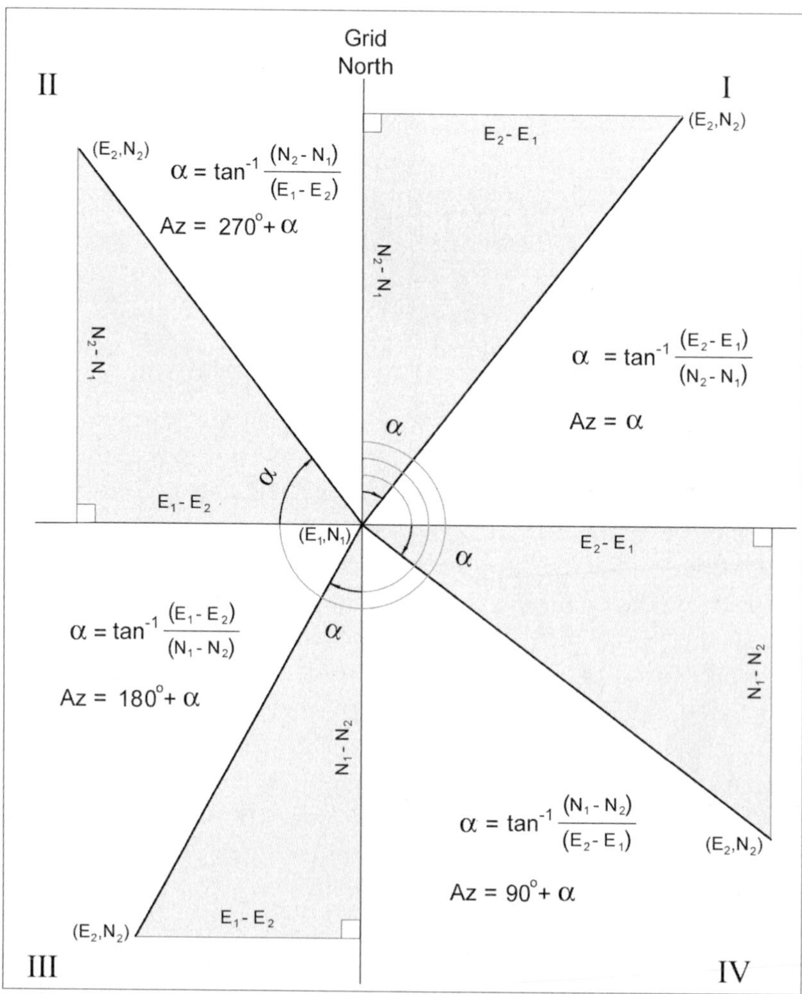

Figure 12.24 Trigonometric basis for computing grid azimuths from grid coordinates.

the bottom of the map. If UTM easting lines are printed on the map, you can align the protractor with one of these vertical lines. Now move the index mark to the start of the direction line, and you can read the grid azimuth from the protractor.

Magnetic azimuths are best measured by finding the true or grid azimuth for the direction line, then converting to a magnetic azimuth using the procedure described earlier in this chapter. You may be tempted to orient the map to the magnetic reference line on the declination diagram and then measure the magnetic azimuth directly with your protractor. Don't do this! Remember that the declination angles are usually so small that the angles between the reference lines in the diagram are increased to make them distinguishable. Only the declination values printed on the map are correct.

Nautical Charts

Accurately determining directions on nautical charts is a critical task in marine navigation. Centuries ago chartmakers simplified the task by putting one or more compass roses on each chart. The modern compass rose has an outer circular angular scale for true azimuths and an inner scale for magnetic azimuths.

Marine navigators use a special straightedge, called a **parallel rule**, to "walk" a direction line until it goes through the center of the compass rose (**Figure 12.23**). A parallel rule consists of two straightedges connected by metal bars that allow the straightedges to remain parallel as they are separated.

To operate the parallel rule, first push the two straightedges together, and align the top or bottom edge with the direction line (Figure 12.23A). Holding the bottom straightedge firmly in place, separate the straightedges so that the top straightedge is closer to the compass rose (Figure 12.23B). You next firmly hold the top straightedge and move the bottom straightedge until it closes the gap between it and the top straightedge (Figure 12.23C). Repeat this holding and moving procedure until you can place the top straightedge at the center of the compass rose (Figure 12.23D). The parallel rule should be parallel to the direction line so that you can read the true or magnetic azimuth from the outer or inner scale on the compass rose.

Computing Directions From Grid Coordinates

You can compute a grid azimuth if you know the grid coordinates (see Chapter 4 for more on grid coordinates) for the endpoints of the direction line. The computation is done with simple trigonometry, as illustrated in **Figure 12.24**. You first need to determine in which **quadrant** the direction line lies. If the beginning point has grid coordinates (E_1,N_1) and the ending point is at (E_2,N_2), the rule for quadrants is:

Quadrant I:	$E_2 > E_1$ and $N_2 > N_1$
Quadrant II:	$E_2 < E_1$ and $N_2 > N_1$
Quadrant III:	$E_2 < E_1$ and $N_2 < N_1$
Quadrant IV:	$E_2 > E_1$ and $N_2 < N_1$

Once you know the quadrant, you can solve the corresponding right triangle for angle α by finding its trigonometric tangent. Remember that the tangent of an angle in a right triangle is the ratio of the opposite and adjacent sides to the angle (rise over run). The lengths of the opposite and adjacent sides are the differences of the eastings and northings for the endpoints of the direction line. Slightly different equations are needed for each quadrant, since the difference in eastings defines the opposite side in quadrants I and III, and the adjacent side in quadrants II and IV. The beginning and ending northings and eastings for the direction line must also be reversed in some quadrants to always have positive distances for the opposite and adjacent sides.

After you find angle α, you need to add 90°, 180°, or 270° for quadrants IV, III, and II, respectively, in order to convert the angle to a grid azimuth.

An example of this calculation is to find the grid azimuth for a direction line from UTM (easting, northing) coordinate (345,630mE, 4,335,480mN) to coordinate (353,287mE, 4,308,592mN). Since the second easting is greater than the first and the second northing is less than the first, the direction line lies in quadrant IV.

Knowing the quadrant, you now solve the quadrant IV azimuth equation:

$$\alpha = \tan^{-1}\left(\frac{(N_1 - N_2)}{(E_2 - E_1)}\right)$$

$$\alpha = \tan^{-1}\left(\frac{(4335480 - 4308592)}{(353287 - 345630)}\right)$$

$$\alpha = \tan^{-1}\left(\frac{26888}{7657}\right) = \tan^{-1}(3.511558)$$

$$\alpha = 74.1°\Lambda \; Az. = 74.1° + 90° = 164.1°$$

DIRECTION FINDING ON SMALL-SCALE MAPS

"Fly north to get east" was Charles Lindbergh's philosophy when he reached Japan by flying over the North Pole. Determining direction on a round earth, as every ship and plane pilot knows, is a far different matter from direction finding over short distances.

Until now, we've defined direction as the angle between a direction line and reference line. But when dealing with directions for points over a hundred miles apart, the flat-earth methods we have just discussed must be modified to account for earth's sphericity. On the spherical earth, there are two types of direction lines—**great-circle routes** between two points and **rhumb lines** of constant compass direction. Let's look at both these types of direction.

Great-Circle Directions

Directions along the great-circle route between two points on the earth's surface are true azimuths because they are measured relative to true north. What makes great-circle routes most valuable to navigators is that they are the shortest possible routes between two locations on the spherical earth. To minimize travel time, navigators traveling long distances want to move along a great-circle path.

Measuring Directions on a Globe

One way to measure true azimuths along a great-circle route is to use a globe (**Figure 12.25**), since all true azimuths along the path are correct. You can hold a string tightly against a globe to find the

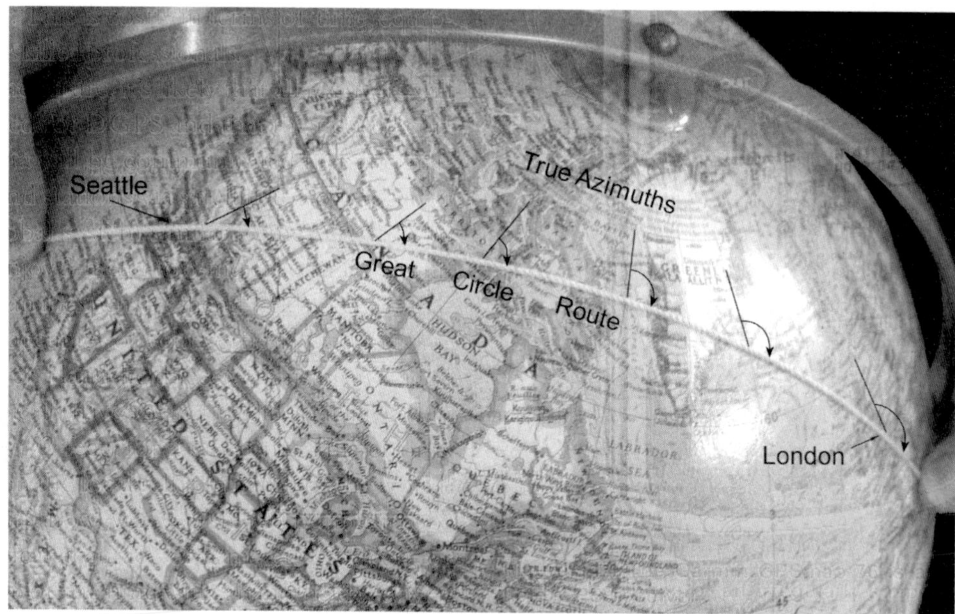

Figure 12.25 True azimuths along a great-circle route are shown correctly on a globe.

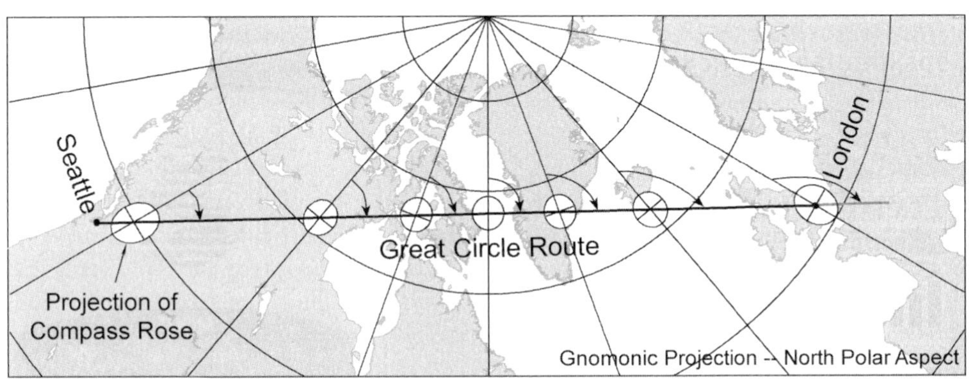

Figure 12.26 The great-circle route from Seattle to London is a straight line on the gnomonic map projection. Circular compass roses at points where the route crosses major meridians are projected as ellipses, showing the distortion of directions that makes it possible to measure true azimuths only roughly along the route.

great-circle route between two locales. A friend can mark the angles from meridians to the great circle, and you can measure these on the globe with your protractor. You will notice that the great-circle route between Seattle and London, for example, has continuously increasing true azimuths from around 30° at Seattle to around 160° as London is approached. This procedure is time consuming and difficult to do accurately, however, so flat maps are used to make better measurements.

Measuring Directions on the Gnomonic Map Projection

The only map projection on which all great circles project as straight lines is the gnomonic (see Chapter 3 for more on this projection). You can use the gnomonic projection to roughly find the true azimuth at a point along the great-circle path between two distant cities like Seattle and London (**Figure 12.26**). Here's how:

1. Draw the straight-line great-circle route between Seattle and London on the gnomonic projection.

2. Find the westernmost meridian that the great-circle route intersects (120°W in this example). Mark the point of intersection with a dot.

3. Place your protractor so that the index mark is on the dot and the zero degree mark on the angle scale is aligned with the meridian.

4. The angle to the great-circle line is roughly the true azimuth.

Notice the projections of compass roses at the intersection of meridians and the great-circle route—all are ellipses! Your measurement with the circular protractor is being done on elliptical direction dials that change in shape along the route. You could make accurate direction measurements if you had an elliptical protractor that would let you constantly change its elongation, but no such device exists. Hence, your protractor only allows rough measurements of true azimuths.

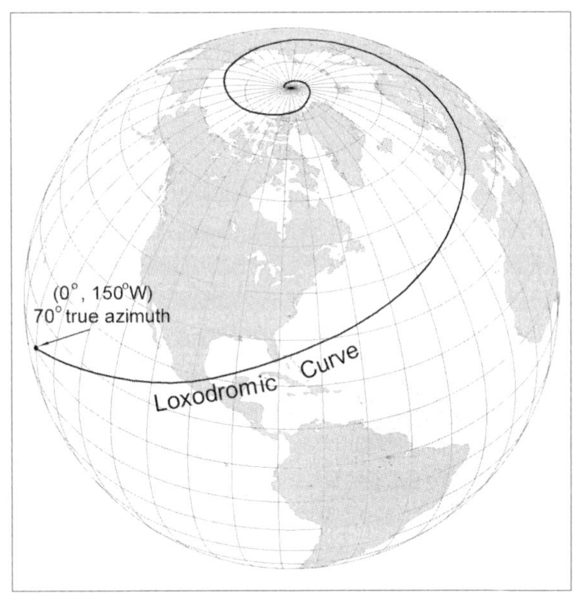

Figure 12.27 A rhumb-line heading of 70 degrees starting at the equator will trace out a loxodromic curve as it converges on the north pole.

Rhumb-Line Directions

When using a compass to navigate, navigators may soon grow weary of continually making directional measurements or computations and steering their craft to keep exactly on a great-circle route. They can alleviate these problems by following a rhumb-line path.

A direction line which is extended so that it crosses each meridian at the same angle is called a **rhumb line**. Rhumb lines are routes of constant compass readings and are therefore extremely useful to navigators. If they follow one of these lines, navigators can maintain a course without constantly figuring out new headings and making turns. They merely check the compass to be sure that they are crossing each meridian at the angle of their rhumb line. Their path may bend, but their compass direction won't change.

Rhumb lines running east-west along the equator or north-south along a meridian return eventually to their points of origin and are also great circles. Those running east-west along parallels other than the equator also close on themselves but are small circles, not great-circle routes.

Rarely, however, are rhumb lines either great or small circles. More commonly they cross meridians at an oblique angle, tracing out an odd-looking path. To cross each meridian at the same angle, the oblique rhumb line has to keep curving on the spherical earth. Its path on the earth forms a spiral, known as a **loxodromic curve**. **Figure 12.27** shows the loxodromic curve that results when a constant 70° direction line (one which intersects every meridian at an angle of 70 degrees) starting at the equator converges on the north pole.

To show all rhumb lines on maps as straight lines, a special projection is required. Mercator solved this problem in 1569, as **Figure 12.28** shows, by pulling the meridians and parallels apart at higher latitudes to create a conformal world projection that preserves directions at any point on the projection surface (see Chapter 3 for more on Mercator projections). On a Mercator projection, then, loxodromic curves have been straightened. This valuable property makes navigation by compass and straightedge straightforward. There are no complicated computations to make, as there are with great-circle routes. The rhumb-line course, however, is the shortest-distance path only along meridians and the equator. The 87° rhumb-line route from Seattle to London is much longer than the great-circle route, although it appears shorter on the Mercator projection. By replacing true azimuths with rhumb lines, navigators make their job easier but lengthen their route.

The Navigator's Dilemma

If you're navigating a long distance, you face a dilemma. Should you use true azimuths along great-circle routes to save travel time, while doing a great

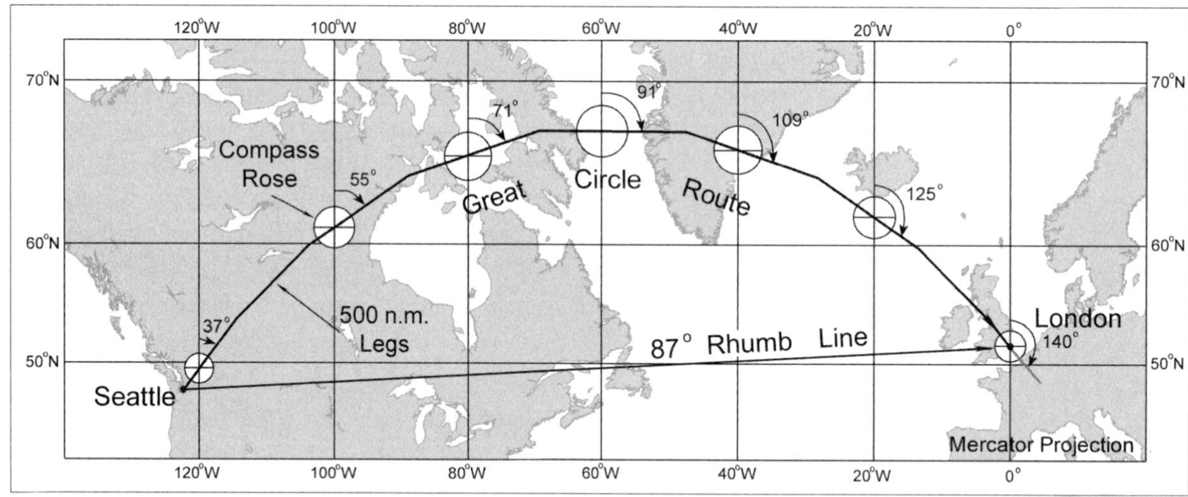

Figure 12.28 Portion of a Mercator world map showing the rhumb-line and great-circle routes from Seattle to London. The great-circle route, obtained from a gnomonic projection, has been divided into 500-nautical-mile legs. Since the Mercator projection is conformal, each compass rose is correctly projected as a circle.

deal of work to determine each azimuth? Or should you use rhumb lines, simplifying navigation planning but lengthening the trip?

There is a solution to the dilemma: use both projections. First, plot the great-circle course as a straight line between your origin and destination on a gnomonic projection (Figure 12.26). Next, transfer the great-circle path to a Mercator projection as a curve (Figure 12.28). Then approximate this curve, which is always concave toward the equator, with a series of straight-line segments called **legs** or **tracks**. Now you can measure the true azimuth at the beginning of each 500-nautical-mile leg with a protractor by finding the azimuth angle between the vertical meridian and the direction line for each leg.

Computing Directions from Geographic Coordinates

You can also compute the true azimuth (Az) at the starting point of the great-circle path. The azimuth computation uses a combination of the **Law of Sines** and the **Law of Cosines** from spherical trigonometry in an equation for the tangent of the true azimuth:

where a and b are the latitudes of the starting and ending points and $\delta\lambda$ is the positive difference in longitude between the two points.

An example of this computation is finding the starting azimuth for a flight from Seattle, Washington (47.5°N, 122.33°W) to London, England (51.5°N, 0°).

SELECTED READINGS

Blandford, P., *Maps & Compasses, A User's Handbook* (Blue Ridge Summit, PA: TAB Books Inc.,1984).

Jonkers, A., *Earth's Magnetism in the Age of Sail* (Baltimore, MD: Johns Hopkins University Press, 2003).

Kjellstrom, B., *Be Expert with Map and Compass* (New York: John Wiley & Sons, 1994).

Maloney, E., *Chapman Piloting,* 64th ed. (New York: Hearst Marine Books, 2003).

Maloney, E., *Dutton's Navigation & Piloting,* 14th ed. (Annapolis, MD: Naval Institute Press, 1988).

Selwyn, V., *Plan Your Route: The New Approach to Map Reading* (London: David & Charles, 1987).

United States Army, Chapter 5 ("Directions") in *Map Reading*, Field Manual, FM 21-26 (Washington, DC: Superintendent of Documents, 1969), pp. 5-1 to 5-27.

$$\tan(Az) = \frac{\cos(b)\times\sin(\delta\lambda)}{(\cos(a)\times\sin(b) - \sin(a)\times\cos(b)\times\cos(\delta\lambda))}$$

$$\tan(Az) = \frac{\cos(51.5°)\times\sin(122.33°)}{(\cos(47.5°)\times\sin(51.5°) - \sin(47.5°)\times\cos(51.5°)\times\cos(122.33°))}$$

$$\tan(Az) = \frac{0.6225\times 0.8450}{(0.6756\times 0.7826 - 0.7373\times 0.6225\times -0.5348)}$$

$$\tan(Az) = \frac{0.5260}{(0.5287 + 0.2455)}$$

$$\tan(Az) = \frac{0.5260}{0.7742}$$

$$\tan(Az) = 0.6794$$

$$Az = 34.2°$$

This navigator is using his map, reference books, and compass to plan a route through the desert.

CHAPTER THIRTEEN
POSITION FINDING AND ROUTE PLANNING

ORIENTING THE MAP

- Inspection Method
  - Terrestrial Features
- Compass Method

FINDING YOUR GROUND POSITION

- Inspection Method
  - Distance Estimation
  - Measurement Instruments
- Resection Method
  - Compass Resection
  - The Fisher's Solution
- Altimeter Method
  - Linear Feature Altimeter Procedure
  - Sight-Line Altimeter Procedure

LOCATING A DISTANT POINT

- Intersection Method
  - Map Inspection
  - Compass Intersection

MAPS USED IN NAVIGATION

- Land Travel
- Water Navigation
- Air Navigation

ROUTE PLANNING AND FOLLOWING

- Dead Reckoning
- Piloting
- Electronic Piloting Systems
- Vehicle Navigation Systems
- Route Planning Software

SELECTED READINGS

"Curse thee, thou quadrant!" dashing it to the deck, "no longer will I guide my earthly way by thee; the level ship's compass, and the level dead-reckoning, by log and by line; these shall conduct me, and show me my place on the sea."
—*Herman Melville, Moby Dick*

It's great being a tourist. Guidebook and camera in my bag, a bottle of water in the car, the map spread out on my knees—what could be finer?
—*Frances Mayes, Bella Tuscany*

13

CHAPTER THIRTEEN

POSITION FINDING AND ROUTE PLANNING

There's no feeling as chilling as realizing you don't know where you are or how to get where you want to go. The most basic aspect of being oriented, then, is to know your position on the ground and where distant features are located in relation to you. Knowing this information also lets you move (navigate) from place to place with confidence.

The need to know your position can be so overwhelming that you hesitate to leave your known environment. But you needn't give in to fears of disorientation. If you know how to compare your surroundings with a map, you can brave new horizons without worrying about getting lost.

People have survived a long time relying solely on their powers of observation. But we have enhanced our natural spatial abilities over the centuries by inventing a variety of technical aids. Clocks, compasses, optical sighting devices, electronic direction and distance finders, inertial navigation systems, and global positioning satellites all fall in this category.

No matter how technically sophisticated our position and path-finding aids, however, they share much in common with longstanding "eyeball" methods. They all use distance or direction information and rely on a few basic geometrical concepts. When our modern technical gadgets fail or aren't at hand, we must fall back on this information and these basic concepts.

So let's start this chapter by discussing traditional observation and compass techniques that have proven useful for centuries and underlie modern satellite-based methods of position finding and route planning. For convenience, we'll begin with orienting the map, then learn about ways to find and map ground positions, and conclude with navigation planning methods. We'll bring these methods up to date with GPS applications in Chapter 14 (GPS and Maps).

ORIENTING THE MAP

To **orient** a map means to turn it so that directions on the ground are lined up with those on the map. The term comes from Medieval Europe where church scholars drew maps of the known world with the Orient (China) at the top, but today most maps are drawn with true north topside.

When traveling, people tend to orient maps in one of two ways. Many people keep the map topside up, no matter which way they're facing. This procedure has the advantage that place names, symbols, and features are easy to read. But it has the disadvantage that map directions aren't usually aligned with ground directions. When you're heading south, right on the map is left in reality. Such reverse thinking can make the mind reel. Imagine trying to make a split-second decision in heavy traffic about which way to turn! Since this may not be much of a problem in familiar settings, it's easy to forget that there is an alternative.

If you're in an unfamiliar, confusing setting, it's usually easier to find your way around if you first orient the map to your direction of travel. Turning the map until ground and map features are aligned has the advantage that you can always determine directions directly. Although you may have to read place names and symbols upside down or sideways, this is easier than trying to unscramble backward directions. The disadvantage is that when following a sinuous route you will have to constantly turn the map to stay aligned with the direction of travel.

Inspection Method

One of the easiest ways to orient a map in the field is by the **inspection method**. With this technique, you don't need to know which way north is. Nor do you need any special tools. Two conditions must be met, however. First, you must be able to see one or more features. Second, you must be able to identify these same features on the map. Various **terrestrial features** satisfy both conditions.

Terrestrial Features

Many landmarks are shown directly on maps. One or two linear features or prominent objects are all you need to orient the map.

Single Linear Feature. There are three forms of alignment with a single linear feature (**Figure 13.1A**). If you can move onto a linear feature such as a road, then you need only turn the map until the mapped road lines up with the real one in front of you. Although this is the most accurate form of alignment, a slight variation of this approach is almost as accurate. With this second method, you assume a position which lies on a straight-line extension of the ground feature. Your third option is to take up a position to either side of the linear ground feature and then to align the map feature so that it is parallel with the ground feature. This last form of map orientation is the least accurate of the three methods, but it often must suffice due to the accessibility problems so characteristic of actual field situations.

The first and third options share one serious problem. When you line up the map road with the ground road, you don't know which direction is which, and you could end up going in the opposite direction from what you intend. Because of this potential **reversal of orientation**, you shouldn't rely on a single linear feature if you can avoid it.

Two Linear Features. A better practice is to rely on two or more linear features when orienting the map by inspection. As with a single feature, you have three options. You can move to a position on either of the two linear features, move to a point which lies on a straight-line extension of either feature, or assume a position off to one side of both features (**Figure 13.1B**). Then you simply turn the map until the two features on the map are aligned with the same features on the ground. Again, the first method is the most accurate, the third approach the least accurate.

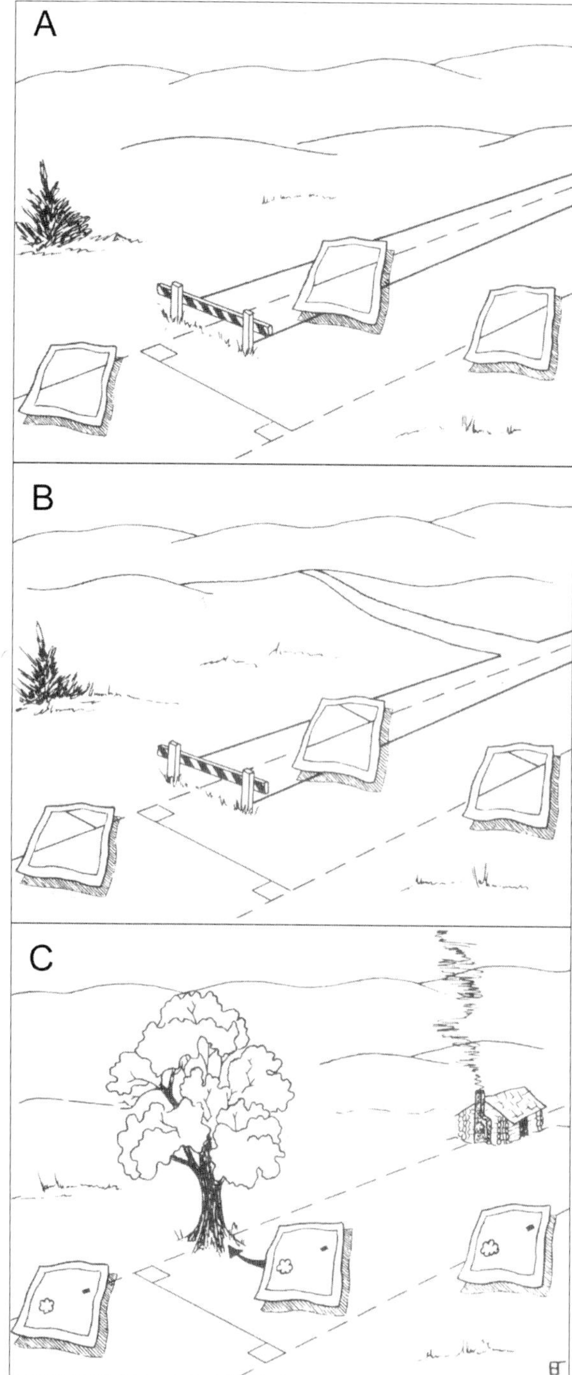

Figure 13.1 You can use a number of methods to orient your map by inspection of one linear feature (A), two linear features (B), or prominent objects (C).

Prominent Objects. Reversal in map orientation can be avoided by using two or more **prominent objects** on the ground that can be found on the map, such as a house, hill, or pond (**Figure 13.1C**). You first move to one of the features or to a position on a line extended through the two features. Next, place a ruler or other straightedge between the features on the map. (If a straightedge isn't available, mentally sighting between the two features will do). Then turn the map until you can sight along the straightedge or sight line to the other visible point (when you have moved to one feature) or to both features (when you have moved to an extension-line position). If you are located off to the side of the features, you will have to position your map so that the straightedge sighting is in parallel alignment to the ground features.

The success of map orientation by the inspection method depends primarily on the ability to identify ground features that can be found on the map. When prominent features are unfamiliar or obscured (by vegetation, fog, or terrain) or when they are locally nonexistent (as on a plain or ocean surface), the method of inspection is of little value. In these special situations, a better method of map orientation is to use a magnetic compass.

Compass Method

To use the **compass method** of map orientation, first be sure you have a compass and a map that shows the direction of magnetic north (see Magnetic North in Chapter 12). Then:

1. Find the magnetic north indicator on the map. This is usually a barb-shaped arrow placed in the margin of the map.

2. Holding the map under the compass, turn the map until the compass needle lines up with magnetic north on the map.

Since this procedure accounts for magnetic declination, your map will now be properly oriented with true north as well.

Figure 13.2 shows why it's so essential to take magnetic declination into account when orienting a map with the compass method. In this example,

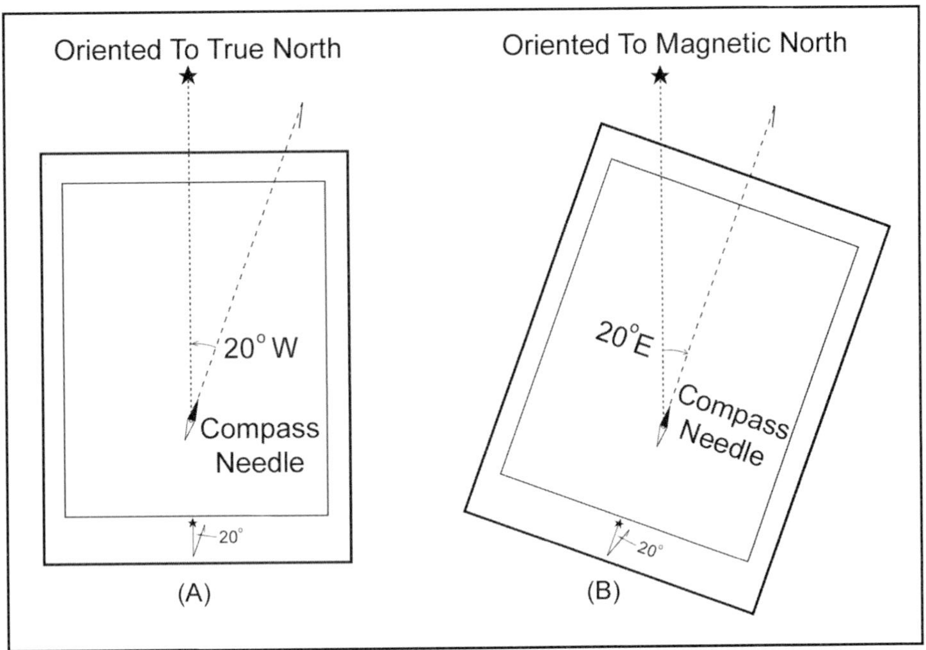

Figure 13.2 When orienting a map to true north (A) or magnetic north (B) with a compass, you must account for magnetic declination.

the magnetic declination is 20° East. When the compass needle is oriented with the magnetic north base line (A), true north is correctly located 20° west of the compass needle. Conversely, when the compass needle is oriented with true north (B), the map is oriented to magnetic north (20° east of true north).

Unfortunately, magnetic north isn't always shown on maps. Often a topographic map sheet will have been cut into sections or have its margins trimmed off to make its size more manageable, with the result that the magnetic north indicator is lost. For these reasons, it makes sense to commit the basic declination pattern to memory. For the contiguous United States, declination varies from approximately 25° West (in the Northeast) to 25° East (in the Pacific Northwest) (see Figure 12.9 in Chapter 12).

If you keep in mind the magnetic declination for the area in which you're traveling, you need never be too far off in estimating the direction of magnetic north. For large portions of the Midwest, the declination is close enough to 0 degrees that true north (indicated by longitude lines) provides a reasonable substitute for magnetic north.

FINDING YOUR GROUND POSITION

At times you'll orient your map on the basis of a known ground position or you'll establish your position in the process of map orientation. At other times, you won't know your ground location even after you've oriented your map. But once your map is oriented, you can then figure out where you are on the map. There are two useful methods: by inspection, and by instruments.

Inspection Method

When you use the **inspection method** to locate your map position, the idea is the same as when you used inspection to orient your map. You are simply looking at (or "inspecting") ground features without any special aids. There are two main inspection techniques. With the first, you find ground features on the map and then estimate their distance from you. With the second, you plot lines that intersect at your position.

Distance Estimation

The most common inspection technique is **distance estimation** (also called **range** estimation). To use this method, first orient your map and select a feature on the ground that you can also identify on the map. Next, estimate the distance from your ground position to the distant feature, and convert this figure to map distance units by using the map scale. Now mark out the computed map distance along the proper direction line and you have established your position (**Figure 13.3A**). You can double-check your work by repeating the procedure with several features, but don't be too discouraged if your results don't agree. Distances are hard to judge accurately, although there are several things you can do to improve your estimates.

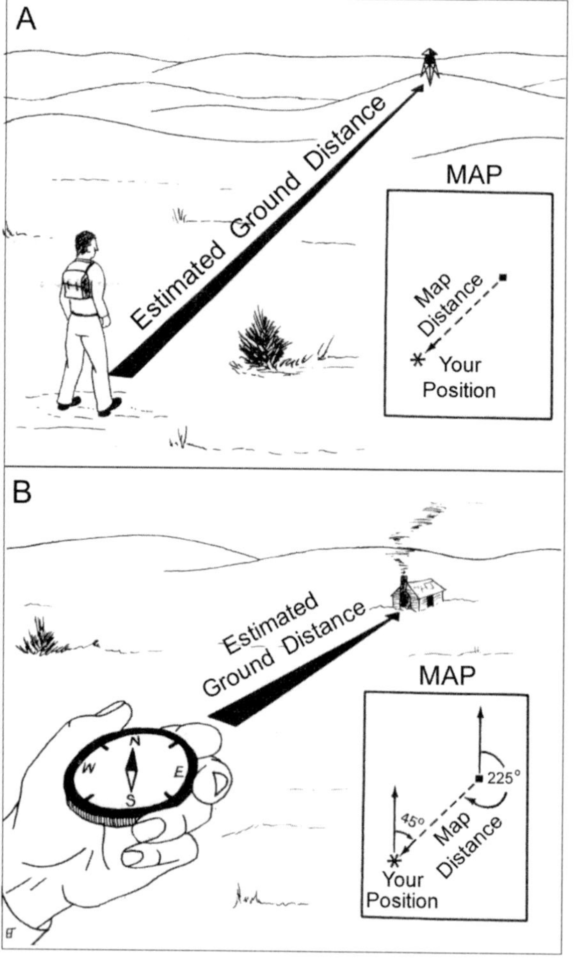

Figure 13.3 One way to find your position is to use range and direction information gained by inspecting your surroundings (A) or using a magnetic compass (B).

One trick is to use **multiples of familiar distance units**, such as a football field (100 yards), or the side of a 40-acre field (440 yards). But most people have trouble visualizing these units. A further complication is that as your vision approaches the vanishing point, it becomes harder to judge distance. The nearest distance unit is easier to estimate than more distant units.

Another trick is to memorize what familiar objects look like at different ranges. Then you can simply compare the size and general appearance of an object, such as a house, with the "template" that you hold in your mind's eye, and you will have a good idea of the range. There are problems with this procedure, however. The object may not be of standard size. Even when it is the correct length or width, troubles may arise. Weather, atmospheric conditions, the relationship of the sun's rays to the object, and the intervening terrain may all compound the difficulties of judging distance on the basis of the size of objects. A feature will appear to be a different distance when seen from a low position over a flat surface than when viewed from one hillside to another. If the object is seen from above or below, it will appear smaller and farther away than it actually is. A back-lighted object will seem farther away than a front-lighted one. A brightly marked feature will appear closer than a dull feature, while both objects will look closer on a bright, dry day than a humid or foggy one.

You can also use a **magnetic compass** to determine direction (**Figure 13.3B**). An advantage of this compass technique is that you don't need to orient your map before finding your position. To perform the range estimation technique, use your compass to sight on a distant feature and note the reading. Then determine the ground distance from your position to that feature using one of the range estimation techniques discussed above. Now, using the map scale, convert this figure to map distance units. Finally, plot the sighting through the target feature on the map, and mark off the estimated distance.

Measurement Instruments

Many gadgets to help estimate distance are on the market. Sophisticated and accurate surveying instruments and hunting scopes that measure distance use the **stadia principle.** These devices have a built-in pair of horizontal wires, called **stadia**, that are spaced to bracket (or subtend) a small angular distance. The angle subtended is usually on the order of **minutes of angle** (MOA). One minute of angle (1/60th of a degree) will subtend approximately 1 inch (actually 1.023 inches) at 300 feet, 2 inches at 600 feet, and so forth. Surveyors use stadia-equipped telescopes to sight at a graduated **stadia rod** and then compute the intervening distance by using simple trigonometry (**Figure 13.4A**). The technique may be far less accurate if an object must be assumed to be of standard size, as is the case in most non-surveying applications.

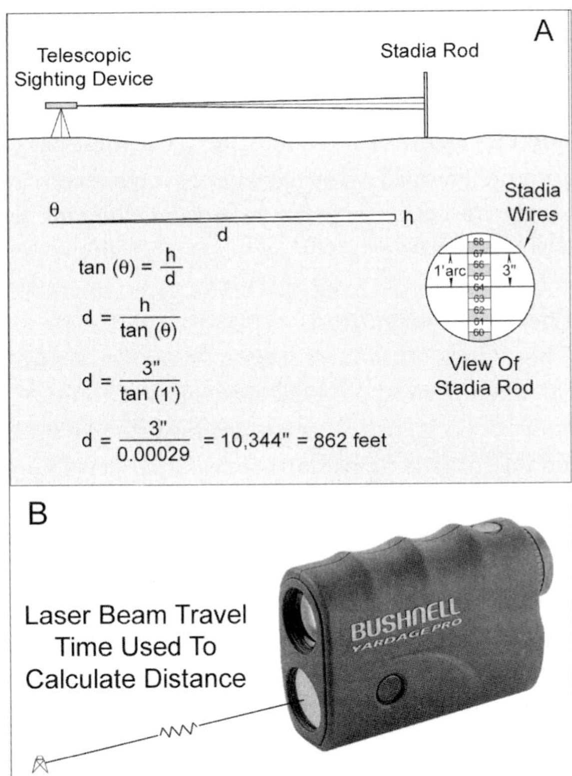

Figure 13.4 Distance estimation instruments include stadia rods and sighting devices (A) as well as laser rangefinders (B).

The latest technology for distance estimation is the **laser rangefinder (Figure 13.4B)**. Although rather expensive, these "point and read" instruments are the most accurate and handy yet invented. Infrared laser beams built into binoculars or a monocular (one eyepiece) measure distance up to 1,000 yards with an accuracy of one yard. These laser rangefinders have become indispensable around construction sites and realtor's offices, where they are known as **electronic rulers**.

Laser rangefinders can be a lot of fun to use, especially in checking the results of your mental distance estimates. Their cost and weight are directly related to their range and accuracy. Varying from 9 ounces to 3 pounds, they're all portable enough to carry.

Resection Method

Unless you're one of the few people who has mastered visual range estimation or has the equipment available to measure distance, you probably should avoid the distance estimation method if accurate position determination is crucial. For most people, a better technique for locating position by inspection is the **resection method**. With this technique, you plot lines that cross, or "resect" at your position. You can make this plot with two or three lines (**Figure 13.5A**).

It is most accurate to use three lines. First, you must be able to find three point features on both the ground and the map. Then, with the map properly oriented, place a straightedge on the line between one of the prominent ground features and the same feature on the map, and draw a line along the straightedge. This line is really a **backsight**, since it's drawn from the known position of a distant feature back to your position. Next, draw lines in the same way for the other two features. You're located where the three lines cross on the map.

You'll get the most reliable position fix when at least two of your sight lines cross at angles close to 90 degrees. If possible, avoid using sight lines which cross at angles smaller than 45 degrees. With small angles, even a slight error in drawing the lines may considerably mislocate the point at which the line should intersect.

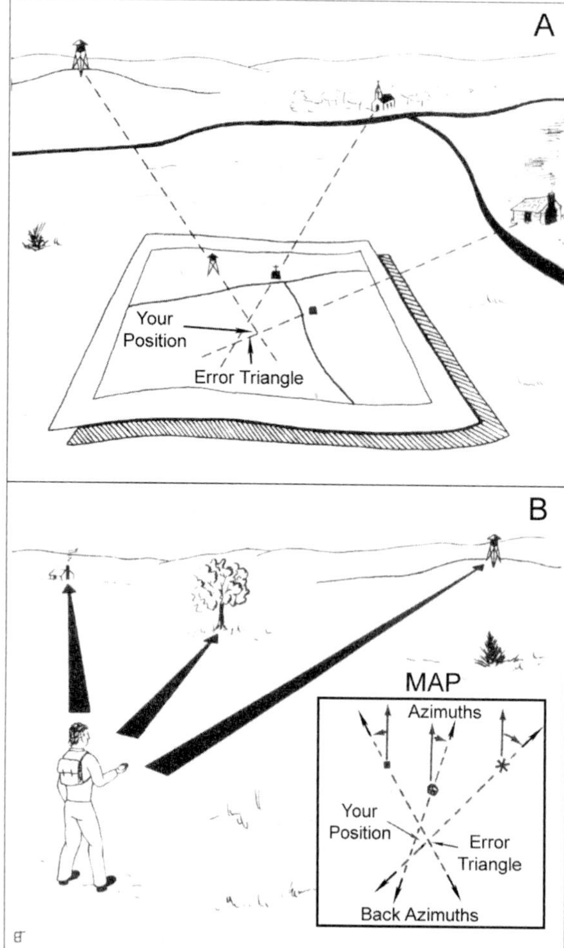

Figure 13.5 Position finding can be carried out by resection based on map inspection (A), or magnetic compass readings (B).

Due to execution inaccuracies, however, even then the three lines will rarely cross at a point but instead will form an **error triangle** within which you're probably located. If this triangle is small, you can feel confident in your results. If the error triangle is large, however, it's advisable to repeat the procedure, taking greater care. It may be that you were sloppy in your sighting. But there's also the chance that you didn't sight to the correct feature or that the map maker misplaced the feature on the map in the first place.

If only two outstanding point features are identifiable on both ground and map, you can still use the resection method, proceeding as you did when three features were available. Because only two lines are constructed, they will cross at a point regardless of drawing errors on your part, giving the illusion of accuracy. Any error you made in either of your sightings won't be evident. Whenever two rather than three lines are used, therefore, you must watch out for this potential **hidden error**.

Compass Resection

The **compass method of resection** makes use of **back azimuths** as resection lines(**Figure 13.5B**). You merely use a compass, rather than a straightedge or visual sighting, to determine the resection lines. Again, you can make your resection plot with two or three lines. To use the three-point resection technique, select three prominent features on the ground that you can also identify on the map. Next, sight on the three distant points with a compass from your ground position and note the azimuths. Plot the back azimuths for the three sightings through their respective map points by using a protractor . Back azimuths are calculated by adding 180° to azimuths less than 180°, or subtracting azimuths greater than 180° from 360°. The three back azimuth lines will come together to form an error triangle, just as your resection lines did when made with a straightedge.

The Fisher's Solution

What if you don't have a map or compass with you when you want to establish your position? Or, what if you want to remember how to get to a certain unmarked position, such as a sunken shipwreck? The **fisher's solution** to either problem is simple and reasonably effective.

Imagine that you find a terrific fishing spot in the middle of a small lake. How will you find the spot next time you go fishing? This is a common problem, often solved by fishers in cartoons by marking an "X" on the side of their boat. There is a much better procedure, however. Simply locate two pairs of features that fall on opposite sides of the lake on imaginary lines that cross at the fishing spot (**Figure 13.6A**). The wider the **angle of separation** between sight lines, the more accurately

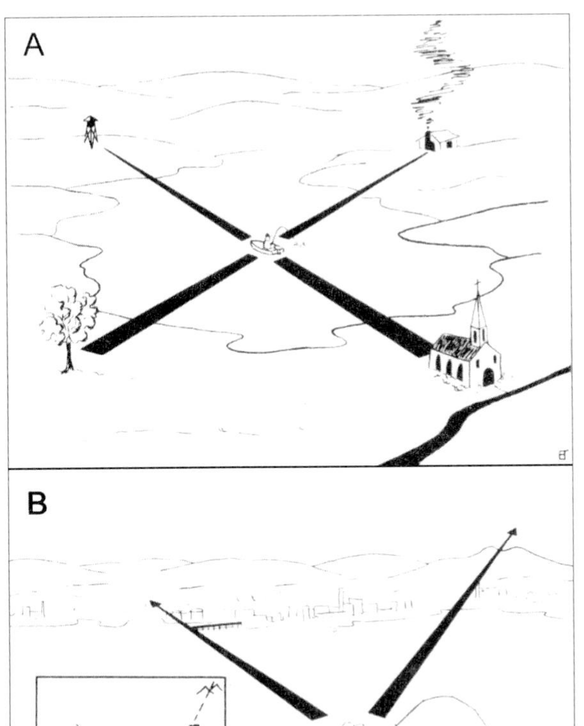

Figure 13.6 As any good fisher knows, position finding doesn't always require the use of a map and compass.

you will be able to return to the spot. A separation of about 45 degrees is probably a good compromise between high positional accuracy and the practical problem of trying to make continuous sightings as you approach the desired position.

Obviously, this technique won't work if you're on a large body of water, since you won't be able to see both shores at once. Another method, which is probably more accurate than the previous one, even for small bodies of water, is to line up two pairs of features along one shoreline. In effect, this procedure establishes your position by crossed backsights and is thus a form of resection. By using this technique to locate a small reef which lies about six miles off the Lake Superior shoreline from Marquette, Michigan (**Figure 13.6B**), some people are able to catch lake trout consistently, while others enjoy only hit-or-miss luck.

Altimeter Method

In mountainous regions, particularly those which are heavily forested or cloud-shrouded much of the time, you may be unable to locate enough features on both the ground and map to use the inspection and compass methods of position finding accurately. In this case, you might think the GPS receiver would be your savior. But you may be wrong. Hand-held GPS receivers in common use have limited capability in rugged, heavily forested terrain (see Chapter 14: GPS and Maps).

A **pocket altimeter** may be the best position-finding aid in such circumstances (**Figure 13.7**). With a topographic map and an altimeter, you can fix your position with the help of only a single feature common to your map and your surroundings. An altimeter position fix is easiest if you are located on or near a linear feature such as a trail, stream, or ridge line. But it's also possible to determine your position with an altimeter if you can make a sighting on a distant feature such as a building, mountain peak, or lake.

Figure 13.7 In heavily forested or cloud-shrouded mountains, a pocket altimeter can be an invaluable position-finding aid.

Before you hike into the wilderness with an altimeter in your pack, there's something you should know. An altimeter's primary drawback in position finding is that an instrument of portable size and weight is difficult to keep calibrated. These calibration problems can be traced to the fact that an altimeter is a form of barometer that determines elevation by measuring air pressure. Unfortunately, the relation between elevation and air pressure isn't a simple one. Since under ideal conditions air pressure decreases systematically with altitude, the altimeter's scale can in theory be calibrated in meters or feet to reflect changes in elevation. In practice, though, air temperature and humidity also influence atmospheric pressure, and these often change rapidly and unpredictably. All things considered, it is best to view pocket altimeter readings as approximate.

You can do several things to increase the accuracy of your altimeter readings, however. One is to pay a little more and obtain **a temperature-compensated altimeter**. Also, always set your altimeter before you start your trip, using your topographic map to obtain accurate elevation data. Finally, reset your altimeter as often as possible during the trip. You can do so whenever you come to a place where you can clearly discern the elevation. A hilltop, a saddle between two peaks, and the point at which a trail branches or crosses a stream are likely spots to calibrate the altimeter. The shorter the time between your altimeter settings, the less chance that changing weather conditions will cause incorrect elevation readings.

Linear-Feature Altimeter Procedure

To establish your position with an altimeter when you're located on a path or other prominent linear feature, there are two steps. First, read the elevation from your altimeter, taking care to tap the device several times to be certain that the pointer hasn't stuck in a wrong position. Next, follow along the appropriate linear feature on your map until you come to the elevation indicated by the altimeter. This will be your approximate ground position.

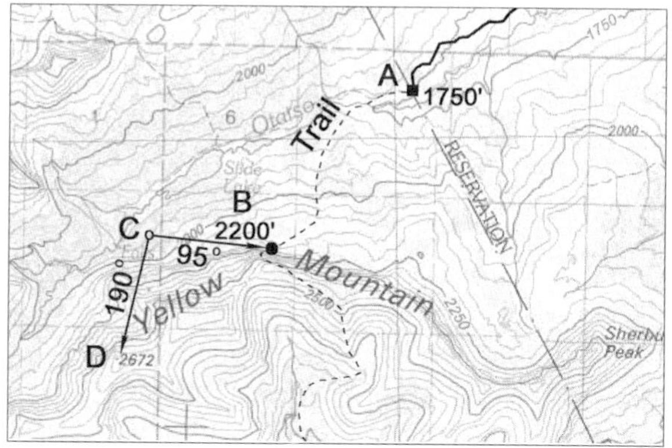

Figure 13.8 Using an altimeter to find your position along a trail and when lost. See text for explanation.

An actual case of position fixing with an altimeter and a linear feature is provided in **Figure 13.8**. Let's assume that you have parked your car at point A, with the intent of hiking up the trail to the south. You note that the parking lot is bisected by the 1,750-foot contour line. Before starting out from your car, therefore, you set your altimeter to this elevation. Later, after hiking several hours through dense fog, you stop and read your altimeter again. The device indicates that you have climbed to an elevation of 2,200 feet. By tracing your route up the trail, you decide that you must be located near point B, where the 2,200 foot contour crosses the trail.

Sight-Line Altimeter Procedure

If you aren't located on a linear feature, you can still use your altimeter to fix your position if you can make a sighting on a distant object. Three steps are required. First, plot the sight line from your position to the visible feature on your map. To do so, you can use one of the inspection methods discussed previously. Next, read the elevation from your altimeter. Finally, visually follow along the sight line until you come to this elevation value. This should be your approximate position.

An example of this sight-line method of position finding is given in Figure 13.8. In this case, suppose that you lost the trail in a snowslide area shortly after making the position fix for point B. After you have searched for an hour or so, the clouds clear enough so that you can see a mountain peak (D) across a valley to the south of your position. With the help of your compass, you determine that the magnetic azimuth to the mountain peak is 190°. At your position, your altimeter indicates an elevation of 1,900 feet. By plotting the sight line on your map, and then following along the line until you get to the point at which it crosses the 1,900-foot contour line, you establish your current position at C. From this point, you decide that the easiest way to reach the trail is by following a magnetic azimuth of 95 degrees.

LOCATING A DISTANT POINT

It isn't always enough to know how to locate your position on the map. What if you want to know the position of something else? A pond, house, or tree, for instance, may be clearly visible but not shown on your map. How do you figure out its correct map location?

Intersection Method

The technique to use here is just the opposite of the method of resection. You use the **method of intersection** to find the map position of something else. As we have seen, resection lines are formed by backsights—lines from a distant feature back to your position. Intersection lines, on the other hand, are made by **foresights**—lines from your position to a distant feature.

Using the intersection method, you sight on the unknown spot from two ground positions whose map locations are known or can be computed. The point at which these foresights intersect establishes the feature's location. As with resection, the accuracy of the method of intersection is improved by using three rather than two known sighting points. Again, the error triangle created by using three sight lines will give you a measure of confidence in how accurately you have determined and plotted the foresights.

To locate a distant point by intersection, you can use techniques similar to those you used to establish your position. The two main techniques are map inspection and compass intersection.

Map Inspection

In intersection by **map inspection**, you first orient the map and determine your position on the map. Next, lay a straightedge (or visually sight) from your map position toward the distant ground feature. Plot this foresight line on your map (**Figure 13.9A**). Now move to a second position that you can find on your map, sight to the same feature, and plot this second sight line. The intersecting foresight lines will establish the location of the feature.

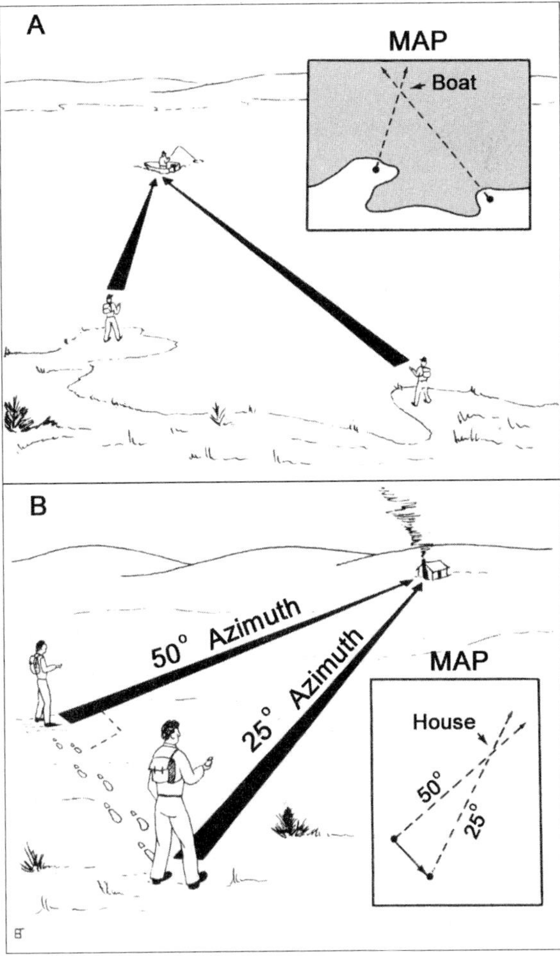

Figure 13.9 The intersection method is commonly used to determine the location of a distant point.

If only a single identifiable ground point is available, you can still use the intersection method if the location of a second point can be computed. Simply follow the above procedure in making a sighting from the known point, and then repeat the procedure from a second point which is a measured distance and direction from the first. As before, the sight lines will intersect on the map at the desired ground position.

Two fixed positions can also be used to determine location of a distant point. Fire towers serve this purpose for firefighters. In this case, one fire station communicates its direction-line information (as measured from the map with a protractor) to the other station to find the location of the fire.

Compass Intersection

If a map and compass are both available, you may determine the location of a distant feature from **compass intersection** by locating your map position, sighting on the distant feature, and recording the foresight azimuth or bearing (**Figure 13.9B**). Next, move to a second known position, sight to the feature, and record the reading of this second foresight. If you plot the two foresight azimuths or bearings from the known positions, the point at which they intersect is the map location of the distant feature. The compass method of intersection can also be used when you're working from two fixed positions or from a fixed position and a computed position. The procedure is similar to the map inspection method discussed above.

MAPS USED IN NAVIGATION

Once you've learned to determine your position and that of distant features, you're ready to determine how best to get from one known location to another. But before we discuss these methods, it is important to consider the types of special maps and charts* available to assist you in navigation. How you travel through the environment will vary depending on what type of map you have at hand and what information it gives you.

With a wide selection of maps available for navigation, your task is to choose those best suited to your needs. Maps used in route finding can be grouped into those designed for land, water, and air travel.

Land Travel

Land travel is often restricted to definite routes such as trails, roads, or railroads. In such cases, travelers are concerned primarily with their route network; they don't much care about the environment as a whole, or about exact compass direction. Maps for such travelers can be greatly simplified, especially if an obvious origin, route, or destination exists.

Making a simple, schematic map that focuses on a particular route isn't a new idea. The Romans simplified their road maps, called **Peutinger tables**, by ignoring exact directions and distances, concentrating instead on showing the road network and cities along the roads (**Figure 13.10, top**).

The distortion of geographic space in schematic mapping that began with the Romans has been carried a step further in recent times. Often there has been a concerted attempt to mislead the map user. For example, the scale and direction relationships on 19th-century **railroad maps** were often carefully arranged to create a favorable impression of the company's service in a region (**Figure 13.10, bottom**). The practice of deliberate map distortion continues today, especially with rapid transit, bus, and airline route maps.

The modern "wilderness" hiking or canoeing guide (**Figure 13.11**) is a similar type of simplified route map. Again, in an effort to make the maps as simple and uncluttered as possible, only the route network and prominent surrounding landmarks are depicted. On these maps, however, an attempt is made to retain correct directions and distances. Such maps are well designed for the amateur outdoorsperson but are generally inadequate for sophisticated map users. Furthermore, there is a danger that some unplanned event such as a damaged canoe will force the user to engage

**By convention, maps used for a special navigational purpose, especially by ship and airplane pilots, are called charts.*

in another mode of transportation for which the map is totally unsuited. The main problem with these simplified route maps, then, is that they aren't flexible. They keep you tied to your route.

You will have more flexibility if you use general-purpose maps on which a route has been marked. One such map, put out by the American Automobile Association, is called a **Triptik (Fig-**

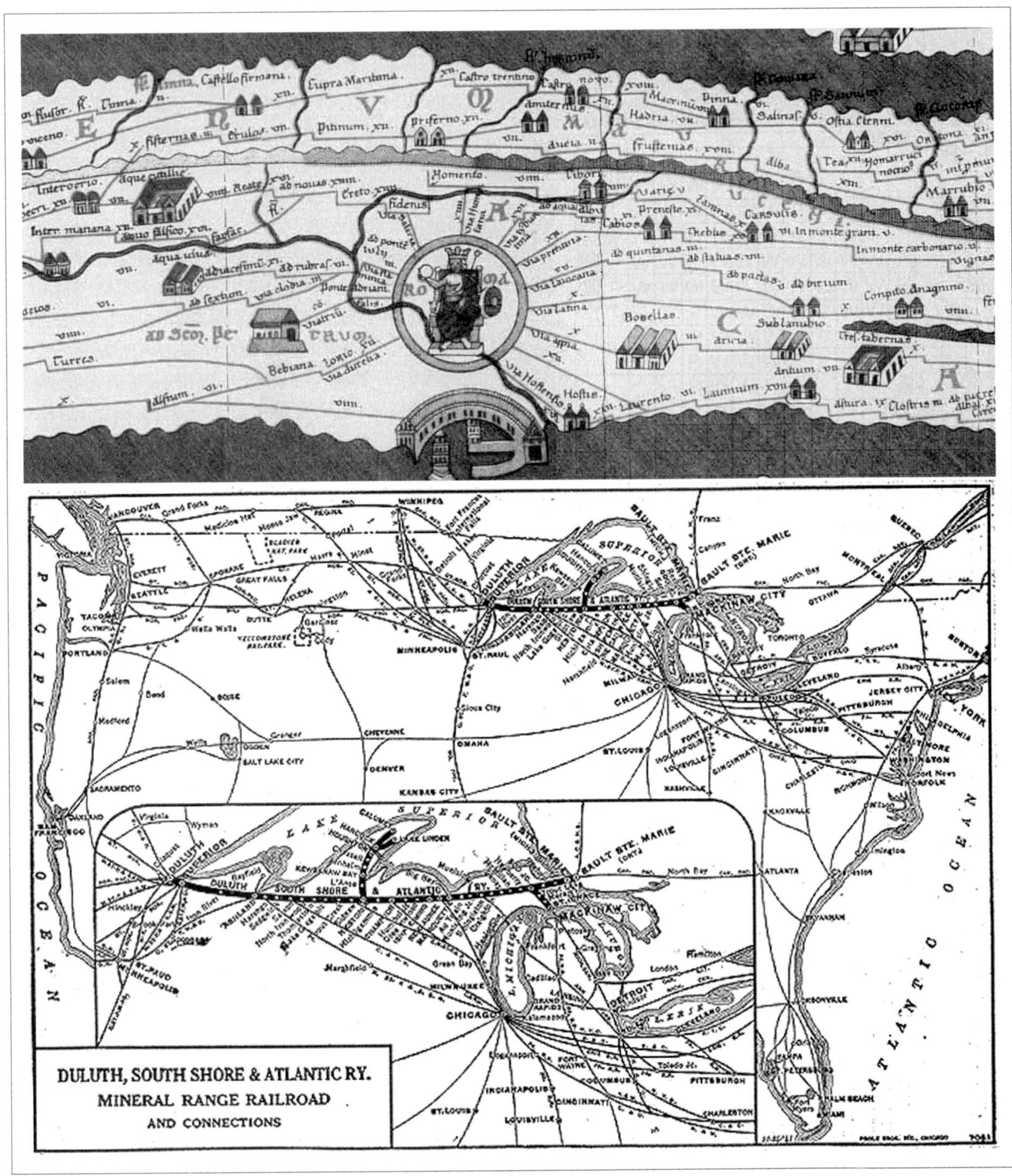

Figure 13.10 A section of a medieval copy of the Roman Peutinger tables (top) and a 19th century railroad map (bottom) are examples of route maps more schematic than planimetrically accurate.

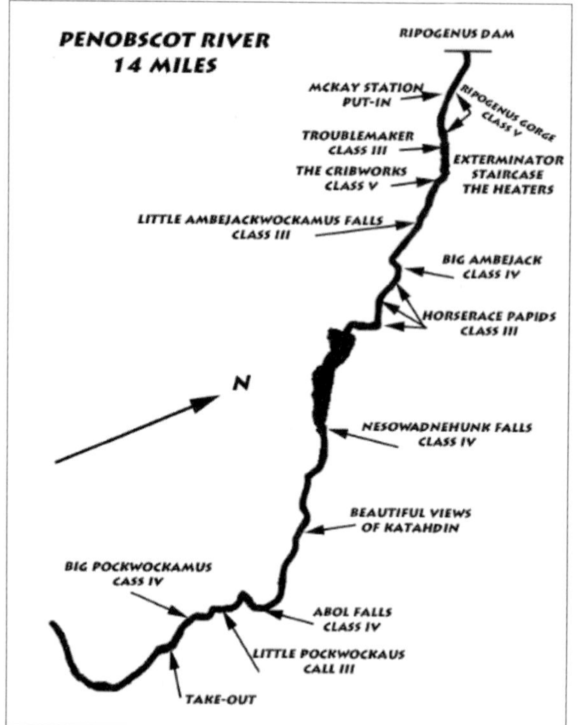

Figure 13.11 Canoeing and rafting map for the Penobscot River, Maine.

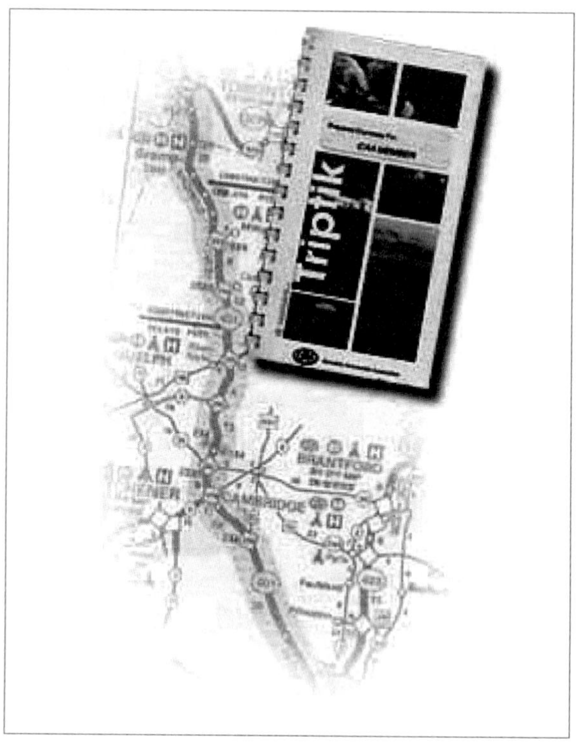

Figure 13.12 The American Automobile Association has popularized a type of route map called a Triptik.

ure 13.12). The Triptik contains a planned route which you can follow, but in the event of an emergency it also includes a complete base map of the region neighboring the route. A major deviation from your planned route is required to thrust you into "unmapped territory."

The **standard road map** provides a still more general picture for route finding, since its coverage is defined by state, region, or country (**Figure 13.13**). A variety of information is available to the traveler, including possible alternate routes such as railroads and river systems. Map information selected for the purposes of highway travel doesn't paint a complete picture of the country, of course. The traveler concerned with environmental details falling much beyond the shoulder of the road will likely find road maps inadequate.

Private companies publish a variety of **road and recreation atlases**. Many travelers carry national road atlases produced by Rand McNally, National Geographic Maps, or other smaller firms. These atlases generally consist of state maps showing different classes of roads, mileage along road segments, cities and towns, counties, rivers, and other features of interest. Recently, larger-scale state road and recreation atlases have been produced by the DeLorme company and Benchmark Maps. Their maps show in greater detail the same types of information as national road atlases, plus relief-shaded and color-tinted topography and detailed land-ownership information (**see Color Plate 13.1**). Closely spaced graticule lines are also printed over the map to assist GPS users.

Large-scale topographic maps are an excellent information source for detailed route finding. A 1:24,000-scale USGS topographic quadrangle shows topography, roads, railroads, streams, buildings, heavily forested areas, and other features that are often important to planning and following a route (even cross-country) on foot. The graticule and grid ticks along the map's margins also are of great value in position finding.

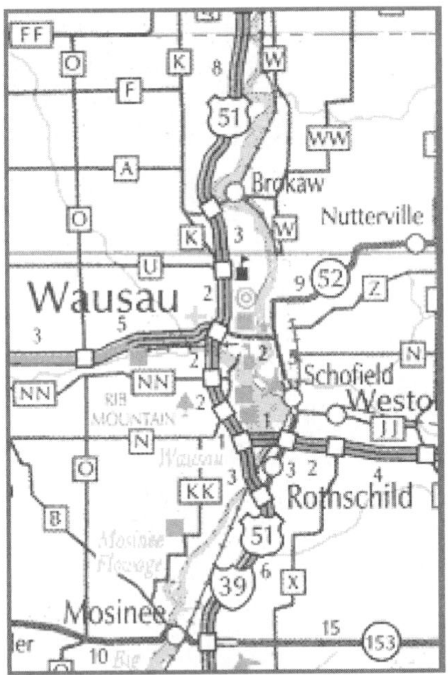

Figure 13.13 State road maps usually show a variety of information in addition to highways, making them useful for general-reference purposes as well as for navigational assistance.

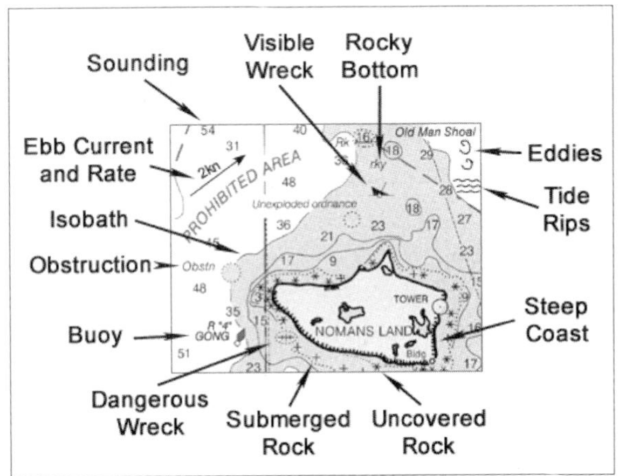

Figure 13.14 Nautical charts contain information specifically for the marine navigator.

Water Navigation

Nautical charts are published primarily for the mariner, although they serve the public interest in many other ways. They are designed to give all available information necessary for safe marine navigation, including soundings, isobaths (bathymetric contours), obstructions and hazards, bottom types, currents, prominent landmarks near shore, and navigational aids such as buoys and lights (**Figure 13.14**).

The scales of nautical charts published for the coastal waters of the United States by the **National Ocean Service** range from 1:2,500 to about 1:500,000. Coverage includes the Atlantic, Pacific, and Gulf coasts, and coastal areas of Alaska, Hawaii, and the United States possessions (Virgin Islands, Guam, Samoa, and Puerto Rico).

Hydrographic charts are also published for certain inland waters. For example, charts for the Great Lakes, the upper Hudson River, Lake Champlain, the New York Barge Canals, and part of the Minnesota-Ontario border lakes are issued at various scales and are designed primarily for navigational use. Most of these charts show the hydrography of water areas, together with the topography of limited areas of adjacent shores and islands, including docks, structures, and landmarks visible from the lakes and channels.

Charts designed for flood control, navigation, and recreation on the Mississippi River and connected waters are also published at several scales. The **U.S. Army Corps of Engineers** is the primary source of these useful charts. In addition, state agencies such as the Department of Natural Resources usually produce hydrographic maps for inland lakes and rivers of significant size or recreational potential.

If you plan to navigate on the water, a good rule is to obtain the largest-scale chart available. This will help ensure that you have the most comprehensive graphic summary of information pertinent to making navigational decisions. Before you use the chart, study the notes, symbols, and abbreviations placed near the title or next to map symbols, for they are essential for effective use of the chart. **Coast and Geodetic Survey Chart No. 1** shows the symbols and abbreviations used on nautical charts and is recommended to the mariner for study.

The date of the chart is of such vital importance to the marine navigator that it warrants special attention. When charted information becomes obsolete, further use of the chart for navigation may be extremely dangerous. Natural and artificial changes, many of them critical, are occurring constantly. It is essential, therefore, that navigators obtain up-to-date charts at regular intervals or hand correct their copies for changes announced in a weekly publication entitled *Notice to Mariners*.

Air Navigation

The National Aeronautical Charting Office (NACO), administered by the Federal Aviation Administration (FAA), publishes and distributes United States government **civil aeronautical charts** and flight information publications (**Figure 13.15**). Aeronautical charts published in the United States are specially designed for use in air navigation, and emphasis is given to features of greatest aeronautical importance (see **Color Plate 13.2**). Five chart series are produced:

Sectional aeronautical charts are designed for visual navigation of slow-moving to medium-speed aircraft. The topographic information consists of the relief and a selection of visual checkpoints used under visual flight rules. The checkpoints include populated places, drainage patterns, roads, railroads, and other distinctive landmarks. The aeronautical information on sectional charts includes visual and radio aids to navigation, airports, controlled airspace, restricted areas, and obstructions.

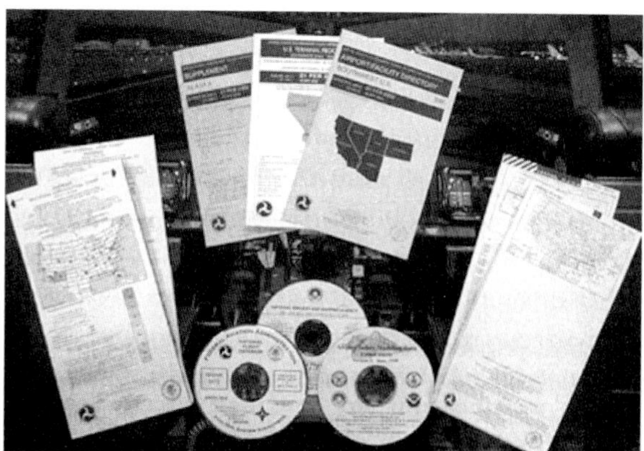

Figure 13.15 U.S. aeronautical chart and flight information is available on charts, flight books, and CD-ROMs.

World aeronautical charts cover land areas at a standard size and scale for navigation by moderate-speed aircraft and aircraft operating at high altitudes. Background information includes cities (shown by color tints), principal roads, railroads, distinctive landmarks, drainage patterns, and relief. Aeronautical information includes visual and radio aids to navigation, airports, airways, restricted areas, and obstructions.

Terminal-area charts depict the airspace around major airports. The information found on these charts is similar to that found on sectional charts, but it's shown in much more detail because the scale is larger.

Instrument flight rules, low-altitude charts provide aeronautical information for navigation under instrument flight rules below 18,000 feet MSL. This chart series includes airways, limits of controlled airspace, VHF radio aids to navigation, airports that have an instrument approach procedure or minimum 3,000' hard-surface runway, off-route obstruction clearance altitudes, airway distances, reporting points, special-use airspace areas, and military training routes.

Instrument flight rules, high-altitude charts are designed for navigation at or above 18,000 feet MSL. Included on these charts are jet route structure, VHF radio aids to navigation, selected airports, and reporting points.

As with nautical charts, once information on an aeronautical chart has become obsolete its further use for navigational purposes becomes a definite hazard. One of the most important things on any chart is its date. On aeronautical charts, the date is usually given in large red type in the lower right margin.

ROUTE PLANNING AND FOLLOWING

Route planning and following is really an extension of position finding. But, instead of determining isolated positions, you're concerned with the sequence of positions that define a route. Special maps and charts are designed to help you move through the environment, as we saw in the previous section. But two special navigational skills are also required: piloting and dead reckoning.

With **piloting**, you plan your intended route and then find your position and direction of movement by paying attention to landmarks, aids to navigation, and water depth. When **dead reckoning**, you are estimating your present postion relative to your last accurately determined location by using direction, speed, distance, and time information. We will discuss these two aspects of navigation separately, realizing that dead reckoning is a key part of piloting. Let's study dead reckoning and piloting by looking at sea navigation in coastal areas.

Dead Reckoning

The term **dead reckoning (DR)** is a shortened form of the phrase "deduced (ded.) reckoning" used in the era of sailing ships. The basic idea is to deduce your current position from the vessel's direction of travel and speed. Dead reckoning is used both when planning a route and steering a boat along the planned route. Let's look at an example of route planning by dead reckoning.

To plan your route, you use large-scale nautical charts to create a **dead reckoning plot** on the charts as a series of **intended dead reckoning tracks** between points. Two track lines are plotted in **Figure 13.16** for the last part of a voyage from Seattle to Flounder Bay on Fidalgo Island, Washington. Assume that your boat has a maximum **cruising speed** of 10 knots (nautical miles/hour) and a **draft** (depth from the water line to the bottom of the keel) of 3 meters.

Before plotting intended dead reckoning tracks, navigators highlight obstructions, hazards to navigation, and navigational aids along the route (circled features in Figure 13.16). Tracks must be plotted to avoid obstructions and minimize hazards. Track 2, for instance, is drawn perpendicular to international shipping lanes in order to minimize the time spent crossing them. Track 3 is the shortest straight line to Flounder Bay that gives safe passage distance around Williamson Rocks, Allan Island, and Young Island while having water depths greater than the boat's 3-meter draft. Dead reckoning does not take into account the effects of currents, winds, vessel traffic, or steering errors on tracks, although the navigator must correct for all these things during the actual voyage.

The **course** (direction) and **distance** for each intended track are now measured on the charts with a parallel rule and dividers, using the methods described in Chapters 11 and 12. Notice that the nautical convention is to write the course (C) and boat **speed** (S) above and below the beginning of each track line, and to write the distance (D) below the center of the line. Track 2, for example, has course C051M (magnetic azimuth* of 51 degrees), distance D3.0 (3 nautical miles), and speed S10.0 (10 knots over the water).

This distance and speed information allows you to calculate the **time** required to complete each track from the equation: T=D×60/S. From this equation, completing Track 2 should take:

$$\frac{3nm \times 60minutes / hr}{10nm / hr} = 18minutes$$

A similar computation gives a crossing time of 26 minutes for Track 3. This means that if you plan to begin Track 2 at 8:00 AM, your **Estimated Time of Arrival (ETA)** at the start of Track 3 is 8:18 AM and at Flounder Bay is 8:44 AM. These times are written on the chart at the start and end of the two tracks as four-digit numbers 0800, 0818, and 0844.

**In strict nautical terminology, the azimuth is called a bearing.*

Piloting

Piloting begins by planning your voyage in advance. You must first acquire the charts and other navigational publications that cover the area you will cross. In sea navigation, you will obtain small- and large-scale nautical charts, tide tables, and current information for the area. You must also learn certain characteristics of your boat, particularly its maximum cruising speed and draft.

The second stage in piloting is to plan the overall voyage on a small-scale chart covering the entire route. Sketching your general route gives you the "big picture" of your voyage, particularly its overall distance and the length of time you will be on the water. The small-scale chart also helps you see how the larger-scale charts upon which you'll do your detailed route planning fit together.

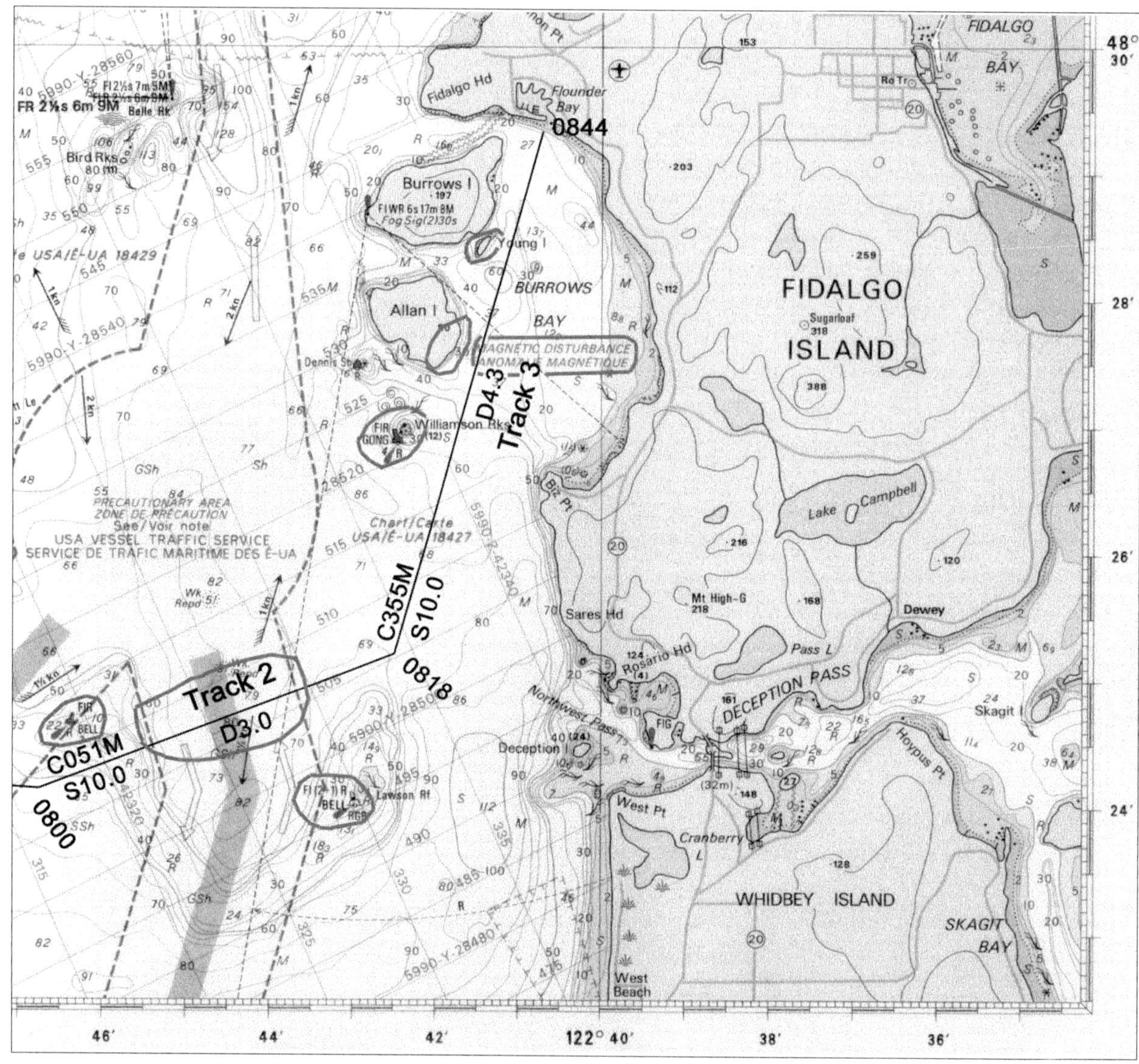

Figure 13.16 Route planning by dead reckoning consists of plotting intended DR tracks on nautical charts. Track information includes the course heading (C) (usually a magnetic azimuth); distance in nautical miles (D); and boat speed over the water in knots (S). Nearby obstructions, navigational aids, and possible hazards to navigation may also be circled on the chart.

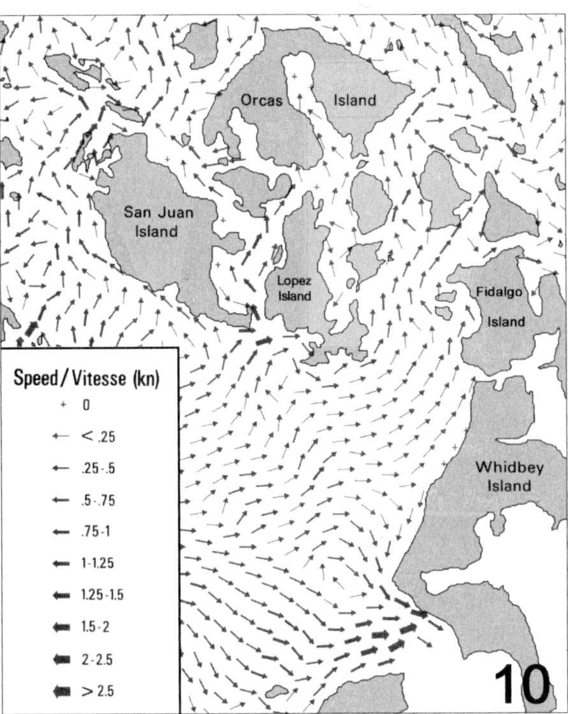

Figure 13.17 Southeast corner of Page 10 (reduced to half-size) from the Current Atlas covering the San Juan Islands. Predicted current directions and speeds are shown with current vector arrows for a one hour period.

Next, turn to your large-scale charts covering coastal areas. Create a dead reckoning plot of your route as a series of intended tracks, as explained in the previous section. Let's use the dead reckoning plot in Figure 13.16 as our example.

Imagine that you're planning a boat trip using the dead reckoning plot in Figure 13.16. You'll notice that this plot doesn't take **water currents** into account. Currents can be strong in this locale, so it's best to look at a map or atlas showing predicted currents at the time of your voyage.

Assume that Page 10 in the *Current Atlas* (produced by the Canadian Hydrographic Service) for the Strait of Juan de Fuca to the Strait of Georgia (**Figure 13.17**) shows the currents predicted at 8:00 AM on the day of your voyage. The arrows on the map show that the current is predicted to be light (<0.25 knots) and at right angles to Track 2, so you can safely ignore that current. However, the arrows in the vicinity of Track 3 indicate a slightly stronger current (0.25-0.5 knots) in the direction of travel. On average, the current will be around 0.4 knots. Adding this current speed to the 10-knot boat speed, you obtain an estimated **speed over the ground (SOG)** of 10.4 knots. At this speed, it should take 4.3×60/10.4, or 25 minutes to complete Track 3. Thus, the current-adjusted ETA at Flounder Bay is 8:43 AM, one minute earlier than the ETA would be if not adjusted for currents. You can ignore this one minute difference due to currents. However, if your boat had a 10-knot maximum speed and the current was 6 knots, you would need to adjust your ETA to take currents into account .

Your route planning is now complete, your voyage is under way, and you have correctly reached the starting point for dead reckoning Track 2. Steering the boat, you set a compass heading of 51° magnetic. You note on the chart that you started the track at 0800, and you adjust your cruising speed to 10 knots (**Figure 13.18**).

At 0806, you estimate that the boat has traveled 1 nautical mile and that you have entered the Traffic Separation Scheme for large tonnage vessels. You must now look and listen intently for ship traffic, first from the southbound and then from the northbound shipping lane, during the 7 minutes that it should take you to cross the 1.2-nautical-mile-wide zone drawn on the chart. No ships have to be avoided, and at 0818 you complete Track 2.

At this time, you use your hand-bearing compass (a special hand-held compass described in Chapter 12) to take a **position fix** using the compass resection method of position finding described earlier in the chapter (mariners call this using two **lines of position**). At 0819 you obtain a magnetic azimuth of 15° to Biz Point and 113° to the center of Deception Island. Plotting the corresponding 195° and 293° magnetic back azimuth lines from these points, you note their intersection as a 0819 fix. Evidently, currents, winds, or steering errors have caused your actual position to differ considerably from that predicted by dead reckoning.

Your course must be adjusted, and you quickly plot a new dead reckoning Track 3 from the fix point to Flounder Bay. Using your parallel rule and dividers, you find the new track to have a course of 351° magnetic and a distance of 4.1 nautical miles. At 10 knots, you should cover this track in 25 minutes, so your Estimated Time of Arrival at Flounder Bay is still 0844.

Setting your compass to 351° magnetic, you motor toward Flounder Bay, visible in the far distance, at 10 knots. At 0827 you see to your left the flashing red light and hear the gong shown on the chart at Williamson Rocks. In another 6 minutes you have the east edge of Allan Island safely to your left. You have also experienced and ignored the slight movement of the compass dial due to the local magnetic disturbance shown on the chart. In another 5 minutes you have traveled nearly a nautical mile and have Young Island at a safe distance to your left. The entrance to Flounder Bay is now clearly in sight and you steer to the entrance, arriving at 0845, almost perfectly on time.

Your voyage is a classic example of daytime piloting under good weather and water-current conditions using a compass, nautical chart and, above all, your eyes for guidance. But what if you are

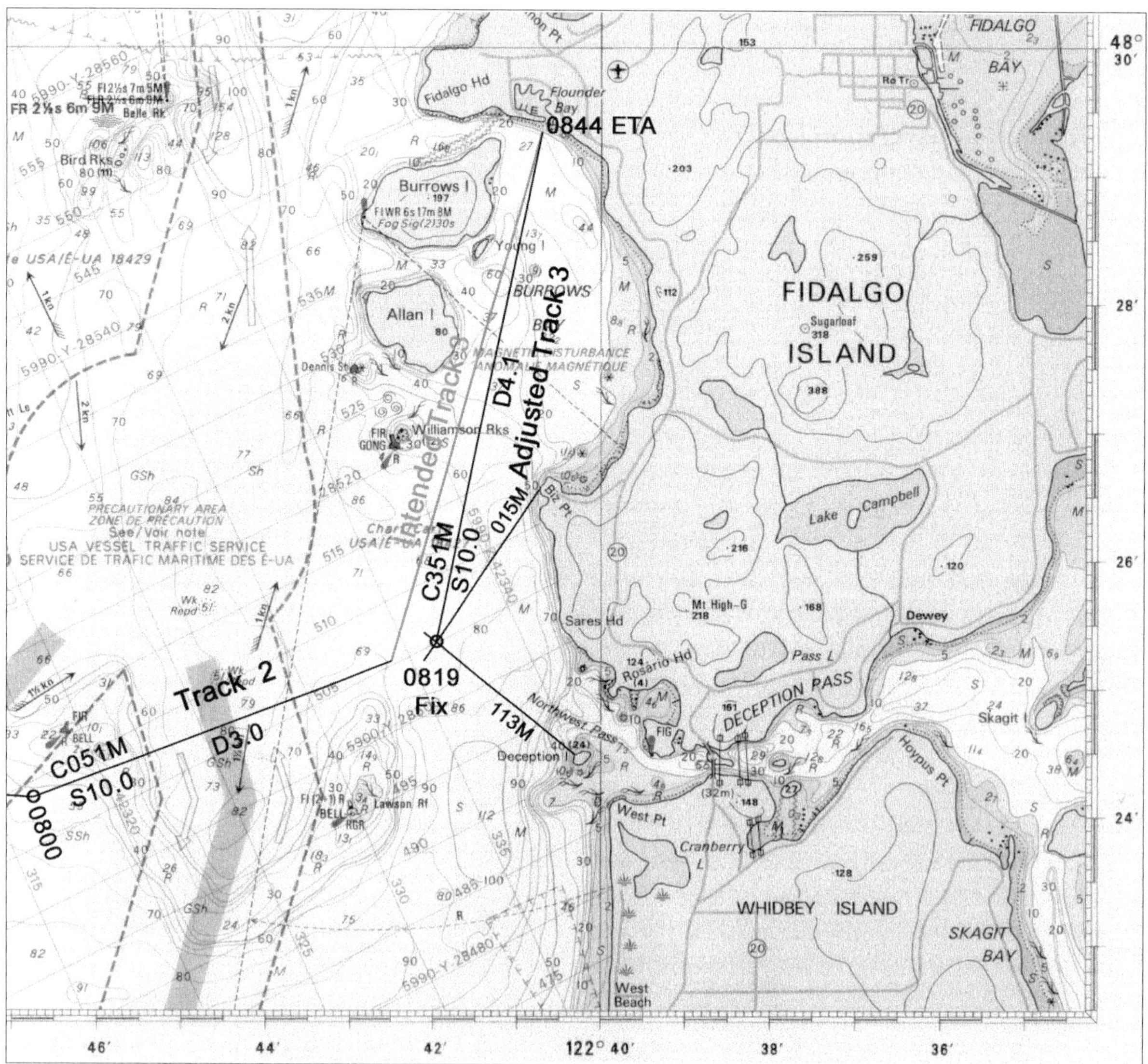

Figure 13.18 Dead reckoning plot showing intended tracks, and adjusted Track 3 necessitated by a position fix.

crossing the open ocean or traveling at night or in heavy fog? Dead reckoning has been the traditional mode of navigation under these conditions, but modern electronic devices have simplified the task.

Electronic Piloting Systems

For several decades, navigators of ships and airplanes have relied on **electronic piloting devices** to maintain a course. Recent developments link maps to radio signals. You can navigate a ship, airplane, or car by observing your progress along a path on a map and then making route decisions on the ground. You can choose from several types of piloting systems. In each case, your changing position is plotted on a map display.

An **inertial navigation system** monitors your vehicle's movements and uses this information to update the position of a vehicle symbol on a map display.* You must initialize the system by properly positioning the cursor on the map at the start of your route. Each distance and direction computation also involves some error. Since each subsequent computation is based on the previous one, errors accumulate, and the estimated position tends to "drift."

With primitive systems, the map backdrop may be a simple screen overlay. But more advanced technology uses detailed digital cartographic data held in some form of disk storage. An inertial navigation add-on option may someday be as popular for automobiles as automatic transmissions.

A second type of navigation aid, and one that seems to hold considerable promise, is based on **radionavigation technology**. Radionavigation has several advantages over inertial navigation. For one thing, radionavigation can provide an initial position fix, as well as subsequent fixes. More important, each new position determination along a route is computed independently of previous ones. Thus, errors don't accumulate as they do with inertial navigation.

**This is actually a hybrid system, since dead-reckoning technology is used to generate positional information, which is then used to update the cursor location on the map display.*

Although ground-based radiobeacons are in widespread use at present, **GPS-linked navigators** are attracting the most attention (see Chapter 14: GPS and Maps). One reason is that they provide grid coordinates that can be used to retrieve the appropriate base map from disk storage. When the vehicle moves off the edge of one map, the next one in the direction of travel is automatically brought up on the display screen.

Vehicle Navigation Systems

Potential applications of GPS technology in route finding stagger the imagination. Route finding will soon be transformed into something hardly recognizable today. GPS companies are selling **vehicle navigation systems** for automobiles. Many trucking, busing, delivery, and car rental companies are using the technology. Compact systems such as the Magellan Roadmate 700 (**Figure 13.19**) are available for less than $1500.

If you provide an origin and destination city, the vehicle navigation system will tell you the shortest-distance, least-time, or most-scenic route. If you specify stop-over points en route, the system will direct you through these points as well. You have the choice of seeing your route marked on a map, or seeing an itinerary giving all pertinent route identification and distance data for each route segment.

In the more sophisticated systems, the map display is linked by cellular phone or radio signals to local databases so that you can receive traffic updates and other useful information as you travel.

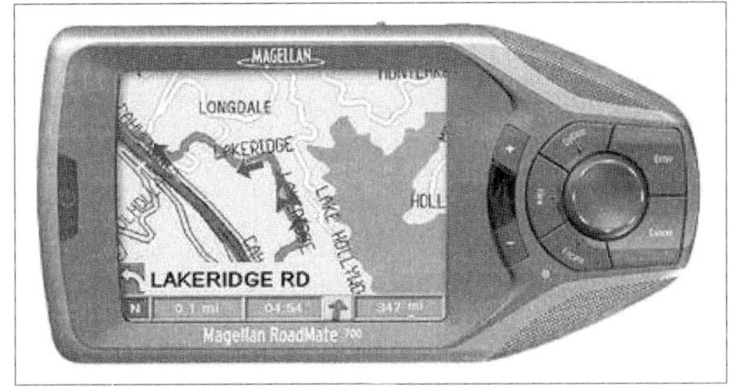

Figure 13.19 The Magellan Roadmate 700 vehicle navigation system displays your map position as you move through the environment.

Vast databases of lodging, restaurant, and other travel information, as well as trip planning software, are also available to assist in your travels.

Route Planning Software

Always knowing your map position can be useful, but sometimes you want to know the location of something on a trip you are planning. **Route planning software** such as DeLorme's Street Atlas USA lets you call up a map with the target location marked with a symbol*. You can make your request by entering a telephone area code, postal zip code, street name, street intersection, building address, or geographic place name (city, national park, and so on). Often these programs are linked with electronic Yellow Pages so that you can find the location of anything in the phone book. Alternatively, you can find locations of target businesses or attractions near an address. The software will also give you the nearest address if you click on a specific map location.

You can view the same location at a wide range of map scales, depending on the amount of geographic detail and extent of geographic coverage you desire. You can customize software settings with a profile of your travel preferences so that only your personal favorites are displayed. Internet links to vendors' web pages and other sites provide access to volumes of additional travel-related information, including road conditions and weather.

**See Appendix B for ordering information and similar products.*

SELECTED READINGS

Ames, G.P., "Forgetting St. Louis and Other Map Mischief," *Railroad History*, 188 (Spring-Summer 2003), pp. 28-41.

Baker, R.R., *Human Navigation and the Sixth Sense* (New York: Simon & Schuster, 1981).

Blandford, P.W., *Maps & Compasses*, 2nd ed. (Blue Ridge Summit, PA: TAB Books, A Division of McGraw-Hill, 1992).

Canadian Hydrographic Service, *Current Atlas: Juan de Fuca Strait to Strait of Georgia* (Sidney, BC: Canadian Hydrographic Service,1999).

Dilke, O.A.W., *Greek and Roman Maps*, Reprint ed. (Baltimore, MD: Johns Hopkins Univ. Press, 1998).

Geary, D., *Using a Map & Compass* (Mechanicsburg, PA: Stackpole Books, 1995).

Hodgson, M.., *Compass & Map Navigator* (Riverton, WY: The Brunton Company, 1997).

Jacobson, C., *The Basic Essentials of Map & Compass*, 2nd ed. (Merrillville, IN: ICS Books, Inc., 1997).

Kjellstrom, B., *Be Expert With Map & Compass: The Complete Orienteering Handbook*, revised ed. (New York: Macmillan General Reference, a Simon & Schuster Macmillan Company, 1994).

Langley, R.B., "The Federal Radionavigation Plan," *GPS World*, 3, 2 (March 1992), pp. 50-53.

Larkin, F.J., *Basic Coastal Navigation: An Introduction to Piloting* (Dobbs Ferry, NY: Sheridan House, 1993).

Maloney, E.S., *Chapman Piloting,* 64th ed. (New York: Hearst Books., 2003).

Randall, G., *The Outward Bound Map & Compass Handbook* (NY: Lyons & Burford, Publishers, 1989).

Seidman, D., *The Essential Wilderness Navigator* (Camden, ME: Ragged Mountain Press, 1995).

United States Army, *Map Reading*, Field Manual, FM 21-26 (Washington, DC: Department of the Army, Headquarters, current ed.).

Wilkes, K. (revised by P. Langley-Price and P. Ouvry), *Ocean Navigation* (London: Adlard Coles Nautical, 1994).

CHAPTER FOURTEEN
GPS AND MAPS

THE GLOBAL POSITIONING SYSTEM

- GPS Terminology
- GPS Design
- Differential GPS
    - Wide Area Augmentation System
- Operating Conditions
- Positional Accuracy

HAND-HELD GPS RECEIVERS

- Tables, Equations, and Databases
    - Datums
    - Coordinate Systems
    - Compass Declination
    - Databases

HAND-HELD GPS FIELD APPLICATIONS

- Find Your Position
- Orient Your Map
- Find a Distant Position
- Plan a Route
- Follow a Route
    - Where Am I Going?
    - Where Have I Been?
    - How Am I Doing?
    - How Do I Get Back?

HAND-HELD GPS LIMITATIONS

- Keep a Notebook
- Keep Your Compass
    - Multi-sensor Receivers
- Warning to GPS Novices

LINKING GPS TO MAPS

- Paper Maps
- Cartographic GPS Units
    - Electronic Chartplotters
- Mobile Electronics
- Laptop and Desktop GPS

SELECTED READINGS

GPS will inevitably contribute to our awareness that we all share the same planet. . . .
—Noel J. Hotchkiss

The prudent mariner will not rely solely on any single aid to navigation. . . .
—Nautical Chart, National Ocean Service

14

CHAPTER FOURTEEN

GPS AND MAPS

This chapter focuses on how you can use a **global positioning system (GPS)** receiver with maps. The aim here is to address the needs of the general (non-professional) user who has a hand-held or cartographic GPS receiver. Since we must be brief, we advise you to consult at least one of the guides under the Selected Readings for this chapter. You'll also find the user's manual that comes with your GPS unit to be an essential reference. Although GPS receivers share many traits, vendors use slightly different designs and terminology. Thus, the manual will explain how to use labeled hard keys on the face of the GPS unit, how to use different key combinations and sequences to activate soft keys (items) in the display menus, and what the menu jargon and cryptic acronyms mean.

THE GLOBAL POSITIONING SYSTEM

The NAVSTAR Global Positioning System (GPS), developed by the U.S. Department of Defense (DOD), became fully operational in 1994. Its **constellation** consists of 24 satellites in approximately 10,000-mile altitude orbits, with four satellites placed in each of six evenly spaced orbital planes. This configuration insures that, from any point on earth, five to eight satellites will usually be visible at all times (**Figure 14.1**).

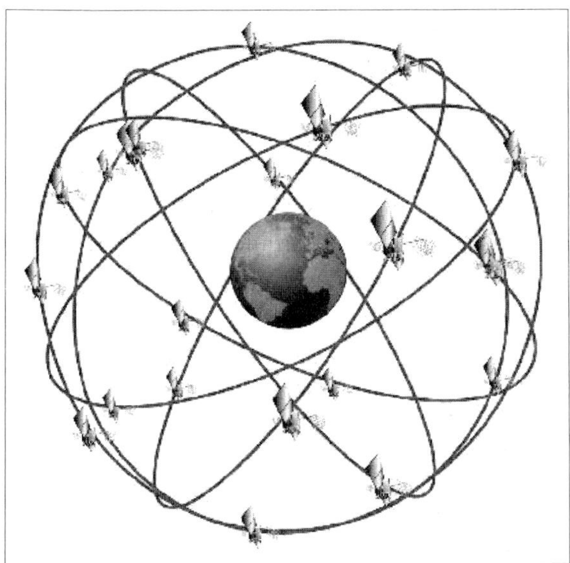

Figure 14.1 The GPS constellation of 24 satellites in six orbital planes (adapted from DOD artwork).

We can gain a general understanding of how GPS works by reducing its complex operating principles to five basic steps:

1. GPS is based on **space trilateration** from four or more of the 24 satellites in the constellation that happen to be in view. The idea is that knowing the precise distance from each satellite to the receiver at the same instant allows us to determine the location of the receiver and then give the position in latitude, longitude, and elevation (see **Figure 14.2**).

2. To trilaterate, the GPS receiver measures the distance to each satellite using the **travel time of radio signals** sent by each satellite.

3. To measure travel time, the GPS receiver needs very accurate timing, which it receives from **atomic clocks** on each satellite, and which it processes using very clever tricks.

4. Along with the distance to each satellite at the same instant in time, the receiver must know where the satellites are in space. High orbits and careful orbital monitoring by the DOD allow each satellite to broadcast its position continuously.

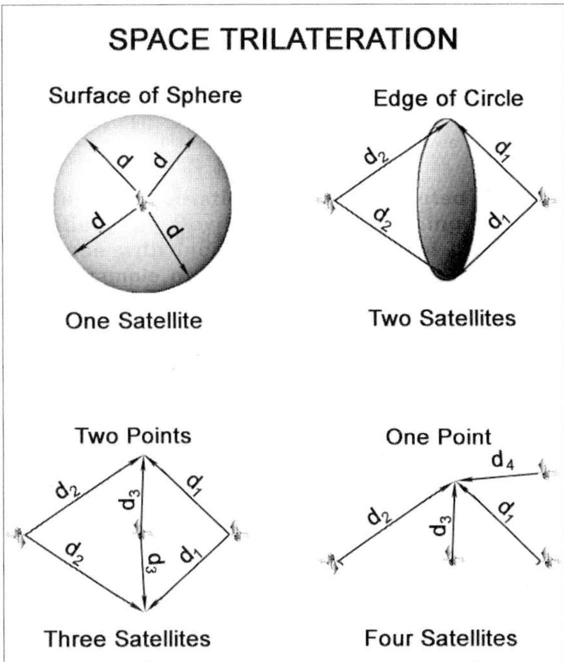

Figure 14.2 A signal at distance d away from a single GPS satellite could be at a location anywhere on the surface of a sphere of radius d. Signals from two satellites at distances d_1 and d_2 intersect and hence define a position anywhere along the edge of a circle. With three satellites, the signals with distances d_1, d_2, and d_3 intersect at two points in space. With four satellites, there is no ambiguity, since the four distance lines intersect at a single point on the earth's surface.

5. Finally, the receiver must correct for any delays the signal experiences from each satellite as it travels through the atmosphere and ionosphere.

GPS Terminology

The global positioning system is, of course, far more complex than these simplified operating principles. There are hundreds of technical terms associated with GPS theory, instruments, operation, accuracy, and use in navigation. Refer to **Table C.1** and **Table C.2** in **Appendix C** for a list of GPS abbreviations, acronyms , and terms. These tables will help you understand the following discussion of GPS design and accuracy.

GPS Design

DOD officials designed two tiers of service into the system. Each satellite broadcasts unique signals of three types: protected or **Precision codes (P-codes)** at two frequencies; **Coarse Acquisition (C/A or CA)** codes at one frequency; and **status information** on satellite condition and orbital position (known as **ephemeris** and **almanac data**). All signals are synchronized to GPS time, called **Universal Time Coordinated (UTC)**, using precise atomic clocks.

The military and other "authorized" parties have access to the more accurate P-code positioning and timing signals. This is called the **Precise Positioning Service (PPS)**. To achieve this higher accuracy, military receivers hold P-codes in memory. With both P-code frequencies available, dual-code military receivers can also make corrections for signal delays caused by changing atmospheric conditions.

Civilians can access only the less accurate C/A codes in the **Standard Positioning Service (SPS)**. With only one frequency available, single-code civilian receivers must rely on less-accurate atmospheric modeling to estimate signal delays. Until May 1, 2000, the DOD further degraded this service by deliberately interfering with signal timing in a random way. This signal degradation process is called **Selective Availability (SA)**.

The DOD's efforts to keep accurate GPS technology out of the hands of potential enemies by providing two levels of service have largely failed. Ingenious ways to circumvent the degraded quality of SPS were developed by private industry and will undoubtedly continue to be used. For example, specialized **codeless receivers** are now used by surveyors when they desire super accurate positioning. These receivers can use P-code information indirectly.

Differential GPS

Similarly, a procedure called **differential GPS (DGPS)** can greatly improve positioning accuracy. This method uses a fixed-position receiver, located

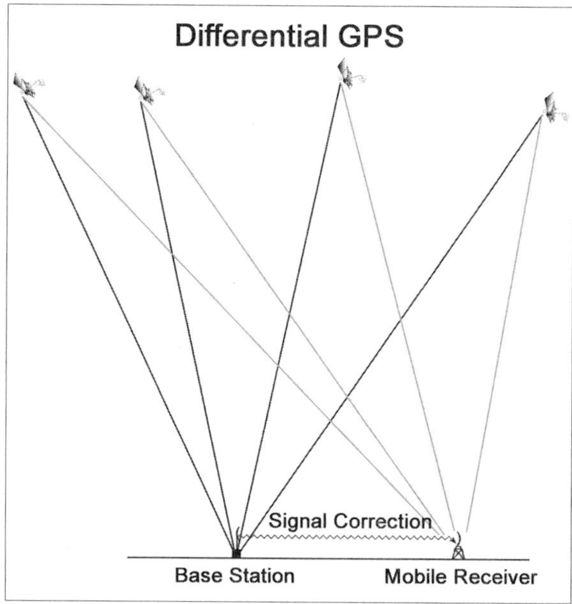

Figure 14.3 By using signals from several satellites, a mobile GPS receiver can quickly compute your latitude, longitude, and elevation coordinates. By using signal correction data from a base station receiver at a surveyed control point, you can greatly improve the accuracy of your positioning.

at a **base station** at a survey control point, in conjunction with a **mobile receiver** (**Figure 14.3**). Since the fixed receiver knows its location precisely from past measurements, it can tell to what extent current atmospheric conditions are affecting satellite signal reception. This information is then communicated in real time by cellular phone or radio to the mobile receiver, which is assumed to be working under similar atmospheric conditions. You can also post-process your GPS readings when you get in from the field, using correction data that you download into your computer.

Differential GPS is of great value to surveyors and has become essential to commercial air and sea navigators. Before long, inexpensive hand-held DGPS receivers will be available for recreational users as well. You can currently either set up your own multiple-receiver system, or you can receive correction data from one of a rapidly growing number of government or commercial DGPS utilities, such as the recently created Wide Area Augmentation System.

Wide Area Augmentation System

The U.S. Federal Aviation Administration and Department of Transportation recently developed the **Wide Area Augmentation System (WAAS)** as a nationwide source of GPS correction data for precision aircraft positioning. Although not yet approved for aviation, boaters and other GPS users already are making use of WAAS data.

Twenty-five ground stations in North America continually collect GPS satellite data. All data are corrected for errors in satellite orbit position, time, and signal delays caused by the atmosphere and ionosphere. Corrected data are transmitted to a communication satellite that then rebroadcasts the data on the same frequency as the GPS signals.

Operating Conditions

GPS positioning accuracy is influenced by operating factors that go beyond receiver design and number. For example, **changing ionospheric and atmospheric conditions** can affect the speed at which signals travel. Signals of different frequencies will be affected differently. Signals can also be reflected from surrounding objects, causing both direct and indirect signal reception from the same satellite at a receiver—a situation known as the **multipath problem**.

The number and **geometric configuration** of the satellites used at any instant also affect positioning accuracy. At least three satellites are needed to make a horizontal fix. A fourth satellite is necessary to make a vertical fix. Even more satellites improve accuracy. Widely spaced satellites are said to have a **strong geometry**, while satellites bunched in the sky have a **weak geometry**.

It's best to have signals reach your position at angles as close to 90° as possible. To understand the logic of this rule, refer to the space trilateration diagram in Figure 14.2. Here you can see how much easier it is to determine the exact point where two sight lines cross when the angles approach 90 degrees. Conversely, the intersection of lines that cross at small angles is difficult to pinpoint.

Another factor affecting positional accuracy is the time it takes to make a fix. A stationary receiver is more accurate than a moving one. If you can stay at one location and take repeated signals, your positioning accuracy is improved. Surveyors often will occupy a point for several hours in an attempt to achieve the best possible accuracy.

Positional Accuracy

Taking all these factors into consideration, what **positional accuracy** is possible using GPS? The stated positional accuracy of GPS receivers varies dramatically from source to source. Part of the problem is that accuracy is defined in two ways: horizontal (a 2-D circle of a given radius), and vertical (height above a datum). So you first want to ask, "What type of accuracy?"

Things get even more confusing because there are several ways to define each type of accuracy. For example, accuracy may be stated with respect to the military design specifications for the system. Since GPS has surpassed design specifications, these figures are conservative. Accuracy may also be stated with respect to the best that can be achieved or by the probability of being within a given distance 50%, 68%, 95%, or 99% of the time. Accuracy is sometimes stated with respect to a single position fix and sometimes with respect to averaging fixes over a period of time ranging up to six hours. Unfortunately, the proper clarification is often missing when you see a statement of GPS accuracy.

If we adopt a 95% rule using what is called the **circular error probable (CEP)** method, we can answer this question by giving the radius of a circle containing 95% of all possible fixes.* Using this method, experts say that hand-held GPS receivers can achieve horizontal accuracies of 20 meters and vertical accuracies of 28 meters. In other

**Beware of vendor hype. You'll see a wide range of numbers given for GPS receiver accuracy. These figures commonly represent the most optimistic case under the best of all conditions. Such luck is rare. The numbers also vary with the definition of accuracy used. CEPs of 50, 68, 95, and 99.9 percent are commonly reported. If vendors adopt a 50% rule, of course, their products may seem to the unwary to be more accurate. You must take care to judge the competition against the same standard.*

words, 95% of the fixes can be expected to fall within 20 meters horizontally of their true position on earth. In practice, greater accuracy is the rule rather than the exception.

If you're willing to average signals over several hours, you can use your hand-held receiver to achieve differential GPS horizontal accuracy as good as three meters (10 feet). This more than matches military specifications for GPS—a fact that has frustrated the Defense Department. A hand-held receiver using differentially-corrected coordinates from WAAS should have a positional accuracy of about 3 meters without averaging signals. Clearly, differential GPS holds great promise. But its added expense and inconvenience may not be justified if you can live with up to 20-meter positioning accuracy.

On the other hand, surveyors and other mapping professionals need DGPS accuracy in the sub-meter range. They are quite willing to put up with the extra effort that this increased accuracy requires. For such people, accuracy in the meter range is now quite routine, and accuracy in the centimeter range is possible under the best of conditions. Such accuracy requires sophisticated equipment and data post-processing using differential GPS and other signal correction technology after returning to the laboratory. This is costly in terms of time, equipment, and skilled professionals.

In the future, it's likely that all receivers will be equipped for DGPS and that the needed correction data will be communicated from permanent ground stations via satellite to your receiver using a global system similar to the WAAS. You will then enjoy 3-meter to 6-meter accuracy worldwide with an inexpensive, hand-held receiver.

The accuracy of your vertical position is another matter. Hand-held receivers, using averaged signals, typically have 95% of readings falling within 28 meters (92 feet) for a given fix. This error is greater than the local relief in much of the world! With DGPS, however, you should be able to obtain a vertical accuracy of 8 meters (26 feet), or better, 95% of the time with a hand-held receiver.

HAND-HELD GPS RECEIVERS

The appearance of a **hand-held GPS receiver**, such as the Garmin GPSmap 76, is usually rather stark (**Figure 14.4**). The receiver has a small (approximately 2"× 3") black-and-white display screen. This screen has rather poor spatial resolution, which explains why a typical screen display consists of only a few characters and a simple graphic. The frequent use of abbreviations and acronyms is a way to increase the amount of information displayed on a screen image.

On the receiver's face, you also find several hard (dedicated function) buttons, including a

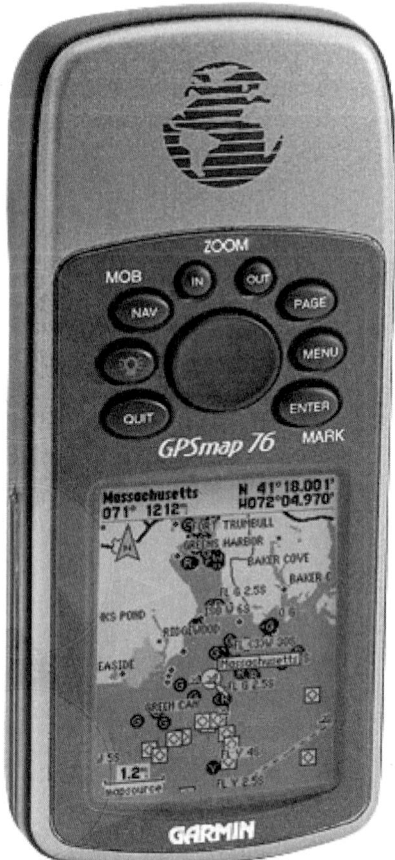

Figure 14.4 The Garmin GPSmap 76 is a typical hand-held GPS receiver.

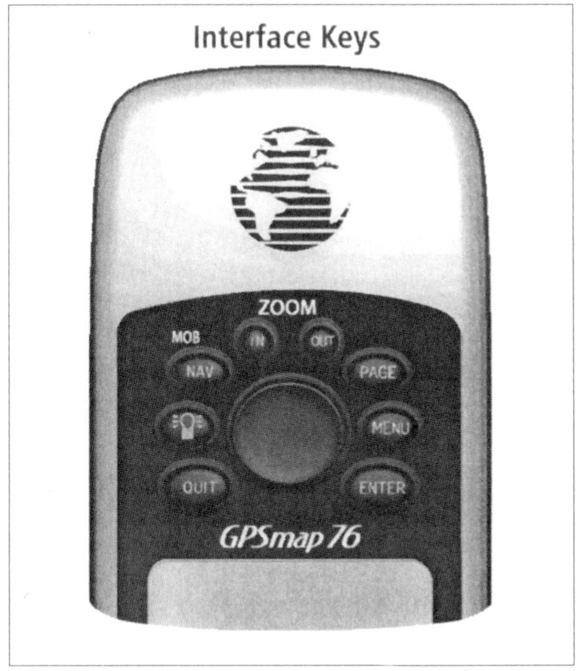

Figure 14.5 Dedicated function buttons you will find on a typical hand-held GPS receiver (Garmin GPSmap 76).

POWER key and a **ROCKER** key (large center button) used to control the horizontal and vertical movement of the cursor on the display pages (**Figure 14.5**). Several additional hard keys, such as **MENU**, **ENTER**, **QUIT**, **PAGE**, Zoom **IN** and **OUT**, and **NAV**, have somewhat self-explanatory functions.

The **PAGE** key lets you browse through a half dozen or so screen pages or menus that give you access to most of the receiver's functions. The Garmin GPSmap 76, for example, has five primary pages:

1. A **GPS Information Page** shows satellite positions and the strength of signals received from each satellite (**Figure 14.6**). Satellite positions are displayed on a north-oriented diagram consisting of two circles and a center dot. The outer circle represents the horizon, the inner circle represents 45 degrees above the horizon, and the center dot represents the point directly overhead. The date and time are displayed below this diagram, along with your current location.

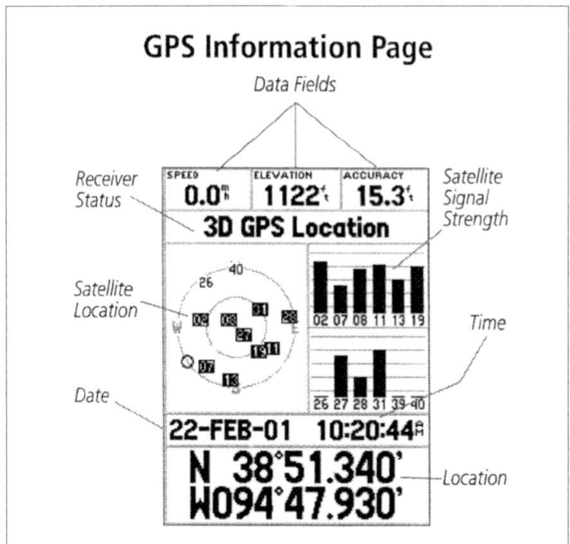

Figure 14.6 The GPS Information Page on the Garmin GPSmap 76 receiver shows the positions of satellites in view, the strengths of their signals, the date and time, and your location.

2. A **Map Page** provides a crude map of your position, the path you have traveled, and nearby features such as streets and highways, cities, railway lines, lakes, rivers, and navigational aids (**Figure 14.7**). Information such as your current heading, speed, or distance to the next waypoint are displayed at the top left and right corners of the map. You can use the Zoom IN and OUT buttons to change the map scale and hence view a larger or smaller area.

3. A **Pointer Page** is used when you can't follow a straight-line course. A compass card rotates as you change your heading. The true azimuth for your current heading is shown by a vertical line at the top of the display (**Figure 14.8**). A large arrow always points toward your waypoint, so you'll know how much your heading deviates from the direction to the waypoint. You can display navigation information, such as your speed and distance to the waypoint, above the compass card.

4. A **Highway Page** is used to navigate a straight-line course to a waypoint (**Figure 14.9**). You simply try to stay in the middle of the highway display

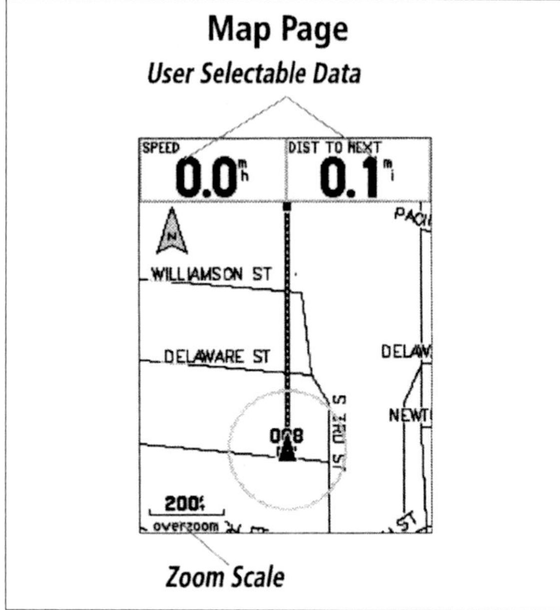

Figure 14.7 The Map Page on the Garmin GPSmap 76 receiver shows a base map with features such as cities, roads, and rivers, along with your position and route traveled.

that moves to the left or right as your heading deviates from the course. If the highway moves to the right, for instance, you must steer to the right until the fixed triangle centered at the top of the display is again aligned with the center of the highway. Your speed, distance to the waypoint, current heading, and the amount you're away from the course line are displayed in boxes above the highway symbol.

5. An **Active Route Page** shows the name of your current waypoint, a list of this point and the other waypoints used on your trip, and the distance to all of these waypoints (**Figure 14.10**).

On each screen page you can scroll up or down to a menu item, or soft key, and then activate that function by pressing ENTER. To enter an alphanumeric character, you must use the ROCKER key to scroll through the alphabet (A-Z) or digits (0-9) until you reach the desired character, and then press ENTER. You must repeat this process for each letter in a word and each digit in a number.

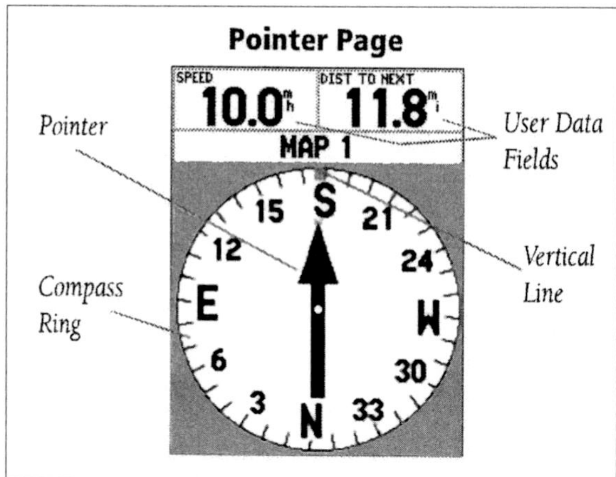

Figure 14.8 The Pointer Page on the Garmin GPSmap 76 receiver guides your steering when you can't follow a straight-line course.

The hand-held GPS receiver interface also includes an antenna. Internal antennas make for a more compact but less flexible unit. External antennas may be fixed to the unit's side and must be rotated into vertical orientation for use. External antennas may also be attached to the unit with a cable so that they can be remotely mounted, say on a vehicle's roof or the top of a backpack. In either case, the antenna must be held upright with a clear line-of-sight to at least three satellites for a two-dimensional fix, or four satellites for three-dimensional positioning.

Tables, Equations, and Databases

The permanent memory in your GPS receiver holds useful equations and tables of data. You can use these equations and tables to process satellite signals. You can also use them to make spatial computations when determining direction (true or magnetic), distance in English or metric units, speed, and position with respect to different grids. These tables and equations also let you process data you enter through the keypad or through a cable link to a stand-alone computer. Let's look more closely at some of these uses.

Datums

The receiver memory holds the data and equations needed to make both **horizontal and vertical**

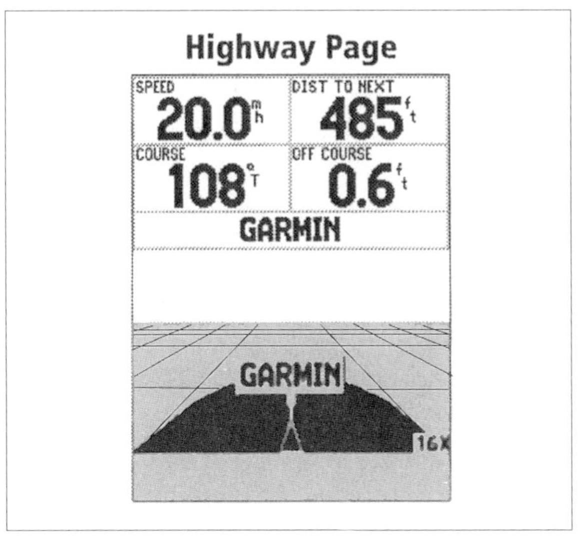

Figure 14.9 The Highway Page on the Garmin GPSmap 76 receiver guides your steering along a straight-line course.

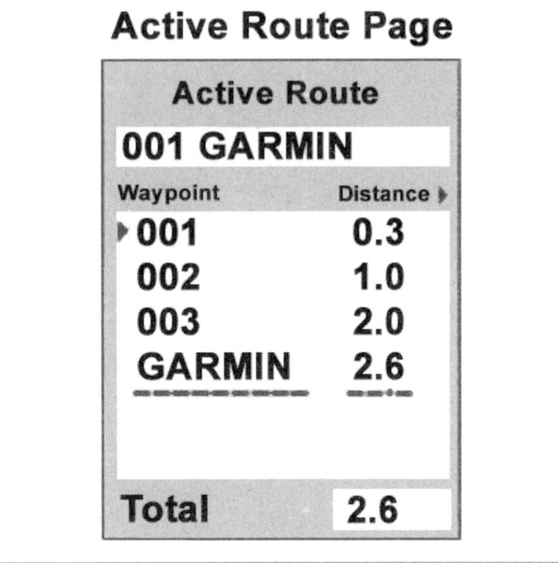

Figure 14.10 The Active Route Page on the Garmin GPSMAP 76 receiver shows all waypoints used on your trip and the distance to each waypoint.

datum calculations (see Chapter 1 for more information on datums). Parameters for over 100 datums used around the world are stored in many hand-held receivers. The computer in the receiver makes the conversions between these datums.

GPS receivers default to the WGS84 horizontal datum. Unfortunately, this datum isn't used on all large-scale maps, particularly older editions. If you're not using a map based on WGS84, the positional discrepancy between your map datum and WGS84 will create positioning errors beyond those associated with the stated accuracy of your receiver. This additional locational error can be as much as 100 meters in the United States and 600 meters worldwide.

To minimize datum errors, you have two choices. You can adjust computed positions to your map manually, which is a laborious task. Or you can enter the datum used to make your map and let the receiver make the datum conversion before displaying position coordinates. This second choice best uses the capabilities of the receiver and is preferred.

Coordinate Systems

The geographic coordinate system (geodetic latitude and longitude) is usually the default. But most GPS receivers can convert latitude and longitude to several types of grid coordinates (see Chapters 1 and 4 for further information on geographic and grid coordinates). All receivers can convert to UTM grid coordinates, and many can also convert to State Plane Coordinates and a variety of regional and proprietary grids. A menu lets you select the grid of your choice. Some receivers even let you define your own grid.

The choice of coordinates usually determines the units of measurement. The UTM grid system, for example, uses metric units. Geographic coordinates are usually displayed in degree, minute, second (dms) units, but can also be in decimal degrees. There normally is a menu option to change to units of your choice.

Compass Declination

GPS receivers give direction with respect to both true and magnetic north. The choice is yours. To make these conversions, the receiver must hold in its permanent memory magnetic declination data for the entire earth. Computations done on these data let the receiver serve as a form of electronic compass. But the standard hand-held GPS receiver is no substitute for a conventional magnetic compass, as we'll discuss later in this chapter.

Databases

More expensive hand-held receivers often hold **databases** of special interest to the GPS user. A database of airport facilities is commonly found in GPS units used in planes, while a database of port facilities and other navigational information is found in units used on boats. A database for highway travel might contain information on local fuel, food, lodging, entertainment, and interesting sites.

HAND-HELD GPS FIELD APPLICATIONS

How does GPS compare with traditional methods of position and route finding? In this section, as we describe what hand-held receivers such as the Garmin GPSmap 76 can do, we invite you to make a comparison with the map-and-compass methods discussed in the previous chapter.

Find Your Position

Position determination is the wonder of GPS. It couldn't be simpler. Merely turn the power on, and the receiver displays your three-dimensional position on one of several pages (see Figures 14.6 and 14.7). In the Positional Accuracy section of this chapter, we saw that the horizontal coordinates on a hand-held receiver will likely be accurate to within 20 meters (66 feet) 95% of the time. If you take continuous readings at one location and average them over several hours, you may achieve 10-meter (33-foot) accuracy. If you are moving, your accuracy is poorest. Conveniently, the receiver will tell you the **estimated position error (EPE)** when it displays your coordinates.

Orient Your Map

1. Turn on your receiver, and either the GPS Information Page or Map page displays the coordinates of your present position. Enter your position as a waypoint.

2. Mark your present position on your map with a dot.

3. Options:

A. Find and mark a prominent distant object on the map and enter the grid coordinates of the object as a waypoint. Press the NAV button, then select the Go To Point option. Change to the Pointer Page. You'll notice that the pointer arrow points to the waypoint for the distant object. Align the pointer arrow with the direction line from your position to the distant object. Your map is now oriented so that straight ahead is at the top center.

B. If you can't identify any prominent objects on your map, switch to the Pointer Page. Then point your receiver in any direction and move (briskly if walking) along a straight path in that direction, keeping your starting point in view. The rotating compass card will display your heading, which then can be used to orient the map to north using the map orientation by compass method described in Chapter 13.

C. As an alternative when faced with the conditions in B, you can move in any direction to a location from which you can see your starting position. Determine the coordinates at your new position and enter them as a waypoint. Press the NAV button, choose the Go To Point option, then select your starting point from the waypoint list. This will give you a backtrack (back-azimuth) reading, the direction back to your starting point. Change this reading to an azimuth by adding or subtracting 180 degrees. You now know the direction from your starting position to your present location. Draw a direction line at this angle on the map, then rotate the map so that the direction line points to your starting position. The map is now oriented to the direction from your present location to your starting position. (See Chapter 13 for further information on orienting maps.)

Find a Distant Position

A GPS receiver can't be used to find the coordinates of a distant position. It only can determine coordinates for its own location. If you know the coordinates for a distant point, you can enter them as waypoints. Once you do so, you can use the Pointer or Highway Pages on your receiver to guide you to the distant position.

Plan a Route

Your GPS unit can be used to **plan a route**, but the receiver depends on you to enter critical data. If coordinates for landmarks are stored as waypoints in your receiver's memory, you can organize these waypoints into a **route sequence**. You can obtain the necessary coordinates from maps, gazetteers, websites, or other geographical sources. It's wise to save coordinate information for routes that you might want to repeat by writing them in a notebook or entering them into a computer file. Remember that coordinates held in a GPS receiver can be lost if the unit is damaged.

The problem with using coordinates from past trips or other sources is that hand-held receivers have limited temporary storage capacity. Current receivers let you store anywhere from 250 to 3,000 waypoints that can be organized into 20 to 200 routes. Once you exceed this capacity, you must clear some coordinates before you can enter new ones. These purged coordinates are lost unless you download them into some other storage device. Some GPS units let you do this to a memory card or disk, directly through a data communication cable plugged into your home computer.

Follow a Route

The awesome power of GPS is revealed when **following routes**. Your GPS unit tells you which way to go, where you've been, how you're doing, and how to get back on track if you're off course. Let's look at each of these functions.

Where Am I Going?

As we discussed earlier, it's essential to plan your route by entering your destination's coordinates into your receiver. Once you've done so, you merely press the NAV button, choose the Go To Point option, and select your destination from the waypoint list. Your receiver will display the direction and distance to your destination on the Pointer or Highway Page.

If your route has several legs, your receiver will automatically shift to the next leg when you approach an upcoming waypoint. The new direction and distance information will be displayed. This process will be repeated until you reach your destination.

Where Have I Been?

The Map Page displays your progress along a route. It shows your starting point and each waypoint you've visited. It also shows the path you took between waypoints to get to your present position. Some units also display landmarks, city locations, and navigation aids stored in the receiver's memory. The plot is crude but sufficient to give you the information you need in the field.

You may want to save information about your route. This might be the case, for example, if you're following a trail or road not found on your map. Later, when you get back to your computer, you can download the route coordinates and plot an overlay. Then you can use the overlay to update your printed map.

How Am I Doing?

Your GPS receiver also provides graphic steering guidance and navigation information en route. This information is displayed on the Pointer and Highway Pages. Compass and Highway Pages commonly include a **course deviation indicator (CDI)**—a graphic display showing how far you've strayed left or right of your desired path. This information is called your **cross track error (XTE or XTR)**. Such a portrayal of navigation error can be very useful in guiding you back on course (see Figure 14.9).

Compass and Highway Pages also display a variety of speed and time information: **Speed (SPD)**, **Speed Over Ground (SOG)**, **Velocity**

Made Good (VMG), **Estimated Time En Route (ETE)**, and **Estimated Time of Arrival (ETA)** are some of these functions (see Table C.2 in Appendix C for definitions). This information may be useful if you're traveling in a vehicle along a fairly straight course at a constant rate of speed. But at slow speed over an irregular course, such as walking, the information is unreliable. Also, remember that the GPS uses straight "as the crow flies" distances in making these calculations.

When you near your destination, your receiver may beep or display a message saying "Arrived." At this point, you should be within viewing distance of your ground destination. It's time to look up and study your surroundings. GPS has done its job. Remember, even experienced navigators complete the final few meters of their journey by eye, not by instrument or map!

How Do I Get Back?

Most GPS receivers have a **backtrack function** that helps you retrace a route back to its starting point. Pressing a few menu keys reverses your route and displays it as a graphic plot. As you follow the route back toward its starting point, the navigation display works the same as when you were outbound on the route.

An interesting variation on backtracking is the **man-over-board (MOB)** function. You might use MOB, for example, if you accidentally drop your fishing rod in the water while trolling across a lake. A couple of quick keystrokes activate the function on most receivers, marking the spot with MOB coordinates. You can quickly navigate back to this position using the Pointer or Highway Pages. If you've ever tried to recover something dropped in a lake while the boat was moving or you were far from shore, you will appreciate the potential of the man-over-board function.

HAND-HELD GPS LIMITATIONS

GPS technology is revolutionary, but it's not magical. A receiver knows coordinates, not geography. It uses these coordinates to compute distance, direction, and speed. It assumes a straight-line path between landmarks when making these computations.

But a GPS receiver lacks the sense of place that makes locations special to us. Since it can't read your mind, its computations aren't tempered by such human factors as needs and desires. It can tell you the shortest distance as measured in miles, but it can't tell you which route is the quickest, safest, or most interesting. You glean such functional information from maps, either those in your head (mental) or those in your hand (cartographic). Maps help you see spatial relations at a glance and put pieces of environmental information together to form a bigger picture. The map suggests alternate places to visit and routes to take. You can then program these positions into your GPS receiver.

Keep a Notebook

We've already discussed the small size and poor resolution of display screens on hand-held GPS receivers. One difficulty with the screens is that many of the displayed terms, graphics, and messages must be abbreviated. Most GPS units will, by default, code waypoints sequentially by number (001, 002, 003, and so on). Having hundreds of numerical identifiers in your receiver's memory is a mental challenge when you want to select a destination or create a route.

Fortunately, receivers have provision for manually entering a short waypoint label in place of the default numerical identifier. A label such as

"CAR," "CAMP," or "PARK" is easier to use than number identifiers, but you soon run out of meaningful short words and recognizable abbreviations. There is no space to say anything significant about a waypoint that you want to recall later, and keying in multiple character identifiers is a laborious process.

You can get around the waypoint entry and recall problems by annotating your map with the proper numerical identifier each time you enter one into your receiver's memory. But this is quite a chore, especially in the field, and it makes a mess of your map if you use it for many trips. Furthermore, you have to add still more annotations to your map to capture the character of the landscape along each leg of your trip. This information is particularly valuable if you decide to backtrack or return at a later time.

A better way to augment waypoint identifiers is to **keep a notebook** or log. In a notebook, you can expand on each short waypoint identifier to your heart's content. You will also know what terrain features to watch for as you approach obscure waypoints. If nothing else, your notebook makes good reading later when you want to daydream about past trips.

Keep Your Compass

We have stressed how maps can help overcome the limitations of GPS technology. The same can be said of the magnetic compass. Your GPS receiver cannot replace your compass. You need both.

True, a GPS receiver can do some of the things compasses and protractors do. For instance, your receiver can give you the true and magnetic directions between any two points for which it has coordinates. This function mimics using a protractor on your map. In the field, your GPS receiver can give you the direction to a distant point for which it has coordinates. This function mimics compass use. If you're moving along at a brisk walk or faster, it can give you your direction of travel. Again, this mirrors using a compass.

But if you aren't moving, your GPS receiver's likeness to a compass breaks down. Under this condition, it doesn't know which way is north or which way you're facing. That is a concern because it makes it difficult to keep your map oriented if you're traveling slowly. It can also be a problem with faster movement over a path that keeps changing direction.

An even greater difference between GPS and compass technology is that GPS uses rather weak satellite signals that are easily blocked. Terrain, buildings, vegetation, and even a boat sail may block the line-of-sight satellite signals that are crucial in making a position fix. Signals can also reflect off nearby objects, confusing the GPS receiver and leading to degraded position calculations.

Other things can happen to the satellite signals as well. Problems can occur with signal transmission at the satellite, resulting in a weak signal or none at all. Satellites must be a certain distance above the horizon or their signals will be weak or blocked. And we learned earlier in the chapter that the satellites' geometrical configuration has an impact on the accuracy of position computations. You don't want the satellites to be bunched together in the sky but to be dispersed rather evenly overhead.

A GPS receiver needs a power supply to run its internal computer. In hand-held units, this power supply is usually a battery. We all know that batteries lose power with time, use, and cold temperatures. Since a loss of power will cause the receiver to fail, batteries must be replaced or recharged after about 24 hours of use. The best way to conserve batteries is to rely primarily on map and compass. Use your GPS receiver only intermittently to check your progress and make navigation adjustments.

In contrast, a magnetic compass uses the earth's magnetic field as its energy source and signal. No electrical power is needed, and magnetic energy is neither blocked nor reflected by landscape features.

GPS and magnetic compass technologies are complementary—one enhances the other. When your GPS receiver fails, is lost, or is damaged, your compass could be life-saving. Carrying both devices is a valuable form of insurance and risk management.

Multi-sensor Receivers

A few manufacturers have recently addressed the stationary-compass and altitude-inaccuracy problems inherent in GPS technology by marketing a **multi-sensor receiver.** The Garmin GPSmap 76S, for instance, includes a WAAS-equipped differential GPS receiver capable of 3-meter horizontal accuracy (**Figure 14.11**). In addition, the unit has a barometric altimeter and electronic compass, so you can obtain accurate horizontal positions, elevations, and heading azimuths when you're standing still. The altimeter still must be calibrated frequently for elevations to be highly accurate (see Chapter 13 for more on altimeters), but even without constant calibration the altimeter values probably will be more reliable than elevations computed by the GPS receiver.

Figure 14.11 The Garmin GPSmap 76S combines a GPS receiver, barometric altimeter, and electronic compass.

Warning to GPS Novices

You may know exactly where you are and where you want to go but still be lost. Your GPS receiver will tell you your location and the direction and distance to your desired destination. It will do this every few seconds for hours—until the batteries drain down. But that information is of little use if you can't move (because of a broken leg, bad storm, or other calamity) and have no way to communicate your location to a rescuer. Before you leave home, then, it's a good idea to arm yourself with a backup device that can let someone know where to find you.

In many parts of the world, a battery-powered cell phone may get your message out. This ground-based system depends on line-of-sight signals, which means you must be located within a region that is served by a transmitter/receiver. The system has the advantage that you can call an existing telephone number, and someone can call you back if you leave a message. The disadvantage of cellular technology is that transmitters are found only in densely populated areas and along major highway routes.

LINKING GPS TO MAPS

How do you best make the connection between GPS and maps? The small, coarse-resolution screen on your hand-held GPS receiver can display only a few landmarks and a simple route or two. It can't display a map of any useful detail. This leaves you with two options—paper maps and cartographic GPS units.

Paper Maps

One option is to carry a conventional large-scale paper map along with your GPS receiver. Whenever you check your position with the receiver, you also visually note the location on your map. Some people prefer to plot positions and make annotations on the map as they move across the landscape. A big advantage of this option is that it is inexpensive. Paper maps cost relatively little, and you can use an inexpensive GPS receiver. Another advantage is that the combination is conveniently portable. Inexpensive receivers weigh only a few ounces, and a map weighs next to nothing.

The disadvantage of using traditional paper maps with your GPS receiver is that they demand the most from you. You must continually keep them oriented. You also must be able to work with the scale and grid coordinates to make sense of the position, distance, direction, and other spatial information supplied by the receiver.

Cartographic GPS Units

This brings us to the second option, which is to link a detailed map to the GPS receiver automatically. A screen of readable size and resolution is required, as is a **digital map database**. The system also must contain the electronics needed to retrieve and display the appropriate map with your present position.

The most convenient method of linking maps to GPS is to purchase a **cartographic GPS unit**. The Garmin GPSmap 2010 a good example. The unit is housed in a 6 × 10 in. (15 × 25 cm.) box, weighing several pounds, with a 4 × 6 in. (10 × 15 cm.) color display screen (**Figure 14.12**). Cartographic GPS units are typically used in boats, airplanes, and highway vehicles where there is ready access to a plug-in source of electrical power. In these vehicles, the added bulk of cartographic units is not a significant factor. But reduced portability is a major obstacle for the person on foot. Indeed, cartographic GPS units are usually permanently mounted.

Figure 14.12 Cartographic GPS units such as the Garmin GPSmap 2010 include a display screen of sufficient size and resolution to display your position on a readable map called up from its memory.

Electronic Chartplotters

Electronic chartplotters such as the Garmin GPSmap 2010 are cartographic GPS units that superimpose the current position of a boat on a nautical chart display screen. You can see the progress you're making toward your destination, the position of your vessel relative to charted features, and a wide variety of navigational data. The display is a moving chart covering several hundred miles of coastline and dozens of conventional printed charts at different scales. Simply pointing to locations on the display screen creates waypoints. The detailed chart information that is displayed helps you to visualize your position and heading relative to navigation hazards. The continual electronic plotting of your position eliminates the time-consuming hand plotting of position fixes on paper charts.

The electronic chart can be entered into the GPS receiver in several ways. You can read into the unit's memory from a digital map database on a CD-ROM before taking the unit onto the water. You can select the geographic area, and in many cases the features you want to load (such as marine aids to navigation) until the memory in the receiver is filled.

More commonly, a data cartridge holding the desired chart is plugged into the unit. After traveling some distance, you may have to insert a new cartridge. These cartridges are often sold by the builders of cartographic GPS units and are much more expensive than paper maps.

Inland and offshore **chart cartridges** can be plugged into your GPS receiver. They are available from several companies on different types of cartridges. **Inland chart cartridges** (examples include Garmin Inland G-chart, Lowrance IMS SmartMap, and Inland C-MAP *NT*) cover all or part of a state. The chart data are in vector format, allowing you to change from very small to very large scales and to pan seamlessly across the map area. As you zoom in, freeways, national and state highways, state boundaries, and large water bodies appear. Zooming in further, minor roads and smaller lakes appear, along with dams, boat ramps, marinas, and public facilities.

Chart information is organized in layers, so that you can selectively add or remove different classes of features from the display. **Offshore chart cartridges** (examples include Offshore C-MAP *NT*, Garmin Offshore G-chart, and Navionics Offshore Cartography) operate like inland charts, but contain sounding, isobath (depth contour), navigational aid, bottom condition, and harbor information.

Some cartographic "**fishfinder**" units are linked to the boat's depth sounder and will show you a sonar depth map as well as an electronic chart (**Figure 14.13**). They do so by splitting a single screen or by alternating between position and depth displays.

Mobile Electronics

The safety and convenience of knowing your location on the road, day or night and in any weather, can be provided by **GPS automobile units** (**Figure 14.14**). These units use a high-performance GPS receiver for quick position determination and reliable signal reception under dense tree cover or next to tall buildings. Your location is continuously plotted on detailed highway maps stored in the unit's memory. You can upload and display street maps and points of interest (restaurants, hotels, gas stations, banks, and shopping areas) from insertible cartridge or CD-ROM databases such as the Garmin US MetroGuide or the Magellan MapSend Streets & Destinations in the United States.

Navigation and route planning is now easier for light aircraft due to the linking of GPS to digital aeronautical charts. A **GPS aviation unit** consists of a high accuracy receiver and a user interface similar in appearance to automobile units (**Figure 14.15**). The display is structured around Satellite Status, Position, Map, **Horizontal Situation Indicator (HSI)**, and Active Route Pages. The Map Page displays aeronautical information from an internally stored database, such as a Jeppesen digital chart, that includes position and facility data for thousands of airports, as well as navigational aids, airspace boundaries, coastlines, lakes, rivers, cities, and highways. An aircraft icon shows your present position on the continuously moving map, and your ground track and route are displayed as a line of dots.

The display screen usually is configured as a split screen with the Horizontal Situation Indicator Page placed to the right of the Map Page. The rotating compass card on the HSI indicates your current heading. The compass arrow and adjacent

Figure 14.13 Cartographic "fishfinder" units, such as the Lowrance LMS-320, show your map position and a sonar chart of underwater features.

Figure 14.14 GPS automobile units like the Garmin StreetPilot III combine satellite tracking technology with detailed electronic road and street maps.

Figure 14.15 GPS aviation units like the Garmin GPSmap 295 link satellite tracking technology to digital aeronautical charts and navigation displays.

course deviation needle point to your desired heading, showing whether you're on the desired course. A "bug" indicator shows your **course to steer (CTS)**, guiding you back to the desired course. Boxes above the compass card can be configured to display flight information such as your altitude, current heading azimuth, course to steer, distance to next waypoint or final destination, speed, and estimated time of arrival.

Battery-operated two-way **Family Radio Service (FRS)** radios have recently been combined with GPS. The Garmin Rino 120 unit (**Figure 14.16**), for example, has WAAS differential-GPS capability for high accuracy horizontal positions. You can call to another radio within a 5-mile radius and give the listener your position to within 3 meters. These radios have a more limited range than cellular phones, and the signals from these unlicensed units can be blocked by landscape obstructions. Furthermore, your message is broadcast on open air waves. Thus, someone needs to be listening on your waveband when you transmit a message. Despite these drawbacks, this combination of GPS and radios can get you help in some circumstances.

Laptop and Desktop GPS

The second method of linking maps to GPS automatically is to connect a hand-held GPS receiver to a general-purpose **laptop** or **desktop computer** (**Figure 14.17**). The computer offers major computational power as well as ease of keyboard data

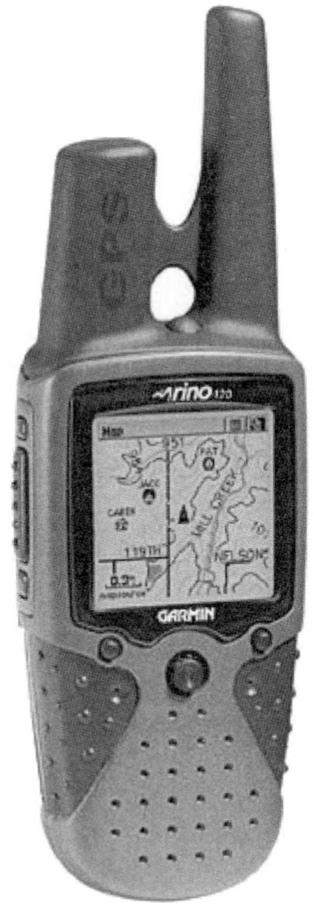

Figure 14.16 The Garmin Rino 120 combines a GPS receiver with a Family Radio Service (FRS) two-way radio.

entry. Since computer memory is vast and the unit can be networked to databases worldwide, all manner of data can be fed into the system. You can also take advantage of the computer display screen, which is bigger, multicolored, and higher in spatial resolution than the screen on most hand-held and cartographic GPS units. This all adds up to a high-quality map display backed up by powerful analytical capabilities. Furthermore, when you're not using the computer with the GPS receiver, you can use it for other things.

A laptop computer has the advantage of portability if you're using it from a vehicle or can move a vehicle near to your desired location. Since the unit isn't permanently mounted, it can be removed from the vehicle when not needed. This may be the most cost-effective way to bring automated positioning technology into your vehicle travels. Furthermore, when you sell your car you don't lose your navigation device as you do when you have an integrated auto navigation system.

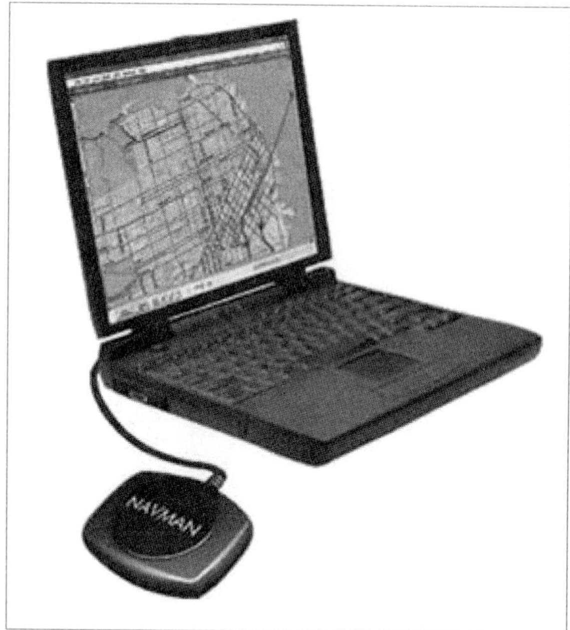

Figure 14.17 Plugging a GPS receiver into a laptop computer creates a powerful unit for analysis and display of positioning data yet is portable enough to use in moving vehicles.

Land, water, and air navigators have discovered the power of this GPS-driven application of digital mapping technology. In each case, the navigation procedure is the same.

First, you use the GPS receiver to determine your grid coordinate position. The computer then uses these coordinates to search a digital cartographic database held on a CD-ROM. Since the corners of each map were geocoded when the database was created, the software can locate the map within whose borders you're located. This map is then displayed with your position marked.

If you preprogrammed a route into your computer or GPS unit, you can display this path. The computer screen will not only show where you've been, but also the path you should take to your destination. By using this "progress" report, you can make route corrections as you go.

Likewise, if you enter a destination, the software can compute and display alternate routes based on your instructions. Common options include the shortest, fastest, or most scenic path. The GPS receiver can then update your position as you move toward your destination.

Over the last few years there has been an increase in the number of personal computer software programs that display nautical chart information combined with GPS data. Programs such as the Nobeltec Visual Mariner and Maptech Pocket Navigator let boaters use their PC or Palm computer onboard like a hand-held or cartographic GPS unit. These programs use raster charts such as the Maptech NOAA Chart CDs and ChartPack Digital Charts or the NDI Digital Charts for Canada. Each CD typically holds up to 50 charts that when viewed look just like the paper source map. Other national hydrographic offices are beginning to use the same raster format so that the software is compatible with foreign chart providers.

The desktop computer lacks portability but has the most processing and graphic display power. Screens as big as 21 inches in full color can be used to display maps. Surveyors and other mapping professionals who process field data in the lab commonly use desktop computers. By making elaborate corrections to field data using information from other sources, experts can make far more precise position determinations than is otherwise possible. This post-processing of DGPS data is essential in geodetic applications and for making the highest-quality maps.

Fleet vehicle companies now commonly use desktop computers linked to multiple GPS receiver/transmitter units. Businesses use this method to monitor the position and movement of each taxi, truck, ship, train, or airplane in their fleet. The military has developed an "electronic battlefield" scenario in which the positions of all friendly troops and vehicles are continuously monitored on desktop electronic maps at a central command center. Field commanders will also have access to these maps on laptop display devices.

SELECTED READINGS

Ackroyd, N., and Lorimer, R., *Global Navigation: A GPS User's Guide*, 2nd ed. (London: Lloyd's of London Press, Ltd., 1994).

Clarke, B., *Aviators' Guide to GPS*, 2nd ed. (New York: TAB/McGraw-Hill, 1996).

Dixon, C., *Using GPS* (Dobbs Ferry, NY: Sheridan, 1995).

Hotchkiss, N.J., *A Comprehensive Guide to Land Navigation with GPS*, 2nd ed. (Herndon, VA: Alexis Publishing, 1995).

Hurn, J., *Differential GPS Explained* (Sunnyvale, CA: Trimble Navigation, Ltd., 1993).

Hurn, J., *GPS: A Guide to the Next Utility* (Sunnyvale, CA: Trimble Navigation, Ltd., 1989).

Kennedy, M., *The Global Positioning System and GPS* (Ann Arbor, MI: Ann Arbor Press, Inc., 1996).

Leick, A., *GPS Satellite Surveying*, 2nd ed. (New York: John Wiley & Sons, 1995).

Letham, L., *GPS Made Easy: Using Global Positioning Systems in the Outdoors* (Seattle, WA: The Mountaineers, 1995).

Sonnentag, B., *Precision GPS Navigation the E-Zutm Way* (Gabbs, NV: GPS International Press, 1997).

Van Sickle, J., *GPS for Land Surveyors* (Ann Arbor, MI: Ann Arbor Press, Inc., 1996).

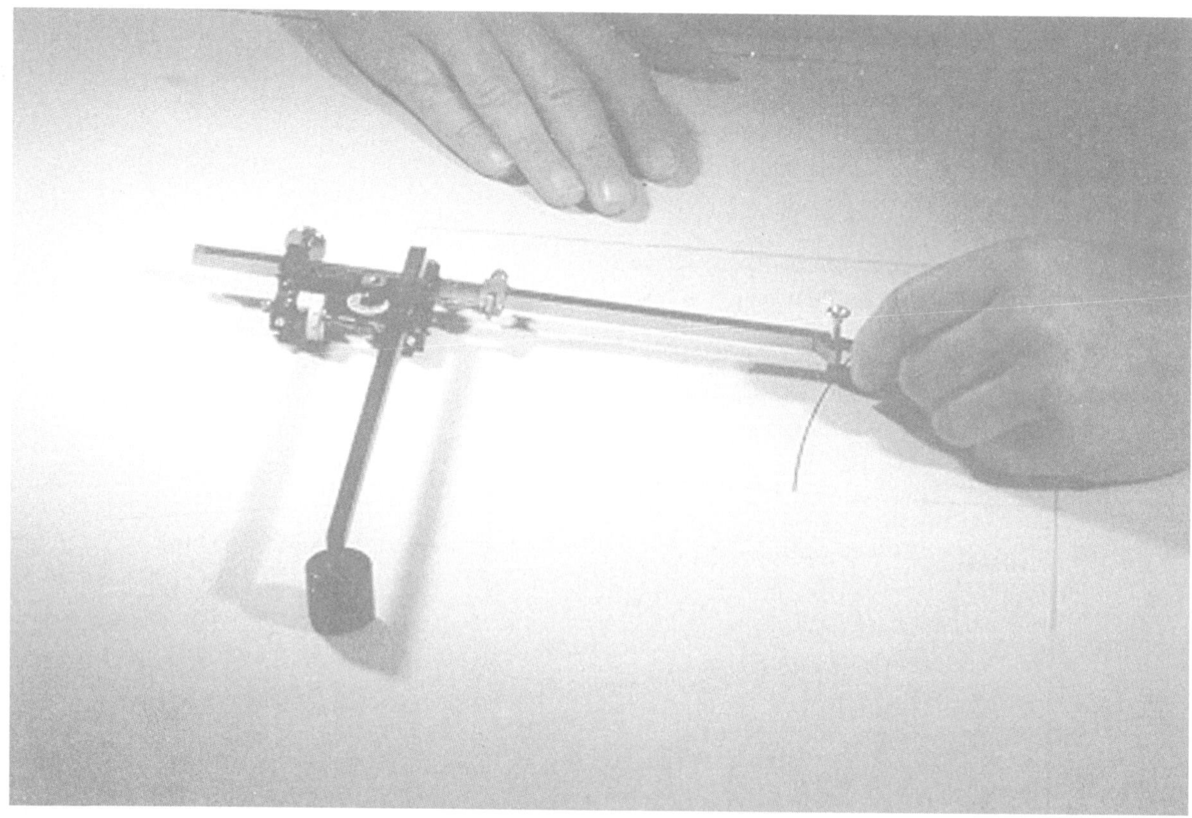

This researcher is measuring map area with a 1950-vintage polar planimeter.

CHAPTER FIFTEEN
DETERMINING AREA, VOLUME, AND SHAPE

I've heard—who knows the truth—
that if you rolled West Virginia out like a flapjack,
it would be as large as Texas.
—William Least Heat-Moon, Blue Highways

15

CHAPTER FIFTEEN

DETERMINING AREA, VOLUME, AND SHAPE

In this chapter we'll look at ways of describing two-dimensional objects or regions called **area features**. The boundaries of many area features (the surface of lakes, for example) are accurately portrayed on large-scale maps. We typically describe these features by their size, but their shape and centroid (center of area) are also sometimes important to know. If the map gives depth or height information, we can measure the volume of features and hence describe their three-dimensional extent.

Estimating the sizes of features in our environment is a basic mental activity important to our survival. We subconsciously estimate the relative sizes of objects as part of our visual perception of the world. But often we need to go further and numerically determine the **areas** of features or regions. Knowing the area of a land parcel, for example, is critical in a real estate transaction and in assessing property taxes. The areas of land parcels can be computed directly from the land survey description for the parcel, but it is often easier to measure the area from a large-scale map or compute the area from grid coordinates read from the map.

The same can be said for determining the **volume** of a feature that has depth or height in addition to area extent. The volume of water in a lake, or the volume of earth to remove in a construction project, for example, are important pieces of information for water managers and civil engineers. Again, although volumes can be computed directly from surveyed depths and heights, it is usually easier and often more accurate to determine volumes from the elevation and water depth information shown on large-scale topographic maps and nautical charts.

Another characteristic of a feature is its center of area, or **centroid**. That the centroid for Oregon is near the city of Prineville, whereas the centroid for Florida lies in the Gulf of Mexico, may be geographic trivia for most people. But there are certain ideas about area features that involve knowing the centroid. One idea is that a certain phenomenon, such as a disease epidemic, disperses outward from the center of the feature. Another is that what is at the center of a feature is the most representative or purest example of that feature. The trees at the center of a forest stand, for instance, may best represent the entire stand.

Measuring the **shape** of a feature may at first seem difficult to do and of little practical value. But shape descriptions are important in a variety of activities. Legislative redistricting is a classic example, since a prime characteristic of districts is their compactness. The original "gerrymander" was created in 1812 by Massachusetts governor Elbridge Gerry, who for political purposes created a long and narrow district that looked like a salamander crawling on the map.

Let's look at methods we can use to measure areas, centroids, volumes, and shapes of features from maps. We'll begin with the measurement of area.

AREA MEASUREMENT

The size of a two-dimensional figure or region is called its **area**. When you want to know the area that lies within a region's boundaries, you can measure the area in several ways. Visual size estimation will suffice if you need only a rough approximation. But if you need a more precise numerical value, you should rely on more rigorous measurement methods. The oldest method relies on grid cell counting.

Grid Cell Counting

The simplest and most common techniques for computing area involve **grid cell counting**. There are two variations, although the idea is the same in both cases.

One procedure is to superimpose a grid of small squares on the map **(Figure 15.1)**. To determine the area of a feature such as a lake, you tally the grid cells that fall completely within its boundary, and then total the cells which fall partially within. You then divide the number of partial cells by 2 and add this value to the number of whole cells.

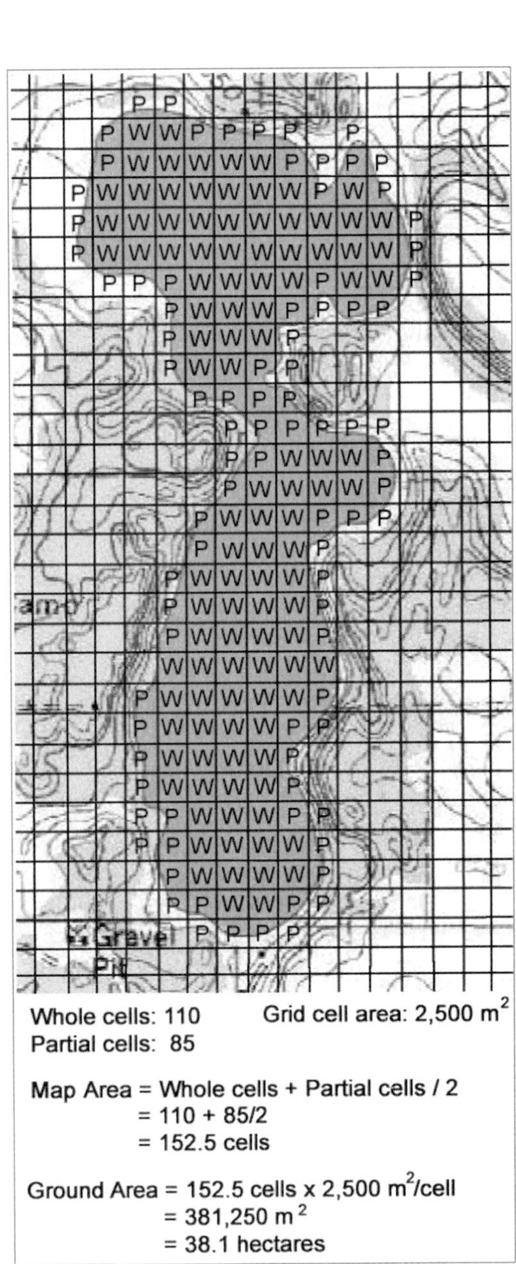

Figure 15.1 The surface area of this lake can be measured in ground units by summing the number of full and partial grid cells falling within its boundary.

Finally, you multiply the resulting sum by the ground area covered by each cell.

Finding the ground area covered by a cell is easy if you know the cell dimensions and the map scale. Say you have 0.1"×0.1" cells on a 1:24,000-scale topographic map. Since this scale can also be stated as 1 inch to 2,000 feet (see Chapter 2 for more on map scale), a grid cell must be 200 by 200 feet on the ground, or 40,000 square feet. You may want to convert square feet to acres, which is easy since an **acre** is defined as a 208.7-foot by 208.7-foot square, or 43,560 square feet*. Each of your grid cells is thus 40,000 ft^2 divided by 43,560 ft^2/acre, or 0.918 acres on the ground. Converting square meters to hectares is easier, since a **hectare** is a 100m by 100m square, or 10,000m^2.

Another method is to find the map area of the feature, then use the map's RF to convert to ground area. In the previous example, each grid square has an area of 0.1"×0.1", or 0.01 square inches. If a feature measures 86.5 grid cells, its map area must be 86.5 cells × 0.01 square inches per cell, or 0.865 square inches. To convert map area to ground area, you must **multiply by the square of the RF**. Hence, 0.865 square inches on a 1:24,000-scale map converts to 0.865 in^2 × 24,000^2 = 0.865 × 576,000,000 = 498,240,000 in^2 on the ground. You will probably convert square inches to square feet, knowing that there are 12×12 or 144 square inches per square foot. Your ground area in square feet is thus 498,240,000 in^2÷144 in^2/ft^2, or 3,460,000 square feet.

You can take advantage of electronic image scanning and digital image processing technology to increase the speed and accuracy of grid cell counting. Such technology is especially helpful if you're measuring features with intricate boundaries, or if you have a large number of features to measure. The data used in digital image processing are stored as a grid of cells, called **pixels** (see Chapter 21 for further information on digital image processing). Area measurement is simply a matter of pixel counting, and most digital image processing systems can tell you the number of pixels on the image that are a certain color or gray tone.

The map containing the features to be measured must be scanned electronically into pixels. You may be able to acquire previously scanned maps, such as USGS **Digital Raster Graphics** (see Appendix A for details), available from a website or on a CD-ROM. Otherwise, you can scan the portion of the map containing the features using your **desktop scanner**. Current inexpensive models scan up to 8.5" by 14" color images at spatial resolutions ranging anywhere from 72 to 1,200 dots (pixels) per inch (dpi). Lower resolution scans are sufficient for measuring the area of all but the smallest features.

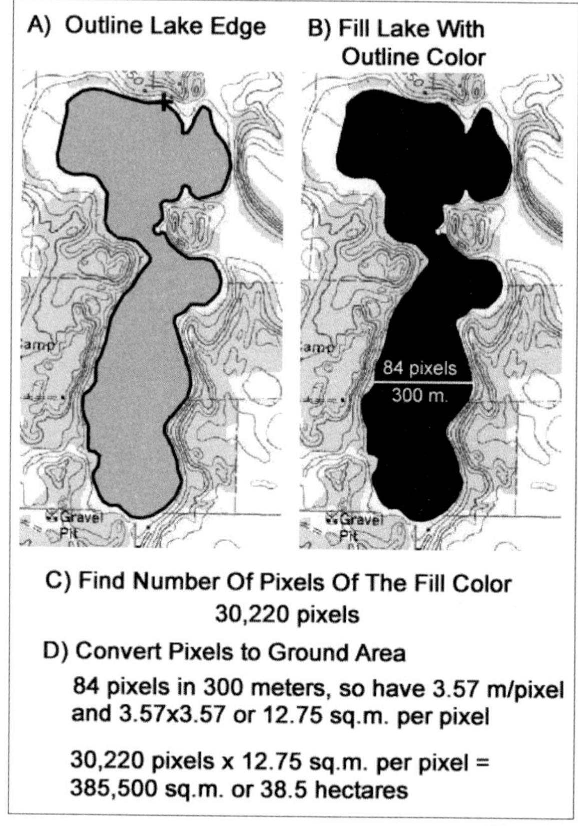

Figure 15.2 Desktop scanners and digital image processing software can be used to generate data for area computation by cell counting.

**Finally*The acre was originally an English unit of measurement that described the area that a yoke of oxen (two oxen) could plow in a day. It originally differed in size from one region to the next, but was ultimately fixed at 4,840 square yards, or 43,560 square feet.*

You must first identify the features on the scanned image displayed on your monitor. You can do so in an electronic version of the traditional way, identifying features by eye and outlining them by hand using your computer's mouse as the tracing tool (**Figure 15.2**). You next fill the area outlined with a unique color that doesn't appear anywhere else on the image. When this is done, area computation is easy—just query the software for the number of pixels of this color (30,220 in the example in Figure 15.2), then multiply by the ground area covered by a pixel. The easiest way to find this area is by counting the number of pixels along a vertical or horizontal line of known ground length. In Figure 15.2, for instance, 84 pixels were found to span the lake where it was 300 meters wide.

Notice that the digital pixel-counting procedure has an all-or-nothing character. You have feature pixels and non-feature pixels, but no in-between pixels along boundaries as you had with manual grid cell counting. In theory, the partial grid cells falling on the boundary of the feature accounted for in manual counting methods should produce a more accurate result. In practice, however, the coarse grids in manual grid-cell counting are actually less accurate than automated high-resolution pixel counting.

Dot Grids

The second graphic measurement technique uses a **dot grid** placed over the map. A dot grid is nothing more than a square grid of alternating solid and open dots (**Figure 15.3**). To measure an area, you count all the dots that fall entirely within the feature's boundary. You then add the number of either open or solid black dots falling on the feature's boundary to this total. Next, multiply the total number of dots by the **unit area value** of each dot (printed on the edge of the grid) to obtain the feature's area in ground units.

In Figure 15.3, for example, 146 dots fell within the lake and 8 solid black dots were found on the boundary line. The unit area value on the dot grid is 2,500 square meters per dot at the scale of the map. The ground area is thus 146 + 8 or 154 dots times 2,500 sq.m. per dot, or 385,000 square meters. This converts to a 38.5 hectare lake.

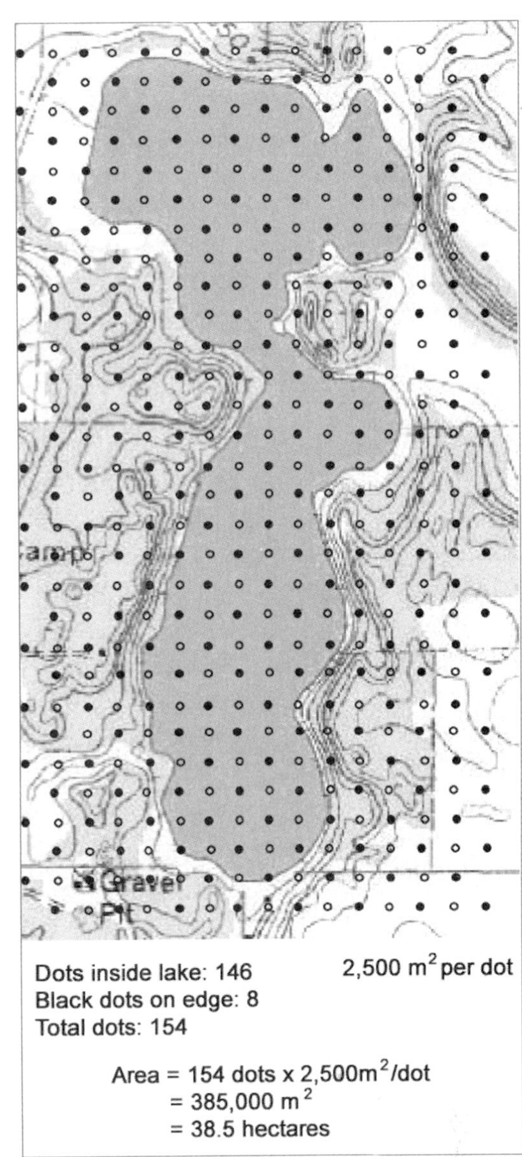

Figure 15.3 A dot grid is used to estimate the area of a feature by counting the number of dots within the feature and the number of solid black dots on its boundary.

Measurement Accuracy

With counting methods, smaller grid cell sizes and more closely spaced dots improve the accuracy of the area computation. But this greater accuracy is attained at the expense of more tedious cell or dot counting. Thus, you should choose a cell size or dot unit value based on how much accuracy you need.

But exactly what grid-cell width or dot-grid spacing should you use? There are no strict rules for these choices, but a few researchers have looked at the problem both theoretically and by experimenting with a variety of feature sizes and shapes.

The first thing this research has shown is that repeating the counting procedure with the grid shifted and rotated differently between each repetition, followed by averaging the measured areas, gives a result closer to the true feature area than the area obtained by a single counting. This makes sense, because at certain grid orientation angles there could be rows of dots aligned parallel to one or more feature edges. In this situation, slightly shifting the grid could cause a large number of grid cells or dots to shift from inside to outside the feature. If you average the area totals obtained by repeating the cell or dot counting at different grid orientations, you'll minimize this type of counting error.

The relationship between the density of dots on a grid, defined by the spacing between dots, and measurement error has also been studied for features of different shapes and areas varying from 1 to 100 square centimeters. The curves in **Figure 15.4** give you a feel of what to expect. The graph shows that, regardless of the dot spacing, measurement error decreases as the area of the feature being measured increases. However, the rate of decrease lessens with increasing feature area, so that using a dot grid with more closely spaced dots would minimally improve measurement accuracy for large features.

This graph also shows you the dot spacing needed to measure features of different approximate sizes with a certain allowable measurement error. For instance, to measure an approximately 10-square-centimeter feature with an allowable error of 1.5% requires a dot grid with 0.2-centimeter dot spacing. **Table 15.1**, derived from the curves in Figure 15.4, gives the maximum dot spacing for several feature area size ranges if the allowable measurement error is 1.5%.

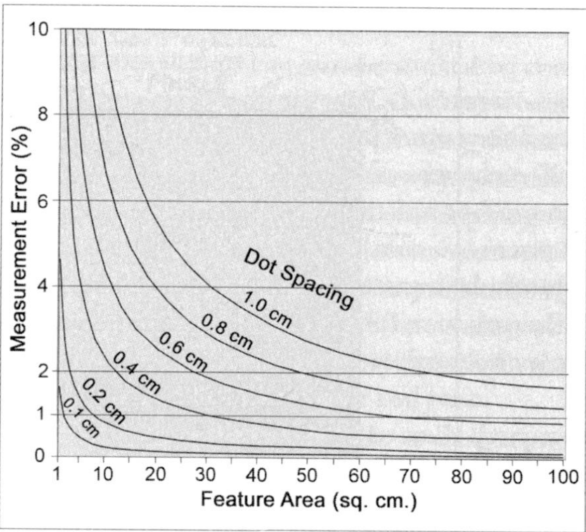

Figure 15.4 Dot grid measurement error (percent of total feature area) decreases exponentially as the size of the feature increases, regardless of the dot spacing on the grid. For any feature size, a point of diminishing returns is reached where further reducing the dot spacing marginally improves measurement accuracy (adapted from Frolov and Maling, 1969).

The recommended dot spacing values tell you that there should be at least 100 dots falling within the feature, regardless of its approximate size, if you want the measured area to be within 1.5% of the true area. To have 100 dots within all features, you will have to use several dot grids of varying densities for different sized features, such as the six grids suggested in Table 15.1.

Table 15.1 Dot Spacing Required to Measure Features in Different Size Ranges with an Allowable Error of 1.5 Percent

Feature Size Range	Maximum Dot Spacing
< 4 cm^2	0.1 cm
4-16 cm^2	0.2 cm
16-36 cm^2	0.4 cm
36-64 cm^2	0.6 cm
64-100 cm^2	0.8 cm
> 100 cm^2	1.0 cm

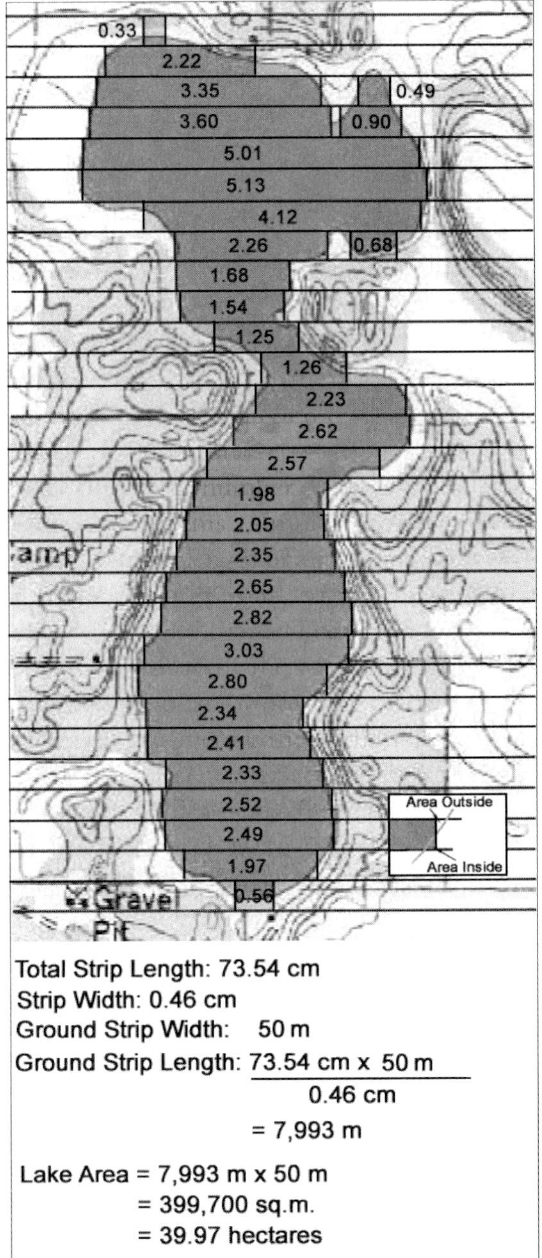

Figure 15.5 The strip method is a less time consuming way to compute the area of irregular features.

These guidelines can also be extended to grid cell counting, as the appropriate grid cell width and height for each feature size range should be the same as the maximum dot spacing in the table. The general rule, then, is that at least 100 grid cells must fall within each feature.

Strip Method

If the tract has an irregular or curved border, you can use a modification of the grid cell counting approach, called the **strip method** (**Figure 15.5**). With this technique, the first step is to position a series of equally spaced parallel lines that define narrow strips across the feature. Make sure there are strips covering the extreme edges of the feature.

Next, for each strip, construct lines perpendicular to the strip at each edge line that crosses the strip. These lines should be drawn where the feature outline intersects the middle of the strip, so that areas falling inside and outside of the feature are approximately equal. For really irregular features, there will probably be more than one set of perpendicular lines for many of the strips. Measure the length of the strip segments between the perpendicular lines, and sum these lengths.

Now, by multiplying the total strip segment length by the strip width, you will have the map area of the region. Using the unit area value determined by the map scale, you can convert the map area to ground area units. Obviously, the more closely spaced the parallel lines, the greater the computational effort, but also the greater the accuracy of your results.

Polar Planimeter

In previous decades, a mechanical instrument called a **polar planimeter (Figure 15.6)** was the tool of choice for area measurement on maps and aerial photographs. A polar planimeter is an interesting type of **analog computer** that measures area through the back-and-forth movements of an integrating wheel. Polar planimeters are much slower and less accurate than modern digital measurement methods, but the devices are still widely available.

You begin by setting up the polar planimeter with the pole weight at the end of the polar arm anchored securely off to the side of the area feature to be measured. You should be able to move the tracing point in the center of the tracer lens attached to the end of the tracer arm freely around the feature boundary. Set the vernier unit area dial to 0, mark a starting point on the feature boundary, then trace the outline of the feature in a clockwise direction. When you come back to the starting point, the dial will tell you the area you've traced. It's a good idea to trace the outline several times to obtain an average reading.

Most polar planimeters give you the area in square centimeters or square inches. This means your final step when using these instruments will be to convert this value into ground units, using the square of the map scale as explained previously. Modern digital polar planimeters make the needed conversions automatically and display the results on a small screen **(Figure 15.7)**.

Coordinate Methods

If you have the (x,y) grid coordinates for the points defining the boundary of a tract of land, you can use this information to calculate the area of the tract. Modern area computation is based on using data files of area feature boundaries, such as State Plane Coordinates, for tracts of land. When UTM or State Plane Coordinate System grid coordinates are used, the tract area will be in square meters or square feet.

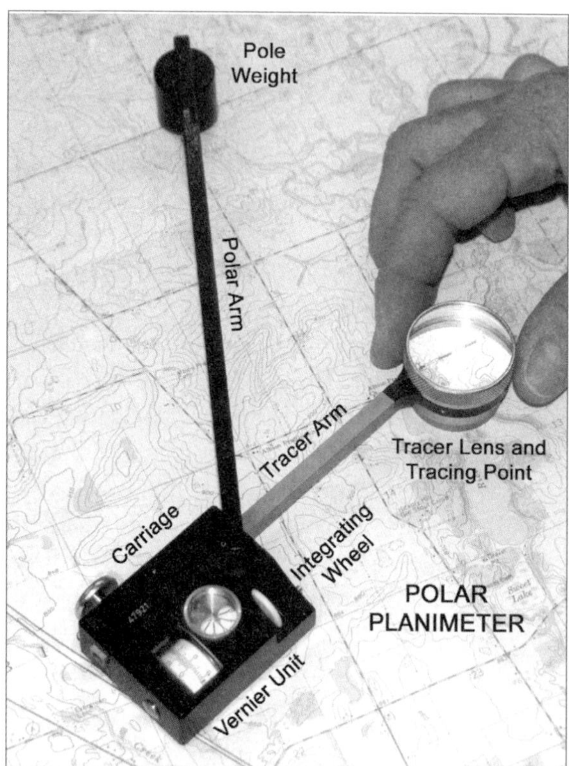

Figure 15.6 Use of a polar planimeter for computing the area of a mapped region requires tracing the region's outline with the instrument's cursor and converting the resulting map reading to ground units.

The **coordinate method** of area measurement is based on finding the areas of trapezoids formed by drawing horizontal lines from the boundary points to the vertical Y-axis. In **Figure 15.8**, for example, the area of tract ABCDE is to be determined from the grid coordinates $(x_1,y_1)\ldots(x_5,y_5)$ for points P_1 through P_5. To compute the area of the tract, five trapezoids must be formed. Trapezoid 1, for example, begins at the intersection of the horizontal line from P_1 and the Y-axis. Its sides are the portion of the Y-axis from this point to the horizontal line from point P_2, then the horizontal line to P_2, the line segment from P_2 to P_1, and finally the horizontal line from P_1 to the Y-axis. The other four trapezoids are constructed in the same manner.

The area of each trapezoid is computed by multiplying the difference in the y-coordinates for the first and second point by the average of the x-coordinates for these two points:

$$area_{trapezoid} = \frac{(x_i + x_{i+1})}{2} \times (y_i - y_{i+1})$$

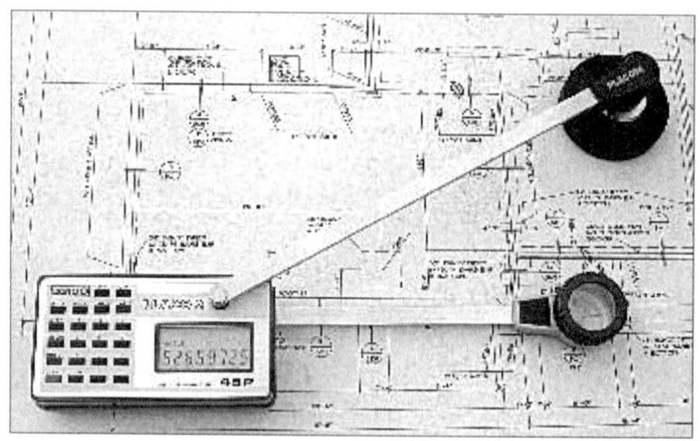

Figure 15.7 A digital polar planimeter converts areas to ground units directly and displays the ground area on a small screen.

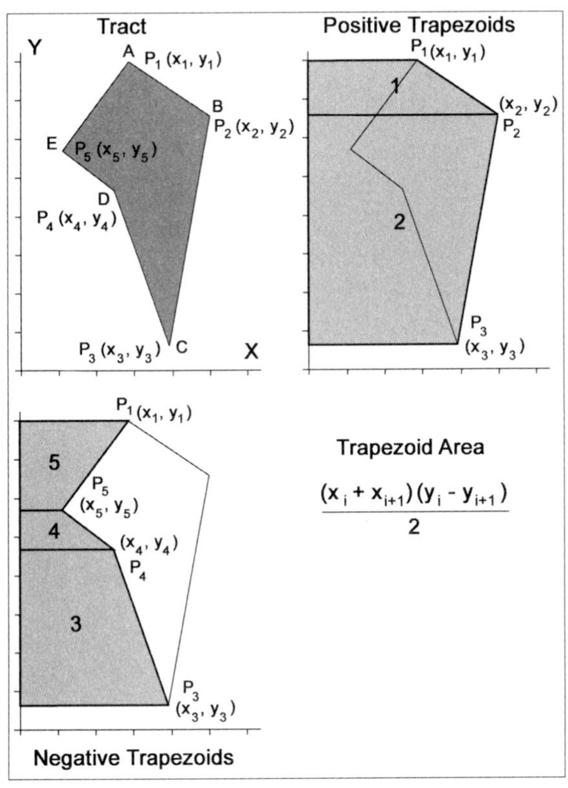

Figure 15.8 The modern way to determine the area of a tract of land or any other area feature is from its boundary coordinates.

Notice that the trapezoid area will be negative when the second y-coordinate is greater than the first. Having positive and negative trapezoid areas is crucial to computing the total tract area. Figure 15.8 shows why*. The negative-area trapezoids are those (3,4, and 5) between the Y-axis and the left side of the tract, whereas the positive-area trapezoids (1 and 2) extend from the Y-axis to the right side of the tract. Thus, summing the positive and negative trapezoids takes away the outside area from the Y-axis to the tract, leaving the area inside the tract.

By combining the individual trapezoid-area equations, the following equation is obtained for the area of the tract:

**This explanation is valid only for simple tracts with a convex shape, but the general computation equation is valid for tracts of any shape and complexity.*

$$\text{Tract area} = 0.5 \times ((x_1+x_2)\times(y_1-y_2) + (x_2+x_3)\times(y_2-y_3) + (x_3+x_4)\times(y_3-y_4) + (x_4+x_5)\times(y_4-y_5) + (x_5+x_1)\times(y_5-y_1))$$

The terms in this equation can be rearranged and the equation can be extended to any number of boundary points:

$$\text{Tract area} = 0.5 \times (y_1(x_n-x_2) + y_2(x_1-x_3) + \ldots + y_n(x_{n-1}-x_1))$$

where n is the number of boundary points. This equation can be stated in words as:

> To determine the area of a tract of land when the coordinates of its corners are known, multiply the ordinate (y-coordinate) of each corner by the difference between the abscissa (x-coordinate) of the following and preceding corners, always subtracting the following corner from the preceding corner. The area of the tract is one half of the sum of the resulting products.

It is also possible to compute the area of a feature from a file of geographic (latitude, longitude) boundary point coordinates. The computation method is similar to that used for grid coordinates, but areas of spherical triangles are computed. In **Figure 15.9**, you can see that the north (or south) pole and two adjacent points along the boundary comprise each spherical triangle. Two of the edges are the angular distances from the pole to the boundary point along meridians (called the co-latitudes of the points). The angle between these edges is the difference in longitude between the two boundary points. Triangle areas are positive or negative depending on whether the longitude of the second boundary point is greater or less than the longitude of the first point. The most commonly used spherical triangle area equation used is:

$$\text{Area} = (\alpha + \beta + \Delta\lambda - 180°) \times R^2$$

where R is the earth's radius (6,371 km), and $\Delta\lambda$ is the absolute value (minus sign dropped) of the dif-

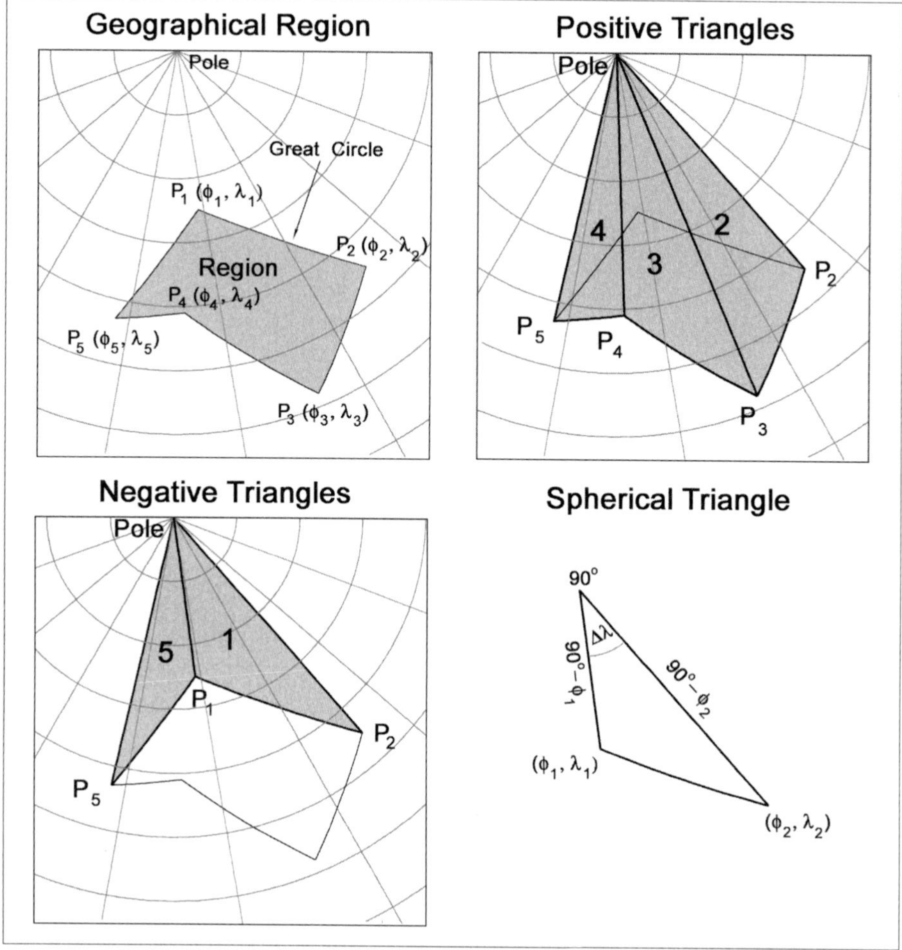

Figure 15.9 Geographic boundary coordinates can also be used in area calculation.

ference in longitude between the two points. The other two interior angles, α and β, are computed from a spherical trigonometry equation that is one of what are called **Napier's Analogies**:

$$\tan\left(\frac{\alpha+\beta}{2}\right) = \frac{\cos\left(0.5\times\left((90^\circ-\phi_1)-(90^\circ-\phi_2)\right)\right)}{\cos\left(0.5\times\left((90^\circ-\phi_1)+(90^\circ-\phi_2)\right)\right)\times\tan(\Delta\lambda/2)}$$

$$\alpha+\beta = 2\times\tan^{-1}\left(\frac{\cos(0.5\times(\phi_2-\phi_1))}{\cos(0.5\times(180^\circ-(\phi_1+\phi_2)))\times\tan(\Delta\lambda/2)}\right)$$

The spherical coordinate method should be used for larger area features spanning more than one grid zone, such as computing the areas of countries or large states. Boundary points for smaller features, such as tracts of land, would have such small differences in latitude and longitude that the area computed would not be nearly as accurate as that from grid coordinates.

Although computing trapezoid or spherical triangle areas is very tedious if done by hand, it is a simple matter to create a computer program for either coordinate method. Such a program will quickly and effortlessly compute the area of any feature. The computer-based coordinate approach is particularly appropriate when the tract's boundary is irregular or involves a large number of boundary points. With curved boundaries, increasing the number of boundary points improves the accuracy of area estimation with a minimal increase in computation time. However, increasing the density of boundary points along nearly straight edges does little to improve the accuracy of area computation. By establishing boundary points only at those positions on the boundary where major angular changes occur, you can approximate the feature's area most efficiently.

Area Measurements on Small-Scale Maps

Counting methods or the use of a polar planimeter to measure the areas of large geographic features on small-scale maps is problematic due to the geometric distortion of the earth's spherical geometry introduced by the map projection. Counting or polar planimeter methods will give accurate areas only if the features are drawn on an **equal-area map projection**. Over a century ago, for instance, the areas of different foreign countries and U.S. states were measured with polar planimeters from boundaries drawn on the Albers conic and other equal-area map projections (see Chapter 3 for more information on equal-area map projections).

An equal-area map projection correctly portrays the relative areas of features on the earth's surface, but how do we convert map area to ground area? On large-scale maps, you only need to multiply by the square of the map's RF, since the scale is essentially constant across the map. But on small-scale maps, the RF printed in the legend is only true at the centerpoint or along the standard parallels. The Albers conic equal-area projection covering the lower 48 states, for example, has standard parallels at 29.5°N and 45.5°N. The scale at the U.S.-Canada border (49°N) and the southern tip of Florida is 1.25% larger in the north-south direction and 1.25% smaller in the east-west direction. This variation in scale is large enough that we must find another way to accurately convert map area to ground area.

The way to obtain accurate ground areas is to measure the map area of a feature of known ground area, such as a quadrilateral bounded by parallels and meridians (quadrilateral areas are listed in **Table D.5** in Appendix D). You can then find the ground area of the feature from the proportion:

Feature ground area = Quadrilateral ground area × Feature map area ÷ Quadrilateral map area.

An example is a feature map area of 4.53 square inches on a map where a 1° by 1° quadrilateral from 44°N to 45°N measures 7.26 square inches. From Table D.5, the ground area of this quadrilateral is 3,412.26 square miles. Hence,

$$\text{Area} = 3{,}412.26 \text{ mi}^2 \times 4.54 \text{ in}^2 \div 7.26 \text{ in}^2$$
$$= 2{,}134 \text{ mi}^2.$$

AREA CENTROID

You may want to find the **centroid** (**center of area**) for an area feature such as a lake. You can think of the centroid as the lake's "balance point" or **center of gravity**. To determine the centroid, assume that the lake's surface is completely flat and without thickness, like the outline of a lake printed on a paper map or displayed on a computer monitor.

If you cut the lake out of a map, and find the point where it balances on the tip of a pencil, you will have found the lake's center of gravity. Mathematically, the centroid of a complex-shaped feature like a lake is determined by subdividing the complex shape into basic shapes. Centroids of simple geometric shapes are easy to find. The centroid of a square or rectangle lies at the midpoint of its height and width (**Figure 15.10**). The centroid of a right triangle is not as obvious, but the rule is that the centroid is 1/3rd of the way along each of its two perpendicular edges. Lines drawn perpendicular to each edge at this location intersect at the centroid.

What about finding the centroid of a more complex shape, such as the lake used earlier in the chapter to illustrate several area computation methods? A basic property of centroids for complex shapes is that they are weighted averages of the centroids for the basic shapes that comprise the

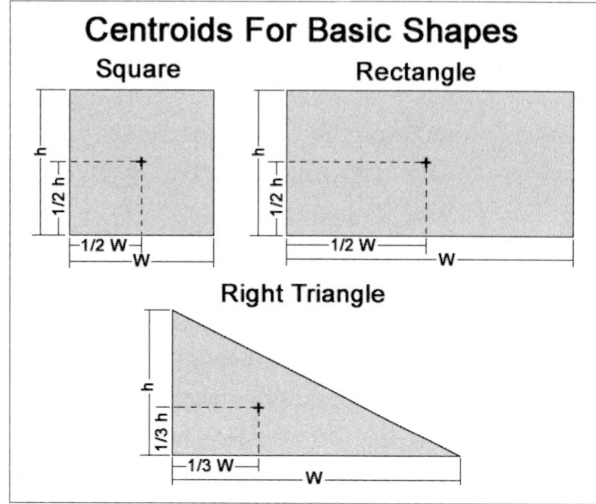

Figure 15.10 Centroids for the basic shapes used to calculate the centroids of complex area features.

complex shape. The weights are simply the areas of the basic shapes.

Centroid locations are defined by (x,y) coordinates. The following equations are used to find the centroid of a complex shape:

$$x = \frac{\sum_{i=1}^{n} x_i \times area_i}{area_{total}} \qquad y = \frac{\sum_{i=1}^{n} y_i \times area_i}{area_{total}}$$

where x_i and y_i are the centroid coordinates for one of the n basic shapes that make up the complex shape.

These equations are easily applied to a feature defined by contiguous grid cells. In the example in **Figure 15.11**, we have simplified the grid by placing its origin at the lower-left corner of the rectangle that bounds the feature. By making each cell 1.0 × 1.0 square units, $area_i$ always is 1.0 and hence can be eliminated from the computations. The x and y centroid coordinates are thus simply the sum of the x and y coordinates of all grid cell centerpoints, divided by the total number of cells making up the feature (n). Figure 15.11 shows an easy computation procedure based on totaling the number of whole and partial grid cells in each row and column.

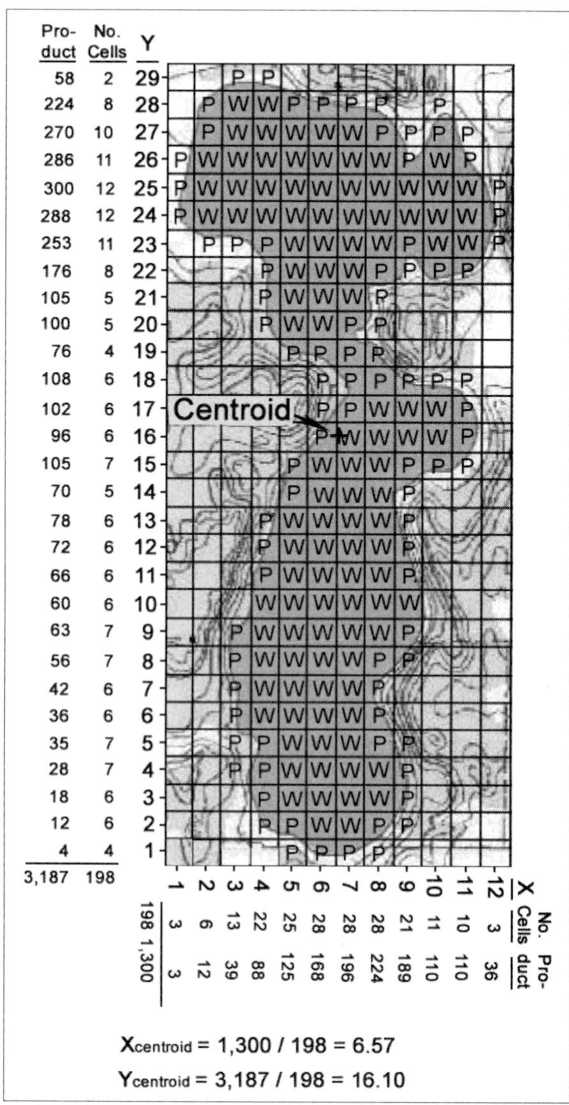

Figure 15.11 The centroid of an area feature such as this lake can be determined by counting the number of square grid cells within and partially within the feature along each row and column. The product of the number of cells and the column and row number (x and y coordinate) is then found and summed. The x and y products are then divided by the number of cells to find the X-centroid and Y-centroid of the feature.

Determining the centroid of an irregularly-shaped area feature defined by a closed string of (x,y) boundary coordinates is more complex. The computation procedure is closely linked to the coordinate method of area calculation described in the previous section. Adding and subtracting trapezoids formed by each line segment and the y-axis

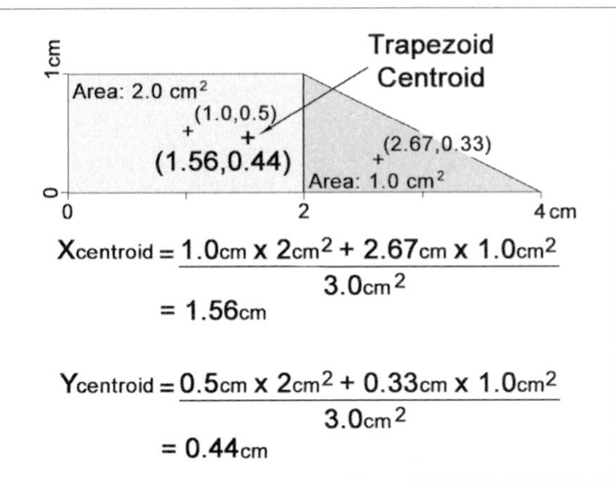

Figure 15.12 The centroid of a trapezoid is computed by dividing it into a rectangle and right triangle. The centroid and area are found for these two basic shapes, then the summation equations described in the text are used to find the x and y coordinates of the centroid.

can be extended to the area weights used in centroid computation.

The first step is to find the area and centroid of each trapezoid by dividing the trapezoid into a rectangle and right triangle (**Figure 15.12**). The centroids of these two basic shapes are found using the formulas given in Figure 15.10. Each centroid location is then converted to an (x,y) coordinate in the system used for the trapezoid. The x-coordinate for the centroid of the right triangle, for instance, is 2 cm (left edge of triangle) plus 1/3rd of the 2-cm-triangle width, or 2.67 cm.

The x and y centroid coordinates are then weighted by their respective areas (height × width, and 0.5 × base height × width). The centroid coordinate equations given above are then used to find the *x* and *y* centroid location for the trapezoid. The computation procedure is illustrated in Figure 15.12.

When the centroid coordinates and area of each trapezoid are determined, the centroid coordinate equations are used again to find the *x* and *y* centroid location for the irregularly-shaped tract such as in **Figure 15.13**. The tract's 12.58 cm² area, computed by subtracting the areas of the three negative trapezoids from the sum of the two positive trapezoids is the $area_{total}$ used in the equations. Applying the equations as shown in Figure 15.13,

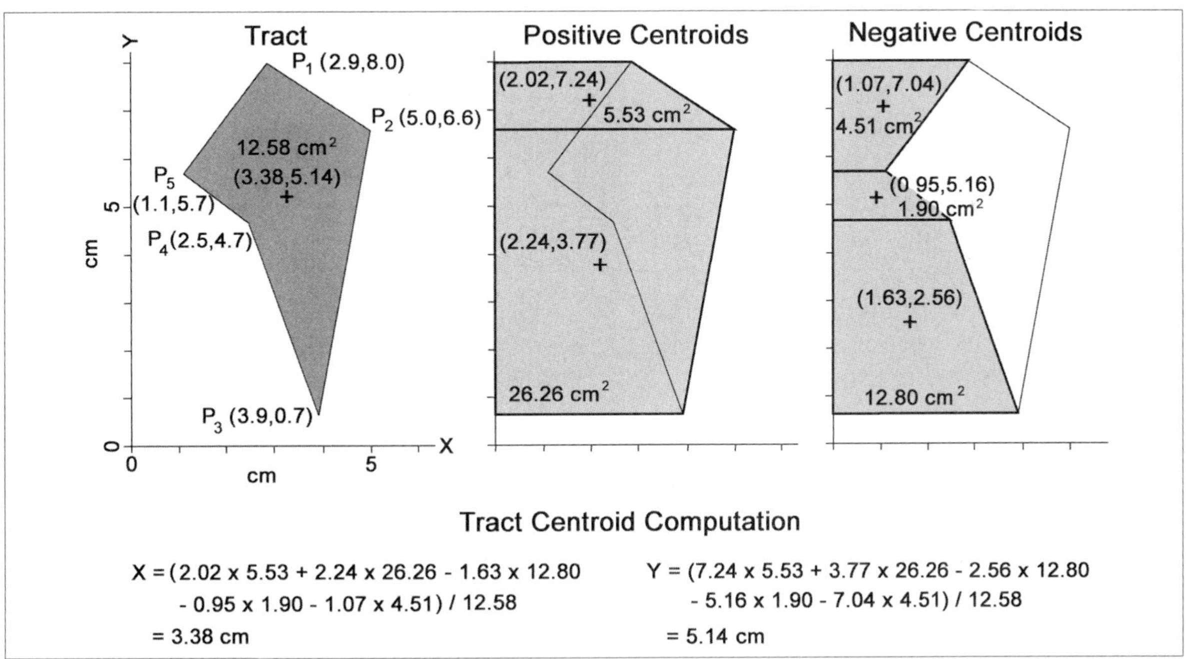

Figure 15.13 The centroid of an irregular tract can be found from its boundary coordinates. Trapezoids are constructed from successive pairs of boundary coordinates. Centroids and areas are computed for each trapezoid, and negative area weights are assigned to trapezoids where the second y-coordinate is larger than the first. The summation equations given in the text are then used to compute the x and y coordinates of the tract centroid.

the tract centroid coordinates are computed as (3.38, 5.14).

Fortunately, this multi-step centroid calculation procedure reduces mathematically to the simple summations:

$$x = \frac{1}{6A}\sum_{i=1}^{n}(x_i + x_{i+1})(x_i y_{i+1} - x_{i+1} y_i)$$

$$y = \frac{1}{6A}\sum_{i=1}^{n}(y_i + y_{i+1})(x_i y_{i+1} - x_{i+1} y_i)$$

where A is the area of the tract computed by the coordinate method, and 1 through n are the tract's (x, y) boundary coordinates (points 1 and $n+1$ are identical). The only complication is that the summations sometimes give negative instead of positive coordinates, so their absolute value should be used.

VOLUME

An object's **volume** is its area times its height or depth. You can find the volume of a feature outlined on a large-scale map if height or depth information is included on the map as contours, isobaths, soundings, or spot elevations (see Chapter 8 for further information on heights and depths). Volume computation is simplified if the base or top of the feature is at a constant height or depth, such as mean sea level or the 500-foot contour line. Let's look at several ways to compute volumes from maps, beginning with the **ordinate method**.

Ordinate Method

With the ordinate method, you first determine the average height or depth of a feature outlined on your map. Then you multiply this value by the feature's area to get the volume. You can combine the area and height determination by laying a square cell grid over the feature. This allows you to determine its area using the cell counting method described earlier in the chapter.

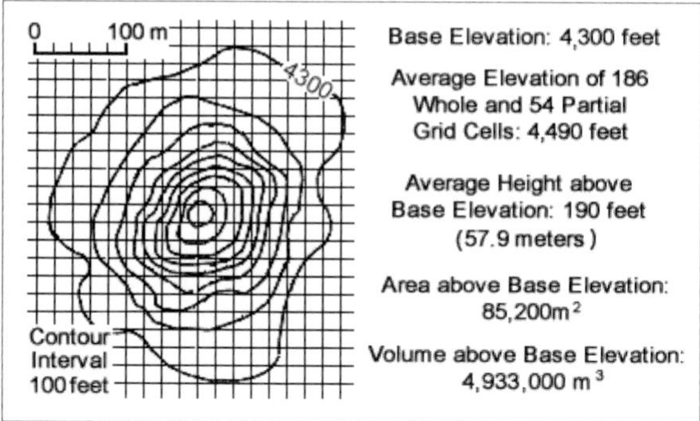

Figure 15.14. You can find the volume of earth material above a base elevation by laying a grid of square cells over your map and following the computation procedure described in the text.

Say you want to determine the volume of volcanic rock above a base elevation of 4,300 feet in Devil's Tower, Wyoming, as depicted on the USGS topographic map segment in **Figure 15.14.** You first count the number of full and partial grid cells bounded by the 4,300-foot contour, then use the cell counting method to find the total area. Next, you estimate the elevation at the center of each cell by linear interpolation between neighboring contours. For example, if the cell center appears to be 1/4th of the way between the 4,400 and 4,500-foot contours, you would estimate the elevation as 4,425 feet. You next use the equation:

$$Avg.elev. = \frac{\sum_{1}^{n} elev._{whole} + \frac{1}{2}\sum_{1}^{m} elev._{part.}}{\left(n + \frac{m}{2}\right)}$$

to compute the average elevation, where n is the number of whole grid cells and m is the number of partial cells. In this example, the average elevation was computed as:

$$Avg.elev. = \frac{840{,}150\,ft. + \frac{1}{2}(232{,}340\,ft.)}{\left(186 + \frac{54}{2}\right)}$$

$$= \frac{840{,}150\,ft. + 116{,}170\,ft.}{213} = 4{,}490\,ft.$$

for the 186 whole and 54 partial cells bounded by the 4,300-foot contour.

You next subtract the 4,300-foot base elevation from the average elevation, giving an average height of 190 feet (57.9 meters) for the area. Finally, you multiply the average height by the ground area to obtain the volume. The area bounded by the 4,300-foot contour was measured as 85,200 square meters, so the volume is 57.9m × 85,200m^2, or 4,933,000 cubic meters.

Using a **sample** of **random ordinates** usually simplifies the volume computation. Using the previous volume problem as an example, you would measure the area bounded by the 4,300-foot contour using any of the area measurement methods described earlier in the chapter. You then randomly place points within this contour line (**Figure 15.15**), then estimate the elevation at each random point by linear interpolation between neighboring contours*. The estimated elevations are then averaged and subtracted from the base elevation (4,300 feet) to obtain the average height within the area. The volume is again obtained by multiplying the average height by the area at the base elevation. In this example, 100 randomly-placed dots had an average height of 204 feet (62 meters), giving a volume of 5,282,000 cubic meters. This value is 7% larger than the volume estimated by the grid cell method. This large difference may be due to an inadequate number of random sample points.

How do you determine the number of random sample points to use? Statisticians would say

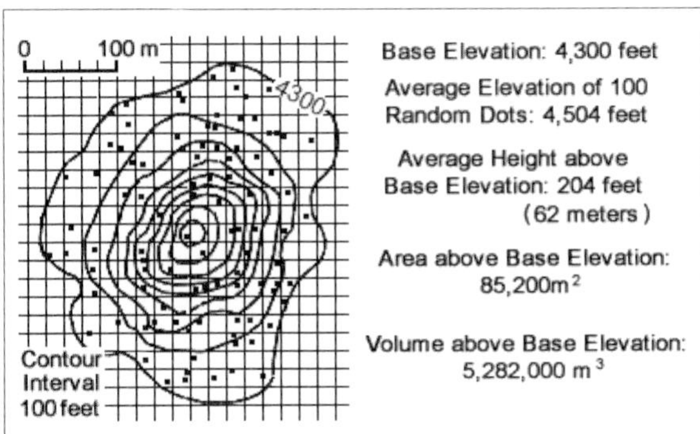

Figure 15.15. Randomly placed sample points can be used to estimate the average elevation within an area.

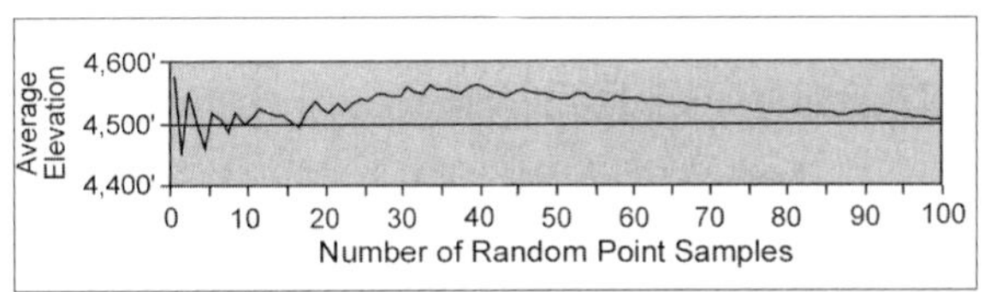

Figure 15.16 Variations in the computed average elevation for Devil's Tower, Wyoming, rapidly decrease with increasing numbers of randomly-placed sample points.

that if the land surface above the base elevation undulates in a random fashion, at least 30 sample points are needed to give a good result. However, land surfaces often vary smoothly and non-randomly. An extreme example would be the top of a flat, horizontal mesa in Arizona or New Mexico, where only one sample point is required to accurately determine its height.

You can see the effect of sample point size on the accuracy of the average elevation by re-computing the average elevation as each new sample point is found. For instance, a graph of average elevation versus number of sample points (**Figure 15.16**) for Devil's Tower, Wyoming, shows a rapid decrease in the variation of computed average elevations with increasing numbers of randomly-placed dots. At 100 sample points there is minimal variation, but the trend in average elevations is still decreasing slightly. This indicates that additional sample points are required to reach a point of minimal variation along a horizontal trend line.

You may be faced with determining the volume of a water body from soundings placed on a nautical chart. These point depths may at first appear to be randomly arranged, but they are probably points taken along transect lines and hence are a **systematic sample.** You can obtain accurate volumes from such systematic height or depth samples if you select at least 30 that are evenly spread across the water feature. Remember that in the U.S., soundings are relative to mean lower low

**In linear interpolation, you assume a constant slope between contour lines. Thus, you would estimate the value at a point midway between contour lines to be onr-half the contour interval value. If the contour lines were labeled 200 and 300, the point midway between them would therefore be 250.*

water (see Chapter 1 for further information on chart datums), so you must add or subtract the difference between mean sea level if you want a volume relative to the datum on topographic maps.

The method of ordinates, using either grid cells or random sample points, can also be applied to an undulating base surface such as the bottom of an irregular ore body. The mine site in **Figure 15.17**, for example, has ore extending from the land surface (shown by black contours) downward to the bottom elevations shown by white contours. For each random sample point, the top and bottom elevations are found by linear interpolation between contour lines. Sample point A, for instance, has a surface elevation of 351 feet and a bottom elevation of 305 feet. This gives an ore body depth of 351-305, or 46 feet at this point. The ore body depths are then averaged and multiplied by the ground area of the mine site, as outlined on the map, to obtain the volume of ore.

Slab Summation Method

You can also determine the volume of an irregular feature outlined on a topographic map by summing the volumes of horizontal slabs whose thickness is the vertical difference between contour lines. To see how the **slab summation method** works, imagine that you have three adjacent closed contours, say at elevations of 200, 220, and 240 feet (**Figure 15.18**). You can estimate the volume of earth material between the 200 and 240-foot contours by measuring the ground area bounded by the 220-foot contour, then multiplying this area by the 40-foot elevation difference between the top and bottom contours. The area within the middle contour is used because we assume that the larger volume below balances the smaller volume above the middle contour.

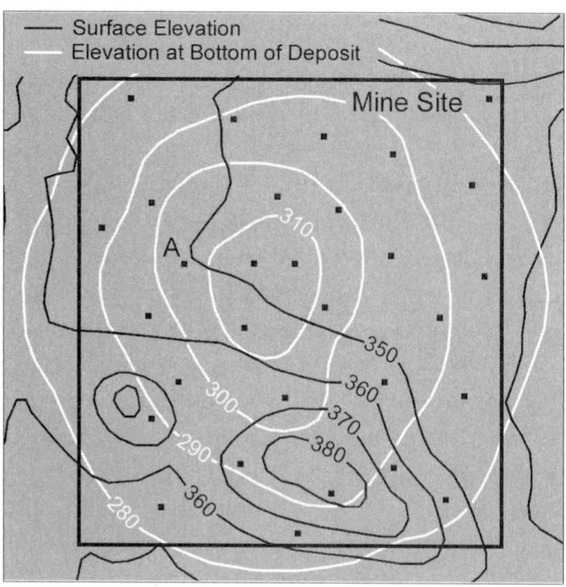

Figure 15.17 The volume of ore within a mine site can be computed from random ordinates if the top and bottom of the deposit can be defined by contour lines.

The only question is how to estimate the volume of the topmost slab. What we do is assume that the top of the feature extends one-half of the contour interval above the last contour. In Figure 15.18, for example, the last contour is at 340 feet, so the top of the feature is assumed to be at 350 feet, one-half contour interval higher.

We next assume that the three-dimensional form of the top slab from its base contour (the 320-foot contour in this example) to the top point can be approximated by a **right circular cone** whose volume is $1/3\pi \times R^2 h$. In this equation, h is the cone height and πR^2 is the area of its circular base. Notice that one-third of the cone height (10 feet in this example) is one-half the contour interval. We can thus restate the equation as: top slab volume equals one-half the contour interval multiplied by the ground area enclosed by the base contour.

SHAPE

An area feature's two-dimensional form is called its **shape**. Shape is one thing that gives each area feature its distinctive geographic character. We use terms such as compact, elongated, or irregular to describe the shapes of area features.

Important as it is to identify the shapes of area features, shape is a difficult thing to commu-

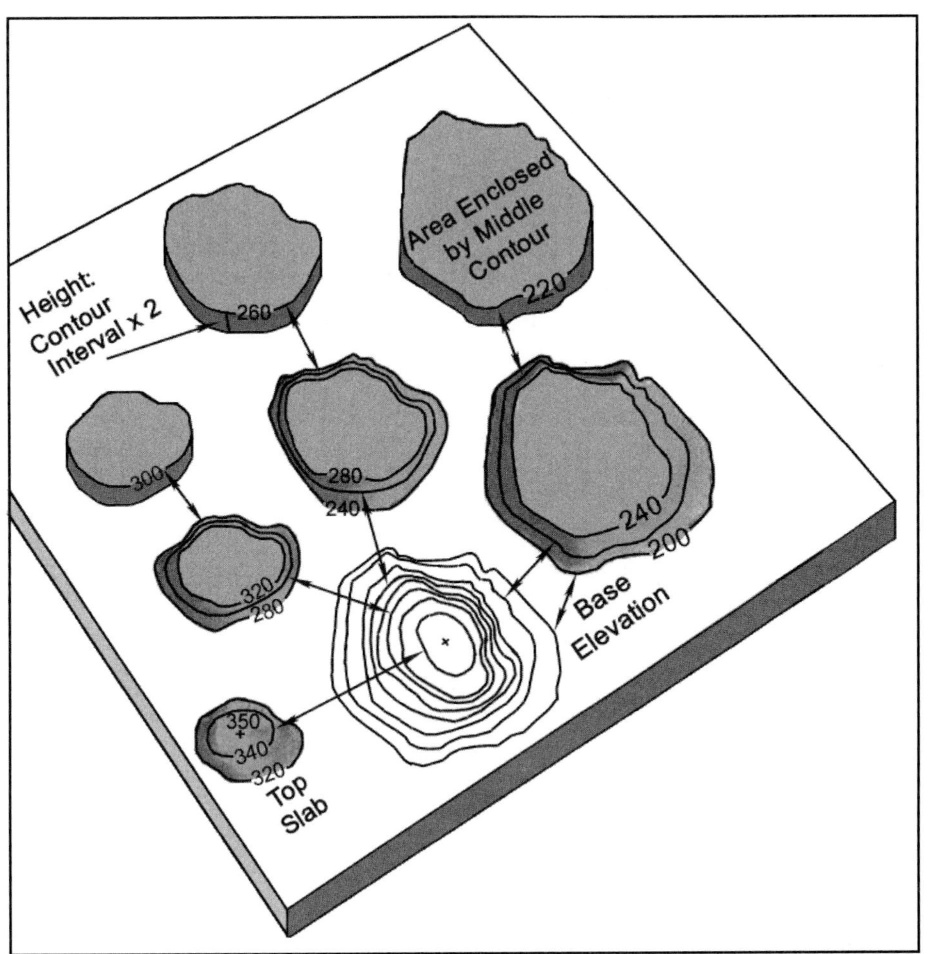

Figure 15.18. The volume of an irregular feature can be determined by slicing the feature into horizontal slabs defined by contour lines. See the text for an explanation of the method.

nicate in words. The outlines or external surfaces of environmental features take so many forms that we can't conveniently attach labels to them all. But we have named a number of simple geometric figures, and we frequently refer to these through comparison. We say that features are somewhat circular, roughly triangular, or approximately square in shape. But the degree of resemblance between the area feature shape (the shape seen on a map) and a standard shape may be difficult to state in words.

While verbal descriptions of different shapes are sufficient for many purposes, the terms used are often so subjective that disagreements arise among map users. Thus, more objective numerical **shape indexes** have been devised.

Shape Indexes

One objective method for describing the shape of an area feature is to state in numerical terms the degree of similarity between a standard two-dimensional shape and the feature. If you want an idea of the circularity of an irregularly-shaped area feature, for example, you can superimpose the feature on a circle of the same map area and compute the **area correspondence** between the two shapes mathematically (**Figure 15.19**). If you repeat the procedure using a square or another standard shape, you can then describe the feature's shape relative to several standards in an objective way.

Although an unlimited number of mathematical procedures could be devised, one example of a shape index should make the procedure clear:

$$Shape = 1.0 - \left(\frac{F \cap S}{F \cup S} \right),$$

where $F \cap S$ is the **intersection** (overlap) area of the feature and standard shape, and $F \cup S$ is the **union** (area in one or the other) of the two shapes.

To compute this shape index, first find the intersection area where the two shapes overlap. You do this by finding the centroid of the irregular shape, then aligning the standard shape so that its centroid location is the same as the irregular shape. You then find the ratio between this intersection area and the total union area covered by the two superimposed shapes. Finally, you subtract this value from 1.0 so that the shape index will range from 0.0 when there is perfect coincidence between the two shapes to 1.0 when there is no overlap.

In Figure 15.19, the irregularly-shaped feature, the circle, and the square all have a map area of 0.634 in^2. For the circle, the intersection area is 0.542 in^2, while the union area is 0.750 in^2. Thus, the shape index is: $1.0 - 0.542 \div 0.750 = 0.272$. For the square, the shape index is: $1.0 - 0.501 \div 0.785 = 0.362$. These shape index values suggest that the irregular shape is slightly closer to a circle than a square. If the index were 0.0, the feature would be perfectly circular.

It's not uncommon to find indexes close to 0.0, especially when determining the shapes of cultural features (those produced by humans). The upper index value of 1.0, however, provides an unreachable limit, for it would mean that the feature and standard shape did not overlap, which is impossible.

In some situations, you might prefer to measure the **compactness** of an area feature rather than comparing it with standard shapes. Compactness of shape often is considered desirable, in part because compact regions are most efficiently serviced and defended. Partitioning space into compact units for administrative and political purposes also conveys a sense of fairness, as suggested by the gerrymandering example at the beginning of the chapter.

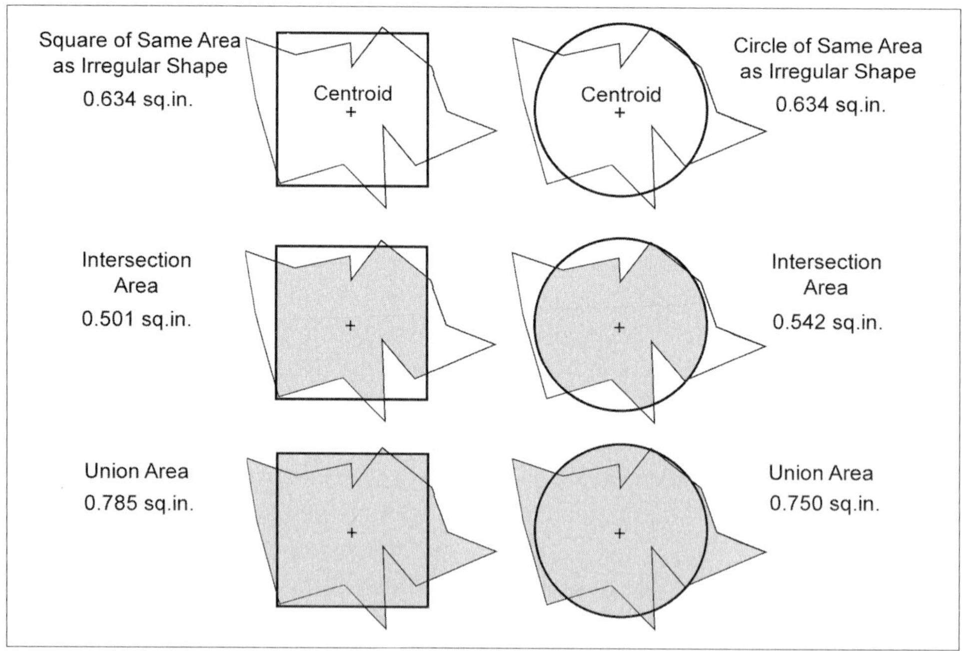

Figure 15.19 A shape index such as the ratio of the intersection and union of an irregularly-shaped feature and standard shapes, such as squares and circles, makes it possible to compare the shapes of different features numerically.

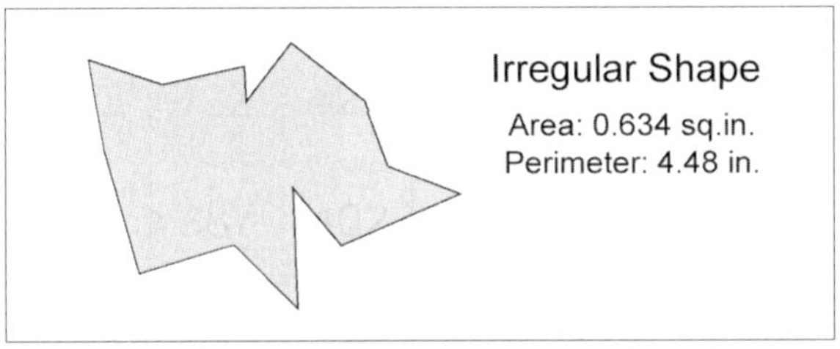

Irregular Shape
Area: 0.634 sq.in.
Perimeter: 4.48 in.

Figure 15.20 Compactness indexes are often based upon the ratio of the area and perimeter of an irregularly-shaped feature.

A compact shape is one in which all points on the boundary are as close as possible to the center. The circle is the most compact two-dimensional figure, because its boundary is everywhere equidistant from its centerpoint. The length of its boundary (perimeter) relative to its area is also minimal. For these reasons, compactness indexes all use the circle in some way as a standard reference figure.

Compactness indexes are derived by forming ratios between such basic figure attributes as area, perimeter, length of longest axis, and the radius of the largest inscribing or smallest circumscribing circle. For example, the ratio of a feature's area (*A*) to its perimeter (*P*) provides a useful compactness index. This ratio usually is modified by multiplying the ratio by 4π and dividing by P, so that a circle has a compactness of 1.0. The compactness index is thus:

$$Compactness = \frac{A \times 4\pi}{P^2}$$

With this index, the more elongated and irregular the feature, the closer to 0.0 its index value will be. As an example, refer to **Figure 15.20**. Since the feature illustrated in this figure has a perimeter of 4.48 in. and an area of 0.634 in^2, its compactness index is $0.634 \times 4\pi / 4.48^2$, or 0.40. This is a medium compactness.

The examples of shape indexes that we've discussed in this section are fairly primitive mathematically, but they do illustrate several attributes of all numerical indexes which you need to consider before putting too much faith in their values. Due to the decisions you must make when determining compactness or comparing a feature with a standard shape, a feature can have several different index values. Shapes that look quite different can also have the same index value. The indexes devised to date don't have unique numerical values for different shapes. Despite these drawbacks, however, shape indexes are still useful in many map analysis situations, especially if they're simple, unit free, independent of the feature's size, and intuitively appealing.

SELECTED READINGS

Barrett, J.P. and Philbrook, J.S., "Dot Grid Area Estimation: Precision by Repeated Trials," *Journal of Forestry*, 68, 3 (1970), pp. 149-151.

Boyce, R.R., and Clark, W.A.V., "The Concept of Shape in Geography," *Geographical Review*, 54 (1964), pp. 561-572.

Dickinson, G.C., "Measurement of Area," Chapter 9 in *Maps and Air Photographs* (London: Edward Arnold Publishers, Ltd., 1969), pp. 132-141.

Dury, G.H., "Geometric Analysis," in *Map Interpretation*, 4th ed. (London: Pitman & Sons, Ltd., 1972), pp. 163-177.

Earickson, R.J., and Harlin, J.M., *Geographical Measurement and Quantitative Analysis* (New York: Macmillan College Publishing Co., 1994).

Frolov, Y.S. and Maling, D.H., "The Accuracy of Area Measurement by Point Counting Techniques," *The Cartographic Journal*, 6, 1 (1969), pp. 21-35.

Gierhart, J.W., "Evaluation of Methods of Area Measurement," *Surveying and Mapping*, 14 (1954), pp. 460-469.

Kimerling, A.J., "Area Computation from Geodetic Coordinates on the Spheroid," *Surveying and Mapping*. Vol. 44, No. 4, 1984, pp. 343-351.

Lawrence, G.R.P., "Measurements from Maps," and "Map Analysis," Chapters 9 and 10 in *Cartographic Methods*, 2nd ed. (London: Methuen & Co., Ltd., 1979), pp. 82-104.

Lee, D.R., and Sallee, G.T., "A Method of Measuring Shape," *Geographical Review*, 60, 4 (1970), pp. 555-563.

Maling, D.H., *Measurement From Maps: The Principles & Methods of Cartometry* (New York: Pergamon Press, Inc., 1988).

Neft, D.S., *Statistical Analysis for Areal Distributions*, Monograph Series No. 2 (Philadelphia: Regional Science Research Institute, 1966).

Proudfoot, M., *The Measurement of Geographic Area* (Washington, DC: U.S. Bureau of the Census, 1946).

CHAPTER SIXTEEN
SLOPE AND PROFILES

SLOPE MEASUREMENT
- Slope Ratio and Angle
- Gradient

SLOPE MAPS

GRADIENT PATH
- Finding Constant Slope Paths

PROFILES

INTERVISIBILITY

CROSS SECTIONS

SELECTED READINGS

Life is most delightful when it is on the downward slope.
—Lucius Annaeus Seneca
Roman philosopher, statesman, and orator
4 BC - AD 65

16

CHAPTER SIXTEEN

SLOPE AND PROFILES

The rise and fall in the ground surface has a major influence on human behavior. We speak of the ease of hiking on a gentle slope, or the effort involved in traversing a steep road. A lake bottom is said to drop off rapidly from shore, and a steep downgrade is a danger to truck drivers. In each case, we are expressing vertical changes across the earth's surface.

These qualitative terms describing vertical change are of limited use, however, because they can take on quite diverse meanings for people under different conditions of age, fitness, or stress. So we turn to maps to provide quantitative information from which we can create mathematical measures and graphical illustrations of the amount of change along lines or across areas.

In this chapter you will see that the amount of **slope** in a particular direction can be computed from the contours on a topographic map or the isobaths on a nautical chart. This slope information allows you to create a **slope map** for an area. Changes in elevation or depth along a line on the map can also be shown graphically by drawing a **profile** of the terrain. You can also use terrain profiles to create **intervisibility maps** that show areas visible and hidden from view at a particular location on the earth. Let's begin by looking at the measurement of slope.

SLOPE MEASUREMENT

The vertical change in the land surface, when determined over a given horizontal distance—along a road or stream, for instance—is known as its **slope**. Slope can only be computed between two points. If you want to know the slope at a specific location, therefore, you must use the elevation at the location and another nearby point in computing the slope. You determine the elevation difference from the contours or isobaths on the map, then measure the map distance between the two points and convert to ground distance using the map scale (**Figure 16.1**).

Slope computations are based on a surface assumed to increase or decrease in height uniformly between two points. Such surfaces are **linear** between the two points. Deviation from a linear surface within the distance over which the slope is computed will result in **slope measurement error**. While the actual slope of the curved surface varies continually in steepness between the two points, the slope computation will give a constant slope value. The greater the distance over which slope is computed and the more curved the surface, the greater the potential slope measurement error.

Although we generally use the term "slope" to refer to the amount of rise or fall of the ground surface, the concept is equally applicable to the change in magnitude with change in distance for any phenomenon. A surface of population density, for example, often slopes steeply downward away from the center of a city.

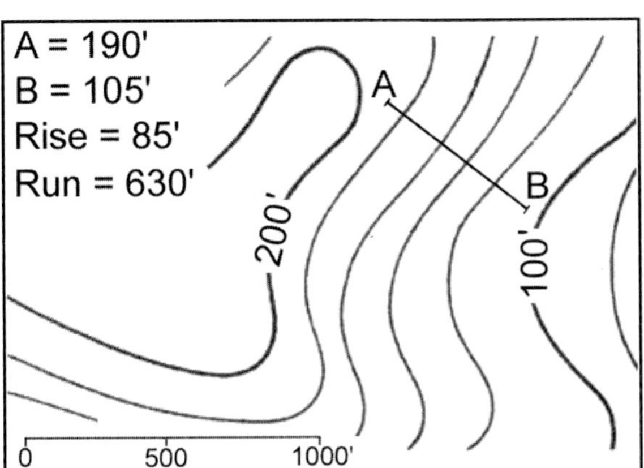

Figure 16.1 Slope is computed from the elevation difference (rise) between two points (A and B) on a topographic map, and the horizontal distance (run) between the two points.

Slope Ratio and Angle

There are several ways to define the slope between two points quantitatively. The simplest is the **slope ratio** between the elevation difference (rise), and the ground distance (run) between the two points (**Figure 16.2A**). Mathematically, this is written as y/x. In Figure 16.1, a rise of 85 feet over a run of 630 feet gives a slope ratio of 85/630, which is 0.13. Slope ratios can also be negative—a fall of 30 feet over a run of 150 feet gives a slope ratio of -30/150, which is -0.2. Notice that the vertical and horizontal distances must always be in the same units of measurement.

You can also express the ratio as a **slope percentage** (**Figure 16.2B**). To do so, simply multiply the slope ratio by 100. In the example above, the slope ratio 0.13 is also 0.13 × 100, or 13%.

Slope can also be defined as a **slope angle**, usually in degrees (**Figure 16.2C**). This way of specifying slope is based on the fact that the slope

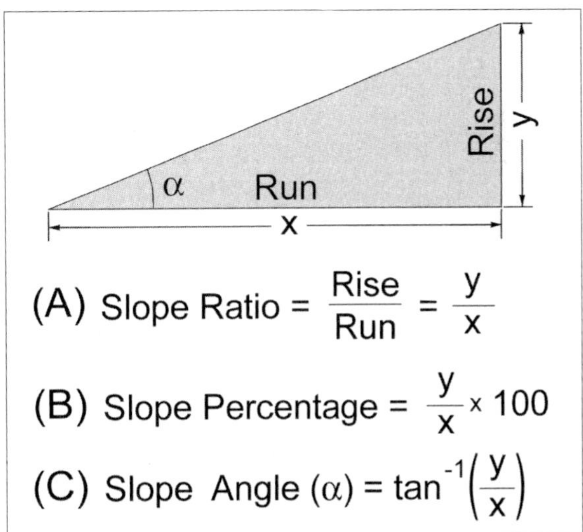

Figure 16.2 The slope of a surface between two points can be specified as a ratio (A), as a percentage (B), or as an angle (C), where $\tan^{-1}$ is read as "angle whose tangent is...."

ratio (y/x) is the **trigonometric tangent** of the slope angle. Consequently, the slope angle is the inverse tangent ($\tan^{-1}$) of the slope ratio (the angle whose tangent is the slope ratio). In the example above, your calculator will give the inverse tangent of 0.13 as 7.4 degrees. Notice that a slope angle of 45° is a 100% slope, since this is the angle whose tangent and slope ratio are 1.0.

Gradient

So far, we have limited our discussion to vertical change between two points on the earth's surface. Sometimes we are interested in finding the maximum amount of vertical change at a point. The maximum slope at a point on a surface, rather than between two points, is known as the **gradient**. In other words, while any downhill road has a slope ratio or angle between any two points along its path, it may not follow a gradient path. It is a gradient path only if from every point along its course it follows the steepest route down the hill (**Figure 16.3**).

Finding the gradient at a point on the earth's surface is a bit more complicated than computing slope ratios and angles since two calculations are necessary. In addition to the slope magnitude, you also have to compute the gradient direction (usually a true azimuth). To make these computations, you determine "partial slopes" in two perpendicular directions.

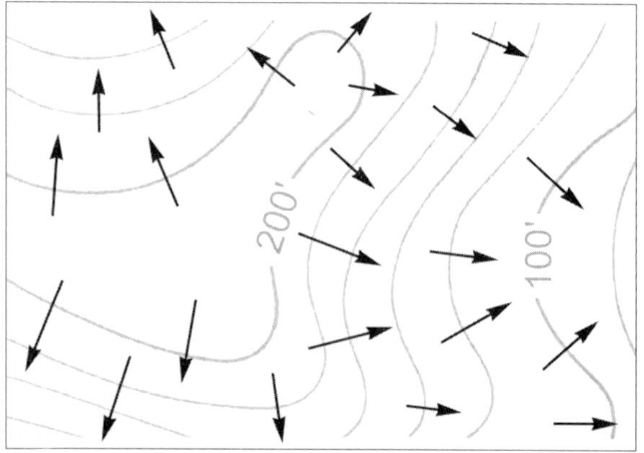

Figure 16.3 The gradient is the steepest downhill route, always perpendicular to the contour lines.

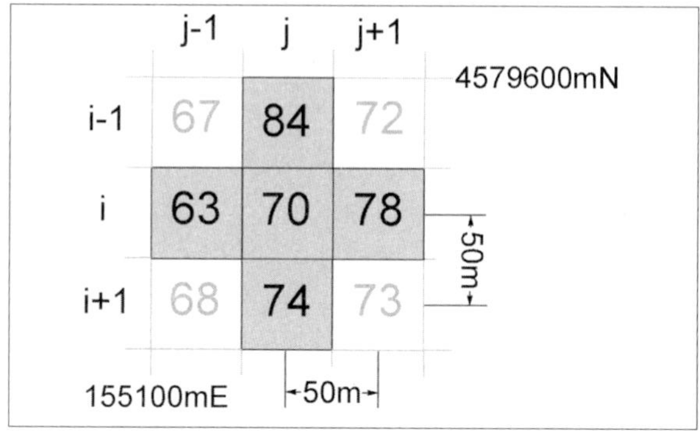

Figure 16.4 The gradient can be computed by finding the elevations for a grid of square cells laid over the map. Here average elevations are given in meters for 50×50 meter cells.

To understand how the gradient is computed, imagine laying a grid of square cells over the map so that the cell boundary lines are equally spaced along the x and y coordinate axes. In **Figure 16.4**, for instance, 50 × 50 meter grid cell boundary lines are defined by UTM grid system easting (x) and northing (y) coordinates (see Chapter 4 for more on the UTM system). You can find either the average elevation within each cell or the elevation at the cell center by interpolating between the contour lines in the vicinity of the cell.

The first step in calculating the gradient at each cell is to find the x-slope in the x (easting) direction and the y-slope in the y (northing) direction. There are several ways to compute the x-slope and y-slope, but a common procedure is to use the elevations of the grid cell and its immediate east-west and north-south neighbors. For example, the x-slope can be calculated as the average slope between the center cell at row i and column j ($Cell_{i,j}$), and the cells immediately to the left ($Cell_{i,j-1}$) and right ($Cell_{i,j+1}$). The y-slope is calculated as the average slope between the center cell ($Cell_{i,j}$) and the cells immediately above ($Cell_{i-1,j}$) and below ($Cell_{i+1,j}$). For a grid cell spacing of *d* meters, the equations used to find the x-slope and y-slope are:

$$x-slope = \frac{1}{2} \times \left(\frac{Cell_{i,j} - Cell_{i,j-1}}{d} + \frac{Cell_{i,j+1} - Cell_{i,j}}{d} \right)$$

$$x-slope = \frac{Cell_{i,j+1} - Cell_{i,j-1}}{2d}$$

$$y-slope=\frac{1}{2}\times\left(\frac{Cell_{i,j}-Cell_{i+1,j}}{d}+\frac{Cell_{i-1,j}-Cell_{i,j}}{d}\right)$$

$$y-slope=\frac{Cell_{i-1,j}-Cell_{i+1,j}}{2d}$$

Notice that although the elevation of $Cell_{i,j}$ is a key part of the initial equations, it cancels out and does not appear in the final equations—only the elevations of the immediate neighbor cells are used in computing the x-slope and y-slope. In Figure 16.4, for instance, $Cell_{i,j}$ = 70m, $Cell_{i,j+1}$ = 78m, $Cell_{i,j-1}$ = 63m, $Cell_{i+1,j}$ = 74m, and $Cell_{i-1,j}$ = 84 meters. For the 50 meter cells (d = 50m), the slope equations are:

$$x-slope=\frac{78m-63m}{100m}=0.15$$

$$y-slope=\frac{84m-74m}{100m}=0.10$$

Once you find the x-slope and y-slope, you can compute the maximum slope ratio, called the **gradient magnitude (G)**, using the following equation:

$$G=\sqrt{(x-slope)^2+(y-slope)^2}$$

In our example, the gradient magnitude at $Cell_{i,j}$ is:

$$G=\sqrt{(0.15)^2+(0.10)^2}=\sqrt{0.0225+0.01}=\sqrt{0.0325}=0.18$$

or an 18% upward slope.

You next find the **gradient azimuth** by using the equation:

$$\theta=\tan^{-1}\left(\frac{x-slope}{y-slope}\right)$$

where θ is the azimuth angle measured from the grid-north reference line, and $\tan^{-1}$ (sometimes called arctan) is shorthand for "angle whose trigonometric tangent is...."

In our example:

$$\theta=\tan^{-1}\left(\frac{0.15}{0.10}\right)=\tan^{-1}(1.5)°=56$$

so the uphill gradient is 18% at a 56° azimuth from grid north. The downhill gradient (signaled by a negative value) is just the opposite: -18% at a 56°+180°, or 236°, grid azimuth.

SLOPE MAPS

By making repeated gradient computations, it is possible to derive a **slope map** from elevation data for an area. Slope maps are useful tools for land use planners and resource managers. They have been used successfully in runoff modeling, urban development (some cities have a slope-zone ordinance), logging, and farming.

Gradient computations become tedious if they must be repeated frequently. For this reason, professionals who create slope maps usually rely on computers to compute the gradient magnitudes from gridded digital elevation model data (see Chapter 8 for more on digital elevation models). The slope map of Mount St. Helens in **Figure 16.5**, for instance, was created by computer from a 30-meter-resolution digital elevation model of the area.

If appropriate slope maps (or the software and data used by professionals to produce them) aren't at hand, you can still come up with a crude slope zone map quickly and cheaply by using **slope templates**. To do so, you first decide on a small number of slope zones: 0-6%, 7-11%, 12-19%, 20-34%, 35-59%, and >60%, for example. You then make a clear plastic template of straight-line contour segments spaced so that their slopes cover the range to be mapped. The template in **Figure 16.6**, for example, has contours spaced increasingly closer so that there is a 1% increase in slope for each succeeding pair of lines. Be sure your slope template is properly matched to the map scale and contour interval.

Next, compare the spacing of lines on the slope template with the spacing of contours across

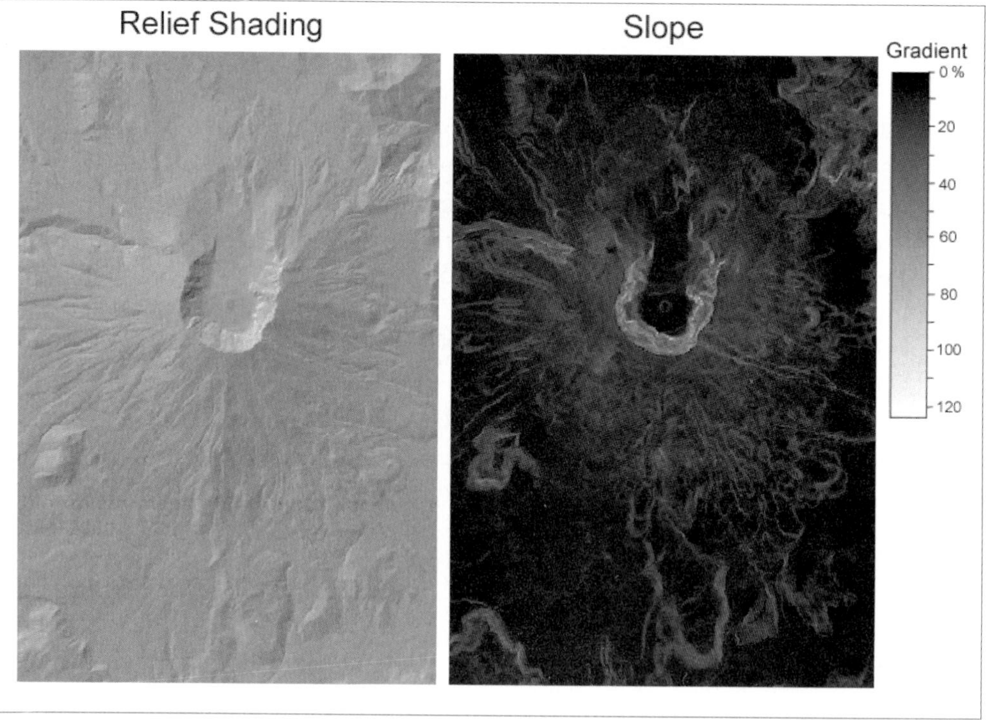

Figure 16.5 Relief shading and slope map for Mount St. Helens, Washington, created in an image processing program from 30-meter-resolution digital elevation model data.

the map. Outline small areas on the map that have slopes falling within a slope zone, so that the entire map ends up divided into different slope zone regions. The hillside in the upper-left corner of Figure 16.6, for instance, has slopes of around 23% that fall within the 20-34% slope zone. **Figure 16.7** is an example of a slope zone map manually produced using a slope template.

Like gradient magnitude computations, gradient azimuth computations are tedious if not done by computer software using digital elevation model data. If such computations have been made, however, it is possible to create a **gradient vector map** (**Figure 16.8**). When working with terrain data, such a map is useful in defining watersheds. With non-terrain data, surface gradient zones and breaks between zones may be suggestive of movement or flow of ideas, goods, or forces. Thus, a gradient vector map of barometric pressure may help to explain the pattern of winds.

GRADIENT PATH

One form of invisible route that has special meaning is the least-effort path from one location to another, called the **gradient path**. To visualize this path, it's helpful to look at a three-dimensional terrain model. You could place a drop of water at the highest point and observe the path the water drop takes moving downward under gravity. If contour traces were drawn on the terrain model surface, you would see the water move downhill along a least-resistance path at right angles to the contours (**Figure 16.9**). This is to be expected, since the maximum gradient always is at right angles to the contour lines. The water merely traces the gradient path (or steepest slope route) from high to low points on the landform.

If contour lines in an area of linear terrain (constant slope) are parallel, the gradient path will be a straight line perpendicular to the contours (Figure 16.9A). Terrain surfaces aren't usually linear, of course. This means that long, straight gradient

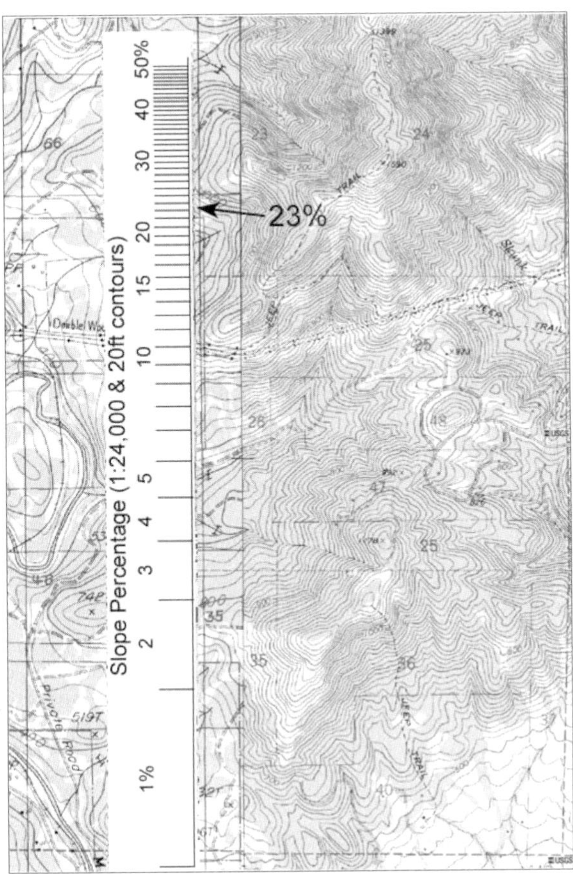

Figure 16.6 Slope templates make it convenient to convert an isoline map into a slope zone map.

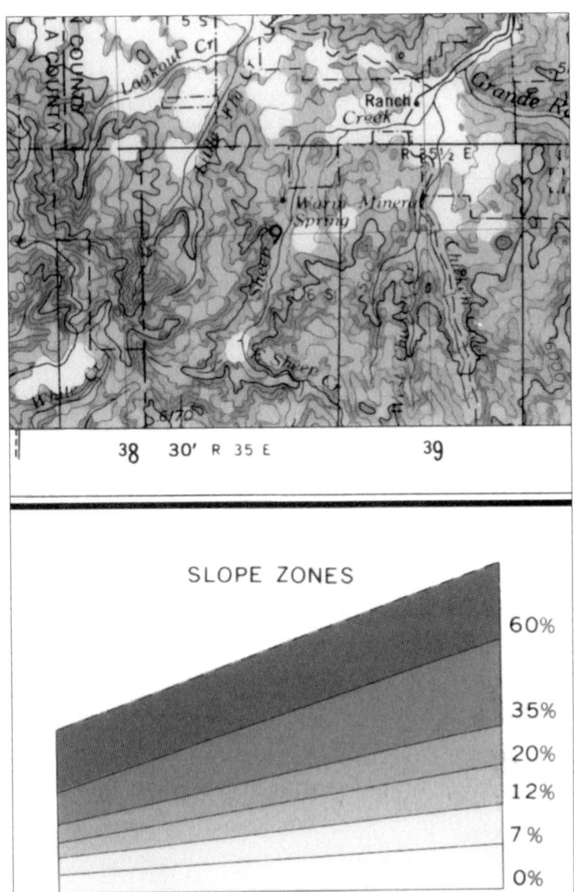

Figure 16.7 Slope templates can be used to create slope zone maps, which are useful land use planning and management tools.

paths aren't all that common, since if water is to flow down a complex terrain surface along a gradient path, its course direction must be altered so that all contours are crossed at right angles (Figure 16.9B).

Finding Constant Slope Paths

Sometimes you may want to determine a **constant slope path**. Suppose, for example, that a road or trail must have a constant slope of five degrees. If you have a contour map available, one way to define this path is to set a pair of dividers at a ground distance equal to the contour interval divided by the tangent of the slope angle. This procedure is illustrated in **Figure 16.10**.

The first step, assuming that your beginning point is located on a contour line, is to place one foot of the dividers at the beginning point and the other foot on the next higher contour line. Mark this second point; then rotate the lower foot of the dividers to the next higher contour line, while keeping the other foot stationary. Mark this third point. Continue the process until you reach the contour line that lies at or just below the elevation of your destination point. Finally, connect the points, including the beginning and destination, with line segments.

A related problem is to determine a **path that cannot exceed a certain slope angle**. The same procedure for finding a constant slope path is used again, but three things can happen. First, the maximum allowable slope line may intersect the destination contour between the destination point and the gradient path from the origin (**Figure 16.11 A**). This means that a straight-line course from ori-

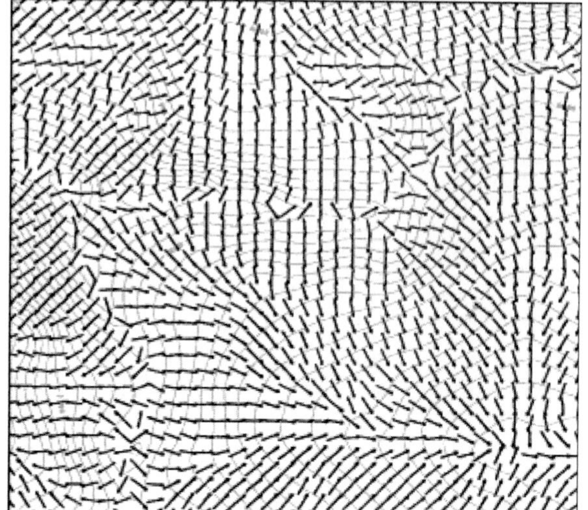

Figure 16.8 Gradient azimuths can be used to generate gradient vector maps which outline ridge lines and basins and suggest patterns of flow associated with surfaces.

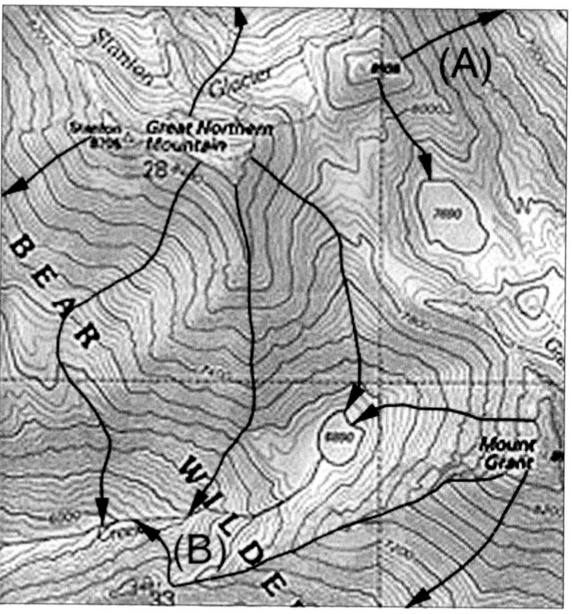

Figure 16.9 The gradient path traces out the least-effort route on a contoured surface. If contour lines are parallel, the gradient path is a straight line perpendicular to the contours (A). Otherwise the gradient path traces out a curved route (B) perpendicular to all contours.

gin to destination will fall within acceptable slope limits. When this happens, you may have a great deal of flexibility in choosing the actual route to take.

The second possibility is that the maximum allowable slope line will connect directly with the destination point (**Figure 16.11 B**). Thus, there will be no flexibility in route location. Such cases are rare.

The most complex situation is when the maximum permissible slope line intersects the destination contour beyond the destination point (**Figure 16.11 C**). This means that a relatively indirect course must be taken between origin and destination to meet the maximum slope restriction. This last case

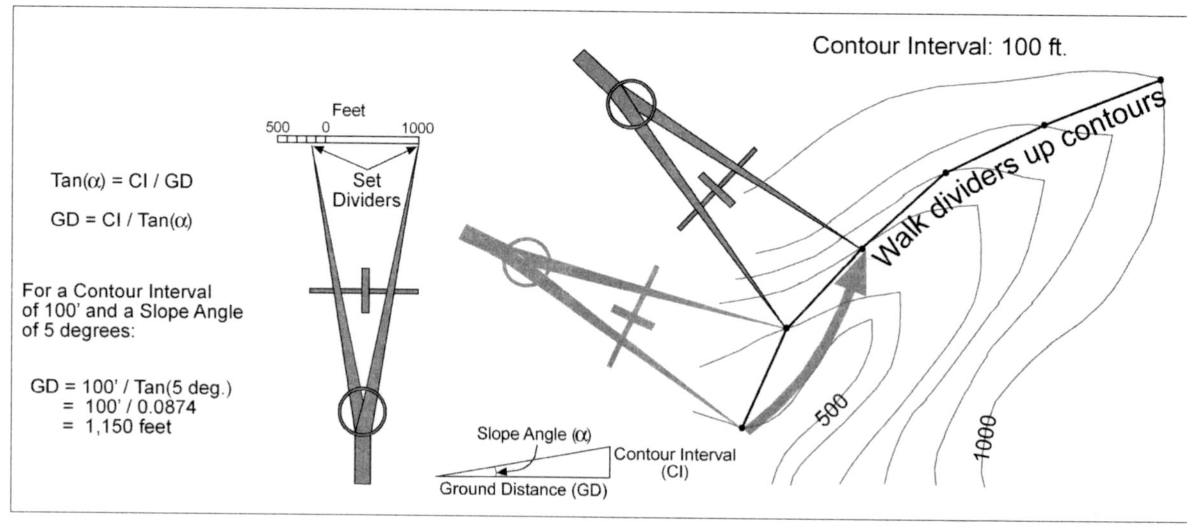

Figure 16.10 You can determine a constant slope path by walking pre-set dividers up the slope.

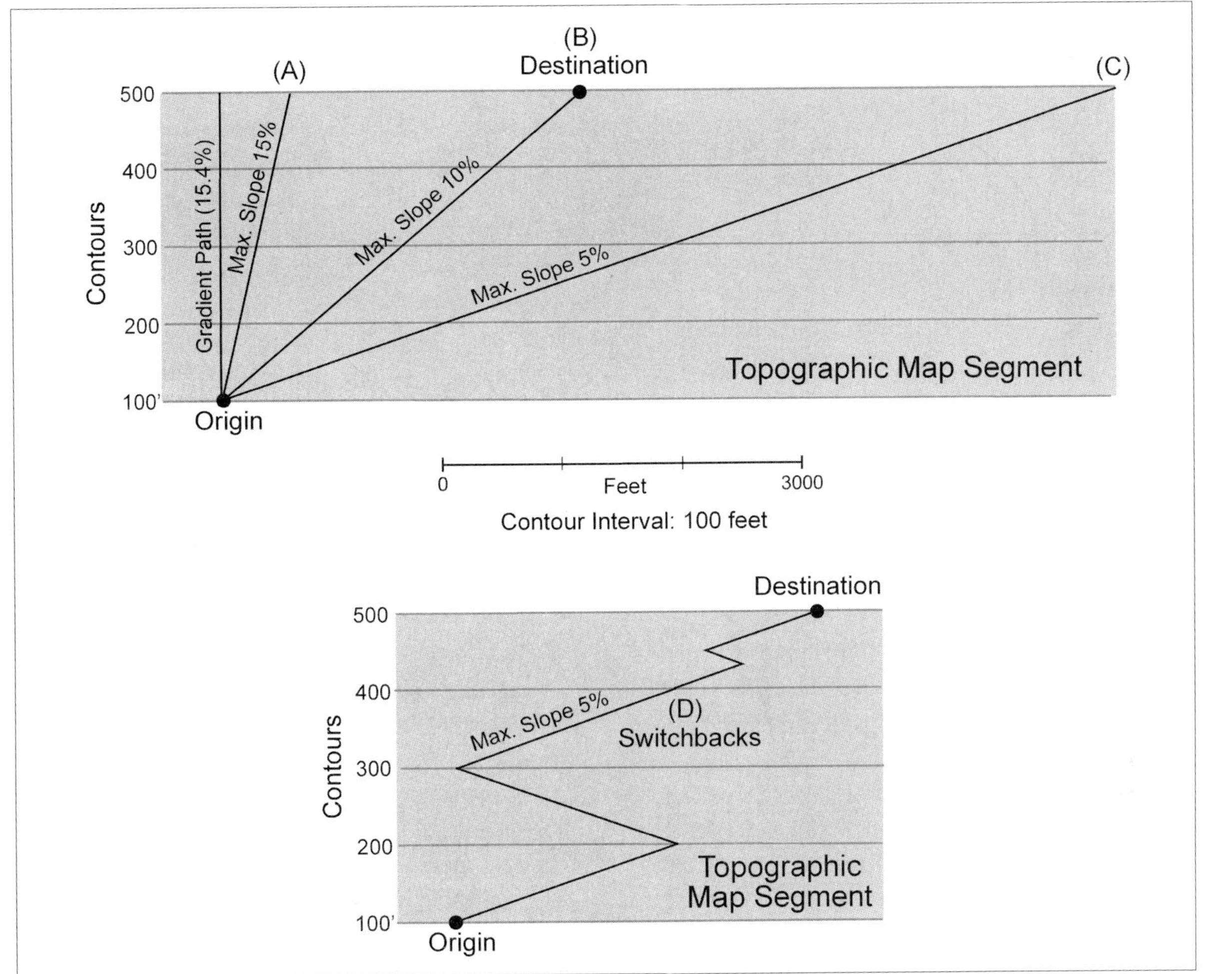

Figure 16.11 Routes laid out with a maximum slope restriction may end up in a series of switchbacks on steep slopes.

explains the prevalence of "switchbacks" on steep mountain hiking trails and roads (**Figure 16.11 D**). Government regulations often specify the maximum slope permissible for such routes.

PROFILES

So far in this chapter we have concentrated on the measurement, calculation, and mapping of slope information. Slope zone and gradient path maps show you changes in these quantities across the map. Knowing the spatial distribution of slopes is important in land management and site planning. But even skilled map users often find it difficult to visualize the three-dimensional nature of changes in the terrain from slope and gradient path maps.

Another way you can visualize changes in slope is to view the surface from the side, using what architects call the **elevation view**. Since you usually can't see a side view of the land surface directly (as you can see the side of a building in an architectural drawing), you must create a **profile** from elevations along a line on the surface. You can construct a profile from contours on topographic maps, or isobath lines on nautical charts, by following these steps:

1. Draw a straight line on the map between the points of interest. This is called the **profile line** (line AB on the map at the top of **Figure 16.12**).

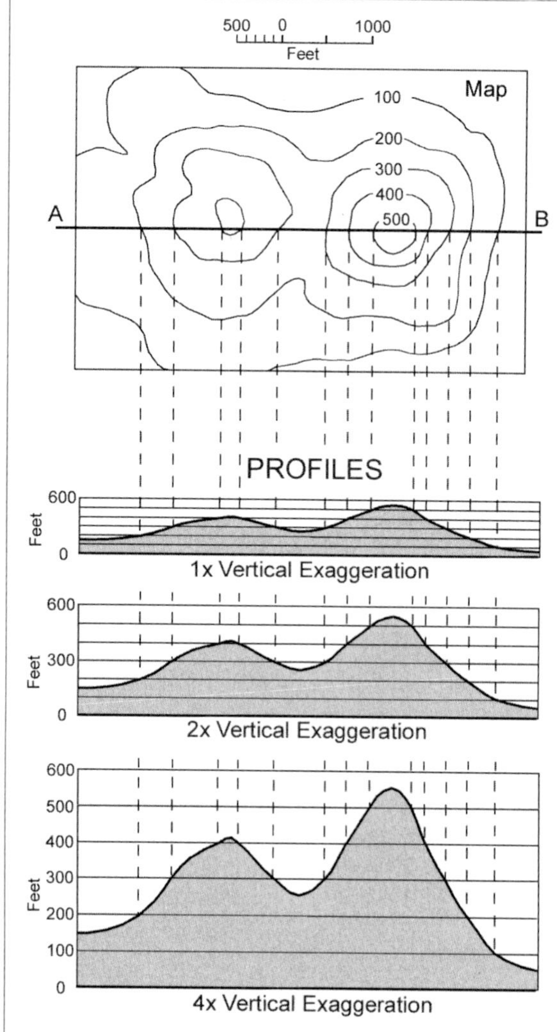

Figure 16.12 A profile can be constructed from a map showing the terrain with contours along any desired profile line, such as from A to B. It is difficult, however, to choose the vertical exaggeration so that the profile gives the same impression of landform variation which the observer would receive in the field.

2. Determine how many contour intervals separate the highest and lowest valued contours that cross or touch the profile line, and add two to this number (totaling seven in this example).

3. On a sheet of paper, draw as many equally-spaced horizontal **construction lines** as the number you determined in the previous step. You can save yourself some work by using commercial graph paper for this purpose.

4. Orient the paper so that the bottom horizontal construction line is aligned directly below the profile line.

5. Label the construction lines with contour elevation values, beginning at the bottom line with the lowest value (one interval below the lowest contour crossed by the profile line) and proceeding to one interval above the highest contour value.

6. From every point at which the profile line is crossed or touched by a contour, draw a vertical dashed line downward to the construction line having the same elevation value.

7. Draw a smooth curve through successive points at which the dashed vertical lines intersect the proper construction lines. Remember that continuous geographic distributions are usually smooth rather than angular as the profile might suggest. When constructing a profile of the terrain surface, you should take local landform conditions into account in modifying the profile. Smoothing off sharp angles in the profile is usually justified.

The top profile's vertical scale is the same as the map scale. It may seem logical to make the vertical scale the same as the horizontal scale. Yet when you do this in constructing a terrain profile, the effect is invariably disappointing. This is because the elevation of a land feature like a hill usually is numerically small when compared to the horizontal extent of the feature. Since terrain variation is so important to people's lives, you usually will have to expand the vertical dimension of your profile to make it appear realistic. Such **vertical exaggeration** not only increases the height of the profile, but also steepens and lengthens the hillsides.

The spacing of the horizontal construction lines defines the scale of the vertical axis on the profile. To exaggerate minor terrain features, you increase the spacing; to de-emphasize features, you decrease the spacing. The unexaggerated top profile in Figure 16.12 is said to have a 1x vertical exaggeration. The middle and bottom profiles in this figure have been vertically exaggerated by factors of two (2x) and four (4x). If the map scale is 1:24,000 (1 inch to 2,000 feet), for example, the vertical scale for the 2x exaggeration will be 1:12,000 (1 inch to 1,000 feet). The 2x profile may appear more realistic than the overly flat 1x and excessively steep 4x profiles. When dealing with a region of high relief, you may occasionally find it necessary to de-emphasize the mountain peaks somewhat (vertical exaggeration <1x) while exaggerating the foothills to make the profile look natural.

A profile line doesn't have to be straight, of course. With a little extra work, you can profile a stream bed or hiking trail as well (**Figure 16.13**). To do so, follow these steps:

1. Determine and clearly mark on the map the irregular profile line.

2. Follow Step 2 in the previous example.

3. Measure the total length of the irregular profile line, and draw a horizontal construction line of this length directly below the map.

4. Beginning at one end of the profile line, measure the length of the first line segment (segment 1-2 in Figure 16.13), mark off this distance from the left end of the construction line with a small tick, and write the line segment endpoint number below the tick.

5. Repeat Step 4 until you reach the end of the profile line (nine line segments were measured, plotted, and labeled in Figure 16.13).

6. Above the initial construction line, draw as many equally-spaced horizontal construction lines as you determined in Step 2. Label these lines from bottom to top as you did in Step 5 of the previous example.

7. Find the elevation of each profile line segment endpoint by interpolating between contour lines, then plot the vertical position of each elevation point directly above the endpoint tick marked on the horizontal axis.

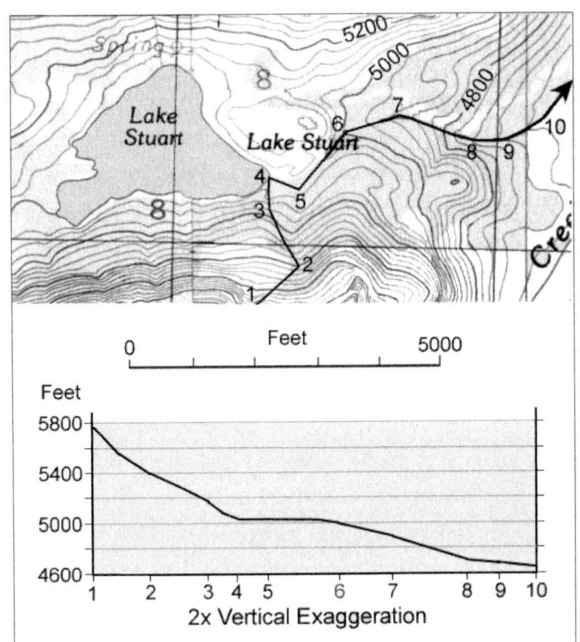

Figure 16.13 The line along which a profile is constructed needn't be straight. For example, the profile of a hiking trail can be constructed by scaling trail distances along the horizontal axis (see text for further explanation).

8. Draw smooth curves through the elevation points plotted in Step 7 to finish the profile.

Scaling the vertical axis of non-topographic profiles is complicated by the fact that the magnitude units aren't comparable to those making up the horizontal dimension. The inch or centimeter units used to measure precipitation, for example, bear no physical relation to the ground units measured in kilometers or miles. This means that there is no such thing as vertical exaggeration with non-topographic profiles. There is, however, such a thing as alternately emphasizing or de-emphasizing aspects of the profile by altering the spacing of the horizontal construction lines. You will have to take special care that you don't end up with a false impression of a distribution based solely on the way a profile is constructed.

Terrain profiles based on contour lines aren't a perfect reconstruction of the surface, of course. Contour lines give elevation information only along the profile line, from which you must infer the complete terrain surface. If contour lines are optimally spaced with respect to terrain undulations, your profile will accurately show the surface. If they're poorly situated, however, your portrayal of the surface will be poor.

The spacing of contour lines is determined by the contour interval. The larger the contour interval, the fewer the number of construction lines you will have available to make the profile and the less topographic detail you will be able to show. The smaller the contour interval, the fewer the topographic features missed by the contour lines. Also be aware that a few topographic maps have a variable contour interval, so that you must adjust the spacing of your horizontal construction lines.

Profiles have a number of practical uses beyond providing a dramatic picture of the vertical or magnitude aspects of geographic distributions. For instance, topographic profiles are used to plan the routing of roads, railroads, pipelines, and canals. When it comes time to determine the earth-moving requirements of such projects, profiles are used to compute the volume of material involved in making surface cuts and fills.

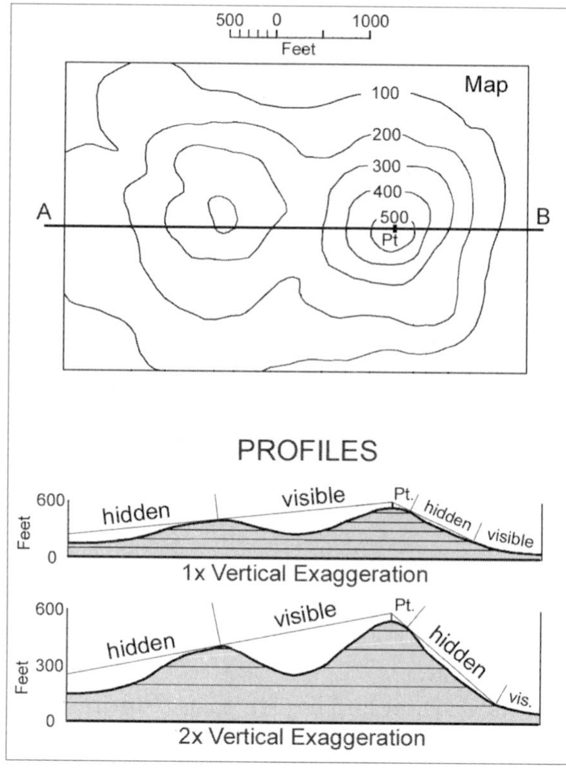

Figure 16.14 Topographic profiles can be used to determine the intervisibility of landscape features from a particular viewpoint along a line of sight. The hidden and visible portions of the landscape are corrected depicted on the profile with no (1x) vertical exaggeration (top profile). Visibility may be shown incorrectly when a vertically exaggerated profile is used (right side of bottom profile).

INTERVISIBILITY

Terrain profiles also provide a way for you to see what environmental features are visible from a given vantage point (**Figure 16.14**). This information, known as **intervisibility**, can be invaluable when orienting yourself in the field. It can also be used in the laboratory to determine whether a certain geographic feature would be visible from a possible building site, thereby saving you a trip into the field.

To determine intervisibility from a point on the profile, you should:

1. Plot your viewpoint on the profile at the correct height above the surface. The viewpoint (Pt.) on the profiles in Figure 16.14 is 50 feet above the top of the hill, for example.

2. Draw lines from the viewpoint that are tangent to (just touch) the profile. Continue each line to where it touches the profile again (right side of Figure 16.14), or to the edge of the profile diagram (left edge of Figure 16.14).

3. Label the visible and hidden portions of the profile.

If profiles are constructed in several directions from a selected viewpoint (or set of viewpoints, such as a trail), visible or hidden areas on the ground can be plotted on an **intervisibility map** (also called a **viewshed map**). Computer programs mathematically create closely-spaced profile lines (**Figure 16.15, left**), determine the visible and

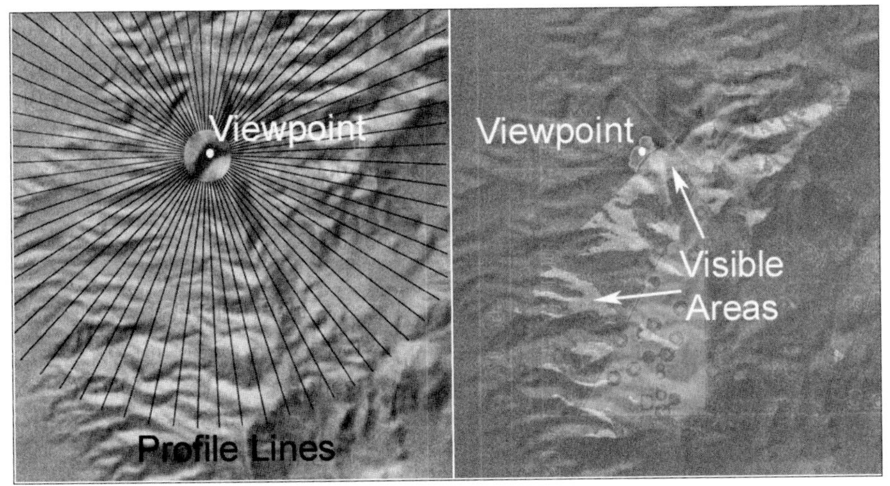

Figure 16.15 A viewshed map is created from a large number of profile lines radiating away from a viewpoint. Visible and hidden areas are inferred from the visible and hidden portions of each line.

hidden portions of each line, then connect the visible-hidden boundary points on adjacent profile lines into visible and hidden areas (**Figure 16.15, right**).

It is often useful to identify areas on the ground that are hidden from view. For instance, trails and campgrounds in a wilderness region might be built to minimize the visual impact of non-wilderness activities, such as clear-cuts, garbage dumps, and quarries.

CROSS SECTIONS

A diagram of the vertical section of the ground surface taken along a profile line is called a **cross section**. Cross sections showing the sub-surface orientation of rock layers are a basic component of a **surficial geology map**. Constructing a cross section from a surficial geology map is an easy matter because contacts between rock layers at the surface are drawn on a topographic base map containing contours (**Figure 16.16**).

Creating a cross section from surficial geology information superimposed on contours involves the following steps:

1. Construct a terrain profile at a given vertical exaggeration from a profile line drawn on the surficial geology map by following the procedure described earlier in the chapter.

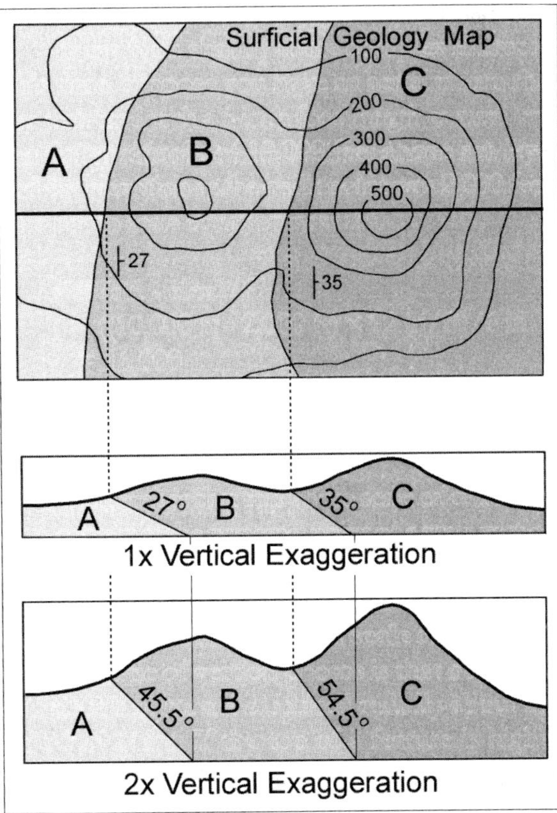

Figure 16.16 Geologic cross sections can be created from surficial geology maps and profiles, as explained in the text.

2. Mark on the profile line the intersection of contact lines between rock layers, such as layers A, B, and C in Figure 16.16.

3. Find the dip angle for each rock layer from the strike-dip symbols on the surficial geology map. For instance, the symbol |- 27 means that the dip angle for rock layer B is 27° downward to the east, assuming the map to be north-oriented.

4. Plot the sub-surface rock layer contacts as straight lines drawn at the dip angle downward from horizontal, then color the sub-surface beds to match the surficial geology map.

Notice that the bottom cross section in Figure 16.16 is drawn with a 2x vertical exaggeration. When the cross section is exaggerated vertically, the dip angles must be adjusted to match the amount of exaggeration. There are two ways to do this.

The first method is to construct a cross section without vertical exaggeration (1x). Below this you draw an exaggerated profile according to the amount of vertical exaggeration . For instance, the 2x cross section in Figure 16.16 is drawn twice as deep as the 1x cross section. You then drop vertical lines downward from both the top (dashed) and bottom (thin solid)of the contact lines on the unexaggerated cross section. Now find the spot at which the line from the top intersects the exaggerated profile and the spot at which the line from the bottom intersects the bottom of the cross section. Those spots define the endpoints of the vertically exaggerated contact line.

The second method is to compute the vertically exaggerated dip angles. The equation to do this is:

$$Angle = \tan^{-1}(\tan(dip) \times v.e.)$$

where *dip* is the dip angle and *v.e.* is the vertical exaggeration. The 27° and 35° dip angles in Figure 16.16, for instance, are 45.5° and 54.5° on a cross section with 2x vertical exaggeration. The first computation is:

$$\tan^{-1}(\tan(27^\circ) \times 2) = \tan^{-1}(0.509 \times 2)$$
$$= \tan^{-1}(1.18) = 45.5^\circ$$

SELECTED READINGS

De Floriani, L., Marzano, P., and Puppo, E., "Line-of-sight Communication on Terrain Models," *International Journal of Geographical Information Systems*, 8 (1994), pp. 329-342.

Evans, I.S., "General Geomorphometry, Derivatives of Altitude and Descriptive Statistics," in: Chorley, R.J. ed., *Spatial Analysis in Geomorphology* (London: Methuen, 1972), pp. 17-90.

Lee J., "Analyses of Visibility Sites on Topographic Surfaces," *International Journal of Geographical Information Systems,* 5 (1991) , pp. 413-429.

Moore, I.D., Grayson,R.B., and Ladson, A.R., "Digital Terrain Modelling: A Review of Hydrological, Geomorphological, and Biological Applications," *Hydrological Processes*, 5 (1991), pp.3-30.

Skidmore, A.K., "A Comparison of Techniques for Calculating Gradient and Aspect from a Gridded Digital Elevation Model," *International Journal of Geographical Information Systems*,4 (1989), pp. 323-334.

Spencer, E.W., *Geologic Maps* (Upper Saddle River, NJ: Prentice Hall, 2000).

Wilson, J.P. and Gallant, J.C., eds., *Terrain Analysis: Principles and Applications* (New York: John Wiley & Sons, 2000).

Zevenbergen, L.W. and Thorne, C.R., "Quantitative Analysis of Land Surface Topography," *Earth Surface Processes and Landforms*, 12 (1987), pp.47-56.

CHAPTER SEVENTEEN
SPATIAL PATTERN ANALYSIS

The facts are available to all, but the patterns they form depend upon the point of view of the observer. Surely the patterns are as valid as the facts themselves,because they make rational and comprehensible a way of life which has too often been considered erratic and strange....Though the pattern is made up of facts, it differs from them as an assembled machine differs from a dismantled one.
—Walter Prescott Webb, The Great Plains

17

CHAPTER SEVENTEEN

SPATIAL PATTERN ANALYSIS

When we look at the landscape or its representation on a map, our attention is drawn to the way features are organized spatially. We call this organization **spatial pattern** on the landscape.

There are several ways to analyze quantitatively the spatial patterns you see on maps. One approach is to divide the landscape into a number of **data collection units**, then make **counts** of the number of features within each unit. Each feature you count can then be **weighted** by an **attribute** of the feature, like its age or height, to give a numerical **value** for each count and a **total value** for each data collection unit. Total values could then be **standardized** by dividing the total value by the area of each data collection unit to obtain the **density** within each unit. Maps of counts, total values, or densities show you the spatial pattern of feature abundance across the landscape.

Another aspect of spatial pattern is the **arrangement** of features across the landscape. You may want to know if features are spaced in a random, regular, or clustered manner. These arrangements may be easy for you to see on the map, but there are mathematical measures of randomness, regularity, and clustering that you can use to describe these types of arrangements. The degree of **spatial autocorrelation** among features is one of the most widely used measures. Other measures of spatial arrangement give you additional information about how features are positioned on the earth. **Connectivity** measures tell you the degree to which line features are interconnected. The **hierarchy** inherent in a network of linear features can also be studied quantitatively. **Fragmentation** and **diversity** measures show you the degree that area features belonging to each category are aggregated (clumped) with respect to each other.

Let's begin our discussion of spatial pattern analysis by looking at counts of point, line, and area features.

FEATURE COUNTS

Counting the number of features within small data collection units on the earth is the beginning point for spatial pattern analysis. Data collection units, such as counties, census tracts, or city lots, often are irregular in size and shape. They can also be identical in size and shape, such as the 24 square cells in **Figure 17.1.** Counts of point, line, and area features are made within each unit.

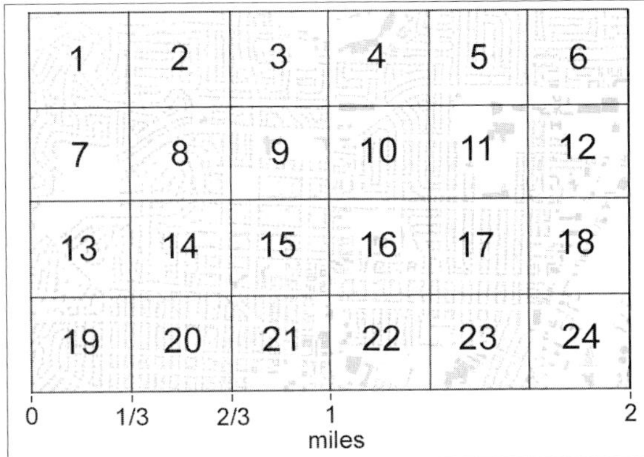

Figure 17.1 Twenty-four data collection units, each one-ninth of a square mile in area, have been placed over a large-scale engineering plan showing building footprints for a portion of Corvallis, Oregon.

Point Counts

Point counts give you information about the **abundance** of features in each data collection unit. When counting point features, you disregard the actual area covered by each. Each building in **Figure 17.2**, for example, is counted as a point (black dot) at its center even though the buildings vary considerably in size. The number printed in the center of each unit is the total number of buildings counted. These counts tell you that there is a wide range (58 to 270) in the abundance of buildings within units. You might next examine the map to see if data collection units with low and high building abundance appear to be clustered together or randomly located on the map.

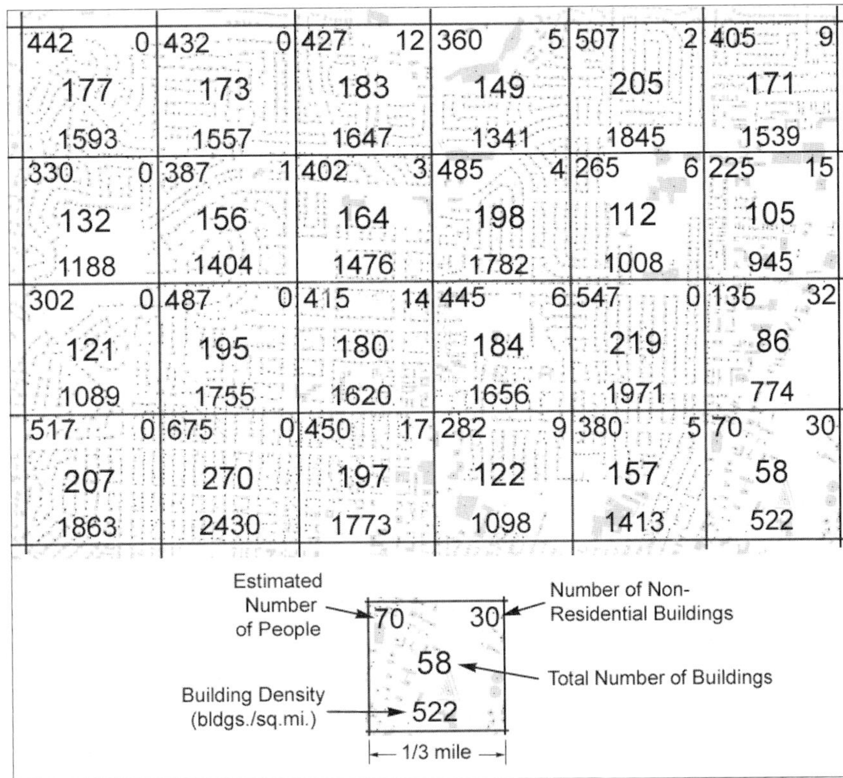

Figure 17.2 Point counts of buildings within data collection units can help you understand the spatial pattern of buildings in a city (see text for explanation).

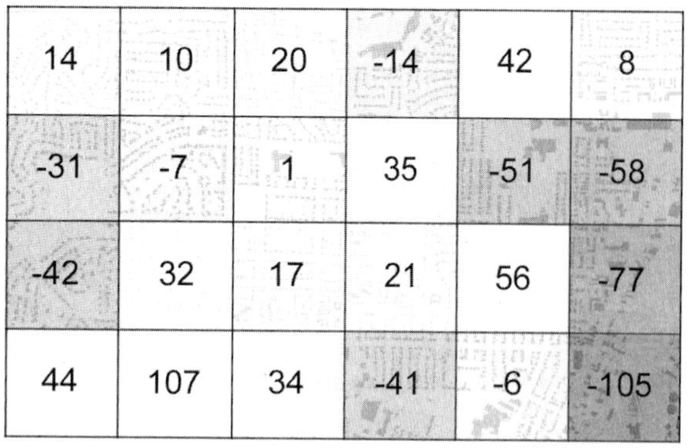

14	10	20	-14	42	8
-31	-7	1	35	-51	-58
-42	32	17	21	56	-77
44	107	34	-41	-6	-105

Figure 17.3 A map of above- and below-average number of buildings in data collection units shows you the relative abundance of buildings. The number in the center of each unit is the positive or negative difference from the average of 163 buildings per unit.

Your search for spatial patterns in the point features on the map may be aided by finding the **relative abundance** of features in each data collection unit. Relative abundance is determined by first finding the average number of features in a unit (163 buildings in this example). You can then identify the above- or below-average units on the map, such as in **Figure 17.3**. There looks to be little spatial clustering of below- and above-average relative building abundance on the map.

You may be able to gain additional information about the features by making point counts of **feature sub-categories**. In our building count example, the sub-categories of residential and non-residential buildings have been counted separately in order to better understand the land use patterns in the city. In Figure 17.2, the number of non-residential buildings is printed in the upper-right corner of each data collection unit. The sub-category counts show you that the largest number of non-residential buildings occur in the two units at the lower-right corner of the map that have the lowest total number of buildings. You can also see that the units with the largest total number of buildings have 0 non-residential buildings, and that there appears to be an inverse relationship between the total number of buildings and the number of non-residential buildings in a data collection unit.

The relationship between residential and non-residential buildings can also be studied by computing the **percentage** of non-residential buildings in each data collection unit. Dividing the number of non-residential buildings by the total number of buildings in a unit, and then multiplying this proportion by 100, you will find that most of the units are between 0 and 10% non-residential. The exception is the two units with the smallest total number of buildings, which are 37% and 52% non-residential.

Another thing you can do is **weight** each point count by the value of some **attribute** of the feature. For example, let's assume that, on average, 2.5 people live in each residential building. You would weight each count by 2.5 (each count now has a value of 2.5), then sum the weighted counts to get an estimate of the number of people residing in each data collection unit. In Figure 17.2, these population estimates are printed in the upper left corner of each unit. This is an example of equal weighting of counts, but for most attributes the weights will be different for each count. The market value of each building rarely will be exactly the same, for instance.

When analyzing feature count data, you normally will adjust for differences in the sizes of data collection units. The square units in Figure 17.1 require no adjustment since each is $1/3^{rd} \times 1/3^{rd}$ mile, or $1/9^{th}$ of a square mile in area. Data collection units such as counties and census tracts vary widely in surface area, however. In either case, you should divide the number of features counted by the area of the data collection unit to get a **feature density** value for the unit. In Figure 17.2, you would divide the number of houses in each unit by $1/9^{th}$ of a square mile to obtain the building density per square mile. These density values are printed at the bottom center of each zone. In this example the building densities are directly proportional to the building count, but density values will be noticeably different for data collection units varying widely in size.

Line Counts

Linear features are counted within data collection units in the same manner as point features. You first disregard the width of each feature and treat it as a one-dimensional straight or curved line. The double-line representation of streets on the left map in **Figure 17.4**, for instance, is replaced by street **centerlines** when making line counts. This simplification of each street is appropriate since the width of each street on the map usually is exaggerated to make streets easily visible on the map. The centerline is a better representation of the actual location of the street on the ground.

Counting the number of streets in each data collection unit seems a simple task, but there is a problem. The full length of a street may cross several data collection units, so you must choose whether to count the street in each unit or only in the unit where most of the street lies. You can get around this problem by breaking each street into **segments**. A segment is the portion of the street between two adjacent intersections, or between the intersection of a dead-end street and its endpoint. In Figure 17.4, we chose to count street segments falling completely or partially within each unit. These are marked with black dots, with the total number printed in the upper-right corner of each data collection unit.

You would expect that the middle-left data collection unit with 19 street segments would have a much lower abundance of streets than the bottom-middle unit with 39 street segments. The 39 count is misleading, however, since it includes numerous small pieces of streets on the boundary of the unit. To lessen this problem, you could define a **minimum distance tolerance**, below which a street segment is not counted.

Linear features like streets can be broken into sub-categories for the purpose of learning more about the spatial nature of the features. You can gain an understanding of the historical development of subdivisions in a city, for instance, by counting the number of dead-end streets in each data collection unit, particularly streets ending in cul-de-sacs. Units with an abundance of dead-end streets were probably constructed from the 1970s to the present, whereas a grid pattern of intersecting streets indicates an earlier approach to subdivision design. In Figure 17.4, counts of dead-end streets are printed in the upper-left corner of each data col-

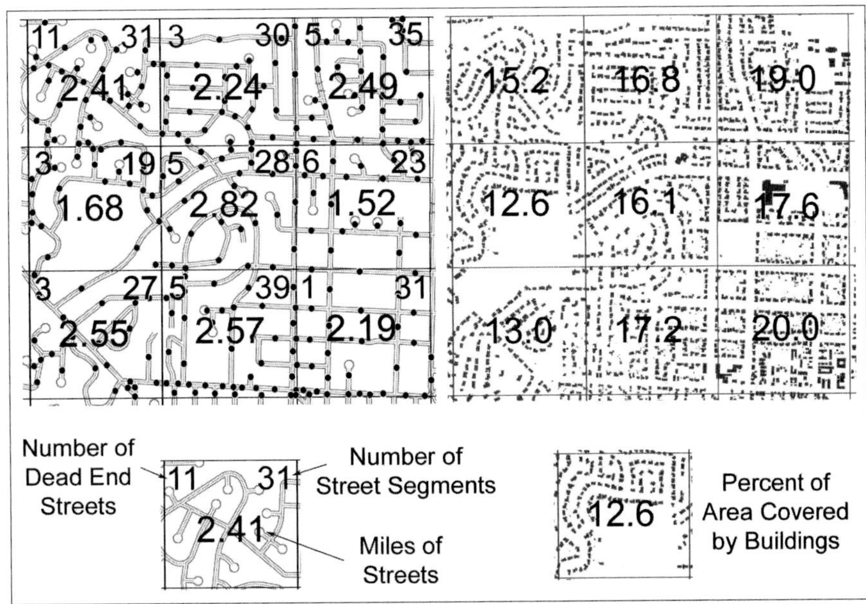

Figure 17.4 Line counts within data collection units include numbers of street segments and total length of streets. The percent of area covered by buildings is a typical area count.

lection unit. Notice the high number in the upper-left unit. This indeed is an area of recent subdivision construction.

Weighting each street segment by its length on the ground may give you more accurate information about the abundance of streets in each data collection unit. If you have determined the street centerlines in a unit, you can use any of the distance measurement methods described in Chapter 11 to determine the length of each street segment in the unit. In Figure 17.4, the total length of street segments is printed in the center of each unit. Notice that the ratio of the difference in total street length (1.68/2.57) is considerably larger than the ratio of total street segments between the units with 19 and 39 street segments (19/39). Weighting the street counts by length appears to have adjusted for the large number of small street segments counted in the bottom-center unit.

You may also want to standardize the street length values to adjust for differences in the sizes of data collection units. To do this, you use the total street length values to compute a **street density** value for each data collection unit. Dividing the street lengths by the area of each unit, you will obtain a street density in miles of street per square mile.

Area Counts

You may be able to determine the total surface area of features having areal extent if they are portrayed on the map without size exaggeration. The building footprints shown on the right side of Figure 17.4 were drawn without exaggeration, for example. Using the area computation methods described in Chapter 15, you can compute the map area of each building, then convert map area to ground area if you know the map scale. Making these measurements and doing the map to ground area conversion for the buildings in each data collection unit, we obtained the total ground area covered by buildings in each unit. The percent coverage value printed in the center of each data collection unit is the total area in buildings divided by the $1/9^{th}$ of a square mile covered by each unit and then multiplied by 100.

You should remember that this method of computing area feature sizes works only if the features are portrayed faithfully on the map. Faithful size portrayal should be expected on very large-scale maps such as engineers' plans in the 1:1,000 to 1:10,000 scale range. Generalized buildings and other features drawn larger than their actual size should be expected at smaller map scales.

SPATIAL ARRANGEMENT

The **spatial arrangement** of features within an area is the second aspect of spatial pattern that we want to consider. To clarify what we mean by spatial arrangement, it is convenient to look first at ways to analyze the arrangement of point features. Later we will look at ways to analyze the arrangement of line and area features.

Point Feature Arrangement

Point features are in theory dimensionless. Thus, if we use them to demonstrate what is meant by spatial arrangement, we can focus solely on direction and distance relationships between points and not have to deal with the added dimensions of length and area. There are three basic arrangements of point features—regular, clustered, and random.

The arrangement of a set of point features is said to be **regular** when there is equal spacing between points—that is, when each point is as far away from its neighbors as possible. Square and equilateral triangular grids of points are the most regular on a flat surface. If, for example, the subsurface structure in an oil field were homogeneous, oil wells would likely be regularly arranged to minimize drilling costs yet maximize the area drilled. You would expect the mapped locations of wells to be arranged in a square or equilateral triangular pattern.

When point features tend to be grouped into one or a few small areas, a **clustered** arrangement results. For instance, if an oil company can lease surface rights only to a few small parcels of land over an oil field, it may decide to drill a number of wells clustered together in each parcel and angle the pipes out in different directions under the surrounding area. The wells will be mapped as clusters of closely spaced point symbols.

When there is no apparent order in the spatial arrangement, it is said to be **random.** There is likely to be some clustering and some regularity in random patterns, but not enough so that the pattern as a whole looks either clustered or regular.

Several quantitative methods have been devised to define randomness, clustering, and regularity in spatial distributions. Let's look at three popular measures: variance/mean ratio, Moran I autocorrelation index, and nearest neighbor statistic.

Variance/Mean Ratio

The **variance/mean ratio** is a measure of spatial arrangement based on superimposing a grid of regularly-shaped data collection units called **quadrats** over the study area on your map. Let's employ the square grid of data collection units used for counts of buildings shown in Figure 17.1 as our quadrats. You count the number of features (x) falling within each quadrat, such as the total number of buildings counted in each data collection unit in Figure 17.2.

You next calculate two basic statistics. The first is the **arithmetic mean** ($\overline{x}$) of the quadrat values or counts. The mean is defined as the sum of the quadrat values ($\sum x$) divided by the number of quadrats (n), and is written mathematically as:

$$\overline{x} = \frac{\sum_{i=1}^{n} x_i}{n}$$

The second statistic required is the **variance,** which is defined as the average of the squared deviations of the individual quadrat values from their mean. The equation for the variance is written as:

$$\text{var.} = \frac{\sum_{i=1}^{n} (x_i - \overline{x})^2}{n}$$

The mean and variance for the building count data in Figure 17.2 are 163.4 and 2,116.0, respectively.

Through experimentation, researchers have found that, for a perfectly random arrangement of points, the variance of quadrat values about their arithmetic mean is equal to the mean itself. Therefore, the ratio of the variance and mean for a random distribution is equal to 1.0. For the variance-mean ratio to be close to 1.0, the pattern must meet three conditions: (1) Only a few quadrats will have no population occurrences. (2) A large number of quadrats will have an intermediate number of occurrences. (3) A few quadrats will have a relatively large number of occurrences.

The upper-right map segment in **Figure 17.5** appears to be a random arrangement of point features. The counts within each quadrat total 81, so the arithmetic mean is 81/9, or 9. The sum of squared deviations is:

$$(7-9)^2 + (6-9)^2 + (13-9)^2 + (10-9)^2 + (11-9)^2 + (12-9)^2 + (6-9)^2 + (9-9)^2 + (7-9)^2 = 56$$

This gives a variance of 56/9, or 6.2. The variance/mean ratio, then, is 6.2/9 or 0.7, so the point arrangement is close to perfectly random.

If the point arrangement is characterized by large numbers of both empty quadrats and quad-

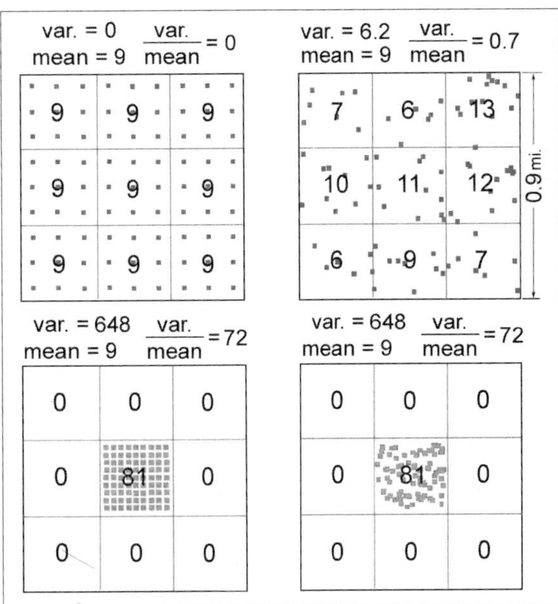

Figure 17.5 Variance/mean ratios for four arrangements of 81 point features within 9 quadrats.

rats containing many individuals, we can say that the distribution is clustered. Since with such a pattern the variance between quadrat values will be greater than the mean of quadrat totals, the variance-mean ratio will become larger than 1. Thus, large variance-mean ratios indicate that individual population occurrences are clumped together in space.

At the opposite extreme from randomness, point features may be arranged in a more regular than random manner. With regular arrangements, the vast majority of quadrats will have similar counts. The variance between quadrat values will thus be less than the mean of quadrat totals, and the variance-mean ratio will be less than 1. Therefore, small variance-mean ratios can be taken as an indication of spatial pattern regularity.

The top-left map in Figure 17.5 has the 81 points arranged in a square grid so that each quadrat contains 9 points. The arithmetic mean is again 9, but the variance is 0 since there are no deviations from the mean in the quadrats. The variance/mean ratio is thus 0/9 or zero, the value expected for a perfectly regular arrangment of point features.

The bottom two maps in Figure 17.5 are the same regular and random arrangements as in the maps above them, but the point spacing has been reduced so that all points fall in the center quadrat. The two arrangements have an arithmetic mean of 9, but the sum of squared deviations is now:

$$8 \times (0\text{-}9)^2 + (81\text{-}9)^2 = 8 \times 81 + 5{,}184 = 5{,}832$$

The variance is now computed as 5,832/9 or 648, giving a variance/mean ratio of 648/9 or 72 for both maps. This high value indicates a tightly clustered arrangement.

Let's now compute the variance/mean ratio for the building counts in Figure 17.2, using the data collection units as quadrats. You will find the arithmetic mean for the 24 quadrats to be 163.4 buildings and the variance to be 2,116. This gives a variance/mean ratio of 13, which indicates a slightly clustered arrangement of buildings in this part of the city.

The variance/mean ratio gives you a mathematical way to describe the arrangement of a spatial pattern, but it does have drawbacks. One criticism is that the terms "random," "clustered," and "regular" are somewhat deceptive since they really refer to variations in the quadrat data values. They don't refer to the spatial pattern of features on the ground from one quadrat to the next, as you might expect. Since the relative location of quadrats having different numbers of population occurrences isn't considered in the computations, the resulting measure of arrangement is non-geographic in nature.

Another criticism of the variance-mean ratio is that its ability to detect non-randomness depends on the quadrat size used in the analysis. In apparently random or regular arrangements, the quadrat analysis may indicate clustering as the size of the quadrats is steadily increased. The most marked demonstration of this problem occurs when the quadrats have an area about the same size as the area of the spatial grouping of population elements, as in the bottom maps in Figure 17.5.

This relationship between quadrat size and the ability to detect clustering can be put to good use, however. Merely by computing the variance/mean ratio several times with quadrats of different sizes, you can determine at what scale clustering occurs. This ability is important because it lets you detect non-randomness in a distribution when visual inspection alone may reveal no sign of clustering. In other words, the human eye seems to use a built-in quadrat size in judging pattern arrangement.

Moran I Autocorrelation Index

There are ways to define uniform, clustered, and random arrangements quantitatively that take the spatial locations of quadrats into account. One commonly used method is to compute the degree of spatial autocorrelation among the features. Spatial autocorrelation deals with the degree to which features on the earth's surface are both spatially and numerically similar to other features located nearby. The notion that there is a high degree of spatial autocorrelation in the arrangement of many features underlies what is called Tobler's First Law of Geography: "Everything is related to everything else, but closer things are more related than distant things."

A commonly used measure of spatial autocorrelation is called the **Moran I** index. As with the variance/mean ratio, you begin by superimposing a grid of regularly-shaped quadrats over the study area on your map. You again count the number of features (x) falling within each quadrat, such as the total number of buildings counted in each data collection unit in Figure 17.2. You then determine the arithmetic mean and variance for your counts.

The next step is to compare the values for each quadrat with values in the other quadrats. If the First Law of Geography is valid, you would expect to see that adjacent quadrats have similar values and that the similarity decreases as the distance between quadrats increases. You can see if this relationship of similarity to distance holds true by measuring what statisticians call the **covariance** between pairs of quadrats.

Covariance is a measure of the degree to which the values for each quadrat deviate from the arithmetic mean for all quadrats. The equation used to compute covariance for quadrats i and j is:

$$\text{cov}_{ij} = \left(x_i - \bar{x}\right)\left(x_j - \bar{x}\right)$$

To find the covariance for the building count values in data collection units 1 and 2, for instance, you would do the following calculation:

$$\text{cov}_{12} = (177 - 163.4)(173 - 163.4) = 130.6$$

Covariance values (rounded to the nearest whole number) for all combinations of the 24 data collection units in Figure 17.1 are presented as a table in **Figure 17.6**. This table is read like the mileage table you may have used on a state highway map or road atlas. The covariance value for units 1 and 2, for example, is read at the top of the leftmost column as 131.

Notice that the covariance values are both positive and negative numbers. Large negative covariances indicate a large difference in quadrat values, with one value above and the other below the average. Large positive covariances are computed when both quadrat values are similar in that both are well above or well below the average.

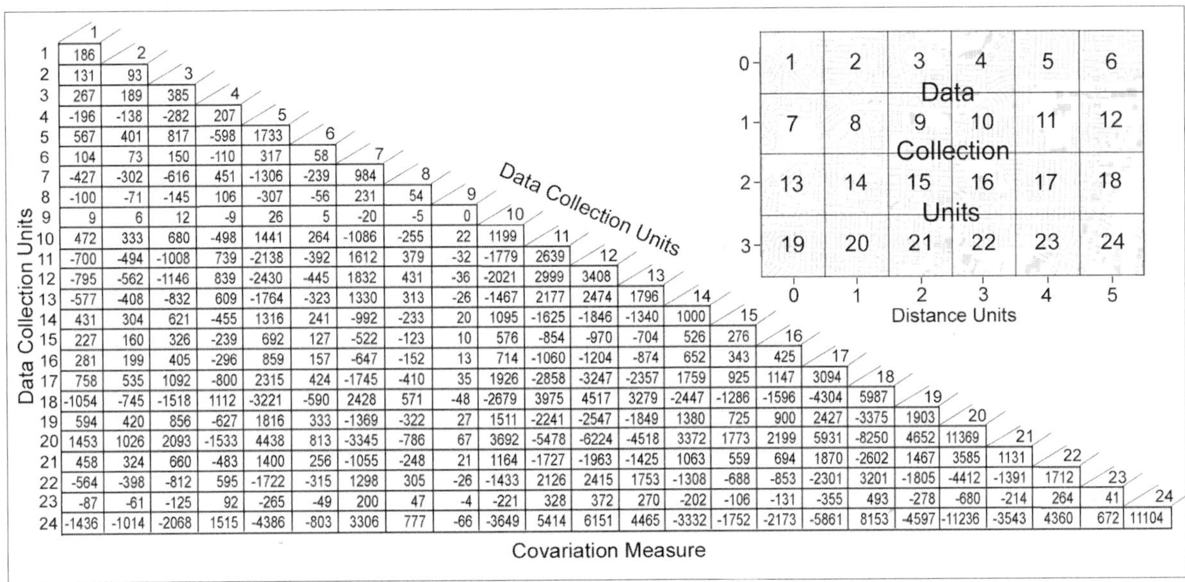

Covariation Measure — Data Collection Units (rows) × Data Collection Units (columns)

	1	2	3	4	5	6	7	8	9	10	11	12	13	14	15	16	17	18	19	20	21	22	23	24
1	186																							
2	131	93																						
3	267	189	385																					
4	-196	-138	-282	207																				
5	567	401	817	-598	1733																			
6	104	73	150	-110	317	58																		
7	-427	-302	-616	451	-1306	-239	984																	
8	-100	-71	-145	106	-307	-56	231	54																
9	9	6	12	-9	26	5	-20	-5	0															
10	472	333	680	-498	1441	264	-1086	-255	22	1199														
11	-700	-494	-1008	739	-2138	-392	1612	379	-32	-1779	2639													
12	-795	-562	-1146	839	-2430	-445	1832	431	-36	-2021	2999	3408												
13	-577	-408	-832	609	-1764	-323	1330	313	-26	-1467	2177	2474	1796											
14	431	304	621	-455	1316	241	-992	-233	20	1095	-1625	-1846	-1340	1000										
15	227	160	326	-239	692	127	-522	-123	10	576	-854	-970	-704	526	276									
16	281	199	405	-296	859	157	-647	-152	13	714	-1060	-1204	-874	652	343	425								
17	758	535	1092	-800	2315	424	-1745	-410	35	1926	-2858	-3247	-2357	1759	925	1147	3094							
18	-1054	-745	-1518	1112	-3221	-590	2428	571	-48	-2679	3975	4517	3279	-2447	-1286	-1596	-4304	5987						
19	594	420	856	-627	1816	333	-1369	-322	27	1511	-2241	-2547	-1849	1380	725	900	2427	-3375	1903					
20	1453	1026	2093	-1533	4438	813	-3345	-786	67	3692	-5478	-6224	-4518	3372	1773	2199	5931	-8250	4652	11369				
21	458	324	660	-483	1400	256	-1055	-248	21	1164	-1727	-1963	-1425	1063	559	694	1870	-2602	1467	3585	1131			
22	-564	-398	-812	595	-1722	-315	1298	305	-26	-1433	2126	2415	1753	-1308	-688	-853	-2301	3201	-1805	-4412	-1391	1712		
23	-87	-61	-125	92	-265	-49	200	47	-4	-221	328	372	270	-202	-106	-131	-355	493	-278	-680	-214	264	41	
24	-1436	-1014	-2068	1515	-4386	-803	3306	777	-66	-3649	5414	6151	4465	-3332	-1752	-2173	-5861	8153	-4597	-11236	-3543	4360	672	11104

Figure 17.6 Covariance values for all combinations of the 24 data collection units used in the building count example. The diagram is read like a mileage table on a road map, with rows being the first unit and columns the second.

The next step in computing the Moran index is to weight the covariance values by the physical distances between the pairs of quadrats. You do this by first computing the distances (*d*) using the coordinate equation form of the Pythagorean theorem described in Chapter 11:

where *col* and *row* are the column and row locations of the two quadrats. It is also easiest to use the coordinate system shown on the map in Figure 17.6, where the centerpoint of quadrat 1 is at (0,0) and the distance between adjacent centerpoints is 1.0.

The distance table in **Figure 17.7** is read in the same manner as the covariance table in Figure 17.6. To find the distances between data collection unit 1 and units 2-6, you read downward from the top of column 1 to see that the distances are 1,2,3,4, and 5.

You next compute **distance weights** from the distances in the table. The First Law of Geography suggests that the distance weight should be inversely related to the distance between quadrats —the smaller the distance, the larger the weight. Two inverse distance weighting functions are commonly used:

$$w_{ij} = \frac{1}{d_{ij}} \qquad w_{ij} = \frac{1}{d_{ij}^{2}}$$

We will use the first (left) inverse distance equation to complete our example of computing the Moran index. The distance weights for data collection unit 1 and units 2-6 are computed as 1.0, 0.5, 0.33, 0.25, and 0.20, for example.

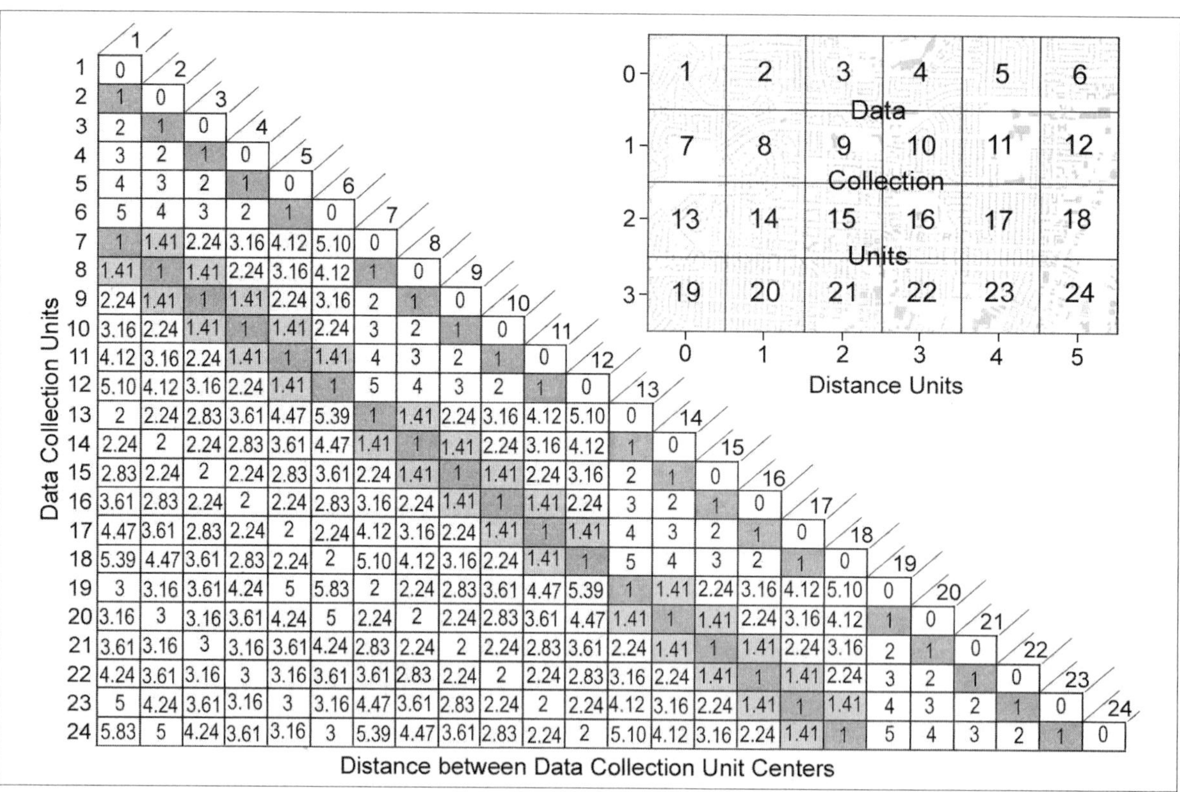

Data Collection Units	1	2	3	4	5	6	7	8	9	10	11	12	13	14	15	16	17	18	19	20	21	22	23	24
1	0																							
2	1	0																						
3	2	1	0																					
4	3	2	1	0																				
5	4	3	2	1	0																			
6	5	4	3	2	1	0																		
7	1	1.41	2.24	3.16	4.12	5.10	0																	
8	1.41	1	1.41	2.24	3.16	4.12	1	0																
9	2.24	1.41	1	1.41	2.24	3.16	2	1	0															
10	3.16	2.24	1.41	1	1.41	2.24	3	2	1	0														
11	4.12	3.16	2.24	1.41	1	1.41	4	3	2	1	0													
12	5.10	4.12	3.16	2.24	1.41	1	5	4	3	2	1	0												
13	2	2.24	2.83	3.61	4.47	5.39	1	1.41	2.24	3.16	4.12	5.10	0											
14	2.24	2	2.24	2.83	3.61	4.47	1.41	1	1.41	2.24	3.16	4.12	1	0										
15	2.83	2.24	2	2.24	2.83	3.61	2.24	1.41	1	1.41	2.24	3.16	2	1	0									
16	3.61	2.83	2.24	2	2.24	2.83	3.16	2.24	1.41	1	1.41	2.24	3	2	1	0								
17	4.47	3.61	2.83	2.24	2	2.24	4.12	3.16	2.24	1.41	1	1.41	4	3	2	1	0							
18	5.39	4.47	3.61	2.83	2.24	2	5.10	4.12	3.16	2.24	1.41	1	5	4	3	2	1	0						
19	3	3.16	3.61	4.24	5	5.83	2	2.24	2.83	3.61	4.47	5.39	1	1.41	2.24	3.16	4.12	5.10	0					
20	3.16	3	3.16	3.61	4.24	5	2.24	2	2.24	2.83	3.61	4.47	1.41	1	1.41	2.24	3.16	4.12	1	0				
21	3.61	3.16	3	3.16	3.61	4.24	2.83	2.24	2	2.24	2.83	3.61	2.24	1.41	1	1.41	2.24	3.16	2	1	0			
22	4.24	3.61	3.16	3	3.16	3.61	3.61	2.83	2.24	2	2.24	2.83	3.16	2.24	1.41	1	1.41	2.24	3	2	1	0		
23	5	4.24	3.61	3.16	3	3.16	4.47	3.61	2.83	2.24	2	2.24	4.12	3.16	2.24	1.41	1	1.41	4	3	2	1	0	
24	5.83	5	4.24	3.61	3.16	3	5.39	4.47	3.61	2.83	2.24	2	5.10	4.12	3.16	2.24	1.41	1	5	4	3	2	1	0

Distance between Data Collection Unit Centers

Figure 17.7 Distance table showing the straight-line distance between each pair of data collection units in the building count example. Centerpoints of adjacent units are 1 distance unit apart. Shaded boxes are distances used in the king's (diagonal) case, and the darker shading indicates distances used in the rook's (row-column) case distance weighting.

The second (right) equation is an inverse distance squared weighting called the **gravity function.** It is given this name because the denominator is identical to that used by Newton in his equation for the strength of gravity between two objects distance *d* apart. The gravity function greatly reduces the weight for distant pairs of quadrats. The weights for unit 1 and units 2-6 are now computed as 1.0, 0.25, 0.11, 0.06, and 0.04, for instance.

The inverse distance weighting is often limited to each quadrat's contiguous neighbors (**Figure 17.8**). Two types of contiguous neighbors are used, named the **rook's case** and the **king's case** because of the similarity to the movements of these two chess pieces. The rook's case is the most restrictive since contiguity is defined by the four adjacent quadrats sharing a row or column edge with the center quadrat. The distances between the centers of the adjacent quadrats are set arbitrarily at 1.0 distance units so that the inverse-distance weights are also 1.0. The king's case includes diagonal neighbors, expanding the neighborhood to eight quadrats. All diagonal distances to adjacent neighbors are the square root of 2, shortened to 1.41 in Figure 17.8. The inverse-distance weights for the diagonal neighbors are thus 1.0/1.41, or 0.707.

All pairs of contiguous quadrats in the our building count example are shaded in Figure 17.7, with the darker shading indicating rook's case neighbors. Notice how few of the total number of quadrat pairs are used in the Moran I index calculation when the neighborhood is restricted to contiguous quadrats.

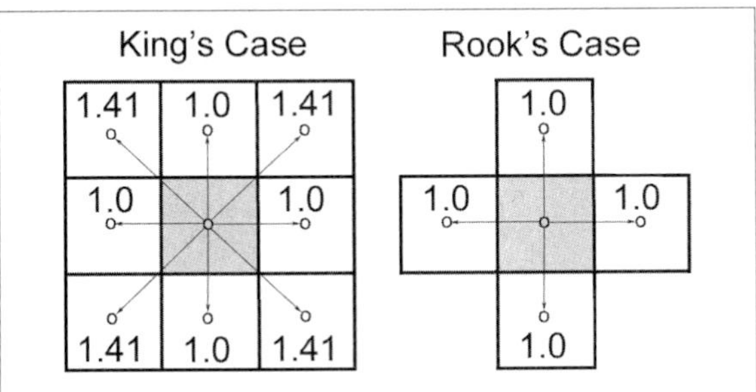

Figure 17.8 Using king's and rook's case nearest neighbors restricts the distance weighting to each quadrat's contiguous neighbors.

The Moran I index is the sum of distance-weighted covariance values for all pairs of quadrats, divided by the sum of distance weights and the variance of the values in all quadrats. The equation used to compute the Moran I index for n quadrats is:

$$I = \frac{\sum_{i=1}^{n}\sum_{j=1}^{n}\left(\text{cov}_{ij} \times w_{ij}\right)}{\left(\text{var} \times \sum_{i=1}^{n}\sum_{j=1}^{n} w_{ij}\right)}$$

Dividing the sum of inverse distance weighted covariance values by the sum of distance weights times the variance is done so that the index can be related to different spatial arrangements. It turns out that the Moran I value expected for a perfectly random arrangement of *n* quadrats is obtained from the equation:

$$\frac{-1}{(n-1)}$$

For large numbers of quadrats, the expected value for a random arrangement approaches 0. Values greater than the expected value are characteristic of clustered arrangements, whereas values less than expected are found with regular "checkerboard" arrangments of high and low quadrat values.

In our building count example, the expected Moran I value is -1/23 or -0.0435. The following values were computed for the four distance weighting options discussed above:

1/d weight for all quadrats:	0.0065
1/d² weight for all quadrats:	0.0549
1/d weight for king's case:	0.0736
1/d weight for rook's case:	0.1781

All of these Moran I values show the spatial arrangement of building counts in the 24 quadrats to be slightly more clustered than random. But notice the large range in the Moran I values computed using the different distance weighting schemes. You can see that the index values increase as the number of quadrats used in the weighting are restricted to contiguous neighbors. This is a drawback of the method—the index values depend on the distance weighting scheme that you use.

Another drawback of the Moran I index is that, like the variance/mean ratio, its ability to detect non-randomness depends on the quadrat size used in the analysis. In an apparently clustered population, the Moran I value may indicate randomness, clustering, and regularity as the size of the quadrats is steadily increased.

A third criticism of the Moran I autocorrelation index is that the spatial arrangement of values within quadrats is being measured, not the actual locations of point features. Studying the spatial arrangement of a set of locations requires the use of another measure, the **nearest neighbor statistic**.

Nearest Neighbor Statistic

A second component of spatial arrangement is **spacing**, defined as the locational arrangement of objects with respect to each other rather than relative to quadrats. Thus, spacing is independent of any boundary one might draw around the points. We can measure spacing by finding the distance between each point feature and its **nearest neighbor.**

The average distance of point features from their neighbors is called the **average spacing**. To compute this statistic, you first have to calculate the distance between all pairs of points using the distance equation (see Determining Distance by Coordinates in Chapter 11). You can then determine which point feature is the nearest neighbor.

Nearest neighbors and distances for seven points are shown in **Figure 17.9**. Notice that the distance from two pairs of points to their nearest neighbors is **reflexive**. This means that point A is the nearest neighbor of point B, and point B is also the nearest neighbor of point A. In this example, points 1 and 2 are reflexive, as are points 4 and 5. Usually, however, point B will have some other nearest neighbor, and the relationship between A and B won't be reflexive.

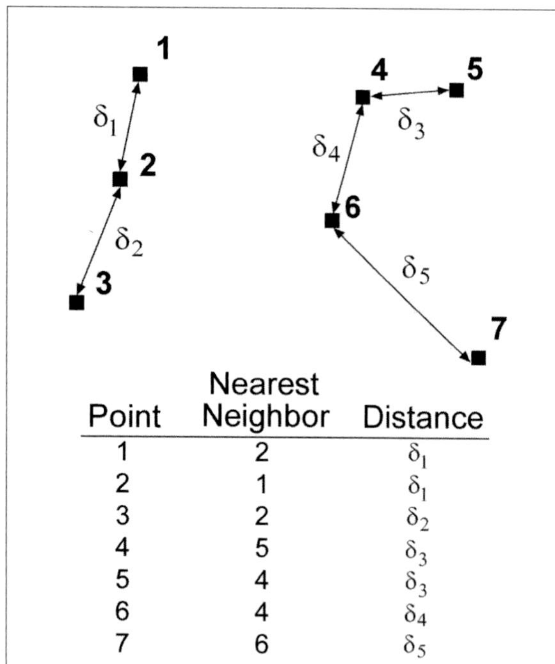

Point	Nearest Neighbor	Distance
1	2	δ_1
2	1	δ_1
3	2	δ_2
4	5	δ_3
5	4	δ_3
6	4	δ_4
7	6	δ_5

Figure 17.9 Nearest neighbors and distances for seven point features.

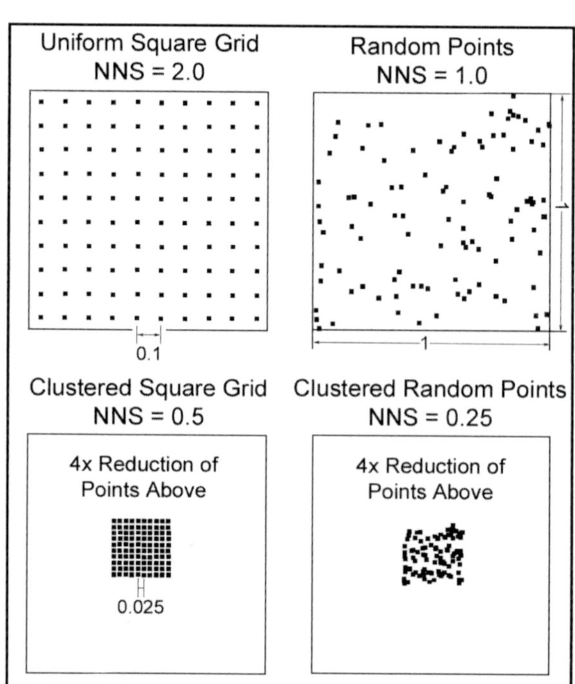

Figure 17.10 Nearest neighbor statistics for four different point patterns, each within a square region 1 square inch in area.

The average spacing (r) is computed by summing the nearest-neighbor distances (δ_i) and dividing the total by the number of points (n). This is written mathematically as:

$$r = \frac{\sum_{i=1}^{n} \delta_i}{n}$$

The nearest neighbor statistic (NNS) compares the average spacing with the expected mean nearest-neighbor distance (*rd*) associated with a random distribution of point features. This distance is computed for *n* points within area *A* using the equation:

$$rd = 0.5 \times \sqrt{\frac{A}{n}}$$

which has been derived by researchers who have studied many random point patterns.

The nearest neighbor statistic equation is the ratio between actual mean distance and expected mean distance for a random arrangement. This is written mathematically as:

$$NNS = \frac{r}{rd}$$

where
NNS = 0 implies maximum clustering,
NNS = 1 indicates a random arrrangment, and
NNS = 2.14 implies maximum regularity (a regular equilateral triangular arrangement).

Applying the nearest neighbor equation to the four point patterns in **Figure 17.10**, we obtain the NNS values shown at the top of each box. Each box is 1 square inch in area and contains 100 point features. The expected mean distance for a random arrangement is computed as:

$$rd = 0.5 \times \sqrt{\frac{1.0in^2}{100}} = 0.5 \times 0.1in = 0.05in$$

The top-left box contains a uniform square grid of points spaced at 0.1 inch increments. The average spacing for these points is:

$$r = \frac{\sum_{i=1}^{100} 0.1in}{100} = \frac{10in}{100} = 0.1in$$

These values give an NNS of 0.1/0.05, or 2.0 for this regular arrangement of point features.

The top-right box contains 100 randomly placed points as determined from a random number generation computer program. This program also found the nearest neighbor and distance for each point from the (x,y) coordinates for the random points. The average spacing was computed as 0.501", giving an NNS of 0.0501"/0.05", or 1.0 for the random point arrangement.

The bottom two boxes contain the same points as the top boxes, but at a 4× scale reduction. The average spacing for the lower-left box is thus 0.025", giving an NNS of 0.025"/0.05", or 0.5. This value is characteristic of a clustered point arrangement. For the lower-right box, the average spacing is 0.0125", giving an NNS of 0.0125"/ 0.05", or 0.25, indicating a tightly clustered arrangement.

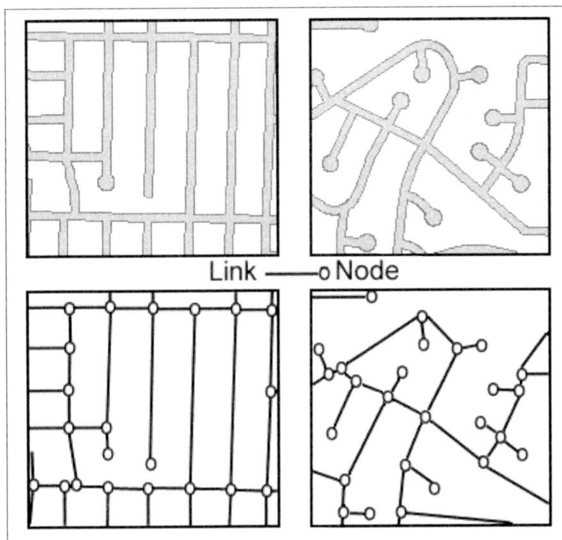

Figure 17.11 Streets, street intersections, and dead ends are links and nodes in a network.

The bottom boxes illustrate the importance of making the bounding area just enclose all point features. If we reduce the boxes at the bottom of Figure 17.10 to 1/16th of their original size so as to just enclose each set of points, the NNS will be 2.0 for the lower-left arrangement and 1.0 for the lower-right arrangment. The arrangements within these smaller regions will now be correctly characterized as regular and random.

Line Feature Arrangement

Line counts or values within quadrats can be used to compute the variance/mean ratio or the Moran I autocorrelation index. In our building count example, you can see if the number of street segments or the total miles of streets in quadrats are arranged in a random, clustered, or regular manner. The number of street segments within each of the nine quadrats in Figure 17.4 have an arithmetic mean of 29.2 and a variance of 31.7. The resulting variance/mean ratio of 1.09 indicates a high degree of randomness in the street segment counts.

There are other aspects of line feature arrangement that you can analyze quantitatively. Let's look at two of these, connectivity and hierarchy.

Connectivity

Many landscape features found on maps are linked to other features through a variety of **linear connections.** Roads, rivers, bus lines, airline routes, and a host of other connections link one place with another. The set of places and connections is called a **network.** Although near things are more likely to be better connected than distant things, juxtaposition alone doesn't ensure connectivity. For example, there may be no road or air linkages between adjoining countries despite their common borders. In contrast, places separated by great distance in space may be closely linked, as people who draw drinking water from a river discover when a toxic chemical spill occurs far upstream.

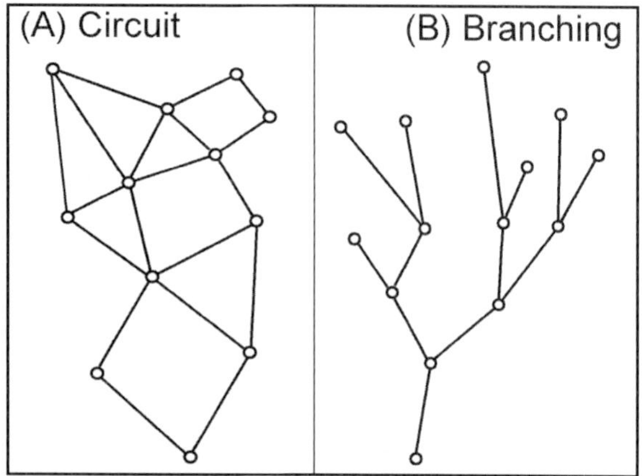

Figure 17.12 Circuit networks (A) are generally more connected than branching networks (B).

In network theory terms, networks consist of **nodes** and **links**. A node is a point at which a line ends or where two or more lines come together or intersect. A link is the linear connection between two nodes. The actual linear connections are represented by straight line links, and nodes are represented by dots (**Figure 17.11**).

Some networks are **totally connected**. In other words, all pairs of nodes are connected by the most direct link. These networks are efficient because direct movements are possible in the greatest degree. Other networks are only **partially connected**. Links between some pairs of nodes pass through at least one additional node and are thus indirect. These networks are relatively inefficient for the traveler because they require indirect movements. Airline "hubs" are a familiar example of partially connected networks: You often find yourself going out of your way to get to a regional hub such as Atlanta or Minneapolis to make "connections" to your destination.

Circuit networks, which have more than one possible path between some pairs of places, are the most connected (**Figure 17.12A**). Least connected are **branching networks** (trees), which have only one possible path between pairs of places (**Figure 17.12B**). When encountering these networks, your curiosity should be aroused so that you seek explanations for why some networks are more connected than others, and what influence these connections will have on communication and hence on other location patterns. Consider, for example, designing residential street networks to minimize through traffic and lower the speed of travel.

There are a number of **connectivity measures** we may use to compare networks with one another and to relate a network's connectivity to the flow of goods and services. One such measure is devised by forming a ratio between the actual number of links between nodes in a network and the maximum possible for a network linking that number of nodes. Often this ratio is multiplied by 100 to provide a measure of the percentage connection in a network:

$$Connectivity(C) = \frac{AL}{PL} \times 100$$

where *AL* is the actual number of links and *PL* is the maximum number possible.

To use this connectivity measure, you need a simple way to determine the maximum possible number of links in a network. You can do so quite readily by counting the number of nodes (n) in the network and then using a formula for the maximum possible number. The problem is that there are three types of networks and hence three different formulas.

In the first type of network, links are **symmetric** (movement occurs in both directions), and links can't intersect without defining a new node. This form is typical of road or railroad networks that don't have one-way segments, overpasses, or underpasses. With such a network, the formula 3(n - 2) defines the maximum possible number of links between n nodes (**Figure 17.13A**).

In a second type of network, links are still symmetric, but they can cross one another without defining a new node. A network of airline routes is a good example, since routes don't connect in mid-air. Overpasses and underpasses in a road network fall in this category as well. With this sort of network, the maximum number of links between n places is given by the expression n(n-1)/2 (**Figure 17.13B**).

A third kind of network is characterized by **asymmetric links**, such as one-way streets, and by links which cross one another without defining a node, as with overpasses or underpasses along a limited-access highway. With such a network, the formula n(n-1) defines the maximum possible number of links between n nodes (**Figure 17.13C**).

Rather than study the connectivity of a network as a whole, you might want to change your focus and determine the connectivity of a particular place with respect to the total network. You may do so, quite simply, by counting the linkages to or from a place. Obviously, in a completely connected network there will be no difference in the connectivity of the various places. In partially connected networks, however, there usually will be variation in the connectivity of individual places: Those with many links will be highly connected to the system, while those having few links will be weakly connected. The next step, of course, is to explain why connectivity varies as it does.

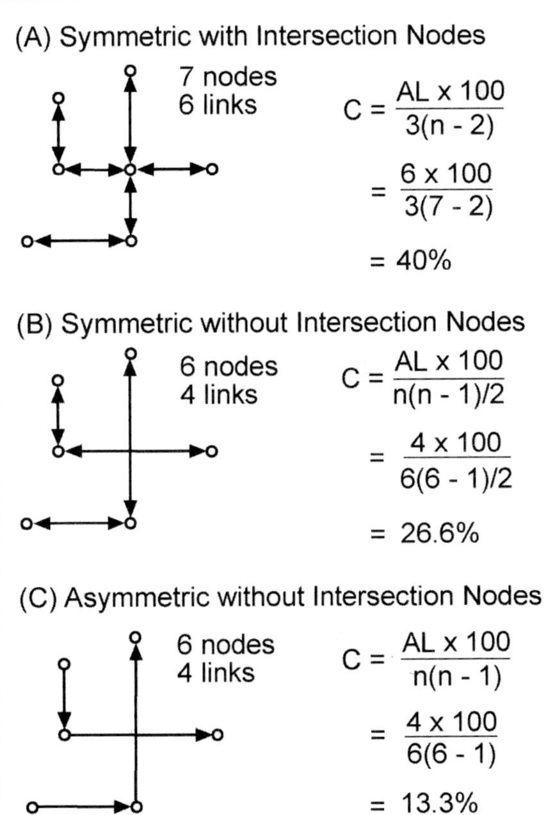

Figure 17.13 By computing the percentage connectivity of different types of networks, we can objectively compare their spatial accessibility.

Hierarchy

The last aspect of line feature arrangement we will discuss is the **hierarchy** of features. Since environmental phenomena differ in size or importance, we can arrange them in a hierarchy. Sometimes this fact is more apparent in the environment than on a map, for maps tend to lump things together and simplify, which masks hierarchical differences. A map may show all roads as thin black lines, for instance, while in reality the roads form a hierarchy from gravel lanes to super highways.

On the other hand, maps sometimes show hierarchies more clearly than the environment does. All railroad tracks look pretty much the same. A map, however, might show railroads in terms of a hierarchy of high to low traffic. Such a map would quickly tell you which tracks accommodated 100 trains a day and which were used by only one train a week.

One way to analyze the hierarchical structure of line networks is to look at the relationship between segments at different **orders of hierarchy** in the network. To do so, it is first convenient to label each level. Stream segments having no tributaries are said to be of the first order (**Figure 17.14**). When two first-order segments join, they form a second-order stream, and so on. In general, the junction of two network links of the same order creates a link one order higher. When two links of different orders join, it doesn't cause a change.

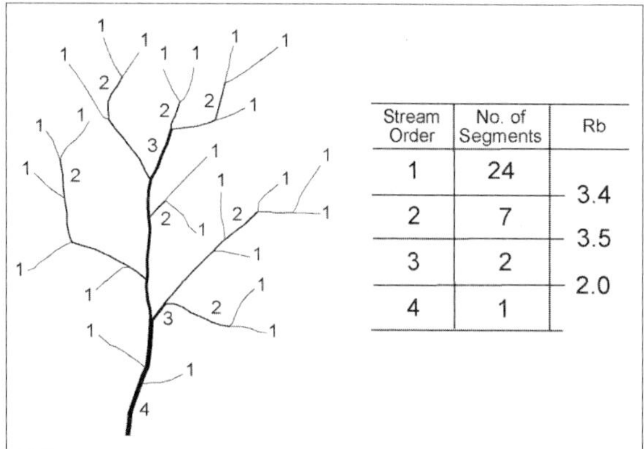

Stream Order	No. of Segments	Rb
1	24	
		3.4
2	7	
		3.5
3	2	
		2.0
4	1	

Figure 17.14 The bifurcation ratio of a branching network provides an objective measure of its hierarchical organization.

Your first step in analyzing a stream network hierarchy is to identify the order of each segment. Colored pencils are useful in differentiating between orders. Once each segment in the network has been classified by its order, your next step is to make a tally of segments falling into each category. This tally will permit you to calculate the **bifurcation ratio (Rb)**, which is defined as the ratio of line segments of one order to the number of line segments of the next higher order. Written symbolically, the bifurcation ratio is:

$$R_b = \frac{N_o}{(N_o + 1)}$$

where N_o is the number of line segments of any order and $N_o + 1$ is the number of line segments of the next higher order. As an example, the bifurcation ratio between first and second order stream segments is found for the drainage basin illustrated in Figure 17.14 by computing the ratio:

$$R_b = \frac{N_1}{N_2} = \frac{24}{7} = 3.4$$

The results of these computations and others in the same drainage system are shown in the table in Figure 17.14. You could compare these results with statistics from other drainage basins to study the nature of different stream systems. The next step would be one of interpretation: You might want to explain any differences that emerge in terms of such factors as geology and climate.

Area Feature Arrangement

The Moran I autocorrelation index can also be used to study the spatial arrangement of area features.The trick is to convert the counts within quadrats into density values. For example, the population estimates for the 24 quadrats in Figure 17.2 can be expressed as number of people per 1/9th square mile.*

**Population densities are usually expressed in people per square mile, but the quadrat area is more meaningful in this example.*

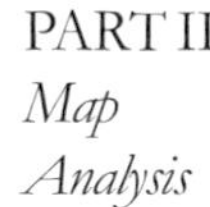

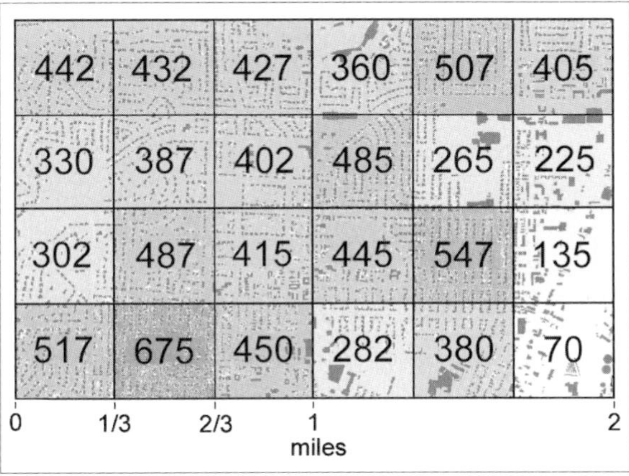

Figure 17.15 Autocorrelation measures can be used to analyze the spatial arrangement of quadrat feature density values, such as these population densities per 1/9th square mile.

Figure 17.16 Section of a landcover map for a forested area north of Corvallis, Oregon.

The resulting population density map (**Figure 17.15**) shows these values with light to dark gray tones representing low to high densities. The density is assumed to be constant within each quadrat. The king's case Moran I index value you would compute for these population densities is 0.0879, which is greater than the -0.0435 expected value for a random arrangement. You would conclude that the quadrat totals have a slightly clustered arrangement, which should agree with the pattern that you see on the map.

Fragmentation

Area feature pattern arrangement can also be studied quantitatively through measures of **fragmentation**. A good example is a landcover map created from remote sensor imagery, such as the map segment in **Figure 17.16**. Each grid cell on the map is placed in one of five landcover categories.

A land manager may want to know the degree of forest fragmentation within the area covered by the landcover map. You can see that some large areas appear to be a single category, whereas other areas seem to be a "salt and pepper" mixture of several categories. You can use a **fragmentation index** to quantify your visual impression of the map.

One widely-used fragmentation index is based on moving a 3 × 3 grid-cell window, or **kernel**, across the gridded map (**Figure 17.17, top left**). At each cell location, the number of different classes found in the neighboring nine-cell kernel is tallied. The total number of categories is then placed in the corresponding center cell to create a **fragmentation map**.

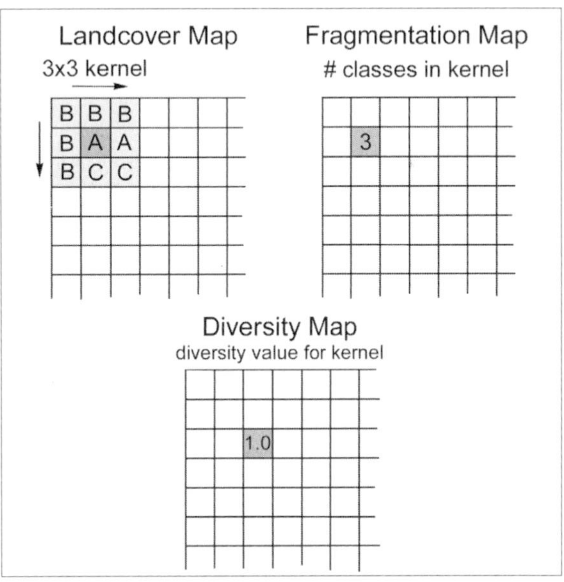

Figure 17.17 A 3 × 3 cell kernel can be systematically moved across a gridded landcover map to obtain the number of classes in the kernel at each cell location on the map. Fragmentation and diversity measures can be computed and mapped from the kernel data.

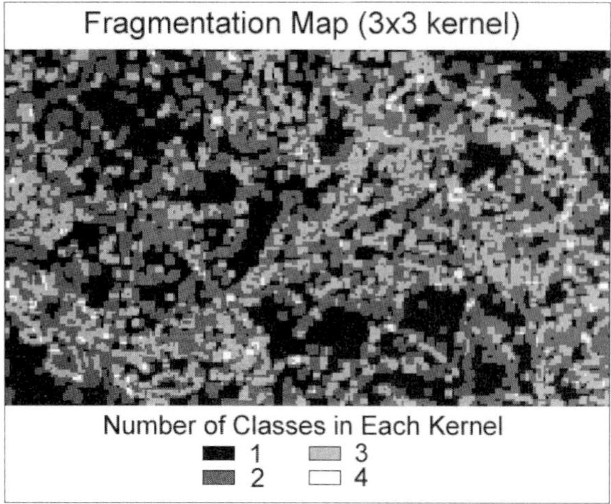

Figure 17.18 A fragmentation map shows the number of map classes found at each kernel position as it is moved across the gridded map.

Sweeping the kernel across the landcover map produced the fragmentation map shown in **Figure 17.18**. Notice that from 1 to 4 classes were found in the different kernel positions, although only 1 or 2 categories were tallied at most positions.

The values in each cell on the fragmentation map are now used to compute an average fragmentation index for the *m* grid cells in the map. The equation used is:

$$F_{avg} = \frac{\sum_{i=1}^{m}(n-1)}{m \times (c-1)}$$

where *c* is the kernel size (9 in this example) and *n* is the number of categories found in the kernel at map position *i*. The equation for our 139 row by 238 column (33,082 grid cell) landcover map example is:

$$F_{avg} = \frac{\sum_{i=1}^{33082}(n-1)}{33082 \times (8)}$$

An average fragmentation of 0.118 was computed for the landcover map. To interpret this number, you must look at the maximum and minimum values possible. It is easy to see that a minimum value of 0.0 is computed when the entire mapped area is of a single landcover category. At the other extreme, a value of 1.0 is reached when 9 or more classes are so fragmented on the map that 9 different classes are tallied at every kernel location.

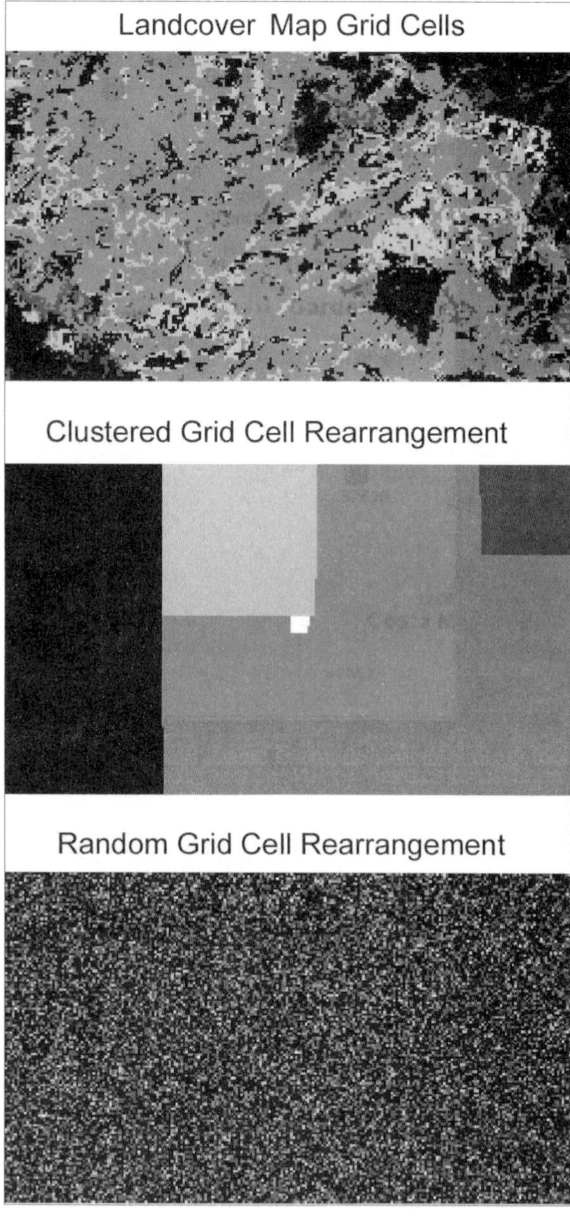

Figure 17.19 An average fragmentation measure value is best interpreted relative to the average values obtained for highly clustered and totally random arrangements of the cells in the landcover map.

A more meaningful interpretation of the average fragmentation index is to compare its value with the minimum and maximum values possible, using the category tally data obtained from the map. The minimum value is estimated by rearranging the cells on the fragmentation map into highly compact regions, such as seen on the middle map in **Figure 17.19**. The value for randomness can be obtained by rearranging the cells into a totally random arrangement, such as on the bottom map in Figure 17.19.

The clustered arrangement has an average fragmentation index value of 0.003 and the random arrangement an average value of 0.247. You can hence interpret the 0.118 average fragmentation for the map as half way between highly clustered and totally random. Does this interpretation of the average fragmentation measure agree with the degree of fragmentation you see on the map?

Diversity

You have seen that the fragmentation index is based on counting the number of categories at each kernel position. A diversity index is a more robust measure of pattern arrangement because the relative abundance of each category is also determined. The widely-used **Shannon diversity** (H) index finds the proportion of each category (p_i) present at each kernel position (Figure 17.17 bottom), then multiplies each proportion by its natural logarithm ($\ln p_i$). These products are then summed and multiplied by -1, using the equation:

$$H = -\sum_{i=1}^{c} p_i \ln p_i$$

for the *c* different categories present at each kernel position.

Figure 17.20 is a diversity map showing Shannon index H values for each grid cell in our land use map example. Notice how similar this map appears to the fragmentation map in Figure 17.18.

The fragmentation map contains the information needed for you to compute the **average diversity** for the mapped area containing *m* grid cells from the formula:

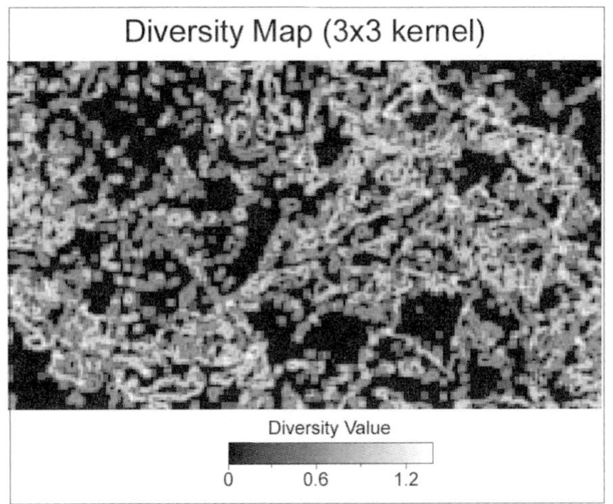

Figure 17.20 Diversity map showing Shannon (H) index values computed in a 3 by 3 kernel for each grid cell in the landcover map in Figure 17.18.

$$H_{avg} = \frac{-\sum_{j=1}^{m}\sum_{i=1}^{c} p_i \ln p_i}{m}$$

The average diversity for our landcover map example is 0.46. The theoretical range of H_{avg} for a 3×3 kernel is from 0.0 where the map is of a single category, to 2.2 where 9 different categories are found at all kernel positions so that p_i is always 1/9. You thus might conclude that the map has a more uniform than diverse grid cell arrangement.

As with the fragmentation index, it is more meaningful to use the diversity range for the collection of categories on the map as the basis for interpreting the diversity value for the map. You could again use the highly clustered and totally random rearrangements of the cells in the landcover map (Figure 17.18, center and bottom) to find this range. If you compute the diversity index for these two maps, you will obtain H values of 0.014 and 0.90. Given the 0.046 average diversity value, you can conclude that the landcover map categories are intermediate in arrangement between tightly clustered and completely random.

In this chapter, we've looked at ways to measure the patterns that features make on our maps. But there's still more to map analysis. Next, we must move our focus from the abundance and arrangement of distributions to spatial associations among different patterns. The comparison of patterns is the topic of the next chapter.

SELECTED READINGS

Barber, G.M., *Elementary Statistics for Geographers* (New York: John Wiley & Sons, 1988).

Boots, B. N., and Getis, A., *Point Pattern Analysis* (Newbury Park, CA: Sage Publications, Inc., 1988).

Davis, J.C., and McCullagh, M.J., eds., *Display and Analysis of Spatial Data* (New York: John Wiley & Sons, 1975).

Ebdon, D., *Statistics in Geography*, 2nd ed. (New York: Basil Backwell, Inc., 1985).

Goodchild, M.F., *Spatial Autocorrelation* (Norwich: Geo Books, 1986).

Haggett, P., and Chorley, R.J., *Network Analysis in Geography* (London: Edward Arnold Publishers, Ltd., 1969).

Lewis, P., *Maps and Statistics* (New York: Halsted Press, 1977).

McGarigal, K., Cushman, S., and Ene, E., *Landscape Metrics: A Comprehensive Guide to Their Use and Interpretation* (2004).

McGrew, J.C., and Monroe, C.B., *An Introduction to Statistical Problem Solving in Geography* (Dubuque, IA: Wm. C. Brown Publishers, 1993).

Monmonier, M.S., "Measures of Pattern Complexity for Choropleth Maps," *The American Cartographer*, 1,2 (1974), pp. 159-169.

Neft, D.S., *Statistical Analysis for Areal Distributions*, Monograph Series No. 2 (Philadelphia: Regional Science Research Institute, 1966).

Rogers, A., *Statistical Analysis of Spatial Dispersion* (London: Pion, 1974).

Taylor, P.J., *Quantitative Methods in Geography: An Introduction to Spatial Analysis* (Boston: Houghton Mifflin Co., 1977).

Wilson, A.G., and Kirby, M.J., *Mathematics for Geographers and Planners* (NY: The Clarendon Press, 1980).

CHAPTER EIGHTEEN
SPATIAL PATTERN COMPARISON

Phenomena intersect; to see but one is to see nothing.
—*Victor Hugo, The Toilers of the Sea*

18

CHAPTER EIGHTEEN

SPATIAL PATTERN COMPARISON

In our analysis of spatial pattern in the previous chapter, the focus was on measuring the abundance and arrangement of a single set of features displayed on a map. We can also compare two or more sets of features found in the same area to determine their degree of **spatial association**. If you can determine where and how environmental features change together across the landscape, you may be able to better explain why this spatial association occurs. When you can describe how environmental features vary together within a geographic area, you can often predict similar associations in other areas.

The suspicion that there is an association between different features located close together is often supported. In some cases the association is direct. Fishermen who realize that underwater features such as weed beds, logs, and large rocks provide protection for fish are likely to have the best "luck", for instance. But the spatial association also may be indirect. Just because two features are found together at the same location doesn't guarantee a meaningful association between them. Both features may be associated with a third phenomenon and not to each other. Continuing our fishing example, trophy fish may be caught along the edge of weed beds because this is where small fish (their food) are found, not because large fish prefer to live close to weeds.

It's difficult to imagine that direct or indirect spatial associations among features in our environment will ever be totally predictable. The ability to predict implies a deep and complete knowledge of the environment that goes beyond what you can see on maps and images. But it may be possible to increase your understanding of how environmental features interact by quantitatively analyzing their degree of spatial association. In this chapter we describe several measures of spatial association between two sets of static features, and then discuss measures of spatial movement and diffusion for dynamic features mapped at several points in time.

TYPES OF SPATIAL ASSOCIATION

There are two basic forms of spatial association. The first is between discrete features. For example, you might look at sets of point, line, or area features in the same geographic area. The closer they are to each other, the greater their spatial association. Or you might detect a spatial association between numerical values computed for features in the same data collection units. When two sets of values increase or decrease similarly within the units, they have a strong **positive spatial association**. A strong **negative spatial association** exists when a high value for the first feature and a low value for the second feature occur in each unit. When there's no systematic spatial relationship between feature values, you can assume there's no spatial association between values for the two features.

The second basic form of spatial association is between continuous phenomena. For instance, you might look at how two or more continuous phenomena, such as elevation and temperature, change in magnitude at the same time. The highest positive spatial association is when the phenomena reach their peaks and valleys at the same locations. The strongest negative spatial association occurs when one phenomenon is highest where the other is lowest, or vice versa. When there's no systematic relation between magnitudes at different locations, you can assume no spatial association between the two phenomena.

When analyzing relationships between sets of features, you need to be aware of **lagged spatial association**. This occurs when there is a positive or negative association between two sets of features, but one set is shifted systematically relative to the other. Perhaps the most familiar lagged spatial association occurs with streets and houses. Houses are associated with streets, but the two features don't coincide spatially (**Figure 18.1**). The systematic setback from the street for houses is the **lag distance**.

Lagged spatial associations are easiest to analyze when only one direction is involved. For instance, the best place for catching large fish consistently might be in deep water close to weed beds. Similarly, paper mills might be found upwind of zones of air pollution, and farmsteads on the Great Plains might be found downwind of shelterbelts.

Lagged associations are more complex and harder to analyze when several directions are involved, which is commonly the case. Lake water quality may be associated with many landscape features in the surrounding watershed. Soils, terrain slope, precipitation, vegetative cover, agricultural practices, urban development, and other factors may contribute to the overall water quality.

JUDGING SPATIAL ASSOCIATION VISUALLY

For centuries, people have used subjective visual judgments to define the spatial association between two sets of point features on maps. The method continues to be popular, largely because it's so natural and easily performed. You might describe relations between two mapped sets of point features

Figure 18.1 Spatial correspondence between two categories of features is often used as an indicator of their degree of association, but it is important to check for lagged spatial association. Notice the systematic shift in position of houses relative to street centerlines.

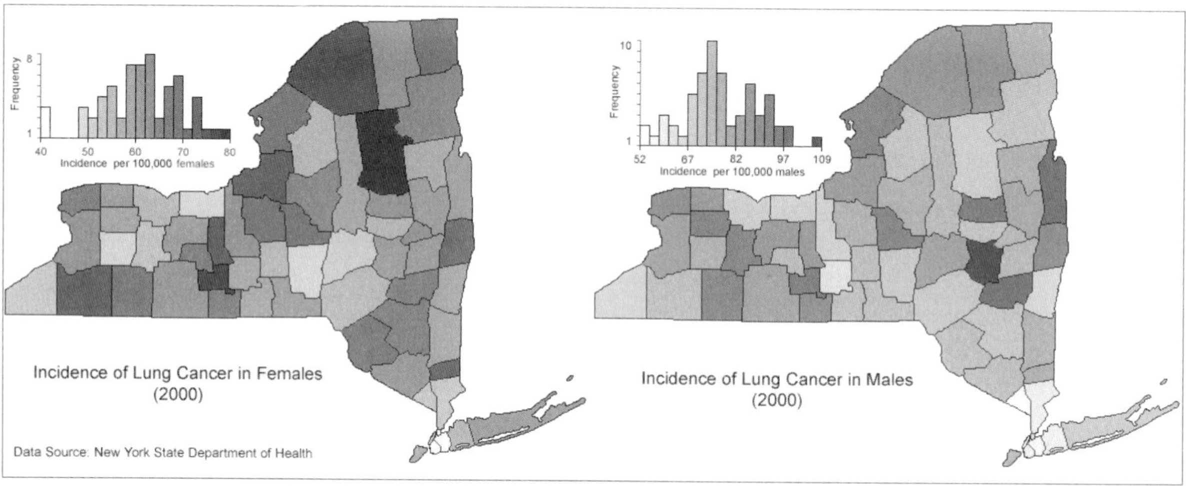

Figure 18.2 Choropleth maps showing the incidence of lung cancer in females (left) and males (right) for New York counties in 2000.

as having a "high correlation," a "poor correspondence," or "a moderate association." Since the meaning of such phrases isn't clear, however, other people won't know exactly what you mean.

Visual judgments of spatial association are easiest to make when the features being compared are superimposed. It makes little difference whether the two sets of features are printed on the same map, or if one set is plotted on a clear medium that is overlaid on the set.

It's not always possible, however, to superimpose the features. It's often necessary to compare maps in a side-by-side arrangement—a chore that requires looking from one map to the other while keeping track of the relative spatial positions of features on the respective maps. Map comparison is simplified, of course, if the maps to be compared are on the same map projection at the same scale and orientation. When this isn't the case, it may be worth your effort to rescale (enlarge or reduce) and reorient one of the maps to match the second.

Another way to compare maps visually is to view them in an alternating time sequence, as when they're toggled on a computer screen. Although the relative effectiveness of this technique isn't known, the method is increasing in popularity as computer map displays have become commonplace.

Make your own visual observations by comparing the two choropleth maps in **Figure 18.2**. These maps of lung cancer incidence in females and males were created from incidence rates published in 2000 by the New York State Department of Health. On these maps, the range of county (including New York City boroughs) lung cancer incidence rates (incidence per 100,000 females or males) was divided into 20 categories for females and 19 categories for males. Notice that on both maps the same light-to-dark gray-tone progression was used to show the categories. Your task is to describe the spatial associations between female and male lung cancer incidence in New York.

What do these maps tell you? First, you probably see that the incidence of lung cancer is higher overall for males, so you must mentally adjust for the difference betweeen males and females on the two maps. You may then see a large number of counties with intermediate lung cancer incidence rates for both males and females. You may next see that there are a few areas where the incidence of lung cancer is low for both females and males. But there also are areas with high incidence rates for both sexes. Finally, you probably notice that there are a number of areas where the incidence rate is high for males or female, but not both.

SPATIAL ASSOCIATION MEASURES

Your list of observations made by comparing the two maps is an important first step in describing spatial associations, but visual observations lack quantitative rigor. The problem is that other people may make different observations when viewing the same maps. Without quantitative measures of spatial association, there's no way to tell how similar people's observations are or if some observations are better than others. Visual observations also often lack repeatability—your descriptions of spatial associations may change the next time you compare the maps.

Many quantitative measures of spatial association have been devised over the years. Each was designed to capture the essence of some logical, intuitive way of comparing spatial patterns for a specific purpose. Some of these measures have become so popular that they're used in many disciplines to serve an even broader range of purposes.

Table 18.1 Lung Cancer Incidence Rates in New York Counties (incidence per 100,000 people)

	Female	Male		Female	Male
Albany	61.8	75.4	Niagara	67.1	86.5
Allegany	69.9	92.7	Oneida	64.9	77.1
Bronx	41.7	62.3	Onondaga	68.3	78.1
Brooklyn	40.1	58.4	Ontario	60.3	85.6
Broome	61.7	74.6	Orange	62.3	75.0
Cattaraugus	72.9	75.7	Orleans	61.3	87.0
Cayuga	63.8	67.8	Oswego	72.1	87.8
Chautaugua	53.3	68.3	Otsego	50.7	82.8
Chemung	67.0	89.3	Putnam	72.3	79.7
Chenango	48.9	70.8	Queens	41.9	55.9
Clinton	68.3	78.2	Rensselar	71.8	91.0
Columbia	58.7	65.0	Richmond	59.2	78.5
Cortland	54.5	74.3	Rockland	53.9	53.1
Delaware	55.5	71.4	St. Lawrence	74.5	86.8
Dutchess	59.3	76.8	Saratoga	61.5	80.1
Erie	63.1	83.2	Schenectady	62.8	74.5
Essex	64.7	72.2	Schoharie	61.3	107.1
Franklin	63.5	87.6	Schuyler	77.6	95.8
Fulton	62.3	94.5	Seneca	72.4	85.5
Genesee	59.7	91.0	Steuben	62.8	83.9
Greene	66.9	98.5	Suffolk	63.7	70.3
Hamilton	79.1	68.3	Sullivan	69.5	74.2
Herkimer	58.9	73.3	Tioga	59.5	74.8
Jefferson	69.4	93.0	Tompkins	58.1	61.3
Lewis	54.0	70.6	Ulster	66.7	70.2
Livingston	53.8	92.1	Warren	57.6	76.8
Madison	69.5	91.2	Washington	62.0	98.8
Manhattan	50.4	53.6	Wayne	48.7	69.2
Monroe	55.1	69.2	Westchester	52.3	58.9
Montgomery	54.6	70.6	Wyoming	48.4	78.7
Nassau	57.4	59.5	Yates	66.1	75.0

Most measures of spatial association require you to go back to the datasets from which the maps were made. In our lung cancer incidence example, we obtained the county totals for 2000 from the website for the New York State Department of Health (**Table 18.1**).

The first thing you could do with the county data is find the **average ($\bar{x}$)** male and female lung cancer incidence rates for the 62 counties in New York. Using the equation:

$$\bar{x} = \frac{\sum_{i=1}^{n} county_i incidence}{62}$$

you will find that the average female incidence rate is 62.1 and the average male incidence rate is 77.6 cases per 100,000 women and men, respectively.

You will also want to know the overall variation in the female and male lung cancer incidence rates for the 62 counties. The **standard deviation (σ)** is one of the most widely used measures of variation within a dataset. It is computed by taking the square root of the variance (see Chapter 17 for information on computing the variance) for the n (62) data collection units:

$$\sigma = \sqrt{\frac{\sum_{i=1}^{n} (x_i - \bar{x})^2}{n}}$$

Using this equation, you'll find the standard deviation for the female and male data to be 8.42 and 11.77, respectively. A beginning statistics book will tell you that if the data values are normally distributed in the familiar bell-shaped curve, 68% of the values will fall within 1 standard deviation ($\pm 1\sigma$) of the average.

Notice that the legends for both maps in Figure 18.2 are **frequency diagrams** (histograms) of the lung cancer incidence rates. A frequency diagram shows you the number of data collection units falling within different ranges of data values. The frequency diagrams in the Figure 18.2 map legends clearly are bell-shaped in appearance, so the standard deviation is an appropriate way to quantitatively summarize the variation within the data. Look again at Table 18.1. You will find that for females, 44 of the 62 counties (71.0%) fall within 1.0 standard deviation of the average (between 52.8 and 69.6). The male cancer incidence data are even closer to the 68% value for a perfect normal distribution—42 counties (67.7%) fall within one standard deviation (between 65.8 and 89.3).

The next step is to find a quantitative measure of the geographic correspondence between the counties with high and low female and male lung cancer incidence rates. To do this, you can use a statistical mapping program or geographic information system (see Chapter 19 for examples) to make maps showing the percentage that each county is above (>100%) or below (<100%) the average for the state. The county maps created in this manner for the female and male data are shown in **Figure 18.3**, using the same percentage ranges for each map category to facilitate visual map comparison.

What do the maps in Figure 18.3 tell you? You may first notice that the range of percentages is greater on the male map, with one county having over 130% of the average male lung cancer incidence. You will also see that counties in the New York city metropolitan area are similarly below average in lung cancer incidence for both females and males. Several counties in the north-central part of the state have above average female and male cancer incidence rates, and many counties have above average female and below average male cancer incidence, and vice versa. These observations, based on average values for the state, quantitatively reinforce what you concluded by comparing the two choropleth maps in Figure 18.2.

You may be able to better see spatial associations between female and male cancer incidence rates if you combine the data on a single map. The female versus male map in **Figure 18.4** shows a simple way to do this by simplifying the data into

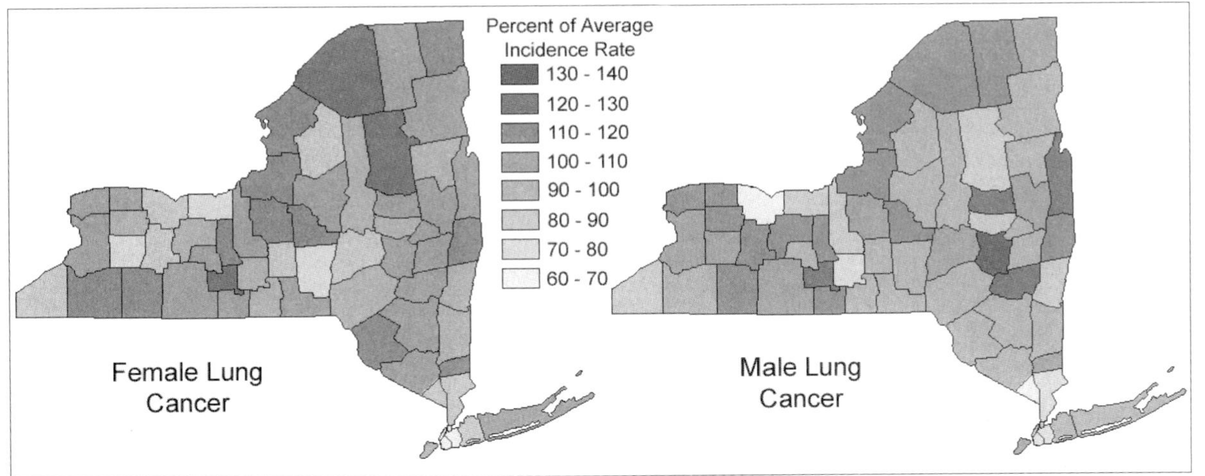

Figure 18.3 Choropleth maps showing the percentage that each New York county is below or above the average female or male lung cancer incidence rate.

four categories. Counties with below-average female and male cancer incidence rates are shown in white. Counties with above-average male and female rates are shown in black. Counties with above-average female and below-average male incidence rates, and vice versa, are shown in two shades of gray. You now clearly see from New York city up the Hudson River Valley a north-south band of below-average counties for both male and female cancer incidence. Counties with above-average male and female cancer rates are concentrated in clusters of counties along the northern, southern, and eastern edges of the state. Between these two bands are many counties that are above average in one gender and below average in the other. Statisticians would say that the counties with either below-average (white) or above-average (black) cancer incidence rates have a **positive spatial association.** Conversely, the gray-toned counties, with high incidence rates for one gender and low rates for the other, have a **negative spatial association**.

The four-category female vs. male map highlights positive and negative spatial associations, but does not tell if the associations are strong or weak. One way to study **strength of association** is to create a **scatterplot** of the data used to make the map. **Figure 18.5** is a scatterplot showing the male and female lung cancer incidence rate data taken from Table 18.1. Notice that the values are clustered in a roughly elliptical area in the top half of the scatterplot. If there was a perfect positive association between the incidence of lung cancer among males and females, their percentages would be identical, and all points would fall along the straight diagonal line defining a perfect positive linear relationship. A perfect negative association would exist if all plotted points fell along the downward sloping diagonal line defining a negative linear relationship. In contrast, a circular, randomly appearing plot indicates that there is no spatial association . The plotted values between male and female lung cancer incidence rates in New York at

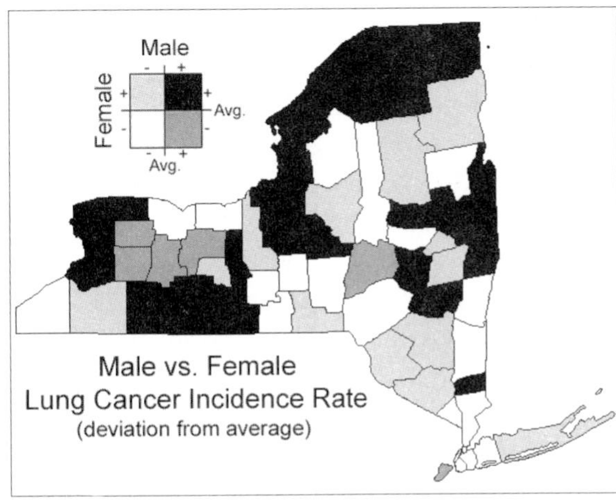

Figure 18.4 This map shows the positive and negative deviation from the average female and male lung cancer incidence rate in each New York county.

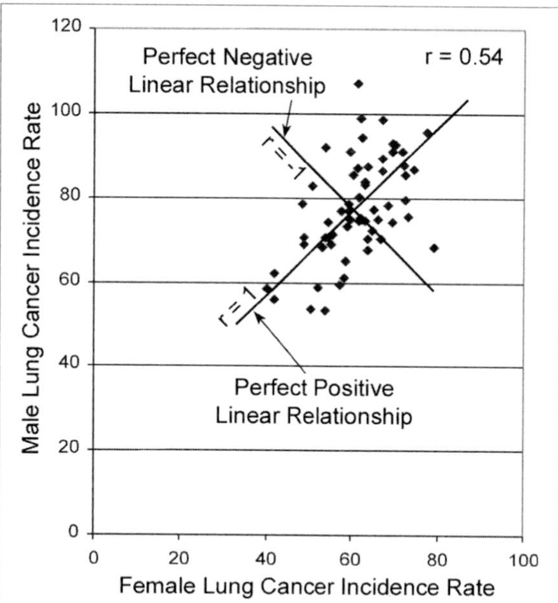

Figure 18.5 A scatterplot of female and male lung cancer incidence data for New York's 62 counties. The correlation coefficient (*r*) indicates the degree of spatial association between the two sets of data.

the county level form an ellipse, with the long axis roughly aligned with the positive relationship line. Thus, you can conclude that, as a whole, there's a definite positive association between female and male lung cancer incidence. This positive association is not surprising, in light of the large number of positively associated counties that you saw in Figure 18.4.

You may now wonder if there is a quantitative measure that shows the overall strength of the spatial association between two sets of point features. Several such **parametric measures** have been developed for normally distributed data like the data in our New York example, but spatial cross-correlation is used most widely.

Spatial Cross-Correlation

Spatial cross-correlation is a measure of the similarity between two different datasets for the same data collection units, such as our lung cancer data for New York counties. The first step in determining the cross-correlation is to compute the amount of **covariance** in the data for each unit. In Chapter 17, you saw that covariance is the product of the amount that the two values for the unit differ from their respective averages. In mathematical terms, the covariance between two data values x and y for a data collection unit is simply:

$$\text{cov.} = (x - \bar{x})(y - \bar{y})$$

The covariance for all data collection units is then summed to obtain the **total covariance**. You then divide this value by the number of data collection units (n) to obtain the **average covariance** for the study area. Finally, the **correlation coefficient** (r) is found by dividing the average covariance by the product of the standard deviations for each dataset:

$$r = \frac{\sum_{i=1}^{n}(x_i - \bar{x})(y_i - \bar{y})}{n\sigma_x\sigma_y}$$

The average covariance is divided by the product of the standard deviations to standardize the correlation coefficient to range between –1 and 1.

Let's do the calculations with the female and male lung cancer incidence data for the 62 New York counties. We have said previously that the average female and male cancer incidence rates are 61.2 and 77.6 with standard deviations of 8.42 and 11.77. Putting numbers into the above equation, we have:

$$r = \frac{\sum_{i=1}^{62}(x_i - 61.2)(y_i - 77.6)}{62 \times 8.42 \times 11.77}$$

From the female and male cancer incidence rates in Table 18.1, you can compute the covariance values for the first three entries, as shown below:

County	Covariance
Albany	(61.8-61.2)×(75.4-77.6) = -1.32
Allegany	(69.9-61.2)×(92.7-77.6) = 131.37
Bronx	(41.7-61.2)×(62.3-77.6) = 298.35

If you compute the covariances for the other counties and sum the numbers, you will find the total covariance for the 62 counties to be 53.25. When you divide this figure by the product of the standard deviations (8.42×11.77) to compute the correlation coefficient, you obtain an *r* value of 0.54.

To see what an *r* value of 0.54 means, let's look at the 1 and –1 limits for the correlation coefficient. For *r* to be 1 for datasets x and y, all pairs of values must be identical and hence fall on an upward-sloping diagonal line defining a positive linear relationship between x and y (see Figure 18.5). Since the equation of this line is $y = x$, the correlation coefficient equation becomes:

$$r = \frac{\sum_{i=1}^{n}(x_i - \bar{x})(x_i - \bar{x})}{n\sigma_x\sigma_x} = \frac{\sum_{i=1}^{n}(x_i - \bar{x})^2}{n\sigma^2} = \frac{\sigma_x^2}{\sigma_x^2} = 1$$

For *r* to be –1, each pair of values is greater and less than the average by the same amount, and thus fall on a perpendicular downward-sloping line defining a negative linear relationship. The equation of this line is $y = -x$, so that $-\bar{y} = \bar{x}$ and:

$$r = \frac{\sum_{i=1}^{n}(x_i - \bar{x})(-x_i + \bar{x})}{n\sigma_x\sigma_x} = \frac{-1\sum_{i=1}^{n}(x_i - \bar{x})^2}{n\sigma_x^2{}_x} = \frac{-\sigma_x^2}{\sigma_x^2} = -1$$

For *r* to be 0.0, the total covariance $(x_i - \bar{x})(y_i - \bar{y})$ must be 0. A covariance of 0 occurs when there is no spatial association between the two sets of values. A scatterplot of values with 0 covariance will look totally random.

Given this understanding of the correlation coefficient, you can conclude that a correlation coefficient $r = 0.54$ indicates a moderate positive spatial relationship between the female and male lung cancer incidence rates for New York counties.

Spearman's Rank Correlation Coefficient

We have seen that cross-correlation is a measure of spatial association based on computing covariance for counts of point features within data collection units. You may wonder if there is a measure based on the individual locations of the two types of features, rather than total feature counts within areas. Statisticians have indeed devised measures of the **independence** between two sets of point features. Let's look at a simple measure based on calculating the distance between nearest neighbors for both sets of features. These measurements allow you to use what is called **Spearman's rank correlation coefficient** to compute their degree of spatial correlation.

Our example (**Figure 18.6**) is a map of a 10×10 mile area that contains 100 point features of category 1 and another 100 features of category 2. Features in both categories appear to be randomly arranged on the map, so you would assume that their locations are not correlated with each other. To measure the actual degree of correlation, you can place a set of random points on the map. In this example, a random number generator computed 100 random sample points, and we have shown the first 20 by open dots on the map.

For each randomly placed point, you must find the nearest neighbors for categories 1 and 2, and then measure the distance from the random point to both nearest neighbors. The straight lines in Figure 18.6 show the nearest neighbors and distances for the first 20 random points. The nearest neighbors in each category are easy to determine visually, and distances can be measured with a ruler, but computer programs that work with digital point location data are normally used to find the neighbors and compute the nearest-neighbor distances. Such a program was used to compute nearest-neighbor distances for the 100 random points. Distances for the first 10 and the 100th random points are listed in **Table 18.2**.

You next sort the distances to find their **ranks**. In our example, the distances were sorted in ascending order, so that the smallest distance is rank 1 and the largest is rank 100 for both categories. The ranks for the first 10 and last random point are listed in columns 4 and 5 of Table 18.2 .

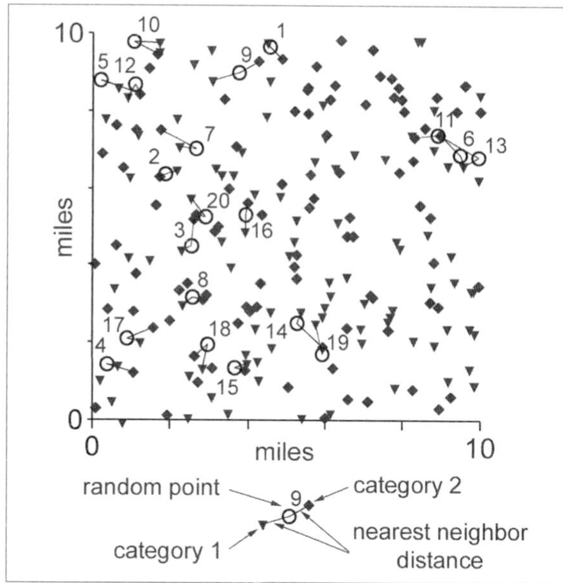

Figure 18.6 Spearman's rank correlation coefficient can be used to measure the spatial association between the 100 point symbols in categories 1 and 2 shown on this map (see text for explanation).

For each random sample point, you next compute the square of the difference between the ranks for the two categories. Column 6 in Table 18.2 shows the equations used to compute each value. These values are then summed to give the total **squared rank difference (D^2)**, which is 181,640 in our example. This (D^2) value is all you need to compute Spearman's rank correlation coefficient.

Spearman's rank correlation coefficient (ρ) is a **non-parametric** measure of correlation. It shows the degree to which the two datasets are spatially independent without having to assume that each dataset has a normal distribution of values. To calculate the ρ coefficient, numerical values must be converted to ranks that are then sorted, just as we have done for the 100 random points.

The equation used for *n* ranks is:

$$\rho = 1.0 - \frac{6\sum_{i=1}^{n} D_i^2}{(n^3 - n)}$$

which for our example is:

$$\rho = 1.0 - \frac{6 \times 181{,}640}{(100^3 - 100)} = 1.0 - \frac{1{,}089{,}140}{999{,}900} = -0.09$$

Table 18.2 Nearest Neighbors, Ranks, and Rank Differences for Computing Spearman's Rank Correlation Coefficient

	Nearest Neighbors Distance		Nearest Neighbors Rank		
Rnd. Pt.	**Cat.1**	**Cat.2**	**Cat.1**	**Cat.2**	**Rank Diff.²**
1	4.26	1.56	53	3	$(53-3)^2 = 2{,}500$
2	2.02	3.46	13	32	$(13-32)^2 = 361$
3	6.26	2.61	77	18	$(77-18)^2 = 3{,}481$
4	6.56	2.65	80	19	$(80-19)^2 = 3{,}721$
5	10.54	4.60	97	46	$(97-46)^2 = 2{,}601$
6	7.84	2.08	86	10	$(86-10)^2 = 5{,}776$
7	10.02	4.89	96	51	$(96-51)^2 = 2{,}025$
8	2.59	2.72	23	22	$(23-22)^2 = 1$
9	5.61	7.29	68	82	$(68-82)^2 = 196$
10	6.24	6.28	76	73	$(76-73)^2 = 9$
.	.	.	.	.	.
.	.	.	.	.	.
.	.	.	.	.	.
100	8.28	3.59	89	36	$(89-36)^2 = 2{,}809$
					$D^2 = \sum_{i=1}^{100}(rank_1 - rank_2)^2 = 181{,}640$

A ρ value of -0.09 is midway in the -1.0 to +1.0 range for ρ This value is very close to the 0.0 value that would be computed for two completely independent datasets. Spatial independence is the expected result, since the positions of all category-1 and category-2 features were determined with a random number generator and thus should be completely independent.

The closer ρ is to 1 or -1, the stronger the positive or negative spatial dependency between the two datasets. A ρ value of 1.0 implies complete **positive spatial dependency**. For ρ to equal 1.0, the total squared rank difference must be 0.0, which happens only when the distance ranks for the two categories are identical. For example, the identical category-1 and category-2 point-feature locations in **Figure 18.7** result in each of the 20 randomly-placed points on the map having identical nearest neighbors. If the nearest-neighbor distances are identical, so are the distance ranks.

Notice that both the regular and random point-feature arrangements in the left and right half of the figure have complete positive spatial dependency. Remember that you are measuring the positional correspondence between two datasets, not spatial arrangement.

A ρ value of -1.0 implies complete **negative spatial dependency** between the locations of features in the two categories. A negative value is obtained only when the ranks are opposite—ascending for category 1 and descending for category 2, and vice versa. Complete negative spatial dependency is rarely found in two sets of point-feature locations, but values of around -0.7 are possible for two regularly-arranged, spatially-lagged datasets.

In **Figure 18.8**, you can see two categories of point features in a square-grid arrangement that are lagged one mile to the east and north. Twenty sample points have been placed randomly on the map so that nearest-neighbor distances can be measured and distance ranks can be determined. You can see that random points close to a category-1 nearest-neighbor location are far away from the category-2 nearest neighbor, and vice versa. **Table**

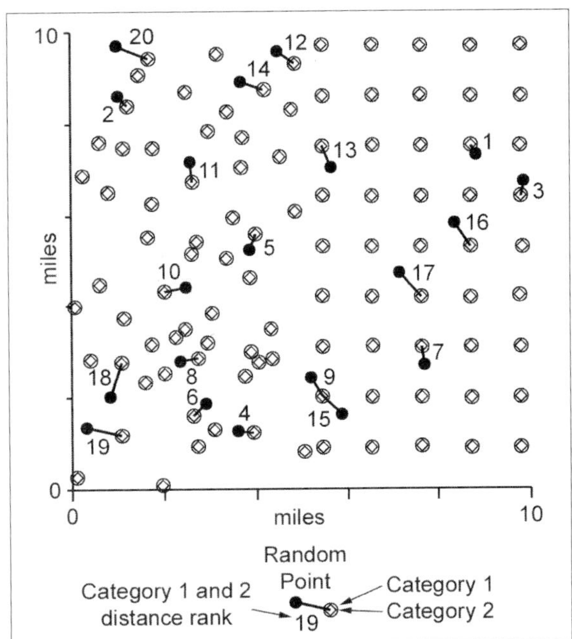

Figure 18.7 When the locations of point features in categories 1 and 2 are identical, the nearest neighbor distances to each randomly placed sample point are identical, as are the distance ranks. This point arrangement gives a Spearman's ρ value of 1.0.

18.3 lists the ranks for the 20 random points, the squared difference in rank values computed from the ranks, and their summed value of 2,252. Notice that the ranks are roughly opposite, but not completely inverse. You can now compute Spearman's rank correlation coefficient as:

$$\rho = 1.0 - \frac{6 \times 2{,}252}{\left(20^3 - 20\right)} = 1.0 - \frac{13{,}512}{7{,}980} = -0.69$$

This ρ value for two regularly-arranged lagged point datasets is probably the greatest negative spatial dependency you can expect to find. The arrangement of real point features on maps is rarely this regular.

LINE-FEATURE SPATIAL ASSOCIATION

You can apply point-feature spatial-association measures to the analysis of two types of line

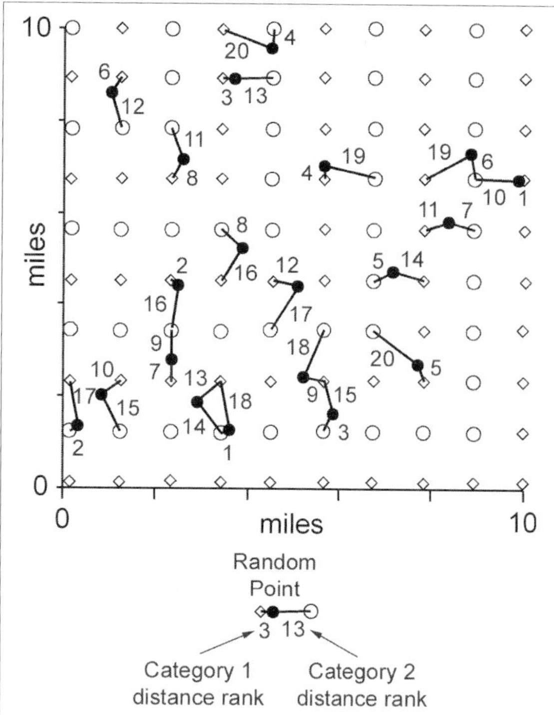

Figure 18.8 Two categories of point features are arranged regularly with a one-mile lag north and east. Notice that when the distance from one of the 20 random sample points to its category 1 nearest neighbor is short, the distance to the category 2 nearest neighbor is long.

Table 18.3 Distance and Rank Data for the 20 Random Sample Points in Figure 18.8

Cat. 1 Dist.	Cat. 1 Rank	Cat. 2 Dist.	Cat. 2 Rank	Rank Diff.²
2.0	1	11.8	10	81
3.1	2	17.3	16	196
4.6	3	14.3	13	100
5.0	4	20.0	19	225
6.8	5	21.0	20	225
6.9	6	13.8	12	36
8.1	7	11.0	9	4
8.2	8	12.4	11	9
8.3	9	19.5	18	81
9.0	10	15.2	15	25
9.1	11	10.0	7	16
9.2	12	19.0	17	25
11.7	13	15.0	14	1
12.1	14	8.1	5	81
12.5	15	7.0	3	144
14.7	16	10.8	8	64
17.0	17	3.7	2	225
18.5	18	3.0	1	289
19.1	19	9.5	6	169
19.8	20	7.7	4	256
			Total	2,252

features shown on separate maps or superimposed on a single map. Seeing associations between line features displayed on maps is again an important first step. If you look at a topographic map of your local area, you may see a high degree of spatial correspondence between line features such as rivers, roads, or Public Land Survey section lines.

Another type of spatial association seen on maps is between different attributes for the same set of line features. For instance, your city's engineering or planning department may have produced a series of street network maps with different features overlaid. Some features may be shown by counts or average values for street segments, usually city blocks. You may be able to find block-by-block information for such things as speed limits, number of parking places, or traffic counts—information that can be compared quantitatively as well as visually.

Let's compare pedestrian and vehicular traffic counts, collected and mapped by city block for downtown Portland, Oregon (**Figure 18.9**). The actual counts have been generalized into five classes that span the range of the pedestrian and vehicle counts. For blocks where counts were taken, thick lines ranging in tone from light to dark show the five classes. The numerical limits for classes aren't the same on the two maps, and not all blocks with pedestrian counts have vehicle counts. Nevertheless, you can visually compare the two maps, looking for positive or negative correspondences between the gray-toned city blocks. You will most likely conclude that there's no spatial association between the pedestrian and vehicular traffic counts.

How can you quantitatively validate (or invalidate) the visual impression that there is no spatial association between pedestrian and vehicle traffic counts? One idea is to identify all the blocks having both pedestrian and vehicle counts (we found 43). You can then think of each map class as a rank from 1 to 5. Treating map classes as ranks allows you to compare pedestrian and vehicle count ranks for the 43 blocks by computing Spearman's rank correlation coefficient. Let's see how to do this.

Pedestrian and vehicle count ranks for the 43 blocks are listed in **Table 18.4**. Unfortunately, you can't use the five ranks as numbers from 1 to 5 because each rank appears several times in the table (a consequence of generalizing the data into five classes). You need to find what is called the **average rank** for each class. To see how to compute average ranks, let's look at the first two pedestrian count classes. Notice that 2 blocks are in class 1, and 14 blocks are in class 2. Placing these blocks in ascending order, the class-1 blocks will now have ranks 1 and 2, followed by the class-2 blocks with ranks 3 through 16. The average rank is one-half the sum of the two ranks, which is $(1+2)/2 = 1.5$ for class 1 and $(3+16)/2 = 9.5$ for class 2. If you repeat this procedure for classes 3-5, you will obtain the average ranks listed in Table 18.4.

You next sum the squared differences between average ranks for each block (see the fifth column in Table 18.4). A value of 13,209 is obtained for the 43 blocks. This value is used in the Spearman rank correlation equation for N = 43:

$$\rho = 1.0 - \frac{6 \times 13{,}209}{\left(43^3 - 43\right)} = 1.0 - \frac{79{,}254}{79{,}464} = 0.003$$

The ρ value of 0.003 indicates that there is no spatial dependency between pedestrian and vehicle traffic counts for the 43 blocks.

You may not be completely satisfied with your Spearman's rank correlation coefficient, due to the fact that only 10 different numerical values were used in the computations, with several of these being used many times in finding the rank differences. A more robust correlation analysis could be carried out if you had the data used to make the maps. Fortunately, traffic counts and many other road network datasets are now readily available on

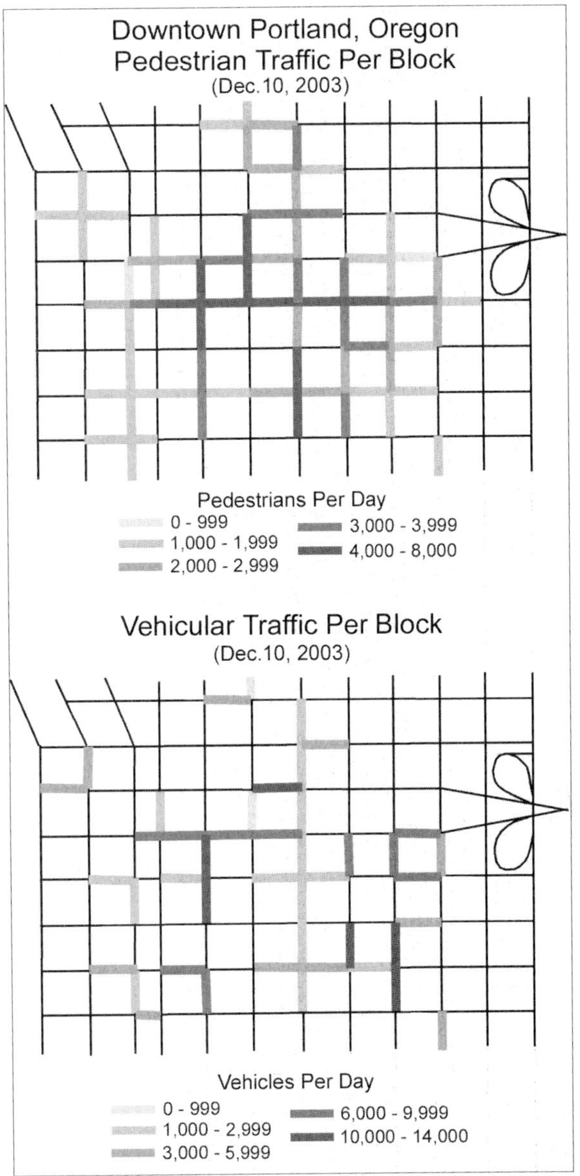

Figure 18.9 Number of pedestrians and vehicles counted for selected city blocks in downtown Portland, Oregon, on December 10, 2003.

the worldwide web, including the traffic counts for downtown Portland. Thus, you can download the actual pedestrian and vehicle traffic counts for the 43 blocks where both were taken and use them to make a scatterplot, like the one shown in **Figure 18.10**.

Looking at the scatterplot, you will see that almost all points fall in a vertical swath on the left half of the pedestrian traffic axis. This arrangement

Table 18.4 Pedestrian and Vehicle Ranks for 43 City Blocks in Downtown Portland, Oregon

Ped. Rank	Veh. Rank	Ped.Avg. Rank	Veh.Avg. Rank	Rank Diff.^{2}
2	1	9.5	1.5	64
2	2	9.5	10.5	1
4	2	31.5	10.5	441
2	3	9.5	23	182.25
3	2	22	10.5	132.25
4	5	31.5	40.5	81
3	2	22	10.5	132.25
4	2	31.5	10.5	441
3	4	22	32.5	110.25
5	1	39.5	1.5	1444
5	2	39.5	10.5	841
3	2	22	10.5	132.25
5	2	39.5	10.5	841
4	4	31.5	32.5	1
5	2	39.5	10.5	841
5	2	39.5	10.5	841
1	4	1.5	32.5	961
2	4	9.5	32.5	529
3	3	22	23	1
4	4	31.5	32.5	1
2	3	9.5	23	182.25
3	5	22	40.5	342.25
2	5	9.5	40.5	961
2	3	9.5	23	182.25
4	2	31.5	10.5	441
3	5	22	40.5	342.25
3	3	22	23	1
4	4	31.5	32.5	1
3	4	22	32.5	110.25
2	2	9.5	10.5	1
3	4	22	32.5	110.25
5	2	39.5	10.5	841
5	5	39.5	40.5	1
5	5	39.5	40.5	1
4	4	31.5	32.5	1
2	4	9.5	32.5	529
2	3	9.5	23	182.25
2	2	9.5	10.5	1
2	3	9.5	23	182.25
3	2	22	10.5	132.25
2	2	9.5	10.5	1
2	3	9.5	23	182.25
1	3	1.5	23	462.25

of points indicates minimal correlation between the pedestrian and vehicle counts. When you enter the two counts for each of the 43 blocks into a statistics program, you will obtain a correlation coefficient (r) of -0.02. This very low r value is a clear indication that there is no spatial correlation between the pedestrian and vehicle counts.

AREA-FEATURE SPATIAL ASSOCIATION

You may be interested in the spatial association between area features shown on maps. For instance, you may wish to compare soil types with vegetation zones, or to correlate climate zones with land use categories. In cases like these, you can think of spatial association as the degree to which two categories overlap on the map. The **coefficient of areal correspondence (CAC)** is a commonly used measure of the amount of overlap between two categories of area features.

The coefficient of areal correspondence is the ratio between the area of overlap and the total areal extent of the two categories A and B, or in mathematical terms:

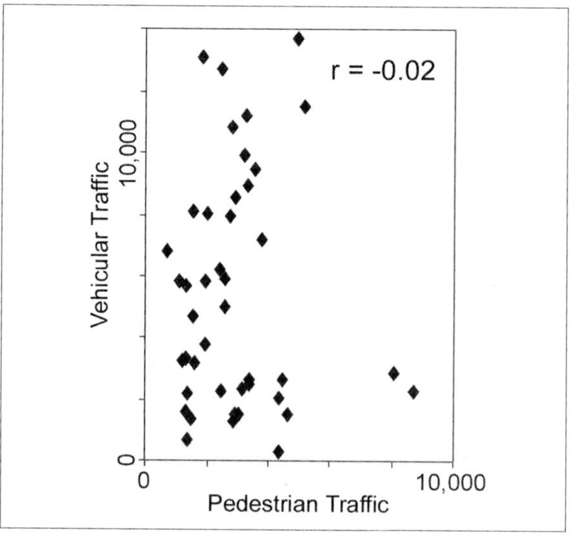

Figure 18.10 Scatterplot of pedestrian and vehicular traffic count data for 43 city blocks in downtown Portland, Oregon.

$$CAC = \frac{A \cap B}{A \cup B}$$

where the symbol ∩ means the **intersection** (overlap) and ∪ means the **union** (total extent) of the two area-feature categories. The coefficient ranges in value from 0 (when there is no overlap) to 1 (when there is perfect areal correspondence) (**Figure 18.11**).

Imagine, for example, that you wish to determine the spatial associations between (1)forest land, (2)agricultural fields, (3)gentle slopes, and (4) steep-slope zones in a portion of the driftless (non-glaciated) region in southwestern Wisconsin (**Figure 18.12, top**). If you place a square grid of 2,500 cells (50 rows by 50 columns) over the map, and then determine the dominant landcover category and slope zone within each cell (see **Figure 18.12, bottom**), you'll find:

1,212 cells in gentle-slope fields
124 cells in steep-slope fields
238 cells in gentle-slope forested land
926 cells in steep-slope forested land

Four coefficients of areal correspondence can be computed from these totals:

$$\frac{Gentle \cap Fields}{Gentle \cup Fields} = \frac{1{,}212}{1{,}574} = 0.77$$

$$\frac{Steep \cap Fields}{Steep \cup Fields} = \frac{124}{2{,}262} = 0.05$$

$$\frac{Gentle \cap Forest}{Gentle \cup Forest} = \frac{238}{2{,}376} = 0.10$$

$$\frac{Steep \cap Forest}{Steep \cup Forest} = \frac{926}{1{,}288} = 0.72$$

These coefficients tell you that there's a high areal correspondence between gentle slopes and agricultural fields, as well as between steep slopes and forest land. Conversely, there is a low correspondence between fields and steep slopes and between gentle slopes and forest lands.

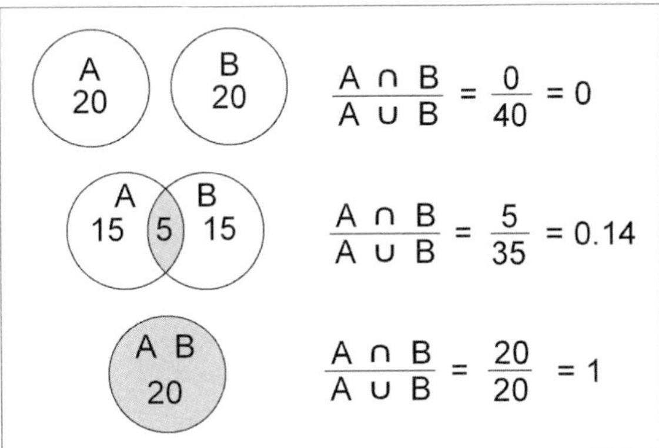

Figure 18.11 The coefficient of areal correspondence provides a simple measure of spatial association which varies between 0 (no overlap) and 1 (complete overlap).

Finding the intersection and union areas for two or more categories is a key function of the **map overlay** analysis tool in a geographic information system. In Chapter 19, you'll see that areas defined by grid cells or (x,y) coordinate outlines can be overlaid digitally to determine intersection and union areas. Using the GIS, you can determine coefficients of areal correspondence between many area features in seconds.

CONTINUOUS-SURFACE SPATIAL ASSOCIATION

Continuous surfaces change smoothly in numerical value across the landscape. Environmental phenomena such as temperature, humidity, or atmospheric pressure are excellent examples of continuous surfaces. Their values change continuously from place to place and also from minute to minute. Ground elevations can be treated as a continuous surface if the surface roughness is smoothed, as happens when contours are created. Another form of continuous surface is a long-term statistical average of something that isn't continuous at a given point in time. Monthly precipitation is a good example, since at any instant it is either raining or not

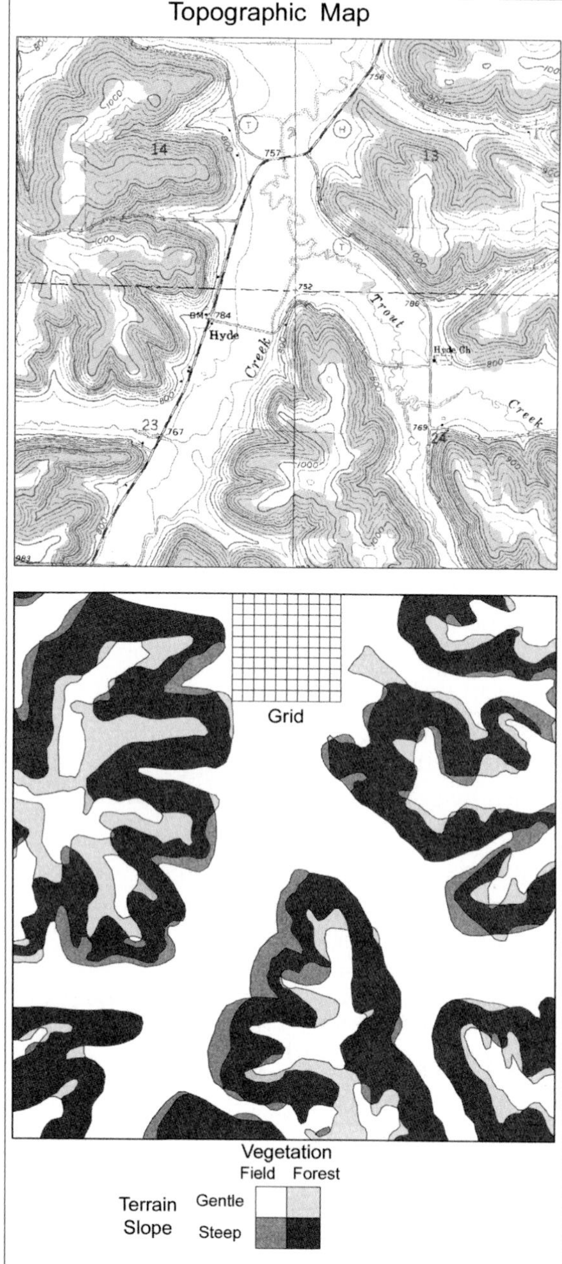

Figure 18.12 Notice the areal correspondence between forest cover and ground slope (shown by close contour spacing) on this portion of the Barneveld, Wisconsin, 1:24,000 USGS topographic quadrangle.The bottom map represents a four-way classification based on forest-cover and ground-slope relations. For data tabulation purposes, the map has been divided into 2,500 grid cells.

raining, but the monthly total can be thought of as a continuous surface.

There are two basic ways to compare continuous surfaces. First, you can compare different features for the same area at the same date. You might compare March precipitation and average temperature data for the same area, for example. Second, you can perform a **temporal change study** for the same feature at different times. For instance, you might compare precipitation values in the same area for December and June.

A common method used to study the spatial association between continuous surfaces that have been mapped is to subdivide the surface into a large number of grid cells (data collection units), then find the average value for each cell or the value at its center. Fortunately, gridded maps in raster format have already been made for many continuous-surface phenomena, and you can use digital image processing software (see Chapter 21 for more on digital image processing) to study their degree of spatial association.

Let's perform a temporal change analysis by looking at Oregon precipitation maps for December, 2002, and June, 2003, (**Figure 18.13, top left and right**). The two monthly precipitation surfaces are approximated by a 128-row by 205-column square grid, with an estimated total precipitation value for each grid cell on land. The range of precipitation for each month is represented by gray tones ranging from black for the lowest value to white for the highest.

Looking at the maps, you can see that there's more precipitation in the western third of Oregon during both months. More detailed visual observations are difficult to make, particularly since the same progression of gray tones on the two maps represent widely differing precipitation ranges.

If you have access to the digital data used to make each map, you can use a GIS or an image processing program to make a new map that is the sum, difference, product, or ratio of the two maps being compared. For instance, you may be able to gain a deeper understanding of winter and summer precipitation differences in Oregon by com-

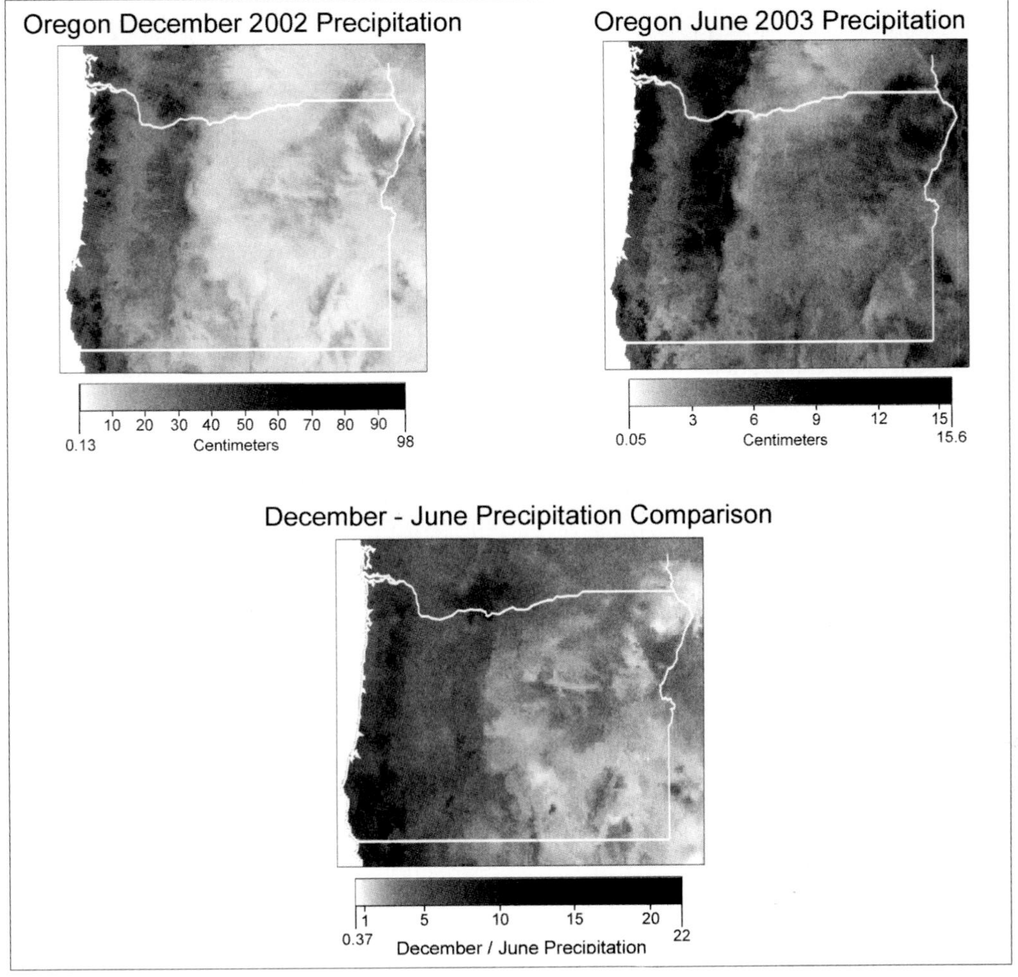

Figure 18.13 The Oregon precipitation surface maps for December, 2002, and June, 2003, can be compared directly, or a single map showing the ratio of December to June precipitation can be created to help understand the seasonal variation.

bining the two monthly maps into a December-June comparison map (**Figure 18.13, bottom**). This map shows the ratio of December to June precipitation for each grid cell. On this map, you can see that the ratio ranges from 22 times wetter in winter in the very southwest corner of Oregon to 0.37 times wetter (better stated as 2.7 times drier) in winter in the high mountains of eastern Oregon. There also appears to be a distinct east-west division between high and low ratio areas, with the dividing line just east of the Cascade range in the middle of the state. A closer examination of the map will show many small anomalous areas within the two broad regions.

The first step in the quantitative comparison of gridded continuous-surface maps is to create **frequency diagrams** (histograms) for the grid-cell values on each map. Frequency diagrams for the December and June precipitation-map grid cell values are shown in **Figure 18.14**. You will want to check for normality in the values. Notice that neither frequency diagram has the bell-shaped curve that characterizes a normal distribution (although the June diagram is closer to normal than the December). Since neither dataset is normally distributed, it is not valid to use summary statistics such as the standard deviation to compare variation in the data.

You can, however, construct a scatterplot for the two datasets and compute their degree of cross-correlation. The scatterplot for the December and June precipitation data (**Figure 18.15**) shows that the 26,240 pairs of values are dispersed in a roughly oval arrangement, with most pairs in the lower-left quarter of the diagram. From this arrangement, you would expect there to be a moderate positive correlation between the December and June precipitation.

The next step is to compute the correlation coefficient (*r*) using the same equation as in the point-feature comparison described earlier in this chapter. A digital image processing program computed an *r* value of 0.702 for the December and June data, a value that indicates a moderate positive correlation between winter and summer precipitation. The correlation analysis program also gives the **regression line** for the scatterplot. A regression line is the straight line of "best fit" drawn through the paired x,y values. The criterion for "best fit" most commonly used is the line that minimizes the squared distances between the y values of the points and the y values on the regression line. This criterion is called the "**least squares criterion.**"

The regression line for the December and June precipitation data is defined by the equation Y = 2.35 + 0.117X. The 2.35-cm. value is the Y-intercept, the place where the regression line crosses the Y-axis of the scatterplot. The 0.117 value is the slope of the regression line, close to horizontal for these data (it appears to be steeper because the two axes are scaled differently). If the data values appear closely clustered along a line so that the correlation coefficient is very close to 1.0, the regression line equation can be used as a predictor of June precipitation for every value of December precipitation. As you might expect, the regression equation rapidly decreases in utility as a predictor as the correlation coefficient lowers.

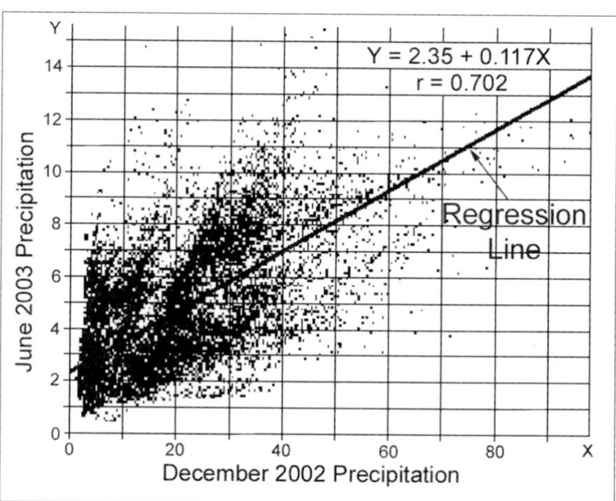

Figure 18.15 Scatterplot of the December and June precipitation data, along with the regression line and equation of best fit.

An advantage of the correlation coefficient r is that it provides you with the positive or negative direction of the correlation and the **degree of linearity** in relations between the datasets. The square of the correlation coefficient, called the **coefficient of determination**, provides a measure of the

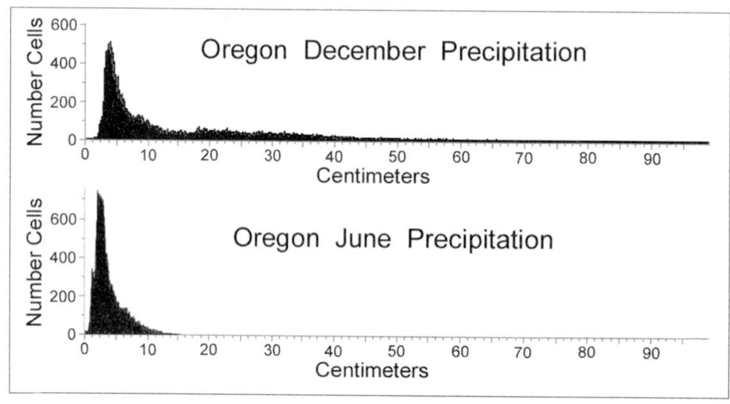

Figure 18.14 Frequency diagrams for the Oregon December and June precipitation data. Notice that neither dataset is normally distributed.

strength of the correlation. Symbolized as r^2, the coefficient of determination can have only positive values ranging from $r^2 = 1.0$ for a perfect correlation (positive or negative) to $r^2 = 0.0$ for a complete absence of correlation. Statisticians say that the coefficient of determination gives the percentage of the explained variation (by the linear regression) compared to the total variation in the data. For instance, the r-value of 0.702 for the December and June precipitation data gives a coefficient of determination of 0.702^2, or 0.49. You can therefore say that 49% of the variability in the December data is explained by the variability in the June data.

MULTIVARIATE SPATIAL ASSOCIATION MEASURES

We have been studying quantitative measures of spatial association between two sets of spatial data, but we are sometimes faced with comparing more than two categories of features at a time. To do so using the methods described so far would require comparing all combinations of feature categories two at a time, an approach that is both inefficient and ineffective. It is also somewhat naive to believe that pairs of complexly interrelated features can be meaningfully analyzed in isolation.

A better approach is to compare all categories of features simultaneously. The spatial analysis functions in a geographic information system are based on overlaying several types of features. You will see in Chapter 19 that you can use Boolean (union and intersection), logical (=, <, >, ...), and arithmetic (+,-,×,÷,...) functions to combine data for each feature. These functions let you create a **mathematical model** for a phenomenon that's related to several feature-category datasets stored in the GIS. For example, a soil scientist might model soil loss as a function of soil composition, precipitation, slope, and vegetation type.

Another approach is to use advanced statistical methods for analyzing **multivariate spatial association**. Some methods involve considering all variables simultaneously by progressively determining the correspondence between pairs of categories while holding the others constant. These measures are referred to as **partial correlation coefficients**.

Other multivariate measures of spatial association involve ranking a set of independent variables in terms of their statistical influence on the dependent variable. For instance, you may wish to correlate crop yield (the independent variable) with various environmental factors (dependent variables). Through multivariate correlation analysis, you may find that soil fertility has a 60% influence, slope has a 25% influence, and all other factors have an influence of 15%. This means that 85% of the crop-yield variation can be explained by variation in only two environmental factors—soil fertility and slope.

What if you want to correlate a single dependent variable with many (say more than 10) patterns representing independent variables? In that case, you'll need to use special numerical techniques. Most of these require an immense number of computations and therefore are practical only when high-speed computers are available. The techniques go by various names, including **cluster analysis**, **factor analysis**, and **multi-dimensional scaling**. But the result is essentially the same regardless of the procedure used. You end up with a sorting of the independent variables into groups representing different dimensions or factors of the spatial association arrangement. The individual dimensions are also ranked in terms of their degree of influence on the dependent variable, as was true with each variable in the multiple correlation analysis mentioned above.

The multivariate measures of spatial association we've been discussing go well beyond unaided visual judgments. Therefore, they provide valuable tools for the sophisticated map user. But they're also non-intuitive. Thus, someone who isn't knowledgeable about the mathematics used and the variables under study may find the results difficult to interpret. For these reasons, the use of multivariate spatial association methods is generally restricted to skilled environmental scientists who understand the mathematics behind the methods and appreciate the insight they may provide.

MOVEMENT AND DIFFUSION

So far in this chapter we've treated the features being compared as static phenomena. In most cases, this assumption is justified, and the pattern comparison methods we've discussed will produce meaningful results. But sometimes we're less interested in spatial association between static features than in the changes in location or diffusion of features over time. Let's look at how you can analyze the movement of a set of point features, realizing you can also use these analysis methods with line and area features.

Measuring Point-Feature Movement

Many physical and cultural features move across the earth as a group—flocks of geese, pods of whales or dolphins, herds of elk, and companies of soldiers, to name a few. You may want to know basic spatial information about their movement, such as the distance and direction traveled by the group as a whole. In addition, you may be interested in knowing the changes in spatial arrangement of the individuals in the group at the beginning and ending locations.

Our example is a hypothetical pod of 18 dolphins tagged with electronic tracking devices so that the geographic position of each dolphin can be determined daily. The position of each dolphin while stopped at a resting or feeding area on days 1 and 2 has been plotted on a large-scale nautical chart (**Figure 18.16**). You can measure the pod's movement from day 1 to day 2 by the distance and direction between the center of the pod on the two days.

You can use a statistic called the **bivariate mean** to find the center of a set of point features such as dolphins in a pod. The bivariate mean, written as $(\bar{x}, \bar{y})$, is the average of the horizontal and vertical coordinates for *n* features:

$$(\bar{x}, \bar{y}) = \left(\frac{\sum_{i=1}^{n} x_i}{n}, \frac{\sum_{i=1}^{n} y_i}{n} \right)$$

We computed the bivariate means for the dolphin locations on the two days by first finding the latitude (ϕ) and longitude (λ) of each dolphin from the electronic tracking system. Since the locations are in geographic coordinates, the equation for the bivariate mean becomes:

$$(\bar{\phi}, \bar{\lambda}) = \left(\frac{\sum_{i=1}^{n} \phi_i}{n}, \frac{\sum_{i=1}^{n} \lambda_i}{n} \right)$$

The bivariate means for the two days are listed and plotted with "+" marks on Figure 18.16. Drawing a grid of parallels and meridians at one-minute increments across the areas holding the dolphins on both days simplifies the measurement of the dolphin locations.

You can use the two bivariate means as summary statistics for the pod location on each day. Plotting the means as points on the nautical chart also makes it easy for you to measure the average distance the pod moved from day 1 to day 2. Remembering that 1 nautical mile equals 1 minute of latitude, you can use the 0.1 minute latitude ticks on the right edge of the chart as a ruler (see Chapter 11 for more on distance measurement). We found the distance between the two bivariate means to be 1.69 nautical miles.

In what direction is the pod of dolphins moving? You can answer this question by first drawing a straight direction line between the two pod centroid locations. Then use a protractor to measure the angle between the meridian (vertical line) at the first pod location and the direction line to the second pod location. The 20° angle you measure is the true azmiuth of the direction between the two pod centers (see Chapter 12 for more on direction measurement.)

You may also want to figure out how much the dolphins shifted their locations within the pod from day 1 to day 2. To do so, first label each dot on the map with the name of the dolphin at this location. Our dolphins were simply given numbers 1 through 18. The labeled dolphin locations for days 1 and 2 (**Figure 18.17, A and B**) can then be superimposed so that the bivariate means coincide exactly (**Figure 18.17, C**). Since each map symbol is labeled by the dolphin's number, you can draw straight lines between pairs of symbols for each dolphin. The length of each line is the amount the dolphin shifted in position from day 1 to day 2 relative to the bivariate mean. Next, measure the length of each line, add these lengths together, and divide the sum of these lengths by the number of dolphins (18). You will find an average spatial shift of 0.13 nautical miles from day 1 to day 2.

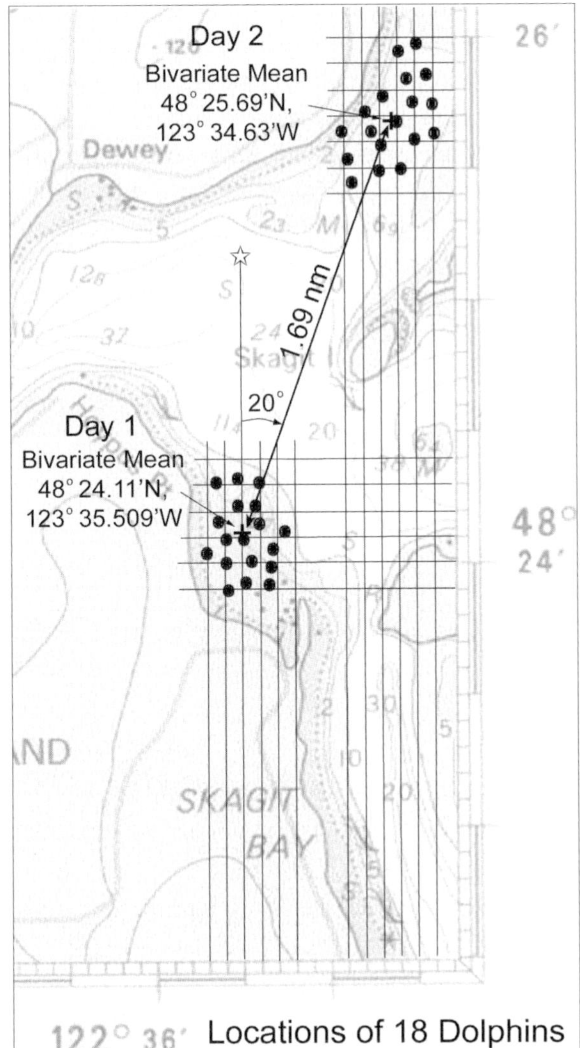

Figure 18.16 The movement of a pod of dolphins from day 1 to day 2 can be mapped if the position of each animal can be tracked.

You can also find angular shifts in position from the shift lines if you plot the center of each shift line at the center of a simple compass rose (**Figure 18.17, D**). This diagram clearly shows that most of the shifts are close to easterly or westerly, and that no shifts are northerly or southerly. A biologist might try to explain this restricted pattern of angular shifts in the relative positions of dolphins by known facts of dolphin pod behavior or by geographic constraints to movement at the two locales.

Measuring Point-Feature Diffusion

Spatial diffusion is the process by which features move outward from a starting position across space over time, continuously decreasing in density. You will find maps showing the spatial diffusion of phenomena such as water pollution from a point source, oil slicks from a grounded oil tanker, or the spread of a forest fire from its point of

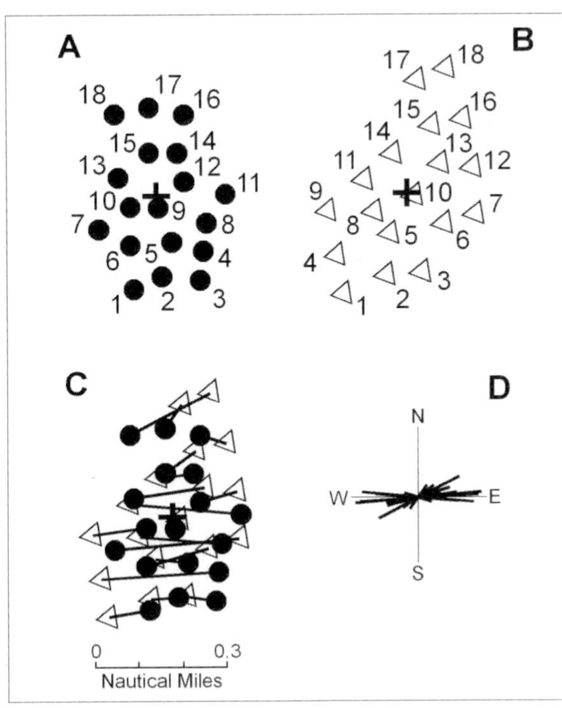

Figure 18.17 You can superimpose the day 1 (A) and day 2 (B) dolphin locations so that you can measure the shifts in position of each animal relative to the bivariate mean (C). Angular shifts can be plotted on a simple compass rose (D).

ignition. The diffusion of a set of point features is easiest to analyze from maps showing their positions at different time intervals.

Your task when analyzing any sort of diffusion map is to understand the dispersal or growth mechanism that lies behind the pattern you see. Professionals use a variety of numerical modeling strategies in diffusion studies, but the high level of statistical expertise required for you to work with these models falls beyond the scope of this book. However, there are simple methods that you can use to analyze the magnitude and direction of diffusion. Let's look at a hypothetical example of point-feature spatial diffusion—the movement of markers outward from an initial point due to the combined influence of coastal currents and winds.

In our example, 30 floating markers equipped with electronic location transmission devices are released from Sandy Point on Waldron Island, one of the San Juan Islands in Washington State. The latitude and longitude of each marker is recorded hourly over a four-hour period, and the location of each marker is plotted on a nautical chart covering the area (**Figure 18.18**). The 30 triangles, squares, pentagons, and circles on the chart show the positions of the 30 markers at 1,2,3, and 4 hours after release from the initial point at the western tip of Waldron Island.

Looking at the hourly positions of the markers plotted on the chart, notice that:

1. The markers appear to have diffused slowly outward from the release point during the first hour, followed by a more rapid diffusion during the second and third hours.
2. Diffusion is not the same in all directions. Land to the east is an obvious barrier to marker movement, and it appears that a combination of coastal current and surface wind has restricted diffusion to the north and south.
3. Marker movement in the west-southwest direction is essentially stopped when markers reach the surf zone of several small islands around three hours after release.
4. By four hours after release, many markers have entered a narrow channel to the west, increasing the density of markers as they pass through the channel.

These observations constitute a *qualitative* analysis of marker diffusion that gives us several insights into the diffusion process. However, it is equally important to conduct a *quantitative* analysis of spatial diffusion. There are several measures of diffusion that will give you further insight into the spatial nature of marker movement. These measures are also evidence for or against conclusions drawn from your qualitative observations. The first set of quantitative measures is based on making point counts within data collection areas.

Notice on Figure 18.18 what appears to be the graticule for a polar-aspect azimuthal equidistant map projection. What you are seeing is actually a polar-coordinate grid centered at the initial point of release. The circles are what we call **range rings**. Range rings serve both as data collection unit boundaries and as a circular distance scale, since the rings are spaced at one nautical mile intervals outward from the initial point. The straight lines are true-azimuth lines radiating outward from the initial point at 30° angular increments. These lines divide the circle into 12 equal **sectors**.

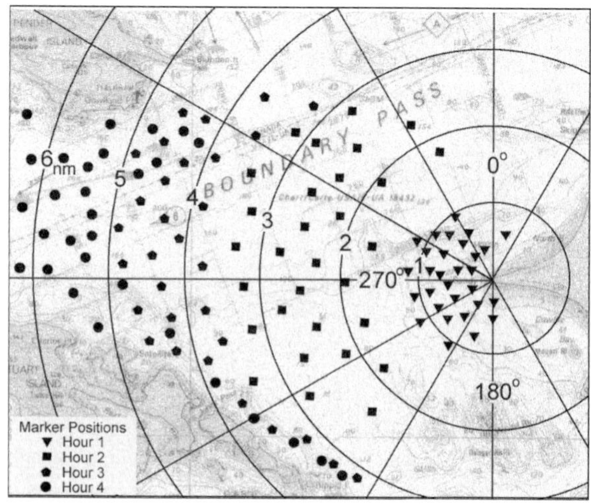

Figure 18.18 Positions of 30 markers at 1,2,3, and 4 hours after their initial release from the western tip of Waldron Island, Washington.

Counting the number of markers within range rings and circle sectors at each hour is straightforward. You can gain further insight into the diffusion process by using a spreadsheet or statistics program to create frequency diagrams of the data. The frequency diagram at the top of **Figure 18.19** shows the number of markers within each range-ring increment. Four rows of raised columns show the number of markers counted in each range-ring increment at the four time intervals. The left column in the first row showing 25 markers to be within 1 nautical mile (1nm) of the initial release point reinforces our visual observation of slow diffusion during the first hour.

The other three rows in this diagram are interesting because the shape formed by the columns roughly resembles a "wave" of diffusion moving outward from the hour-1 marker positions during the next three hours. The three waves peak at 2-3nm, 4-5nm, and 5-6nm, which indicates a steady diffusion rate for two hours, followed by a slowdown in the movement of markers during the fourth hour.

The frequency diagram at the bottom of Figure 18.19 shows the number of markers in each circle sector during each time period. What stands out on this diagram is the reduction in the angular range of the markers over the four hours. Notice the increasing number of markers in the two western sectors over time. The data on this graph correspond well with the visual observation of an increased concentration of markers in the channel to the west during hours 3 and 4.

Maps showing the movement of each point feature give you additional details about the diffusion process. The map in **Figure 18.20**, for example, shows the movement of each marker over the four-hour time period. The straight lines connecting the marker positions at each hour are only rough approximations of the actual path followed, since shorter time interval positional information was not collected.

The map looks like a maze of intersecting lines, but you can see the overall westerly drift of the markers after their initial outward diffusion from the release point. Notice that there is little angular difference among lines after the first hour. This tells you that the westerly currents or winds responsible for the motion must have been fairly steady in intensity. Also apparent is the variable amount of movement among markers, particularly the very slow movement of the markers that drifted close to the shore of nearby islands.

Measuring the length of each straight line gives you more detailed information about individual marker movement. These measurements allow you to compute the average amount of marker movement for each hour. We converted the 30 line lengths for each hour into nautical miles, then summed the lengths and divided each sum by 30 to obtain average movements of 0.73, 2.00, 1.65, and 1.20 nautical miles for hours 1-4. These values

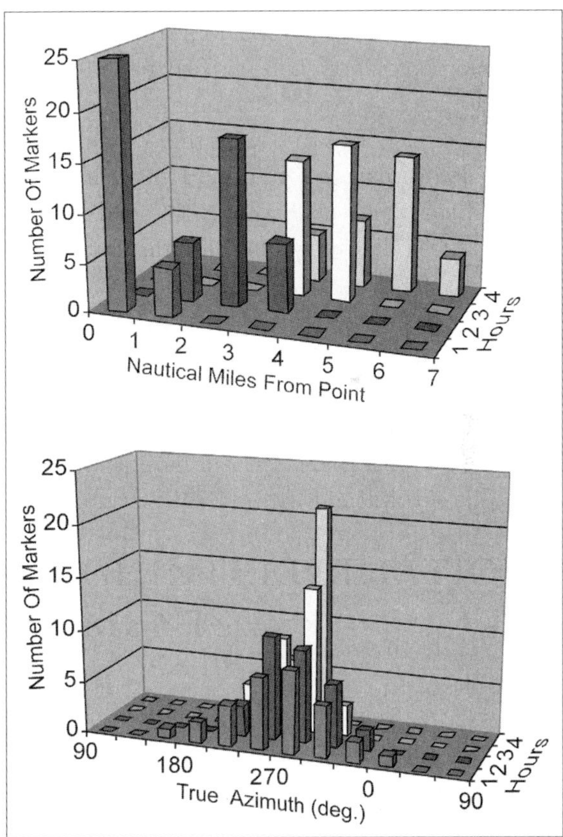

Figure 18.19 Frequency diagrams showing the number of markers within each 1 nautical mile (nm) range increment (top) and within each 30° sector at the end of hours 1-4.

are the speeds of movement for each hour in knots, since a knot is one nautical mile per hour. The four speeds support the visual observation of slower diffusion during the first hour followed by more rapid diffusion.

You can learn more about the details of the hour-to-hour movement of the markers by making a composite frequency diagram for the line length data. The frequency diagram in **Figure 18.21** shows the number of lines that fall in 0.2 nautical mile increments for each hour. The first row shows that a roughly equal number of markers moved from 0.2 to 1.2 nautical miles during the first hour. Rows for hours 2 through 4 show the longer distances to be close to normally distributed about the average value, particularly in the last two hours. You can use the standard deviation and other statistics based on a normal distribution of values to describe these data.

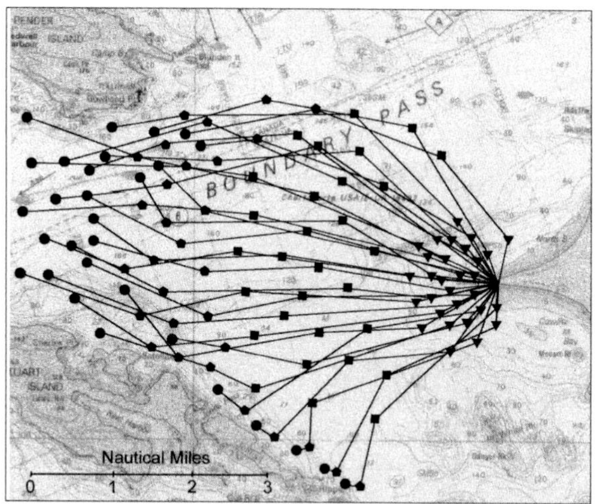

Figure 18.20 This map shows you the approximate paths followed by each of the 30 markers during the four hours after release.

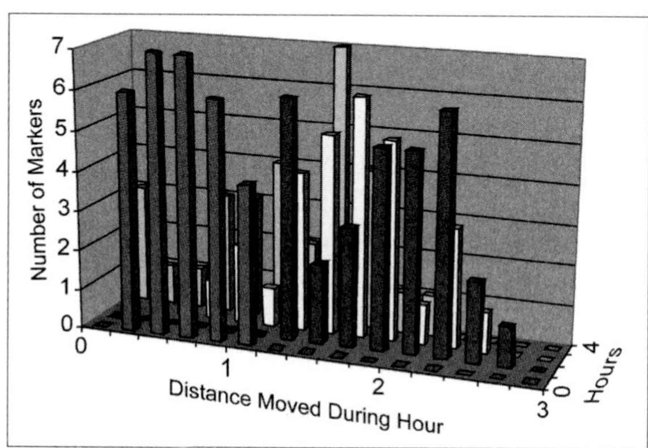

Figure 18.21 Frequency diagram showing the number of path lines falling within 0.2 nautical mile (nm) distance increments at the end of each hour.

SELECTED READINGS

Bailey, T.C., and Gatrell, A.C., *Interactive Spatial Data Analysis* (New York: John Wiley & Sons, 1995).

Clark, W.A.V., and Hosking, P.C., *Statistical Methods for Geographers* (New York: John Wiley & Sons, 1986).

Dunteman, G.H, *Introduction to Multivariate Analysis* (Beverly Hills, CA: Sage Publications, 1984).

Griffith, D.A., and Armheim, C.G., *Multivariate Statistical Analysis for Geographers* (Upper Saddle River, NJ: Prentice-Hall, 1997).

Griffith, D.A., Armheim, C.G., and Desloges, J.R., *Statistical Analysis for Geographers* (Englewood Cliffs, NJ: Prentice-Hall, 1991).

Haining, R., *Spatial Data Analysis in the Social and Environmental Sciences* (New York: Cambridge University Press, 1990).

Johnston, R.J., *Multivariate Statistical Analysis in Geography* (New York: Longman, Inc., 1980).

Morrill, R., Gaile, G.L., and Thrall, G.I., *Spatial Diffusion* (Newbury Park, CA: Sage Publications, 1988).

Shaw, G., and Wheeler, D., *Statistical Techniques in Geographical Analysis* (New York: John Wiley & Sons, 1985).

Walford, N., *Geographical Data Analysis* (New York: John Wiley & Sons, 1995).

CHAPTER NINETEEN
GIS AND MAP ANALYSIS SOFTWARE

STAND-ALONE PACKAGES

- Cartometrics
- Address Matching
- Route Finding
- Statistical Mapping
- Terrain Analysis
  - Elevation Determination
  - Surface Profiles
  - Slope and Gradient
- Spatial Optimization
  - Optimal Route Selection
  - Facility Selection

GEOGRAPHIC INFORMATION SYSTEMS

- Data Sources
- Data Conversion
- Spatial Analysis
  - Search Window
  - Buffer
  - Overlay
  - Modeling

LINKING GIS AND GPS

- Precision Farming

SELECTED READINGS

The computer . . . can be asked by us to "think the unthinkable" and the previously unthought.
—Alvin Toffler, The Third Wave

19

CHAPTER NINETEEN

GIS AND MAP ANALYSIS SOFTWARE

Computers are made for numbers and equations. Thus, to the joy of map users, map analysis is now largely automated. Commercial products are available to perform most common map analysis tasks. These commercial products require a fully-configured computer system and basic computer literacy on the part of the map user.

The basic computer system needed for map analysis must be more robust than that used for map retrieval. The hardware must be more powerful. The software must be expanded to include analytical functions. And the database must be structured with extensive cross-referencing among different data entries.

No matter what software vendors say, we're still far from the point at which a single software package is a complete solution. Making map analysis easy and inexpensive enough for a novice working on entry-level computer hardware means you can't begin to satisfy the needs of professional users. Conversely, making software powerful enough to please a skilled professional with a high-end computer system means you're going to overload low-end hardware and bury the novice in confusing options. Given this situation, the market is filled with a multitude of products targeted at different users.

In this chapter we will describe several types of stand-alone map analysis packages, followed by a general description of more robust geographic information systems (GIS). The names and addresses of the companies or organizations producing the software mentioned in this chapter are listed in Appendix B.

STAND-ALONE PACKAGES

The most direct way to enlist computers in map analysis is to attack one problem at a time. The idea is to do one thing well. Software designed to solve a specific problem is generally simpler, easier to use, and less expensive than multifunctional programs.* In most cases, software packages that stand alone also place the least demands on database design and computer hardware. Individual software packages range widely in both scope and depth, as we'll see in the following examples.

Cartometrics

Computers are admirably suited to search a database for information and perform analyses such as those outlined in Chapters 11 and 12. At the simplest level, computer software for two-dimensional cartometric analysis should help you to determine such things as the latitude-longitude coordinates of a position, the distance between two cities, the direction from a plane crash site to the nearest road, the size of an urban area, and the change in elevation between you and a mountain top.

As an example, the inexpensive **3-D TopoQuads** software and 7.5-minute topographic quad data by **Delorme** are well-suited to these tasks (**Figure 19.1**). After calling up the relevant portion of a USGS topographic quadrangle on your computer screen, you merely point, click, drag, or trace to perform the desired cartometric tasks. This is both quicker and more accurate than traditional manual map measurement methods. But a computer system can go far beyond these simple analysis tasks.

Software for **three-dimensional cartometric analysis** is also available. Representative of this software is a package called **Surfer**.

**Many packages that began as single-function software now are multifunction, so distinctions between the two categories of software are blurred. Competition between vendors contributes to "option creep" as each tries to gain market share by outdoing the functionality of the other's program. The result is bloated software that demands more computer resources to operate effectively.*

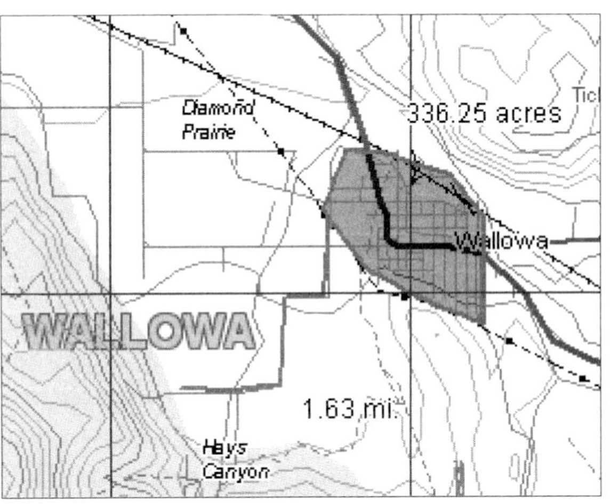

Figure 19.1 Simple two-dimensional cartometric analysis is both quick and accurate when using a software-database bundle such as 3-D TopoQuads, which is designed specifically for position, direction, distance, and area analysis.

You might use this software to determine the volume of water in a reservoir, the size of a mineral deposit, or the amount of earth removed in a quarrying operation. To do so, you need a three-dimensional database. We discuss this topic in further detail under Terrain Analysis later in this chapter.

Address Matching

Position finding is one of the most basic tasks we perform with maps. In the parlance of the computer age, we call this **address matching**. We're using "address" here in the broadest sense of the term. Any spatial identifier will do, such as latitude-longitude coordinates, geographic names, house numbers, zip codes, and telephone area codes. To support effective address matching, you need a database that includes cross-references among as many of these locational aliases as possible.

There are several needs for address matching. You may want to give an address and have the computer show its location on a map. Alternatively, you may wish to point to a spot on the map and have the computer give its address. A few products have either **address-to-map** or **map-to-address** capability, but most software has both capabilities (**Figure 19.2**).

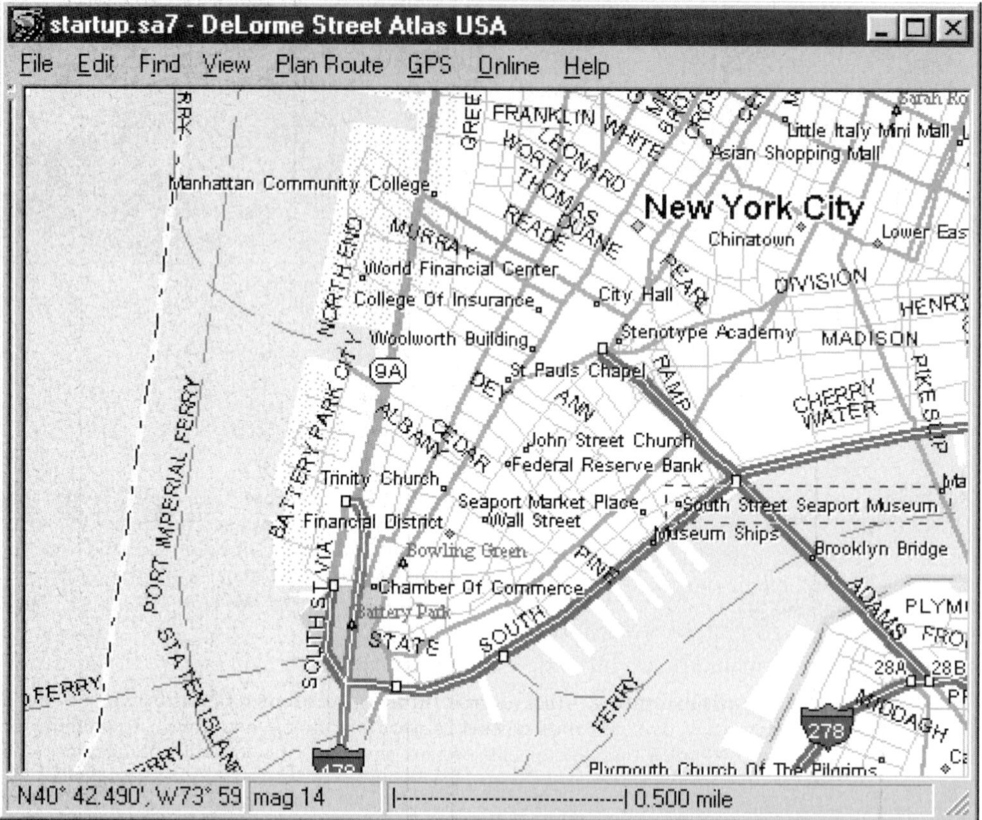

Figure 19.2 Street Atlas USA draws on a massive street-level cartographic database for the entire United States on a CD-ROM.

Address-matching software serves many needs. Of special importance is providing emergency services. Fire, ambulance, and police personnel benefit by being able to pinpoint the location of a distress call. Their next concern is reaching the location as quickly as possible, which is a route finding problem.

Route Finding

You may want to go beyond position finding and determine the **route** between places. Computer programs that provide this capability build upon address-matching. Route-finding software varies in sophistication, depending on the type of information and extent of cross-referencing included in its database (**Figure 19.3**). These databases have become larger with each new software version. But keeping large databases up to date is difficult and expensive, so choose your vendor carefully. Competition in this market is fierce, and the cheapest software is usually not the best buy.

Depending on the software you're using, you start the program by entering the street address, zip code, or latitude-longitude of your origin and destination. The package will then automatically determine the shortest travel route, taking into consideration one-way streets, overpasses, freeway exits, and speed settings for different types of roads and streets. Some software can also read your travel agenda and then sort the order of stops to minimize travel distance or time. In addition to displaying the travel route, you can generate written directions and provide distance and travel time information (Figure 19.3, top). You can even estimate fuel requirements from travel time.

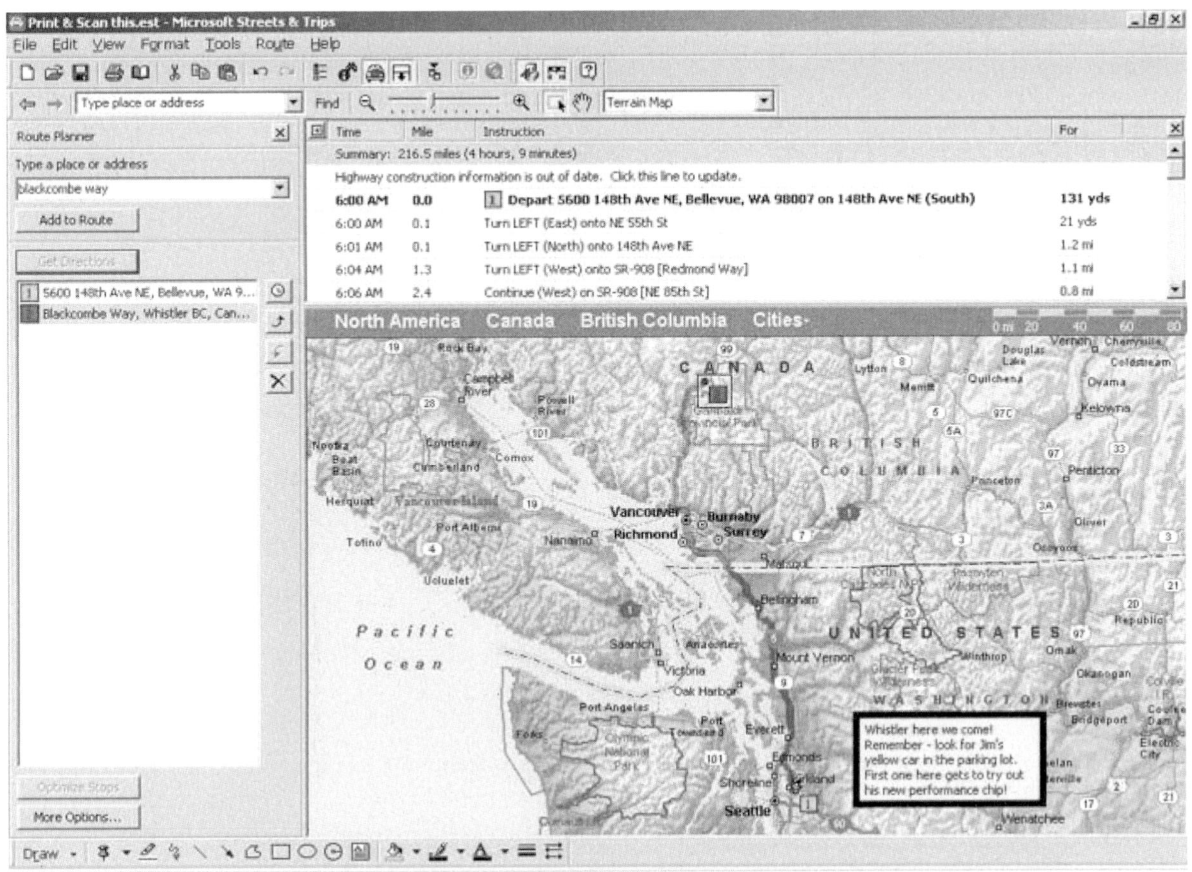

Figure 19.3 Microsoft Streets & Trips lets you work with a map display and menu bar to determine the best route between places, and then highlights your selected route.

Statistical Mapping

Software for cartographic analysis of statistical data is available at several levels of sophistication. Spreadsheet programs such as Microsoft **Excel**, **Maplinx**, and **Business Map** come with limited statistical mapping features. More comprehensive add-on cartographic and statistical databases greatly enhance spreadsheet mapping capabilities. One such product is **MapPoint,** which with **Excel** is part of **Microsoft Office (Figure 19.4).** In both cases, maps are usually restricted to the "value by area" type that we call choropleth maps.

More specialized stand-alone statistical mapping software is also available. Packages such as **MapViewer**, **MapInfo**, and **Proximity** provide a choice of analysis and display methods (**Figure 19.5**). You can expect to find maps using proportional point symbols, stepped surfaces (choropleth and 3-D histograms), and smooth surfaces (isolines and 3-D fishnets). We discuss these methods in Chapter 7.

Finally, you can find statistical mapping capabilities in general-purpose software marketed to the business community. You may hear these packages referred to as **business geographics** software. More commonly, however, they carry the GIS (geographic information systems) label. We discuss this important category of analytical mapping software under **Geographic Information Systems (GIS)** later in the chapter.

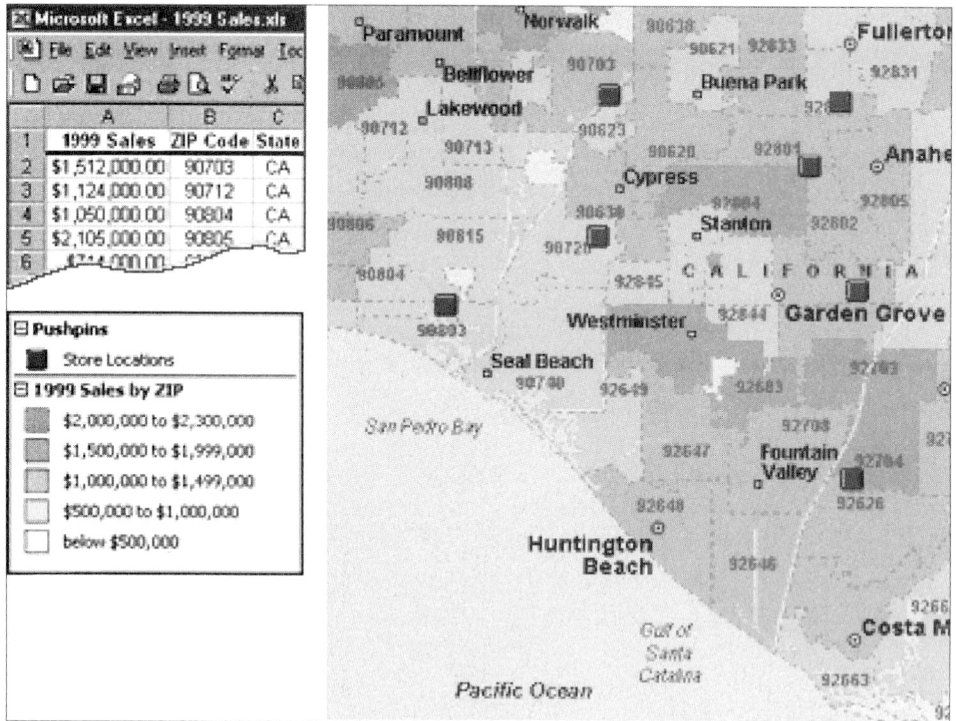

Figure 19.4 Microsoft MapPoint allows you to select data in a Microsoft Excel spreadsheet and drag the selection to MapPoint, where a choropleth map is made.

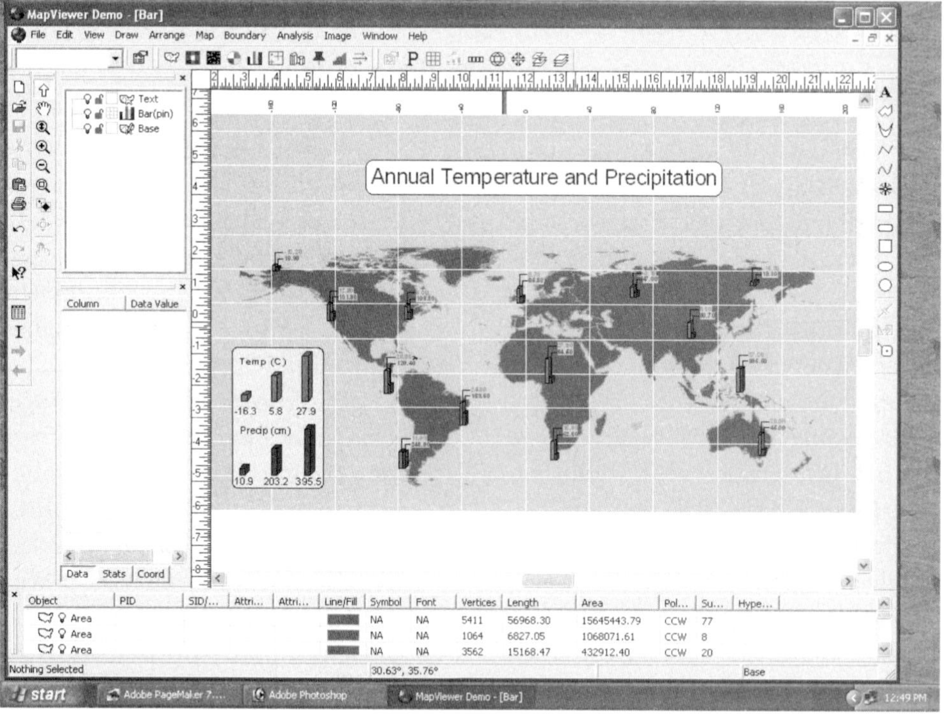

Figure 19.5 You can easily manipulate and display statistical data in a variety of map forms using software such as MapViewer.

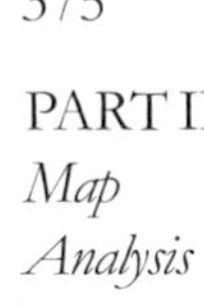

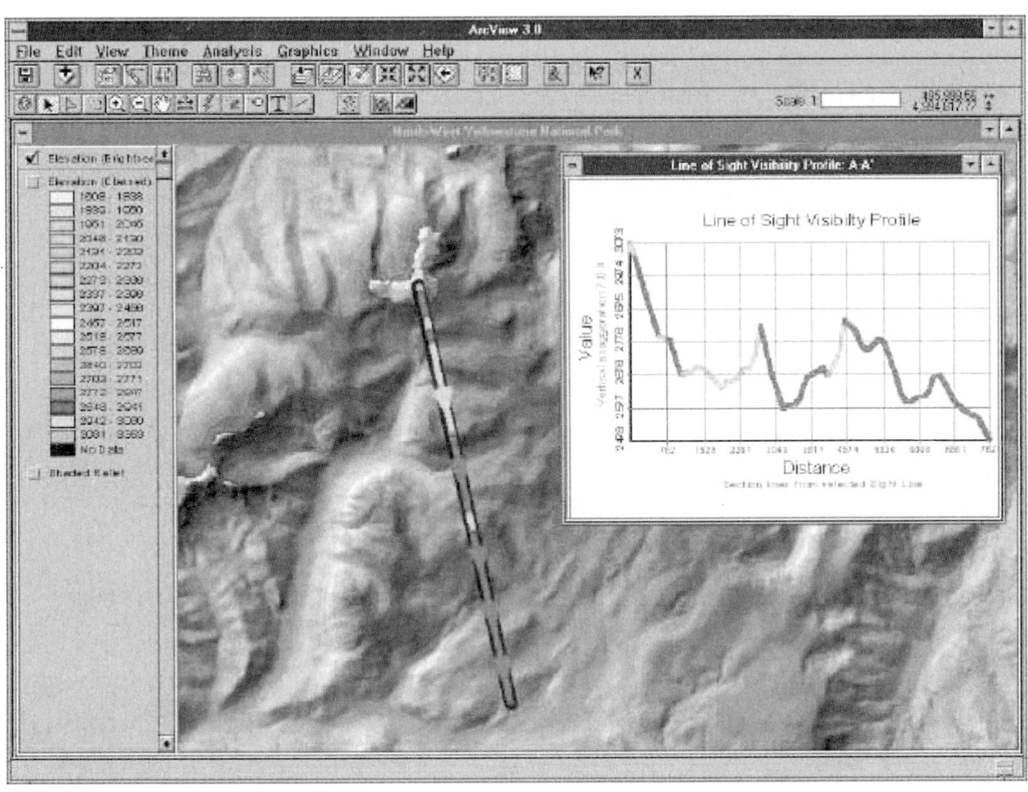

Figure 19.6 Terrain profiling software such as ArcView Spatial Analyst can do in seconds what it takes hours to do manually. Repetitive, point-and-click terrain profiling is also an excellent way to gain a feel for the landscape surface.

Terrain Analysis

Printed maps are inherently two-dimensional, so it makes sense that they are used to make horizontal measurements of position, distance, and direction. But what if we need to consider the third environmental dimension, as in measuring elevation or depth? Three-dimensional analysis has always been more challenging, because it requires extracting information from quantitative symbols such as contour lines or interpreting some other way of representing the surface.

Mapping software and three-dimensional digital databases greatly ease the task of three-dimensional map analysis. We'll use a terrain example to illustrate this point, but anything mapped as a continuous surface can be handled in the same fashion.

Software such as **Surfer**, **Arcview Spatial Analyst**, and **Arcview 3D Analyst** used for digital-terrain analysis must be used with a database of elevation values. The database is usually a digital elevation model (DEM), or a triangulated irregular network (TIN).* The software makes all terrain calculations based on values in the DEM or TIN. Although there are many terrain-analysis applications, all begin with determining the elevation at one or more locations.

**A triangulated irregular network (TIN) is used by some terrain-analysis software. Whereas a DEM approximates the terrain surface with a square grid of the same values, a TIN captures the surface with a network of triangular facets of varying size and shape, depending on the roughness of the surface. Each facet has a constant slope. A TIN is considered a more efficient way of storing terrain data than a DEM, but it is more difficult to create and its use requires more sophisticated software.*

Elevation Determination

Software such as **3-D TopoQuads, ArcView Spatial Analyst**, and **ArcView 3-D Analyst**, lets you determine the elevation at a location by pointing and clicking the mouse. These programs have to be quite sophisticated because they must interpolate between known data points to answer your query. If you find yourself frequently needing to determine elevations, it's easy to justify the extra cost of this software.

Surface Profiles

Most terrain-analysis software will let you create a **terrain profile**. The least-sophisticated packages restrict the profile to rows or columns in the DEM. But more robust software, such as **ArcView Spatial Analyst**, lets you choose any two locations as the endpoints of a profile (**Figure 19.6**). The software may also allow you to define a complex profile, such as along a curved road or river.

A digital-terrain profile is handy for making related calculations, such as the amount of cut and fill needed in a road construction project. You can also compute the intervisibility between different locations, which is useful in selecting sites with view restrictions (potential building sites) or in hiding unattractive sites (such as quarries or clearcuts).

Slope and Gradient

You can use terrain-analysis software to determine the steepness and direction of ground slope at any given location from DEM data. Repeat the calculations, and you can trace the gradient (least-effort path) that water or eroded soil will take (see Chapter 16 for details on slope and gradient calculations). Make enough calculations and you have a runoff map, from which you can define watersheds. The angle at which the sun strikes the landscape has an important influence on vegetation and is critical in orienting solar collectors for heating purposes. The ground slope and aspect are essential information for solar angle calculations.

Automated slope analysis has other applications as well. Construction in mountainous areas is commonly restricted by ground slope. Similarly, slope data are critical inputs to erosion prevention, and stormwater runoff models such as the **WMS Watershed Modeling System** are used in managing such activities as agriculture, logging, and urban development.

Spatial Optimization

We often want to do something in the environment in the best way possible. Doing so requires an optimization strategy with respect to certain spatial factors. Since an optimization procedure involves a great deal of computation, it is easiest done with the help of computer software and spatial databases. Let's look at procedures for selecting optimal routes, sites, and political districts.

Optimal Route Selection

How to best get from one place to another in an optimal manner is a common problem. We discussed the simple "here to there" case previously under Route Finding. Let's now explore the more complex situation in which you would use routing software such as **ArcView Network Analyst** to choose a route to connect a number of locations involving pickup and delivery of varying amounts of goods.

Optimal route selection is an important problem for truckers delivering commodities from facilities such as dairy plants. To be competitive, management must minimize production expenses, including the cost of trucks, driver wages, and truck maintenance. In this example, the commodity to transport is fresh milk, which is perishable, bulky, and low in value for its weight. Milk is produced in different amounts and grades by farmers scattered across the landscape. Road conditions, bridge capacity, and traffic volume also vary from place to place.

So how is a milk truck to be routed to client farmers and back to the plant in order to minimize capital investment in trucks, driver time, and truck maintenance? Routing software tackles this task. Spatial inputs include a digital description of the transportation network and the location, volume, and grade of farm production. The computer

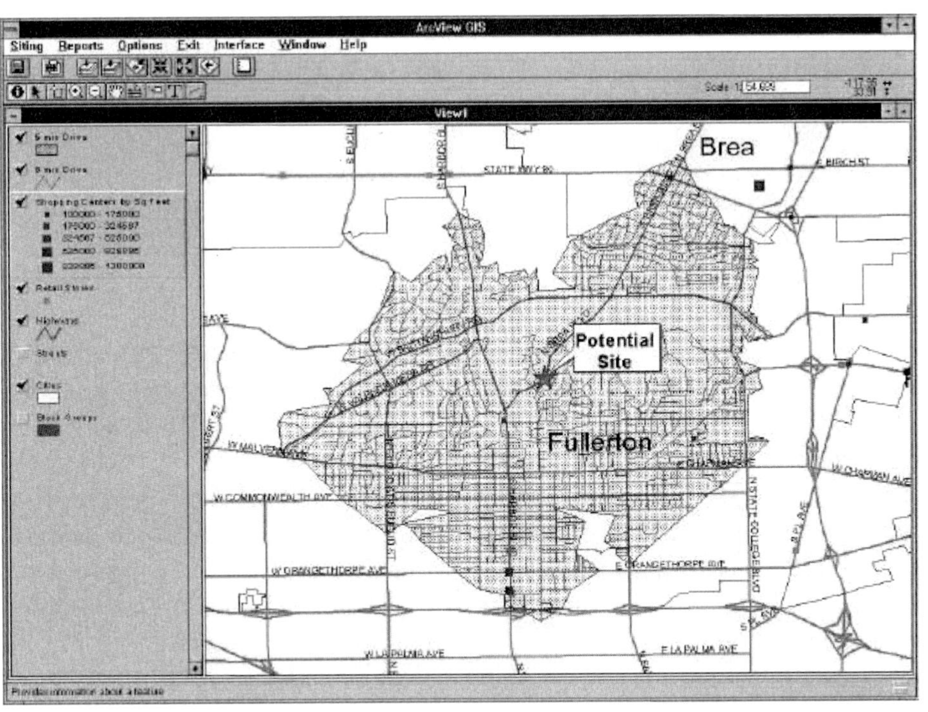

Figure 19.7 Routing software such as ArcView Network Analyst greatly eases the task of site selection. Selecting a good site for a new restaurant is illustrated here.

searches all possible alternatives to come up with the optimal sequence of paths for the given conditions. The route can then be plotted on a map, making it easy for a driver to follow. When a farm goes out of business or a new farm becomes a client, the software can quickly recalculate a new optimal route.

Facility Selection

Where to best locate a facility in the environment is another common map analysis problem. The list of facilities includes factories, sawmills, smelters, communication towers, airports, warehouses, retail businesses, hospitals, schools, churches, police and fire stations, government buildings, residences, and countless others. The location chosen often has a crucial impact on the effectiveness, the efficiency, and even the ultimate survival of the facility.

Some facility locations depend primarily on local conditions. An ideal airport site might be within 20 miles of the city boundary, have at least four square miles of nearly level land, be within two miles of an expressway, and be at least three miles from a waterfowl area or other site (such as a landfill) that might attract birds. Problems of this type are best tackled with the aid of GIS software (discussed later in this chapter).

Other facility sites depend primarily on access or connections to distant places. This would be the case with a factory. Rarely are factories and distributors at the same locations, and the factory usually has many suppliers. Furthermore, supplies and products are seldom moved in a straight line "as the crow flies" but, rather, routed through a network of roads, railroads, and rivers.

To maximize product or service delivery under these conditions, the costs of moving supplies and products along transportation routes must be factored into site selection (**Figure 19.7**). Local access to an expressway, railroad, or airport might be critical. Vendors offer site selection software such as **Compass** and **ArcView Network Analyst**, databases, and services to help solve this complex problem. The payoff can be immense, since a well-chosen site can save much of the operating expense that would result from a poor location.

GEOGRAPHIC INFORMATION SYSTEMS

Stand-alone software for map analysis has its drawbacks. Since each vendor introduces its own special jargon and procedures, learning to use a new package can be a major chore. Data format requirements also differ among software packages. These different standards cause data compatibility conflicts when you try to analyze the same information with more than one software package.

Frustration with stand-alone software has led to development of integrated map-analysis packages, called **geographic information systems (GIS)**. A GIS aims to facilitate environmental data-handling by combining data collection, storage, manipulation (both numerical and graphical), and display into a single integrated system (**Figure 19.8**). Most of the analytical techniques we've discussed in this and previous chapters are now included in geographic information systems.

Perhaps the most ambitious, unique, and widely used system for GIS development is **ArcInfo**. A second major GIS is **Intergraph MGE.** Image processing programs with extensive GIS functions include **IDRISI** and **ERDAS Imagine.**

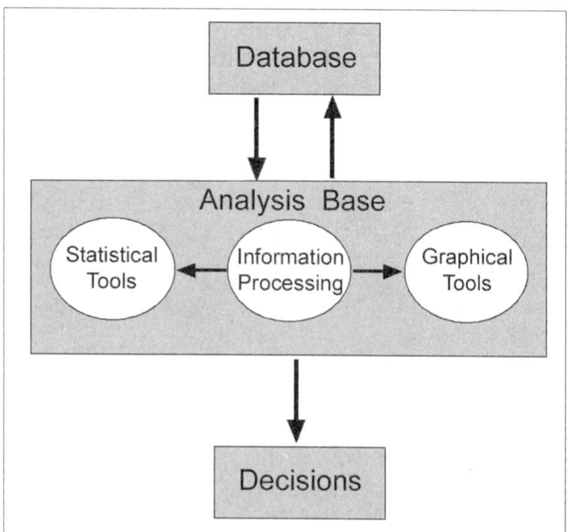

Figure 19.8 In a geographic information system (GIS), a database is integrated with powerful statistical and graphical tools of analysis to provide maps and other information needed in making environmental decisions.

GIS Data Sources

Data for GIS come from a wide variety of sources. The vector and raster data described in Appendix A can be used in most systems, particularly the TIGER and US GeoData vector files, digital elevation models (DEMs), and digital orthophoto quads. Tabular data from spreadsheets, text files, and other sources are a second major data source. Display-oriented systems allow the inclusion of graphs and diagrams, ground photos, and movie clips. A geographic location for each data element is all that is needed.

It is important that vector GIS data represent earth features either as points, lines, or polygons (closed lines and interior areas). Lines are defined by strings of points connected by straight-line segments, or by mathematical equations defining small sections of each line. Lengths of lines and areas of polygons are typically computed by the GIS and stored as part of the database. Topological relationships must be encoded in the data, specifically the beginning and ending points of each line and the polygon numbers to the right and left of the line. This allows the system to determine which lines are connected and which polygons are adjacent (**Figure 19.9**).

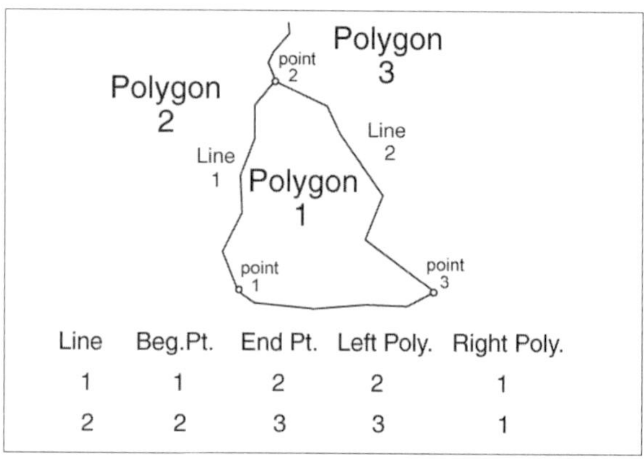

Line	Beg.Pt.	End Pt.	Left Poly.	Right Poly.
1	1	2	2	1
2	2	3	3	1

Figure 19.9 Vector GIS databases store features as points, lines, or polygons, along with their beginning/end point and right/left polygon topological information.

GIS data typically are organized by **theme**, and themes are also called **data layers** or **coverages**. Themes are often stored in separate data files that are shared among users or purchased from data vendors. Elevation, landcover, and satellite images are common raster themes. Typical vector themes include political boundaries, hydrography, transportation networks, property boundaries, and utility lines. The great thing about GIS, though, is that anything you can assign locations to can be made into a data theme with proper data conversion.

Data Conversion

A great deal of data processing may be required to make data for geographic information systems compatible. When maps of different scales and projections are scanned or digitized, the resulting data are recorded in arbitrary machine coordinates. These data have to be converted to a common geographic reference system before they can be used in a GIS. Geographic coordinates, such as latitude and longitude, UTM, or State Plane, are usually chosen for this purpose. Raster data not only must be converted to the same map projection and scale, but also to the same pixel resolution so that pixel centers for all themes are in the same ground location. When data conversion is complete, the data are identically **georeferenced**, and we can think of the data layers as correctly stacked over each other on the ground (**Figure 19.10**).

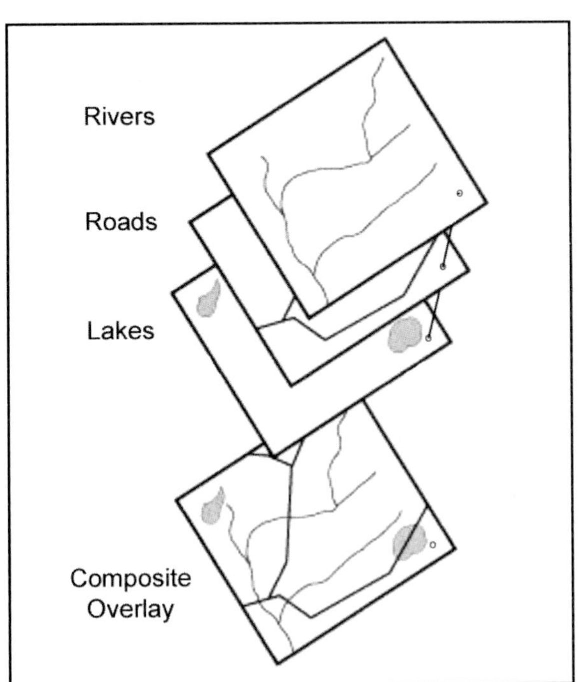

Figure 19.10 Environmental data that have been converted to a common coordinate system can be stacked in layers for spatial analysis.

Spatial Analysis

Spatial analysis is at the heart of GIS. Many map and image analysis problems can be reduced to answering one or more basic geographical questions dealing with spatial relationships among features. Six important questions are listed below:

- How far apart are features?
- How big is a feature?
- Which and how many features are adjacent to a feature?
- Which and how many features are within a certain distance of a feature?
- What is the average value of features within an area?
- Which and how many features share the same space?

These questions are answered using GIS spatial analysis tools we call Search Window, Buffer, Overlay, and Modeling.

Search Window

In theory, digital databases are seamless.* That is, they extend continuously in all directions from a point. When you want to see a particular region or analyze data within a certain area, you must open a **viewing** or **search window**. You may do so in several ways.

One way to specify a viewing window is to give a position and a search radius (**Figure 19.11A**). For example, you might instruct the computer to

**The database may be seamless, but the maps used to build the database are not. A displayed map may be based on parts of three printed maps differing by decades in their original production dates. So map borders do live on as database artifacts.*

show the region within 50 miles of a resort town. Alternatively, you might specify the borders of a rectangular viewing window by giving its southwest and northeast corners (**Figure 19.11B**). In the same fashion, you might create a less regular viewing window by specifying key border points (**Figure 19.11C**).

Search windows are defined the same way as viewing windows. But, in this case, the program goes beyond displaying a map to performing some numerical operation on the data within the specified region. Someone looking for a new business location might want to know, for example, how many people live in a square block or within a certain distance of a street intersection.

Buffer

Environmental decision makers are often interested in the zone, called an **offset** or **buffer**, surrounding features. To protect water quality, for example, environmental managers might create a buffer along lakes and streams within which logging is prohibited. Likewise, rural zoning laws may mandate that agricultural pesticides can't be used within 200 yards of a drinking-water well. Zoning laws may specify that buildings and other constructions (such as fences) must be offset at least 25 feet from the center of the street or highway. In each example, a GIS can display the buffer (**Figure 19.12**).

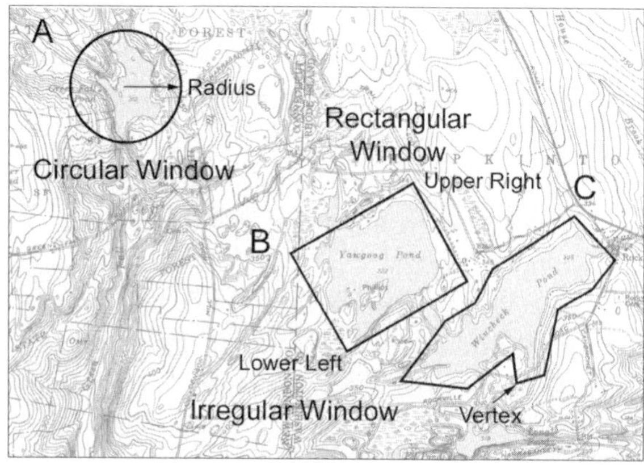

Figure 19.11 GIS users must create a window within which to display or analyze information held in the database.

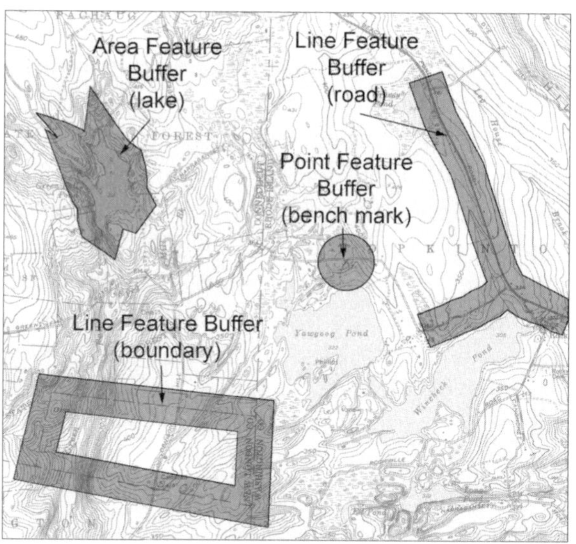

Figure 19.12 Buffer creation, which involves simple proximity analysis with respect to points, lines, and surfaces, is one of the most useful GIS functions.

A GIS also lets you **inventory** features or areas falling within a buffer. Thus, you can determine the number of acres in which logging or pesticide-based agriculture can't be practiced. If you want to know how much agricultural land or how many board feet of lumber are to be taken from production by the buffer, you can overlay the buffered features on the appropriate resource maps.

Overlay

To carry out their decision-making responsibilities, environmental managers must often consider combinations of variables. They might need to know, for example, how many people live in a floodplain or how many acres of an endangered species' habitat were destroyed by forest fires. To answer such questions, they must determine the extent of overlap between two distributions (**Figure 19.13**). The process is called **map overlay**, although it is carried out numerically in a GIS. The numerical operations are based on finding the **intersection** or **union** of two themes. You would, for example, answer the second question by determining the intersection of burned areas *and* habitat areas for the endangered species. The union of these two themes would be all burned areas *or* endangered species habitat.

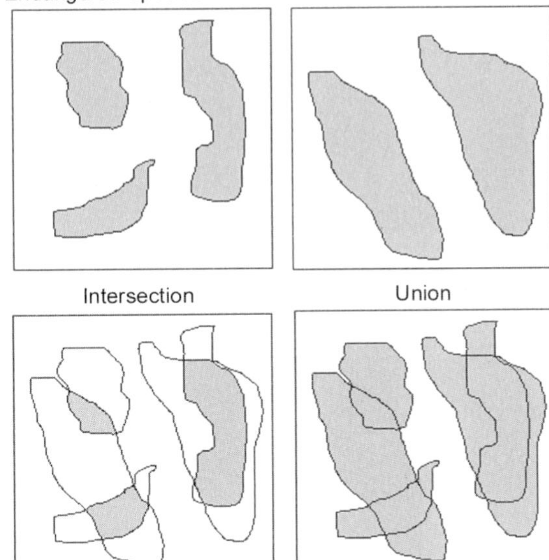

Figure 19.13 The extent of the intersection and the union between two or more distributions can be determined through a procedure called map-overlay analysis.

Overlay problems can involve more than two features, of course. Sometimes dozens of variables must be analyzed. Highway planners, for example, might need to consider such factors as terrain slope, soil, vegetation, land-parcel configuration, groundwater, and location of rivers and lakes. Progressive overlay of maps showing each variable would reveal those corridors most suitable for highway construction. Further analysis could then be used to choose the optimal corridor (see Spatial Optimization earlier in this chapter).

Even multiple-variable overlay procedures don't satisfy the needs of all land-information professionals. Despite the many repetitive calculations involved, overlay analysis is nothing more than the simple manipulation of raw data values. What we need is a modeling procedure that lets us weight individual variables to form composite measures. Let's consider these more sophisticated products of GIS analysis.

Modeling

Complex environmental problems lead to attempts to **model** spatial situations and processes. For instance, we might simulate atmospheric dispersion of radioactive gas from a damaged nuclear power plant under different weather conditions. Such information would be useful in planning evacuation routes in case of an accident. This modeling activity involves selecting variables perceived to be relevant and giving each of them a priority rating or weight.

The **weighted-composite measures** resulting from this activity have a meaning quite different from that of the simple analytical measures we discussed previously. There is a vast difference in the subjectivity of composite-variable analysis. To clarify weighted-composite analysis, let's look first at relatively value-free measures that characterize objective modeling, and then consider the more subjective case of value-laden measures.

Value-Free Measures. Some composite measures derived through GIS analysis are technologically weighted and, therefore, relatively value free. Environmental sensitivity, sustainability, or vulnerability measures are of this type. The computation and mapping of trafficability measures also fall into this class. Here, vehicle weight, traction, and dimensions are used with environmental measures of slope steepness, soil firmness, vegetation size and density, and other factors to determine the potential for cross-country vehicular movement. Although trafficability maps are primarily of military interest, they are also used in disaster relief operations, logging, and agriculture. A farmer planning a spring planting schedule might want to know, for example, how great an implement load each field could support in light of its soil and slope characteristics and recent weather conditions.

There are two main concerns with maps based on weighted-composite measures. One is that the data for each factor can vary greatly in quality. Soil, vegetation, slope, and similar distribution maps are themselves highly conceptual and generalized in nature. Composites made with these data can be only as good as the poorest component map—and may actually be worse due to the compounding effects of errors.

The second concern is the proper weight to be given each variable. In other words, how much should each variable contribute to the composite index? This is a matter of judgment. The farmer, for instance, in deciding whether to risk moving heavy equipment into a field where it might get bogged down and further delay spring planting, has to determine whether recent weather conditions should override inherent soil characteristics.

A key advantage of GIS modeling is the ease of changing the weights and running the model again. It is possible to create a number of alternative composite measures that can be analyzed to see how well each predicts actual ground conditions. You may find that additional variables need to be added to the model to increase its performance. It may also be that a variable like temperature does not play a significant role in the model and can be safely deleted. You can also test the sensitivity of each variable—that is, how do slight changes in the weights given to variables affect the composite index?

Value-Laden Measures. Weighting relatively value-free variables involves judgments concerning a variety of physical, economic, social, and technological factors. These judgments can be refined as knowledge of the factors improves. Thus, once the farmer learns the capabilities of the new tractor, determining trafficability of each field under different weather conditions will be enhanced.

Many weighted composites, however, involve human values as well. For instance, land managers may use a GIS to partition a region into zones most suitable for urban, recreational, industrial, agricultural, and waste-disposal uses. The results of such an analysis are displayed on a **land-suitability map** (**Figure 19.14**). Other value-laden composite measures include those that address issues of sustainability, susceptibility, desirability, and accessibility.

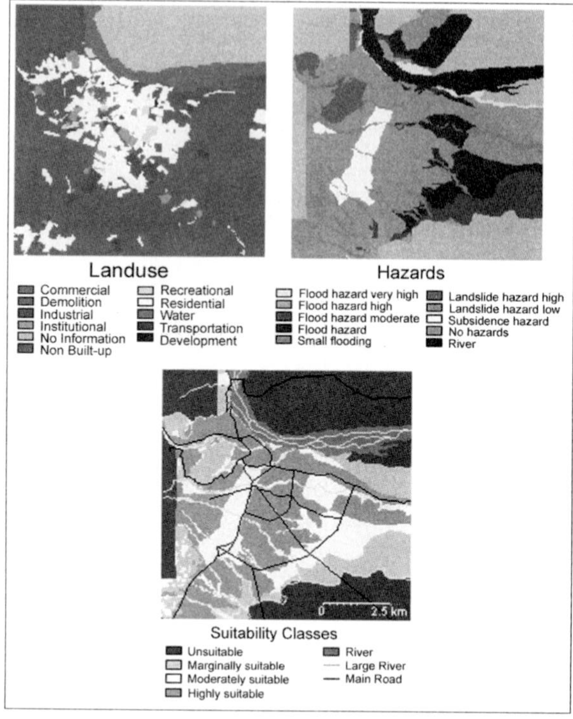

Figure 19.14 Partitioning land into zones most suitable for different uses involves values concerning which features are to be preserved, modified, and destroyed.

No matter how hard the analyst tries to be objective, the final composite measure will reflect values placed on such environmental factors as clean air, pure water, undisturbed soil, and healthy natural vegetation. Likewise, it will reflect values placed on such human factors as health, individual rights, taxation, and profit making. The land suitability map represents a balance between environmental and human factors. As such, it is as much the product of current environmental perception as of actual environmental conditions.

Care is needed when using maps based on value-laden composite measures. If different indexes were created at different times, by people of different cultural backgrounds, or for agencies with different responsibilities, the variable weightings and therefore the composite measure might well be different. We need only look at how greatly values can change from one time to another. Just 25 years ago in the United States, for instance, it was legal to dump toxic industrial wastes into lakes and streams; asbestos was being used to insulate school buildings; cars burned leaded gasoline; and nuclear power plants were thought to be the answer to low-cost energy production.

LINKING GIS AND GPS

Map analysis can be moved from the laboratory into the field with the help of GPS technology (see Chapter 14: GPS and Maps). You use the GPS receiver to determine the coordinates of your current position, and then use these coordinates to display your position, route, and destination. You can also use GPS technology to attach coordinates to data being gathered as you traverse the landscape, thereby producing a **geocoded database** directly in the field. This can be done with a laptop computer running a GIS capable of recording the geographic positions and structuring the locational data into points, lines, or polygons for the map theme. You can later use this geocoded database to guide environmental activities. Let's look at how GPS and GIS have been linked to create a new form of agricultural management—precision farming.

Precision Farming

In precision farming, you attach a GPS unit to a computer loaded with your GIS. The GIS serves as a **crop-yield monitor** linked to your harvesting equipment. As you harvest your crop, the GIS geocodes the yield data every meter or so, producing a precise yield map of the field.

The next step is to produce an equally detailed soils map of the field and to map other significant factors, such as past management practices, ground slope, and the groundwater table. The GIS is then used to analyze the yield map in relation to these factors. A crop management plan will emerge from this analysis. During the next cropping season, the farmer will use this plan to guide soil preparation, planting, and chemical applications.

Chemical and seed applications are made with equipment guided by a computer with a GIS and a GPS receiver. The GPS unit keeps track of where the equipment is in the field and the optimum mix of chemicals and seeds is at each location. Since treatments may vary from one location to the next, the equipment must be capable of variable rate applications.

Precision agriculture makes possible the farming of individual soils in a field. The economic benefit is that precision farming minimizes expenses while maximizing profits. The environmental benefit is that applications of chemicals that go beyond crop needs are minimized, so that chemicals aren't left in the landscape to contaminate the soil and water.

SELECTED READINGS

Berry, J.K., *Spatial Reasoning for Effective GIS* (Fort Collins, CO: GIS World, 1995).

Chou, T.H., *Exploring Spatial Analysis in Geographic Information Systems* (Santa Fe: On Word Press, 1997).

Chrisman, N., *Exploring Geographic Information Systems* (New York: John Wiley & Sons, 1997).

Clarke, K.C., *Getting Started with Geographic Information Systems* (Upper Saddle River, NJ: Prentice-Hall, 1997).

Greene, R.W., *GIS in Public Policy* (Redlands, CA: Environmental Systems Research Institute, 2000).

Heit, M., and Shortreid, A., eds., *GIS Applications in Natural Resources* (Fort Collins, CO: GIS World Inc., 1991).

Johnson, A.I., et al., eds. *Geographic Information Systems and Mapping: Practices and Standards* (Philadelphia: American Society for Testing & Materials, 1992).

Lang, L., *Managing Natural Resources with GIS* (Redlands, CA: Environmental Systems Research Institute, 1998).

Laserna, R., and Landis, J., *Desktop Mapping for Planning and Strategic Decision Making* (San Jose, CA: Strategic Mapping, 1990).

Longley, P.A., Goodchild, M.F., and Maguire, D.J., *Geographical Information Systems: Principles and Applications* (New York: John Wiley & Sons, 1999).

Steede-Terry, K., *Integrating GIS and the Global Positioning System*, Redlands, CA: Environmental Systems Research Institure, 2000).

Taylor, D.R.F., ed., *Geographic Information Systems: The Microcomputer and Modern Cartography* (New York: Pergamon Press, 1991).

Tomlin, C.D., *Geographic Information Systems and Cartographic Modelling* (Englewood Cliffs, NJ: Prentice-Hall, 1990).

CHAPTER TWENTY
AERIAL PHOTO ANALYSIS

20

CHAPTER TWENTY

AERIAL PHOTO ANALYSIS

We saw in Chapter 9 that aerial photographs are a rich source of detailed information about features on the earth's surface. You can obtain much of this information by making measurements on the photos. You can make measurements of feature length, area, and volume using the methods in Chapter 15. You can also use special methods to measure object heights from photos, as you'll see in this chapter.. These measurements depend on knowing the scale of the aerial photo, so let's first look at how you can determine the photo scale.

FINDING THE PHOTO SCALE

In Chapter 9 we saw that standard 9 × 9 inch vertical aerial photographs have **fiducial marks** inserted at each corner and at the midpoint of each edge (**Figure 20.1**). If you draw straight lines connecting opposite pairs of fiducial marks, the point where the lines intersect is called the **principal point** of the photo. If the aircraft isn't tilted at the instant the photo is taken, a truly vertical photo is acquired and the principal point corresponds to the point directly under the camera. We call this the **nadir point**.

The first method for finding the scale of a vertical aerial photograph at the nadir point depends on knowing the **focal length** (f) of the aerial camera and the **flying height** (H) above the nadir. A typical 9 × 9 inch aerial mapping camera has a 6-inch focal length lens, although high-altitude aerial photography is sometimes taken with a 12-inch focal length lens.

Modern aircraft have laser altimeters that continuously record the flying height above the ground at the nadir. The flying height or altitude may be printed on the edge of the photo, or obtained for each frame from the company or agency that flew the photography.

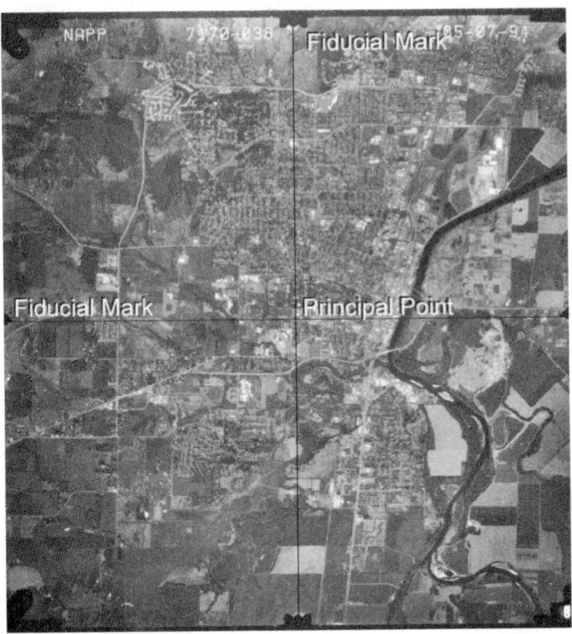

Figure 20.1 The principal point of an aerial photo is the intersection point of straight lines connecting opposite pairs of fiducial marks.

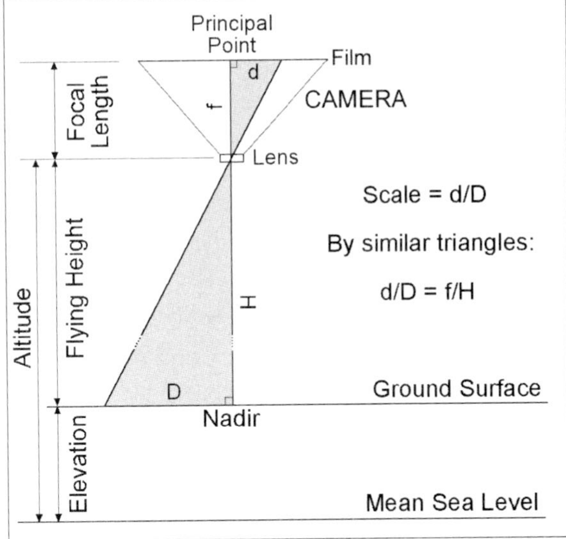

Figure 20.2 The equation Photo Scale = f/H is obtained from the geometry of similar triangles relating positions on the ground and aerial photo.

Older aerial photos may have heights based on altitude above sea level. On these older photos, you will need to measure the elevation of the nadir point from a topographic map or go out into the field and check the elevation with a GPS receiver. To obtain the flying height, you subtract the elevation from the altitude.

Once you know the focal length and flying height, you can determine the photo scale at the nadir point by using the simple geometry of similar triangles. As **Figure 20.2** shows, the ratio of photo distance to ground distance (f/H) is used to find the RF. Hence, the RF can be computed from the equation $1/x = f/H$, and the scale denominator from $x = H/f$.

Here's a simple example of how you can determine scale. Imagine that you have an aerial photo that was obtained with a 6-inch focal length camera lens at a flying height of 10,000 feet above the ground at the nadir point. Remembering that f and H must be in the same units of measurement, you can calculate the scale denominator at the nadir point as follows:

$$x = H/f = (10{,}000 \text{ ft} \times 12 \text{ in/ft})/ 6 \text{ in} = 20{,}000$$

so that the photo RF is 1/20,000.

Now for a slightly more complex example. This time, suppose you have an aerial photo that was obtained with a 6-inch focal length camera lens at a flying altitude of 10,000 feet above sea level and the elevation at the nadir point was 2,000 feet. The photo scale equation now is:

$$\begin{aligned} x &= (\text{alt. - elev.})/f \\ &= ((10{,}000 \text{ ft} - 2{,}000 \text{ ft}) \times 12 \text{ in/ft})/6 \text{ in} \\ &= 16{,}000 \end{aligned}$$

so that the photo RF is 1/16,000 at the nadir point.

Remember that this photo scale calculation is only correct at the principal point of a truly vertical aerial photo, since the scale will most likely differ as we move away from the ground nadir point. The primary reason that this **radial scale distortion** is characteristic of vertical photos is that objects of different heights are displaced radially about the principal point. If the top of a feature is higher than average ground level, it will be displaced outward. Inward displacement occurs with objects lying below average ground level. The geometric explanation for this pattern of radial displacement

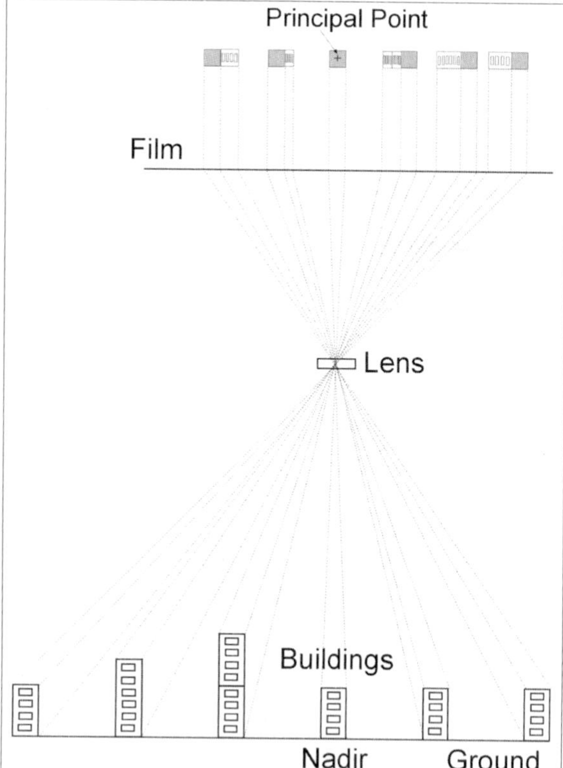

Figure 20.3 Radial scale distortion on aerial photos causes tops of buildings and other tall features to be displaced outward from the principal point of the photo. The amount of displacement varies with the distance from the principal point and the height of the feature.

is provided in **Figure 20.3**. Notice the relation between the position of features on the ground and on the film. The greater the height or depth of features relative to the ground, and the farther features are from the center of the photo, the greater their radial displacement.

What if you don't know the camera focal length or the flying height, or if you need to find the exact photo scale at a location away from the center of the photo? When faced with these common situations, you can use the **measured length of a known terrestrial feature** (see Chapter 2) to determine scale. Lengths and widths for several of the relatively few features of standard dimensions that are visible on aerial photos are given in **Table 20.1**. For any of these features, you can compute the photo RF from the following equation, remembering that the units of measurement must be the same in the numerator and denominator:

Table 20.1 Standard Lengths and Widths of Ground Features

Feature	Dimension
U.S. Football Field	160 ft wide
	300 ft long (goal lines)
	360 ft long (end zones)
Baseball Field	90 ft (adjacent bases)
	127.5 ft (home to 2nd)
	60 ft (home to mound)
Tennis Court	78 ft long
	27 ft wide (singles)
	36 ft wide (doubles)
Olympic Swim Pool	50 m long
	25 m wide
Olympic Track	70 m infield width
	90 m infield length
	35 m semicircle radius
	1 m lane width
U.S. Freeways	12 ft lane widths
U.S. Railways	4.7 ft between rails

$$\frac{1}{x} = \frac{\text{measured length or width}}{\text{standard length or width}}$$

You may want to invert this equation to first determine the scale denominator. For instance, if you see a baseball field on the photo and measure the distance from home plate to second base as 0.12 inches, you can calculate the photo RF as follows:

$$1/x = 0.12 \text{ in} \,/\, (127.25 \text{ ft} \times 12 \text{ in/ft}) \text{ or}$$
$$x = 127.25 \times 12 \,/\, 0.12 = 12{,}725$$
$$RF = 1{:}12{,}275$$

There's another, more common way to determine the photo scale. You can simply measure the distance between two points on the photo and a map or image of known scale. Using this method, you would find the RF for the photo as follows:

$$\frac{\frac{1}{x}}{\frac{1}{msd}} = \frac{pd}{md} \qquad x = \frac{msd \times md}{pd}$$

where msd is the map scale denominator, md is the map distance, and pd is the photo distance.

For example, suppose the distance between the same two road intersections is measured as 0.3 inches on the aerial photo and 0.6 inches on a 1:24,000 scale topographic map. In this case:

$$x = 24{,}000 \times 0.6 \text{ in}/\ 0.3 \text{ in} = 48{,}000$$

so that the photo RF is 1:48,000.

MEASURING OBJECT HEIGHTS

Sometimes you may want to know the heights of ground features, such as trees or buildings. There are three common ways to find the heights of features from measurements made on aerial photos. We call these the radial displacement, shadow length, and parallax methods.

Radial Displacement Method

You may be able to determine the height of a vertical feature like an apartment building or telephone pole quite accurately using a single large-scale, vertical aerial photograph by measuring its **radial displacement** outward from the photo center.

Using this method, you determine object heights by the following geometrical relationship (see **Figure 20.4**):

$$\text{Height of object } (h_o) = H \times d/r$$

where:
d = the length of the displaced image on the photo.
r = the radial distance from the principal point to the top of the displaced image. (This must be measured in the same units as d.)
H = the aircraft flying height above the base of the displaced object. (This number must be given in the units desired for the object's height.)

Figure 20.4 You can determine the height of a feature such as the U.S. Steel building in New York City from its radial displacement on a vertical aerial photograph.

For example, if you assume that the original 9 inch × 9 inch photo of the World Trade Center site (reduced by two-thirds in Figure 20.4) was taken from a flying height of 3,000 ft. with d and r measured as 0.7 and 2.8 inches, you can compute the U.S. Steel building height as follows:

$$h_o = 3{,}000 \text{ ft.} \times 0.7 \text{ in.} / 2.8 \text{ in.} = 750 \text{ ft.}$$

Notice that d was measured as 0.7 inches from the bottom to top of the feature along the radial line from the principal point to the bottom, as was the 2.8 inch measurement for r.

The accuracy of this height determination depends on several factors. The photo must be truly vertical (non-tilted) so that you can accept the principal point as the nadir point. You must know the precise flight altitude above the base of the object. Both the base and top of the displaced object must be clearly visible. And, finally, the degree of image displacement must be great enough to be measured with available equipment (such as an engineer's scale). If any of these conditions is open to question, you should regard resulting height determinations as approximate only.

Shadow Length Method

You can also compute the heights of objects by measuring shadow lengths on a vertical photo if several conditions are met:

✎ The object must be vertical (perpendicular to the earth's surface) and its bottom must be visible.

✎ The object's shadow must be cast from its top, not its side.

✎ The shadow must fall on open ground at the level of the object's base, where it is undistorted and easily measured.

✎ You must know the height of another vertical feature whose shadow can be measured precisely on the photo.

If these conditions are satisfied, you can determine the object's height by using the fact that the **length of an object's shadow is directly proportional to its height**. As you can see in **Figure 20.5**, height computations involve the basic geometry of similar triangles:

$$\text{Height of object } (h_x) = h_o \times S_x / S_o.$$

For example, if the 24-foot vertical light pole in **Figure 20.6** casts a 0.16 inch shadow on level ground, the adjacent seven-story building casting a 0.57 inch shadow would be:

$$h_x = 24 \text{ ft} \times 0.57 \text{ in} / 0.16 \text{ in} = 86 \text{ feet tall.}$$

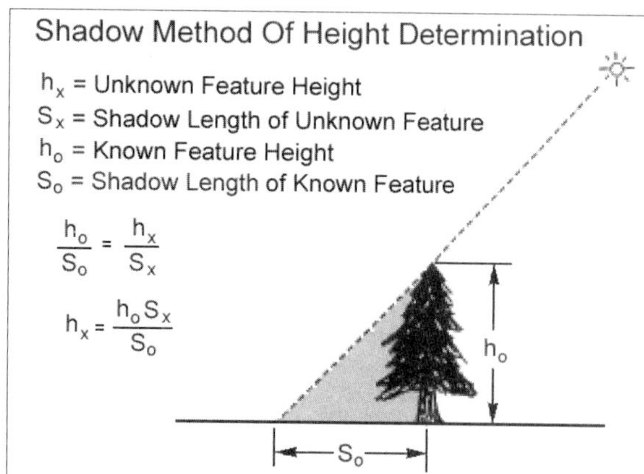

Figure 20.5 Under special conditions, you can determine the height of an object on a vertical aerial photograph from its shadow length and the ratio of height to shadow length for a known feature.

Figure 20.6 Shadow length measurements for a 24 foot light pole and building of unknown height.

To obtain accurate results, you should measure shadow length to the nearest 0.01 inch or less. In the previous illustration, for example, an error of only 0.01 inch in measuring the light pole shadow length on the photo would lead to a 5-foot difference in the calculated building height.

Parallax Method

Although the radial displacement and shadow length methods of object height determination are useful when only a single photo is available, they depend on so many hard-to-control factors that they don't always provide reliable height measurements. A valuable alternative to use when adjacent overlapping photographs are available is the **parallax method of height determination**. "Parallax" is the term given to the apparent displacement of objects when viewed from the perspective of different vantage points.

It is common to take aerial photos with a single camera pointed straight down from a moving airplane.These photos are usually taken so that successive photos along the flightline overlap. Thus, all features appear on at least two images (**Figure 20.7**). Each pair of overlapping photos is called a **stereopair**. Since the two photos in a stereopair are taken of the same landform from slightly different observation points, parallax is a normal characteristic of these overlapping vertical photographs.

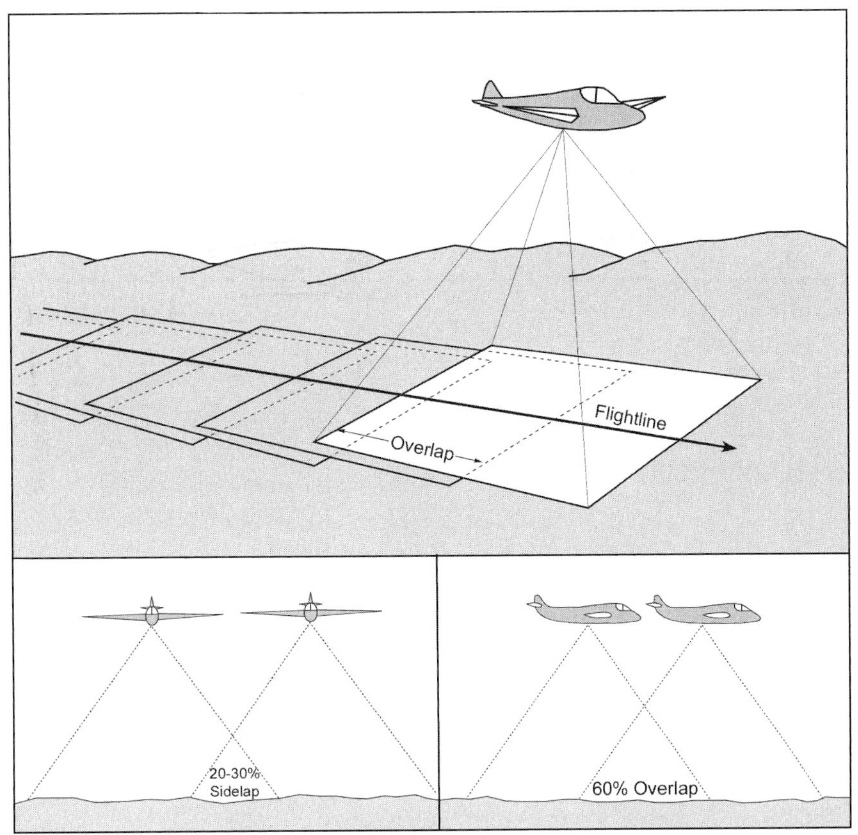

Figure 20.7 Adjacent aerial photos are taken so as to overlap 60 percent along the flightline and 20 to 30 percent between flightlines (sidelap) to ensure overlapping ground coverage.

To determine an object's height using the parallax method, you must first obtain two parallax measurements. Before making these measurements, first align the stereopair along the flightline, as illustrated in **Figure 20.8**. To find the flightline, you must determine the principal point (PP) for each photo, then find what are called the **conjugate principal points** (CPPs). A CPP is the location of the principal point on the first photo located and plotted as a point on the second photo. Hence, each overlapping photo should have a CPP plotted for the principal points of the preceding and succeeding photos. Assuming that the aircraft flew in a straight line between each photo that was taken, a straight line between the PP and each CPP defines the flightline. The photos must be aligned so that the plotted flightlines fall on a horizontal line.

Once the photos are properly aligned, you're ready to determine the object's height using the parallax method. The first step is to compute the **absolute parallax** (P). You can do so by summing the distance (measured along the horizontal flightline) from the principal point to the bottom of the object on each photo. An alternate way to find the absolute parallax is to find the average of the distance between the principal point and conjugate principal point on the two photos, each measured along the flightline.

The second step in finding the object's height is to compute the **differential parallax** (dP). The differential parallax is simply the difference in absolute parallax at the top and bottom of the object being measured. The easiest way to calculate the differential parallax is to measure the distance (along the flightline) between the top of the object on the first photo and the top of the object on the second photo. Then measure the distance between the bottom of the object on the first photo and the

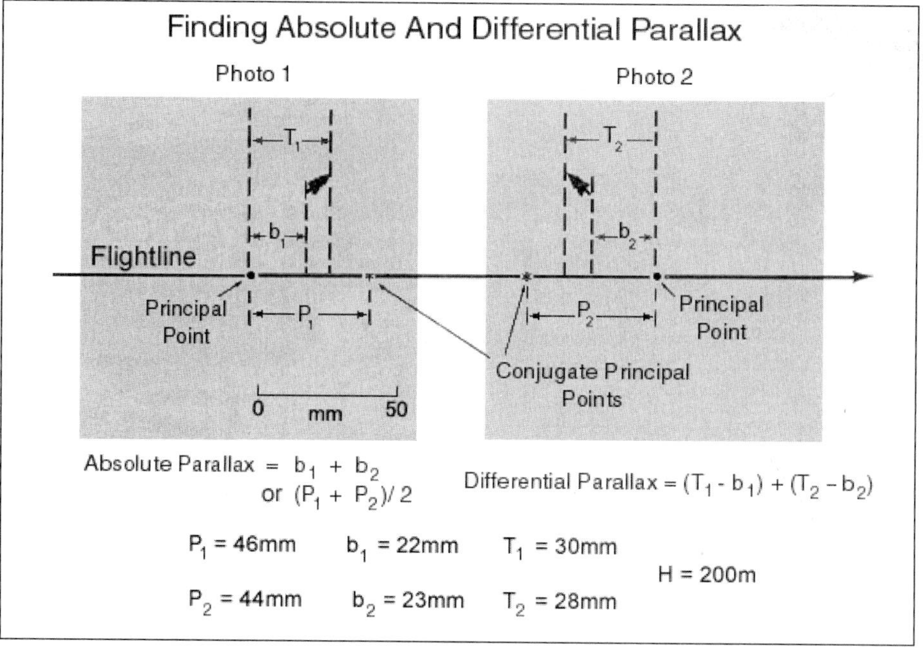

Figure 20.8 You can determine an object's height from a pair of overlapping vertical aerial photographs by lining the photos up along their flightline and then measuring the object's absolute and differential parallax.

bottom of the object on the second photo. To find the differential parallax, you simply subtract the top distance from the bottom distance.

With these two parallax measurements completed, you can determine the object's height by applying the following equation:

$$\text{Height of object } (h_o) = H \times dP / (P + dP)$$

where H is the aircraft's height above the object's base (expressed in the units desired for the object height, usually feet or meters), and dP (differential parallax) and P (absolute parallax) are expressed in the same units (usually hundredths of inches or millimeters).

In Figure 20.8, the flying height of the aircraft is given as 200 meters. The absolute parallax of the tree is measured as 22 mm + 23 mm = 45 mm, while the differential parallax is computed to be 8 + 5 = 13 mm. Thus, by substitution:

$$h_o = 200 \text{ m} \times 13 \text{ mm} / (45 \text{ mm} + 13 \text{ mm}) = 45 \text{ meters}$$

The accuracy of this object height estimate depends on how precisely you can make the two parallax measurements and how close the true flying height is to 200 meters.

STEREOVIEWING AND HEIGHT MEASUREMENT

Depth perception is based on your eyes capturing two slightly offset images of the environment. Through a process called "cortical fusion," your brain converts the parallax differences in the two images into a three-dimensional perception of the world.

Stereoviewing is the process whereby you view the area of overlap on two adjacent aerial photos separately with each eye to create a three-dimensional image of the environment in your mind. The standard method is to view the overlap area on each photo through one of the two lenses in a **stereoscope** viewing device (**Figure 20.9**).

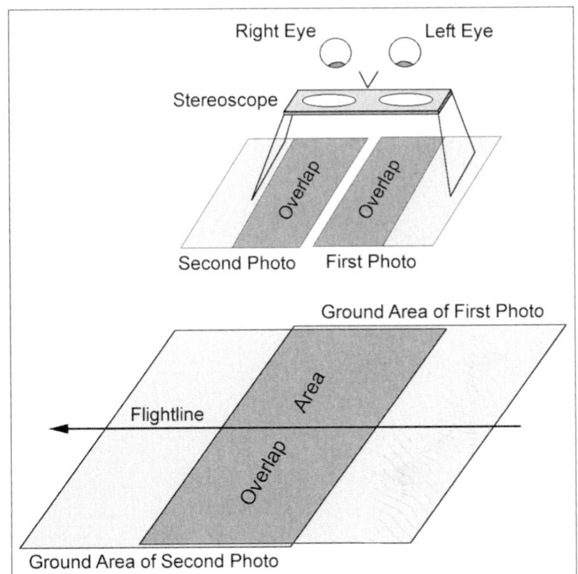

Figure 20.9 A stereoscope is used to view separately the area of overlap on two adjacent air photos.

Using the Parallax Bar

To improve measurement precision, it helps to measure the differential parallax **stereoscopically** with a **parallax bar** (**Figure 20.10**). The parallax bar has two small glass plates attached, each with a "floating dot" in the center. The left dot is fixed, but you can move the right dot horizontally by turning the dial at the right end of the bar. A vernier scale on the dial allows you to make measurements to a precision of one tenth the smallest division on the main scale of the instrument. The parallax bar in Figure 20.10 gives measurements of one-hundredth of a millimeter precision, for example.

To obtain a reading, align the stereoscope and attached parallax bar with the flightline. Then move the stereoscope so that the left dot is at the base of the object. Viewing the photo through the stereoscope, turn the dial until you see the right and left dots fuse, then read the vernier scale to make the precise measurement.

Now, repeat the procedure so that both dots appear to "float" at the top of the object. Take a second vernier scale reading. The difference of the two measurements gives the differential parallax.

The precision of stereoscopically determined measurement depends on your ability to see the top and bottom of the object on both photos. It helps immensely to have an object clearly imaged on high-resolution photos of known scale and flight altitude.

Figure 20.10 A parallax bar attached to a stereoscope is used to precisely measure differential parallax.

SELECTED READINGS

Avery, T.E. and Berlin, G.L., *Fundamentals of Remote Sensing and Airphoto Interpretation* (Upper Saddle River, NJ: Prentice Hall, 1992).

Campbell, J.B., *Introduction to Remote Sensing*, 2nd ed. (New York: The Guilford Press, 1996).

Ciciarelli, J.A., *Practical Guide to Aerial Photography: With an Introduction to Surveying* (New York: Van Nostrand Reinhold, 1991).

Jensen, J.R., *Remote Sensing of the Environment: An Earth Resource Perspective* (Upper Saddle River, NJ: Prentice Hall, 2000).

Lillesand, T.M. and Kiefer, R.W., *Remote Sensing and Image Interpretation*, 3rd.ed. (New York: John Wiley & Sons, 1994).

III

PART THREE
MAP INTERPRETATION

You practice interpretation every day. When you notice that things seem to form a pattern, you ask yourself, "Why?" If you come into class and find everybody crowded into one corner, you'll be struck by this unusual arrangement of students. You can describe their grouping as a clustered distribution, but that won't explain why they're clumped over there. Are they looking at something fascinating or trying to hide from something terrible? Has there been an accident or a great discovery? Your curiosity will likely be aroused to find the answer.

When you interpret a map, you do the same thing. You notice unusual or interesting patterns and seek explanations for them. The difference is that in map interpretation there is a buffer between you and your environment. Features and distributions are generalized and symbolized. Thus, the answers to your questions won't often be immediately obvious. The map can include only enough clues to provide you with touchstones, starting points for discovery. Maps are springboards for the imagination, trigger devices to set you questioning and inspire you to search for answers.

As we emphasized in our discussion of map reading (*Part I*), the relationship between reality and its map representation is not one-to-one. It requires a creative effort to move from the static, simplified map to the vibrancy and detail of the environment. The distinction between map reading and interpretation is analogous to the difference between reading a book for its obvious story line and interpreting the book's symbolism to discover what the author was trying to show. With a book or a map, one must learn to "read between the lines."

Intuition is an important part of map interpretation, just as it is in interpreting a book, a poem, or a painting. Therefore, the validity of your inferences depends on your ability to let the map serve as a surrogate for your environment. As your mental map improves, so will your skill at interpretation.

You can approach map interpretation in two ways. You can look at one map and seek explanations for the patterns you see. Or you can compare several maps from different periods and speculate on what processes might have produced the changes that have taken place over time.

Even if you use just one map, you are looking at time as well as space. Present environmental forms are the result of past environmental processes. Since these "results" are what maps depict, map interpretation rests upon inferences about the past. Thus, time should never be overlooked as a possible factor in map interpretation. When a pattern differs from one place to another, it may be due to varying conditions in different areas at the same time, or it may be due to the fact that the patterns developed under the same conditions but at different times.

It is also important to be aware that a variety of different processes can lead to the same result. This is known as the **principle of equifinity**. There may be a lack of trees in an area, for example, because the climate isn't conducive to vegetation, or because there has been a forest fire, or because the trees have been cut down. The map interpreter must decide which of these or other possible explanations applies in a particular case.

The opposite is also true. A single process can end in a number of different results. The process of building a city, for instance, can lead to a wide variety of city patterns.

Map interpretation, then, is a complex, creative act. Everything you've learned so far about map reading and analysis will be put to use. In fact, everything you've learned throughout your life will be helpful. For interpretation requires an understanding of more than maps. You must also have some knowledge of the features depicted on the map. To explain the pattern of soils on a map, you must know a number of things about the area, such as its climate, bedrock geology, and whether it has been glaciated.

Obviously, it is impossible to include all these potentially important factors on one map. The resulting portrayal would be cluttered and complex beyond human comprehension. Consequently, interpretation requires going beyond the map itself and seeking additional information elsewhere. The best source of such information may be other maps. Many patterns will become clear as you compare one map to another and study the patterns of related phenomena.

As you gain proficiency in map interpretation, you'll be amazed at your ability to generalize from situation to situation. The explanation of some small detail of the environment will often provide the basis for understanding many other features in the surrounding area as well. Similarly, the clues you use to explain phenomena in your local area can help you to understand things in other parts of the world and even on other planets.

Map interpretation is a skill that comes with practice, a skill that can't really be taught in a book. All we can do here is to give examples of interpretation and describe some general procedures that might be used. For convenience, we'll deal first with the interpretation of air photos and other remote sensor images (Chapter 21). We'll then look at using maps to interpret landforms and geology (Chapter 22), the atmosphere and biosphere (Chapter 23), and then the human landscape (Chapter 24). Finally, in Chapter 25, we'll discuss pitfalls associated with treating maps as reality and reality as a map.

The examples of map interpretation given in these chapters are by no means exhaustive. They merely represent a selection of interpretative situations and problems you may encounter. As you go through them, you'll notice that there are a few basic methods which are used repeatedly. Also, since the interpretation of a map often requires finding other maps to study and compare, many of these examples use other maps in the explanation.

Interpretation is open-ended. Comprehension is never complete. Each new experience you have, in every facet of life, will give you new understanding and allow you to extract new meaning. If you have ever reread a book years later, you found that you gained different insights from it than you did the first time, because you had grown. So it is with a map. The more you bring to it, the more you will gain from it.

Of all the aspects of map use, interpretation requires the most from the map user. You must give all of yourself. Every subject you have studied, every experience you have ever had, every thought process you have mastered, contributes to your interpretation of a map. Interpretation is the most demanding of all map use endeavors.

It is also the most exciting. You can spend hours lost in an interesting map, just as you can in a good book. Everyone loves a mystery, they say, and a map is as enthralling as any detective story. Hidden within that pattern of map symbols is the very essence of the environment. The map interpreter's challenge is to search out those buried meanings, to piece together the fragments of mapped information and come up with a picture of vibrant, ever-changing reality. Once you have met that challenge and discovered the rewards of interpretation, you'll look at all maps in a new way, picking out intriguing patterns and asking yourself, "Why?"

CHAPTER 21
IMAGE INTERPRETATION

THE NATURE OF IMAGE INTERPRETATION

IMAGE INTERPRETATION ELEMENTS

- Shape
- Tone
  - Panchromatic Imagery
  - Near-Infrared Imagery
  - Thermal-Infrared Imagery
  - Radar Imagery
- Color
- Size
- Height
- Shadow
- Pattern
- Texture
- Site and Situation

SCALE GRADIENT

INTERPRETATION STRATEGY

- Checklist
- 20 Questions
- Quotas
- Meaning

MENTAL TEMPLATES

SMALL-SCALE SATELLITE IMAGE INTERPRETATION

DIGITAL IMAGE CLASSIFICATION

- Supervised Classification

SELECTED READINGS

It is a hieroglyphical and shadowed lesson of the whole world.
—Sir Thomas Browne

21

CHAPTER 21

IMAGE INTERPRETATION

As a map interpreter, you can think of conventional maps as value-added products. The cartographer has separated environmental features by category so that you see different symbols for roads, buildings, water, and so forth. If the meaning of a symbol isn't obvious, you merely look it up in the map's legend. With feature identification so simplified, you can devote your attention to problems of interpretation.

The simplicity of conventional maps does have a price, however. For one thing, a cartographer has determined what features in the environment to represent on the map, and what symbols to use for each feature. These cartographic decisions may not suit your needs. You must make do with the cartographer's generalized version of the environment, unless you have access to an aerial photo or other image of the area.

Another problem is that the process of making a map is costly. It demands time, labor, and capital. For this reason, conventional maps of the features you want to see may not be available at large map scales or frequent time intervals. Images often serve as a substitute for conventional maps in these situations.

So, for these reasons, it's helpful to learn to interpret aerial photos and other images. They will prove the ultimate test of your interpretation ability. You'll be dealing with an image made up of different tones, colors, textures, patterns, and shapes.

Images contain a detailed record of the environment at the time the image was created. But they aren't a complete document of the environment. What they contain depends on sensor sensitivity (spectral, spatial, radiometric) and vantage point. Within the constraints set by these factors, images usually provide less of a buffer between reality and map user than do conventional maps. The person using an image is in a sense closer to the environment than when using conventional maps. There has been less cartographic intervention in the representation of the environment.

Image interpretation is based on visual clues provided by the different tones, colors, sizes, and shapes seen on the image. These clues lead to visual detection, then to visual differentiation, and finally to feature recognition.

Image interpretation has been used in many fields, including agriculture, forestry, geology, meteorology, archeology, oceanography, soil science, ecology, civil engineering, planning, medicine, astronomy, and military intelligence. No matter what the field, the same visual elements and procedures form the basis for interpretation.

THE NATURE OF IMAGE INTERPRETATION

Image interpretation may seem strange at first, because it forces you to conjure up features for yourself, and try to identify what you're seeing. Most people have had little training in this type of picture-based thinking and, therefore, feel more comfortable with word-based thought. But with some guidance and experience, you'll be amazed at how much you can learn from an image map.

Expert image map interpreters seem to work effortlessly, with no apparent rules. They "just know" what something is at a glance. If you look at **Figure 21.1**, you can experience this for yourself. If you instantly recognize a road, house, river, or some other feature, you know that "expert" feeling of just knowing. If asked how you knew the identity of a feature, you might first say, "I just knew." If questioned further, you probably could come up with a list of reasons to support your answer.

Expert image interpretation requires that you meld analytical and holistic thinking into a single, integrated approach. Perhaps most important, experts have learned to use the image as a trigger to dredge up tacit knowledge from their subconscious. They are able to imagine how things they have experienced in day-to-day living might look when viewed from a distant oblique or vertical vantage point, with little side-view information to provide familiar identification cues.

Figure 21.1 Even a novice can usually identify some features on a conventional aerial photo at a glance. See how you do.

While such expert skills don't come automatically, there are strategies that will help you learn them. First, you may need to enrich your language of spatial terms. **Feature identification elements** include: shape, tone, color, size, height, shadow, pattern, texture, and site/situation. This list provides a useful spatial vocabulary and can be applied to all forms of image interpretation. Only the meaning of the elements differs from field to field. Thus, what you see on an aerial photo as a dark patch of evergreen trees in a lighter-toned deciduous forest, a radiologist might see as a dark clump of cancer cells against a background of healthy tissue.

IMAGE INTERPRETATION ELEMENTS

The following discussion considers image interpretation elements separately. Ultimately, however, you must recognize that these elements are different aspects of a feature. When you integrate these elements into a full understanding of the feature, you'll move from a novice to an expert image interpreter.

Shape

An object's **shape** is the most fundamental identification clue. Your eyes are inherently drawn to the edges of features. Indeed, your brain has a special mechanism for processing these edges.

When interpreting shapes on an image, first decide if a shape is likely of natural or human origin (see **Figure 21.2**). Natural features tend to have irregular shapes. In contrast, features resulting from human activity tend to have simple geometric forms (straight sides, sharp angles, smooth curves).

This division into natural vs. human is only a general guideline, however. Natural features can sometimes have regular shapes, as is the case with a smooth sandy coastline, a river running along a fault line, or vegetation stopping abruptly at a break between bedrock types.

Conversely, human activity can sometimes result in deceptively irregular shapes, as when a strip mine follows an outcrop of coal along a valley, or a farm field conforms to a fertile soil region in otherwise infertile soils.

Tone

Tone refers to an object's lightness or darkness on the image. Although different colors vary in lightness, we'll focus here on the achromatic gray-tone range from black to white. (We'll explore the two other dimensions of color, hue and saturation, when we examine the element of color later in this chapter.)

Tone is an important visual cue because tonal differences create contrasts which are fundamental to feature detection and identification. Since the interpretation of tonal variation differs from one type of image to another, let's look first at tones on panchromatic aerial photos. Then we'll compare these with the interpretation of tones on near-infrared, thermal-infrared, and radar images.

Figure 21.2 Features of natural and human origin on this aerial photo of The Breakers, Newport, R.I. You can tell that most of the features are of human origin because of their regular shapes.

Panchromatic Imagery

On black-and-white panchromatic aerial photography and other images recording visible light, tones are determined by the amount of light reflected from each object on the ground. An object's reflectance depends, first, on its surface characteristics and, second, on how it is positioned in the environment.

A smooth, shiny surface is highly reflective, like a mirror. The reflected light leaves the surface at the same angle as it arrives from its source but in the opposite direction (see the left diagram in **Figure 21.3**). You can think of these shiny surfaces as **mirror reflectors** (also called **specular reflectors** in remote sensing).

It's important to note that the tone on the photo may be more than a simple matter of surface smoothness. Tone also depends on the position of the sun and the aerial camera. Thus, a highly reflective surface such as a lake on a calm day may appear black on one part of the photo and white on another, depending on where the light is reflected specularly relative to the camera position. Ocean and lake waves are also commonly identified by alternating light and dark lines across the image that correspond to high and low specular reflection from each wave (**Figure 21.4**).

In contrast to mirror reflectors are objects with uniformly rough surfaces that scatter or diffuse light in many directions (see the middle diagram in Figure 21.3). These **diffuse reflectors** (also

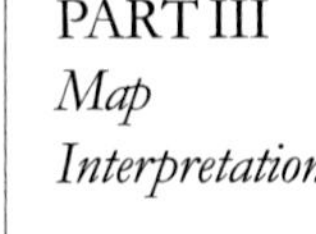

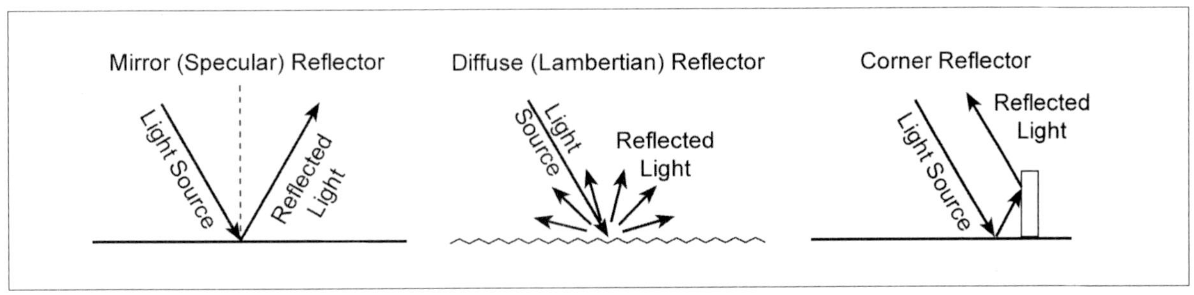

Figure 21.3 Image tones depend on features' reflective character. Some features reflect in mirror fashion (left diagram). Some reflect diffusely (middle diagram). And, in some cases, light bounces off horizontal and vertical features that serve as corner reflectors (right diagram).

called Lambertian surfaces) appear about the same mid-range tone no matter what the angle of incoming light or position of the camera. Most ground objects are diffuse reflectors. However, there may be one or more directions from which ground objects show slightly less or greater reflectance (Figure 21.4).

Highly reflective objects will usually appear light toned (although they can assume a full range of tones from light to dark depending on the orientation of the sun and the sensor relative to their position). Objects that absorb most of the visible light hitting their surface almost always will appear dark toned.

Sand, dry soil, and rock usually appear light in tone on a panchromatic photo, while wet soil appears dark. Roads made of cement and gravel usually appear light, whereas asphalt roads appear medium gray. Water usually is dark, but may be lightened by aquatic vegetation or suspended sediments. Buildings vary widely in tone depending on roofing material.

Figure 21.4 Tone isn't a reliable indicator of feature type, as this photo shows. Note how the ocean waves vary in tone from white to black across the photo, with very high mirror reflection of solar radiation at the upper center of the photo.

Vegetation rarely appears white or black, but varies in tone from light to dark depending on type. Evergreen conifers tend to be darker than broadleaf deciduous vegetation. Grass varies in tone with the seasons more than evergreen shrubs and trees. Farm crops are especially prone to vary in tone through the seasonal cycle of growth, maturation, and dormancy.

Vegetation is a good example of features that change tone through the cycle of seasons. What appears as a light tone in the spring may be a dark tone in the summer and a light tone again in the fall. Thus, it's crucial to know the date of the image.

A third type of reflection occurs when perpendicular objects are close together and thus create special reflection effects. For instance, light reflecting from water may bounce off the side of a vertical metal boathouse and be directed back to the camera, creating an unusually bright spot on the photo (see the right diagram in Figure 21.3). These objects are referred to as **corner reflectors**.

Near-Infrared Imagery

You'll see different tonal variations on near-infrared images from what you see on panchromatic photos. For one thing, the longer wavelengths of near-infrared energy are absorbed by water more completely than the shorter wavelengths of visible

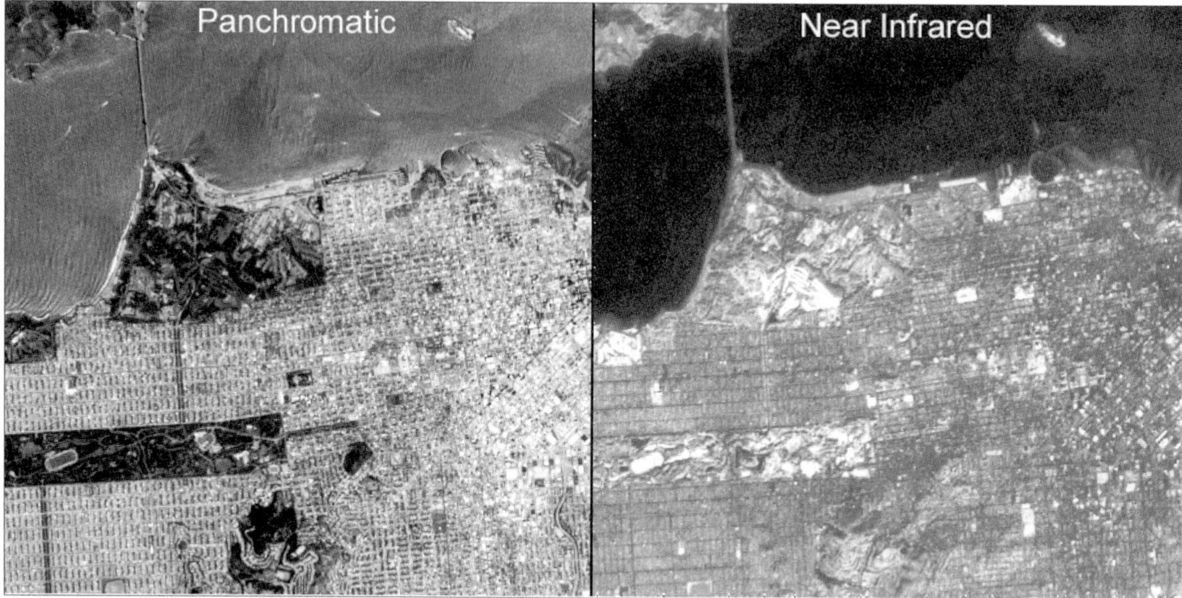

Figure 21.5 Note the tonal differences between the same features on these panchromatic (left) and near-infrared (right) black-and-white images of San Franciso, California.

light. The result is that water features such as lakes and streams tend to appear dark gray to black on near-infrared images. Also, you won't find the mirror reflection from water bodies that is common on panchromatic aerial photos.

An even more pronounced difference between conventional photos and near-infrared images is the appearance of vegetation. Healthy vegetation reflects far more in the near-infrared than in the visible waveband. Due to this higher reflectance, vegetation appears lighter on a near-infrared image than on a panchromatic aerial photograph (**Figure 21.5**).

More important, differences in vegetation types lead to more pronounced tonal variation on near-infrared images than on panchromatic photos. In particular, conifers tend to be darker than deciduous trees. This fact makes it possible to distinguish between these tree groups.

Thermal-Infrared Imagery

Interpreting tonal variation on thermal scanner imagery is even less intuitive than with near-infrared images. On thermal imagery, lighter tones are associated with warmer objects, darker tones with colder objects (see **Figure 21.6**).

On thermal images, an object's tone is related to three characteristics: (1) its **thermal capacity** (the amount of energy it can store); (2) its **conductivity** (its resistance to heating or cooling); and (3) its **inertia** (the rate at which it gains or loses heat).

Water, for example, has low conductivity but high thermal capacity and inertia. In contrast, rock has moderate conductivity and capacity but low inertia. Thus, water features tend to be warmer (lighter) than land features at night, but cooler (darker) than land features during the day when the sun is shining (**Figure 21.7**)

On thermal images, the time of image creation is even more significant than on conventional photos. The reason is that thermal images don't depend on sunlight and, therefore, can be taken at any time of day or night. What makes matters confusing is that tonal contrast between features may change **diurnally** (throughout the day). For instance, the lake that looks darker than the surrounding land at noon but lighter than the land on a nighttime image must appear the same temperature (therefore tone) twice a day (morning and evening). These times are referred to as **thermal crossover** times.

Figure 21.6 Thermal-infrared imagery makes it possible to distinguish between warm and cold features, as you can see by the thermal plume from a power generating plant (bottom) and burning trees in a forest fire (top).

Similar tone variations occur with changes in the seasons. Again, not all features heat up and cool down at the same rate. Water, for example, heats more slowly in the spring and cools more slowly in the fall than the surrounding land. To avoid misinterpretation, you must be aware of the seasonal effect on tonal relations between land and water.

Radar Imagery

Several factors cause tonal variation on a Side Looking Airborne Radar (SLAR) image. First, tonal variation depends on the surface character relative to microwave-energy reflection. Rough surfaces scatter microwave signals, resulting in mid-range tones. Smooth surfaces (mirror reflectors) reflect microwave energy with strong directional characteristics. Thus, these surfaces may appear light or dark depending on the sensor's position relative to the object (**Figure 21.8**).

When smooth horizontal and vertical surfaces are close together, they may serve as corner reflectors, creating a very high-intensity SLAR signal. When studying radar images, be careful of bright spots created by corner reflectors. Because these spots tend to be disproportionately large, you may be tempted to think an object is bigger than it really is.

Second, tonal variation on SLAR images depends on a surface's orientation relative to the SLAR sensor. Surfaces at right angles to incoming microwaves will send back the strongest signal (commonly called the **return signal** or **return**), while those oriented away from outgoing microwaves will be weak. Areas blocked from the outgoing radar signal will appear black (see Shadow, later in this chapter).

Color

For most people, the word **color** means red, green, blue, and so forth. Technically, the sensation of red or any other color is caused by the dominant wavelengths of visible spectral energy received by our eye. The term **hue** refers to this spectral aspect of the phenomenon we call color.

The hue of features on true-color images is one of the most straightforward interpretation cues and can be a very helpful aid. What surprises novice interpreters, however, is the weakness or washed-out nature of image colors. This dimension of color is called **saturation** (also known as purity or chroma), referring to the "brightness" or

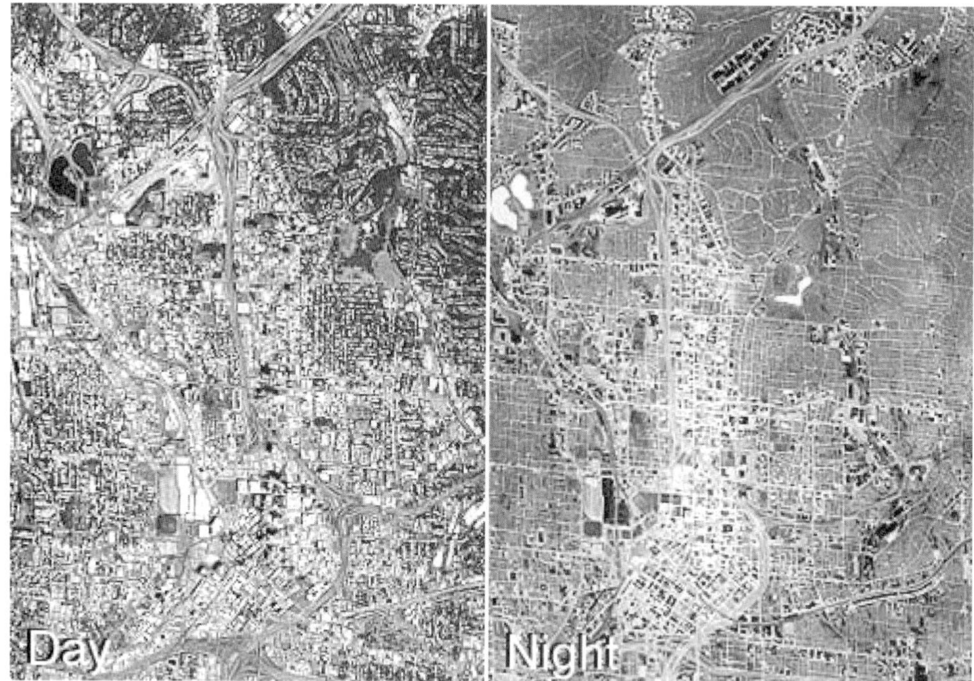

Figure 21.7 Environmental features change temperature at different rates from day to night on these images of downtown Atlanta, Georgia. Notice that the two water bodies at the upper left edge of each image appear dark (cooler) on the day image and light (warmer) on the night image.

"intensity" of a hue. Thus, one feature might be described as bright red, another as dull red.

The richness and intensity of color aren't nearly so great on an image as on the ground. Colors become more and more muted with increasing distance between the sensor and the ground. You experience this effect in day-to-day activity, where views of distant landscapes lack crisp color definition. It's also obvious to anyone who has looked out an airplane window that color decreases with distance. But it still comes as a shock to find that the colors on true-color images leave much to be desired (see **Color Plate 9.1**).

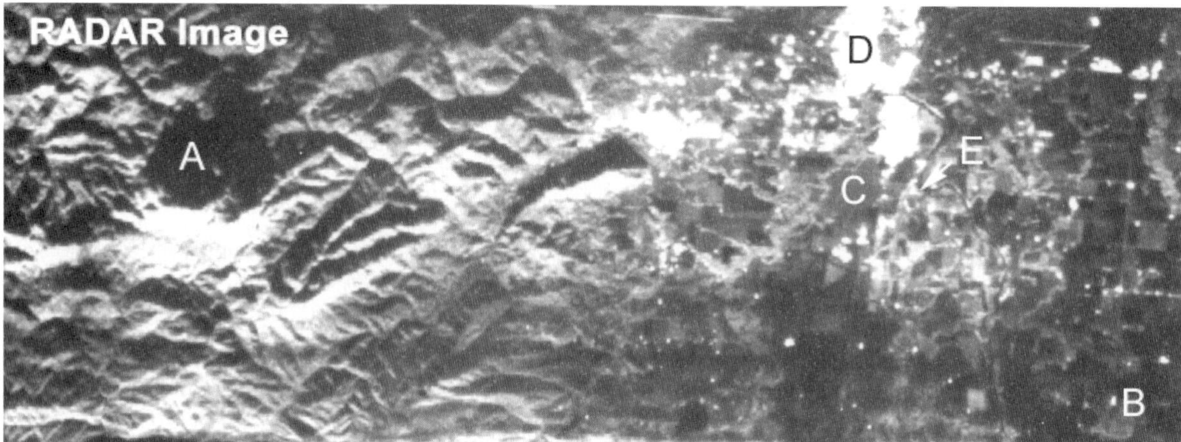

Figure 21.8 This SLAR image of the area southwest of Corvallis, Oregon, shows a great amount of environmental detail. Notice the characteristic black radar "shadows" (A), white corner reflection from a farm building (B), smooth gray medium reflection from agricultural fields (C), strong reflection from the Corvallis urban area (D), and dark areas of mirror reflection from the Willamette River (E).

The colors of features on images don't always look natural. When images are created from radiation other than visible light, there is no such thing as natural color. In these cases, any association between image color and the environment is arbitrary. This explains why the adjective **false-color** is applied to these images.

Since humans are most sensitive to the red portion of visible light, red is commonly used in creating false-color images. The choice of red as the dominant hue ensures that you can see the maximum amount of image detail.

You'll find the most dramatic example of false-color technology in color-infrared images (see **Color Plate 9.2**). Here, red is used to represent electromagnetic energy just beyond visible red wavelengths. Since healthy vegetation is highly reflective in the near-infrared, the red component of these images represents plant health. Deciduous trees will generally be a brighter red than conifer species. Roads, buildings, and parking lots look blue due to their low red and near-infrared reflectance. Water absorbs all wavelengths from green through near-infrared and hence appears black, unless contaminated with sediments or supporting considerable plant life.

Thermal-infrared and SLAR images, normally black-and-white, may also be displayed in a variety of colors. Since choice of color is arbitrary, it's up to you to determine this information from the image legend. Once you've done so, you can interpret different colors as indicators of the energy intensity recorded within the associated waveband. Different environmental features will have different spectral responses and will thus be represented by different hues and saturations.

Size

An object's **size** can be an important identification clue. Look at the rectangular shapes on the large-scale aerial photo in **Figure 21.9,** for example. You can interpret the smallest shape as a trailer, the slightly larger shape as a house, the next larger shape as an apartment building, the still larger shape as a commercial building, and the largest shape as an industrial building. Notice, however, that the commercial building at the lower left of the image is as large as the industrial plant and that several of the commercial buildings are the same size as buildings in the apartment complex. A strict assignment of building size to function isn't possible, and you must look for further clues when making these kinds of identifications.

Another potential problem is that images are available at a variety of scales. Thus, the same-sized rectangular object may turn out to be a house on a large-scale image and a farm field on a small-scale image.

You can usually solve this problem by finding some easily identified feature on the image, such as a house or road, whose size on the ground is standard. You can then compare your target feature with one of these features of known size. If you can't find a feature of known size on the image, then you'll have to determine the image scale (see Chapter 20 for more on scale computation). Once you know the image scale, you can easily determine the ground size of an object on the image.

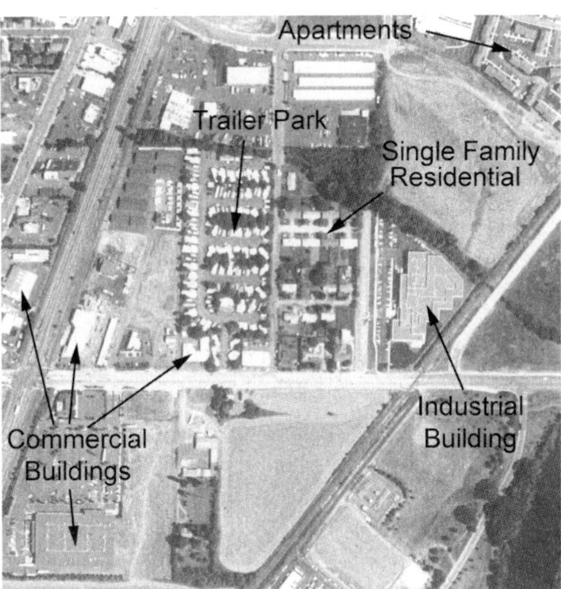

Figure 21.9 Increasing sizes of rectangular shapes for trailers in trailer parks, single-family residences, apartment houses, commercial buildings, and industrial plants.

Avoid taking a shortcut here. Low-contrast images, and objects which contrast little with their background, can make it difficult to determine an object's size. Although you may feel a scale check is too much effort, it is time well spent. Novice interpreters often ignore size or make unjustified size assumptions. But unless you make at least a rough size approximation, you risk becoming hopelessly confused when identifying features.

Height

On images such as **Figure 21.10** where buildings and other features are viewed obliquely, you can easily determine the **relative heights** of the features. Knowing the relative heights of features may be crucial to your identification of their function and their setting. Houses usually aren't as tall as commercial buildings, for instance, and different tree species reach different heights at maturity.

You saw in Chapter 20 that you can view the overlapping portions of aerial photos through a stereoscope to create a three-dimensional mental image of the ground area. The relative heights of features seen stereoscopically, although typically exaggerated vertically, may be important identification clues since features may have characteristic heights. Look at **Color Plate 21.1** with a stereoscope to see exaggerated building heights.

Figure 21.10 The differences in building heights apparent on this Quickbird satellite image of San Francisco, California, allow you to separate the central business district from the surrounding commercial area.

Stereoscopic viewing also lets you determine the **relative position** of an object located on the side of a tall feature like a mountain. This relative position may be essential information for feature identification, since certain features, such as plant species, may exist only at the top or bottom of the mountain. You can guess, for instance, that trees near the tree line on a Colorado mountain are spruce or fir, while those at lower altitude are oaks or aspen. Certain human activities visible on images also depend on the elevation. Agriculture is an obvious example, since farmers can grow only a limited number of crops at high elevations.

Shadow

The **shadows** cast by environmental features are important image interpretation cues. On aerial photos, the tone of a shadow is usually darker than the tone of an object. Objects that occur within shadows reflect less light and will be harder to discern than similar objects not in shadows. In this respect, shadows hinder feature recognition.

But shadows can also make it easier to recognize objects. A shadow gives a vertical profile of an object, indicating the object's shape and relative height. For instance, on a vertical image, a water tower might appear as a circle. You could have trouble distinguishing it from a round building, tank, or pool. The water tower's shadow would provide the information needed to identify it. Likewise, you can use shadow information to differentiate between conifer and deciduous trees (**Figure 21.11**). Notice in Figure 21.10 that you can deduce the relative heights of buildings by their shadow lengths (see Chapter 20 for the shadow method of computing their exact heights). Remember, however, that shadow length is directly related to the time of day the image was taken. Long shadows may indicate tall objects, but they may also be the result of a low sun angle.

On non-photographic images, shadows have a different meaning. On thermal-infrared images, shadows may represent the cooling that occurs

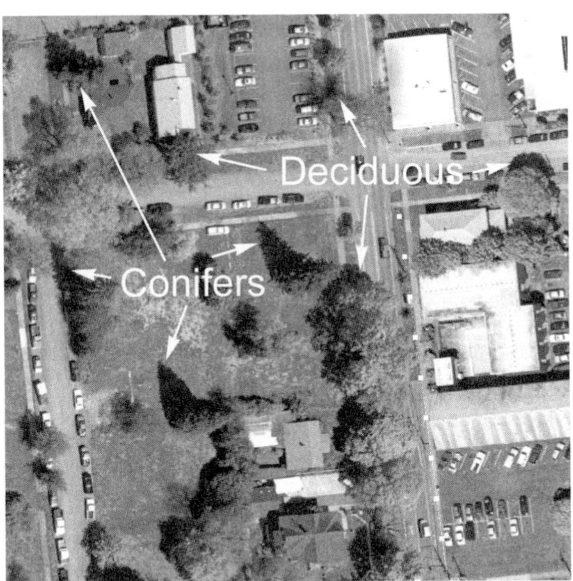

Figure 21.11 Conifer and deciduous trees can be distinguished by the shadows they cast.

when sunlight is blocked. For instance, although clouds won't be visible because the long thermal wavelengths easily penetrate them, the "cool" shadow of clouds may indeed be noticeable. This can be particularly confusing on images taken when a scattering of isolated but dense clouds is present.

On radar images, shadows represent areas in which microwave energy from the sensor was blocked. These shadows are completely black, unlike the somewhat transparent shadows on conventional photos (see Figure 21.8). Radar shadows are cast from raised objects in a direction perpendicular (at right angles) to the flightline. The lower the aircraft or satellite altitude and the higher the relief, the longer the shadows.

Shadows can have a curious effect on the interpretation of relief features. In order to see raised features and maximize the relief effect, you must view the image with the shadows falling to your lower-right. In other words, you want to face the source of illumination. To do otherwise is to risk getting the impression that raised objects are depressed, and vice versa. This apparent reversal of relief is called the **pseudoscopic effect** (see **Figure 21.12**).

The people who produce aerial photographs have established conventions which unwittingly encourage relief reversal. The problem arises because photos taken in the northern hemisphere are commonly labeled along their north edge. Since in this hemisphere the sun is usually located to the south, holding these images with the labeling at the top means that the shadows fall away, not toward, the observer. The likely consequence is relief reversal. To overcome this possibility, it is good practice to rotate an image until the relief effect is maximized before you interpret the image.

Pattern

Repetition of certain spatial forms or relationships is characteristic of many environmental features. This repetition across an area creates a **pattern**, which can be a helpful aid in recognizing objects.

Pattern is valuable because it may signal an underlying process. Pattern represents order, and order has a cause. If you can figure out what process led to the pattern, your image interpretation task will be simplified. Since natural processes typically create different patterns than human processes, it is convenient to separate the two for purposes of discussion.

Figure 21.12 This north-oriented aerial photo shows the pseudoscopic effect. Turn the book upside-down to see the landforms correctly.

Examples of natural patterns abound (**Figure 21.13**). Parallel light and dark lines on glaciers and lava flows, for instance, reflect movement of ice and molten lava (Figure 21.13A) . Beach ridges along a water body whose surface level has dropped are identified by a series of parallel old-beach lines that are easily recognized (Figure 21.13B). Sand dune fields, both on Earth and Mars, have a characteristic pattern of crescent-shaped dunes (Figure 21.13C). A meandering river in a broad, flat valley, with its sinuous pattern of cut-off meanders and ox-bow lakes, is equally easy to identify (Figure 21.13D).

In contrast to these natural patterns, human patterns tend to have a simple form, with sharp angles, straight lines, and smooth curves. See, for example, the human patterns in **Figure 21.14**.

Patterns of human origin aren't always uniform, however. Sometimes people create irregular patterns on purpose, as with golf courses and winding streets in subdivisions. More commonly, human activity that takes on an irregular structure has been influenced by the natural environment. For instance, a strip mine may follow the mineral outcrop around the sides of a valley. Or a road may follow the irregular ridge or valley line in a region of highly dissected terrain.

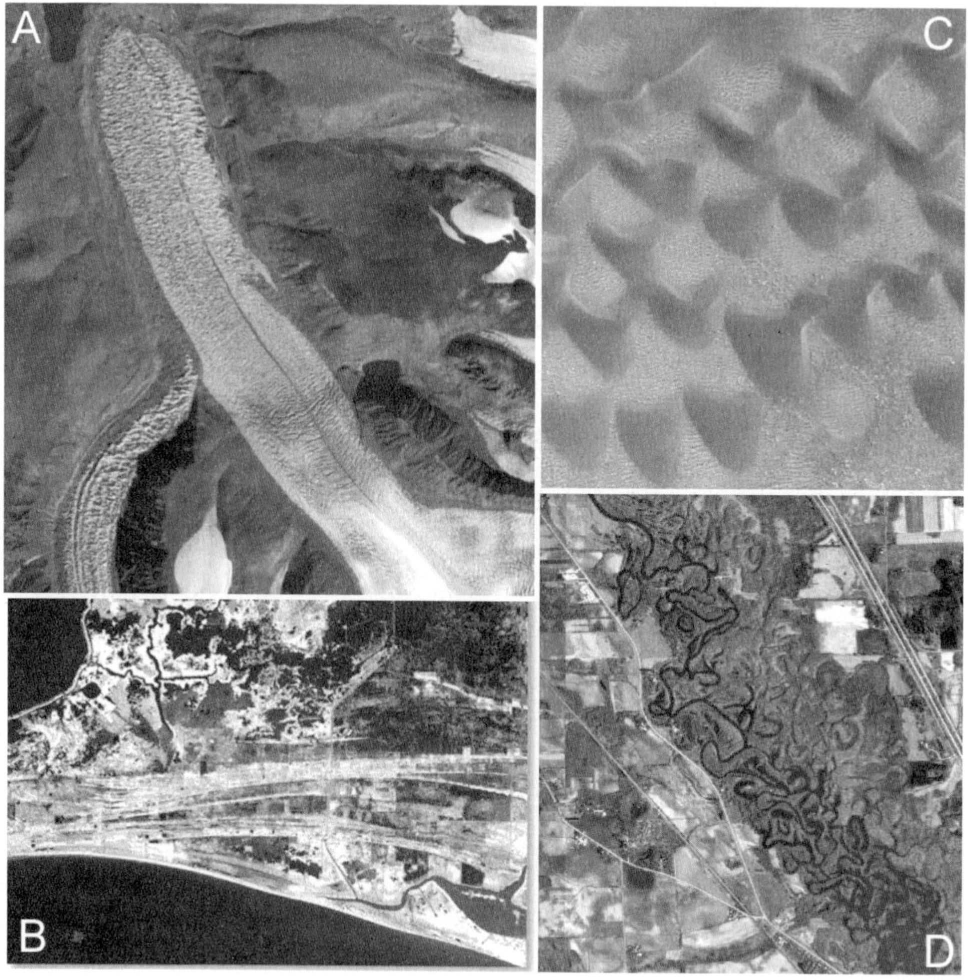

Figure 21.13 Natural features such as glaciers in Bhutan (A), beach ridges in southwestern Louisiana (B), sand dunes on Mars (C), and river meanders north of Madison, Wisconsin (D) are often easy to identify by their characteristic pattern on images.

Texture

Many environmental features are too small to be perceived individually on an image. Together, however, their shape, size, arrangement, shadow, and tone combine to create a pattern of tonal variation. The frequency of tonal change is referred to as **texture** (see **Figure 21.15**).

Texture ranges from coarse (in the case of mature trees with broad crowns) to fine (in the case of plowed fields or mowed grass on golf courses). As an image's scale becomes smaller, a feature's texture becomes finer. Eventually, of course, smaller scales will cause the feature's texture to disappear.

Figure 21.14 Human modifications of the landscape are reflected in characteristic patterns for features such as: railroad switching yards (A), residential developments with parallel streets (B), parking lots (C), center pivot irrigation (D), orchards (E), combine tracks in harvested fields (F), golf courses (G), residential areas with curved streets and cul de sacs (H), and trailer courts with curved streets (I).

Figure 21.15 Features range in texture from fine to coarse at a particular image scale.

This relationship between texture and scale is a key factor in image interpretation. When using texture as an interpretation clue, the first step is to determine the image scale. Then imagine what size an object must be to create a given texture at that scale.

Texture is an excellent aid in identifying crops and vegetation types. The texture of corn is quite different from that of alfalfa. Similarly, the crowns of spruce and pine trees have different textures.

Site and Situation

The relation of an object to surrounding features can provide useful hints to its identity, and may be the only way to recognize some objects. Many features are closely linked and therefore occur in association with each other. For example, you can distinguish high schools from elementary schools on an image by looking at surrounding features . Near high schools, you'll find football fields, baseball diamonds, running tracks, and parking lots for students and teachers (**Figure 21.16A**). Near elementary schools, you'll see playground equipment, open playing fields with painted game lines, and parking for teachers only (**Figure 21.16B**).

You can differentiate between various industrial facilities because they're served by different forms of transportation . For example, a building served by railroad tracks is likely to be a factory (**Figure 21.17A**). A grouping of large cylindrical tanks adjacent to a water body where ships are docked could well be a chemical storage site (**Figure 21.17B**).

Vegetation types are found in association with certain landscape features (**Figure 21.18**). Along streams you would expect to find willows and other riparian vegetation, whereas lily pads, reeds, and cattails line many shallow lakes.

The **geographical situation** provides a means of anticipating what to look for on an image. For example, you would expect to find a stor-

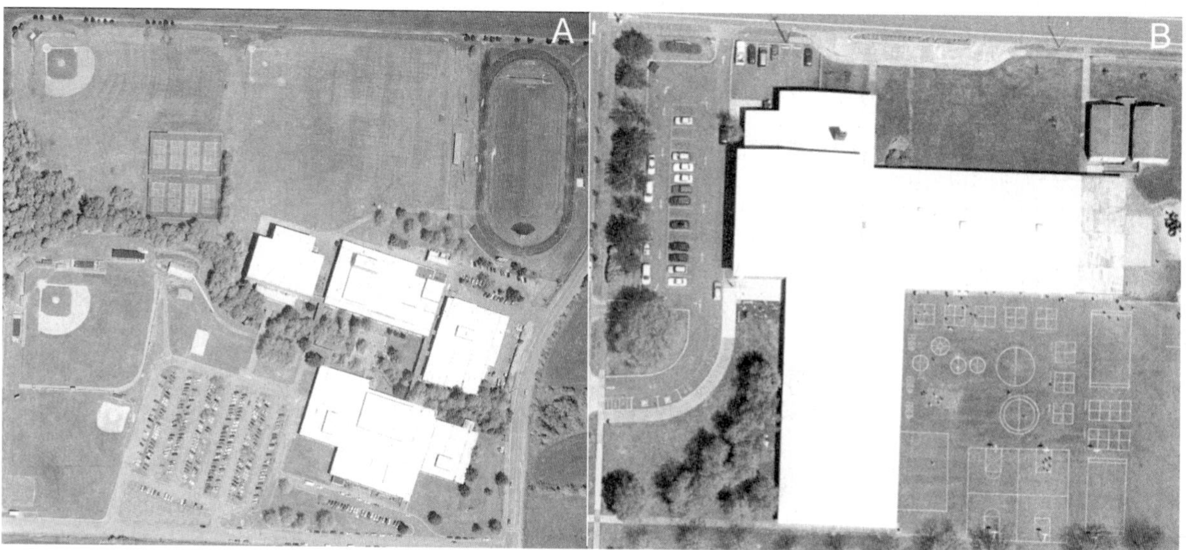

Figure 21.16 Surrounding features like football fields, tracks, baseball diamonds, and large parking lots for students distinguish a high school (A) from an elementary school (B).

Figure 21.17 You can use the relations between site and situation to determine the function of buildings, such as a factory (A), and a port chemical storage tank facility (B).

age area for boats along a lakeshore (**Figure 21.19**). Thus, a boat storage shed near a freeway will be more difficult to identify than one located near a lake. Likewise, a ferris wheel stored in a farm field during the "off season" will be harder to recognize than one in an amusement park.

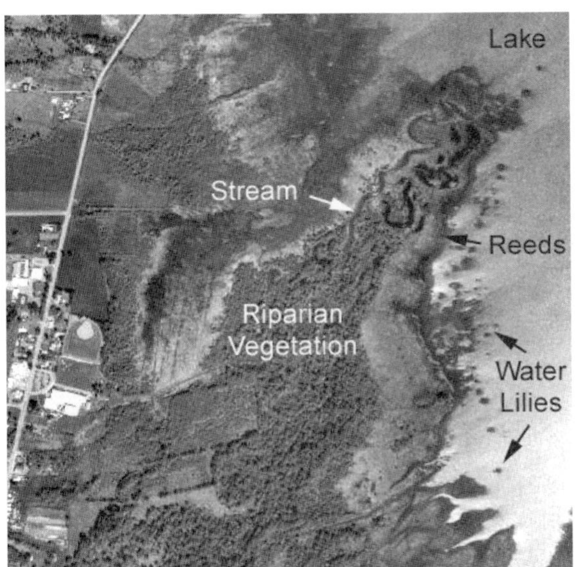

Figure 21.18 Different vegetation types are found next to lakes and streams.

In some cases a feature may be barely visible on the image, but you can predict its location on the basis of its situation. The pattern of roads, tanks, and well sites that suggest an oil field may all be visible, even though the oil pumps themselves aren't clear (**Figure 21.20A**). Parallel rows of propeller-shaped objects accessed by short side roads on a ridgetop indicate a wind energy facility (**Figure 21.20B**).

So far we've considered site and situation only where there is a connection between a site and its

Figure 21.19 Boat storage areas are normally found next to a water body, often close to boat docks.

Figure 21.20 The pattern of roads, tanks, powerlines, and well sites on photo A all suggest an oil field, even though the pumps themselves aren't obvious. In photo B, the short side roads and propeller-shaped objects aligned parallel to each other on a ridgetop suggest a wind energy facility.

situation. The reverse condition can also yield insights. If there appears to be no connection between a feature and its surroundings, you can guess that the setting will provide relatively little interpretative information (**Figure 21.21**). You can thus conclude that the situation of the feature is at a more regional level. Examples include roads, pipelines, powerlines, railroads, communication transmission towers, and similar features that serve a regional rather than a local purpose.

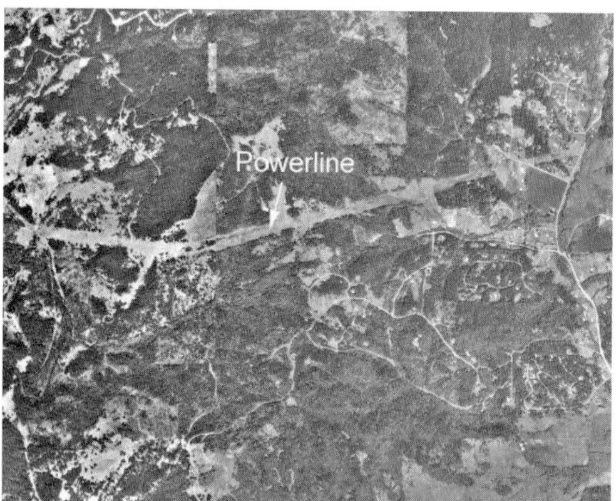

Figure 21.21 There appears to be no connection between this powerline and its surroundings other than a straight line corridor which has been cut through the surrounding vegetation.

SCALE GRADIENT

Earlier (see Size), we discussed image scale. We noted that scale is important in identifying features because it determines the apparent (or image) size of an object.

Scale is also important in image interpretation for other reasons. Large-scale images are easy to interpret because they provide details familiar from your daily experience. On these images, there are strong visual cues such as tonal differences, shadows, size, shape, and texture to help distinguish between features. Indeed, large-scale images can appear so realistic and familiar that you almost feel you are there (**Figure 21.22, top**).

This familiarity is quickly lost as image scale decreases. The smaller an image's scale, the fewer environmental details are visible (**Figure 21.22, middle and bottom**). There is a progressive loss of cues, such as shadows, and a general degradation of feature definition. As the small features that make up most of what you see in day-to-day living disappear, the image becomes less and less familiar.

What emerges at smaller image scales is a picture of the relations between features—something you may not be aware of in daily living. Size, pattern, and particularly site and situation cues become more important in recognizing features as the image scale decreases.

Figure 21.22 Large-scale images provide the best feature detail (top), but small-scale images are more useful for studying regional patterns in the landscape (bottom). Notice how the appearance of the golf course changes as the photo scale reduces from top to bottom.

INTERPRETATION STRATEGY

Image interpretation draws on a wide range of skills. The most successful interpreters are those with keen powers of observation and a rich and varied environmental experience. Image interpretation success depends on imagining what everyday features might look like if viewed from a distant vertical or oblique vantage point. Here are several strategies to help you polish your image interpretation skills.

Checklist

The image interpretation elements that we've been discussing serve as your conceptual tools. When you consciously apply them to an image, they will help you distinguish features and see their graphic characteristics. These elements extend and enrich your image interpretation vocabulary.

When you want to identify a feature on an image, run down the list of elements. You'll be surprised how easily this triggers ideas. The identity of many features will become apparent well before you reach the end of the checklist.

What you're doing is getting in touch with the tacit knowledge you've acquired over your lifetime. Your goal is to use the image to help you recall this knowledge.

Guard against using only size, or shape, or any other element by itself or in combination with only one or two other cues. These elements only represent concepts we can use to stimulate the way we think about the environment. The environment is a single whole, in which everything occurs simultaneously. Objects can best be recognized by integrating information from all of the interpretation elements.

20 Questions

A second interpretation strategy is to play a game similar to "20 Questions." Ask yourself, first: Is the feature primarily of natural or human origin?

If the feature is primarily human, does it reflect agriculture, recreation, mineral exploitation, forestry, or transportation (pipelines, railroads, roads, airports, canals, power transmission, telecommunication)? Does it represent residential, commercial, or industrial land use?

If natural, is the feature associated with the atmosphere, biosphere, lithosphere, or hydrosphere (lakes, rivers)? Does it represent the combined effect of these spheres (such as climate)?

Remember, of course, that many features are the result of physical impact on human activity, human impact on physical features, or complex interactions between human activities and physical processes.

Quotas

Patience is also important in image interpretation. You must guard against leaping to conclusions at the first hint of a feature's identity.

A good strategy is to set an idea quota. For example, you might set yourself a quota of three ideas. You then refrain from making a judgment until you've come up with three possible interpretations. These possibilities may be as off-the-wall as you like, because your only goal at this point is to meet the quota.

Once you've used intuition to meet your quota, it's time to release the power of analytical thinking. Analyze the pros and cons of each idea. Eliminate any idea that doesn't stand up to rational scrutiny. This will leave you with the most plausible interpretation or, at worst, several possible identifications. Go back to your checklist if you want more insight.

Now let's test this quota strategy. Study **Figure 21.23**. Before reading further, make up a list of possible explanations for the strips of missing vegetation running from the top to bottom of the photo. After you've filled your quota of ideas, go back and logically determine which is the most plausible. After you're satisfied with your answer, check the footnote at the bottom of the page.*

Meaning

Often you'll recognize a feature on an image map but have no ready answer for why it is found where it is. This is particularly true when the feature is of human origin, since its location will be influenced by political, social, technological, and economic activities. To correctly interpret such features, it helps to understand human motivation, especially how people use the land.

Consider, for example, the image provided in **Figure 21.24**. A marsh with a number of ponds is evident. The rectangular shape and regular spacing of the ponds suggest a human origin. But why would people spend valuable resources making ponds in a marsh? No roads or trails to the ponds are evident, so it is unlikely that people use the ponds

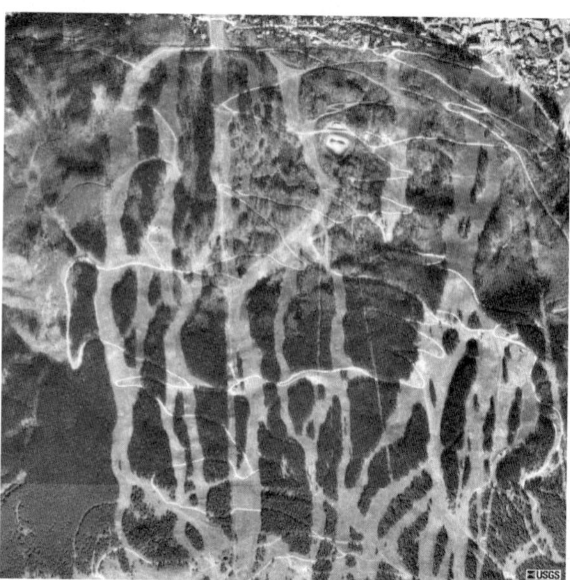

Figure 21.23 Can you identify the wide, treeless linear features running from top to bottom on this aerial photo?

**The straight-line geometry of the target features suggests they are human creations. Your quota of ideas might include such guesses as golf fairways, roadways, powerline corridors, clearcut logging, ski runs, and so forth. Notice that the linear paths of the target features are not altered by terrain and have no connection to other features on the image. They seem merely to pass through the region. Since it doesn't make sense to log such narrow, long strips of land, clearcut logging can be assigned a low probability. Since roads are evident elsewhere on the photo and look quite different from our target features, these also get a low probability. Powerline corridors are usually single swaths far more linear than those on the photo. This leaves ski runs as the most likely idea. Indeed, the features are ski runs at Vail Mountain, Colorado. Look closely and you'll see shadows from ski lift towers.*

for recreation. The ponds are obviously not needed as a source of irrigation or domestic water. So what are we seeing?

The answer is obvious if you're tuned in to modern wetland management ideas. The ponds were made with the aid of special "wildlife funds" in an attempt to improve waterfowl habitat. This activity is intended to compensate for the widespread destruction of wetlands due to urban growth, industry, and agriculture.

Notice how our explanation came from focusing on the question "Why would people spend scarce resources building ponds in a marsh?" It's easier to explain a cultural feature if you remember that people have reasons for doing what they do at different locations. It takes time, energy, and money to create visible impressions on the landscape. Thus, little that you see of human origin on an image "just happened."

Something similar can be said for physical features. You may find that the effects of wind, gravity, sunshine, precipitation, and so on are key elements in explaining different physical features on the image.

Beware, however, of features that are byproducts of other processes or activities. Novice image interpreters often have trouble explaining coincidental features, such as a pond in a gravel pit. In **Figure 21.25**, for example, the pond (the dark feature in the center of the image) wasn't the aim but, rather, the byproduct of mining.

Always consider the possibility that the feature you're studying is best explained by some related activity. Sometimes, as in the case of a cleared strip through a forest for a powerline right-of-way, the associated activity (in this case, the powerline) may not even be visible at the image scale.

MENTAL TEMPLATES

It's easier to recognize something familiar than something new. Once you've identified a feature on one image, then, you'll recognize it faster next time.

Classes of features have distinctive characteristics. Once you've seen one trailer park, you have in a sense seen them all. These class prototypes are stored in your brain as **mental templates**, to be recalled and matched to image features.

Take advantage of your successful identifications. After you've recognized a feature, review in your mind the information that led you to this conclusion. Become conscious of the decision path you

Figure 21.24 The regular shape and pattern of these wildlife ponds, dug in a wetland area, provide useful interpretation cues.

Figure 21.25 Sometimes features, such as this pond in a gravel pit, are the byproduct rather than the aim of human activity.

followed. By doing so, you'll make it easier to identify the same type of feature next time. Also, your decision-making will become more and more intuitive as you repeat your successful strategies.

The value of experience is that it shifts feature identification from mainly analytical to mostly intuitive. The more experience you have, the more intuitive you will become and the fewer analytical cues you'll need to identify features.

Even the novice will intuitively recognize familiar features, of course. Similarly, experts have to become more analytical when they encounter an unfamiliar feature. Thus, the relative importance of analysis and intuition in feature identification will vary from situation to situation.

Mental template building will help you increase your image interpretation skill rapidly with experience. But you always face the problem of encountering something you've never before seen. To get around this lack of direct experience, you can train with the aid of **feature templates**. Many of the figures in this chapter are feature templates. More such templates can be found in standard image interpretation texts. Many times these templates are pen-and-ink drawings of how the features look when viewed vertically (see **Figure 21.26**). By studying these and similar examples, you'll build your store of mental templates.

SMALL-SCALE SATELLITE IMAGE INTERPRETATION

You can manually interpret Landsat, SPOT, or other digital satellite images to create medium-scale to small-scale maps of a scene. The most common maps are of landcover categories for cities, counties, or entire states.

There are three methods you can use to interpret the satellite image and create a landcover map:

✐ Place a sheet of tracing paper over a hard-copy print of the image. Then draw boundary lines between landcover categories on the tracing paper.

✐ Use an optical image transfer device like a **Zoom Transfer Scope** (see **Figure 21.27**) to trace the class boundaries onto a base map of the area. To do so, place the hard-copy image onto a clear glass plate at the top of the instrument. Then view the image through a binocular eyepiece. You can optically scale and rotate the image until it appears to overlay correctly on the base map, which you can also see in the eyepiece.

✐ Display the image on a computer monitor. Then use the computer's mouse to manually trace the boundary lines between landcover categories.

What makes this type of image interpretation different from the identification of individual objects is that the entire image must be subdivided into areas that are assigned one of the landcover categories.

Figure 21.28 is a black-and-white rendition of a false-color Landsat Thematic Mapper image with manually determined landcover class boundaries. (See Chapter 9 for more on Landsat and remote sensing). Notice that most of the categories are general terms like forest, agriculture, and urban. In addition, a few more specific categories, like golf course and riparian forest, could also be identified and mapped at the 30-meter spatial resolution of the Landsat image data.

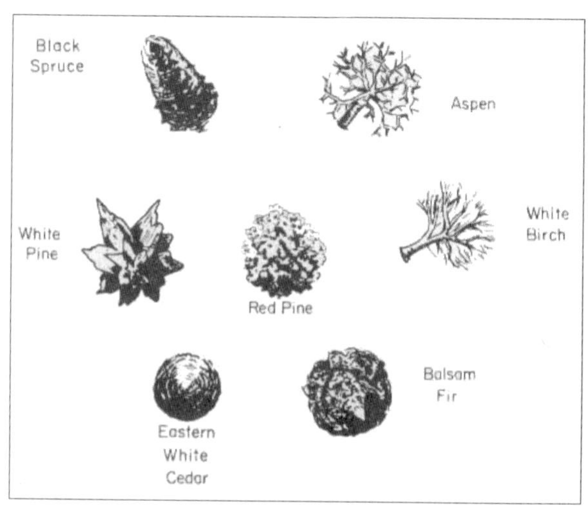

Figure 21.26 This tree identification template consists of sketches of different tree crowns as seen from above.

An image interpreter familiar with Corvallis, Oregon, and vicinity drew the landcover boundary lines in Figure 21.28 by relying on different interpretation elements for different categories:

✎ water—black, smoothly-curving lines and elongated areas.
✎ forest—mixture of highly-saturated, irregularly-shaped, medium and dark toned red areas with coarse texture in the dark red areas.
✎ urban—a regular pattern of small white to light blue areas with occasional bright-red areas intermixed to form a coarse texture.
✎ agriculture—finely-textured, large, rectangular areas ranging in color from light blue to light pink.
✎ pasture—irregularly-shaped, low-saturation, tan areas of medium texture.
✎ golf courses—an irregular pattern of closely-spaced, highly-saturated, elongated and smoothly curved red areas.

Notice that the image interpreter has made many arbitrary decisions when drawing the class boundary lines. For one thing, there may be transition zones rather than abrupt changes between classes on the ground. The interpreter must decide where to place the boundary line within the transition zone, resulting in parts of the area outlined being more "purely" of the class than others.

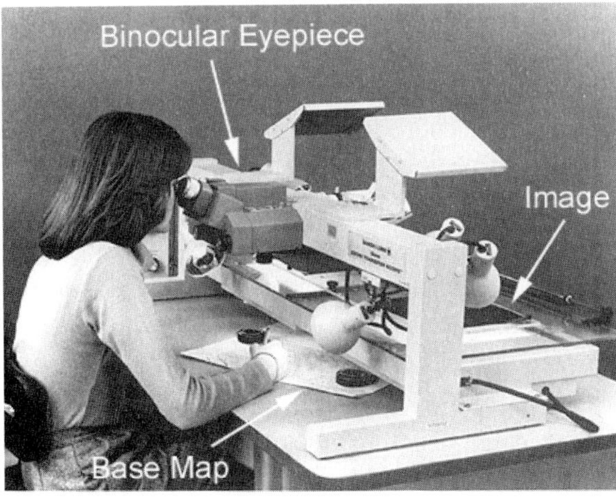

Figure 21.27 You can use a Zoom Transfer Scope to view an image and base map simultaneously so you can trace features seen on the image onto the base map.

You will also see that the interpreter had to generalize the detail on the ground into a limited number of areas for each category. Small islands in the river, for instance, have been included in the water category. There are also many small areas of other categories that have been included in each of the outlined classes, including features not named in the classification scheme.

These arbitrary decisions produce a map of the **dominant landcover** in each outlined area. It's usually not possible to outline homogeneous areas of each category completely.

DIGITAL IMAGE CLASSIFICATION

The basic requirement for digital image classification is a powerful microcomputer and **image processing software.** Examples of image processing programs include ERDAS Imagine, ER Map-

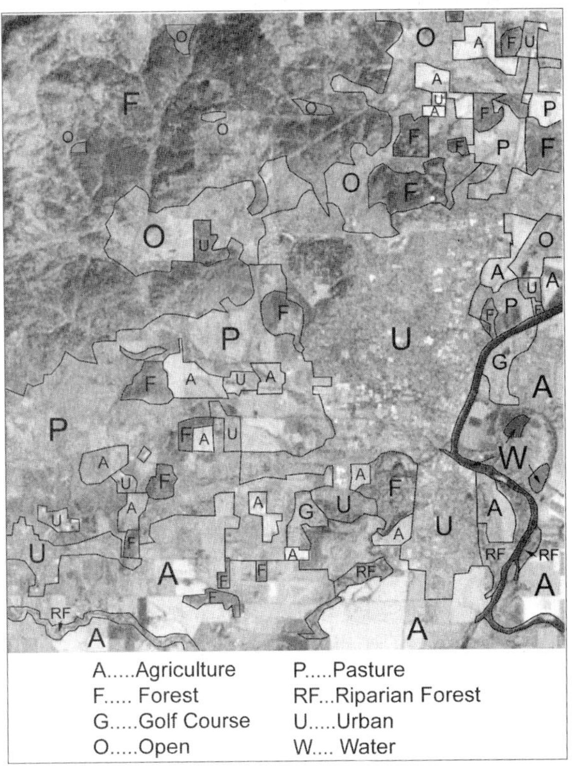

Figure 21.28 Landcover map of Corvallis, Oregon, with categories manually interpreted from a false-color Landsat TM scene (shown in black and white).

per, ENVI, IDRISI, and ArcView Image Analysis*. These programs are designed for professional use and take some effort to master. But their capability goes well beyond that of image editors. You can import and export digital remote sensor images described in one of many graphic file formats. Most important, you can set rules for enhancing the appearance, classifying and geometrically correcting the entire image automatically.

Whatever computer configuration is used, the image must first be available in digital form. The tones you see on digital images are graphic displays of the digital brightness values recorded by the sensor at each pixel. Today most digital imagery comes directly from electronic sensing systems. But existing images can also be converted to digital form in the laboratory, using a video recorder, digital still camera, film recorder, or scanner.

All image processing programs available commercially today manipulate the digital brightness values of individual pixels, usually in several different spectral bands. The image classification logic is far more sophisticated in some programs than in others, and their classification accuracy varies accordingly.

Let's look at supervised image classification, one of the most commonly used methods in remote sensing.

Supervised Classification

Supervised image classification is based on the program user having prior knowledge of small "**training areas**" on the image for each feature category. The idea is to travel to the area covered by the image, determine the landcover at a number of sites, and then look at these same areas on the image. In **Color Plate 21.2, top right**, for instance, training areas for agriculture, forest, golf course, pasture, urban, and water areas have been outlined. The digital brightness values within each training area are extracted for all spectral bands used in the classification (TM Bands 1,2, and 4 in this example). Summary statistics, particularly the mean and standard deviation, are computed for each band and a frequency diagram of the values is often displayed (**Color Plate 21.2 left**).

A classification rule is next defined. A form of supervised classification, called **minimum distance to means**, uses a simple rule. Each pixel in the image is assigned the landcover class that has mean values lying closest to the brightness values for the pixel.

A landcover map for Corvallis, Oregon, and vicinity created through minimum distance to means supervised classification is seen in **Color Plate 21.2, bottom right**. Although the map looks quite detailed and accurate, the technique suffers from the problem that environmental features don't always have the same brightness values in different locations on the image. Water bodies illustrate this point well, since they may be light-toned in one part of the image and dark-toned in another, depending on the positions of the sun, the sensor, and the reflectivity of the water surface.

Another problem is that the training area means for each class may be close to each other with a large spread of values about the mean, even when the classification is extended to multiple bands. This problem was particularly severe for the pasture and open categories, which were merged into pasture for the landcover map.

The digitally classified landcover map also lacks the generalization performed on the manually produced map in Figure 21.28. Since the classification is done pixel-by-pixel, the large areas in each category are peppered with pixels of other categories, some correct but many incorrectly classified.

The best image processing programs can achieve 80% to 90% landcover classification accuracies for categories like water using multispectral satellite imagery of 30-meter spatial resolution and a mapping scale of 1:100,000. If multispectral imagery of 10-meter spatial resolution is used, similar results can be achieved at a mapping scale of 1:24,000.

**See Appendix B for information on how to order these products.*

Notice that we have used the term "landcover classification" in the previous paragraphs. Existing image classification programs identify such features as vegetation zones, bare soil, crop types, water bodies, urban areas, and so forth. They don't identify schools, beaver dams, railroads, and other individual features that are associated with detailed use of the land. You might learn that a feature is a water body, but have no indication whether it is used for stock watering, human drinking, fish breeding, waterfowl nesting, or sewage treatment. In other words, true interpretation that gets at the "why?" aspect of the image is missing.

SELECTED READINGS

Arnold, R.H., *Interpretation of Airphotos and Remotely Sensed Imagery* (Englewood Cliffs, NJ: Prentice-Hall, 1997).

Avery, T.E., *Forester's Guide to Aerial Photo Interpretation* (Washington, DC: USDA Forest Service, 1969).

Avery, T. E., *Interpretation of Aerial Photographs*, 4th ed. (Minneapolis: Burgess Publishing Co., 1985).

Avery, T.E., and Berlin, G.L., *Fundamentals of Remote Sensing and Airphoto Interpretation*, 5th ed. (Englewood Cliffs, NJ: Prentice-Hall, 1992).

Blair, C.L., and Gutsell, B.V., *The American Landscape: Map and Air Photo Interpretation* (New York: McGraw-Hill Book Co., 1974).

Blair, C.L., Frid, B.R., and Day, E.E.D., *Canadian Landscape: Map and Air Photo Interpretation*, 3rd ed. (Toronto, ON: Copp Clark Pitman, 1990).

Brugioni, D.A., "The Art and Science of Photoreconnaissance," *Scientific American* (March 1996), pp. 78-85.

Buisseret, D., ed., *From Sea Charts to Satellite Images: Interpreting North American History through Maps* (Chicago: The University of Chicago Press, 1990).

Denegre, J., ed., *Thematic Mapping from Satellite Imagery* (London: Elsevier Applied Science Publishers, Ltd., 1988).

Doane, J., *America: An Aerial View* (New York: Crescent Books, 1978).

Drury, S.A., *A Guide to Remote Sensing: Interpreting Images of the Earth* (New York: Oxford University Press, 1990).

El-Baz, F., "Space Age Archaeology," *Scientific American* (August 1997), pp. 60-65.

Erickson, J., *Exploring Earth from Space* (Blue Ridge Summit, PA: TAB Books, Inc., 1989).

Frohn, R.C., *Remote Sensing for Landscape Ecology* (Boca Raton, FL: Lewis Publishers, 1997).

Hock, T.K., and Brown, E.D.R., *Geographical Interpretation Through Photographs* (London: George Allen & Unwin, 1972).

Jensen, J.R., *Introductory Digital Image Processing: A Remote Sensing Perspective*, 2nd ed. (Upper Saddle River, NJ: Prentice-Hall, 1996).

Lillesand, T.M., and Kiefer, R.W., *Remote Sensing and Image Interpretation*, 3rd ed. (New York: John Wiley & Sons, 1994).

Muller, J.P., *Digital Image Processing in Remote Sensing* (London: Taylor & Francis, 1988).

Rabenhorst, T.D., and McDermott, R.D., *Applied Cartography: Introduction to Remote Sensing* (Columbus, OH: Merrill Publishing Co., 1989).

Stephens, N., *Natural Landscapes of Britain from the Air* (New York, Cambridge University Press, 1990).

Stone, K.H., "A Guide to the Interpretation and Analysis of Aerial Photos, *Annals of the Association of American Geographers*, 54, 3 (September, 1964), pp. 318-328.

Ungar, S.G., *The Earth's Surface Studied from Space* (Oxford: Pergamon Press, 1985).

Verbyla, D.L., *Satellite Remote Sensing of Natural Resources* (Boca Raton, FL: Lewis Publishers, 1995).

Wanless, H.R., *Aerial Stereo Photographs* (Northbrook, IL: Hubbard Press, 1973).

Williams, J., *Geographic Information from Space: Processing and Application of Geocoded Satellite Images* (New York: John Wiley & Sons, 1995).

Wood, E.A., *Science from Your Airplane Window*, 2nd ed. (New York: Dover Publications, Inc., 1975).

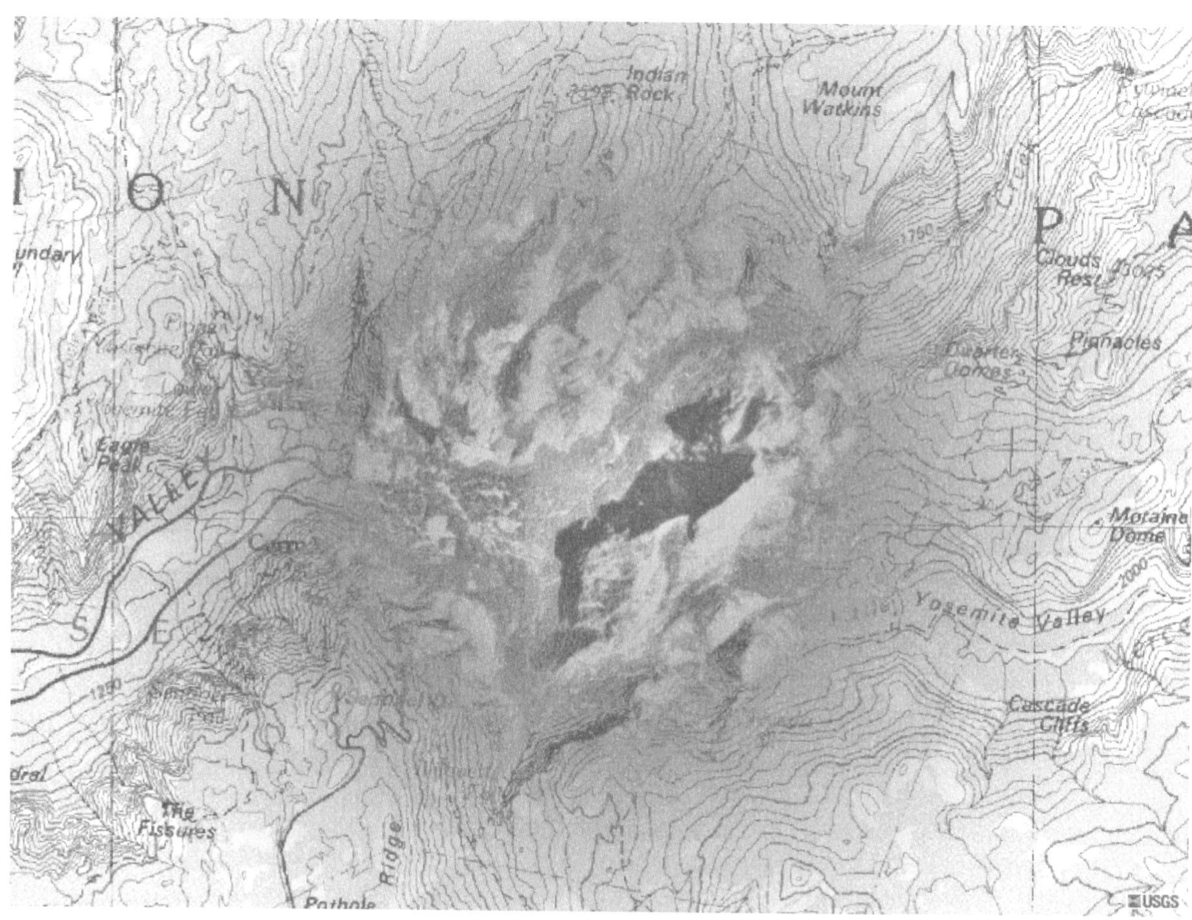

The Half Dome area in Yosemite National Park, California, is shown in this topographic map-orthophoto blend.

CHAPTER 22
INTERPRETING THE LITHOSPHERE

BASIC LANDFORM FEATURES

MAJOR LANDFORM TYPES

- Volcano
- Dissected Plateau
- Uniformly Sloping Plain
- Ridge and Valley Topography
- Dome
- Floodplain
- Braided River Channel
- Alluvial Fan
- Karst Topography
- Alpine Glaciation
- Continental Glaciation

GEOLOGY

- Geologic Maps
    - Rock Units
    - Geologic Cross Sections
    - Strike and Dip
    - Faults
- Regional Geology

SELECTED READINGS

But the hills that we climbed were just seasons out of time
—Westlife lyrics, Seasons In The Sun

22

CHAPTER 22

INTERPRETING THE LITHOSPHERE

The most prominent aspect of the physical environment is the **lithosphere**—the land surface upon which we live. Its changing form is everywhere evident. It also provides the stage upon which other aspects of the physical environment operate. For these reasons, understanding the landforms that make up the lithosphere is fundamental to interpreting the physical environment from maps.

To understand landforms, you must consider the great forces of land building and destruction. Volcanic processes force molten rock to the surface from deep within the earth. The solid crust of the earth is folded and faulted by the stress set up by tectonic (land shifting) processes. Less dramatic but equally powerful agents of erosion are running water, glaciers, and wind. Land is continually being torn down by erosion and built up by sediment deposition and tectonic uplift.

In this chapter, you'll see how interpreting maps and images can help you understand an area's landforms and surface geology. A **landform feature** is a distinctive three-dimensional object on the earth's surface created by erosion or deposition of rocks, silt, clay, or other sediments. Landform features play such an important role in human activity that we have a variety of names for them—hills, mountains, peaks, valleys, ravines, saddles, cliffs, depressions, and so on. Larger landforms are composed of individual features and the set of streams that drain the area. Distinctive combinations of landform features and drainage patterns are given names such as floodplains, volcanoes, glaciated mountain ranges, domes, and many others. Different landform features and drainage patterns are identified by characteristic geometric patterns of contours and hydrographic features (streams and lakes) seen on topographic maps. You can also identify landforms by their appearance on aerial photographs or satellite images, particularly if you can view the photos stereoscopically.

Landforms are closely linked to the underlying geologic materials. **Geologic maps** are a primary tool for understanding the composition and age of earth materials. The tectonic features (faults and folds) shown on geologic maps also help you understand how landforms were created over time and how they may change in the future.

Let's begin our interpretation of the lithosphere by studying the distinctive arrangement of contours for basic landform features.

BASIC LANDFORM FEATURES

Contour arrangements for several **basic landform features** taken from topographic maps are shown in **Figure 22.1**, along with a perspective-view drawing of each feature. One of the most basic landform features is a **hill** (**Figure 22.1A**), which you can think of as a rounded surface rising above its immediate surroundings. The **hilltop** is the point of highest elevation. The ground slopes downward from the hilltop in all directions. A series of increasing small, closed contours at higher elevations indicates a hill. You can assume that the center of the smallest contour at the highest elevation is the location of the hilltop. A long and narrow hillside is called a **ridge**. A land mass that projects well above its surroundings, higher than a hill, is called a **mountain**.

The separation between contours tells you the **relative steepness** of hillsides, assuming the contour interval to be the same on the topographic maps showing the features. Widely separated contours equally spaced on the map (**Figure 22.1B**) tell you that the hillside has a uniformly gentle slope. Compare this illustration with the evenly spaced, more closely separated contours in (**Figure 22.1C**). You can see these contours are showing a uniformly steep slope.

Hillsides are often eroded into concave or convex forms. An inward curving **concave hillside** (**Figure 22.1D**) will have contours more closely spaced at the top of the hill, with a progressive widening between contours down-slope. Notice that the contours for the ridge shown in this illustration are "U" shaped, and that the bottom of each "U" is on the slope gradient (maximum down-slope direction) line. Standing at the top of the hill, you should be able to see the entire concave hillside if your viewpoint isn't obstructed by vegetation or other objects.

An outwardly curving **convex hillside** (**Figure 22.1E**) has the opposite down-slope contour arrangement—more widely spaced at the top of the hill and more closely spaced down the hillside. The bottoms of the "U"-shaped contours defining the hillside point down-slope, but you'll be able to see only the top part of the convex hillside when standing at the hilltop.

The steepest hillside, of course, is a vertical **cliff** (**Figure 22.1F**). If the cliff slope is truly vertical, the contour lines on the slope will overlay each other, appearing to merge into a single line. Map makers add small ticks perpendicular to the single line, oriented so that the ticks point toward the bottom of the cliff. If the cliff is overhanging, such as for the waterfall in this illustration, the lower-elevation contours will cross behind those at the top of the cliff. In this special situation, the lower-elevation contours in the undercut are shown with dotted lines indicating that they aren't visible from the top of the cliff.

Another very common landform feature is a **valley** (**Figure 22.1G**)—a relatively long and narrow area, often containing a stream, that is bounded by two areas of higher elevation. Contours in a valley are "V"-shaped and parallel the stream until they cross it at the base of each "V". You can see that the base of each "V" always points upstream. The more level the valley, the longer each contour will parallel the stream before crossing it. In a very flat valley, the contour may parallel the stream across the topographic map without crossing, making it difficult to determine the direction of water flow.

A **ravine** (or draw) is a deep, narrow, steep-sided valley formed by water erosion on a hillside. Ravines are often found on the sides of ridges, perpendicular to the valley. A series of contours with "V"-shaped notches, one above the other, indicate a ravine. Notice that the base of each "V" always points upstream.

A lower-elevation pass that slopes gently between two higher-elevation hills or peaks is called a **saddle** (**Figure 22.1H**). A saddle may also simply be a dip in elevation along a level ridge crest. Contours curve away from the pass on both sides, looking roughly like the outline of a horse saddle.

Depressions (**Figure 22.1I**) are low areas surrounded on all sides by higher ground. Depressions may be human-made like the rock quarry in

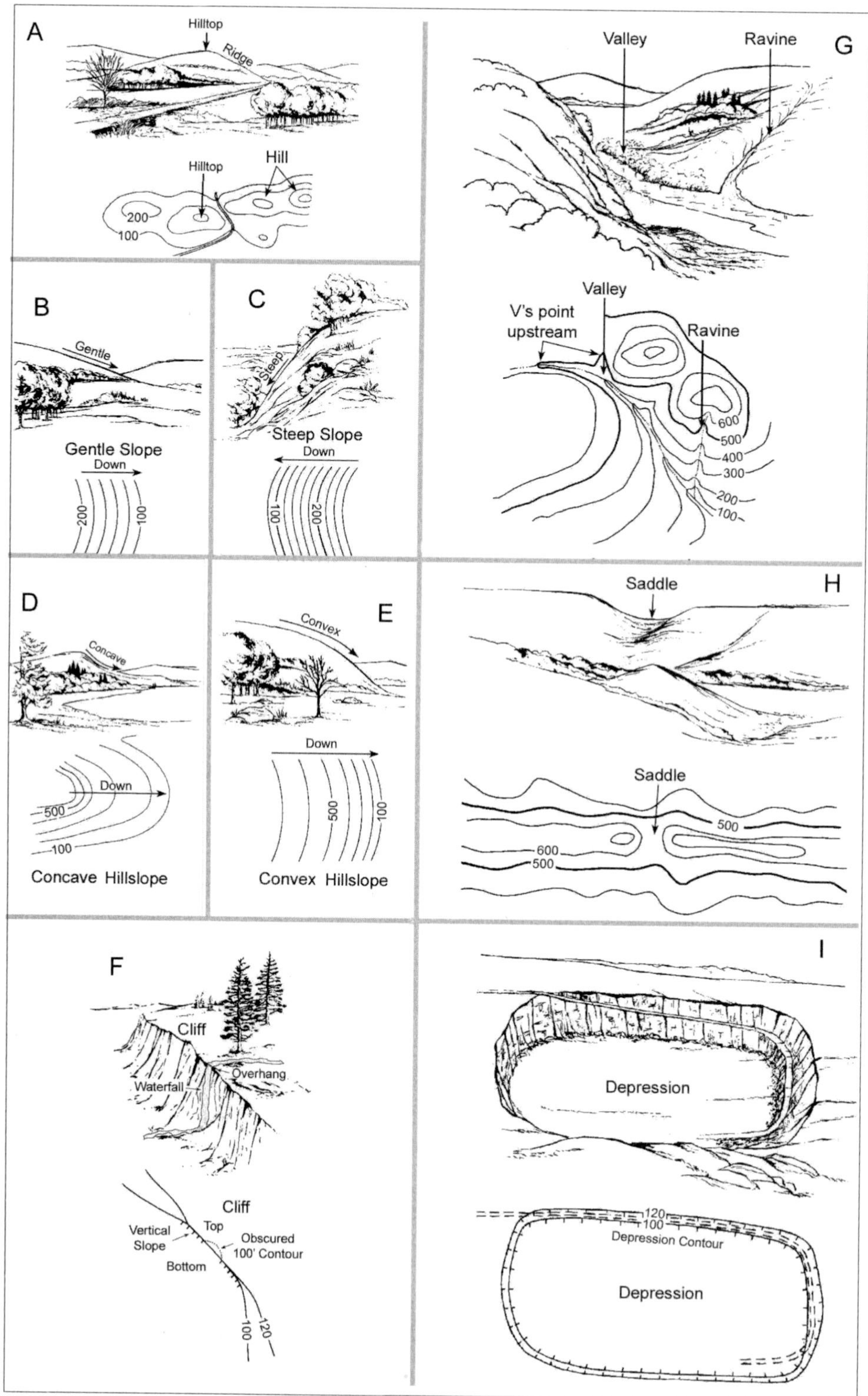

Figure 22.1 Basic landform features can be identified on topographic maps by distinctive arrangements of contours and by the use of special contour symbols (based on illustrations in U.S. Army FM 21-26, Map Reading).

the illustration, or natural features such as craters and sinkholes. In either case, map makers use **depression contours** to show the feature. Depression contours have small perpendicular tick marks added to the contour. The ticks always point in the downhill direction.

MAJOR LANDFORM TYPES

Basic landform features are the elements used to describe larger and more complex types of landforms. In this section, we'll look at 11 major landform types that occur in the United States: volcanoes, dissected plateaus, uniformly sloping plains, ridge and valley topography, domes, floodplains, braided river channels, alluvial fans, karst topography, alpine glaciation, and continental glaciation. These landforms are the result of different geological processes ranging from volcanism to glaciation. River erosion and deposition, along with groundwater leaching, create a distinct set of fluvial landforms.

Each landform type has a characteristic assemblage of basic landform features and one of the distinctive drainage patterns shown in **Figure 22.2**. The landform illustrations on the following pages blend from an aerial photo to a topographic map of the area. This blending allows you to see how the same landform appears on an air photo and topographic map, and in the middle of each blend you will see the contours overlaid on the photo. This overlay area will help you understand how contours represent landforms.

Basic landform features and drainage characteristics mentioned in the text description are labeled on the topographic map and air photo portions of each illustration. A small diagram showing a highly simplified drawing of the drainage pattern characteristically associated with the landform type is placed in the corner of each illustration to help you understand its geometrical form.

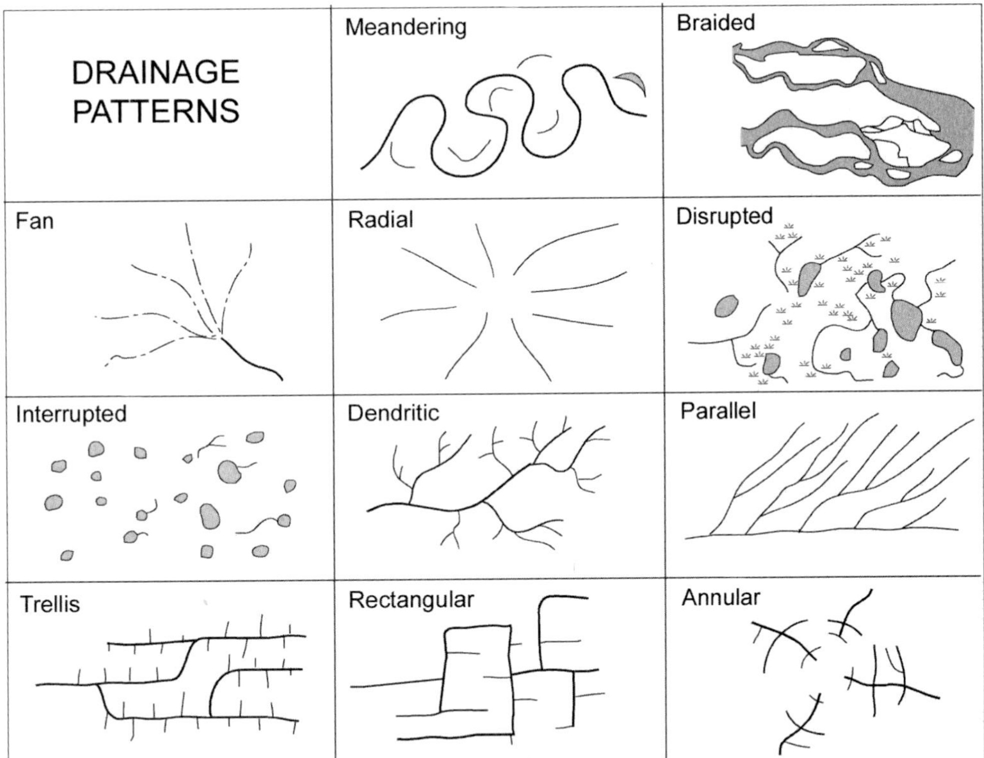

Figure 22.2 These drainage patterns are associated with different types of landforms.

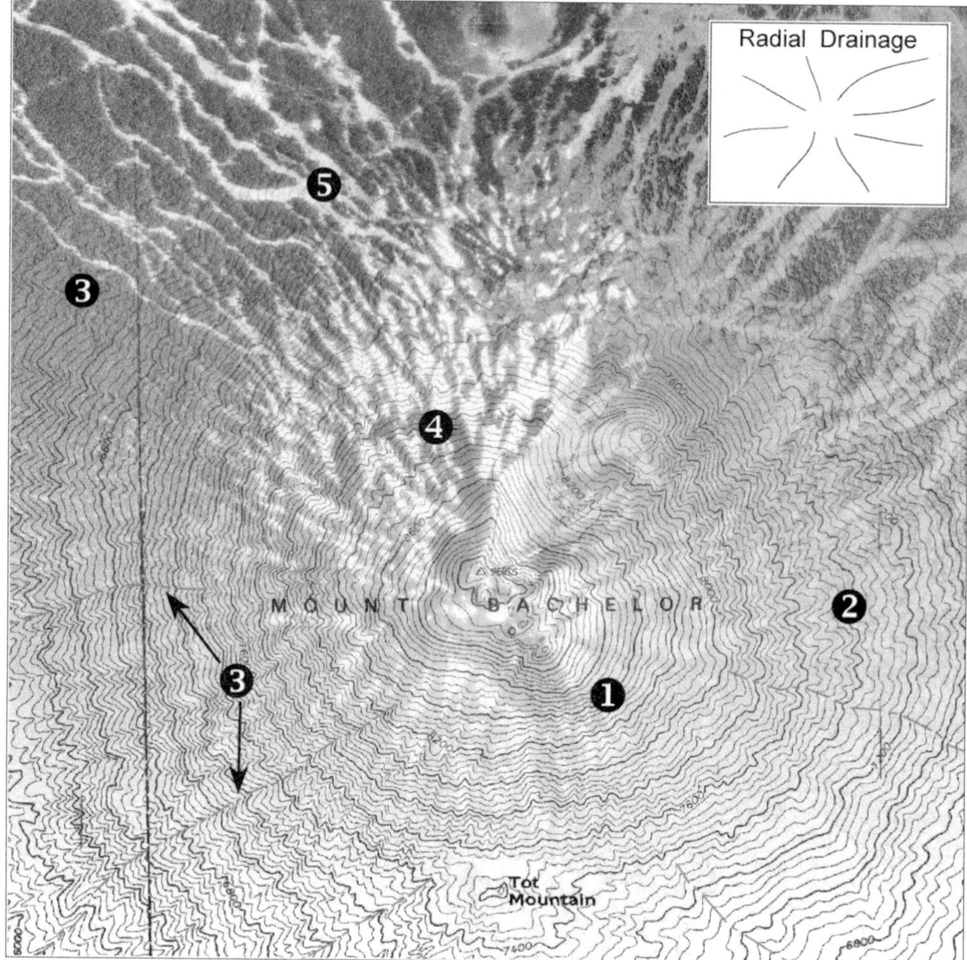

Figure 22.3 Mt. Bachelor, Oregon, is a young volcano in the Cascade Range.

Volcano

Mt. Bachelor, near Bend, Oregon, is a classic cone-shaped volcano. You can identify a volcano on a topographic map, such as the one on the bottom of **Figure 22.3**, by the pattern of ever-smaller, roughly circular, concentric contours (1) that end at the summit. The slopes of a young volcano are uniformly steep from its summit to lower elevations, as the uniformly spaced contours on the map (2) illustrate.

Water flowing down the sides of the volcano form a **radial drainage pattern** (3) of straight streams that radiate outward from the summit. Snowfields near the summit are often visible on an air photo of the volcano (4). You may also see a radial pattern of roughly straight ski runs as cuts through the forest (5) if the volcano is also a ski resort.

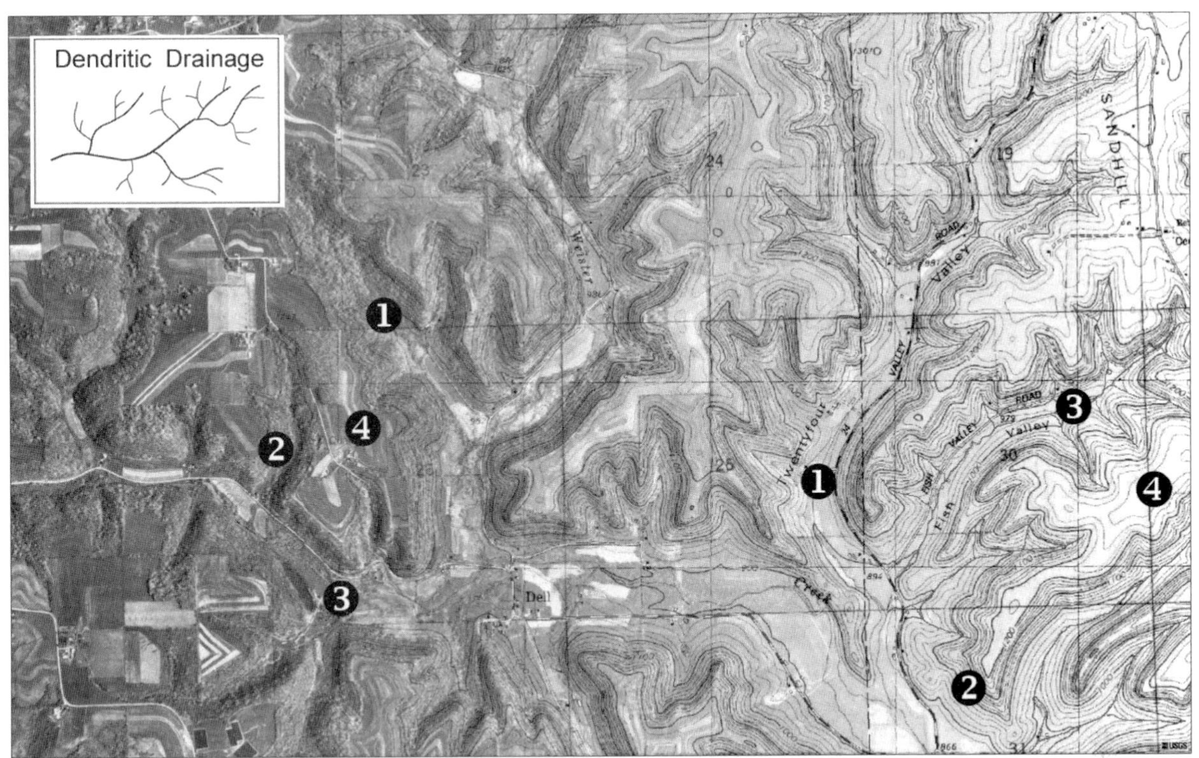

Figure 22.4 The "driftless area" in southwestern Wisconsin is a dissected plateau eroded by a dendritic drainage system.

Dissected Plateau

The air photo on the left and the contour map on the right side of **Figure 22.4** cover a small portion of the "driftless area" in southwestern Wisconsin. The driftless area was never subject to continental glaciation, and hence is a remnant of the **dissected plateau** that wasn't leveled by massive Pleistocene ice sheets. This portion of Wisconsin is a horizontal plateau of sedimentary rock layers that has been severely eroded by streams over millions of years. The pattern of contours on the map tells you that the area is now covered by gently sloping valleys (1), steep ridges (2), and gently sloping ridge tops. Notice the classic arrangement of V-shaped contours outlining valleys and ravines, and the closely spaced U-shaped contours on the ridges. These shapes are also easy to spot on the air photo, partly due to the shadows in the valleys when the photo was taken.

The **dendritic drainage pattern** seen on the map and air photo (3) is typical of dissected plateaus. A geologist would tell you that horizontal layers of soft sedimentary rock such as shale often erode in a dendritic manner, so that the stream basin is shaped roughly like a leaf and the streams look like its veins. The ridge tops that remain (4) usually are sedimentary rock layers more resistant to erosion, such as sandstone or limestone.

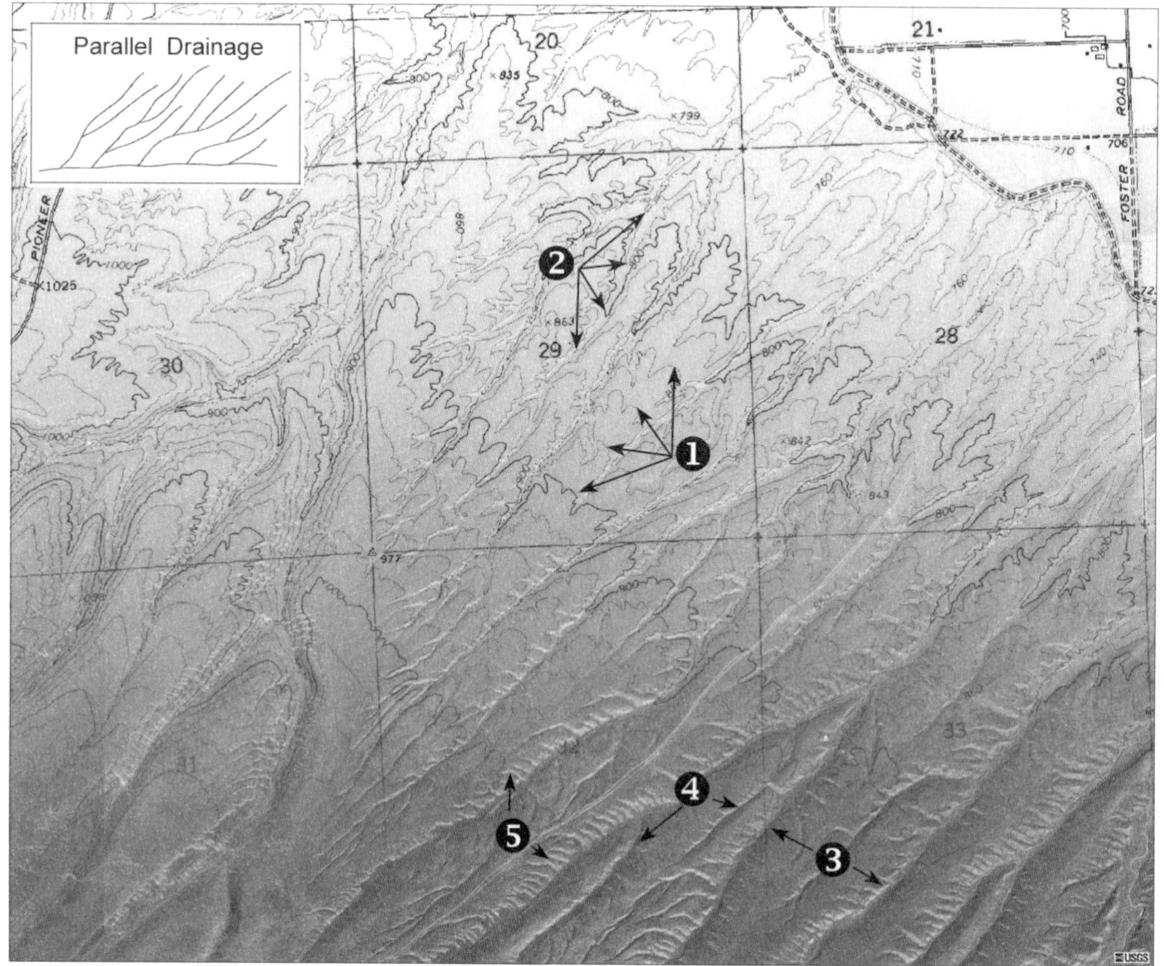

Figure 22.5 This area just north of a ridge in the Horse Heaven Hills near Sunnyside, Washington, is a uniformly sloping plain with parallel drainage.

Uniformly Sloping Plain

The area shown in **Figure 22.5** is just to the north of one of the east-west trending ridges in the Horse Heaven Hills near Sunnyside, Washington. The equally spaced contours (1) that are zigzag in form yet run diagonally across the map tell you that this is a uniform plain that gently slopes downward toward the northeast. Notice that the V's on each contour are aligned perpendicular to the general contour direction (2). You will also see that the V's along each stream course are aligned with the downward slope direction, indicating that the streams are flowing parallel to each other. The air photo clearly shows this **parallel drainage pattern** (3) on the uniformly sloping plain.

A parallel drainage pattern forms where the surface has a pronounced uniform slope. Tributary streams tend to stretch out in a parallel-like fashion, following the slope of the surface (4). Notice that very small tributary gullies tend to form in a perpendicular direction to the main stream (5).

A parallel drainage pattern often develops in regions of parallel, elongated landforms. The Horse Heaven Hills were created several million years ago by lava eruptions followed by buckling of the lava flows into elongated ridges as they were compressed from the north and south. Sediments eroded from each ridge form the uniformly sloping plain.

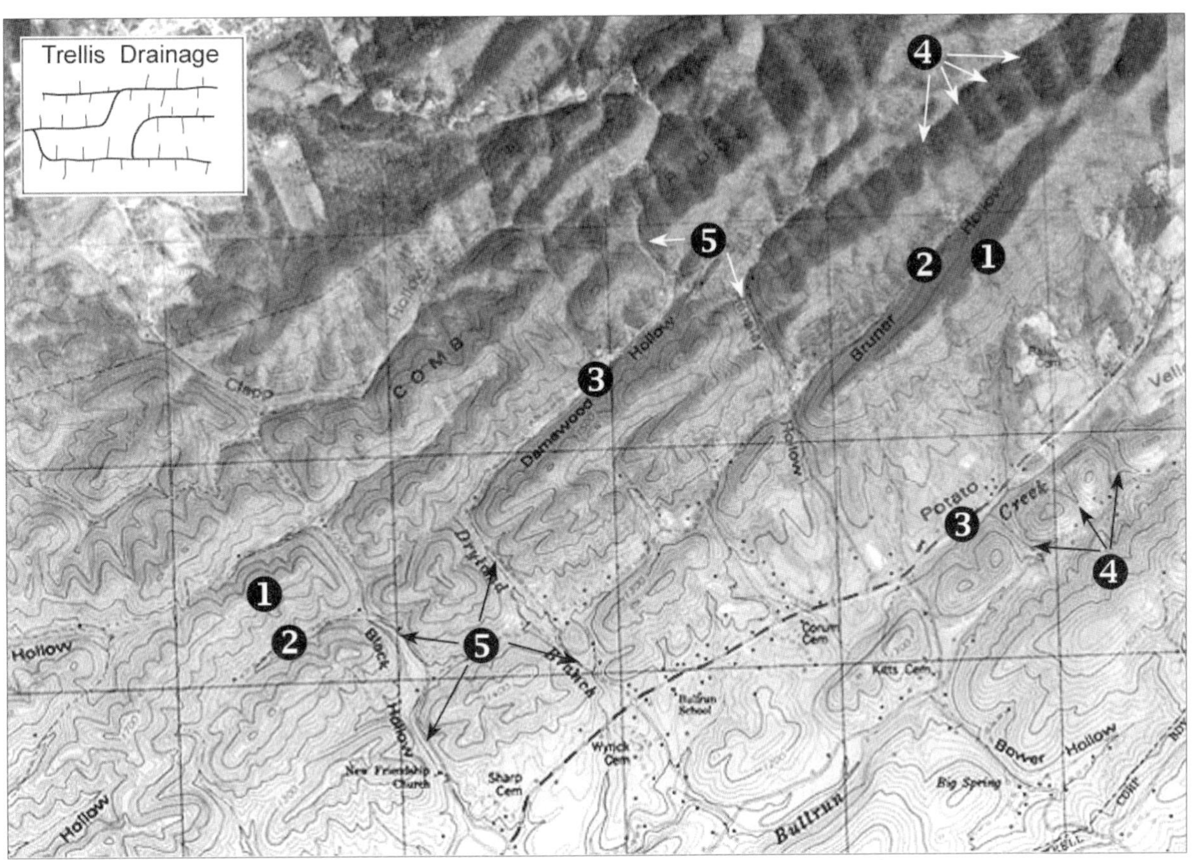

Figure 22.6 Ridge and valley topography is characteristic of the Appalachian Mountains. A trellis drainage pattern develops to drain the valleys.

Ridge and Valley Topography

The area near Maynardville, Tennessee, shown in **Figure 22.6** is an example of the **ridge and valley topography** found throughout the Appalachian Mountains that run from Alabama to New York. The northeast-trending ridges (1) and valleys (2) seen on the topographic map and air photo are the roots of a much taller, ancient mountain range. This range was formed several hundred million years ago when North America, Africa, and Europe collided, forming a super-continent that geologists call Pangaea. As the continents collided, the sedimentary rock layers on the east coast of North America were folded and uplifted to form a long narrow mountain range. Around 200 million years ago, the continents split and began drifting apart to their current locations. Two hundred million years of erosion have reduced the mountain range to about half of its original height and exposed its folded roots.

A **trellis drainage pattern** develops in ridge and valley topography. The down-turned folds, called **synclines**, form long, straight, narrow valleys in which the major streams flow (3). Small tributary streams run straight down the sides of the up-turned parallel ridges (4), called **anticlines**, and join the main stream at right angles. Here and there, the main streams have eroded through the ridges at right angles (5), forming **watergaps**. Seen together, the stream pattern resembles a garden trellis.

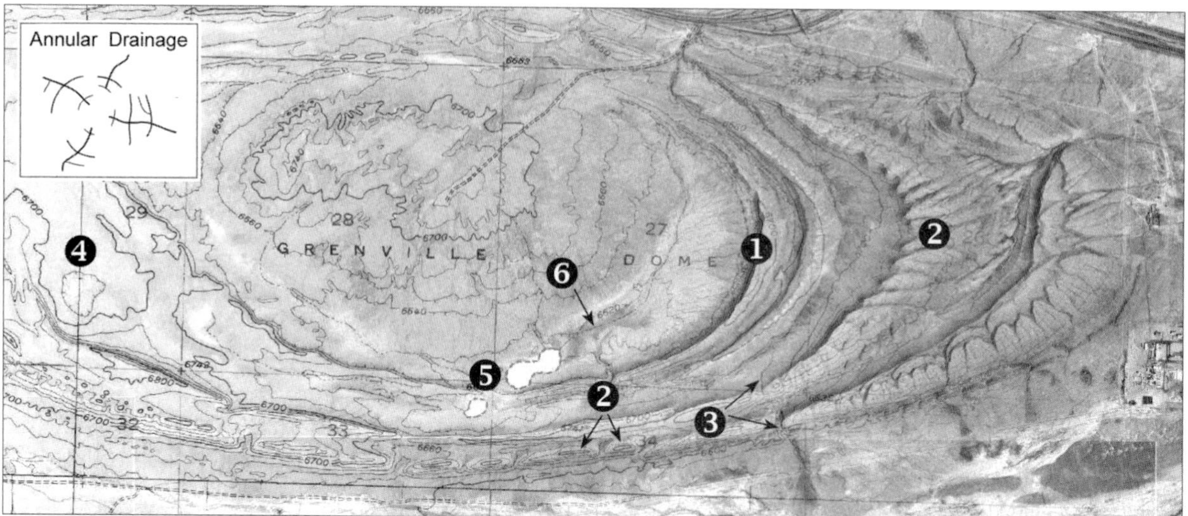

Figure 22.7 The Grenville Dome near Sinclair, Wyoming, is a classic anticlinal dome with a well developed annular drainage system.

Dome

The Grenville Dome, near Sinclair, Wyoming, is a classic **anticlinal dome** (shown on the air photo on the left and the topographic map on the right of **Figure 22.7**). The area initially was a flat plain underlain by horizontal sedimentary rocks. Tectonic activity beneath the crust bowed the rock layers upward into an ellipse-shaped anticline. As the rock layers rose upward, most of each layer eroded away, leaving gentle, smoothly curving ridges called **cuestas** (1), and steeper, serrated ridges called **hogbacks** (2) that encircle the dome. You can easily pick out the hogbacks on the air photo by their serrations, and you can identify them on the topographic map as a series of parallel, low, elongated hills.

As erosion proceeds, a characteristic **annular drainage pattern** develops. Streams flow parallel to the narrow, curving valleys between cuestas and hogbacks, then break through them at right angles to join the stream in the adjacent valley (3). Softer rock in the center of the dome may be eroded to the point that shallow depressions are created (4), shown by closed depression contours on the map. Playa lakes (5) sometimes form at the center of a depression, with intermittent streams flowing into the lake (6).

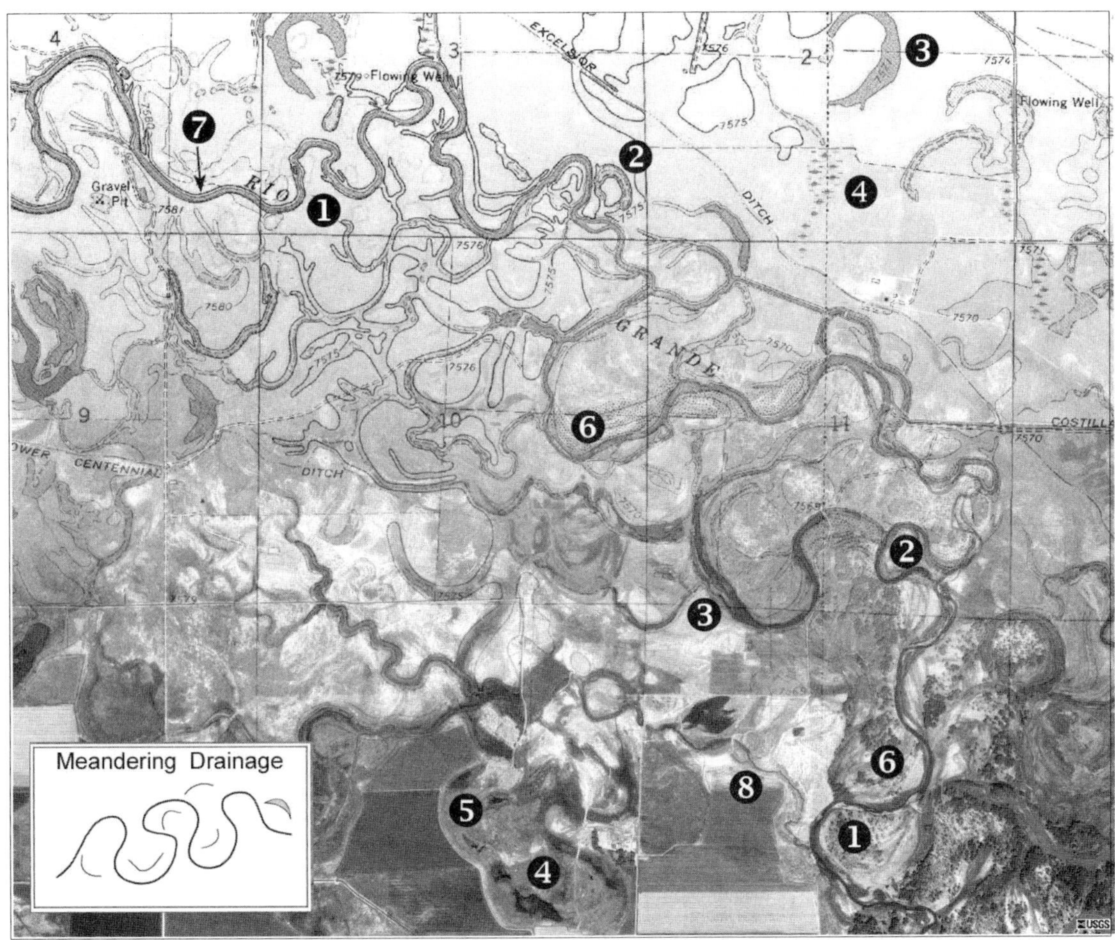

Figure 22.8 The Rio Grande meanders in its floodplain near Alamosa, Colorado.

Floodplain

The Rio Grande flows easterly in its **floodplain** through the San Luis Valley near Alamosa, Colorado. The five-foot contour interval and the few contours on the map in **Figure 22.8** tell you that the valley must be nearly flat. In nearly flat valleys, the river develops a **meandering drainage pattern** with a **sinuous channel** (1) that meanders across its wide floodplain. Over time, the channel often closes back on itself, forming a **cutoff meander** (2). The floodplain is defined by the cutoff meanders that develop into the many curved, crescent-shaped **oxbow lakes** (3) seen on the map and aerial photo. Each oxbow lake was once part of the river channel. Over time, many of the oxbows fill in with sediment from floods, forming marshy areas, identified by marsh-area symbols on the map and by partially filled oxbows on the photo (4).

Meander scars (5) are formed when the river cuts a curve into higher ground, forming a river terratce at the edge of the floodplain. You can see the path of the channel's eroding edge in the appearance of sandbars deposited on the opposite edge (6). Recently deposited sandbars appear white or light gray on the photo, whereas older sandbars are darker in tone due to riparian vegetation growing on them.

Contours adjacent to the river channel (7) tell you that the river has formed a **natural levee** from the sediment deposited on its banks during floods. Natural levees may force tributary streams to parallel the main channel for a considerable distance (8) before cutting through the natural levee and joining the river.

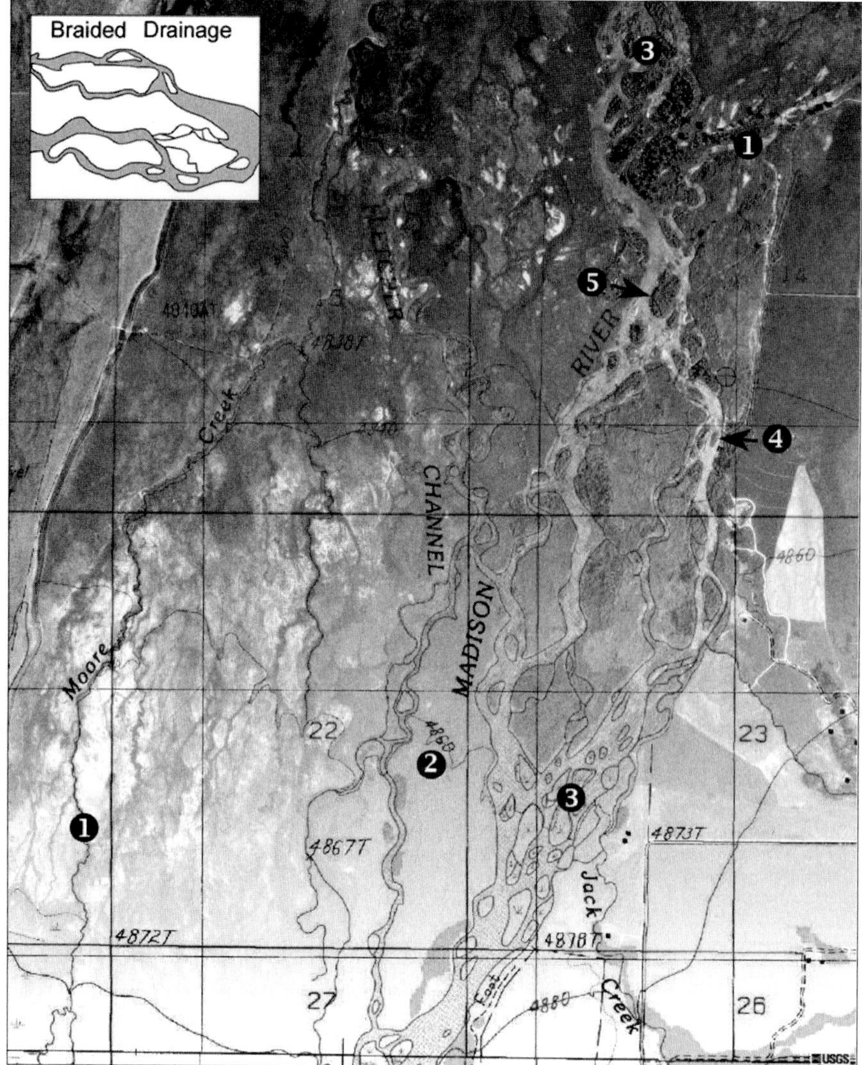

Figure 22.9 The Madison River near Ennis, Montana, has a braided river channel.

Braided River Channel

The Madison River near Ennis, Montana, has a **braided drainage pattern** within its floodplain (**Figure 22.9**). Braided drainage occurs when tributary streams (1) bring in more sediment than the main channel can transport. Channel braiding is common in areas with long periods of low stream flow interspersed with short periods of high stream flow. Such conditions are found in arid areas with sporadic, heavy precipitation from large thunderstorms, and in alpine or polar areas drained by seasonal, glacial-meltwater streams.

A braided channel is formed by the heavy deposition of sand and gravel, which gives the stream a broad, shallow channel. The few contour lines seen on the topographic map (2) show you the flatness of the channel. The river divides into several channels (3) that merge and subdivide repeatedly in a seemingly random manner within the floodplain. Sand and gravel bars are commonly found in the channels and are often visible on an air photo (4). Small islands between the braided channels (5) may exist long enough to be covered by shrubs, small trees, and other riparian vegetation.

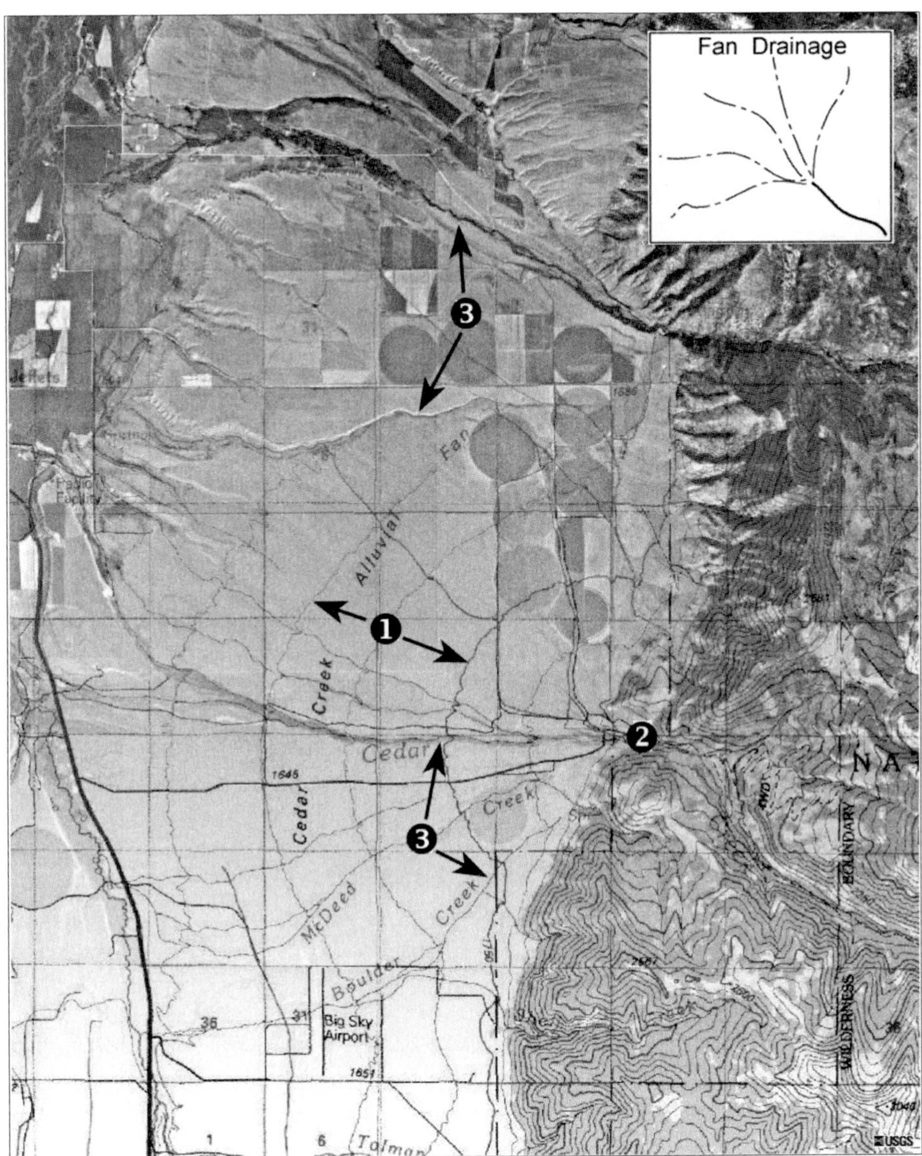

Figure 22.10 The Cedar Creek alluvial fan, near Ennis, Montana.

Alluvial Fan

The air photo and topographic map in **Figure 22.10** show a depositional landform called an **alluvial fan**. Streams carrying high sediment loads from mountainous areas to a flat valley bottom, particularly during infrequent, intense rainstorms in arid areas, build alluvial fans. Over time, the stream deposits the sediments on the valley floor as a low cone of sand and gravel that resembles an open Japanese fan when the feature is viewed from above. On a topographic map, you can identify an alluvial fan by the widely separated, evenly spaced, semi-circular contour lines (1) that indicate a uniform, gently sloping conical landform.

The apex of an alluvial fan is at the end of a canyon or ravine (2) at the edge of the valley. Streams radiate outward from the apex in a **fan drainage pattern** (3), with each stream resembling a rib of the fan. Several stream courses are visible on the map and photo. These stream courses tell you that the channel shifts position with each major rainstorm.

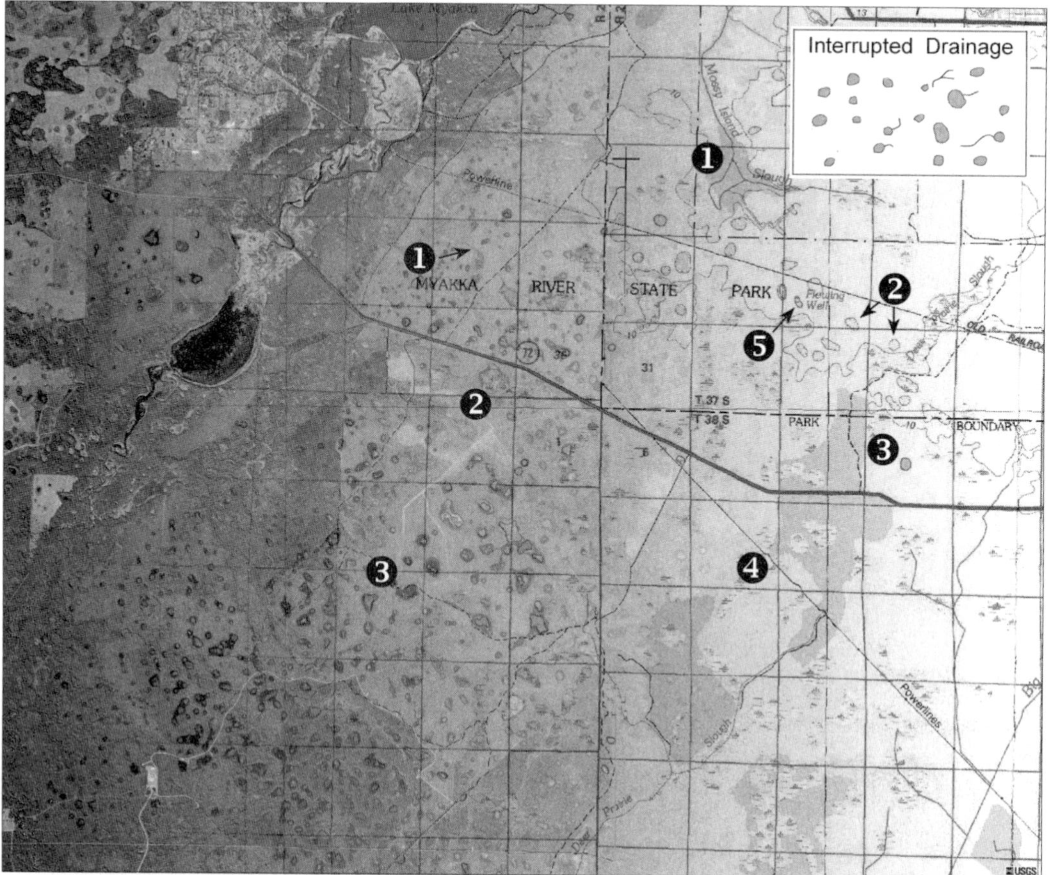

Figure 22.11 Myakka River State Park near Sarasota, Florida, is an excellent example of karst topography.

Karst Topography

Myakka River State Park, near Sarasota, Florida (**Figure 22.11**), is an area of **karst topography**. Karst is a distinctive topography in which the landscape is largely shaped by the dissolving action of water on carbonate bedrock (usually limestone, dolomite, or marble). Karst is formed when rainwater picks up carbon dioxide from the air and dead plant debris in the soil, then percolates through cracks, dissolving the rock. This geological process, occurring over many thousands of years, results in unusual surface and sub-surface features, including well-eroded rolling hills, deep hollows, sinkholes, vertical shafts, natural bridges, disappearing streams, and springs. Underground, there will be a complex drainage system and caves.

One way you can identify an area of karst topography is by the few surface streams visible on the map or air photo. You may see **disappearing streams** (1) where surface water flow suddenly disappears into the groundwater system. A multitude of small, round **sinkholes** will be seen as circular depression contours on the map (2). A sinkhole is a collapsed portion of bedrock above a void. A sink may be a sheer vertical opening into a cave or a shallow depression of many acres.

Many sinkholes fill with water to form the small, circular lakes dotting the air photo and map (3). Other sinkholes have been filled with sediment, forming the marshes seen on the topographic map (4). You may also see **springs** or **natural wells** on the map (5). These are natural resurgences of groundwater, usually along a hillside or from a valley floor. Disappearing streams, sinkhole lakes, and springs together give areas of karst topography an **interrupted drainage pattern**.

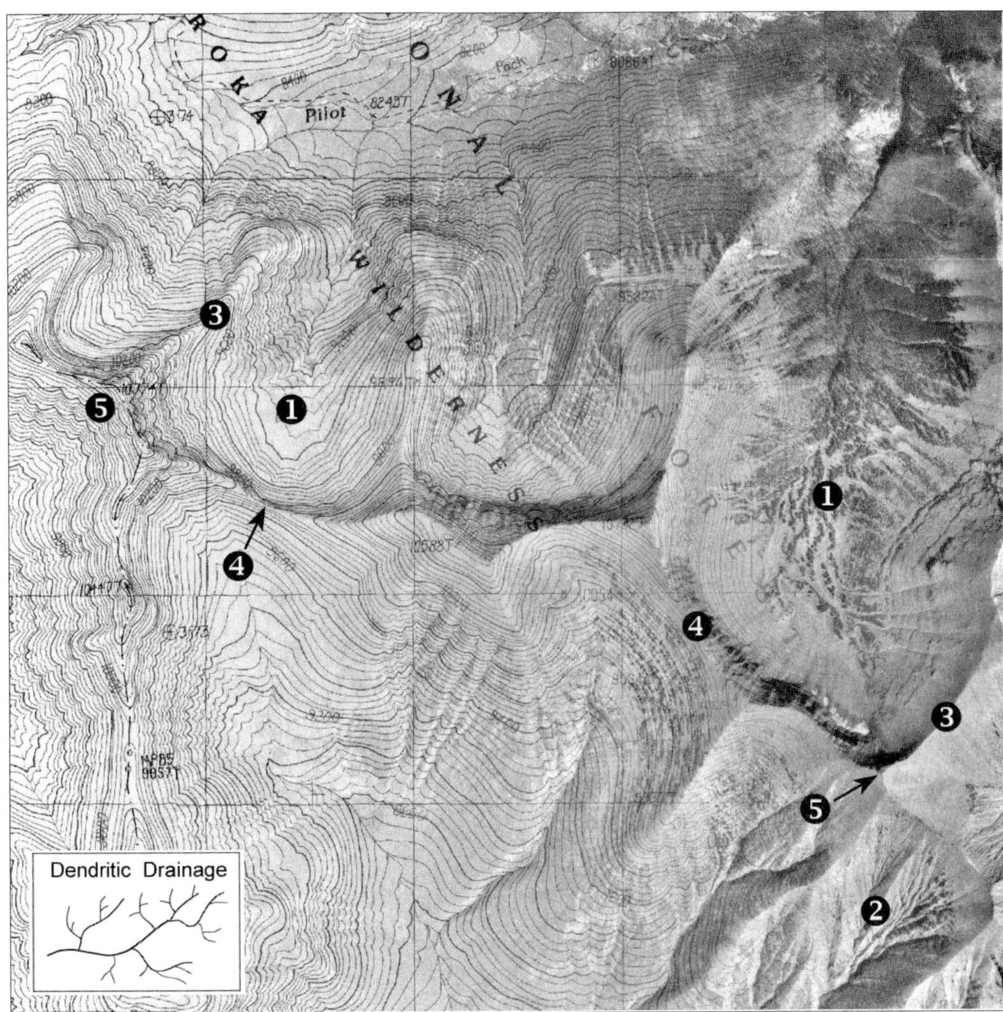

Figure 22.12 This area in Wyoming just east of Yellowstone National Park was formed by alpine glaciation. The photo is a clear example of apparent relief reversal. Try turning the page upside-down to gain an even better impression of the landforms.

Alpine Glaciation

The area in Wyoming just east of Yellowstone National Park, shown in **Figure 22.12**, is one of the best examples of **alpine glaciation** in the conterminous United States. During the Pleistocene (around 20,000 years ago), alpine glaciers covered the area. Ice fields at higher elevations grew into lobe-shaped glaciers whose downward movement eroded bowl-shaped **cirques** (1) into the mountains. You can identify a cirque on a topographic map by the closely spaced U-shaped contours at higher elevations that show its steep, curved walls. The contour spacing often increases in the middle of the cirque, where the surface slopes gently enough for small **tarn lakes** to be formed after the glacier has melted. A **dendritic drainage pattern** typically develops within each cirque, and on an air photo you'll see the dendritic branching of streams that resembles the pattern of veins in a leaf (2).

As glaciation continues, adjacent cirques expand until they intersect, forming steep, narrow ridges called **arêtes** (3). You will often see a saddle, called a **col** (4), in the middle of the arête. Three cirques will sometimes converge to form a steep, rocky peak called a **horn** at their intersection point (5). The horn's triangular shape is easily identified on the air photo, as are the set of ever-smaller, closed, triangular contours that end at the top of the horn.

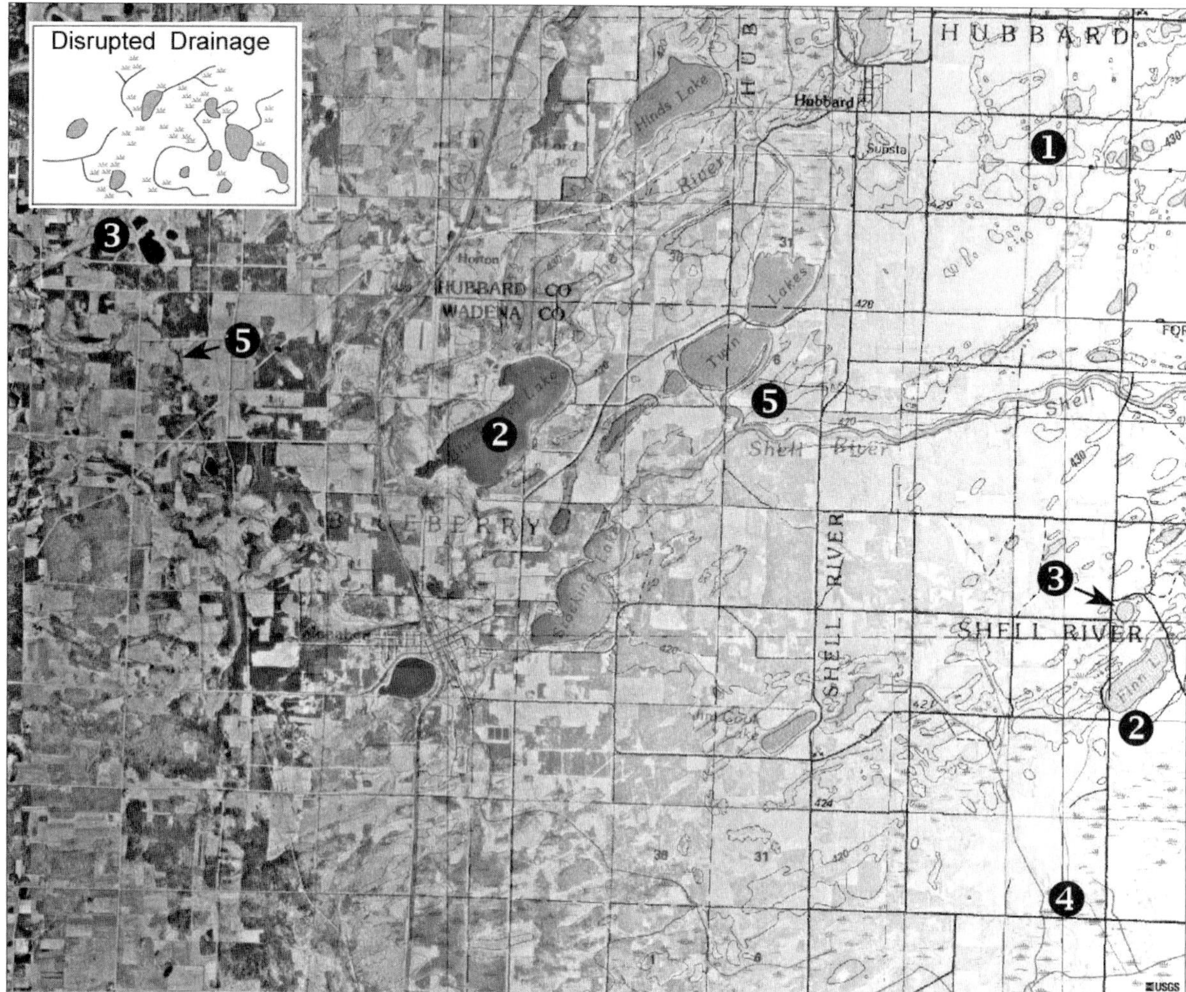

Figure 22.13 The landscape around Menahga, Minnesota, was created by Pleistocene continental glaciation.

Continental Glaciation

The area around Menahga, Minnesota, shown in **Figure 22.13**, was sculpted by **continental glaciation**. During the Pleistocene, mile-high ice sheets covered most of the upper Midwest, including Minnesota. As the ice sheets advanced and retreated, their sheer weight and slow movement eroded the bedrock into a flat plain. Notice that the relatively few contour lines depicting the low topography appear unorganized and randomly placed on the map (1).

As the last ice sheet retreated, a **disrupted drainage pattern** developed on the glaciated plain. You'll find numerous lakes (2) in shallow depressions scoured out by the ice. Small **kettle lakes** (3), identified by their small, round shape on topographic maps and aerial photos, were created by detached chunks of buried ice that left a round depression when they melted. As the depressions fill in with sediment, **marsh** areas develop. These areas are shown on the topographic map with the standard **marsh-area** symbol (4). Streams appear to wander across the landscape, connecting marshes and lakes in a haphazard, seemingly random manner (5). This arrangement of lakes, marshes, and streams indicates that the surface is very young geologically, and that the original drainage pattern was completely disrupted by the continental glaciation.

GEOLOGY

The geology in your area affects your life in many ways. You may live in an area where natural hazards such as landslides, earthquakes, or volcanic activity threaten your safety. The local geology may determine the availability and quality of groundwater in wells and the ease of constructing buildings and roads. Your area's economy may be based on the mining of minerals or the extraction of oil and natural gas.

In addition to the practical importance of understanding your local area's geology, the geologic features are clues helping you understand the earth's long history of sediment deposition, erosion, volcanic activity, and deformation of rock layers by faults and folds. Interpreting geologic maps helps you piece together the puzzle of how your local geology has developed over long periods of time.

Geologic Maps

Let's examine a small part of one of the earth's most spectacular landforms—the Grand Canyon in Arizona. You may have visited the canyon's south rim and been awestruck by the view to the north. The ground photo in **Figure 22.14** cannot do justice to the grandeur of what you saw, but it does capture the horizontal rock layers that appear to have been eroded away like an intricately carved layer cake. A **geologic map** will help you understand how this landform came to be.

Figure 22.14 Ground photo of the Grand Canyon in Arizona looking northwest from Maricopa Point near the south rim village.

Figure 22.15A shows a portion of a geologic map of the area around the south rim canyon village produced by the U.S. Geological Survey. We have reproduced the map in monochrome, but the areas of different bedrock types are shown with different pastel colors on the original. The map shows the distribution of different types of bedrock and tectonic features such as faults and folds. The geologic information is usually printed on top of a large-scale topographic base map to help you locate the geologic features on the ground. The topographic base map is printed in light gray so it doesn't interfere with seeing the geologic features on the map. Colored areas, lines, and special point symbols and labels unique to geologic maps represent the geology. Correctly interpreting these symbols will allow you to understand the geology shown on any standard geologic map.

Rock Units

The first thing the geologic map in Figure 22.15A shows you is the location of different **rock units** of various ages. Rock units vary in composition, texture, and geologic age. A **formation** is a type of rock unit that has a unique composition and stratigraphic position (above or below other formations). The area on the surface covered by a rock unit or formation is shown on the geologic map by a particular color or pattern, as well as by a label that identifies its geologic age and name. Rock units are named by the geologists who make the map, based on their observations of the kinds and ages of the rocks.

The boundary between two different rock units is called a **contact**, and is represented by different kinds of lines on the geologic map. Depositional contacts are shown on most geologic maps. All rock units are formed over, under, or beside other units. For example, lava from a volcano flows over the landscape, and when the lava hardens into rock, the place where the lava rests on the rocks underneath is a depositional contact. Where the original depositional contact between rock units is visible on the surface, it is shown on the geologic

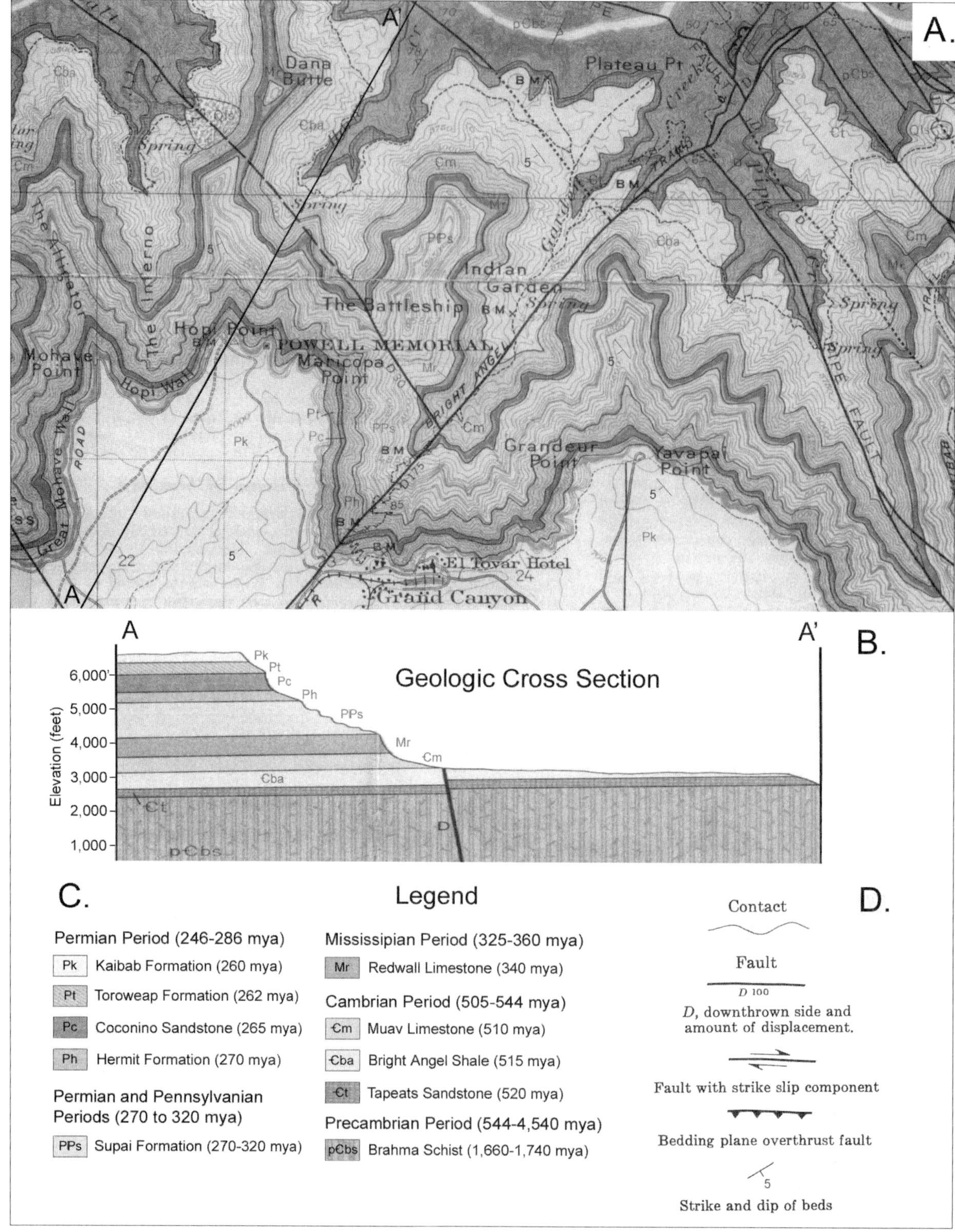

Figure 22.15 This portion of the geologic map (A) and cross section (B) for a portion of the Bright Angel quadrangle in Grand Canyon National Park (A) contains the variety of geologic information found on this type of map. The map legend describes the rock units (C) and tectonic features (D) found on the map.

map as a solid, thin line shown in **Figure 22.15D**. If the location of the contact is only approximately known, it is shown by a thin, dashed line. The shorter the dash, the more uncertain the location. A dotted line is the most uncertain of all, because the contact is concealed at the surface, so no amount of searching at the surface could ever locate it.

The rock layers that you can see on the photo in Figure 22.14 are shown on the geologic map by solid contact lines and colored bands identified by letter codes such as Pk or Mr. Notice that the horizontal rock layers coincide with contour lines, allowing you to estimate the thickness of each layer. The geologic map legend (**Figure 22.15C**) tells you that 10 rock units ranging in age from Permian to Precambrian geologic periods are found on the map. Geologists divide the history of the earth into a hierarchy of **eons** (the largest time division), **eras**, **periods**, and **epochs**, primarily based on the types of fossils found in rocks. The period is the most common division of time used to define the age of creation for rock units.

The time scale for geologic periods in the map legend tells you that the topmost rock unit, the Kaibab Formation, is the youngest at around 260 million years old. Each succeeding rock unit is an earlier page in the geologic record, ending with the billion-year-old Precambrian Brahma Schist, which is reached at the bottom of the canyon. Notice that there are three time gaps in the geologic record—a 260-million-year gap from the present to the Kaibab Formation, a 160-million-year gap between the Redwall and Muav limestone formation, and a one-billion-year gap between the Tapeats Sandstone and Brahma Schist. Why do these gaps occur? There are two possible hypotheses: (1) No sediments were deposited during these periods. (2) Rocks of these ages have disappeared due to surface erosion. The second hypothesis is true for the Kaibab Formation, since geologic maps of the Grand Canyon region show a few places where younger rock layers were not eroded and are found on top of the Kaibab unit.

Geologic Cross Sections

A **geologic cross section** gives you the geologist's idea of the vertical position and extent of rock units and faults that you would see if you could view a vertical slice through the ground along a line of the section. A cross section for the line of section A-A' in Figure 22.15A is shown in **Figure 22.15B**. Cross sections are annotated terrain profiles that are vertically exaggerated (see Chapter 16 for instructions on creating a vertically exaggerated profile).

To add the cross section to the profile, geologists first find the points at which rock unit contacts and fault lines intersect with the line of cross section. They project these intersection points vertically from the cross-section line to the top of the profile. Then they use the strike and dip symbol information for rock units in the vicinity of the cross-section line, plus fault orientation and form information, to infer the sub-surface orientation and extent of all rock units. Estimates of vertical and horizontal offsets in rock units due to faults are critical to creating the cross section.

The finished cross section looks detailed and exact, but in truth it will fall somewhere between a very good guess and a very poor approximation of the actual sub-surface geology. Its accuracy depends on the quality of the geologic map, how familiar the geologists are with the area, and how complex and detailed the geology is.

You can see that the cross section in Figure 22.15B shows all rock units to be essentially horizontal, as you guessed from the ground photo in Figure 22.14. The **stratigraphic position** (above or below position) of each rock unit in the cross section also matches its position on the geologic map. But what the cross section shows especially well is the thickness and elevation of each rock unit. Notice that the total thickness of rock beds above the Precambrian basement rock is almost 4,000 feet, and that the rock units range from 2,700 to 6,500 feet in elevation.

You could place the nine rock units above the Precambrian into three thickness categories: thin (Pk, Pt, Ph, and Ct), medium (Pc, Mr, Cm, and Cba), and thick (PPs). Comparing the rock unit thicknesses with their geologic ages, notice that thickness generally correlates with the age ranges implied in the map legend. For instance, the Supai (PPs) unit is thickest and was formed over 50 million years, while the thin Pk and Pt layers were formed in 2 to 3 million years.

Geologic cross sections also show the relative steepness of each rock unit's exposed face. Notice in Figure 22.15B that the Pc and Mr units are very steep, for example, while the Ph and PPs units are more gentle. You might correctly guess that the steepness of the face is related to the material that composes each rock unit. Your reasoning would be that rock units more resistant to erosion by water have steeper faces.

The geologic map legend and explanatory notes accompanying the map tell you the composition of each rock unit. The map legend for our map shows that the Coconino (Pc) and Tapeats (Ct) formations are sandstone, for example, whereas the Redwall (Mr) and Muav (Cm) units are limestone formations. The explanatory notes tell you that these hard sandstone and limestone rocks are more resistant to erosion in an arid environment than the softer, less erosion-resistant materials that compose the other rock units.

Geologists may have also described the depositional environment for each sedimentary rock unit. Most of the formations on our geologic map are described as being formed in a shallow marine environment like what now exists on the Atlantic coast of the United States. However, the Coconino sandstone was created from sand dunes formed on dry land, and part of the Toroweap formation was formed in a coastal desert.

You now know that rock layers formed at sea level must have been uplifted over a mile, nearly maintaining their initial horizontal form, and then were eroded into what you see in Grand Canyon National Park. Accounts of the geological history of the area explain that the uplift must have begun about 40 million years ago (hence there are no rock units younger than this). The Colorado River and smaller tributary streams began to erode the Grand Canyon about 6 million years ago, and erosion has been continuous until the present.

Strike and Dip

Many rock units form in broad, flat layers called **beds.** In areas like northern Arizona, thick stacks of rock beds that have built up over millions of years remain in their original horizontal orientation. In other places, however, tectonic forces bend and tilt the beds.

Information collected by geologists on the orientation of tilted rock beds is shown on a geologic map with **strike and dip** symbols (**Figure 22.15D**). A strike and dip symbol consists of three parts:

- A long line, called the **strike line**. It shows the direction in which the bed intersects the horizontal surface. This direction is perpendicular to the maximum tilt direction.
- A short line, called the **dip line**. This line shows the direction of maximum tilt.
- A number, called the **dip**. This number shows how much the bed is tilted, in degrees, from flat.

Notice the strike and dip symbols on Figure 22.15A on the Kaibab Formation to the west and east of the canyon village (labeled Grand Canyon on the map). These and the other strike and dip symbols on the map have a northwest-southeast strike and a 5 degree downward dip from horizontal to the southwest. If you look carefully at the geologic cross section, you can see this slight westerly dip in the rock units.

Faults

Rock units are often fractured and moved along cracks called **faults**. When different rock units have been moved next to one another after they were formed, their contact is a fault, shown on the geologic map by a thick line. Faults can also cut through a single rock unit. These faults are shown with the same thick line on the map, but have the same rock unit on both sides.

Several kinds of faults are shown on geologic maps. A **normal fault (Figure 22.15D)** is a block of ground that has been ruptured vertically. The fault line is typically labeled with the letters U and D, indicating the up-thrown and down-thrown sides. A **thrust fault** is a low-angle fault formed by compression, whereby the upper block of ground is thrust over the lower block, causing the crust to shorten in length. The "saw teeth" added to the fault line symbol show the side of the upper block. A **strike-slip fault** occurs where the adjacent surfaces appear to have moved horizontally. Arrows placed parallel to the fault line show their relative direction of movement.

Notice the normal fault in Figure 22.15A that crosses the section line. The cross section shows that the rock units to the west have dropped to the west, and the fault line on the map shows this drop to be 30 feet. The map notes explain that this faulting is associated with the uplift millions of years ago, and that most of the faults are currently inactive. They are the part of geologic history that you can easily see in canyon walls and roadcuts.

Regional Geology

The ability to think of landform-building processes in terms of geologic time is crucial in understanding how the terrain in a large region has developed. Changes which are imperceptible during our lifetime can result in gross alterations of the surface and sub-surface when accumulated over millions of years. Let's take as an example the interpretation of a landform map of the Great Lakes region. The question for the map interpreter is why the region is shaped as it is.

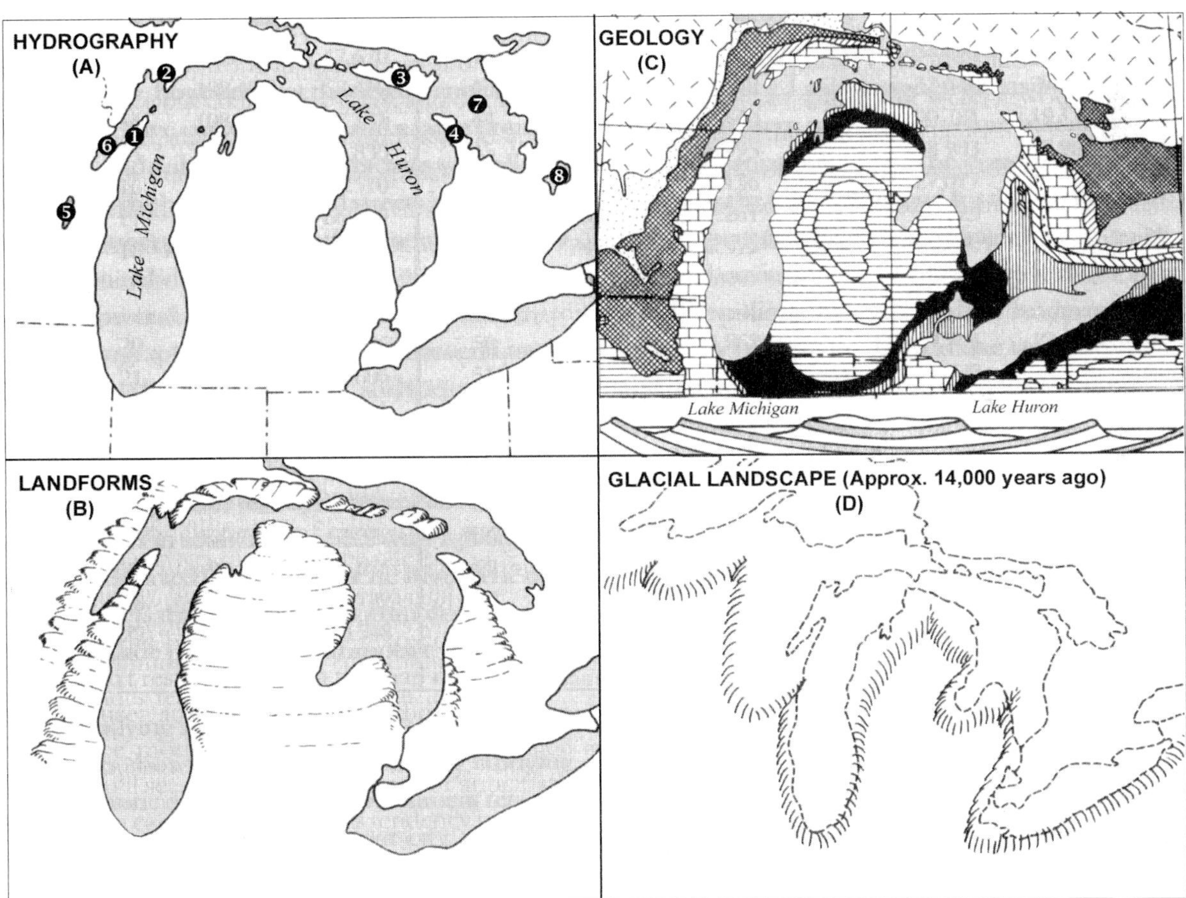

Figure 22.16 The Michigan Basin (A) provides an excellent example of how landforms (B), geology (C), and glacial activity (D) are all interrelated.

If you look closely at the small-scale hydrography map in **Figure 22.16A**, you will notice a curious thing. There is a rough symmetry about the central part of the southern peninsula of Michigan. Specifically, there appear to be concentric rings of remarkably similar features. Lake Michigan on the west is matched by Lake Huron on the east. The Door Peninsula (1), Garden and Stonington Peninsulas (2), Manitoulin Islands (3), and the Bruce Peninsula (4) form the second ring. These features are flanked by Lake Winnebago (5) and Green Bay (6) on the west and Georgian Bay (7) and Lake Simcoe (8) on the east.

This remarkably circular pattern of nested features is a map interpreter's dream. Not only is there order to the landforms, but the elements of the topography are intimately related. This means that if you can explain one of the rings, or even one feature such as a lake or peninsula, the chances are that you will have found the key to the entire structure.

We can begin our interpretation of the Great Lakes region by studying its topography, as depicted in **Figure 22.16B**. This admittedly "exaggerated" illustration looks much as if several different-sized saucers have been piled on top of one another, from largest at the bottom to smallest at the top of the stack. The circular pattern of peninsulas and islands represents erosional remnants of the edges of these saucer-like strata, while water bodies occupy the belts of lower land that lie between the saucer rims. But what could have caused these saucer-shaped layers of rock?

If there is a structural explanation, this can easily be confirmed by studying a map of the region's geology. Therefore, let's turn next to the geologic map and cross section in **Figure 22.16C**. This figure reveals that the geologic structure is that of a basin. Geologically speaking, the entire region was inundated for millions of years by a prehistoric ocean. During this period, thick beds of sediments were deposited in layers of sand, mud, and seashells. With time, these horizontal sediment layers were slowly transformed into beds of sedimentary rock (sandstone, shale, and limestone), which subsequently were warped up at their margins, forming a giant basin structure. The structure's uplifted edges were then eroded, leveling out the whole region. The rate of erosion varied with the strength of the alternate rock layers, however. Beds of weaker rock eroded the most, leaving lowlands separated by intervening high belts (cuestas) of more resistant rock.

But this scenario still doesn't explain how the Great Lakes were formed. The missing scrap of information we need is the fact that a thick continental ice sheet moved through this region on at least four occasions. According to the glacier theory, the region was molded by immense forces of moving ice several miles thick. The last glacier (which melted only some 12,000 years ago) gouged out the Great Lakes and, by alternately scouring and depositing material, disrupted the region's surface form in countless other ways (**Figure 22.16D**). The effect was to disguise the basic geologic structure in some places and accentuate it in others.

SELECTED READINGS

Blair, C.L., and Gutsell, B.V., *The American Landscape: Map and Air Photo Interpretation* (New York: McGraw-Hill Book Co., 1974).

Catacosinos, P.A. and Daniels, P.A., 'Early Sedimentary Evolution of the Michigan Basin," *The Geological Society of America*, Special Papers, No. 256, 1991.

DeBruin, R., 100 *Topographic Maps Illustrating Physiographic Features* (Northbrook, IL: Hubbard Press, 1992).

Gersmehl, P.J., "Maps in Landscape Interpretation," *Cartographica*, Monograph 271, 18, 2 (Summer, 1981), pp. 79-114.

Lisle, R.J., *Geological Structures and Maps: A Practical Guide*, 3rd ed. (New York: Butterworth Heinemann, 2003).

Miller, V.C., and Westerback, M.E., *Interpretation of Topographic Maps* (Upper Saddle River, NJ: Prentice Hall, 1989).

Schneider, A.F. and Fraser, G.S., *Late Quaternary History of the Michigan Basin* (Geological Society of America, 1990).

Spencer, E.W., *Geologic Maps*, 2nd ed. (Upper Saddle River, NJ: Prentice Hall, 2000).

Strahler, A.N. and Strahler, A., *Introducing Physical Geography* (New York: John Wiley & Sons, 2003).

United States Army, *Map Reading, Field Manual*, FM 21-26 (Washington, DC: Department of the Army, Headquarters, current ed.).

Way, D.S., *Terrain Analysis* (Stroudsburg, PA: Hutchinson Ross, 1982).

CHAPTER 23

INTERPRETING THE ATMOSPHERE AND BIOSPHERE

ATMOSPHERIC CONDITIONS

- Weather Maps
- Weather Satellite Images
- Doppler Radar Maps
- Wind Velocity Maps

CLIMATE MAPS

- Average Annual Precipitation
  - Precipitation in Washington State
- Monthly Climate Maps
- Climate Types
- Heating Degree-Days
- Solar Radiation

BIOSPHERE

- Species Distribution Maps
  - Plant Specimen and Observation Maps
  - Individual Animal Maps
  - Migratory Route Maps
- Species Range Maps
  - Natural Vegetation Zone Maps

One of the best paying professions is getting ahold of pieces of country in your mind,
learning their smell and their moods, sorting out the pieces of a view,
deciding what grows there and there and why....
This is the best kind of ownership, and the most permanent.
—Jerry & Renny Russell, On the Loose

23

CHAPTER 23

INTERPRETING THE ATMOSPHERE AND BIOSPHERE

In this chapter you'll see how to interpret maps that show aspects of the atmosphere and biosphere. The **atmosphere** is the thin mass of air surrounding the earth. Maps display **atmospheric conditions**, such as temperature, precipitation, and wind velocity, that directly affect your day-to-day living. **Weather maps** show current atmospheric conditions and predictions for the next few days. **Climate maps** reveal long-term average monthly or yearly atmospheric conditions, such as average annual precipitation, temperature, pressure, wind flow, and solar radiation received.

The **biosphere** encompasses all regions on the earth's surface (and in the atmosphere) where living organisms exist. Mapping the **flora** (plants) and **fauna** (animals) that live in different regions is a key activity for biogeographers, botanists, and zoologists. These maps help you understand the **range** and **habitat** for a species and its **migration** or **dispersal** patterns. You can find a region's degree of **biodiversity** by aggregating the information from species range or migration maps.

ATMOSPHERIC CONDITIONS

To understand current and predicted atmospheric conditions, you need information about temperature, precipitation, wind velocity, and atmospheric pressure that has been collected on the ground at meteorological stations and obtained from weather satellite images. You can find this information on a variety of weather maps. The weather maps in this section were collected July 5-6, 2004, to help you see how the information shown on each map is interrelated. Let's see what you can learn from these maps about current and future atmospheric conditions.

Weather Maps

The basic U.S. **weather map** (**Figure 23.1**) shows the values of several types of **surface observations** taken at hourly intervals for major meteorological stations across the country. The map in Figure 23.1 shows observed temperature, pressure, wind, and cloud cover data at 00Z on July 6, 2004. 00Z is midnight "Zulu" time, the hour at the Greenwich prime meridian. Since the conterminous United States falls in time zones from 6 to 9 hours west of the prime meridian, the map shows observations from 3:00 p.m. on the west coast to 6:00 p.m. on the east coast of the country.

The upper-left number on each meteorological station symbol is the **surface temperature** in degrees Fahrenheit (F) (degrees Celsius (C) in other countries). You might expect these July temperatures to decrease from west to east across the map, since the east coast observations are taken three hours later in the day. That there is little variation in temperature across the country tells you either that there is a heat wave in the eastern U.S. (or a cold spell in the West), or that there is much higher hu-

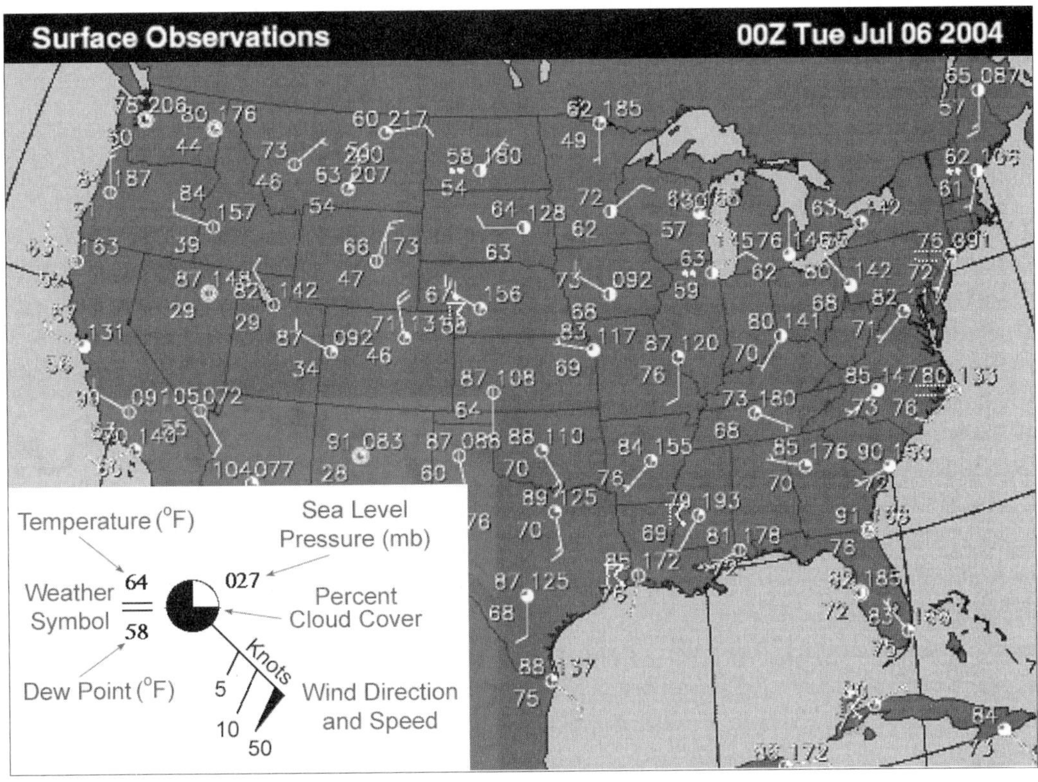

Figure 23.1 The basic daily weather map shows surface observations of temperature, precipitation, air pressure, and wind velocity taken at meteorological stations.

midity on the eastern half of the country, allowing the atmosphere to retain more heat in the evening hours.

The lower-left number on the station symbol is the **dew point temperature**. The dew point is the temperature to which air must cool in order to reach a state of saturation, where the air is holding the maximum possible amount of water vapor for its temperature and atmospheric pressure. **Condensation** in the form of clouds, fog, or frost occurs when the air temperature reaches the dew point.

The higher the dew point, the greater the moisture content of the air. When the air temperature is close to the dew point, the air has a high **relative humidity**. Meteorological stations reporting both high air and dew point temperatures are most likely uncomfortably humid, while a much lower dew point temperature is characteristic of dry, comfortable air. The high air and dew point temperatures on the right half of the map tell you that this must have been a hot, humid day. On the other hand, the much lower dew point temperatures reported at stations in the mountain and arid southwestern states indicate dry air and warm to hot afternoon temperatures.

The weather symbol between the air and dew point temperatures tells you the **type of weather** currently occurring at the meteorological station. The "=" sign in the map legend signifies fog, for example. The two dots on the Chicago station symbol mean moderate rain. The R-shaped symbol for the station near the Texas-Louisiana border means that a thunderstorm is present.

The pie diagram in the center of the station symbol indicates the **percent cloud cover** to the nearest 25%. Thus, the solid, dark circle on the Las Vegas, Nevada, station symbol means clear skies. The white quarter-circle in the legend shows 25% cloud cover (scattered clouds). A completely white circle means that the skies are totally overcast. The map in Figure 23.1 shows that most of the country is under clear skies or broken clouds.

The complex symbol at the lower right is the "**wind barb,**" showing **surface wind direction and speed**. The orientation of the wind barb's pole shows you the direction from which the wind is blowing. For instance, the wind barb in Figure 23.1's legend shows wind from the southeast, while at San Antonio, Texas, the wind is from the south. The "barbs" tell you the wind speed in knots (nautical miles per hour). Each short barb stands for 5 knots, each long barb means 10 knots, and a pennant indicates 50 knots. You find the station wind speed by adding these values. Thus, the wind barb in Figure 23.1's legend shows 5+10+50, or a 65-knot gale-force wind. The map shows that the wind at most stations is light, with a few stations reporting 20-knot breezes. Where winds are calm, you'll find a larger, open circle around the cloud-cover pie diagram, as you see at the Winnemucca, Nevada, station.

The number in the upper-right corner of the station symbol gives the **air pressure** in millibars (mb), adjusted to what the air pressure would be at sea level. These numbers are tricky to read. The rule is that if the number is less than 500, you add 10,000, then divide by 10 to find the pressure in millibars. Therefore, the air pressure for Figure 23.1's legend symbol (027) is 10,027/10, or 1,002.7 mb. If the number is greater than 500, you add 9,000 and divide by 10. A value of 938, then, stands for a pressure of 9,938/10, or 993.8 mb.

Standard (average) **sea level atmospheric pressure** is 1,013.2 mb (its map symbol would be 132), so most stations are reporting above-average pressure. A notable exception is the below-average pressure at the Des Moines, Iowa, station in the center of the circling wind barbs.

The weather map you've seen on television and in your newspaper (**Figure 23.2**) is the meteorologist's interpretation of temperature and air-pressure variations, as well as frontal activity, across the country at a certain time. This interpretation is based on meteorological station data and weather satellite imagery.

Areas colored from blue to red (shown in gray tones in Figure 23.2) to show cold to hot surface temperatures stand out prominently on the map. Each colored area is the zone between lines

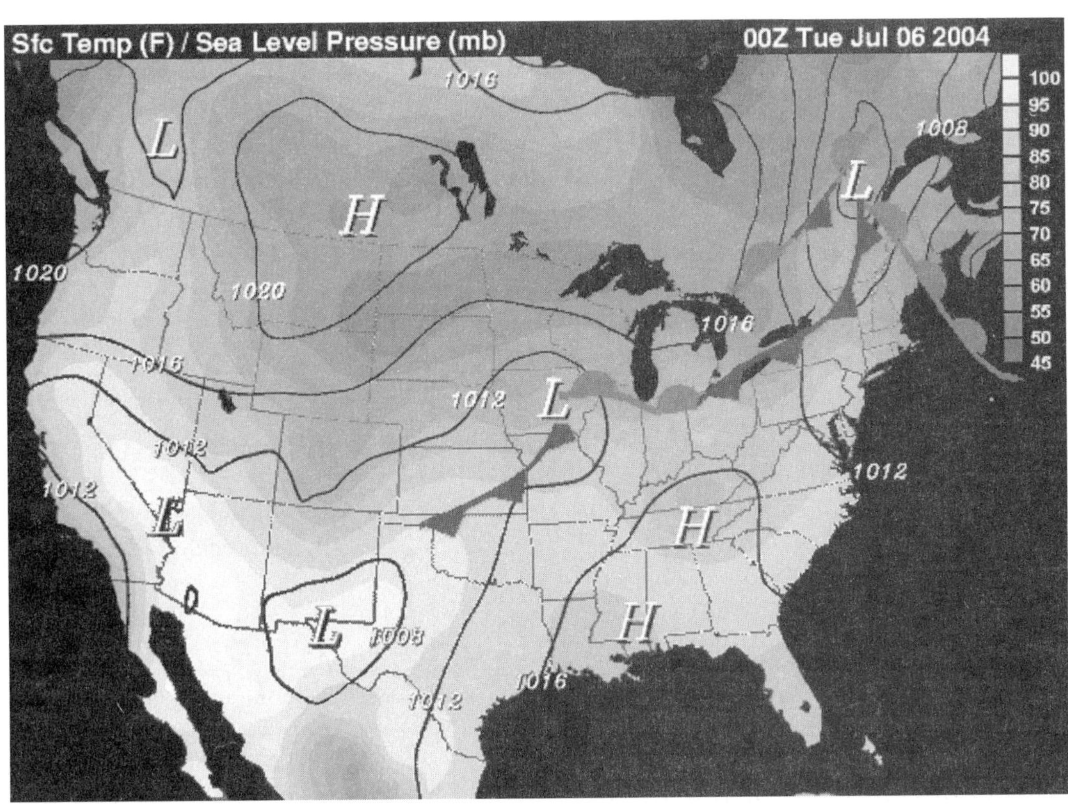

Figure 23.2 Television or newspaper weather maps typically show temperature zones, isobars of atmospheric pressure, locations of pressure centers, and weather fronts.

of equal temperature called **isotherms**. The meteorologist thinks of surface temperature data from meteorological stations as sample points taken from a continuous temperature surface. Computer mapping software interpolates between temperature readings to find the locations of isotherms, and the **temperature zones** between isotherms are colored. Figure 23.2 shows isotherms at 5°F increments.

What do the temperature zones tell you about the day recorded on the map in Figure 23.2? You can see that most of the United States experienced warm to hot afternoon temperatures, with cool air only in the north-central region and the east half of Maine. The temperature-zone widths indicate the steepness of the **temperature gradients** from one place to another. Notice the very steep temperature gradient at the bottom left of the map. You would feel a rapid increase in temperature when driving eastward out of the mountains in north-central Mexico toward Texas.

The thick, black lines in Figure 23.2 are **isobars**, which represent the continuous air-pressure surface at sea level. The isobars at four-millibar increments were interpolated from ground observations at meteorological stations using computer mapping software. Although the large isobar increment used for the map gives you only a general view of the pressure surface, large areas of above and below average pressure stand out on the map.

The location of the highest pressure recorded in each high-pressure area is a **high-pressure center**, also called an **anticyclone**, shown by a large "H" on the map. The area around a high-pressure center should have clear skies and dry air. The reason for this is that air from the upper atmosphere is descending, warming and drying as it descends. In the northern hemisphere, clockwise-flowing surface winds carry this air outward from the high pressure center to the surrounding area.

The lowest air pressure in each low-pressure area is a **low-pressure center**, also called a **cyclone**, shown by a large "L" on the map. Areas around low-pressure centers often have clouds and precipitation. This is because surface air around a low-pressure center is rising toward the upper atmosphere, cooling as it rises. As the air cools, its humidity increases until it reaches full saturation and cloud droplets form through condensation. These droplets grow into the raindrops, hail, snow, or sleet that falls in the low-pressure area.

Surface winds in the northern hemisphere flow counterclockwise as they spiral into the low-pressure center. Notice in Figure 23.1 that the wind directions at stations in the upper Midwest aren't random but, rather, appear to circle counterclockwise around a point in eastern Iowa. This circular pattern indicates surface winds flowing into the low-pressure center that you see in Figure 23.2.

Air flowing into the low-pressure center typically isn't uniform in temperature and humidity, since **air masses** from different source areas are spiraling into the center. The edge of an air mass is called a **front**.

On a weather map, a thick line marks the edge of a front. Solid triangles along this line show the **cold front** of a relatively cold, dry air mass. Semicircles along the line indicate a **warm front** at the edge of a relatively warm, moist air mass .

In Figure 23.2, notice the cold and warm fronts radiating outward from the low-pressure center in eastern Iowa. The cold-front triangles tell you that cold, dry air from the north is rotating into the low-pressure center. Cold air is denser and heavier than warm air. Consequently, air masses from the north displace warmer air moving from the south. Friction with the earth's surface slows the movement of the heavy, cool air, creating a steep temperature-pressure gradient along the cold front at the forward edge of the air mass (**Figure 23.3**). The warmer and lighter air lying in the cold front's path is forced up over the cold air mass, creating heavy clouds and sometimes violent but usually short-lived storms (thunderstorms, blizzards, tornadoes).

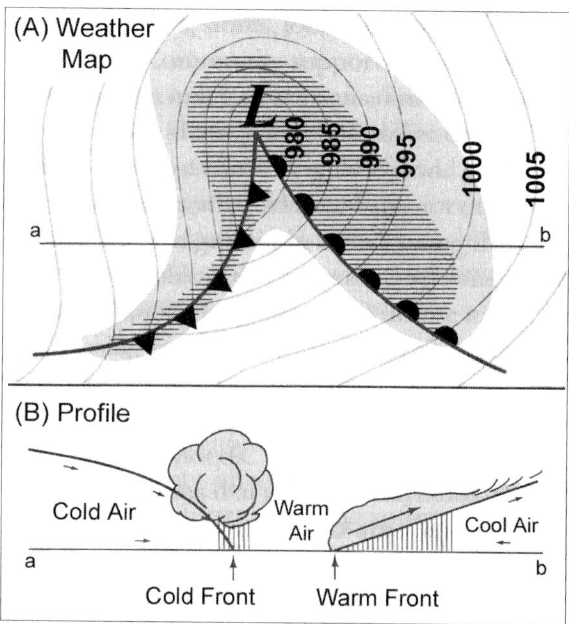

Figure 23.3 Cold and warm fronts around a low pressure center bring different kinds of weather to the area.

In contrast to the steep gradient on the leading edge of a cool air mass, friction with the ground draws out the temperature-pressure gradient along the slower-moving tailing edge of the air mass. Because lighter, warm air moves across the country faster than cool, heavy air, moist air from the south often pushes up the gentle back slope of cold air masses, creating a warm front. This front is characterized by light to heavy clouds and gentle but steady (often lingering for days) precipitation.

Weather Satellite Images

The two weather maps in Figures 23.1 and 23.2 give you enough air pressure, wind velocity, cloud cover, and frontal position information for you to make educated guesses as to where heavy cloud cover and precipitation are occurring. But to see the actual extent and moisture content of the clouds, you must look at **weather satellite images**. Your local television or newspaper weather report probably uses one or more composite satellite images of the United States created from Geostationary

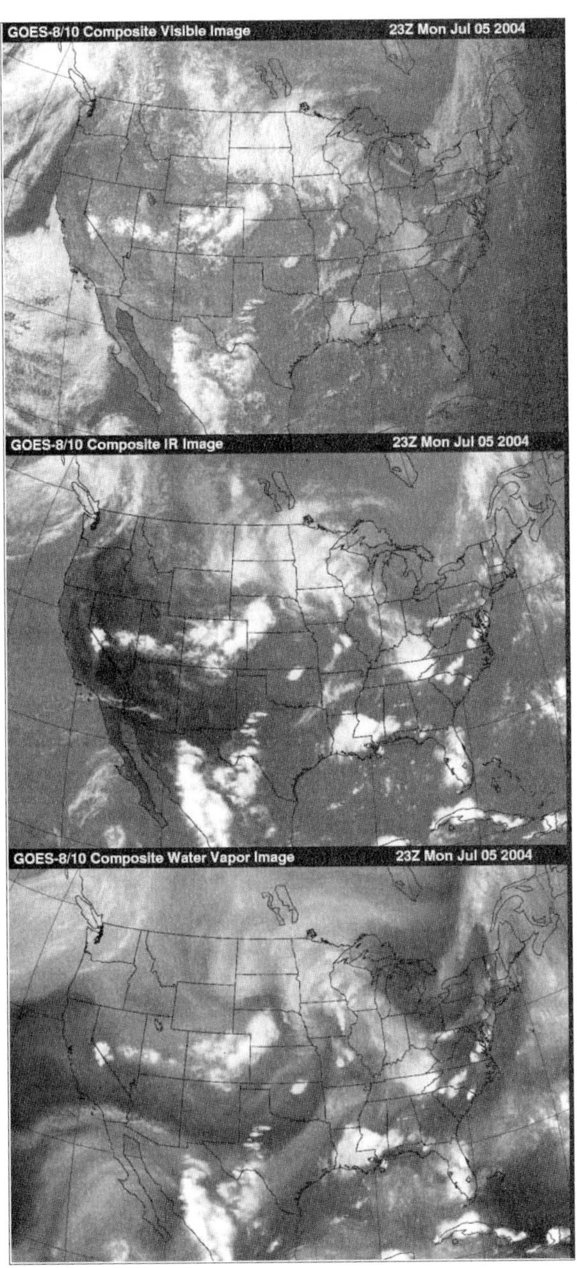

Figure 23.4 GOES weather satellite visible (top), infrared (middle), and water vapor (bottom) images of the United States allow you to see the cloud and moisture conditions.

Operational Environmental Satellite (GOES) 8 and 10 imagery (see Chapter 9 for a detailed description of these weather satellites).

GOES composite **visible satellite images** (**Figure 23.4, top**) show you the amount of visible sunlight reflected back to the satellite sensor by clouds, the land surface, and water bodies. Thicker clouds reflect more light than thinner clouds and hence appear lighter on the image. However, you can't distinguish among low, middle, and high-level clouds, which is important for predicting the location and intensity of precipitation.

Compare the cloud patterns in the map at the top of Figure 23.4 with the frontal line shown in Figure 23.2. Concentrating on the area around the low-pressure center in eastern Iowa, you can see thick clouds at the low-pressure center and behind the cold front. The only clouds to the north of the warm front are in southern Wisconsin. That's what you would expect, since the warm front is very short and turns into a cold front coming from the low-pressure center in eastern Quebec.

The **infrared weather satellite image** (**Figure 23.4, middle**) allows you to distinguish low, middle, and high-level clouds by their gray tone on the image. Warmer objects appear darker than colder objects on the image. Since the temperature drops as you go higher into the atmosphere, high-level cirrus clouds or thunderheads (cumulus clouds associated with thunderstorms) will appear white.

The image shows white to light-gray clouds around the eastern Iowa low-pressure center. These are most likely tall thunderheads intermixed with mid-level cumulus clouds. Notice the barely-visible gray clouds off the California coast that are probably a low-level fog layer.

On the **GOES water vapor image** (**Figure 23.4, bottom**), the lighter the cloud, the more moisture it contains. The white cloud plumes in eastern Iowa and southern Minnesota indicate moisture-laden thunderheads. The other clouds in the area contain less moisture and thus are slightly darker.

Compare the top image in Figure 23.4 (the visible satellite image) with the bottom one (the water vapor image). You'll see the most striking tonal difference off the California coast, where the dark gray, moisture-barren clouds are consistent with a thin layer of fog covering the ocean.

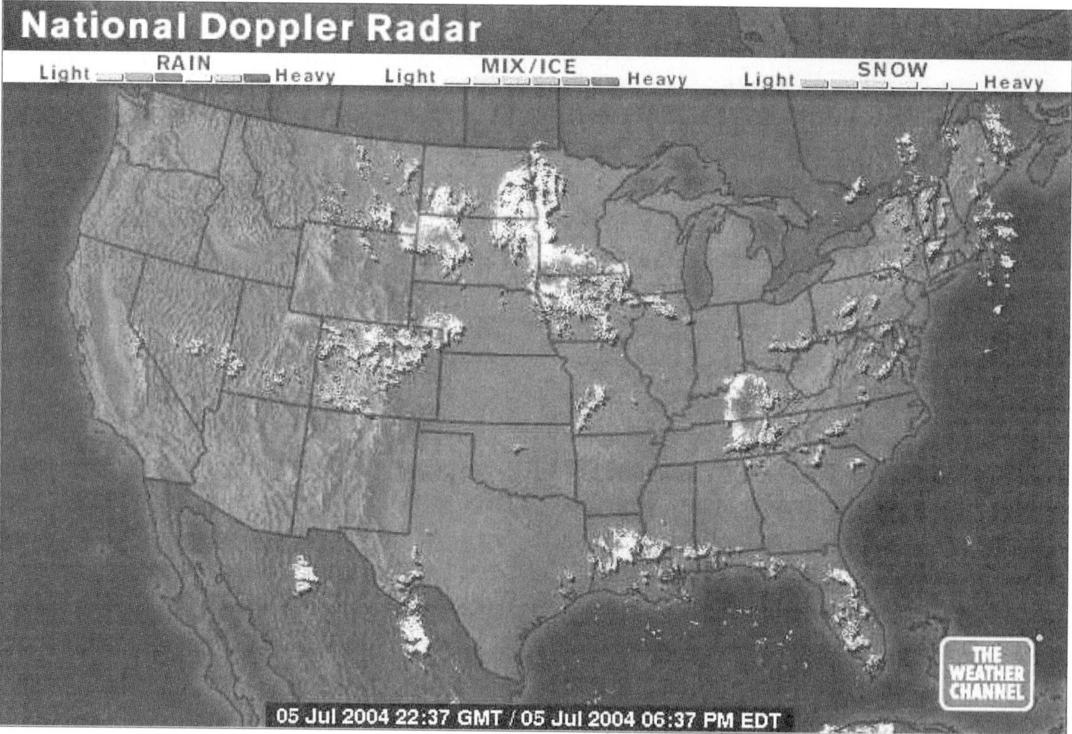

Figure 23.5 The national Doppler radar map seen on the weather channel shows you areas under light to heavy precipitation.

Doppler Radar Maps

You've used the weather maps and satellite images in Figures 23.1 through 23.4 to outline areas where different kinds of clouds with different moisture content are likely to be present. So far, however, you have scant information about the amount and type of precipitation that is falling. For such information, you need to look at a **Doppler radar map.** Doppler maps show areas where it is raining, snowing, or hailing as well as the severity of the precipitation.

The precipitation type and intensity map you see on the weather channel (**Figure 23.5**) is an excellent example of Doppler weather radar data overlaid on a relief-shaded base map. The radar information on the map is a mosaic of images collected from a network of ground radar facilities placed at airports and other strategic locations. Each Doppler radar device sends out circular pulses of radio wave energy into the atmosphere. If a portion of a pulse intercepts precipitation, some of the energy from this part of the pulse is scattered back to the radar device as a "radar echo" whose ground position can be mapped. Radar echos are digitally analyzed to determine the type (rain, snow, or a mixture of rain and ice) and intensity of the precipitation that was detected. This information is displayed on the base map using different colors (shown as gray tones in Figure 23.5) to reveal the types and intensities of precipitation.

The Doppler radar map in Figure 23.5 shows medium-intensity rainfall along the Iowa-Minnesota border, with a few small areas of heavy rain in northeastern Iowa. Light rainfall is occurring throughout northern Iowa and along borders between Minnesota and North and South Dakota. This rainfall pattern is consistent with what you learned about the weather in this area from the other maps and images. The only thing missing is what is happening in the upper atmosphere.

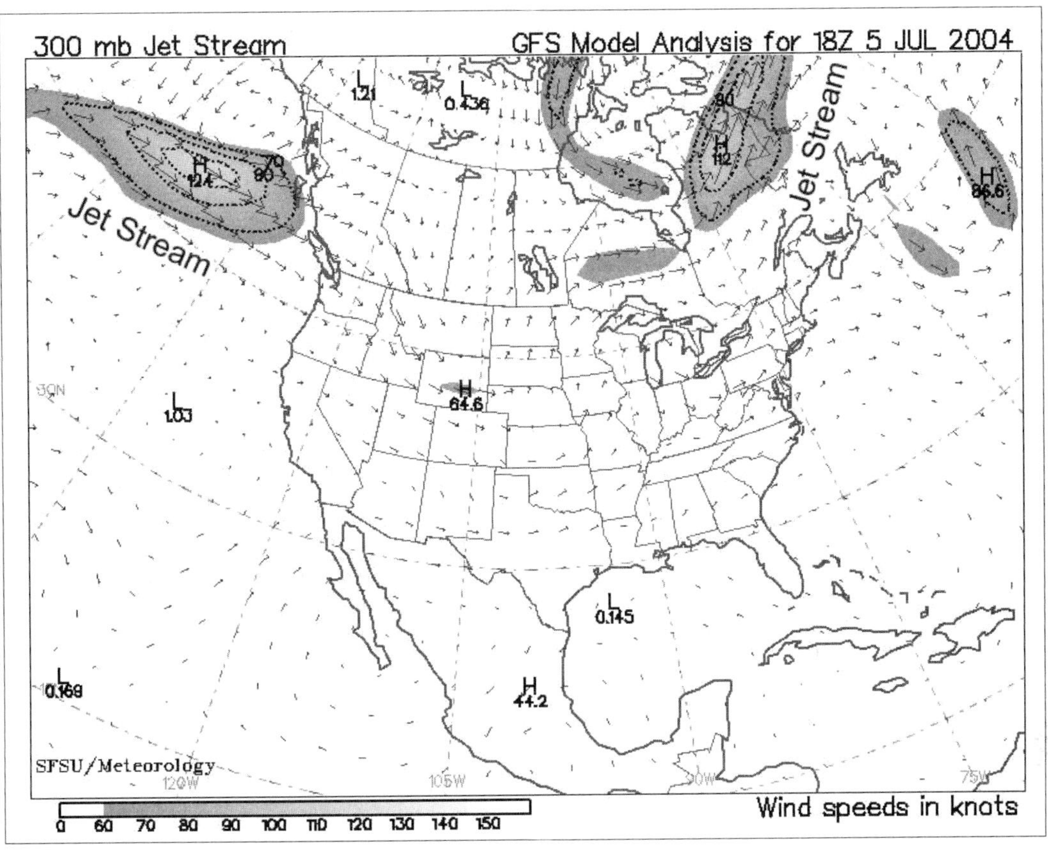

Figure 23.6 Upper-level wind maps show wind velocities with arrows and areas with high wind speeds, particularly the jet stream, as a shaded surface.

Wind Velocity Maps

Wind velocity (speed and direction) is the upper-level atmospheric condition that helps you most to understand weather conditions at the surface. You can download maps from government and university websites that show upper-level wind speeds and directions for North America (**Figure 23.6**). These maps are produced by computer models that use upper-level wind data. This information is collected by balloon-borne instrument packages, and from ground antennas that transmit and receive acoustic (sound) pulses. Wind velocity is calculated from shifts in the frequency of the acoustic pulses caused by the motion of clouds in the upper atmosphere.

Upper-level winds typically are mapped on the 300-millibar (mb) atmospheric-pressure surface, at an altitude of roughly 30,000 feet. **Wind vectors** are calculated by atmospheric modeling software for 5° increments of latitude and longitude. Each vector is shown on the map with an arrow whose length gives the wind speed in knots. Areas on the 300-mb surface with wind speeds greater than 60 knots are shown by gray tones that lighten as the speeds increase. These areas are also depicted as a continuous surface defined by lines of equal wind speed called **isotachs**.

The gray-toned areas and isotachs show the position and intensity of the **jet stream**. The jet stream is a ribbon of fast moving upper-level air that usually occurs six to nine miles above the surface. It is often thousands of miles long, a few hundred miles wide, and only about a mile thick. The jet stream sits above ground locations having the greatest temperature gradients, typically at the boundary between cold and warm air masses.

Strong jet stream winds tend to "steer" low-pressure centers, so that storms follow the jet stream path.

You've probably seen the jet stream shown as a narrow moving band (see Figure 6.13, for example), but the upper-level wind map gives you more information about its extent and strength. The gray-toned areas in Figure 23.6 show the jet stream over North America on July 5, 2004. You can see that on this day the jet stream consists of two short segments, neither over the United States. Neither segment has wind speeds over 100 knots, which is typical of summer months when surface temperature gradients are low. During the winter months, the upper-level wind map would show a strong, continuous jet stream across North America, positioned at the boundary between warm tropical and cold Arctic air masses.

CLIMATE MAPS

The **climate** of your area is defined by its average monthly and yearly atmospheric conditions. Data are collected for many atmospheric conditions, but precipitation and temperature averages are most important for defining and mapping different types of climates. These averages are computed for a three-decade period, currently 1971-2000, from meteorological station records across the world. To produce detailed **climate maps**, the station averages and digital elevation model data are input into a computer climate modeling program, such as the PRISM model produced by the Spatial Cliimate Analysis Service, Oregon State University (see Appendix B). The model creates a grid of estimated average monthly or yearly average precipitation and temperature values, from which national

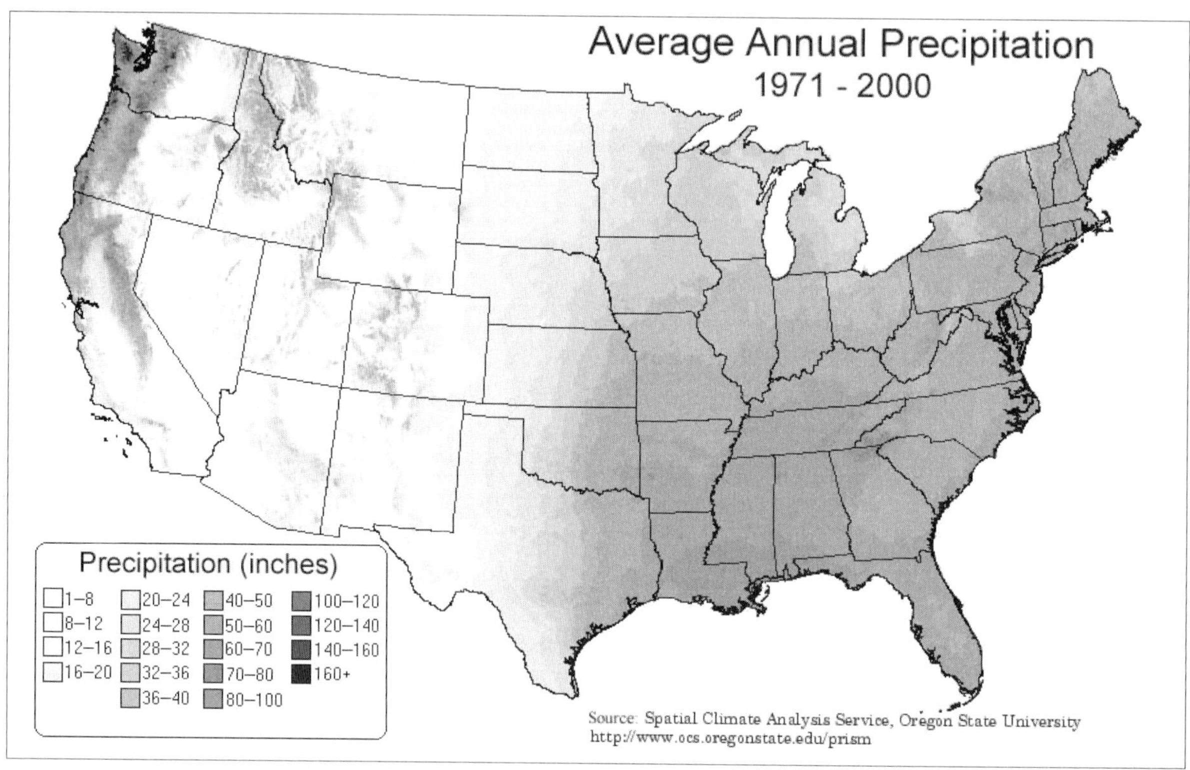

Figure 23.7 Average annual precipitation map created using the PRISM model by the Spatial Climate Analysis Service, Oregon State University.

and state maps are made. Let's look at several national maps created from PRISM model grid cells at a 2.5-minute latitude-longitude spatial resolution. This spatial resolution provides enough detail for you to see how major landform features influence the pattern of precipitation and temperatures in the United States.

Average Annual Precipitation

The **average annual precipitation** map in **Figure 23.7** shows you four things about the spatial pattern of precipitation across the country:

1. The highest average yearly rainfall is in the coastal mountains and Cascade Range of the Pacific Northwest.
2. Other mountainous areas across the country receive greater rainfall than their surrounding valleys or lowlands.
3. Other than the mountainous areas, the western half of the country receives lower annual precipitation than the eastern half. Notice the steady eastward increase in rainfall from the Colorado Front Range through the Great Plains to the Midwest. Geographers say that the division between the arid west and humid east is where annual precipitation exceeds evaporation, near the 100°W meridian in the center of this precipitation gradient.
4. The southeastern part of the nation, from eastern Texas and Arkansas to Florida, Alabama, and Tennessee, has much greater rainfall than does the eastern seaboard stretching from Georgia to Maine.

To understand the physical processes responsible for these four observations, you need to look at climate-related information shown on other maps. Let's begin with the first observation by looking carefully at the relationship between average annual precipitation and major landforms in Washington State.

Annual Precipitation in Washington State

Notice on the Washington average annual precipitation map (**Figure 23.8, top**) that the amount of rainfall changes dramatically in north-south bands corresponding to the Olympic Mountains and Coast Range and then the Cascade Range. This implies that local rather than regional climate controls are in force. Indeed, precipitation in much of the state is known as **orographic**, meaning that it is related to mountains. A map of precipitation is a good substitute for a landform map of the state (**Figure 23.8, middle**), but notice that the highest rainfall is on the west side of the mountain ranges.

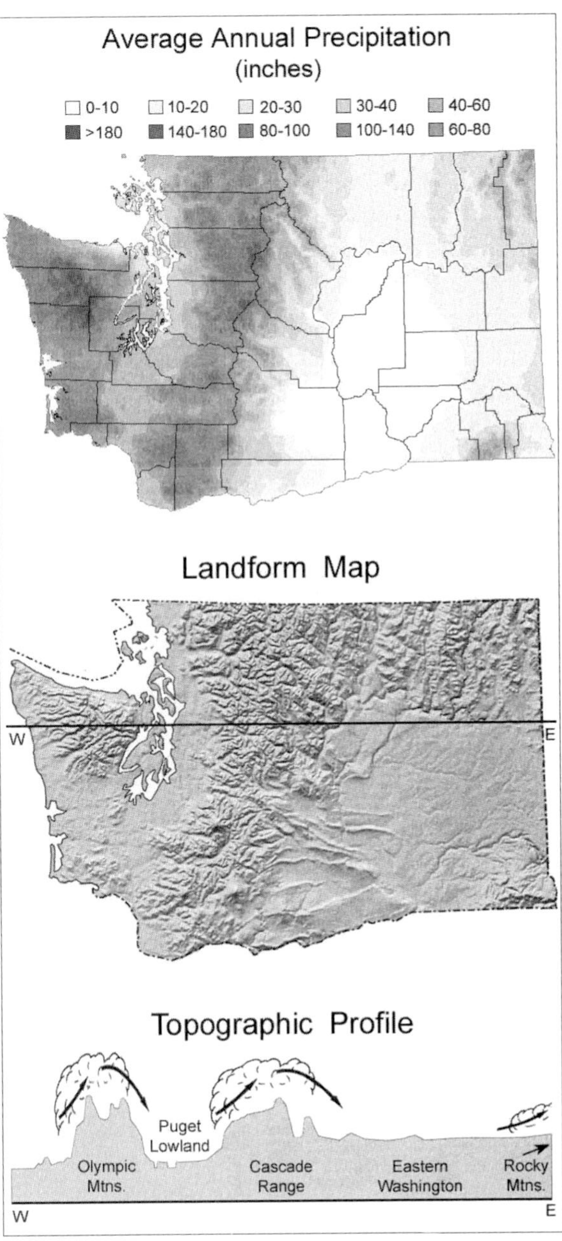

Figure 23.8 Relationships among landforms, prevailing winds, and orographic precipitation are well illustrated in Washington state.

The **orographic effect** is most pronounced in the winter months when prevailing westerly winds carry low-level, cool, very moist air inland from the Pacific Ocean and force the air to flow over the Olympic Mountains, the Cascade Range, and then the Rocky Mountains (**Figure 23.8, bottom**). As air rises up the windward, west side of these ranges, it cools further, causing water vapor to condense into clouds that drop heavy amounts of precipitation.

After crossing the mountain range crest, the now-drier air descends the leeward, east side of the ranges, warming and further drying in the process. Consequently, the east sides of the mountains are under a relatively dry "**rain shadow.**" These long, north-south, wet and dry belts are characteristic of the Pacific Northwest.

Since the moisture-laden air rises over the coastal mountain barrier first, the potential for precipitation is greatest in this region. As you can see on the precipitation map, annual rainfall on the Olympic Mountains' western flanks can exceed 180 inches (500 cm.). This pattern is muted on the map, however, because the coastal range's southern portion is relatively low in elevation compared to the Olympic Mountains, causing the coastal range to receive less rainfall on its western flanks.

The Cascade Range is the next topographic barrier. These mountains are fairly uniform in elevation from north to south. You can see on the map that the west side of the Cascades receives about the same amount of precipitation throughout their north-south extent. The total west-side precipitation is less than the Olympic Mountains, since the air has lost some of its moisture to the west flanks of the Olympics and coastal range. This less-humid air warms and dries further as it descends the east side of the Cascades, creating a narrow rain-shadow area with very low precipitation. The air remains dry as it moves inland, until it reaches

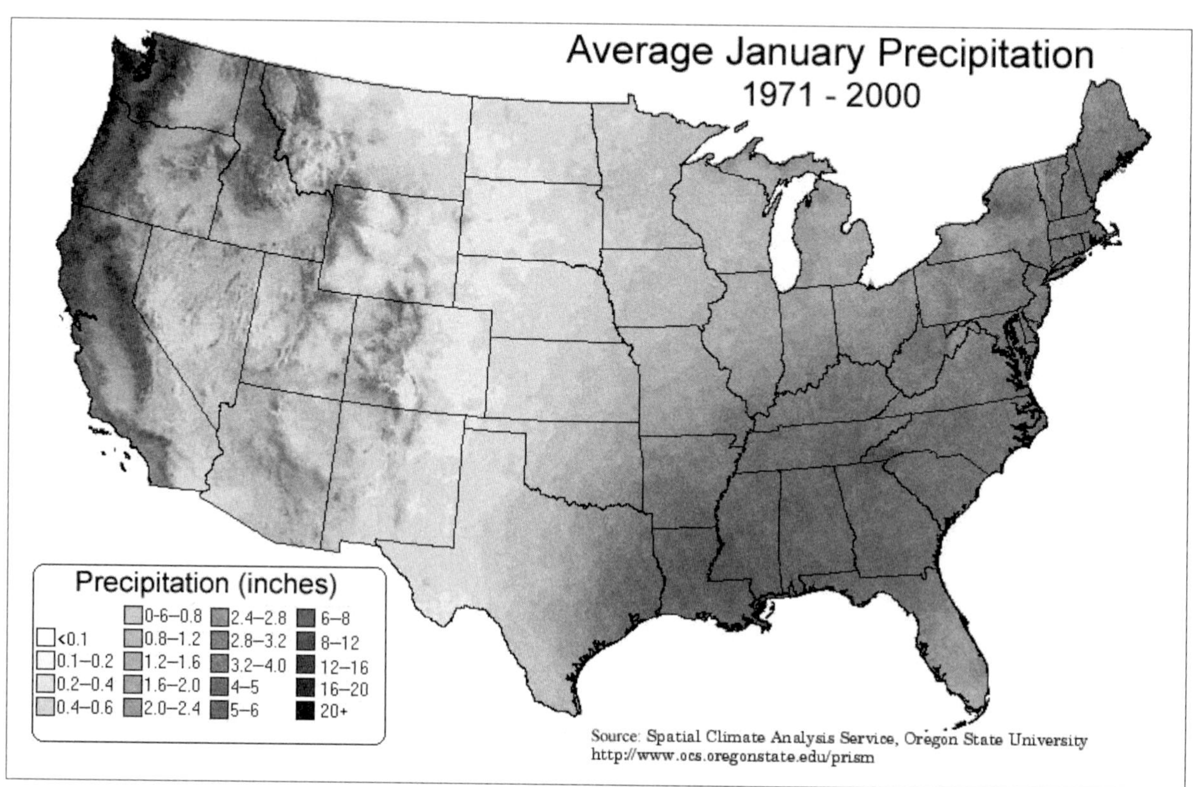

Figure 23.9 Average January precipitation map created using the PRISM model by the Spatial Climate Analysis Service, Oregon State University.

the Rocky Mountain foothills at the east edge of the state. The rising and cooling repeats, but with less annual precipitation released because the air has been twice wrung of moisture by the orographic effect.

The orographic effect also helps explain our second observation—that mountain ranges generally receive more annual rainfall than their lower-elevation surroundings. Notice in Figure 23.7 that the west sides of the Sierra Nevada in California and the northern Rocky Mountain ranges in Idaho and Montana receive more precipitation than do their east sides. You can also see smaller orographic effects in the middle and southern Rocky Mountains in Colorado and New Mexico, the Ozarks in Arkansas, the Adirondacks in New York State, and the Appalachian Range on the eastern seaboard. But notice that the west sides of the mountain range don't always receive the highest annual rainfall. You need to look at winter and summer monthly precipitation and wind flow maps to understand these directional differences in the windward sides of mountain ranges.

Monthly Climate Maps

Monthly climate maps are often produced for January and July, since these months are most representative of winter and summer conditions. Let's begin with average January precipitation (**Figure 23.9**). Notice how similar this map is to the average annual precipitation map in Figure 23.7. You'll see that the heaviest rainfall is on the windward side of the high mountain ranges in the West, with heavy precipitation in the western lowlands of Oregon, Washington, and northern California and in an west-east swath from eastern Texas to southern Virginia. Also visible is a broad area of low precipitation from the leeward flanks of the Cascade Range and Sierra Nevada through the lower portions of the mountain states, the Great Plains, the Midwest, and into western New York state.

The maps show you that in most areas winter precipitation is the most important component of the annual total. But what physical processes are causing the variations in precipitation? Maps showing the positions of air masses, high and low pressure centers, and wind flow patterns help you understand the processes involved in winter months.

Maps of North American air-mass sources and January surface winds (**Figure 23.10, top and**

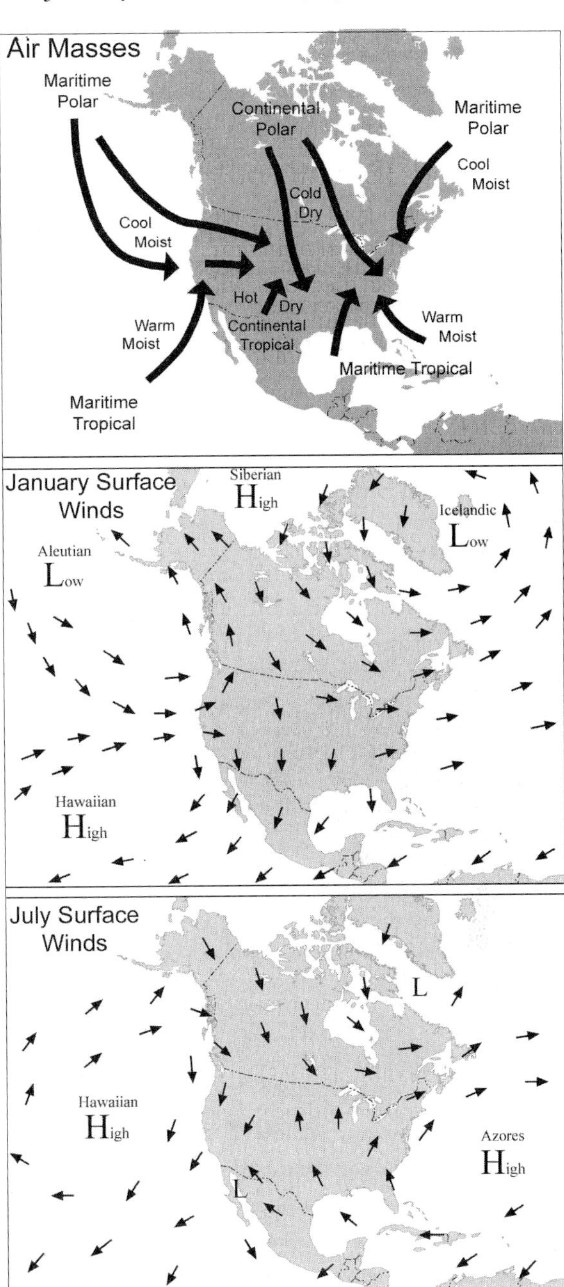

Figure 23.10 Maps of North American air-mass sources (top), January surface winds (middle), and July surface winds (bottom) help you understand the winter and summer temperatures and precipitation in the United States.

middle) show how polar and tropical air masses correspond with January low- and high-pressure centers. Notice that the Aleutian Low corresponds with the center of a cool, moist, maritime polar air mass. This air flows counterclockwise eastward around the Aleutian Low until it strikes the west coast of North America, anywhere from southern California to British Columbia. These westerly surface winds are the driving force behind the heavy winter orographic precipitation along the Pacific coast and inland to the Rocky Mountains. You can see that warm, moist air originating from a maritime tropical air mass centered west of Mexico is also carried by the eastward flow to southern California, bringing heavy winter precipitation to coastal areas as the air rises over the high mountain ranges to the east and north.

Look again at the air-mass map at the top of Figure 23.10. Notice the cold, dry, continental polar air centered in northern Canada. Southerly winds moving counterclockwise around the Icelandic Low and Siberian High push tongues of polar air into the region from the Rocky Mountains to New England. These polar outbreaks can reach the southern states and are responsible for winter freezes as far south as Florida. A map of average January maximum temperatures (**Figure 23.11**) shows a broad band of sub-freezing temperatures across these areas and into New England—temperatures matched only in the high-elevation areas of the Rocky Mountains. The mountain states, Great Plains, and Midwest are under this dry polar air much of the winter, which is why the average January precipitation is so low in these areas.

The band of heavy January precipitation in the Southeast is due to frontal activity along the jet stream where continental polar air meets warm, moist maritime tropical air centered in the Gulf of Mexico. The band of warm January maximum temperatures from eastern Texas to South Carolina is a result of maritime tropical air moving over this coastal swath throughout the winter.

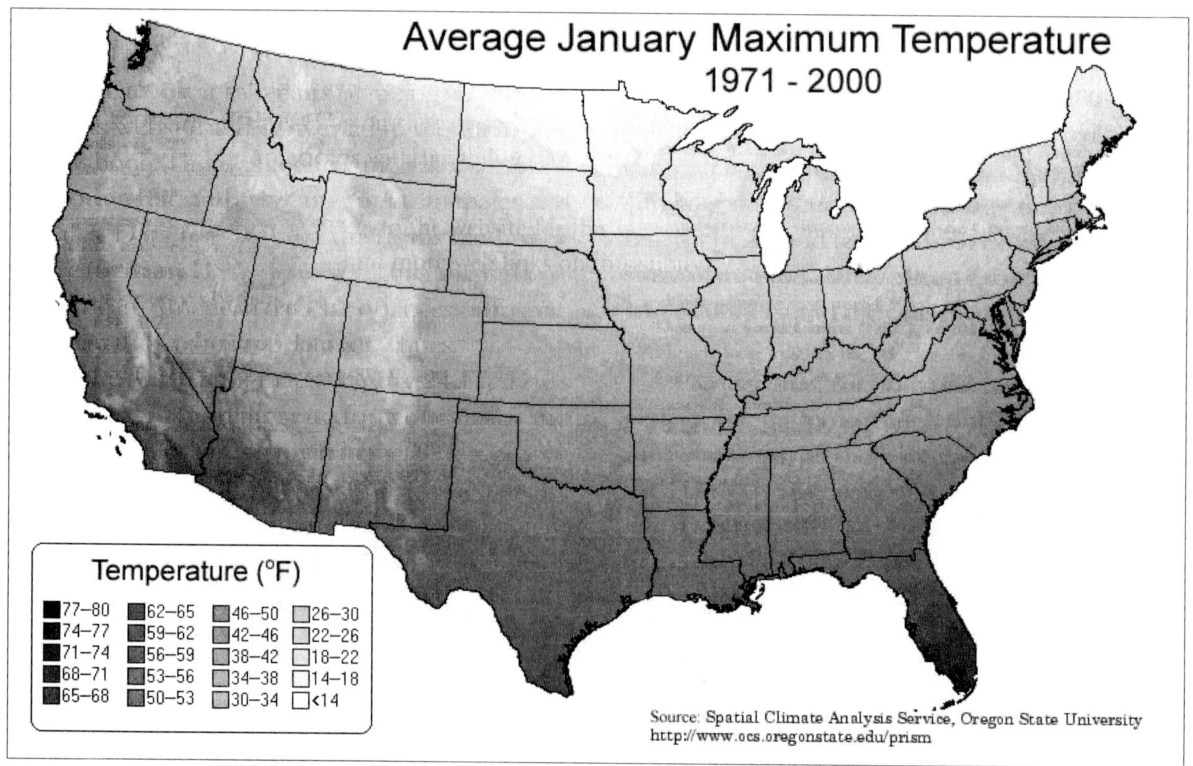

Figure 23.11 Average January maximum-temperature map created using the PRISM model by the Spatial Climate Analysis Service, Oregon State University.

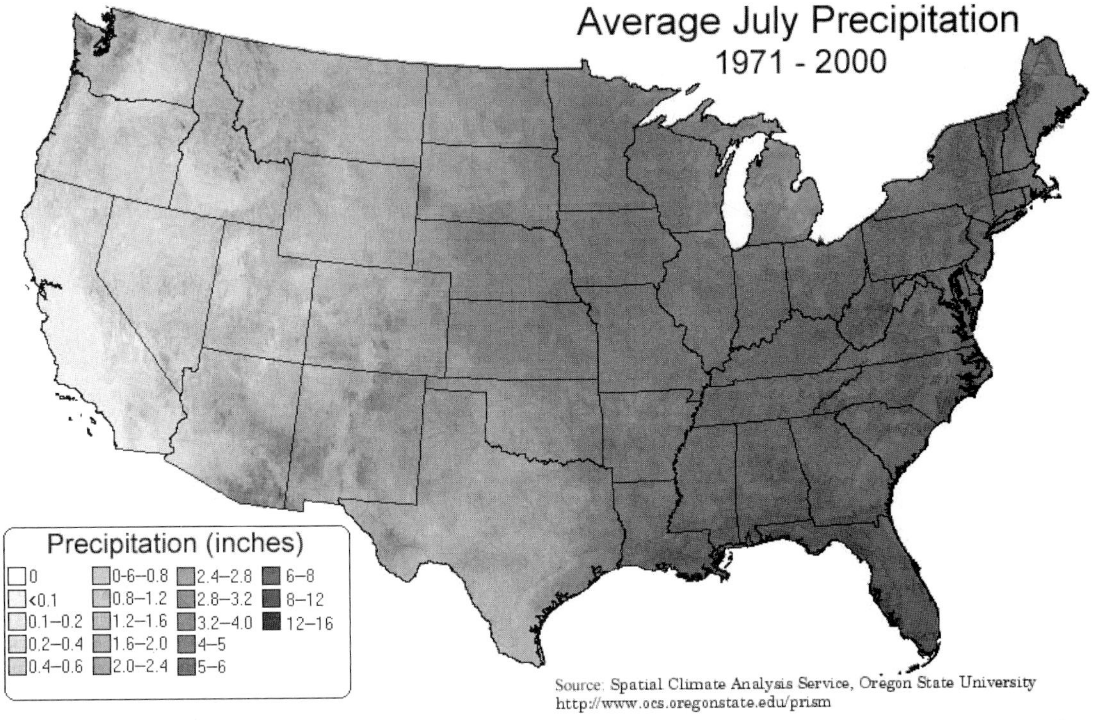

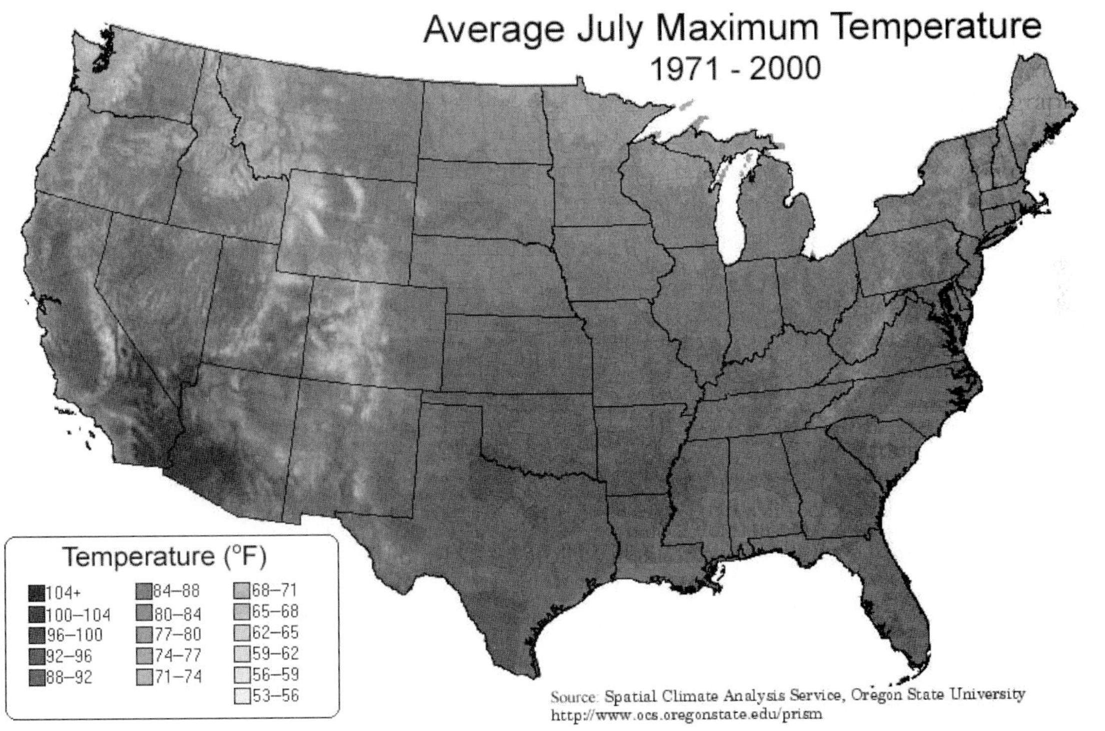

Average July Precipitation
1971 - 2000

Precipitation (inches)

0
<0.1
0.1–0.2
0.2–0.4
0.4–0.6
0-6–0.8
0.8–1.2
1.2–1.6
1.6–2.0
2.0–2.4
2.4–2.8
2.8–3.2
3.2–4.0
4–5
5–6
6–8
8–12
12–16

Source: Spatial Climate Analysis Service, Oregon State University
http://www.ocs.oregonstate.edu/prism

Average July Maximum Temperature
1971 - 2000

Temperature (°F)

104+
100–104
96–100
92–96
88–92
84–88
80–84
77–80
74–77
71–74
68–71
65–68
62–65
59–62
56–59
53–56

Source: Spatial Climate Analysis Service, Oregon State University
http://www.ocs.oregonstate.edu/prism

Figure 23.12 Average July precipitation (top) and maximum-temperature (bottom) maps created using the PRISM model by the Spatial Climate Analysis Service, Oregon State University.

A final thing to notice is the lack of precipitation in the low-elevation regions of the Southwest. The January surface-wind map in the middle of Figure 23.10 shows you that the Southwest is under the influence of southerly winds at the eastern limits of the Hawaiian High. These winds warm and dry as they descend, creating the very dry conditions and warm winter days indicated on the January maximum-temperature map in Figure 23.11.

The average July precipitation map (**Figure 23.12, top**) shows a pattern of rainfall distinctly different from both January and the annual average. Note that precipitation is heaviest across the eastern half of the country, as well as in the higher-elevation portions of the Southwest. The air-mass map at the top of Figure 23.10 and the July surface-wind map (**Figure 23.10, bottom**) help you understand the summer precipitation pattern.

The first thing to see is that the Hawaiian High has shifted northward. This summertime shift causes the west coast to be under warm, dry, descending air at the east edge of the high-pressure center. A map of average July maximum temperatures (**Figure 23.12, bottom**) shows that all but the mountainous portions of the west coast have very warm temperatures, which is characteristic of the warm and dry summers in this region.

In contrast, you can see that the eastern half of the country is dominated by warm, moist maritime tropical air carried inland from the Gulf of Mexico by southerly winds at the western edge of the Azores High. During the summer, this tropical air repeatedly meets cool, dry air from the north along cold fronts that spawn large thunderstorms, bringing heavy precipitation to the region.

Notice that a low-pressure center develops in July over the northern Gulf of California in Mexico. The very hot temperatures that you see in this area on the July maximum-temperature map in Figure 23.12 creates a summer "thermal low." The July surface-wind map in Figure 23.10 shows warm, moist air from the Gulf of Mexico being drawn inland by the low pressure. As this air reaches higher-elevation mountains, orographic precipitation in the form of thunderstorms provides most of the annual rainfall in this arid region.

**They base these climate types on the numerical ranges of seasonal rainfall, temperature, and evapotranspiration (the moisture given off to the atmosphere through evaporation, and through transpiration from plants. (Vegetation types are used in defining climate zones.)*

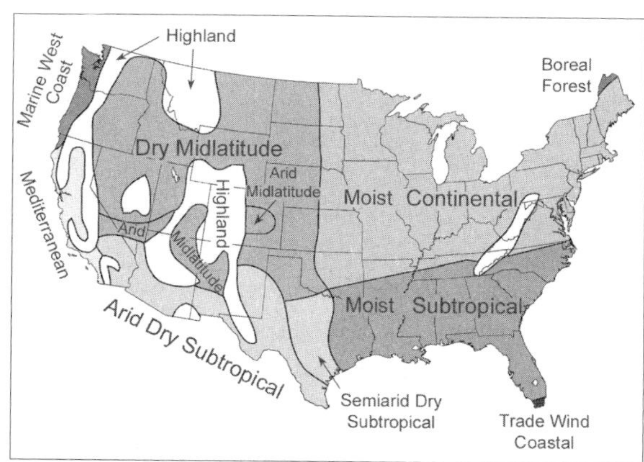

Figure 23.13 Climate types for the United States, redrawn from the Strahler World Climates Map.

Climate Types

Climatologists use the information on average monthly precipitation and temperature maps when classifying the earth into distinctive **climate types.*** One of the most useful climate classification systems was developed by the physical geographer Arthur Strahler. We have redrawn in black and white the section of the multicolor Strahler World Climates Map covering the United States (**Figure 23.13**).

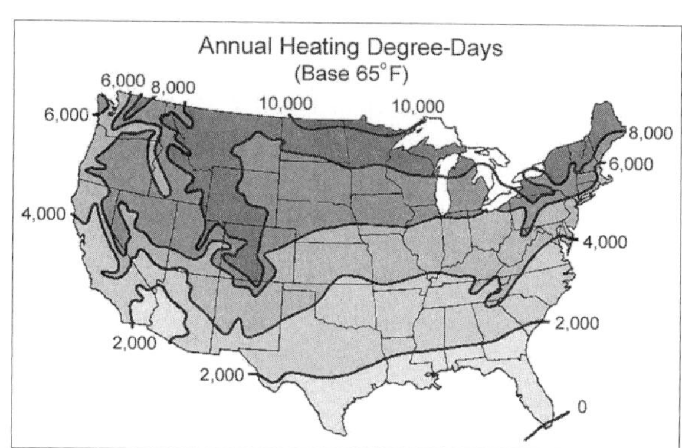

Figure 23.14 Total annual heating degree-days vary dramatically within the United States.

Notice that eight major climate types are found in the conterminous United States, ranging from Trade Wind Coastal in southern Florida to Boreal Forest in northern Maine. The map legend (not copied here) gives the general seasonal temperature and precipitation characteristics for each climate type. If you live in the Moist Continental climate of the Midwest, for example, you experience cold winters, warm summers, and ample precipitation in all months. In contrast, the Mediterranean Climate found in the Central Valley and coastal areas of California is characterized by hot, dry summers and cool, rainy winters.

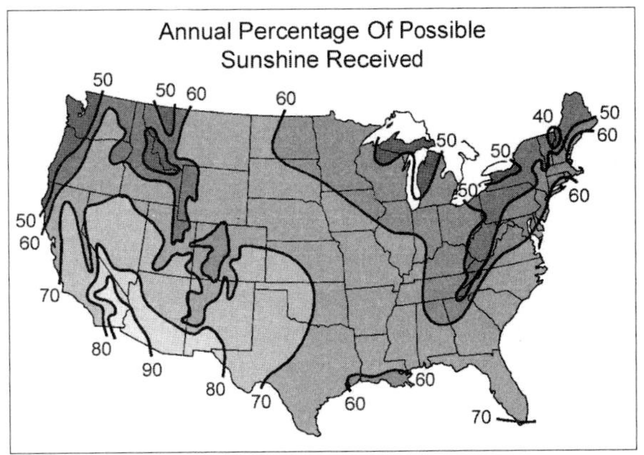

Figure 23.16 The annual percentage of possible sunshine received at different locations in the United States varies dramatically.

Heating Degree-Days

You can use the information on daily average temperature maps to compute and map annual **heating degree-days** (**Figure 23.14**). Heating degree-days are the number of degrees (Fahrenheit) by which the average temperature for a day falls short of 65°F. If the average temperature for a given day is 50°F, for instance, that day contributes 15 degree-days to the annual total. The heating degree-days map provides a useful indication of possible heating-fuel consumption, necessary heating-system capacity, and desirable amounts of home insulation.

The map in Figure 23.14 shows you that heating degree-days generally increase from south to north, but also vary with elevation. You can correctly surmise that heating requirements are minimal in the southern "Sun Belt" and extreme in northern Minnesota. The high-elevation areas of the West also appear to have higher heating requirements than the low-elevation regions of the eastern United States at the same latitude. These heating degree-day patterns on the map are closely related to the amount of solar radiation received at different locations.

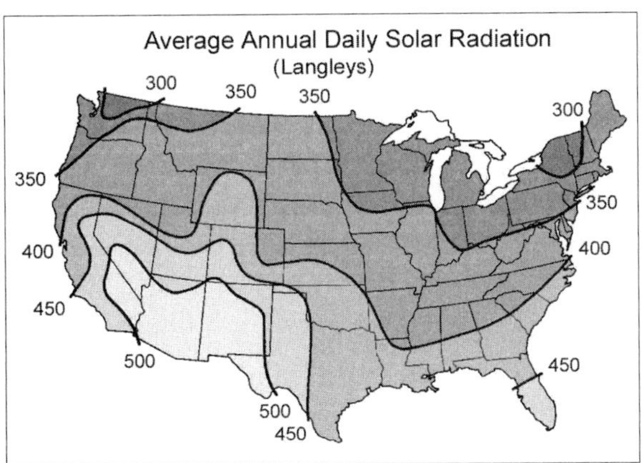

Figure 23.15 Average daily solar radiation received at the ground surface on an annual basis (measured in Langleys).

Solar Radiation

Although it has been said that solar energy is everywhere available and free, this is only partly true. The amount of **solar radiation** reaching different parts of the earth varies immensely, and the cost of collecting it in sufficient amounts varies in direct proportion to the amount received. Thus, if you can determine the amount of solar energy reaching the earth across the United States, you will know to a large degree where it is practical to install solar energy collectors.

Determining the amount of solar radiation you receive is fairly complex. First of all, the amount of energy reaching your location on earth is determined by two factors. One factor is the duration of sunshine. This depends on the length of day, which is related to the latitude of your location. As latitude increases, summer days are longer and winter days are shorter.

But the length of day is only one aspect of solar energy potential. The other factor is the angle of the sun above the horizon—the higher the latitude, the lower the average annual sun angle. The average sun angle in Miami, Florida, is 64°, while in Seattle, Washington, it is only 42°. The reason sun angle differences are important is that the lower the angle is, the farther the sun's rays have to travel through the atmosphere to reach the earth's surface. Since the atmosphere absorbs, reflects, and scatters the sun's rays, the amount of solar energy eventually reaching a location on the earth is inversely related to the amount of atmosphere that must be traversed.

The distance a sun's ray must travel through the atmosphere to reach your position also depends on your elevation. Denver is a mile higher in elevation than San Francisco and other coastal cities. Since the atmosphere is densest near sea level, this difference in elevation alone can have a substantial influence on the amount of solar radiation reaching the earth.

Climatologists can use data from meteorological stations to map the **average daily solar radiation** received in the United States. The map in **Figure 23.15** shows a continuous surface defined by lines of equal radiation, with gray tones added between lines to accentuate high and low radiation areas. Notice the progressive decrease in solar energy from south to north, which is what you would expect. Also as you would expect, mountainous regions are exceptions to the south-north pattern of solar energy increase. You can see a "ridge" of higher solar radiation coinciding with the mountains of Colorado and Wyoming. As anyone who has ever received a high-elevation sunburn knows, the thin, less polluted atmosphere at mountainous locations lets more solar energy reach the earth than is the case at lower elevations. Clouds, dust, and air pollutants also may obscure the sun for much of the day, substantially reducing the amount of solar radiation recorded at a meteorological station on the ground.

The measured average daily solar radiation may differ greatly from the **potential solar radiation** received, which can be estimated by accounting for length of day, sun angle, and elevation. If the average daily solar radiation received is divided by the average potential solar radiation for locations across the United States, the result is a map of the **annual percentage of possible sunshine** (**Figure 23.16**). This is really a cloud-cover and air-pollution map in reverse. In other words, a place falling in the 70% to 80% zone would experience obscuring cloud cover, dust, or air pollution 20% to 30% of the time.

BIOSPHERE

The maps you have seen so far have demonstrated the interdependence of landforms, short-term atmospheric conditions, and long-term climate differences. The biological realm we call the **biosphere** has shaped and been shaped by landforms and climate. Plants and animals have evolved in close association with their inorganic surroundings, as well as with each other. Specialization and adaptation to different physical settings are pronounced. In both the plant and animal communities, there is a great range in size and form. At one extreme are whales and redwoods, at the other countless varieties of invisible microorganisms.

Because of their high degree of environmental sensitivity, both plants and animals provide powerful clues for interpreting the physical setting from maps. Plant types reflect soil moisture conditions. Animal populations suggest nearby water sources. The vigor of plants and animals reflects mineral nutrients in soil and water. Climate conditions are indicated by the existence of certain species of plants and animals. Thus, understanding the workings of the biosphere is a major step toward becoming a skilled map interpreter.

Species Distribution Maps

A variety of ecological factors influence the vegetation and animals found in your area. These include climate, topography, soil, plant-animal interaction, and disturbance events (fire, disease, etc.) We will look at examples of several of these influ-

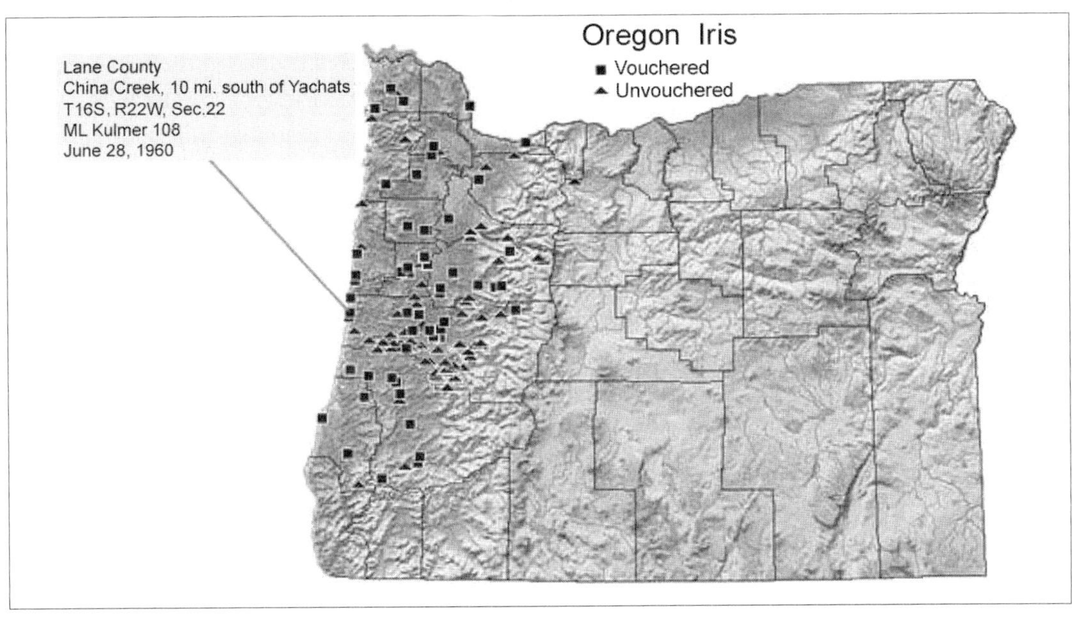

Figure 23.17 This map from the *Oregon Plant Atlas* project shows locations of vouchered specimens and unvouchered observations of the Oregon iris. The map is interactive in that you can click on a location to obtain more detailed information from a herbarium database.

ences by examining different types of maps that show the distribution of plants and animals.

Plant Specimen and Observation Maps

The most fundamental information on plants and animals is obtained by field observations of different species made by amateur and professional botanists and zoologists. Many of these field observations have been placed on **plant specimen and observation maps** that you can view on the Internet. Species habitat, climate, and landform data have also been combined to map **ecoregions** at the global, national, and regional levels.

The Oregon iris map in **Figure 23.17** is an example from the *Oregon Plant Atlas* project. The atlas contains locality maps for each plant species, showing where it has been collected or observed in Oregon. You can view these locations on different base maps of the state showing landforms, ecoregions, mean annual precipitation, or vegetation types. When you click on a location, a box appears, giving the U.S. Public Land Survey location to the section, the name of the collector and observer, and the date of collection. Each location is mapped as vouchered (from a herbarium specimen) or unvouchered (observations that don't have a collected specimen, often recorded by an amateur). This information helps you judge the relative reliability of each mapped location.

The small-scale base map upon which the locations are mapped (a multicolor map on the plant atlas website) allows you to make general statements about the plant's habitat. For instance, you might guess that the Oregon iris lives in the Marine West Coast climate of western Oregon at low elevations in river valleys. Professional biologists use these interpretations from maps, coupled with detailed habitat research in the field, to make species range maps.

Individual Animal Maps

Spatially, the main difference between plants and animals is their mobility. Plants move about primarily through their offspring: Wind, water, and animals carry seeds to distant places. Otherwise, plants are fairly well rooted in space.* For this reason, plants make good map subjects. They are likely to be found where maps show them to be.

**Exceptions must be made, of course, for such vegetative types as plankton floating in the ocean currents.*

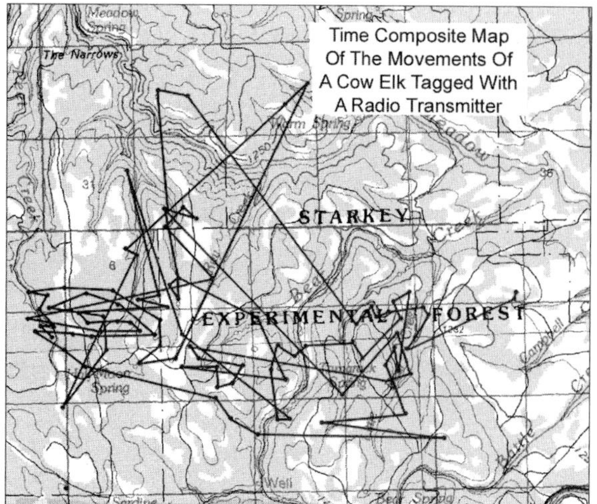

Figure 23.18 Time composite plot of the movements of a cow elk tagged with a radio transmitter.

In contrast, animals are highly mobile, and maps of animal populations usually have a strong temporal bias. Most animals have a diurnal (daily) pattern of movement, and many also exhibit a seasonal migration pattern. In the case of some mammals (whales), birds (waterfowl), fish (salmon), reptiles (turtles), and insects (butterflies), the annual migration cycle may span several thousand miles.

Wildlife biologists map the **movement of individual animals** to gain information used to determine their range. Increasing use of radio telemetry and GPS transmitters by wildlife researchers in animal tracking studies has made such maps rather common. In telemetry research, an animal is captured and fitted with a radio transmitter. After the animal is released, a researcher equipped with an appropriate radio receiver plots the animal's movements. It is assumed, of course, that the capture and transmitter fitting process hasn't affected the animal's movement. Movements of individual whales, turtles, birds, elk, and even insects have been made visible by plotting telemetry data over a base map.

This type of map can be insightful but can also be difficult to interpret. Part of the problem is the loss of environmental context. You can gain useful insights into the range of an individual from the map in **Figure 23.18** by comparing the elk's movements with landforms, water sources, roads, and other features found on the topographic base map. But most base maps won't include such meaningful factors as seasonal availability of food supplies, changing weather conditions, predators, human disturbances, and the presence of other members of the same species.

Thus, this type of map may have little but historical validity for times other than when it was made. Such maps may be too individual and time-specific to be useful in determining a species range. Furthermore, you have no idea how representative the monitored animal was of herd or species behavior at the time.

Migratory Route Maps

Migratory route mapping is another way of capturing the movement of animal species on maps. Consider the map of migratory bird flyways in **Figure 23.19**. After millions of observations, scientists concluded that migration routes could be generalized into four general paths called the At-

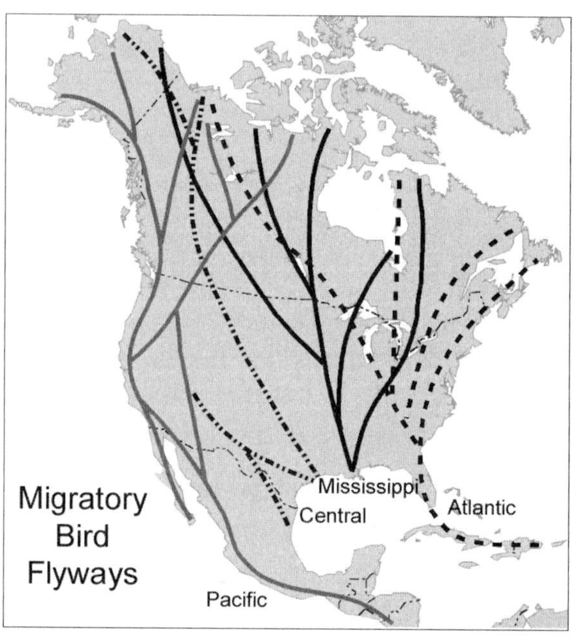

Figure 23.19 The routes taken by migratory birds in North America have been classed into four flyways: Atlantic, Mississippi, Central, and Pacific. A host of environmental factors contribute to these general patterns.

lantic, Mississippi, Central, and Pacific flyways. The migration route taken by an individual bird is classified as being along one of these flyways.

You are looking at a highly conceptualized map, since it's the general pattern, not the route of an individual bird, that is relevant. The map indicates that flyway boundaries are vaguely defined, with a great deal of interaction occurring among the separate flyways. This interaction is most pronounced on the northern breeding grounds. From about latitude 45° southward, the flyways become much more distinct. The spatial complexity of the flyways also tends to decrease from east to west.

Why do we have this flyway pattern? Its north-south character undoubtedly reflects a seasonal adjustment to food supplies and weather conditions. The individual migration routes further represent adjustments to such environmental factors as the landform configuration, suitable resting sites, and prevailing winds. On a species by species basis, limiting factors such as parasites, disease, and predators also help explain why birds choose some locations over others for breeding and wintering.

Species Range Maps

Considering the problems discussed above, a general mapping of species is often more useful than a mapping of individual animal movements. A good example of a general species map is the **species range map**. Range is defined as the region that a species could inhabit at some time. When map makers translate this concept into map symbols, they draw boundaries to segment space into range and non-range. Presumably, a species may exist on one side of a boundary and not on the other.

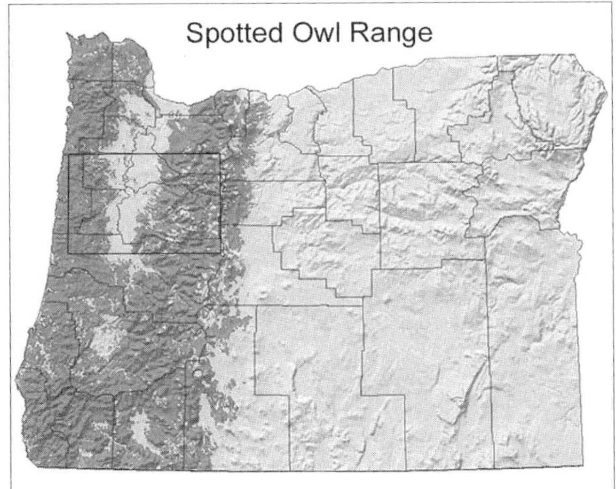

Figure 23.20 Range map of the spotted owl, taken from the *Atlas of Oregon Wildlife* (Corvallis: Oregon State University Press, 1997).

Since a species range is two dimensional, you need to interpret the range's location, size, shape, and orientation. Using the range of Oregon's spotted owl as an example (see **Figure 23.20**), scientists have found that around 2,000 breeding pairs occupy the entire area. Furthermore, species densities within the range vary markedly. Thus, if we randomly checked a dozen sites within the range boundary, we probably wouldn't see an owl.

This is understandable given the abstract nature of the species range concept. The range boundary was generalized from a scattering of past sighting locations and is somewhat biased toward regions of high accessibility and visibility. The species range was probably changing (most likely contracting) during the time that sightings were gathered. Thus, there is a historical lag or friction factor built into the range boundary's location.

In addition, the spotted owl's range is based on its **habitat**. A map of **wildlife habitat types** (**Figure 23.21**) was made from a detailed map of actual landcover. In Oregon, 30 wildlife habitat types were determined, and two of these—type 21 (mixed conifer-deciduous) and 18 (mountain hemlock)—were found to be the spotted owl's habitat.

The next step was to lay a grid of hexagonal data collection cells over the habitat map and determine which cells contained past sighting locations. Finally, areas classed as habitat types 18 or 21 that fell into a grid cell containing one or more past sightings were placed on the range map.

Mapped in this way, the spotted owl's range includes almost all of the coast and Cascades. You are looking at a politically sensitive map, since the spotted owl is an endangered species that has been used in court battles as a major reason for blocking logging of old-growth trees on national forest

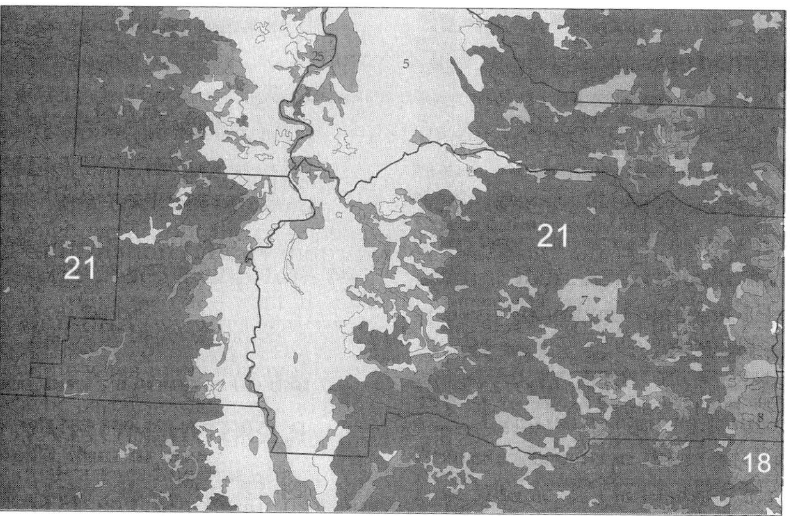

Figure 23.21 This monochrome copy of the southern Willamette valley portion of the multicolor Oregon Wildlife Habitat Types Map (see boxed area in Figure 23.20 for location) serves as the basis for creating species range maps for individual animals. The spotted owl's prime habitat includes types 18 (mountain hemlock) and 21 (mixed conifer-deciduous).

lands. Logging opponents argue that much of the owl's lower-elevation habitat shown on the map in Figure 23.21 is already lost due to clear-cut logging, and that all remaining old-growth forest (not shown on the habitat map) must be preserved. Their reasoning is that spotted owls have large home ranges and build their nests 1-2 miles apart in large stands of old-growth Douglas fir. Neither of these critical habitat requirements is shown on the range map, and the suitable habitat is much smaller if these requirements are taken into account.

Natural Vegetation Zone Maps

Vegetation zones are areas that would have a certain plant cover in the absence of human activity such as logging, agriculture, industrial development, and urbanization. Natural vegetation maps don't show you the actual types of plants currently in an area. Instead, such maps show **climax vegetation.** Climax vegetation is defined as the dominant vegetation that would exist if plant growth occurred over a long time period of constant climate conditions and lack of disturbance by human activity or natural disturbances such as fires and floods.

Take a look at **Color Plate 23.1**. It shows the Washington state portion of a vegetation-zone map for the Pacific Northwest. Notice that vegetation zones are identified either by tree-species names or geographic locales. Each vegetation zone includes several plant communities that would exist together as the climax vegetation. For example, the western-hemlock zone in the Puget Sound lowland has this tall, shade-tolerant tree as a climax species, but currently the dominant tree is the commercially harvested Douglas fir. You'll also find communities of western red cedar, red alder, and big leaf maple trees within this vegetation zone.

The differences in climax vegetation within each of the 11 zones seen in Color Plate 23.1 are due to such physical factors as precipitation, elevation, and soil types. To see how these factors interact from the Pacific shore to the Idaho border, look at **Color Plate 23.2**. This map of natural influences on vegetation in Washington is a classic multivariate map. Notice the four west-east elevation profiles placed over the precipitation base map. You can see how elevation relates to precipitation, how precipitation relates to soil types, and how the dominant climax vegetation relates to elevation, precipitation, and soil.

The relationship between vegetation zones and climate couldn't be more direct. Plant life depends on two things: (1) enough water to meet the plant's immediate needs and to compensate for moisture transpired in the form of water vapor, and (2) a temperature range which favors cell reproduction and growth. The higher the temperature, the greater the potential for evaporation of soil moisture and transpiration of plant fluids. Higher temperatures diminish the effectiveness of precipitation. Wind speeds up the processes of evaporation and transpiration, while high humidity reduces them. What all this means is that precipitation alone isn't always a good predictor of the type of vegetation you'll find in a region.

Note that you'll pass through five vegetation zones on a trip eastward from Seattle to central Washington. The rapid changes in winter and summer average maximum temperatures and the orographic precipitation pattern that you saw on the maps earlier in this chapter are responsible for these vegetation zones. A botanist would say that the systematic north-south latitude variation in vegetation zones from tropical to tundra is disrupted in the mountainous regions of the United States, due to the progressive cooling which occurs as altitude increases. The altitude-cooling effect is the same as the cooling at higher latitudes. The alpine vegetation zone at the highest elevations in the Olympic Mountains and Cascade Range is a classic example, since this is the same type of vegetation found at low elevations in northern Canada and Alaska.

SELECTED READINGS

Chaston, P.R., *Weather Maps: How to Read and Interpret All Basic Weather Charts* (Kearney, MO: Chaston Scientific, Inc., 1995).

Climatic Atlas of the United States, Environmental Sciences Services Administration, U.S. Department of Commerce, 1992.

Cloud, P., "The Biosphere," *Scientific American*, 249, 3 (September 1983), pp. 176-189.

Csuti, B. et al., *Atlas of Oregon Wildlife* (Corvallis, OR: Oregon State University Press, 1997).

Dingle, H., *Migration : the Biology of Life on the Move* (New York : Oxford University Press, 1996).

Furley, P.A., and Newey, W.W., *Geography of the Biosphere* (London: Butterworths, 1983).

Ingersoll, A.P., "The Atmosphere," *Scientific American*, 249, 3 (September 1983), pp. 162-174.

Jackson, P.L., and Kimerling, A.J, *Atlas of The Pacific Northwest*, 9th ed. (Corvallis, OR: Oregon State University Press, 2003).

Kuchler, A.W., *Potential Natural Vegetation of the Conterminous United States*, American Geographical Society Special Publication No. 36, 1964.

Priede, I.G. and Swift, S.M. eds. *Wildlife Telemetry : Remote Monitoring and Tracking of Animals* (New York : Ellis Horwood, 1992).

Scott, R.C., *Essentials of Physical Geography* (St. Paul, MN: West Publishing Co., 1991).

Strahler, A. and Strahler, A., *Physical Geography*, 2nd ed. (New York: John Wiley & Sons, 2002).

Large-scale orthophotos and street maps, such as these for Washington, D.C., are useful tools for interpreting the human environment.

CHAPTER 24
INTERPRETING THE HUMAN LANDSCAPE

HUMAN FACTORS

- Administrative Factors
- Technological Factors
- Cultural Factors
- Economic Factors

HUMAN LANDSCAPE FEATURES

- Urban Settlement
- Land Use and Zoning
- Rural Land Use
  - Agriculture and Forestry
    - Types of Crops
    - Field Structure
    - Commercial Forestry

DEMOGRAPHICS

- Population Density
- Minority Population Concentrations
- Ethnic Neighborhoods
- Population Age
- Education, Income, and Unemployment
- Housing Characteristics

DISEASE AND MORTALITY

SELECTED READINGS

Indeed it is well said, "in every object there is inexhaustible meaning; the eye sees in it what the eye brings means of seeing."
—Thomas Carlyle, History of the French Revolution

24

CHAPTER 24
INTERPRETING THE HUMAN LANDSCAPE

Although the physical environment sets the stage for human activity, we spend most of our lives in an environment of our own making. This **human landscape** is intimately entwined with the physical realms, yet it remains mostly the product of the human mind and hand.

To interpret the human landscape from maps, we must search for distinctive patterns of human activity. Yet much of the information needed to truly understand how the human landscape has developed may not be on maps. The logic underlying decisions made by politicians and other administrators is often better explained by psychologists, sociologists, and historians than by environmental scientists such as geographers. You may see the effects of these decisions on maps, but the decision-making logic so crucial to understanding what you see cannot be shown on maps. Thus, map interpretation of human features on the landscape is usually challenging. The task is further complicated by the fact that the social and cultural mechanisms underlying human organization and communication aren't well understood.

Human factors are responsible for more features seen on maps than you probably realize. To become effective in recognizing these human landscape features, you'll have to isolate the factors that underlie human activity and see how they have contributed to creating the human landscape. Let's look first at four basic human factors.

HUMAN FACTORS

When we examined the physical landscape in Chapter 22, we looked at the factors that molded the environment. We can apply the same strategy to the human landscape. In doing so, we can classify human activity into four broad realms: administrative, technological, cultural, and economic (**Figure 24.1**). After introducing these human factors, we'll discuss several examples of human landscape features that reflect the influence of one or several of the factors.

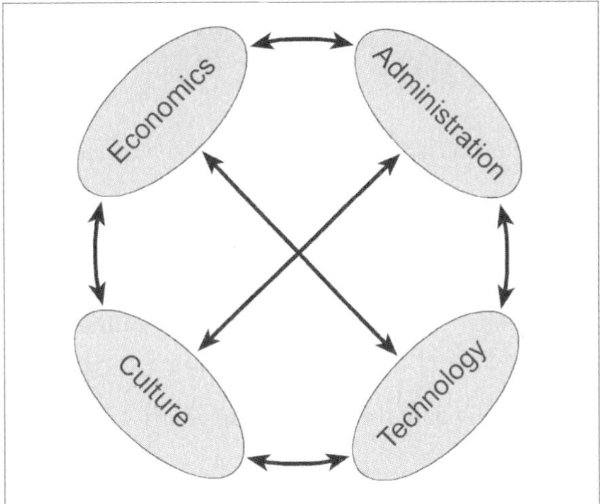

Figure 24.1 The human landscape is molded by a mixture of technological, cultural, economic, and administrative factors.

Administrative Factors

The complex workings of human societies require structure at all levels. Indeed, this structure is the essence of civilization. Since the job of managing falls on the governmental sector, it is understandable that bureaucratic and administrative factors will strongly affect the character of the human landscape. Later in this chapter, we'll interpret maps dealing with urban settlement, land use, and zoning. In each case, we'll discover that administrative factors are an important force behind these mapped patterns.

Technological Factors

The design of tools and machines is in part a matter of function and in part a matter of human imagination and aesthetics. Our technological inventions leave a unique imprint on the pattern of human activity viewed on a map. Furthermore, this imprint changes almost as readily as technology itself. We can tell a great deal about a society's technological development by interpreting a map of its human landscape. Later in this chapter, we'll look at maps of urban settlement to demonstrate the impact of technology upon the human landscape.

Cultural Factors

Administrative and technological factors are primarily responsible for many human landscape features. But these factors alone are insufficient to explain the pattern of human activity, because they don't account for the variety of social and cultural factors that guide our lives. Attitudes, values, aesthetics, styles, heritage, and wealth are just a few of the many cultural factors that influence our work and leisure activities. These factors are expressed in such diverse human features as the geometry of street grids and the segmentation of a city into ethnic neighborhoods. We'll examine maps showing these features later in this chapter.

Economic Factors

Accountants like to point out that, in general, all human activity is governed by economic viability. There are exceptions, of course, since we make errors in judgment, attach non-monetary value to things, and forego economic considerations altogether if recreation or entertainment is our goal. But it is probably fair to say that our environmental behavior reflects at least the perception of economic prudence. It is natural, then, that the character of the human landscape will represent adjustments to these economic factors. Later in this chapter, you'll see maps that show the impact of economic factors on the pattern of timber harvesting and on spatial distribution of college-educated and unemployed people in a city.

HUMAN LANDSCAPE FEATURES

The administrative, technological, cultural, and economic factors we've discussed influence the form in which human features appear in the landscape. We can classify human features in terms of the human activities that create them. Thus, human features are largely due to urban settlement, agriculture, forestry, and other rural land uses. Let's look at each of these types of human landscape features and the factors that helped mold them. The few examples we present in this chapter are only intended to provide ideas on how a skilled map interpreter might proceed. Countless other forms of human activity on the landscape would be equally instructive.

Urban Settlement

Maps can help you understand how an urban area develops over time. Let's take Corvallis, Oregon, as an example. Several types of maps available in printed and digital form from the city planning department and university library show you many things about how Corvallis has grown over the past 150 years.

General Land Office **township survey maps** from the early 1850s (**Figure 24.2**) are a rich source of information on the initial settlement of an area. These maps show U.S. Public Land Survey township, section, and fractional section lines, and also Donation Land Claim boundaries, types of terrain, vegetation, roads and trails, cultivated fields, and houses. The Corvallis area is shown as a low, rolling prairie bounded on the north and west by oak-covered hills. You can see on the maps that the first settlers staked out much of the prairie as Donation Land Claims (see Chapter 5 for more information on these claims). But notice that the town of Marysville (soon renamed Corvallis) has been platted (in 1851) next to the Willamette River from parts of the Avery and Dixon Donation Land Claims.

Avery and Dixon platted the original streets in Corvallis parallel and perpendicular to the Willamette River, at an angle to the north-south boundaries of their land claims. This placement of streets is a common initial urban settlement pattern in the United States, as settlers frequently aligned the street system with physical features such as rivers, bays, or lakeshores. Downtown sections of cities

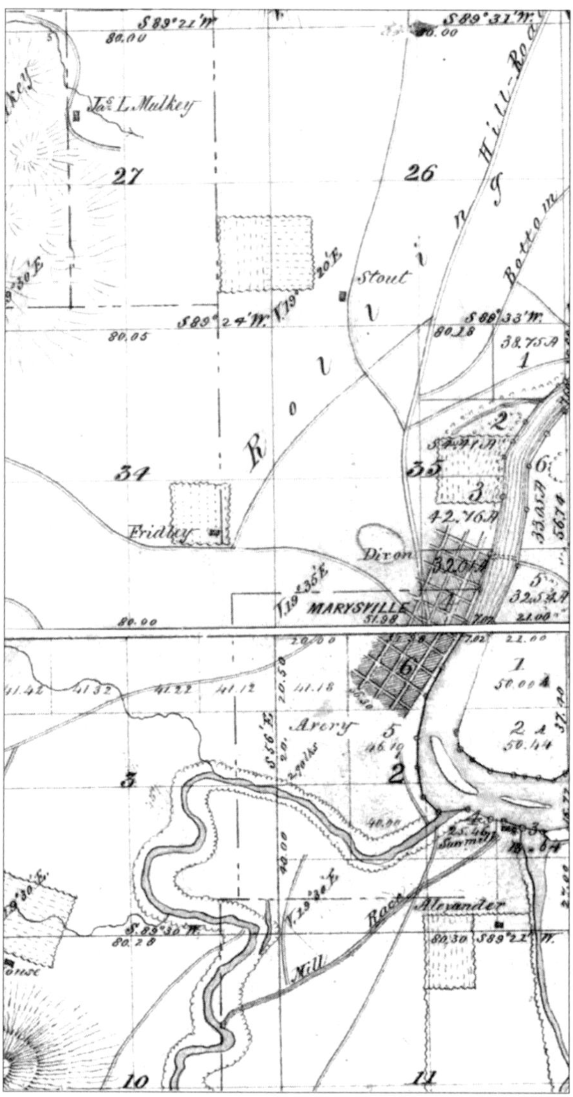

Figure 24.2 Portions of two 1852 General Land Office township survey maps showing the Marysville (now Corvallis) town plat carved from the Avery and Dixon Donation Land Claims (dashed boundary lines). Streets are straight lines running parallel and perpendicular to the Willamette River, but were drawn at slightly different orientations on the two maps.

such as Detroit, New Orleans, and Seattle reflect this early method of street orientation. As cities expand, their street networks must be adjusted to physical obstacles such as rivers, lakes, swamps, and rough terrain. Indeed, the street network alone often gives you major clues to the nature of the surrounding physical environment.

The township survey maps also show the Marys River entering the Willamette River just south of the town site. Historians have written that the Marys River contributed enough water to the Willamette to make Corvallis the southern limit of year-round steamboat navigation. The town site was hence well placed from an economic viewpoint, but also from a physical viewpoint. The Corvallis topographic quadrangle shows the west bank of the Willamette River to be higher than the east bank, making the town far less vulnerable to flooding.

Since cities expand through annexations, you can learn about urban settlement patterns by looking at annexation date information. Corvallis, like many cities, has annexation boundaries stored as a GIS data layer that includes the date the land was annexed. From this information, you can make a map showing areas annexed during different time periods, such as the seven periods from 1851 to 2000 shown in **Figure 24.3**.

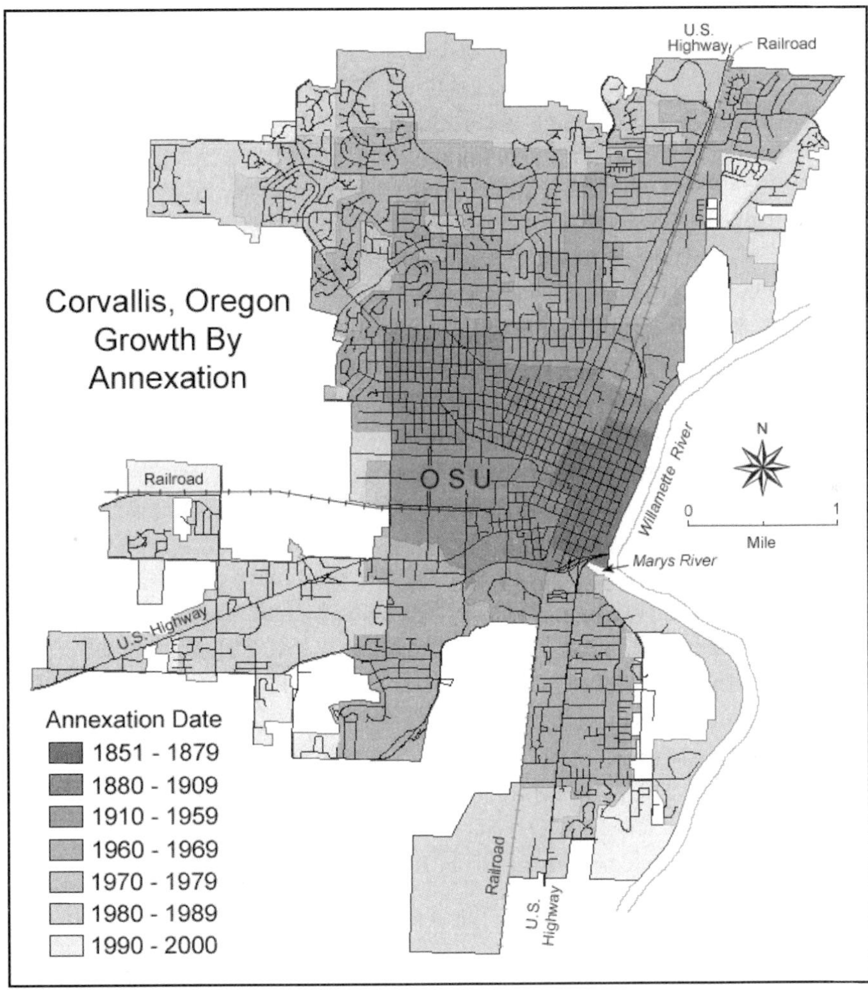

Figure 24.3 This map of annexation dates shows that Corvallis grew steadily in land area from 1851 to 2000.

Comparing the town plat of 1851 with the annexations to Corvallis by 1879, you can see that the town grew slowly during these 28 years, adding streets in a semi-circular pattern around the original plat. The Willamette River was, and still is, a barrier to eastward expansion, but neither map shows the low-lying land to the east of the river that cannot be built upon due to frequent flooding. Only from written historical records will you learn that a large flood in 1861 washed away the competing town of Orleans on the east bank of the river.

Notice that streets within the annexations were aligned with those in the original town plat. The city historical records indicate that there was no compelling reason to change their orientation, particularly since this period was the height of steamboat transportation, and easy access to the many docks lining the riverfront was important to the settlers.

The map in Figure 24.3 shows three distinct annexations to Corvallis between 1880 and 1909, and two events in the city history bear this out. The first event was the completion in 1880 of the railroad from the north that you see in the top center of the map. The railroad tracks were aligned with the town plat, running through the city in the middle of a street six blocks west of the waterfront. The railroad brought greater wealth and many new residents to the city, but also hastened the demise of steamboat transportation on the Willamette River. To accommodate the new residents, blocks to the west of the railroad were built in alignment with the original town plat. Continuing the original street alignment gave the new residents easy access to the railroad and the city's commercial center, which was moving westward away from the rapidly declining riverfront.

The second event was the city's purchase of land in the 1880s for Corvallis College (now Oregon State University) and the subsequent construction of campus streets and buildings. The college wasn't tied to the riverfront or the railroad, and campus streets were aligned with the cardinal directions (north-south and east-west). This new street orientation pattern coincided with the U.S. Public Land Survey fractional section lines and the Donation Land Claim boundary line that you can see in Figure 24.2. The railroad that reached Corvallis from the west in 1880 was aligned parallel to one of the campus streets, and the annexation to the north of the campus continued this new cardinal-direction street orientation. Notice in Figure 24.2 that the original road you see in the west half of Section 34 wasn't abandoned when the subdivision was constructed. Instead, it cuts diagonally through the new streets.

The 1910-1959 period is the early era of the automobile, which affected the settlement of the Corvallis area in many ways. To begin, the railroad you see in Figure 24.3 entering the city from the south was completed in 1908, and in the 1920s the federally funded Pacific Highway was constructed parallel to this rail line and to the line entering the city from the north. This paved highway, along with highway links from the west and east that you see on the map, caused the demise of passenger train service to Corvallis. No more rail lines were constructed, and railroads ceased to be a factor in planning the alignment of new streets.

City engineering department records show that most streets in the city were paved by 1920, as the automobile replaced the horse-drawn carriage as the main means of transportation. Maps produced by the city showing the dates of land subdivisions show that hundreds of large residential lots in the center of the city were partitioned during this time period. Historians note that homeowners no longer needed large back lots for horse barns and outbuildings, so subdividing their land and selling the back lot as a new home site was a wise move economically.

The 1910-1959 time period is a single category on the annexation date map because few additions to the city were made during these five decades. The population records for the city, however, show a continual slow growth in the number of residents and an increase in the population density around the city center as houses were built on the partitioned original lots. Annexations that did occur reflect the fact that automobile transportation allowed people to live farther away from the city center and commute to work. The subdivisions platted to the north and west had wider streets designed for the automobile, and continued the cardinal-direction street alignments to maximize the ease of driving through residential neighborhoods. The curved streets you see on the map were in subdivisions platted in the foothills, where streets had to be built along the contour of the hill.

Annexations to Corvallis from 1960 to 2000 reflect the later era of the automobile. The annexation date map shows that the city more than doubled in land area in this 40-year period. Earlier subdivisions were annexed, as were several subdivisions in the remaining flat prairie to the north. In both areas, streets were again aligned with the Public Land Survey fractional section and Donation Land Claim boundary lines.

Notice, however, that the newest annexations to the city have curved streets and a large number of dead-end cul-de-sacs. Contractors will tell you that this is the best way to build streets in hilly areas. But this street pattern also reflects new ideas about suburban subdivision design that stress reduced traffic flow and car speeds in residential areas.

Geographers have developed several models of how cities grow spatially, and the concentric zone model best fits Corvallis. You can see that the central business district is in the oldest part of the city, and that growth through annexation occurred more or less in semicircular arcs with full circular growth restricted by the Willamette River. The outermost arc is the most recent commuter's zone of homes, made possible by automobile transportation.

Studying how Corvallis grew over the past 150 years shows what you can learn by studying maps, historic documents, and government records. Similar maps likely exist for your city, or can be made from GIS data layers.

Our picture of Corvallis is still incomplete, however, because we haven't seen how land is currently used and zoned for future use. Let's look next at the role of this important factor in interpreting the human landscape.

Land Use and Zoning

The **land use pattern** within cities often reflects people's adjustment to physical, administrative, economic, and cultural factors. Commercial and industrial land use is generally tied closely to the terrain and transportation networks. For large shopping centers or intensive industry, a broad, flat area close to freeways is ideal. Residential land use, in contrast, is far less sensitive to the physical setting. Houses are built on flat areas if land is available, but can also be built up steep slopes if necessary. In fact, sloping hillsides may be preferred for the view they afford.

Administrative policies affect the pattern of human habitation through land use planning and zoning policy. Laws designed to ensure a sensible land use pattern generally structure human activity in an organized society. The common aim is to optimize the long-term good for the greatest number of people while minimizing damage to the physical environment. The first step in developing land use policy is to inventory how land parcels are currently being used. A **land use map** produced by your city or county planning department shows this inventory.

Let's take the land use map for Corvallis, most of which is shown in **Color Plate 24.1**, as our example. City planners defined a limited number of land use categories, then placed city blocks and large undeveloped parcels into the category that best characterized each area.

Notice the correspondence between the types of current land use and the historical pattern of annexations to the city. The original town plat remains the central business district, but the riverfront blocks are now parkland. Oregon State University is in the public institution category, and you can see that its original annexation boundaries have changed little. What has changed is land use in the two residential annexations during the late 1800s. Many of the low-density, single-family residences have been replaced by medium- to high-density housing units to serve the growing student population.

You can see that low-density residential land use dominates the newer annexations to the city farther away from the university housing area. As in many cities, the low-density residential area is interspersed with small shopping centers at major street intersections. But the major commercial area consists of two strips along the U.S. highways entering the city from the north and south. You will probably see such a commercial strip on the land use map for your city.

The final thing to notice is that Corvallis has very little industrial land use. Lack of manufacturing industries and a large research technology center tells you that Corvallis is likely a "white collar" city dominated by professional employment.

Zoning is the city or county regulation of land use through the creation and enforcement of **zoning codes** under local law. If the city **zoning map** (**Color Plate 24.2**) is brought into the picture, the explanation for the land use pattern becomes much clearer. The map shows you that a city is divided into a number of **zoning districts**. The basic districts are residential, commercial, industrial, and open space, with sub-categories for each. Notice, for example, that there are low, medium, and high-density residential districts. Cryptic identifiers like RS-3.5, RS-9, and RS-20 are all that you see in most zoning map legends. We have added information to the legend to show you how the districts differ. The three residential densities, for instance, are defined by the number of housing units per acre and the types of units that are allowed. The low-density residential category is further divided into RS-3.5, RS-5, and RS-6 sub-categories that allow the same number of units per acre, but specify whether duplexes, townhouses, and smaller lot sizes are permissible. Detailed regulations for each type of district comprise the zoning code for the city.

Notice how closely the zoning district map resembles the land use map for Corvallis. Their close correspondence should not be a surprise, since land subdivided and buildings constructed in the past either had to comply with the zoning code, or the code was changed to accommodate a different type of land development. The zoning district map guides future developments in the city, but districts on the map are not set in stone.

The zoning code for a city or county reflects various aspects of the physical landscape, but it is also sensitive to human wishes and needs, including food production, shopping, journey to work, recreation, clean air and drinking water, and high-quality residential areas. Planners do the best they can under difficult conditions to zone for land uses that will serve all these often-conflicting needs. Explaining the reasoning behind individual zoning decisions is a challenge for even the most adept map interpreter.

Rural Land Use

Over the past few decades, many maps have been made to show types of landcover in areas that are mostly rural. These maps show the geographic patterns of rural landcover at different scales and with different levels of detail, but many are similar to the small-scale map of Oregon's Willamette Basin in **Figure 24.4**. Landcover in the basin is placed into the general categories of urban, agricultural, forested, and water. Remote sensing specialists digitally classify satellite images of an area into these general landcover categories to create the map.

The map indicates that most of the land in the Willamette Basin is forested, that the Willamette Valley in the center of the basin is predominantly agricultural, and that urban development is centered at the north and south ends of the valley. More detailed maps at larger scales will show you more about the human use of the forested and agricultural lands. For example, you will see categories for irrigated and non-irrigated fields, and forested land may be divided into commercial forests and wilderness areas off limits to logging.

You can learn more about how land is used in your local area by interpreting similar maps. Combined with written records of your area, such landcover maps will help you understand how these land uses have evolved over time into the geographical patterns you see today.

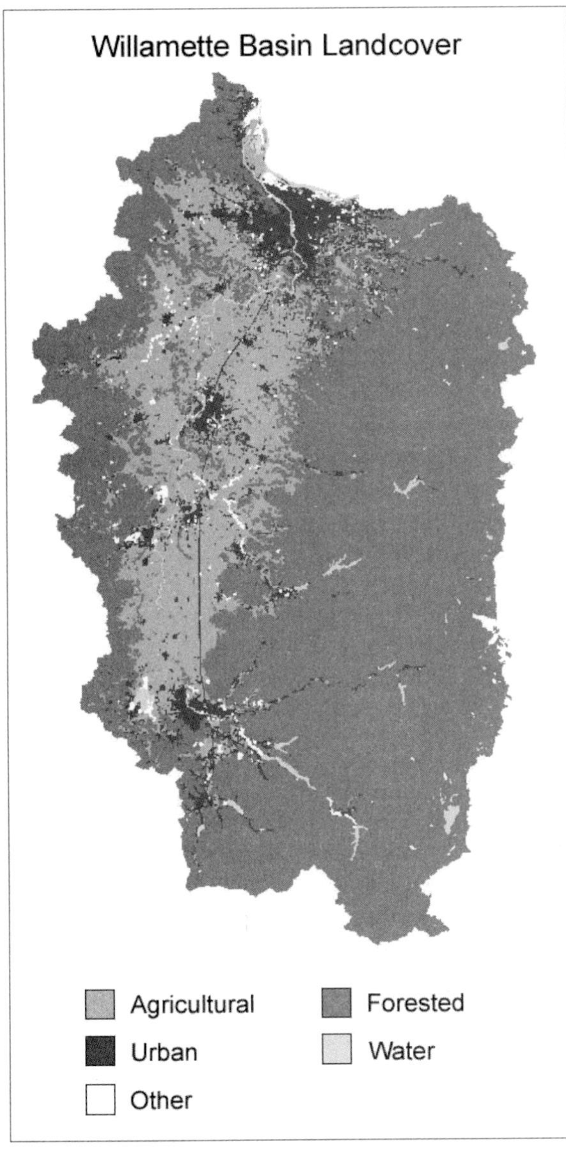

Figure 24.4 Landcover map for the Willamette Basin, with categories determined by digitally classifying satellite images of the area.

Agriculture and Forestry

Variations in agricultural land use are often due to the physical environment. This is true of the type of crops grown in an area, and of the geometrical form of farm fields used to raise these crops. We will look at examples of these two aspects of agriculture.

Types of Crops. Let's begin by considering a map of agricultural practices in the narrow zone along the shores of Lake Michigan (Figure 24.5A). This map reveals that a wide variety of fruit is grown around the lake. It also indicates that there are definite concentrations of fruit types on opposite shores of the lake. Apples are grown west of the lake, while such crops as peaches, grapes, and blueberries are raised east of the lake. At the lake's northern end, cherries are grown along both shores. Why, you may wonder, is fruit-growing clustered along the shores of the lake in the first place? And why are different types of fruits grown on different sides of the lake?

The answer to the first question is found in the special type of climate caused by the lake. Large water bodies influence the local climate by warming up more slowly than the neighboring land in warm periods and cooling down more slowly than the surrounding land in cool periods. Through constant mixing and circulation, the mass of water in the lake serves as a large reservoir of thermal energy. Thus, winter temperatures are generally warmer along the shores of a large lake, while summer temperatures are cooler. The more moderate winter serves the fruit trees' need for a cold dormant period, but isn't so cold that blossom buds and other delicate plant tissue are damaged. Large bodies of water are also likely to increase the average annual precipitation and reduce the range in monthly precipitation. Of special importance for this example is the fact that the incidence of late spring frosts is reduced at the vulnerable blossoming stage of the fruiting cycle. Together, these conditions create a climate conducive to growing fruit in the middle latitudes.

This moderating lake effect explains why fruit-growing is clustered near the shores of Lake Michigan. But it doesn't provide insight into the concentration of different fruit crops around the lake. To explain why different fruits are grown on opposite shores of the lake, we must look at the general weather pattern in the Great Lakes region.

Notice that with the exception of cherries in the north, only hardy fruits such as apples are successfully grown on the west sides of the lake, whereas less hardy crops, such as peaches and

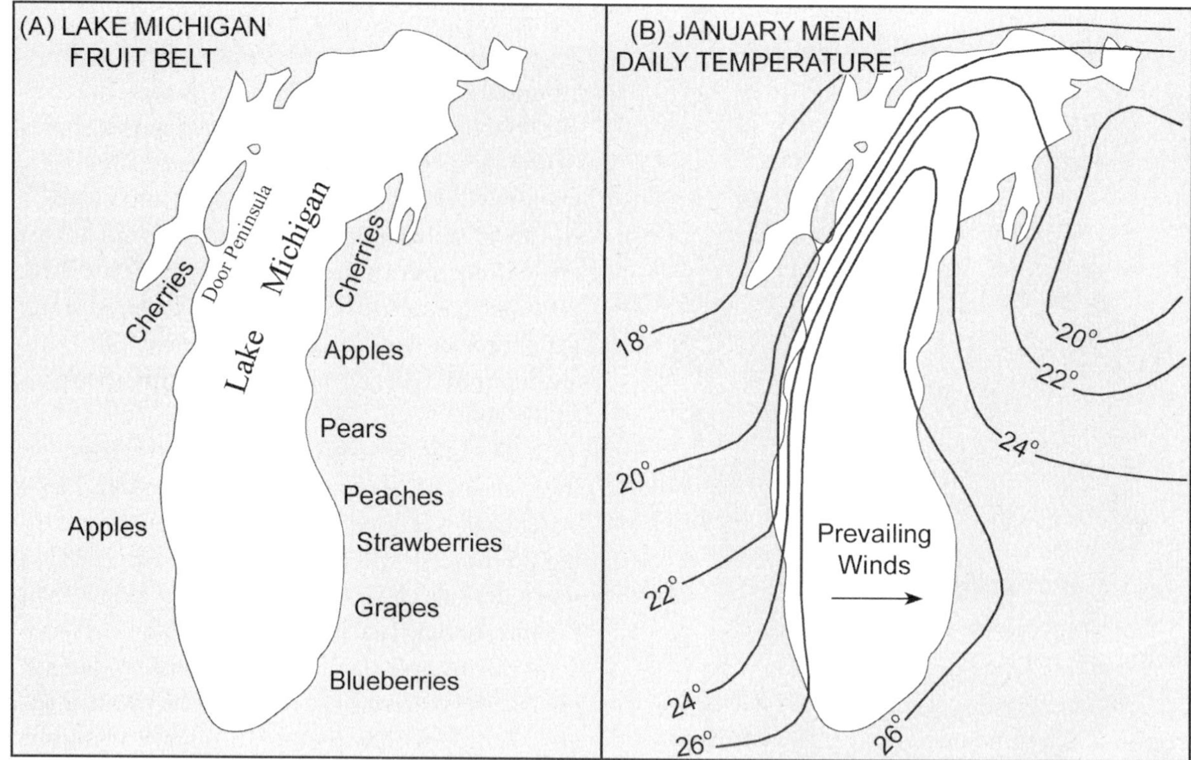

Figure 24.5 Fruit production around the shores of Lake Michigan are influenced by the moderating lake effect on the local climate.

grapes, are grown on the east side. These crop differences suggest that the moderating lake effect is greatest to the east, which in turn implies that the prevailing winds are probably coming from the west. Data shown on monthly temperature, precipitation, and wind vector maps for the Lake Michigan region (**Figure 24.5B**) confirm this suspicion. These maps show that the east shore is indeed more moderate than the west, and that both are more moderate than inland locations.

At first glance, cherries appear to be an exception to the upwind-downwind explanation, because they are grown on both sides of the lake. But these areas of cherry production can be explained by the fact that Wiconsin's Door Peninsula is itself under the moderating effect of Green Bay to the west.

Field Structure. The physical environment is a primary factor in determining not only the type of crops grown, but also the shape of farm fields. If land is flat, it's simplest for the farmer to make rectangular fields of fairly uniform size and orientation. On rough terrain and land segmented by a stream network, farmers often create fields of irregular shape, size, and orientation. In areas of flat and rough terrain, the field pattern may clearly identify the type of terrain. Notice in **Figure 24.6**, for example, how the parallel pattern of fields (A) sharply defines three linear beach ridges. Similarly, small drainage systems that might otherwise be indistinguishable on the air photo (B) are made obvious by breaks in the field planting.

Even when field shapes don't reflect the form of the topography, the manner in which the fields are cropped might. Contour planting and strip cropping can sometimes create a vivid picture of the terrain. With contour planting, farmers work the land along the contour of the terrain to minimize runoff and erosion.

In some regions, contour strip cropping is so widely used and landform features are so localized that on an air photo the terrain looks as though it

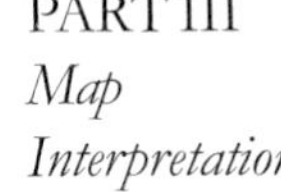

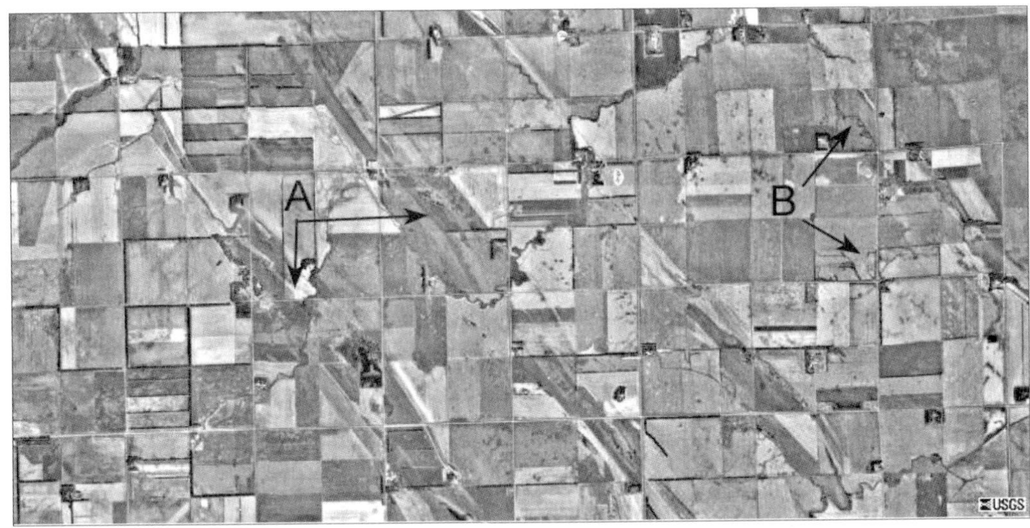

Figure 24.6 In this area 15 miles south of Grand Forks, North Dakota, the pattern of agriculture fields reflects the presence of glacial lake beach ridges (A) and small streams (B).

has been portrayed with layer tints. The region near Black Earth, Wisconsin (**Figure 24.7**) is an excellent example. In most cases, however, the contour cropping is fragmented, and we are left to piece together the form of the underlying terrain. This often involves looking beyond the rows and crop strips to the drainage, forest, and highway patterns.

The absence of contour planting on an air photo is a good indication that the area has relatively flat terrain. This isn't always the case, however, because contour planting is usually voluntary, requiring foresight and extra work on the part of the farmer. Therefore, the presence of contour cropping on an air photo is an almost certain indicator of hilly terrain.

Figure 24.7 Contour planting is an attempt to adjust agricultural practices to the physical environment.

Commercial Forestry. Commercial forestry is shaped by the physical environment, but also by administrative factors. Take the Oregon Coast Range, for example. Here the mild, wet Marine West Coast climate (see Chapter 23 for a description of this climate) is ideal for growing commercially-valuable Douglas fir trees. Logging these low but steeply sloped mountains has always been a mainstay of Oregon's economy.

Figure 24.8 is an air photo of a small piece of the Coast Range forest southwest of Eugene, Oregon. To interpret the timber harvest patterns visible on the photo, you first have to understand the history of the area's land ownership. Notice that the land appears broken into squares, with sharp differences in gray tone along their edges. You are looking at U.S. Public Land Survey sections and quarter-sections that were surveyed in the 1860s.

The checkerboard pattern on the landscape reflects the alternating private and public land ownership that you would discover on the tax assessor's map for the area. Researching the historical land ownership records for western Oregon, you would find that shortly after the Civil War, Congress authorized a land grant for the construction of a railroad from Portland southward to the California border. The land grant comprised all odd-numbered sections of public land 20 miles on either

Figure 24.8 These clear-cuts southwest of Eugene, Oregon, reflect historical legislative and legal decisions, as well as Oregon's forest practice laws.

side of the proposed railroad line. The purpose of the land grant was to cover the "up-front" expenses of the private company building the railroad. The grant stipulated that land had to be sold to settlers and that no more than 160 acres could be sold to an individual—hence the quarter-sections that you see on the air photo.

The General Land Office sold the land not granted to the railroad company to settlers, many of whom were bought out by private timber companies during the Great Depression. The railroad company sold some of its land, but violated every stipulation of the grant when doing so. Consequently, in the early 1900s it was forced to return its unsold land to the government, where the Bureau of Land Management (BLM) administers it today. You can easily see the private and BLM lands on the air photo. The rightmost sixth of the photo is BLM land, and the heavily fragmented forest on the rest of the photo is in private ownership.

The 1971 Oregon Forest Practices Act, the first of its kind in the nation, regulates timber harvest on private land. In Figure 24.8, you can see the effects of the Act's logging rules. Private companies consider clear-cutting the most economical way to harvest trees, and a patchwork of clear-cuts is easy to see on the photo. The logging rules state that every clear-cut must be replanted, and the different tones you see in the clear-cuts tell you the relative age of this regrowth—the darker the older. Loggers also must leave a "riparian buffer" of trees on either side of a stream, and you can see these buffers as dark narrow sinuous strips cutting through clear-cuts.

Economic factors also play a major role in timber harvesting. The irregular-shaped clear-cuts are designed to minimize the cost of moving felled trees from the hillside to a central collection point called a landing. Landings are usually located on the top of ridges, connected by the logging roads that you see as wavy, thin, white lines on the photo. Clear-cuts and landings are planned so as to minimize the total cost of bringing logs from the hillside to the lumber mill.

DEMOGRAPHICS

Maps showing annexations, land use, and zoning help you understand how land is settled over time, but tell you little about the **demographics** of your city or county. Demographics is the study of socioeconomic groups that differ in gender, age, race, ethnicity, income, or occupation. **Demographic maps** show where different socioeconomic groups reside.

The United States Census of Population and Housing, conducted at the end of each decade (see Chapter 7 for further details on census data collection), is a rich source of demographic information for your area. The data collected at residences are aggregated into totals for census blocks, census tracts, cities, counties, and states. Demographic maps are made at each of these levels, but you'll see the most detailed information on the census block and tract maps. Let's look at several demographic maps of the metropolitan Chicago area that show socioeconomic data at the tract level.

Population Density

The choropleth map in **Figure 24.9** shows **population densities** in Chicago census tracts, with the density range divided into quartiles (each legend category contains one-quarter of the census tracts in the metropolitan area). As in most U.S. cities, the central business district (CBD) has a low population density. You can see that the highest population densities are in a ring of census tracts that surround the CBD. Population density decreases rapidly in all directions toward the low-density residential districts in the suburbs.

The population density pattern mirrors the concentric ring model of urban development described earlier in the chapter, but notice the sparsely populated industrial corridors along the Chicago River and Ship Canal that cut through the concentric rings like narrow sectors of a circle. The high-density ring also is wider to the north of the CBD. A demographer would tell you that the prosperous neighborhoods on the North Side lakefront are more densely populated than the many problem-ridden neighborhoods on the city's South and West sides.

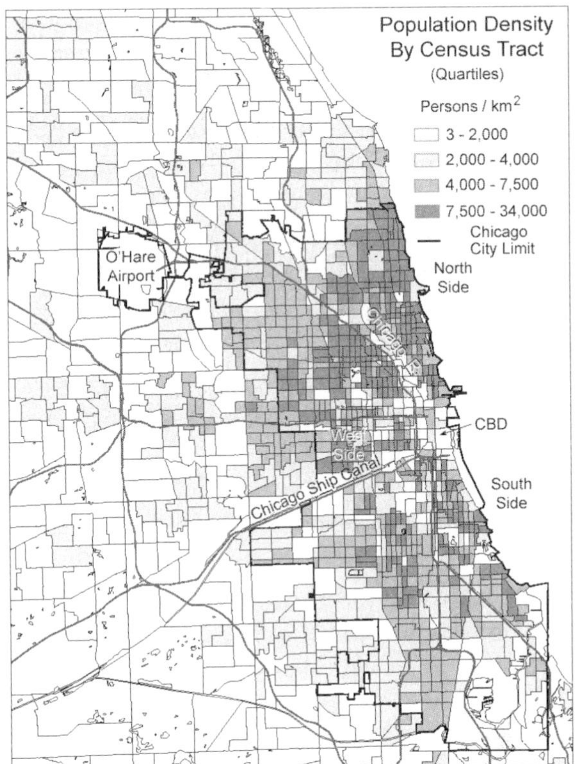

Figure 24.9 Population density by census tract in the Chicago metropolitan area [adapted from a University of Chicago Map Collection digital map of 1990 population density].

Minority Population Concentrations

The clustering of individuals with similar racial heritage into **minority population concentrations** is another important aspect of the human landscape. Continuing with the Chicago example, a map of minority concentrations (**Figure 24.10A**) shows you that many of the South Side and West Side census tracts have a majority of African-American or Hispanic residents. In contrast, the North Side has very few census tracts dominated by minorities.

Notice that the predominantly African-American and Hispanic census tracts aren't interspersed but instead cover large contiguous sections of the metropolitan area. Demographers report that large parts of the South and West Sides of Chicago have become essentially all African-American. This clustered spatial pattern of minority residences hints strongly at being of economic and cultural rather than physical origin.

The map shows a large African-American-dominated census tract at the northwest corner of the city. It seems strange to have this concentration of minorities in the suburbs, until you notice in Figure 24.9 that this is a low-population-density tract containing most of the Chicago O'Hare international airport. You can now guess that this census tract includes a small number of residences occupied by mostly African-American airport employees.

Ethnic Neighborhoods

Individuals of similar ethnic background also cluster into **ethnic neighborhoods** within a city. Chicago is known for its ethnic neighborhoods, but there are now hardly any census tracts in the city or its inner suburbs where a majority of residents are of the same European ancestry. There are, however, certain parts of the metropolitan area where a particular ethnic group comprises more than a quarter of the total population. The ethnic neighborhood map (**Figure 24.10B**) shows census tracts containing the two largest ethnic groups—Polish and Italian. Notice that there appears to be one Italian neighborhood, but the Polish community resides in three distinct neighborhoods ringing the city center.

Overt government districting or zoning might be suspected as the cause of minority or ethnic concentration in some countries, but not in the United States. If governmental factors are responsible here, they are likely to be expressed in subtle ways. They may show up, for instance, in the provision of services which encourage concentration and in bureaucratic red tape which discourages movement into other neighborhoods.

Indeed, cultural factors most likely have had the biggest influence on the creation and perpetuation of minority and ethnic neighborhoods in U.S. cities. Cultural forces can encourage movement into and discourage movement out of these ethnic zones. High on the list of positive influences is cultural continuity. New immigrants face less cultural shock by joining people who share their ethnic heritage. Faces, churches, stores, jobs, and language will all be familiar. Community support is also available. It makes for a much easier transition for an immigrant to start life in a new, unfamiliar country by settling first in an ethnic neighborhood.

On the negative side, the behavior of outsiders can discourage people from leaving their socially comfortable neighborhoods. Sometimes there is overt prejudice, as when people refuse to rent or sell housing to others. Or the behavior may take the more subtle form of making people feel uncomfortable socially when out of their more familiar neighborhoods.

The reasons that minority and ethnic neighborhoods develop and persist are obviously very complex. But the influencing factors almost always are of human origin. The map interpreter thus should concentrate on cultural factors when attempting to explain such patterns in the human landscape.

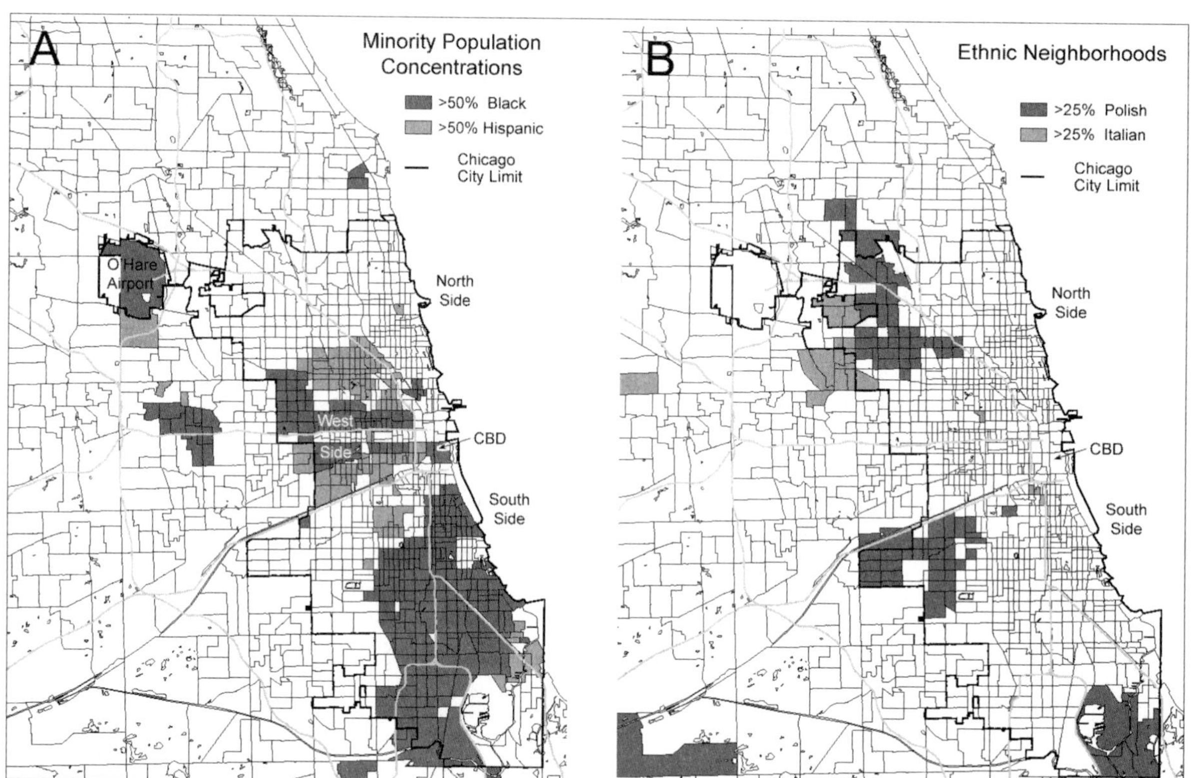

Figure 24.10 The partitioning of Chicago, Illinois, into minority concentrations (A) and ethnic neighborhoods (B) is a spatial manifestation of a host of social influences on immigrant settlement [adapted from University of Chicago Map Collection digital maps of 1990 African-Americans, Asians and Pacific Islanders, and Hispanics(A); and ethnic groups of European origin(B)].

Population Age

Economic and cultural conditions can create large variations in the percentage of children, young adults, and mature people living in different parts of a city. A map showing the percentage of the total population in a certain age range living in each census tract can help you understand age structure variations within your city. Let's continue with the Chicago metropolitan area example by looking at population age maps for children and young adults.

The percentage of total census tract population under 18 years old is shown in quartiles on the map in **Figure 24.11A**. Notice that children and teenagers comprise from 30% to 60% of the population in most South Side and West Side census tracts. This high percentage of youth is in sharp contrast to the North Side and the suburbs surrounding the city, where most tracts have less than 25% of the population in this age group. Comparing this map with the previous three, you'll see that census tracts with high percentages of children under 18 correspond closely to high-population-density tracts where most residents are African-American or Hispanic. Also, notice that the Polish and Italian ethnic neighborhoods have a much lower percentage of children than adjacent minority population concentrations.

The spatial distribution of young adults 25-34 years old (**Figure 24.11B**) looks completely different from the distribution of children. Notice the concentration of young adults along the North Side lakefront, where almost all census tracts have from 20% to 50% of the total population in this age range. You'll also see census tracts with high percentages of young adults interspersed through the suburban area ringing the city.

Let's now compare this map with the others. First, notice that children and young adults are concentrated in different sections of the city. You could say that there is a negative visual correlation be-

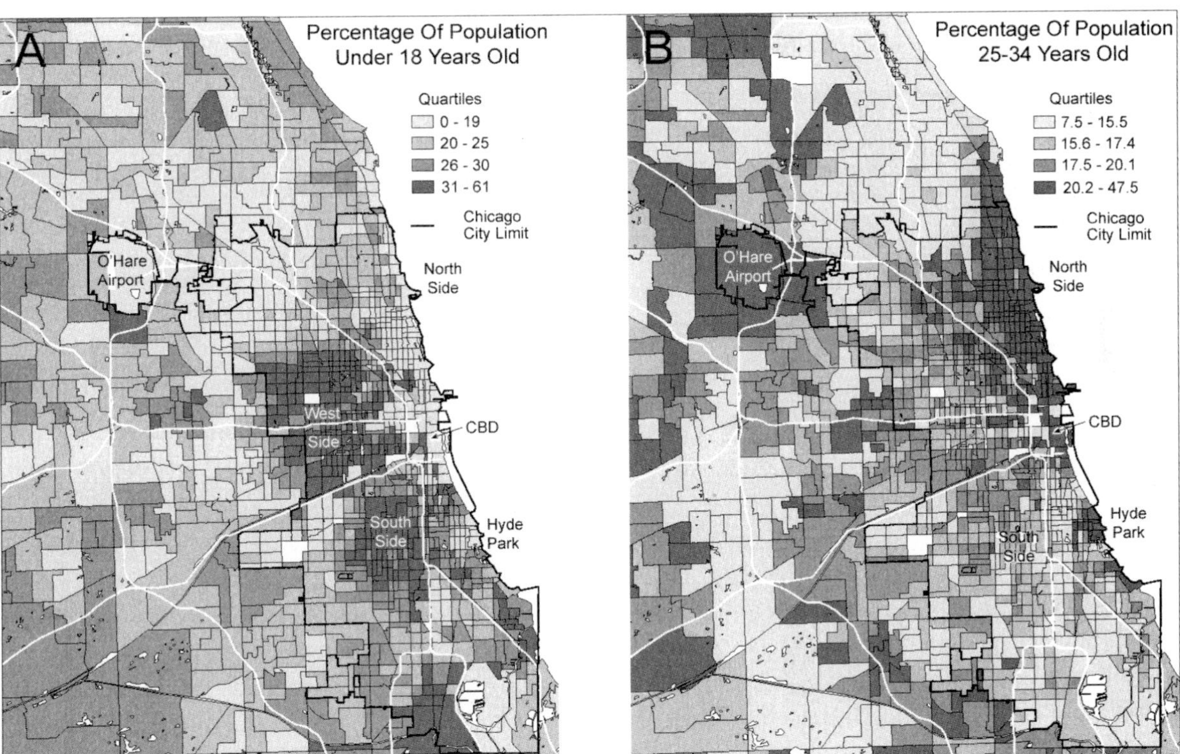

Figure 24.11 Chicago metropolitan area percentage of population under 18 years old (A) and 25-34 years old (B) [adapted from University of Chicago Map Collection digital maps of 1990 college-educated population and per capita income].

tween the two maps in Figure 24.11. The population-density map shows you that the North Side census tracts dominated by young adults have high population densities, whereas the suburban tracts have lower population densities. The minority concentration and ethnic neighborhood maps tell you that young adults aren't concentrated in minority or ethnic neighborhoods but, rather, in areas with high percentages of white residents.

Education, Income, and Unemployment

Someone may have told you that in the United States a college education is the key to financial stability and good living conditions. Maps of the Chicago metropolitan area showing the percentage of adults over 25 with a college education and per capita income (**Figure 24.12 A and B**) give strong evidence for the link between education and financial success. Notice on the college education map that over 50% of adults over 25 have a college education in most North Side census tracts, in Hyde Park on the South Side lakefront, and in certain suburbs, particularly north of the city.

In stark contrast, you can see that no more than one-eighth of the adults over 25 have a college education in most South and West Side census tracts. This lack of higher education is particularly apparent in the densely populated tracts in these areas that are dominated by minorities. Most of these census tracts are in the lowest quintile (one-fifth of census tracts), with 6% or less of the adult residents college educated. Look again at Figure 24.11 and you will see that the census tracts with the lowest percentage of college-educated adults also tend to have the highest percentage of children under 18—an unfortunate social condition for any city.

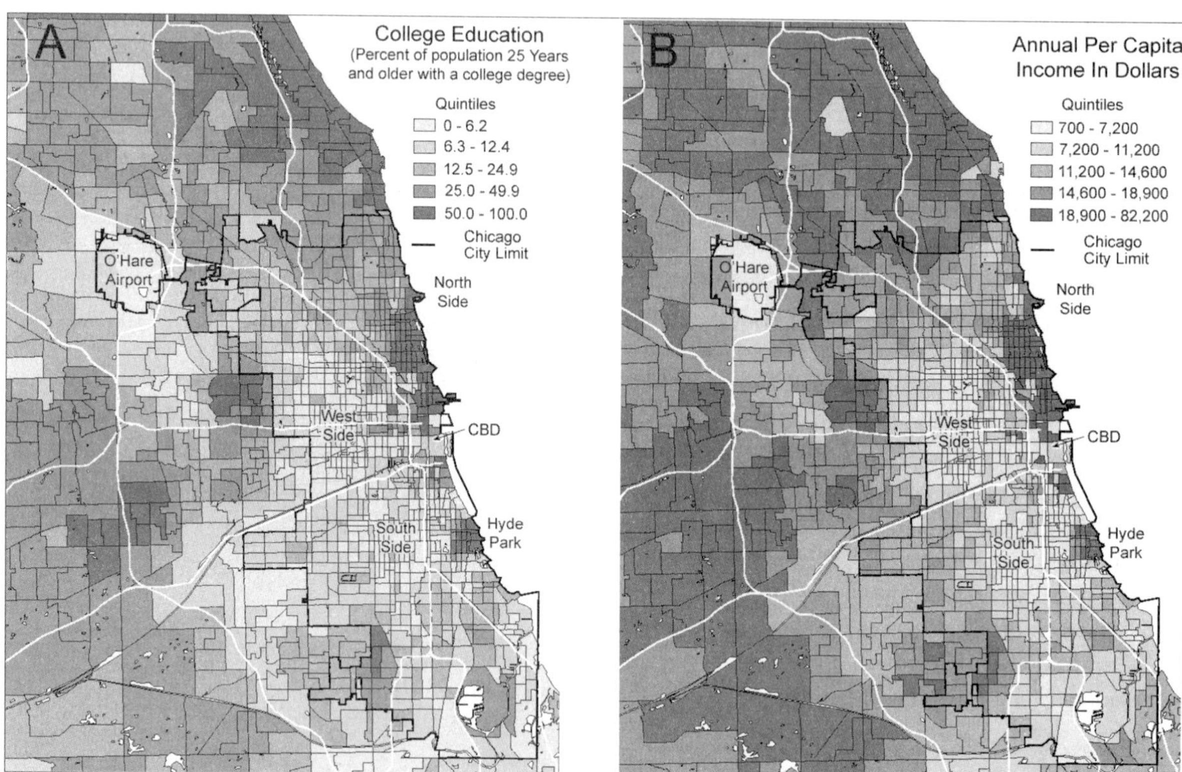

Figure 24.12 Chicago metropolitan area percentage of population with a college education (A) and annual per capita income (B) [adapted from University of Chicago Map Collection digital maps of 1990 college-educated population and per capita income].

The map of annual per capita income by census tract (Figure 24.12B) looks nearly identical to the college education map. If you were to perform a cross-correlation analysis on the two maps (see Chapter 18 for a description of this statistical test of map pattern similarity), you would find that the two maps are highly correlated in the positive sense. The map is telling you that where the percentage of college-educated people is greater, the annual per capita income is higher.

Putting together what you've learned from the maps so far, you can conclude that the high proportion of predominantly white, college-educated adults living in North Side lakeshore census tracts have the highest annual incomes in the metropolitan area. Also, the prosperous, well-educated white residents of the Hyde Park neighborhood on the South Side lakefront stand out dramatically from the surrounding areas. That's because the census tracts on the South and West Sides are densely populated by less-educated, minority residents with low annual income. The income map legend shows you that there is a very large difference in income level between these two parts of the city. The average annual income in the poorest census tract is about 1% of that in the richest tract.

The per capita income map suggests that poverty is an important part of the Chicago human landscape. The U.S. Census Bureau defines the **poverty level** as a minimum family income that varies with the size of the family unit. For instance, the poverty level in 2000 for a family of four was $17,761. Maps have been made for major metropolitan areas showing the percentage of population with family incomes below the poverty level. Let's take a look at a graduated circle map showing the percentage of people below the poverty level for Chicago metropolitan area census tracts (**Figure 24.13**). This map is based on a multicolor map of the same title produced in 1998 by Dr. William Bowen.

The large black circles on the map represent census tracts where 75% or more of the population has a family income below the poverty level. These truly impoverished areas appear to be in the heart of the minority-dominated parts of the city's South and West Sides. These are the areas that would stand out on maps showing crime rates, unemployment, and public expenditures on welfare.

Looking at the pattern of graduated circles for the next two lower poverty classes (which include census tracts where 25%-75% of the people fall below the poverty level), you can see that poverty permeates the city's South and West Sides. The map also clearly shows the striking differences in financial well being between these poor sections of Chicago and the affluent North Side and suburban neighborhoods, where most census tracts have less than 10% of their population below the poverty level.

Let's now look at a map of the unemployment rate (**Figure 24.14**) to see how closely pov-

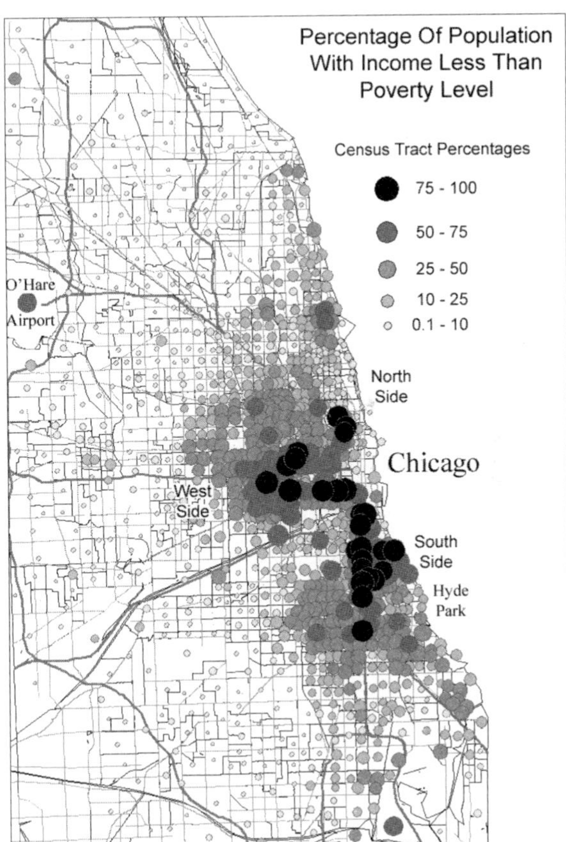

Figure 24.13 Chicago metropolitan area percentage of population with income less than the poverty level [adapted from a multicolor map of the same title produced by Dr. William Bowen].

erty and unemployment are related in the Chicago metropolitan area. If you were to superimpose the poverty level and unemployment rate maps, you would see just how closely they correspond. The unemployment rate appears to define the degree of poverty, or vice versa. Notice again the stark difference in poverty and unemployment between Hyde Park and its surrounding census tracts, a dramatic example of the vast differences in education and wealth found in adjacent neighborhoods.

Housing Characteristics

Poverty and wealth are also reflected in maps of **housing characteristics**. The U.S. Census Bureau collects data on the age and type of housing within census tracts, and maps have been made from the data for the Chicago metropolitan area. **Figure 24.15A** shows the **age of housing** as defined by the time period when most houses in a census tract were built. Twenty-year time increments between 1940 and 2000 were used to show the pace of new home construction and urban renewal in different parts of the metropolitan area.

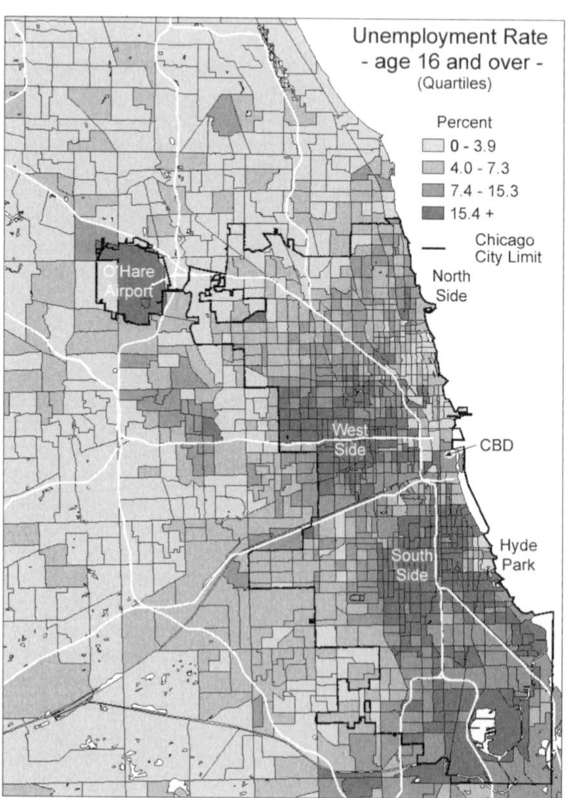

Figure 24.14 Chicago metropolitan area unemployment rate [adapted from a University of Chicago Map Collection digital map of unemployment].

The map indicates that the majority of housing units in a broad semi-circular "age ring" around Chicago's central business district were built before 1940. You can see the next age ring in the inner suburbs, where the majority of houses in most census tracts appear to have been built from 1940 to 1980. A third age ring is visible in the outer suburbs, where most houses are shown as more recent than 1980.

Notice that the age rings aren't uniformly of a single time period. An urban planner would tell you that the rings have been broken by more recent redevelopment projects that often involved tearing down older homes. The lakefront area is also an exception to the age ring model. You can see that housing units older than 1940 dominate the north shore census tracts, as well as Hyde Park on the south shore. The map also displays the age of housing only for tracts with more than 25 housing units, and the age rings might well appear more uniform if this arbitrary map display limit were eliminated.

Another important piece of demographic information is the **type of housing** in different parts of a city. A map showing census tracts dominated by single-family or multi-unit housing (**Figure 24.15B**) helps you understand housing patterns in the Chicago metropolitan area.

Notice that the entire lakefront within the Chicago city limit is greater than 75% multi-unit housing. The housing age map indicates that most of these large units have been built from 1960 to the present. An urban planner will tell you that Chicago's stock of multi-unit, high-rise apartment buildings on or near the lakefront includes some of the most expensive housing in the city—and also many of the most wretched public housing projects. As you might expect from the income and poverty maps, the most expensive multi-unit housing is on the north shore and, except for Hyde Park, the most dilapidated housing units are on the south shore.

The map also shows you that single-family, detached homes dominate Chicago's suburbs, as in most large American cities. Only in the southwestern corner of the city do you see a concentration of census tracts that are greater than 75% single-family residences. Most of Chicago is in neither map category, meaning that there must be a more even mix of single-family and multi-unit housing throughout most of the city's South and West sides.

This demographic map interpretation exercise for Chicago shows what you can learn about an area's economic and cultural conditions by carefully viewing and comparing maps. You can see that map comparison is simplified when each map is at the same scale and map projection and is based on the same data collection units, such as census tracts. When comparing maps, it's also important to look at data collected by the same agency or organization so you can be sure the same data collection procedures were used for all map themes. U.S. Census Bureau demographic data are an excellent example of consistent collection methods. Finally, if you are to obtain an unbiased picture of the data, the mapping method used for each map should be as similar as possible. The Chicago maps are again a good example, because map makers used the same gray-tone scheme and the quartile or quintile method of defining class intervals to depict each range of numerical data.

DISEASE AND MORTALITY

Disease and mortality always lurk in the human landscape. Since the mid-1800s, maps have played a fundamental role in **epidemiology**, the study of the incidence, distribution, and control of disease in a population. Dr. John Snow's map of the terrible cholera outbreak in central London during the summer of 1854 is one of the first **epidemiological maps** (the center section of the map is

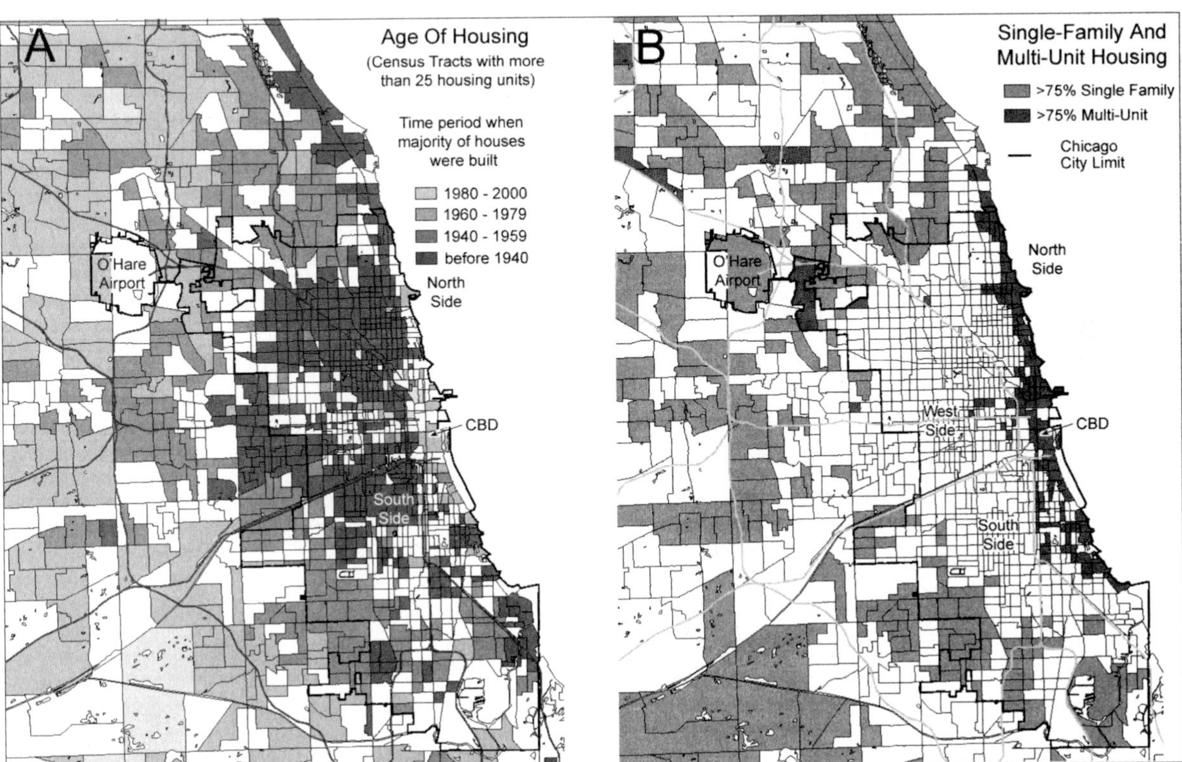

Figure 24.15 Chicago metropolitan area age of housing (A) and single-family and multi-unit housing (B) [adapted from University of Chicago Map Collection digital maps of 1990 age of housing, single-family housing, and multi-unit dwellings].

shown in **Figure 24.16**). The popular story is that Snow discovered the source of the epidemic to be a particular water pump by plotting the locations of deaths and pumps and seeing which pump was in the center of the deaths. Snow's personal account of the outbreak, published in 1855, paints a more accurate picture of how the map was used:

> As soon as I became acquainted with the situation and extent of this irruption of cholera, I suspected some contamination of the water of the much-frequented street-pump in Broad Street, near the end of Cambridge Street; but on examining the water, on the evening of the 3rd September, I found so little impurity in it of an organic nature, that I hesitated to come to a conclusion. Further inquiry, however, showed me that there was no other circumstance or agent common to the circumscribed locality in which this sudden increase of cholera occurred, and not extending beyond it, except the water of the above mentioned pump....
>
> On proceeding to the spot, I found that nearly all the deaths had taken place within a short distance of the pump. There were only ten deaths in houses situated decidedly nearer to another street pump. In five of these cases the families of the deceased persons informed me that they always sent to the pump in Broad Street, as they preferred the water to that of the pump which was nearer. In three other cases, the deceased were children who went to school near the pump in Broad Street. Two of

Figure 24.16 Center section of Dr. John Snow's 1855 map of the 1854 cholera epidemic in central London.

them were known to drink the water; and the parents of the third think it probable that it did so. The other two deaths, beyond the district which this pump supplies, represent only the amount of mortality from cholera that was occurring before the irruption took place.

With regard to the deaths occurring in the locality belonging to the pump, there were sixty-one instances in which I was informed that the deceased persons used to drink the pump-water from Broad Street, either constantly, or occasionally. In six instances I could get no information, owing to the death or departure of every one connected with the deceased individuals; and in six cases I was informed that the deceased persons did not drink the pump-water before their illness.

The result of the inquiry then was, that there had been no particular outbreak or increase of cholera, in this part of London, except among the persons who were in the habit of drinking the water of the above-mentioned pump-well…

The deaths which occurred during this fatal outbreak of cholera are indicated in the accompanying map, [Figure 24.16] as far as I could ascertain them. …

The pump in Broad Street is indicated on the map, as well as all the surrounding pumps to which the public had access at the time.

It requires to be stated that the water of the pump in Marlborough Street, at the end of Carnaby Street, was so impure that many people avoided using it. And I found that the persons who died near this pump in the beginning of September, had water from the Broad Street pump. With regard to the pump in Rupert Street, it will be noticed that some streets which are near to it on the map, are in fact a good way removed, on account of the circuitous road to it. These circumstances being taken into account, it will be observed that the deaths either very much diminished, or ceased altogether, at every point where it becomes decidedly nearer to send to another pump than to the one in Broad Street. It may also be noticed that the deaths are most numerous near to the pump where the water could be more readily obtained. The wide open street in which the pump is situated suffered most, and next the streets branching from it, and especially those parts of them which are nearest to Broad Street. If there have been fewer deaths in the south half of Poland Street than in some other streets leading from Broad Street, it is no doubt because this street is less densely inhabited.

Snow's account clearly shows that he did not use his map to discover the likely source of the cholera epidemic, since from the beginning he suspected water contamination from the Broad Street pump. This suspicion came from his previously held belief that cholera is a gastrointestinal disease transmitted by polluted drinking water. Rather, his map is a record of his investigation into the locations of the cholera deaths and water pumps. The map helped him explain to the public that the polluted water had to be from the Broad Street pump because it was the closest source for the victims.

The real story behind Snow's cholera map is a valuable lesson for those who believe that cause and effect relationships can be determined by comparing maps alone. Visual and statistical correlations among mapped information have helped epidemiologists test biologically plausible hypotheses about the causes of disease and death. But without a sound hypothesis, the associations interpreted from maps may lure you into believing that you have learned something about the cause. The resulting claims that you may hear about disease and mortality "red zones" often create needless worry and distract epidemiologists from the actual causes of disease and death.

Snow's 1855 cholera map initiated the use of maps in studying geographic patterns of disease and mortality. For the next 100 years, mapping of disease in the United States was either in similar small areas or at the state level. By the late 1970s, computer mapping systems had developed to the point that county-level mortality data could be quickly drawn on choropleth maps. Epidemiologists interpreting these maps found previously unnoticed concentrations of counties with unusually high mortality rates for a certain disease. Public health officials visited these areas and found interesting links between mortality and personal habits or working conditions. For instance, a cluster of counties with above-average oral cancer mortality also had a high percentage of tobacco-chewing males.

The *Atlas of United States Mortality*, published in paper, CD, and web-accessible form by the U.S. Department of Health and Human Services, is the most recent collection of national epidemiological maps. Mortality rates were calculated from place and cause of death information recorded on U.S. death certificates. County census data from 1990 were used to compute the mortality rate (deaths per 100,000 population) for each cause of death shown in the atlas. For this atlas, mortality rates have been determined for data collection units called Health Service Areas (HSAs). HSAs are defined as relatively self-contained entities in terms of health care. Most HSAs are composed of several counties serviced by a regional health care facility. The 3,141 counties in the United States are aggregated into 802 HSAs.

Let's look at two pairs of maps taken from the atlas website and converted to monochrome for this book. The atlas contains mortality rate maps for both white and African-American males and females. Data for African-Americans tend to be sparse for many HSAs, however. Thus, maps showing African-American data are often less informative than those showing data for whites.

The first pair of maps (**Figure 24.17**) shows differences in mortality rate for white males and females for all causes shown in the atlas—cancer, heart disease, stroke, pulmonary disease, diabetes, liver disease, HIV, suicide, homicide, and unintentional injury. You might think that a map showing the combined mortality rate from all these causes would reveal little variation across the nation, but this is not the case.

The two maps show that several sections of the country have a considerably higher mortality rate from the combined causes. Notice the band of higher mortality for both males and females stretching from eastern Texas through most of the southeastern U.S., except for Florida and the higher elevation portions of the Appalachian Mountains. The highest rates for both genders appear to be in West Virginia, eastern Kentucky, the Atlantic coastal plain from Georgia through southern Virginia, and along the Mississippi River. On the white female map, you can see additional areas of higher mortality in the Nevada-Utah-Arizona border area and the northwestern corner of California. In contrast, most HSAs in the upper Midwest and Great Plains have male and female mortality rates one-third lower than in the southeast. Southern Florida, Hawaii, and a swath of HSAs from central Utah to northwestern Montana also have lower mortality rates.

These maps show you interesting geographic patterns of higher and lower mortality from a large number of causes other than old age, but tell you nothing about the cultural, economic, or physical conditions that might be responsible for the mortality variations. To gain this deeper understanding of probable cause and effect, you need to find a map for each cause of death and look at the results from epidemiological studies focused on each cause. The second pair of maps (**Figure 24.18**) showing differences in the lung cancer mortality rate for males and females is an excellent example, since many studies have been carried out in an effort to understand the causes of this dreaded disease.

Notice that, for both males and females, the geographic pattern of high and low lung cancer mortality mirrors the pattern for all causes. This correlation between the two sets of maps is in part due to the fact that lung cancer is the second leading cause of death (heart disease is substantially greater) for males and females in the United States. Understanding variations in lung cancer mortality helps explain the pattern of mortality from all causes.

When explaining regional variations in lung cancer mortality, epidemiologists begin with a basic medical fact: The dominant cause of lung can-

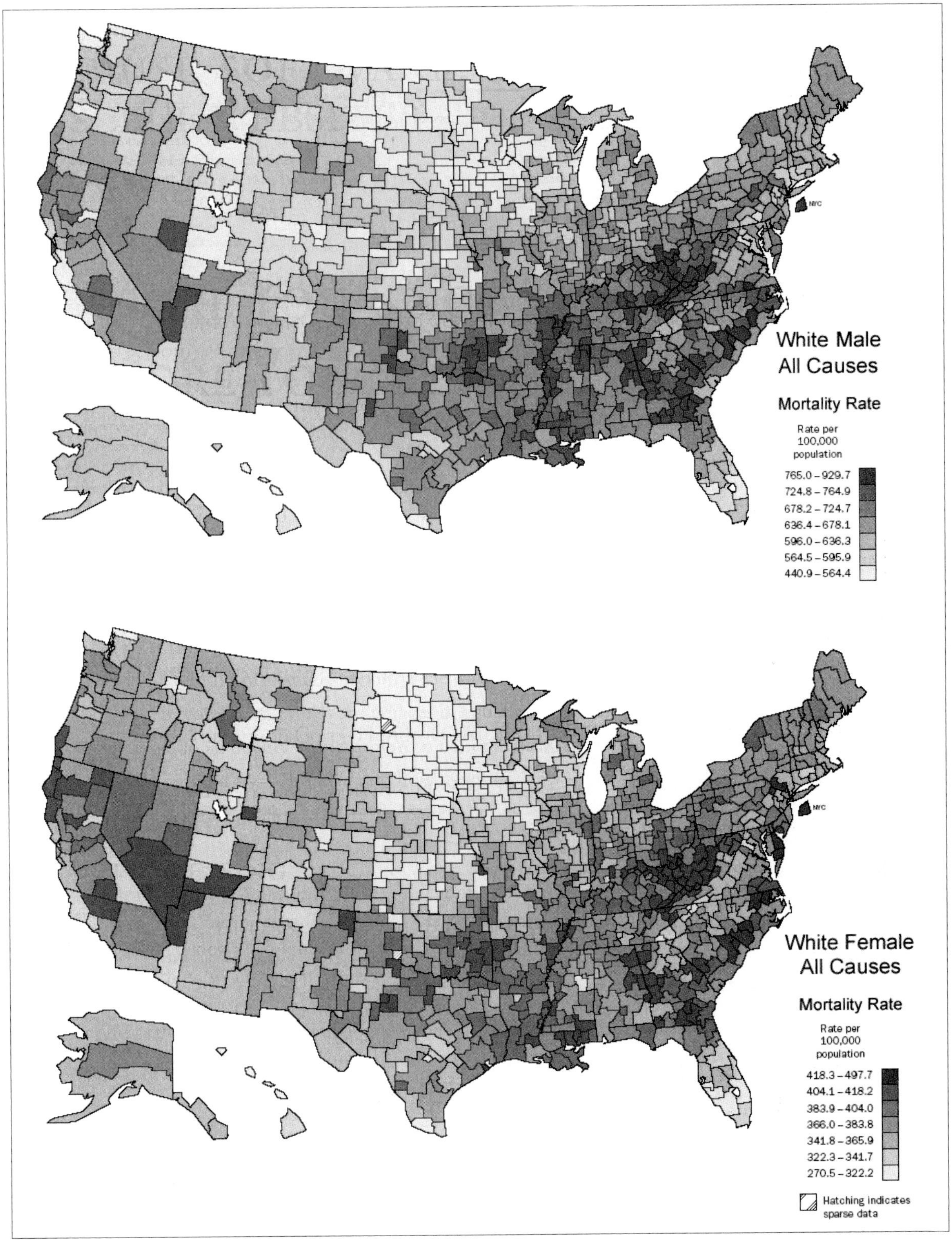

NYC

White Male
All Causes

Mortality Rate

Rate per
100,000
population

765.0 – 929.7
724.8 – 764.9
678.2 – 724.7
636.4 – 678.1
596.0 – 636.3
564.5 – 595.9
440.9 – 564.4

NYC

White Female
All Causes

Mortality Rate

Rate per
100,000
population

418.3 – 497.7
404.1 – 418.2
383.9 – 404.0
366.0 – 383.8
341.8 – 365.9
322.3 – 341.7
270.5 – 322.2

Hatching indicates
sparse data

Figure 24.17 Mortality rates by Health Service Areas for all causes for white males and females [adapted from multicolor maps of the same title in the *Atlas of United States Mortality*].

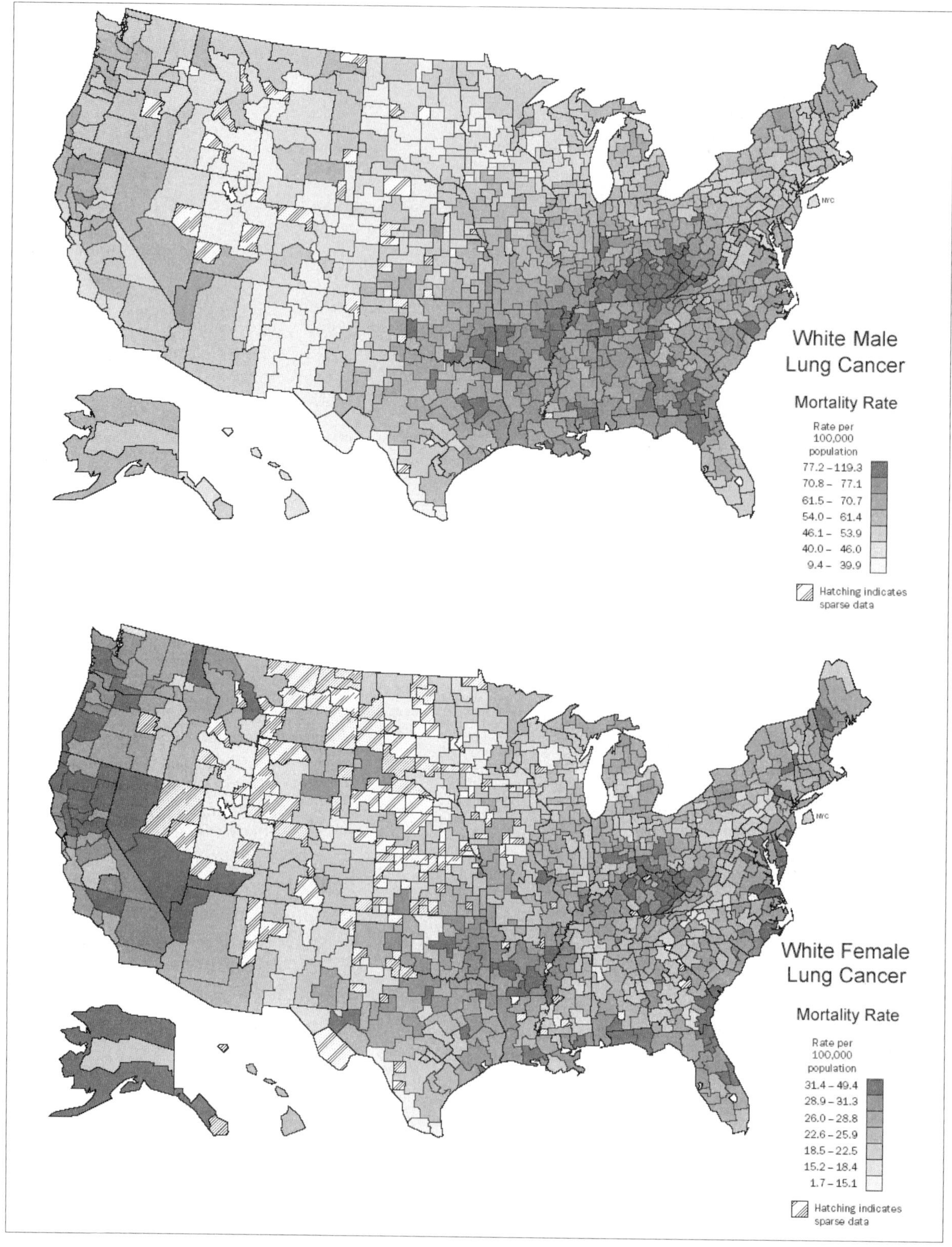

Figure 24.18 Mortality rates by Health Service Areas for lung cancer in white males and females [adapted from multicolor maps of the same title in the *Atlas of United States Mortality*].

cer in the United States is cigarette smoking. Hence, the spatial pattern of smoking should be positively correlated with the pattern of lung cancer mortality. Notice that this correlation helps explain the patterns on the map, but tells you nothing new about the causes of the disease.

Epidemiological field studies show that by the late 1970s, the highest proportion of male smokers was in the South, and by the 1980s the South led the nation in the percentage of adult male smokers at all ages. Hence, smoking trends over the last few decades fit well with the elevated lung cancer mortality across broad portions of the South that you see on the map.

Current mortality rates often are more a reflection of conditions in the near past than in the present. A classic example is white female smoking, which in the 1950s was most prevalent in the West and lowest in the South. But by the 1980s, females in the Pacific Coast and Rocky Mountain states had the lowest smoking rates in the country. The higher lung cancer mortality rates that you see on the west coast are thus more likely associated with earlier than later differences in white female smoking. This time lag is consistent with medical evidence that lung cancer develops slowly over several decades of smoking.

Epidemiologists are certain that the frequency of smoking largely accounts for regional variations in lung cancer mortality. Certain smaller areas with higher mortality rates are associated with dangerous working conditions as well. For instance, the higher male and female mortality in coastal Virginia and Georgia has been associated with asbestos exposure from work in shipyards during World War II. The combination of asbestos exposure and smoking appears to have produced the unusually high lung cancer mortality in these areas.

SELECTED READINGS

Brody, H., et al., "Map-making and myth-making in Broad Street: the London cholera epidemic, 1854", *The Lancet,* 356 (2000), pp. 64-68.

Clay, G., *Close-Up: How to Read the American City* (Chicago: The University of Chicago Press, 1980).

Earle, C., Mathewson, K., and Kenzer, M.S., eds., *Concepts in Human Geography* (Lanham, MD: Rowman & Littlefield Publishers, Inc., 1996).

Hamnett, C., ed., *Social Geography: A Reader* (London: Edward Arnold, 1996).

Hardwick, S.W., and Holtgrieve, D.G., *Patterns on Our Planet* (New York: Macmillan Publishing Co., 1990).

Hart, J.F., *The Look of the Land* (Englewood Cliffs, NJ: Prentice-Hall, 1975).

Hartshorn, T.A., and Alexander, J.W., *Economic Geography*, 3rd ed. (Englewood Cliffs, NJ: Prentice-Hall, 1988).

Jackson, R.H., and Hudman, L.E., *Cultural Geography: People, Places and Environment* (St. Paul, MN: West Publishing Co., 1990).

Jordon, T.G., and Rowntree, L., *The Human Mosaic*, 5th ed. (New York: Harper & Row, Publishers, 1990).

Meining, D.W., *The Interpretation of Ordinary Landscapes: Geographical Essays* (New York: Oxford University Press, 1979).

Pickle, L.W. et al., *Atlas of United States Mortality* (Hyattsville, MD: U.S. Department of Health and Human Services, 1996).

Raitz, K.B., and Hart, J.F., *Cultural Geography on Topographic Maps* (New York: John Wiley & Sons, 1975).

Richardson, B.F., *Atlas of Cultural Features: A Comparative Study With Topographic Maps and Aerial Photographs of Man's Imprint on the Land* (Northbrook, IL: Hubbard Press, 1973).

Snow, J., *On the Mode of Communication of Cholera*, 2nd ed. (London: John Churchill, 1855).

Watts, M.T., *Reading the Landscape of America*, revised ed. (New York: Collier Books, 1975).

White, P.T., "This Land of Ours—How Are We Using It?", *The National Geographic Magazine*, 150, 1 (July 1976), pp. 20-67.

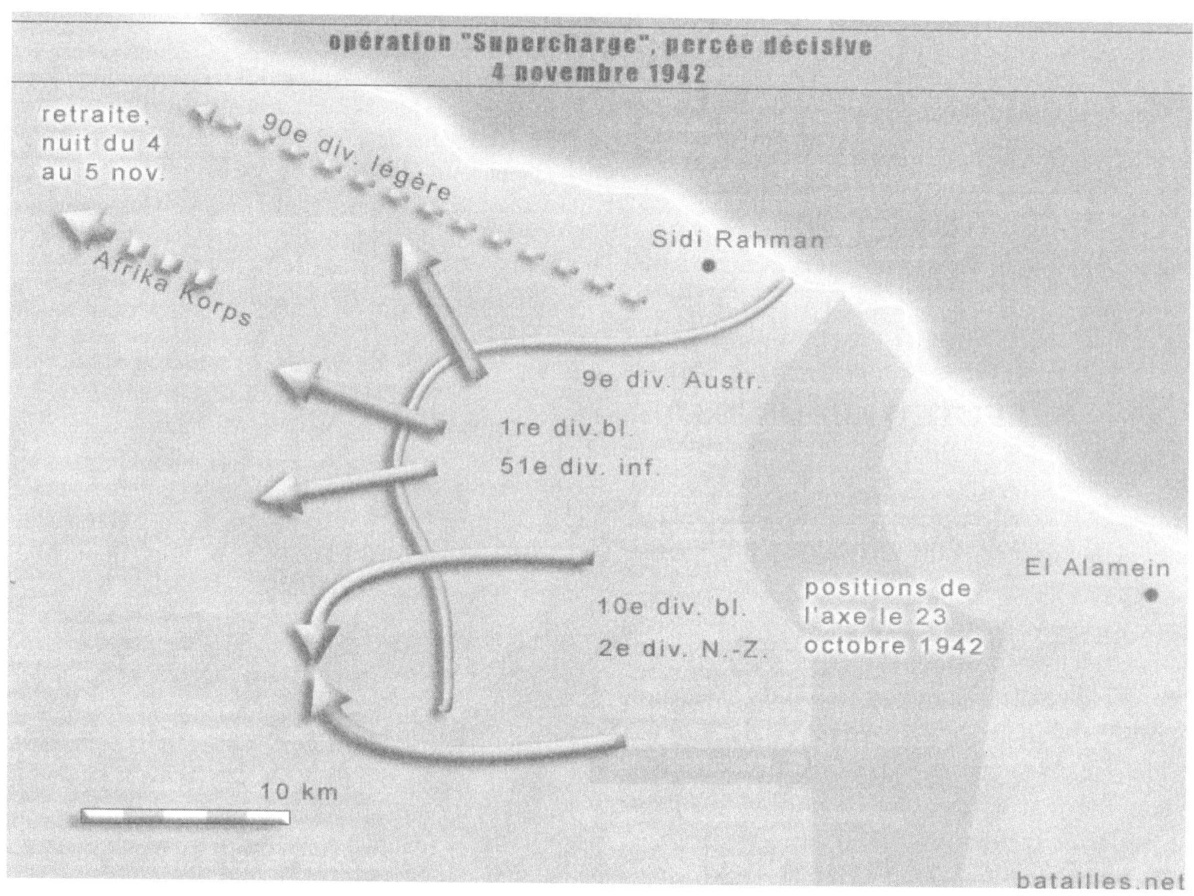

This World War II military map shows the desired, not actual, movement of troops and battle outcome.

CHAPTER TWENTY-FIVE
MAPS AND REALITY

It is not down on any map: true places never are.
—Herman Melville, Moby Dick

25

CHAPTER TWENTY-FIVE

MAPS AND REALITY

. . . the very best map-reader has to suffer some severe shocks when he comes face to face with reality.
(Josephine Tey, *The Man in the Queue*, p. 138)

This observation about map use, disquieting though it may be, is as important as anything you've learned about maps. Your ultimate aim, after all, is not to understand maps. Maps are just one means to your real goal—understanding the world.

If you don't look beyond map symbols to the reality they represent, you may defeat your purpose and end up with a warped view of your surroundings. The gravest accusation we can make of maps is that they may taint our judgments about the environment. In this chapter, then, we will look at the hazards of putting too much faith in maps, of not realizing their limitations, and of forgetting to look beyond symbols to the real world.

THE MAP AS REALITY

We began this book with the statement that maps mirror the world. Therefore, we suggested, the better your knowledge of maps, the wiser your spatial behavior. If we carry this analogy further, we see that some cautions are built in. A mirror is a useful tool, but it shows only a piece of reality. No one would confuse its reflection with the real thing. Yet a surprising number of people treat the map's reflection of the world as if it were reality.

Substituting maps for reality encourages a mechanical rather than humane view. A statement such as "the explosion wiped the town off the map" ignores the fact that a real town has suffered. Such fuzzy thinking can cause a confusion of cause and effect. How often do you hear people speak of "the changing map" when they're referring to a changing world? They see maps as actors rather than reflectors of the world. This viewpoint suggests that if we could keep maps from changing, we could keep the world from changing—or that by changing a map, we could change the world.

The extremes to which such faulty reasoning can carry us are portrayed in the novel *Catch-22*. The men in a bomb squadron have been ordered to bomb Bologna the next day. They stare pleadingly at the bomb line on the map, as if that mapped line were itself to blame.

> "I really can't believe it," Clevinger exclaimed to Yossarian in a voice rising and falling in protest and wonder.
>
> "It's a complete reversion to primitive superstition. They're confusing cause and effect. It makes as much sense as knocking on wood or crossing your fingers. They really believe that we wouldn't have to fly that mission tomorrow if someone would only tiptoe up to the map in the middle of the night and move the bomb line over Bologna. Can you imagine? You and I must be the only rational ones left."
>
> In the middle of the night Yossarian knocked on wood, crossed his fingers, and tiptoed out of his tent to move the bomb line up over Bologna.
>
> (Heller, p. 117)

The next morning the men consult the map. Sure enough, it shows that Bologna has been captured. The mission is canceled, and everyone is happy.

The outcome here is a pleasant one. Usually, though, you get in trouble when you substitute maps for reality. Sometimes the result is merely inconvenience and narrow-mindedness. But the consequences can be more serious, as you will see.

Cartographic Artifacts

When you look beyond maps and come face to face with the real world, as Josephine Tey pointed out in the quote beginning this chapter, you're in for some shocks. One shock you have to face is that much of what you see on a map doesn't exist in reality. Many map features are pure cartographic fiction—the result of the mapping process. The first time you realize this, you may react as indignantly as Huck Finn did while on a balloon trip with Tom Sawyer. When Huck commented that they were flying over Illinois, Tom asked how he could be sure. Huck replied:

> "I know by the color. We're right over Illinois yet. And you can see for yourself that Indiana ain't in sight."
>
> "I wonder what's the matter with you, Huck. You know by the color?"
>
> "Yes, of course I do."
>
> "What's the color got to do with it?"
>
> "It's got everything to do with it. Illinois is green, Indiana is pink. You show me any pink down there, if you can. No sir; it's green."
>
> "Indiana pink? Why, what a lie!"
>
> "It ain't no lie; I've seen it on the map, and it's pink."

> You never see a person so aggravated and disgusted. He says:
>
> "Well, if I was such a numskull as you, Huck Finn, I would jump over. Seen it on the map! Huck Finn, did you reckon the states was the same color out-of-doors as they are on the map?"
>
> "Tom Sawyer, what's a map for? Ain't it to learn you facts?"
>
> "Of course."
>
> "Well, then, how's it going to do that if it tells lies?
>
> That's what I want to know."
>
> (Twain, *Tom Sawyer Abroad*, pp. 42-43)

Huck's question is a good one: How can a map give you facts if it tells lies? The answer is central to an understanding of maps. To tell the truth, a map must lie. As you saw in Chapter 10, generalization is required to transform reality to a map. Generalization is a helpful way to organize and reduce the detail in the environment. But the generalization process adds cartographic artifacts that bear little or no relation to reality. The danger is that the artifacts will so dominate the map that you'll mistake them for real aspects of the environment.

Most map readers aren't as naive as Huck. Few of us expect a map's colors to be the same on the ground or a tree's symbol to look like its leafy real-life counterpart. It's obvious that colors and other symbols are artifacts of the mapping process and have nothing to do with the environment. Yet even sophisticated map users can mistake cartographic artifacts for real geographical features.

Image maps, created from aerial photographs, are a good example, since many people don't think of them as maps at all. Photos, they reason, can't contain misleading artifacts because they show the environment exactly as it is. This is one of the biggest map misconceptions. Photos, like all maps, contain distortions and artifacts of the methods used to make them.

For one thing, atmospheric and light conditions can alter tones and textures on photos. As you saw in Chapter 9, this problem is especially clear on mosaics, made by fitting several photos together. A mosaic of air photos often shows the mottled effect of different tones and textures. Some lines joining the photos will be unnoticeable, while others will stand out clearly. If you don't realize how the image map was made, you could confuse these artifacts from mosaic-making with real environmental patterns. Like Huck, you could expect to see in reality what was only the map maker's technique.

Even on a single air photo, features can vary dramatically in tone. A lake in one corner of a photo may appear as a light tone, for example, while a similar lake in another corner appears dark. You might jump to the conclusion that these variations indicate different water depths, turbidity levels, or algae growth. But if the map's other lakes show the same light-to-dark trend, you can assume that light reflection, not water quality, provides the explanation.

Flaws in the photographic process cause other artifacts. It's common, for instance, to find streaks across an image map. For you, the map user, it doesn't matter whether these streaks are caused by the film, camera, development, or reproduction. The effect is the same. You just want to be sure you don't come up with some exotic interpretation for a feature that doesn't exist.

You can't anticipate every possible artifact. The best defense is to learn to recognize the effects of various mapping methods. Envision these methods' impact on the map's appearance. This will keep you from interpreting something as reality that in fact is only a cartographic artifact.

The Missing Essence

The fact that many things on maps don't exist in reality is only one side of the coin. Even more serious is the fact that many things in reality are missing from maps. Indeed, it seems to be the most beautiful and humanizing parts of our lives that are absent from maps. In his *Diary* (November 10, 1860), Thoreau laments the inadequacy of a map:

> How little there is on an ordinary map! How little, I mean, that concerns the walker and the lover of nature. Between the lines indicating roads is a plain blank space in the form of a square or triangle or polygon or segment of a circle, and there is naught to distinguish this from another area of similar size and form. Yet the one may be covered, in fact, with a primitive oak wood, like that of Boxboro, waving and creaking in the wind, such as may make the reputation of a county, while the other is a stretching plain with scarcely a tree on it. The wauling woods, the dells and glades and green banks and smiling fields, the huge boulders, etc., etc., are not on the map. . . .

By condensing geographical phenomena into symbols, we make the environment easy to study, but we also make it sterile. The essence of life, that which is most crucial, rarely is found on a map. In *Travels With Charley* (p. 71), Steinbeck records which highways he took on his cross-country trip and adds:

> I can report this because I have a map before me, but what I remember has no reference to the numbers and colored lines and squiggles.

Maps seldom capture life's vivid, meaningful experiences—the touches, sounds, smells, and linkages between people and their surroundings. The price of losing these traits is that we may forget the relation between a feature or activity and its map symbol.

Imaginative Map Use

To gain the most from maps, you must be willing to stretch your imagination, allowing symbols to conjure up their full meaning in your mind. Map symbols are meaningless in themselves. They are meant to direct your thought beyond the map to the environment. Here, for example, is what an imaginative map reader saw in one line symbol:

> Finally, there was the fact that this was a frontier region. That meant far more than a line on a map. It meant all the treachery, the corruption, the bravado, and the watchfulness of such a confrontation.
>
> (Drummond, *Cable Car*, p. 73)

Every symbol holds such hidden meanings if you look for them. It's up to you to step from map to real world—and a giant step it is. Getting at realities beneath appearances is never easy. Can you imagine a map that evokes images of disaster less than the "disaster map" in **Figure 25.1**? At a glance, you'd never know it portrays floods, tornados, and other disasters. The matter-of-fact symbols don't begin to show the devastated fields, shattered towns, homeless people, and ruined lives caused by these disasters. It takes a vast imaginative leap to look at such symbols and picture reality.

One person who has perfected the technique of using imagination to look beyond map symbols is the armchair traveler. Before travel was as widespread as it is today, writers often remarked that those who had never traveled could have exciting journeys by map. In *Don Quixote* (Vol. 3, p. 80), Cervantes commented that one can "journey all over the universe in a map, without the expense and fatigue of traveling, without suffering the inconveniences of heat, cold, hunger, and thirst."

A map can inspire an imaginative person to enter the reality it depicts. Joseph Conrad (*Heart of Darkness*, p. 33) has noted the imaginative appeal of maps:

> Now when I was a little chap I had a passion for maps. I would look for hours at South America, or Africa, or Australia, and lose myself in all the glories of exploration. At that time there were many blank spaces on the earth, and when I saw one that looked particularly inviting on a map (but they all look that) I would put my finger on it and say, "When I grow up I will go there."

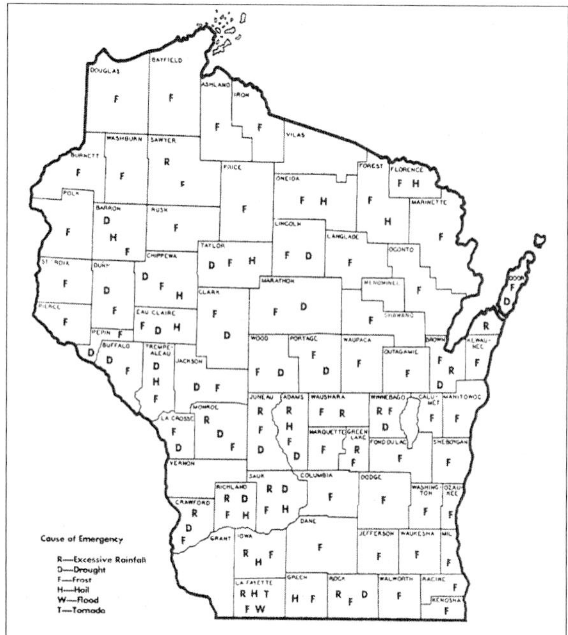

Figure 25.1 This map shows the 68 counties in Wisconsin which were designated "disaster areas" because of crop loss in 1974. Note how hard it is to achieve a visual impression due to the poor graphic design.

The fact that even blank spaces can generate excitement underscores the imagination's power to give maps depth. As Aldo Leopold put it:

> To those devoid of imagination, a blank place on the map is a useless waste; to others, the most valuable part.

In *Deliverance*, James Dickey (pp. 7-8) also suggests a map's ability to evoke more than the composite of its symbols. In the novel, some friends plan a trip down a river that will soon be obliterated by a new dam. For Ed, the narrator, the map has a power and vitality—almost a life of its own.

> "When they take another survey and rework this map," Lewis said, "all this in here will be blue. . . ."
>
> I leaned forward and concentrated down into the invisible shape he had drawn, trying to see the changes that would come, the nighttime rising of dammed water bringing a new lake up with its choice lots, its marinas and beer cans, and also trying to visualize the land as Lewis said it was at that moment, unvisited and free. . . . I looked around the bar and then back into the map, picking up the river where we would enter it. . . .

The author's wording gives life to the map; we can almost see the river running. By using such phrases as "looked into the map," Dickey suggests that a map isn't just something at which you glance but something into which you can see. For Ed, the map holds an unknown dimension, wonder, and excitement. He can see a crooked blue line on paper and at the same time a raging river. As he studies the map, he sees even more (p.13):

> It [the map] was certainly not much from the standpoint of design. The high ground, in tan and an even paler tone of brown, meandered in and out of various shades and shapes of green, and there was nothing to call you or stop you on one place or the other. Yet the eye could not leave the whole; there was a harmony of some kind. Maybe, I thought, it's because this tries to show what exists. And also because it represents something that is going to change, for good. There, near my left hand, a new color, a blue, would seep upward into the paper, and I tried to move my mind there and nowhere else and imagine a single detail that, if I didn't see it that weekend, I never would; tried to make out a deer's eye in the leaves, tried to pick up a single stone.

This ability to let your imagination carry you from map to reality is the sign of skilled map use. Once you have this knack, maps will be truly beautiful and useful to you, evoking images and emotions beyond the printed paper or computer screen. But if you lack the imagination to move from a map's abstract image to the concrete world, you will never realize the map's full value.

Map Abuses

When you treat maps as reality, it becomes easy to view the environment in impersonal, machine-like terms. Environmental features are dwarfed on maps. People are invisible. The cultural environment (farms, cities, roads) looks like a child's board game. The world is reduced to an unchanging background against which you play out your life. If you don't remind yourself how limited maps are, you can lose sight of that "missing essence" which is found on no map but only in reality.

In *I Was a Savage*, a Nigerian educated in the United States describes his eagerness to return to his people and share the wonders of maps. To his surprise, his father was less than enthusiastic:

> Maps are liars, he told me briefly. . . . The things that hurt do not show on the map. The truth of a place is in the joy and the hurt that come from it. I had best not put my trust in anything as inadequate as a map, he counseled.
>
> (Prince Modupe, p. 147)

Many preliterate people share this distrust of maps, and with good reason. Maps separate you from the environment. If you see yourself as part of your environment, you know you can't harm it without harming yourself. If you reduce your environment to symbols on a map, however, you're more apt to abuse it. You can then misuse maps just as you can mutilate a person's photo while you wouldn't think of injuring the real person. There's an important difference, though: When you paint a mustache on a political poster, the politician doesn't suffer. But when your behavior results from abusive map use, reality may bear the consequences.

When environmental decision makers treat a map as mere symbols and disregard the real-life emotions it represents, the results can be disastrous. City planners, for instance, may be tempted to build a new freeway along the line that looks straightest and most convenient on the map. But the route may disrupt thousands of people's lives or the ecology of an area where an endangered animal species lives. Thus, it might be better to take a more roundabout path, along which there are no homes or animals facing extinction. The map way isn't always the best way.

It can't be overstressed that the reason for studying maps is to understand the real world, not the map world. When you make plans based on maps, it's not the map but reality which stands to gain or lose. This fact may seem obvious. Yet time and again, people draw map boundaries for a project without regard for the people or region to be affected. Subdivisions are constructed, dams built, neighborhoods "renewed," all without due thought for those who will suffer.

This is also one of the tragedies of war. Many people die needlessly because the way that looked simplest on the map wasn't the wisest way in the field. A commander may study a map, decide that a certain spot would make a good observation point, and give the order to march. While peering at symbols on a map, it's convenient to ignore such things as terrain or climate or morale. Yet these factors will influence the soldiers who must obey the orders. While it takes only a second to put that X on the map, it may take millions of dollars of equipment, weeks of time, and a terrible toll of lives to carry out the mission.

People who surround themselves with maps are liable to arrive at cold strategies, untempered by feelings, if they forget who or what will bear the consequences of their decisions. In *The Naked and the Dead* (p. 567), Norman Mailer describes such an unimaginative map reader. Major Dalleson, making strategy decisions with maps during the war, "had a picture for a moment of the troops moving sullenly along a jungle trail, swearing at the heat, but he couldn't connect that to the figures on the map. An insect crawled sluggishly over his desk and he flicked it off." As casually as this, as casually as he brushes an insect from his desk, a decision is made and people's fate decided.

Major General Cummings, another *Naked and the Dead* character, wanted to reduce reality to mere "figures on the map." He was frustrated that soldiers' emotions kept his plans from being as effective in real life as in theory. At one point (p. 277), Cummings threw down his pencil and "stared with febrile loathing at the map board by his cot. By now, it was a taunt to him." He could control the map world but not the reality.

War encourages military officers to substitute maps for reality. Miles from the battlefield, surrounded by "complete" map intelligence, they find the consequences of their actions easy to ignore. To make a few lines on a map is painless. To visualize the soldiers and their loved ones, the landscapes and ecosystems whose doom is sealed by those mapped lines is another matter. How different it would be if the decision makers were there when their decisions were carried out!

Even the soldiers who carry out these decisions aren't always in direct touch with reality, as an article about bomb crews over Vietnam tells us:

> The maps used by the crews show almost no place names. One general said that kept the maps uncluttered. It also keeps them impersonal. The targets are given code numbers and are marked by intersecting map coordinates. "For all you know," one pilot said, "you could be bombing New York City."
>
> (The *New York Times*, October 13, 1972, p. 12)

In this case, technology has removed military personnel from the reality of fighting and killing and made possible warfare by remote control. The bomb crew, with only their maps to go by, need never face the destruction they have caused.

Likewise, the media referred to the Persian Gulf War as the "Nintendo war" and praised "smart" bombs for their "surgical strikes." As *Newsweek* (January 28, 1991) described it:

> It all seemed effortless, antiseptic and surreal: casualties were very light, at least among the attackers, and the high-tech gadgets in America's multibillion-dollar arsenal seemed to work with surgical lethality. Like a day at the office, one pilot said.

Map abuses are by no means solely responsible for war's atrocities. But we can trace many military difficulties to maps' insensitivity to crucial human and environmental features—and to map users' failure to take this missing essence into account.

All maps aren't equally insensitive, of course. Since some types represent reality better than others, decisions based on one map won't be the same as those based on another. Image maps, for instance, show much more information than conventional maps and therefore aren't as likely to be abused. The consequences of military actions are also more evident on an image map, providing more information for decision making.

Degraded Environmental Image

Another result of treating maps as reality may be to hinder us from experiencing a rich, full life, as Steinbeck (*Travels With Charley*, p. 23) reminds us:

> For weeks I had studied maps, large-scale and small, but maps are not reality at all—they can be tyrants. I know people who are so immersed in road maps that they never see the countryside they pass through, and others who, having traced a route, are held to it as though held by flanged wheels to rails.

You would be wise to adopt Steinbeck's suspicion of maps as complete records of reality. As he notes, a map represents only a few of many truths. Its purpose is to help us see more, but if you expect too much of it, it may keep you from seeing anything.

> There are map people whose joy is to lavish more attention on the sheets of colored paper than on the colored land rolling by. I have listened to accounts by such travelers in which every road number was remembered, every mileage recalled, and every little countryside discovered. Another kind of traveler requires to know in terms of maps exactly where he is pin-pointed every moment, as

> though there were some kind of safety in black and red lines, in dotted indications and squirming blue of lakes and the shadings that indicate mountains.
>
> (*Travels With Charley*, p. 70)

By realizing a map's limitations, Steinbeck found his cross-country trip far more satisfying than his friends who were slaves to maps. For him, a map was useful as a framework for his memories. Maps enhanced rather than detracted from his enjoyment because he was wisely aware that "maps are not reality at all."

Abstract Decision Making

Although there are dangers in treating maps as reality, at times such a viewpoint has advantages. Decision makers who deal with emotional issues (and pressure groups) may find it easier to do their jobs when they can work with symbols. Our values and feelings are less aroused when working with abstractions than when confronting ugly or distasteful issues directly. Thus, an objective, removed position may be desirable; otherwise, short-term satisfaction might compromise the long-range good.

In *Night Flight*, Saint-Exupéry describes a decision maker who has learned that only by treating maps as reality can he do his duty. The character Riviére has the job of tracing the flights of pilots who carry the mail at night. In the pioneering days of air mail delivery depicted in this novel, such flights involved great hazard, and Riviére knows that each time he sends a plane into the darkness, he risks a pilot's life. As he stares at the map with the airlines traced in red, he muses (p. 48):

> "On the face of it, a pretty scheme enough—but it's ruthless. When one thinks of all the lives, young fellows' lives, it has cost us! It's a fine, solid thing and we must bow to its authority, of course; but what a host of problems it presents!" With Riviére, however, nothing mattered save the end in view.

For a moment Riviére has allowed his imagination to make the leap from the cold, solid "face" of the map to the reality it symbolizes. To accomplish "the end in view," however, he must veer abruptly from this reality and think of the map as an abstract thing. Otherwise, he couldn't keep sending pilots into such danger. He would be better off, perhaps, would suffer less, if he were a more unimaginative map reader.

Map readers are, in a way, like doctors, who must put emotional distance between themselves and their patients. Otherwise, tragic cases may impair their judgment. Some doctors succeed so well that patients complain they're treated as diseases or broken bones, not as the frightened people they are. We would hope our doctors would strike a balance between emotion and rationality. When we use maps to make decisions that affect other people, we must achieve just such a balance. Overly emotional decisions are as undesirable as overly insensitive ones. When we need to transcend our human limitations, maps can provide a useful counter-balancing perspective.

REALITY AS A MAP

We've seen how dangerous it is to treat maps as reality. Just as dangerous is the mistake of treating reality as if it were a map—of thinking that the world is laid out in map-like form. How many people look down at the earth from an airplane and say, "It looks exactly like a map"? Such a statement is comparable to gazing at the Grand Canyon and remarking, "It looks just like a postcard"; this attitude strips an incredible sight of its grandeur. Likewise, when we view the world as a map, the land becomes a thing—fragmented, split, weakened, drained.

Regrettably, confusing reality with maps is a common occurrence. We all know people who claim to have visited nearly every state in the nation; when pressed, they admit that all they saw of many states was an airport or freeway. Even business executives who cross the United States hundreds of times may be familiar with little more than the views from Holiday Inns. Although the map says they're in a distant state, in reality they may as well be at the Holiday Inn in their hometown.

Marlowe, Joseph Conrad's narrator in *Heart of Darkness* (p. 48), describes the map-like way we often view an unfamiliar environment:

> "Next day I left that station at last, with a caravan of sixty men, for a two-hundred-mile tramp.
>
> No use telling you much about that. Paths, paths, everywhere; a stamped-in network of paths spreading over the empty land, through long grass, through burnt grass, through thickets, down and up chilly ravines, up and down stony hills ablaze with heat; and a solitude, a solitude, nobody, not a hut."

To maintain his sanity in the African jungle, Marlowe reduces the environment to a series of connected pathways, like lines on a map. The abundance of plant and animal life between those paths he dismisses as "empty land."

Many people simplify the world this way when thrust into an unfamiliar setting. But it's a bad habit to develop. With this map-like conception of reality, it's easy to lose your orientation. Whatever is unknown becomes, as it did for Marlowe, a wilderness to be avoided.

"Wilderness" doesn't have to be the backwoods kind, of course; for some people, a trip to the central city is as adventuresome as a journey to the Yukon. We fear what we don't understand. If we would stop infusing our world with the structure of a map and explore its true variety, we might find many of our fears unfounded.

The error of treating reality as a map can affect your whole perception of yourself and your world. The following warning about photographs applies to all types of maps:

> Photography as art has had a lot to do with the way we perceive the world and react to it, and to some extent the accepted image of our environment is one that the art of photography has given us.
>
> They (photographers) have taught us a way to look at the world, and in turn, we see the world their way.
>
> And that is the rub. The curious thing about images of the environment is that they inevitably structure reality. Our perception is trained by them. . . .
>
> In architecture and urbanism the photograph has become as valid as the thing itself.
>
> (Ada Louise Huxtable, *The New York Times*, Nov. 25, 1973, Section 2, p. 26)

So it is with a map-like view of reality. Maps are no more objective than photographs; they reflect the way we view the world.

SURVIVAL

The deficiency of both treating the "map as reality" and "reality as a map" is that both separate you from your environment. These views encourage you to ignore the interrelationships upon which your quality of life and your survival depend.

Maps are a metaphor for a limited kind of experience. Mapped features may have as little relation to the world as a telephone number to its subscriber. You must place maps in perspective as a limited communication device, only one of many. To put too much emphasis on maps is to screen out much of what is crucial to environmental behavior.

Rather than see the environment as map makers do, biased by the tools of their profession, take an omniscient viewpoint. Unite yourself and the environment in all phases of experience. Only when you see the whole environment as one system, as events separate but united in time and space, will you appreciate all that maps have to offer. While viewing a map, you can then bridge the distance between you and the environment and look *into* rather than *at* map symbols.

This task of visualizing mapped features in all their depth won't be simple. It will take effort and experience. The job will be hardest when you're sitting in an environmentally controlled room scrutinizing artificial map symbols, far removed from the phenomena under study and the procedures used to create the map. In addition, your job is complicated by an obvious but often overlooked fact: We all are human.

We All Are Human

Mapping, as a communication process, is influenced by human shortcomings throughout. We, map maker and map user alike, are fallible. We crave simplicity; we are strong in some areas and weak in others; we are biased in many ways; and our integrity, judgment, and insight are never beyond question. We are human, and the mapping process is built around this fact.

Every map is a reflection of a myriad of decisions made by the map maker. It's not a copy but a semblance of reality, filtered by the map maker's motives and perceptions. The map is partly a representation of reality and partly a product of its maker. The map maker's knowledge, skill, and integrity all enter the map design. If 10 map makers were given the same mapping task, the results would vary widely. Some of their maps would be effective and pleasing, while others would fail to communicate or would actually mislead.

But the blame for poor map communication doesn't rest entirely with the map maker. You, the map user, approach maps with the bias of your experience, motives, and skill. Your biggest danger is that you'll see what you want to see or anticipate seeing. You can guard against this tendency by keeping an open mind.

Sometimes the penalty for being a human link in map use is disaster. A pilot misreads a map, and an airplane crashes. Deadly accidents occur when drivers miss their freeway exit and try to turn back. Soldiers are bombed by their own comrades when map coordinates are misunderstood.

Luckily, the price of misusing maps is usually more frustrating than disastrous for most of us. And even this frustration can be reduced if you understand the nature of maps. There's no way to eliminate human failings or map limitations, but once you know they exist you can learn to live with them.

Living With Map Limitations

You've seen how maps' abstract, generalized nature introduces the potential for error and abuse. Yet these same qualities are what make maps so valuable for showing the big picture. If a map's strengths are also its weaknesses, the opposite is true as well. A map is remarkably useful as long as you don't ask it to do things for which it wasn't designed. You mustn't, for instance, ask a map to be the same as reality; if it were, it would lose its unique clarifying function.

One problem with maps is that they are rarely tailored to the requirements of the individual user. Therefore, they are seldom perfect for specific needs. Most map makers have only a vague idea of who will use their maps. But you can learn to live with this map weakness, too. Maps are available in infinite variety. You can save yourself grief by finding the best map available for each situation, rather than using one map for all purposes.

If you're aware of map limitations, it's usually easy to make up for them. It makes sense to bring as much experience and information as possible to bear on map interpretation. The best navigators are those who augment map information with all the direct "ground truth" they can. Pilots don't land their planes or dock their ships with maps; they rely on direct visual or instrumental contact during those final, crucial moments. Part of using maps shrewdly is knowing when to go beyond them.

Every map represents just one way of looking at reality. If one map doesn't serve your needs, don't become disenchanted with all maps. Perhaps you can find another map that better fits your requirements. Or maybe you need to supplement your map or turn to another source of information. But if you give up on maps entirely, you are cheating yourself, for at some other time they may be exactly what you need. You must strike a balance between too much faith and not enough faith in maps.

In this chapter, we have stressed that maps are incomplete, limited, and often faulty. But maps needn't be perfect to be useful, as Alvin Toffler points out in *Future Shock* (p. 6):

> Even error has its uses. The maps of the world drawn by the medieval cartographers were so hopelessly inaccurate, so filled with factual error, that they elicit condescending smiles today when almost the entire surface of the earth has been charted. Yet the great explorers could never have discovered the New World without them. Nor could the better, more accurate maps of today been drawn until men, working with the limited evidence available to them, set down on paper their bold conceptions of worlds they had never seen.

Those old maps, so pitifully lacking, served an indispensable function by moving us the next step to something better. Our maps of today serve the same purpose. We are on a long path toward understanding the world, and every new map, imperfect though it may be, carries us one step closer to our goal.

SELECTED READINGS

Henrickson, A.K., "The Map as an 'Idea': The Role of Cartographic Imagery During the Second World War," *The American Cartographer*, 2, 1 (April 1975), pp.19-53.

Keates, J.S., "Symbols and Meaning in Topographic Maps," *International Yearbook of Cartography*, 12 (1972), pp. 168-180.

Monmonier, M., *How to Lie With Maps* (Chicago: University of Chicago Press, 1991).

Monmonier, M., *Maps, Distortion & Meaning*, Resource Paper No. 77 (Washington, DC: Association of American Geographers, 1977).

Muehrcke, P.C., "Beyond Abstract Map Symbols," *Journal of Geography*, 73, 8 (November 1973), pp. 35-52.

Muehrcke, P.C., "Map Reading and Abuse," *Journal of Geography*, 73, 5 (May 1974), pp. 11-23.

Muehrcke, P.C., and Muehrcke, J.O., "Maps in Literature," *Geographical Review*, 64, 3 (July 1974), pp. 317-338.

Pickles, J., ed., *Ground Truth: The Social Implications of Geographic Information Systems* (New York: The Guilford Press, 1995).

Quam, L.O., "The Use of Maps in Propaganda," *Journal of Geography*, 42, 1 (January 1943), pp. 21-32.

Ristow, W.W., "Journalistic Cartography," *Surveying and Mapping*, 17, 4 (October-December 1957), pp. 369-390.

Robinson, A.H., and Bartz-Petchenik, B., *The Nature of Maps: Essays Toward Understanding Maps and Mapping* (Chicago: University of Chicago Press, 1976).

Wood, D., and Fels, J., "Designs on Signs: Myth and Meaning in Maps," *Cartographica*, 23, 3 (1986), pp. 54-103.

Wright, J.K., "Map Makers Are Human: Comments on the Subjective in Maps," *Geographical Review*, 32, 4 (October 1942), pp. 527-544.

APPENDIX A
DIGITAL CARTOGRAPHIC DATABASES

RASTER DATA

- Scanned Topographic Maps
- Digital Elevation Models
  - High-Resolution DEMs
  - Medium-Resolution DEMs
  - Low-Resolution DEMs
- Raster Thematic Maps
  - Weather-Climate Maps
  - Landcover Maps
  - Global Population Maps

VECTOR DATA

- TIGER
- The National Map
- Digital Line Graphs
- WDBII
- Digital Chart of the World
- Commercial Databases

APPENDIX A

DIGITAL CARTOGRAPHIC DATABASES

Digital data are the foundation of computer mapping systems. Each year, more geographical information is gathered in digital form directly in the field. But, for the most part, numerical information suitable for computer mapping is the result of converting existing printed maps into digital files. Since different data formats have been used in developing digital cartographic databases, mapping software must be matched to these different ways of organizing the data.

There are two fundamentally different data formats. Digital scanning and printing technology uses a matrix or grid of tiny cells called **pixels**. In this **raster format**, data are recorded, stored, and processed on a pixel-by-pixel basis.

The alternative to the raster format is to think of the environment as being a collection of **features** of varying geometrical character. These features may be represented in a database as points, lines, areas, and continuous surfaces defined by x,y, and sometimes z coordinates. We use the term **vector format** when referring to coordinate data describing features.

RASTER DATA

The simplest way map makers convert existing maps to digital form is to scan the map as a whole. Many raster databases are available. Some were made using a camcorder or digital camera set up to download individual image frames to a computer. Others were made by scanning maps with desktop electronic scanners capable of recording the full range of colors found on a printed map. Because this process is so straightforward, raster cartographic databases are common.

The advantage of raster databases is that they can be created relatively quickly and inexpensively from existing maps. A disadvantage is that only the information on the original map is included in the database. The original map design dominates subsequent displays of the information. Furthermore, the map is represented in the database as a single layer. Since individual features on the map can't be manipulated separately, data flexibility is limited.

Let's look at several widely used raster databases based on topographic maps. These are examples of databases created in two ways: scanning maps and extracting raster data from existing maps.

Scanned Topographic Maps

The USGS decided in the mid-1990s to scan its topographic map coverage of the United States. The product is called a **Digital Raster Graphic** (**DRG**). The USGS began producing DRGs of its 1:24,000 maps in the mid-1990s, with plans to do all its topographic maps, including the 1:100,000 and 1:250,000 series. The DRG project at 1:24,000-scale is now complete for all states, as are the 1:63,360-scale maps for Alaska.

Topographic quadrangles are scanned at 250-dpi spatial resolution, converted to an 8-bit color image, and then compressed into a Tagged Image File Format (TIFF). Compressed files for a 7½-minute quadrangle range from 5 to 15 megabytes of data, so you need a robust computer to display the maps. DRGs are available on CD-ROM and on-line through the USGS Earth Explorer System.

The Delorme company also sells scanned USGS quads as seamlessly mosaicked DRGs on a state-by-state basis as its **3-D TopoQuads™** product. Maptech competes in this market with its **Terrain Navigator** digital topographic map series. CDs contain blocks of scanned quads that cover entire states or national parks within a region. The National Geographic Society has produced a similar product for selected regions called **Topo**.

Digital Elevation Models

Digital Elevation Models (DEMs) are created by extracting raster data from existing topographic maps. The contours on the maps are digitized and interpolated to a regular grid of elevations. In the United States, DEMs are available at several spatial resolutions through the USGS's U.S. Geodata program. Let's look at the fine, medium, and coarse resolution data available.

High-Resolution DEMs

The USGS has produced DEMs from its 1:24,000-scale topographic quadrangles, using a ground distance sampling interval of 30 meters. The data are derived from digitized contours or from a scanned stereo-model of high-altitude photographs. Most of the 7.5-minute quads have been completed for the contiguous United States, Hawaii, and Puerto Rico. A small part of Alaska is also finished. In addition, 10-meter-resolution grids covering 1:24,000-scale quads are being created in certain parts of the country.

The USGS has recently created the **National Elevation Dataset (NED)**. This is a 1-arc-second (approximately 30-meter) resolution grid for the contiguous United States, Hawaii, and Puerto Rico, as well as a 2-arc-second grid for Alaska*.

Medium-Resolution DEMs

In most of Alaska, DEMs covering the 1:63,360-scale, 15-minute quads have been completed at a grid spacing of 2 by 3 arc-seconds (about 200 by 150 feet in Alaska). Scanned contour and hydrographic data from each quad were used to interpolate the DEM grid.

Contour lines for U.S. states and territories have been digitized from 1-degree by 2-degree 1:250,000-scale topographic maps. This information was then interpolated to grids with a 3-arc-second sampling interval. Two 1° × 1° tiles cover each map, one for the east and one for the west half.

Low-Resolution DEMs

The **Global 30-Arc-Second DEM project (GTOPO30)** was completed in 1997 as the result of an international effort led by the USGS. The entire land surface of the earth is now covered by a 30-arc-second-resolution DEM (all ocean waters are given a special numeric code) broken into 33 tiles. Except for Antarctica, each tile covers 50° of latitude by 40° of longitude (6000 × 4800 cell data file). You will be able to use these data for map scales as large as 1:3,000,000.

The **Global Land One-kilometer Base Elevation (GLOBE)** project is another 30-arc-second-resolution DEM covering the land surface of the earth. The earth is divided into 17 tiles. Each tile covers 90° of longitude (180°W-90°W, 90°W-0°, 0°-90°E, 90°E-180°E) and either 40° or 50° of latitude (0°-50° N and S, 50°-90° N and S).

The **Earth Topography 2-minute-resolution (ETOPO2)** digital land-elevation and sea-depths project is currently the highest-resolution DEM depicting the entire surface of the earth. One file of 5,400 rows by 10,800 columns (116.64 megabytes) covers the whole earth. You can use this file to create maps with scales 1:10,000,000 or smaller.

Raster Thematic Maps

We are witnessing a huge increase in the availability of raster-format thematic map data. The diversity of map themes and Internet sites where they can

**Note how cells vary in size with latitude.*

be obtained is truly astounding. People from all professions have made their collections of scanned paper thematic maps available on-line. More important, however, are thematic maps created initially in digital form from original source data such as satellite imagery or census information. Let's look at three examples: raster thematic maps of weather/climate, landcover, and global human population.

Weather-Climate Maps

If you visit the USA Today website weather page (see Appendix B for this and other useful website addresses), you will be able to select from a menu of digital weather maps derived from recent observations and satellite images. You can view and download the current temperature and precipitation map for the nation or your region. Additional national maps show current thunderstorm activity and severe weather alerts.

Climate maps show the average value of weather variables such as precipitation. The average may be monthly, seasonal, or annual. The Oregon Climate Service has developed a complex climate prediction model that combines weather station and DEM data to create two-kilometer-resolution grids of average monthly and annual precipitation, temperature, degree-days, and snowfall for each state. Grids for the nation or one state can be downloaded.

Landcover Maps

The **Global Land Cover Characterization (GLCC)** project led by the USGS has created several one-kilometer-resolution raster landcover maps based on unsupervised classification of AVHRR satellite data. Each continent has a separate grid on the interrupted Goode homolosine and Lambert azimuthal equal-area map projection surfaces (see Chapter 3 for map projection details). Maps with seven different landcover classification schemes may be downloaded. These include the Global Ecosystems and USGS Land Use/Land Cover classification systems.

The **National Landcover Characterization Project** used a variety of information—including satellite imagery, topography, census data, agricultural statistics, soil characteristics, other landcover maps, and wetlands data— to determine 21 classes of landcover for the United States at 30-meter resolution. The landcover dataset is being used for a wide variety of national and regional applications, including watershed management, environmental inventories, transportation modeling, fire risk assessment, and land management.

Global Population Maps

The **LandScan Global Population Project**, led by Oak Ridge National Laboratory, has created a 30-arc-second-resolution global grid of estimated population. The number of people within each cell is derived from census data from larger tracts that are distributed to cells based on digital maps of landcover, slope, distance to roads, and number of nighttime lights. This is by far the most detailed and accurate mapping of global population, particularly in rural areas.

VECTOR DATA

Cartographers also create databases by converting existing maps to digital form on an feature-by-feature basis. They digitize roads, rivers, political boundaries, and other features as layers of x,y coordinates, called vector data, in separate data files. The resulting databases are complex in structure but more flexible to use than raster databases.

The problem with vector databases is that data gathering is time-consuming and expensive. The extra cost is often justified, however, because individual features as well as feature layers in the database can be manipulated and tailored to a wide variety of user needs. Let's look at some of the better-known vector databases.

TIGER

The **Topologically Integrated Geographic Encoding and Referencing (TIGER)** database was created by the U.S. Census Bureau to support the extensive large-scale mapping effort for the 1990 Census of Population and Housing. TIGER is based on planimetric data from USGS 1:100,000 quadrangles and was developed with USGS assistance. Features include roads, addresses, hydrography, railroads, miscellaneous transportation, and census unit boundaries. TIGER data used for the 2000 census are available from the Census Bureau as downloadable scanned maps or boundary files. The full TIGER database, usually in upgraded form, is widely used by private vendors in their digital mapping products.

The National Map

USGS Geography (a division of USGS) uses the term **"the National Map"** in reference to its system for providing public access to high-quality spatial data from multiple partners to help support decision making by resource managers and the public. Digitizing of spatial data began in the 1960s. The first database effort was to digitize 1:250,000 and 1:100,000-scale land-use and landcover maps. Digital planimetric coverage of the entire United States was completed from *National Atlas* reference maps at 1:2,000,000-scale in 1982. In 1997, the USGS and partners began to develop a new digital *National Atlas* displaying environmental, resource, demographic, economic, social, political, and historical information in traditional static and animated map form. Hundreds of map feature files can now be downloaded from the National Map website.

Digital Line Graphs

The USGS began digitizing planimetric data from its topographic maps in the early 1980s. These files were called **Digital Line Graphs** (**DLG**), in reference to their **topological structure**. Each line in the database has its beginning and ending **node** (point), and the **polygon** (area) to its right and left defined in a separate topology file.

Large-scale DLG data files produced in 7.5 × 7.5 minute blocks are partially complete for conterminous U.S. 1:24,000 and Alaska 1:63,360-scale topographic quadrangles. Data layers include boundaries, hydrography, hypsography (contours), transportation, and U.S. Public Land Survey lines. Intermediate scale (1:100,000) DLG files for these same features are nearly complete for all states except Alaska. These data are available in 30 × 30 minute blocks that correspond to the west or east half of each 1:100,000-scale quadrangle. The 21 *National Atlas* sectional reference maps at 1:2,000,000 are available as boundary, hydrography, and transportation DLGs. You can download this information from the USGS EROS Data Center website.

World Data Bank II

The original **World Data Bank II (WDBII)** was completed by the Central Intelligence Agency in 1977 by digitizing air navigation chart sheets at scales from 1:2,000,000 to 1:4,000,000. This database includes over six million latitude-longitude coordinates and covers international boundaries, hydrography, coastlines, and U.S. state boundaries.

WDBII is the basis for many digital mapping products sold by private vendors. The original ASCII files that filled 122 megabytes have been compressed into 100 files that take a little over 12 megabytes. These are widely used in PC mapping programs to create small-scale, page-size reference maps.

Digital Chart of the World

The **Digital Chart of the World (DCW)** was developed by the U.S. Defense Mapping Agency (now National Geospatial-Intelligence Agency), in conjunction with private contractors. Originally released in 1992, the DCW is the most detailed worldwide cartographic database.

To create the database, a series of 1:1,000,000 maps that cover the world, called Operational Navigation Charts (ONC), were scanned at 1,000 dots per inch. These raster files were then divided into 5 × 5 degree tiles and converted to ESRI's PC ARC/INFO vector format. The data were sorted by feature type into 17 information layers, including coastlines, international boundaries, cities, airports, contours, roads, railroads, water features, cultural landmarks, and other base-map information. The database totals 1.7 gigabytes in size and comes on 4 CD-ROMs. The DCW data, and special desktop software for using the data, are available from ESRI (see contact information in Appendix B).

Commercial Databases

Several private firms now distribute proprietary vector cartographic databases. Some of these commercial databases have been developed from scratch. Others are modifications and updates of public-domain databases such as those discussed previously. The two examples we discuss here are chosen because they're used by so many developers and providers of digital mapping products.

1. One of the oldest commercial suppliers of cartographic databases is Geographic Data Technology (GDT). Its highly regarded **Dynamap** products include a street network database (streets, addresses), postal (zip code) boundaries, political boundaries, census district boundaries, landmark layers (airports, railroads, parks, recreation areas, transportation terminals, institutions, major retail centers, large urban landmarks), insurance rate territories, hydrography, coastal windstorm areas, postal carrier routes, and other features. GDT has had a long and intimate relation with the U.S. Census Bureau's TIGER file development.

2. Environmental Systems Research Institute (ESRI) markets **ESRI Data & Maps 2003**, a CD-ROM database ready to use with its ArcGIS and ArcView software. Base-map information includes political boundaries, cities, rivers, and roads at several levels of detail for the world, Europe, Canada, Mexico, the United States, and 54 European countries. World ecological regions and a color image of the world created by combining hundreds of satellite images are also included. The United States data are more comprehensive, containing additional themes such as census tract and block boundaries, zip code boundaries, parks and public lands, landmarks and points of interest, market areas, and congressional district boundaries.

APPENDIX B
MAP USE SOFTWARE, DATA SOURCES, AND USEFUL WEBSITES

SOFTWARE

GIS

3-D TopoQuads, DeLorme, P.O. Box 298, Two Delorme Drive, Yarmouth, ME 04096, 207-846-7000 (www.delorme.com).

ArcInfo, Environmental Systems Research Institute, Inc., 380 New York Street, Redlands, CA 92373-8100, 909-793-2853 (www.esri.com).

ArcView, Environmental Systems Research Institute, Inc., 380 New York Street, Redlands, CA 92373-8100, 909-793-2853 (www.esri.com).

Atlas GIS, Environmental Systems Research Institute, Inc., 380 New York Street, Redlands, CA 92373-8100, 909-793-2853 (www.esri.com).

Business Map, Environmental Systems Research Institute, Inc., 380 New York Street, Redlands, CA 92373-8100, 909-793-2853 (www.esri.com).

Intergraph MGE, Intergraph Corp., Huntsville, Al 35894-0001, 256-730-9000 (www.intergraph.com).

Compass, Claritas, Inc., 5375 Mira Sorrento Pl., San Diego, CA 92121, 800-234-5973 (www.claritas.com).

IMAGE PROCESSING

ERDAS Imagine, ERDAS, Inc., 2801 Buford Highway, Atlanta, GA 30329, 404-248-9000 (www.erdas.com).

IDRISI, The IDRISI Project, The Clark Labs for Cartographic Technology and Geographic Analysis, Clark University, 950 Main St., Worcester, MA 01610-1477, 508-793-7526 (www.clarklabs.org).

ER Mapper, Earth Resource Mapping, 4370 La Jolla Village Drive, San Diego, CA 92122, 858-558-4709 (www.ermapper.com).

ENVI, Research Systems, Inc., 4990 Pearl East Circle, Boulder, CO 80301 (www.envi-sw.com).

ArcView Image Analysis, ESRI, 380 New York Street, Redlands, CA 92373, 714-793-2853 (www.esri.com).

DATA DISPLAY AND ANALYSIS

MapInfo, One Global View, Troy, NY 12180, 800-327-8627 (www.mapinfo.com).

MapLinx, IMSI, 75 Rowland Way, Novato, CA 94949 (www.imsisoft.com).

MapPoint, Microsoft (www.microsoft.com/office/mappoint).

MapViewer, Golden Software, Inc., 809 14th Street, Golden, CO 80401-1866, 303-279-1021 (www.goldensoftware.com).

Surfer, Golden Software, Inc., 809 14th Street, Golden, CO 80401-1866, 303-279-1021 (www.goldensoftware.com).

Proximity, Decisionmark Corp., 200 Second Ave., S.E., Cedar Rapids, IA 52401, 800-365-7629 (www.decisionmark.com).

ReMap 2000™, Election Data Services, 1401 K Street, Washington, DC 20005, 202-789-2004 (www.electiondataservices.com).

Terrain Navigator, Maptech (www.maptech.com).

Topo, National Geographic Society through Rand McNally (www.randmcnally.com).

WMS Watershed Modeling System, Scientific Software Group, P.O. Box 23041, Washington, DC 20026, 703-620-9214 (www.scisoftware.com).

MAP FINISHING

Illustrator, Adobe Systems, Inc., 345 Park Ave., San Jose, CA 95110, 408-536-6000 (www.adobe.com).

CorelDRAW, Corel Systems Corp., 1600 Carling Ave., Ottawa, Ontario K1Z 8R7, 613-728-8200 (www.corel.com).

Freehand, Macromedia Inc., 600 Townsend St., San Francisco, CA 94103, 415-252-2000 (www.macromedia.com).

ROUTE PLANNING

Street Atlas USA, DeLorme, P.O. Box 298, Two Delorme Drive, Yarmouth, ME 04096, 207-846-7000 (www.delorme.com/streetatlasusa).

Streetfinder and **Trip Planner**, Rand McNally, 8255 N. Central Park Ave., Skokie, IL 60076, 800-275-7263 (www.randmcnally.com/store).

Streets & Trips, Microsoft (www.microsoft.com/Streets).

IMAGE EDITING

Paint Shop Pro, JASC Software, 7905 Fuller Road, Eden Prairie, MN 55344 (www.jasc.com).

Photoshop, Adobe Systems Inc. (www.adobe.com/products/photoshop/main.html).

PhotoSuite, Roxio, Inc., 455 El Camino Real, Santa Clara, CA 95050 (www.roxio.com/en/products/index.jhtml).

PhotoImpact, Ulead Systems (www.ulead.com).

CLIP-ART MAPS

Digital Maps, Cartesia Software, 80 Lambert Lane, P.O. Box 757, Lambertville, NJ 08530, 609-397-1611 (www.mapresources.com).

Mountain High Maps, Digital Wisdom, P.O. Box 2070, 300 Jeanette Dr., Tappahannock, VA 22560, 800-800-8560 (www.digiwis.com).

DIGITAL ATLASES AND ENCYCLOPEDIAS

Hammond Atlas of the World, Hammond World Atlas Co. (www.hammondmaps.com).

Rand McNally New Millennium World Atlas, Rand McNally (www.randmcnally.com).

Encarta Encyclopedia, Microsoft (www.microsoft.com).

Compton's Encyclopedia (www.broderbund.com).

Grolier Multimedia Encyclopedia, Grolier Electronic Publishing (www.broderbund.com).

DATA

DIGITAL RASTER GRAPHICS

U.S. Geological Survey (http://topomaps.usgs.gov/drg).

California Spatial Information Library (http://gis.ca.gov/casil/gis.ca.gov/drg).

Tennessee Valley Authority (www.tva.gov/river/mapstore/map_digital.htm).

DIGITAL ELEVATION MODELS

National Elevation Dataset (http://edc.usgs.gov/geodata).

ETOPO2 (www.ngdc.noaa.gov/mgg/fliers/01mgg04.html).

GTOPO30 (http://edcdaac.usgs.gov/gtopo30/gtopo30.asp).

GLOBE (www.ngdc.noaa.gov/seg/topo/globe.shtml).

WEATHER/CLIMATE MAPS AND DATA

USA Today (http://asp.usatoday.com/weather/weatherfront.aspx).

Oregon Climate Service (www.ocs.orst.edu/prism).

LANDCOVER MAPS

Global Land Cover Characterization (http://edcdaac.usgs.gov/glcc/glcc.asp).

National Land Cover Characterization (http://landcover.usgs.gov/nationallandcover.asp).

POPULATION MAPS AND DATA

LandScan Global Population Project (www.ornl.gov/gist/projects/LandScan).

VECTOR REFERENCE DATA

TIGER Files (www.census.gov/ftp/pub/geo/www/tiger).

APPENDIX C
GPS TERMINOLOGY

TABLE C.1
GUIDE TO GPS ABBREVIATIONS & ACRONYMS

Abbreviation	Meaning
ALT:	Altitude (also EL)
BRG:	Bearing (also azimuth)
C/A:	Coarse (Course) Acquisition Code (unprotected civilian use)
CDI:	Course Deviation Indicator
CMG:	Course Made Good
COG:	Course Over the Ground
CTS:	Course to Steer
DMG:	Distance Made Good
DOP:	Dilution of Precision
DST:	Distance
DTG:	Distance to Go
DTK:	Desired Track
E:	East
EL:	Elevation (also ELEV and ALT)
EPE:	Estimated Position Error
ETA:	Estimated Time of Arrival
ETE:	Estimated Time En Route
FT:	Feet
GMT:	Greenwich Mean Time
GQ:	Geometric Quality
GRI:	Grid
HDG:	Heading
K:	Kilometers or Knots
LFX:	Last Fix
LMK:	Landmark
M:	Meters or Magnetic
MAG:	Magnetic (north)
MGRS:	Military Grid Reference System
MOB:	Man Over Board
MPH:	Miles per Hour
N:	North
NAV:	Navigation
ODOM:	Odometer
P Code:	Protected (Precision) Code (military use)
PPS:	Precise Positioning Service
S:	South
SA:	Selective Availability
SOA:	Speed of Advance or Speed of Approach
SOG:	Speed Over Ground
SQ:	Signal Quality (strength)
SPD:	Speed
SPS:	Standard Positioning Service (civilian use)
STM:	Statute Miles
STR:	HDG - BRG (Heading minus Bearing)
2D Fix:	Two-Dimensional Fix (latitude-longitude)
2D NAV:	Two-Dimensional Navigation
3D Fix:	Three-Dimensional Fix (latitude-longitude-elevation)
3D NAV:	Three-Dimensional Navigation
TFF:	Time to First Fix
TRK:	Track
TTG:	Time to Go
TTFF:	Time to First Fix
UTC:	Universal Time Coordinated
VMG:	Velocity Made Good
VOG:	Velocity Over the Ground
W:	West
WGS84:	World Geodetic System—84
WPT:	Waypoint
XTE:	Cross Track Error (also XTK)

TABLE C.2
GUIDE TO GPS TERMS

Acquisition: The satellite receiver's process of locating the source of the satellite signal and starting to collect data from the satellites.
Almanac Data: Satellite constellation information transmitted by each satellite to the GPS receiver so that the receiver can determine its position.
Anywhere Fix: A fix made by a GPS receiver when you don't first initialize it (or tell it approximately where you are in terms of latitude and longitude).
Auto Mag: Adjustment that can be made to a GPS receiver so that it automatically gives magnetic courses and bearings.
Azimuth: See bearing.
Base Station: GPS receiver that's fixed over a known control point that provides correction data for differential GPS.
Bearing (BRG): The direction measured clockwise in degrees from north. This is technically the "azimuth," but most GPS receivers use the term "bearing" instead of azimuth. GPS receivers use either true north or magnetic north, whichever you select in your setup menu.
Channel: The part of the satellite receiver that tunes in on a satellite's signal and sends the information to the receiver's processor to calculate your position.
Checkpoint: Same as waypoint and landmark.
Coarse (or Course) Acquisition Code (C/A): One of two types of signals sent out by GPS satellites. The other is the Precision (P) code. The CA code is the one sent to civilians and is not as precise as the P code used by the military.
Course: Same as courseline or track.
Course Deviation Indicator (CDI): A graphic way of showing the amount and direction of Cross Track Error (XTE or XTK) in your course.
Course Made Good (CMG): The compass heading from your starting point to your present position.
Course Over the Ground (COG): The direction of travel achieved from your starting point to your present location.
Course to Steer (CTS): The recommended heading to reach your destination most efficiently.
Cross Track Error (XTE or XTK): The distance from your current location to your desired track (DTK).
Courseline: Your planned line of travel from departure point to destination.
Default: The setting automatically chosen by the GPS unit.
Desired Track (DTK): The course you want to travel as given by your "from" and "to" waypoints.
Differential GPS (DGPS): A method in which a base station sends GPS correction signals to your receiver, thus improving the accuracy of Coarse Acquisition Codes for civilian use.
Dilution of Precision (DOP): Measurement of the accuracy of a fix on a scale of 1 to 10, with 1 the most accurate and 10 the least accurate.
Distance Made Good (DMG): Distance from your last position to your present position.
Distance to Go (DTG): The distance you have yet to travel to reach your destination.
Estimated Position Error (EPE): Estimate of the error of a fix, given in feet.

continued...

Table C.2 *continued*

Estimated Time of Arrival (ETA): The time you should reach your destination, based on your current speed.
Estimated Time En Route (ETE): The amount of time remaining to arrive at your destination, based on your current speed.
Fix: A position given in latitude and longitude (for a two-dimensional fix). A three-dimensional fix gives latitude, longitude, and elevation.
Geometric Quality (GQ): Same as Dilution of Precision.
Global Positioning System (GPS): A system of 24 satellites that can be used with receivers to fix a position.
GoTo Function: A function that lets you use a display screen to point the direction you want to travel while your GPS receiver guides you to your destination.
Ground Speed (SPD): The speed you're traveling over the ground (as opposed to speed through the water).
Heading (HDG): The direction in which you're moving with respect to either true or magnetic north.
Initialization: The initial act of telling your GPS receiver approximately where you are in terms of latitude and longitude.
Lock-on Time: The time between turning on your GPS receiver and receiving a good signal.
Man Over Board (MOB): A simple keystroke combination you can use to mark a spot quickly so that you can return to it.
Mark: A hard key on some receivers that lets you activate the Man Over Board function directly.
Precise Positioning Service (PPS): The accuracy provided by Protected (P) Codes for military use.
Protected (or Precision) Code (P Code): One of two types of signals sent out by GPS satellites. The other is the Coarse Acquisition (C/A) code. The P code, which gives far more accurate fixes than the C/A code, may be used only by the military.
Rover: GPS receiver that can be moved about, in contrast to a fixed base station.
Selective Availability: Method the U.S. Department of Defense uses to deliberately make civilian GPS receivers less accurate by causing an apparent clock error.
Signal Quality (SQ): The strength of the signals from a satellite.
Speed (SPD): The speed at which you're moving with respect to the earth.
Speed of Advance (SOA): Your speed in the direction of your destination. If you're heading directly toward your destination, your SOA is the same as your ground speed. If you're not on course, your SOA is less than your ground speed. The GPS receiver shows a negative SOA as a blank line.
Speed of Approach (SOA): Same as Speed of Advance.
Speed Over Ground (SOG): Same as Ground Speed.
Standard Positioning Service: The accuracy provided by Coarse Acquisition Codes for civilian use.
Status: Estimate of the combined impact of Dilution of Precision (DOP) and Signal Quality (SQ).

continued...

Table C.2 ***continued***

Time to First Fix (TTFF or TFF): The time it takes a GPS receiver to make its first position fix after you turn it on. This is the time it takes the receiver to collect position information from every satellite.
Time to Go (TTG): Estimate of the time from your current location to your next waypoint, based on your current speed.
Track (TRK): Your direction of movement relative to a ground position.
Universal Time Coordinated (UTC or UT): The time obtained from GPS satellites, adjusted to Greenwich Mean Time.
Velocity Made Good (VMG): Same as Speed of Advance.
Velocity Over the Ground (VOG): Same as Ground Speed.
Waypoint: The coordinates of a place you want to reach.
World Geodetic System—84 (WGS84): A satellite-based global datum for making horizontal measurements on the earth's surface.

APPENDIX D
TABLES

D.1 METRIC AND ENGLISH EQUIVALENTS
D.2 VARIATION IN THE LENGTH OF A DEGREE OF LATITUDE
D.3 VARIATION IN THE LENGTH OF A DEGREE OF LONGITUDE
D.4 LATITUDE-LONGITUDE VALUES FOR THE LARGEST CITY IN EACH STATE
D.5 AREAS OF QUADRILATERALS OF 1° EXTENT

Table D.1
Metric and English Equivalents

METRIC	ENGLISH
1 micrometer (micron)	0.00003937 inch (in)
1 millimeter (mm)	0.03937 inch
2.54 mm	0.1 inch
1 centimeter (cm) [10 mm]	0.3937 inch
2.54 cm	1 inch
1 decimeter (dm) [10 cm]	3.937 inches
30.48 cm	1 foot (ft) [12 inches]
91.44 cm	1 yard (yd) [3 feet]
1 meter (m) [100 cm]	39.37 inches [3.281 ft] [1.094 yd]
1 decameter (dm) [10 m]	32.81 feet
1 hectometer (hm) [100 m]	328.1 feet
1 kilometer (km) [1,000 m]	0.6214 mile (mi) [3,281 ft] [39,372 in]
1.609 km	1 statute mile [5,280 ft] [63,360 in]
1.852 km	1 nautical mile (nm) [6076.1 ft]
1 cm^2	0.155 in^2
6.45 cm^2	1 in^2
0.092 m^2	1 ft^2
0.836 m^2	1 yd^2
1 m^2	1.196 yd^2 [10.764 ft^2]
0.405 hectare (ha)	1 acre [43,560 ft^2]
1 hectare [10,000 m^2]	2.471 acres
16.188 hectares	40 acres
1 km^2 [1,000,000 m^2]	0.386 mi^2
2.59 km^2	1 mi^2 [640 acres]

Table D.2
Variation in the Length of a Degree of Latitude
(measured along the meridian on the WGS 84 ellipsoid)

Latitude	Meters	Statute Miles	Latitude	Meters	Statute Miles	Latitude	Meters	Statute Miles
0-1°	110 567.3	68.703	30-31°	110 857.0	68.883	60-61°	111 423.1	69.235
1-2	110 568.0	68.704	31-32	110 874.4	68.894	61-62	111 439.9	69.246
2-3	110 569.4	68.705	32-33	110 892.1	68.905	62-63	111 456.4	69.256
3-4	110 571.4	68.706	33-34	110 910.1	68.916	63-64	111 472.4	69.266
4-5	110 574.1	68.708	34-35	110 928.3	68.928	64-65	111 488.1	69.275
5-6	110 577.6	68.710	35-36	110 946.9	68.939	65-66	111 503.3	69.285
6-7	110 581.6	68.712	36-37	110 965.6	68.951	66-67	111 518.0	69.294
7-8	110 586.4	68.715	37-38	110 984.5	68.962	67-68	111 532.3	69.303
8-9	110 591.8	68.718	38-39	111 003.7	68.974	68-69	111 546.2	69.311
9-10	110 597.8	68.722	39-40	111 023.0	68.986	69-70	111 559.5	69.320
10-11	110 604.5	68.726	40-41	111 042.4	68.998	70-71	111 572.2	69.328
11-12	110 611.9	68.731	41-42	111 061.9	69.011	71-72	111 584.5	69.335
12-13	110 619.8	68.736	42-43	111 081.6	69.023	72-73	111 596.2	69.343
13-14	110 628.4	68.741	43-44	111 101.3	69.035	73-74	111 607.3	69.349
14-15	110 637.6	68.747	44-45	111 121.0	69.047	74-75	111 617.9	69.356
15-16	110 647.5	68.753	45-46	111 140.8	69.060	75-76	111 627.8	69.362
16-17	110 657.8	68.759	46-47	111 160.5	69.072	76-77	111 637.1	69.368
17-18	110 668.8	68.766	47-48	111 180.2	69.084	77-78	111 645.9	69.373
18-19	110 680.4	68.773	48-49	111 199.9	69.096	78-79	111 653.9	69.378
19-20	110 692.4	68.781	49-50	111 219.5	69.108	79-80	111 661.4	69.383
20-21	110 705.1	68.789	50-51	111 239.0	69.121	80-81	111 668.2	69.387
21-22	110 718.2	68.797	51-52	111 258.3	69.133	81-82	111 674.4	69.391
22-23	110 731.8	68.805	52-53	111 277.6	69.145	82-83	111 679.9	69.395
23-24	110 746.0	68.814	53-54	111 296.6	69.156	83-84	111 684.7	69.398
24-25	110 760.6	68.823	54-55	111 315.4	69.168	84-85	111 688.9	69.400
25-26	110 775.6	68.833	55-56	111 334.0	69.180	85-86	111 692.3	69.402
26-27	110 791.1	68.842	56-57	111 352.4	69.191	86-87	111 695.1	69.404
27-28	110 807.0	68.852	57-58	111 370.5	69.202	87-88	111 697.2	69.405
28-29	111 823.3	68.862	58-59	111 388.4	69.213	88-89	111 698.6	69.406
29-30	111 840.0	68.873	59-60	111 405.9	69.224	89-90	111 699.3	69.407

Table D.3
Variation in the Length of a Degree of Longitude
(measured along the parallel on the WGS 84 ellipsoid)

Latitude	Meters	Statute Miles	Latitude	Meters	Statute Miles	Latitude	Meters	Statute Miles
0°	111 321	69.172	30°	96 488	59.956	60°	55 802	34.674
1	111 304	69.162	31	95 506	59.345	61	54 110	33.623
2	111 253	69.130	32	94 495	58.716	62	52 400	32.560
3	111 169	69.078	33	93 455	58.071	63	50 675	31.488
4	111 051	69.005	34	92 387	57.407	64	48 934	30.406
5	110 900	68.911	35	91 290	56.725	65	47 177	29.315
6	110 715	68.795	36	90 166	56.027	66	45 407	28.218
7	110 497	68.660	37	89 014	55.311	67	43 622	27.106
8	110 245	68.504	38	87 835	54.579	68	41 823	25.988
9	109 959	68.326	39	86 629	53.829	69	40.012	24.862
10	109 641	68.129	40	85 396	53.063	70	38 188	23.729
11	109 289	67.910	41	84 137	52.281	71	36 353	22.589
12	108 904	67.670	42	82 853	51.483	72	34 506	21.441
13	108 486	67.410	43	81 543	50.669	73	32 648	20.287
14	108 036	67.131	44	80 208	49.840	74	30 781	19.127
15	107 553	66.830	45	78 849	48.995	75	28 903	17.960
16	107 036	66.510	46	77 466	48.136	76	27 017	16.788
17	106 487	66.169	47	76 058	47.261	77	25 123	15.611
18	105 906	65.808	48	74 628	46.372	78	23 220	14.428
19	105 294	65.427	49	73 174	45.469	79	21 311	13.242
20	104 649	65.026	50	71 698	44.552	80	19 394	12.051
21	103 972	64.606	51	70 200	43.621	81	17 472	10.857
22	103 264	64.166	52	68 680	42.676	82	15 545	9.659
23	102 524	63.706	53	67 140	41.719	83	13 612	8.458
24	101 754	63.228	54	65 578	40.749	84	11 675	7.255
25	100 952	62.729	55	63 996	39.766	85	9 735	6.049
26	100 119	62.212	56	62 395	38.771	86	7 792	4.842
27	99 257	61.676	57	60 774	37.764	87	5 846	3.632
28	98 364	61.122	58	59 135	36.745	88	3 898	2.422
29	97 441	60.548	59	57 478	35.716	89	1 949	1.211
						90	0	0

Table D.4
Latitude-Longitude Values for the Largest City in Each State

CITY & STATE	LATITUDE	LONGITUDE
Birmingham, Alabama	33° 25′ N	86° 52′ W
Anchorage, Alaska	61 20	149 55
Phoenix, Arizona	33 22	112 05
Little Rock, Arkansas	34 45	92 15
Los Angeles, California	34 15	118 15
Denver, Colorado	39 46	104 59
Hartford, Connecticut	41 53	72 45
Wilmington, Delaware	39 45	75 23
Miami, Florida	25 45	80 11
Atlanta, Georgia	33 45	84 21
Honolulu, Hawai'i	21 20	157 50
Boise, Idaho	43 37	116 10
Chicago, Illinois	41 49	87 37
Indianapolis, Indiana	39 50	86 10
Des Moines, Iowa	41 37	93 30
Wichita, Kansas	37 35	97 20
Lousiville, Kentucky	38 16	85 30
New Orleans, Louisiana	30 00	90 04
Portland, Maine	43 31	70 20
Baltimore, Maryland	39 22	76 30
Boston, Massachusetts	42 15	71 07
Detroit, Michigan	42 23	83 05
Minneapolis, Minnesota	45 00	93 10
Jackson, Mississippi	32 20	90 10
St. Louis, Missouri	38 40	90 10
Billings, Montana	45 47	108 29
Omaha, Nebraska	41 15	96 05
Las Vegas, Nevada	36 10	115 10
Manchester, New Hampshire	43 00	71 30
Newark, New Jersey	40 40	74 05
Albuquerque, New Mexico	35 06	106 40
New York, New York	40 40	73 58
Charlotte, North Carolina	35 14	81 53
Fargo, North Dakota	46 52	97 00
Cleveland, Ohio	41 30	81 45
Oklahoma City, Oklahoma	35 30	97 30
Portland, Oregon	45 29	122 48
Philadelphia, Pennsylvania	44 00	75 05
Providence, Rhode Island	41 52	71 30
Columbia, South Carolina	34 00	81 00
Sioux Falls, South Dakota	43 30	96 50
Memphis, Tennessee	35 08	90 03
Houston, Texas	29 46	95 21
Salt Lake City, Utah	40 46	111 57
Burlington, Vermont	44 30	73 15
Norfolk, Virginia	36 49	76 15
Seattle, Washington	47 36	122 20
Charleston, West Virginia	38 23	81 30
Milwaukee, Wisconsin	43 05	88 00
Cheyenne, Wyoming	41 08	104 47

Table D.5
Areas of Quadrilaterals of 1° Extent

Lower Latitude	Area in Square Kilometers	Area in Square Miles	Lower Latitude	Area in Square Kilometers	Area in Square Miles
0°	12308.09	4752.16	45°	8686.89	3354.01
1	12304.44	4750.75	46	8533.30	3294.71
2	12297.14	4747.93	47	8377.07	3234.39
3	12286.21	4743.71	48	8218.17	3173.04
4	12271.63	4738.08	49	8056.69	3110.69
5	12253.39	4731.04	50	7892.69	3047.37
6	12231.56	4722.61	51	7726.18	2983.08
7	12206.05	4712.76	52	7557.23	2917.85
8	12176.94	4701.52	53	7385.85	2851.68
9	12144.23	4688.89	54	7212.17	2784.62
10	12107.89	4674.86	55	7036.18	2716.67
11	12067.92	4659.43	56	6857.93	2647.85
12	12024.41	4642.63	57	6677.51	2578.19
13	11977.30	4624.44	58	6494.94	2507.70
14	11926.61	4604.87	59	6310.33	2436.42
15	11872.35	4583.92	60	6123.64	2364.34
16	11814.57	4561.61	61	5935.01	2291.51
17	11753.24	4537.93	62	5744.46	2217.94
18	11688.41	4512.90	63	5552.08	2143.66
19	11620.06	4486.51	64	5357.88	2068.68
20	11548.24	4458.78	65	5161.97	1993.04
21	11472.95	4429.71	66	4964.38	1916.75
22	11394.19	4399.30	67	4765.19	1839.84
23	11312.01	4367.57	68	4564.44	1762.33
24	11278.21	4334.52	69	4362.18	1684.24
25	11137.44	4300.17	70	4158.56	1605.62
26	11045.08	4264.51	71	3953.53	1526.46
27	10949.38	4227.56	72	3747.24	1446.81
28	10850.36	4189.33	73	3539.73	1366.69
29	10748.06	4149.83	74	3331.05	1286.12
30	10642.47	4109.06	75	3121.29	1205.13
31	10533.66	4067.05	76	2910.51	1123.75
32	10421.62	4023.79	77	2698.75	1041.99
33	10306.39	3979.30	78	2486.14	959.90
34	10188.00	3933.59	79	2272.70	877.49
35	10066.48	3886.67	80	2058.51	794.79
36	9941.87	3838.56	81	1843.64	711.83
37	9814.18	3789.26	82	1628.17	628.64
38	9683.49	3738.80	83	1412.17	545.24
39	9549.80	3687.18	84	1195.70	461.66
40	9413.15	3634.42	85	978.84	377.93
41	9273.60	3580.54	86	761.67	294.08
42	9131.15	3525.54	87	544.21	210.12
43	8985.85	3469.44	88	326.60	126.10
44	8837.75	3412.26	89	108.88	42.04

BIBLIOGRAPHY OF QUOTATIONS

Boorstin, Daniel J., *The Discovers* (New York: Random House, 1983).

Carlyle, Thomas, *The French Revolution: A History* (London, Chapman and Hall, 1837).

Carroll, Lewis, *Alice's Adventures in Wonderland*; and *Through the Looking Glass* (New York: Three Sirens Press, 1930).

Cervantes, Miguel de, *Don Quixote of La Mancha* (Edinburgh: John Grant, 1902).

Conrad, Joseph, *Heart of Darkness and The Secret Sharer* (New York: The New American Library, 1960).

Dickey, James, *Deliverance* (Boston: Houghton Mifflin Co., 1970).

Drummond, June, *Cable Car* (New York: Holt, Rinehart & Winston, 1967).

Gregory, R.L., *The Intelligent Eye* (New York: McGraw-Hill, 1970).

Heller, Joseph, *Catch-22* (New York: Simon & Schuster, 1961).

Huff, Darrell, *How to Lie with Statistics* (New York: Norton, 1993).

Hugo, Victor, *The Toilers of the Sea?* (Boston: Little Brown and Co., 1888).

Huxtable, Ada Louise, *The New York Times* (November 25, 1973), Section 2, p.26.

Least Heat-Moon, William, *Blue Highways: A Journey into America* (Boston: Little, Brown, 1982).

Mailer, Norman, *The Naked and the Dead* (New York: Holt, Rinehart & Winston, 1948).

Mayes, Frances, *Bella Tuscany* (New York: Broadway Books, 1998).

Melville, Herman, *Moby Dick* (New York: Charles Scribners' sons, 1899).

Nadolny, Sten, *The Discovery of Slowness* (New York: Viking, 1987).

Nautical Chart, National Ocean Service (NOS), U.S. Dept. of Commerce.

Newsweek, material in issues dated January 22, 1973 and January 21, 1991 (page 12).

New York Times, material in the issue dated October 13, 1972.

Patton, Francis Gray, *Good Morning, Miss Dove* (New York: Pocket Books, 1956).

Pelletier, Cathie, *The Funeral Makers* (New York: Macmillan, 1986).

Prince Modupe, *I Was A Savage* (New York: Frederick A. Praeger, 1957).

Russell, Jerry & Renny, *On The Loose* (New York: Ballantine Books, 1967).

Saint-Exupéry, Antoine de, *Night Flight* (New York: The New American Library, 1961).

Shakespeare, William, *King Lear* (New York: Washington Square Press, 2004).

Snow, John, *On the Mode of Communication of Cholera*, 2nd. ed. (London: John Churchill, 1855).

Steinbeck, John, *Travels with Charley* (New York: Bantam Books, 1963).

Tey, Josephine (Elizabeth Mackintosh), *The Man in the Queue* (London: Peter Davies, 1927).

Thoreau, Henry David, *The Journal of Henry D. Thoreau* (Thoreau's diaries), two volumes, edited by Bradford Torrey & Francis Allen (New York: Dover Publications, 1963), pp.228-229.

Toffler, Alvin, *Future Shock* (New York: Bantam Books, 1971).

Toffler, Alvin, *The Third Wave* (New York: Bantam Books, 1981).

Twain, Mark (Samuel Clemens), *Tom Sawyer Abroad* (New York: Charles L. Webster & Co., 1894).

Webb, Walter P., *The Great Plains* (Waltham, MA: Blaisdell Pub. Co., 1959).

CREDITS

A. Jon Kimerling created all maps, graphs, and diagrams not noted below.

INTRODUCTION

Figure I.1, courtesy Register and Tribune Syndicate; Figure I.2, courtesy Eugene S. Sinervo (Sand River, MI); Figure I.4, globe illustration courtesy National Geographic Society, wall map photo courtesy Terra Grande; Figure I.5, Oregon maps courtesy of Oregon Climate Service and Oregon State University Press; Figure I.7, from MIFTAH.org Palestine map library; Figure I.10 from Columbia City, Indiana, Internet advertisement; Figure I.11 adapted from Pickles, et al., *Atlas of United States Mortality*.

PART I

CHAPTER 1

Figure 1.6 from digital color photography by U.K. Science Museum; Figure 1.11 Bureau of Land Management photograph; Figure 1.12 courtesy U.S. Geological Survey; Figure 1.14 courtesy National Ocean Service; Figure 1.15 courtesy National Aeronautical Charting Office.

CHAPTER 3

Figure 3.1, digital photo courtesy Replogle Globes ; Figure 3.19, from map produced by Oxfam.org.

CHAPTER 4

Figures 4.9,4.11,4.13, 4.16,and 4.18, topographic map segments courtesy USGS; Figures 4.12 and 4.15, redrawn from Department of the Army TM 241-8.

CHAPTER 5

Figures 5.2,5.3,5.4,5.5,5.12, topographic map segments courtesy USGS; Figure 5.6, photo courtesy Bureau of Land Management; Figure 5.16, engineering plan section courtesy City of Corvallis, Oregon, Public Works Dept.

CHAPTER 6

Figure 6.5 and 6.7 adapted from the Atlas of the Pacific Northwest, Oregon State University Press; Figure 6.8 soil map segment courtesy U.S. Soil Conservation Service; Figure 6.10 adapted from a flyway map produced by The Nature Society; Figure 6.12 adapted from National Park Service maps of the Gettysburg National Military Park; Figure 6.13, adapted from www.weatherbank.com jet stream maps; Figure 6.15 topographic map segments courtesy USGS; Figure 6.16A based on map published by *USA Today*.

CHAPTER 7

Figure 7.4, map segment courtesy Washington State Department of Transportation; Figure 7.5, adapted from web map courtesy Washington State Department of Transportation; Figure 7.6, adapted from map courtesy Georgia Water Resources Department; Figures 7.10, 7.14, 7.18, 7.19, 7.20 and 7.26, adapted from maps in the Atlas of the Pacific Northwest, 9th ed., Oregon State University Press; Figure 7.12, courtesy NCGIA Cartogram Central; Figure 7.22, after map prepared by the USGS; Figure 7.23, map prepared by Eugene Turner using data from the Los Angeles Community Analysis Bureau (Northridge, CA); Figure 7.27, courtesy Instructional Technology, College of Education, University of Georgia.

CHAPTER 8

Figures 8.1, 8.4 and 8.21, topographic map segments courtesy USGS; Figure 8.2, photo courtesy www.a2zgorge.info; Figure 8.3, nautical chart segment courtesy National Ocean Service; Figure 8.8, photo courtesy NutriSystems Raised Relief Globes; Figure 8.10, photo courtesy Raisedreliefmaps; Figure 8.12, from a post card by Richard A. Pargeter; Figure 8.13, courtesy Terragraphics; Figure 8.15, block diagram by William Morris Davis; Figure 8.18, map segment courtesy Library of Congress; Figure 8.22, map section courtesy National Park Service; Figure 8.23, taken from Tanaka, K. "The Relief Contour Method of Representing Topography on Maps," *Geographical Review*, Vol. 40, pp. 444-456, 1950; Figure 8.24, adapted from web map by Map Illustrations.

.

CHAPTER 9

Figure 9.5, cropped photo from NOAA Photo Library; Figure 9.7, courtesy USGS National Aerial Photography Program; Figures 9.8, 9.9, and 9.17, courtesy City of Corvallis Public Works Dept.; Figure 9.10, from NASA Manned Space Flight photo library; Figure 9.11, courtesy J.L. Rich, Virginia Division of Mineral Resources; Figure 9.13, courtesy NASA National High Altitude Photography Program; Figure 9.14, courtesy USGS Digital Orthophotoquad program; Figure 9.15, from T.E. Avery, *Interpretation of Aerial Photographs*, 1st ed.; Figures 9.19 and 9.21, courtesy Oregon Army National Guard; Figure 9.22 from JPL Public Information Office; Figure 9.23, from Ohio State University RADARSAT-1 Antarctic Mapping Project; Figure 9.25, adapted from NASA Landsat MSS Handbook; Figures 9.26, 9.27 and 9.28 from NASA image galleries on the web; Figures 9.29 and 9.30 from SPOT image galleries; Figure 9.31, from IRS image gallery; Figure 9.32, from Ikonos image gallery; Figure 9.33, from Quickbird image gallery; Figures 9.34 and 9.35, courtesy National Ocean Service; Figure 9.36, from MODIS image gallery; Figure 9.37, courtesy USGS; Figure 9.38, courtesy NASA Jet Propulsion Laboratory; Color Plate 9.1, courtesy NOAA; Color Plate 9.2, courtesy USGS NAPP; Color Plate 9.3, from NASA Remote Sensing Tutorial; Color Plates 9.4, 9.12 and 9.14, courtesy USGS; Color Plate 9.5, courtesy NASA Jet Propulsion Laboratory; Color Plate 9.6, courtesy USGS Eros Data Center; Color Plate 9.7, courtesy USGS National Wetlands Research Center; Color Plate 9.8, from SPOT image galleries; Color Plate 9.9, from IRS image gallery; Color Plate 9.10; from Ikonos image gallery; Color Plate 9.11; from Quickbird image gallery; Color Plate 9.13, from MODIS image gallery.

CHAPTER 10

Boxes 10.1, 10.2, and 10.3, courtesy Morris Thompson, *Maps for America*, 2nd ed. (Reston, VA: USGS, 1982); Figures 10.1, 10.2 and 10.3, topographic map segments courtesy USGS.

PART II

CHAPTER 11

Figure 11.1, diagrams courtesy U.S. Army (from *Map Reading*, FM 2126, 1965); Figure 11.2, from Topocompanion advertisement on web; Figure 11.3, from Silva Map Measure and Scalex Map Wheel ads on web; Figure 11.5, topographic map segment courtesy USGS; Figure 11.12, from www.travelportland.com Mileage Map; Figure 11.3, courtesy Alaska Dept. of Transportation; Figure 11.5, adapted from J.C. Muller, "The Mapping of Travel Time in Edmonton, Alberta," *The Canadian Geographer*, Vol. 22, 1978.

CHAPTER 12

Figure 12.9, data from map titled "Magnetic Declination in the United States1990," courtesy USGS; Figure 12.10 courtesy National Ocean Service; Figure 12.11 courtesy USGS; Figure 12.16 and 12.19, courtesy the Brunton Co. (Riverton, WY); Figure 12.17 top and 12.18 B, courtesy Silva Co. (LaPorte, IN); Figure 12.18 A and C, courtesy Ritchie Navigation (Pembroke, MA); Figure 12.18 D, courtesy Davis Instruments, Inc. (Hayward, CA); Figure 12.20 right, courtesy Boat Owners Association of the United States;

CHAPTER 13

Figures 13.1, 13.3, 13.5,13.6 and 13.9 created by Robert Tucker; Figure 13.4 B, range finder photo courtesy Bushnell Performance Optics, (Overland Park, KS); Figure 13.7, photo courtesy The Science Company; Figure 13.10 top, from Conrad Miller facsimile, 1887; Figure 13.11, courtesy of Raft Maine (Bethel, ME); Figure 13.12, courtesy American Automobile Association; Figure 13.13, courtesy Wisconsin Department of Transportation; Figure 13.14, nautical chart segment courtesy National Ocean Service; Figure 13.15, courtesy National Aeronautical Charting Office; Figures 13.16, 13.17 and 13.18, nautical chart segment courtesy Canadian Hydrographic Office; Figure 13.19, courtesy Magellan Systems Corporation (San Dimas, CA); Color Plate 13.1, courtesy Raven Maps and Images, Medford, Oregon; Color Plate 13.2, courtesy National Aeronautical Charting Office.

CHAPTER 14

Figures 14.4, 14.5, 14.6, 14.7, 14.8, 14.9, 14.10, 14.11, 14.12, 14.14, 14.15 and 14.16, courtesy Garmin International (Olathe, KS); Figure 14.13, courtesy Lowrance Electronics, Inc. (Tulsa, OK); Figure 14.17, courtesy Navman NZ Ltd. (Auckland, NZ).

CHAPTER 15

Figure 15.1, adapted from Y.S. Frolov and D.H. Maling, "The Accuracy of Area Measurement by Point Counting Techniques," The Cartographic Journal, Vol 6, 1969; Figure 15.7, courtesy Topcon America Corporation (Paramus, NJ).

CHAPTER 16

Figure 16.7, slope map segment courtesy USGS; Figure 16.8, from examples of graphical output from SCOP program, Inst. of Photogrammetry and Remote Sensing, Technical Univ. of Vienna; Figure 16.10, topographic map section courtesy USGS; Figure 16.15, images from MicroDem program.

CHAPTER 18

Figure 18.2, from *Atlas of the Pacific Northwest*, 9th ed., Oregon State University Press.

CHAPTER 19

Figures 19.1 and 19.2, courtesy DeLorme (Yarmouth, ME); Figures 19.3 and 19.4, courtesy Microsoft Corporation (Redmond, WA); Figure 19.5, courtesy Golden Software (Golden, CO); Figures 19.6 and 19.7, courtesy ESRI (Redlands, CA); Figure 19.14, adapted from ITC ILWIS example on web.

CHAPTER 20

Figure 20.4, photo segment courtesy USGS.

PART III

CHAPTER 21

Figures 21.1, 21.9, 21.15, 21.16, 21.17 A, and 21.22, courtesy City of Corvallis Public Works Dept.; Figures 21.2, 21.4, 21.12, 21.13 A,B, and D, 21.17 B, 21.18, 21.19, 21.20, 21.21, 21.23, 21.24 and 21.25, from Microsoft Terraserver; Figure 21.5, photo from USGS NHAP program; Figure 21.8, courtesy Oregon Army National Guard; Figure 21.10, from Quickbird image gallery; Figure 21.13 C, courtesy Malin Space Science Systems; Figure 21.26, from T.E. Avery, Forester's Guide to Aerial Photo Interpretation; Figure 21.27, photo courtesy Bausch & Lomb; Color Plate 21.1, photos from UC Berkeley Earth Science & Map Library.

CHAPTER 22

Figure 22.1, diagrams courtesy U.S. Army (from *Map Reading*, FM 2126, 1965); Figures 22.3, 22.4, 22.5, 22.6, 22.7, 22.8, 22.9, 22.10, 22.11, 22.12, and 22.13, original photo and map segments from Microsoft Terraserver; Figure 22.15, geologic map segments courtesy USGS.

CHAPTER 23

Figures 23.1 and 23.2, adapted from map courtesy Atmospheric Sciences Dept., University of Illinois; Figure 23.4, images courtesy National Ocean Service; Figure 23.5, courtesy The Weather Channel; Figure 23.6, courtesy San Francisco State University, Meteorology Dept.; Figure 23.7, 23.8 top, 23.9, 23.11 and 23.12, courtesy Spatial Climate Analysis Service, Oregon State University.

CHAPTER 24

Figure 24.3, data for map courtesy of City of Corvallis Public Works Dept.; Figure 24.4, courtesy USGS National Water Quality Assessment Program; Figures 24.6, 24.7 and 24.8 , from Microsoft Terraserver; Figures 24.9, 24.20, 24.11, 24.12, 24.14 and 24.15, adapted from maps courtesy University of Chicago Library Map Collection; Figure 24.13, adapted from map courtesy William Bowen, California State Univ. at Northridge; Figure 24.16, digital copy of original map courtesy UCLA Dept. of Epidemiology; Figures 24.17 and 24.18, adapted from maps in L.W. Pickle, et al., *Atlas of United States Mortality*; Color Plates 24.1 and 24.2, adapted from maps courtesy City of Corvallis Public Works Department.

CHAPTER 25

Figure 25.1, courtesy *Wisconsin State Journal*, Madison Newspapers, Inc.

APPENDIX D

Tables D.2 and D.3, courtesy U.S. Coast and Geodetic Survey; Table D.5, from Smithsonian Geographical Tables.

INDEX

ORDER FORM

SEND TO: JP Publications
P.O. Box 44173
Madison, WI 53744-4173

_____I enclose check or money order for ____copies of MAP USE at U.S. $50 per copy (includes postage and handling). From Canada, please send U.S. $75 per copy (U.S. funds, drawn on U.S. banks only, please).

Name____

Address____

____

____

- -

ORDER FORM

SEND TO: JP Publications
P.O. Box 44173
Madison, WI 53744-4173

_____I enclose check or money order for ____copies of MAP USE at U.S. $50 per copy (includes postage and handling). From Canada, please send U.S. $75 per copy (U.S. funds, drawn on U.S. banks only, please).

Name____

Address____

____

____

ORDER FORM

SEND TO: JP Publications
P.O. Box 44173
Madison, WI 53744-4173

_____I enclose check or money order for ____copies of MAP USE at U.S. $50 per copy (includes postage and handling). From Canada, please send U.S. $75 per copy (U.S. funds, drawn on U.S. banks only, please).

Name____

Address____

____

____

- -

ORDER FORM

SEND TO: JP Publications
P.O. Box 44173
Madison, WI 53744-4173

_____I enclose check or money order for ____copies of MAP USE at U.S. $50 per copy (includes postage and handling). From Canada, please send U.S. $75 per copy (U.S. funds, drawn on U.S. banks only, please).

Name____

Address____

____

____